Twentieth-Century
Literary Criticism

Guide to Thomson Gale Literary Criticism Series

For criticism on	Consult these Thomson Gale series
Authors now living or who died after December 31, 1999	*CONTEMPORARY LITERARY CRITICISM (CLC)*
Authors who died between 1900 and 1999	*TWENTIETH-CENTURY LITERARY CRITICISM (TCLC)*
Authors who died between 1800 and 1899	*NINETEENTH-CENTURY LITERATURE CRITICISM (NCLC)*
Authors who died between 1400 and 1799	*LITERATURE CRITICISM FROM 1400 TO 1800 (LC)* *SHAKESPEAREAN CRITICISM (SC)*
Authors who died before 1400	*CLASSICAL AND MEDIEVAL LITERATURE CRITICISM (CMLC)*
Authors of books for children and young adults	*CHILDREN'S LITERATURE REVIEW (CLR)*
Dramatists	*DRAMA CRITICISM (DC)*
Poets	*POETRY CRITICISM (PC)*
Short story writers	*SHORT STORY CRITICISM (SSC)*
Literary topics and movements	*HARLEM RENAISSANCE: A GALE CRITICAL COMPANION (HR)* *THE BEAT GENERATION: A GALE CRITICAL COMPANION (BG)* *FEMINISM IN LITERATURE: A GALE CRITICAL COMPANION (FL)* *GOTHIC LITERATURE: A GALE CRITICAL COMPANION (GL)*
Asian American writers of the last two hundred years	*ASIAN AMERICAN LITERATURE (AAL)*
Black writers of the past two hundred years	*BLACK LITERATURE CRITICISM (BLC)* *BLACK LITERATURE CRITICISM SUPPLEMENT (BLCS)*
Hispanic writers of the late nineteenth and twentieth centuries	*HISPANIC LITERATURE CRITICISM (HLC)* *HISPANIC LITERATURE CRITICISM SUPPLEMENT (HLCS)*
Native North American writers and orators of the eighteenth, nineteenth, and twentieth centuries	*NATIVE NORTH AMERICAN LITERATURE (NNAL)*
Major authors from the Renaissance to the present	*WORLD LITERATURE CRITICISM, 1500 TO THE PRESENT (WLC)* *WORLD LITERATURE CRITICISM SUPPLEMENT (WLCS)*

ISSN 0276-8178

Volume 189

Twentieth-Century Literary Criticism

**Criticism of the
Works of Novelists, Poets, Playwrights,
Short Story Writers, and Other Creative Writers
Who Lived between 1900 and 1999,
from the First Published Critical
Appraisals to Current Evaluations**

Thomas J. Schoenberg
Lawrence J. Trudeau
Project Editors

THOMSON

GALE

Detroit • New York • San Francisco • New Haven, Conn. • Waterville, Maine • London

Twentieth-Century Literary Criticism, Vol. 189

Project Editors
Thomas J. Schoenberg and Lawrence J. Trudeau

Editorial
Kathy D. Darrow, Jeffrey W. Hunter, Jelena O. Krstović, Michelle Lee, Russel Whitaker

Data Capture
Frances Monroe, Gwen Tucker

Indexing Services
Laurie Andriot

Rights and Acquisitions
Margaret Chamberlain-Gaston, Margaret Abendroth, Jacqueline Jones

Imaging and Multimedia
Dean Dauphinais, Robert Duncan, Leitha Etheridge-Sims, Mary Grimes, Lezlie Light, Michael Logusz, Dan Newell, Denay Wilding

Composition and Electronic Capture
Tracey L. Matthews

Manufacturing
Rhonda Dover

Associate Product Manager
Marc Cormier

LIBRARY OF CONGRESS CATALOG CARD NUMBER 76-46132

ISBN-13: 978-0-7876-9964-2
ISBN-10: 0-7876-9964-0
ISSN 0276-8178

Printed in the United States of America
10 9 8 7 6 5 4 3 2 1

Contents

Preface vii

Acknowledgments xi

Literary Criticism Series Advisory Board xiii

Preface

Since its inception *Twentieth-Century Literary Criticism* (*TCLC*) has been purchased and used by some 10,000 school, public, and college or university libraries. *TCLC* has covered more than 1000 authors, representing over 60 nationalities and nearly 50,000 titles. No other reference source has surveyed the critical response to twentieth-century authors and literature as thoroughly as *TCLC*. In the words of one reviewer, "there is nothing comparable available." *TCLC* "is a gold mine of information—dates, pseudonyms, biographical information, and criticism from books and periodicals—which many librarians would have difficulty assembling on their own."

Scope of the Series

TCLC is designed to serve as an introduction to authors who died between 1900 and 1999 and to the most significant interpretations of these author's works. Volumes published from 1978 through 1999 included authors who died between 1900 and 1960. The great poets, novelists, short story writers, playwrights, and philosophers of the period are frequently studied in high school and college literature courses. In organizing and reprinting the vast amount of critical material written on these authors, *TCLC* helps students develop valuable insight into literary history, promotes a better understanding of the texts, and sparks ideas for papers and assignments. Each entry in *TCLC* presents a comprehensive survey on an author's career or an individual work of literature and provides the user with a multiplicity of interpretations and assessments. Such variety allows students to pursue their own interests; furthermore, it fosters an awareness that literature is dynamic and responsive to many different opinions.

Every fourth volume of *TCLC* is devoted to literary topics. These topics widen the focus of the series from the individual authors to such broader subjects as literary movements, prominent themes in twentieth-century literature, literary reaction to political and historical events, significant eras in literary history, prominent literary anniversaries, and the literatures of cultures that are often overlooked by English-speaking readers.

TCLC is designed as a companion series to Thomson Gale's *Contemporary Literary Criticism*, (*CLC*) which reprints commentary on authors who died after 1999. Because of the different time periods under consideration, there is no duplication of material between *CLC* and *TCLC*.

Organization of the Book

A *TCLC* entry consists of the following elements:

- The **Author Heading** cites the name under which the author most commonly wrote, followed by birth and death dates. Also located here are any name variations under which an author wrote, including transliterated forms for authors whose native languages use nonroman alphabets. If the author wrote consistently under a pseudonym, the pseudonym is listed in the author heading and the author's actual name is given in parenthesis on the first line of the biographical and critical information. Uncertain birth or death dates are indicated by question marks. Single-work entries are preceded by a heading that consists of the most common form of the title in English translation (if applicable) and the name of its author.

- The **Introduction** contains background information that introduces the reader to the author, work, or topic that is the subject of the entry.

- The list of **Principal Works** is ordered chronologically by date of first publication and lists the most important works by the author. The genre and publication date of each work is given. In the case of foreign authors whose works have been translated into English, the English-language version of the title follows in brackets. Unless otherwise indicated, dramas are dated by first performance, not first publication. Lists of **Representative Works** by different authors appear with topic entries.

■ Reprinted **Criticism** is arranged chronologically in each entry to provide a useful perspective on changes in critical evaluation over time. The critic's name and the date of composition or publication of the critical work are given at the beginning of each piece of criticism. Unsigned criticism is preceded by the title of the source in which it originally appeared. All titles by the author featured in the text are printed in boldface type. Footnotes are reprinted at the end of each essay or excerpt. In the case of excerpted criticism, only those footnotes that pertain to the excerpted texts are included. Criticism in topic entries is arranged chronologically under a variety of subheadings to facilitate the study of different aspects of the topic.

■ A complete **Bibliographical Citation** of the original essay or book precedes each piece of criticism. Source citations in the Literary Criticism Series follow University of Chicago Press style, as outlined in *The Chicago Manual of Style,* 15th ed. (Chicago: The University of Chicago Press, 2003).

■ Critical essays are prefaced by brief **Annotations** explicating each piece.

■ An annotated bibliography of **Further Reading** appears at the end of each entry and suggests resources for additional study. In some cases, significant essays for which the editors could not obtain reprint rights are included here. Boxed material following the further reading list provides references to other biographical and critical sources on the author in series published by Thomson Gale.

Indexes

A **Cumulative Author Index** lists all of the authors that appear in a wide variety of reference sources published by Thomson Gale, including *TCLC.* A complete list of these sources is found facing the first page of the Author Index. The index also includes birth and death dates and cross references between pseudonyms and actual names.

A **Cumulative Topic Index** lists the literary themes and topics treated in *TCLC* as well as other Literature Criticism series.

A **Cumulative Nationality Index** lists all authors featured in *TCLC* by nationality, followed by the numbers of the *TCLC* volumes in which their entries appear.

An alphabetical **Title Index** accompanies each volume of *TCLC.* Listings of titles by authors covered in the given volume are followed by the author's name and the corresponding page numbers where the titles are discussed. English translations of foreign titles and variations of titles are cross-referenced to the title under which a work was originally published. Titles of novels, dramas, nonfiction books, and poetry, short story, or essay collections are printed in italics, while individual poems, short stories, and essays are printed in roman type within quotation marks.

In response to numerous suggestions from librarians, Thomson Gale also produces a paperbound edition of the *TCLC* cumulative title index. This annual cumulation, which alphabetically lists all titles reviewed in the series, is available to all customers. Additional copies of this index are available upon request. Librarians and patrons will welcome this separate index; it saves shelf space, is easy to use, and is recyclable upon receipt of the next edition.

Citing *Twentieth-Century Literary Criticism*

When citing criticism reprinted in the Literary Criticism Series, students should provide complete bibliographic information so that the cited essay can be located in the original print or electronic source. Students who quote directly from reprinted criticism may use any accepted bibliographic format, such as University of Chicago Press style or Modern Language Association (MLA) style. Both the MLA and the University of Chicago formats are acceptable and recognized as being the current standards for citations. It is important, however, to choose one format for all citations; do not mix the two formats within a list of citations.

The examples below follow recommendations for preparing a bibliography set forth in *The Chicago Manual of Style,* 15th ed. (Chicago: The University of Chicago Press, (2003); the first example pertains to material drawn from periodicals, the-second to material reprinted from books:

Morrison, Jago. "Narration and Unease in Ian McEwan's Later Fiction." *Critique* 42, no. 3 (spring 2001): 253-68. Reprinted in *Twentieth-Century Literary Criticism.* Vol. 127, edited by Janet Witalec, 212-20. Detroit: Thomson Gale, 2003.

Brossard, Nicole. "Poetic Politics." In *The Politics of Poetic Form: Poetry and Public Policy,* edited by Charles Bernstein, 73-82. New York: Roof Books, 1990. Reprinted in *Twentieth-Century Literary Criticism.* Vol. 127, edited by Janet Witalec, 3-8. Detroit: Thomson Gale, 2003.

The examples below follow recommendations for preparing a works cited list set forth in the *MLA Handbook for Writers of Research Papers,* 5th ed. (New York: The Modern Language Association of America, 1999); the first example pertains to material drawn from periodicals, the second to material reprinted from books:

Morrison, Jago. "Narration and Unease in Ian McEwan's Later Fiction." *Critique* 42.3 (spring 2001): 253-68. Reprinted in *Twentieth-Century Literary Criticism.* Ed. Janet Witalec. Vol. 127. Detroit: Thomson Gale, 2003. 212-20.

Brossard, Nicole. "Poetic Politics." *The Politics of Poetic Form: Poetry and Public Policy.* Ed. Charles Bernstein. New York: Roof Books, 1990. 73-82. Reprinted in *Twentieth-Century Literary Criticism.* Ed. Janet Witalec. Vol. 127. Detroit: Thomson Gale, 2003. 3-8.

Suggestions are Welcome

Readers who wish to suggest new features, topics, or authors to appear in future volumes, or who have other suggestions or comments are cordially invited to call, write, or fax the Associate Product Manager:

Associate Product Manager, Literary Criticism Series
Thomson Gale
27500 Drake Road
Farmington Hills, MI 48331-3535
1-800-347-4253 (GALE)
Fax: 248-699-8054

Acknowledgments

The editors wish to thank the copyright holders of the criticism included in this volume and the permissions managers of many book and magazine publishing companies for assisting us in securing reproduction rights. Following is a list of the copyright holders who have granted us permission to reproduce material in this volume of *TCLC*. Every effort has been made to trace copyright, but if omissions have been made, please let us know.

COPYRIGHTED MATERIAL IN *TCLC*, VOLUME 189, WAS REPRODUCED FROM THE FOLLOWING PERIODICALS:

College Literature, v. 21, June, 1994. Copyright © 1994 by West Chester University. Reproduced by permission.—*Contemporary Literature,* v. 33, spring, 1992. Copyright © 1992 by the Board of Regents of the University of Wisconsin System. Reproduced by permission.—*Criticism,* v. 17, summer, 1975. Copyright © 1975 Wayne State University Press. Reproduced with permission of the Wayne State University Press.—*Encounter,* v. 19, October, 1962 for "Vladimir Nabokov's 'Pale Fire'" by Mary McCarthy. Copyright © 1962 by Encounter Ltd. Reproduced by permission of the author.—*Essays in Literature,* v. 2, fall, 1975; v. 14, spring, 1987. Copyright 1975, 1987 by Western Illinois University. All reproduced by permission.—*Forum for Modern Language Studies,* v. 41, October, 2005 for "Death and the Virgin Martyr: Re Writing Hagiography in *Dulce Dueño*," by Kathy Bacon. Copyright © The Author, 2005. Published by Oxford University Press for Court of the University of St. Andrews. Republished with permission of the author and Oxford University Press, conveyed through Copyright Clearance Center, Inc.—*Hispania,* v. 52, March, 1969; v. 59, December, 1976. © 1969, 1976 The American Association of Teachers of Spanish and Portuguese, Inc. Both reproduced by permission—*Hispanic Journal,* v. 3, fall, 1981; v. 9, spring, 1988; v. 20, fall, 1999. Copyright © 1981, 1988, 1999 IUP Indiana University of Pennsylvania. All reproduced by permission.—*Hispanofila,* v. 64, 1978; v. 142, September, 2004. All reproduced by permission.—*The Journal of Narrative Technique,* v. 17, winter, 1987. Copyright © 1987 by *The Journal of Narrative Technique.* Reproduced by permission.—*Letras Peninsulares,* v. 11, fall, 1998. Copyright © 1998 *Letras Peninsulares.* Reproduced by permission.—*Literature Interpretation Theory,* v. 13, 2002 for "The Riddle of/in *Pale Fire*" by Neil D. Isaacs. Copyright © 2002 Taylor & Francis. Reproduced by permission of Taylor & Francis Group, LLC., http://www.taylorandfrancis.com and the author.—*Modern Drama,* v. 7, February, 1965; v. 21, June, 1978; v. 22, June, 1979. Copyright © 1965, 1978, 1979 by the University of Toronto, Graduate Centre for Study of Drama. All reproduced by permission.—*Nottingham French Studies,* v. 17, May, 1978. Copyright © The University of Nottingham 1978. Reproduced by permission.—*Papers on Language and Literature,* v. 4, spring, 1968. Copyright © 1968 by The Board of Trustees, Southern Illinois University at Edwardsville. Reproduced by permission.—*Revista Canadiense de Estudios Hispánicos,* v. 5, winter, 1981 for "The Antithesis between Religion and Nature in *Los pazos de Ulloa*: A Different Perspective" by R. C. Boland. Reproduced by permission of the publisher and author.—*Romance Quarterly,* v. 39, May, 1992. Copyright © 1992 by Helen Dwight Reid Educational Foundation. Reproduced with permission of the Helen Dwight Reid Educational Foundation, published by Heldref Publications, 1319 18th Street, NW, Washington, DC 20036-1802.—*Studies in American Fiction,* v. 4, autumn, 1976. Copyright © 1976 Northeastern University. Reproduced by permission.—*Symposium,* v. 43, summer, 1989. Copyright © 1989 by Helen Dwight Reid Educational Foundation. Reproduced with permission of the Helen Dwight Reid Educational Foundation, published by Heldref Publications, 1319 18th Street, NW, Washington, DC 20036-1802.—*Texas Studies in Literature and Language,* v. 26, winter, 1984 for "The Author as Reader as Nabokov: Text and Pretext in *Pale Fire*" by John Haegert. Copyright © 1984 by the University of Texas Press. Reproduced by permission of the publisher and author.

COPYRIGHTED MATERIAL IN *TCLC*, VOLUME 189, WAS REPRODUCED FROM THE FOLLOWING BOOKS:

Boyd, Brian. From *Nabokov's* **Pale Fire:** *The Magic of Artistic Discovery.* Princeton University Press, 1999. Copyright © 1999 by Brian Boyd. Reprinted by permission of Princeton University Press.—Couturier, Maurice. From "The Near-Tyranny of the Author: *Pale Fire*," in **Nabokov and His Fiction: New Perspectives.** Edited by Julian W. Connolly. Cambridge University Press, 1999. Copyright © 1999 Cambridge University Press. Reprinted with the permission of Cambridge University Press.—Edelstein, Marilyn. From "*Pale Fire*: The Art of Consciousness," in **Nabokov's Fifth Arc: Nabokov and Others on His Life's Work.** Edited by J. E. Rivers and Charles Nicol. University of Texas Press, 1982. Copyright © 1982 by the University of Texas Press. All rights reserved. Reproduced by permission of the University of Texas Press.—

Thomson Gale Literature Product Advisory Board

Arthur Adamov
1908-1970

(Full name Arthur Sourenovitch Adamov) Russian-born French playwright, essayist, editor, and translator.

The following entry provides an overview of Adamov's life and works. For additional information on his career, see *CLC*, Volumes 4 and 25.

INTRODUCTION

Arthur Adamov is recognized as an important and influential figure in modern French drama. Along with Eugène Ionesco and Samuel Beckett, he helped shape the Theater of the Absurd movement in France during the 1950s and 1960s. Many of the psychological themes that recur in Adamov's plays, such as human isolation, self-destruction, and the inevitability of death, have been connected with the playwright's own neuroses and obsessions. His dramatic works, characterized by a bleak and nightmarish atmosphere, were often difficult to produce because of their reliance on strong visual imagery and unusual physical objects on stage to communicate meaning to audiences. Although Adamov was considered a pioneer of Absurdist Theater, he eventually rejected his own early plays in favor of a more politically engaged drama, one that blended contemporary social concerns with the psychological and existential themes of his earlier work. Adamov's literary career was ultimately eclipsed by the more popular plays of Ionesco and Beckett, and as a result he never experienced sustained critical and popular acclaim during his lifetime. In recent years, however, scholars have praised him as an innovative and influential figure in the development of twentieth-century theater.

BIOGRAPHICAL INFORMATION

Adamov was born August 23, 1908, in Kislovodsk, Russia. At the beginning of World War I he moved with his parents, Helene Bagaturov Adamov and Sourene Adamov, a wealthy businessman, to Geneva, Switzerland. After the Russian revolution the Soviet Union confiscated the Adamov estate. This left the family impoverished and forced them to sell off their personal belongings to survive. In 1922 they moved to Wiesbaden, Germany, and Adamov began taking classes at the International French Lycée at Mainz. Two years later the family relocated to Paris, where Adamov attended high

school at the Lycée Lakanal and encountered several young artists and writers, including André Breton and Alberto Giacometti. Many of the artists he mingled with during the 1920s and 1930s had begun questioning traditional modes of expression and experimenting with new forms of art, such as Surrealism. Antonin Artaud, who emphasized the metaphysical significance of drama, was among the most influential of these artists. From an early age, Adamov suffered from anxiety and self-destructive tendencies. When he was twenty, he attempted suicide. His life was also filled with personal tragedy: his father committed suicide in 1933, and his mother died from tuberculosis in 1942. Although he was not actively involved with the French Resistance, Adamov was interned by the Nazis during World War II.

Although Adamov had experimented with poetry early in his literary career, his first publication was an autobiographical work titled *L'aveu* (1946; partially translated as *The Endless Humiliation*). In the late 1940s Adamov began writing plays, and in 1950 his first original dramas—*La grande et la petite manoeuvre* and *L'invasion* (*The Invasion*)—were produced in Paris. In 1952 *La parodie* was performed on stage at the Théâtre Lancry. With the production of these plays, Adamov emerged as one of the pioneers of Absurdist Theater in France. He produced several more Absurdist plays before writing *Le professeur Taranne* (1953; *Professor Taranne*), a transitional work that sent his literary career in a new direction. Influenced by the more politically engaged work of playwright Bertolt Brecht, Adamov became increasingly frustrated with his early plays and with Absurdist Theater in general. He turned his attentions to social issues in such later plays as *Le ping-pong* (1955), *Paolo Paoli* (1957), and *Le printemps 71* (1963; *Spring 71*). In the late 1960s Adamov began incorporating both political and psychological elements in his plays, a synthesis which many critics consider his greatest contribution to the theater. Such works as *Off Limits* (1969) and his last play, *Si l'été revenait* (1972), were representative of this period in his theatrical career. Adamov did not live to see his final play produced. On March 15, 1970, he committed suicide by ingesting an overdose of barbiturates.

MAJOR WORKS

Professor Taranne is considered the most significant of Adamov's early plays, and the first in which he began moving away from the mechanical language and characterization of his purely Absurdist works. According to Adamov, the play was a direct transcription of one of his nightmares. The action begins when the police accuse the protagonist, Professor Taranne, of undressing in front of a group of children on the beach. He denies the accusations on the basis that he is a known and respected university professor. When no one can confirm his story, the professor's identity is called into question. Through the use of subtle set changes, the scene shifts, and Professor Taranne is once again questioned, this time in his hotel room. In addition to the dominant themes of self-destruction, fear, and the quest for identity, the play explores the issues of isolation, futility, and the nature of existence. The professor's repeated attempts to assert his identity and defend his reputation are thwarted by several characters; he even receives a letter from the university accusing him of plagiarism and posing as another scholar named Professor Menard. As with several of Adamov's other plays, *Professor Taranne* utilizes a failure of communication to create a nightmarish atmosphere and sense of hopelessness for the main character. The professor's attempts to assert his innocence are ineffectual and his isolation complete. The play ends ambiguously—in the final scene, the professor slowly undresses as the curtain falls. The image alludes to the initial accusation of exhibitionism raised against Taranne and casts doubt on his character. Scholars have noted that *Professor Taranne* is one of the first of Adamov's plays to employ a fully realized, three-dimensional main character.

Of Adamov's later plays, *Le ping-pong* is his best known and most commercially successful. The focal point of the play is a visual object, a pinball machine that is located in Madame Duranty's café. The machine not only occupies the visual focus of the stage but draws the attention and energies of the characters, as well. The lives of Arthur, an art student, and Victor, a medical student, along with several other characters, revolve around the pinball machine, and they dedicate their resources to its governing consortium. Arthur eventually takes over the consortium, while Victor continues his studies and becomes a physician. Many years later, Arthur and Victor meet again and play a game of ping-pong. The game progresses and becomes increasingly chaotic as the friends invent new rules. They stop using paddles and hit the ball with their hands. As the pace of the game quickens, Victor dies suddenly from the exertion. Many critics consider Adamov's characterization of the pinball consortium a harsh critique of capitalism. The degenerative power of materialism is another significant theme in *Le ping-pong* The obsession that the characters exhibit for material objects, and their desire for monetary gain exist at the cost of authentic relationships. Indeed, the ping-pong game itself becomes Adamov's vision of a materialistic and corrupted society.

Adamov's final play, *Si l'été revenait*, is set in Stockholm and relates the dreams of four interconnected characters: Lars, the protagonist; his wife, Brit; his sister, Thea, with whom he is incestuously involved; and a hermaphrodite named Alma who first introduced Lars and Brit. The four dreams reveal the complex relationships between the characters and, in particular, the failings of Lars as a husband and brother. As each character dreams, the other characters act out hidden meanings of their subconscious visions. As in his other plays, Adamov uses a significant visual object on stage to convey meaning. A seesaw occupies part of the stage and symbolizes, according to some scholars, the instability and ambivalence of the relationships between the dreamers. Other critics have interpreted the image as connoting a desire for balance in human affairs. *Si l'été revenait* was completed just a few months before Adamov committed suicide and is often considered an expression of his despair and sense of failure as a playwright.

CRITICAL RECEPTION

Critics often note the difficulty in assessing Adamov's place in French literature because his work, even in his more socially and politically engaged plays, is so closely linked to the personal obsessions and neuroses of the author himself. According to most commentators, it is nearly impossible to comprehend meaning in Adamov's plays without an understanding of the playwright's own psyche. For this reason, Adamov has been faulted for failing to transcend the subjective and translate the personal into truly universal literature. Critics have also disagreed over the ultimate success of Adamov's inventive use of the physical and visual elements of the stage to reflect theme and convey meaning. While some have complained that his interest in objects, gestures, and symbols overpower the role of dialogue and action in his plays, others, such as John J. McCann, have discerned a more unifying effect, claiming that this is perhaps Adamov's greatest contribution to the modern stage.

Although his contemporaries Beckett and Ionesco have eclipsed him as the major playwrights of the French Absurdist theater, critics today still regard Adamov as a significant and influential figure of the period. As many scholars note, in his greatest works, including *Professor Taranne, Le ping-pong* and *Si l'été revenait*, Adamov managed to restrain his hermeticism and present dramas of universal power. In these, as well as his more accomplished "social" plays, such as *Paolo Paoli, Spring 71,* and *Off Limits,* Adamov succeeded in depicting the complexity of reality and the existential, social, and political dilemmas of the human condition.

PRINCIPAL WORKS

*L'aveu (autobiography) 1946

La mort de Danton [adaptor; from the play *Danton's Tod* by Georg Büchner] (play) 1948

La grande et la petite manoeuvre (play) 1950

L'invasion [*The Invasion*] (play) 1950

La parodie (play) 1952

Le professeur Taranne [*Professor Taranne*] (play) 1953

Le sens de la marche (play) 1953

Théâtre I (plays) 1953

Tous contre tous (play) 1953

Comme nous avons été (play) 1954

Auguste Strindberg, dramaturge [with Maurice Gravier] (criticism) 1955

Le ping-pong (play) 1955

Théâtre II (plays) 1955

Paolo Paoli [*Paolo Paoli: The Years of the Butterfly*] (play) 1957

Les ames mortes (play) 1960

La politique des restes [*Scavengers*] (play) 1963

Le printemps 71 [*Spring 71*] (play) 1963

Ici et maintenant (autobiography) 1964

Théâtre III (plays) 1966

L'homme et l'enfant [*Man and Child*] (autobiography) 1968

M. le Modéré (play) 1968

Théâtre IV (plays) 1968

Off Limits (play) 1969

Si l'été revenait (play) 1972

*This work was partially translated into English as *The Endless Humiliation*.

CRITICISM

Martin Esslin (essay date 1961)

SOURCE: Esslin, Martin. "Arthur Adamov: The Curable and the Incurable." In *The Theatre of the Absurd*, pp. 92-127. New York: Vintage Books, 2001.

[*In the following essay, originally published in 1961, Esslin discusses Adamov's existential vision of life—specifically his belief in "the futility of human endeavor"—and traces his development as a playwright.*]

Arthur Adamov, the author of some of the most powerful plays in the Theatre of the Absurd, later rejected all his work that might be classified under that heading. The development that led him toward this type of drama, however, and the development that led him away from it again, are of particular interest to any inquiry into its nature. Adamov, who was not only a remarkable dramatist but also a remarkable thinker, has provided us with a well-documented case history of the preoccupations and obsessions that made him write plays depicting a senseless and brutal nightmare world, the theoretical considerations that led him to formulate an aesthetic of the absurd, and, finally, the process by which he gradually returned to a theatre based on reality, the representation of social conditions, and a definite social purpose. How did it happen that a dramatist who in the late nineteen-forties so thoroughly rejected the naturalistic theatre that to use even the name of a town that could actually be found on a map would have appeared to him as 'unspeakably vulgar' could by 1960 be engaged in writing a full-scale historical drama firmly situated in place and time—the Paris Commune of 1871?

Arthur Adamov, born in Kislovodsk, in the Caucasus, in 1908, the son of a wealthy oil-well proprietor of Armenian origin, left Russia at the age of four. His parents could afford to travel, and, like the children of many well-to-do Russian families, Adamov was brought up in France, a fact that explains his mastery of French literary style. The first book he ever read was Balzac's *Eugénie Grandet,* at the age of seven. The outbreak of the First World War found Adamov's family at Freudenstadt, a resort in the Black Forest. It was only through the special intervention of the King of Württemberg, who was acquainted with Adamov's father, that the family escaped internment as enemy citizens, and were given special permission to leave for Switzerland, where they settled in Geneva.

Adamov received his early education in Switzerland and later in Germany (at Mainz). In 1924, at the age of sixteen, he went to Paris and was drawn into Surrealist circles. He wrote Surrealist poetry, edited an avant-garde periodical, *Discontinuité,* became a friend of Paul Eluard, and led the life of the Parisian nonconformists.

Gradually he stopped writing, or at least stopped publishing what he had written. He himself later described the severe spiritual and psychological crisis that he went through in a small book that must be among the most terrifying and ruthless documents of self-revelation in world literature, *L'Aveu* (*The Confession*). The earliest section of this Dostoevskian masterpiece, dated 'Paris, 1938', opens with a brilliant statement of the metaphysical anguish that forms the basis of Existentialist literature and of the Theatre of the Absurd:

> What is there? I know first of all that I am. But who am I? All I know of myself is that I suffer. And if I suffer it is because at the origin of myself there is mutilation, separation.
>
> I am separated. What I am separated from—I cannot name it. But I am separated.

In a footnote Adamov adds, 'Formerly it was called God. Today it no longer has any name.'[1]

A deep sense of alienation, the feeling that time weighs on him 'with its enormous liquid mass, with all its dark power',[2] a deep feeling of passivity—these are some of the symptoms of his spiritual sickness.

> Everything happens as though I were only one of the particular existences of some great incomprehensible and central being. . . . Sometimes this great totality of life appears to me so dramatically beautiful that it plunges me into ecstasy. But more often it seems like a monstrous beast that penetrates and surpasses me and which is everywhere, within me and outside me. . . . And terror grips and envelops me more powerfully from moment to moment. . . . My only way out is to write, to make others aware of it, so as not to have to feel all of it alone, to get rid of however small a portion of it.[3]

It is in dreams and in prayer that the writer of this haunting confession seeks escape—in dreams that are 'the great silent movement of the soul through the night'[4]; in prayer that is the 'desperate need of man, immersed in time, to seek refuge in the only entity that could save him, the projection outward from himself of that in him which partakes of eternity'.[5] Yet what is there to pray to? 'The name of God should no longer come from the mouth of man. This word that has so long been degraded by usage no longer means anything. . . . To use the word God is more than sloth, it is a refusal to think, a kind of short cut, a hideous shorthand. . . .'[6] Thus the crisis of faith is also a crisis of language. 'The words in our ageing vocabularies are like very sick people. Some may be able to survive, others are incurable.'[7]

In the next section of *L'Aveu,* dated 'Paris, 1939' (it has been published in English, under the title ***The endless humiliation***)[8] Adamov gives a ruthlessly frank description of his own sickness, his desire to be humiliated by the lowest of prostitutes, his 'incapacity to complete the act of carnal possession'.[9] Fully aware of the nature of his neurosis—he was well versed in modern psychology and even translated one of Jung's works into French[10]—Adamov was also aware of the *value* of neurosis, which 'grants its victim a peracute lucidity, inaccessible to the so-called normal man',[11] and which may thus give him the vision that 'permits him, through the singularity of his sickness, to accede to the great general laws by which the loftiest comprehension of the world is expressed. And since the particular is always a symbolic expression of the universal, it follows that the universal is most effectively symbolized by the extreme of the particular, so that the neurosis which exaggerates a man's particularity of vision defines that much more completely his universal significance.'[12]

Having given a brutally detailed description, itself a symptom of masochism by the violence of its self-humiliation, of his neurosis, with its obsessions, rites, and automatisms, Adamov returns to a diagnosis of our epoch in a section entitled 'Le temps de l'ignominie'. He defines ignominy as that which has no name, the *unnamable,* and the poet's task is not only to call each thing by its name but also to 'denounce . . . the degenerated concepts, the dried-up abstractions that have usurped . . . the dead remnants of the old sacred names'.[13] The degradation of language in our time becomes the expression of its deepest sickness. What has been lost is the sense of the sacred, 'the unfathomable wisdom of the myths and rites of the dead old world'.[14]

The disappearance of meaning in the world is clearly linked to the degradation of language, and both, in turn, to the loss of faith, the disappearance of sacred rites and sacred myths. But perhaps this degradation and despair are necessary steps toward a renewal: 'Perhaps the sad and empty language that today's flabby humanity pours forth, will, in all its horror, in all its boundless absurdity, re-echo in the heart of a solitary man who is awake, and then perhaps that man, suddenly realizing that he does not understand, will begin to understand.'[15] Therefore the only task left to man is to tear off all that dead skin until 'he finds himself in the hour of the great nakedness.'[16]

In this document of ruthless self-revelation, Adamov outlined a whole philosophy of the Theatre of the Absurd, long before he started to write his first play.

In the pages of *L'Aveu,* we can follow him through the war years—still in Paris in May and June 1940; in Cassis in July; in Marseille by August; then, between December 1940 and November 1941, at the internment camp of Agelès, months passed in a stupor of dejection; back in Marseille at the end of 1941; returning to Paris in the last month of 1942. The last section of *L'Aveu* and the preface are dated 1943.

In reading this astonishing book, we are witnessing a mind laying the foundations of its salvation through self-examination and a merciless recognition of its own predicament. In his contributions to the short-lived literary review *L'Heure Nouvelle,* of which he became editor shortly after the end of the war in Europe, Adamov returned to the same themes, but already in a spirit of detachment, in the posture of a thinker called upon, at a great turning point in history, to work out a programme of action for a new beginning in a new epoch.

It is a programme characterized by a complete absence of illusions and easy solutions: 'We are accused of pessimism, as though pessimism were but one among a number of possible attitudes, as if man were capable of choosing between two alternatives—optimism and pessimism.'[17] Such a programme would of necessity be destructive in its rejection of all existing dogmatisms. It insists on the artist's duty to avoid selecting just one aspect of the world—'religious, psychological, scientific, social—but to evoke behind each of these the shadow of the whole in which they must merge.'[18] And again this search for wholeness, for the reality underlying the bewildering multiplicity of appearances, is seen as a search for the sacred: 'the crisis of our time is essentially a religious crisis. It is a matter of life or death.'[19] Yet the concept of God is dead. We are on the threshold of an era of impersonal aspects of the absolute, hence the revival of creeds like Taoism and Buddhism. This is the tragic impasse in which modern man finds himself: 'From whatever point he starts, whatever path he follows, modern man comes to the same conclusion: behind its visible appearances, life hides a meaning that is eternally inaccessible to penetration by the spirit that seeks for its discovery, caught in the dilemma of being aware that it is impossible to find it, and yet also impossible to renounce the hopeless quest.'[20] Adamov points out that this is not, strictly speaking, a philosophy of the absurd, because it still presupposes the conviction that the world *has* a meaning, although it is of necessity outside the reach of human consciousness. The awareness that there may be a meaning but that it will never be found is tragic. Any conviction that the world is wholly absurd would lack this tragic element.

In the social and political sphere, Adamov finds the solution in Communism. But his is a very personal form of support for the Communist cause. He finds in Communism no supernatural, sacred element. Its ideology confines itself to purely human terms, and for him it remains open to question 'whether anything that confines itself to the human sphere could ever attain anything but the subhuman.'[21] If this is the case, why support Communism?

> If we turn to Communism nevertheless, it is merely because one day, when it will seem quite close to the realization of its highest aim—the victory over all the contradictions that impede the exchange of goods among men—it will meet, inevitably, the great 'no' of the nature of things, which it thought it could ignore in its struggle. When the material obstacles are overcome, when man will no longer be able to deceive himself as to the nature of his unhappiness, then there will arise an anxiety all the more powerful, all the more fruitful for being stripped of anything that might have hindered its realization. It goes without saying that such a purely negative hope does not seem to us to entail an adherence that, to be complete, would have to manifest itself in action.[22]

This was Adamov's position in 1946. Later, largely as a consequence of the emergence of General de Gaulle after the events of May 1958, he took a more active line in support of the extreme Left. Yet when asked in 1960 whether he had changed his attitude since 1946, Adamov confirmed that he still subscribed to what he had written fourteen years earlier.

It was towards the end of the Second World War that Adamov began to write for the theatre. He was reading Strindberg at the time, and under the influence of Strindberg's plays, notably *A Dream Play,* he began to discover the stuff of drama all around him, in 'the most ordinary everyday happenings, particularly street scenes. What struck me above all were the lines of passers-by, their loneliness in the crowd, the terrifying diversity of their utterance, of which I would please myself by hearing only snatches that, linked with other snatches of conversation, seemed to grow into a composite entity the very fragmentariness of which became a guarantee of its symbolic truth.'[23] One day he witnessed a scene that confronted him, in a sudden flash, with the dramatic reality he had wanted to express. A blind beggar passed by two pretty girls singing a refrain from some popular song: 'I had closed my eyes, it was wonderful!' This gave him the idea of showing 'on the stage, as crudely and as visibly as possible, the loneliness of man, the absence of communication'.[24]

La Parodie, Adamov's first play, is the fruit of this idea. In a succession of rapidly sketched scenes, it shows two men infatuated with the same empty-headed, commonplace girl, Lili. One of them, the 'employee', is brisk, businesslike, and ever optimistic, while the other, 'N', is passive, helpless, and despondent. The employee, who, in a chance meeting, has gained the wholly erroneous impression that he has a date with Lili, never loses his hope and constantly turns up at imagined rendezvous. N, on the other hand, spends his time lying in the street, waiting for Lili to pass by chance. In the end the optimistic, buoyant attitude of the employee and the abject passivity of N lead to precisely the same result— nothing. Lili cannot even tell her two rival suitors apart. The employee lands in prison, where he goes on making plans for the future and still hopes to maintain his position, although he has gone blind. N is run over by a car and swept into the garbage by the street-cleaners. Lili is flanked by relatively successful men—a journalist with whom she seems in love and who keeps her waiting when they have a date, and the editor of his paper, who treats her as his kept mistress. The editor also takes the place, as and when the action requires it, of a number of other persons in authority—the manager of a restaurant, the director of a firm for which the employee works as a salesman, the receptionist of a hotel where he fails to get a room. While N and the employee are seen, as it were, from their own point of view, the journalist and the editor are seen wholly from the outside, as 'the other people', who, inexplicably, seem to be able to master the human situation, to whom nothing calamitous ever happens. Two identical and interchangeable couples act as a kind of chorus, the faceless crowd that surrounds us; they age as the action proceeds, but remain anonymous and interchangeable throughout.

Time is constantly evoked: the characters keep on asking each other the time without ever receiving an answer. A clock without hands is a recurring feature of the décor. The action of time is also illustrated by the gradual shrinkage of space. A dance hall shown in the beginning appears again in scene II—but now the set has become much narrower.

At one point, N is shown with a prostitute whom he begs to humiliate him. As Adamov himself has pointed out, *La Parodie* served to justify his own attitude: 'Even if I am like N, I shall not be punished any more than the employee.'[25] Buoyant activity is as pointless as cringing apathy and self-humiliation.

La Parodie is an attempt to come to terms with neurosis, to make psychological states visible in concrete terms. As Adamov defines it in the introduction to the first edition, the performance of a play of this type is 'the projection into the world of sensations of states of mind and images that constitute its hidden content. A stage play ought to be the point of intersection between the visible and invisible worlds, or, in other words, the display, the manifestation of the hidden, latent contents that form the shell around the seeds of drama.'[26]

In its determined rejection of individuality in favour of schematic types—in which it resembles German Expressionist drama—*La Parodie* represents a revolt against the complexities of the psychological theatre. It is a deliberate return to primitivism. Adamov does not want to represent the world, he wants to parody it. 'When I arraign the world around me, I often reproach it for being nothing more than a parody. But the sickness I admit to—is it anything more than a parody?'[27] Parody is direct, harsh, and oversimplified. *La Parodie* deliberately eschews all subtleties of plot, characterization, or language. This is a theatre of gesture—N lying in the road, the employee bustling about, the interchangeable couples going through the motions of human existence without being recognizable individuals.

Adamov felt that, having parodied the world in such simple terms, he had reached a dead end. In his next play, *L'Invasion,* he took the first steps toward portraying real characters in real human relationships. The isolated, lonely individuals of *La Parodie* are replaced by a family. It is still a family composed of lonely individuals, unable to communicate. But they are strongly linked together nevertheless—curiously enough, by a shared loyalty to a dead hero.

This hero is a dead writer, Jean, who has left an enormous mass of undeciphered papers to his friend and disciple, Pierre, the husband of the dead man's sister Agnes. The apartment where they live, together with Pierre's mother, is in a state of complete disorder, which expresses the disorder reigning in the minds of the char-acters. The task of deciphering Jean's literary remains is an impossible one. His writing is not only illegible but the characters themselves have faded. One can never know what he really wrote, and there is a constant danger that the literary executor will simply invent what he thinks the master ought to have written. And even if a scrap of paper, a single sentence, is finally deciphered, it still must be placed in the context of the vast mass of disordered papers.

There is another disciple of Jean's who tries to help, Tradel, but he is suspect precisely because he tends to read things into Jean's writing. The disorder within the room where the action takes place is matched by the disorder of the whole country: immigrants are streaming across the frontiers, the social structure is disintegrating. In the second act the disorder in the room, now cluttered up with furniture, has increased. Pierre finds it ever more difficult to understand the meaning of the manuscripts. A man who is looking for someone in the apartment next door enters and strikes up a conversation with Agnes. He is 'the first one who comes along' with whom Agnes will run away. In the third act, this man has become a fixture in the room, and Pierre wants to retire to his own private den downstairs to work in peace. Agnes duly leaves him and goes off with the 'first one who comes along'. In act IV the room has been cleaned up, the papers are neatly stacked. Order has also returned in the country. Pierre has decided to give up his work. He begins to tear up the manuscripts. Agnes appears—she wants to borrow the typewriter. Her lover is ill, she is unable to manage his business. Pierre, who has gone down to his den, is found there by Tradel; he is dead.

L'Invasion is a play about the hopeless search for meaning, the quest for a message that will make sense in a jumble of undecipherable papers; but it is concerned with order and disorder in society as well as in the family. It almost seems that Agnes stands for disorder. Has Pierre, in marrying her, not at the same time married her dead brother with his confused manuscripts? When she leaves, order returns, and disorder and business failure enter the household of the man whose mistress she has become. Yet when Pierre abandons his work on the manuscripts, he dies. He loses Agnes to the first man who comes along because he is withdrawing more and more from human contact. The disorder that Agnes brings also represents the bewildering nature of reality and of relationships with other human beings, which Pierre is unable to cope with. He withdraws from contact with others, because he finds communication more and more difficult. Language is disintegrating before his eyes: 'Why does one say, "It happens?" Who is that "it", what does it want from me? Why does one say "on the ground" rather than "at" or "over"? I have lost too much time thinking about these things. What I want is not the meaning of words, but their volume and their moving body. I shall no longer search for anything. . . . I'll wait in silence, motionless.'[28]

Pierre begs his mother, who will bring him his food in his den, never to speak to him—a sign of his complete withdrawal. It is when he abandons his attitude of withdrawal, when he decides that he wants to lead a life like everybody else, that he learns that Agnes has left him. 'She left too late, or too soon. Had she had a little more patience, we could have started all over again,'[29] he says, and returns to his den—to die, just missing Agnes, who comes to ask 'to borrow the typewriter', yet is clearly begging to be taken back. But Pierre's mother does not, or does not want to, understand, and fails to call Pierre upstairs.

Here the tragedy turns on a misunderstanding. Had Pierre's mother not taken Agnes's demand for the typewriter literally, rather than as a symbolic request to be taken back and participate in the work of the family, Pierre might not have died rejected and unloved. Adamov has described how he thought that he had found an important new dramatic device—indirect dialogue, the characters' oblique reference to the subject under discussion, since they cannot find the courage to display their feelings openly and thereby expose themselves to tragic misunderstandings. Later he realized that he had merely reinvented a technique already used by other dramatists, notably by Chekhov.

L'Invasion is a haunting play. André Gide was deeply impressed by it; he felt that it dealt with the greatness of a dead writer and the process by which his influence and power gradually fade away—surely a curious misunderstanding on the part of the venerable old man of letters, applying the conceptions of his own generation to the works of a new age. To a contemporary reader, the most striking feature of *L'Invasion* is precisely the unreality of the dead hero, the fact that his much vaunted message is essentially meaningless—absurd.

Jean Vilar, the great French director, who had produced Adamov's adaptation of Büchner's *Danton's Death* at the Avignon Festival of 1948, saw *L'Invasion* with the eyes of a contemporary. He praised Adamov for renouncing 'the lace ornaments of dialogue and intrigue, for having given back to the drama its stark purity'[30] of clear and simple stage symbols. He contrasted this stark modern theatre with that of Claudel, 'which borrows its effect from the alcohols of faith and the grand word'[31] and, posing the alternatives Adamov or Claudel, clearly answered—Adamov.

Gide's and Vilar's tributes to Adamov, together with comments by other distinguished literary and stage figures like René Char, Jacques Prévert, and Roger Blin, are contained in the slim volume in which Adamov, having failed to get them performed on the stage, presented his first two plays to the reading public in the spring of 1950. The response to this publication had the desired effect; on 14 November, 1950, *L'Invasion,* directed by Jean Vilar, opened at the Studio des Champs-Elysées. Three days earlier, Adamov's third play, *La Grande et la Petite Manœuvre,* had been presented at the Théâtre des Noctambules, directed by another of the outstanding pioneers of the French avant-garde, Jean-Marie Serreau, and with Roger Blin in the leading part.

Adamov himself has explained the title of *La Grande et la Petite Manœuvre* as referring to the small manoeuvre of the social disorder depicted in the play, in contrast to the large manoeuvre of the human condition itself, which envelops and dwarfs the former,[32] the word 'manoeuvre' in this context having a double military and psychological sense.

La Grande et la Petite Manœuvre combines the theme of the parallel lives of *La Parodie* with that of the social and political disorders in the background of *L'Invasion.* The active, self-sacrificing struggle of a revolutionary leader is shown to be as futile as the passivity of a tormented victim of hidden psychological forces, who is compelled to execute the shouted orders of invisible monitors who drive him to the gradual loss of all his limbs. The action takes place in a country oppressed by a brutal dictatorship. The active character, *le militant,* leads the victorious struggle against the forces of the police state; in the end he collapses while making a speech admitting that the revolutionaries have been compelled to use methods of brutal terror to gain their victory. Moreover, the *militant* has caused the death of his own child, because the disorders he himself had provoked made it impossible for the doctor to reach its sickbed. Once again the activist has achieved no more than the passive character, *le mutilé,* who, a legless, armless cripple, on a pushcart, is kicked into the road by the woman he adores, to be crushed in the crowd.

The *mutilé,* who must obey the orders of the voices that compel him to put his hands into the machine that will cut them off, to walk in front of the car that will run him over, is clearly the chief character in the play, embodying the author's own attitude. His mutilations, like the deaths of N and Pierre in the earlier plays, are the direct outcome, and the expression, of his inability to make human contact, his incapacity for love. He himself says that if he could live with a woman and have a child by her, the voices of his monitors would lose their power over him[33]; the accidents in which he loses limb after limb usually follow his repeated failures to hold the affection of the woman he loves, Erna, who at times suggests that she really cares for him, while at others she appears to be merely spying on him on behalf of a secret-police agent who is her lover.

Adamov himself has interpreted the play, which is based on a particularly vivid and terrifying dream, as an attempt to justify himself for his failure to take a more active part in the political struggle of the Left. To the outside observer, this may seem an incomplete account of the complex content of *La Grande et la Petite Manœuvre*. The play not only argues (as Adamov later believed, unfairly) that the efforts of the revolutionary to eliminate political terror are vain because all power is ultimately based on the exercise of brute force; it also shows, very graphically, that there is an essential similarity between the activist fighter for justice and the passive slave of the irrational forces of his own subconscious mind. The categorical imperative that forces the *militant* to risk his life, to leave his wife in fear and trembling and ultimately to cause the death of his sick child, is shown as springing, basically, from the same inability to love as the implacable self-destructive commands of the subconscious mind that force the *mutilé* into masochistic self-destruction. The aggressive impulses of the *militant* are merely the reverse side of the *mutilé*'s aggression against himself.

The very ambivalence of possible interpretations is an indication of the power of *La Grande et la Petite Manœuvre* as a dramatic projection of an intense and tormented experience of fundamental human dilemmas. This play also shows Adamov in full command of the technical resources he needed to put his ideas into practice. The action not only moves forward in a succession of effectively contrasted scenes that follow each other with the flow of cinematic montage, it is also a perfect realization of Adamov's conception that the theatre should be able to translate ideas and psychological realities into simple and concrete images, so that 'the manifestation of . . . content should literally, concretely, *corporally* coincide with that content itself.'[34] This leads to a shift of emphasis from the language of drama toward visible action. The language of the play ceases to be the main vehicle of poetry, as it is in the theatre of Claudel, with which Vilar contrasted Adamov's work. As Adamov defines this shift, 'It is in this growth of gesture in its own right . . . that I see the emergence of a dimension to which language by itself would be unable to do justice, but, in turn, when language is carried along by the rhythm of bodily action that has become autonomous, the most ordinary, everyday speech will regain a power that might still be called poetry, but that I shall be content merely to call functionally effective.'[35] In *La Grande et la Petite Manœuvre* the transmutation of content into visible, literal outward expression is completely realized.

The instrument he had perfected seemed available to Adamov to be used at will. Its only drawback was the narrowness of its field of application; there are relatively few basic human situations that can be expressed in such simple and general terms. Yet while his next

play, *Le Sens de la Marche* (*The Direction of the March*), contains many of the elements and themes of its predecessors, Adamov again succeeded in finding a new expression for his basic preoccupation, while introducing an important new element indicating his progress in mastering his obsessions. In *Le Sens de la Marche,* the hero for the first time refuses to submit, and counterattacks. That action may not be directed against the real author of his troubles, but it is an action nevertheless. The hero, Henri, the son of a tyrannical father, goes through a number of episodes in which he confronts that father figure in a whole series of incarnations: in the commanding officer of the barracks where he goes for his military service, in the leader of a religious sect whose daughter is his fiancée for a time, in the headmaster of a school where he becomes a teacher. He submits to all these, but when he returns to his old home and finds his dead father's sinister *masseur* installed as the domestic tyrant and lover of his sister, he strangles him. As Adamov has pointed out, the idea from which he started was that 'in this life of which the basic circumstances themselves are terrifying, where the same situations fatally recur, all we can do is destroy, and too late at that, what we consider, mistakenly, to be the real obstacle, but what in fact is merely the last item in a maleficent series.'[36] This is a very original idea, and it is most imaginatively realized. Some of the themes of earlier plays recur, such as the revolutionaries, who are again unsuccessful; the hero's inability to love; and the sister figure.

Adamov was dissatisfied with *Le Sens de la Marche* and had put it aside for a while when another dream presented him not only with an idea for a play but with an entire, almost ready-made play itself. And this play, *Le Professeur Taranne,* became a turning point in Adamov's development.

The professor of the title is accused of indecent exposure on a beach. He denies the allegation by indignantly pointing out that he is a distinguished scholar who has even been invited to lecture abroad, in Belgium. But the more he protests his innocence, the more deeply he becomes involved in contradictions that make his guilt more probable. A lady who comes into the police station seems to recognize him, she addresses him as Professor—but she has taken him for another professor, Menard, whom Taranne superficially resembles. The scene changes to the hotel where he is staying. Again Taranne is accused of an offence, that of having left litter in a bathing cabin at the seaside. He protests that he did not undress in a cabin at all—and thus confirms the earlier allegation. The policemen produce a notebook that has been found. Taranne eagerly recognizes it as his, but is unable to read the handwriting. What is more, the notebook consists mostly of empty pages, although Taranne insists that he had used it up entirely. A roll of paper is delivered to the professor—it is the seating plan of the dining-room of an ocean liner, with his place marked at the table of honour. Jeanne, a woman relative or secretary, brings a letter that has arrived for the professor. It is from Belgium, from the rector of the University. This will confirm Taranne's claims! But in fact it is an angry refusal to invite him again. His lectures have been found to have been plagiarisms of those of the famous professor Menard. Taranne remains alone. He hangs the seating plan of the liner's dining-room on a hook on the wall—it is a perfectly blank piece of paper. Slowly the professor begins to undress, performing the very act of indecent exposure of which he was accused at the beginning. Having been exposed as a fraud, he exposes himself. It is the nightmare of man trying to hold on to his identity, unable to establish conclusive proof of it.

In his dream, which the play transcribes as it was dreamed, without any attempt to 'give it a general meaning, to prove anything',[37] everything that happens to Taranne happened to Adamov himself, the only difference being that instead of shouting, 'I am Professor Taranne,' he exclaimed, 'I am the author of *La Parodie*!'[38]

Adamov considered *Le Professeur Taranne* of particular importance in his progress as a playwright. In transcribing an actual dream he was, as it were, forced to cross a decisive threshold. For the first time in one of his plays, he named an actual place, a place existing in the real world. Taranne claims that he has lectured abroad, *in Belgium,* and he receives a letter that is recognized as coming from that country by its stamp, which bears the Belgian Lion. 'This looks like a trifle, but it was, nevertheless, the first time that I emerged from the no man's land of poetry and dared to call things by their name.'[39]

And indeed for the tormented author of *L'Aveu,* suffering from the sense of loneliness and separation described in that book, it was a tremendous step forward to have established a link, however tenuous, with reality, the reality of the world outside his own nightmares, even if at first it appears only in the form of the name of a real country heard within a nightmare. Of course, in *L'Aveu* itself Adamov had described real scenes from his own life. But there is a vast difference between the deliberate humiliating *exposure* of his own suffering (reminiscent of Taranne's indecent exposure) and the ability to deal with the real world in the process of creative imaginative writing, which implies the ability to confront and master a reality outside oneself.

As Maurice Regnaut has pointed out in a penetrating essay on Adamov,[40] *Le Professeur Taranne* also marks another important stage in Adamov's development. In previous plays, to express his sense of the futility and absurdity of life, Adamov had projected the two basically contradictory attitudes that in the end amount to the same thing—namely, nothing—in pairs of characters: the employee and N, Pierre and his complacent mother, the *militant* and the *mutilé,* Henri and the revolutionaries. The dream on which *Le Professeur Taranne* is based showed him, for the first time, the way in which affirmative and self-destructive attitudes can be fused in a single character simultaneously—in the very act of asserting his worth as a citizen, his achievements as a scholar, Taranne reveals these claims to be fraudulent. And it is by no means clear whether the play is meant to show a fraud unmasked, or an innocent man confronted by a monstrous conspiracy of circumstances engineered to destroy his claims. In fact, as Adamov identifies himself with Taranne, the latter is the more tenable view; after all, in his dream Adamov cried out, 'I am the author of *La Parodie,*' which he undoubtedly was, and yet his claim was disproved by a succession of nightmare confrontations. Of course, if all activity is futile and absurd, then the claim to have written a play or to have lectured in Belgium is, in the final reckoning, a claim to nothing; death and oblivion will blot out all achievements. Thus, in *Le Professeur Taranne,* the hero is both an active scholar and a fraud, a respectable citizen and an exhibitionist, an optimistic hard-working paragon and a self-destructive, slothful pessimist. This opened a way for Adamov toward the creation of ambivalent, three-dimensional characters to take the place of schematic expressions of clearly defined psychological forces.

Adamov wrote *Le Professeur Taranne* in two days in 1951. It had taken him several years to complete his first two plays—a clear indication of how far he had succeeded in mastering his neurosis by harnessing it to a creative effort.

After completing *Le Sens de la Marche,* the writing of which he had interrupted to note down his nightmare of *Le Professeur Taranne,* Adamov returned to a subject that had preoccupied him before: the disorder of the times, social upheaval, and persecution. In *Tous Contre Tous,* we are again in a country that has been flooded by refugees from abroad; they are easily identifiable because they all limp. The hero, Jean Rist, loses his wife to one of the refugees and becomes a demagogue ranting against them. For a brief moment he is in power but when the wheel of political fortune turns and the persecutors become the persecuted, he escapes arrest by assuming a limp himself and pretending to be a refugee. He lives in obscurity, upheld by the love of a refugee girl. When there is another upheaval and the refugees are again persecuted, he might perhaps escape death by declaring his true identity. But in confirming that he is the well-known hater of refugees, he would lose the love of the girl. He refuses to do so, and goes to his death.

In Jean Rist, the persecutor and the victim of persecution, Adamov again fused two opposite tendencies in one character, not simultaneously, as in *Le Professeur Taranne,* but consecutively, in the ups and downs of the passage of time, and thus less successfully. The ending, with its self-sacrifice for the sake of love, has been criticized as a lapse into the sentimental heroics of a quite different, romantic convention of drama. This may be unjust: Jean Rist's refusal to save himself might also be interpreted as an act of resignation; of suicide in the face of an absurd, circular destiny. What the play does suffer from (in Adamov's own view) is its failure to come to grips with the reality of the problem it deals with. It is fairly obvious that this is the Jewish problem, or at least the problem of racial persecution. Yet by not situating his characters within a clearly defined social framework at one particular moment in history, at one particular point on the map, the author has deprived himself of the opportunity to do justice to the subject; he is unable to provide the background that would explain the rights and wrongs at issue: Why have the refugees taken away the jobs of the inhabitants of the country in question? Are those inhabitants justified in trying to exclude them again? Adamov himself recognized these flaws. On the one hand, he said, he wanted to show that all sides are equally reprehensible in such a conflict, yet he acknowledged that he made a larger number of the victims 'good' characters, simply because they are made to suffer innocently. But, he added, 'I suffered from the limitation imposed on me by the vagueness of the place, the schematization of the characters, the symbolism of the situations, but I did not feel that I had the power to tackle a social conflict, and to see it as such, detached from the world of archetypes.'[41]

In *Le Professeur Taranne* he had found the courage to let in a glimpse of the real world, if only in a dream. So he decided to return to a world of dreams in two plays with very similar themes: *Comme Nous Avons Eté (As We Were,* published in the *Nouvelle Revue Française* in March 1953) and *Les Retrouvailles* (undated, but written *c.* 1952). Both plays deal with a grown man's regression to childhood, just when he is on the threshold of marriage. In *Comme Nous Avons Eté,* the character A is having a nap in his room just before setting out to get married. Two women, mother and aunt, enter in search of a little boy who, they believe, must have wandered into the house. A does not know them, but as the play proceeds he himself gradually turns into the little boy the two women have been looking for. In *Les Retrouvailles,* Edgar is about to leave Montpellier, where he is reading law, to return to his home near the Belgian frontier, when he encounters two ladies, one elderly, the other young, and is persuaded to stay in the house of the elderly woman while becoming engaged to the younger. He neglects his new fiancée, and she is killed in a train accident. Having finally returned home,

he hears that his former fiancée, who had been waiting for him there, has also been killed in a train accident. His mother forces him into a perambulator and pushes him offstage.

These are dream plays with very obvious psychological implications; they are both attacks against the mother figure, who is trying to keep the son from establishing an adult relationship with another woman. Adamov completely repudiated *Comme Nous Avons Eté,* to the point of not having given it a place in the edition of his collected plays (although he allowed it to be published in an English translation in 1957).[42] *Les Retrouvailles,* technically most intriguing in the way it establishes the dream atmosphere by gradual scene changes and by the reduplication of the two pairs of mother-fiancée characters, has been published in Adamov's collected plays. But in his preface, Adamov rejects the play as a dream that he did not have but merely constructed. Yet he declares, '*Les Retrouvailles* has been most important for me; for, having finished the play, having reread it and examined it well, I understood that the time had come to put an end to the exploitation of the half-dream and the old family conflict. Or, to put it in more general terms, I think that thanks to *Les Retrouvailles* I have liquidated all that which, after having made it possible for me to write, now had become a hindrance to my writing.'[43]

In other words, Adamov had reached a stage where he felt capable of writing a play that, though still an expression of his vision of the human condition, could people the stage not with mere emanations of his own psyche but with characters existing in their own right as objective human beings observed from the outside. This play is *Le Ping-Pong,* one of the masterpieces of the Theatre of the Absurd.

Le Ping-Pong presents the life story of two men—Victor, a medical student when the play starts, and Arthur, an art student. They meet at Mme Duranty's café and play the pinball machine installed there. The machine fascinates them as a business proposition, for they observe the employee of the company coming to collect the coins that have been dropped into it; as a technical problem, for it has flaws that could surely be eliminated; and even as a challenge to their poetic instinct—the machine has a poetry of its own, flashing lights, and is in some ways a work of art. Victor and Arthur suggest an improvement in the machine. They penetrate to the headquarters of the consortium that controls it, and gradually the machine becomes the dominating influence in their lives, controlling their dreams and their emotions. If they fall in love, it is with the girl who works at the headquarters of the consortium. If they have quarrels between themselves, they are about that girl and the machine. If they fear anyone, it is the boss of the consortium. Their interest in the society around them is dictated by the relevance of political and social developments to the rise or fall of pinball machines.

And so they grow old. In the last scene we see them as two old men, playing ping-pong, a contest as childish and as futile as their lifelong preoccupation with a plaything. Victor collapses and dies. Arthur remains alone.

Le Ping-Pong, like Adamov's first play, *La Parodie,* is concerned with the futility of human endeavour. But while *La Parodie* merely asserted that whatever you do, in the end you die, *Le Ping-Pong* provides a powerful and closely integrated argument to back that proposition—it also shows *how* so much of human endeavour becomes futile, and *why.* It is in losing themselves to a *thing,* a machine that promises them power, money, influence over the woman they desire, that Victor and Arthur waste their lives in the futile pursuit of shadows. By making a machine, a means to an end, an end in itself, they pervert all those values of their lives that are genuine ends in themselves—their creative instinct, their capacity to love, their sense of being part of a community. *Le Ping-Pong* is a powerful image of the alienation of man through the worship of a false objective, the deification of a machine, an ambition, or an ideology.

The pinball machine in *Le Ping-Pong* is more than just a machine; it is the centre-piece of an organization and of a body of thought. The moment the objective—the improvement of pinball machines—becomes an ideal, it embodies itself in an organization with its own struggles for power, its own intrigues and politics, its own tactics and strategies. As such it becomes a matter of life and death for all who serve the ideal. A number of the characters in the play are destroyed in the service of the organization, or in its internal struggle for power. All this is conducted with the utmost fervour, seriousness, and intensity. And what is it all about? A childish game, a pinball machine—nothing. But are most of the objectives men devote their lives to in the real world—the world of business, politics, the arts, or scholarship—essentially different from Arthur's and Victor's dominating obsession? It is the power and beauty of *Le Ping-Pong* that it very graphically raises this very question. Adamov achieves the difficult feat of elevating the pinball machine to a convincing image of the objectives of *all* human endeavour. He does so by the poetic intensity with which he invests his characters when they talk about the most absurd aspects of that absurd apparatus with a conviction and obsessive concentration that sound utterly true.

The play contains the elements of reality and fantasy in exactly the right dosage; time and place are sufficiently real to carry conviction, yet the world in which the action takes place is hermetically sealed off from anything outside the characters' field of preoccupation. This is not because of a lack of realism on the part of the playwright; it springs directly from the obsession of the characters, which effectively confines them in so narrow a segment of the real world that we see the world through their confined field of vision.

The characters in *Le Ping-Pong* are fully realized individuals. No longer merely compelled by forces outside their control, or moving through the action like somnambulists, they have an element of freedom in determining their lives—we actually watch Arthur and Victor making the decision to devote themselves to pinball machines. And although Victor is the more practical of the two, and Arthur a poet, they are no longer merely personifications of complementary characteristics.

What is perhaps the most original feature of *Le Ping-Pong* is the way in which an inner contradiction, a dialectical relationship, is established between the action and the dialogue. This is a play that may well appear completely meaningless if it is merely read. The speeches about improvements in the construction of pinball machines may seem trivial nonsense: the meaning of the play emerges precisely at the moment when the actor delivers these nonsensical lines with a depth of conviction worthy of the loftiest flights of poetry. It is a play that has to be acted *against* the text rather than with it. This is a technique analogous to the indirect dialogue Adamov thought he had invented for *L'Invasion* and later discovered in Chekhov, but it is here raised to quite a different level. Chekhov used indirect dialogue in situations where the characters are too shy to express their real thoughts and hide their emotions behind trivial subjects. Here the characters believe in absurd propositions, with such intensity that they put forward their nonsensical ideas with the fervour of prophetic vision. In Chekhov, real feelings are suppressed behind meaningless politeness; in *Le Ping-Pong* absurd ideas are proclaimed as if they were eternal truths.

Adamov has given an interesting account of the genesis of *Le Ping-Pong.* He started with the final scene of the two old men playing ping-pong before he had even decided what the subject of the rest of the play would be. All he knew was that he wanted once more to show how, in the end, all human endeavour comes down to the same futility—senile whiling away of the remaining time before death reduces everything to final absurdity. But, Adamov said, 'this peculiar method of work, paradoxically enough, saved me. Once I was sure that, as usual, I should be able to show the identity of all human destiny . . . I found myself free to make the characters act, to create situations. . . .'[44] Once he had decided to put a pinball machine into the centre of the action, moreover, he was compelled to specify the time (the present) and the place (a city very much like Paris) of the action.

Nevertheless *Le Ping-Pong* belongs in the category of the Theatre of the Absurd; it shows man engaged in purposeless exertions, in a futile frenzy of activity that is bound to end in senility and death. The pinball machine has all the fascinating ambiguity of a symbol. It may stand for capitalism and big business, but it may equally well stand for any religious or political ideology that secretes its own organization and apparatus of power, that demands devotion and loyalty from its adherents.

Yet while he was working on the play, Adamov was moving away from the idea of a theatre dealing with such general human questions. He has criticized *Le Ping-Pong* on two counts—the last scene, which, having been written before the rest of the play, as it were, prejudged the issue and cramped his style; and, second, the schematic nature of the consortium, which remains

> incompletely detached from allegory. In fact, the social developments that, in the course of years, modify the internal organization of the consortium are not really indicated, so that one does not sufficiently feel the state of society on the one hand, the flow of time on the other. If I had gone so far as to tackle the 'coin-operated machine', I had to examine the wheels of the great social machine with the same thoroughness that I examined the bumpers and flippers of the pinball machine. This is the examination I am trying to carry out in a new play, even more clearly situated in a specific time and milieu than *Le Ping-Pong.*[45]

This play on which Adamov was working at the beginning of 1955, when he wrote his introduction to the second volume of his collected plays, was *Paolo Paoli,* completed the next year and performed by Roger Planchon's brilliant young company at Lyon on 17 May 1957. It marks Adamov's abandonment of the Theatre of the Absurd and his adherence to another, equally significant movement of the modern stage—the Brechtian 'epic theatre'. He came to regard Brecht as the greatest of contemporary playwrights and put him next to Shakespeare, Chekhov, and Büchner among the dramatists of world literature he admired most. Having freed himself from compulsions and obsessions, he felt at liberty to follow models outside his own experience. (He had previously translated and adapted works by Büchner and Chekhov.)

Paolo Paoli is an epic drama depicting the social and political causes of the outbreak of the First World War and examining the relationship between a society based on profit and the forces of destruction to which it gives rise. The play spans the period from 1900 to 1914. Each of the twelve scenes is preceded by a survey of the social background of its period—quotations from the newspapers of the time are projected on to a screen, accompanied by current popular tunes.

The characters are most ingeniously chosen to represent a whole microcosm of the political, religious, national, and social forces involved in the origins of the First World War. Adamov's brilliance as a dramatist is shown by the astonishing ingenuity with which he has condensed all this—and extremely convincingly—into a cast of only seven characters.

Paolo Paoli is a dealer in rare butterflies; Florent Hulot-Vasseur, a collector of rare butterflies and Paolo's customer, is an importer and manufacturer of ostrich feathers. He also becomes the lover of Paolo's German-born wife, Stella. An abbé and a captain's wife represent clericalism and chauvinist nationalism. A worker and trade unionist, Robert Marpeaux, and his young wife, Rose, complete the cast.

The role played by pinball machines in *Le Ping-Pong* is in *Paolo Paoli* taken by commodities no less absurd—butterflies and ostrich feathers. Yet these objects of trade and manufacture have far greater reality. As one of the newspaper projections before the first scene points out, ostrich feathers and products manufactured from them formed France's fourth largest export in 1900. Adamov brilliantly shows the far-reaching social and political ramifications and implications of the trade in these absurd articles: Paolo's business is founded on the fact that his father, a small Corsican civil servant, served in the public-works department on Devil's Island. This enabled the young man to organize the convicts there as part-time and ill-paid butterfly hunters. Marpeaux, the young workman who was serving a sentence for a petty theft, has escaped to the mainland and the swamps of Venezuela; he is wholly at Paolo's mercy, depending on the butterflies he catches for his livelihood. When troubles break out in China, butterfly hunting becomes more difficult there and the price of rare Chinese specimens goes up. The abbé, whose brother is a missionary in China, is able to provide Paolo with these precious goods. And so, in a few strokes, Adamov has shown the connection between the seemingly absurd object of trade and the penal system of French society, foreign politics, and the workings of the Church. The same is true of Hulot-Vasseur's ostrich feathers in relation to the Boer War, and, as the plot develops, the labour and trade-union troubles of his factory and his fight against German competition are very convincingly made explicit within the narrow circle of the play.

As in *Le Ping-Pong,* the characters are obsessed with their pursuit of money and power, represented by the absurd commodities they deal in. Paolo grows rich, for a time at least, by becoming a manufacturer of knick-knacks made from butterflies' wings—ashtrays, tea trays, even religious pictures, which flourish in a period of clericalism and slump when clericalism fades and German competition raises its ugly head. He loses his wife when he sets her up as a milliner, which makes her dependent for her supplies of ostrich feathers on Hulot-Vasseur, whose mistress she becomes. Stella, the German-born woman, also embodies the absurdities of

European nationalism; she leaves France at the height of the anti-German feeling over Morocco, because people hate her as a German, and returns on the eve of the First World War, when her German neighbours persecute her as the wife of a Frenchman.

The only characters free of these obsessions are Marpeaux and his wife, Rose (though she for a time becomes Paolo's mistress). When Marpeaux returns, illegally, from Venezuela, Paolo suggests that he should spend the time till his pardon is granted by going to Morocco to hunt butterflies. (The crisis over Morocco has driven the prices up.) Of course, Morocco has become very dangerous; the French are fighting the natives. And here lies the moral of the play—the commodity that seems the object of trade is absurd, mere butterflies, but the commodity that is *really* traded is man, who has to sell his health and safety in the pursuit of butterflies. The ultimate object of trade is man, who himself becomes a commodity. (This is also the point of Adamov's very effective dramatization of Gogol's novel *Dead Souls*.) Moreover, the commodities are being bought and sold in deadly earnest; trade leads to war.

Marpeaux, the victim of the social system, realizes what is at stake. After he has received his pardon (at a time when war between France and Germany seemed imminent over Morocco, and volunteers could gain amnesty), he returns to France and joins the Socialists. Working in Hulot-Vasseur's factory, he opposes the 'yellow' Catholic unions managed by the abbé and also distributes pacifist pamphlets to the soldiers in their barracks. To get rid of him, the abbé denounces him for subverting the fighting forces. As the first troops march off to war, Rose tells Paolo that Marpeaux has been arrested, and this leads to a somewhat unconvincing change of heart in Paolo, who, in the closing speech of the play, vows that henceforth he will use his money to help the hungry and needy, rather than let it circulate in the endless, iniquitous cycle of exchange, the buying and selling of useless commodities.

Paolo Paoli is a political play, brilliantly constructed and executed as a drama, not very original as a political argument. (Paolo's last speech certainly makes little sense even in terms of Marxist economics: money spent on food for the victims of Right Wing persecution is by no means effectively withdrawn from the cycle of capitalist exchange.) Nevertheless, as a *tour de force* the play shows Adamov as the sovereign master of his material, handling it with remarkable powers of invention, construction, and compression.

The question arises—does this piece of powerfully constructed didactic special pleading equal the haunting, dream-like poetry of far less cleverly structured plays like *La Parodie, La Grande et la Petite Manœuvre,* or *Le Professeur Taranne*? Is the highly explicit social framework of *Paolo Paoli,* for all the virtuosity with which it is handled, equal in depth, or even in its power to convince, to the vaguer, more general, but therefore all-embracing images of *Le Ping-Pong*?

There can be no doubt that for Adamov the development from *La Parodie* to *Paolo Paoli* represented a gradual liberation, through the artist's creative power, from the incubus of neurosis and deep personal suffering. In the whole history of literature it will be difficult to find a more triumphant example of the healing power of the creative processes of sublimation. It is fascinating to watch the gradual breaking down of the barriers that keep the writer of this series of plays from dealing with the realities of everyday life; to watch him gain the confidence that he needs to turn the nightmares that mastered him into mere material that *he* can mould and master. His early plays are, as it were, emanations of his subconscious mind, projected on to the stage as faithful transcripts of terrifying fantasies. *Paolo Paoli* is consciously planned and rationally controlled. Yet it might be argued that this gain in rationality and conscious control represents a loss of the fine frenzy, the haunting power of neurosis that gave the earlier plays their magnetic, poetical impact. What is more, by concentrating his attack on the political and social front, Adamov narrowed his field of vision.

If in *La Grande et la Petite Manœuvre* it was the revolutionaries' futile struggle that represented the small manoeuvre, and the all-enveloping absurdity of the human condition dwarfing the social struggle that stood for the big manoeuvre, then in *Paolo Paoli* the small manoeuvre looms large and the large manoeuvre has receded into a barely perceptible background. 'We all know,' says the revolutionary leader in the earlier play, 'that death surrounds us. But if we do not have the courage to detach ourselves from that idea, we shall retreat from the demands of the future, and all our sacrifices will have been in vain.'[46] This is the argument that Paolo Paoli represents. In the earlier play Adamov had supplied his own bitterly ironical comment on it: at the very moment when the revolutionary leader speaks these defiant words, his voice becomes slower, the pace of his delivery slackens, and he collapses.

Adamov was far too acute a thinker to be unaware of the implications of his later position. Having in his earlier phase concentrated on the absurdity of the human condition, he later maintained that 'the theatre must show, simultaneously but well-differentiated, both the curable and the incurable aspect of things. The incurable aspect, we all know, is that of the inevitability of death. The curable aspect is the social one.'[47]

It is precisely because it does succeed in maintaining the extremely delicate balance between the incurable and the curable aspects of the human condition that *Le*

Ping-Pong must be regarded as Adamov's finest achievement. The pinball machine stands for all illusory objectives, material and ideological, the pursuit of which secretes ambition, self-seeking, and the urge to dominate other human beings. There is no necessity to fall victim to such illusory aims, so there *is* a social lesson in the play. And yet the absurdity of all human endeavour in the face of death is never quite forgotten, and is finally put before our eyes by a telling and compelling image. *Paolo Paoli,* on the other hand, is marred not only by the intrusion of oversimplified economic and social theories, but, above all, by the introduction of a wholly positive and therefore less than human character, Marpeaux, and by the even less credible conversion of a hitherto negative character, Paolo, to provide a climax and a solution. This noble character and this noble action are clearly the consequence of the author's special pleading for the curable aspect of things, which leads to an underplaying of the incurable side of the human situation. Marpeaux's efforts, in the last resort, are as futile as those of the employee in *La Parodie*—he is arrested and the war breaks out in spite of him. Yet the author has to make this into a noble failure, due to the special wickedness of individual enemies, or of social conditions, at a given period of history. And that is the point at which the pathetic fallacy enters a politically biased theatre. Brecht, who was well aware of this danger, avoided similar pitfalls by forgoing all positive characters in some of his more successful plays (*Mother Courage, Galileo*), so that the positive message might emerge by inference rather than by concrete demonstration—but with the result that the effect on the audience tends to be one of a negative theatre that concentrates on the incurable aspect of things.

In some respects, *Paolo Paoli* contains an important promise—it shows the way in which some of the elements of the Theatre of the Absurd can be combined with those of the conventional well-made play to produce a very fruitful fusion of two different traditions. In the simplicity of its construction, the boldness of its characterization, the use of butterflies and ostrich feathers as symbols that are at the same time perfectly valid in the world of economic realities, *Paolo Paoli* contained some useful lessons for the future development of a theatre combining elements of both the didactic epic style and the Theatre of the Absurd.

Nor was Adamov's rejection of a nonrealistic style as complete as it might appear. It is surely significant that in the autumn of 1958, when he felt himself called upon to take an active part in the campaign against the new Gaullist constitution, Adamov found it easier to resort to allegorical techniques than to make his point in the form of realistic didactic drama. Of the three short pieces he contributed to the volume *Théâtre de Société,*[48] two are allegorical and only one is realistic—and an acknowledged failure.

The most ambitious of these three sketches, *Intimité,* uses personified collective concepts rather like those we find in medieval mystery plays—de Gaulle is caricatured as The Cause Incarnate, the Socialists as Cause's servile and stupid lackey, the young bloods among the Algerian *colons* as a bullying ruffian labelled The Elite. The Cause Incarnate is protected by a bodyguard of brutal strong-arm men; they are called The Effects of the Cause. In the short monologue *La Complainte du Ridicule,* the personification of ridicule laments the sad fact that it seems to have lost the power to kill it possessed in former, happier times in France. Both these playlets, although clearly ephemeral *pièces d'occasion,* are successful as robust topical satire. The third, *Je ne Suis pas Francais,* fails even on this level; it shows the way French parachutists in Algiers were reported to have coerced the Moslem population into demonstrating for France in May 1958, but remains unconvincing in spite, or because, of its documentary technique. The political purpose is so obvious that the more realistically the subject is presented, the more it seems to lose the effect of reality.

Realism and fantasy are also combined in the radio play *En Fiacre* (1959), by the device of presenting a real, historically authenticated event involving characters who are demented—three old ladies who, having lost the house they lived in, spend the night in horse-drawn cabs they hire to drive around and around the streets of old-time Paris. The incident, presented as based on the casebook of a psychiatrist, and as having actually happened in February 1902, might well have sprung from the dream world of one of Adamov's early plays. One of the three sisters is killed when she falls out of the moving cab. Has she been pushed out by the other two? And why have these three old women become homeless wanderers in the night? It appears that they learned only after their father died that the house they lived in had been the headquarters of a chain of brothels. There is also a suggestion that the dead sister, the youngest of the three, might have been in on the secret, that she might have been involved in what went on in those brothels, that she had a lover, that she was in the habit of occasionally paying the cabdrivers for those nightly journeys in currency other than mere money. But then all this may be the outcome of the fantasies of insane old women. *En Fiacre* is strictly documentary, but, in the nature of a scientific case-book, it does not seek to explain too much; it merely sets down what has been reported, leaving the motives of the action as unexplained as the solution. And while the treatment is naturalistic, the theme is madness, fantasies, dreams, irrational fears, and jealousies. The streets of Paris at night, pitiful victims of neurosis exposed to the insults of cabdrivers—this is a world not too far removed from that of *L'Aveu.*

In *Le Printemps '71* (*Spring '71,* 1961), a vast canvas of the Paris Commune in twenty-six scenes, nine interludes, and an epilogue, Adamov finally broke through to the large-scale portrayal of historical reality. The tragic suppression of the revolutionary city government of Paris is shown in an intricate mosaic of minutely observed scenes involving dozens of characters. But even here Adamov could not do without the grotesquely allegorical element; the nine interludes, which he himself calls *guignols* (puppet shows), point the moral of the action through the grotesque cavortings of historical and allegorical personages: Bismarck, Thiers, the Commune itself, the Bank of France sitting inside her vaults, the National Assembly, a sleepy old woman knitting socks, and so on. These are the cartoons of Daumier come to life, and while the realistic action, impressive as it is, appears somewhat diffuse, these allegorical cartoon scenes are concise, witty, and make their point with astonishing force.

Adamov's next major play, *Sainte Europe* (1966), was an immense political cartoon in which Charles de Gaulle merges into the Emperor Charlemagne. It is an attempt to marry political realism with the dream world of political nightmare. I personally, however, doubt very much whether it succeeds as drama.

In the last years of his life Adamov was greatly hampered by persistent serious illness not unconnected with bouts of alcoholism. His last plays show a distinct falling-off of his powers. They mingle elements of his old neuroses with his political and propagandist preoccupations. *La Politique des Restes* (written 1961-2; first performed 1967) deals with racial oppression in the United States; *M. le Modéré* (1967) shows the futility of a moderate attitude in politics. *Off Limits* (1968) is a further bitter attack against the American style of life, while *Si l'Été Revenait* (1969) is situated in an affluent bourgeois Sweden and explores guilt in a middle-class family.

On 15 March 1970 Arthur Adamov died from an overdose of barbiturates, probably suicide.

Adamov's development from a tormented, deeply neurotic individual who haunted the streets where prostitutes congregate in order to provoke them into insulting and beating him, to a highly respected militant of the left, is one of the most fascinating and best-documented case histories in European literature. (He added a second part to *L'Aveu* and republished it as *Je . . . Ils* in 1969; another autobiographical volume, *L'Homme et l'Enfant,* appeared in 1968.) His early absurdist plays exorcized his neurosis, so that he gradually became able to deal with the real world. In *Le Ping-Pong* and *Paolo Paoli* he found the ideal synthesis between his poetic and his political commitment. In the later, highly tendentious plays, the needs of political commitment

and partisanship again, ironically, removed him from the real world; now he merely dramatized the clichés and myths of the totalitarian left, and the political fanaticism which drove him could be seen as merely another—and a less productive—aspect of his neurosis. The difference lies precisely in the fact that while the plays which reflect his personal neurosis spring from a soul in torment and thus communicate powerful insights into the human condition, the fanaticism of his political drama merely reflects the ready-made truisms of a political machine. In the output of his last years, when he was in constant pain and in deep psychological anguish, the personal neurosis occasionally came to the surface, but by this time his creative powers had been eroded.

Adamov was a fascinating human being: slight, dark, with enormous piercing, probing eyes in a saturnine, unshaven face, always most raggedly dressed, he was the archetypal Paris Bohemian and *poète maudit*. He was a man of immense erudition, widely read in psychology and psychopathology, translator of Jung, Rilke, Dostoevski (*Crime and Punishment*), Strindberg (*The Father*), Gogol, Büchner, Gorki, and Chekhov, author of an excellent monograph on Strindberg, compiler of an anthology of the Paris Commune. He was the friend of Artaud and played an important part in liberating him from the asylum; a man of immense charm, passion and commitment. His work for the theatre is uneven, but his best plays will surely endure.

Notes

1. Arthur Adamov, *L'Aveu* (Paris: Éditions du Sagittaire, 1946), p. 19.

2. ibid., p. 23.

3. ibid., pp. 25-6.

4. ibid., p. 28.

5. ibid., p. 42.

6. ibid., p. 45.

7. ibid.

8. Adamov, 'The endless humiliation', trans. Richard Howard, *Evergreen Review,* New York, II, 8, 1959, pp. 64-95.

9. *L'Aveu,* p. 69; 'The endless humiliation', loc. cit., p. 75.

10. Carl Gustav Jung, *Le Moi et l'Inconscient,* trans. Adamov (Paris: 1938).

11. *L'Aveu,* p. 37; 'The endless humiliation', loc. cit., p. 67.

12. *L'Aveu,* p. 58; 'The endless humiliation', loc. cit., p. 67.

13. *L'Aveu,* p. 106.

14. ibid., p. 110.

15. ibid., p. 114.

16. ibid., p. 115.

17. Adamov, '*Une fin et un commencement*', *L'Heure Nouvelle,* no. II (Paris: Editions du Sagittaire, 1946), p. 17.

18. Adamov, '*Assignation*', *L'Heure Nouvelle,* no. I, p. 3.

19. ibid., footnote on p. 6.

20. '*Le refus*', *L'Heure Nouvelle,* no. II, footnote on p. 6.

21. '*Une fin et un commencement*', loc. cit., p. 16.

22. ibid.

23. Adamov, *Théâtre II* (Paris: Gallimard, 1955), '*Note préliminaire*', p. 8.

24. ibid.

25. ibid., p. 9.

26. Adamov, *La Parodie, L'Invasion* (Paris: Charlot, 1950), p. 22.

27. *L'Aveu,* p. 85; 'The endless humiliation', loc. cit., p. 85.

28. Adamov, *Théâtre I* (Paris: Gallimard, 1953), p. 86.

29. ibid., p. 94.

30. *La Parodie, L'Invasion,* p. 16.

31. *La Parodie, L'Invasion,* p. 16.

32. Adamov, quoted by Carlos Lynes, Jr, 'Adamov or "*le sens littéral*" in the theatre', *Yale French Studies,* no. 14, Winter 1954-5.

33. *Théâtre I,* p. 107.

34. *La Parodie, L'Invasion,* p. 22.

35. ibid., p. 23.

36. *Théâtre II,* p. 11.

37. ibid., p. 12.

38. ibid., p. 12.

39. ibid., p. 13.

40. Maurice Regnaut, '*Arthur Adamov et le sens du fétichisme*', *Cahiers de la Compagnie Madeleine Renaud—Jean-Louis Barrault,* Paris, nos. 22-3, May 1958.

41. *Théâtre II,* p. 14.

42. Adamov, *As We Were,* trans. Richard Howard, *Evergreen Review, I,* 4, 1957.

43. *Théâtre II,* p. 15.

44. ibid.

45. ibid., p. 17.

46. *Théâtre I,* p. 136.

47. '*Qui êtes-vous Arthur Adamov?*', *Cité Panorama* (programme bulletin of Planchon's Théâtre de la Cité), Villeurbanne, no. 9, 1960.

48. *Théâtre de Société. Scènes d'Actualité* (Paris: Les Editeurs Français Réunis, 1958).

Bibliography

PLAYS

Théâtre, 4 vols., Paris: Gallimard, vol. I, 1953, vol. II, 1955, vol. III, 1966, vol. IV, 1968.

Vol. I contains: *La Parodie, L'Invasion, La Grande et la Petite Manœuvre, Le Professeur Taranne, Tous Contre Tous.* (*Le Professeur Taranne* trans. by A. Bermel in *Four Modern French Comedies,* New York: Capricorn Press, 1960; by Peter Meyer in *Absurd Drama,* Harmondsworth: Penguin Books, 1965)

Vol. II contains: *Le Sens de la Marche, Les Retrouvailles, Le Ping-Pong.* (*Le Ping-Pong* trans. by Richard Howard, New York: Grove Press, 1959)

Vol. III contains: *Paolo Paoli, La Politique des Restes, Sainte Europe*

Vol. IV contains: *M. le Módéré, Le Printemps '71*

SEPARATELY PUBLISHED PLAYS

La Parodie, L'Invasion, précédées d'une lettre d'André Gide, et de témoignages de René Char, Jacques Prévert, Henri Thomas, Jacques Lemarchand, Jean Vilar, Roger Blin, Paris: Charlot, 1950

Paolo Paoli, Paris: Gallimard 1957 (English trans. by Geoffrey Brereton, London: Calder, 1959)

Les Ames Mortes, d'après le poème de Nicolas Gogol, Paris: Gallimard, 1960

Comme Nous Avons Eté, Paris: *Nouvelle Revue Française,* March 1953 (trans. by Richard Howard, *As We Were,* New York: *Evergreen Review, I,* 4, 1957)

Théâtre de Société. Scènes d'Actualité, Paris: Les Editeurs Français Réunis, 1958, contains three short sketches by Adamov: *Intimité, Je ne Suis pas Français, La Complainte du Ridicule.*

En Fiacre (radio play), unpublished ms., 1959

Le Printemps '71, Paris: Gallimard, 1961

Si l'Été Revenait, Paris: Gallimard, 1970

OTHER WRITINGS

L'Aveu, Paris: Sagittaire, 1946 (one section of this autobiographical confession trans. by Richard Howard, 'The endless humiliation', New York: *Evergreen Review,* II, 8, 1959)

'*Assignation*', Paris: *L'Heure Nouvelle,* no. II, 1945

'*Le Refus*', Paris: *L'Heure Nouvelle,* no. II, 1946

Auguste Strindberg, Dramaturge, Paris: L'Arche, 1955

'*Théâtre, argent et politique*', Paris: *Théâtre Populaire,* no. 17, 1956

'*Parce que je l'ai beaucoup aimé . . .*' (on Artaud), Paris: *Cahiers de la Compagnie M. Renaud-J.-L. Barrault,* nos. 22-3, May 1958

Anthologie de la Commune (ed. Adamov), Paris: Editions Sociales, 1959

Ici et Maintenant (collected essays), Paris: Gallimard, 1964

L'Homme et l'Enfant (diaries), Paris: Gallimard, 1968

Je . . . Ils (reissue of *L'Aveu* and new memoirs), Paris: Gallimard, 1969

TRANSLATIONS BY ADAMOV

Rilke, *Le Livre de la Pauvreté et de la Mort,* Algiers: 1941

Büchner, *Théâtre Complet,* trans. by Adamov and Marthe Robert

Dostoevsky, *Crime et Châtiment*

Jung, *Le Moi et l'Inconscient,* Paris: 1938

Gogol, *Les Ames Mortes,* Lausanne: La Guilde du Livre

Chekhov, *L'Esprit des Bois,* Paris: Gallimard (in the series 'Le Manteau d'Arlequin')

Chekhov, *Théâtre,* Paris: Club Français du Livre

Strindberg, *Le Pélican,* Paris: *Théâtre Populaire,* no. 17, 1956

Strindberg, *Père,* Paris: L'Arche, 1958

Kleist, *La Cruche Cassée,* Paris: *Théâtre Populaire,* no. 6, 1954

Gorki, *Théâtre,* Paris: L'Arche

ON ADAMOV

Gaudy, René, *Arthur Adamov,* Paris: Stock, 1971

Lynes, Carlos, Jr, 'Adamov or "*le sens littéral*" in the theatre', *Yale French Studies,* no. 14, Winter 1954-5

Regnaut, Maurice, '*Arthur Adamov et le sens du fétichisme*', Paris: *Cahiers de la Compagnie M. Renaud-J.-L. Barrault,* nos. 22-3, May 1958

Richard E. Sherrell (essay date February 1965)

SOURCE: Sherrell, Richard E. "Arthur Adamov and Invaded Man." *Modern Drama* 7, no. 4 (February 1965): 399-404.

[*In the following essay, Sherrell explores how Adamov's personal neurosis and his "sense of separation" are manifested in his second play,* The Invasion.]

Arthur Adamov's critics are in general agreement that his early plays (those included in *Théâtre,* Vols. 1 and 2)[1] are in many ways the direct result of his effort at what Leonard C. Pronko calls "an exorcism of private terrors."[2] In his self-revelatory work, *L'Aveu,* a portion of which is translated into English, Adamov admits that by expressing his neurosis he exorcises himself.[3] As a result of *L'Aveu* the dimensions and motifs of Adamov's "disease" are well known and we see these contents gaining expression in his plays. Martin Esslin in his book, *The Theatre of the Absurd,*[4] has given a lengthy review of *L'Aveu* together with helpful insights as to some of the relationships between Adamov's neurosis and his activity as a playwright. I do not propose to recapitulate this review. Rather, I want to point up what are for me some interesting expressions of Adamov's neurosis and insight which I find in his second play, *L'Invasion.*

Immediately following the Second World War Adamov became editor of the short-lived literary magazine, *L'Heure Nouvelle.* In the first issue he included an article, entitled **"Une Fin et un Commencement,"** in which he said:

> From whatever point he starts, whatever path he follows, modern man comes to the same conclusion: behind its visible appearances, life hides a meaning that is eternally inaccessible to penetration by the spirit that seeks for its discovery, caught in the dilemma of being aware that it is impossible to find it, and yet also impossible to renounce the hopeless quest.[5]

In Adamov's view the impossibility of either fulfilment or abandonment of this quest describes the tragic situation of man. This conceptualization of modern man's plight had been given concrete expression in the earlier *L'Aveu* in reference to himself. There we find:

> Hence it is only too obvious that the sickness binding me is governed by guilt, the consciousness of a fault, and that this fault is related to the mystery of sex. . . . There is no escape; I must expiate a fault which seems to have fallen on my very flesh. But the flesh is only a

link in the endless chain of realities symbolizing each other. We must discover what is hidden behind the last of such symbols.

> The overwhelming evidence must become apparent to all eyes: This fault is not ultimately *my* fault, it transcends me, greater than even the sickness within me. I want to make this truth contagious, virulent: every private fault, every individual guilt, whether the guilty person is conscious of it or not, transcends the individual to identify itself with the fault of all men everywhere and forever—the great original prevarication which is named Separation. (In the word *fault* there is on the one hand the sense of *failure* and on the other the sense of *falling.* Fault is thus absence and fall, which are precisely the terrible aspects of Separation.)[6]

Thus we see that even in 1939 (the date of this portion of *L'Aveu*) Adamov was not only aware of his own deep alienation but was able to place his personal experience into a universalistic framework in which all men are guilty and hence separated. The problem is: separated from what? To this question which he addressed to himself, Adamov wrote:

> I do not know. All I know is that I am suffering, and that if I am suffering it is because at the source of myself there is mutiliation, separation. I do not know what name to give what I am separated from, but I am separated from it. Once it was called God. Now there is no longer any name.[7]

This is remarkable documentation of what modern existential ontologists, such as Martin Heidegger and Paul Tillich, are talking about when they speak of man's separation from the ground of being. My concern, however, is not to make a philosopher out of Adamov, but to try to indicate how his sense of separation manifests itself in *L'Invasion.*

There is one other dimension of Adamov's neurosis which needs some notation before we go on to discuss the play. This is the role played by woman in Adamov's dream-world. As he mentions in the long quotation above, his sickness is related to the "mystery of sex." Specifically, Adamov, in *L'Aveu,* feels a need to be humiliated by women who represent "the Other," the contrary of himself. "Woman is the image of everything which, deriving from the depths, possesses the attraction of the abyss."[8] In Adamov's self-exorcism he must plumb his own depths in order to find the meaning or the sense of his separation. In this process woman becomes the agent of self-investigation, and, as such, woman symbolizes both the attraction of death (with attendant fears of castration) and the possibilities of renewal.

It is thus noteworthy that within Adamov's felt relationship to woman are to be found reflections of classic mythical understandings of woman as symbol of both death (whether through a return to the womb by way of regression, or as sacrifice to the Terrible Mother goddess of fertility) and of renewal of male vitality through sexual relations. As I will try to show, both these elements of death and renewal in relation to woman are manifested in *L'Invasion.*

In the play, *L'Invasion,* the action centers in the effort by a group of people to decipher and edit the message of one Jean, deceased friend of Pierre and brother of Agnes. Pierre and Agnes are married, and besides them the group includes Pierre's mother and his friend, Tradel. Jean has left behind an immense manuscript. As the play begins the stage is literally full of pages of the manuscript. The group, led by Pierre, is deep in the struggle to put this vast amount of material together. Unfortunately, Jean never numbered his pages. What is more, his writing is nearly illegible and the ink is now fast fading into dim obscurity. If a phrase or sentence is discovered which seems to contain a connected thought or expression, the task still remains to fit it into the mass of yet undecipherable material. Pierre and Tradel have different methods of approaching the task. Pierre is unwilling to guess at what is written, while Tradel feels he has an inerrant intuition which can grasp the sense of indistinct and uncertain sections. This difference leads Pierre, who feels the task is properly his own anyway, to reject Tradel's help. In time the struggle to read the manuscript leads Pierre to question the meaning of everything said by anyone, including himself. As he says:

> Pourquoi dit-on: "Il arrive?" Qui est ce "il," que veut-il de moi? Pourquoi dit-on "par" terre, plutôt que "à" ou "sur"? J'ai perdu trop de temps à réfléchir sur ces choses. Ce qu'il me faut, ce n'est pas le sens des mots, c'est leur volume et leur corps mouvant. Je ne chercherai plus rien. J'attendrai dans le silence, immobile. Je deviendrai très attentif. Il faut que je parte le plus vite possible.[9]

Finally he does retire from the group entirely to meditate and wait.

Nowhere that I have found does Adamov explain the title of this play. At the very least we can say that Pierre's life, and to a lesser extent the lives of the others, is invaded by the indecipherable legacy of Jean. There is a real question, however, as to whether Jean even knew what he was writing. Thus it seems to me that we are entirely justified in seeing the manuscript as a symbol of the undiscernable meaning which invades life at its core, as Adamov has noted in his article, **"Une Fin et un Commencement."** This meaning brings with it the necessity both of discovering its content and of communicating in language what is discovered. Pierre thus becomes a type of the modern man who is caught in the task of trying to discover the meaning of life, which remains obscure, and who is at the same time unable to leave off the struggle. Pierre's strategy is to forsake all communal efforts and pursue a kind of ascetic way alone. His personal quest thus takes on much of the character of the religious quest which is pursued in hermitic isolation. He refuses to speak to anyone while he is alone in his room apart. His mother brings his food on a tray but does not converse with him.

While he is alone his mother piles up the sheets of the manuscript and restores order to the room. Finally Pierre gives up his isolated struggle and returns to the stage to tear up the manuscript. He creates an even greater mess than before, almost becoming buried in the scraps of paper. He then returns to his room apart and later is discovered there dead.

Can we say that for Pierre to give up the struggle, regardless of its futility, means that he must die? I think we can, but not without first inquiring into his relationships with both his mother and his wife, Agnes.

Pierre's mother, La Mère, holds a prominent place in the household. Her position is symbolized by her chair: a large, imposing armchair which is always present and evident. This chair is placed slightly to one side until the last act when order is restored to the room and La Mère's chair is placed in the very center, facing the audience. The position of La Mère in Pierre's life moves similarly until she is central as the dominant woman. Her "silver cord" attachment to him has been evident throughout. She worries about his eyes as he strains to read the manuscript. She takes him his food when he is isolated. She is clearly a type of dominating mother.

Adamov depicts such a mother elsewhere in his theater, as for instance La Mère in *Tous Contre Tous.* But in *L'Invasion* her character and her place on the stage and her relationship with Agnes all combine to make of her a type of the woman who gives birth and who also lures to death. While Pierre is in his room apart, his wife, Agnes, goes off with Le Premier Venu (The First One Who Comes Along) and later returns to borrow the typewriter. La Mère seems to deliberately misunderstand that Agnes is really seeking readmission to the family. La Mère does not call Pierre to come see Agnes who asks after him. Instead she remains enthroned in her chair, center stage front, and Agnes finally leaves again without seeing Pierre. When Pierre does come out of isolation, La Mère tells him that Agnes had just been there and had gone off again. Pierre tears up the manuscript and returns to his room apart which is located at the rear of the set directly and visually, now, behind La Mère's chair. This room apart, a kind of hermit's cave, has the symbolic value of a womb, as all such "caves" do. Thus, both in terms of which woman reigns supreme in his life at the end and in terms of the stage action, we see Pierre returning to the womb and death.

It is in Pierre's relationship to Agnes that the other pole of the woman symbol is revealed. Agnes' presence always represents possibilities for renewal. In the first scenes she is the one who works at the typewriter, an instrument of communication. The room is messy when she is around but the feeling is one of creative possibilities within the mess. However, as Pierre increasingly withdraws from his relationship with Agnes, these possibilities are reduced. Agnes' sexual significance is then transferred to Le Premier Venu when Pierre retires into isolation, and Agnes leaves with her new man. We learn when she comes back for the typewriter that Le Premier Venu has taken sick, and she is left with trying to hold his business together. Thus, perhaps, disintegration as well as renewal are symbolized in her, but so far as her relationship to Pierre is concerned renewal remains a possibility. Such a possibility is underlined when Pierre comments to his mother at the end that if only Agnes had had more patience, the two of them could have made a new beginning on the manuscript, an April renewal if you will. But this possibility had been finally frustrated by La Mère, and Pierre's doom is sealed.

Reflections of Adamov's neurosis are clearly evident in the characters of many of his plays. For instance, N in *La Parodie* grovels about in the gutter waiting for Lili to come along and humiliate him by rejection. Similarly Le Mutilé in *La Grande et la Petite Manoeuvre* responds to his "moniteurs" by masochistic self-mutilation. Also Edgar in *Les Retrouvailles* regresses to infantilism and is finally pushed off stage in a perambulator by his mother, another La Mère. But nowhere are the metaphysical implications of Adamov's sense of separation, together with his intense relationship to woman, so successfully related and revealed as in *L'Invasion.*

I am quite willing to grant the legitimacy of interpretations of this play which remain with the problem of communication between people, or with Pierre's inability to love. But I think the play gains significance when interpreted in the light of Adamov's self-analysis and description of modern man's predicament, as I have tried to do here.

It is clear that Adamov has not only turned away from concern with his own sickness in his later plays, *Le Ping Pong* and *Paolo Paoli,* but has probably succeeded in sublimating his neurosis to the creative imagination as Esslin and others suggest. Nevertheless, in my mind his most distinctive contribution to contemporary theater remains with the earlier plays and their depiction of modern man who is afraid and alone. Somehow Adamov's fears are more profound and representative of us all than anything he can say about modern social and national conflicts. In this regard he really speaks best for himself.

> I am afraid, and from the depths of my fear rises a pitiful prayer, the heavy stammering of anguish: "Obscure powers, forces of shadow fastened on the surface of

myself, take pity on my desperate efforts, on the frenzied energy I unremittingly expend with the single purpose of appeasing you. Beyond the movements of my guilty hands—to satisfy you they obey the meticulous fury of all things subject to you. I pledge in sacrifice to you all the time of my life, my heart which beats throughout duration. I give you my time as the most precious of all human treasures, the only gift I can never have back again. In return my need, my demand is not great. I do not ask that the threat which weighs upon me be repealed but only that it be a little lightened, a little postponed."[10]

Notes

1. Arthur Adamov, *Théâtre* (Paris, 1953), Vol. 1; Arthur Adamov, *Théâtre* (Paris, 1955), Vol. 2.

2. Leonard C. Pronko, *Avant-Garde: The Experimental Theatre in France* (Berkeley and Los Angeles, 1962), p. 131.

3. Arthur Adamov, "The Endless Humiliation," *Evergreen Review,* Vol. 2, No. 8, Spring 1959 (Translated by Richard Howard), p. 64.

4. Martin Esslin, *The Theatre of the Absurd* (Garden City, N. Y., 1961), pp. 47ff.

5. Quoted in Esslin, *op. cit.*

6. Arthur Adamov, "The Endless Humiliation," p. 66.

7. *Ibid.,* pp. 66-7.

8. *Ibid.,* p. 70.

9. Arthur Adamov, *Théâtre.* Vol. 1, p. 86.

10. Arthur Adamov, "The Endless Humiliation," p. 80.

John H. Reilly (essay date 1974)

SOURCE: Reilly, John H. "The Curable Evil." In *Arthur Adamov,* pp. 83-119. New York: Twayne Publishers, Inc., 1974.

[*In the following excerpt, Reilly offers close readings of what many critics consider two of Adamov's greatest plays:* Le ping-pong *and* Paolo Paoli*; he refers to the former as a transitional work and the latter as the first play in which Adamov demonstrates political commitment.*]

Arthur Adamov was now ready to move on to another development in his writing. Having utilized the stage as an expression of his neuroses, he had managed at this point in his life to find a way to cope with his obsessions.[1] Noticing with some satisfaction that the critics had a tendency to join his name with those of Beckett and Ionesco, he at first experienced a certain pleasure.

However, he soon added, "I began to judge my first plays severely and, very sincerely, I criticized *Waiting for Godot* and *The Chairs* for the same reasons. I already saw in the 'avant-garde' an easy escape, a diversion from the real problems, the words 'absurd theater' already irritated me. Life was not absurd—only difficult, very difficult" (***HE*** [***L'Homme et l'enfant***], p. 111). The author was thus in the unusual position of repudiating his early works. It must be pointed out, however, that, as was often the case in Adamov's writing, this extreme reaction on his part was not a true reflection of the situation. As his neuroses came under some form of control, he had the opportunity to expand the political and social interests which had always been present since the beginning, although in a lesser way. He was now of the opinion that life contained more than the cruel hand of fate and that man was able to be responsible to himself and to others. This was the curable evil with which he must deal: "The theater must show, simultaneously but well differentiated, both the curable and the incurable aspect of things. The incurable aspect, we all know, is that of the inevitability of death. The curable aspect is the social one."[2]

The Perfect Balance: *Le Ping-Pong*

In this second phase of his writing, Adamov went to another extreme: In plays such as ***Paolo Paoli*** and ***Le Printemps 71,*** he emphasized the political and social realities to such an extent that his theater became almost a diatribe and harangue. However, before he plunged entirely into this second period, in 1954-1955 he composed ***Le Ping-Pong,*** a transitional work and considered by some critics to be the best play that he ever wrote.[3] At this particular point in his progress as a writer, the dramatist seemed to have controlled his neuroses sufficiently to provide a broader, more concrete, more universal expression to his anguish and torment. At the same time, he had not yet adopted the overwhelmingly Marxist or political orientation which many of his later plays contained. It is precisely because ***Ping-Pong*** is a transitional work which avoids extremes that the play succeeds so well.

In this work, the futility of human action is presented in counterpoint to the effects on the individual of the capitalist system: "Here the how and the why of human Failure are precisely situated; it is now a matter of the particular failure of two young men who are victims both of their own phantasms and of the temptations offered by a certain society organized with profit as the goal."[4] In twelve tableaux, almost as episodic as a novel, ***Ping-Pong*** traces the lives of two men from youth to old age, as they dissipate their energies on an obsession for a pinball machine. At the beginning, Arthur is a young art student, Victor is studying to be a doctor.[5] Both men are intrigued by a pinball machine at Madame Duranty's café, and soon their involvement with the machine is so great that it becomes the center of their lives, virtually their only goal. They see it for its various possibilities: as a business venture, for they are aware that Sutter, an employee of the company that owns the machines, comes to collect the coins which are deposited and Victor and Arthur dreamily imagine the profits involved; as a technical challenge, providing them with the opportunity to improve the apparatus; and finally as a poetic endeavor, allowing Arthur to make use of his creative and imaginative talents.

Because of their suggestions they manage to enter the consortium which controls the operation of the machines. There they are introduced to the treachery and deceit of big business, which is interested only in obtaining money. Arthur and, in part, Victor are now dominated by the machine and exist only in their connection to it. Their human contacts are also based upon this same obsession: Each of the characters in the play revolves around the apparatus and the resultant love, friendship, fear, and hatred of daily living develop as a consequence of the characters' interrelationships with each other and with the machine. In so doing, they destroy their lives through a wasteful commitment, betraying their more genuine and honest human values. As all of the characters grow older and it becomes evident that their associations with the pinball machine have ruined them, Victor and Arthur are seen in the final, compelling tableau, this time playing table tennis, a new obsession as absurd and foolish as their previous preoccupation. Even at this point, each man continues to change the rules and perfect the game to such an extent that the whole project becomes a farce. Victor collapses and dies, leaving Arthur alone.

Adamov's first inspiration for the play was the image of two old men playing table tennis. He did not know what the subject of his work would be, but he knew how he would end it, having the perfect opportunity to show that all human action results in the same wastefulness, eventually leading to death. Once he had the overall image in mind, the playwright then took a specific incident from his own life: "The first concrete idea of *Ping-Pong* came at the Mabillon [a café in the Saint-Germain des Prés section in Paris], while playing a pinball machine named 'The Rocket and the Moon.' The player was supposed to operate it in such a way that the rocket reached the moon. The machine then lighted up, the game was won" (*HE,* p. 112). From this pastime in his personal life, Adamov saw how his work could be enlarged, preferring to use the pinball machine as the main image of his play, rather than the game of table tennis, because of the former's closer links to the business world and the capitalist system. The theme of this play was very personal to Adamov, who had seen his

father fritter away and destroy his life because of his exaggerated preoccupation with gambling, an exercise in futility similar to that experienced by Victor and Arthur.

Once he began the writing, Adamov made the pinball machine the center around which everything turned, like Lili in *The Parody*: "*Ping-Pong,* with its purposely deceptive title, has the pinball machine as its real subject. I wanted the play to revolve around the obsession for this pinball machine. I wanted it to be the center of all the concerns, yearnings, ambitions" (*HE,* p. 112). In a sense, the pinball apparatus replaces the fatality of the former plays. As a result, the characters have greater freedom, or as Adamov termed it, "indecision," than in previous works. In spite of the givens of the situation in which each one will inevitably fail, they do have a certain independence. They are fighting a machine, a part of the capitalist system, not simply the destiny that awaits all men. This time the enemy is not the uncontrollable disturbance of the psyche brought about by the fatality of life. Arthur and Victor can avoid what is happening to them: "Contrary to what takes place in my other plays . . . the threat does not come only from outside; the characters secrete their own poison, prepare their own unhappiness; and this unhappiness, not having exactly the same cause for each one, does not have the same results" (*Th.* [*Théâtre*], II, 16-17). In *Combat,* Adamov commented on the greater degree of complexity and individualization of his characters: "My machine is not a symbol. Rather, it is a center of interest for each one, according to his age, character, or social position. For some, it is an object that they want to keep, to protect. For others, it is an instrument of domination. For Sutter, the possibility of impressing the world. For Arthur, an escape from this world, a trapeze for the acrobatics of his brain. For Victor, a simple pastime."[6]

In fact, each of the characters is defined or distinguished by his relation to and utilization of the machine. Annette, who is the principal female figure, sees the instrument as an opportunity to achieve a better position in life. To that end, she uses the men around her who can help her gain entrance to the consortium. In spite of her goal, she often seems to share Arthur's enthusiasm for the creative possibilities of the machine, and Adamov endows her with more sympathy than he normally does his women characters. For Madame Duranty, the mother figure, the apparatus is only an overt indication of how life has treated her badly. When it breaks down, she loses money. Existence becomes a perpetual complaint because of her inability to get the machine repaired and to put her affairs back in order. In this context, Madame Duranty is basically the same as the whining mother figures of the previous plays.

Those who work at the consortium reflect Adamov's contemptuous view of the world of big business. Sutter and Roger are both employed by the company, but neither one has any real interest in the pinball operation; their work is simply a means to an end, a way to power, fame, and money. But it is the director of the consortium, *Le Vieux* (The Old Man), for whom Adamov reserves his greatest scorn. Seeing the whole operation not only as a money-making proposition, but as a close link to sexual conquests, *Le Vieux* manipulates people for his own purposes. He asks Annette to become a spy for his group, promises Madame Duranty that he will fix her machine if she will sign a petition for him, accepts Arthur's and Victor's ideas, planning to use them and to keep the credit to himself. In short, the playwright suggests that *Le Vieux* represents the capitalist system, exploiting others for its own profitable goals. The Old Man is willing to sacrifice quality for quantity in his frenzied desire for money. At the same time, he is willing to sacrifice people in his quest for power, a prefiguration of the characters in **Paolo Paoli**.

The two principal figures, who were inspired in part by Flaubert's *Bouvard et Pécuchet*,[7] are also presented in their interreaction with the pinball machine. Victor, in a lesser way, shares many of the same business ideals of *Le Vieux*. He views the enterprise as a moneymaking proposition and participates in it to the extent that it can prove useful to him. Other than that, his interest is superficial and passing and yet even he cannot avoid an obsessive involvement. The more practical of the two men, he has gone on to become a doctor. Nevertheless, in spite of his detachment, he is unable to separate himself from the machine's influence, finding that he can obtain his patients by going to the places where people play the game.

On the other hand, Arthur, presumably Adamov himself, is the poet, the visionary. Of all of the characters, Arthur is the most truly interested in the pinball machine for its creative possibilities. Although, like Victor, he may appreciate its moneymaking aspects, he can also relish the infinite variations which the instrument has to provide, with the reduction of its side flippers, the addition of the extra ball, the rocket reaching the moon. For him, the game becomes such an obsession that it dominates his life. In his own way, Arthur uses this preoccupation as a means of escape from the world surrounding him. He becomes the very image of man's alienation, virtually deifying a machine, while distorting his human relationships. Even his friendship with Victor suffers when the latter becomes less interested in the game.

Arthur becomes the exaggeration of those who are entrapped in the orbit of the machine, his situation only a magnification of what is happening to the other characters. Since he has given each character a certain degree of differentiation, Adamov reveals an even more pronounced pessimism about life. In the previous works, there was nothing that man *could* do. In this play, there is nothing that man *will* do. Each character fails to cope with reality, continually striving to reach his own paradise via the machine, allowing the capitalist system to use him. Each personage could manipulate his destiny in a limited way, but does not; each one is at least partially responsible for what happens to him. Sutter becomes a virtual beggar, Roger disappears, Madame Duranty is reduced to poverty and senile complaining, *Le Vieux* dies—a victim of his own emotions, Annette is killed by a taxi, either a suicide or an accident victim, Victor dies while foolishly pursuing his game of table tennis, and Arthur remains alone after having devoted his life to a wasteful and destructive goal, a life now empty and hollow.[8]

Yet in spite of their individualization and greater complexity, the characters in the play are not meant to exist as psychologically-developed beings, as they would in the naturalistic theater. They do not possess a soul, and are identified mainly through their connection with the machine. Since the situations in which they find themselves are spurious, their language must also be false: Their words are clichés, stereotypes, and truisms, they sound as if they are reciting something which they have memorized, something lifeless. Roland Barthes, calling the play a series of *situations de langage,* comments: "**Ping-Pong** is entirely constituted by a block of language under glass, analogous, if you wish, to those frozen vegetables which allow the English to enjoy the tartness of spring in their winter."[9] Since man has not really accepted the freedom of his responsibility, his language is not free. Language is thus an indication of his refusal to face reality: There is no sense of spontaneity, everything is thought out before it is spoken. Because the speeches do not allow for deviation from the set pattern which has been learned, there can be no communication.

The language represents the position in which the characters find themselves. Placed in situations which are clearly wasteful—situations in which they use enormous amounts of energy, time, and thought on the refinement of a game which is mere child's play—the characters are required to use a speech pattern which carries the same distortion, becoming a parody of their actions. As Martin Esslin points out, in an interesting comment on the use of language in the work, "This is a play that may well appear completely meaningless if it is merely read. The speeches about improvements in the construction of pinball machines may seem trivial nonsense; the meaning of the play emerges precisely at the moment that the actor delivers these nonsensical lines with a depth of conviction worthy of the loftiest flights of poetry. It is a play that has to be acted *against* the text rather than with it."[10] The mission of the characters is inane, but they engage in it seriously and persistently, revealing the absurdity of their world. In *The Invasion,* Adamov had utilized indirect language in cases where the characters did not express their real opinions but hid their feelings behind idle conversation, a technique used by Chekhov. But in *Ping-Pong,* the characters proclaim their foolish notions with religious intensity: "In Chekhov, real feelings are suppressed behind meaningless politeness, in *Le Ping-Pong* absurd ideas are proclaimed as if they were eternal truths."[11] In Adamov's work, language is one of the signs of man's sense of estrangement—mankind is doomed to failure because there is no point of human contact.

Yet, the weakness of the individual human being is not the only cause of the isolation which we all suffer. Adamov now suggests more strongly than in previous works that the *strength* of other human beings working toward their own perverted goals creates the capitalist system, which must also share a great deal of the blame: "Alienation . . . of man captive in a society in which the pinball machine sparkles, rules, sits in state. It [the pinball machine] does not yet clearly specify the society of which it is the image, but my half-willed, half-involuntary imprecision does not prevent one from recognizing the guilty party: the capitalist system" (*HE,* p. 112). Unlike the procedure in his later plays, Adamov does not place the blame entirely on the world of big business but, for the first time, he does make it one of the specific enemies in man's struggle. The director of the consortium typifies the system's craftiness and willful disregard for people, its exploitation of others. Adamov wants to stress that all those involved in the system lack any real interest in the project for itself: They want only the power and money which can be derived from it. Thus the basis for all the activity springs from a society that is false and a goal founded on twisted premises.

Rather than a frontal assault on the capitalist system, however, *Ping-Pong* shows that when man allows himself to be controlled by any idea or ideology, he loses his freedom and becomes a slave to the organization which develops around it. The pinball machine is the image of man's objective—a silly, childish game. But for all those involved in the project, it is a serious question of their existence, eventually even a matter of life and death. Because of their obsession with the machine, an entire network of interrelationships and structures has developed, involving, implies Adamov, those who exploit and those who are exploited. By giving their lives over to a machine, by hoping that it will give them power and love, Victor, Arthur, and the others have let themselves be manipulated. This foolish project, very much a part of the capitalist world, has become the real enslaver. At this particular moment in his writing, the playwright had not yet placed the full responsibility on the capitalist system. Victor and Arthur

can still pull themselves out of the quicksand into which they are sinking. Yet, like the playwright's father, they cannot help what they do and the system draws them in even more deeply. While each character is provided with some "indecision," it is clear that he cannot liberate himself entirely from his obsessions, he cannot face the world as it really is. Adamov's theater is still one of general human considerations; in spite of the dramatist's turn toward the outer world, he has not yet left the realm of the inner being.

It is precisely because he remained too much in this realm that Adamov later criticized the play. He felt that he had not sufficiently developed the workings of the consortium and that he had left that aspect too detached from the piece as a whole. Although he recognized that he had made an ever greater step toward reality by placing the action in a fixed time and place, he nevertheless noted that "the social events which, in the course of the years, change the internal organization of the consortium, are not truly indicated, so that one does not really feel the state of society on the one hand and the passage of time on the other. . . . I should have tried to examine the wheels of the great social machine as carefully and as minutely as I had examined the bumpers and side flippers of the pinball machine. This is the examination I am trying to undertake today in a new play, situated even more firmly in a time and place than *Ping-Pong*" (*Th.,* II, 17).[12]

In spite of the playwright's disclaimer, *Ping-Pong* is one of Adamov's best works and he has been unfair in his judgment. Although he is still depicting the same theme, we are now confronted with the how and the why of life's situations, to use Madame Serreau's terms. The effect of the analysis allows us to understand the workings behind the feelings; the theme is no longer so closely allied with the dramatist's own psyche that, as in many of his earlier plays, the spectator cannot appreciate it. Now we can comprehend the efforts behind man's foolish actions. The image of the pinball apparatus is surely one of the most striking in his theater: The ridiculous aberrations of the characters around the machine become the visual representation of the truly tragic meaning of life's wastefulness.

In the final analysis, it was a wise decision on Adamov's part not to emphasize the workings of the consortium. As the play stands, it contains the right combination of the inner and outer worlds, the psyche and reality. Although it is true that the world which he has created deals only with the preoccupations of the characters and has little in common with the normal routine of living, this is not a weakness—it is rather an effective structural device that reflects the narrow vision of the people involved. What we see in *Ping-Pong* reveals the very limited arena in which Victor and Arthur operate. If Adamov had stressed the economic and social situation, he would have destroyed the very delicate balance which he had created. Having made his own terror more specific, but having not yet introduced the strongly Marxist overtones of his following works, the playwright succeeded in finding an excellent blend of the personal and historical elements which would henceforth constitute the basis of his theater. In addition, **Ping-Pong,** along with **Professor Taranne,** is one of the two works by the playwright which seem to be faithful to the spirit in which they were composed. All of his other plays, including those which follow **Ping-Pong,** reveal an exaggerated involvement on the dramatist's part which becomes almost as neurotic and obsessed as the principal characters in the plays.

Ping-Pong has remained one of Adamov's more popular dramas. It was first presented in Paris at the Théâtre des Noctambules on March 2, 1955, under the direction of Jacques Mauclair, who comments: "The creation of **Ping-Pong** constituted an important step in Adamov's career and in his relationship with the public. He came out of the ghetto of the authors of the damned, condemned to clandestine theaters. Adamov no longer, understandably, wanted to hear one speak of the 'Tuesdays at the *Oeuvre*' or of performances given at 6 o'clock stealthily before three spectators. Performed at the Noctambules at 9 P.M., he was well received by the press and the play had, if I remember correctly, more than 150 performances, which was an unhoped-for number."[13]

In this transitional work, Adamov created one of his most accessible plays, one which has been performed numerous times around the world, including productions in New York, London, West Berlin, and Stockholm. At this point in his career, the dramatist was concerned with both the incurable and the curable elements in life. However, as he continued to write over the next few years, he would turn particularly to the social or curable elements for his subject matter.

· · · · ·

HISTORY AND POLITICAL COMMITMENT: *PAOLO PAOLI*

Paolo Paoli is the first play written in Adamov's "new" style. Perhaps his favorite work (in **Man and Child,** he devotes an entire chapter to it), this is his first attempt to take a specific, factual subject, placing it in an historical context. The play represents an abandonment of some of the philosophical principles of Adamov's first phase of writing and an acceptance of an ideological, political commitment; life's incurable element is only one part of the total picture. The dramatist now emphasizes the curable aspects, studying the workings of society, analyzing its defects, and suggesting improvements.

An ambitious play, with a rich, complex, sometimes confusing mingling of social, economic, and historical background, **Paolo Paoli** deals with the circulation of merchandise in the capitalist system in France and its overseas territories during the *belle époque,* the "banquet years," from 1900-1914. Ostensibly, the merchandise for sale is the comically absurd selection of butterflies and ostrich feathers. In actual fact, Adamov wants the audience to see that the real product being manipulated is man, who is exploited and utilized by his fellowmen in their quest for financial gain. The playwright links the fate of the individual to the times and background of which he is a part: "**Paolo Paoli** is, in fact, situated very precisely in this period [1900-1914], and the evolution of the characters is conditioned by the unfolding of the events of the world in which they live."[14] No longer is his theater placed in an indefinite period with characters detached from the world around them; the theater is to be the realm of the specific. For the first time, Adamov will attempt a political and social satire of the twentieth century.

The dramatist came upon the subject of his play by accident. In order to make a living, since his theater could not provide him with a substantial enough income, he had taken on a number of writing chores, especially translations into French of works like Georg Büchner's *Danton's Death,* Heinrich von Kleist's *The Broken Pitcher,* and Strindberg's *The Pelican.* In the Spring of 1955, with the aid of his wife, he agreed to "rewrite" the memoirs of Eugène Le Moult, an entomologist who had made his fortune by utilizing the convicts in Cayenne[15] to find butterflies for his business: "Le Moult is a scoundrel, but it does not matter since, by listening to him evoke his past, the idea came to me for my play, **Paolo Paoli**" (**HE,** p. 117). Adamov was immediately attracted to both the comic and tragic elements of the portrait of the convict chasing after butterflies with his net. He realized that this picturesque image was only a diversion from the real, bitter truth: The butterfly for the entomologist was not an *objet d'art,* but an object of business; the convict was not an amusing figure but a horrifying example of exploitation. Since these events took place in 1900-1914, Adamov had found the period for his play. He next decided that the entomologist should have a business associate to whom he would sell his products and, after some research, he found the proper complement: a merchant in the feather industry, which, until 1912, was the fourth largest French export trade. Upon further study into the period, he became interested in the separation of church and state and the idea of a priest as a major character came to his mind. He was further helped in the development of his play by reading that certain missionaries in China had also ventured into the butterfly industry, using schoolchildren to seek out the insects for them. The idea of the priest became even clearer when he happened to come upon a brochure in the National Library in Paris written by an abbot in the 1900's. This abbot strongly defended the feather industry, arguing that it was not a crime to kill birds, otherwise why would God have permitted them to fly in the sky? In any case, reported Adamov, the priest felt that it was not such a terrible fate to end up on a lady's hat (*HE,* p. 118).

With these images in mind, the dramatist set about creating a play which would say something about the "curable" situation of man, in which men would be seen in direct relation to the world around them. Dealing with an apparently frivolous topic, the playwright wanted to show the truly tragic dimensions of the human condition. And this was another reason that he chose the "banquet years," for the silliness of the prewar years collided with the reality of World War I: "And if I chose the period before 1914, it is because it was a period which went from the most obvious frivolity to the most dramatic events. So much so that the movement of private life, under the circumstances, could be linked particularly well to that of public life."[16]

In essence, Adamov attempted to provide an accounting of the system of exchange which society had established. The play is so structured that it is the economic mechanism of exchange which determines the movement of the work rather than individual persons. The characters are caught in a network of socioeconomic requirements, trapped in an endless pattern of bargaining and merchandising: They begin by exchanging butterflies and end up by exchanging men. These individuals are, first, a microcosm of society and, then, of nations, struggling and competing for markets, eventually leading to a class fight and finally to World War I. Adamov particularly wanted to stress the circular aspect of such a situation, showing that societies (or the individuals in the societies) allow themselves to be caught in a constant repetition of events which he called *tourbillons circulaires* (circular whirlwinds). In this same context, the dramatist also hoped that the audience would grasp the parallels to be drawn with modern France, which was repeating the same mistakes and committing the same ignominies.[17]

The most remarkable achievement of Adamov's ambitious undertaking is that he managed to portray the religious, political, social, and national complexities of this society by means of only seven characters: Paolo Paoli, a collector and dealer of rare butterflies; Florent Hulot-Vasseur, also a collector of butterflies and an importer and manufacturer of ostrich feathers; the Abbé Saulnier, cunning and devious, a willing accomplice in all the business ventures; Madame de Saint-Sauveur, a captain's wife, the chauvinist, blind to everything but the jingoistic militarism of France; Stella, Paolo's German-born wife, who becomes Hulot-Vasseur's mistress; and finally, the victims, Robert Marpeaux, the convict utilized by Paolo and Hulot-Vasseur for their own commercial purposes, the "commodity," and his wife, Rose, another martyr of exploitation.

Curiously, in spite of Adamov's new approach to theater, the structure of the play is quite similar to that of his previous works. At first *Paolo Paoli* seems like a simple repetition of the construction of *Ping-Pong.* The butterflies and ostrich feathers around which all the characters gravitate and which have become their obsessions are used exactly like the pinball machine of the previous play. In both works, the ridiculousness and absurdity of man's actions are underscored. In addition, the theme of human beings trapped in a web from which they cannot escape had served as the basis of all of his earlier "dream" works, and, once again, two of the major characters—Paolo and Hulot-Vasseur—appear to be heading toward a similar fate.

This time, however, there are some significant differences in the content. While man is still the helpless pawn in the struggles of existence, he is no longer controlled principally by his obsession or by fate: There is a new, "curable" element. The capitalist system and man himself must bear the burden of responsibility. The system is composed of human beings and they must accept the blame for the situation of their fellowmen. At the same time, implies Adamov, man can change this situation through his will, his desires, and his awareness. Although Paolo and Hulot-Vasseur share similar experiences, they are really designed to represent two poles of the economic system, the two ends necessary for the trading and exchanging. Their structural use is no longer meant to convey the essential sameness of man's fate, but the polarity which is the basis of business. Nor do they share the same final role: Paolo rebels against the system and everything represented by Hulot-Vasseur.

Paolo,[18] based on Eugène Le Moult, the original inspiration of the work, is a dealer in butterflies. His father, like Le Moult's, was a minor Corsican civil servant at Cayenne. Recognizing the opportunities for financial gain at the expense of others, Paolo organizes the convicts in the city to work as poorly-paid butterfly hunters for his business in France. One of the young convicts, Marpeaux, serving a sentence for a minor crime, escapes to Venezuela, where he is completely dependent upon Paolo for his livelihood and he must continue to hunt butterflies. Paolo is encouraged in his business ventures by Hulot-Vasseur, the other part of the organization, for Hulot-Vasseur purchases the butterflies for his own commercial undertakings. A shrewd and ruthless industrialist, he is beset with many problems, brought about by the labor conflicts in his factory and his struggle with German competitors. The third member of this unholy trio, Abbé Saulnier, is drawn most willingly into the web of business: His brother is a missionary in China, and when the market becomes difficult for Paolo in that country, the abbot offers his brother's services in obtaining some rare butterfly specimens for Paolo. In the first few scenes, Adamov thus effectively conveys the cruel absurdities as well as the inter-relationships of the economic, religious, and penal systems, all against the background of historical events.

In his portrait of Paolo, Hulot-Vasseur, and the priest, Adamov is especially interested in presenting the conniving and treacherousness which he considers a part of the capitalist system. Paolo is a foolish, small-time businessman, making his fortune by selling objects made from butterfly wings—religious pictures, ashtrays, saucers, trays. Hulot-Vasseur exists only for the money and power which he holds, coldly indifferent to human beings as individuals; Paolo, the abbot, and Marpeaux are only pieces to be used in Hulot-Vasseur's overall pursuit of financial success. The priest loses all of his religious trappings and turns into a businessman, becoming probably the most unpleasant character in the play—hypocritical and devious. What is particularly striking about Adamov's picture of Abbé Saulnier is that the priest has no concept of morality or decency. At the very moment that he is approaching Hulot-Vasseur to ask him to aid Marpeaux (a project which his later actions show that he cares nothing about), it develops that he is really asking the industrialist to buy some butterfly specimens from his brother in China, thereby betraying Paolo, to whom he had previously promised the specimens.[19]

The playwright is underlining his point that only the strongest, the most ruthless, the most deceitful can survive in the jungle of the economic system. As the play progresses, Paolo loses most of his business because he is basically a somewhat anarchical, second-rate entrepreneur whose interests clash with the much more concerted and ambitious efforts of major industry. It is Adamov's view that those who are victorious succeed because they know how to make alliances at the right moment, alliances which oftentimes create strange bedfellows: "Finally, what I especially had to show.. was the monstrous alliance, constantly renewed, of the so-called Christians and the so-called anticlericals."[20] Hulot-Vasseur, a militant anticlerical, joins forces with the abbot when it becomes economically profitable for him to do so. Both sides unite to fight against the one whom Adamov sees as the victim in the affair, the worker Marpeaux. Essentially, adds the playwright, it is the worker who is the major threat to the capitalists and their system and they will bury any personal differences in this class struggle in order to keep him subjugated.

Marpeaux, the pawn in the system, has returned from Venezuela to seek pardon from the government. Since the pardon may be some time in coming, Paolo sends him to Morocco in the interval, completely indifferent to the fact that the country has become dangerous because the French are still waging a battle against the natives. It is obvious that Marpeaux is an object to be used, a commodity to be exploited. Upon his return from Morocco, after having obtained his pardon, he joins the Socialist party and opposes the *jaunes,* a militant Catholic organization run by Abbé Saulnier. Working in Hulot-Vasseur's factory, Marpeaux distributes pacifist pamphlets urging soldiers to desert. The abbot, Marpeaux's former protector as long as he was not a threat to the priest's interests, denounces him for subverting the troops and Marpeaux is then arrested. As soon as Paolo hears of this, he has a sudden change of heart and vows that he will no longer help the system, his money will be used for those who really need it: "Mark it well, my friend Saulnier, you can say goodbye to that money. That money will no longer be a part of your dirty little circuit. . . . It will go directly to those who need it to eat, clothe themselves, and to annoy you, which comes to the same thing" (*Th.,* III, 141).

This is the first play in which Adamov has created a "positive" major character (Marpeaux) and a "noble" action (Paolo's attempt to take money out of the capitalist system and turn it over to the needy.[21] Interestingly, both of these aspects are the weakest points in the play. Marpeaux's characterization is not successful because of the one-sidedness of the portrait, the lack of complexity in his makeup. He is so totally "good" that he is less than believable. Although Adamov intended that Marpeaux represent an ideological point of view—the worker struggling against the system—and the author did not want the spectator to identify with the character, it is clear that his own sympathies lay very strongly with Marpeaux. As a result, Adamov has developed a characterization in spite of himself and, unfortunately, a characterization lacking in dimension.

A more serious criticism can be made of the abrupt and unconvincing change of attitude expressed by Paolo at the end. This admirable gesture, found very rarely in Adamov's theater, is utterly unbelievable, especially in view of Paolo's generally negative portrait throughout the rest of the work. It is also hardly likely that Paolo's action will take the money out of circulation as he claims. In any event, he has nothing to lose by his action. It is principally an act of anger against Hulot-Vasseur and Abbé Saulnier who have deserted him now that his business has been ruined by the war. Yet Paolo's gesture is important to the theme of the play because it allows Adamov to show that human beings can do something, that their situations are "curable." By their will power and by their determination, suggests the playwright, they can triumph over the workings of the capitalist system. This is Adamov's call for a limited revolt, based upon human strength and represents the dramatist's hopes for mankind.

It is probable that the author intended to use this final scene as a vivid contrast to the rest of the play. In this last part, Paolo is meant to depict man at his best, working for the betterment of all. For the first time, his words and his deeds coincide. Earlier Paolo and the others of the capitalist system mouthed false, hypocritical words to cover up what they were really doing, the playwright stressing the opposition between "what the characters do and what they say." It is the dramatist's contention that people like Paolo, Hulot-Vasseur, and the abbot speak of "eternal" values but have only temporal interests in mind—their own commercial gains. In this comedy of disproportion, the spectator is meant to recognize the situation of men relentlessly pursuing their business interests, to laugh at the absurdity of their endeavor, and, finally, to realize that this is more than just grotesque foolishness. It is a tragic representation of man's hypocrisy and his exploitation of others. The spectator is to understand that, in this type of system, those who succeed do so at the expense of others. The audience is then expected to take its observations one step further, associating the individual actions to the historical incidents which provide the background, "transposing" the ideas generated in the play from men to nations, finally realizing that wars are simply further extensions of this same distortion of life.

In order to make the connection between the individual actions occurring on stage and the historical events, Adamov precedes each of his twelve scenes with brief comments from the 1900-1914 period. Using the methods of the political theater of Erwin Piscator, quotations from the newspapers and photographs of the major figures of the time are projected onto a screen, a technique which also functions as a means of "distancing" the action, breaking the illusion, and reminding the audience that it is in a theater. Each projection provides the necessary historical situation in which the characters move. As Paolo, Hulot-Vasseur, and Saulnier go through their paces, the spectator can link their actions to those related incidents on the social and political fronts; as the main characters proceed through their dramas, the spectator is able to connect them with the information he is given on the Boer War, the troubles in China, the struggle in Morocco, the Dreyfus affair, the Balkan War, the strikes in France, the effort to break the power of the unions. It is an easy step to relate Paolo's efforts to send Marpeaux from Venezuela to Morocco for his own business purposes to that of England exchanging Morocco for Egypt, both people and nations being used as articles of exchange. Most important, the projections on the screen help to convey the seriousness of the situation against which the frivolity of the people is contrasted. In his own remarks on the staging of *Paolo Paoli,* Adamov observed: "Do not forget the photos of Krupp and of Schneider. . . . I only placed butterflies and feathers on stage, but the screen must come forth with the representatives of capitalism, the faces of those responsible, visible, identified, named."[22] All of this culminates in the final set of projections, representing August, 1914, when Nicholas II of Russia is reported as saying to his cousin William II of Germany: "I imagine that you will be forced to mobilize," signifying the start of World War I.

In order to deal with this complex historical plot, Adamov adopted an entirely new method of work: He undertook extensive research and documentation on his subject. Up to this time, the playwright had drawn largely upon his own inner world and external matters were not probed. Starting with *Paolo Paoli* and continuing with his next few plays, Adamov concentrated on enriching his theater through a careful study of the people and their historical period: "I feared for a while that I was going to drown in documentation. Reading *The Century, The Free World, The Cross,* of course, *The Figaro* [newspapers of the period] in massive doses is rather maddening. But, little by little, a main idea asserted itself: exchange, merchandise."[23] The dramatist no longer felt that his work could advance without some external awareness, because, by now, he was arriving at a new concept of poetry which would come from facts, details which no imagination could supply: "Poetry, the true poetry, is always linked to the most extreme particularization."[24] In his view the allegorical aspects of the avant-garde and his former theater represented the opposite of what art should be; the true aesthetics of drama come from a study of time, place, and background.

His research led him into a deeper understanding not only of the capitalist system, but of those whom he saw as its victims: the powerless, the politically and economically impotent. In his new phase, the author came into contact with two groups which he considered to be the only audience capable of appreciating his writings: the workers and the youth. In his future plays he would keep these people in mind and, at times, they would play a central role in the works.

Paolo Paoli was first presented in Lyon at the Théâtre de la Comédie by Roger Planchon on May 24, 1957. Planchon, who had previously directed *Professor Taranne* and *The Direction of the March,* was actually Jacquie's choice. The playwright was enormously pleased with the final results, admiring the inventive creativity of the director as well as the effectiveness of the acting and the sets. It was at this time that the close association of the director and dramatist developed. The production, unfortunately, was not without its troubles. Planchon had at first been advised by one of the members of the Commission of Arts and Letters not to perform the play, with the veiled threat that Planchon would not obtain the subsidy needed to open up a theater which he had been planning in Villeurbanne, outside Lyon (*HE,* pp. 122-23). However, thanks to the intervention of Jacques Lemarchand, the drama critic of the *Figaro Littéraire,* the performance was permitted. Similar problems awaited the play in Paris, where it was the first such spectacle put on by Planchon in that city. Roger Martin du Gard, a major novelist and former Nobel Prize winner, had to intervene to insure the presentation. Despite the succession of obstacles, Adamov saw the production as a great triumph: "Public success of **Paolo Paoli.** The C.G.T.[25] and the Communists help us, it is true. All the seats are taken 10 days ahead of time. But the bourgeoisie, for its part, is impressed and attends" (**HE,** pp. 124-25).

In his new style, Adamov did not completely abandon the theater of the absurd, still retaining the grotesque and ridiculous situations, the exaggeration of detail, the inventive use of time. What he achieved, rather, was a fusion of the avant-garde with the epic, historical play, emphasizing the latter. As he indicated, he was well aware that the human condition contained both that which could be corrected by man's will and that which could not be changed. In his view, the only true theater was one which would take into account both aspects of life to create a total picture. Is this new approach more valid than his previous style? It seems likely that it is not, if the final answer is to be found in the effectiveness of the plays as presented in a theater. The early plays, whatever their deficiencies, conveyed a genuine expression of anguish and possessed a ring of truth which came from the depths of his soul. **Paolo Paoli** is an often brilliantly conceived and executed drama, providing incisive reflections on man in a social, political, and economic world, but it is also a strident, somewhat didactic, politically-biased theater. As such, it loses much of its power.

Notes

Four volumes of Adamov's plays have been grouped together under the title *Théatre*. Hereafter, references to any one of the four volumes will be incorporated into the text of this study and referred to by the abbreviation *Th.* and the indication of the volume number.

1. This apparent resolution of his difficulties would not last long. In his final phase of writing, the neuroses would reappear and once again become a major part of his theater.

2. "Qui êtes-vous Arthur Adamov?" *Cité Panorama* (Program Bulletin of Planchon's Théâtre de la Cité), Villeurbanne, No. 9, 1960. As cited in Esslin, *Absurd,* p. 94.

3. Esslin calls it "one of the masterpieces of the Theatre of the Absurd" (p. 86), and Serreau also views the work as Adamov's supreme accomplishment (p. 82).

4. Serreau, p. 75.

5. Arthur is Adamov himself and Victor is the name of his close childhood friend.

6. Jean Carlier, "Adamov apporte deux billards électriques: un pour les acteurs, un pour le public," *Combat,* February 3, 1955.

7. Arthur and Victor also bring to mind the wasted lives of Frédéric and Deslauriers in Flaubert's *L'Education sentimentale.*

8. At the same time, however, Arthur does not share the total defeat experienced by the others, probably because he is the only character in the play who is interested in the machine for its imaginative aspects.

9. *Mythologies* (Paris: Editions du Seuil, 1957), p. 100.

10. *Absurd,* p. 88.

11. *Ibid.*

12. This play is *Paolo Paoli.*

13. Gaudy, p. 59.

14. Claude Olivier, "'Paolo Paoli,' c'est la demi-conscience," *Les Lettres Françaises,* January 16, 1958. As cited in [Arthur Adamov] *Ici et maintenant* [(Paris: Gallimard, 1964)] p. 52.

15. The capital of French Guiana.

16. "Le théâtre pêut-il aborder l'actualité politique?" *France-Observateur,* No. 405, February 13, 1958. As cited in *Ici et maintenant,* p. 70.

17. "Quand les critiques sont dans la pièce . . . ," *La Nouvelle Critique,* No. 94, March, 1958. As cited in *Ici et maintenant,* p. 87.

18. The title and name of the central character, Paolo Paoli, came from a play which Adamov had written a few years earlier and had then destroyed (Mélèse, p. 56).

19. The portrait of the priest is so vehement that Adamov later felt obliged to state that he considered the characterization of the abbot suitable and that the anticlerical tone of the work was not excessive.

20. "A propos de 'Paolo Paoli,'" *Théâtre Populaire,* January, 1958. As cited in *Ici et maintenant,* p. 60.

21. The actions of the characters in *One Against Another* are too suspect to be listed as "noble."

22. "Courtes remarques sur la mise en scène de 'Paolo Paoli,'" *Paolo Paoli* (Paris: Gallimard, 1960). As cited in *Ici et maintenant,* p. 96.

23. "Les papillons du bagne," *Les Lettres Françaises,* March 21, 1957. As cited in *Ici et maintenant,* p. 48.

24. Claude Sarraute, "Arthur Adamov définit un nouvel art poétique," *Le Monde,* January 19, 1958.

25. *Confédération Générale du Travail,* the workers' union.

Selected Bibliography

PRIMARY SOURCES

A listing of Adamov's works in order of first published editions. In cases where the first published edition is not readily available and was not cited in this study, the most readily available edition follows in brackets. In some cases the only published version has been in a journal or review and this has been so indicated.

1. PLAYS

La Parodie. Paris: Charlot, 1950. [*Théâtre I*—Paris: Gallimard, 1953.]

L'Invasion. Paris: Charlot, 1950. [*Théâtre I*—Paris: Gallimard, 1953.]

Le Professeur Taranne. Théâtre I—Paris: Gallimard, 1953.

Le Sens de la marche. Théâtre II—Paris: Gallimard, 1955.

Le Ping-Pong. Théâtre II—Paris: Gallimard, 1955.

Paolo Paoli. Paris: Gallimard ("Le Manteau d'Arlequin"), 1957. [*Théatre III*—Paris: Gallimard, 1966.]

Le Printemps 71. Paris: Gallimard, 1961. [*Théâtre IV*—Paris: Gallimard, 1968.]

2. ENGLISH TRANSLATIONS

The Invasion, trans. Robert Doan. University Park: University of Pennsylvania Press, 1968.

Paolo Paoli, trans. Geoffrey Brereton. London: Calder, 1959.

Ping-pong, trans. Richard Howard. New York: Grove Press, 1959.

Professor Taranne in *Four Modern French Comedies,* trans. A. Bermel. New York: Capricorn Press, 1960.

Professor Taranne in *Absurd Drama,* trans. Peter Meyer. Harmondsworth: Penguin Books, 1965.

Two Plays: Professor Taranne and Ping pong. Professor Taranne, trans. Peter Meyer; and *Ping pong,* trans. Derek Prouse. London: J. Calder, 1962.

3. OTHER WORKS

L'Homme et l'enfant. Paris: Gallimard, 1968.

SECONDARY SOURCES

1. BOOKS

Barthes, Roland. *Mythologies.* Paris: Editions du Seuil, 1957. A brief but incisive account of Adamov and his use of language (pp. 99-102).

Esslin, Martin. *The Theatre of the Absurd.* Rev. Ed. Garden City, N. Y.: Anchor Books (Doubleday), 1969. A very perceptive, intelligent, and scholarly chapter on the playwright and his work (pp. 66-99).

Gaudy, René. *Arthur Adamov.* Paris: Théâtre Ouvert (Stock), 1971. The first book to appear on Adamov and a useful study on the dramatist from the point of view of background.

Mélèse, Pierre. *Arthur Adamov.* Paris: Théâtre de tous les temps (Seghers), 1973. A good work, particularly helpful on background details. Excellent plot summaries.

Serreau, Genevieve. *Histoire du "nouveau théâtre."* Paris: Gallimard, 1966. An excellent and sensitive chapter on Adamov, studying his works up to *La Politique des restes* (pp. 66-82).

John J. McCann (essay date 1975)

SOURCE: McCann, John J. "The Political Plays." In *The Theater of Arthur Adamov,* pp. 94-121. Chapel Hill: North Carolina Studies in the Romance Languages and Literatures, 1975.

[*In the following essay, McCann analyzes Adamov's political plays written between 1958 and 1961, maintaining that these works reveal two basic paradigms: the human struggle within a political context and an essentially social theatrical world.*]

The elusive quality of Adamov's theater is that it never seems to be what it is, but rather seems to be eternally becoming something other or more than what it is or has been. As Marc Beigbeder wrote just after the production of *Paolo Paoli* in 1957, Adamov's plays always announce another, each play is a promise of something to come:

> A vrai dire, comme il arrive quelquefois, chacune des pièces d'Adamov en annonce une autre, promet le chef-d'œuvre, la plénitude, pour le lendemain. Il n'y a pas de création sans, chez le créateur, insatisfaction. Mais il est des créateurs dont, en quelque sorte, elle est la vraie et seule création. Dont les œuvres courent pathétiquement, et avec qualité, génie, après l'œuvre-qui ne sera jamais.[1]

This explains to a large degree why there is no one play in the theater of Adamov which can stand as a prototype or basic invariant for the rest of the plays. Rather each play is a variant of the other, a restructuring and reviewing of an essentially similar yet superficially different universe. For no one play can sum up or envelop the playwright's total view; no one statement can exhaust the reality of a given subject. This was a lesson learned from the two apparently contradictory major influences on Adamov's work, the expressionist theater of Strindberg, what Adamov defined as a "jeu de fragiles surprises dans un édifice de monotonie,"[2] and the epic-realist, socially committed theater of Bertolt Brecht, from which Adamov claims to learn the peril of seeking an all enveloping formula for the expression of his duel consciousness before the havoc of human reality:

> Et j'ai même vu là une leçon, encore, que nous donne Brecht: ne pas chercher à dire dans une seule pièce tout ce qu'on a à dire, fût-ce sur un seul sujet. Rien de plus dangereux, de plus faux intellectuellement, que la recherche de la formule qui enveloppe tout, de la phrase philosophale.[3]

But it is not surprising that a lesson learned from Strindberg is relearned from Brecht, for Adamov's theater is perhaps the most effective synthesis in France of these two major contemporary traditions, a perpetually developing theater that incorporates the best elements of the two orientations. *Le Ping-Pong* and *Paolo Paoli* had marked a moment of fusion in the theater of Adamov. Rejecting some of the limitations of his early schematic plays situated in a no-man's land of eternal conflict, he had sought to concretize man's struggle within its social, political and historical context. This process of fusion or synthesis continues in the later plays with some plays accentuating the political more than the social dimension. But as Guicharnaud points out, the process is consistent and Adamov was persistent in his search for a fuller, more complete portrayal of man's condition:

> Finding the no-man's land of the plays during the 1950's too limited because it obliged the writers to go round in circles within their eternal commonplaces, Adamov wanted to give man a more complete and more concrete image, that is, to restore his social and historical dimensions by means of a synthesis of the two visions, thus achieving a total portrayal of man's condition. Obviously, his evolution consists less in repudiating past experiences than in criticizing them, in order to recover them for use on another level.[4]

It is then a matter of degree, of perspective and not change, for the theater of Adamov is continually absorbed with both the "grande" and the "petite manœuvre," man's human condition and man's social, political, and historical situation. Thus having stressed the "grande manœuvre" in the early plays' Adamov's theater moves to the foreground of our interest the "petite manœuvre," the "mal curable" of man's dual dilemma. But as Martin Esslin points out, the one aspect is never totally excluded in favor of the other:

> If in *La grande et la petite manœuvre* it was the revolutionaries' futile struggle that represented the small manœuvre, and the all-enveloping absurdity of the human condition dwarfing the social struggle that stood for the big manoeuvre, then in *Paolo Paoli* the small manoeuvre looms large and the large manoeuvre has receded into a barely perceptible background.[5]

This shift in emphasis, first perceptible in *Le Ping-Pong,* more obvious in *Paolo Paoli,* continues in the later plays, but even within this shift there are varying emphases, various aspects of man's situation which are predominant. However, when viewed in its totality and in retrospect, the later orientation of Adamov's theater reveals two basic directions or observable paradigms; (1) those plays wherein man struggles within a primarily political context and (2) those plays whose dimensions are essentially social.

The "political" plays, 1958-1961, represent Adamov's effort to deal with his recognition that death, the ultimate ignominy and humiliation, does not obviate man's need to battle the historical forces of life that would crush him. His theater exhibits a need to go beyond the statement of life's essential "absurdity" that we find in his early plays towards a working-out of man's political and social problems. In speaking of his "metamorphosis," Adamov says:

> Le fait que l'homme soit mortel-et redoute la mort, et que cette crainte souvent l'obsède-ne l'empêche pas de vivre, donc de lutter. Et pas d'histoire: on sait toujours contre quoi on lutte, et pourquoi.[6]

Thus his "political" theater in no way denies his vision of man's ultimate helplessness in an unrecognizable and hostile universe, but in addition it posits a need to react within this given context against the curable aspects of the situation. His theater of revolt evolves toward a theater of revolution. Nor does his political theater abandon the formal considerations so important to his earlier work. Like Brecht before him, he recognizes that form is inseparable from substance, that, as Guicharnaud says of the "new" committed playwrights:

> . . . it is not enough to offer a traditional presentation of the conflicts between worthy proletarians and nasty bosses, but that the very structure of the play must also be a revolutionary act.[7]

Not only do we see the carry-over of many avant-garde techniques and procedures in Adamov's political theater, but more importantly we witness an ever-present concern for the individual, the particular, the human element. The dual-dilemma of man's consciousness both of himself as an individual in an absurd universe and of his role as a political and historical object in a given situation is preserved with delicate balance. It is in sustaining this equilibrium that Adamov's political theater avoids for the most part the dangers of traditional committed theater, a danger he was acutely aware of and that he describes in *Ici et Maintenant,* a collection of his essays on theater:

> Je vois un danger . . . dans un théâtre politique qui, à force de refuser les particularités, aboutirait, par un autre chemin, au symbolisme qu'il s'efforce de combattre.[8]

Just as in the earlier plays Adamov's characters were the images of individuals while at the same time they represented man in general, so in his later theater his characters react differently to the same situations because they are individuals, specific and complex human beings, as well as workers, peasants, revolutionaries:

> Deux ouvriers travaillent à la même chaîne, leur condition est la même; mais à aliénation égale, leur comportement sera différent, selon leur physique-l'un est beau, l'autre est laid, l'un grand, l'autre petit—leur vie familiale, leurs amours. . . .[9]

Théâtre de Société, "(scènes d'actualité)," is a collection of five "saynètes politiques," short plays of obvious political orientation: *La vedette* of Guy Demoy, *La nouvelle constitution* of Maurice Regnaut, **Intimité, Je ne suis pas Français,** and **La complainte du ridicule** of Arthur Adamov.

As early as 13 May 1958 Adamov notes in his journal *L'Homme et L'Enfant* the rise of "fascism" in France and Algeria and adds:

> Nous essayons d'écrire des saynètes politiques, dénonçant l'imposture qui vient, mais nous y arrivons mal, le recul manque.[10]

The three short plays represent Adamov's first efforts to deal with what he calls: "a difficult but tempting genre," to find a form wherein man's political role and essential being are balanced cohesively. That each play varies in its approach, tone and techniques bears witness to the continuing evolution of Adamov's theater. But the unifying structural principle of these plays as well as **Les Ames mortes** and **Le Printemps 71** is the representation of man's political and existential struggle within a specific time, place and situation as literally and as grossly as possible. The plays seek to deal then with a current predicament—an obvious departure from the early plays—but in a familiar manner. Adamov explains in the **"Avant-Propos"**:

> Le "théâtre de société," pour ne pas dire le théâtre politique, est un genre ardu mais tentant. La situation française actuelle (1958), par exemple, avec ses paradoxes apparents, ses retournements grotesques dissimulant l'impeccable logique des intérêts de classe, demande à être *représentée,* et cela le plus littéralement, donc le plus grossièrement possible.[11]

Thus Adamov does not limit himself to a purely "political" theater in the traditional sense of the term, but rather seeks to dramatize man's struggle within an historical and political context, simultaneously aware of man's eternal human condition as well as his specific role or roles in particular social and political situations:

> Beaucoup croient que je veux me borner à un théâtre politique. Ce n'est pas vrai. Ce qui est vrai, c'est la haine que je voue aujourd'hui à des "histoires" coupées de leur contexte social, mutilées, soi-disant "éternelles."[12]

Intimité (1958), the first of the three political sketches, is highly allegorical in style, using personified collective concepts as characters, as well as highly satirical in intent, exposing the manipulations and degradation of power politics. Adamov is rather explicit in the **"Avant-Propos"** in stating his intentions:

> J'ai commencé par écrire **Intimité,** où j'essaie de résumer sous une forme délibérément allégorique la connivence réelle du général de Gaulle avec les factieux et le grand capital.[13]

The short play is divided into two almost equal parts. In the opening section *La Cause incarnée* is the principal guest at an intimate dinner at the home of M. de Ponteville. Others present are M. de Ponteville's friend M. Royal, his nephew L'Élite, and the lackey M. Le Pupille. They are first of all a tightly knit group of people bound together in intimacy by selfish interest. While individually they jockey for more favorable positions within the group, collectively they maintain a strong posture of mutual protection against outside disruptive influences. It is a world wherein people use people to their own advantage, a society in which a person's importance is predicated on his ability to be of use. They are individual stars within a self-contained galaxy, parts of a whole whose sustaining gravitational force is *La Cause incarnée.* His unique importance is quickly established by the opening lines of the play, which are not spoken by the character *La Cause incarnée,* but rather by a record of his voice. *La Cause incarnée* is France, the duty, honor, and destiny of France. The record announces, in what is an obvious and fairly heavy-handed caricature of De Gaulle:

> Français, Françaises, la Cause incarnée, qui n'appartient à personne sinon à la France, a su, au moment le plus terrible de l'Histoire de France, assumer la France. Et, assumant la France, elle est absolument, elle est intégralement, devenue la France.[14]

The respective roles of the others present at the dinner quickly fall in line. M. de Ponteville represents capital, the financial underpinnings of the state, anxious to put the glorious speeches aside so as to discuss the important economic situation. M. Royal personifies the elitist spirit of nobility, monarchy, and tradition recognizing the need of the state for the support of the masses, but only as a support, "Oui, les masses dirigées par l'élite, l'élite soutenue par les masses."[15] His nephew, L'Élite, dressed in para-military fashion, represents the storm troopers of totalitarianism, the military solution to the complexities of political and social life. M. le Pupille, the lackey is the subservient socialist republicanism of the Fourth Republic, admitted to the intimate inner circle only because he is needed to serve. He is still learning—and a very willing pupil—from the older more traditional forces of the state, continually compromising himself to curry favor, to stay within the privileged group. He is perhaps the most powerful symbol of the resultant degradation of power politics because in him we see the degradation in process. We see his corruption not as a finished product but as being accomplished. When M. le Pupille is released from the closet by L'Élite because, "On a encore besoin de toi, on te cassera la binette plus tard," he is ecstatic, "C'est le plus beau jour de ma vie!"[16]

Into this lion's den of intrigues and power walks L'Homme qui voit les causes et ressent les effets, a worker in overalls, carrying the sign *Vive la République.* The second part of the play is a dramatic confrontation between the proletariat and the tightly knit group of selfish interests that hides hypocritically behind the banners of nationalism and patriotism. The worker's very presence in the room exposes the machinery of the politics of arrangement which crushes the common man with its greed, its drive for financial, social, and political power. The others are defenseless before the honesty and purity of his laugh. M. de Ponteville feels threatened by his mocking presence and calls on force, Effet de la Cause, to subside the revolutionary laugh. A battle ensues and when L'Homme seems to be gaining the upper-hand and M. le Pupille falters in his support of totalitarian methods, other Effets de la Cause are quickly summoned up to defeat L'Homme. Now La Cause Incarnée can continue uninterrupted the meal in which the privileged castes of the unified front of capital, nobility, and subservient socialism share. For now not only is there a style of government, but even a rhythm of government, a relentless pounding of the individual into subservience and degradation. In one of his many "inspired" moments La Cause Incarnée pontificates:

> L'intervention de la destinée humaine dans l'enchaînement des circonstances a quelque chose d'irrévocable.[17]

The hypocritical machinery of "state" has been set in motion. Only the worker is free to revolt against its nefarious corruption and degradation. The original statement of power politics at the dinner party in the opening part of the play is intensified by a series of repetitious demonstrations of that power at work corrupting, degrading at an accelerated pace until it reaches its paroxysm in the necessary destruction of L'Homme.

The familiar structure of intensification reappears in this first of a series of political plays as a natural instrument for unveiling the hidden hypocrisy of a Cause that sacrifices its people for itself. Man is the victim of the play, the object manoeuvered, bought, and sold. And yet man is the only one capable of halting the machinery, of revolting against it by throwing himself into the very machine itself to stop its relentlessly crushing motion. Man, the bartered object of *Le Ping-Pong* and of

Paolo Paoli, will be the bartered object of *Les Ames mortes* and other plays to come, but now with the added difference that within his given social, political, and historical context he will revolt, he will seek to halt the degrading, destructive machinery of state and system. Thus, while *Intimité* is in itself inferior in many respects to Adamov's other plays, it is important historically in that it marks the playwright's first step in a direction that becomes increasingly more central to his theater.

Je ne suis pas Français, while distinctly "realistic" in style in contrast to the more allegorical *Intimité,* makes fundamentally the same statement as the first play regarding power politics while employing the same basic structure of intensification by repetition. The play depicts Algiers in May of 1958, just after the De Gaulle proclamation of Franco-Mussulman solidarity, and the way in which the French military coerce the Moslems into displaying support of the government. Adamov describes in the "Avant-Propos" to *Théâtre de Société* the need he felt to dramatize this subject even though he himself had not been in Algeria:

> *Je ne suis pas Français* est peut-être trop schématique, trop'avant-garde'au sens où je n'aime plus ce terme. Mais je voulais absolument parler de cette "fraternisation" franco-musulmane, et, n'ayant pas été en Algérie, j'ai dû me référer aux temoignages de ceux qui en revenaient. Le tableau final m'a été effectivement inspiré par le récit d'un journaliste étranger (libéral).[18]

The short play is divided into three tableaux each of which demonstrates the same persecution and manipulation of the Arabs, but with each tableau growing in intensity by virtue of its parallelism reinforced by moderate variation. The typically bourgeois and chauvinistic Famille-Pied-Noir which insults the Algerian selling peanuts in the opening tableau anticipates the two French paratroopers who coerce the same Algerian to take part in a demonstration for the government of De Gaulle in the second tableau. And interestingly enough this repeated harassment of the manipulated Arab is framed within terms of language. The obstinate silence of the Arab provokes Papa-Pied-Noir:

> Tu sais pas le français, peut-être? Si tu ne sais pas le français, moi, je peux te l'apprendre.[19]

Just as it provokes the two paratroopers:

> Tu ne sais pas le français, peut-être? On peut te l'apprendre, si tu veux?[20]

It is only in the third and final tableau when questioned about franco-mussulman solidarity by the two English journalists that the Arab breaks silence. His only words, repeated with finality and total revolt, are, "Je ne suis pas Français."[21]

But it is more than the silence of the Arab which is the ultimate act of his revolt against and rejection of the totalitarian system being foisted on him. For just as the worker's laugh in *Intimité* had such a disconcerting effect on the powers of state and had to be silenced, so the Arab's look unsettles Papa-Pied-Noir, who wiping his sweaty brow in Tableau I says:

> Moi, je suis Français, et puis je n'aime pas qu'on me regarde comme ce type-là m'a regardé. J'y peux rien, je n'aime pas ça.[22]

He is helpless before "that look" as is the Premier Para of the second tableau who stands paralyzed in front of the Algerian:

> Pourquoi que tu nous regardes comme ça? J'aime pas moi, qu'on nous regarde comme ça![23]

It is the same look which instills fear even in the relatively neutral English newspaper man:

> A votre place, Harry, je n'interrogerais plus ces musulmans. Vous n'avez peut-être pas remarqué l'étrange regard que cet homme nous a jeté, mais moi, qui suis observateur, je l'ai remarqué. . . .[24]

The crushing machinery of totalitarianism must be halted, the play tells us. The degrading ignominy of a system wherein people are made objects to be manipulated or bartered must be balanced by the simple yet heroic "Je ne suis pas Français" of the persecuted Arab. The laugh of the worker in *Intimité,* the look of the Algerian in *Je ne suis pas Français* is the hope of the future, the rebellion of the present, the necessary stand that man must take if he is ever to live justly. For the imperfect social and political system of which he is the victim is not inherent in the human condition. Thus the fear and paralysis of Papa-Pied-Noir, the Premier Para, and the Premier Journaliste are the first cracks in the mask of ignominious persecution, the beginning of the unmasking of those terrible powers that seem to control man's destiny but in fact are only permitted by man's loss of a sustaining and unifying spiritual dimension.

The power of the Arab to unsettle the paralyzing totalitarianism of the situation rests in the simple yet heroic dignity of his refusal to accept the system. His rejection couched in the simple terms, "Je ne suis pas Français," makes him more than just an object of hate and persecution, a victim put-upon by the selfishness of those in power. He becomes a positive point of departure in a universe of uncertainty. And as David Grossvogel points out in his *20th Century French Drama,* this is true of many of Adamov's characters:

> As usual, his human is hardly more than a negative quantity, a victim whose capacity to exist is real only to the extent that the physical instruments of his torture

are real and will be used on him: it is only by comparison with these instruments that he is found to have significance greater than that of the rudimentary and static object.[25]

In *La Complainte du Ridicule,* the final playlet of *Théâtre de Société,* it is again language which occupies the central place, which is used, in this case, to contradict and battle against the false language of propaganda and suppression. Adamov describes in the "Avant-Propos" his intention and approach:

> *La Complainte du Ridicule* joue sur les mots. Je me suis demandé si souvent pourquoi le ridicule ne tuait plus que j'ai fini par faire du Ridicule un personnage fatigué. Et puisque la propagande gouvernementale use continuellement d'un langage truqué, pourquoi ne pas lutter contre elle à l'aide du vrai langage?[26]

They play is shaped in the form of a short monologue in which the personification of ridicule, alone on the stage, is being teased and stoned by his supporters offstage because he is no longer capable of killing. His speech, at first tearful and apologetic, then growing more firm and forceful in tone, is both an explanation of his reduced effectiveness against the political stupidities of the present as well as a plea for the support of others in his necessary work against pretention and suppression.

The entire speech is divided into three equal parts: (1) a statement of his glorious effectiveness in the past, (2) an explanation for his reduced efficiency in the present, and finally (3) a plea for help against the false republic, war and dire poverty. In the opening section Le Ridicule cites examples from history—Général Boulenger, Colonel de la Rocque, Badinguet and his plebiscite, Maréchal Lebœuf, Monsieur Thiers—as indicative of his energetic youthful pursuit and destruction of enemies of the people by exposure of the falsity, pomposity and ridiculousness of their pretentions:

> Et vous savez aussi combien j'ai travaillé, combien je me suis démené . . . Vraiment, j'ai la conscience tranquille. Vraiment, j'ai tué tous ceux que j'ai pu . . .[27]

The central section of the tripartite division concentrates on the present, principally France of 1958, France of the new constitution and Général de Gaulle. Le Ridicule explains the complexity of a situation wherein the ridiculous and the hypocritical are so prevalent amongst both political leaders and their followers that he is at a loss as to where to begin his attack:

> Seulement aujourd'hui, surtout depuis cette nouvelle constitution, j'ai trop à faire, que voulez-vous? Et quand on a trop à faire, quand on est débordé, on est perdu . . . Frapper, tuer même, au besoin, d'accord! Mais par où commencer, par qui?[28]

Numerous people deserving of his destructive attention are cited, De Gaulle, socialist deputies of a certain type, hypocritical supporters of the referendum, Pineau, Pompidou, Rothschild, Général Chassin. There are so many, just in France alone, that the aging, tiring le Ridicule is incapable of doing the job alone. The ridiculous is so omnipresent that he is even obligated to travel abroad from time to time:

> Sans compter que je suis bien obligé d'aller à l'étranger quelquefois, pour entendre Franco parler de la Démocratie, ou voir se casser le nez une quelconque petite fusée américaine . . .[29]

In the closing section, he calls upon the aid of his allies in the battle against hypocrisy, totalitarianism and degradation. Le Ridicule cites a recent example of his success, the interruption of De Gaulle's "tournée présidentielle," and credits his minor master-stroke to the support he received from sympathetic forces. For when things become truly serious, when there is shooting or killing, he needs collaboration, friends, and extra effort in order to expose the ridiculous fraud of his enemies to the eyes of the world:

> Quand les choses deviennent sérieuses, quand au truquage des paroles s'ajoute, comme en Algérie, la torture des corps, comment voulez-vous que tout seul . . . ?[30]

The long, entreating harangue, a parody of a typical De Gaulle speech in its phrasing, organization, and emotional appeal, fatigues le Ridicule and he begins to collapse. But the urgency, conviction, and good sense of his words prevail upon the very people who had been casting stones at him at the opening of the play. They come to his rescue, support and maintain him. The fight will go on.

The obvious political content of *La Complainte du Ridicule* as well as the two other "saynètes politiques" of *Théâtre de Société* is rescued from banality and heavy-handedness by a core of humor that punctures the political pretentiousness of those that it attacks. To the degree that this humor is lacking *Je ne suis pas Français* is the least successful of the three plays. In its "realistic" approach, it is the play which takes itself most seriously and forfeits the aesthetic distancing achieved by the humor and caricature of *Intimité* and *La Complainte du Ridicule.* For humor, in the theater of Adamov, is an element, which while perceptible in the early plays, grows in importance in the later plays, reaching its highest point in *M. le Modéré.* It is a humor born of despair, a gesture of defiance against the humiliating ignominy of life, a last defense against life's ultimate degradation, death, or as Adamov himself describes, an antidote against suicide: "Cerné par le malheur, il fallait que j'éclate de rire ou me suicide."[31]

The political playlets of *Théâtre de Société,* while circumscribed in scope, schematic in structure, and limited in objective, point the way in the theater of Adamov towards the more ambitious, complex, fleshed-out political dramas of *Les Ames mortes* and *Le Printemps 71.*

Les Ames mortes, 1960, is an adaptation for the stage of Gogol's famous novel *Dead Souls.* It is both interesting and informative that Adamov chose to adapt a novel for his first full-length political play. Being the capable critic that he was, Adamov was fully aware of the perils of adaptation:

> Les dimensions de la prose ne sont pas celles du théâtre, et vouloir rendre littéralement, dans l'espace physique, les actes qui se déroulent dans un autre espace me semble presque toujours aberrant.[32]

But Adamov, always the playwright, constantly in search of how best to utilize the physical space of the stage and always acutely conscious of the genre in which he worked and by which he sought to represent "literally" his vision of man in the world, recognized, like Gogol himself, the poetic dimensions of *Dead Souls:*

> . . . *les Ames mortes* ne sont pas un roman, mais, comme Gogol l'indiquait lui-même, un poème. Je traduis en langage du XXe siècle, et je dis: une épopée. C'est en effet parce que les aventures de Tchitchikov débordent, et de loin, le cadre romanesque, que je me suis permis de les en faire sortir.[33]

But perhaps most importantly it was the dual-orientation of Gogol's work, its fusion of sharp social and political criticism with intense, personal poetry that captivated Adamov and led him to find in *Dead Souls* a synthesis parallel to that toward which his own work was striving:

> De plus, *Les Ames mortes* se situant constamment au point d'intersection d'une critique sociale aiguë et de la poésie qui, dans la multiplicité des faits, choisit le fait révélateur, il m'est apparu qu'elles ne sont pas étrangères au théâtre dont nous avons actuellement le plus besoin: un théâtre épique et critique.[34]

Les Ames mortes, while an adaptation, achieves its own originality of form and statement; unlike Adamov's translations, *La Mort de Danton* of Büchner in 1948 and *Les Petits Bourgeois* of Gorki in 1959, it deserves inclusion as an authentic and personal dramatic statement in any systematic study of Adamovian dramaturgy.

The long play which centers around the adventures of Tchitchikov in Czarist Russia of the nineteenth century is divided into two parts of approximately the same length with seven and eight tableaux respectively. The "Première Partie," which describes the arrival of Tchitchikov in a small Russian town, his social and economic conquests, and his strange pursuit of "dead souls" might be sub-titled "The Rise of Tchitchikov." He is the polished, sophisticated outsider, the city man come to the provinces, the new center of attraction and emulation. The limited social universe of the play revolves around him: women want to dance with him, the important men of the society, the Gouverneur, wealthy landowners, the Président du Tribunal, the Directeur des Postes want to talk to him. But underneath the attractive veneer of civilization Tchitchikov is a man possessed, a man whose energies are controlled by a singular obsession, that of buying up the "dead souls" of the region. Adamov explains the play on words of the title on which the play is built:

> La pièce (comme le roman) repose sur un terrible "jeu de mots." Dans la Russie tsariste, on appelait "ames mortes" les serfs de sexe masculin sur lesquels les propriétaires fonciers payaient un impôt.[35]

This tax had to be paid for each serf on the census rolls, whether he was living or not. Thus the political system of the time had created a situation whereby, for whatever his own personal reasons, Tchitchikov found most landowners eager to sell at a low price the dead "dead souls" for which they were accountable.

Five of the opening seven tableaux are variations of the same basic quest, Tchitchikov's buying of dead souls, his exploitation of a currupt system for his own benefit. But throughout the entire "Première Partie" we, like the landowners of the play, are never permitted to fathom his true motive, to understand why it would be advantageous for him to "own" dead serfs for whom he would be forced to pay a tax. What we see, however, are the avaricious landowners eager to benefit from Tchitchikov's strange obsession, bargaining as though the commodity where real, dealing in people as though they were products. Korobatchka hesitates to sell, fearing that perhaps the market for dead souls will rise. Nozdriov prefers to gamble over them and even cheats at play. Sobakievitch hints at the illegality of the sale so as to raise the price. And as they try, each in his own way to use Tchitchikov and his obsession to their advantage, so Tchitchikov slowly, coldly, and with intense calculation manipulates the landowners to serve his own needs. Moreover, there is always lurking in the background the ultimate morbid irony of their dealings, the fact that the product of exchange is dead souls.

As Tchitchikov's fortunes rise with increasing regularity from tableau to tableau in the "Première Partie," so they begin to fall and disintegrate in the "Deuxième Partie." Once his scheme has been exposed as formally illegal, there is a direct parallelism-in-reverse between his descent towards disgrace and his earlier rise to fame and fortune. Just as each tableau of the "Première Partie" repeatedly portrayed an increasingly successful deal for dead souls, so each tableau of the "Deuxième Partie" exposes a Tchitchikov more and more humiliated, the object of more and more pernicious rumors.

And as the first ball at the Gouverneur's house in the "Première Partie" marked the beginning of Tchitchikov's ascent to power and wealth, so it is the second ball at the Gouverneur's house in the "Deuxième Partie" that signals the beginning of his fall from grace. For it is at this social gathering, Tchitchikov's moment of triumph, that the drunken Nozdriov exposes Tchitchikov's clever game in front of the Gouverneurs and other notables. Each succeeding scene announces a new rumor, increasingly greater in scope and more pernicious in nature, to explain the mystery of his buying of dead souls. The women Anna Grigorievna and Sofia Ivanova interpret his dealings as a subterfuge whereby to make off with the Gouverneur's daughter. The town officials fear that Tchitchikov is really an inspector sent by the Gouverneur General and traveling incognito to check the irregularities of their district. The Directeur des Postes and Bégouchkine see in Tchitchikov the unidentified counterfeiter known to be at large in their district. Each interprets Tchitchikov and his plan differently and in keeping with his own fears and frustrations. But they are all agreed that the buying of dead souls was only a strategy.

Rumor leads to rumor as rumor contradicts rumor and leads to general confusion:

LE MAÎTRE DE POLICE

> Arrêter Tchitchikov, comme suspect.

L'INSPECTEUR DES SERVICES D'HYGIÈNE

> Et si c'était tout de même l'envoyé du Gouverneur Général?

LE MAÎTRE DE POLICE

> Ce qui, après tout, n'est pas absolument impossible. Exact.

LE PROCUREUR

> Mais si Tchitchikov n'est . . . ni l'envoyé du Gouverneur . . . ni un vrai conseiller de collège . . . ni un vrai faux-monnayeur . . . ni . . . ni un bandit, alors que peut-il bien . . . ?[36]

The rumors and resultant confusion continue to mount from tableau to tableau. Some declare that Tchitchikov is really le capitaine Kopékine, a hero of the campaign of 1812, who unlike Tchitchikov, however, had only one leg and one arm. Others think it is more likely that he is really Napoleon set loose in Russia by the English. They take their confusion to Nozdriov who explains that Tchitchikov is (1) a spy, (2) a counterfeiter, (3) a man who intended to seduce the Gouverneur's daughter and (4) that their suspicions that he is Napoleon might just be the right explanation for Tchitchikov's frequent absences as a boy from school.

Confusion creates fear and the Procureur dies of fright. When Tchitchikov realizes the seriousness of his predicament, he prepares to flee, but is then put under arrest to appear before the Gouverneur Général. Once in prison Tchitchikov begs the Protopope for aid, revealing at the same time his true motive for dealing in dead souls:

> Bien sûr, se faire prêter de l'argent, beaucoup d'argent par le Conseil de tutelle sur des âmes . . . inexistantes . . . n'est ni . . . licite . . . ni moral.[37]

But he also makes clear that his plot was spawned by a corrupt system that failed to take into account a man's life, that looked upon serfs as numbers to be taxed whether living or dead:

> Oui, est-ce de ma faute si un jour, quand j'étais fondé de pouvoir, et que, employé consciencieux, je m'inquiétais de savoir quels serfs étaient vivants et quels autres morts, le secrétaire m'a dit: (Prenant une voix froide, administrative.) "D'accord, les uns naissent, les autres meurent, mais pourquoi vous inquiéter, Pavel Ivanovitch? Puisqu'ils figurent tous sur la liste de recensement, et que le compte se retrouve toujours. Le secrétaire était estimé par ses supérieurs, je voulais l'être aussi. Oui, tout . . . tout le mal vient de ce secrétaire.[38]

A promise of repentence and the offer of financial reimbursement convince the Protopope of Tchitchikov's sincerity and elicit from him a guarantee of help. But it is finally the Maître de Police, in league with the other town notables, who frees Tchitchikov, returns him his money-box, tears up the evidence of the confiscated acts of sale, and advises him to flee as quickly and as far off as possible. He does all this in the name of order, harmony, friendship and thirty thousand roubles.

Thus the rise and fall of Tchitchikov is complete. His short-lived passage through the provincial Russian town has changed nothing. The system has simply absorbed another experience, another victim. The final scene of the play testifies to Adamov's dramatic acuity, for not only does it bring the adventures of Tchitchikov full circle within the confines of the play, but it anticipates the encompassing circular pattern of Tchitchikov's subsequent life from province to province. Adamov explains his choice of ending in *Ici et Maintenant*:

> Chacun sait que *Les Ames mortes* n'ont pas de fin. Or, au théâtre, il faut bien finir, et je n'ai pas trouvé de fin qui me paraisse à la fois plus scénique et plus *juste* que l'arrestation dérisoire de Tchitchikov, rapidement suivie d'une libération obtenue à prix d'or. Cette fin ne laisse-t-elle pas supposer, d'ailleurs, le prochain recommencement du voyage, des tractations, des victoires, des dangers, et une autre arrestation, dans une autre petite ville de l'immense Russie?[39]

The repetitive structure of intensification which is the informing principle of Adamov's theater is ideally suited to translate from one medium to another the poetry of Gogol's novel. The rising crescendo of the "Première Partie," the systematic buying of dead souls, financial security and social prestige intensifies by its repetition with variation the sameness of the quest with its concomitant absence of human values in the bargaining for souls. Adamov explains how the structure of the play reinforces its thematic statement:

> Même si l'on me reproche une progression trop linéaire, je crois qu'il était nécessaire de faire défiler systématiquement ces propriétaires apparement différents les uns des autres, mais semblables du seul fait de leur souci commun: s'enrichir au maximum, exploiter *tout ce qui peut être exploitable*.[40]

This series of deals for dead souls in the "Première Partie," this initial pattern of repetition whose intensity is heightened by virtue of the varying but increasingly successful results, is further intensified by the parallelism of the decrescendo of the "Deuxième Partie." Here the scenes become in effect repetitions or semi-repetitions of each other, variations of the initial accusation against Tchitchikov growing in seriousness and to such ridiculous proportions as to become ludicrous. Yet it is this pattern of accusation which causes his ultimate downfall, disgrace, imprisonment and reprieve. A victim of the system, Tchitchikov supports the system so as to be free to victimize others. Thus the circular patterns within the play are further reinforced by our awareness that they are but the first in a hypothetical series of circular patterns throughout the apparently infinite spaces of Czarist Russia.

The play, by using the "epic" structure of Tchitchikov's odyssey in search of dead souls, accuses a system so corrupt, so inhuman as to permit such a person as Tchitchikov, a character who in turn exposes the system by pushing to its ultimate absurdity or illogicality the apparently acceptable established political order of Czarist Russia. It is a political system of servitude, of bondage of man by man, a system wherein the principal product of exchange is implicitly and explicitly man, wherein peasants whether dead or alive are referred to as "dead souls," a system wherein there could be no authentic life. In a sense Tchitchikov is the most sympathetic of the manipulators in this political and social order because he is the least successful. In trying to be part of the ruling elite, he fails, but in so doing, he pushes to the extreme the consequences of this inherently vicious system and thus becomes its greatest critic.

The play is then a political play, for not only does it condemn man's use of man for his own ends as do *Le Ping-Pong* and *Paolo Paoli,* where man was only implicitly the real product of exchange, but it indicts a system, an established order where man as product of exchange was both politically and morally acceptable. The play succeeds in denouncing this "legitimate" system by showing its ultimate consequences and inherent absurdity, by demonstrating literally and in concrete images the ultimate viciousness of a system which man in his inhumanity had grown accustomed to accepting as natural and logical.

In the final analysis the "dead souls" of the play are then not only the serfs bought and sold, but the dead in spirit who deal in these dead souls. The illegitimate quest of Tchitchikov to buy dead "dead souls" is the ultimate irony of a system whose corruption is so complete that the purchase of living "dead souls" is legitimate. To preserve itself, the political system gives the appearances of absorbing and invalidating the adventures of Tchitchikov, while in reality it frees him to victimize others. Therein lies the ultimate victory of the existing political order. For rather than collapse before the onslaught of Tchitchikov's *reduction ad absurdum,* it temporarily anesthetizes its victim-accuser by permitting him to play a minor role in the system, albeit somewhere else, and thereby permitting the political order to propagate itself. To the extent that **Les Ames mortes** describes an historically accurate form of exploitation and dehumanization in Czarist Russia of the nineteenth century, the play is historical. But its appeal reaches beyond the purely descriptive level. While grounded in history, **Les Ames mortes** with its symbolic overtones speaks to our own age wherein men and systems still exploit and dehumanize other men.

The seriousness of the play's statement on man's inhuman use of man and the trenchant criticism of a political system wherein man is the chief product for sale is at one and the same time thematically intensified but tonally alleviated by the humor and poetry of many of the play's images. The use of film projections of Tchitchikov traveling across the immense open spaces of Russia and its desolate countryside spotted occasionally with isolated villages adds a dimension of timelessness and continuity to his odyssey. They reinforce poetically the empty but relentless quest of man for domination over man. The opening and closing images of the play, Tchitchikov's troika against a void of immense, desolate space, encircle spatially and temporally his adventures within the immense, desolate spaces of human degradation and absence of authentic human values of the play's universe just as the images of desolate countryside between tableaux in the "Première Partie" encircle his separate adventures into individual, desolate domains.

The play on words on which the play is built is sustained and deepened by the growing humor of Adamov which, though "black," rescues the play from a deadening gravity inimical to the play's dual thrust. It makes of **Les Ames mortes** a political play which avoids the pitfalls of its genre. Humor raises **Les Ames mortes** above the simple but heavy-handed formula of "class against class" melodrama by preserving the humanity and complexity of its characters. It makes them more than one-dimensional political beings. The humor springs for the most part from the familiar Adamovian device of using exalted language to describe banal proceedings, or the exact reverse, ordinary, banal terminology to describe extraordinary situations. The crafty, bargaining Korobotchka, anxious to reap even greater profits, hesitates to sell her dead souls and uses a typical formula of sale's resistance, "D'autres marchands viendront."[41] It is only when we realize what is the subject of sale that the incongruity of the words demands our critical but amused appraisal. Familiar expressions are sometimes inverted to achieve unfamiliar and humorous effect. In a fit of impatience to close a deal, Tchitchikov reworks to his own advantage a traditional Christian expression, "Laissez donc en paix les vivants, Dieu les bénisse! Je vous parle des morts."[42] Not only is the inversion humorous, but it transmits the inverted values of the play's universe. It sums up and exposes by caricature and poetic distance the absurdity of the norms people live by. Humor in language in **Les Ames mortes** is the key to this mechanism of critical exposure while at the same time it keeps the play from being a fruitless and heavy-handed exercise in political satire.

Le Printemps 71 marks the final stage of Adamov's development within the political plays of the years 1958-1961. Of all his major plays it is the most overtly political in nature while at the same time it represents his most advanced and complex attempt to synthesize techniques from the two major orientations within his work, the avant-garde theater of derision and the Brechtian epic-realist theater.

The play is based on the history of the short-lived Paris Commune of 1871, when the working classes seized control of Paris, the Bank of France, and means of production on the 18th of March. It describes the rise and fall of the Commune with its eventual destruction on the 28th of May of the same year by the regular French army of the government of Thiers with the assistance of Bismarck, his Prussian troops, as well as sympathetic French reactionaries working inside the city. Within this broad historical framework, Adamov creates a play which, while basically simple in structure, is extremely rich in texture. It portrays some thirty-six possible political positions, ranging from cautious liberalism to the militant marxism of the late nineteenth century, as well as numerous personal dramas intertwined within the major political drama.

The play, Adamov's longest, is divided into three acts which in turn are divided into 26 tableaux. Act I represents the Commune triumphant, her enemies provisionally in flight to Versailles. Act II is the Commune in its first stages of disintegration, slowly losing control of the city and its people by a series of political errors and betrayals. Act III shows the dissolution and destruction of the Commune, its ultimate victimization by the system. This broad historical outline is, however, only the canvas on which Adamov paints the essential dramas of man's struggle within history and against the systems he has created. It is the "petite manœuvre" enlarged but still symbolic rather than essential to his statement of man's oppression of man. For though historical, the play does not concentrate on the grand designs of its period, spotlighting the famous and infamous leaders known to the conventional history texts. It is rather a play about the political evolution of the little people who made up the Commune, their understanding of its political significance, and the drama of their relationship to the Commune's efforts to throw off the shackles of subjugation and political ignominy.

This dual orientation of the play is advanced and formally defined by a repetitive structure of intensification created by the juxtaposition of the numerous "realistic" tableaux depicting personal or individual dramas of relationship and political evolution and the nine "allegorical" interludes or "guignols" which outline the political and historical thrust of the play. It is only in the "guignols," for example, that the principal historical characters of the Commune and its suppression appear—Thiers, Bismarck, etc.—while at the same time the societal and political forces of the period such as the Bank of France, the National Assembly and even the Commune itself appear as allegorical characters. The "guignols" are frequently humorous but principally they depict the grand historical lines of the three-month Commune, thereby freeing the tableaux for the play's dominant concern, the study of the people, their personal dilemmas, their relationships to each other, and of course, their evolving relationship to the Commune and its principles. It is they who elicit, as Geneviève Serreau points out in her *Histoire du nouveau théâtre,* our interest, sympathy and pity:

> Adamov mit sur scène dans **Le Printemps 71** le petit peuple de la Commune, les ouvriers de Paris "tels qu'ils étaient, gais, travailleurs, turbulents, héroïques," requérant du spectateur et son adhésion et sa sympathie et sa pitié. En contrepoint, les "guignols" versaillais, inspirés par les dessins de Daumier, apparaissent en des "intermèdes allégoriques" chargés surtout de faire le point des événements qui précipitèrent le sanglant affrontement.[43]

The people, the citizens of Paris, are not only those like Robert, Jeanne-Marie, and Pierre who are willing to give their life so that the idea of freedom might live, but they are also those like Anatole who worry only about the possible destruction of their personal possessions. They are people who fall in love and people who become jealous and hate. There are those who make political decisions based on political considerations and those who act politically for personal or sentimental reasons. Pierre explains to Robert the truth of his decision to go to defend the Préfecture:

> Tu vas à la Préfecture parce que Polia y va, et Polia parce qu'elle s'inquiète pour Sofia.[44]

There are those like Sofia and Polia for whom the ultimate importance is the continued struggle of the working classes for liberation, and those like the bourgeois Pécheteau for whom the major concern is:

> . . . que les ateliers Pécheteau passent des mains de Pécheteau père aux mains de Pécheteau fils.[45]

They are a people confused and giddy with the expectation of success, citizens who are incapable of recognizing the truth of their political and military situation. A soldier of the Commune, wounded in the battle at Clamart, is at the center of the deception when he says:

> Je n'ai pas peur . . . Mais je pense à Clamart, tout le temps. Si tu savais! . . . quelle déroute . . . Et à Paris, on parlait de nos victoires.[46]

When the collapse of the city is imminent, there is not only despair and faultfinding, courage and fear, but vanity and frivolity. The baroness Sibylle excitedly searches for Monsieur Beaubourg of the newspaper *Le Figaro*:

> Il m'a promis que j'aurais ma binette dans *Le Figaro*: la première petite baronne dans Paris encore insurgé.[47]

The man who once sold newspapers sympathetic to the Commune now sells reactionary papers that herald the triumph of Thiers and the forces of Versailles. He excuses his defection of grounds of practical necessity:

> J'ai deux petits à la maison, et ils ont faim.[48]

The Commune, the people of the Commune, turns inward in a moment of agonizing reappraisal and soul-searching to discover its mistakes. It is a time of second-guessing, fault-finding, and eventually self-recrimination. It is Jeanne-Marie, always zealous but frequently critical who now best sums up the situation:

> On a tous fait des fautes. Moi, la première. Si on avait osé occuper la Banque, ils n'auraient jamais, jamais . . . osé occuper Paris. C'est Sofia qui avait raison.[49]

All these individual dramas of relationship and evolution which take place within and become part of the great historical conflict of the future against the past, of the Republic against the Monarchy are victimized not only by the tyranny of the political system that crushes them, but also by the tyranny of time, a time much too brief for the numerous tasks confided to the Commune and its partisans. The drama of this exemplary moment in the history of man's struggle upward is intensified and humanized by its temporal dimension, its built-in "theatrical" time of only 73 days, by the contraction of so much political, historical and human drama into such a short period of time. Adamov underlines the importance of the temporal dimension as he explains in *Ici et maintenant* his attraction to the Commune:

> La Commune me paraît un événement particulièrement important, tant du point de vue politique que du point de vue strictement dramatique. Tant de grands pressentiments, d'erreurs, de combats *sur tous les fronts,* et en si peu de temps . . . C'est peut-être cette question du temps, du manque de temps, ce resserrement terrible des choses, en soixante-treize jours, qui m'a le plus intéressé, le plus frappé.[50]

Thus we see that Adamov regarded the Commune of 1871 as important from a political point of view as well as dramatically captivating. The "poésie folle" of the Commune, its heroism, its abortive and naive attempt to cure political and social evils, *le mal curable,* was inspirational but also instructive. For the first time in history, Adamov observed, men defended their own fate, power was held by the working classes over the means of production:

> Le premier gouvernment ouvrier, le courage, l'intelligence, puis l'héroïsme qui ont fait de Paris durant trois mois la capitale du monde, n'y a-t-il pas là l'un des plus grands sujects de théâtre?[51]

But the play is not only an heroic hymn to the Commune and the "little people" of Paris. It is also a realistic play which criticizes their errors as well, errors which we see depicted in the squabblings, indecisions and petty jealousies within the tableaux:

> En d'autres termes, j'ai tenu donc à ce que *Le Printemps 71* soit une pièce critique, et qui tienne compte de tout ce que nous avons appris depuis, et en grande partie grâce à la Commune.[52]

Yet even in this most advanced of "political" plays in which the *mal curable* is most obviously the central concern, the play continues to mingle Adamov's two dominant preoccupations of inner and exterior conflict, of the psychological as well as the political dimension, and of the individual as well as the class struggle. And once again it is this concern for the lost unifying spiritual dimension of man—along with certain technical procedures—which saves the play from that particular sort of simplistic symbolism so common to historico-political drama and which Adamov so consciously sought to avoid:

> . . . j'ai essayé de bannir le symbolisme et de raconter une très simple histoire qui tienne compte à la fois des éléments psychologiques et aussi des éléments politiques. Ce qui m'a attiré dans la Commune, c'est le rapport qui existait alors entre la vie privée et la vie politique.[53]

The drama of the Commune is the drama of the people, of the individual men and women who collectively created the political evolution of France in 1871. The emphasis within the play is therefore not on the celebrated heroes and villains of history, but on the particular evolution of each and every man within the general political situation.

In a very real sense the drama of the Commune is the drama of Robert Marpeaux multiplied, for *Le Printemps 71* is that "political" play of Adamov which promotes most the direction outlined by the transitional work *Paolo Paoli.* The solitary, evolutionary character of Marpeaux is here more extensively defined and developed as the working class in revolt against its suppression. The commodities of *Paolo Paoli,* both real and apparent, are more specifically political in *Le Printemps 71* as are the terms of the conflict. The individual Communards are made more believeable and sympathetic. Yet *Le Printemps 71* fulfills to a great degree the promise contained in *Paolo Paoli.* It combines on both a thematic and formal level and with a certain degree of success elements of the Theater of the Absurd as well as components of the epic-realist theater of criticism.

Moreover, man is still the victim and therefore, ultimately, the oppressor. The system which dehumanizes him is man-made—*le mal curable*—and is an extension of the inner conflict proceeding from man's loss of the spiritual or unifying dimension. The thematic evolution of Adamov's theater within the "political plays" lies in man's refusal to accept the blind victimization and dehumanization that he once endured as inescapable. He now mobilizes his forces against those aspects of life which can be challenged. For from the earliest plays to the very last the theater of Adamov never varies from its core, man's victimization and ignominy. It is only the attitude toward his condition which evolves and becomes the redeeming factor, as Guicharnaud notes in his *Modern French Theater*:

> If the individual is a victim, it is because the social system can be maintained only by anti-Kantian procedure. Adamov's plays are all centered on that blind victimization (*La grande et la petite manœuvre,* for example) or on a refusal of it (*Le Printemps 71*) as well as on an aesthetic revenge: The playwright himself transforms into objects—that is, into puppets—the social forces that feed on the dehumanization of man.[54]

Notes

1. Marc Beigbeder, *Le Théâtre en France depuis la libération* (Paris, 1959), p. 182.

2. Arthur Adamov, *Auguste Strindberg, Dramaturge* (Paris, 1955), p. 62.

3. Arthur Adamov, *Ici et maintenant* (Paris, 1964), p. 165.

4. Jacques Guicharnaud in collaboration with June Guicharnaud, *Modern French Theatre from Giraudoux to Genet* (New Haven and London, 1967), pp. 198-99.

5. Martin Esslin, *The Theatre of the Absurd* (New York, 1961), pp. 72-73.

6. *Ici et maintenant,* p. 143.

7. Guicharnaud, p. 206.

8. *Ici et maintenant,* p. 163.

9. *Ici et maintenant,* p. 163.

10. Arthur Adamov, *L'Homme et L'Enfant* (Paris, 1968), p. 128.

11. Arthur Adamov, *Avant-Propos* in *Théâtre de Société* (Paris, 1958),

12. *Ici et maintenant,* p. 167.

13. *Avant-Propos* in *Théâtre de Société,* p. 9.

14. Arthur Adamov, *Intimité* in *Théâtre de Société* (Paris, 1958), p. 14.

15. *Intimité,* p. 16.

16. *Intimité,* p. 20.

17. *Intimité,* p. 17.

18. *Avant-Propos* in *Théâtre de Société,* pp. 9-10.

19. Arthur Adamov, *Je ne suis pas Français* in *Théâtre de Société* (Paris, 1958), pp. 34-35.

20. *Je ne suis pas Français,* p. 38.

21. *Je ne suis pas Français,* p. 44.

22. *Je ne suis pas Français,* pp. 37-38.

23. *Je ne suis pas Français,* p. 40.

24. *Je ne suis pas Français,* p. 45.

25. David I. Grossvogel, *20th Century French Drama* (New York, 1961), p. 323.

26. *Avant-Propos* in *Théâtre de Société,* p. 9.

27. Arthur Adamov, *La complainte du ridicule* in *Théâtre de Société* (Paris, 1958), p. 50.

28. *La complainte du ridicule,* p. 50.

29. *La complainte du ridicule,* p. 50.

30. *La complainte du ridicule,* pp. 51-52.

31. Arthur Adamov, *Note préliminaire* in *Théâtre IV* (Paris, 1968), p. 11.

32. Arthur Adamov, *Introduction* in *Les ames mortes* (Paris, 1960), p. 7.

33. *Introduction* in *Les ames mortes,* p. 7.

34. *Introduction* in *Les ames mortes,* pp. 7-8.

35. *Ici et maintenant,* p. 115.

36. Arthur Adamov, *Les ames mortes* (Paris, 1960), p. 185.

37. *Les ames mortes,* p. 216.

38. *Les ames mortes,* p. 217.

39. *Ici et maintenant,* p. 114.

40. *Ici et maintenant,* p. 113.

41. *Les ames mortes,* p. 68.

42. *Les ames mortes,* p. 66.

43. Geneviève Serreau, *Histoire du "nouveau théâtre"* (Paris, 1966), p. 79.

44. Arthur Adamov, *Le Printemps 71* (Paris, 1961), p. 113.

45. *Le Printemps 71,* p. 154.

46. *Le Printemps 71,* p. 162.

47. *Le Printemps 71,* p. 219.

48. *Le Printemps 71,* p. 223.

49. *Le Printemps 71,* p. 211.

50. *Ici et maintenant,* p. 118.

51. *Ici et maintenant,* p. 145.

52. *Ici et maintenant,* p. 122.

53. *Ici et maintenant,* p. 129.

54. Guicharnaud, p. 202.

Bibliography

I

Adamov, Arthur: *Les Ames mortes,* Paris: Gallimard, 1960.

———: *L'Homme et L'Enfant,* Paris: Gallimard, 1968.

———: *Ici et maintenant,* Paris: Gallimard, 1964.

———: *Paolo Paoli,* Paris: Gallimard, 1957.

———: *Le Printemps 71,* Paris: Gallimard, 1961.

———: *Théâtre IV,* Paris: Gallimard, 1968.

———: *Théâtre de Société,* Paris: Les Editeurs Français Réunis, 1958.

II

Beigbeder, Marc: *Le Théâtre en France depuis la libération,* Paris: Bordas, 1959.

Esslin, Martin: *The Theatre of the Absurd,* New York: Doubleday and Company, 1961.

Grossvogel, David I.: *20th Century Drama,* New York: Columbia University Press, 1961.

Guicharnaud, Jacques, in collaboration with June Guicharnaud: *Modern French Theatre from Giraudoux to Genet.* Revised ed. New Haven and London: Yale University Press, 1967.

Serreau, Geneviève: *Histoire du "nouveau théâtre"*, Paris: Gallimard, 1966.

Michael Worton (essay date May 1978)

SOURCE: Worton, Michael. "Obsessional Theatre? The Role of the Father-Figure in Arthur Adamov's Early Plays." *Nottingham French Studies* 17, no. 1 (May 1978): 71-7.

[*In the following essay, Worton argues that Adamov's early plays reveal the author's obsession with father figures.*]

Of all the post-war French dramatists, Arthur Adamov most defiantly proclaims his obsessions, neuroses and sexual perversions.[1] In his introduction to *L'Aveu* Adamov emphasizes the positive value which he accords to neurosis:

> La névrose étant, par nature, grossissement et exagération d'une tare universelle qui existe à l'état embryonnaire en tout être humain, mais dont elle multiplie et renforce les effets, mon mal, de par son caractère propre, devient exemplaire.[2]

Adamov thus considers his own suffering to be representative of that of all humanity, but he insists on his need to struggle against it—and, while he may not be fully aware of the therapeutic potential of acting out one's obsessions,[3] he finds hope in the act of writing his plays:

> Mon seul recours est d'écrire, coûte, que coûte, en dépit de tous et de tout. Car si je cessais d'écrire, tout s'écroulerait.[4]

Adamov's writing and method of creation are closely linked with his own life—he himself informs us, for example, that the Victor in *Le Ping-Pong* is a childhood friend actually called Victor[5] and that *Le Professeur Taranne* is the direct transposition of a dream, in which he has changed only one sentence, modifying "Je suis l'auteur de *La Parodie*" to "Je suis le professeur Taranne".[6]

Adamov would therefore seem to exemplify Freud's view that the work of art arises directly out of the personal experiences of the artist[7] and, when one remembers that he read much of Freud and of Jung (even translating one of Jung's works into French[8]), one may conclude that he was consciously constructing theatre out of his neuroses.

The aim of this article is not to impose a Freudian/Jungian interpretation on Adamov's plays but rather to suggest that his early plays[9] reveal a dominant theme—his obsession with father-figures. Strangely, while recent research emphasizes the importance of the dominating, castrating Mother,[10] the Father has hitherto escaped the attention of critics, despite the fact that Adamov makes no significant reference to his mother in his frank autobiographical works but makes many revelatory remarks about his father.

It is clear that Adamov, even in early childhood, was subject to feelings of insecurity:

> Mes parents possédaient une bonne partie des pétroles de la Caspienne. Cela ne m'empêcha pas, à quatre ans déjà, de trembler à la seule idée de la pauvreté . . .
>
> Ma seconde complainte . . . a été: Je ne veux pas grandir. Ce n'est pas par hasard si j'ai eu tant de mal à me comporter en homme à l'âge d'homme.[11]

These fears, common to many children, were never dispelled for Adamov—and were, in fact, aggravated by his father who imposed on his son a sense of sexual guilt which was to haunt his later life:

> Mon père venu spécialement pour m'annoncer que mon sexe était une pierre noire, que cela voulait dire que je me masturbais. Si je continuais, je deviendrais fou.[12]

The father fulfils the patriarchal role of suppressing a manifestation of genital sexuality in his child and this suppression results in a permanent maiming of Adamov's development, leading to his inability to achieve sexual maturity.[13] His father remained always a figure of authority for Adamov: his decision, at the age of twenty, to defy his father and live with Irene[14] suggests an act of rebellion, but in 1936, at the age of twenty-eight, he conceives a hatred for his friend Cramer in whom he sees his (now dead) father who continues to persecute him.[15]

Although Adamov clearly fears his father, even as a child he is unable to feel respect for him:

> Mon père me fait honte: dans une réunion où se trouvaient précisément les Pitoëff [friends of the Adamov parents], il ose, la main dans la poche du gilet, déclamer: Etre ou ne pas être. Je ne sais où me mettre.[16]

This embarrassment is understandable in a young boy, but Adamov also recounts how between the ages of fourteen and sixteen he had to go every second evening to the casino to try in vain to persuade his father to return home. His father now appears to him as "menteur, lâche"[17] and throughout his life Adamov both recognizes his father as the custodian of power and despises him as a weakling who ultimately demonstrates his weakness by committing suicide in 1933.

Adamov's immediate reaction to the death is one of guilt:

> Je détestais mon père, c'est donc moi qui l'ai tué. Pendant au moins une année, j'en étais sûr. Je ne suis jusqu'à présent sûr du contraire.[18]

It is patent that Adamov's hateful fear of his father burdens him with guilt[19] but his very contempt for this figure of authority becomes a positive force for him preventing him from the suicide which, he reveals, tempted him throughout his life. Adamov is afraid of suicide, but perhaps more important is his reluctance to imitate his father and thus join the ranks of those in authority whom he so detests:

> 4 mars [1967]
> Vais-je me tuer ou pas?
>
> Mon corps écrabouillé contre le sol, loque sanglante?
> Cela finira-t-il ainsi?
> Je ne m'en cache pas, le saut me fait peur.
> Et puis il y a mon père. Me suicidant,
> je fais comme lui, j'entre dans le rang.[20]

If, as has been suggested above, Adamov's neuroses serve as a creative impulse, his attitude to the father-figure is an especially rich source of inspiration. The playwright repeatedly presents an isolated individual living within a society which crushes him and which is quintessentially patriarchal, in that social positions are determined in relation to male figures. In *La Parodie* (1947) N. (who is almost a cipher for Adamov[21]) loves the fickle Lili but has a rival in the weak editor of the newspaper "L'Avenir".[22] Significantly, Lili, if she abandons N., also deserts the Editor; the puppet-master/playwright is thus able to attack his father and all authoritarian figures through a form of self-humiliation:

> Dans un tout autre domaine, je voulais aussi me venger;
> Lili me permit cette vengeance.[23]

If, in *La Parodie,* Adamov is attacking and avenging himself on a patriarchal system which has destined him to impotence, it is interesting that in his second play *L'Invasion* (1949) where the reader is confronted with a desperate quest for meaning and truth, the dominant social figure is La Mère who is incapable of bringing order to the chaotic world in which the characters live. Only the dead Jean can offer truth and, in an Oedipean search, Pierre must eventually commit suicide in an attempt to rejoin brother-in-law Jean whose oppressive presence permeates the play: like Adamov's father who pursued the writer throughout his life, Jean is considered as the custodian of authority who continues to dominate all the characters from the grave.

In *Le Professeur Taranne* (1951), the only one of the early plays which Adamov did not later repudiate, Adamov consciously creates an exemplar of social values in order to destroy it. As an internationally renowned scholar (for so he describes himself[24]), Taranne represents the didactic father who during the course of the play is exposed as a charlatan, despised by the society on whose values he depends (while also flouting them, as in his acts, alleged *and* witnessed, of indecent exposure). Adamov would here seem to be exorcising his scorn of his own weak, untruthful father; more than this, though, he is rejecting the standards of education and morality—and of justice—which support society, but which betray themselves as much as Taranne as the play progresses. Taranne himself is, in short, a hypocritical weakling functioning as a paradigmatic version of the father-figure but also, paradoxically, representing the persecuted victim of society.

In all of the plays society is a force of oppression but *La Grande et la Petite Manœuvre* (1950) and *Tous contre tous* (1952) may be seen as the most overtly political plays. Here Adamov concentrates solely on the social expression of persecution and directs his attack at the police who persecute in a less personal way than the father-figure. In *Le Sens de la Marche* (1951), however, he interestingly makes an attempt to juxtapose (in human form) the two powers he most fears. It soon becomes apparent that Berne's (or the police's) attitude to crime is different from that of the father:

Berne

> —Les mécontents en prison! C'est comme ça qu'on assure l'ordre.

Le Père, soulevant la tête

> —Non, ce n'est pas comme ça! Ce qu'il faut, c'est étouffer le mal dans le germe, c'est ne pas permettre . . .[25]

Berne clearly represents the social oppressor who imposes order on a society by removing all rebellious forces, while the Father believes that one must simply never allow insurrection to begin—there is a clear parallel here with Adamov's own father who stifled his son's sexual development. Le Père both hates and fears disorder ("Ce désordre, c'est ce désordre qui me tue"[26]); this loathing serves as the explicit link between the Father and his successive reincarnations, le Commandant, le Prédicateur and le Directeur de l'Ecole, each of whom voices his horror of disorder.[27] So, although the Father dies between the Prologue and Act I, he continues to dominate his son, Henri, who eventually returns home to find that Berne has become his sister's lover/master as well as assuming the role of Father. The social and personal tyrants have therefore united in Berne, and Henri, in a final desperate act, kills him. For once, in Adamov's theatre, the individual succeeds in defeating the forces of oppression.

In *Comme nous avons été* (1953) formative elements from the dramatist's past determine the significance of the play as the double character André/A. is described as visiting the casino to fetch his father and as haunted by his father's suicide. In the re-enactment of the last father/son conversation, A. plays both roles, revealing the betrayal by the son and his subsequent guilt. When A. is then reduced to a helpless child undressed by the dominant Mother, we may see this as a symbolic, theatrical admission of Adamov's own immaturity: the exorcism effected in *Le Sens de la Marche* has not proved durable, the father-figure continues to obsess him.

Adamov makes another attempt, in *Les Retrouvailles* (1953), to examine his identity with reference to the absence of the father, which, peculiarly, seems to be equivalent to the absence of manhood and liberty.[28] As elsewhere, he feels obliged to create a "castrating" mother who fulfils the role of father. Indeed, one may justifiably suggest that this Mother is merely another reincarnation of the father-figure, since she is both dominant and weak and is obsessed by the need for order:

EDGAR

—Cette manie qu'ont toutes les femmes de toujours vouloir fair de l'ordre! Parce qu'elles n'en ont pas dans la tête.[29]

Edgar (Adamov) here propounds an interesting theory: that it is the lack of personal, internal coherence which forces the individual to search obsessively for order. This trait, perceptible in the writer himself, is singularly important in any consideration of Adamov's attitude to his father who lacked unity and self-discipline and thus prevented his son from finding coherence in social systems.

It should not be assumed, however, that every Mother in Adamov's play is a cipher for the father-figure, since she rarely has the *social* authority that the Father possesses, although she often has great control over her offspring whom she subjugates by treating him as a small child. It is interesting to note also that Adamov's filial relationships are always son to father or son to mother: the concept of the parental couple is consistently excluded from the plays. Adamov is quite different, in this respect, from another obsessional playwright, Arrabal, in whose works the Mother frequently loathes the Father and obliges the child to espouse her hatred: in *Les Deux Bourreaux,* for example, Françoise delights in the agonies of her tortured husband and, after his death, obliges the "disobedient" son, Maurice to renounce his attachment to the Father. Here the Mother is clearly the oppressive figure whereas the Father is both lost and betrayed; Arrabal uses the relationship of tension between the parents to explain his loathing of the matriarchal figure.

Arthur Adamov, on the other hand, refuses to present couples and this refusal to present husband-wife/father-mother couplings in his early plays would seem to suggest that, for him, the parent-figure must be essentially a patriarchal being: the intrusion of a tender, caring parent-figure is inconceivable in Adamov's theatre, both in psycho-analytical terms and in theatrical terms since persecution, which becomes the main-spring of his work, was at the heart of his relationship with his father. The early plays are essentially personal, even introspective and egocentric; they all demonstrate the close relationship between Adamov's neuroses and his theatre, as he admitted when speaking of Genet:

". . . je ne dis pas supprimer ses névroses, car enfin, sur quel autre terrain pouvons-nous bâtir?"[30]

If one of the writer's major neuroses is his obsession with the father who both formed and deformed Adamov, the man, and Adamov, the playwright, it is clear that this figure functions above all as the wielder of power, as a symbol of the authority which the dramatist so hates. The continual reappearance of the father in the plays reveals Adamov's inability to separate himself from him and also suggests that Adamov views *external* forces of repression (such as the police) as developments of that primal source of oppression which is created and maintained by an essentially and eternally patriarchal society.

When the playwright changes direction with *Le Ping-Pong* (1955), he claims that this is because "j'ai appris à me méfier des archétypes dont l'emploi, en fin de compte, permet d'éluder l'histoire à des fins bien suspectes".[31] The father-figure patently operates as an archetypal force in the early plays, but Adamov's move into a more consciously political theatre is perhaps largely due to an acceptance of the impossibility of escaping from the domination of his father. He therefore places his theatre in a more widely social context since, as in *Le Sens de la Marche,* it is only when the oppressor of his neurosis is fused with an external repressive force, when the writer can lose himself in the role of an individual struggling against society, that he can envisage the possibility of a triumph over authority and an escape into liberty and manhood.

Notes

1. Notably in the autobiographical *L'Aveu* but also in *Ils,* a collection of "récits"; both published in *Je . . . Ils* (Paris, 1969).

2. *Je . . . Ils* p. 19.

3. See, in this context, the theories and doctrines of the founder of psychodrama, Dr. J. L. Moreno, in, for example, J. L. Moreno *Psychodrama, vol. I* (revised), New York, 1964 and *Psychodrama, vol. II,* New York, 1959.

4. *Je . . . Ils* p. 33.

5. Adamov, *L'Homme et l'Enfant,* Paris, 1968, p. 204.

6. Adamov, *Théâtre II,* Paris, 1955, p. 12.

7. See Freud's essay on Jensen's "Gradiva", *Delusion & Dream* (London, 1921) and his essay, *Leonardo da Vinci* (London, 1948).

8. C. G. Jung, *Le Moi et l'Inconscient* (trans. A. Adamov), Paris, 1938.

9. Adamov himself, in the "Note préliminaire" to *Théâtre II,* states that *Le Ping-Pong* (1955) is a new departure in his writing: he emphasizes this by rejecting all earlier works except *Le Professeur Taranne.*

10. Notably John M. McCann, *The Theatre of Arthur Adamov,* Chapel Hill, 1975 and Richard E. Sherrell "Arthur Adamov and Invaded Man" in *Modern Drama* No. 7, 1964-65, pp. 399-404.

11. *L'Homme et l'Enfant* pp. 13-14.

12. Ibid. p. 14.

13. Adamov's case illustrates Wilhelm Reichs theory, expounded in *The Mass Psychology of Fascism* (New York, 1946) and *Sexual Revolution* (New York, 1962), that, by suppressing the natural sexuality of children, the patriarchal system renders the child submissive, fearful of authority and incapable of rebellion.

14. See *L'Homme et l'Enfant* p. 38.

15. See ibid. p. 60.

16. Ibid. p. 21.

17. Ibid. pp. 24-25.

18. Ibid. p. 45.

19. An interesting parallel is to be found in Freud's assertion: "Parricide . . . is the principal and primal crime of humanity as well as of the individual. It is in any case the main source of the sense of guilt, though we do not know if it is the only one." (Sigmund Freud, *Collected Papers vol. V,* London, 1950, p. 202).

20. See *L'Homme et l'Enfant,* p. 14.

21. Adamov's attitude to N. is made clear in his "Note préliminaire" to *Théâtre II*: "*La Parodie* n'a pas été seulement pour moi une tentative de justification ('j'ai beau être comme N., je ne serai pas plus puni que l'Employé'), mais aussi un acte de rébellion." (p. 9.)

22. The other figures of authority who appear in the play are "reincarnations" of the Editor: especially important is the Gérant of the dance-hall who, when brutally expelling the Employé, demonstrates that, in Adamov's world, figures of authority wield undeservedly great power, even though they themselves are weak—this ambivalence is at the heart of Adamov's attitude to his father.

23. *Théâtre II,* p. 9.

24. Arthur Adamov *Théâtre I,* Paris, 1953, p. 218.

25. *Théâtre Ii,* p. 23.

26. Ibid. p. 25.

27. This loathing, visible in many of the early plays, is the central theme of *La Politique des Restes* (1962) where the psychotic Johnny Brown transforms his neurosis into a social weapon.

28. Adamov was haunted by the spectre of his father from whom he could not free himself and who therefore prevented Adamov from achieving independence and possible maturity.

29. *Théâtre II,* p. 77.

30. Arthur Adamov, *Ici et Maintenant,* Paris, 1964, p. 156.

31. Ibid. p. 46.

Alexander Fischler (essay date June 1978)

SOURCE: Fischler, Alexander. "The Absurd Professor in the Theater of the Absurd." *Modern Drama* 21, no. 2 (June 1978): 137-52.

[*In the following excerpt, taken from a broader discussion of the stock figure of the professor in French drama, Fischler describes the ways in which Adamov adapted the professor character type in his play* Professor Taranne.]

> "Cher docteur imprévisible et routinier. Certainement nous cultiverons votre mémoire."
>
> Robert Pinget, *Identité* [Paris, 1971] (I, v)

Since incongruity characterizes the professor whenever he appears on a conventional Western stage, one wonders what happens to this traditionally absurd figure when he enters the theater of the absurd with Ionesco and Adamov. One anticipates an answer based on the algebraic model of two "negatives" combining to yield a "positive." But this proves to be absurd mathematical reasoning worthy of Ionesco's professor, that is, mostly, though not entirely, false. Negative and positive poles are particularly hard to determine in this case. The professor resists congruity even when he is featured in a sentimental or happy ending. His incongruity is congenital and absolute; he is at odds not only with his surroundings, but with his own self; he is a two-sided figure, combining, for instance, the character of victim with that of executioner, or concealing an intensely active nature under a contemplative mask; his absurdity is a function of his ambiguity; being a simulacrum, all words and pose, he is ideally suited to any theater and can make the most contrived action around him on stage pass for real life. The theater of the absurd could not make the absurd professor seem logical any more than it could make him blend harmoniously with his surroundings. However, by accentuating and accelerating the disjointedness of character, setting and situation, the displacement, as Simone Benmussa would call it,[1] the theater of the absurd turned the professor into a central figure for the representation of man's condition in the modern world, in a way neither Mr. Chips nor his cousins, Molière's Docteurs, could have represented it.

Ionesco's Professor and Adamov's Taranne, the central figures considered here, are obviously steeped in the tradition of the stage professor, a tradition which for both its comic and tragic effects supposes a link with everyday life and reality. This link survives, though it has become extremely tenuous, and though the figures on stage now seem to re-enact everyday nightmare in patterns that are as unlife-like as possible, yet more compelling than ever for all involved. Overcoming the grotesque distortion of displacement and acceleration, this new professor holds the center of the stage and shows disturbing marks of kinship with the more heroic figures whose place he has usurped.

How does a professor talk about his own demonstrably absurd type without seeming to re-enact Ionesco's *Lesson,* down to the rape-murder of the audience, or without revealing, like Taranne, unforgivable and inexplicable lacunae? Is it possible to go back, even armed with scholarly detachment, and re-examine the adventures of a type who is subjected to ridicule and made to seem grotesque all along the line, who arrives with a pomp no circumstance could warrant and indulges in or is subjected to a humiliation that only pathology could excuse? Professors in fiction (I place under this heading all colleagues appearing in literature, on stage and, more recently, on screen) form an ever-receding line, akin to Baudelaire's "Sept Vieillards" (obviously encountered somewhere in the neighborhood of the Rue des Écoles). The strip tease of Adamov's Taranne is symbolic of the inevitable end of any inquiry into the professor's identity, whether conducted by another professor or not: to be left exposed, not merely hollow, but with a dubious past, a suspicious present, and no future whatever. Yet it seems, and this may be justification for the inquiry, that it is precisely from such an ambiguous stance that the professor has traditionally derived his powers. Beckett, Ionesco and Adamov (at least during the fifties, while they were creating what came to be called the theater of the absurd) tried to destroy once and for all both message and identity in the theater. The stage professor or, rather, professor-doctor, turned out

to be rather well-suited for their attack. For armed with an identity—one which implied a role in the real world—he nevertheless invariably operates on the fringes. Characteristically, the professor inscribes himself on a non-existent blackboard in Ionesco and on a *tabula rasa* in Adamov. But non-messages from an ambiguous character are our habitual fare in this theater, and we have learned, absurdly enough, that they do communicate so long as we are willing to accept them on their own ground, a disquieting stage on which is performed the drama of the liberated "whole man" taken from the Surrealist tradition, that is, without the conventional devices which allow us to distinguish conscious from unconscious, waking from dream, and so-called serious activity from play.

The professor-doctor comes to the theater of the absurd with antecedents going back to the origins of the genre, and an extremely diversified role, generally secondary. He is familiar to all under a variety of names: Dottore, Graziano, Faustus, the Professor, the Logician, the Pedant, and so forth. "He is," says Maurice Sand, "a member of the Academia della Crusca, a philosopher, an astronomer, a grammarian, a rhetorician, a cabalist and diplomatist. He can talk upon any subject, pronounce upon any subject, but not withstanding that his studies were abnormally prolonged, he knows absolutely nothing, which, however, does not hinder him from citing inappropriately the Latin tags which he garbles." He quotes with aplomb and intrepidity. "When he is a lawyer, he is clear-sighted only in those affairs with which he is not entrusted." He puts the court to sleep. He can be a miser and a lecher. "If he inclines to pleasantries, such pleasantries invariably have their root in ill-will." When he is a physician, his expertise extends beyond medicine to alchemy and the occult sciences; he is avaricious, egotistical, weak in resisting his own appetites; he consults the pulse and other parts of the female anatomy.[2]

This is the type as consecrated by the 16th and 17th centuries. Taken back via his medieval corollaries, his Roman antecedents, all the way down to a likely prototype in Doric comedy, he remains remarkably consistent in his main lines, notably in the coexistence of opposites within his character, the derisory and the disturbing, the diurnal and the nocturnal. Of particular relevance here is a subtype who combines the professor, the doctor and the actor, namely, the mountebank. His particular origins, too, evidently go back into antiquity and survive until the present era. At the height of his popularity, in the Middle Ages, he is "quack doctor, half astrologer, half magician," selling often deadly remedies, with a show of tricks, much fake Latin, and an ever-ready store of platitudes. We learn that when he did join professional shows, "the oldest theme in which he found his place is the struggle between winter and summer, personified in the Contrasto between Master

Carnival and Lent. . . ."[3] He does not cure, of course; he merely helps Carnival die his inevitable death. As doctor, pedant, lawyer or executioner, he is a great crowd pleaser, a one-man show. His character can be ambiguous or double. His symbol is usually the owl.[4]

The modern theater has been able to assume the traditional professor-doctor fairly intact. Reinhardt Kuhn, in a study called "The Debasement of the Intellectual in Contemporary Continental Drama," reviewed the situation ten years ago with the conclusion implicit in his title.[5] Nothing has changed since then, of course: plays like Simon Gray's *Butley* (1971) and Tom Stoppard's *Jumpers* (1972) feature professors still classifiable somewhere between Tesman and Frankenstein; and the protagonist of Obaldia's *Monsieur Klebs et Rozalie* (1974) is a contemporary Faust. In Pinget's *Identité* (1971), a "grand mouvement d'osmose" allows the professor, the doctor and the maid to fuse into one universal type; evidently, this great heir of the theater of the absurd saw that not the least theatrical of the professor's paradoxical attributes is his ability to seem universal by the very fact of his oddity.

The main objective of this study, however, is not to establish the consistency of the type, but to see why Ionesco and Adamov, two *avant-garde* authors, resorted to a traditional theatrical figure like the professor at precisely the time when their avowed purpose was to modernize the theater, to force it back to anonymous origins whence communication could start afresh, based on the images and archetypes yielded by intensely personal experience, vision or dream. (Both authors rely on a combination of Jung and Artaud to explain communication in the new theater.) Ionesco, at the time of *La Leçon* (1950, 1951), his second play, and Adamov, at the time of *Le Professeur Taranne* (1951, 1953), his fourth, are engaged in a polemic to justify their radical departure from conventional theater. Adamov was to lose interest fairly soon, turning to political arguments, but Ionesco's debate went on unabated, culminating in the *Impromptu de l'Alma* (1956), where he appears on stage in person to take on three professor-doctors of theatrology, Bartholoméus I, II and III, in a pseudo-discussion at the end of which he himself is invested with doctoral role and title by Marie, the maid: "Car ne pas être docteur, c'est encore être docteur."

The defense in the madcap *Impromptu* is consistent with the arguments gathered in Ionesco's *Notes,* in his *Journals* and in the *Entretiens*. It asserts the playwright's freedom to choose his own methods and argues the existence of "la propre mythologie de l'oeuvre, [. . .] son univers."

> Le théâtre est, pour moi, la projection sur scène du monde du dedans: c'est dans mes rêves, dans mes angoisses, dans mes désirs obscurs, dans mes contradictions intérieures que, pour ma part, je me réserve le droit de prendre cette matière théâtrale. Comme je ne suis pas seul au monde, comme chacun de nous, au plus profond de son être, est en même temps tous les autres, mes rêves, mes désirs, mes angoisses, mes obsessions ne m'appartiennent pas en propre; cela fait partie d'un héritage ancestral, un très ancien dépôt, constituant le domaine de toute l'humanité.

([*Notes et contre-notes*] II, pp. 56-57)[6]

Ionesco has continued to be faithful to this conception of theater as a universe where the archetype has a privileged position and the intensely private blends with the commonplace. He evidently feels that even if this theater no longer has reasonable answers or truths to deliver in the form of a message, and cannot offer a norm in the device of a happy ending, it can present the ongoing, absurd quest for answers and truths, and the inhuman obstacles along the way. Furthermore, even before a public which has heard, repeated *ad nauseam,* the existentialist lesson that identity comes with ill-faith and tyranny, this theater can accentuate role-playing and show ill-faith as a pathetic exercise on all levels of consciousness, as inevitable as death. There is room here for the types derived from tradition, for those created and cast by the author, for the author himself, should he choose to associate with them, and, of course, for "chacun de nous." The traditional types, like the professor-doctor, the maid or the student, merely benefit from special associative ability: they link "la propre mythologie de l'oeuvre" with traditional patterns which continue to fascinate even when they no longer seem to hold. The case of the professor in *La Leçon* is, in this respect, particularly interesting, for it recalls not only the mountebank, but, with him, the tradition of the Carnival *contrasto*; as a result, "la propre mythologie de l'oeuvre" emerges by contrast with the Dionysian myth, going against the grain of Western drama. This, in itself, should help assess and explain the impact of the little play.

. . . . .

When we turn to Adamov's *Le Professeur Taranne* (1951, 1953), we find a character who, from the outset, cannot be defined by reference to anything or anyone outside himself, in a play representing his attempts to find definition. Taranne is scarcely playing the part of the stock professor-doctor, even though he has obviously retained some of his attributes. Furthermore, he has no antagonist on stage in the conventional sense which still applied to Ionesco's student; and to acquire mythic significance, albeit negatively, by reference to a traditional pattern, his drama would have to be apprehended as passion at the final stage, beyond hope. Indeed, from his first appearance he is hovering over a background of rumor, shifting figures, and imprecise events with which his connections are tenuous. If he is not, as his author claims, a pure product of nightmare, he can only be the Pascalian man, tottering on the abyss.

Adamov recalled on several occasions the ease with which he transcribed during two days and three nights the wealth of detail offered to him in that one dream: almost nothing needed to be added. The adaptation for the stage taught him, he claims, that experience, in order to be communicable, need not be mediated by allegory: life and art could be linked with only minor changes; theater at last could be called true ([*Théâtre*] II, pp. 12-14; *IM* [*Ici et maintenant*], pp. 28-29; *HE* [*L'Homme et l'enfant*], pp. 100-101). Actually, obsessed as he was by the need to assert the intensely personal and even exhibitionist character of his dramatizations, Adamov was prone to overstate the case for identity between his life and his art; *Le Professeur Taranne,* as we have it, is so carefully structured for the stage that its origins in dream have to be established explicitly for a reader or spectator.

The most remarkable feature of the play is, in fact, its rigorous construction: it sets up a modified *structure en abîme* in which the chain of presentation is replaced by a sequence of outward acts inextricably linked to inner revelations; the whole has the effect of closing in on Taranne (and on Adamov, if we agree to identify him with the professor) even more mercilessly than the receding boxes of Quaker Oats close in on the Quaker.

Taranne must disculpate himself from accusations of public exhibitionism. An inquest to determine identity, integrity and merit, which is conducted as the play proceeds on the stage (it would be hard to say "as the plot unravels"), occurs simultaneously in his own mind; but whereas the external inquirers invariably seem to lose interest, Taranne's search becomes more and more obsessive, and its conclusions more and more threatening. The evidence offered or suggested in the case turns out to be either open to doubt, or the result of probably mistaken identity, or else inconclusive, fragmentary, and ultimately unimportant. Outside interest in the case ceases two-thirds of the way through the play, and, not long afterwards, outside interest in Taranne, past, present and future, is denied. He is not to be invited again to lecture in Belgium. Even his last chance, an ocean voyage during which he would have had a place of honor at the captain's table, literally fades away at the end of the play as he goes to the back of an empty stage to hang up what was supposed to have been a seating chart, but turns out to be a blank, a *tabula rasa,* grey in color, like the potential evidence, the suggested guilt, and the likelihood of innocence.[7]

The professor was a novelty in Adamov's theater. His predecessors, N., Pierre, le Mutilé, and Zenno were projections of the author having only the barest of identities of their own. Taranne, however, comes with a title which, he assumes, clearly designates for him a place in society and all the rights and privileges appertaining thereto. By the time the play is over, however, it is likely that both his title and his position were assumed or plagiarized from a rival, le Professeur Ménard; Taranne is left alone on the stage, stripping off his clothes so as to offer his body, the only remaining confirmation of an identity and a place, against a background of grey nothingness.

In the "Introduction" he wrote for a 1963 edition of the play, Adamov suggests that Taranne's effectiveness as a dramatic figure is due to the fact that his plight is one with which the spectator can identify but his title necessitates a distance from him, or, as Adamov puts it characteristically, prevents solidarity with him: "Nous ne sommes pas tous des professeurs d'Université, vaniteux et plagiaires"; and he concludes: "Il fallait sans doute cette désolidarisation, pour permettre l'émotion et, en même temps, le rire qui la rend supportable" (*IM,* pp. 28-29).

I do not propose to answer the questions concerning Taranne's identity and the relation of dreamer to dreamed. None the less, I should like to point out that when they invested Taranne with a university professorship, the dark forces of dream gave Adamov not only one of his most effective protagonists, but an ideal figure to incarnate his own pathological obsessions and his deviant behavior, for the eminently theatrical professor could incarnate guilt as well as innocence, be an exhibitionist, a sadist and a masochist all in one, and seem grotesquely impotent yet none the less terrifying. If indeed the dream featuring Taranne and its transcription had revealed to Adamov a new harmony and a way of creating theater in which life and art coexisted, it was largely due to the fact that this protagonist had, since the beginnings of theater, been a figure mediating between everyday routines and fantasy, wearing two opposite masks, and seeming thereby to incarnate theater. Taranne was the perfect intermediary between the avowed exhibitionist Adamov and his public.

The masochism of N., the protagonist of Adamov's first play, was a function of the character: the extent to which it seemed appropriate depended on the success of the dramatization. The masochism and exhibitionism of Taranne, however, were a function of the history of drama: so long as professors, doctors, pedants, and their like appear on stage, they will have a propensity for subjecting themselves and others to ridicule and pain.

Both as a figure in a dream and as a professor, Taranne at once belongs and does not fit. He is thus a perfect scapegoat figure, and, if anything, theatrical tradition has served to make his behavior and the behavior of others toward him seem appropriate. Appearing in a theater of dream and displacement, he offers relief by being a reassuring sight, as he was no doubt in the Carnival *contrasto,* providing a link with "reality," being a figure in whom outlandishness is "normal"; his manner is, on the whole, rather entertaining, and, as Adamov saw it, he allows us to remain *désolidarisés,* that is to say, he gets us off the hook.

Ionesco and Adamov tell us repeatedly in their autobiographical writings that giving form to one's obsessions, recording significant images and disturbing dreams, establishes a framework for analogy, for correspondence in what amounts to the Baudelairian sense (whether or not the "Sept Vieillards" who come out of the mist and pass, leaving the poet "blessé par le mystère et par L'Absurdité," were actually professors, they formed a "cortège infernal," a progression and a potential road to infinity; similarly, in Ionesco and Adamov, figures recede or are absorbed by infernal cycles and assorted machines representing the dark of the abyss[8]). Though it explains nothing, answers nothing, formulation seems terribly important: it situates significant fragments and figures in a context which might, eventually, suggest wholes by analogy. Professors are such significant figures: aside from their traditional associations in the theater, they tend to incarnate authority. Simone Benmussa associated long ago Ionesco's professors with the other authority figures in his theater, the fathers, the policemen, the guards, the rhinoceroses.[9] No doubt, in the context of Adamov's theater as well, the professor is an authority figure with the father, the judge, the capitalist, the politician, anyone who can serve as a point of reference and lend significance to humiliation. And the professor is, of course, also the subject of authority, turning readily into the victim, a singularly apt figure to incarnate self and others or self in others. Dottore, the professor, becoming the intelligent but ineffectual analyst whom they repeatedly meet in the clinic, is precisely the figure Ionesco and Adamov seek in the nightmares which their journals transcribe, and it is, perhaps, as they suggest, the best they can hope for in their own "cité pleine de rêves."

It is much easier to assess the role of the professor in the theater of the absurd with respect to the spectators than to follow the two playwrights into the maze of their autobiographical works and establish, if possible or necessary, what intimate links exist between them and their characters. One such role has already emerged: the familiar figure, in whom the absurd is "normal," makes the displaced setting and action almost tolerable and certainly easier to assimilate. But another function was suggested as well, underlined, in fact, by the insistence of the masochist Adamov that Taranne is an ideal projection (not just for himself, but, if we recall *L'Aveu,* for the modern world): the professor not only makes the displaced context familiar, but also makes the disquieting action admissible (which is not to say acceptable or understandable). When he is the scapegoat, the professor in the theater of the absurd is not very different from when he is the executioner, or when he tries to cure the incurable; the carnival atmosphere suits all, es-

pecially when no relief is in sight. For catharsis here, if it is to take place at all, cannot follow Aristotelian lines, as Serge Doubrovsky pointed out with particular reference to Ionesco: laughter here has replaced the catharsis of pity and fear.[10] No doctor of theatrology has satisfactorily explained how purgation occurs in the theater. If Doubrovsky is right in arguing that only laughter occurs and this laughter does not conquer absurdity but merely stresses it and revels in it, then we can understand why our authors resorted to the figure of the professor in creating a new non-cathartic theater: he elicits a combination of pity and fear, and calls forth laughter, or, at the very least, the smile which accompanies the consolation of the *déjà vu.* We can also understand why the playwrights subsequently avoided giving him the center of the stage, since he commands only a limited attention span, and our defenses against him are so firmly established that it is easy to dismiss him as a comfortable stereotype. But the professor had also had one more talent, paradoxical like the rest: though a master of obfuscation, he remained a means to formulate a relevant question here and there. The figure of Taranne raised before us by Adamov was indeed (as has been pointed out before) a wonderful symbol for the new theater in its self-conscious phase, standing before an endgame world in which suggestive images are operative, in which there is, however, no organic cycle, in which progressions have replaced logical sequences, in which there can be no real continuity except on stage, and even there only from one performance to the next: a world without hope for explanations and, in fact, without a sustained desire to obtain them. Dramatization of the questions in plays like **Le Professeur Taranne** forces the obsessive perspective on the spectator without quite pushing him towards the *abîme;* in a world in which engagement has been established as the only justifiable course of action, the position of the spectator becomes quite uncomfortable. The questions he raises about the professor have an obsessive quality for him too. What is the relation between exhibitionism and desire to be recognized? Are these necessarily attended by paranoia also, as in the case of Taranne, who alternates between compulsive search for witnesses and fear of being surrounded or pursued? Does man write or is he written, and how does one account for the *lacune,* the hole in the text, the blank pages which must be examined and which always seem to condemn? (It is interesting to set next to Taranne's double-entry system and his inexplicable blank pages the obsession with filling lacunae in Ionesco's theater, most notably dramatized in *Victimes du devoir* [1952] and in the short play effectively entitled *La Lacune* [1966] in which a distinguished academician finds that all his titles and degrees are annulled and his career ruined because, on learning that he had failed to take the second half of the *bachot,* he felt compelled to go back and try to fill the gap.)

Obviously, those of us who are professors have a special stake in these plays, and the questions they raise have a special pertinence in our lives. For us, blank pages are inscribed with the words "publish and/or perish"; being called upon to perform every day, we understand the fear generated by the lack or the presence of an audience; we know the ordeal of performing a text which must be given without even the aid of the plot outline available to *Dottore* in the *Commedia*; we know also that when we resort to stock phrases which we think belong to the repertory, there is a danger that one of our audience, far from being comforted by recurrence of the familiar, will write to the Rector and denounce us for plagiarizing some "leading" figure, a Professor Ménard. We always entertain a suspicion that what takes place in our classroom is indeed rape or murder, as in *La Leçon*; though we console ourselves with another suspicion, namely, that we were the victims or that, indeed, the students had asked for it! So what is true of the professor's effect on others in the theater of the absurd does not really apply to us: *il ne nous désolidarise pas*. He merely reassures us about our ridiculous tenure in history. *Ionesqua qui malum habet in pansa*.

Notes

1. There are almost as many definitions of the term "absurd," applied to the theater of the fifties, as there are arguments against its applicability. For the sake of convenience, I have followed Simone Benmussa, who, instead of concentrating on the lack of conventional sense, finds the distinguishing trait of the new theater in the displacement of everything that occurs on stage. See: "La Déréalisation par la mise en scène," in *L'Onirisme et l'insolite dans le théâtre français contemporain*, Actes du Colloque de Strasbourg [1972] présentés par Paul Vernois (Paris, 1974), pp. 28-29, 34-35.

2. *History of the Harlequinade* (London, 1915), pp. 31-34.

3. Winifred Smith, *The Commedia dell'Arte* (New York, 1964), pp. 35-39.

4. It is easy to recognize here a model for the doctor in *Le Roi se meurt* (1962), Le Médecin "qui est aussi chirurgien, bourreau, bactériologue et astrologue"; but the mountebank is already an ancestor to the professor in *La Leçon* (1951).

5. *Modern Drama*, 7 (Feb. 1965), 454-462.

6. All page references to the plays of Ionesco and Adamov are to the collected editions published by Gallimard; roman numerals indicate the volume. Standard designations will also be used for the other works. For Ionesco: *Notes et contre-notes* (Paris, 1966)—*NCN; Journal en miettes* (Paris, 1967)—*JEM; Présent passé Passé présent* (Paris, 1968)—*PPPP;* for Adamov: *Ici et maintenant* (Paris, 1964)—*IM; L'Homme et l'enfant* (Paris, 1968)—*HE.*

7. Jacqueline Adamov, the playwright's widow, suggests that the chart bears the inscriptions of both crime and punishment ("Censure et représentation dans le théâtre d'Arthur Adamov," in *L'Onirisme et l'insolite, op. cit.,* p. 218).

8. Vernois compares Ionesco's association techniques with a "jeu de correspondances tel que l'a défini Baudelaire" (*op. cit.,* p. 170).

9. *Eugène Ionesco* (Paris, 1966), p. 43.

10. "Ionesco and the Comic of Absurdity" ["Le Rire de Ionesco"], in Rosette C. Lamont, ed., *Ionesco* (Englewood Cliffs, N. J., 1973) pp. 11-20; originally in *YFS,* 23 (Summer 1959), 3-10. See also Simone Benmussa in "La Déréalisation par la mise en scène," *op. cit.*: "En effet, autant le théâtre traditionnel, parce qu'il met en scène la projection d'un moi idéal permet une catharsis chez le spectateur, autant les structures éclatées du théâtre onirique, seul cadre possible, parce que brisé et mouvant de la représentation 'bigarrée' du fantasme, s'en éloignent et mettent le spectateur en lutte contre le spectacle et l'obligent à renouveler ses défenses" (p. 33).

Gerhard Fischer (essay date June 1979)

SOURCE: Fischer, Gerhard. "The Ideologies of *Le Printemps 71*: Adamov's 'Metamorphosis' Reconsidered." *Modern Drama* 22, no. 1 (June 1979): 97-108.

[*In the following essay, Fischer contends that* Spring 71, *rather than being a strictly Marxist play, exhibits both Marxist and Absurdist-Existentialist ideologies.*]

I.

Arthur Adamov's career as a dramatist is generally interpreted as the development of an existentialist avant-garde author to a politically committed, left-wing writer with clear Marxist preferences. His early plays, from *La Parodie* to *Tous contre Tous,* all written between 1947 and 1953, belong to the first dramatic expressions of what later came to be called Theatre of the Absurd; in fact, Adamov was one of the pioneers of this new theatrical form together with, but independent of, Samuel Beckett and Eugène Ionesco. The next two works, *Ping Pong* (1955) and *Paolo Paoli* (1957), which established Adamov's international reputation, already constitute a turning point in his career, a first break away from the absurd theatre to a more concretely political, social and historical drama. *Le Printemps 71*

(1960) is usually considered the work that marks the completion of the playwright's "conversion" to Marxism: a play with an evident leftist political tendency, treating an historical topic which is of central importance to Marxist theories of the state and the revolution, i.e., the Paris Commune of 1871.

The same Marxist tendency appears already in a publication by Adamov that came out in 1959; entitled *Anthologie de la Commune,*[1] this collection of documents, essays, eye-witness accounts of the Commune also includes a selection of texts by Marx, Engels and Lenin. Adamov's own statements, concerning both his artistic and intellectual development and his interpretation of the Commune, likewise leave no doubt as to his ideological position.[2] He writes that he undertook the study of this period almost as "un devoir envers le premier gouvernement de la classe ouvrière dans le monde,"[3] and he comments on the aim and purpose of *Le Printemps 71*: "Une pièce sur la Commune de Paris, si elle est réussie, peut aider, doit aider, ceux qui auront la possibilité de la lire ou de la voir, à comprendre la lutte de la classe ouvrière. Et cette lutte n'est pas finie."[4] The play certainly seems to bear out the author's objective. One only has to look at a few of the play's *guignols,* dramatic interludes set with symmetric regularity between the scenes (*tableaux*) of the drama, in order to realize how Adamov has tried to present his ideological conviction. The *guignols* add up to an allegorical mime-show of the historical events in which the enemies of the Commune are savagely caricatured whereas the figure of La Commune is heroically idealized. Perhaps the clearest indication of the play's political implication and of Adamov's view of the Commune is the final scene: an epilogue reveals a map of the world in which all "socialist and progressive countries"[5] appear in red; at the same time the International is being played. This scenic solution is evidently designed to furnish what is called the "optimistic perspective" in orthodox socialist literary theory, i.e., a device to suggest the continuing and eventually successful revolutionary struggle of the international proletariat. This interpretation of the Commune emphasizes the Marxist view of history according to which the example of the Parisian revolutionaries, even in their defeat, shows the way to the victory of the working-class movement in the future.

It is no surprise, then, that critics have unanimously subscribed to the theory of Adamov's conversion to Marxism; according to the generally held view, Adamov was an "avowed Marxist at the time he wrote this last play [*Paolo Paoli,* G.F.]," who has repudiated "the philosophy of the absurd" and whose "theatre is thus committed and openly Marxist."[6] Given the prima facie evidence of *Le Printemps 71* and the remarks of its author about his artistic and intellectual development, given Adamov's interpretation of the Commune and his editorial emphasis in his *Anthologie de la Commune,*

there seems to be little point in questioning this assessment. However, a careful consideration of the play reveals a number of inconsistencies in Adamov's dramatization of the Commune that can hardly be reconciled with his statements concerning the political implications of his play. A strictly Marxist interpretation of *Le Printemps 71* is not altogether conclusive or convincing. I should like to suggest in this paper that the play exhibits, in fact, two ideologies, one Marxist and one absurdist—existentialist;[7] and I wish to show the existence of elements in *Le Printemps 71* which can only be understood as remnants of Adamov's pre-Marxist consciousness, in terms both of existentialist ideas and of the dramatic forms of the absurd theatre in which these ideas found their artistic expression. My argument is based on the interpretation of three aspects of the play: the role and dramatic treatment of time; the function of the marginal characters, particularly The Poor Girl; the structural division of the drama, or rather the effect of this division on Adamov's presentation of historical change. It can be shown that each of these aspects is part of an ideological undercurrent that runs contrary to the play's professed Marxist interpretation.

II.

Margaret Dietemann has defined *Le Printemps 71* as "a play about time" or more precisely about "the time gap between event and knowledge."[8] The source of this observation must be attributed to Adamov himself. He writes in *Ici et Maintenant* about his interest in a dramatization of the Commune: "C'est peut-être cette question du temps, du manque de temps, ce resserrement terrible des choses, . . . qui m'a le plus intéressé."[9] The lack of time which did not allow the Commune to carry out any of its measures or to work out a comprehensive program of social change was already noted by Lenin as one of the reasons for the defeat of the Paris Commune,[10] and the author of *Le Printemps 71* thus seems to be only echoing another point of Marxist historical analysis. However, it is not the objective issue of the lack of time which is emphasized in the play, but rather a feeling of time as experienced by the dramatic characters, namely a subjective notion of the individual's perception of his position within the historical process. Adamov puts it this way: "Mais ce qui m'a, je crois, le plus intéressé, c'est de faire que les personnages n'en soient jamais au point où en sont les événements: ils sont en deçà ou au-delà. Montmartre est déjà pris (trahison ou pas) et tout leur espoir réside encore dans cette conviction: rien n'est perdu tant que Montmartre n'est pas pris, et Montmartre est imprenable."[11]

This is exactly how the fall of Montmartre is reported in the play. A proclamation of the Commune read in *tableau* 7 assures that Paris defended by its barricades is invincible; at the beginning of the following scene, a National Guardsman reports that the red flag is still flying over Montmartre, and at the end of the scene, this is revealed as mere rumour or wishful thinking: Oudet sadly confirms that Montmartre has long since fallen. This technique of presenting the progress of historical development in the form of conflicting or contradictory reports is repeatedly employed in *Le Printemps 71,* most prominently perhaps in *tableau* 11: while the Communards are celebrating the victory of General Dombrowski at Asnières, a Versaillese agent is distributing a pro-government newspaper announcing the recapturing of the fort by Thiers's troops. In *tableau* 16, the fall of Issy is presented in a very similar manner.

It is all but impossible to evaluate this dramatic pattern on an historical basis. There certainly have been incidents similar to the ones described by Adamov, but whether they deserve to be elevated to an historical principle is highly doubtful, and, in terms of the overall historical experience, they are hardly significant. The author's emphasis on this discrepancy between event and knowledge creates a very curious, deterministic and rather un-Marxist impression: the fight of the Commune seems to be doomed from the very beginning because the revolution is confronted with an invisible enemy, time, that appears as some abstract, absolute entity outside of human control and that is of necessity always ahead of any human effort. Adamov presents lastly the futility of the Communards' fight for existence and for a better world: their defense measures are useless because they apply to situations which no longer prevail, and their socio-economic decrees are already outdated upon publication because of the changed political balance of power. The Commune thus does not control the pace of historical progress, i.e., time; it is always seen reacting against developments imposed upon it.

This conclusion does not apply only to the military situation where, in fact, the aggressive initiative of Versailles puts the Parisian troops in a position of relative passivity and helplessness. The example of the pawnshop decree also proves the inability of the Commune to manage and to control the historical development it has envisioned: the "leftist" Versaillese Martin-Bernard convinces The Poor Girl that the measure cannot be enforced for reasons of time, the distribution of all pawned objects would take at least a whole year. The National Guards violently oppose this interpretation, but they fail to give a convincing argument in support of the Commune's policies. Here again time appears as an important dramatic topic, presented as an obscure autonomous force that invariably turns against the revolution and that confronts the individual with an overpowering notion of futility.

From an ideological point of view, Adamov's presentation of this theme reminds one more of existentialist or absurdist thoughts than of Marxism; the whole idea of a group of men desperately struggling to adjust to the chronological process of historical change that they cannot control certainly contains an element of absurdity. The dramatic pattern of introducing items of news that are later found to be incorrect rumours or outdated facts, ending many of his scenes on a note of pessimistic reversal, may well be compared to the favourite myth of the existentialists, Sisyphus. It also attests to a failure of communication, one of the key issues of the absurd theatre. In each of these scenes, the final experience is that of total frustration of man's endeavours in view of an incomprehensible and uncontrollable development in time, utterly destroying the notion of historical progress.

III.

The function of some of the marginal characters in the play similarly reminds of an absurdist philosophy. There is above all the role of The Poor Girl, the "ouvrière désemparée,"[12] who appears in four scenes and is mentioned in one other. She is also involved in a subplot, a counter-revolutionary scheme thought up by the Abbé de Villedieu and Widow Legros concerning the sewing of brassards for the government soldiers. At the end of the play, the Poor Girl finds herself in the street after her house has been set on fire. She puts all the blame on the Commune, calling Oudet an arsonist. However, this incident does not prevent her from being arrested in the very next scene as a *pétroleuse* herself and from being shot by the soldiers who are wearing the arm-badges she has sewn. The Poor Girl's function is much more prominent than her limited presence on stage would suggest. She is dramatically linked to the two main groups of characters: to the reactionaries (Martin-Bernard, the Abbé, Widow Legros), by whom she is used for their purposes and against her own real interests; and to the adherents of the Commune (Fournier, Oudet), who realize the futility of their efforts by the example of her case. The Poor Girl thus stands exactly in the centre of the dramatic conflict: her fate illustrates the oppressive, dehumanizing nature of the old regime and the failure of the new system to establish social conditions that put an end to the exploitation of man.

As a dramatic character, the Poor Girl is endowed with a good deal of allegorical quality, and her name already points to this fact. Being a member of the lowest social stratum, she seems to offer an excellent test case for the effectiveness of the Commune to better the lot of the underprivileged. This test, however, turns out to be negative. The Poor Girl does not profit at all from the new social order, losing her house and finally her life also. She falls victim to the very forces that meant to liberate her. The pawnshop decree not only fails to accord her a minimum of material benefit; with its abstract because unrealistic and unenforceable meaning, it also contributes to her mental confusion. The promises of the revolution prove to be illusory, and the historical event is totally without consequence. The reality of this figure is that of a suffering, helpless victim who at all times during the play remains the object of political forces she cannot comprehend.

It is not too difficult to see in the part of the Poor Girl remnants characteristic of Adamov's absurd theatre, a theme namely that could be described as the reification of the human individual, his or her social role as a mere object. David Grossvogel, who has also pointed out the close relation of many of Adamov's characters to allegorical figures, has given the following interpretation of the early plays: "As usual, his human is hardly more than a negative quantity, a victim whose capacity to exist is real only to the extent that the physical instruments of his torture are real and will be used on him: it is only by comparison with these instruments that he is found to have significance greater than that of the rudimentary and static object."[13] Jacques Guicharnaud has made a similar point, stating that "the theme of the man-object as a victim is . . . [a] constant in Adamov's works" which feature as a central thematic concern "the tragedy of conscious and irreplaceable subjectivity being incomprehensibly massacred, humiliated, or mutilated by the world."[14] He adds: "Adamov's plays are all centered on that blind victimization (*La Grande et la Petite Manoeuvre,* for example) or on a refusal of it (*Le Printemps 71*) as well as on an aesthetic revenge; the playwright himself transforms into objects—that is, into puppets—the social forces that feed on the dehumanization of man."[15]

These observations could equally well have been made with reference to the role of the Poor Girl, but Guicharnaud's remark that *Le Printemps 71* contains as a theme the refusal of man's victimization certainly needs to be qualified. The Poor Girl, who appears as a victim of the old and of the new socio-political order, and who symbolizes the futility of well-meaning but lastly unrealistic efforts to achieve historical change, demonstrates very clearly that Adamov has not made a complete break with his earlier dramatic productions. Nor is the Poor Girl the only character in *Le Printemps 71* to fit the thematic pattern of the man-object as victim. The Old Worker in *tableau* 6 who wants to submit a petition to the Municipal Commission set up by the Commune makes two unavailing attempts to present his case; both times he is ignored by the Communards in charge of the office. Similarly, the Old Man in *tableau* 8 is seen throughout the scene as quietly laughing to himself, muttering always the same words: "Le siège recommence."[16] The implications of both episodes are evident: history repeats itself, any political change is bound to bring only new injustice and suffering to individual people, historical progress is illusory. To be sure, these two figures appear only once in the very long play and have only marginal importance; however, together with the part of the Poor Girl, they point to a significant

ideological undercurrent in Adamov's view of history. Next to the Marxist convictions of the author, the play exhibits a parallel, or maybe lower, level of consciousness which can only be called absurdist: a dramatic presentation of human futility, of the uselessness of revolutionary efforts to create conditions of social progress. Adamov's use of impersonal type-characters with allegorical qualities in *Le Printemps 71,* a distinctive feature of his earlier dramas, also points to the persistence of elements of the absurd theatre, with regard both to dramatic form and to the philosophical notion it expresses.

IV.

A final ideological inconsistency of *Le Printemps 71* lies in the very structure of the play, i.e., in its presentation of the historical material on two different levels of action. The *guignols,* which have an informative as well as a distantiating function, furnish the "cadre historique,"[17] as Adamov has put it, to the fictitious intrigue of the dramatic action unfolded in the *tableaux;* the *guignols* are satirical caricatures of *la haute politique,* while the *tableaux* offer realistic frescoes of the daily lives of the Communards. In the interludes, Adamov presents the leaders, the historical facts and developments, the proclamations and decrees of the Commune parallel with the decisions and moves of the Thiers government; the dramatic scenes of the fictitious level, on the other hand, show the effects and consequences of the historical events on the people.[18]

A few examples may show that this division between cause and effect is indeed the overriding structural principle of the play. *Guignol* 1, for instance, gives a dramatic if stylized rendering of the uprising of March 18; the following *tableau* describes the reaction of various people to this event. *Guignol* 4, in which the rent decree is proclaimed and which features the government's attack on Paris (Thiers kicks the figure of La Commune), is followed by *tableau* 8, in which Tonton is seen moving out of his house, leaving the landlord to worry about the unpaid rent, and in which Riri and Julot swear revenge after hearing the news of the army's attack. In *guignol* 6, the actress representing La Commune kicks over a small replica of the Vendôme column, and in the following *tableau* 17, Fournier and Sofia quarrel about the significance of this act: she thinks it is a politically useless waste of energy, while he defends the destruction of the column as a blow to tyranny in the minds of the people.

From an historical and especially from a Marxist point of view, this kind of structural relationship raises a number of questions. In Adamov's dramatic view of the Commune, the political decisions and events take place in the allegorical interludes, while the realistic scenes are limited to a description of the reaction of the people.

This creates a curiously fatalistic result: the characters of *Le Printemps 71,* the Communards and the people of Paris, appear as objects of the historical development. They seem to be affected only by events outside their control rather than affecting the course of history. Furthermore, the particular nature of the *guignols,* i.e., the grotesque and over-simplified allegorical presentation of complex political circumstances, does not lend itself to a differentiated and precise historical analysis. The Commune is represented by a single figure; consequently, the process of decision-making is not shown, just as it is not present in the *tableaux,* which feature neither the leadership of the Commune nor its administrative structure through which political decisions are implemented. The characters of the *tableaux* are thus not only shown as reacting to events that seem to be completely out of their reach; they are also viewed as objects of a political process which remains largely undefined and obscure. The analysis of the dramatic structure of *Le Printemps 71* therefore leads again to a discovery of absurdist ideas in the play: the notion of the individual as the object of history, and the conception of history as an unintelligible, autonomous and apparently self-motivated force.

It is interesting in this context to quote an observation made by Jean Vannier about Adamov's approach to the dramatization of history in an earlier play, *Paolo Paoli.* Vannier writes in *Théâtre Populaire*: "Dans *Paolo Paoli* . . . le rapport des personnages à l'Histoire n'est pas vraiment dialectique; c'est un rapport de *répétition,* dans la mesure où les relations et les combinaisons nouées entre eux par les personnages, en dépit de leur plasticité apparente, sont comme pétrifiées dans leur forme même, qui est la forme des rapports humains dans une société fondée sur le troc et le marchandage."[19] This observation fits *Le Printemps 71* equally well. The structure of the play does not correspond to a dialectical process of history; it rather expresses a static rapport of repetition or reaction.[20] One could even quote Adamov himself in support of this interpretation: "J'ai essayé, au cours de toute la pièce, de bien faire voir la précipitation des nouvelles contradictoires, et la manière dont réagissent à ces nouvelles les protagonistes du jeu."[21] Here the contradiction to a Marxist presentation of historical change is quite clearly spelled out, although Adamov was seemingly not aware of any such inconsistency: his dramatic characters only react to political decisions and events, or enact decrees which have come about without their understanding and participation; they are moved instead of being movers. Adamov does not show changes in individual characters or demonstrate their role in the making of the new society. He fails to express in his play that the Commune constitutes a qualitatively new beginning—in Marxist theory anyway—the nucleus of a socialist state in which a way is shown to overcome the traditional roles imposed on man by the socio-economic system of a capitalist soci-ety based on, to use Vannier's expression, commerce and exchange. The structure of *Le Printemps 71* increases thus the doubts about its ideological implications. The division of the play into historical allegory and a fictitious intrigue only obscures the central Marxist notion about the significance of the Commune, i.e., the historical fact of workers "storming heavens," of becoming the subject of history by taking over the state and smashing what Marx called its "bureaucratic-military machine."[22]

Most of the critics who have written about *Le Printemps 71* have evaluated the *guignols* quite positively. René Gaudy, for instance, who is very critical of the play in general, concludes that only the *guignols* are fully convincing: "Mais la pièce possède aussi des qualités burlesques grâce aux 'guignols' inspirés de Daumier, qui tout a la fois nous informent et nous amusent."[23] The burlesque, grotesque quality of the interludes is also praised by Raymond Temkine, while Konrad Schoell has described the faculty of parody as one of Adamov's special talents.[24] It is not too difficult to see in the mode of buffoonery a typical ingredient of the absurd theatre, and it is probably not wrong to agree that the *guignols* are successful (and popular with non-Marxist critics) precisely because Adamov is "at home" in this field. The exceptional dramatic qualities of the play lie, in fact, in the devastating satirical comments on the bourgeois enemies of the Commune and in the hilarious effect, created by the *guignols,* of the great spectacle of history reduced to a hurly-burly circus-show. The ideological problem, here again, concerns the place value of the interludes within the whole structural framework of the play and their historical and political relevance. Maurice Regnault has clearly detected the contradiction inherent in the structure of the play: "J'ai aimé le spectacle [the production of *Le Printemps 71* at Saint-Denis, G.F.], je l'ai aimé sans en être pleinement satisfait. Je pense à présent que la faute en est aux guignols. Ils sont en soi une haute réussite; dans la pièce, ils sont à la source d'une grande erreur. . . . En choisissant le caricatural comme arme de combat, ce qui conditionnait la structure de l'oeuvre entière, Adamov ne fait que remporter, et nous avec lui, une victoire morale."[25]

Adamov has rejected this criticism without, however, being able to elaborate on his disagreement or to give reasons for his refusal to accept this view.[26] In my opinion, Maurice Regnault has precisely identified the crucial dilemma of Adamov's political and historical intentions. *Le Printemps 71* constitutes a moral but not a political victory; its author describes the bourgeoisie as bloodthirsty, treacherous and ridiculous, the Communards as heroic, generous and dedicated fighters for a better world. While there is no doubt about Adamov's well-meaning engagement in favour of the socialist revolution or about the essential correctness of his historical interpretation, his drama fails to convince the audience of the political lessons that are to be drawn out of the experience of the Commune. The epilogue of *Le Printemps 71,* which suggests the optimistic perspective of a Marxist interpretation, i.e., the existence of numerous socialist countries arising out of the historical experiment of the Paris Commune, has a symbolic quality that finds no correlative in the course of the play. It is grafted on the action, as it were, but does not logically and organically develop out of the drama itself. *Le Printemps 71* does not show how the sufferings and the defeat of the Parisian workers of 1871 point the way to an eventual victory over the "historical monsters"[27] of the bourgeoisie, as Adamov wants his readers and spectators to believe. There remains, in the final analysis, a fundamental discrepancy between the reality of the play and the political views and dramatic objectives of its author.

V.

It would go beyond the limits of this essay to attempt to give an explanation of the inconsistency between Adamov's expressed aims and the reality of his literary product. A full assessment of this question clearly requires more evidence, and it would have to include an interpretation of his later writings together with a careful consideration of his biographic development, both of his personal circumstances and his reaction to the socio-political situation in France during the last years of his life. However, a few suggestions may be proposed at this point. One obvious reason may be that Adamov's "metamorphosis" to Marxism was a too recent and short-lived affair to produce a complete change of values and opinions. This process had begun in the early 1950's as a result of the defeat of the French colonial army in Vietnam (Dien-Bien-Phu, 1954) and the Algerian war of independence, which led to a sharply antagonistic ideological polarization of public opinion and concurrently to the destabilization of the IVth Republic. It is doubtful whether in 1960, at the height of the Algerian crisis and at the time of his writing *Le Printemps 71,* Adamov had discarded all his previously held doubts and apprehensions about historical progress, as he was apparently not prepared to sacrifice the complexity of his artistic and political imagination in order to make his play ideologically coherent.

On the other hand, while the atrocities committed by the French troops in Algeria doubtlessly served to remind Adamov of the bloody repression of the Paris Commune by the Thiers government, it is difficult to see how the historical parallel could have been made productive in any other way with regard to the French political scene around 1960. It is thus possible that Adamov's Marxism remained basically academic because he was never involved in a revolutionary situation in which the Paris Commune could have become a model for concrete political action, except in the sense of a legitimate defense against a repressive colonial government, as in the case of the Algerian resistance which led to a revolutionary situation in Algiers but not in Paris. Another possible explanation may be that Adamov's awareness of the historical development in Russia and other Communist countries had made him question the validity of a revolutionary model—the Paris Commune—that has definitely been abused by its self-professed successors in order to legitimatize new oppression and exploitation. A final point, and one which could be considered with reference to all these explanations, may well be that the internal contradictions reveal a case of repressed consciousness: Adamov wants to believe in the Marxist interpretation of the Commune and its historical significance, and emotionally he prefers to believe in it, but he expresses his innermost doubts in his literary creation.

Notes

1. Paris, 1959.

2. Adamov himself has spoken of his "metamorphosis" with regard to his artistic and intellectual development. See *Ici et Maintenant* (Paris, 1964), pp. 142-146.

3. "A duty towards the first government of the working class in the world," preface of *Le Printemps 71* (Paris, 1961), p. 6. All translations are mine.

4. "A play on the Paris Commune, if it is to be successful, can help and must help those who have the chance to read it or to see it to understand the struggle of the working class. And this struggle is not over." Quoted by Pierre Mélèse, *Adamov* (Paris, 1973), p. 70.

5. *Le Printemps 71,* p. 231.

6. Ruby Cohn, *Currents in Contemporary Drama* (Bloomington, 1969), p. 29; Margaret Dietemann, "Departure from the Absurd: Adamov's Last Plays," *Yale French Studies,* 46 (1971), 48; Jacques Guicharnaud, *Modern French Theatre from Giraudoux to Genet* (New Haven, 1967), p. 203.

7. I am using the terms "absurdist" and "existentialist" as synonyms to suggest Adamov's affinity to the philosophical and socio-political ideas of the dramatists of the absurd theatre, as developed, for instance, by Martin Esslin in his introductory chapter "The Absurdity of the Absurd" of his *The Theatre of the Absurd* (New York, 1961), pp. xv-xxiv.

8. Dietemann, p. 52.

9. "It is perhaps this question of time, or lack of time, this terrible contraction of things, which has interested me most." *Ici et Maintenant,* p. 118; see also p. 125.

10. See V.I. Lenin, *On the Paris Commune* (Moscow, 1970), p. 26.

11. "But what has interested me most, I think, is to show that the characters are never in tune with the events: they are behind or ahead. Montmartre has already been taken (treason or not) and all their hope still lies in this conviction: nothing is lost as long as Montmartre is not taken, and Montmartre is impregnable." *Ici et Maintenant,* pp. 120-121.

12. "Distressed worker," *Le Printemps 71,* p. 11.

13. David Grossvogel, *20th Century French Drama* (New York, 1961), p. 323.

14. Guicharnaud, p. 202.

15. *Ibid.,* p. 203.

16. "The siege begins again," *Le Printemps 71,* p. 104.

17. "Historical framework," *Ici et Maintenant,* p. 128.

18. See also Konrad Schoell, *Das französische Drama seit dem zweiten Weltkrieg* (Göttingen, 1970), II, p. 70.

19. "In *Paolo Paoli* . . . the connection of the characters to History is not really dialectical; it is rather a connection of *repetition* in so far as the relationships of the characters among one another appear, in spite of their seeming plasticity, as petrified in their very form, which is the form of human relationships in a society based on exchange and commerce." Quoted by Adamov, *Ici et Maintenant,* pp. 85-86.

20. See also André Gisselbrecht, "Brecht in Frankreich," *Sinn und Form,* 20 (1968), 1003, and Heinz Heller, *Untersuchungen zur Theorie und Praxis des dialektischen Theaters: Brecht und Adamov* (Bern/Frankfurt, 1975), pp. 97-101. Both come to similar conclusions but from a different approach and point of view, namely a comparison with Brecht.

21. "I have tried, in the course of the play, to show very clearly the precipitation of contradictory news, and the way in which the protagonists of the play react to these news." *Ici et Maintenant,* p. 121.

22. This is most clearly expressed by Marx in his letter to Kugelmann of July 12th, 1871. See Karl Marx, *Briefe an Kugelmann* (Berlin, 1952), p. 124.

23. "But the play has also a burlesque quality thanks to the *guignols,* which are inspired by Daumier, and which inform and entertain at the same time." René Gaudy, *Arthur Adamov* (Paris, 1971), p. 70.

24. Raymond Temkine, "La Commune au Théâtre," *Europe,* 48, No. 499-500, p. 220; Schoell, p. 87.

25. "I have loved the show [the production of *Le Printemps 71* at Saint-Denis, G.F.], I have loved it without being fully satisfied. I now think that the fault lies with the *guignols.* By themselves they are highly successful but in the play they constitute the basis of a great error. . . . By choosing caricature as a weapon of combat, which then conditioned the structure of the entire work, Adamov achieves to win, and we his spectators with him, only a moral victory." Quoted by Pierre Mélèse, p. 166.

26. See *Ici et Maintenant,* p. 147.

27. Dietemann, p. 53.

Deborah B. Gaensbauer (essay date 1991)

SOURCE: Gaensbauer, Deborah B. "Arthur Adamov." In *The French Theater of the Absurd,* pp. 66-78. Boston: Twayne Publishers, 1991.

[*In the following excerpt, Gaensbauer surveys Adamov's career as a dramatist, from the works of his Absurdist period, to his transitional phase, to his Brechtian socialist and political plays, and finally to his return to the principles of Absurdism his late plays.*]

THE ABSURDIST PERIOD: FROM *THE PARODY* TO *PING PONG*

When Adamov began his career as a playwright, it was Artaud who represented for him "the truth of the theater" (*IM* [*Ici et Maintenant*], 84). Even when he later rejected the theater of the absurd, he continued to draw inspiration from Artaud: "When Antonin Artaud, in the middle of a poem, suddenly has an old woman say: 'how difficult, very difficult!' attempting thus to express very simply, very 'stupidly' the *real* difficulty of life, I find that much more true, much more tragic than when one speaks of the *absurdity* of life" (*IM,* 131-32). Like Artaud, Adamov was preoccupied with the debasement of language and attempted to renew the language of theater by emphasizing the physicality of the stage: "The theater as I conceive it is bound entirely and absolutely to representation" (*IM,* 13). Adamov's, like Artaud's, is a cruel theater, making extensive use of the Artaudian concept of the double.

Adamov's conviction that "a play ought to be the place where the visible world and the invisible world touch and collide with one another," also reflects a debt to Strindberg, the Swedish playwright acclaimed by the German expressionists as one of their masters (*IM,* 14). Adamov credited Artaud's 1927 production of Strindberg's *A Dream Play* with steering him to write for the theater. "What does Strindberg want essentially," Adamov asked, finding the answer to the question in the mirror of his own psyche: "to affirm, exhibit, prove and hide himself all at once. Where could he better satisfy these desires than on stage."[1] Inspired by what he described as "the appearance of a new time on the stage, a shorter time, the time of a dream" and the "visible changes of decor which are at the same time instantaneous changes of interior states" (*S* [Eugene Ionesco, *A Stroll in the Air* and *Frenzy for Two,* trans. Donald Watson (New York: Grove Press, 1965)] 61-62), in Strindberg's theater, Adamov experimented with oneirically condensed time and fluid stage imagery.

LA PARODIE (THE PARODY)

Adamov often recounted the incident that was the source of his first play: "A blind man was begging. Two young girls pass without seeing him, bump into him inadvertently; they were singing: 'I closed my eyes, it was wonderful'" (*IM,* 17). The characters in **The Parody,** which begins with the sounds of an offstage eye examination, can neither "see" nor "hear" one another. Blindly narcissistic, they create such different languages from the same words that each becomes deaf to the others' meaning. Their dialogue becomes a parody of communication.

The Parody juxtaposes four nameless male characters— N., the Employee, the Journalist, and the Director—and a female character, almost as impersonally named Lily.[2] Each of the men wants Lily. Both N. and the Employee are wrongly persuaded that Lily has promised a rendezvous and waste away in a grimly comical pursuit. "I started from a general idea . . . all destinies are equivalent, the refusal of life (N.) and its complacent acceptance (the Employee) both end in inevitable failure, in total destruction" (*IM,* 18). The Employee, who is initially as obtusely optimistic and agitated as N. is pessimistic and lethargic, winds up a literally blind, broken prisoner of an unseen but noisily omnipresent police force. N., very clearly a shadow of his creator, spends much of the time lying about in the street. In his first encounter with Lily, he begs her to kill him since he is already dead: "Everybody is dead, not only me. Look at them blink their eyes, as if they were always getting cold rain in the face. They pretend to be walking, and at each step it is like two brooms balancing to the left and right."[3] N.'s death finally comes in a manner reminiscent of Adamov's suicidal gesture in 1928. He is run over by a car. When the curtain comes up on the last tableau, N.'s bloody body is lying onstage, arms stretched out in a cross. Lily doesn't see it and bumps into it. Two sanitation workers appear and matter-of-factly sweep N. from the stage like ordinary trash. The brightest light of the play is reserved for this brutal moment, illuminating the emptiness of human existence. The stage directions indicate that the moment the broom touches N., the lighting is to become as harsh and bright

as possible and a background is to appear that seems as real as possible and "perfectly empty, raw and cold."

Martin Esslin notes that the original meaning of the word *absurd* is "out of harmony" (Esslin, 23). All the elements of **The Parody,** linguistic and physical, are out of harmony. Set against a blurry, circular black-and-white photograph at the back of the stage and accompanied by the discordant sounds of impersonal city life, voices, police sirens, and typewriters, the action unfolds in rushed, jerky, dreamlike sequences of puppetlike agitation and missed cues. A municipal clock without hands, which grows bigger from one part to the next, stands at the side of the stage. Characters constantly ask each other for the time but receive either no answer or a brusque command to look at the clock. Time in this parody of human expectations is measured by abrupt physical decay and by the shrinking of hopes, a phenomenon that Adamov renders concretely by shrinking the stage sets from part 1 to part 2, in contrast to the "growing" clock. The characters visibly decay, succumbing to disabilities and a telescopic aging process. Only the Director, who plays three different roles and is a prototype of the unsavory capitalist chameleons in Adamov's theater, resists the progressive collapse. N.'s degradation represents most graphically the paralyzing absurdity of human existence. He regresses from exhausted stumbling to complete immobility before being impersonally crushed to death. His fate is foreshadowed in an earlier scene, in which the Director becomes so busy signing his name that he drowns the immobile N. in the papers that are spilling from his desk onto the office floor.

Roger Blin directed the premiere of **The Parody** in June 1952 in the small theater where Ionesco's *The Chairs* had opened just six weeks before. It folded quickly, drawing only about 15 people a night. One of the prefatory essays to the 1950 edition had predicted that "when **The Parody,** where the figures of desire and anguish led by time destroy themselves in their journey toward an unattainable escape, finds a place on stage, then it will be understood that a profoundly modern theater . . . is affirming and explaining itself."[4] This did not turn out to be the case in 1952. "Adamov," according to a reviewer for *Le Figaro,* "is one of these painters who paint boredom with boredom . . . he creates absurd theater by placing shorthand sentences end to end. There is, on the whole, in this spectacle a taste for the infamous, a pleasure in vileness that is rightly unbearable" (Latour, 262).

LA GRANDE ET LA PETITE MANOEUVRE (THE GREAT AND THE SMALL MANEUVER)

The Great and the Small Maneuver (1950) is perhaps the best illustration of the goal Adamov set for himself in his early plays: to make the staging "coincide literally, *concretely, corporally*" with the contents of the play (*IM,* 14). Like **The Parody,** it involves a passive victim, the Mutilé, and an activist, the Militant. In this Kafkaesque play both are maneuvered to failure, victims of their own psyches (the "great maneuver") and politics (the "small maneuver").[5] Adamov chose the title because, he claimed, "it is more correct to say of threatened man that he is in reality *maneuvered*: each of my characters is persecuted but without being able to say from what side the persecution comes. It comes from everywhere and men *maneuver* all along fear" (Latour, 59).

The source of **Maneuver** was a terrifying dream in which Adamov was summoned to self-destructive activities by voices from loudspeakers. The phantasmagoric effect is recaptured in the play in the rapidity and abruptness with which the 10 short tableaux follow one another, and in the nightmarish grip created by the staging, which from the opening moments of the first tableau establishes a context of blind manipulation and brutality. The curtain rises on a dark, empty stage. Cold, even voices from the loudspeakers issue orders to an unidentified victim. From offstage comes a noise of clapping hands, a sound whose savage irony is later revealed when the Mutilé begins to lose his limbs. As the lights come up, the Militant is brought onstage and roughed up by two policemen. In tandem with the physical battering taking place on stage, Adamov continues to assault the audience acoustically with the monitors' voices, the clapping, and the sound of hostile laughter coming from the wings.

In dreamlike shifts of time and place, the subsequent tableaux, which Adamov conceived as having "an almost cinematic linking," present the destruction of the Mutilé and his brother-in-law, the Militant, a member of a revolutionary group called the Partisans. The Militant, whose blind adherence to the demands of the revolutionary movement causes the death of his son and ruins his marriage, is essentially destroyed by his own rhetoric. Articulating the eternal untruths of demagogues, the victorious Partisans adopt the same power-hungry behavior as that of the reactionary government they replaced. Adamov's recurring theme of the degeneration of language is broadened in **Maneuver** to encompass linguistic manipulation for political ends. In a parallel but more graphically horrifying phenomenon, the Mutilé is progressively dismembered in response to mysterious orders from monitors, which no one else hears. Adamov, as cruelly as Beckett, uses physical degradation to portray the debilitating effect of modern society. As soon as the Mutilé hears the monitors' voices, he begins to shake. After minimal resistance, he simply crosses his arms, an action that becomes particularly grotesque when they have been reduced to stumps, and slinks away to submit. The inadmissibly brutal mutilation becomes a source of cruel humor, both when the Mutilé attempts to cross his ineffective stumps and when he enrolls in a typing course for the disabled. As the typing students struggle, the director and her assistant engage in constant hand play and make tactless references to hands. Laughing, however uncomfortably, at the inappropriate words and gestures, the spectator or reader is forced to acknowledge an unwitting alliance with the persecuting "others" in the play. This is precisely the kind of cruel theater promoted by Artaud.

The first of Adamov's plays to be performed, **Maneuver** received mixed reviews and had only 25 performances. Camus congratulated Adamov for **Maneuver,** but Adamov's approach in this play was deliberately anti-Sartrean and anti-Camusian. Defending his theater, which he expected to be judged "puerile" in contrast to the philosophical theater then in vogue, Adamov maintained, "If the drama of a man consists in any kind of a mutilation of his person, I do not see a better means to render the truth of such a mutilation dramatically than to represent it physically on stage . . . for me it is precisely in this puerility that all the resources of a living theater reside" (*IM,* 22).

LE PROFESSEUR TARANNE (PROFESSOR TARANNE)

Adamov created the two short tableaux of **Professor Taranne** very rapidly in 1951 from another dream. In **Taranne,** according to Adamov, for the first time he was able simply to transcribe a dream without distorting it for ulterior motives. The naturalness with which he captures a dream's fluid time and settings and its capacity to condense complex webs of fear and desire into a few indelible images makes **Taranne** an exceptional play. He described Taranne as "a premonitory text. My fear of being nothing but a lecturer, a traveling salesman, the author invited abroad, ignored in France" (**HE** [**L'Homme et l'enfant**], 101).

The play opens with the professor in a police station, defending himself in an ineffective rush of words against the charge of appearing naked on the beach. He bases his defense on the fact that he is Professor Taranne, known by everyone. No one in the police station has heard of him, however. The one person who thinks she recognizes Taranne mistakes him for a Professor Menard. A journalist familiar with the university not only claims not to know Taranne but essentially denies his existence by turning away from him when he tries to introduce himself. Abandoned in the police station, Taranne rushes off, frantic because he hasn't signed the necessary papers. His terrified voice can be heard from the wings: "I don't understand."[6] Taranne joins the many Adamovian characters for whom imposing one's existence, even just enough to be recognized as physically present, is an insurmountable obstacle.

A dreamlike shift, brought about by the appearance of a hotel manageress who slightly adjusts the furniture and hangs a rack of keys on the wall, transforms the police station into the reception area of Taranne's hotel. His key is missing. Two policemen enter looking for Taranne, now accused of strewing papers in beach cabins. Taranne undertakes another rambling, implausible defense, in which his identity becomes even more questionable. While Taranne loses himself in unlikely excuses, the policemen slip offstage. The hotel manageress returns and hands Taranne an enormous roll of paper. Spreading it out in the middle of the stage, Taranne reveals a dining room seating plan for a steamship on which he had failed to book passage. He has been assigned a place at the head table. Taranne's sister appears and reads a letter from the rector at the university where Taranne claims to be so highly regarded denouncing his incompetence and accusing him of plagiarizing a Professor Menard and even stealing his eyeglasses. Literally staggering from the blow, Taranne grasps at the table to keep from falling as he asks: "Why tell me this now, after all these years? Why hasn't he told me sooner? Why haven't they all told me? Because it's obvious! You can see it immediately!" (**TP** [**Professor Taranne**], 29). But Taranne, although accused in the first act of watching all the time and seeing too much, inhabits, like the other characters in Adamov's early plays, a world in which people cannot or will not see.

The sister disappears. The hotel manager comes in and, without looking at Taranne, empties the stage of all its properties except for an incriminating notebook, the letter, and the seating plan. Taranne doesn't notice. He tacks the seating plan to the wall, revealing only a large empty surface. Taranne has no visible place, not even on paper. With his back turned to the audience, he stares at the blank plan for a long moment and then very slowly begins to undress as the curtain falls. It is an ambiguous ending typical of the theater of the absurd. Taranne is the kind of alienated individual for whom the terms *guilty* or *innocent* make no sense, since he has been allotted no place among the smug ranks of people sure enough of their own roles to be willing to make that kind of judgment.

In **Professor Taranne** Adamov achieved an effect he had admired much earlier in a scene in Strindberg's *The Road to Damascus*: "To translate the painful impression . . . of a rapid transformation and degradation of places and beings, impression of half-sleep but also the reality of fear and discouragement" (**AS** [**Auguste Strindberg**], 61). As in a dream, it is primarily the physical language that tells the story, usually in contradiction to Taranne's words. Taranne is unable to defend himself against the solid, accusatory muteness of the stage properties. Stripped of his words, the doubly naked, ridiculous, and probably dishonest Taranne becomes one of the most unforgettable Nobody-as-Everyman figures to appear on the twentieth-century stage. With **Taranne,** Adamov had accomplished what he once claimed was the only task left: "to tear away all the dead skin, to strip oneself

to the point of finding oneself at the hour of the great nakedness."[7] Unfortunately, Adamov had no more luck with his **Taranne** in Paris, where it opened in May 1954, than with his previous plays, although by then the theater of the absurd was becoming a more familiar phenomenon.

TRANSITION: LE PING-PONG (PING-PONG)

Increasingly frustrated by the contrast between the growing success of Beckett and Ionesco and his own continued condemnation to offnight performances, Adamov began to chafe at the limits of his absurdist theater. In **Ping-Pong,** completed in 1955, he made a transition to a more politicized theater by introducing multidimensional characters who are crushed not by a vague but inexorable fate but by a fixation on pinball machines and a desire to "make it" that drops them in the maw of a capitalist corporation. Adamov conceived the title image—"two old men . . . whose deplorable habit of complicating everything pushes them to complicate even the game of Ping-Pong" (Latour, 68-69)—before he knew what he would make of it in the play. Instead of Ping-Pong, pinball became the controlling image: "I wanted everything in the play to revolve around the pinball machine . . . every worry, every nostalgia, every ambition" (**HE,** 112). Each of the characters sacrifices whatever limited financial or creative resources he or she possesses to a consortium that controls the economics of the pinball industry. The destructively mesmerizing behavior of the unreliable pinball machines and the consortium that controls them is mirrored in the progressively dehumanized mechanical relationships of the characters. In the last scene of the play, the main characters, Arthur and Victor, who were young at the beginning of the play, are white-haired old men. Still quarrelling over points and procedures as they used to during the pinball games in their youth, they play the Ping-Pong match that gives the play its title. The game grows progressively madder as they invent new rules. The net is thrown away, then the paddles. Shouting in anger, they leap about, using their hands as paddles, until Victor suddenly falls dead. The comically degenerate but tragically lethal Ping-Pong game is Adamov's mirror image of a society in which scheming has replaced intelligence, and addiction and rapaciousness have replaced desire.

Ping-Pong, which Adamov considered the most comic of his plays—"comedy a little grinding, no doubt, but a deliberate turning of the back to the falsely tragic expressionism of my first plays" (Latour, 68)—is tied to the theater of the absurd by the treatment of language. In the sometimes humorous, sometimes irritating, stilted, and inflated dialogues, words become the empty, addictive equivalent of a pinball game. The lines addressed to a snoring old woman by a down-and-out former employee of the consortium reflects a world held captive by the machinery of its language: "Yes," he exclaims, walking about like a madman and knocking a dead body that has been laid out on chairs to the floor, "the sleeping traveler inside me awakened and called and I answered, 'Here!' Import-export, U.S.A. How does that sound to you? . . . In the States they have big ideas. They see things on a big scale. Ideas have consequences, people take action, the bidding rises, people put money on you, double or nothing, the winner and still champ, drive, it's all drive. Once you've got drive, the machine runs itself and it runs and runs."[8]

The most successful of Adamov's plays to date, **Ping-Pong** was still not the theatrical victory Adamov dreamed of nor the financial success he so desperately needed. After **Ping-Pong** he severed his ties with the theater of the absurd for several years. "Little by little, writing **Ping-Pong,** I began to judge my first plays severely and, very sincerely, criticized *Waiting for Godot* and *The Chairs* for the same reasons. I already saw in the 'avant-garde' an easy escape, a diversion from real problems. . . . Life wasn't absurd, but difficult, very difficult" (*HE,* 111).

BRECHTIAN THEATER

Adamov's discouragement with his absurdist theater coincided with an increasingly indignant awareness of the politics of the Fifth Republic and his discovery of Brecht, who replaced Strindberg, Artaud, and Kafka as the dominant influences on his theater. *Paolo Paoli,* the first of Adamov's Brechtian plays, satirizes the speculative greed of pre-World War I society. Brecht's influence is evident in *Paolo Paoli* in both the often humorous treatment of the political topic and in the distancing effect of the staging, which calls for the breaking up of the tableaux by projections of historical photographs and newspaper excerpts from the days just before World War I. *Paolo Paoli* was followed by *Le Printemps '71* (*Spring '71*), a massive historical epic depicting the insurrection and brutal repression of the Paris Communards in 1871. Adamov's debt to Brecht, who had written a play on the same topic, is again evident in the alienating device of allegorical "Guignol" interludes, where real actors, not puppets, adopt exaggeratedly repellent styles to portray repressive historical figures or institutions. Made up of 26 scenes, interspersed with nine allegorical "Guignols," and an epilogue, it is a forerunner of the vast spectacles that came into vogue in the French theater in the 1970s.

La Politique des restes (*The Politics of Waste*), completed in 1962, is set in South Africa but was inspired by Adamov's discovery of Harlem during a trip to New York City. In the 1967 Paris production, images of poor black neighborhoods in American cities and slums in the Paris environs were projected between the scenes.[9] Adamov made two trips to the United States, the first in 1959 for a disastrous New York production of **Ping-Pong,** the second when he was invited to be a visiting lecturer at Cornell University in the fall of 1964. In 1968 he wrote **Off Limits,** another harshly anti-American play. Using a party given by a wealthy New Yorker as his framework, he breaks the episodes into a series of happenings, allowing him to take on both the politics of the Vietnam War era and the society responsible for a generation lost to drugs.

THE ABSURD RENEWED

Although the years that correspond to Adamov's political theater continued to be difficult, this period was the most successful of his career. His left-leaning theater brought new audiences, more sympathetic than Left Bank audiences had been to his absurdist plays. Several of his plays were performed outside of France. Toward the end of his career, however, still discouraged by the reception of his plays in France, and suffering the effects of years of alcohol and drug addiction, Adamov renewed some of his ties to the theater of the absurd: "I wanted to go back to my former 'absurd' theater. . . . But I believe that in these last plays I have united, reunited, a little better than in the past individual psychology and the general political line" (*Théâtre,* 3:9). With the exception of his last play, *Si l'été revenait* (*If Summer Were to Return*), none of these plays is as powerful as his early works, nor were they particularly successful.

The ironically named *Sainte Europe* (*Holy Europe*), completed in 1966, is a burlesque epic in which actors alternate between allegorical dreams and realistic waking scenes, playing caricatural dual roles as medieval figures and modern political dignitaries. In *M. le Modéré* (*Mr. Moderate,* 1967) which Adamov called a "clownerie," he again attacks the decadence of contemporary European politics, particularly the role of the moderates, and the intrusive role of American policy in European affairs, but scales the stature of the main characters and their political ambitions to *Ubu*esque dimensions. Through comically implausible circumstances involving an American agent, the narcissistic and excessively moderate M. le Modéré, a hotel keeper in Paris, becomes the chief officer of the Jura in Switzerland and is charged with putting down a rebellion. His devices for income-generating methods of punishment, although a little gentler than Ubu's, involve the same kind of pernicious, self-centered logic and bombastic rhetoric. He is exiled finally to London, where he is confined to a wheelchair by a stroke and becomes an alcoholic. This cruel play represented a moment of reckoning for Adamov, who was once more in the hospital suffering from drug and alcohol abuse when he wrote it: "Hemmed in by misery, I had to either burst out laughing or commit suicide" (*Théâtre,* 4:11). When it was staged in Paris in 1968, the director set the action in a hospital, putting M. le Modéré in pajamas for the entire play. The scenery was changed by nurses to the sound of ambulance sirens (Gaudy, 87).

If Summer Were to Return, a final, Strindbergian reworking of Adamov's neuroses and his failure as a playwright, is presented as a series of four dreams. The central figure, Lars, is a repressed and brutal son; a failure as a brother, husband, and friend; and a failure at any profession. Like his desperately ill creator, he wears pajamas during much of the play. Each of the four dream sequences alters the perspective on Lars. As one character dreams, the others stand to the side of the stage acting out the dream's hidden meaning. A seesaw onstage physically captures the ambivalence and instability of the characters' relationships. *If Summer Were to Return* was completed two and a half months before Adamov's death, in 1970, from an overdose of barbiturates.

Paying homage to Adamov's theater in 1976, Roger Planchon, a director who worked closely with Adamov for many years, described it as "fundamental for all those who are interested in the adventure of theater," and, although he worried that Adamov was in danger of becoming "an author for authors the way some poets exist only for other poets," he forecast that "future generations might one day be more drawn by the hesitations and imperfections in Adamov's theater than to the perfections of Beckett's."[10] There has been a renewed interest in the last decade in Adamov's experiments with stage language and their adaptability to both absurdist and political themes. In 1975 Planchon created a very successful spectacle entitled *A.A.: Théâtres d'Arthur Adamov,* a collage of episodes from his early plays and autobiographical writings. Consummate exhibitionist, masochist, and ironist that Adamov was, he might have found a perverse pleasure in the fact that Planchon had a greater box office success with his *A.A.* than Adamov had had with most of his own plays. "When I arrange the world around me," Adamov wrote, "I often reproach it for being nothing more than a parody."[11]

Notes

1. Arthur Adamov, *August Strindberg, dramaturge* (Paris: L'Arché, 1955), 61-62; hereafter cited in the text as *AS.*

2. Lily, according to Adamov, has a "name which suits her, as it does every woman, a flighty name" (*Théâtre* [Paris: Gallimard, 1953-68], 1:9). She inaugurates a long list of pretty young female characters in his theater who, although they are selfish and quick to betray, are subject in the long run to the same degradation and defeat as the male characters.

3. Arthur Adamov, *Théâtre,* 1:17.

4. Arthur Adamov, *La Parodie, L'Invasion* (Paris: Charlot, 1950), 17.

5. Carlos Lynes, Jr., "Adamov or le sens littéral in the Theatre," *Yale French Studies* 14 (1954-55):52.

6. Arthur Adamov, *Professor Taranne,* trans. Peter Meyer, in *Two Plays* (London: John Calder, 1962), 17; hereafter cited in the text as *TP.*

7. Arthur Adamov, *Je . . . ils* (Paris: Gallimard, 1969), 115.

8. Arthur Adamov, *Ping-Pong,* trans. Richard Howard (New York: Grove Press, 1959), 143.

9. Pierre Mélèse, *Arthur Adamov* (Paris: Seghers, 1973), 85.

10. Roger Planchon, "Le Sens de la marche d'Adamov," in *Les Nouvelles littéraires* 2563 (16-23 December 1976):16.

11. Arthur Adamov, "The Endless Humiliation," trans. Richard Howard, *Evergreen Review* 2, No. 8 (1959):85.

Selected Bibliography

PRIMARY WORKS

ARTHUR ADAMOV

Plays in French

La Parodie. L'Invasion. Paris: Charlot, 1950.

Théâtre. Vol. 1. *La Parodie. L'Invasion. La Grande et la Petite Manoeuvre. Le Professeur Taranne.* Paris: Gallimard, 1953, 1970.

———. Vol. 2. *Le Sens de la marche. Les Retrouvailles. Le Ping-Pong.* Paris: Gallimard, 1955.

———. Vol. 3. *Paolo Paoli. La Politique des restes. Sainte Europe.* Paris: Gallimard, 1966.

———. Vol. 4. *Le Printemps 71. M. le Modéré.* Paris: Gallimard, 1968.

Théâtre de société: Intimité. Je ne suis pas Française. La Complainte du ridicule. Paris: Les Editeurs Français Réunis, 1958.

Off Limits. Paris: Gallimard, 1969.

Si l'été revenait. Paris: Gallimard, 1970.

Le Professor Taranne. In *"Le Professor Taranne"* and *"Pique-Nique en campagne,"* edited by Peter Norrish. London: Routledge, Chapman and Hall, 1989.

English Translations

Paolo Paoli. Translated by Geoffrey Bereton. London: Calder, 1959.

Ping-Pong. Translated by Richard Howard. New York: Grove Press, 1959.

Two Plays: Professor Taranne and *Ping-Pong.* Translated by Peter Meyer and Derek Prouse. London: Calder, 1962.

Essays, Memoirs, Journals

Auguste Strindberg. Paris: l'Arché, 1955, 1982.

L'Homme et l'enfant. Paris: Gallimard, 1958.

Ici et maintenant. Paris: Gallimard, 1964.

Je . . . ils. Paris: Gallimard, 1969.

SECONDARY WORKS

WORKS TREATING MORE THAN ONE AUTHOR

Esslin, Martin. *The Theatre of the Absurd.* 3d ed. New York: Pelican Books, 1983. Updated version of the work that introduced the concept of the theater of the absurd.

Latour, Geneviève, ed. *Petites scènes, grand théâtre.* Paris: La Délégation à l'Action Artistique de la Ville de Paris, 1986. Invaluable collection of excerpts from interviews and newspaper reviews, 1944-60.

ARTHUR ADAMOV

Gaudy, René. *Arthur Adamov.* Paris: Stock, 1971. Brief general study; includes essays by directors who worked with Adamov.

Mélèse, Pierre. *Adamov.* Paris: Séghers, 1973. Critical survey supplemented by interviews and excerpts from the press.

Les Nouvelles Littéraires 2563 (16-23 December 1976). Special issue on Adamov.

FURTHER READING

Bibliography

Bradby, David. *Adamov,* London: Grant & Cutler Ltd., 1975, 77 p.
> Comprehensive bibliography of Adamov's plays and other writings, as well as a listing of criticism of his works.

Biography

Pruks, Inge. "Arthur Adamov and the Business of Living." *Meanjin Quarterly* 29, no. 3 (1970): 338-45.
> Briefly surveys Adamov's life and career as a writer, including commentary on a number of his major works.

Criticism

Adamov, Arthur, and Emmanuel C. Jacquart. "A Last Interview with Arthur Adamov." *Drama and Theatre* 9, no. 2 (winter 1970-71): 73-4.
> Interview with Adamov conducted a few weeks before his death in March, 1970.

Barthes, Roland. "Adamov and Language." In *The Eiffel Tower and Other Mythologies,* translated by Richard Howard, pp. 55-8. New York: Hill and Wang, 1979.
> Disagrees with the prevailing critical view that the pinball machine in Adamov's *Le ping-pong* is meant to be symbolic, claiming that it is "not a key" but "an object which generates language."

Bishop, Tom. "Pirandello and French Theater." In *From the Left Bank: Reflections on the Modern French Theater and Novel,* pp. 41-63. New York: New York University Press, 1997.
> Discusses the influence of the Italian playwright Luigi Pirandello on a number of Adamov's early works, including *La grande et la petite manoeuvre, The Invasion,* and *La parodie.*

Fischer, Gerhard. "Arthur Adamov, *Le Printemps 71* (1960)." In *The Paris Commune on the Stage: Vallès, Grieg, Brecht, Adamov,* pp. 147-206. Frankfurt am Main: Peter Lang, 1981.
> Examines Adamov's treatment of the Paris commune and its conflict with Versailles in 1871 in his play *Spring 71.*

Norrish, Peter. Introduction to *Arthur Adamov,* Le Professeur Taranne *and Fernando Arrabal,* Pique-nique en Campagne, edited by Peter Norrish, pp. 1-53. London: Routledge, 1988.
> Examines the dreamlike action and atmosphere of Adamov's *Professor Taranne,* praising the play as the first work in which the dramatist created an individual protagonist, with relevance for his audience, rather than a character type.

Additional coverage of Adamov's life and career is contained in the following sources published by Thomson Gale: *Contemporary Authors,* Vols. 17-18, 25-28R; *Contemporary Authors Permanent Series,* Vol. 2; *Contemporary Literary Criticism,* Vols. 4, 25; *Dictionary of Literary Biography,* Vol. 321; *DISCovering Authors Modules: Dramatists*; *Encyclopedia of World Literature in the 20th Century,* Ed. 3; *Guide to French Literature: 1789 to the Present*; *Literature Resource Center*; *Major 20th-Century Writers,* Ed. 1; and *Reference Guide to World Literature,* Eds. 2, 3.

Pale Fire

Vladmir Nabokov

The following entry presents criticism of Nabokov's novel *Pale Fire* (1962). For discussion of Nabokov's complete career, see *CLC*, Volumes 1, 2, 3, 6, 8, 11, 15, 23, 44, and 46, and *TCLC*, Volume 108; for discussion of the novel *Lolita*, see *CLC*, Volume 64.

INTRODUCTION

Pale Fire is widely considered one of the most unconventional and innovative novels of the twentieth century, and one of Vladimir Nabokov's greatest fictional works. In its critique of traditional narrative forms and the authenticity of language, *Pale Fire* has been described by a number of critics as a landmark work that heralded the ascent of postmodernism in American literature. The book, which includes a long poem, explores issues of mortality, art, and the differences between reality and perception. *Pale Fire* has also been the subject of much critical debate, with scholars offering various views on its form and plot, as well as Nabokov's intention in writing the novel. In an assessment of the book written in 1962, Mary McCarthy argued that "this centaur-work of Nabokov's, half-poem, half-prose, this merman of the deep, is a creation of perfect beauty, symmetry, strangeness, originality, and moral truth. Pretending to be a curio, it cannot disguise the fact that it is one of the very great works of art of this century, the modern novel that everyone thought was dead and that was only playing possum."

PLOT AND MAJOR CHARACTERS

Pale Fire owes a great deal of its reputation to its unique structure. The novel is composed of the fabricated posthumous publication of a poem and accompanying material. The foreword, commentary, and index to the poem were written by the novel's protagonist, Charles Kinbote, who claims to be a refugee from a country called Zembla. The poem itself was written by Kinbote's neighbor and colleague, a poet and professor named John Shade. Before finishing his poem, Shade was murdered by a man named Jack Grey, who had escaped from an insane asylum.

The poem itself, titled "Pale Fire," represents Shade's attempts through verse to understand and make peace with mortality, partly in reaction to the death of his daughter, Hazel, whom he believes has committed suicide. The poem is 999 lines long, written in heroic couplets, and reveals Shade's philosophy of life and art, as well as his love for his wife, Sybil, and their daughter. In the poem, Shade ruminates on reality and perception, asserts that art is the only response to the reality of death, and discusses the patterns in life and the interconnectedness of humanity. The poem closes as Shade reiterates the importance of art, the creation of which he believes gives meaning to existence.

In his foreword to "Pale Fire," Kinbote claims that Shade's poem is incomprehensible without his own illuminating remarks. Kinbote has fled his native country and settled in America, where he develops a relationship with Shade. He maintains that they became best friends, but his resentment toward Shade's wife, Sybil, is evident, and he admits to having spied on the couple. He believes that "Pale Fire" is actually inspired by his own tale of King Charles the Beloved of Zembla, who is exiled because of his homosexual preferences and refusal to produce an heir. Kinbote's notes and cross-references are only loosely related to the poem; more often, they merely provide him an opportunity to tell his own story. Kinbote further asserts that he is, in fact, the exiled King Charles, and that Shade's murderer, Jack Grey, is really Jakob Gradus, an assassin hired by Zembla's secret police force to kill Kinbote. By the end of the commentary, it seems likely that Kinbote has completely fabricated his claims, and that he is really a refugee scholar, dismissed by most of the academic community, but pitied and tolerated by Shade. It also becomes clear that Shade's murder was caused by mistaken identity. Shade's killer, Jack Grey, sought revenge on Kinbote's landlord, the judge who had sent him to the asylum. Because Shade bore a resemblance to the judge, Grey accidentally killed Shade instead of his intended target.

MAJOR THEMES

Human mortality and the nature of existence are central themes in Shade's poem, "Pale Fire." The preoccupation with death is evident in the first lines of the poem, in which a bird crashes into a window and dies after trying to fly to freedom. Shade presents a more intimate portrait of mortality through his descriptions of the suffering and deaths of his Aunt Maud and daughter, Hazel, both of whom die after experiencing emotional pain. Shade then reflects on the possibility of an afterlife, but concludes that the existence of life after death is beyond his knowledge. He instead finds comfort through several epiphanies, including his recognition of the inherent patterns in life, even within events or situations that seem accidental. These patterns indicate for Shade the possible existence of a higher power. Shade also finds comfort in his aesthetic endeavors and regards art as the only knowable means of achieving immortality. For Shade, the creation of art is not only an assertion of life but a means of combating despair associated with the inevitability of death.

Doubles and mirror images recur throughout *Pale Fire*. Several of the characters have aliases, even multiple identities. Charles Kinbote equates himself with King Charles the Beloved; he is also linked to professor Botykin, whose last name is the syllabic inverse of Kinbote. Jack Grey is referred to as Jakob Gradus. While John Shade is never given an alias, he closely resembles Judge Goldsworth, a fact that leads to his accidental murder. The image of the butterfly, which recurs in Shade's poem and in Kinbote's commentary, is also tied to the mirroring and doubling that takes place in *Pale Fire*. The body of the butterfly is perfectly symmetrical, and the wings carry identical designs, which are mirror images of the other. Mirroring also takes place on the linguistic level of the book, as seen in the word play that Kinbote uses throughout his commentary.

Perhaps the most important theme of *Pale Fire* is the disparity between reality and perception. Shade's poem, though primarily concerned with mortality, addresses this relationship. Images in the poem are often reflected or juxtaposed with other incongruous images in the glass of a window pane or a mirror, creating the appearance of a different reality. Confusions between reality and perception pervade the frame story of the novel, as well. Kinbote's delusions are the most obvious example of this discrepancy. He misinterprets his relationship with Shade, as well as the meaning of Shade's poem, and creates a new reality for himself by adopting the persona of King Charles the Beloved. Even Shade's death at the hands of Grey is a result of mistaken identity, an error based on a misperception. Finally, the puzzle-like formal construction of *Pale Fire* creates ambiguity concerning plot and character identity, and as a result obscures from the reader the reality of the fictional world that the novel establishes.

CRITICAL RECEPTION

Pale Fire was generally praised by critics following its publication in 1962, though some reviewers found it difficult to assess the novel's experimental form. Indeed, debate over the narrative's formal structure dominated early criticism of *Pale Fire*. While some scholars argued that the elaborate construction of the book obscured its content, others thought that the work's complexities contributed to its artistic merit. In a definitive essay published in 1962, Mary McCarthy described Nabokov's *Pale Fire* as "a Jack-in-the-box, a Fabergé gem, a clockwork toy, a chess problem, an infernal machine, a trap to catch reviewers, a cat-and-mouse game, a do-it-yourself novel" that reveals itself on several different levels. Since then, many commentators have maintained that Nabokov introduced a new novel-form with his innovative narrative, one that requires the imagination of the reader to interpret the author's design. Writing in 1982, Marilyn Edelstein echoed this point when she stated that "the novel makes the reader into an artist, an active participant in the creation of sense and meaning." Still other critics suggested that Nabokov's structuring of the novel should be interpreted as a parody of the poetic commentary form.

The question of authorship is another central concern among scholars of *Pale Fire*. While some accept the general premise of the novel, in which John Shade wrote a poem titled "Pale Fire" and Charles Kinbote wrote a commentary on that poem, others propose that either Shade or Kinbote invented the other as a fictional character within their metafictional world, or that Shade, Kinbote, and Grey/Gradus are partial entities that only when taken together form a complete persona. On the theme of authorship, Neil D. Isaacs averred that Nabokov's intent in his book "includes drawing attention to the concept of artist as magician or conjuror, to the theme of appearance/reality, and to innovations in points of view, personae, filters, and removes. By employing dual artists and dual lives, interacting and refracting, he newly lights up the old dialectic of life and art, the working out of art as plot, and the concern with artist as subject."

All of these issues reflect what many critics consider the central concern of *Pale Fire,* the nature of the self and the relation of identity and language. As Patrick O'Donnell concluded in his 1986 study of the novel, "For Nabokov, in *Pale Fire*, the self is textual and mortal: an entity who comes into being by establishing its relation to the elements of the language in which it is born, through which it is identified, to which it dies. His novel is ultimately a celebration of our legibility, our being readable within the confinements of language—that 'currency' of the human world."

PRINCIPAL WORKS

Stikhi (poetry) 1916

Al'manakh: Dva puti. Stikhi [with Andrei Balashov] (poetry) 1918

Grozd': Stikhi [as Vladimir Sirin] (poetry) 1922

Gornii put' [as Vladimir Sirin] (poetry) 1923

Chelovek iz SSSR [as Vladimir Sirin] (play) 1926

Mashen'ka [as Vladimir Sirin; *Mary*] (novel) 1926

Korol', dama, valet [as Vladimir Sirin; *King, Queen, Knave*] (novel) 1928

Vozvrashchenie Chorba [as Vladimir Sirin] (short stories) 1930

Zashchita Luzhina [as Vladimir Sirin; *The Defense*] (novel) 1930

Kamera obskura [as Vladimir Sirin; *Laughter in the Dark*] (novel) 1932; published in journal *Sovremennye Zapiski*

Podvig [as Vladimir Sirin; *Glory*] (novel) 1932; published in journal *Sovremennye Zapiski*

Otchaianie [as Vladimir Sirin; *Despair*] (novel) 1936

Dar [*The Gift*] (novel) 1937-38; published in journal *Sovremennye Zapiski*

Priglashenie na kazn' [as Vladimir Sirin; *Invitation to a Beheading*] (novel) 1938

Sobytie [as Vladimir Sirin] (play) 1938

Sogliadatai [as Vladimir Sirin; *The Eye*] (novel) 1938

The Real Life of Sebastian Knight (novel) 1941

Nikolai Gogol (criticism) 1944

Bend Sinister (novel) 1947

Nine Stories (short stories) 1947

*Conclusive Evidence: A Memoir (autobiography) 1951

Stikhotvoreniia 1929-1951 (poetry) 1952

Lolita (novel) 1955

Vesna v Fial'te i drugie rasskazy (short stories) 1956

Pnin (novel) 1957

Nabokov's Dozen: A Collection of Thirteen Stories (short stories) 1958; also published as *Spring in Fialta,* 1959

Poems (poetry) 1959

Lolita (screenplay) 1962

Pale Fire (novel) 1962

Notes on Prosody: From the Commentary to His Translation of Pushkin's Eugene Onegin (criticism) 1963

Eugene Onegin: A Novel in Verse [translator; from novel by Aleksandr Pushkin] (novel) 1964

Nabokov's Quartet (short stories) 1966

Izobretenie Val'sa [*The Waltz Invention: A Play in Three Acts*] (play) 1968

Ada or Ardor: A Family Chronicle (novel) 1969

Poems and Problems (poetry) 1970

Transparent Things (novella) 1972

A Russian Beauty and Other Stories (short stories) 1973

Strong Opinions (essays) 1973

Look at the Harlequins! (novel) 1974

Tyrants Destroyed and Other Stories (short stories) 1975

Details of a Sunset and Other Stories (short stories) 1976

The Man from the USSR and Other Plays (plays) 1985

The Enchanter (short stories) 1986

Selected Letters (letters) 1989

The Stories of Vladimir Nabokov (short stories) 1995

Nabokov's Butterflies: Unpublished and Uncollected Writings (prose and poetry) 2000

*This work was revised and republished as *Speak, Memory: An Autobiography Revisited* in 1967.

CRITICISM

Mary McCarthy (essay date October 1962)

SOURCE: McCarthy, Mary. "Vladimir Nabokov's 'Pale Fire'." *Encounter* 19, no. 4 (October 1962): 71-84.

[*In the following essay, McCarthy provides an overview of* Pale Fire, *focusing on the imagery and themes that contribute to the novel's complexity.*]

Pale Fire[1] is a Jack-in-the-box, a Fabergé gem, a clockwork toy, a chess problem, an infernal machine, a trap to catch reviewers, a cat-and-mouse game, a do-it-yourself novel. It consists of a 999-line poem of four cantos in heroic couplets together with an editor's preface, notes, and index. When the separate parts are assembled, according to the manufacturer's directions, and fitted together with the help of clues and cross-references, which must be hunted down as in a paper-chase, a novel on several levels is revealed, and these "levels" are not the customary "levels of meaning" of modernist criticism but planes in a fictive space, rather like those houses of memory in medieval mnemonic science, where words, facts, and numbers were stored till wanted in various rooms and attics, or like the houses of astrology into which the heavens are divided.

The poem has been written by a sixty-one-year-old American poet of the homely, deceptively homely, Robert Frost-type who teaches at Wordsmith College in New Wye, Appalachia; his name is John Shade, his wife is called Sybil, née Irondell or Swallow; his parents were ornithologists; he and his wife had a fat, plain daughter, Hazel, who killed herself young by drowning in a lake near the campus. Shade's academic "field" is Pope, and his poem, **"Pale Fire,"** is in Pope's heroic measure; in content, it is closer to Wordsworthian pastures—rambling, autobiographical, full of childhood memories, gleanings from Nature, interrogations of the universe: a kind of American *Prelude*. The commentator is Shade's colleague, a refugee professor from Zembla, a mythical country north of Russia. His name is Charles Kinbote; he lives next door to Shade in a house he has rented from Judge Goldsworth, of the law faculty, absent on sabbatical leave. (If, as the commentator points out, you recombine the syllables of "Wordsmith" and "Goldsworth," you get Goldsmith and Wordsworth, two masters of the heroic couplet.) At the moment of writing, Kinbote has fled Appalachia and is living in a log cabin in a motor court at Cedarn in the Southwest; Shade has been murdered, fortuitously, by a killer calling himself Jack Grey, and Kinbote, with the widow's permission, has taken his manuscript to edit in hiding, far from the machinations of two rival Shadians on the faculty. Kinbote, known on the campus as the Great Beaver, is a bearded vegetarian pederast, who has had bad luck with his youthful "ping-pong partners"; a lonely philologue and long-standing admirer of the poet (he has translated him into Zemblan), he has the unfortunate habit of "dropping in" on the Shades, spying on them (they don't draw theirs) with binoculars from a post at a window or in the shrubbery; jealous of Mrs. Shade, he is always available for a game of chess or a "good ramble" with the tolerant poet, whom he tirelessly entertains with his Zemblan reminiscences. "I don't see how John and Sybil can stand you," a faculty wife hisses at him in the grocery store. "What's more, you are insane."

That is the plots' ground floor. Then comes the *piano nobile.* Kinbote believes that he has inspired his friend with his tales of his native Zembla, of its exiled king, Charles the Beloved, and the Revolution that started in the Glass Works; indeed, he has convinced himself that the poem is in a sense *his* poem—the occupational mania of commentators—and cannot be properly understood without his gloss, which narrates Zemblan events paralleling the poet's composition. What at once irresistibly peeps out from Kinbote's notes is that he himself is none other than Charles the Beloved, disguised in a beaver as an academic; he escaped from Zembla in a motor-boat and flew to America after a short stay on the Riviera; an American sympathiser, a trustee of Wordsmith, Mrs. Sylvia O'Donnell, has found a post on the language faculty. His colleagues (read "mortal enemies") include—besides burly Professor Hurley, head of the department and an adherent of *"engazhay"* literature—Professor C., a literary Freudian and owner of an ultra-modern villa, a certain Professor Pnin, and an instructor, Mr. Gerald Emerald, a young man in a bow tie and green velvet jacket. Meanwhile the Shadows, the Secret Police of Zembla, have hired a gunman, Jakob Gradus, alias Jacques d'Argus, alias Jacques Degré, alias Jack Grey, to do away with the royal exile. Gradus' slow descent on Wordsmith synchronises, move by move, with Shade's composition of **"Pale Fire"**; the thug, wearing a brown suit, a trilby, and carrying a Browning, alights on the campus the day the poem is finished. In the library he converges with Mr. Gerald Emerald, who obligingly gives him a lift to Professor Kinbote's house. There, firing at the king, he kills the

poet; when the police take him, he masks his real purpose and identity by claiming to be a lunatic escaped from a local asylum.

This second story, the *piano nobile,* is the "real" story as it appears to Kinbote of the events leading to the poet's death. But the real, real story, the story underneath, has been transpiring gradually, by degrees, to the reader. Kinbote is mad. He is a harmless refugee pedant named Botkin who teaches in the Russian department and who fancies himself to be the exiled king of Zembla. This delusion, which he supposes to be his secret, is known to the poet, who pities him, and to the campus at large, which does not—the insensate woman in the grocery store was expressing the general opinion. The killer is just what he claims to be—Jack Grey, an escaped criminal lunatic, who has been sent to the State Asylum for the Insane by, precisely, Judge Goldsworth, Botkin's landlord. It is Judge Goldsworth that the madman intended to murder, not Botkin, alias Kinbote, alias Charles the Beloved; the slain poet was the victim of a case of double mistaken identity (his poem too is murdered by its editor, who mistakes it for something else). The clue to Gradus-Grey, moreover, was in Botkin's hands when, early in the narrative, he leafed through a sentimental album kept by the judge containing photographs of the killers he had sent to prison or condemned to death: ". . . a strangler's quite ordinary-looking hands, a self-made widow, the close-set merciless eyes of a homicidal maniac (somewhat resembling, I admit, the late Jacques d'Argus), a bright little parricide aged seven. . . ." He got, as it were, a preview of the coming film—a frequent occurrence in this kind of case. Projected on to Zembla, in fact, are the daily events of the campus. Gradus' boss, Uzumrudov, one of the higher Shadows, met on the Riviera in a green velvet jacket, is slowly recognised to be "little Mr. Anon.," alias Gerald Emerald, alias Reginald Emerald, a teacher of freshman English, who has made advances to (read in reverse "had advances made to him by") Professor Botkin, and who is also the author of a rude anonymous note suggesting that Professor Botkin has halitosis. The paranoid political structure called Zembla in Botkin's exiled fantasy—with its Extremist government and secret agents—is a transliteration of a pederast's persecution complex, complicated by the commonplace conspiracy-mania of a faculty common-room.

But there is in fact a "Zembla," behind the Iron Curtain. The real, real story, the plane of ordinary sanity and common sense, the reader's presumed plane, cannot be accepted as final. The explanation that Botkin is mad will totally satisfy only Professors H. and C. and their consorts, who can put aside *Pale Fire* as a detective story, with the reader racing the author to the solution. *Pale Fire* is not a detective story, though it includes one. Each plane or level in its shadow box proves to be a false bottom; there is an infinite perspective regression, for the book is a book of mirrors.

Shade's poem begins with a very beautiful image, of a bird that has flown against a window and smashed itself, mistaking the reflected sky in the glass for the true azure.

> *I was the shadow of the waxwing slain*
> *By the false azure of the window pane.*

This image is followed by another, still more beautiful and poignant, a picture of that trick of optics whereby a room at night when the shades have not been drawn, is reflected in the dark landscape outside.

> *Uncurtaining the night I'd let dark glass*
> *Hang all the furniture above the grass*
> *And how delightful when a fall of snow*
> *Covered my glimpse of lawn and reached up so*
> *As to make chair and bed exactly stand*
> *Upon that snow, out in that crystal land!*

"That crystal land," notes the commentator, loony Professor Botkin. "Perhaps an allusion to Zembla, my dear country." On the plane of everyday sanity, he errs. But on the plane of poetry and magic, he is speaking the simple truth, for Zembla is Semblance, Appearance, the mirror-realm, the Looking Glass of Alice. This is the first clue in the treasure-hunt, pointing the reader to the dual or punning nature of the whole work's composition. **"Pale Fire,"** a reflective poem, is also a prism of reflections. Zembla, the land of seeming, now governed by the Extremists, is the antipodes of Appalachia, in real homespun democratic America, but it is also the *semblable*, the twin, as seen in a distorting glass. Semblance becomes resemblance. John Shade and Gradus have the same birthday—July 5th.

The word Zembla can be found in Pope's *Essay on Man* (Epistle 2, v); there it signifies the fabulous extreme north, the Hyperborean land of the polar star.

> *But where the Extreme of Vice was ne'er agreed.*
> *Ask where's the North? At York, 'tis on the*
> *Tweed;*
> *In Scotland, at the Oroades, and there,*
> *At Greenland, Zembla, or the Lord knows where;*
> *No creature owns it in the first degree,*
> *But thinks his neighbour farther gone than he.*

Pope is saying that vice, when you start to look for it, is always somewhere else—a will-o'-the-wisp. This somewhere else is Zembla, but it is also next door, at your neighbour's. Now Botkin is Shade's neighbour and *vice versa*; moreover, people who live in glass houses. . . . Shade has a vice, the bottle, the festive glass, and Botkin's vice is that he is an *invert, i.e.,* turned upside down, as the antipodes are, relative to

each other. Further, the reader will notice that the word Extreme, with a capital (Zemblan Extremists) and the word degree (Gradus is degree in Russian), both occur in these verses, in the neighbourhood of Zembla, pre-mirroring **Pale Fire,** as though by second sight. Reading on, you find (lines 267-268), the following lines quoted by John Shade in a discarded variant:

> *See the blind beggar dance, the cripple sing,*
> *The sot a hero, lunatic a king. . . .*

The second line is **Pale Fire** in a nutshell. Pope continues (lines 267-270):

> *The starving chemist in his golden views*
> *Supremely blest, the poet in his muse.*

Supremely Blest is the title of John Shade's book on Pope. In this section of the poem, Pope is playing on the light and shade antithesis and on what an editor calls the "pattern of paradoxical attitudes" to which man's dual nature is subject. The lunatic Botkin, incidentally, playing king, *inverts* his name.

To leave Pope momentarily and return to Zembla, there is an actual Nova Zembla, a group of islands in the Arctic Ocean, north of Archangel. The name is derived from the Russian Novaya Zemlya, which means "new land." Or *terre neuve,* Newfoundland, the New World. Therefore, Appalachia=Zembla. But since for Pope Zembla was roughly equal to Greenland, then Zembla must be a green land, an Arcadia. Arcady is a name often bestowed by Professor Botkin on New Wye, Appalachia, which also gets the epithet "green," and he quotes *Et in Arcadia ego,"* for Death has come to Arcady in the shape of Gradus, ex-glazier and killer, the emissary of Zembla on the other side of the world. Green-jacketed Gerald Emerald gives Death a lift in his car.

The complementary colour to green is red. Zembla has turned red after the revolution that began in the Glass Factory. Green and red flash on and off in the narrative like traffic signals and sometimes reverse their message. Green appears to be the colour of death and red the colour of life; red is the king's colour and green the colour of his enemies. Green is pre-eminently the colour of seeming (the theatrical greenroom), the colour, too, of camouflage, for Nature, being green at least in summer, can hide a green-clad figure in her verdure. But red is a colour that is dangerous to a wearer who is trying to melt into the surroundings. The king escapes from his royal prison wearing a red wool cap and sweater (donned in the dark) and he is only saved by the fact that forty loyal Karlists, his supporters, put on red wool caps and sweaters too (red wool yarn—yarn comes from Latin "soothsayer"—is protective Russian folk magic) and confuse the Shadows with a multitude of false kings. Yet when the king arrives in America, he floats down with a green silk parachute (because he is in disguise?), and his gardener at New Wye, a Negro whom he calls Balthasar (the black king of the three Magi), has a green thumb, a red sweater, and is seen on a green ladder; it is the gardener who saves the king's life when Gradus, alias Grey, appears.

Now when Alice went through the looking-glass she entered a chess game as a white pawn. There is surely a chess game or chess problem in *Pale Fire,* played on a board of green and red squares. The poet describes his residence as "the frame-house between Goldsworth and Wordsmith on its square of green"; the Rose Court in the royal palace in Onhava (Far Away), the Zemblan capital, is a sectile mosaic with rose petals cut out of red stone and large thorns cut out of green marble. There is much stress, in place-descriptions, on framing, and reference is made to chess problems of "the solus rex type." The royal fugitive may be likened to a lone king running away on the board. But in problems of the solus rex type, the king, though outnumbered, is, curiously enough, not always at a disadvantage; for example, a king and two knights cannot checkmate a lone king—the game is stalemated or drawn. All the chess games played by characters in the story are draws. The plot of the novel ends in a kind of draw, if not a stalemate. The king's escape from the castle is doubtless castling.

Chess is the perfect mirror-game, with the pieces drawn up confronting each other as in a looking-glass; moreover, castles, knights, and bishops have their twins as well as their opposite numbers. The piece, by the way, called the bishop in English is in French *"le fou"* or madman. In the book there are two opposed lunatics at large: Gradus and Kinbote. The moves made by Gradus from the Zemblan capital to Wordsmith in New Wye parallel spatially the moves made in time by the poet toward the completion of his poem; at the zero hour, there is a convergence of space and time. What is shadowed forth here may be a game of three-dimensional chess—three simultaneous games played by a pair of chess wizards on three transparent boards arranged vertically. A framed crystal land, the depth-echo of the bedroom projected on to the snow.

The moves of Gradus and Botkin also hint some astrological progression. Botkin reached Judge Goldsworth's "chateau" on February 5, 1959; on Monday, February 16, he was introduced to the poet at lunch at the Faculty Club; on March 14, he dined at the Shades', etc. Shade's *magnum opus* was begun on July 1, under the sign of Cancer; he walks sideways, like a crab. The poem is completed (except for the last line) the day of Gradus' arrival, July 21, on the cusp between Cancer and Leo. As the poet walks to his death, the sound of horseshoes is heard from a neighbouring yard

(Horseshoe Crabs?). The fateful conjunction of three planets seems to be indicated, and the old astrological notion of events on earth mirroring the movements of the stars in the sky.

The twinning and doubling proliferate; the multiplication of levels refracts a prismatic, opaline light on Faculty Row. Zembla is not just land but earth—"Terra the Fair, an orbicle of jasp," as John Shade names the globe; a Zemblan feuilletonist had fancifully dubbed its capital Uranograd—"Sky City." The fate of Charles the Beloved is a rippling reflection of the fate of Charles II of England on his travels, of Bonnie Prince Charlie, and of the deposed Shakespearean rulers for whom streets are named in Onhava—Coriolanus Lane, Timon Alley. Prospero of *The Tempest* pops in and out of the commentary, like a Fata Morgana, to mislead the reader into looking for "pale fire" in Shakespeare's swansong. It is not there, but *The Tempest* is in *Pale Fire*: Prospero's emerald isle, called the Ile of Divels, in the New World, Iris and Juno's peacock, sea caves, the chess game of Ferdinand and Miranda, Prospero's enchantments, his lost kingdom, and Caliban, whom he taught language, that supreme miracle of mirroring.

Nature's imitations of Nature are also evoked—echo, the mocking-bird perched on a television aerial ("TV's huge paper-clip"), the iridescent eyes of the peacock's fan, the cicada's emerald case, a poplar tree's rabbit-foot—all the "natural shams" of so-called protective mimicry by which, as Shade says in his poem,

> *The reed becomes a bird, the knobby twig*
> *An inchworm and the cobra head, a big*
> *Wickedly folded moth.*

These disguises are not different from the exiled king's red cap and sweater (like the markings of a bird) or the impersonation of an actor. Not only Nature's shams but Nature's freaks dance in and out of the lines: rings around the moon, rainbows and sun-dogs (bright spots of light, often coloured, sometimes seen on the ring of the solar halo), the heliotrope or sun-turner, which, by a trick of language, is also the bloodstone, Muscovy glass (mica), phosphorescence (named for Venus, the Morning Star), mirages, the roundlet of pale light called the *ignis fatuus,* everything speckled, freckled, curiously patterned, dappled, quaint (as in Hopkins' poem, "Pied Beauty"). The arrowy tracks of the pheasant, the red heraldic barrings of the Vanessa butterfly, snow crystals. And the imitation of natural effects in manufactures: stained glass, paperweights containing snowstorms and mountain views, glass eyes. Not to mention other curios like the bull's eye lantern, glass giraffes, Cartesian devils. Botkin, the bearded urning, is himself a prime "freak of Nature," like Humbert Humbert. And the freakish puns of language ("Red Sox wins 5/4 on Chapman's Homer"), "muscat" (a cat-and-mouse game), anagrams, mirror-writing, such words as versipel. The author loves the ampersand and dainty diminutives ending in "let" or "et" (nymphet). Rugged John Shade is addicted to "word-golf," which he induces Botkin to play with him. Botkin's best scores are hate-love in three (late-lave-love), lass-male in four (last-mast-malt-male), live-dead in five. If you play word-golf with the title words, you can get pale-hate in two and fire-love in three. Or pale-love in three and fire-hate in three.

The misunderstandings of scholarship, cases of mistaken word-identity, also enchant this dear author. *E.g.,* "alderwood" and "alderking" keep cropping up in the gloss with overtones of northern forest magic. What can an alderking be, excluding chief or ruler, which would give king-king, a redundancy? "Erle" is the German word for alder, and the alder tree, which grows in wet places, has the curious property of not rotting under water. Hence it is a kind of magic tree, very useful for piles supporting bridges. And John Shade, writing of the loss of his daughter, echoes Goethe's "The Erl-King."

> Who rides so late in the night and the wind?
> It is the writer's grief. It is the wild
> March wind. It is the father with his child.

Now the German scholar, Herder, in translating the elf-king story from the Danish, mistook the word for elf for the word for alder. So it is not really the alderking but the elf- or goblin-king, but the word alder touched by the enchanted word elf becomes enchanted itself and dangerous. Goethe's erl-king, notes Kinbote, fell in love with the traveller's little boy. Therefore alderking means an eerie, dangerous invert found in northern forest-countries.

Similar sorcerer's tricks are played with the word stone. The king in his red cap escaping through the Zemblan mountains is compared to a *Steinmann,* which, as Kinbote explains, is a pile of stones erected by alpinists to commemorate an ascent; these *Steinmensch,* apparently, like snowmen, were finished off with a red cap and scarf. The *Steinmann,* then, becomes a synonym for one of the king's disguised followers in red cap and sweater (*e.g., Julius Steinmann, Zemblan patriot*). But the *Steinmann* has another meaning, not divulged by Kinbote; it is the *homme de pierre* or *homme de St. Pierre* of Pushkin's poem about Don Giovanni, in short the stone statue, the Commendatore of the opera. Anyone who sups with the stone-man, St. Peter's deputy, will be carried off to hell. The mountain that the *Steinmann*-king has to cross is wooded by Mandevil Forest; toward the end of his journey he meets a disguised figure, Baron Mandevil, man of fashion, catamite, and Zemblan patriot. Read man-devil, but read also Sir John Mandeville, medieval impostor and author of a book of voyages who posed as an English knight (perhaps a chess

move is indicated?). Finally the stone (glancing by glass-houses) is simply the stone thrown into a pool or lake and starting the tremulous magic of widening ripples that distort the clear mirroring of the image—as the word stone itself, cast into the pool of this paragraph has sent out wavelets in a widening circle.

Lakes—the original mirrors of primeval man—play an important part in the story. There are three lakes near the campus, Omega, Ozero, and Zero (Indian names, notes Botkin, garbled by the early settlers); the last time the king saw his consort, Disa, Duchess of Payn (sadism; theirs was a "white" marriage) she was mirrored in an Italian lake. The poet's daughter has drowned herself in Lake Omega; her name (". . . in lone Glenartney's hazel shade") is taken from *The Lady of the Lake.* But a hazel wand is also a divining-rod, used to find water; in her girlhood, the poor child, witch Hazel, was a poltergeist.

Trees, lakes, butterflies, stones, peacocks—there is also the waxwing, the poet's alter ego, which appears in the first line of the poem (duplicated in the last, unwritten line). If you look up the waxwing in the *O.E.D.,* you will find that it is "a passerine bird of the genus Ampelis, esp. A. garrulus, the Bohemian waxwing. Detached from the chatterers by Monsieur Vieillot." The poet, a Bohemian, is detached from the chatterers of the world. The waxwing (belonging to the king's party) has red-tipped quills like sealing-wax. Another kind of waxwing is the Cedar Waxwing. Botkin has fled to Cedarn. The anagram of Cedarn is nacred.

More suggestively (in the leering, popular sense), the anal canal or "back door" or *"porte étroite"* is linked with a secret passage leading by green-carpeted stairs to a green door (which in turn leads to the green-room of the Onhava National Theatre), discovered by the king and a boyhood bed-fellow. It is through this secret passage (made for Iris Acht, a leading actress) that the king makes his escape from the castle. Elsewhere a "throne," in the child's sense of "the toilet," is identified naughtily with the king. When gluttonous Gradus arrives in Appalachia, he is suffering from a severe case of diarrhœa, induced by a conflict of "French" fries, consumed in a Broadway restaurant, with a genuine French ham sandwich, which he had saved from his Nice-Paris railway trip. The discharge of his bowels is horribly paralleled with the discharge of the automatic pistol he is carrying; he is the modern automatic man. In discharging the chamber of his pistol he is exercising what to him is a "natural" function; earlier the slight sensory pleasure he derives from the act of murder is compared to the pleasure a man gets from squeezing a blackhead.

This is no giggling, high-pitched, literary camp. The repetitions, reflections, misprints, and quirks of Nature are taken as signs of the presence of a pattern, the stamp or watermark of a god or an intelligence. There is a web of sense in creation, old John Shade decides—not text but texture, the warp and woof of coincidence. He hopes to find

> *Some kind of correlated pattern in the game,*
> *Plexed artistry, and something of the same*
> *Pleasure in it as they who played it found.*

The world is a sportive work of art, a mosaic, an iridescent tissue. Appearance and "reality" are interchangeable; all appearance, however deceptive, is real. Indeed it is just this faculty of deceptiveness (natural mimicry, *trompe l'oeil,* imposture), this power of imitation, that provides the key to Nature's cipher. Nature has "the artistic temperament"; the galaxies, if scanned, will be an iambic line.

Kinbote and Shade (and the author) agree in a detestation of symbols, except those of typography and, no doubt, natural science ("H$_2$O is a symbol for water"). They are believers in signs, pointers, blazes, notches, clues, all of which point into a forest of associations, a forest in which other woodmen have left half-obliterated traces. All genuine works contain pre-cognitions of other works or reminiscences of them (and the two are the same), just as the flying lizard already possessed a parachute, a fold of skin enabling it to glide through the air.

Shade, as an American, is naturally an agnostic, and Kinbote, a European, is a vague sort of Christian who speaks of accepting "God's presence—a faint phosphorescence at first, a pale light in the dimness of bodily life, and a dazzling radiance after it." Or, more concessively, "Somehow Mind is involved as a main factor in the making of the universe." This Mind of Kinbote's seems to express itself most lucidly in dualities, pairs, twins, puns, couplets, like the plots of Shakespeare's early comedies. But this is only to be expected if one recalls that to make a cut-out heart or lacy design for Valentine's Day all a child needs is scissors and a folded piece of paper—the fold makes the pattern, which, unfolded, appears as a miracle. It is the quaint principle of the butterfly. Similarly, Renaissance artificers used to make wondrous "natural" patterns by bisecting a veined stone, an agate or a carnelian, as you would bisect an orange. Another kind of magic design is the child's trick of putting a piece of paper on the cover of a school book and shading it with a pencil; wonderfully, the stamped title, CAESAR'S GALLIC WARS, emerges, as though embossed, in white letters. This, upside down, is the principle of the pheasant's hieroglyph in the snow or the ripple marks on the sand, to which we cry "How beautiful!" There is no doubt that duplication, stamping, printing (children's transfers), is one of the chief forms of magic, a magic we also see in Jack Frost's writing on the window, in jet trails in the sky—an intelligent spirit seems to have signed them. But it is not only in symmetry and reproduction that the magic signature of Mind is discerned, but in the very imperfections of Nature's work, which appear as guarantees of authentic, hand-knit manufacture. That is, in those blemishes and freckles and streakings and moles already mentioned that are the sports of creation, and what is a vice but a mole?

Nabokov's tenderness for human eccentricity, for the freak, the "deviate," is partly the naturalist's taste for the curious. But his fond, wry compassion for the lone black piece on the board goes deeper than classificatory science or the collector's chop-licking. Love is the burden of **Pale Fire,** love and loss. Love is felt as a kind of home-sickness, that yearning for union described by Plato, the pining for the other half of a once-whole body, the straining of the soul's black horse to unite with the white. The sense of loss in love, of separation (the room *beyond,* projected on to the snow, the phantom moves of the chess knight, that deviate piece, *off* the board's edge on to ghostly squares), binds mortal men in a common pattern—the elderly couple watching TV in a lighted room, and the "queer" neighbour watching *them* from his window. But it is most poignant in the outsider: the homely daughter stood up by her date, the refugee, the "queen," the bird smashed on the window pane.

Pity is the password, says Shade, in a philosophical discussion with Kinbote; for the agnostic poet, there are only two sins—murder and the deliberate infliction of pain. In the exuberant high spirits, the wild laughter of the book, there is a cry of pure pain. The compassion of Nabokov stops violently short of Gradus, that grey, degraded being, the shadow of a Shade. The modern, mass-produced, jet-propelled, newspaper-digesting automatic killer is described with a fury of intimate hatred; he is Death on the prowl. Unnatural Death is the natural enemy of the delicate gauzy ephemerids who are under Nabokov's special protection, like the nymphet ephemerida who "died" to Humbert Humbert when she passed puberty. Kinbote makes an "anti-Darwinian" aphorism: "The killer is *always* his victim's inferior."

Gradus in his broad-brimmed hat, with his umbrella and black travelling bag, figures as a kind of Bat-Man out of children's comic books, whirring darkly through space; yet he is also Mercury (the mercury stands at so many *degrees* in the thermometer; there is a headless statue of Mercury in the secret passage leading from the palace to the theatre), conductor of souls to the underworld, Zeus's undercover agent, god of commerce, travel, manual skill, and thievery. In short, a "Jack of small trades and a killer," as Kinbote calls Jacques d'Argus, who was a pharmacology student at one time (the caduceus) and a messenger boy for a firm of cardboard box manufacturers; Mercury or Hermes was the slayer of the giant *Argus* set to watch on Io by Juno-Hera; the hundred eyes of Argus were set in the tail of the peacock, Juno's familiar. Hermes, born in Arcady, is simply a stone or herm; he is thought to have been in early times the *daimon* that haunted a heap of stones (the *Steinmann* or grave-ghost), also the place-spirit of a roadside marker or milestone; as a road god, he was the obvious patron of traders and robbers. He was often represented as a rudimentary stock or stone with a human head carved on top and a phallus half-way up. The ancient Hermes-Mercury was the god of eloquence and letters, but the beheaded Gradus-d'Argus has reverted to a rudimentary state of insentient stoniness—he has given up sex too and once tried to castrate himself.

Not only Hermes-Mercury, all the gods of Arcady are glimpsed in *Pale Fire,* transformed, metamorphosed into animal or human shapes. Botkin is identified by Sybil Shade with the botfly, which is a kind of parasitic horsefly that infests sheep and cattle too. Io, in cow form, was tormented by a gadfly, sent by Hera; one of the Vanessa butterflies is the Vanessa Io, marked with peacock eyes. Another of the Vanessids is the Limenitis Sibylla, the White Admiral, and the Red Admiral is the Vanessa Atalanta, which feeds on wounded tree stems, like the scarred hickory in Shade's bosky garden. Atalanta was born in Arcadia. The sibyls are connected with Apollo, and Shade with his laurel trees is an Apollonian figure. Sibyl was born Swallow; the land of Arcady was drained by swallow-holes. The Hyperboreans (read Zemblans) were a northern legendary people sacred to Apollo. Zeus, the sky-king, reigned on Mount Lycaeon in Arcadia with his thunderbolts, and he is heard in the thunderstorms that occur at crucial moments in the Zemblan story—at the arrival of Gradus in America and in Mandevil Forest, on Mount Mandevil, when the king is making his escape; Zeus's thunderbolts, in classical times, were stones too, by which oaths were sworn.

The Arcadian gods of *Pale Fire* are meteoric fugitives, like the deposed Kinbote, fitfully apprehended in a name, a passing allusion. Shade's ornithologist mother was called Caroline Lukin—a triple reference to the Carolina waxwing, to Apollo Lukeios, and to the sacred wood, *lucus* in Latin, full of singing birds. A reference to the Pléiade edition of Proust conjures up the Pleiades, daughters of Atlas, who, fleeing from Orion, were turned into stars and set in the constellation Taurus. One of the seven Pleiades is Electra, "the shining one," born in Arcadia; the word electricity in Greek was the word for amber, which was sent to Delphian Apollo by his Hyperboreans in the north. But the Pleiad was also a group of seven poets who sought to revive tragedy at the court of Ptolemy Philadelphus in Alexandria, one of whom, Lykophron, was the author of a curious riddling

poem, like *Pale Fire* one of the hermetic puzzles of its time, called the *Alexandra*—another name for Cassandra, Priam's daughter, who was loved by Apollo.

With the myriads of references to sacred belief there is hardly a glance at Christian myth and legend—a remarkable feat in itself. I have found only two: the oblique allusion to St. Peter as gatekeeper of Heaven and the chess-jesting one to the Black King of the Magi. The book is adamantly classical, magical, and scientific. The author's attitude toward the mystery of the universe is nearer to the old herborist's charmed wonder than to the modern physicist's mystic "faith." His practical morality is not far from Kant's, while his practical pantheism contains Platonic gleams: Kinbote's "phosphorescence" recalls the cave myth, and Shade, in a poem about electricity, discusses metempsychosis, Plato's favourite doctrine. Kinbote concedes in his final remarks that Shade's **"Pale Fire,"** for all its deficiencies, has "echoes and wavelets of fire and pale phosphorescent hints" of the real Zemblan magic. This madman's concession may also be taken as the author's apologia for his own work, in relation to the fiery Beyond of the pure imagination—Plato's Empyrean, the sphere of pure light or fire. But Plato's Empyrean is finished, a celestial storehouse or vault of models from which the forms of earthly life are copied. In Nabokov's view (see Shade's couplet, "Man's life as commentary to abstruse / Unfinished poem. Note for future use"), the celestial Poem itself is incomplete.

The source of "pale fire" is *Timon of Athens,* Act IV, Scene 3, Timon speaking to the thieves:

> "... *I'll example you with thievery*:
> *The sun's a thief, and with his great attraction*
> *Robs the vast sea; the moon's an arrant thief,*
> *And her pale fire she snatches from the sun*;
> *The sea's a thief. ..."*

This idea of natural thievery is bound up with the mirror-theme, for a mirror is held by primitive people to "steal" the image of the man it reflects, and all reflection, including poetic mimesis, can be regarded as a theft from reality, which in turn is always stealing ideas and plagiarising from itself. It is only appropriate that thieving Mercury, "that transcendental tramp," as Kinbote calls Gradus, should be one of the work's principal characters. Botkin, in effect, has stolen Shade's poem. The moon, shining with her borrowed rays, appears in the Luna moth; Io, the cow, was originally a moon goddess, as can be seen from her crescent horns. Shade's Aunt Maud had a verse book kept open at the index ("Moon, Moonrise, Moor, moral"), and Shade's *Webster* is open at *M*. The sky-god Zeus's love-affairs with various moon goddesses—*e.g.,* Europa as well as Io— are adumbrated. Finally, the Red Admiral Vanessa butterfly, which accompanies the poet Shade, like a herald of death, to his doom, is often seen, as on that fatal day, at sunset; it has the unusual habit of flying at night, looking for its home, which is often a hollow tree; in other words, the Red Admiral is a butterfly that acts like its nocturnal double, a moth.

Pale Fire itself circles like a moth, or a moon, around Shakespeare's mighty flame. There are many allusions to Shakespeare's plays, to his biography, to the trees mentioned in Shakespeare, hiding in the lines, and it occurs to me that the treacherous colour green may betray the presence of Shakespeare's enemy, the poet Robert Greene, who described the Bard as an upstart crow dressed in other's feathers; the crow, of course, is a thief. It is also the southernmost constellation, at the other extreme from Zembla.

The pale fire of the title spreads beyond its original Shakespearean source and beacons toward a number of odd corners. In the commentary there is an account of the poet burning his rejected drafts in "the pale fire of the incinerator." An amusing sidelight is provided by the word ingle, used by Kinbote to mean a catamite or boy favourite, but which also means blaze, from the Gaelic word for fire. Helena Rubinstein has a lipstick and nail polish named "Pale Fire." I think too of the pale fire of opals and of Shelley, whose "incandescent soul" is mentioned in Shade's poem:

> *Life like a dome of many-coloured glass*
> *Stains the white radiance of eternity.*

Whether the visible world, for Nabokov, is a prismatic reflection of eternity or the other way around is a central question that begs itself but that remains, for that very reason, moot and troubling. In the game of signalling back and forth with mirrors, which may be man's relation with the cosmos, there is perhaps no before or after, first or second, only distance—separation—and across it, the agitated flashing of the semaphore.

In any case, this centaur-work of Nabokov's, half-poem, half-prose, this merman of the deep, is a creation of perfect beauty, symmetry, strangeness, originality, and moral truth. Pretending to be a curio, it cannot disguise the fact that it is one of the very great works of art of this century, the modern novel that everyone thought was dead and that was only playing possum.

Note

1. *Pale Fire.* By VLADIMIR NABOKOV. *Weidenfeld & Nicolson,* 21s.

Timothy F. Flower (essay date summer 1975)

SOURCE: Flower, Timothy F. "The Scientific Art of Nabokov's 'Pale Fire'." *Criticism* 17, no. 3 (summer 1975): 223-33.

[*In the following essay, Flower maintains that in* Pale Fire *Nabokov combines scientific description with literary allusion as a way of drawing attention to the nature of reality.*]

Most readers have noticed the personal and unusually fictional qualities of Nabokov's non-fictional work—notably his book on Gogol, his various articles on lepidoptera, his Cornell lectures on European novels, his criticism of nineteenth-century Russian literature in *The Gift,* and his heavily meticulous edition of *Eugene Onegin.* But his scholarly and scientific interests are seldom recognized in his fiction, except for a general acknowledgement of his learned allusiveness and of the lepidopteral imagery in his stories. Like Kinbote reading Shade's poem **"Pale Fire,"** we dutifully note the pretty butterflies and moths flitting about, but we are unsure what they "mean." We may recognize them as Nabokov's literary trademarks and as reflections of his scientific interests, as well as useful metaphors for his fiction—as mimics, metaphoric being, double images, and elusive, beautiful creatures. But what remains generally unrecognized is Nabokov's interest in combining the qualities of art with those of science.[1]

Of all Nabokov's scientific interests, lepidopterology suits his fiction particularly well, because both lepidopterology and his fiction repeatedly invesigate processes of camouflage, mimicry, metamorphosis, hunting, and capture, all of which require acute perception, close observation, and accurate classification. The object, whether fictional or lepidopteral, is usually fragile, fleeting, deceptive, and beautiful.[2] Besides offering a highly appropriate analogue or metaphor for Nabokov's fiction, lepidopterology also indicates the empirical, somewhat old-fashioned nature of Nabokov's version of science. Seldom are his scientific or other writings concerned with theories and experiments, hypotheses, statistics, mathematics, research projects, or the apparatus and methodology of modern technology. Instead, Nabokov is more concerned with field work and taxonomy—work which demands a keen eye, a great deal of legwork and patience in locating and accumulating the right specimens, followed by extensive, accurate classifying and naming according to an exacting system which has an extensive and highly precise technical vocabulary. The emphasis in Nabokov is on discovery and description, both of which rely heavily on observation.[3]

To this scientific style Nabokov adds a scholar's bookish interests in languages, research, criticism, teaching, the philosophy and aesthetics of his subjects, and the history and major practitioners in these fields, whether the field is science, translation, chess, or literature. These qualities make Nabokov's fiction scholarly as well as scientific, and they presuppose a reader who is able to read fiction the way a scholarly scientist might. Nabokov's ideal reader, sometimes described as "a little Nabokov," would be a scholar especially expert in languages and literatures, and a natural scientist expert in taxonomy, geography, ornithology, entomology, and lepidopterology. Nabokov once offered a definition of "reality" in which this ideal reader emerges as the bridge between the partly subjective perceptiveness of art and the objective reality of nature:

> Reality is a very subjective affair. I can only define it as a kind of gradual accumulation of information; and as specialization. If we take a lily, for instance, or any other kind of natural object, a lily is more real to a naturalist than it is to an ordinary person. But it is still more real to a botanist. And any further stage of reality is reached with that botanist who is a specialist in lilies.[4]

Reality, for Nabokov and his ideal reader, would seem to be relative yet finally objectively verifiable, since it is based on the assumption that he who empirically observes something most often and in most detail, and with the most extensive specialized training and experience in such observation, knows its nature best. Although one cannot become a specialist in reality itself or nature itself (Nabokov often equates the two), one can learn how best to go about understanding an aspect of reality.

Applied to fiction, Nabokov's scientific attitude becomes a scientific aesthetic in which, ideally, both author and reader are specialists in their subject. They both perceive reality, or at least the reality of a novel, by means of "gradual accumulation of information." In *Pale Fire* we perceive Gradus's precisely synchronized, gradual emergence through just such "accumulation," whereas in more conventional modes of fiction characters are typically introduced by "block" description, dramatic dialogue, significant action, or withholding followed by revelation. Gradus's reality is directly proportionate to what we quantitatively discover about him as we gradually see more of him, if we observe him carefully as he emerges bit by bit. In Nabokov's terms, we become "specialists" in Gradus as we read. Yet Gradus is not nature or reality or a lily; he is a fiction, invented, exaggerated, and distorted by Kinbote, who is in turn carefully controlled by Nabokov. The subject of Nabokov's art, then, can be seen as the interrelation or dialectic between the natural scientist's empirically verifiable reality and art as a created response to this reality. Gradus has no provable reality apart from *Pale Fire,* yet he is created by means of techniques analagous to science, and he is perceived by readers' similar techniques. Gradus, then, is on the one hand pure invention, having no finite objective existence apart from Kinbote's imagination or Nabokov's novel. On the other hand, even though we eventually discover that Gradus is Kinbote's cleverly invented disguise for Jack Grey, Gradus is finally far "more real" than Grey can ever be, because we encounter Gradus by means of "a kind of gradual accumulation of information; and . . . specialization" akin to scientific knowledge.

Natural science, which is what Nabokov means when he speaks of science, is basically empirical: "the study of visible and palpable nature."[5] In translating his scientific values to his aesthetic works, Nabokov appropriately emphasizes sensory experiences, especially by means of his extraordinary sense of sight. What it means to *see* and thereby understand fiction as an empirical scientist might—and as I think Nabokov wants us to—is particularly clear in the articles about lepidoptera he wrote when he was a research fellow in Harvard University's Museum of Comparative Zoology from 1942 to 1948. In these highly technical studies Nabokov is concerned far less with the originality of his discoveries than he is with the importance of accuracy in precise taxonomic description—his scientific speciality, and one of his greatest fictional skills. His frequently harsh criticisms of other lepidopterists, like his better known criticisms of imprecise translators, generally concern problems of absolute precision in observation and definition.[6] His entomological descriptions, like his translations, are usually corrective and definitive rather than experimental, tentative, or generalized. As in his *Onegin* commentaries and his biographical works, Nabokov repeatedly chastises his predecessors for not examining their subjects carefully enough (e. g., in a Kinbote-like voice he berates "W. H. Edwards, working, it may be assumed in a bad light. . . . The description of the male is worthless for all purposes of determination and I have ignored it in my bibliographical summary").[7] He is particularly critical of incorrect nomenclature and sloppy definitions. In an article which foreshadows the complicated patterns of identities and resemblances in *Pale Fire,* Nabokov first defines the taxonomic meanings of the terms "repetition," "isomorphism," "parallelism," and "analogy." When he finds these terms too imprecise for what he wants to define (the same impetus generated his *Notes on Prosody*), he coins his his own term, "homopsis," then qualifies *that* term by making it *interspecific homopsis,* to be precise."[8]

This precision in dealing with complex and confusing data is partly reversed in *Pale Fire,* where Nabokov deliberately shows how "resemblances are the shadows of differences" and confuses us with Shades, Degrees, and "Zemblances," thus forcing *us* to make careful distinctions and avoid the simple either/or labeling that separates *Pale Fire* and its Commentary as poetry and prose, or takes Shade and Kinbote to be either opposites or the same.

The reader of Nabokov's fiction, like the scientist, the scholar, the memoirist, or the translator, must experience deception or difficulty in perceiving, in order to learn the resemblance-difference lesson ex-professor Nabokov often teaches. Analogous to these difficulties in understanding a book like *Pale Fire* is the scientist's problem in understanding his "reality"—a problem Nabokov often describes as a game of deception involving both "false resemblances" and "false dissimilarities"— terms which also characterize *Pale Fire.*[9] In much the same way that Shade depicts Father Time, in these technical articles Nabokov personifies Mother Nature as a diabolically clever opponent who tries to deceive him and who flirts with him in a game of hide-and-seek played on the microscope's glass slide (e. g., "Even in the most zebroid species . . . the macules peep through their linear disguise").[10] In *Pale Fire* he partly reverses the roles in this game of perception, in that he generally takes the part of Nature, while we become the Enchanted Hunters, now confronted by Nabokovian nature as well as the nature Shade struggles with and Kinbote attempts to surpass. Nabokov combines scientific allusions and characteristics with literary ones because his most basic themes and methods describing relationships between art and nature, not just between art and art. Literary allusions and parodies direct *Pale Fire* toward its author and toward other literature; but scientific allusions go much farther, by relating Nabokov's art to nature's art—a relation in which Nabokov sees that nature, his rival, can be more artificial than art.[11] *Pale Fire* continually calls attention to seeming absurdities and Kinbotian exaggerations, but in contexts arranged to contradict our easy impression that Kinbote's wonder-filled art is that of an amusing but pathological liar. Typically Kinbote's imagined past is made "more real" (as the lily is more real to the botanist who devotes himself to lilies) than his present is, in that his imaginary universe is far richer, ampler, more extensive, and more detailed than are the merely actual or near-actual worlds represented in the novel by New Wye and New York—worlds which are "there" mainly to remind us of art's power to re-create and transform them. Nabokov typically shows us this interrelationship by calling our attention to the factual amid the fanciful, or vice-versa, and especially by "planting" facts and accurate allusions in the midst of Kinbote's wildest fancies and most ridiculous pedantries. For instance, Kinbote's seemingly precise dating of events in Zemblan "history" is counterbalanced by his completely accurate references to individual *Life* magazines. Such techniques help us see *Pale Fire* as a dialectic between fact and fiction, not fiction "using" fact or "based on" fact; nor "pure fiction" of the art-for-art's-sake with which Nabokov is too often associated.

Nabokov the scientist and Nabokov the novelist meet continually in his evident delight in using exotic and highly precise terms (e. g., "demilune," "alin," and "luciola," all on one page).[12] Such words almost enable him literally to pin down elusive phenomena, especially when these words are combined with a wealth of carefully structured close observations. This pinning down is characteristic of both Shade and Kinbote, and a reminder of Humbert Humbert's attempt to "fix the perilous magic of nymphets" in *Lolita*.[13]

All Nabokov's artist-figures attempt this verbal capture and control, often in the form of a maddening "paper chase" pursuit of something unattainably perfect. In this sort of pursuit, Kinbote sometimes seems to fumble with scientific names, allusions and judgements of Shade's poem, and this apparent ignorance suggests that he lacks Shade's special skills. Actually he only lacks some of Shade's specific interests. His vocabulary, for instance, is if anything more extensive, esoteric, and scientifically precise than Shade's, and his eye is as sharp too, though focused on different objects. By the end of the book, when his similarities to Shade have emerged, Kinbote describes in his note to lines 993-995 the same scene Shade describes in those lines, though Kinbote's version is richer in puns and metaphors. Each description is similarly poetic and equally accurate; the first and second re-creation, and re-creator, of the scene have merged, and the two genres—Shade's poem and Kinbote's prose—have coincided.[14]

Because Kinbote's voice dominates *Pale Fire,* the novel's style is a deliberately confusing mixture of the language of fantasy (derived from Kinbote's splendid dreams of his beloved Zemblan past, and his paranoid nightmares about his present) intermixed with the precisely formal languages of highly controlled, often documentary, observation, narration, research, and editing. This stylistic mixture and paradox occurs because in his attempt to "fix the perilous magic" of Zembla, Kinbote must make his fiction seem real, or seem more than real, because its reality is continually threatened by time, mortality, formlessness, and antagonists like Gradus, Gerald Emerald and Mrs Hurley. What Kinbote calls his "blue magic" is not his ability to create any fanciful thing, but to virtually out-do nature by making his Zembla seem more real than New Wye or New York. On the other hand, Kinbote's language is also highly fantastic. Because he mainly wants to evoke the fairy-tale romance of "distant" Zembla and the glamorous adventures of its last King, he exploits the lyrical language of romance, the hyperbole and excitement of discovery, escape, and pursuit; and the sensuous spectacle of castles, costumes, landscapes, and impossibly glamorous personages. The three authors of *Pale Fire*—Kinbote, Shade, and Nabokov—are dealing with abstractions and elusive phenomena (time, space, death, reality, memory, illusion, emotion, metamorphosis, fantasy). This means a fiction characterized on the one hand by elusive subject matter, and on the other hand by what I have called "scientific" methods of representing these elusive realities objectively: close observation of a wealth of detail, extensive and esoteric technical vocabulary, careful definitions and redefinitions, and a wary eye for "false resemblances" and equally "false dissimilarities."[15] Hence *Pale Fire's* extraordinary wealth of visual detail, its vast number of named people, places, and things; its encyclopedic creation of a world within a world—which involves the Adam-like naming or renaming of everything; its half-new language; its highly precise, almost too artificial diction, and its esoteric words like "lemniscate," which are seldom used except by specialists and by persons intent upon the *mot juste* no matter how awkward or obscure that technically correct word may be; its mazes of illusion and disguise; its thorough mixture of "our" world (Geneva, Shakespeare, and the real V. Botkin) with its own world (Onhava, Conmal, and the pseudonym, V. Botkin); and its attempts to rival reality and out-do nature by imitating them, mocking them, and suggesting that they are at least as artificial as art.

Nabokov combines the poetic and the scientific in his fiction because he wants us to react to his *art,* not only to his imitation of reality or his ability to supply Rorschach blots for our fantasies. He draws attention to the extremes combined in his art: the qualities we identify both with the lyric poet and with the natural scientist. Surely Nabokov delights in mimicry, especially parody or the kind of verbal precision which enables the reader to re-create an experience. But in both these kinds of imitation Nabokov reveals his own hand, reminding us of the special literary nature of the imitation. Sometimes this is done by making the parody or the detailed observation a *tour de force*—an exercise in imitation in which we admire the artistry more than its ostensible object, as in the description of the Goldsworths' house, or the brilliant "stop-time" scene culminating in the news of Queen Blenda's demise.[16] Such performances are always autographed by stylistic details, as in the following sentence, which I think typifies the special combination of prose, poetry, precision, and fantasy in *Pale Fire*:

> So here was Otar, looking with a puzzled expression at the distant windows of the Queen's quarters, and there were the two girls, side by side, thin-legged, in shimmering wraps, their kitten noses pink, their eyes green and sleepy, their earrings catching and loosing the fire of the sun.[17]

The sentence begins in narrative cliché ("So here was . . . and there were"), but this crude parallelism introduces more subtle structural patterns which in their syntactical pairings and interlinkings reflect the twin nature of their subject: the two sisters. Also notice the poetic sound patterns: alliteration ("Queen's quarters," "side by side"), consonance (mainly the terminal "s" sounds), assonance (short "i" sounds and "green and sleepy"), and the use of "s", "t" and "th" sounds throughout the sentence. Notice too how certain sensuous details suggest the chilly after-party dawn atmosphere and the girls' fairy-tale adolescent beauty: their child-like side by side stance, thin legs, pink kitten noses, and sleepiness—half contrasting with the more adult and elegant romantic associations evoked by their shimmering wraps, green eyes, and flashing earrings. Also typical of Nabokov, particularly of *Pale Fire,* are the possible puns (on "catching and loosing" the sun's reflected pale "fire") and the "something hidden"—in this case the association of Otar, the Queen, the new King, and the twins—a conjunction in which Otar may be a Tarot card figure.

In other words, we can usually see Nabokov's fingerprints on the mirrors he seems to hold up to life. Like Kinbote, Nabokov is never quite satisfied to let things simply be themselves; he is constantly revising experience, transmuting it, adding a touch here, a flourish there, until it is clearly *his* art.

The artificiality of Nabokov's "scientifically poetic" prose, then, provides a kind of running commentary on itself, calling attention to the sheer artistry of the art, preventing us from making our own fictions out of Nabokov's, making us *see,* and in general revealing Nabokov's hand and asserting his ultimate control over his fiction.

Nabokov's scientist's viewpoint and skills turn us outward in "live specific impressions."[18] The specifically visual and verbal nature of his art depends on details and on our perceptions of differences, not on our ability to lable or synthesize generally. As Nabokov says in a footnote in the **Annotated Lolita,** "I was really born a landscape painter, not a landless escape novelist as some think."[19] His peculiar glass-enclosed landscapes do include his mind, but his "landscape painter" aphorism is, I think, meant as a corrective insistence on the objective, even scientific qualities of his art, as opposed to art as the mere re-creation of personal experiences in private fantasies. The autobiographical escapist and solipsist in **Pale Fire** is Kinbote, not Nabokov. Only Kinbote tries to escape from realities by equating his life with his art, involuting even reality, by confusing similarity with identity, and by seeing "Zemblances" of himself everywhere. Appropriately enough, Kinbote's brilliant but technically false recreation of the nonexistent concludes as it began, with death, exile, and madness.

Shade, on the other hand, is like Shade's Aunt Maud and like Nabokov, who discover art in life instead of trying to make life do what only art can do. Instead of substituting a fictional world for the real world they see and know, they perceive the artistic patterns in life. (Not that Kinbote fails to see art in life; he sees his life *too much* as art, while pretending to write only nonfiction. A matter of Degree.) When Shade says he understands his existence only through the "combination delight" of his art (lines 971-77), he is not saying that he completely involutes existence into private artistic terms, but that he understands existence by discovering its relationships to what he understands—that is, his art. He knows nature on nature's terms, not as a pale reflection of his imagined self; and he is pleased by nature's correspondences to art, which brings the two together in what he calls "combinational delight."

If we accept this view, the game Nabokov plays and asks us to play has "something of the same / Pleasure" as actual experience does, and is equally justified. Hence

Nabokov's extraordinary emphasis on the visible, the palpable, the provable. His magic has very specific sources. Puns, for example, are based on conventional lexical meanings and can therefore be looked up. Yet they are also language, or languages, set loose for new creations and fantasy, since a pun reflects itself, its "double" (homonym), and implies limitless uses of word relationships rather than a fixed set of meanings for each word, or a single language for each person.

Pale Fire is Nabokov's freest and most fantastic book, in this sense, yet it has countless "real" roots. It mirrors his *Eugene Onegin* work, and its most extreme artifices—puns, allusions, parodies, anagrams, autoplagiarisms, coincidences, and Zemblan neologisms—are all based on undeniably real sources in other literature, real languages, and the real world. Nabokov's struggle in his art, then, is sometimes reflected in fantasy worlds, or words, and the games he plays with his readers; but these are mainly "Kinbotian" trademarks and ways of drawing us toward Nabokov's central concerns with problems of time, perception, memory, language, and the nature of reality as seen in the reality of nature and, above all, in the nature of art.

Notes

1. Compare Nabokov's phrase "the passion of the scientist and the precision of the artist," quoted by Ross Wetzteon, "Nabokov as a Teacher," *TriQuarterly* No. 17 (Winter, 1970), 242. Also see Peter Duval Smith's interview with Nabokov, *The Listener,* LXVIII (Nov., 22, 1962), 856, ("the precision of poetry and the excitement of pure science"), and "On Translating 'Eugene Onegin,'" *Poems* (New York: Doubleday, 1955), 36 ("This is my task—a poet's patience / And scholiastic passion blent").

2. The main butterfly in *Pale Fire* is the Vanessa Atalanta, a real butterfly which Nabokov uses for its resemblances to the novel. The Vanessa Atalanta wears "Kinbote's" colors but has a grayish underside; it is found in three of "Kinbote's" geographic locales, has two generations, and feeds on both nettle and false nettle; the solitary larva (cf. "solus rex") devours its nest and forms another, and its rapid but erratic flight makes it extremely difficult to capture.

3. Additional possibilities along these lines are described by Alfred Appel in *The Annotated Lolita,* ed. Alfred Appel, Jr., (New York: McGraw, 1970), pp. 340-41.

4. Duval Smith interview, *Listener,* 856. Presumably this progression toward knowledge if applied to a Nabokov novel might be: common reader, Nabokov reader, specialized Nabokov reader, and Nabokov himself.

5. "Playboy Interview: Vladimir Nabokov," *Playboy, XI* (Jan., 1964), 45. Also see *Speak, Memory: An Autobiography Revisited* (New York: Putnam's, 1966), pp. 166-67, 218. *Pale Fire* sometimes approximates the scientist's use of microscopes, cameras, and X-rays; e. g., *Pale Fire* (New York: Putnam's 1962), pp. 277-78 (all subsequent references to *Pale Fire* are to this edition).

6. See *The Annotated Lolita,* pp. 405, 425.

7. "Some New or Little Known Nearctic Neonympha," *Psyche: A Journal of Entomology,* XLIX (Sept.-Dec., 1944) Nos. 3-4 (bound as one), 73.

8. "Notes on the Morphology of the Genus Lycaeides (Lycaenidae, Lepidoptera)," *Psyche,* LI (Sept-Dec., 1944) Nos. 3-4 (bound as one), 137. Compare Nabokov's eleven-part definition of "romanticism" in his *Eugene Onegin* Commentary: Aleksandr Pushkin, *Eugene Onegin,* translated from the Russian, with a Commentary by Vladimir Nabokov, 4 vols. (New York: Pantheon, 1964), Vol. III, 32-36; and his "Notes on Prosody" (in Vol. III, 448-540), as well as the highly literalistic precision of his translation (discussed in Vol. I, vii-xii and defended at great length in a series of articles reprinted in *Strong Opinions* [New York: McGraw, 1973], pp. 231-67).

9. "Notes on Neotropical Plebedjinae," *Psyche,* LII (Mar.-June, 1955), Nos. 1-2, 4. Also see Notes 10 and 11, below.

10. "Notes on the Morphology of the Genus Lycaeides (Lycaenidae, Lepidoptera)," 120. These phrases occur in a discussion of "the illusion of a stripe" in a long section of the article dealing with illusions and the mistakes likely to be made by an incautious, imprecise observer. Compare *Speak, Memory,* p. 298, and *Strong Opinions,* pp. 320, 334.

11. See, for example, *Speak, Memory,* pp. 77, 125; *TriQuarterly* No. 17 ("Life is the least realistic of fictions"); *The Gift* (New York: Putnam's, 1963), p. 9 ("life finding itself obliged to imitate art"); *Nikolai Gogol* (New York: New Directions, 1941), p. 148 ("all reality is a mask"); and "Vladimir Nabokov Talks About Nabokov," *Vogue* (Dec., 1969), 190.

12. *Pale Fire,* p. 106.

13. Regarding Nabokov's interest in this kind of "pinning down," see "A Discovery" (*Poems,* pp. 15-16), *Speak, Memory,* p. 121, and "Some New or Little Known Nearctic Neonympha," 74. Also see Diana Butler, "Lolita Lepidoptera," *New World Writing,* No. 16 (1960), 50-84.

14. Shade seems to be the book's naturalist (e. g., p. 185), but see pages 139 and 184. Kinbote also

pretends to dislike word games (pp. 188-89, 193, 222, 260, 262).

15. This combination of the scientifically objective and the poetically subjective (or the scientifically subjective and the poetically objective) is especially characteristic of *Mary, The Gift, Speak, Memory,* and *Ada,* as well as Nabokov's poems, translations, and *Pale Fire.*

16. *Pale Fire,* pp. 82-85, 105-6.

17. *Ibid.,* p. 105.

18. *The Annotated Lolita,* p. 362.

19. *Ibid.,* p. 406. The phrase "landless escape novelist" fits Kinbote better, I think, as would the phrase "land-escaping novelist."

Phyllis A. Roth (essay date fall 1975)

SOURCE: Roth, Phyllis A. "The Psychology of the Double in Nabokov's *Pale Fire*." *Essays in Literature* 2, no. 2 (fall 1975): 209-29.

[*In the following essay, Roth offers a psychoanalytic reading of* Pale Fire, *emphasizing Nabokov's use of "doubling" and "tripling" as a means of structuring and unifying his novel.*]

Critics and admirers of Nabokov's fiction have been so concerned to heed the author's admonitions and, as a result, to avoid any sort of psychological approach to the novels that a major object of Nabokov's parody has been overlooked. Those who entertain the subject of Nabokov and psychology do so only to quote one or many of Nabokov's numerous slaps at the "Viennese Delegation" and, specifically, at "Dr. Sig-Heiler," as Freud is called in *Ada.* While recognizing that Nabokov explicitly mocks Freudianism, most critics have failed to recognize the extent to which Nabokov knows whereof he speaks, the extent to which psychoanalytic theories underlie the disastrous failures of central characters. While some have seen this possibility, notably Alfred Appel, Jr. in his work on the doubling of Humbert and Quilty, and Claire Rosenfield in *"Despair and the Lust for Immortality,"*[1] the full extent to which Nabokov parodies psychoanalytic techniques has, on the whole, remained undocumented. For example, in an interview with Nabokov, Appel remarked, "The parodies of Freud in *Lolita* and *Pale Fire* suggest a wider familiarity with the good doctor than you have ever publicly granted. Would you comment on this?" But there may be more in Nabokov's answer than Appel seems to see: "He is not worthy of more attention," Nabokov responds, "than I have granted him in my novels and in *Speak, Memory.*"[2] The question is, how much attention is that?

Elsewhere,[3] Nabokov has said, "All novelists of any worth are psychological novelists, I guess." To understand the way in which Nabokov employs psychoanalytic theory, particularly as it pertains to the psychology of the double, is not to commit the Nabokovian heresy either of producing a straightforward psychoanalysis of the fiction or of Nabokov himself. Nor is it to assume that the novels are populated by "real doubles," an interpretation Nabokov forestalls.[4] Rather, it provides a means of further appreciating that Nabokov is a novelist of worth, and of recognizing the extent both of erudition and parody in the novels: in this case, especially in *Pale Fire.*

Pale Fire appears in some respects at least to be Nabokov's most complicated novel involving the use of the double, if only because any major doubling is not immediately evident to a reader unfamiliar with Nabokovian twists, turns, and false trails. The Table of Contents of *Pale Fire* indicates that the book in hand is not a novel but a text consisting of a Foreword, a poem in four cantos entitled **"Pale Fire,"** a Commentary, and an Index. The reader who is well-schooled in willing suspension of disbelief will begin to read the Foreword with a certain degree of naive trust. But his faith in the editor, "Charles Kinbote," will be tried on the very first page when, amid tedious scholarly detailing of not only the poet's birth and death dates, but the colors of the lines on notecards used by the poet, he finds, "There is a very loud amusement park right in front of my present lodgings."[5] Alerted to the unusual, the reader will observe that the scholarship of the Foreword is interrupted by other intrusions of a personal nature which undermine the relationship of the editor to the poem: the editor raises the controversy of his right to the manuscript, and takes potshots at the poet's wife for her interference. He digresses at length to describe the Goldsworth house in New Wye where he lived in proximity to the poet, John Shade, and Shade's wife Sybil. He provides dark intimations not only of his own homosexuality, but also regarding the "true" source of the poem, which seems to be, in Kinbote's mind, not the poet but the editor—Kinbote himself. More and more curious. The Foreword appears to be its "own cancellation," as Kinbote says of Shade (p. 26), for while contentiously asserting that "John Shade valued [his] society above that of all other people" (p. 24), Kinbote also reveals that the poet never showed his manuscript to the editor and that Shade's wife and academic colleagues deny Kinbote's claims both to the friendship of the poet and to the poem. Indeed, they suggest that Kinbote is insane.

Following this the reader may turn with some relief to the 999-line poem which by itself is a relatively uncomplicated autobiographical presentation of the poet's attempt to confront death—his Aunt Maud's, his daughter's suicide, his own mortality—and to come to terms with or discover intimations of immortality. The form of the poem, which implies that for the thousandth line one returns to the first, suggests that the poet may have succeeded in his efforts. We shall see differently. The poem contains some lovely lines and passages, some pathos, and evidence of a sense of humor which is directed by the poet toward himself. But as Kinbote says, John Shade is not Robert Frost. He does, however, seem to be sane, especially in comparison with Kinbote, and the wise reader turns to the editor's Commentary with some wariness. In this frame of mind, one can only interpret the Commentary as, at best, a parody of biographical criticism, of scholarly irrelevancies, of symbol-mongering, of critical solipsism. For example, Kinbote introduces a variant to the poem which he admits may not be correct and which he later advises the reader to ignore, and others which one suspects he wrote himself. Perhaps most striking in the disjunction between poem and Commentary is that the notes refer back and forth to one another, not usually to the poem. As a result, the reader finds himself enmeshed in the story of a "Zemblan king" called Charles the Beloved, exiled from his land and throne because, as a homosexual, he was unable and unwilling to produce an heir to the throne. Charles escaped incarceration with the assistance of hundreds of Karlists, the royalists, who dressed themselves in the red garb the king was wearing when last seen and who doubled for him all over the countryside. The Shadows, or anti-Karlists, were in hot pursuit and had locked up hundreds of fleeing kings before they discovered that the "real" Charles had escaped to America where he was teaching at Wordsmith University, living next to John Shade, and attempting to thrust on the poet as the subject for his poem the adventures of Charles Xavier, king-in-exile of a northernland called Zembla. To complete the circle of solipsism which the reader gradually discerns, Kinbote "knows" that the Shadows have sent his way an assassin, a would-be regicide named Jakob Gradus whose journey Kinbote synchronizes line-by-line with the writing of Shade's poem. When Shade completes the poem, "Gradus" arrives, and kills, not Kinbote—or Charles II—but John Shade who resembles Judge Goldsworth (remember: Kinbote is renting his house) who convicted and sentenced a criminally ill man named Jack Grey!

Despite all this involution, the reader is certain of a number of "facts" when he both completes the Commentary and, in increasing disbelief, attempts to correlate poem and notes. He knows that Kinbote believes he is both Charles II of Zembla and John Shade's best friend; he knows that Kinbote is neither of these and that Grey, alias Gradus, no more attempted to kill an exiled king than John Shade tried to write one into existence. Nevertheless, the questions that remain are of a piece: what is the relation between poem and Commentary; between Shade and Kinbote; and among Shade, Kinbote, Gradus, and Nabokov?

Kinbote's own repetition of synonyms for "pale fire" reminds us that he could not find those lines in his copy of a Zemblan translation of *Timon of Athens,* the play from which Shade took his title:

> The sun's a thief, and with his great attraction
> Robs the vast sea. The moon's an arrant thief,
> And her pale fire she snatches from the sun.
> The sea's a thief, whose liquid surge resolves
> The moon into salt tears. . . .
>
> ([*Pale Fire*] IV.iii.443-47)

Critics of the novel have found the passage, however, and have, since the novel's publication, attempted to debate the question of narration (although the passage from Shakespeare suggests there is no reductionist answer): who is the "waxwing," who the "shadow" introduced in the poem's first lines; which part of the novel is the moon whose pale fire is stolen from the sun, and which is the sun? In other words, who is the "author," Kinbote or Shade?

Like *The Real Life of Sebastian Knight, Pale Fire* is composed of the literary achievements of two characters and their author, Nabokov; however, whereas the interrelationships among Sebastian's novels and V's experiences and biography are clear in the former, the apparent unrelatedness of the Foreword, poem, Commentary, and Index which comprise *Pale Fire* is what first strikes the reader. Furthermore, at the end of *Sebastian Knight,* the synthesis of Sebastian and V is a *fait accompli* and their relationship to their author is explicitly stated. *Pale Fire* does not at first glance appear even to suggest any major doubling beyond Kinbote's assertion that he is Charles of Zembla; nor is there any statement of relationship between the characters and the author. Nevertheless, *Pale Fire* illustrates precisely V's description of the "methods of composition" used by Nabokov and employing doubling:

> the heroes of the book are what can be loosely called "methods of composition." It is as if a painter said: look, here I'm going to show you not the painting of a landscape, but the painting of different ways of painting a certain landscape, and I trust their harmonious fusion will disclose the landscape as I intend you to see it.[6]

Throughout *Pale Fire* Nabokov subtly, deceptively, some may feel diabolically,[7] manipulates characters and relationships in such a way as constantly to disclose the painting of the landscape: that is, the creation of the fictional reality. Once the reader sees this texture in the novel—sees the brushstrokes of the artist—the harmonious fusion into a unified landscape seems both inevitable and miraculous. Furthermore, he will then recognize that the painting of different ways of painting is not only the method of composition of *Pale Fire* but the subject of *Pale Fire.* Shade's poem and Kinbote's

Foreword, Commentary and Index are attempts at creating their landscapes, or "realities," but only Nabokov fully succeeds. As we shall see, Shade, Kinbote, and Nabokov are all concerned with the creation of what Shade calls some sort of "correlated pattern in the game" of existence. Nabokov signals this urge common to him and his characters by deliberately creating resemblances between himself and Shade, himself and Kinbote. For example, like Kinbote, Nabokov has written an extended commentary to a poem. Kinbote's Commentary must be taken then, in part, as evidence of Nabokov's well-known sense of humor and self-allusiveness (see also the reference in *Pale Fire* [p. 243] to Hurricane Lolita). Nabokov and Kinbote also share a profound loathing of stupidity, of generalized ideas (p. 152), and of the bestiality represented by the likes of Gradus. Shade bears a stronger resemblance to his author in his photographic memory, in the extraordinary significance colors and reflections have for him, in his knowledge of nature, in his criticism of students and critics, in his use of notecards, in his collaborative intimacy with his wife, in his hatred of

> abstractist bric-a-brac;
> Primitivist folk-masks; progressive schools;
> Music in supermarkets; swimming pools;
> Brutes, bores, class-conscious Philistines, Freud,
>   Marx,
> Fake thinkers, puffed-up poets, frauds and sharks.
>
>   (ll. 926-30)

Above all, and as we shall examine at length, the three are concerned with mortality and questions of the survival of consciousness.

But, as Shade puts it, "resemblances are the shadows of differences" (p. 265),[8] and woe to the critic who falls into the trap of assuming on the basis of certain resemblances that Shade is the author's "persona" in the novel. The method of composition is directed toward revealing the artist's control, what the Russian formalists call the technique of "laying bare." Alfred Appel, Jr. once asked Nabokov whether, like other novelists, he felt that after a certain point his characters took over and wrote themselves, as it were. Nabokov's answer is noteworthy:

> I have never experienced this. What a preposterous experience! Writers who have had it must be very minor or insane. No, the design of my novel is fixed in my imagination and every character follows the course I imagine for him. I am the perfect dictator in that private world insofar as I alone am responsible for its stability and truth. Whether I reproduce it as fully and faithfully as I would wish, is another question.[9]

To give characters their own lives is to destroy the artist's control, a control which is essential to Nabokov's battle against the "two darknesses" surrounding life—

against non-conscious being.[10] For in his art, Nabokov has found "the only immortality you and I shall know," as Humbert puts it. And to make characters doubles of one another or of their author is both the Nabokovian heresy and the trap laid for the unwary in *Pale Fire.* The following analysis attempts to demonstrate how the trap is laid *and* laid bare.

The key to this analysis is to recognize that multiple sets of doubling are at work in the novel. First, of course, is Kinbote's unremitting identification of himself with Charles of Zembla. Next is his obsession with John Shade, his belief that Shade is affirming and immortalizing the Charles identity. Third is the equally obsessive conviction that Gradus is out to get him; that is, out to destroy Charles the Beloved. These beliefs are as wrong-headed as Kinbote's conviction that he and Shade are close friends. The achievement (and the complexity) of *Pale Fire* lies in the distinctions between Kinbote's delusions and the few "facts" presented in opposition, and the ways in which all the delusions are tied together and eventually the novel as a whole is unified. To appreciate all these aspects of *Pale Fire* we must recognize in order: Kinbote's fantasy of Zembla, including the fantasy of the regicide Gradus, and its implications; Kinbote's fantasy regarding Shade, which creates out of Shade the poet a false double who is writing "Solus Rex," the adventures of Charles II; finally, Nabokov's synthesis of Kinbote and Shade, which structures *Pale Fire* and creates Jack Grey, homicidal maniac.

Kinbote's fantasy of Charles II is an expression of wish-fulfillment on his part, a means of gaining fame, immortality, approbation for his behavior, and a self he likes. But much like Smurov of *The Eye* and Hermann of *Despair,* Kinbote's ego-ideal is unrealized in two significant ways: first, he attempts to re-create himself as Charles, but his reign is ultimately a failure, since he cannot reign as a homosexual and he is incapable of providing an heir to the throne; secondly, since that identity is a failure, Kinbote attempts to find a more flattering reflection by having the manual labor—as it were—of creation done by John Shade. He tries to get Shade to write "Solus Rex."

If we look more closely at the two failures of Kinbote's existence the novel can be brought into focus for the remaining analysis. We need only ask why is it that Kinbote's fantasy is a failure, to approach the key to the doubling and to the novel. Since the Zemblan world is Kinbote's creation, it is he who determined that his reign as a homosexual was doomed. He did so because, in part, he feels guilty for the homosexuality and wants to punish himself for it. To do so, he chooses a convenient homicidal maniac, projects onto him the desire to punish himself, and creates Gradus, the "evil self" or punishing double. Similarly, because of his guilt and insecurity resulting from the homosexuality, Kinbote also needs evidence of approval. This need finds expression in the creation of the "good father" double, John Shade, whom Kinbote wants to "father" Charles of Zembla. Thus, Shade and Gradus are the result of a battle between two conflicting drives in Kinbote: desire and guilt, self-love and self-hatred. It is only logical that one overcome the other; in this case the guilt is the stronger and destroys its antithesis. The destruction of Shade by Gradus is not a resolution for Kinbote; rather it is an indication of imminent self-destruction on Kinbote's part. At the end of the Commentary Kinbote says that a bigger and better Gradus is setting out after him and, in the Foreword, that he fears he will have to destroy himself to be rid of the assassins.

Simply speaking, this is the basic psychology of Kinbote's perception. Apparent in the working out of the delusions is the pattern of the creation of doubles by the character and the repudiation of the doubling by Nabokov. Since his Zemblan identity is a fantasy, it is safe to assume that Kinbote did not arrive in America or anywhere else by parachute. What is possible to infer from the fantasy, however, is that Kinbote has been homosexual in the past, as well as possibly unsuccessfully married (as the fantasy Charles is unsuccessfully to his Queen Disa). His arrival at Wordsmith College is the beginning of a new "incarnation" for him which he signals by what Field has called "a homosexual's homosexual fantasy,"[11] that of Zembla. Possibly, too, Kinbote selected both Wordsmith and the Goldsworth house for the access to Shade provided by them; his fantasy includes an attempt to translate Shade's verses into Zemblan (p. 19), which, along with his eagerness to meet the poet, indicates prior knowledge of Shade. Once installed as Shade's neighbor, Kinbote's life revolves around the poet's; he is as obsessed with the creation and identification of Shade's poem as V is with Sebastian Knight, and Smurov in *The Eye* with himself.

Step by step Kinbote's Commentary reveals that he has taken every opportunity to give Shade his theme and his subject for a poem Kinbote believes will be "Solus Rex." What is finally revealed by the Commentary, however, is that Kinbote not only did not influence Shade's poem, he did not even deceive Shade about his identity. Ironically, Kinbote has believed that perhaps Shade guessed his great secret—that he is Charles the Beloved. In fact, Shade knows both that Kinbote believes himself to be the exiled king and that this belief is a fantasy.

According to Claire Rosenfield, "With Shade's death Kinbote loses at once his *raison d'être* and any hope of eventual recovery."[12] Actually, Shade's death provides the impetus for a new incarnation, since at one stroke Kinbote both receives the poem and discovers he has lost the identity the poem was to provide him. In support of this understanding of Kinbote's motivation is his view of Shade's death as a laying on of hands: "I felt—I still feel—John's hand fumbling at mine, seeking my fingertips, finding them, only to abandon them at once as if passing to me, in a sublime relay race, the baton of life" (p. 294). At this point he begins his Commentary to rectify the omissions of the poem, to assert that in fact the doubling does exist—Shade was writing of him.

The Commentary, then, is at least a third "incarnation," and represents an attempt—again, similar to V's biography—to describe "the real life" of the poem or of Charles the Beloved. What the Commentary describes, rather, is neither the poem, nor Shade, nor the Zemblan fantasy, but an imaginative re-creation of a life which, at that point, is the life Kinbote believes he is living. Evidence of a continued decomposition is the Index, yet another version of the Charles-Zembla-Shade-**"Pale Fire"** story, a version even more to Kinbote's liking since it omits most of the uncomfortable events and people included in the Commentary, such as Gerald Emerald and the Hurleys. Indeed, it omits all reference to New Wye except the Shades, and assumes the many connections between the poem and Charles the Beloved which are contrived in the Commentary. Obviously, Kinbote is attempting to re-create the original Zemblan fantasy in purer form, but just as obviously, the final version is no more successful: the result is inevitably more fantastic as Kinbote attempts to purify his fantasy.

Nabokov has stated that "Kinbote committed suicide . . . after putting the last touches to his edition of the poem. . . ."[13] What is apparent from within the novel is that Kinbote moves closer and closer to non-existence as he attempts more and more frantically to create a world in the image of his fantasy.

Nabokov signals to the reader that the "incarnations" I have been discussing are taking place by sending onto the stage of the novel one of his agents, the butterfly. The butterfly appears at the turning points of the incarnations, in the Foreword, in the poem, in the Commentary, and in the Index, and since the butterfly signifies doubling, its appearance in the novel is pertinent to this analysis. First of all, part of the fascination and beauty of these creatures derives from the way in which their wings are mirror images of one another; secondly, in the metamorphosis of the butterfly, each stage doubles the former insofar as it is simultaneously the same insect and an apparently independent, separate individual. *Pale Fire,* ostensibly composed by two authors who are mirror reversals of one another,[14] is simultaneously undergoing a process of metamorphosis, as we have seen, in which one stage generates the next—and in which at least one of the stages, the poem, is independent of the others and another, the Commentary, seems irrelevant to the poem. Two of the stages, the poem and the novel as a whole, have the same name, but they are not even remotely equivalent to one another. Thus the lives of Shade and Kinbote are stages in the metamorphosis of a single creature, *Pale Fire,* a synthesis of apparently antithetical stages.

The death of Shade is the beginning of Kinbote's stage in the Commentary. As in the metamorphosis of the butterfly, each stage signals both death and rebirth, mortality and immortality. The Red Admirable appears at the end of the poem:

> A dark Vanessa with a crimson band
> Wheels in the low sun, settles on the sand
> And shows its ink-blue wingtips flecked with white.
>
> (ll. 993-96)

Kinbote includes in the appropriate place in the Commentary, also at the end of a stage, or of one of his incarnations, the following gloss:

> One minute before his death, as we were crossing from his demesne to mine and had begun working up between the junipers and ornamental shrubs, a Red Admirable (see note to line 270) came dizzily whirling around us like a colored flame. Once or twice before we had already noticed the same individual, at that same time, on that same spot, where the low sun finding an aperture in the foliage splashed the brown sand with a last radiance while the evening's shade covered the rest of the path. One's eyes could not follow the rapid butterfly in the sunbeams as it flashed and vanished, and flashed again, with an almost frightening imitation of conscious play which now culminated in its settling upon my delighted friend's sleeve. It took off, and we saw it next moment sporting in an ecstasy of frivolous haste around a laurel shrub, every now and then perching on a lacquered leaf and sliding down its grooved middle like a boy down the banisters on his birthday. Then the tide of the shade reached the laurels, and the magnificent, velvet-and-flame creature dissolved in it.
>
> (p. 290)

Not only are the two passages thoroughly different recreations of the same scene, which illustrate the different personalities of the authors, they also reflect different stages of the metamorphosis. Kinbote knows that Shade died immediately following this scene. In his description, the butterfly, a traditional mythic representation of the soul, lights on Shade, and prefigures that death. Furthermore, Kinbote is very much like the butterfly at this stage. In his note to line 270, Kinbote describes having seen a Red Admirable in its parasitic role, "feasting on oozy plums. . . . It is a most frolicsome fly" (p. 172). Kinbote himself is suggested by the role of the parasite, even more so since the note immediately preceding that to line 270, refers to the fact that Sybil spoke of Kinbote as "'an elephantine tick; a king-sized botfly; a macaco worm; the monstrous parasite of a genius'" (pp. 171-72). Thus, in one sense, the analogy

between the butterfly sliding down the leaf to the boy sliding down the banister on his birthday alludes to Kinbote: Shade's death just subsequent to the butterfly vignette is a birthday gift for Kinbote. He receives **"Pale Fire"** and then is born again in a new form in writing the Commentary.

In several ways, then, the butterfly signals Shade's death, and the beginning of a new stage in the metamorphosis of Kinbote. Shortly after the note on the butterfly in the Commentary, Kinbote begins the Index. And even in the Foreword he refers to "wind-borne black butterflies," the ashes of early drafts Shade burned "in the pale fire of the incinerator before which he stood with bent head like an official mourner" (p. 15), thus tying together poem, death, and butterfly. At each stage of the metamorphosis, Kinbote stops to see if he has found himself, if he is identified; but, like the butterfly, he is not equal to only one of his stages. Thus Kinbote is not equal to Shade, or even to his own Commentary taken by itself, as the Commentary is not equivalent to the poem. Each is a stage in the life of Nabokov's *Pale Fire.* The doubling of Shade and Kinbote as manifested in the structure of the novel is a method of composition, similar to that employed in *Despair,* by which Nabokov presents a character who is attempting to reduce himself to a false identity at the same time that his author is synthesizing the whole to reveal the failure of the reduction.

Up to now we have examined the motivation underlying Kinbote's attempted creation of two doubles for himself—Charles the Beloved and John Shade—primarily as the motivation is manifested on the surface of the narrative. We have seen both how Kinbote fails to achieve his goal of immortalizing a fantasized identity and how Nabokov succeeds in structuring the novel to portray Kinbote's failure. The next task is to demonstrate that in **"Pale Fire"** Shade attempts to act out a similar fantasy and that again Nabokov's synthesis, to which the character of Gradus/Grey is essential, reveals Shade's failure. Once these points are made, we can come to terms with Nabokov's most technical employment of the psychology of the double.

The most striking similarity between Kinbote and Shade is to be found in their quests for meaningful existence, motivated in both cases by the need to transcend mortality, and attempted in both cases by means of artistic creativity.[15] Kinbote rightly identifies "true" artistry as the ability to "pounce upon the forgotten butterfly of revelation, [to] wean [oneself] abruptly from the habit of things, [to] see the web of the world, and the warp and the weft of that web" (p. 289). John Shade expresses the same thought in verse:

> all at once it dawned on me that *this*
> Was the real point, the contrapuntal theme;

Just this: not text, but texture; not the dream
But topsy-turvical coincidence,
Not flimsy nonsense, but a web of sense.
Yes! It sufficed that I in life could find
Some kind of link-and-bobolink, some kind
Of correlated pattern in the game,
Plexed artistry, and something of the same
Pleasure in it as they who played it found.

(ll. 806-15)

Field argues that "death . . . is the unifying bond between the poem and the Commentary—in a word, the subject of *Pale Fire*."[16] As he observes,[17] all four cantos of **"Pale Fire"** center around death and Shade's attempts to come to terms with what the character Van Veen in *Ada* calls "the final tragic triumph of human cogitation: I am because I die."[18] Like Nabokov himself, Shade recognizes that his life is bounded on each end solely by the bars of time's prison:

Infinite foretime and
Infinite aftertime: above your head
They close like giant wings, and you are dead.

(ll. 122-24)

Nonetheless, and also like his author, Shade perceives and delights in the productions of nature: "For we are most artistically caged" (l. 114).[19]

Most significantly for an understanding of Shade's relation to Kinbote and to Gradus, Shade's sense of his own mortality is present to him, from childhood, in terms of "How fully [he] felt nature glued to [him]" (l. 102). Indeed, throughout **"Pale Fire"** Shade reveals himself as tripped up by what he sees as his grotesque animal nature. Discussing his childhood, he asserts,

Then as now
I walked at my own risk: whipped by the bough,
Tripped by the stump. Asthmatic, lame and fat,
I never bounced a ball or swung a bat.

(ll. 127-30)

That this animal nature of Shade's provides his intimations of mortality is most clearly evidenced by his description of his childhood apocalypses:

A thread of subtle pain,
Tugged at by playful death, released again,
But always present, ran through me. One day,
When I'd just turned eleven, as I lay
Prone on the floor and watched a clockwork toy-
A tin wheelbarrow pushed by a tin boy-
Bypass chair legs and stray beneath the bed,
There was a sudden sunburst in my head.

And then black night. That blackness was sublime.
I felt distributed through space and time:
One foot upon a mountaintop, one hand
Under the pebbles of a panting strand,
One ear in Italy, one eye in Spain,

In caves, my blood, and in the stars, my brain.
There were dull throbs in my Triassic; green
Optical spots in Upper Pleistocene,
An icy shiver down my Age of Stone,
And all tomorrows in my funnybone.

During one winter every afternoon
I'd sink into that momentary swoon.
And then it ceased. Its memory grew dim.
My health improved. I even learned to swim.
But like some little lad forced by a wench
With his pure tongue her abject thirst to quench,
I was corrupted, terrified, allured,
And though old doctor Colt pronounced me cured
Of what, he said, were mainly growing pains,
The wonder lingers and the shame remains.

(ll. 139-66)

Thus, John Shade, like so many of the characters in Nabokov's fiction, finds himself face-to-face with the prison of mortality. Shade seeks an answer to the questions he raises about mortality and what he arrives at is a result of a physical dissolution which echoes his childhood experiences. Following his lecture at the Crashaw Club on "Why Poetry Is Meaningful to Us," Shade is addressed by

One of those peevish people who attend
Such talks only to say they disagree [who]
Stood up and pointed with his pipe at me.

And then it happened—the attack, the trance,
Or one of my old fits. There sat by chance
A doctor in the front row. At his feet
Patly I fell. My heart had stopped to beat,
It seems, and several moments passed before
I heaved and went on trudging to a more
Conclusive destination. . . .
              I can't tell you how
I knew—but I did know that I had crossed
The border. Everything I loved was lost. . . .
And blood-black nothingness began to spin
A system of cells interlinked within
Cells interlinked within cells interlinked
Within one stem. And dreadfully distinct
Against the dark, a tall white fountain played.

I realized, of course, that it was made
Not of our atoms; that the sense behind
The scene was not our sense.

(ll. 688-710)

What Shade experiences is his own type of decomposition, even when he does not have an attack, and the fissure along which he splits is one frequently found in Nabokov characters—for example, in Pnin, in Sebastian Knight, and in Cincinnatus—the split between the spiritual and the physical.

The famous opening lines of the poem can now bring some diverse elements into focus:

I was the shadow of the waxwing slain
By the false azure in the windowpane;

I was the smudge of ashen fluff—and I
Lived on, flew on, in the reflected sky.

(ll. 1-4)

Shade sees himself as the shadow of a bird (signifying the soul); in other words, a self or double which survives the death of the physical self. Thus, Shade begins his poem with a doubling of selves, implying immortality, his quest for which the rest of the poem documents. The dichotomy between the physical and the spiritual selves apparent in the first lines is, as we have seen, reiterated throughout the poem. Indeed, his childhood Whitmanesque apocalypses occur by means of a physical disintegration touched off by watching that clockwork toy. The correlated patterns of these doublings of physical and spiritual selves emerge with the creation of Gradus/Grey, the mechanical man who is the embodiment of mortality in the novel.

In documenting the identity of Gradus as the mechanical toy which touches off physical disintegration and spiritual transcendence, we are clarifying the relation of **"Pale Fire"** to the rest of the novel. Indeed, in affirming that Gradus/Grey represents Shade's mortality within the poem, we are correlating the descriptions within the poem with Kinbote's descriptions of Gradus in the Commentary. Furthermore, since Kinbote also insists that Gradus was actually after Charles II, our understanding of the poem indicates the organic unity of the novel.

First, Gradus is described by Kinbote as follows: "Mere springs and coils produced the inward movements of our clockwork man" (p. 152). Gradus' journey to New Wye is synchronized, with mechanical precision, with the progress of Shade's poem. In addition, Shade's revelation of the link-and-bobolink of existence, of what is immortal, is touched off by the vision of a man pointing a pipe at him, which we cannot but associate with Gradus pointing a gun. In the poem's last written line, Shade observes the gardener "Trundling an empty barrow up the lane," an echo of the "tin wheelbarrow pushed by a tin boy" which set him off as a child, and which is, for the reader, associated with Gradus.

Gradus is also the embodiment of the grotesque, physical side of existence that Shade needs to transcend, and no evidence more clearly indicates this about Gradus that Kinbote's excremental vision of the state of Gradus' bowels as he gets closer and closer to the murder of Shade. Indeed, the correlation Kinbote makes between Gradus' need to fire his gun and Gradus' need to find a bathroom explicitly connects mortality with the gross, animalistic side of man: "One finds it hard to decide what Gradus alias Grey wanted more at that minute: discharge his gun or rid himself of the inexhaustible lava in his bowels" (p. 283). Gradus, the "pri-

mate" with "the chimpanzee slouch" (p. 277), is thus the personification of the animal in man. And, of course, it is *homo naturalis,* biological man who dies.

Simply speaking, then, Gradus is the embodiment of Shade's mortality—the physical nature which must die—just as he is of Kinbote's, as Kinbote makes clear by indicating that he is awaiting "a bigger, more respectable, more competent Gradus" (p. 301). Both Shade and Kinbote are confronted by the fact of their own mortality, and each in a way which parodies their expectations: Kinbote because he falsely believes Gradus to be after him; Shade because, as we are about to see, the arrival and actions of Gradus undercut the philosophical system Shade has come to in **"Pale Fire."**

We have said that in his poem Shade traces his progress in understanding his own mortality as best he can; further, he comes to what is for him a satisfactory conclusion:

> I feel I understand
> Existence, or at least a minute part
> Of my existence, only through my art,
> In terms of combinational delight;
> And if my private universe scans right,
> So does the verse of galaxies divine
> Which I suspect is an iambic line.
> I'm reasonably sure that we survive
> And that my darling somewhere is alive,
> As I am reasonably sure that I
> Shall wake at six tomorrow, on July
> The twenty-second, nineteen fifty-nine,
> And that the day will probably be fine;
> So this alarm clock let me set myself,
> Yawn, and put back Shade's "Poems" on their shelf.

(ll. 971-84)

For Shade, existence is a large scale model of his poem and the "combinational delight" of his poem represents the link-and-bobolink of something timeless and enduring in existence. Thus, the poem affirms its initial image of immortality and we can safely assume that line 1000 would be the same as line one. This is not to say as some have[20] that Shade commits suicide by going out to meet Grey/Gradus whom he could not possibly have expected, but that his poem is completed insofar as it immortalizes his life to this point within his own, obviously limited, scheme of things. That he remarks

> *Man's life as commentary to abstruse*
> *Unfinished poem.* Note for further use.

(ll. 939-40)

does not refute this interpretation. It merely corroborates the obvious fact that Shade is unaware of his imminent death. Furthermore, as we shall find, Shade's life is used by Nabokov as a commentary to the poem which is unfinished by itself without the rest of **Pale Fire,** without Gradus.

John Shade believes then that he has found some sort of satisfactory answer to his life by doubling art and mortality. It remains to be seen that the comfort he finds by doubling his life, his physical mortality (which we recognize to be Gradus) with his immortalizing poem, is but "the simple thetic solution"[21] Nabokov repudiates. In other words, Nabokov undercuts Shade's analysis of his life just as we saw earlier that Kinbote's interpretation of his life is undercut by the structure of the novel.

The way in which Shade's analysis is sabotaged is most clearly revealed within the poem itself in Canto Four, deriving from the disjunction between heroic verse and subject matter and Shade's verse and subject matter. Previously, in Canto Three, Shade feels that he has found sense in the universe, even if only the sense in nonsense. This aperçu is revealed to him as he ponders the relation of his mystically perceived fountain to Mrs. Z's mountain, also mystically perceived; the reader will recall that Mrs. Z's mountain appeared, through a newspaper misprint, as "fountain." ("Life Everlasting—based on a misprint!" [l. 803].) Immediately after Shade's great aperçu, his assertion of a "faint hope," Canto Four begins forcefully,

> Now I shall spy on beauty as none has
> Spied on it yet. Now I shall cry out as
> None has cried out. Now I shall try what none
> Has tried. Now I shall do what none has done.

> (ll. 835-38)

This is a heroic dedication indeed. Yet the very next line creates a disjunction which can only be called mock-heroic:

> And speaking of this wonderful machine:
> I'm puzzled by the difference between
> Two methods of composing: *A*, the kind
> Which goes on solely in the poet's mind,
> A testing of performing words, while he
> Is soaping a third time one leg, and *B*,
> The other kind, much more decorous, when
> He's in his study writing with a pen.

> (ll. 839-46)

Shade goes on to question the nature and value of these methods as well as to a description of shaving and bleeding in the bathtub (Marat/Shade?), television commercials, and a comparison of the efficacy in shaving of "Our Cream" with the thrill of "The sudden image, the immediate phrase" (l. 918). A very oozy step behind Frost, as even Shade himself recognizes. Certainly, this description fails of a successful spying on beauty. The opening lines of the Canto prepare us for another *Paradise Lost* or, at least, a second *Essay on Man*, but not only is the promise never kept, the poet is also distracted by irrelevancies (almost as if Milton had digressed into a discussion of the moulting habits of the

dove which broods over the vast abyss). Again, Shade says, "Now I shall speak of evil as none has / Spoken before" (ll. 923-24) and, included in his quasi-epic listing of things he loathes is, for example, music in supermarkets. This is Ginsberg, perhaps; Alexander Pope or John Milton—or Robert Frost—definitely not. Even Kinbote recognizes that "With all his excellent gifts, John Shade could never make *his* snowflakes settle that way" (p. 204).[22]

Even Shade's several epiphanies which result from the physical disintegrations he describes are undercut by the very descriptions of them. For instance, it is difficult to entertain seriously the image of "One ear in Italy, one eye in Spain"; nor is it possible totally to ignore the suggestion of autoeroticism about the "momentary swoons" the poet experienced every day one childhood winter and because of which he feels "corrupted," "allured," and forever shameful for something compared to seduction by a "wench," but which the doctor describes as "mainly growing pains" (ll. 150-66).

Kinbote himself discerns the ridiculous as well as the sublime in Shade:

> My sublime neighbor's face had something about it that might have appealed to the eye, had it been only leonine or only Iroquoian; but unfortunately, by combining the two it merely reminded one of a fleshy Hogarthian tippler of indeterminate sex. His misshapen body, that gray mop of abundant hair, the yellow nails of his pudgy fingers, the bags under his lusterless eyes, were only intelligible if regarded as the waste products eliminated from his intrinsic self by the same forces of perfection which purified and chiseled his verse. He was his own cancellation.

> (p. 26)

Recalling the narrator's comments in *Pnin* on Pnin's seizures (Shade has "a wobbly heart" [p. 22] also), which begin with feelings of divestment and communion and which are alien to the health of the ego and to sanity, the possibility that Shade's vision is not so sublime is not farfetched. The sublimity is further deflated by the "half a Shade" pun which occurs after Shade's swoon at the Crashaw Club: the doctor tells Shade he was not dead, "'Not quite: just half a shade,' he said" (l. 728).

It is possible that Shade recognizes the mock-heroic nature of his "transparent thingum" (l. 961). What he fails to recognize, however, is that whatever correlated pattern he is able to make of his art and his existence, that correlation is still contained within the vicious circle of mortality. His poem ends on a hopeful note, that he will live to see the following day, which Nabokov dispels by bringing death onto the scene at this precise moment. Shade's attempt to create for himself an intimation of immortality in the link-and-bobolink of existence is a failure. Indeed, rather than discovering a sign of immortality in the poem, the reader locates the agent of mortality. Thus, one element of the Nabokovian dialectic of *Pale Fire* is the thematic spiral which questions who it is Gradus exists to destroy: thesis, it is Charles the Beloved as Kinbote contends; antithesis, it is Judge Goldsworth as the facts indicate; synthesis, it is John Shade both as he is mistaken for the Judge and as he is correctly taken as one whose mortality Gradus represents. As a result, the correlation made by Kinbote between Gradus' journey and Shade's poem is not as arbitrary as it seems. The final lap of the journey as described by Kinbote takes on an additional resonance when the equation between Shade's mortality and Gradus is made:[23]

> Who could have guessed that on the very day (July 7) Shade penned this lambent line (the last one on his twenty-third card) Gradus, alias Degré, had flown from Copenhagen to Paris, thus completing the second lap of his sinister journey! Even in Arcady am I, says Death in the tombal scripture.
>
> (p. 174)

The Nabokovian synthesis is not completely revealed, however, until we understand the tripling of Shade, Gradus, and Kinbote. Carol Williams summarizes part of this complicated synthesis when she says: "In *Pale Fire* the man who is a poet, John Shade, and his mortal fate, Gradus, a man in his intestines, a machine in his mind, are synthesized in King Charles-Kinbote, a balance between the holy muse and the pitiful voyeur."[24] To do such an incorporation, we must employ psychoanalytic tools, tools Nabokov is fully aware of and for which he has provided all the evidence. We must turn first to the evidence planted in the descriptions of Kinbote's relationship to the Shades.

Nabokov's objection to Freudian reductionism has as one of its complaints the psychoanalytic perception of a neurotic child in every man. In *Pale Fire* Kinbote invites psychoanalysis of his problem as a neurotic "adjustment" to an Oedipal situation, an "adjustment" which, in fact, is typical of the homosexual and integral to perceiving the doppelgänger.

The evidence of the Oedipal situation in the novel is extensive. To begin, Kinbote sees himself as the child of Sybil and John. The most apparent manifestation of this is his rivalry with their deceased daughter Hazel Shade. Kinbote literally identifies himself with Shade's child when he speaks of Hazel's delight in playing word games:

> One of the examples her father gives is odd. I am quite sure it was I who one day, when we were discussing "mirror words," observed (and I recall the poet's expression of stupefaction) that "spider" in reverse is "redips," and "T. S. Eliot," "toilest." But then it is also true that Hazel Shade resembled me in certain respects.
>
> (p. 193)

And, as could be expected, Kinbote feels rivalry with Hazel for a place in **"Pale Fire"**; he describes Shade's depiction of his daughter as "maybe a little too complete, architectonically, since the reader cannot help feeling that it has been expanded and elaborated to the detriment of certain other richer and rarer matters ousted by it" (p. 164)—most notably, of course, the Zemblan fantasies of Kinbote.

Such jealousy for the attention of Shade in the poem appears also with regard to Sybil and occurs in the context of Kinbote's distaste for heterosexuality: Kinbote wishes that Shade would "spare his reader the embarrassing intimacies that follow" (p. 174) his description of Sybil in the poem. These "embarrassing intimacies" consist of Shade's enumeration of the times he and Sybil have slept together. Nonetheless, Kinbote counts these moments also (p. 157) in his obsession with the events of the Shade home. And, in his jealousy, he maligns his "friend" and the marriage in a note which, like so many others, bears no relation either to the text or to "reality":

> Far from me be it to hint at the existence of some other woman in my friend's life. Serenely he played the part of exemplary husband assigned to him by his small-town admirers and was, besides, mortally afraid of his wife. More than once did I stop the gossipmongers who linked his name with that of one of his students (see Foreword).
>
> (p. 228)

It will be apparent to the psychoanalytically informed reader that such remarks evidence both Kinbote's anxieties and his desires: he is anxious about Shade's heterosexuality (to be read as unfaithfulness to Kinbote), and he would like to imagine, at the same time, that Shade is unfaithful to Sybil and that the marriage is a failure. Kinbote, then, not only describes other possible rivals to Sybil, but explicitly describes himself as the primary rival: "I had just met Sybil speeding townward and therefore nursed some hopes for the evening. I grant you I very much resembled a lean wary lover taking advantage of a young husband's being alone in the house!" (p. 287).[25]

One must recognize that what Kinbote seeks from Shade is analogous to a father's approval—a father's exclusive attention—for which the mother is the rival. This behavior is typical, in the psychoanalytic view, of the neurotic response to the Oedipal dilemma which frequently leads to homosexuality. The mechanism by which this is said to occur originates in the child's initial desire for the mother, his desire to reciprocate the love and warmth she represents; however, the recognition of the father as rival and of the physical differences between the sexes leads to the fear of castration at the hands of the father-rival. This can be allayed by an unconscious "resolve" to save himself by identifying himself with the mother rather than with the father, and then by seeking the love of the father. The result is that the child now finds the mother to be a rival, a situation which is the direct opposite of the initial libidinal impulse, and which has developed as a way of dealing with castration anxiety.

Perhaps the clearest evidence that Nabokov is self-consciously employing psychoanalytic conceptions and terms is provided by Kinbote's description of a series of scenes in which he depicts himself behaving as if he were the three-year-old enmeshed in the Oedipal dilemma: the scenes in which Kinbote acts out his version of a "primal scene fantasy"[26] and of the child's attempted viewing of such a scene. The "primal scene fantasy" is an integral part of the psychoanalytic delineation of the Oedipal situation and results from the initial stages of confrontation with "reality" which I have distinguished as part of the Oedipal development. Once the child connects his mother's leaving him to the existence of the father, and once the child is preoccupied with his own and his father's masculinity, and once he begins to question where he came from, he envisions nightmare activities between the mother and father.

In a like manner, Kinbote not only envisions but, like the child, attempts to witness what goes on between his "parents." And so, in the Commentary, Kinbote admits his habit of peeping into the Shade home at all hours of the day and night in order to determine what was going on between the poet and his wife:

> . . . I was granted now and then scraps of happy hunting. When my casement window ceased to function because of an elm's gross growth, I found, at the end of the veranda, an ivied corner from which I could view rather amply the front of the poet's house. If I wanted to see its south side I could go down to the back of my garage and look from behind a tulip tree across the curving downhill road at several precious bright windows, for he never pulled down the shades (*she* did). If I yearned for the opposite side, all I had to do was walk uphill to the top of my garden. . . .
>
> (p. 87)

The most exciting and important of the scenes witnessed by Kinbote occurs, as one might expect, at night.

> It was a hot, black, blustery night. I stole through the shrubbery to the rear of their house. At first I thought that this fourth side was also dark, thus clinching the matter, and had time to experience a queer sense of relief [like the child, Kinbote does not want confirmation of his worst fears] before noticing a faint square of light under the window of a little back parlor where I had never been. It was wide open. A tall lamp with a parchment-like shade illuminated the bottom of the room where I could see Sybil and John, her on the edge of a divan, sidesaddle, with her back to me, and him on a hassock near the divan upon which he seemed

to be slowly collecting and stacking scattered playing cards left after a game of patience. Sybil was alternately huddle-shaking and blowing her nose; John's face was all blotchy and wet. Not being aware at the time of the exact type of writing paper my friend used, I could not help wondering what on earth could be so tear-provoking about the outcome of a game of cards.

> (p. 90)

Kinbote, like the child, has witnessed more than he can comprehend at the moment and, indeed, even later when he realizes that John was reading sections of **"Pale Fire"** to Sybil. This later realization is in itself important for this analysis because, again, Kinbote phrases it in terms not only of rivalry with Sybil (she sees what he cannot), but of the supposed removal of his Zembla from the poem:

> Not only did I understand *then* that Shade regularly read to Sybil cumulative parts of his poem but it also dawns upon me *now* that, just as regularly, she made him tone down or remove from his Fair Copy everything connected with the magnificent Zemblan theme with which I kept furnishing him and which, without knowing much about the growing work, I fondly believed would become the main rich thread in its weave!
>
> (p. 91)

Kinbote overlooks some important evidence with which he has, in fact, provided the reader. The explanation of the poem being read to Sybil still does not explain the tears of the scene Kinbote witnesses, but, just prior to the witnessing, Kinbote dates the evening as "July 11, the date of Shade's completing his Second Canto" (pp. 89-90). The Second Canto concludes with the description of Hazel's suicide, and this explains the tears. Again, the rivalry of Kinbote with Hazel is indicated; it can be expressed as the desire to witness the act which conceived *him* but which results instead in the ironic witnessing of the act which gives poetic conception to *Hazel*.

To summarize this analysis, Kinbote's self-portrayal requires a psychoanalytic reading which reveals in his situation at New Wye—the situation of an alienated and ridiculed homosexual seeking approval from a poet whom he wishes to have immortalize his fantasies—the presence of a paradigmatic Oedipal dilemma, a forced adjustment which leads from self-preoccupation, narcissim, and homoeroticism, to hatred of women and heterosexuality. Significantly, these are precisely the stages delineated by Otto Rank and others as the origins of many conceptions of the doppelgänger.[27] Furthermore, as Rank indicates, it is not at all unusual for the double to be depicted as the father, and Kinbote attempts to employ Shade as the "good" father, a double who immortalizes.

More often, the father is seen as a "bad" or punishing self. The punishing double is typically associated with the father because, in psychoanalytic terms, the fear of punishment is based on the initial fear of castration at the hands of the father. Gradus is, then, a parody of the punishing double. The situation set up in the Zemblan fantasy is an idyllic homosexual reign disrupted and destroyed by the realistic demands of a portion of the population: namely, that their king provide them with an heir to the throne and that he renounce his homosexuality. Gradus is the current representative of those who have decided that Charles must be destroyed for his refusal to do so. That the fantasy and the persecuting double are Kinbote's creations is evidence that he feels guilt for his homosexuality.

The identity of Gradus as "bad father" is suggested early in the Commentary, in fact in connection with Kinbote's primal scene fantasies. It will be recalled that Kinbote remarks on "the very special and very private fears . . . discussed elsewhere" and refers the reader to note 62. Note 62 in turn refers directly and indirectly to the Shadows, the Zemblan organization allegedly dedicated to Charles' destruction:

> Were those phantom thugs coming for me? Would they shoot me at once—or would they smuggle the chloroformed scholar back to Zembla, Rodnaya Zembla, to face there a dazzling decanter and a row of judges exulting in their inquisitorial chairs?
>
> At times I thought that only by self-destruction could I hope to cheat the relentlessly advancing assassins who were in me, in my eardrums, in my pulse, in my skull, rather than on that constant highway looping up over me and around my heart as I dozed off. . . .
>
> (pp. 96-97)

The most distinct, increasingly distinct,[28] Shadow of them all is Gradus. The role which Kinbote creates for Gradus, the role of the pursuer, of the punishing father, is as much a projection of his own anxieties onto a conveniently placed person as Shade's writing of "Souls Rex" rather than **"Pale Fire"** is a projection of Kinbote's desires. As several critics have noted, "the murderer is really [sic] an escaped criminal lunatic who seeks revenge on the judge who committed him, and whose house Kinbote has rented; he shoots Shade in mistake for the judge."[29] Kinbote tells us that Gradus "gave his name as Jack Grey, no fixed abode, except the Institute for the Criminal Insane . . . which the police thought he had just escaped from" (p. 295). As Mary McCarthy points out,

> The clue to Gradus-Grey, moreover, was in Botkin's hands when, early in the narrative, he leafed through a sentimental album kept by the judge containing photographs of the killers he had sent to prison or condemned to death: ". . . a strangler's quite ordinary-looking hands, a self-made widow, the close-set merciless eyes of a homicidal maniac (somewhat resembling, I admit, the late Jacques d'Argus). . . ."[30]

Despite all of the evidence to the contrary, the paranoid egotism of Kinbote insists on Grey as Gradus, insists that he, as Charles II, was the target. Indeed, Kinbote

even goes to the lengths of visiting Grey in jail: "By making him believe I could help him at his trial I forced him to confess his heinous crime—his deceiving the police and the nation by posing as Jack Grey, escapee from an asylum, who mistook Shade for the man who sent him there" (p. 299).

Again, what is given in **Pale Fire** is that Kinbote is narcissistic and paranoid. His narcissism is expressed in a self-preoccupation and self-glorification which he projects onto Shade, making Shade his double, his guardian angel, the function the primitive conception of the double is meant to serve, according to Rank.[31] As Rank explains, however, the narcissism also results in a behavior—homosexuality—with which the self is not totally secure; this explanation further clarifies the obsessive need for a guardian angel, or the sort of approval which "Solus Rex" would have afforded Kinbote. In attempting to dispell his insecurity, Kinbote seeks Shade's approval but does not find it. Shade does not write "Solus Rex"; he is neither Kinbote's double nor his father, and as a false double of Kinbote, he cannot approve of Kinbote any more than Kinbote does of himself.

The paranoid projection of Gradus is the evidence that Kinbote does not approve of himself; since he cannot tolerate his own self-criticism, he projects it outward onto a punishing, pursuing figure. Thus, both Shade and Gradus function for Kinbote as means of separating the two sides of himself which are at war with one another.

This understanding also clarifies the fact that while Gradus' destruction of Shade might seem to serve Kinbote's ends—the death of Shade puts the poem into Kinbote's hands—it actually works to Kinbote's destruction as well. First, the poem turns out most disappointingly for Kinbote and, secondly, the death of the guardian angel is certainly a bad omen. Kinbote is left where he began, with the obsessive insistence upon himself as Charles the Beloved, including both aspects of the ambivalance realized in Shade and Gradus, the Karlists and the Shadows: the self-love and the self-hatred. Kinbote says that "Shade is his own cancellation." It is perhaps more accurate, at least in this context, to see that Kinbote is his own cancellation—the ambivalence in his own nature is manifested by his doubling of Shade and Gradus for the two sides of himself.

The ambivalence is never resolved. Kinbote's failure to affirm even an assumed identity is the failure of the reductionism of the doppelgänger vision: the resolution of the battle between Shade and Grey cannot be reduced to a resolution for Kinbote. Kinbote cannot exorcise his self-criticizing shadow any more than he can find the approval and immortality he desires from Shade's poem. Kinbote had said "that only by self-destruction" could he "hope to cheat the relentlessly advancing assassins" (p. 97). He ends his Commentary with these words:

> But whatever happens, wherever the scene is laid, somebody, somewhere, will quietly set out—somebody has already set out, somebody still rather far away is buying a ticket, is boarding a bus, a ship, a plane, has landed, is walking toward a million photographers, and presently he will ring at my door—a bigger, more respectable, more competent Gradus.
>
> (p. 301)

Kinbote is right: the relentless assassins are projections of his own guilt. Only by self-destruction can that guilt be exorcised for him.

This analysis of **Pale Fire** has aimed at indicating several outstanding features of the novel: the parodic employment of the doppelgänger; the sophistication of the psychoanalytically accurate portrayal of the doppelgänger; the significance of Gradus and the tripling in the novel which indicates that the novel cannot be fully understood when the critic is concerned only with the doubling of Kinbote and Shade, or with any reductionist approach. Indeed, such simplification is to fall into the trap Nabokov has described as the nemesis of both Kinbote and Shade.

The consummate image of the tripling is, of course, the magical mirror of Sudarg of Bokay, the mirrored incarnation of Gradus (Sudarg of Bokay is Yakob Gradus spelled backwards), appropriate because, as we have seen, Gradus is the key to the novel as a unified whole, both psychologically and structurally. Thus, **Pale Fire** is best described in one image: the "cheval glass, a triptych of bottomless light, a really fantastic mirror." The "secret device of reflection" (p. 111) of the novel as well as of the mirror multiplies the number of characters within it and then reduces them to nothing, extends the reflections throughout time and space, defying time and space and then reduces time and space to nothing. The true "mirror maker of genius," the artist whose "life span [is] not known" (p. 314), is Nabokov, and the only reality is his art: "'reality' is neither the subject nor the object of true art which creates its own special reality having nothing to do with the average 'reality' perceived by the communal eye" (p. 130).

Notes

1. *Nabokov: The Man and His Work*, ed. L. S. Dembo (Madison: Univ. of Wisconsin Press, 1967), pp. 66-84.

2. "An Interview with Vladimir Nabokov," *Nabokov: The Man and His Work*, p. 22.

3. Alfred Appel, Jr., "Conversations with Nabokov," *Novel*, 4 (1971), 216.

4. Appel, "An Interview with Vladimir Nabokov," p. 37.

5. *Pale Fire* (New York: Putnam's, 1962), p. 13. All subsequent references are to this edition and will appear in parentheses.

6. Vladimir Nabokov, *The Real Life of Sebastian Knight* (Middlesex, Eng.: Penguin, 1964), p. 79. At one time early in his life, Nabokov thought he would be a painter.

7. In describing in *Speak, Memory* the types of chess problems he created, Nabokov describes his narrative strategy as well:

> Deceit, to the point of diabolism, and originality, verging upon the grotesque, were my notions of strategy; and although in matters of construction I tried to conform, whenever possible, to classical rules, such as economy of force, unity, weeding out of loose ends, I was always ready to sacrifice purity of form to the exigencies of fantastic content, causing form to bulge and burst like a sponge-bag containing a small furious devil.
>
> (New York: Putnam's, 1966, pp. 289-90)

8. With this in mind, Kinbote's explanation that "the name Zembla is a corruption not of the Russian *zemlya,* but of Semblerland, a land of reflections, of 'resemblers'" (p. 265), results in signifying the opposite of what he intends.

9. "An Interview with Vladimir Nabokov," p. 25.

10. See Chapter One of *Speak, Memory.*

11. Andrew Field, *Nabokov: His Life in Art* (Boston: Little, Brown, 1967), p. 320.

12. "The Shadow Within: The Conscious and Unconscious Use of the Double," *Daedalus,* 92 (1963), 341.

13. "An Interview with Vladimir Nabokov," p. 29.

14. Kinbote is a homosexual, Shade heterosexual; Kinbote is a vegetarian, Shade hates vegetables; Kinbote is ignorant about nature, Shade knowledgeable; Kinbote is attractive, Shade is ugly, at least according to himself and to Kinbote; Kinbote styles himself a pious Christian, Shade is an atheist who attains a certain belief in design; Kinbote writes only prose, Shade poetry as well.

15. These similarities extend to the structures of the sections belonging to Shade and Kinbote. In both sections, the first is the last. The poem's first line becomes the last; the Foreword was the last section written by Kinbote. In each case what is suggested is a dog chasing its own tail: in Nabokov's terms, the vicious circle of mortality.

16. *Nabokov: His Life in Art,* p. 300.

17. Ibid., pp. 106-13.

18. *Ada* (New York: McGraw-Hill, 1969), p. 153.

19. Since Nabokov's descriptions of his own sense of time and mortality are well known, I do not quote them here. The reader is again referred to Nabokov's autobiography, *Speak, Memory,* especially to Chapter One.

20. Julian Moynahan, *Vladimir Nabokov,* Minnesota Pamphlets on Amer. Writers (Minneapolis: Univ. of Minnesota Press, 1971), p. 44.

21. *Speak Memory,* p. 291.

22. That Nabokov has indicated similarities between his tastes and experiences and those of Shade described here (see *Strong Opinions* [New York: McGraw-Hill, 1973], pp. 68-69, 311) does not preclude the possibility of their being used as elements of parody in such a context as *Pale Fire.* After all, this novel employs satirically the "wrong-man-murdered" theme which is possibly the most poignant theme in Nabokov's life: on "a certain night in 1922, at a public lecture in Berlin . . . [his] father shielded the lecturer (his old friend Milyukov) from the bullets of two Russian Fascists and, while vigorously knocking down one of the assassins, was fatally shot by the other" (*Speak, Memory,* p. 193).

23. Furthermore, in John Stark's words, "'Gradus' is Russian for degree, which in turn is a synonym of 'shade'" (*The Literature of Exhaustion* [Durham, N. C.: Duke Univ. Press, 1974], p. 107). As a result, the name "Gradus" implies all of the functions of the character in the novel: "shade" as death, or shadow (of a waxwing), the Shadow trailing the exiled king, the shadow as double of both Kinbote and Shade and, especially, the shadow created by Kinbote's imagination.

24. "Nabokov's Dialectical Structure," *Nabokov: The Man and His Work,* p. 169.

25. Sybil Shade is presented to the reader in two ways. The reader knows, for example, despite Kinbote's interpretation of events, that Sybil is the loving and protective wife of the poet, completely in his confidence. And Shade presents her this way in the poem. But Kinbote's depiction of her is as a woman incapable of truly understanding her husband, who only blocks his way to his true muse, namely Kinbote himself. This second view of Sybil must be seen as a delusion—indeed, as a projection of Kinbote's feelings about Sybil's treatment of him. Sybil, as depicted by Kinbote, is a character blocking his way to his soul-mate. The Commentary abounds with references to Sybil's diabolical exclusion of Kinbote from the society of his poet, as well as to her attempts to keep the poem's manuscript from him: "who is to blame, dear S. S?" (p. 204). The way in which Kinbote is denied an invitation to Shade's birthday party, for instance, is poignantly rendered by the commentator. Kinbote feels that Shade understands him and that Sybil does not.

26. See Norman Holland, *The Dynamics of Literary Response* (New York: Oxford Univ. Press, 1968), pp. 45 ff. "Primal Scene" appears in *Pale Fire* as a variant to Line 57 (p. 94) which Kinbote provides and, most likely, wrote himself. Both *Lolita* and *Speak, Memory* provide further evidence of Nabokov's knowledge of and contempt for "primal scene fantasies." *Lolita* includes two direct references—(pp. 36 and 174 in Appel's *The Annotated Lolita* (New York: McGraw-Hill, 1970)— and the autobiography speaks of uterine fantasies (for Nabokov undoubtedly the *reductio ad absurdum* of primal scene fantasies): "bitter little embryos spying, from their natural nooks, upon the love life of their parents" (p. 14).

27. See especially, Otto Rank's *The Double: A Psychoanalytic Study,* trans. Harry Tucker, Jr. (Chapel Hill: Univ. of North Carolina Press, 1971). Readers interested in pursuing the theme of the double in literature are also referred to Robert Rogers' *A Psychoanalytic Study of the Double in Literature* (Detroit: Wayne State Univ. Press, 1970), and to Ralph Tymms, *Doubles in Literary Psychology* (Cambridge: Bowes and Bowes, 1949), among others.

28. Kinbote remarks: "I have staggered the notes referring to him in such a fashion that the first (see note to line 17 where some of his other activities are adumbrated) is the vaguest while those that follow become gradually clearer as gradual Gradus approaches in space and time" (p. 152).

29. Frank Kermode, "Zemblances," *New Statesman,* 9 Nov. 1962, 671.

30. "A Bolt from the Blue," *New Republic,* June 1962, p. 22.

31. "The Double as Immortal Self," *Beyond Psychology* (New York: Dover, 1958), p. 62.

David Walker (essay date autumn 1976)

SOURCE: Walker, David. "'The Viewer and the View': Chance and Choice in *Pale Fire.*" *Studies in American Fiction* 4, no. 2 (autumn 1976): 203-21.

[*In the following essay, Walker explores the significance of linguistic patterns and imagery in Nabokov's* Pale Fire.]

Vladimir Nabokov is an artist obsessed with pattern. The fabric of each of his books is woven with a dense texture of mirrors, doubles, parodies, games, riddles, masks, and disguises. An important part of the reason for this emphasis is the aesthetic pleasure which the perception of such patterning affords. In his afterword to *Lolita,* Nabokov claims, "for me a work of fiction exists only insofar as it affords me what I shall bluntly call aesthetic bliss, that is a sense of being somehow, somewhere connected with other states of being where art (curiosity, tenderness, kindness, ecstasy) is the norm."[1] In his supremely anti-naturalistic, involuted novels, such games of perception help celebrate with great joy the very artificiality of the fictional world that transforms experience into art.

Highly complex patterning is not confined to the realms of art; its existence in nature, in the "real world," is also of great importance to Nabokov. Perceiving natural patterning results in the same kind of exhilaration; it clarifies and extends an intuition of the world. But its meaning is different in an important way because it involves the idea of coincidence. Nabokov's fiction acknowledges repeatedly its fictional nature; the author is everywhere apparent, making Hitchcockian appearances and winking at the camera. Nature, on the other hand, is governed not by choice but by chance—or so the customary thinking goes. For Nabokov this is too easy a distinction:

> The mysteries of mimicry had a special attraction for me. Its phenomena showed an artistic perfection usually associated with man-wrought things. . . . I discovered in nature the non-utilitarian delights that I sought in art. Both were a form of magic, both were a game of intricate enchantment and deception.[2]

Suddenly the world begins to seem a work of art, perfectly patterned, controlled, designed. Yet for Nabokov this second scheme is also false and incomplete; to deny the boundary between life and art, the difference between an object and its reflection in a mirror, is to miss the point entirely. Nature does not consistently demonstrate artistic principles; its games of "intricate enchantment and deception" have meaning only when they are revealed by human aesthetic perception. The artist who refuses to accept this distinction, who denies the reality of human existence apart from his own conception of it, enters the dangerous province of mad solipsism. Only the artist who focuses his perception on the world to reveal its significant textures and forms, without mistaking these forms for the only true reality, finds the necessary balance. The reconciliation of life and art, the attempt to penetrate the double truth of chance and choice, is the core of all of Nabokov's writing. But none of his books explores the idea of combinational fate, of the role of design both in life and in art, as thoroughly or as brilliantly as does *Pale Fire.*

The structure of *Pale Fire* may appear fairly straightforward. It is composed of a meditation in verse on death and the fate of consciousness by John Shade, a baggy, venerated poet, and notes on the poem (plus Foreword and Index) by Charles Kinbote, a mad scholar who completely misunderstands what the poem is about, tries to convert it to his own devices, and loses all control in the process. But *Pale Fire* is no mere twentieth-century *Tale of a Tub* or paranoid *Dunciad*; it is in fact a radically experimental novel.

At first the commentary seems unrelated to the concerns of the poem, and Shade and Kinbote appear to be riding different breeds of hobbyhorse. But that perception, coupled with the assumptions one normally brings to a scholarly critical edition, illuminates the underlying structure of *Pale Fire.* One doesn't expect the set of notes to a poem to have its own integrity, any significant order, sequence, or movement apart from the form of the poem it mirrors. And if the notes do not really reflect the poem at all, then one might expect total chaos, a sort of insane omnium-gatherum. But the reader of *Pale Fire* soon begins to notice correspondences and coincidences, not only from note to note but from notes to poem, and the sense of organic unity—of a web of sense that exists almost in spite of itself—seems more and more clear.

Even this construction, this assembling of parts into a multifaceted, coherent whole, is not *Pale Fire*'s ultimate formal achievement. Eventually its principle of fragmentation leads the reader to the same conclusions that Shade and Kinbote find. The novel explores the idea that the essence of art lies not in its "text" but in its "texture," not in the authority of images themselves but in the correspondences the mind can perceive or invent between them. And the experience of reading *Pale Fire* mirrors this idea; its puzzles force the reader to become an active participant, to find or create the connections that unify the fiction and the world, and in the process it illuminates and extends a sense of the pleasures and possibilities of aesthetic form.

The dominant image of the book is the mirror; trapped in a prison of reflections, the characters are doomed to see, or think they see, everything as reflected image. Twins, doubles, dualities, imitations abound. But these are no ordinary mirrors; all the images are in some way altered or distorted. "There are no 'real' doubles in my novels."[3] In *Invitation to a Beheading,* Cincinnatus C.'s mother describes a toy consisting of two parts: a set of unrecognizable objects called *nonnons,* and a special mirror that completely distorts ordinary objects. Neither by itself is more than a curious oddity. But

> when you placed one of these incomprehensible, monstrous objects so that it was reflected in the incomprehensible, monstrous mirror, a marvelous thing happened; minus by minus equaled plus, everything was restored, and the shapeless speckledness became in the mirror a wonderful, sensible image . . . a charming picture, so very, very clear.[4]

This is roughly the structure of *Pale Fire.* Certainly neither poem nor commentary is shapeless or incomprehensible, but only when they are read as mirror-images of each other does the full pattern of Nabokov's art emerge.

The first stanza of John Shade's **"Pale Fire"** is extremely complex; it suggests all the major themes of the poem—and of the novel:

> I was the shadow of the waxwing slain
> By the false azure in the windowpane;
> I was the smudge of ashen fluff—and I
> Lived on, flew on, in the reflected sky.

The waxwing's fate is only the first of a number of violent accidental deaths in the novel, and it results from mistaking the mirrored reflection of the sky for actual freedom. Flight through the impenetrable looking-glass is impossible; the apparent safety that the mirror promises is illusory and destructive. Yet in the moment of impact the waxwing seems to divide, to become both the dead "smudge of ashen fluff" and a figure that flies on in a world obviously different in kind from the natural scene. It is an important clue, one that Kinbote apparently doesn't notice, that Shade says "I was the shadow of the waxwing," rather than "I was the waxwing." This is highly ambiguous, but it suggests that the shadow (the illusory, half-real double) *can* penetrate the looking-glass, can transcend the boundaries of time and space, into the shadow world of illusion and art. The rest of the stanza demonstrates that on the other side of the glass there is also a reality reflected, a projected shadow-world. The idea of combinational fate is introduced here: "how delightful" when snow happens to fall outside to exactly the right level to meet the reflected furniture, when the inner and outer realities chance to mesh exactly into a single perfect image, when "night unites the viewer and the view."

"We are most artistically caged," says Shade. The clearest boundaries are the temporal ones that engender the pain of a finite consciousness in an infinite world. But this awareness is only one of the causes of human suffering. Shade says that he was miserable as a child: orphaned early, "asthmatic, lame, and fat," "a cloutish freak." His response to this misfortune was to retreat into fantasy, pure aesthetics, the pleasures of the natural world, and the perception of pattern. He became "a preterist: one who collects cold nests," for whom the recaptured, recollected world is a primary source of pleasure and comfort. This reliance on memory and imagination is for Nabokov—as well as for Shade—the necessary chemistry of the artist; to recreate remembered and imagined details by fixing them in aesthetic form is to transcend ignorance, brutality, suffering, the limits of mortality.

The second canto enlarges and extends these themes. Maud Shade is for the poet a grotesque example of suffering. In Shade's youth, she at least had pretensions to art. But at eighty, when "a sudden hush / Fell on her life," she was incapable either of finding any aesthetic solace or of gaining any control over her suffering ("her look / Spelt imploration as she sought in vain / To reason with the monsters in her brain"). Fat, ugly, psoriatic Hazel Shade experienced a similar fate; she was as isolated and unhappy as her equally misfortunate father. "She hardly ever laughed, and when she did, / It was a sign of pain." But she was not capable of aesthetic defenses; though strangely drawn to supernatural forces and mysteries, she failed finally to achieve any meaningful relationship with the imaginative world. The terrors of the physical world finally overwhelmed her, and, unable to find a refuge in art, she chose the only other possible escape: suicide, the deliberate flight into the mirror surface of the lake.

Two other themes are repeated here. First, the impossibility of penetrating the opaque mirror-surface of death, of knowing the fate of consciousness on the other side, is challenged by Shade's decision to devote all his "twisted life" to exploring the question. He declares that the poem is his attempt at an answer, though it seems ludicrous to try to translate "into one's private tongue a public fate." And second, the idea of combinational fate appears again, though this time not as nature's perfect pattern of chance (the snow rising to meet the furniture), but as the artist's conscious arrangement of details for their aesthetic effect. Shade's use of what Kinbote calls "the synchronization device" to stylize the alternation of two sets of events that actually did occur simultaneously emphasizes the delicate and shifting relationship between natural coincidence and aesthetic design.

Shade's third and most important canto continues to explore the question of "death's abyss." His term at I. P. H. taught him only what to ignore in his investigation: unable to accept the Institute's firm belief in the existence of another conscious realm beyond death or to scorn "a hereafter none can verify," he concludes that the only thing he can be certain of is that death is an impenetrable mirror that prevents a view of any possible existence beyond, and through which there can be no communication. Given such an eternity, though, Shade would only accept it if its rules included all the aesthetic processes that make this life bearable: memory, the perception of natural beauty, the immortality of art. And he repeats, more explicitly here than in any other passage, his belief that the only intelligent response to human pain is an aesthetic one. It is important to recognize that Shade does not claim that such a response can help evade fate, the horror of execution, the inexorable advance of death. But style, control, a sense of the dramatic, can help to make such ugly moments into theatrical events and thus perhaps to avoid total despair.

The second half of the canto illuminates Shade's most important discovery, the idea of a web of sense connecting all experience. The attack which mirrors his childhood fits plunges him through the looking-glass, into the "blood-black nothingness" on the other side of death—and he discovers what seems a coherent system of interlocking cells. Obsessed by this image, but unable to decipher its meaning, at last he discovers in Mrs. Z.'s account of "The Land Beyond the Veil" an experience that seems to duplicate his. The connection between the accounts, the single perfect point of conjunction, turns out to be only a typographical error: "Life Everlasting—based on a misprint!" But suddenly he realizes that this is exactly the point: that in such accidental conjunctions lies significant pattern, that not the text but the texture of life (and art) is the necessary evidence for the existence of larger design and order. "Accidents and possibilities" may be seen in purely aesthetic terms; Shade imagines mysterious beings playing with human destiny on a chessboard, "kindling a long life here, extinguishing / A short one there." But he is not affirming total determinism; his discovery leads him only to "faint hope." Though convinced of the existence of perceived pattern, he cannot tell whether such pattern is the result of choice or chance, whether there are in fact intelligent beings "playing a game of worlds," or if it is only his own artistic perception making connections between actually random, unplanned occurrences that makes "a web of sense" appear.

None of these questions is resolved in the fourth canto, where Shade recapitulates his reliance on artistic forms to give intelligible meaning to his existence. The couplet *"Man's life as commentary to abstruse / Unfinished poem.* Note for further use" inverts the usual relationship, and suggests that life may be a reflection of art. But given the novel's plot, the observation is also strikingly ironic. It seems to suggest that Shade knows his poem will remain unfinished and that a commentary will be written. And since the poem is nearly complete, it raises the possibility that Shade anticipates his own death—which undermines any reductive "solution" to the puzzle of the relationship between him and Kinbote. On the other hand, it is possible that the irony is entirely accidental and "revealed" only by hindsight. In any case, surely the ambiguity is intentional. Just as Shade never allows his vision of fatal agents to be a conclusive answer to the question of death's abyss, so is it impossible to be sure whether the irony of his observation results from accident or deliberate design.

Charles Kinbote's commentary is the perfect mirror for Shade's rambling, discursive *nonnon*. His objections notwithstanding, poem and notes do merge to form the "monstrous semblance of a novel."[5] *Pale Fire*'s primary structural emphasis is that in very different ways Shade and Kinbote discover truths that are not antithetical but identical. The notes to **"Pale Fire,"** like Humbert Humbert's fifty-six-day memoir, were ostensibly written at near breakneck pace: less than three months from the poet's death to their completion. Kinbote repeatedly maintains that they are only "an unambiguous *apparatus criticus*" (p. 62), "short notes to a poem" (p. 77) whose only purpose is to clarify and illuminate its meaning. Yet, also like Humbert's memoir, the notes are densely textured with rich patterns of images: butterflies, birds, windows, mirrors, theaters, masks. It is clear that one has to look deeper than the surface of Kinbote's narrative, to examine its texture as well as the text. Having done so, it will be clear that Shade's concerns (the nature of the world, the importance of perceived pattern and conjunction, the necessary balance between life and art) are Kinbote's as well.

LINE 175: WHAT DAWN, WHAT DEATH, WHAT DOOM

It is misreading **Pale Fire** to suggest, as numerous critics have, that Jakob Gradus represents a further doubling, or tripling, of Shade and Kinbote.[6] Gradus is a crucial figure, both in the structure and the meaning of the book, but this "automatic man" (p. 197) is not nearly as complex or elusive a character as Shade or his shadow. He is the agent of fate; his methodical descent on New Wye represents the inexorable advance of doom. "The one who kills is *always* his victim's inferior" (p. 166), and Gradus is clearly also an inferior Shadow. His assignment "was decided by a show of cards"—chance!—"but let us not forget that it was Nodo who shuffled and dealt them out" (p. 108). "The contrapuntal genius of human fate" (*SM* [*Speak, Memory*], p. 139) works in mysterious ways, and the question of design surfaces here once again.

The figure of Gradus becomes even more interesting considering that everything that is known about him comes from Kinbote. Kinbote's personified version of fate is more "objectified" than Shade's but no less ambiguous. Gradus's advance is perfectly schematized, timed, deliberate—thus supporting the idea of plexed artists in control—but he depends upon such fortuitous circumstances as Gerald Emerald's generosity, and the whole scheme is overthrown when the wrong bird (at least in Kinbote's version) is bagged. If "the rule of a supernal game . . . the immutable fable of fate" (p. 173) can only be completed when "a bigger, more respectable, more competent Gradus" (p. 213) rings at the door, it is difficult to see how this can be called fate at all. "Who is the Judge of life, and the Designer of death?" (p. 160). Both Shade and Kinbote are highly concerned with questions of fate, pattern, choice and chance; that the *surface* of the commentary seems irrelevant to the poem is itself an irrelevant observation.

LINE 998: SOME NEIGHBOR

Kinbote's awareness of the constant approach of Gradus is no less strong than Shade's sense of the temporal and spatial limits of mortality, but, as for Shade, this awareness is not the only source of his despair. He is at great pains, in both the foreword and the notes, to stress his close friendship with Shade, but it soon becomes apparent that Shade's is not only "feigned remoteness." A New Wye housewife hisses at Kinbote in the grocery store, "You are a remarkably disagreeable person. I fail to see how John and Sybil can stand you" (p. 16); in fact, Sybil cannot, and John's attitude is clearly one of tolerance rather than of affection. The password is pity, says Shade; "more than anything on earth he loathed Vulgarity and Brutality" (p. 153), and, rather than deliberately inflict pain on Charles, he endures his persistent prying and fawning. But, though Kinbote apparently tries to conceal it, he obviously perceives what Shade tries to hide from him. He recognizes that "Shade was very kind to the unsuccessful" (p. 168); his constant insistence on the intimacy of the bond gives him away. The lane that divides their houses forms as impenetrable a barrier as any mirror's surface. Finally Kinbote admits, "Solitude is the playfield of Satan. I cannot describe the depths of my loneliness and distress" (p. 69), and in desperation he hopes for Shade to suffer another heart attack, for the "great warm burst of sympathy" (p. 70) it would provoke. Because he cannot force Shade to discuss **"Pale Fire"** with him, he resorts to "peeps and glimpses, and window-framed opportunities" (p. 62), which evolve into "an orgy of spying which no considerations of pride could stop" (p. 63).

The clearest demonstration of his loneliness is the scene of Shade's birthday party, the honored guests arriving in style while "through the golden veil of evening and through the black lacery of night" Kinbote watches "that lawn, that drive, that fanlight, those jewel-bright windows" (p. 115). The next morning, hurt and pathetic, he crosses the lane and delivers his present and the news that it had been his birthday too. "'Would he ever come for me?' I used to wonder waiting and waiting, in certain amber-and-rose crepuscules, for a ping-pong friend, or for old John Shade" (p. 132). Kinbote's desperate need to escape loneliness, which drives him both to hound Shade and to pursue a long series of empty, unfulfilling affairs, is thus an important mirror of Shade's own ugliness, awkwardness, and isolation.

LINE 456: THE SOFT FORM DISSOLVING

Disa, Duchess of Payn, Charles's "lovely, pale, melancholy Queen" (p. 216), has gone largely unexamined by the critics, but the scene of her final meeting with him is highly important because of what it reveals about Kinbote and because it links several important ideas. Contrary to common critical opinion, Kinbote's homo-

sexuality is primarily important *not* as an emblem of inversion (the mirror image of heterosexual Shade) or perversion (the distorting mirror, the poem misread), but as the source of great unhappiness: his own, Fleur de Fyler's, and especially Disa's.

Kinbote says that his sentiments toward Disa had never amounted to more than "friendly indifference and bleak respect" (p. 149); their life together had been largely painful. Charles's casual heartlessness and Disa's "great show of sarcastic sophistication" (p. 149) preclude any possibility of tenderness or excitement in the relationship. But he dreams of her, both before and after she is banished to Cap Turc, in quite a different light:

> These heart-rending dreams transformed the drab prose of his feelings for her into strong and strange poetry. . . . The gist, rather than the actual plot of the dream, was a constant refutation of his not loving her. His dream-love for her exceeded in emotional tone, in spiritual passion and depth, anything he had experienced in his surface existence. . . . They were, in a sense, amorous dreams, for they were permeated with tenderness, with a longing to sink his head onto her lap and sob away the monstrous past. Everything had changed, everyone was happy.
>
> (pp. 149, 150, 151)

This tendency to abandon himself to fantasy, to retreat from the agonies of the present and the bitterness of memory into a realm where he is capable of rich and poignant feelings, parallels exactly Shade's flight into aesthetics. But there is an important difference. Shade is able to use his artistic sensibility to transform the "real world" of pain and suffering, to change the nature of the circumstances of this world by casting them in aesthetic form. Kinbote's dreams, however, remain isolated "in the heart of his dreaming self" (p. 149); they are so much "purer than his life" (p. 150) that they cannot affect "at all his attitude toward the real Disa" (p. 149). At least, that is what he says. But his last visit to Villa Disa is charged with pain and frustration; his casualness is obviously only a mask for his awareness of Disa's loneliness and grief. As he leaves,

> he glanced back and saw in the distance her white figure with the listless grace of ineffable grief bending over the garden table, and suddenly a fragile bridge was suspended between waking indifference and dream-love.
>
> (p. 153)

For an instant he is able to see through the glass. But the image moves, and he recognizes it as only an illusory Disa, "only poor Fleur de Fyler collecting the documents left among the tea things" (p. 153).

That suspended bridge, the meaningful balance between artistic creation and actual experience, is the heart of the novel. In an earlier passage, Kinbote notes the resemblance between Shade's portrait of Sybil in **"Pale Fire"** and Disa; what is important, he says, is that the "idealized and stylized" image of Sybil corresponds to Disa in "a plain unretouched likeness" (p. 148). "I trust the reader appreciates the strangeness of this, because if he does not, there is no sense in writing poems, or notes to poems, or anything else at all" (p. 148). As always, when Kinbote sounds most lucid he is being most ambiguous. His observation seems to have two meanings. The resemblance is "strange" because it is so coincidental; it underscores the novel's repeated emphasis on chance, on perceived correspondence. But it is also "strange" that Kinbote, who so consistently denies (both through such scenes as the one with Disa and through direct observation) that he is ever able to bridge the abyss, to see through the glass, demonstrates here that he is in fact able to make meaningful connections between the real circumstance and its transformed reflzction.

LINE 22: IN WINTER'S CODE

John Shade's last canto reaffirms that the only way he can understand his existence is through his art, "in terms of combinational delight." Implicit in this artistic process is the idea of seeing the world as artifice, of seeing a snowy road as a blank page on which a pheasant's tracks spell out a coded message. Perceiving natural mimicry is a part of this process as is the idea that pure coincidence can be read as significant pattern. Viewing natural phenomena in artistic terms introduces order into an otherwise chaotic universe.

Kinbote's world is not as baldly artificial as that of *Invitation to a Beheading,* whose two-dimensional sets literally fall apart at its conclusion. Nor is the narrator as omnipresent and obviously manipulative as in *Bend Sinister,* where Nabokov imperiously interrupts the narrative at its climax. But Kinbote obviously delights in seeing nature as artifice. "How serene were the mountains, how tenderly painted on the western vault of the sky!" (p. 86). Indeed, Kinbote often becomes positively Nabokovian in his flaunting of anti-naturalistic devices. And his statement of faith in God—as, in fact, all the references to religious faith in the book—can be read most meaningfully as his affirmation of the role of the artist in the universe:

> When the soul adores Him Who guides it through mortal life, when it distinguishes His sign at every turn of the trail, painted on the boulder and notched in the fir trunk, when every page in the book of one's personal fate bears His watermark, how can one doubt that He will also preserve us through all eternity?
>
> (p. 158)

The effect of seeing the world as artifice, "when the lamp of art is made to shine through life's foolscap" (*SM,* p. 25), is to reveal that watermark, to infuse into nature a sense of order and form, and thus to achieve a measure of control over the forces that cage and torment humanity.

LINE 235: LIFE IS A MESSAGE SCRIBBLED IN THE DARK

The cryptic message that Hazel Shade transcribes from the dictation of the luminous circlet in the haunted barn illuminates further the role of pattern and perception in Kinbote's world. It raises the tantalizing question of whether the "short line of simple letter-groups" is in fact only a "jumble of broken words and meaningless syllables" (p. 135) or whether there is actually a "secret design in the abracadabra," some meaningful pattern in the barn ghost's speech. Kinbote abhors such games, but, faithful commentator that he is, he spends hours poring over the text, forming lexical units, searching for the correlated patten, only to conclude that there is none.

It is clear that Kinbote is a master at perceiving hidden patterns—at least, those he wants to see. His eagerness to see the allusions to Zembla and Gradus in **"Pale Fire,"** the ones that Sybil failed to weed out, makes that apparent. Disgusted at the futility of his labors, he reports that he could not discover

> the least allusion to the poor girl's fate. Not one hint did I find. Neither old Hentzner's specter, nor an ambushed scamp's toy flashlight, nor her own imaginative hysteria, express anything here that might be construed, however remotely, as containing a warning, or having some bearing on the circumstances of her soon-coming death.
>
> (p. 135)

He seems to be absolutely right. There does not appear to be any way to decode the message to relate it to Hazel's suicide. But perhaps Kinbote is searching for the wrong design in her game. Perhaps the message that this strange, superstitious girl left behind refers not to her own death, but "pada ata lane pad not ogo old wart alan ther tale feur far rant lant tal told." Suddenly a pattern begins to emerge, not perfectly lucid, certainly not provable, only "a faint phosphorescence at first, a pale light in the dimness of bodily light" (p. 161). Still, it certainly seems possible that this *is* a warning, that Hazel is telling her father not to cross the lane to Judge Goldsworth's house, where she knows he will meet the pale fire ("tale feur"?) of Gradus's revolver. And perhaps "far rant lant tal told" specifies the time of Shade's death, when he has completed telling the tale of Zembla, that foreign land. Such tentative suggestions embody the same kind of possibility that Kinbote's loony, eccentric, but quite meaningful reading of the poem contains. And this is precisely the point: if a meaningful pattern can be perceived in the texture of life or art, it is not important whether that pattern has been deliberately woven into the fabric, or whether perception itself has created it. What matters is the perception, the secret design, and what is done with it; "the decoding of the undulation of things"[7] is another way of seeing the disordered universe in the ordered terms of art.

LINE 809: TOPSY-TURVICAL COINCIDENCE

Kinbote is as conscious of coincidence, of the role of combinational fate in natural and artistic design, as Shade. "The synchronization device" operates often in Shade's poem, and both chance and deliberate design contribute to such instances of symmetry; the same ambiguity persists in Kinbote's world. Some cases of correlated pattern seem obvious elements of the "chaos of chance" (p. 161); others are clearly consciously created. But the commentary's primary example of symmetry, the coordination between Shade's composition and Gradus's approach, is problematical. Kinbote constantly proclaims his wonder at how closely their movements correspond; his meticulous documentation and apparently scrupulous honesty ("Shade composed these lines on Thursday, July 14th. What was Gradus doing that day? Nothing. Combinational fate rests on its laurels" [p. 165]) might begin to lend an air of authenticity were Kinbote's inventive hand not quite so obvious. If Gradus is Kinbote's figure for immutable fate, it might seem perfectly clear that all the coordination is deliberate, imposed, artificial. But this solution is complicated by Kinbote's frequent assertion that Gradus's movement depends upon Shade's poem: "The force propelling him is the magic action of Shade's poem itself, the very mechanism and sweep of verse, the powerful iambic motor" (p. 98). In short, Kinbote describes his role here, not as a creative artist, but as a sensitive critic; he insists that he has not created the patterns of correspondence, merely perceived them. And unlikely as this may seem, it cannot be dismissed as a possibility. One is again left suspended in the delicate balance between chance and choice: viewer and view, perceiver and pattern, are inextricably meshed.

LINE 2: THE FALSE AZURE IN THE WINDOWPANE

Kinbote's assertion that "There is, moreover, a symptomatic family resemblance in the coloration of both poem and story" (p. 58) does not begin to suggest how closely they mirror each other. **Pale Fire** is a chamber of mirrors—verbal, visual, episodic—as these notes attempt to demonstrate. "The name Zembla is a corruption not of the Russian *zemlya,* but of Semberland, a land of reflections, of 'resemblers'" (p. 187); Zemblan is "the tongue of the mirror" (p. 172). Kinbote glosses "the crystal land": "Perhaps an allusion to Zembla, my dear country" (p. 54), and certainly it is; Zembla is the realm of the mirror, of appearance, illusion, Alice's Looking-Glass.

The importance of the image of the slain waxwing is to suggest that to mistake the "false azure" for the real, to

be deceived by "the illusion of continued space" (p. 53), is to risk destruction. The mirror image is highly significant, it is the key to truth, but it is not "real"—at least, not in the same way as the object it reflects. The idea of the mirror's destructiveness is given weight by a set of related images in the notes. It is no accident, for example, that Shade is constantly described as "a big bird" (p. 183), or that after death he lies "with open dead eyes directed up at the sunny evening azure" (p. 208). King Charles's father, absent-minded Alfin the Vague, was highly prone to crash landings, and a "very special monoplane" became "his bird of doom" (p. 75). Alfin has the illusion of safety: "just before the white-blurred shattering crash," he raises "one arm in triumph and reassurance" (p. 75). But man is never master of gravity (doom, fate); inventions for circumventing the rules are valid only until the rules change, or until one mistakes the order they establish for the only true reality. In another instance of the pattern, Kinbote expresses his desire for "the perfect safety of wooed death" (p. 158); if his religious images may all be read as references to art, then his urge toward "destruction in the Lap of the Lord" parallels the waxwing's destruction in the mirrored azure. Kinbote has destroyed King Charles by sinking "his identity in the mirror of exile" (p. 189). Shade dies when he encounters the minor Shadow whose life has mirrored his own during the composition of his poem. And Gradus, too, "is to meet, in his urgent and blind flight, a reflection that will shatter him" (p. 98). The mirror, clearly, can be a dangerous and destructive force, if one fails to recognize that its images are of a completely different material from those of this world. To mistake human artifice for the "artifice of eternity" (to quote another visionary), to trust the ordered constructions of art and ignore the chaos that lurks outside them, is to be vulnerable to the threat of Gradus and his fellow Shadows.

LINE 962: HELP ME, WILL! *PALE FIRE*

Shade's title comes, of course, from the very passage in *Timon of Athens* that Kinbote quotes (in a re-Englishing of Conmal's mangled translation) early in the commentary:

> The sun's a thief, and with his great attraction
> Robs the vast sea. The moon's an arrant thief
> And her pale fire she snatches from the sun.
>
> (IV, ii, 442-44)

Timon, with its proud, mad, exiled king, is an important reference, and Kinbote *has,* in a sense, stolen Shade's poem. But this passage is more important as a description of the nature of art than of the universality of theft. The moon is the primary natural mirror, and light is the medium of mirroring. But the moon also suggests lunacy, metamorphosis, imaginative transformation, so that the moon's illumination is of a wholly different kind from the sun's penetrating rays. Lunar reflection is not essentially mimetic but recreative; like all the mirrors in this novel, the moon's pale fire distorts the reality it reflects.

The title is also relevant to the relationship between the poem and the commentary. The novel's two parts, like life and art, are necessary and complementary mirrors, but it is impossible to identify one as the primary object and the other as its mirror. Here is another deliberate ambiguity: world and art, sane and insane, are constantly and paradoxically inverted and reversed. When Shade is writing, Kinbote perceives "a blaze of bliss . . . of that spiritual energy and divine wisdom . . . reflected upon" his "rugged and homely face" (p. 64)—thus casting him as the moon—but Sylvia O'Donnell calls him "our brightest sun" (p. 176). Similarly, Kinbote admits that he has "caught myself borrowing a kind of opalescent light from my poet's fiery orb" (p. 59), but later calls **"Pale Fire"** "oh, pale, indeed!" (p. 126) and "pale and diaphanous" (p. 58)—implying that the poem is only a reflection of the glorious radiance of Zembla. The ambiguity, the inversion, is important; the delicate balance that this model of prismatic fiction achieves helps to portray "somewhere beyond the throes of an entangled and inept nightmare, the ordered reality of the waking hour" (*SM*, p. 39).

Pale Fire often resembles a three-dimensional game of chess whose three boards may be described as follows:

The Story: John Shade, an elderly Frostian poet, writes a long, rambling poem, at the end of which he is murdered by a killer calling himself Jack Grey. Shade's neighbor and colleague, a refugee professor from Zembla named Charles Kinbote, takes the poem into hiding, and writes a long, illuminating commentary.

The real story: Kinbote is convinced that he has inspired the poem with his account of his native Zembla and its exiled king, Charles the Beloved, that the poem is *his* poem, incomprehensible without his gloss. Moreover, Kinbote is none other than King Charles incognito. The Shadows, Zembla's anti-Karlist secret police, have hired a professional killer, Jakob Gradus, to track down the exile: his advance on New Wye parallels Shade's work on **"Pale Fire."** Poem finished, thug arrives, shoots at king, fells poet, and claims to be a lunatic escapee from a mental hospital.

The real real story: Kinbote is a mad refugee scholar who imagines himself the exiled king of Zembla, pitied and tolerated by Shade. The killer is, in fact, Jack Grey, an escaped criminal madman who had reached Kinbote's house to kill—not him, not Shade, but Judge Goldsworth, Kinbote's landlord, who bore a striking resemblance to Shade and had sent Grey to the asylum. Kinbote's commentary is an attempt to link Shade's poem to his fantasy, but is totally unconvincing.

This, fortunately, is only the novel's framework. Much critical energy has been expended trying to untangle the web of correspondences that unites Shade and Kinbote, but that web and its attendant ambiguities are perfectly intentional. Van Veen suggests that "some law of logic should fix the number of coincidences in a given domain, after which they cease to be coincidences, and form, instead, the living organism of a new truth,"[8] and in *Pale Fire* the network of correlation is clearly pervasive enough to establish such an organism. But to jump from this perception to the equation $S + K = N$, as several critics have, is to ignore an important part of the book, the further exploration of that relationship.

"Real" and "unreal" are continually being inverted in *Pale Fire.* The reader comes to the work prepared for the commentary to be that element which "explains" the poem, ties its imaginative fabric to the "real life" that inspired it. Kinbote's foreword asserts that

> without my notes Shade's text simply has no human reality at all since the human reality of such a poem as his . . . has to depend entirely on the reality of its author and his surroundings, attachments and so forth, a reality that only my notes can provide.
>
> (pp. 18-19)

and this claim (though not its tone) is one that the reader is generally ready to accept. Instead he finds that the poem, while evidence of a genuinely artistic perception at work, grows rather specifically (and often in quite a pedestrian way) out of the "real life" of New Wye, while Kinbote's memory and references to Zembla are wholly fictitious. Ultimately, of course, there is no intrinsic reason to assume that Zembla is any less real than New Wye (or Jefferson, Mississippi). Because *Pale Fire* is a great work of art, every approach is instructive; here, as elsewhere, ambiguity is to be enjoyed. Even the bare chessboards are not to be abandoned; it is possible, however improbable, that the thematic bond, the web of correlation between poem and notes exists wholly through coincidence, that Kinbote really does not understand what the poem is about and is only attempting precisely what he says: "to sort out those echoes and wavelets of fire, and pale phosphorescent hints" (p. 210) of Zembla. To deny such a possibility is to ignore an important part of the truth Shade finds. But such an explanation is clearly a limited view.

Andrew Field is the principal spokesman for what is apparently the dominant critical perspective: "the primary author . . . must be John Shade." This is a distinct possibility, but Field's arguments are specious. He reads the book as an "allegorical portrait of 'the literary process'": Kinbote represents Shade's muse (the unharnessed imagination, "the 'outward extension' of insanity") and his creation (the "huge moon" circling "the pale and staid planet"). This is unnecessarily reductive. The commentary blazes with imagination, vivid language, "strong and strange poetry" (p. 149), fantastic and moving scenes. In Field's allegorical view, the artistic process becomes one of taming the madness, subduing the imaginative vision into often mediocre suburban verse. If Shade is the controlling author—and is thus capable of the rich texture of Zembla—then it is unclear why he would write the inferior poem. There is, of course, the answer that the poem is deliberately inferior, but this blurs Shade with Nabokov in a way that does not seem valuable. Field's theory, that Shade is central to both poem and notes, depends upon such observations as this: "that Shade is the intended victim is made evident by the perfect synchronization of Gradus' advance on him." But he fails to account for the fact that it is Kinbote who *arranges* this synchronization and to explain what he thinks this means. In fact, Field's refutation of the idea of Kinbote as primary author seems wholly unconvincing:

> There are many compellingly logical reasons to place John Shade before Charles Kinbote. A sane man may invent an insane character, and we call him an artist; an insane man who invents a perfectly sane character is also an artist, but *ipso facto* no longer insane in the way that Kinbote is. What sort of an Alice would the Mad Hatter make for us?

But Field has perhaps concluded too hastily "the way that Kinbote is" insane; he fails to recognize that the Mad Hatter may be most interesting if he is only dissembling madness. Field understands **The Eye** as a "narrative in which it is unclear whether the narrator is an uncontrolled neurotic or a fantastically clever artist *pretending* to be that neurotic."[9] Surely such a reading is equally possible here.

It is useful to compare Kinbote to the hero of **Despair.** In that novel, Hermann Karlovich meets a tramp who appears to resemble him perfectly, and the likeness becomes for him an obsessive symbol of his superior vision; he murders the tramp and assumes his identity, to fix the likeness permanently. Unfortunately, his attempt fails completely, because, as it turns out, the resemblance is apparent only to Hermann. Trapped in the solipsist's prison of mirrors, he writes **Despair** to justify his vision, to demonstrate the artistry of his scheme to an insensitive world. This is, of course, ironic; he convinces no one. But, paradoxically, the comic record of his failure achieves precisely what the murder could not; it fixes Hermann's imaginative construction, gives it authenticity through form. His book rescues him from "the hollow hum of blank eternity" whether or not he *intends* it as a second, separate attempt to gain the immortality of art. Charles Kinbote resembles Hermann in interesting ways: they are both obsessed with mirrors, they both disguise themselves in thick brown beards, they both argue with the paranoia and conviction of madmen. But they share much deeper affinities: despite Kinbote's far superior imaginative capabilities, it is possible to read his book in much the same terms as Hermann's, to see him as the controlling author, without blurring the distinction between him and Nabokov.

A professor of Russian named Botkin[10] (who is mentioned only fleetingly in the novel) "deliberately peels off a drab and unhappy past and replaces it with a brilliant invention" (p. 169), a series of adventures concerning a mysterious country named Zembla and its exiled king. But his imaginative construct is, like Hermann's, too imaginative, too absorbing, and New Wye dismisses him as a madman. His only sympathetic ear is his neighbor and "fellow poet" (p. 169), John Shade, to whom he relates the adventures in extensive detail, carefully hiding "an ultimate truth, an extraordinary secret" (p. 153): that he thinks he is the exiled King Charles himself. His rambles with Shade are selfishly motivated; he is obsessed by "the utter degradation, ridicule, and horror of having developed an infinity of sensation and thought within a finite existence" (**SM,** p. 297), and since he does not consider himself a true artist, the only way he can assure the immortality of "the dazzling Zembla burning in my brain" (p. 58) is to persuade Shade to recreate it in a poem, to fix it in aesthetic form. "Once transmuted by you, the stuff *will* be true, and the people *will* come alive" (p. 153). When he discovers that Shade is writing a long poem, he assumes that he is "reassembling my Zembla" (p. 184).

The poet is murdered, and Botkin discovers that "treacherous old Shade" (p. 192) has written a poem that does not seem to be about Zembla at all. It requires a commentary "to sort out those echoes and wavelets of fire, and pale phosphorescent hints, and all the many subliminal debts to me" (p. 210). And to write this commentary, Botkin invents for himself a third identity, that of Charles Kinbote; like Hermann's crime, Botkin's first attempt at artistry fails, but his second effort succeeds magnificently. The poem *is* in fact about Zembla (the mirror realm of resemblance and deception); it is because Botkin/Kinbote "can do what only a true artist can do—pounce upon the forgotten butterfly of revelation, wean myself abruptly from the habit of things, see the web of the world, and the warp and the weft of that web" (p. 204) that the poem and commentary merge to form "the monstrous semblance of a novel" (p. 62).

The possibility must be granted that Botkin is really a mad solipsist crashing against the mirrors of his cell, that he writes the commentary solely

> to make people calmly see—without having them immediately scream and hustle me—the truth of the tragedy—a tragedy in which I had been not a "chance witness" but the protagonist, and the main, if only potential, victim,
>
> (p. 211)

that all the subtle connections beneath the surface exist accidentally, in spite of his failure to understand the poem. To deny this possibility would be a serious violation of the novel's themes. There is certainly considerable evidence that Botkin is mad, perhaps even confined in an asylum. But, as always, the reader is wholly at the mercy of the narrator, and there is good reason for seeing Botkin as a rational, conscious artist. He frequently emphasizes the design of the notes: "I have staggered the notes referring to him" (p. 109), "the orderly course of these comments" (p. 111). His concept of God is strikingly similar to Shade's idea of the omnipotent artist: "somehow Mind is involved as a main factor in the making of the universe" (p. 162). Masterful control is suggested by the gradual revelation of levels of meaning. Primarily, of course, Botkin *does* seem to have understood the poem and mirrored its patterns and concerns in his notes.

What tips the scales in favor of choice over chance, finally, is the role of Gradus in the novel. Botkin's desire is to demonstrate the ascendency of order over disorder by fixing his imaginative vision into the immortality of art. But even after he has woven an amazingly complex web of correspondences that demonstrate that the subject of Shade's poem *is* "wild, misty, almost legendary Zembla" (p. 180), the accidental murder of Shade by a madman would certainly thwart that desire. The only way Botkin can "plunge back into his chaos and drag out of it, with all its wet stars, his cosmos" (p. 184) is by making Shade's death a part of that pattern. And by creating the character of Gradus he does precisely that, conjugates the Shadows of Zembla with Shade of New Wye, correlates the method of Gradus's advance on Kinbote with Shade's composition, and asserts his control over that advance. Gradus is the shared fate of Shade and Kinbote; his inexorable progress "through the entire length of the poem" (p. 56) *and* the commentary weaves through the fabric of the book a clear, ordered pattern, and makes "the whole involuted, boggling thing one beautiful straight line" (p. 185).

This is only one possible way to read **Pale Fire**. Any discussion of the question of a controlling author must recognize the possibility of every degree of artistic duplicity, up to and including Nabokov's own: Botkin mad, Botkin giving the illusion of madness, Shade giving the illusion of Botkin mad, and so on. Any attempt to fix a schematic reading of the novel to the exclusion of others must be reductive; it is the range of simultaneous possibilities, in which the reader must perceive significant patterns, that gives **Pale Fire** its rich texture of meaning. Ultimately, of course, in such a web of possibilities all distinctions dissolve; the "master thumb" of Nabokov is seen most clearly in the way Shade and Kinbote seem to merge. **Pale Fire** is finally a fiction, and the existence of Shade and Kinbote is, of course, an imaginative one; indeed, their "reality" is explicitly identified with that of the text: "my left hand still holding the poem, still clutching the inviolable shade'" (p. 207), "My notes and self are petering out" (p. 212), "My work is finished. My poet is dead" (p.

212). This does not resolve the ambiguities of the novel, but it encloses them in a system whose controlling author is, clearly, achieving his effects through deliberate artistic choice.[11] This, then, is the final remove, the one bottom which is not false, and it is here that the novel finds clearest expression of its moral truth: artistic perception and design can transcend human fortunes and misfortunes; chaos can be ordered by transforming the world into significant aesthetic form. Perhaps Nabokov would not subscribe to such an unambiguous reading of his most complex and labyrinthine novel, but, for better or worse, it is the commentator who has the last word.

Notes

1. Vladimir Nabokov, *Lolita* (New York: Putnam, 1955), pp. 316-17.

2. Vladimir Nabokov, *Speak, Memory* (New York Putnam, 1966), pp. 124-25. Subsequent references are to this edition and are included in the text, identified *SM*.

3. Alfred Appel, Jr., "An Interview with Vladimir Nabokov," in *Nabokov: The Man and His Work,* ed. L. S. Dembo (Madison: Univ. of Wisconsin Press, 1967), p. 37.

4. Vladimir Nabokov, *Invitation to a Beheading* (New York Putnam, 1959), pp. 135-36.

5. Vladimir Nabokov, *Pale Fire* (New York: Berkley paperback, 1968), p. 62. Subsequent references are to this edition and are included in the text.

6. See Phyllis A. Roth's excellent "The Psychology of the Double in Nabokov's *Pale Fire," Essays in Literature,* 2 (1975), 209-29, which I read in manuscript after completing my article. Of particular interest is her treatment of the relationship between Kinbote and Gradus ("a parody of the punishing double"). Although her psychological approach is quite different from my interest in structure and pattern, we move toward many of the same conclusions.

7. Vladimir Nabokov, "Signs and Symbols," in *Nabokov's Dozen* (New York: Doubleday, 1958), p. 70.

8. Vladimir Nabokov, *Ada* (New York: McGraw-Hill, 1969), p. 383.

9. Andrew Field, *Nabokov: His Life in Art* (Boston: Little, Brown, 1967), pp. 300, 317, 307, 316, 303, 317, 210.

10. *"Botken, -kin,* obs. forms of BODKIN. . . ." *"Bodkin. . . . 6. transf. (colloq.)* A person wedged in between two others where there is proper room for two only" *(OED).*

11. See R. H. W. Dillard's important "Not Text, But Texture: The Novels of Vladimir Nabokov," in

The Sounder Few, ed. R. H. W. Dillard, George Garrett, and John Rees Moore (Athens: Univ. of Georgia Press, 1971), pp. 139-65.

Marilyn Edelstein (essay date 1982)

SOURCE: Edelstein, Marilyn. "*Pale Fire*: The Art of Consciousness." In *Nabokov's Fifth Arc: Nabokov and Others on His Life's Work,* edited by J. E. Rivers and Charles Nicol, pp. 213-23. Austin: University of Texas Press, 1982.

[*In the following essay, Edelstein argues that in* Pale Fire *Nabokov constructs his characters, language, and plot in such a way as to force readers to participate in "the creation of sense and meaning."*]

Pale Fire is the supreme manifestation of the indivisibility of style and meaning in the work of Vladimir Nabokov. The novel's narrative consciousness, plot, and structure, as well as its ultimate significance, can only be discerned through the reader's own efforts; it thus becomes a paradigm of Roland Barthes's reader-created text. Critics uniformly recognize the playfulness of Nabokov's technique; few recognize the aesthetic and philosophical purpose of such literary sleight-of-hand. By placing the fictional process in the foreground of a novel, where the narrative human presence once was, Nabokov forces the reader to examine the similarity between fictional creation and self-creation.

In *Pale Fire* we are presented a poem with a critical commentary, including foreword and index. The poem was written by a homely American poet named John Shade, in largely autobiographical style. The commentary, we soon discover, is largely autobiographical too, with the "auto-" in this case somewhat harder to identify, ostensibly being one Charles Kinbote, who in reality is the exiled King Charles of Zembla, but who might also be V. Botkin, American scholar of Russian descent. Whoever the author of the commentary may be, on the very first page of the foreword the reader realizes that his work is not going to be an objective apparatus criticus. Kinbote is too personal, too anecdotal, and too absurd to be believed as a scholar. He constructs a complicated scenario for the events leading to Shade's demise, an almost paranoid plot that revolves around King Charles's overthrow in his kingdom of Zembla, a hired assassin named Jakob Gradus, and the murder of Shade—either as accidental victim of Gradus, out to kill King Charles (incognito in America as Charles Kinbote); or as accidental victim of Jack Grey, out for revenge on Judge Goldsworth, who sentenced Grey to the Institute for the Criminally Insane and whose house Kinbote is subletting. Soon one realizes that an integral component of the novel is this very confusion and multiplicity of plot, character, reality.

Pale Fire is concerned with "how each individual mind filters reality, recreates it."[1] We see the different patterns of sense that can be created out of the same set of events by different minds. Nabokov is aware of the reductionism necessary for people to perceive order in a chaotic world and of the further reductionism implicit in linguistic formulations of experience. Nabokov believes that seeing one static reality, perceiving facts without imagination, is like death (and like Gradus). Why should fictional characters be static and easily differentiable when life itself is not? Patterns of sense are personal creations, not universal givens. Nabokov constantly tricks the reader into believing in one possible interpretation of the facts, only to throw all "facts" into doubt, showing thereby that only individually created realities are possible. Nabokov constantly enters *Pale Fire* (with, for instance, his self-reflecting references to Hurricane Lolita, an émigré professor of Russian, and butterflies). These intrusions of the author's personality reinforce the artificiality of the fiction by emphasizing its maker's constant presence. They also stress that there is one undeniable human presence in the novel: the author himself. His is the controlling, unifying consciousness, and in that functional sense Nabokov's is the ultimate self of this book.

Each of the three main characters—Shade, Kinbote, and Gradus—can be seen as constituting one aspect of a whole human self. Gradus is the least conscious character. He can be seen as the repressed shadow of Shade, as the dark aspect of the unconscious, and, most importantly, as the darkness of death against which the artist struggles. He is almost a mechanical man, endowed with a sense of purpose (as assister of the plot) and little else. He is simply a killing device, a fictional tool; since he has no imagination, he cannot be a man in the Nabokovian schema. Charles Kinbote represents the solipsistic subjectivity of a not-quite-conscious self—like the surrealistic subconscious, where dreams, fantasy, and reality are indistinguishable. Yet he is also wildly imaginative, and thus creative, so he meets a basic Nabokovian criterion for humanity. Shade is objective and compassionate, as he presents himself in the poem and as he appears in Kinbote's commentary. He seems the most individuated and substantive character of the three. He is an artist, with the imaginative power to construct a reality and the awareness that reality *is* a construct: he is thus the most like his own author, Nabokov, and therefore the most like a man. Carol Williams has suggested that Shade, Kinbote, and Gradus are aspects of one whole artist who is centered in Shade.[2] Yet even he does not quite stand on his own as a fully developed fictional character or as the artistic equivalent of a fully realized human self. Shade's poem, the part of the book that manifests his identity, exists in the novel surrounded by the words of another man. Although critics point out that Shade's poem can stand alone, whereas Kinbote's commentary cannot, the fact remains that the poem *does not* stand alone. All the verbal elements in the book are interconnected in much the same way that the characters' identities are interlinked. Standing over all his inferior creations is the artificer-god Nabokov, playing a "game of worlds" with his creations.

One can clearly see the intermingling of the characters through an analysis of their respective names. "Gradus, Jakob, 1915-1959; alias Jack Degree, de Grey, d'Argus, Vinogradus, Leningradus, etc."[3] Bader tells us:

> Gradus in Latin means "step, *degree*." A *Gradus ad Parnassum* is a dictionary used as an aid in writing poetry, and literally means "a step to the place where the Muses live." "Shade" is defined by the dictionary as "shadow, *degree* of darkness; a disembodied spirit; to undergo and exhibit difference or variation." There is thus a specific connection between Gradus and Shade, and the suggestion that the two characters are aspects of a single consciousness—that Gradus is a creation of the poet, a degree of Shade, or a step in the structure. Gradus, who is repeatedly identified with the inevitable ending of the poem—indeed he arrives at the very last line—may be the final tool used by the poet to complete his work and arrive at Parnassus.[4]

Shade has also written a poem called "The Sacred Tree" which Disa, exiled queen of Zembla, has translated. *Grados* means "tree" in Zemblan. Kinbote says that Shade "shared with the English masters the noble knack of transplanting trees into verse with their sap and shade" (p. 93). Kinbote is actually the one who transplants Gradus into the poem, through synchronizing his approach with the poem's progress. There is therefore an element of godlike power—over life and death—in Gradus' purpose in the story. Through Kinbote's eyes, we see Gradus arrive at the poem's completion, and we see him complete the *process* of the poem's growth by destroying its creator. Perhaps Shade is made to die in order to show the necessity of at least attempting to outwit the tyranny of death through art, or perhaps death comes to him simply to display the absolute authority of the novel's ultimate god—Nabokov—over him. Although both Gradus (Sudarg of Bokay) and Nabokov make mirrors, Gradus is anti-life, anti-art, and he has the demonic power of unimaginative unconsciousness. Gradus awaits the end of Shade's artistic process just as death awaits the end of Nabokov's deceitful illuminations. Both Degree and Gradus, as process, as steps toward something, are appropriate names for a character whose very being is viewed by Kinbote as almost created by the processes of aesthetic motion (p. 78).

> We shall accompany Gradus in constant thought, as he makes his way from distant dim Zembla to green Appalachia [from Z to A, alphabetically], through the entire length of the poem, following the road of its rhythm, riding past in a rhyme, skidding around the corner of a run-on, breathing with the caesura, swinging down to the foot of the page from line to line as from branch to branch, hiding between two words . . . , reappearing on the horizon of a new canto, steadily marching nearer in iambic motion, crossing streets, moving up with his valise on the escalator of the pentameter, stepping off, boarding a new train of thought, entering the hall of a hotel, putting out the bedlight, while Shade blots out a word, and falling asleep as the poet lays down his pen for the night.

As Grey, Gradus not only represents the grayness of death, but also the gray of the printed page, where black and white combine. He is also a gray being, relatively unconscious, "endowed with a modicum of self-awareness (with which he did not know what to do), some duration consciousness, and a good memory for faces, names, dates, and the like. Spiritually he did not exist. Morally he was a dummy pursuing another dummy" (p. 278). Gradus exists in a barely human, preconscious state, where a creature can obtain faint sensual pleasure, of the sort appropriate to an "anticomedoist," from the extinction of a human life, from the murder of a fellow "dummy." He is a fiction destroying another fiction within a fiction, and he is a degree of the same shade that Shade is "most artistically caged" within—the netherworld of fictional existence, subject to the whims of its creator.

"Shade" and its related words, "umbra" "ombre," and "shadow," have various connotations relevant to this discussion. An "umbra" is a ghost, a phantom, a shadow, a vestige. A shadow can be a reflected image, or one who tags along with another, or watches closely in a secret manner—much as Kinbote shadows (maintains surveillance on) Shade through his window. "Shade" itself is partial or relative darkness caused by the intervention of an opaque body between the space contemplated and the source of light: absence of complete illumination. Shade is not fully conscious, not fully illuminated, not totally aware of himself. Opacity is Cincinnatus C.'s "crime" in Nabokov's *Invitation to a Beheading,* since in his terrifyingly absurd society to be normal is to be transparent and without a self. Shade seeks self-knowledge, but he also seeks freedom from the dark knowledge of death. Though his imperfect creation of flesh—Hazel—dies, his beautiful linguistic creation will live on beyond even his own mortal existence. An "ombre" is a European *gray*ling, demonstrating yet another connection between Shade and Jack Grey/Gradus. The grayling called "ombre" is a type of fish; but "grayling" can also denote a butterfly of the family Satyridae, thus hinting at the controlling presence of Nabokov. "Ombre" is also a three-handed card game and the player in this game who elects to name the trump and oppose the other two players. There is certainly a three-handed game going on here, either with Shade calling the trump (in the sense of creating the aesthetic playing field), or with Nabokov calling the trump on all three of his characters. Shade is the closest thing we have to *un hombre*—a man—in the novel; we know far more about him *as* a man, through his poem and through the poem's distorted reflection in Kinbote's commentary, than we do about the other characters.

Kinbote/Botkin/King Charles is another multi-faceted character. The "-bote" in "Kinbote" seems to derive partly from the word "bot" or "botfly"—a parasite which lives in mammals. Shade's wife calls Kinbote "the monstrous parasite of a genius" (p. 172). A "kinbote" is also a bote given by a homicide to the kin of his victim—a bote being a compensation paid for a wrong done. This definition has intriguing implications, insofar as it appears to be a clue to Kinbote's contribution to Shade's death and to the subsequent "murder" of Shade's poem through the self-aggrandizing commentary. Gradus, Shade's shadow, has indirectly allowed Kinbote to acquire Shade's poem. Kinbote is thus compensated for the loss of a friend and potential Karlist court poet through his possession of Shade's poem and through his creation of a new hybrid literary entity from his friend's life and his own real or imagined life. Kinbote discusses suicide and speaks of "a bare botkin (note the correct spelling)" (p. 220). Apart from the intended meaning of a sharp dagger, there is "bodkin," the alternate spelling, which means a person wedged in between two others where there is proper room for only two. Kinbote attempts to wedge himself between Shade and Gradus' bullets; metaphorically, Kinbote's commentary stands between the created object and destruction. Kinbote lives somewhere between Nabokov, master-creator, and Shade, apprentice-creator. The story of Shade, Zembla, and King Charles is conveyed through Kinbote's eyes, filtered through his intermediary vision. A "bot," in addition to being a parasite, is an inveterate borrower or cadger, a sponger. Kinbote shines with the reflected glory of Shade's light through his own commentary, although Shade's poem is actually "pale and diaphanous" in imaginative power compared to Kinbote's story of Zembla. Kinbote is aware of "borrowing a kind of opalescent light from my poet's fiery orb" (p. 81). The relationship between Shade and Kinbote is more symbiotic than parasitic, suggesting once again that they are really facets of one *ur*-personality: Shade is orderly, rational, sublime; Kinbote is imaginative (to excess), fantastic, Dionysiac. Kinbote's commentary can be seen as the dark underside of the poem, just as Kinbote may be the dark underside of Shade. "Kinbote" also means regicide in Zemblan, which links Kinbote to Gradus. Of course, Gradus, as death and unconsciousness, awaits the madman as well as the poet.

There is also a set of surface connections among the three characters. All three have the same birthday (the day Nabokov—their artistic daddy—began the work). Shade and Kinbote both lost their fathers at the age of three, and neither boy knew his father (do characters ever really *know* their author?). And all three characters die at the end: Shade is shot by Gradus; Gradus takes his own life with a rusty razor; and, as Nabokov says in an interview, Kinbote commits suicide, too.[5] Kinbote knows: "My notes and self are petering out" (p. 300). They would necessarily end simultaneously, for even if Kinbote had not committed suicide, he would "die" at the end of the novel the same way he was "born" at its inception. His fictional self is only viable as long as his presence is aesthetically necessary. Aesthetic life, we are reminded, is artificial and at the whim of the author. The remark also seems to equate Kinbote's notes with his selfhood, and his selfhood with his writing and that of Nabokov. In fact, Kinbote and the other characters all exist merely as a series of written signs on paper.

We thus see each individual character as composite: Kinbote is also King Charles and Botkin the scholar; Shade looks like Samuel Johnson and an old hag who works in a cafeteria and Judge Goldsworth; Gradus is also Jack Grey, Jacques d'Argus, a Shadow, and a glassmaker.

The sense in which we should perceive these similarities and other "links and bobolinks" in the tale is rendered in a comment by Kinbote. He is considering the similarity between Shade's portrait of a younger Sybil and his own young Queen Disa; it seems a "strangeness" without whose full comprehension "there is no sense in writing poems, or notes to poems, or anything at all" (p. 207). One must perceive the integral relationship of events and people within the microcosmic world of the novel to understand the fundamental artifice of both nature and art. As Kinbote also says, "'reality' is neither the subject nor the object of true art which creates its own special reality having nothing to do with the average 'reality' perceived by the communal eye" (p. 130). Nabokov strips away layer after layer of reality, and beneath them all reside magic and artifice.

Even the title of the novel has multiple layers of meaning and importance. Though Kinbote fails to locate the phrase "pale fire" in his only volume of Shakespeare ("having no library in his Timonian cave," index, p. 308), and though he says that it would have been a "statistical monster" (p. 285) if the allusion *had* been in *Timon of Athens,* it is, indeed, there, in lines he quotes in a distorted and incomplete re-Englishing of a Zemblan translation. Such possibilities do come true in the world of **Pale Fire**: the "monstrous semblance of a novel" (p. 86) is actualized, and this staggering coincidence confirms the possibility of patterns in a chaotic world. The passage from *Timon* (in act 4, scene 3) describes the infinite reflection of objects upon each other, and implies that the borrowing of light and life is a cyclical process and a sign of interdependence:

> The sun's a thief, and with his great attraction
> Robs the vast sea: the moon's an arrant thief,
> And her pale fire she snatches from the sun:

The sea's a thief, whose liquid surge resolves
The moon into salt tears: the earth's a thief,
That feeds and breeds by a composture stolen
From general excrement: each thing's a thief. . . .

Timon of Athens is considered by some scholars to be unfinished and botched by a later hand. And we are told repeatedly, in the foreword and in the commentary, of various efforts by critics, editors, and even Shade's widow to extricate the poem from Kinbote's possession, lest it be botched by his hand. Ironically, the poem itself is left intact by Kinbote; he merely appends his wildly imaginative commentary to it. Some scholars regard Shakespeare's *Timon* as an incomplete rough draft, just as Shade's poem is regarded as an incomplete rough draft by its other potential editors and commentators, as Kinbote tells us in the foreword.[6] Still other critics think *Timon* was a rough draft for *King Lear,* just as Kinbote thinks **"Pale Fire"** a rough draft of the epic *Solus Rex* (itself an epic Nabokov once began). *Timon* falls naturally into two halves—the part before Timon's fall and the part after it; *Pale Fire* is essentially divided into the part written before Shade's death, by Shade, and the part written after his death, by Kinbote. Timon does not arrive at self-knowledge as Lear does; even at the end of the play he does not really know himself. Kinbote does not know himself either, and Shade has only partial self-knowledge. Furthermore, *Timon of Athens* may be a work that to some extent reveals Shakespeare's artistic *process,* since it is possibly a rough draft. And the artistic process is certainly a central concern in **Pale Fire.**

Analysis of **Pale Fire** which stops at the elucidation of the tricks and games and allusions within the novel is superficial, although not as fruitless as it might be with an author who, unlike Nabokov, does not place language in the foreground. The essential point about Nabokov's playful authorial omnipotence is that the trickery serves a function beyond mere aesthetic pleasure. Nabokov's incredibly rich use of language, his tricks of plot, his games with characterization, style, and structure act upon the reader. We are allowed to watch consciousness in action—the consciousness of two artists and a mad creative genius (Shade, Nabokov, and Kinbote, respectively) in the process of creating, and the consciousnesses of various "human" selves in the process of being created. The patterning that Shade seeks in life we discover in the book—but we must at least help to create it. The carpet may sometimes be pulled out from under us as it is pulled out from under Shade for a moment in the mountain/fountain episode. But such toppling of expectation is a medium for a message about the nature of reality. Since deception is an integral part of nature (as with Nabokov's beloved mimetic butterflies, who masquerade as bark), a writer who points out the deceptive potential of the world is doing the reader a service. If one adheres to a single

version of reality, one runs the risk of being gravely misled. Nabokov demonstrates how different patterns are produced by different minds—Kinbote's, Shade's, Gradus', Nabokov's, each reader's—even when viewing the same events. This interplay of patterns, of processes of creation, of "webs of sense," shows that there is no one overriding pattern to be discerned; we must each create our own pattern, using our own imaginative consciousness. Awareness of the power of deception is necessary to understand this fluidity of reality; being allowed to watch the characters in the novel as they attempt to bring order out of chaos is also an important aid. Nabokov tricks us into believing temporarily in many different versions of reality and thus forces us to revise our perceptions, our presuppositions about fiction, reality, and language. To do this he must present a fiction which does not allow complacent reading and happy identification with safely human, substantive characters. Nabokov "assumes that the proper goal of an artist is to create timelessness; the realists err in thinking that they should recreate time by imitating real, or at least plausible actions."[7] He has said:

> A creative writer must study carefully the works of his rivals, including the Almighty. He must possess the inborn capacity not only of recombining but of recreating the given world. In order to do this adequately, avoiding duplication of labor, the artist should *know* the given world. . . . Art is never simple. . . . Art at its greatest is fantastically deceitful and complex.

> The fake move in a chess problem, the illusion of a solution or the conjuror's magic: I used to be a little conjuror when I was a boy. I loved doing simple tricks—turning water into wine, that kind of thing [he has said elsewhere that "Vladimir" rhymes with "redeemer"]; but I think I'm in good company because all art is deception and so is nature; all is deception in that good cheat, from the insect that mimics a leaf to the popular enticements of procreation.[8]

As long as reality is a question of perception and interpretation by its beholder, deception will be possible. Some think of art as creating a static reality; Nabokov seems to think of it as an ongoing process that engages the reader in a revelatory hermeneutical event.

John Shade is the only character in **Pale Fire** conscious of the Nabokovian tenet that we each devise our own reality; thus, he is the most conscious character, and the artist figure in the novel. Shade learns that we cannot look to outside sources for the "correlated pattern"; if we do, we are tricked into mistaking "humdrummery" for reality. But Shade, in spite of all his attempts at creation of a perceptible pattern, is still at the mercy of his aesthetic captor/creator, Nabokov. Shade at least is aware that he is "artistically caged," and, as a practicing poet, he is of all the characters the most conscious of the power of art and artifice to shape reality. Reality, even if only *a* reality, is formed in the process of transmutation from event to word. The dark abyss of death and of meaninglessness (as manifested by Gradus) surrounds the attempt to achieve full consciousness; but the products of that attempt survive. "Dead is the mandible, alive the song" (p. 42). The instrument through which poetry passes is mortal; the poem is not. Shade converts life into art: he makes the rooms in which he, his wife, and his daughter sit into "a tryptich [*sic*] or a three-act play / In which portrayed events forever stay" (p. 46). Shade wants to carry the fruits of human consciousness with him into whatever lies beyond this life, a desire Nabokov has often expressed. Since Shade is an artist, he is aware, as is Nabokov, of the power of imagination to make, or remake, a world. Yet, as F. W. Dupee has pointed out, "In *Pale Fire,* as so often in our author's work, it takes two men to make a proper Nabokovian man—two men who, however, rarely succeed in uniting."[9] Kinbote has the disordered power of pure imagination; this is necessary to the artist, but it must be tempered by insight, order, and lucid detachment, which Shade possesses. Together, Kinbote and Shade possess elements of the artist as Nabokov conceives, creates, and embodies him. Gradus lurks as the power of death, demonic unconsciousness, anti-imagination. Ironically, when Shade completes the poem, it does not fall into the hands of a dispassionate critic but into the hands of a fantasy-ridden, creative genius. But the mad genius and the sensitive poet are both dispensed with when Nabokov no longer needs them in his aesthetic process.

When Shade asks Kinbote how Kinbote can know intimate details about King Charles and how these details can be printed if they are true, Kinbote says, "Once transmuted by you into poetry, the stuff *will* be true, and the people *will* come alive" (p. 214). This statement seems applicable to the question of who is who, or who is "real" in the novel. It is ultimately irrelevant if "in fact" Kinbote has produced Shade and Zembla, as Stegner thinks, or if Shade has produced Kinbote and the rest, as Bader and Field think, or if any other possible permutation of the combinations might be "true."[10] Within the fiction, the characters are equally real, and they all only exist in words. If art and imagination are as real as facts in Nabokov's world, then these characters are also real. The characters' intermingling and interdependence are intentional, and the characters are definitely aesthetic tools of the author, made to combine and recombine for an aesthetic purpose. Nabokov created all of them, and he created them purposely to be difficult to differentiate.

Pale Fire is an assault on our "brutish routine acceptance" of the "miracle of a few written signs being able to contain immortal imagery, involutions of thought, new worlds with live people, speaking, weeping, laughing" (p. 289). Nabokov creates fragmented or schizophrenic narrators and characters precisely to inhibit an unthinking identification with the people of the book, thereby forcing the reader to grapple with the epistemological complexities of life. The idea of linear, discursive language and plot, of cause and effect, the whole set of Cartesian presuppositions that are the unconscious baggage of most of us are bombarded with refutation after refutation, in favor of a vision of correlations, patterns, and rhythms which each reader must discern for himself or herself. The novel makes the reader into an artist, an active participant in the creation of sense and meaning. Just as *Finnegans Wake* uses "verbal pyrotechnics" as part of a thematic purpose—breaking down barriers between unconscious and conscious, between illusion and reality, and ultimately between individual and individual—so *Pale Fire's* amazing articulateness is part of an aesthetic reordering and re-creation of reality through artifice. Both books make claims on the reader's consciousness and imagination, and both books are, finally, consciousness-expanding or consciousness-altering fictions. From notes rejected when writing *Pale Fire,* Nabokov reads: "Time without consciousness—lower animal world; time with consciousness—man; consciousness without time—some still higher state."[11] It may be this higher state that the fragmented self in *Pale Fire* attempts to find in the timeless, fluid realm of imagination.

Notes

1. Robert Alter, *Partial Magic,* p. 215.

2. Carol T. Williams, "'Web of Sense': *Pale Fire* in the Nabokov Canon," *Critique* 6 (1963-1964), 29-45.

3. Nabokov, *Pale Fire,* p. 307. Hereafter cited in text.

4. Julia Bader, *Crystal Land,* p. 34.

5. Nabokov, *Strong Opinions,* p. 74.

6. There is, however, a reference to Shade's poem "The Nature of Electricity" (p. 192), wherein he refers to his fondness for the number 999 (the number of lines in "Pale Fire" as it stands), so there is some likelihood that the poem is after all complete. Even Kinbote thinks the poem is missing line 1000, which he believes was to be a repeat of the first line—a nice cyclical touch. Of course, Nabokov prefers spirals, with their openendedness, to closed circles.

7. John O. Stark, *The Literature of Exhaustion,* p. 90.

8. Nabokov, *Strong Opinions,* pp. 32-33, 11.

9. F. W. Dupee, *The King of the Cats and Other Remarks on Writers and Writing,* p. 141.

10. Page Stegner, *Escape into Aesthetics,* pp. 129-30; Bader, *Crystal Land,* p. 35; Andrew Field, *Nabokov: His Life in Art,* pp. 316-17.

11. Nabokov, *Strong Opinions,* p. 30.

Bibliography

PRIMARY SOURCES

Invitation to a Beheading (novel: English translation by Nabokov and Dmitri Nabokov of *Priglashenie na kazn'*). New York: Putnam's, 1959.

Pale Fire (novel). New York: Putnam's, 1962.

Strong Opinions (occasional prose). New York: McGraw-Hill, 1973.

SECONDARY SOURCES

Alter, Robert. *Partial Magic: The Novel as a Self-Conscious Genre.* Berkeley: University of California Press, 1975.

Bader, Julia. *Crystal Land: Artifice in Nabokov's English Novels.* Berkeley: University of California Press, 1972.

Dupee, F. W. *The King of the Cats and Other Remarks on Writers and Writing.* New York: Farrar, 1965.

Field, Andrew. *Nabokov: His Life in Art.* Boston: Little, 1967.

Stark, John O. *The Literature of Exhaustion: Borges, Nabokov, Barth.* Durham: Duke University Press, 1974.

Stegner, Page. *Escape into Aesthetics: The Art of Vladimir Nabokov.* New York: Dial, 1966.

Williams, Carol T. "'Web of Sense': *Pale Fire* in the Nabokov Canon." *Critique* 6 (1963-1964), 29-45.

Austin M. Wright (essay date 1982)

SOURCE: Wright, Austin M. "Creative Plot: *Pale Fire.*" In *The Formal Principle in the Novel,* pp. 260-87. Ithaca, N.Y.: Cornell University Press, 1982.

[*In the following essay, Wright explores the narrative structure, complex characterization, and riddles, secrets, and jokes in* Pale Fire, *contending that these devices all contribute to the challenge of reading and interpreting Nabokov's novel.*]

Two problems make Vladimir Nabokov's **Pale Fire** a challenge to the formal critic. One is its unorthodox narrative structure. At first glance there seems to be no narrative at all: instead, a poem (999 lines long, in heroic couplets), and a much longer commentary, the whole preceded by a foreword and followed by an index. What, we may ask, is novelistic about a structure like this, and how can we talk about a plot?

Since both the poet, John Shade, and the commentator, Charles Kinbote, are fictitious, the method suggests parody—possibly of two kinds: parody of a poem and parody of the scholarly enterprise. The reader quickly discovers, however, that parody is only part of the whole. The lives of both poet and commentator are developed, partly in the poem and at greater length in the commentary, and this development makes the work into a novel. It is a peculiar one. Not only are the characters and action embedded in the literary enterprise of poem and commentary, they emerge in an organization calculatedly designed, it would seem, to do away with the sequential arrangement of plot. In an arrangement of poem and commentary, the two parts are usually intimately dovetailed. We would, as we read the poem, pick up the notes as we go along. If we do read **Pale Fire** in this way, its plot is organized by a backtracking process in which the two big sections are read together—simultaneously. The idea is supported by the numerous cross-references which, if followed, would lead us through a still more complex weave, back and forth, in and out and around, with frequent returns, as we work our way gradually through the text. The whole picture is complicated still more by the astonishing suggestion in the foreword that the reader would do best to "consult them [these notes] first and then study the poem with their help."[1]

As it turns out, the reader's movement isn't nearly so back and forth as my description suggests. Most of the notes in the commentary, except the short ones, relate only very loosely to the poem. Kinbote has his own stories to tell, and he seizes upon any excuse to tell them. Many of the cross-references are to minor connections: they serve the parody and the characterization of Kinbote rather than the actual process of reading. Others become meaningful only on second reading. The natural way to read this text is in its order of presentation, after all—foreword, poem, commentary, index. The organization of these four parts is an order that is *not* interchangeable. The cross-references—notes to poem and notes to notes—make connections explicit, but though every reader will often want to check them, I do not think they reorganize the text or dictate a specific change in the order of reading. They call explicit attention, rather, to links of a kind which exist in all novels and which readers discover, generally, in no determined order.[2]

The progression of the novel is carried by several distinguishable sequences, some implied at the start, others with origins in the poem or the commentary. All are developed in the commentary, intertwined or interwoven with each other, through the so-called notes, many of which are really narrative segments, often quite long. Part of the brilliance of the novel depends on this interweaving, the contrasts and juxtapositions such a method gives rise to, not to speak of the rich range of interests brought together. The formal problem consists, then, in relating these sequences to each other by some unifying principle.

The second formal challenge in *Pale Fire* concerns the nature of the commentator, Charles Kinbote himself. How do we interpret his claim to be the exiled King of Zembla—a "distant northern land," somewhere near Finland, perhaps—in disguise? The claim is central in his commentary; he lives by it and had hoped Shade's poem would be about it. Since the poem is not about it, he has filled his commentary with his claim. The description of his life as King and his escape from the revolution is concrete and circumstantial. If it seems extraordinary that such a figure should end up on the faculty of Wordsmith College in New Wye, state of Appalachia, there is at any rate an explanation for everything—the college trustee with an interest in Zembla; the long-standing literary and pedagogical interests of the King. If Zembla itself seems fanciful, its reality is recognized at Wordsmith: Professor Nattochdag teaches Zemblan there; the Faculty discusses Zembla at the Faculty Club, and one faculty member insists on the close resemblance of Kinbote to the exiled King. Finally, there is Gradus, who comes out of Zembla to kill him but misses and kills Shade instead.

Critics are almost unanimously agreed, however, that Kinbote is mad and the whole story of his kingship is a fabrication. There are good reasons for this judgment—hints that grow strongest toward the end of the book. We know from the start that many of the faculty at Wordsmith consider him a madman. Near the end there is Shade's overheard remark to Mrs. Hurley: "One should not apply it [the word loony] to a person who deliberately peels off a drab and unhappy past and replaces it with a brilliant invention" (p. 238). Though another explanation is offered, the reader cannot avoid concluding that it is a reference to Kinbote. Again, there is the way in which all the witnesses to the activities of the killer are permitted to adjust their stories to make Gradus seem to be really only Jack Grey from the local Institute for the Criminal Insane, who has mistaken Shade for Judge Goldsworth, owner of the house Kinbote was occupying. Even Kinbote himself, when speaking of possible future incognitos at the end, describes a play he might write, about "a lunatic who intends to kill an imaginary king, another lunatic who imagines himself to be that king, and a distinguished old poet who stumbles by chance into the line of fire, and perishes in the clash between the two figments" (p. 301). The name Zembla, he tells us, "is a corruption . . . of Semblerland, a land of reflections, of 'resemblers'" (p. 265); he refers to his story as a "kind of *romaunt*" displaying a "rich streak of magical madness." Most critics have accepted Mary McCarthy's suggestion that Kinbote is really V. Botkin, "American scholar of Russian descent," mentioned only in the index, and that Zembla is a purely fantasy land. Some

have concluded also that Kinbote is writing his commentary not in a trailer camp, as he says, but in an asylum, and even that the commentary is addressed to a doctor.[3]

Yet there are difficulties with these ideas, as we shall see. By no means should we allow ourselves to assume at the start that Kinbote's story of the King is necessarily any less "real" or more "imaginary" than, say, the story of Shade's life or of Kinbote's own during his stay at Wordsmith College in Judge Goldsworth's house. We start with an ambiguity on this point. Our analysis of the plot will have to deal with this ambiguity; the efficacy of the hypothesis will depend to some extent on how well it does so.

Besides the formal problems, *Pale Fire* presents another challenge which for many readers comes first. This is the challenge of details, involving the accurate perception of the parts without regard to the whole they form. We are challenged by the trickiness and game playing that characterize Nabokov's manner and the special erudition he brings to it. The text is full of buried secrets, jokes, traps, riddles. (A good example is the concealment of the source of the title by a misquotation from *Timon of Athens*.)[4] This aspect has given critics for the last nineteen years much work to do. Unlike the riddles of *The Waste Land* or *Finnegans Wake*, however, those of *Pale Fire* do not obstruct a fairly well advanced perception of the form even at an early stage of perusal. The secrets in the text enhance the "progressing visibility of the form," not by heavily blocking the initial view, but by offering new subtleties for continued study. In our analysis of the plot we may assume that these challenges are on their way to being solved but will continue to reveal themselves.

There are other problems, too, in this problem-rich novel: the unreliability of the narrator, the judgment of Shade's poem, for instance. These will show up naturally as we try to analyze whatever the plot must be.

"Narrative in the form of commentary upon a poem" is the primary presentational commitment in *Pale Fire*. It offers a natural starting point for an analysis of the germinal principle. The work gives us two narratives and two narrators, one (John Shade's, the poem) contained within the other (Charles Kinbote's, the foreword, commentary, and index). It combines direct narrative and dramatic method: the former in the poem and many parts of the commentary; the latter in the display to the reader of poem against commentary: the reader can observe for himself the adequacy of the narrator's perception of the poem. The narrative becomes dramatic also when we perceive the various manifestations of Kinbote's unreliability as a narrator:[5] in his strained interpretation of events which invite more natural interpretations (for example, his failure to recognize that he is making a pest of himself with the Shades), in his displays of ignorance of matters familiar to any American reader (for example, that "Chapman's Homer" in an article about baseball would not refer to Keats's poem), in the recognizable language of his various obsessions, putting his narrative objectivity in doubt (the language of his homosexual obsession and of his paranoia, as, for example of the latter, this early warning, in the foreword: "she suddenly shot me a wire, requesting me to accept Prof. H(!) and Prof. C(!!) as co-editors of her husband's poem. How deeply this surprised and pained me! Naturally, it precluded collaboration with my friend's misguided widow" [p. 18]). His unreliability is associated in part with his parodic role as a pedant, his pedantic lack of sense of proportion and, for the rest, in his judgments of himself and others. In abstract matters such as psychiatry, Marxism, and to some extent art (in theory—though not, evidently, in practical criticism), he is probably trustworthy (that is, the implied author agrees with him), though less so than Shade.

Shade himself as narrator (in his poem) appears to be reliable—at least with regard to what he tells us and how he interprets it. His judgment of his own work may be shakier, since the poem, despite its good qualities, its clarity, readability, vividness, genuine emotion, and good sense, does ramble, does fall into triviality, does fall short of claims it makes for itself ("Now I shall spy on beauty as none has / Spied on it yet" [p. 64]. "Now I shall speak of evil as none has / Spoken before" [p. 67])—unless we are to read such claims not as Nabokov's mockery of Shade but as Shade's own self-mockery,[6] a distinct possibility, to be sure, for the poem is unquestionably self-mocking in many places. In most respects Shade provides a standard of skeptical, good-humored sanity that throws Kinbote's excesses into sharp relief.

We must also note briefly the other primary commitments which the germinal principle covers. The linguistic instrument in both the poem and Kinbote's prose is a flexible, informal, idiomatic, and often colloquial language, conversational in its quality. It is capable in both writers of strong narrative thrust and of vivid concrete descriptive imagery and metaphor. Kinbote's prose shows also some distinctive features: a caustic ironic wit; a tendency to overstate, using epithets and adjectives (as, for example, in the characterizations of Gradus as subhuman); a tendency to reiterate epithets ("my powerful car"); to exploit his obsessions until the reader recognizes them in the most minimal reminders; and in general to suggest innuendo and irony constantly at work. His language reflects an interest in language as such—in language sounds, as in the alpine scene with the gnarled farmer (a *grunter* [mountain farmer] whose name was Griff, with a guttural call and a daughter named Garh), in names (all the names he finds for Gradus), in word games (see Word Golf), in translation. It is flexible enough to parody the sound of American academics in faculty clubs. It is a language well adapted to dramatize his character (his nastiness, his nerves, his sensitivity, his enthusiasms). And it is capable both of evoking the ecstatic and "magical madness" of his Zembla story and of parodying his own stuffy pedantic quality.

As for the fictional world, in the foreground it is literary: that is, occupied by an explicitly literary text, through which we can behold a middle ground or background realistic and contemporary, though marked by a division into two rather different looking parts. There is the familiar American world of New Wye and Wordsmith College—the world native to Shade, in which Kinbote is a plausible foreigner, a world of college faculties, students, townspeople, nature walks, well within the norms of modern realism. There is also the world of Zembla, not to be found on any real map, lying indefinitely within the real enough world of Europe. It is true that the central places of both worlds have fictitious and sometimes absurd names and are surrounded by places with real names (besides New Wye, in the state of Appalachia, there is New York; besides Zembla, there are the great cities of Europe). One can fly from Zembla to Copenhagen or Stockholm. The oddness begins not with Zembla as such but with the fact that our view into Zembla is through the eyes of its King, and that this King (Charles the Beloved) is none other than the academic Kinbote himself—if indeed he is. It is true that certain northern countries still have kings and queens. The conventions of modern realism do not generally adopt a king's point of view, however; it is contrary to the interest in the familiar, the near at hand, the "life as it is" which is so central to realism. And of course the events in Zembla—the King's escape, with its secret tunnel, its mysterious disguised spies, its secret signs, its parachute leap, all so squarely in the tradition of high adventure tales—create a distance from New Wye that is more than merely geographical. It is indeed like the division one might expect in a novel about a poem and its commentary, except that it reverses that expectation, since the poem and the poet's world are realistic, whereas the commentary is romantic.[7] The difference between these worlds is of course a reflection of the problematical ambiguity noted at the start, the most important feature of this fictional world, with implications that we shall consider later on.

The first step in the analysis of the plot proper is to distinguish the various sequences which develop through the novel. First, there is the progression of the text itself, through foreword, poem, commentary, and index. It is a movement in which one text (the poem) can be said to give rise to the rest. It is produced by the combined work of Shade and Kinbote, the latter building upon, perhaps to correct or revise or create anew, what the former has done. If the commentary, with its various narratives, is regarded as a "poem" in its own right, the essentials of this sequence might be reduced to a process in which one poem is born out of another.

The other sequences are all visible within this first one, running through it. First among these is John Shade's story—revealed mainly in his poem but enlarged upon and completed in the commentary. It is a life Kinbote calls "singularly uneventful." There are, to be sure, events—most notably the suicide of his unhappy daughter Hazel—yet it is mostly a comfortable, happy, successful life: it includes his growth from childhood and his love for his wife Sybil. There are certain childhood fits, and later a mild heart attack. The most striking feature, apart from the general impression of settled stability and establishment success is the uncomfortable quest, indicated in the poem, for something significant in his life: he looks for signs of life after death and finds nothing. He spies on beauty but is distracted; he considers evil and finds irritations, certain matters of taste and stupidity.[8] He is wise, skeptical, a lover of nature and his past. He is humane (kind to Kinbote). He finds his hope in patterns of coincidence and in art: "I feel I understand / Existence . . . only through my art, / In terms of combinational delight" (pp. 68-69). In the poem he is "the shadow of the waxwing slain / By the false azure in the windowpane; / I was the smudge of ashen fluff—and I / Lived on, flew on, in the reflected sky" (p. 33). He is driven into art by the need—for life, for beauty—which this expresses. He is in a sense prosaic; his poem, autobiographical and realistic, is more prosaic, despite its skillfully handled meter, than the narrative Kinbote introduces into the commentary. The outcome of Shade's story is his killing by Gradus—an accident, a mistake, whether seen as Gradus missing the King or Jack Grey aiming at Judge Goldsworth—and it is totally unforeseen by Shade. This outcome is known from the beginning, though the manner in which it takes place becomes an increasingly strong question of suspense through the book.

Shade's daughter's part should be noted. She is involved in a quest in some ways similar, though without the aid of art: she seeks and finds possibly evil spirits in a barn, but is unable to persuade her skeptical parents to believe. In view of the resemblance "in certain respects" to Kinbote, which he notes in the commentary, her case—the suicide associated with her social and sexual failures and suggesting some failure or shortcoming in Shade's comfortable fatherly love, some lack of efficacy—points up Shade's possible parallel limitation in relation to Kinbote, not in love or sympathy, to be sure, but in the adequacy of his art—as we shall consider further below.

A second major strand is the story Kinbote had hoped would be told in the poem: the story of himself as King Charles of Zembla—his life and escape from the revolution, culminating with his taking the position at Wordsmith under the incognito of Kinbote. This story is told largely in narrative segments in the notes, mostly in chronological order, with some flash-forwards and flashbacks. The outcome here, too, is known early in the book. The action unfolds as a great romantic adventure, as we have seen, with conventional adventure trappings. It is enriched by the comic treatment of his troubles with beautiful young women who try to seduce him, a wife whom he can love only in memory or dream, hosts of compliant page boys, and the like. This story rests upon the central ambiguity, of course: is it "real" or is it someone's fantasy? Accordingly, there lurks beneath it, most shadowy, an alternative—a mad inventor, perhaps Botkin, perhaps writing in an insane asylum, perhaps revealing fragments of another life, even an unhappy marriage, with dim clues. The obvious suspense of the King's story concerns the question of how this King finally managed to wind up as professor in such a college and commentator on such a poem. The question is carefully answered before the end. Another suspense, arising out of the shadow alternative, develops the ambiguity itself: it grows as the novel develops and is never answered.

A third sequence, though this could also be considered a part of the King's story, is the approach of the killer Gradus. This, too, is developed chronologically by narratives in the commentary, linked to lines in the poem according not to what they say but to when they were written. As Kinbote points out: "We shall accompany Gradus in constant thought, as he makes his way from distant dim Zembla to green Appalachia, through the entire length of the poem, following the road of its rhythm, riding past in a rhyme . . ." (p. 78). Like the King's story, this, too, is based upon an ambiguity, and we can discern the alternative—Jack Grey pursuing Judge Goldsworth—at the end. The narrative in this sequence emphasizes the process of constructing an action. Thus Kinbote calls attention to the increasing specificity and detail as Gradus draws near: the first note "is the vaguest while those that follow become gradually clearer as gradual Gradus approaches in space and time" (p. 152). The sinister aspect of Gradus's approach is modified by the comic stress on his stupidity and ineptitude, enriched by the wit in the narrator's outrage and contempt. Again, the primary suspense concerns the mistake we know he is going to make: how does he manage to kill Shade instead of Kinbote? Another suspense concerns the nature of the shadow alternative, which is not revealed until after the shooting itself.

A fourth sequence is the unfolding of Kinbote's relationship with John Shade. This also develops through narrative segments in the commentary, but it is a non-chronological (disclosure) process, revealed through inferences we draw as we recognize the blindness or obfuscation of Kinbote's account. Though it is possible to reconstruct a chronology of Kinbote's relationship to Shade, the sequence is organized rather to break down gradually the initial view of a close and dear friendship. Step by step this reduction proceeds: we learn first that Shade's wife is hostile to Kinbote (so he thinks); then we begin to notice Kinbote's attempts to dismiss with excuses the rebuffs he receives in response to his excessive demands. Then the narratives begin to admit the hurt he feels (clear in the episode of Shade's birthday party, to which he was not invited). Finally we see clearly Shade's efforts to be kind, in response to Kinbote's hysterical need, by taking walks with him; it is during such a moment of kindness that he meets his unexpected death. The most important aspect of this relationship is of course Kinbote's hope that Shade will tell the King's story in his long poem. The frustration of this hope is the incentive for writing the commentary—the creation of the text as a whole. The reader's perception changes in the early stages: only gradually is Kinbote brought to admit that the poem does not secretly tell the Zemblan story or that he was bitterly disappointed to discover that it did not.

Kinbote's relation to Shade is part of the broader problem of his relation to the whole New Wye community. His unawareness of the effect he has on others is a rich source of comedy throughout—again, his plan to surprise the Shades at their summer retreat is a case in point. Yet there are signs gradually emerging that he really does know, that to some extent his behavior is deliberate and provocative. His attitude to most of the people in New Wye is contemptuous. This hostility and selfimposed outcasting are pretty much evident from the beginning. He knows he is being ridiculed. He strikes back.

Still another sequence, of lesser importance, is the account of the actual writing of poem and commentary. The record of Shade's work is fairly detailed; the dates on which he writes are specified; we watch Kinbote as he spies on Shade at work, following his actions through the narratives in the commentary. The dates are, as we have seen, correlated with the approach of Gradus. The record of the writing of the commentary is not so specific, but we do have some description of Kinbote's life in the Utah motel during the process of composition. This setting, too, may have a shadowy alternative, if those critics who detect the signs of an asylum are not mistaken.

Finally, there is the rich and important sequence of judgments and observations on general matters. Some of these are Shade's, in the poem and in discussions with Kinbote in the commentary; others are Kinbote's, directly presented. They are interspersed among the longer narrative segments in the commentary. As comments, the observations have a closer connection to lines and words in the poem than the others, although even these are for the most part but loosely linked. They cover a broad range of topics. Some deal with literature, some with language, or with language games, or with pronunciation, or names, or aphorisms, or criticism. Some deal with translations, with examples of various kinds. There are examples of other poems by Shade and short lyrics on a variety of subjects, as well as variant lines to those in the poem. There are discussions of prejudice, of religion, of suicide. There are a great variety of judgments on tastes and manners, American trivia and American vulgarity. There are discussions of butterflies and their names and other facets of nature. And there are critical judgments on the poem, appreciations of certain effects, objections to others. A great many of these judgments are parodic or charged with authorial irony, although some (especially those contributed by Shade) appear to be quite straight.

The ordering of these comments depends in part on the other sequences and is otherwise random or arbitrary. It is clear that often they are used to break up the other narratives, set them off in high relief. This purpose is especially evident near the end, where the comments serve a classic function of intensification by delay and by contrast of interests. Often they relate to the other sequences by producing startling effects of juxtaposition and metaphor. They reinforce the literary foreground of the fictional world, keeping the other sequences in touch with this context and providing a constant substratum of brilliance, subtlety, and wit.

The next step in the plot analysis is to seek the unifying principle. We must consider now the question of the status of the King, the question of Kinbote's sanity. The prevailing view, as I have said, is that Kinbote is mad, the story of his kingship (and perhaps of Zembla itself) a fabrication. By this view (with Kinbote the presumed protagonist) the primary plot process is probably the victory of the madman over the sane one, demonstrated by his conversion of the poem into the tale of the King. This process is accompanied by secondary actions whose ultimate function is to establish the fact that Kinbote indeed suffers from a case of madness. Since the victory consists of Kinbote's finding a place for his fantasy in Shade's poem and is accomplished by the act of writing the commentary and the rest, the plot is essentially dynamic (and dramatically represented by the unfolding of the text itself), though supported or qualified by some secondary disclosure processes. It is of course a severely flawed victory, marred by the madness which shows through despite Kinbote's efforts.

The most obvious difficulties with this theory concern the limits of Kinbote's fantasy. If, as some claim, he is really Botkin ("of Russian descent") and Zembla itself is fantasy, we are obliged to extend the range of his fantasy into New Wye and Wordsmith itself, far beyond the bounds of the obviously unreliable elements in his account of his life there. For as we have seen, Zembla is known in the Wordsmith College which he presents to us: there are Professor Nattochdag and the scenes in the Faculty Club. If these events are to be questioned, we begin to question everything he tells us: the whole thing becomes "fantasy," and then where are we? We have at any rate lost the crucial distinction that the madman theory is attempting to set up. Instead, we may choose to distinguish between Zembla as "real" (in the fictional world, of course) and the King's adventures as imaginary.[9] The latter distinction casts our Botkin connection in doubt, of course. It is also peculiarly cumbersome, without any evidence I have been able to discover to support it. It gives to Kinbote's madness a peculiar specialized quality (for if there is a Zembla, there must have been a deposed King, too, only he is not, by this theory, Kinbote. Why, then, has Kinbote chosen to identify with him? And why are we given no signs of how this King must have looked to him, Kinbote, as a citizen or admirer?). This, too, makes the line between the imaginary and the real seem arbitrary—as if imposed by us upon the book. In addition to such difficulties, there is the question of the interest which this explanation finds in the plot. It is true, the novel has been described as presenting "the irrational through the rational by probing the world of madness,"[10] and Kinbote has been described as the "bearer of a whole wasteland of cultural fragments which he has shored against his ruin—myths of a decayed and deposed aristocracy, the ghost of the mind of Europe."[11] Yet as long as Kinbote's revision of (or confrontation with) Shade's poem is seen as simply a manifestation of some hallucinatory madness, it seems legitimate to ask to what extent this madness, even creative madness, is an interesting explanation? Is it not a banal explanation, an "unrewarding" one, as one critic has said,[12] a disappointing reduction of this fascinating material?

No doubt for this reason, some readers have attempted to turn Kinbote himself into a figment of the imagination of the poet, John Shade.[13] This interpretation would give us a plot of a completely different kind. It would have the advantage of bringing Shade and "Kinbote" into a more integral relation: it emphasizes the parallels and oppositions between them (Kinbote as alter ego) and implies strongly the incompleteness of Shade in himself both artistically and psychologically. The plot by this view is a dynamic unfolding, through the text, of the inner drama of the opposite sides of Shade's personality: the completion of the commentary establishes the needed balance.

The obvious difficulty with this theory is that Shade is killed and lives to tell about it, a turn of events that of course echoes the third and fourth lines of his poem, quoted above. It has been said that "Shade . . . has perpetrated his own 'stylistic' death within the novel, and he has then given us a new aspect of himself in the guise of another soul and another artwork." Again, it is a "recurrent idea in *Pale Fire* that the artist momentarily perishes with each of his creations, in order to give life to a work of art." Gradus (the connection to *gradus ad Parnassum* is noted: a dictionary, a "step to the place where the Muses live") is the "final tool used by the poet to complete his work and arrive at Parnassus."[14] Obviously the only way to account for Shade's death is to treat it allegorically—and once again we run into the problem of the limits to fantasy. For it is not only his own death that Shade has presumably invented here; it is also his whole description of life in New Wye, as seen through "Kinbote's" eyes. Has he invented also Kinbote spying on him, Kinbote hurt because he was not invited to Shade's birthday party; has he invented his own kindness to Kinbote to make up for slights? It seems obvious that if once we absorb Kinbote into Shade, we turn everything into fantasy by Shade, and the distinction between Shade and Nabokov himself disappears. And if this happens we are back where we started, and the same problems confront us all over again.

Recognizing this difficulty, some critics have dismissed the controversy as a false issue, insisting rather that all fictional levels in the text are equally real and that the characters Kinbote and Shade are expressions of Nabokov himself.[15] The truth seems to be that the novel does not permit us to decide whether the Zemblan exile is "true" or "fantasy," whether Kinbote is psychotically hallucinating or only neurotically trying to preserve some memorial to his past. The hints of madness cannot be confirmed, they cannot be supported in all parts of the novel. On the other hand, the story of the King's conversion into Kinbote can be supported, it does cohere, but it is challenged by those hints of madness and the strange imbalance it creates. The novel moves toward the disclosure not of Kinbote's madness, nor of his sanity, but of the ambiguity, the balance between the two possibilities, which we reach when Kinbote discusses his future incognitos at the end of his final note before the index. The index itself reinforces the point. The suspense of what I have called the "shadow alternatives"—suspense as to the truth of the King's story—ends in ambiguity. We are made to accept *both* the "real" and the "imaginary" interpretations of the King's adventures. We allow to them the qualities of imaginary projection without forfeiting their grounding in the fictional reality of the work. But in so doing we find we have moved into a so-called narrator-controlled fictional world, and the plot, which must incorporate this construction, seems to be a creative plot.

The world is narrator controlled because the integration of the King's story with the others is made coherent, made "probable" in the Aristotelian sense, not by the mimetic principles of the Zemblan world (a King in danger in such a country under such conditions) nor by the different mimetic principles of an unhappy scholar building a fantasy, but by the coexistence of both sets of principles, both sets of probabilities. Two different worlds are brought together and forced to merge, not by resolving the incompatibility between them but by forcing them to coexist—as if by command of the narrator. (For explanation of why I attribute this kind of disruption to the narrator, see chapter 4 and, in the same chapter, n. 14.) By narrator here I do not mean either Kinbote or Shade but the unseen narrator-in-charge behind them both. The discontinuity or incoherence which is the mark of the narrator-controlled fictional world lies here in the fact that *within the fictional world* fantasy is real; the barrier between what is real and what is not real is broken down. (This world is similar to that of *Absalom, Absalom!*, where the imaginings of Quentin and Shreve are taken for real—real and imagined at once.) Seen in this light, the emphasis on creating Gradus becomes an important clue to our reading of the whole book.

The plot is *creative* because this principle—namely, the collapsing of the real and the imagined—underlies the construction and becomes the chief organizer of the plot. It creates the simultaneous separation and identity of Kinbote and the King. The central action of this plot is the making of the text, the incorporation of one poem (Shade's) into another (Kinbote's); its outcome is not simply the completion of the text, however, but the revelation which emerges from it—namely, the establishment of this unresolvable ambiguity.

Now, if the plot is the making of the text, the protagonist of this plot is the maker. But if the text is made by Kinbote and Shade (a compound protagonist), it ends by questioning its own authorship. The true maker, creator of that ambiguity itself, is this unseen narrator-in-charge, who controls the narrator-controlled world. This narrator is the "latent protagonist." We need the concept of the latent protagonist here, since the ambiguity, the uncertain ontology of the manifest protagonist, can be made intelligible only by referring it to something else, some source from which it arises. (We could refer to an "implied author," but then we would have to find some other way to describe the difference between this and a traditional mimetic plot.) As there is a latent protagonist, so there is a latent, or underlying, plot, in which we can find the principle that unifies and organizes the "manifest" plot. The manifest plot and its manifest protagonist are the creations of the latent protagonist; they are "projections" of his interests. The latent plot is the intelligibility of the manifest plot.

How can we describe that intelligibility? We can discover it, in a case like this, by regarding the manifest plot as an exemplification of a general process. We translate it into general terms, we seek its symbolic significance. We cannot stop with a single symbolic interpretation, to be sure; we must seek all that are relevant. There must be a limit, of course, which we can express by saying that any symbolic reading of the manifest action is legitimate if it increases our perception of its coherence and unity. The underlying plot is an abstract unity of symbolized general possibilities visible only through the manifest action—so that if the plot gives to that manifest action an effect of unity, it also finds unity, as well as visibility, only in it.[16]

What is the general process exemplified by this manifest one? The novel has been said to be "about the full process of artistic creation," and the essentials have been analyzed in a variety of ways by many critics.[17] This formulation could easily be misinterpreted to imply a didactic or rhetorical plot. The differences are several: one could say that the emphasis is on the exemplification of the creative process rather than the development of the concept, on the latent protagonist's personal perception of it, his struggle with it, perhaps, rather than on an attempt to persuade the reader of its truth. The crucial difference, however, is the multiplicity of possible symbolic interpretations of the manifest process, as we have just observed—the fact that the underlying process, though we called it "general," resists reduction to a formulable statement or proposition, that it can in fact be exemplified only by this one case and can be described only by a combination or convergence of a variety of symbolic interpretations.

In this necessarily abbreviated analysis, I must limit myself, in examining the possibilities, only to those which the construction of the plot renders most obvious. Two aspects of the manifest process seem to be primary. One is the fact that a text or work of art is created from the interaction of the subplots we have noticed, activity which involves, as actors, Shade, Kinbote, the King, and Gradus, and as creators, Shade and Kinbote. The other aspect is the outcome we have just considered: the disclosure in the work of art of the ambiguity between Kinbote and the King, which is finally revealed by the work of art. Questioning the ambiguity first, we see, fairly obviously, that it signifies—it demonstrates or affirms—the power of the imagination (and art) to create reality. It shows the ability of the maker to turn the figmentary into the real by giving to the object (the King) the qualities of both. This point is amply supported by parallels and other suggestions throughout the text. "Once transmuted by you into poetry, the stuff *will* be true, and the people *will* come alive," as Kinbote tells Shade with reference to his Zemblan material (p. 214). The point is driven home in the treatment of Gradus's approach.

If this is the dominant process of the underlying plot, we have a disclosure plot—for the King (in contrast to Gradus) is not dynamically "created" through the processes of the text but is *discovered* as having been so created in an organization which moves toward the revelation of his true ambiguity. This is really a disclosure of the nature of the manifest protagonist which, as we have just suggested, would be the manifest maker of the text: a compound, the unity of Kinbote and Shade. If the outcome, however, is the establishment of the King's and hence Kinbote's ambiguous identity, we will find it more useful to regard the true manifest protagonist (the center into which the latent protagonist projects his vision) as a tripartite compound of Kinbote, Shade, and the King. Why should we add the King to the combination? Because adding him acknowledges the important point (in this novel) that the work of art is created not only by the writers but by the figures they write about—that is to say, into whom they project their imaginations. Shade is both writer and hero of his own poem. Kinbote as Kinbote is unwitting and comic hero of one subplot of his poem; as King he is romantic hero of the other. The tripartite protagonist projects these relationships. It also projects the power of artistic projection itself: Kinbote's protagonist is the King, the latent protagonist's protagonist is the relationship between writer and protagonist.

The other symbolically significant aspect of the manifest plot is the interaction of the members of the manifest protagonist to create the work of art. This interaction starts perhaps with Shade, the established poet, recognized as such by the others, with all the honors such a poet can receive. As we have already seen, he sees himself as shadow or reflector of beauty. He seems to be seeking a worthy subject for poetry, and looks for strangeness, but the poem he writes is prosaic and realistic and cannot pass beyond his own uneventful life for subject and his sane solid skepticism for attitude. We notice also two visionaries seeking something from him and failing to find it—Kinbote and his daughter Hazel.

In relation to Shade, Kinbote is first of all a reader—commentary and criticism being expressions of reading. He is in a sense a parasite of the poet and is so developed at comic length and in comic detail in the subplot of his relationship to Shade. Still, he is a radically dissatisfied reader. He would rather read about the romantic adventures of the King, a life opposite to the dull shaded normality of Shade's. As "reader" Kinbote identifies with this romantic subject, projects himself into it. His commentary becomes an extravagant "misreading" (anticipating the critics of misreading by a good many years), into which he projects an ideal image of himself.

The simple picture of reader, poet, and romantic hero as compound protagonist is complicated by the approach of Gradus and the killing of Shade. Symbolically it would appear that the poet is killed by the reader's story—that is, by his misreading—an amusing enough

idea. If Gradus is also plain Jack Grey, then the reader (Kinbote) has in effect tried to rob the poet of his own death. Here again we see Kinbote's grab for adventure as like a scavenger he tries to absorb into his own life every kind of experience. Perhaps also the attempt expresses his craving for order, for "explanations," since Shade's death is such a mischance. The reader is voracious for experience and for order—that is to say, for story. He appropriates everything of the poet's, his poem and even his death, and makes it express himself. Is this not a kind of madness, normal though it is?

We must pay full attention in this interpretation to the emphasis on Gradus. He is seen by Kinbote at the end as one of the three figures in the story he expects to keep on telling. He becomes almost archetypal in Kinbote's continued expectation of being pursued by a "bigger, more respectable, more competent Gradus." Who is this Gradus? If he is, in the interpretation earlier noted, a step on the way to Parnassus, he is also, and more obviously, the epitome of the enemy, the destroyer, death. But he is necessary. In terms of the story of which he is a part, he is the cause of the adventure, the incentive, the negative disrupter of harmony, which makes the story go. If there is a protagonist, there must also be a Gradus—the story requires it. He is the motivator of Kinbote and the King; his neglect by Shade (seen also in Shade's poem) is fatal.

The limits of this symbolism appear if we ask why Kinbote the reader is presented as so alienated a figure, a notion concretized in his nationality—he is literally alien. But his distancing from the society, including his homosexuality, as well as his misunderstood relationship with Shade, expresses a general alienation from what is normal and conventional everywhere. There is an inversion of stereotyped notions: here it is the poet, traditionally and romantically the alienated one, who epitomizes the establishment; it is the reader, the commentator, who is outside.

Again, it is Kinbote who wears the masks: his appearance at New Wye is incognito, and his future life, he tells us, will continue incognito—in disguises he will be retelling his story in various ways. Kinbote is the artist here and Shade merely a character in the repeating story.

In a second symbolic interpretation, then, Shade and Kinbote appear as two different kinds of poets. The one is a sane, realistic establishment poet, the other is a mad, neurotic, romantic one. The first cannot see a subject beyond himself; the second can't bear himself and creates another subject, a glamorous exile to glorify his alienation. They are opposites, mirror images of each other—as men (socially, sexually, emotionally), as writers (poem, commentary), and in the works they write. As such they complement each other: neither is complete without the other. When Gradus emerges from the romantic poet's poem to kill the establishment poet, he provides a vindication of the romantic, in spite of his madness—he shows him as close in some sense to the poetic truth—unless (the ambiguity again) that closeness was really only an unfortunate accident of chance. But why, then, is the romantic poem parasitical to the other, attached to it as "commentary"? Does this relationship signify perhaps the necessity of tradition in the development of art? Does the alienated romantic, original though he may be, need to build his original poem on a base of traditional and conventional poetry? The new grows from the old, revises it (and as it does so, the old poet dies).

The two symbolic readings are not alternatives that we must choose between; one does not replace the other. Each is a reasonable analogy to the manifest action, an aspect, a set of implications, by which the manifest becomes meaningful, coherent as a projection of something. They work together. Both are weak, however, in their explanations of Kinbote as exile. And they ignore another feature of the novel which bears on the question of exile, the deliberate exploitation of knowledge of Nabokov's own biography. To be sure, the presence of authorial biography in fiction sometimes confronts formal critics with difficulties. Yet there is really no reason why the image of the implied author might not include some biography, why an author might not include among his conventions some knowledge of himself. The practice is common in poetry. The problem for the reader is to know how much he ought to know. Once again, the best test is probably this: if the introduction of such knowledge into the form appreciably strengthens that form (strengthens, not merely alters—for conceivably some biographical material, so introduced, might undermine it),[18] then it is relevant.

In the case of *Pale Fire,* there are a number of direct Nabokovian allusions—the reference to Hurricane Lolita, to Professor Pnin, to nymphets, for instance—sly references which tell us that knowledge of the author may be pertinent. More significant is the way in which we are reminded of Nabokov the Russian émigré and public personality. The Russian language is prominent throughout: Gradus under pressure speaks Russian; in the entry headed "two tongues," among the seventeen pairs of languages listed, English and Russian form the only pair that is repeated, and it appears four times. The revolution against the King has Soviet support. There is the allusion to the "old, happy, healthy, heterosexual Russian, a writer in exile," among Kinbote's future incognitos. There are the celebrated Nabokovian opinions on psychiatry and Marxism, projected by Shade and Kinbote. There is Shade's interest in butterflies. Such matters and others bring the figure of Vladimir Nabokov prominently into the form of this work.

Nabokov appears there as an aspect of the latent protagonist—and thereby a shaping force for the fiction. If the Kinbote-Shade-Charles combination projects this latent protagonist's perception of an artistic process, the alienation which is so important in this process may also project the Nabokovian consciousness of exile. Here, then, is a third symbolic reading. Kinbote now becomes a comic (self-mocking? or disguising?) projection of the exile's alienation in the land to which he has been exiled, Charles is a somewhat mocking projection of the glamor and nostalgia of the exile's memory (the exile as hero), Shade is the projection of the exile's view of the sanity and security but confined range of the art of his new home. The exile seeks the shelter of the American Shade, he seeks to find himself (to read himself) in the Shade. He is the exiled poet seeking entry perhaps into the Shade of American literature.[19] This reading, like the others, acts as an implied subplot, metaphor or comment, qualifying the rest and qualified by it: it tells us that the artistic process delineated here is the Nabokovian one, and the discomfort and need that give rise to art, as represented by Kinbote's alienation, consist in the alienation of the Nabokovian exile. The "romaunt" he wants told is the romaunt of the exile. It includes not only the adventures of the King but also the absurdities of Kinbote making a crotchety pest of himself in New Wye. And there is Gradus, of course, destroyer and motivator. In this symbolic reading, the manifest story is "like" Nabokov's own story, stringently, sternly, comically depersonalized and projected.

None of these symbolic readings adequately incorporates the high development of the commentary device itself—the sequence of opinions, judgments, games, in the direct comments, a separate subplot. Apart from its general function of intensification, which I have already commented upon, this subplot constitutes the most explicit projection of the latent protagonist's general literary interests. Thereby it qualifies all the more specific narrative and dramatized projections: it distances them and to some extent undermines the claims of all our symbolic readings, putting them in a more hypothetical light. The subplot further establishes a governing attitude, skeptical, playful, wondering, ridiculing in many aspects—a judgment on the literary enterprise itself, its possibilities and limitations. It provides a context rich in incidental subtlety and implication, which calls attention to these qualities throughout and colors everything with its brilliant glow.

Although other relevant symbolic readings may certainly be added, the three I have considered, qualified by the context of the developed commentary, seem to me (at this stage of my perception) to be chiefly responsible for unifying the manifest plot and for articulating the underlying one. This plot could be summed up as a creative disclosure plot which reveals a personal (latent protagonist's) image (projection) of a kind of artistic process, a specifically Nabokovian one. It is creative rather than rhetorical or didactic because the projection is personal; the interest is in the creation of the image that projects it rather than in a concept or judgment served by it. It is disclosure rather than dynamic because the organization does not unfold the projected artistic process directly but moves rather to a revelation of the nature of the compound protagonist—that is, to the nature of the projection.

The projection gives a vision of certain powers in that artistic process and of certain conditions giving rise to it. Central among the conditions is the opposition of the romantic, imaginative, "mad" vision to the realistic, relatively prosaic, "sane" one. The incentive for artistic creation arises from the alienation of the poet (or the reader—the two are ultimately collapsed and collapsed with the critic as well). This alienation (which reveals itself nonartistically in foolishness, vanity, and self-deception) is symbolized in one aspect by the windowpane (alienation from nature) and epitomized in another by exile (from humanity or society). Along with alienation is the necessary consciousness of what Gradus represents—time, change, and death, motivators both within the fiction and outside it, which eventually will kill both poet and protagonist. This vision of art focuses finally on its power to create its own reality (and the probable corollary, suggested in the poem and implicit in Kinbote's desperation, that only through art can reality be made tolerable). Poetic creation is also seen as transcending the misery and foolishness from which it comes—in general through the vitality of the intelligence with which it criticizes that foolishness and more specifically by the combinations of qualities which the true work of art unites. The former is seen in the comedy of the latent protagonist's treatment of Kinbote and in the wit and subtlety of the incidental commentary. The latter is seen in the balance of the two "poems"—for of course the true artistic achievement is not the romantic poem alone but the interaction of the two; though the romantic shows up the limits of the realistic, it, too, is implicitly criticized (as is Kinbote by Shade) by the juxtaposed reality and sanity of the other, and the final poise is between imaginative madness and common sanity.

The analysis is not complete without consideration of the effect. As this is a creative plot, the effect can be equated with the implied attitude of the latent protagonist toward his creation. It includes, first of all, a clear appreciation of the constructional virtuosity which the creative plot displays. This kind of effect, as I suggested earlier, might be called "felicity," generally apparent in the zestful quality of the whole, especially in the interaction of the various sequences, and culminating in the powerful exhilaration of Kinbote's last narrative, where the ambiguity of his role as creator of his stories becomes most explicit. In general, however, the

virtuoso aspect is integrated with more specific attitudes attached to the manifest actions as fictions, and the dominant effect is finally defined by these attitudes.

The effect of the manifest actions is, as I have suggested, for the most part clearly and strongly, delightfully and richly comic, mainly at Kinbote's expense. The potential pathos of Kinbote in the last few pages as he recognizes his possible madness is overshadowed by the evident exhilaration. The potential tragedy in the death of Shade is nullified; the event is kept well within the confines of comedy by its long preparation, the absurdities in its execution, and the way our attention is directed away from it, during and after the moment.

We may ask, however, whether a comic attitude is appropriate to what we have described as the underlying plot—the latent protagonist's perception of the achievement of art, its transcendence of foolishness and misery. If the latent protagonist is laughing at his Kinbote figure, is he also laughing at his compound protagonist and at the artistic process in which it is involved? The implied attitude toward the balanced artistic achievement which this plot projects seems more likely to be not ridicule but appreciation or approval. This, intensified by the unmentioned suffering of the Nabokovian exile and the implied general suffering that gives rise to art, checks the ridicule at the underlying level, limits its scope. Yet the ridicule is not thereby dismissed; the work is not finally a romance in which we find the latent protagonist lost in admiration for what Kinbote-Shade-Charles represent. Rather, that judgment is suspended—ridicule and admiration are arrested in balance, and we have a final effect (once again) of *wonder*. Our attention is fixed upon the strangeness—what is surprising, incredible—of the artistic process which the disclosure plot has revealed, but without judgment good or bad. The comic absurdity is found, as we so clearly see, in the conditions that give rise to art (they must be recognized in the art itself) distancing their unspoken pain; the value of the art does not cancel the absurdity but balances it. The balance—this totally involved and interested perception of distance—is wonder.

Such an analysis finds further support, curiously, in a theory of poetry which is suggested in the text, fragmentarily, in several places. With regard to the supposed likeness between Shade's description of Sybil Shade and the appearance of Queen Disa, Kinbote remarks: "I trust the reader appreciates the strangeness of this, because if he does not, there is no sense in writing poems, or notes to poems, or anything at all" (p. 207). And more clearly: "By the very act of brutish routine acceptance [of a poem], we undo the work of the ages, the history of the gradual elaboration of poetical description and construction, from the treeman to Browning, from the caveman to Keats. . . . I can do what only a true artist can do—pounce upon the forgotten butterfly of revelation, wean myself abruptly from the habit of things, see the web of the world, and the warp and the weft of that web" (p. 289). The dry modern name for the critical idea expressed here is "defamiliarization." The proper effect of art is strangeness, amazement: to see things as we have forgotten how. (Notice how often Kinbote uses the word "magic.") We see the efforts to achieve amazement running through all the ways of this book. It marks the language which fixes attention through wit and innuendo, as well as the constructive tendency to overturn clichés and stereotypes everywhere. Amazement is one of the main effects Kinbote seeks with his narrative of the King; Shade seeks it, too, and tends to miss it, which is no doubt one of the reasons why his poem must be completed by another.

In the theory of this book, the wonder of defamiliarization is a general effect of all art, characterizing the perception of every form until it becomes banal. It is an aesthetic rather than a specific fictional effect and will exist in any good work along with whatever kind of tragic, comic, ironic, or other attitude the work displays. But wonder can be a specific fictional effect, too, an extension of the general artistic attitude into the presented material of the work itself. Wonder itself is held up to display—to be wondered at. We have seen in *The Portrait of a Lady* and *The Sound and the Fury* such displayed wonder applied to fictional characters and behavior. In **Pale Fire** it is directed to the artistic process itself, the absurdity and the magic.

Finally, let us consider just briefly the index, which I suggested at the start was part of the whole. Its most obvious function is to reestablish the distance which has been threatened by the intensities of Kinbote's last narrative. It puts everything in order, bringing narrative progression to a full stop, buried in alphabetical order and cross-reference. In the process the index reviews the subplots. It also introduces new things, enlarged or revised explanations of details indicated only obliquely before. One of these is Botkin—it thus brings the "shadow alternative" into some dim view and fortifies the final ambiguity. It reveals also that Kinbote has contributed "variant readings" to Shade's poem which in the commentary he had attributed to Shade—reinforcing the distance between Zembla and Shade. The index also distinguishes Kinbote and the King by separate entries, a matter relevant to our conception of the compound protagonist. It contains some games, as we see if we follow the cross-references from Crown Jewels and Word Golf. It clarifies certain relationships, such as Odon's ancestry, and adds other interesting secondary details, such as Kinbote's relations with his neighbors in the Utah trailer camp. Several items in the index have no page references at all. Like the appendix in *The Sound and the Fury,* it is an epilogue; though all essential revelations have been completed, the index brings the disclosure plot to an end by reaffirming the narrator's character as academic and pedant, the ambiguous quality of much of the action, and the dominantly comic tone of the manifest plot. More than anything else it compels us to look closely at the details again. The net effect is to insist on our attention and to remind us that our attention has been demanded all along. In such ways the index reiterates the importance of amazement and surprise and confirms the true wonder of this quite wonderful book.

Notes

1. Vladimir Nabokov, *Pale Fire* (New York, 1962), p. 28. Page references in the text refer to this edition.

2. For other views on the order of reading *Pale Fire,* see June Perry Levine, "Vladimir Nabokov's *Pale Fire*: 'The Method of Composition' as Hero," *International Fiction Review* 5 (July 1978), pp. 103-8.

3. Mary McCarthy, "Vladimir Nabokov's 'Pale Fire,'" *Encounter* 19 (October 1962), pp. 71-84. Nina Berberova claims that after the reference to "doctor" on p. 279, "no doubts are possible" as to the madness and confinement in an asylum of Kinbote ("The Mechanics of *Pale Fire*," in *Nabokov: Criticism, Reminiscences, Translations, and Tributes,* ed. Alfred Appel, Jr., and Charles Newman [Evanston, Ill., 1970], p. 152).

4. On p. 80 Kinbote translates back into English a passage from *Timon of Athens* previously translated into Zemblan. In the process the words "pale fire," in the original, have been dropped out, though Kinbote is unaware of the omission.

5. Barbara J. Eckstein suggests that Kinbote is a parody of the unreliable narrator of realistic fiction ("Conventions of Irony in Some American Novels about Art" [Ph.D. dissertation, University of Cincinnati, 1980]).

6. Critics differ somewhat as to the merits of Shade's poem. Julia Bader regards it as excellent, for instance; it "can be read alone; the commentary cannot" (*Crystal Land: Artifice in Nabokov's English Novels* [Berkeley, 1972], p. 55). Page Stegner (*Escape into Aesthetics: The Art of Vladimir Nabokov* [New York, 1966], p. 117) finds the poem a "serious meditation on death . . . and the artist's escape from the consequences of physical deformity and decay into the realm of pure aesthetic delight." Richard Pearce ("Nabokov's Black [Hole] Humor: *Lolita* and *Pale Fire,*" in *Comic Relief: Humor in Contemporary American Literature,* ed. Sarah Blacher Cohen [Urbana, Ill., 1979], p. 42) finds the poem "neither elegant nor stupid. It is wildly comic but capable of constraining the

most ornate diction and the most mundane perceptions, the most sophisticated allusions and the most slapstick descriptions within its tightly controlled meter." See also note 8.

7. John O. Stark observes that we tend to read Shade's portion "as if it came from a realistic novel" and Kinbote's "as if it came from a nonrealistic novel" (*The Literature of Exhaustion: Borges, Nabokov, and Barth* [Durham, N.C., 1974], p. 69).

8. This point seems evident, even though in an interview Nabokov quoted the lines about evil from memory "without" as Fowler puts it, "any qualification as to their judgment" (Douglas Fowler, *Reading Nabokov* [Ithaca, 1974], p. 105.

9. Andrew Field suggests this possibility: "two Zemblas—the thing itself and the tale as told" (*Nabokov: His Life in Art: A Critical Narrative* [Boston, 1967], p. 294).

10. L. L. Lee, *Vladimir Nabokov* (Boson, 1976), p. 137.

11. G. M. Hyde, *Vladimir Nabokov: America's Russian Novelist* (London, 1977), p. 177.

12. Robert Merrill, "Nabokov and Fictional Artifice," *Modern Fiction Studies,* 25:3, p. 458.

13. Bader and Field see Kinbote as having been created by Shade. It has also been suggested that Kinbote created Shade, but this possibility seems even more difficult to support.

14. Bader, *Crystal Land,* pp. 31, 39, 34.

15. Lee: "My point is that each level is quite as true as the next" (*Vladimir Nabokov,* p. 135). Stark: "Any layer inside them [the author and his book]—actually *in* the novel—is imaginary, and none of these inside layers has more reality than any other" (*The Literature of Exhaustion,* p. 65). Eckstein: "Each character's world in the series of worlds which exist in both novels [*Pale Fire* and *The Turn of the Screw*] is at once 'real' and fictional. Each is 'real' because it asserts validity within its own fictional frame" ("Conventions of Irony," p. 181).

16. This method of unifying creative plots needs to be used carefully; otherwise we'll find that we have turned all creative plots into didactic ones. Strictly speaking, we begin to generalize just the fictional incoherence that makes for a creative plot, and where we go from there depends on the nature of that incoherence. In *Second Skin,* for example, the significant generalization is simply the recognition that all events are embodiments of Skipper's fears and wishes. Skipper's experiences can then be treated as a projection of a personal vision of wishes and fears. In an allegory (*Pilgrim's Progress*) the generalization is a recognition that all events are governed by a continuing correspondence between two lines of action. The interest of the latent protagonist is creative: to maintain that correspondence as consistently and completely as possible. In the case of *Pale Fire* the incoherence is in the nature of the manifest protagonist, a compound protagonist engaged in artistic activity; our symbolic readings all relate to the question of this protagonist's nature.

17. Eckstein, "Conventions of Irony," p. 182. See also Bader, *Crystal Land,* Stark, *The Literature of Exhaustion,* and Field, *Nabokov.*

18. The genetic fallacy: if we bring too much knowledge about Lawrence, for instance, to *Sons and Lovers,* we may obscure our perception of the novel—asking the "false question," for example, of whether the novel is being "fair" to Paul Morel's father.

19. In his postscript to *Lolita,* Nabokov spoke of wishing to become an American writer: "I chose American motels instead of Swiss hotels or English inns only because I am trying to be an American writer and claim only the same rights that other American writers enjoy." Also: "An American critic suggested that *Lolita* was the record of my love affair with the romantic novel. The substitution 'English language' for 'romantic novel' would make this elegant formula more correct" (*Lolita* [New York, 1955], pp. 317, 318).

John Haegert (essay date winter 1984)

SOURCE: Haegert, John. "The Author as Reader as Nabokov: Text and Pretext in *Pale Fire.*" *Texas Studies in Literature and Language* 26, no. 4 (winter 1984): 405-24.

[In the following essay, Haegert relates the experiences of Kinbote and Shade to the reader's interpretive process.]

[In memoriam *Gwin J. Kolb*]

Perhaps no chance remark in modern literature has occasioned more amusement or prompted more perplexity than that of Charles Kinbote, Nabokov's incurable pederast and lunatic commentator in ***Pale Fire*** (1962). It occurs at the end of his ostensible introduction to the 999-line autobiographical poem by his good "friend" and colleague, John Francis Shade, a poem Kinbote has edited for publication after the poet's death. "[W]ithout my notes," Kinbote blithely asserts, "Shade's text simply has no human reality at all since the human reality of such a poem as his . . . has to depend entirely on the reality of its author . . . , a reality that only my notes can provide."[1] Kinbote's exalted claims of editorial authority, of a privileged intimacy with the poet's life and intentions, are of course unjustified by anything save his invulnerable egotism and megalomania; and readers have hastened to point out not only the tenuousness of the textual connection between his "crazy" commentary and Shade's poem, but his (and presumably Nabokov's) attitude of imperial disdain toward this very lack of connection. At first glance, Nabokov appears to have fulfilled the flamboyant role assigned him by many of his critics. *Pale Fire* would seem to be the work of a master illusionist largely indifferent to the coarse reality of human problems, concerned only with—as he implies in his Afterword to *Lolita*—the suave satisfactions afforded by "aesthetic bliss."[2] A more prolonged contemplation of Kinbote's role, however, elicits responses which are not so easily categorized. As I hope to demonstrate in my discussion of the book, Kinbote's elaborately prepared misreading of Shade's poem—as well as Shade's "misreading" of his own life—offers us fresh perceptions of our own interpretive acts and the way they are structured. Employing the techniques of parody and artifice, Nabokov estranges us from our accustomed view of the author and his text; in doing so he illuminates the unavoidable role we as readers play in the creation of fictional, as well as everyday, reality.

I

The history of Nabokov criticism has always revealed an endless fascination for the redoubtable energy and resourcefulness of Kinbote's madness, although the exact nature of his madness, not to mention its comic force, has often been eclipsed by various discussions of his status within the work itself. Is he to be regarded primarily as a mere *fantouche* and authorial mouthpiece? Or is he to be viewed as an autonomous and fully rounded character, the Dionysian mirror image of Shade's sober Apollonian self? In one sense, of course, such preliminary questions are both pertinent and inevitable. Given Nabokov's undeniable penchant for ostentatious artifice and verbal sleight of hand, it is perhaps to be expected that his readers now question even the most basic "facts" of his fiction. (The problematic residue produced by this last phrase already indicates something of the difficulty in reading his works.) In its labyrinthine complexity and artifice, in its almost compulsive literariness, *Pale Fire* remains one of the most difficult novels yet published in a century notorious for difficult novels. As Robert Adams suggests, not altogether approvingly: "At first glance, [it] seems to be a novel in spite of itself." Despite the numerous critical studies devoted to its explication, each has tended to confirm rather than clarify Nabokov's sly remark, in 1968, that "one of the functions of all my novels is to prove that the novel in general does not exist. The book I make is a specific and subjective affair. I have no purpose at all

when composing the stuff except to compose it. I work hard, I work long, until it grants me complete possession and pleasure."[3]

A "possession and pleasure," one might add, that is often denied to readers accustomed to the usual coordinates of more traditional fiction. For in *Pale Fire,* as has often been noted, we cannot even be sure of what is notionally real or what is only illusion or sport; nor, I would submit, of what is most deeply comic or what is merely verbal horseplay. The structural idiosyncrasy of its story of the aging poet and his mad amanuensis has been nicely defined by Nina Berberova: "There is in *Pale Fire* a structural surprise: the symbolic level, the fantastic, the poetic, lies on the surface and is obvious, while the factual, the realistic is only slightly hinted at, and may be approached as a riddle."[4] Considered as a piece of realistic fiction or as a conventional character study, the work is indeed unpromising. Divided into the component texts of a scholarly edition, it would consist of Shade's amiably undistinguished last poem in iambic couplets, supplemented by the botched and irrelevant critical apparatus supplied by Kinbote: the fantastic Foreword, Commentary, and Index which have aroused in every reader, academic and otherwise, a sense of imaginative complexity bordering on chaos. In the Commentary, especially, it soon becomes apparent that Shade's poem is not simply being misinterpreted by Kinbote; it serves him primarily as a pretext for recasting his secret life as King Charles-Xavier of Zembla, whose once illustrious reign and now inglorious exile from his beloved European homeland he fervently believes to be the real inspiration—as well as the implicit subject—of Shade's autobiographical work. Subsequent revelations, however, strongly suggest that Kinbote is neither an intimate of Shade's nor a king of anything, but only a deluded émigré instructor named Botkin to whom Shade—a distinguished colleague and next-door neighbor—has been unavoidably kind.

Telling a pair of converging stories across these several obstacles and through incongruous angles of consciousness is a tour de force in itself, and most readers, after recognizing the book's rather obvious academic parody, have sought to clarify the continuing mystery of its comic structure in one of two ways. Either they have emphasized the more conventional elements of Nabokov's work, stressing its participation in the traditional allegiance of novels to empirical reality and representational realism; or they have focused on its self-reflexive character and flaunted artifice, regarding it not as a novel, in any representational sense, but as a spirited apologue or metafiction—a nonmimetic work in which the element of character is suppressed in order to emphasize artistic design for its own sake or for the didactic ends we associate with fables, parables, and allegories.[5] The ambiguities arising from Nabokov's art are real and undoubted. We may sympathize with those who have attempted to resolve them, but the two approaches to his work outlined above have often taken a confusing turn. Instead of rendering its mystery more accessible, many of the supposed "reconstructions" of *Pale Fire* have only reduced and simplified the power and complexity of Nabokov's masterful imaginative achievement.

Stressing the narrative unity of *Pale Fire,* for example, Andrew Field has suggested that we have a choice as to the author of the Commentary: "The primary author—even without Nabokov's acknowledgment that Kinbote really does not know what is going on in the poem—must be John Shade." Page Stegner, on the other hand, has argued in *Escape into Aesthetics* (1966) that if Kinbote is able to invent an exotic kingdom full of "fantastic, though imaginary, personalities, he is certainly able to dream up John and Sybil Shade and their daughter Hazel, and create a fictitious poem as well." Diametrically opposed in their conclusions, both critics remain firm in their determination to tighten and intensify the story line, to give a consistent credibility and depth to a central consciousness underlying Nabokov's elaborate fictional artifice. Recently, Ellen Pifer has made another effort to simplify Nabokov's intentions, as if she were determined to rehabilitate *Pale Fire* within the conventional terms of realistic fiction. In *Nabokov and the Novel* (1980), she interprets the book as if it were really a novel called *The New Neighbor in New Wye,* toning down the metafictive element, treating the relationship between Shade and Kinbote as evidence of Nabokov's supreme desire to celebrate the human complexity of his central characters. Unlike Field and Stegner, Pifer cherishes the characters as individual identities, but she does not allow them any larger significance. She insists upon psychological motive, cause, and specific effect, and she stresses the "essential singularity" of each character's individual perceptions.[6]

The merit of such readings—whomever we regard as the "primary author" (Shade, Kinbote, or Nabokov himself)—is that it attends to major elements in the book which we ignore at our peril, such as the rich and suggestive realities of New Wye and Zembla or the intense inner life of its central characters; its defect is that, in its haste to underline these elements, it ignores other elements no less central to the book's design, such as the recurrent tension between two opposing modes of imagination "represented" by Shade and Kinbote respectively. Like Field and Stegner, Pifer is concerned with particle at some cost to principle. If we read the book as the perversely obfuscated tale of John and Sybil Shade, Kinbote (or Botkin), and Shade's assassin, Gradus (or Jack Grey), we find many stretches of narrative answering to these assumptions; but we are likely to miss the larger demands—as well as the different intellectual pleasures—arising from Nabokov's epistemological quandaries. Indeed, if we experience them

at all, we are apt to regard them, as Douglas Fowler does, as disturbing contradictions and impediments in an otherwise amusing tale of Nabokovian "doubles."[7] So it is not enough, and it might be seriously misleading, to decide that *Pale Fire* is simply a traditional novel overlaid by elaborate verbal trickery.

Other readers have run to the other extreme. In his Introduction to *The Annotated Lolita* (1970), Alfred Appel has made a case for the inevitably self-reflexive nature of Nabokov's fiction, declaring that Nabokov's art is "artifice or nothing," that it everywhere exhibits the "fantastic, a-realistic, and involuted form which even his earliest fictions evolve." Appel has not written of *Pale Fire* in detail, but he has implied a reading of the book which is, I think, clear enough. Indeed, some of the detail is available in Mary McCarthy's early appreciation of the work that regaled it as a beautiful game of chess, a book of mirrors in "fictive space," rather than, in the empirical sense, as a novel. In this view the characterizations of Shade and Kinbote, as of Sybil and Gradus, or of New Wye and Zembla are to be savored not for their own sake but for their participation in an ulterior intellectual enterprise: the careful elaboration of Nabokov's ideas about artistic perception and literary form. What is rounded characterization for one reader is inspired "puppetry" for another. Whether we agree that the true subject of *Pale Fire* is the thematic interplay of death and art, or imagination and reality, the natural tendency of such readings is to transform Nabokov's highly individualized characters into "verbal figurations"—rhetorical instruments who exist to prove and illustrate the author's thesis. That Nabokov's characters *are* so highly individualized, often in exuberant excess of their apparent meanings, is perhaps the most persuasive argument against their suppression.[8]

II

Is there a way of moderating these critical extremes, thereby making epistemological sense of the work while respecting the unique integrity of its central characters? My own solution to the "problem" of *Pale Fire* is at once simpler and more complex than the various reconstructions offered by its recent critics: I propose that we take *at face value* the radical indeterminacy and disorder of the work itself. Such a proposal obviously runs counter to our critical instincts and even our critical faith. Normally we suppress our awareness of a work's residual anomalies whenever these threaten our sense of its underlying unity and coherence. Indeed, not to do so is almost an act of critical malfeasance: a tacit admission that the finished text is not really finished, that it has not altogether emerged from its raw, unresolved, pregeneric state. Yet unless we study the manner in which Nabokov contrived to keep *Pale Fire* "unfinished," our understanding of his overall achievement is certain to be impoverished.

Indeterminacy, disorder, incompleteness—to judge from most critical reactions, these are almost the last qualities associated with *Pale Fire.* Implausible as it seems, Nabokov's most baffling and elusive book is in some immediate peril everywhere of being "overstood"—rather than understood—by its most admiring readers. The whole question of genre is a striking case in point, but it is by no means the only one. Evidence of critical "overstanding" abounds even in the most preliminary reconstructions of the work—those designed to forge a "single shared thematic bond" between Shade's poem and Kinbote's Commentary.[9] Given the notorious incongruity of the Commentary, it is scarcely surprising that most readers have tried to locate the controlling principle of the book outside the farcical configuration of its texts. The parody of a critical edition is so broad, moreover, beginning with the first page of Kinbote's unlikely Introduction, that we are immediately confronted with the question of what this book is really *about.* The question becomes all the more compelling as we doggedly persist through its component parts and discover that there is virtually *no* connection between poem and Commentary. For example, in Canto Two of his creation, Shade refers to "An imbecile with sideburns" brandishing "his gun" (p. 49, ll. 468-69). The reference is actually a harmless allusion to a television thriller he and Sybil happened to be watching on the night of their daughter's death. In the lawless conversions supplied by the Commentary, however, "his gun" is unquestionably assumed to be an allusion to Gradus: the anti-Karlist assassin bent on Kinbote's destruction (pp. 215-16).

As a critical summary of Shade's **"Pale Fire,"** Kinbote's fanciful remarks are of course absolute rubbish. Not only are they hopelessly muddled and off the mark, but in the end they actually reverse the normally self-effacing protocol of scholarly editing, treating Shade's autobiographical work as a mere subtext for the more exotic life of its editor. But the trouble with this observation—as Andrew Field and others have rightly contended—is that many readers have been very much taken with Kinbote's spirited tale of the fantastic Zemblan revolution. The Commentary may have no exegetical bearing on **"Pale Fire,"** but it can be seen as a considerable imaginative achievement in its own right. Indeed, it can almost be viewed as a work of art. Here, of course, we arrive at the "single shared thematic bond" hopefully supplied by critics as a way of organizing and completing Nabokov's deeply divided work. Incommensurable as they are in other ways, the texts of *Pale Fire* can nonetheless be related as works of art, "the products of two radically different yet equally compelling artistic imaginations."[10]

Once this initial and determining step has been taken, everything else seems to fall neatly into place. The usual result of this procedure—whether one later conceives of the work as a novel or as a metafiction—has been to regard Shade and Kinbote as antithetical doubles, "fellow poets" engaged in the common and ultimately specious task of confronting through their art alone the chaos of their own existence. In this unified perspective, Shade is pursued by the idea of death, the extinction of self; and he tries to imagine poetry as a vehicle of transcendence, a way of inscribing on the darkened universe the iambic orderliness of his own personality. The buoyant optimism of his artistic faith is conveyed in the penultimate stanza of Canto Four:

> I feel I understand
> Existence, or at least a minute part
> Of my existence, only through my art,
> In terms of combinational delight;
> And if my private universe scans right,
> So does the verse of galaxies divine
> Which I suspect is an iambic line.
> I'm reasonable sure that we survive
> And that my darling somewhere is alive,
> As I am reasonably sure that I
> Shall wake at six tomorrow, on July
> The twenty-second, nineteen fifty nine,
> And that the day will probably be fine . . .
>
> (pp. 68-69, ll. 971-83)

For Field and subsequent critics, the passage has always held considerable canonical power, since the "combinational delight," celebrated here with some ambivalence (Shade's modernity is no doubt reflected in his "reasonably sure"), seems to be related to Nabokov's earlier and more emphatic valorizations of art in books like *Invitation to a Beheading* and *Bend Sinister*—works in which the power of "aesthetic bliss" is made triumphant over the gross literalism of totalitarian repression. It anticipates as well Nabokov's own later pronouncements on the nature of our human condition, especially our need to "fight the utter degradation, ridicule, and horror of having developed an infinity of sensation and thought within a finite existence."[11] As Nabokov goes on to say in this passage from his autobiography, *Speak, Memory,* love is one of our most important "weapons" in such a fight; art is obviously another. There would seem to be every reason to suppose, then, that art or at least the aesthetic imagination is of considerable thematic importance in *Pale Fire.*

Is it the book's *controlling* theme, however? Does it really allow us to reconstruct *Pale Fire* in a way which intelligibly harmonizes poem and Commentary? Certainly in Shade's poem the consoling power of art is paramount. The reference to "my darling" in the quoted passage is to Hazel, Shade's monumentally ugly daughter, who has committed suicide. Shade's poem is inspired by this death and constitutes an extended meditation on our finite existence. Here Shade's calm assumption of equivalence between his "private universe" and "galaxies divine" leads to an assertion of personal immortality—the "combinational" survival of the "wax-wing" poet adumbrated in the poem's opening lines. If art is indeed a weapon in our fight against the extinction of all sensation and thought, Shade and his poem proclaim that this contest can be won. It can be won because life ultimately reveals a "web of sense," not the "flimsy nonsense" it appears to be. Shade's confident conclusion underlies the often repeated view that in *Pale File* Nabokov means to assert that "artistic perception and design can transcend human fortunes and misfortunes; chaos can be ordered by transforming the world into significant aesthetic form."[12]

Whether this optimistic view is actually shared by Nabokov is open to serious question. But there can be no doubt that critics have consistently employed it as a thematic focus for understanding the "real" significance of Kinbote and his Commentary. Shade himself seems to offer some warrant for this view when defending Kinbote. After a colleague calls Kinbote a madman, Shade replies, "That is the wrong word. . . . One should not apply it to a person who deliberately peels off a drab and unhappy past and replaces it with a brilliant invention." Such a person is actually a "fellow poet" (p. 238). No less than Shade's **"Pale Fire,"** Kinbote's crazy Commentary has come to be read as an artistic response to the otiose realities of our human estate. Recast as a "fellow poet" rather than as a madman, he can thus be seen to participate in the same illustrious enterprise as his beloved master; he replicates with his inverted left hand the miraculous transformations performed by Shade with his right. For if Shade is haunted by intimations of immortality, Kinbote is pursued by his own derangement ("the frozen mud and horror in my heart," p. 258), that is, a radical isolation of the self. And each man's response to his "drab and unhappy" lot is to recast reality with an aesthetically consoling fiction: one by writing a poem to commemorate his faith in a providential universe; the other by writing a commentary to that poem to correspond to his own sense of imperial exile and self-imposed severance from the commonplace.

This, or something like it, has been the dominant critical perspective on *Pale Fire* for quite some time. Its value is that it provides a stable and consistent focus for the book's otherwise discrepant parts; it offers a secure thematic center which allows the reader to proceed outward, as it were, in his search for resemblances and repetitions that are not readily supplied by the texts themselves. Thus, for example, the irrelevant notes and trivial commentary about Disa, Charles's queen (pp. 204-14), are made "relevant" by virtue of their reconstructed meanings within the fantasy life of V. Botkin, who in turn has *his* significance through his association with Shade: a relationship expressive of Nabokov's perennial preoccupation with the ways of the imagination. In short, the strategic value of this reconstructive reading is that it permits us to make sense of a literary work which in its most obvious and original form seems to defy all sense, all meaning.

The problem with it, however, is that it violates one of the basic fictional data of the book. The assumption that Kinbote's Commentary is a work of art flies in the face of a prosaic but immutable fact—one which cannot be willed away however hard we try to restructure the book to conform to our predilection for formal unity and intellectual coherence. Within the putative framework of *Pale Fire,* Kinbote's Zemblan narrative is first and foremost a *critical* commentary, that is, an exegetical work whose subsidiary status is defined and sustained by the prior existence of another work. While it does seem a "brilliant invention," it hardly seems deliberately patterned in the way that Shade's poem is patterned. Nor is it designed to "create a whole world . . . and to people it with dramatically vivid figures,"[13] even though an unwitting consequence of its glorious ineptitude is the creation of such a world. Indeed, Kinbote's Commentary seems to be precisely what it "really" is—a willfully perverse misreading of a work of art prompted by the paranoid fantasy of one V. Botkin, who projects his petty academic quarrels onto the fabulous fictional landscape of Zembla, "a distant northern land" (p. 315). The limitations of Kinbote's Commentary are so obvious and abundant that it is easy to understand why readers have come to see it as a work of art, if only by default. I would argue that the limitations of Kinbote's so-called "art" are even more obvious, for it is quite impossible to imagine that his Commentary was *consciously* contrived to assert anything, let alone the value of an infinity of sensation and thought. Those who contrast his "Shakespearean" qualities with Shade's "Popean" ones do not mean to impute an undeserved originality to either character, but they do imply a shared aesthetic intention which is simply misleading.[14]

III

It is rather more to the point, and rather more difficult, to define Kinbote's role in the "real" world, which is to say, the world of the unreconstructed fiction. Kinbote's fantasy life is sufficiently rich and circumstantial that it is all too easy to overlook his primary function in *Pale Fire*: that of reader and interpreter. To recall that function is often ponderous, but the effort is justified by our entry into a new relationship with the text and its characters, one in which we become acutely aware of our own creative role as readers. Whether in the last analysis we regard *Pale Fire* primarily as a novel or as a metafiction, it is clearly of the first importance that we always see it as the thing it pretends to be: a scholarly edition that is designed to elucidate a poem, but which scandalously falls apart as a result of its editor's gross ineptitude and indefatigable egotism. I sometimes wish it were possible to recover and retain through successive readings the original shock every reader feels on first encountering this scandal.[15] An important element of our overall experience with the work is inevitably lost to us if we overcome its strangeness too quickly, calmly assimilate its disjunctions, and compensate for its discrepancies by supplying thematic linkages which the texts themselves do not provide. On another level, the texts "themselves" do provide these things, but only in retrospect and in collaboration with a reader determined to dominate their unfamiliar shapes rather than be taken over by them. In this crucial regard *Pale Fire* is not merely the story of John Shade and Charles Kinbote. Nor is it only an "apologue" on the mysterious ways of art. On its most literal level, *Pale Fire* is also the story of our own experience as readers: a parody (as well as a paradigm) of the interpretive process we all undergo as we confront the essential strangeness of new and difficult texts and attempt to reconcile them to the familiar patterns of our literary experience.

In the widest sense, of course, this is a process common to all hermeneutical acts—though most especially in the case of revolutionary works, by now the acknowledged classics of our literary heritage. In the shadow of the intervening years, we forget how much sheer intellectual guesswork, confusion, tension, arbitrariness, and egoism had gone into the "combinational delights" we all enjoy now that the problem plays have been made less problematic, or *Tristram Shandy* more fashionably modern, or *Ulysses* and *The Wasteland* more safely "characteristic" of other twentieth-century works that we have come to know and admire. At our secure remove from the muddled actualities of our inspired first readings, we forget how alone we truly were when we first encountered these works of idiosyncratic genius, just as we tend to forget how thoroughly all our critical sorties were then piloted by the seat of our pants rather than by any prearranged plan or signal. My metaphors are mixed, but I trust my meaning is clear. What I am here suggesting with regard to *Pale Fire* is that Nabokov deliberately prolongs and intensifies this initial experience of indeterminacy and so forces us to acknowledge the active role we invariably play in shaping the literary texts we read. Like Stevens's Canon Asperin in *Notes toward a Supreme Fiction,* we "impose" as much as we "discover" the unseen order of things. And if, as Humbert Humbert suggests, one of the functions of art is to provide a refuge from reality, another—suggested by *Pale Fire*—is to assess the fictions whereby we make sense of reality. Making sense of *Pale Fire,* within the dizzying domain of its fictional reality, has become a creative activity as well as an academic industry which shows no sign of letting up.

Here the madness of Kinbote (rather than his "artistry") is especially illuminating, not only for what it tells us of his own character but for what it has to say about our own discomposure when initially confronted with works like *Pale Fire.* That Kinbote is a narcissist and a madman is well known, but it is perhaps the first rather than the last thing that must be said of him. For the more closely one examines his career throughout the book, the more one realizes that there is a kind of luminous integrity, indeed a heroism, in his continuous self-projection. As Charles-Xavier of Zembla, he is not only the perfect subject for an academic poet but is also a "poet" himself (as well as an exiled king), regally surveying his fantasies, inhabiting his private realms. Indeed, in the extremity of his imagination, he is remarkably true to the Romantic archetype that Georges Poulet describes in *The Metamorphoses of the Circle*:

> Perhaps there could be no better definition, if not of Romanticism, at least one of its most important aspects, than to say that it is a taking possession by consciousness of the basically subjective character of the mind. The Romantic is one who discovers himself to be a center. It does not matter very much that the world of objects may be out of reach; the Romantic knows that deep within himself there is something which cannot be assimilated to an object. That is the subjective and most authentic part of the self, the part which he most willingly recognizes as his own. Deprived of the periphery, the Romantic will gradually familiarize himself with the self, the center.[16]

Applying this to Kinbote, we might say that he is all center and no circumference. One important way of describing his hapless Commentary is to say that it represents the continuous rediscovery, on his part, that the true periphery is lost, the world of objects a deceit or a disappointment. And rather than be "assimilated" to the lackluster world of New Wye and Sybil Shade, he will assimilate that world into the radiant realm which occupies the center of his being.

Much of the mock-heroic tension of Kinbote's character inheres precisely in this unwavering commitment to his own center, in his fierce if sometimes frenzied struggle to protect the interior authenticity of his dreams from the encircling menaces of everyday life—including, of course, the ever present menace of Shade's inhospitable poem. To those readers who would deny that Kinbote is a truly novelistic character, in the sense of encountering real obstacles and represented instabilities, I would argue that the poem itself—in its very indifference to his Zemblan existence—offers innumerable challenges to his self-interpretive powers. But the important point is that Kinbote's relation to the poem and to Shade himself mirrors the moment of cognitive tension undergone by all readers before a text lying just outside the familiar boundaries of their literary experience. It is no accident that the climax of his Commentary is very precisely portrayed as a moment of textual quandary in which Kinbote, confronting **"Pale Fire"** for the very first time, must overcome his sense of the poem's incongruity and irrelevance before incorporating it into the familiar patterns of his fantasy life:

> Gradually I regained my usual composure. I reread **"Pale Fire"** more carefully. I liked it better when expecting less. And what was that? What was that dim distant music, those vestiges of color in the air? Here and there I discovered in it and especially, especially in the invaluable variants, echoes and spangles of my mind, a long ripplewake of my glory. I now felt a new, pitiful tenderness toward the poem as one has for a fickle young creature who has been stolen and brutally enjoyed by a black giant but now again is safe in our hall and park, whistling with the stableboys, swimming with the tame seal.

(p. 297)

Objective text has become personal pretext, in the double sense of a hidden motive and of a further creative opportunity, for expanding the center of one's interpretive needs to include the alien material outside. In retrieving from Shade's poem the "dim distant music" of an older, more familiar "glory," the mad Kinbote speaks for any sane and responsive reader who has ever attempted to wring a sense of continuity and order from the gross inconsistencies of literary history.

John Shade, wiser than Kinbote and less inclined to imperial avarice, acknowledges the inevitable duplicity and self-deception of most interpretive acts. *"Life is a message scribbled in the dark"* (p. 41, l. 235), he writes at one point; later he is reported to have said, "Resemblances are the shadows of differences. Different people see different similarities and similar differences" (p. 265). Like Nabokov himself, Shade realizes that between two people, as between two literary works or between a literary work and a work of criticism, there can never be a perfect congruence of sympathies and signifiers—only the pretext of one, in whose name we nevertheless strive to find "Some kind of link-and-bobolink, some kind / Of correlated pattern in the game" (p. 63, ll. 812-13). Yet even Shade is motivated by a need for meaningful "resemblances," immemorial patterns that may withstand the corrosive force of time. In a crucial reminiscence he recalls the period of his heart attack when, lying close to death, he had observed a "tall white fountain" playing "dreadfully distinct" against the darkness (p. 59, ll. 706-07). Convalescing later, he discovers a magazine article in which it is revealed that a certain Mrs. Z. has undergone a similar experience, complete with the treasured vision he himself has witnessed. Seemingly, their shared perception of the fountain is a "signpost" offering objective evidence of eternal life; and upon its "robust truth" Shade reposes the entire burden of his providential faith—his belief that the individual soul survives the ravages of time and death. Only later does he realize the folly of this simplistic "proof." Subsequent inquiries reveal that the magazine has in part misprinted the true report of Mrs. Z.'s experience: in her deathlike state she had seen not a tall white *fountain* but a tall white *mountain*!

The irony of the episode is complex and suggestive, depending as it does not only on the comedy of the misprint but on Shade's irrepressible desire to impose some sort of order on the chaotic flux of experience. The point to stress, however, is that the misprint itself constitutes for Shade a moment of religious crisis that repeats, even as it varies, Kinbote's interpretive crisis later. We have just seen how Kinbote, in the climactic moment of his Commentary, subverts **"Pale Fire"** to his own advantage. Rather than relinquish his belief that the poem is about himself, Kinbote sets out systematically to "improve upon" its clarity, finding oblique references where there had been only differences, until, suffusing the entire poem with his Zemblan existence, he can absorb its resistant realities into his own egoistic orbit. The stolidity and balance of Shade's character have usually prevented readers from seeing that he is here engaged in a similar act of appropriation. Thus in the climactic moment of the poem, the cold factuality of the misprint serves as an equally rude disclaimer, exposing his providential faith to potential ridicule and a charge of wishful thinking. Rather than renounce his faith, however, Shade turns incontrovertible fact into imperial advantage. If the misprint impugns the ontological authority of his dream, then it is still possible to ask: why *this* misprint rather than some other? What design, if any, accounts for *this* set of circumstances, *this* particular coincidence? This Shade does; with growing confidence and elation he goes on to conclude that the true "signpost" of his faith is the "contrapuntal theme" of the misprint itself. Not his dream per se but a "topsy turvical coincidence" (of dream *and* misprint) points to the reality of an immanently purposive universe and the presence in it of mysterious divinities intent on "Making ornaments / Of accidents and possibilities" (p. 63, ll. 828-29).

I have dwelled at length on Shade's strategy of self-recovery because, though generally unremarked, it suggests an approach to **Pale Fire** which is both truer to its form and more accurately reflective of our reading experience than the thematic reconstructions offered by earlier critics. In the first place, it underscores an essential affinity between the central characters which cuts clean across their alleged "artistic" differences.[17] In most readings of the work it is Shade who is regarded as the reliable, and Kinbote the unreliable, spokesman for reality. The basis for this judgment is of course the Commentary, which in its open defiance of the real and the factual seems to be engaged in the purest kind of fabulation. (The poem, by contrast, since it is the *central* fact from which the Commentary departs, seems all the more securely rooted in reality.) But as Shade's interpretation of the misprint suggests, both men are embarked on an effort of assimilation that is clearly in excess of the facts alone. If Shade resembles Nabokov in subscribing to the sanctity of individual difference, he also resembles Kinbote in his compulsive search for likeness; that is, for meaningful repetitions that will substantiate his own version of reality. Shade's presiding "version," as we have seen, entails a fiercely held belief in a providential universe; and to uphold this belief, to ensure its integrity against any possible contravention, Shade marshals all the supporting evidence at his command—all the contributive hints, "signposts," and signals which testify, however tenuously, to his vision of a "Life Everlasting" beyond the brute contingency of the grave. No less than Kinbote, then, Shade struggles valiantly to maintain the supremacy of a personal fiction over the felt illusion of human circumstance. But there is another likeness between them— one seldom noticed by Nabokov's critics but clearly crucial to our understanding of the book's notorious difficulty. In their common pursuit of a sustaining fiction, each character is conspicuously engaged in ad hoc responses to apparently objective facts; something that I can only call, in a crudely impressionistic way, a creative revision of reality.

We may examine this process in greater detail by noting, first, that it is implicitly an act of reparation and self-assertion; and second, that it is not dependent on absolute notions of accuracy and error: not dependent, that is, on the idea of objective fact and correspondent truth which has virtually dominated traditional Western thinking. A classic example of such thinking, in the critical sphere, is Arnold's often repeated assertion that the "aim of criticism is to see the object as in itself it really is."[18] This statement went with his demand for disinterested curiosity as the mark of the critic; its inadvertent effect was to put the critic on his knees before the object he was discussing. Not everyone enjoyed this position—least of all a writer like Nabokov. Almost a century later, his emphatic strictures against the "average reality" of passive impressions alert us to the potential tyranny of the Arnoldian ideal.[19] They also shift the center of attention from the rock of the object to the winds of the perceiver's responses.

In this context of expanded reader involvement, we must assess again the various "misreadings" performed by Shade and Kinbote. When Kinbote announces in his Foreword that without his notes Shade's poem has no "human reality," he is informing us in advance of at least two things: first, that his Commentary is an untrustworthy and unreliable guide to Shade's poem, but second, that Shade's poem is an inadequate and unreliable foundation for his Commentary. Rather than surrender to its "facts," therefore, he will impose dominion on them; he will repair and unify its fragments until they reassert themselves as his beloved Zemblan narrative. Shade applies roughly the same procedure to the magazine misprint. Viewed as an isolated and elemental fact, the misprint constitutes an insurmountable challenge to his faith, one whose pitiless dismissal of his vision renders his belief in an afterlife "untrue." Reconceived as a symbolic event, however, its implications can be reversed and lead to the discovery of a deeper truth: the "topsy turvical coincidence" that for Shade affirms the existence of an inscrutable Deity invisibly operative in the visible world. That Shade's discovery is actually an invention—a reinter-pretation generated by a desperate need for resemblances (or indeed any "correlated pattern")—has hardly been noticed by most readers. But surely it undercuts the popular view that in *Pale Fire* it is only Kinbote who "misreads" and recycles facts, pieces things together to suit his own advantage, defers to alternate "drafts" as occasion or need demands, or who otherwise subverts everyday reality to his own subjective vision. For all their differences in temperament, Shade and Kinbote finally join hands in their determination to resist the craven power of fact embodied in Gradus: the book's "average reality" principle and quintessential expression of anti-imaginative man.

To call this conquest of fact an "artistic" achievement, however, or to regard "art" as the unifying theme of the book is, as I have suggested, doubly misleading. Not only is it at odds with the ad hoc nature of Shade's and Kinbote's responses (which are, after all, as human as they are artistic), but it also runs counter to the prevailing spirit of anomaly and disorder that pervades *Pale Fire* itself: a work which more than any other by its author appeals to the reader's own ingenuity at reconceiving facts and piecing things together. The unusually close relation between the reader's role and the characters' underscores the issue here and ultimately leads back to the mystery implicit in the title of the book. The phrase "pale fire" is taken from Shakespeare's *Timon of Athens* (but not from IV.iii, as Kinbote asserts):

> I'll example you with thievery:
> The sun's a thief, and with his great attraction
> Robs the vast sea; the moon's an arrant thief,
> And her pale fire she snatches from the sun.
>
> (IV.ii.441-44)

The pale fire of art, in the usual view, reflects the fierce sun of reality; but as most readers have observed, Nabokov overturns this traditional formulation to reveal a further paradox, and another mirroring: art may itself become a magical source of undying illumination for its beholders, rivaling and even displacing in its brilliance that of the natural sun. To this familiar modern paradox, Nabokov joins another, postmodern one: in *Pale Fire* the light-thieving critic and commentator—like Kinbote vis-à-vis Shade—might in turn become his own sun, generating from within the recesses of his febrile imagination a radiance as compelling as the original work of art. In this context both critic and artist, lunar thief and solar source, are said to assume an equal authority and complementary importance, one equidistant between them, as it were, yet finally dependent upon their mutually reflecting surfaces. The pale fire produced by this circular process, so the paradox goes, is no reflection at all but an original source of light: a third illumination generated by the complex clash and lively interaction of two sensibilities separated in time and space.

The aesthetic paradoxes so brilliantly on display in *Pale Fire* have been cited repeatedly by recent critics; indeed, they underlie the critical position outlined in the second section of this essay. Suggestive as they are, however, they finally seem of rather limited value in dealing with the parodic nature of Nabokov's text. For in spite of the obvious inventiveness of the poem and its commentary, and apart from the fact that they were both written by Nabokov, it remains true that they have nothing else in common whatsoever. They do not, as it were, speak to each other; nor are they even distantly related. Between their impervious integuments there is no equidistant point of reference—no membrane of resemblance—only an unbridgeable gulf of difference. As a parodic commentary, Kinbote's farcical notes do not even remotely criticize any possible original reading that we might imagine—in the revisionist manner, say, of Harold Bloom on Yeats, Hillis Miller on Hardy, or more recently, of James E. Miller, Jr., on T. S. Eliot.[20] To the contrary, as we have seen, Kinbote's Commentary serves no other rhetorical purpose than to draw the unwary reader into its own fantastic depths. In the final analysis, it does not complement Shade's poem at all; it simply competes with it.

In what conceivable context, then, does **"Pale Fire"** serve as an appropriate and effective title? What illumination does it bring to this obscurely disjointed work, this "monstrous semblance of a novel" (p. 86) which has the appearance also of an apologue or a metafiction? To some extent, the significance of the question corresponds to our alternating sense of the book as a work both written and read. On the one hand, the indeterminacy of the text compels us to intervene as readers and complete the totalizing task "intended" by its author. Depending on what we choose to discover, therefore, the work will always reflect the kind of order we have given it. Yet at the same time, the work as written will also mirror the inadequacy of our responses, exposing our nostalgic need for unity and our desire to fashion a consistent totality out of its mutually discrepant parts. In this expanded context the title phrase refers not to a specific theme or determinate order within the work itself but alludes instead to the constant and tantalizing promise of such an order—a promise which Nabokov's text repeatedly suggests but which it persistently withholds. Hence the ultimate paradox of the book: *Pale Fire* is a work of art that is—as Peter Rabinowitz suggests—permanently enshrouded in ambiguity, oscillating uncertainly between what he calls its "authorial audience," on the one hand, and its "narrative audience," on the other;[21] yet for that very reason it

remains permanently susceptible to our reconstructions, to our successive visions and revisions of its final form and meaning. The reconstructed text that emerges from our readings, the version of its unity that we ourselves create—as a reflection of the "real" one underlying its parodic fragments—is the "pale fire" ultimately referred to in the title of Nabokov's playfully subversive book.

For in the final analysis, it is the art of reading (or better, misreading) which is the principal focus of *Pale Fire.* The interpretive process whereby as readers we attempt to organize literature's irreducible anomalies into recognizable wholes—this is what Nabokov's work is most fundamentally about; as we have seen, it is a process fully descriptive also of its central characters, who, for different reasons and in different tones of voice, are no less vitally concerned to demonstrate the power of "resemblance" over the authority of fact. This shared activity, at once so playful and so serious, is the key to the "contrapuntal theme" enunciated by Shade a few days before his absurd and untimely death:

> Life Everlasting—based on a misprint!
> I mused as I drove homeward: take the hint,
> And stop investigating my abyss?
> But all at once it dawned on me that *this*
> Was the real point, the contrapuntal theme;
> Just this: not text, but texture; not the dream
> But a topsy-turvical coincidence,
> Not flimsy nonsense, but a web of sense.
>
> (pp. 62-63, ll. 803-10)

Knowing full well that any everlasting truth or theory is always to some extent "based on a misprint," Shade, like the rest of us, nonetheless continues his self-deception, continues "to keep sane in spiral types of space"—which, in the context of our response to *Pale Fire,* most certainly means that he continues to read and interpret, to unify the anomalous "texts" of his own experience.

Notes

1. Vladimir Nabokov, *Pale Fire* (New York: G. P. Putnam's Sons, 1962), pp. 28-29. Future references to this edition will be incorporated into the text.

2. In the frequently quoted passage from his Afterword to the 1958 edition of *Lolita,* Nabokov said: "For me a work of fiction exists only insofar as it affords me what I shall bluntly call aesthetic bliss, that is a sense of being somehow, somewhere, connected with other states of being where art . . . is the norm" ("On a Book Entitled *Lolita,*" in *The Annotated Lolita,* ed. with preface, introduction, and notes by Alfred Appel, Jr. [New York: McGraw-Hill, 1970], pp. 316-17). The number of critics who have approached Nabokov as a master illusionist and aesthete indifferent to the struggles

of ordinary humanity would seem to be inexhaustible, but even a partial list of them would have to include Appel's own influential introduction to *The Annotated Lolita.* See also Frank Kermode's review of *Bend Sinister,* "Aesthetic Bliss," *Encounter,* 14 (June 1960), 81-86, and Joyce Carol Oates, "A Personal View of Nabokov," *Saturday Review,* January 1973, pp. 36-37.

3. Robert M. Adams, *Afterjoyce: Studies in Fiction after Ulysses* (New York: Oxford University Press, 1977), p. 151, and Vladimir Nabokov, *Strong Opinions* (New York: McGraw-Hill, 1973), p. 115.

4. Nina Berberova, "The Mechanics of *Pale Fire,*" *Triquarterly,* 17 (Winter 1970), 147-48.

5. The theoretical differences underlying these two approaches are ventilated, respectively, by George Levine, "Realism Reconsidered," in *The Theory of the Novel: New Essays,* ed. John Halperin (New York: Oxford University Press, 1974), pp. 233-53, and Robert Scholes, *Fabulation and Metafiction* (Urbana: University of Illinois Press, 1979), esp. pp. 103-38. The term "apologue" is taken from the late Sheldon Sacks, who applies it to works of narrative fiction which are dominated more by "a development of ideas" than by a concern for "characters and their fates." See especially the first and last chapters of his *Fiction and the Shape of Belief* (Berkeley and Los Angeles: University of California Press, 1964).

6. Andrew Field, *Nabokov: His Life in Art* (Boston: Little, Brown, 1967), p. 300; Page Stegner, *Escape into Aesthetics: The Art of Vladimir Nabokov* (New York: Dial Press, 1966), pp. 129-30; and Ellen Pifer, *Nabokov and the Novel* (Cambridge: Harvard University Press, 1980), pp. 110-18.

7. Douglas Fowler, *Reading Nabokov* (Ithaca: Cornell University Press, 1974), pp. 112-21.

8. Appel, Introduction to *The Annotated Lolita,* p. xviii, and Mary McCarthy, "Vladimir Nabokov's *Pale Fire,*" *Encounter,* 19 (October 1962), 71-84.

9. Field, p. 297.

10. Robert Merrill, "Nabokov and Fictional Artifice," *Modern Fiction Studies,* 25 (Autumn 1979), 458. Merrill's general position, that *Pale Fire* is an a-realistic work unified by Nabokov's ideas about art, is the predominant point of view in recent Nabokov criticism. See, e.g., John O. Lyons, "*Pale Fire* and the Fine Art of Annotation," in *Nabokov: The Man and His Work,* ed. L. S. Dembo (Madison: University of Wisconsin Press, 1967), pp. 157-64; Julia Bader, *Crystal Land: Artifice in*

Nabokov's English Novels (Berkeley and Los Angeles: University of California Press, 1972), pp. 31-56; and L. L. Lee, *Vladimir Nabokov* (Boston: G. K. Hall, 1976), pp. 132-44.

11. Vladimir Nabokov, *Speak, Memory: An Autobiography Revisited,* rev. ed. (New York: G. P. Putnam's Sons, 1966), p. 297.

12. David Walker, "'The Viewer and the View': Chance and Choice in *Pale Fire,*" *Studies in American Fiction,* 4 (Autumn 1976), 220.

13. Robert Alter, *Partial Magic: The Novel as a Self-Conscious Genre* (Berkeley and Los Angeles: University of California Press, 1975), p. 203.

14. Ibid., p. 204.

15. That Nabokov himself was fully aware of the "parodic" shock produced by editorial intervention is evident from his comments concerning his own experience editing and translating Pushkin's *Eugene Onegin*—an effort of erudition concurrent with the composition of *Pale Fire*: "The term 'literal translation' is tautological since anything but that is not truly a translation but an imitation, an adaptation or a parody" ("Problems of Translation: *Onegin* in English," *Partisan Review,* 22 [1955], 504).

16. Translated by the author from Georges poulet, *Les metamorphoses du cercle* (Paris: Librairie Plon, 1961), p. 136.

17. See Daniel Albright, e.g., on the contrast between Shade's "truthful" and Kinbote's "nonsensical" imaginations, in *Representation and the Imagination* (Chicago: University of Chicago Press, 1981), p. 84.

18. Matthew Arnold, "The Function of Criticism at the Present Time," in *Poetry and Criticism of Matthew Arnold,* ed. A. Dwight Culler (Boston: Houghton Mifflin, 1961), p. 237.

19. In *Strong Opinions,* p. 118, Nabokov averred that "average reality begins to rot and stink as soon as the act of individual creation ceases to animate a subjectively perceived texture."

20. Harold Bloom, *Yeats* (New York: Oxford University Press, 1970); J. Hillis Miller, *Thomas Hardy: Distance and Desire* (Cambridge: Harvard University Press, 1970); and James E. Miller, Jr., *T. S. Eliot's Personal Waste Land: Exorcism of the Demons* (University Park: Pennsylvania State University Press, 1977).

21. Peter J. Rabinowitz, "Truth in Fiction: A Reexamination of Audiences," *Critical Inquiry,* 4 (Autumn 1977), 121-41.

Patrick O'Donnell (essay date 1986)

SOURCE: O'Donnell, Patrick. "Nabokov's Watermark: Writing the Self in *Pale Fire*." In *Passionate Doubts: Designs of Interpretation in Contemporary American Fiction,* pp. 3-22. Iowa City: University of Iowa Press, 1986.

[*In the following essay, O'Donnell identifies elements of reflexivity in Nabokov's* Pale Fire, *claiming that the novel is representative of "self-critical" fiction.*]

> The words of a dead man
> Are modified in the guts of the living.
>
> W. H. Auden, "In Memory of W. B. Yeats"

According to Mikhail Bakhtin, one of the novel's primary generic traits incorporates a commentary upon the semantic conditions that prevail when a given text is produced. Bakhtin writes that "the novel . . . emerges consciously and unambiguously as a genre that is both critical and self-critical, one fated to revise the fundamental concepts of literariness and poeticalness dominant at the time."[1] It is in the nature of the novel he argues, to recognize and criticize the complex of discourses (philosophical, social, literary) in which it is born, as well as to be critical of itself, thus self-reflexive. In the present era of intensive self-scrutiny and the novel's dominance, it seems fitting that one of the reigning hallmarks of contemporary fiction is its complication of "reflexivity." The notion of reflexivity in fiction is certainly more problematic than a term often associated with it, "self-consciousness," and its existence, Bakhtin suggests, is hardly coterminous with the advent of contemporary literature. As Robert Alter has shown, reflexivity has manifested itself as a quality of fictions since (at least) *Don Quixote*.[2] The understanding of reflexivity as a determining element of those contemporary novels which concern me here must be tied to a contemporaneous concept of the "self-critical" which goes beyond Bakhtin's understanding of the traditional, generic critique of established literary modes and discourses. This concept differs from mere self-consciousness in a notable way. "Self-conscious" fiction is aware of itself *as* fiction and thus indulges in speculations about the relations between narrative and "reality"; it is, above all, concerned about its own fictive status or the rhetorical successes and failures of its own narrative operations. As Alter demonstrates, *Don Quixote* is unquestionably self-conscious in this regard, as are *Vanity Fair* and *Herzog*. "Self-critical" fiction, I suggest, is more interrogative and not only in its intense self-awareness as it directly questions the principles of its own composition or reflects ironically upon relations to the discourse of "reality" which it, by turns, mirrors, transmutes, fragments, and distorts. Doubly reflexive, self-critical fiction ponders the very conditions of its reflexivity as it, more specifically, raises questions about

its *own* language, the substance and vehicle of its expression. Moreover, these questions are asked from within the texts where they appear, as if the text was an echo chamber that reproduced in endless variation the soundings of its own title or table of contents—those expressions which name what it is and define what it contains.

The rhetoric of my definition of the self-critical text exhibits the kind of hyperinteriority characteristic of reflexive fictions, which many readers find merely precious or annoyingly solipsistic. And, too, this self-critical fiction is not only a contemporary phenomenon: *Tristram Shandy, Gargantua and Pantagruel,* or *Moby-Dick* could, conceivably, render examples of my definition as easily as the particular instance of a contemporary self-critical novel to be considered shortly, Vladimir Nabokov's **Pale Fire.** Regarding the question about the validity of these reflexive forms, it may be said that the interior scrutiny they perform is a crucial alternative and corrective to a culture (any, not just ours) that assumes the merely instrumental, functional aspects of language and builds world views upon these. The contemporary nature and attitude of self-critical fiction are not so much historically unique as they are compounded by the novel's place *in* history. Contemporary narrative is written in a culture obsessed with the origins and ends of history, with the reflexive nature of its own "contemporaneity," and with its own confinement in the languages through which it makes itself known. Given this context, the ironic, questioning, disruptive function of self-critical fiction must be balanced against its opposite. While these fictions play language games and deconstruct the philosophical assumptions that lie behind enabling stories about the world, they also *construct* their own semiologies. They are engaged, thematically, structurally, and stylistically, in generating fictive sign systems that designate their status as self-questioned discourses. They stand as linguistic topographies that proclaim their emergence from a realm of silence into a noisy, contradictory, sign-filled world which is that of the text.

In this broad definition, self-critical fiction can be seen to dwell more narrowly on the first term of my hyphenated label—the nature of the "self," as that entity which writes itself into existence through the complex, interwoven language of a given fictional text.[3] The narrating "I" of *Tristram Shandy,* "HCE" of *Finnegans Wake,* and the Barth-like, letter-writing "Author" of John Barth's Letters can all be seen as verbal, even alphabetic inscriptions who doubtfully construct a "self" in narrative through the reflexive manipulation of narrative signs. These constructions reflect a concern with the identity of texts paralleled with an anxiety about the origins and identities of selves in texts. As one of these self-critical fictions, **Pale Fire,** which most surely is a parody of the critical act and a compendious examination of paranoia, is also a presentation of the autobiographical self as a sign within a textual system of signs: the mad commentator, Charles Kinbote, finds "himself" within the seemingly irrelevant markings of John Shade's poem, **"Pale Fire."** In so doing, Kinbote creates a language—his interpretation of the poem—that in its structuring of linguistic relations, samenesses and differences, defines the writing, interpreting self. The subject of the novel may be seen as a process rather than a theme; indeed, the subject of *Pale Fire* is the dethroned "subject," Kinbote, seen watermarking the text with the sign of his own identity.[4] That this identity is a fiction which reflects upon the operations of language and the creation of linguistic kingdoms suggests the larger purposes of Nabokov's hermeneutic parody and of self-critical fiction in general: to discover the limits of the self conceived in language, as well as its constructive possibilities.

Ostensibly, *Pale Fire* is the annotated text of an autobiographical poem. Perhaps an exercise in self-irony, it was published only two years before the appearance of Nabokov's own lengthy translation and annotation of Pushkin's *Eugene Onegin*. The reader does not have to venture far into Kinbote's annotations of Shade's **"Pale Fire"** to discover that the novel is more Kinbote's autobiography than a scholarly edition of Shade's confessional poem. *Pale Fire* is actually comprised of four separate texts, the central two being Shade's poem and Kinbote's "commentary" on the poem. Kinbote's function as editor is made suspect immediately when we discover that the incomplete poem has come into his hands as a bundle of index cards, which he removed from the dead poet's body and hid in his own house. These texts are flanked by two others, Kinbote's foreword and index. Nabokov thus creates in *Pale Fire* the visible effect of "intertextuality": the four texts mirror each other and reverberate against one another so that our attention is diverted from assessing the truth or informational value of the poem or the commentary. Instead, as one reader states, we are compelled to note "correspondences and coincidences, not only from note to note but from notes to poem," resulting in the revelation of "the correspondences the mind can perceive or invent between them."[5] The whole novel reflects Shade's discovery in his search for empirical evidence of an afterlife: it is not the proof of divinity itself which is important but the associations one can see between life and afterlife, or the real and the imaginary, or (later, for Kinbote) poem and commentary. As Shade writes:

> But all at once it dawned on me that *this*
> Was the real point, the contrapuntal theme;
> Just this: not text, but texture; not the dream
> But topsy-turvical coincidence,
> Not flimsy nonsense, but a web of sense.
> Yes! It sufficed that I in life could find
> Some kind of link-and-bobolink, some kind
> Of correlated pattern in the game,

> Plexed artistry, and something of the same
> Pleasure in it as they who played it found.

> ([*Pale Fire*] C. III, ll. 806-15)[6]

This much-cited passage imitates through its verbalizations Shade's discovery that life is a matter of pattern and relation. The phonic interplays between "text" and "texture," "sense" and "nonsense," "link-and-bobolink," "plexed" and "pleasure" immediately suggest what Kinbote, in his commentary, will confirm as the primary concern of *Pale Fire*: to enact a scene of writing, where significance is achieved through the creation of sonorous pleasure and alphabetical correspondences.

In his poem, Shade recounts his search, after a near-fatal stroke during which he has had an eschatological vision of a luminous fountain, for a corresponding validation of his having "crossed the border" (C. III, ll. 699-700). He thinks he finds it when he reads a newspaper account of a woman who has also "died" for several seconds and who has seen a vision with a fountain in it. His conception of life as an aesthetic game, a "web of sense," where not the linear exposition of "text" but the spatial correspondences of "texture" are the objects of the search for truth, arrives after his now infamous discovery that what he thought was proof of the afterlife is based on a misprint, evidence of a misreading: the woman has seen a mountain, not a fountain. Shade concludes that whatever truths are to be found about the ultimacies of existence rest upon coincidences and imposed patterns of perception; the truth becomes for him a matter of cross-reference, correspondence, and analogy rather than a statement of fact or a proposition.

To go no further in this analysis of Shade's discovery would be to reiterate the standard critical positions regarding Nabokov's mannerist vision of artful intricacies and verbal prisons. But a closer reading with an eye to phonic, alphabetic "texture" reveals that Shade's discovery is based upon a correspondence that is, essentially, a linguistic pattern of sameness and difference. "Mountain" and "fountain" are nearly identical, save for the difference in their initial letters. Both words designate elemental phenomena that rise into the air, but one is constituted of earth, the other of water; one is natural, the other usually artificial. Both are backlighted in Shade's vision by the pale fires of life's fading so that, together, they establish a tableau of the primary elements of the universe (air, earth, fire, water); yet, in the difference of initials, they designate the sexual distinctions, male and female, that regenerate the "life" of this elemental world. The effort may seem Kinbotian, but the text of *Pale Fire* encourages us to make such construals. Out of the misread and misprinted relations between events, a wholly constituted, structured universe of elemental and sexual identities can be detected, within which Shade proclaims that the pattern of his own life can be traced.

Earlier in the poem, Shade parodically evokes Wallace Stevens in lines on the remembered pleasures of mortal life:

> And I'll turn down eternity unless
> The melancholy and the tenderness
> Of mortal life; the passion and the pain;
> The claret taillight of that dwindling plane
> Off Hesperus; your gesture of dismay
> On running out of cigarettes; the way
> You smile at dogs; the trail of silver slime
> Snails leave on flagstones; this good ink, this rhyme,
> This index card, this slender rubber band
> Which always forms, when dropped, an ampersand,
> Are found in Heaven by the newlydead,
> Stored in its strongholds through the years.
>
> (C. III, ll. 525-36)

Much of this is hilariously bad poetry, but it is notable that Shade translates experience into sign as he recalls the ephemera of domestic life. A disquisition on the ineffability of human passion turns to more concrete notions—reflections of light, gestures, mollusk trails—and ends with a reference to the very cards upon which the poem is presently being written. Even the rubber band that binds these fragments inevitably forms, when dropped, a symbol that looks suspiciously like the mirrored, cursive letter of Shade's initial; as an ampersand, it represents the unfinished, metonymical etceteras of his incomplete poem and quest for certainty. The passage suggests that the perceptions and desires of the autobiographical self are transcribed into letters on the page; thus, it often seems, as in the first lines of **"Pale Fire,"** that it is not the "I" of Shade who speaks but the poem itself, giving voice to its own tenuous existence:

> I was the shadow of the waxwing slain
> By the false azure in the windowpane;
> I was the smudge of ashen fluff—and I
> Lived on, flew on, in the reflected sky.
>
> (C. I, ll. 1-4)

Similar to the floating, butterflylike ashes of the variants to the poem which Kinbote describes Shade burning, **"Pale Fire"** is the self's remnant and supplement, Shade's shadow, the inscribed mark of the fingerprint that survives as the writing, reflected self. Shade's poem is an enactment of self-inscription, down to the letter, as it generates a universe of signs bound together by the emerging trace element, the "S" that designates the poet's name and self. From the "text" of experience or the misprintings of existence, the poet traces the design of the self and reinscribes it in the text of his poem.

If **"Pale Fire"** enacts a process of self-inscription, Kinbote's commentary does so doubly. For Kinbote, Shade's rambling poem about his life, his daughter's suicide, and his acceptance of uncertainty concerning the nature of eternity is a secondary text into which are

woven the "wavelets of fire" and the "pale phosphorescent hints" of Kinbote's former life as the king (now exiled) of Zembla, land of shadows and mirrors (297). Kinbote's remembered or fantasized life in Zembla is transcribed by him into the commentary which, on first reading, bears only marginal resemblance to the poem. He hopes that Shade will "recreate in a poem the dazzling Zembla burning in my brain" (80). But when he first scans the text after his prodigious, obsessive efforts to provide the poet with information about Zembla during the writing of the poem, he is distraught: "Instead of the wild glorious romance—what did I have? An autobiographical, eminently Appalachian, rather old-fashioned narrative in a neo-Popian prosodic style . . . void of my magic, of that special rich streak of magical madness which I was sure would run through it and make it transcend its time" (296-97). However, a second reading convinces Kinbote that the poem's "dim distant music," "vestiges of color," and "invaluable variants" reflect the "echoes and spangles of my mind" (297). The poem, rather than being a perfect mirror reflecting his Zemblan past, becomes for him a *deflection,* a scattering of signs and clues to be regathered in the commentary's autobiography. The poem is the novel's pale fire or lamp, which "in its pale and diaphanous final phase" (81) dimly illuminates the commentator's past.[7] We are thus exposed to the comically vertiginous spectacle of Shade creating a text, **"Pale Fire,"** inspired by another text (the misprinted newspaper), which delineates the hieroglyphic signature of the poet's "self." This is used by Kinbote as a cipher or Rosetta stone that translates, if obscurely, Appalachian into Zemblan, wherein he detects the sign of a personal past that mixes memory and desire.

Accordingly, in much of his commentary, Kinbote is anxious about matters of translation and concerned about the authenticity of several specious variants to the poem which he claims he has discovered. These, he argues, can be construed as a "refuge" for the story of Charles Xavier, king of Zembla, which has almost disappeared from the poem, "drained of every trace" of the king's presence, bearing now only as a "minute but genuine star ghost" the "specific imprint of my theme" (81-82). The unrevised or discarded variants which survive to tell Charles' story emerge as shadows, traces, or ghostly imprints, which are also descriptions of the relation of the commentary to the poem. Kinbote often mentions Conmal, the Zemblan translator of Shakespeare, whose rendition of *Timon of Athens* the misanthropic Kinbote awkwardly retranslates into English as he comments upon an obscure variant in lines 39-40 of Shade's poem. Kinbote's notable mistranslated translation reads:

> The sun is a thief: she lures the sea
> and robs it. The moon is a thief:

he steals his silvery light from the sun.
The sea is a thief: it dissolves the moon.

(80)

The original from *Timon of Athens* reads:

The sun's a thief, and with his great attraction
Robs the vast sea; the moon's an arrant thief,
And her pale fire she snatches from the sun;
The sea's a thief, whose liquid surge resolves
The moon into salt tears;

(IV, iii, ll. 432-36)

What Kinbote obviously misses in these crucial lines is the title of Shade's poem, which he fails to translate and upon which he offers no comment—this certainly undercuts his reliability as an editor. But of more importance is the texture of similarities and differences which a comparison of the original to its doubly rendered translation offers: Kinbote, via Conmal, has made the sun female, the moon male, an "m/f" transliteration that parallels Shade's own "mountain/fountain" skewing. As the suspicious variants are to the canonical text of Shade's poem, so this translation is a reversal and a shadow of the original, Shakespeare's "pale fire" transformed into Kinbote's "silvery light," a linguistic alchemy which transmutes gold into base silver, fire into diffuse moonlight. Through this translation, Kinbote writes himself into the text, though only as a seemingly irrelevant supplement to **"Pale Fire."** His sun becomes "she," the homophonous "son" becomes female, inscribing the inversions of his flagrant, comic homosexuality; the "silvery light" inscribes the shadowland of Kinbote's Zembla and the refracted, illuminating element by which he detects the mark of the self in Shade's text.

Moreover, like sun, moon, and sea, Kinbote's retranslated translation robs the "original" of its poetic power: the fluid and verbal richness of Shakespeare's poetry becomes, in Kinbote's hands, monotonous repetition. However, both texts share a vision of elemental thievery that undermines the very notion of "origin," since for both even the sun's power is entropic and derivative. The Shakespearean metaphor, applied to Kinbote's commentary and Shade's poem, suggests that there is no "authoritative" text in **Pale Fire,** no ultimate fount or source of significance, just as in nature there is no beginning to the cycle that transfers power from sun to moon to sea and back again. Instead, we have Kinbote's annotations, which scan a poem in order to refract the pale fire of its title. The poem itself is incomplete, a stack of index cards which, arranged in some varied manner, may tell the story of an exiled king or the poet's attempt to find mirrored in the "text" of his life the pale fires of life's supplement, the reflected glow of the afterlife.

As his name implies, the "Shade" caught in the poem is the self's shadow, an "otherness" translated into language and defined by the poem's dull illumination; at a further remove, Kinbote exists as a thieflike Hermes, a commentator and interpreter who, in the act of comic transference, generates the image of the self in a process that both violates and recreates the "original."[8] So as Shade and Kinbote are sun and moon to each other, every text in **Pale Fire**—foreword, poem, commentary, and index—is supplementary to the others, a corruption and thieflike translation. The novel enacts what Jacques Derrida, in an analysis of the difference between writing and speech, cites as a mythical instance of "supplementarity" evidenced by the story of the Egyptian god of writing, Thoth:

As the god of language second and of linguistic difference, Thoth can become the god of the creative word only by metonymic substitution, by historical displacement, and sometimes by violent subversion. . . . This type of substitution thus puts Thoth *in Ra's place* as the moon takes the place of the sun. The god of writing thus supplies the place of Ra, supplementing him and supplanting him in his absence and essential disappearance. Such is the origin of the moon as supplement to the sun, of night light as supplement to daylight. And of writing as the supplement of speech.[9]

Derrida's translation of the Thoth story into an allegory of the scene of writing infers a mythological "origin" in the sun, Ra, or speech, from which writing is a falling away, a second-rate substitution for the full presence of the spoken word or the blinding light of the sun. All of **Pale Fire** speaks its own supplementarity in this regard: it is an inscription of the yearning for lost kingdoms and the manifestations of divinity, a realization of their absence, and a translation of this loss into a system of signs which marks the history of the self's desire.

The novel is concerned with matters of translation in the less usual sense of the word: to transfer, to cross or carry over. **Pale Fire** is replete with physical analogues of this sense, from the underground passages and overland passes which Charles must traverse in order to escape from Zembla, to the fatal, frozen lake that Hazel Shade unsuccessfully walks upon "at Lochan Neck where zesty skaters crossed / From Exe to Wye" (C. II, ll. 489-90). In the novel-long metaphor which equates the writing of texts with the creation of worlds, topography comes to represent textual and metaphysical anxieties. While Shade in his poem worries about "crossing the border" to preexistence or afterlife, Kinbote is paranoiacally anxious about his ability to show the "crossings"—the web of not-so-coincidental similarities—between poem and commentary. Crossings and borders, the "lemniscate" pattern of a bicycle tire or the footprints of a pheasant left on "the blank page of the road" in a winter landscape (C. I, l. 21), all resonate with significance as the locations where the act of writing is seen as a "translation," or where the marks of the self's transference appear within the text. In Kinbote's commentary, the seemingly insignificant lane that runs between his and Shade's houses acts as the space that separates the critic's vision from the poet's, as well as the sign of the common thread that runs between their lives via their interconnected texts. Like all of the transverse, intersecting streets of the novel, the lane can be seen as a line (to be fatally crossed for the last time by Shade seconds before his death) that marks the distance between and the reciprocity of **"Pale Fire"** and its annotations.

The significance of this demarcation of sameness and difference is dramatized by another "lane" in the novel. Late in his commentary, Kinbote makes an obscure reference to the letters of Franklin Lane, particularly to one fragment from those written by Lane on the eve of his death, which reads: "And if I had passed into that other land, whom would I have sought? . . . Aristotle!—Ah, there would be a man to talk with! What satisfaction to see him take, like reins from between his fingers, the long ribbon of a man's life and trace it through the mystifying maze of all the wonderful adventure. . . . The crooked made straight. The Dedalian plan simplified by a look from above—smeared out as it were by the splotch of some master thumb that made the whole involuted, boggling thing one beautiful straight line" (185; Kinbote's ellipses). As June Perry Levine has noted, Franklin Lane is not an invention of Kinbote's or Nabokov's but a real historical personage, as authentic as the passage that Kinbote quotes. When combined with the obsessive concern for reading the patterns of nature and divinity promoted in Shade's poem, Levine suggests, Lane's vision of "crossing the border" connotes the possibility of viewing the self in the novel as "a moebius strip ribbon whose Shade side and Kinbote side are revealed as one."[10] In this sense, the whole of **Pale Fire** is a "lane," line, or "inky maze" (C. IV, l. 852), a tracing of "the long ribbon of a man's life," but hardly the "crooked made straight" or the "Dedalian plan simplified," as Kinbote hopes his commentary will make Shade's poem. Instead, as variant, translation, and labyrinth, the novel mixes the interweaving voices of Kinbote and Shade; it skews the "one beautiful straight line" and reveals the fictionalized, textual self as a collation of incongruities and specious similarities. Thus, the "lane" that exists between Kinbote and Shade is the text: the sign of their botched relation and the language that inculcates it.

In another sense, the amount of attention that Kinbote gives in his commentary to his escape from Zembla (as King Charles the Good) signifies the novel's concern with a "translation" whereby a language, which serves as a discrete articulation of the self, emerges out of a realm of perfect resemblances. At one point during the escape, Kinbote describes Charles looking back on the northern mountains of Zembla as he traverses a westward pass:

Great fallen crags diversified the wayside. The *nippern* (domed rocks or "reeks") to the south were broken by a rock and glass slope into light and shadow. Northward melted the green, gray, bluish mountains—Falkberg with its hood of snow, Mutraberg with the fan of its avalanche, Paberg (Mt. Peacock), and others,—separated by narrow dim valleys with intercalated cotton-wool bits of cloud that seemed placed between the receding sets of ridges to prevent their flanks from scraping against one another. Beyond them, in the final blue, loomed Mt. Glitterntin, a serrated edge of bright foil; and southward, a tender haze enveloped more distant ridges which led to one another in an endless array, through every grade of soft evanescence.

(143-44)

Like many of the descriptive passages in Kinbote's commentary—the portrayal of Charles' castle, the secret tunnel that runs from the king's bedroom closet to a dressing room in the state theater, the landscape of Wordsmith College—this celebration of Zembla's topography is a replication of Kinbote's self, emerging from the linguistic prison by which the commentator/king is defined and from which he unsuccessfully flees. The view of the mountains reveals a panorama of ssamenesses and differences that reenact the repetitions and variations of Kinbote's language throughout his commentary. The "reeks" to the south are broken into "light and shadow," the primary "colors" of Kinbote's world which form a pure opposition that creates a meaningful correspondence between its elements in terms of their placement against each other. There would be no understanding of light without the shadow cast by the reflected pale fire of objects, and there would be only undifferentiated darkness without the light that breaks it into sun and shadow.

The description of the mountains is analogous to the symbiotic relationship that exists between poem and commentary, original and translation. The latter is the shadow of Shade's poem; the former is the illuminating light (which, paradoxically, maintains its status as the phantom of Shade's self) that casts this shadow over the commentary as its rays are intercepted by the opaque markings of Kinbote's self-inscriptions. The ridges of the mountains in the distance seem to fade into one another as the vista of an "endless array" unfolds, yet they remain distinct, passing through "every grade of soft evanescence." Arising from this geographical grid of repetitions and gradations are Zembla's great peaks, including Mutraberg and Paberg, whose names are guttural and vernacular echoes of the familial past Charles is leaving behind, as well as repetitions of the primary sexual and typographical oppositions—father/mother, m/f, sun/moon, mountain/fountain—that elsewhere mark the text. Essentially, Charles' (or Kinbote's) flight from Zembla and his passage through the mountains are illusory, since the peaks mark the linguistic boundaries of his past and self, never to be traversed but always reinscribed at every turn in his autobiographical commentary.

Charles' view of the peaks is also a linguistic revelation of the adversary who chases him out of Zembla and who pursues him into exile. Paberg is, Englished by Kinbote, Mt. Peacock, a name that recalls Argus, the Greek monster of self-reflection who was transformed into the many-eyed peacock. Hence the mountain also recalls the name of Jack D'Argus, a pseudonym of Gradus', the hired assassin who hunts down the exiled king within the commentary as **"Pale Fire"** is written:

> We shall accompany Gradus . . . through the entire length of the poem, following the road of its rhythm, riding past in a rhyme, skidding around the corner of a run-on . . . reappearing on the horizon of a new canto, steadily marching nearer in iambic motion, crossing streets, moving up with his valise on the escalator of the pentameter, stepping off, boarding a new train of thought, entering the hall of a hotel, putting out the bedlight, while Shade blots out a word, and falling asleep as the poet lays down his pen for the night.
>
> (78)

Gradus is a member of an antiroyalist cadre, the Shadows, and here he is the elusive shadow of Kinbote's poetic double, his second self, who, like Conrad's secret sharer, is a manifestation of self-destructiveness as well as the uncanny "other" whom the writing of the commentary seeks to circumscribe and pin down.[11] Gradus is also associated with Mt. Glitterntin, as he is a glazier and mirror maker who corresponds, in Kinbote's mind, to a tin clockwork toy of a man pushing a wheelbarrow which belongs to Shade. To complete the circle of relations, the last lines of **"Pale Fire"** read: "And through the flowing shade and ebbing light / A man, unheedful of the butterfly— / Some neighbor's gardener, I guess— goes by / Trundling an empty barrow up the lane" (C. IV, ll. 996-99). The gardener is closely connected by events with Gradus, who finally tracks down the exiled king but kills Shade by mistake, instead of Kinbote, and who is felled in the act by Kinbote's wheelbarrow-trundling gardener; it is equally possible, of course, that "Gradus" is really Jack Grey, a vengeful madman of this world rather than a Zemblan assassin.

For the reader, Gradus' ambivalent status (escaped lunatic or assassin?) reduplicates the interpretive difficulties faced throughout the novel, for how can "Gradus" be Gradus and Grey at the same time? Forced to choose between Shade's version of "reality" (in which Grey would be a madman who mistakenly kills the poet, thinking he's a hanging judge) and Kinbote's (in which Gradus is a Zemblan conspirator), we may feel compelled to focus our attention on the novel's accidents, rather than noting its phonic overdeterminations. The

game Nabokov constructs here is one in which he plays off our readerly expectation and desire for noncontradictory meanings against our ability to "hear" the phonetic, graphic differentiations of the novel, from which these readings arise. The verbal movement between Mt. Peacock, Argus, Mt. Glitterntin, a tin toy, the Shadows, Gradus, and the gardener (who is black) creates an area of linguistic "gradation" that encourages us to indulge in the forging of linguistic chains and punning relations, while revealing the nondeterminative nature of these. We could as easily perceive the shadowy aspects of this description, as well as notice its reflective tendencies. The scene of traversing the mountains formulates a partial language, a complex interweaving of verbal associations wherein discrete words—"shadow," "haze," "tin," "glitter," "light," "grade"—become coordinated into a narrated world that inscribes the storytelling self, Kinbote. His past and his future, his hope for an eternal life (even if it is the "afterlife" of an exiled king living in the shadow of his former brilliance), and his anxiety about the "serrated edge" of the assassin's blade are erected into the topographies of text and the system of signs from which the self emerges, as the intercalation of that system.

Appropriately, it is from Zembla, the realm of resemblance, "a land of reflections" (265), that Charles attempts to escape. More specifically, he runs from Gradus, to whom "generality was godly, the specific diabolical," for whom "difference itself was unfair" (152). Kinbote's story arises as a flight from the landscape of perfect similitude, narrated in a language that annotates the self through the relations of difference and paradox; these are especially notable when he tells us that "resemblances are the shadows of differences" (265) and that the name of the hater of differences, Gradus, connotes the gradations of variation. Significantly, Gradus, who has participated in the construction of an elaborate, unworkable code system for the revolutionary party, is often associated with noise and mistranslation. In one scene, Kinbote imagines him in a Nice hotel on "a transverse street, between two thoroughfares parallel to the quay, and the ceaseless roar of crisscross traffic mingling with the grinding and banging of construction work proceeding under the auspices of a crane opposite the hotel (which had been surrounded by a stagnant calm two decades earlier) was a delightful surprise for Gradus, who always liked a little noise to keep his mind off things" (251). The noise of construction and crisscrossing traffic on a transverse street is matched by the noises and crossings of the passage itself, with its harsh assonances and meandering descriptiveness.

Later, aboard a plane going to America, suffering from acute indigestion, Gradus is exposed to another kind of noise: "he found himself wedged among several belated delegates to the New Wye Linguistic Conference, all of them lapel-labeled, and representing the same foreign language, but none being able to speak it, so that conversation was conducted (across our hunched-up killer and on all sides of his immobile face) in rather ordinary Anglo-American" (279-80). No doubt Nabokov the translator and master of many languages is mocking at the linguistic competence of academicians in this passage, but its real importance is to present Gradus, maker of reflective surfaces, as a contradiction: a foe of difference and a lover of order, yet liking noisy surroundings and acting, here, as a kind of "translator" across which the language of these polyglot monolinguists is spoken. As such, Gradus represents Kinbote's contradictory anxieties and desires as he constructs his verbal topography—for what Kinbote wishes to see in Shade's poem is his own perfect, mirrored image, his Zembla/emblem; what he fears is the utter difference between poem and commentary. What he manages to create is a textual self related as a network of words that sonorously echo each other yet reveal their alphabetic, imagistic differences in the play of the novel's sun and shadow. Gradus, who parasitically pursues the parasitical Kinbote through the text, acts as the site or occasion for this construction, which is known by its noisy rumblings and crossed connections.

Gradus serves as a textual catalyst in a most elaborate scene that reveals the disguised seams of Kinbote's linguistic tapestry. This occurs during the assassin's visit to Libitina, a Swiss villa owned by a "Karlist" where King Charles is thought to be hiding in exile. Gradus does not find Charles there, but Kinbote, who is reconstructing this visit to the province of Lex, marks the text with the words of his being. Comically, he invokes the vision of an adolescent boy, Gordon, who conducts Gradus about the villa while undergoing a series of miraculous costume changes, and who doubtless reflects Kinbote's own sexuality. A close look at the patina of the villa's description reveals the verbal dimensions of the world of Lex. Kinbote writes that the sun over Libitina "found a weak spot among the rain clouds and next moment a ragged blue hole in them grew a radiant rim" (198); that the owner of the villa collects pornographic scenes painted on lampshades, called *ombrioles*; that Gradus and Gordon walk "through light and shade" (200); that Gradus, driving away from the villa, comes to a promontory where Charles once stood, observing "on a misty and luminous September day, with the diagonal of the first silver filament crossing the space between two balusters . . . the twinkling ripples of Lake Geneva and . . . their antiphonal response, the flashing of tinfoil scares in the hillside vineyards" (201-02). Kinbote notes that at Libitina, which is the name for the Roman goddess of corpses and tombs, Gradus is barely able to communicate with a footman even though he speaks in three different languages.

This is to cite only a few examples from the baroque patternings of the world of Lex, which effect, for us, an

elaborate series of verbal correspondences. Sun and shade intersect, the diagonal filaments of the sunlight appear as the markings of a pen, the reflections of the lake serve as responses to the reflections of the tin scarecrows in the vineyards, all observed by a "tin man" whose alias is, among others, Vinogradus. The multiple reverberations and mirrorings of the description are set against a background of noisy miscommunications, presided over by the reflective name of a goddess (Libi*tin*a) who commemorates the inscriptions of the self-entombed. Kinbote thus makes a world of words at Lex which doubly reflects the sign of his own self and that of the text out of which the self arises. As he sees the desired relation between poem and commentary represented by an intricate play of teasing reflexivity, so the textual language of this passage is a play of similarities and differences, descriptions of black engravings on white spaces, chance echoes, and punning relations. At the poles of this scene of inscription are, on the one hand, the scriptural commemoration of death and silence and, on the other, meaningless noise. Kinbote's description infers that in between noise and silence, utter dissemination and utter similitude, language and self, departing from these extremes, are generated.

Ultimately, everything in the world of *Pale Fire* is made to correspond to the exigencies of Kinbote's personal destiny and to bear his autobiographical stamp as commentator. The irony and reflexivity inherent in a series of annotations turned to self-revelation are illuminated by Nabokov's comments on self-knowledge in his own autobiography, *Speak, Memory.* There, he equates the function of art as self-discovery to a mechanical process of inscription: "Neither in environment nor in heredity can I find the exact instrument that fashioned me, the anonymous roller that pressed upon my life a certain watermark whose unique design becomes visible when the lamp of art is made to shine through life's foolscap."[12] At first glance, Nabokov seems to indulge in a pseudoreligious metaphor for inspiration and individuality, grounded in Plato with overtones of Augustine and Pope. The "anonymous roller" appears as a godlike aesthetic authority who impresses upon the artist the watermark of selfhood, to be discovered in a process of self-divination. The image appears to agree with the crucial watermark analogy of Kinbote's commentary, which proclaims that the self of the believer, detecting the signs of "our Lord," knows infinity: "When the soul adores Him Who guides it through mortal life, when it distinguishes His sign at every turn of the trail, painted on the boulder and notched in the fir trunk, when every page in the book of one's personal fate bears His watermark, how can one doubt that He will also preserve us through all eternity?" (221-22). Kinbote's watermark is one more expression of his desire as a reader of texts to find in the book of his own past the markings of eternal life, the divinity of his kinghood, and his accession (as "Xavier" or "savior") to godhead. It is an inscription, he realizes elsewhere, never to be found in human life or worldly books.

A closer look at the artistic metaphor of *Speak, Memory* shows that it is a complex analogy for the connection to be made between the act of writing and the inscription of the self, annotated, into the world's text. For this anonymous authority who authenticates and forges the mark of selfhood, this "roller" or "instrument," is but another version of the artistic self implicated in the quest for self-knowledge that is charted by the "graph" of autobiography. We can imagine Nabokov, inscribing the words of *Speak, Memory* upon the blank page, conceiving of the creation of personality as another inscription upon another unmarked page. This inscribed self (the watermark) is revealed only through an act of interpretation (the shining of art's lamp upon the page) which mediates between the self writing and the self as written. In Nabokov's metaphor, these separate movements become unified into the act of writing as such, which is at once self-creation, interpretation, and demarcation, all of which designate their coming into being *as* writing. To return to the problem of originality discussed earlier, the watermark analogy of *Speak, Memory* illuminates the act of writing as a quest for the "original" self, pregiven in nature—an unimaginable "self" that exists prior to life, writing, and consciousness, whose shadow is all that writing is able to embody.

In *Pale Fire,* this "original" self is King Charles, last monarch of Zembla, not as he exists via the annotations of Shade's poem or the imposed anxieties of Kinbote's transliterations but as he inconceivably *was* in the timelessness of his youth and the power of his kinghood. In this sense, Charles is Kinbote's "original," but one who never existed in time or space and whose continued existence comes about only through the glimmerings of a faulty memory or the misinterpretations of an obsessed imagination. There is also the "original" text of **"Pale Fire,"** but by the time we read it, its originality has been translated into the secondariness of commentary by Kinbote. Moreover, the poem subverts its own origin and authority (God, the self) in portraying Shade interrogating the marks of divinity he vainly searches for, finding only the incomplete, accidental correlations and patterns of his partially inscribed existence. The discoveries of Shade's autobiography and the translation of Kinbote's commentary can be seen as "the process of indirect reconstruction" which Claude Lévi-Strauss defines as the mark of writing and culture or which Jonathan Culler calls "the 'reactivation' of modes of intelligibility: that which is natural is brought to consciousness and revealed as a process, a construct."[13] In this view, writing becomes a deformation of the "original" self as it passes into the time of narrative, exiled from the land of perfect identifications and exact mirror resemblances, into the realm of the sign, where the text is the texture of misreadings, translations, and noise that work to define the "self." The process of inscription in *Pale Fire* thus marks the articulation of a writing/interpreting/written self into a system of signs and a "history" that does not exist before this process but is realized by it. As the Nabokovian metaphor suggests, this textual self is the sign of its own creation.

Many commentators have remarked that *Pale Fire* is a game wherein reader and author are engaged in a complex, frustrating, but ultimately pleasurable battle of wits that relates the playing of language games to the construction of fictions.[14] More precisely, *Pale Fire* indulges the "game" of self-creation—that of our readerly selves as well as of Kinbote's comic mirrored image arising within the crosshatchings of the text. As we have seen, this game is one of imprecise rules. The novel's roads, paths, branches, labyrinths, barriers, passages, bridges, crossings, tunnels, maps, and topographies, with their twistings and inversions, are analogous to the "noise" of Kinbote's commentary: its "interferences" with the text and its obscurations of the imagined encoded message of **"Pale Fire."** Moreover, it is through such unruliness that the outline of a world and the king who is imprisoned within it appears. Misprision, superimposition of legend upon poem, red herrings, detected designs and frames of reference form the intertwined paths of communication braided into a language world founded upon the disasters of a personal history.[15]

Pale Fire both performs and judges this translation of the dim past into the present. Its "subject" is the blazoning of the self into time and narrative, but the judgment that falls upon Kinbote's self-inscribed world is the knowledge that it is mutable and entropic. At one point, Kinbote describes this wordy, textual kingdom as a "miracle" of readability, a product of "blue magic," an artistic opportunity to "pounce upon the forgotten butterfly of revelation, wean himself abruptly from the habit of things, see the web of the world, and the warp and the weft of that web" (289). Miraculous as this world may be, it comes about only through "warp," defamiliarization, and the pain of exile: "I found myself enriched with an indescribable amazement as if informed that fireflies were making decodable signals on behalf of stranded spirits, or that a bat was writing a legible tale of torture in the bruised and branded sky" (289). So the world reflects Kinbote and his self-tortured translation of being into writing—an inscription that inevitably commemorates the mortality of words and worlds.

Pale Fire is an elegy in this sense: it marks a highly mutable world in which the premise for its writing, Shade's poem, remains unfinished, now a bundle of index cards in the dead poet's hands, subject to Kinbote's mishandlings. The legendary Zembla erodes before our eyes as it drifts back into the haze of Kinbote's memory, its glass towers destroyed by revolutionaries, its palaces gutted, its magical tunnel collapsing under the weight of the earth. And even though the commentator is, finally, a self-confessed failure as he awaits a "bigger, more respectable, more competent Gradus" (301)—a true repressor of differences—Kinbote does write himself into existence, if not immortally, then fully implicated in a temporary and temporal design now given over to our only partially competent hands. There, Nabokov demands, in the annotated pages of the book, we must engage in the construction and watermarking of our own interpreting selves as we pull together the fragments of a broken, time-bound world. There, as David Packman argues, we are compelled to fulfill our readerly desire to resolve "the tension between progression and simultaneity" as we observe the workings of a text that hedges against, while fully realizing, its own mortality.[16] For Nabokov, in **Pale Fire,** the self is textual and mortal: an entity who comes into being by establishing its relation to the elements of the language in which it is born, through which it is identified, to which it dies. His novel is ultimately a celebration of our legibility, our being readable within the confinements of language—that "currency" of the human world.

Notes

1. Mikhail Bakhtin, "Epic and Novel," in *The Dialogic Imagination: Four Essays,* introd. Michael Holquist, trans. Caryl Emerson and Michael Holquist (Austin: University of Texas Press, 1981), p. 10.

2. See Alter, *Partial Magic,* for a historical/critical account of reflexivity in the tradition of the novel. I am, as any commentator on present-day fiction must be, indebted to Alter's discussion, though I am more concerned here than he with the semiotic remifications of reflexivity in *Pale Fire.* For a larger, anthropological conception of reflexivity as a self-critical concept, see the special issue of *Semiotica,* 30 (1980), on the reflexivity of signs in culture, ed. Barbara A. Babcock, and her introductory essay, "Reflexivity: Definitions and Discriminations," pp. 1-14.

3. As with the notion of reflexivity in fiction, the fictive presentation of the self has always been an integral part of narrative traditions. For relevant critical discussions of the history of self-presentation in Anglo-American literature, see Stephen J. Greenblatt, *Renaissance Self-Fashioning: From More to Shakespeare* (Chicago: University of Chicago Press, 1980); Arnold Weinstein, *Fictions of the Self: 1550-1800* (Princeton: Princeton University Press, 1981); Robert Langbaum, *The Mysteries of Identity: A Theme in Modern Literature* (New York: Oxford University

Press, 1977); and Poirier, *Performing Self.* Again, my discussion dwells more on a semiotic conception of the self than these, as does a recent analysis of the self as sign in nineteenth-century American literature to which I am indebted, John T. Irwin, *American Hieroglyphics: The Symbol of the Egyptian Hieroglyph in the American Renaissance* (New Haven: Yale University Press, 1980), especially pp. 114-235.

4. Both Lucy Maddox, *Nabokov's Novels in English* (Athens: University of Georgia Press, 1983), p. 29, and Marilyn Edelstein, "*Pale Fire*: The Art of Consciousness," in J. E. Rivers and Charles Nicol, eds., *Nabokov's Fifth Arc: Nabokov and Others on His Life's Work* (Austin: University of Texas Press, 1982), p. 218, mention in their discussions of *Pale Fire* that Nabokov is interested in the presentation of the self as a written sign, but they do not pursue the subject to the point of discussing how self-inscription and textuality form parallel concerns in the novel.

5. David Walker, "'The Viewer and the View': Chance and Choice in Pale Fire," *Studies in American Fiction,* 4 (1976), 204. I am in basic agreement with Walker on the critical controversy over the novel as to whose voice—Shade's or Kinbote's—is the authoritative one. For Walker, the question is moot, since it is the drive to create correspondences *between* texts that forms the novel's main interest. But for dissenting views, see Julia Bader, *Crystal Land: Artifice in Nabokov's English Novels* (Berkeley and Los Angeles: University of California Press, 1972), p. 31, where she argues that Shade writes both poem and commentary, projecting Gradus, Kinbote, and himself as aspects of the artist's multiple personality. See also Page Stegner, *Escape into Aesthetics: The Art of Vladimir Nabokov* (New York: Dial Press, 1966), p. 129, who argues that Gradus, Shade, and Kinbote are all figments of Kinbote's imagination—projections, like Zembla, of a mind obsessed with chance and coincidence.

6. Vladimir Nabokov, *Pale Fire* (New York: G. P. Putnam's Sons, 1962), pp. 62-63. All future references will be to this edition and will be noted parenthetically in the text.

7. The familiar distinction is that of M. H. Abrahms, *The Mirror and the Lamp: Romantic Theory and the Critical Tradition* (New York: Oxford University Press, 1953). Nabokov's frequent comparisons of lamps, suns, and fire with the aesthetic act in *Pale Fire,* and his use of mirrors as distortive rather than purely reflective devices, place him in the tradition Abrahms defines as romantic and antimimetic.

8. This analysis of translation, exchange, and interpretive thievery is based upon Michel Serres' compelling "The Apparition of Hermes: *Don Juan*," in his collection of translated essays, *Hermes: Literature, Science, Philosophy,* ed. Josué V. Harari and David F. Bell (Baltimore: Johns Hopkins University Press, 1982), pp. 3-14.

9. Jacques Derrida, *Dissemination,* trans. and introd. Barbara Johnson (Chicago: University of Chicago Press, 1981), p. 89.

10. June Perry Levine, "Vladimir Nabokov's *Pale Fire*: 'The Method of Composition' as Hero," *International Fiction Review,* 5 (1978), 105.

11. Nabokov is notorious for his doubling and mirroring motifs; these are investigated for *Pale Fire* by Phyllis A. Roth, "The Psychology of the Double in Nabokov's *Pale Fire*," *Essays in Literature,* 2 (1975), 209-29.

12. Vladimir Nabokov, *Speak, Memory: An Autobiography Revisited,* rev. ed. (New York: G. P. Putnam's Sons, 1966), p. 25.

13. Claude Lévi-Strauss, *Structural Anthropology,* quoted in Terence Hawkes, *Structuralism and Semiotics* (London: Methuen, 1977), p. 50; Culler, *Structuralist Poetics,* p. 190.

14. For explications of this view and its thematic results, see Douglas Fowler, *Reading Nabokov* (Ithaca: Cornell University Press, 1974), p. 17; Bader, *Crystal Land,* pp. 4-8; Walker, "'The Viewer and the View,'" pp. 205-20; and Tanner, *City of Words,* pp. 33-39.

15. The term "misprision" I take from Harold Bloom, who defines it as the deliberate misreading of the poetic father or original by son or commentator, so that the latter may establish his own originality. *Pale Fire* might be seen as a parody of misprision, in which the swerving or clinamen of the son's text from the father's original becomes, in Kinbote's case, a wild careening, a comic chase after the elusive Gradus (shadows cast by the poetic father/double) in the text. Bloom's theory is clearly informed by a series of patrilineal metaphors that, themselves, deserve thoroughgoing questioning as evidences of self-inscription. See Harold Bloom, *The Anxiety of Influence: A Theory of Poetry* (New York: Oxford University Press, 1973), pp. 19-45.

16. David Packman, *Vladimir Nabokov: The Structure of Literary Desire* (Columbia: University of Missouri Press, 1982), p. 89. Packman's book appeared as I was completing this analysis of *Pale Fire*; I share its views of several matters discussed here, particularly of the text's inculcation of its

own temporality and its desire for immortality, reflected in the narrative line; see especially pp. 74-89.

Peggy Ward Corn (essay date winter 1987)

SOURCE: Corn, Peggy Ward. "'Combinational Delight': The Uses of the Story Within a Story in *Pale Fire*." *The Journal of Narrative Technique* 17, no. 1 (winter 1987): 83-90.

[*In the following essay, Corn posits that a new level of meaning is created by the interplay of the "nested" narratives in Nabokov's* Pale Fire.]

Embedding a story within a second story is not a new narrative technique: it goes back as far as the stories of the Arabian Nights, and figures in *The Canterbury Tales* and many Renaissance and Jacobean plays. The twentieth century has witnessed the revival and flourishing of the story within a story. John Barth's novels often employ the technique, as to Tom Stoppard's plays, most recently *The Real Thing.* Doris Lessing's *The Golden Notebook,* Gilbert Sorrentino's *Mulligan Stew,* and Luigi Pirandello's *Six Characters in Search of an Author* also employ the story within a story, to various ends. In the last few years the use of this technique has increased; it can be found in such diverse and popular works as Calvino's *If on a winter's night a traveler,* Vargas Llosa's *Aunt Julia and the Scriptwriter,* Thomas's *The White Hotel,* and Frayn's *Noises Off.*

Traditionally, works employing the story within a story have consisted of a frame story introducing but almost never concluding the "real" or main story. The frame is a fragment in these works, often quickly forgotten: *The Taming of the Shrew,* for instance, is quite often performed without its Induction. Another type of story within a story reverses the emphasis: in this second type the outer story is the main one, and the inner story is the fragment. *Hamlet* and *A Midsummer Night's Dream* are two famous examples of this type. Of the works written before this century that employ the story within a story, almost all fall into one of these two categories.

A third type is what I call Russian doll fictions, after the wooden nesting dolls made in Russia. Like the first two types, it consists of two distinct narrative planes, on which reside two distinct stories. But unlike the first two, each Russian doll story is substantial, developed at length, and neither exists merely to frame the other. The meaning of such a novel or play emerges from the interplay between narrative planes. The essence of the Russian doll work lies in its doubleness, in the way it compels a reader to shuttle between the two stories and somehow synthesize them. Unlike the first two types of stories within stories, the Russian doll novel or play is almost always characterized by interruption; the narratives are interleaved.[1]

The structure of most Russian doll works maintains the narrative envelope that we find in the frame story, with the outer story acting as a container for the inner; however, each is much more substantial than a frame or short interpolated story. The quantitative difference in number of pages devoted to each narrative becomes a qualitative difference when the reader comes to understand that the meaning of the work as a whole resides in transactions between narrative levels. This is the case with Nabokov's *Pale Fire,* a Russian doll work which does not rely on a container-contained relationship between its parts. In that novel, John Shade's poem is accompanied but not framed by Charles Kinbote's Commentary. In *Pale Fire,* Nabokov makes the most of the interplay between the two narratives to create a whole greater than the sum of its parts. Nabokov's masterful use of the Russian doll device affords a reader both an account of and an opportunity to participate in the quest for what Shade calls "Some kind of link-and-bobolink, some kind / Of correlated pattern in the game"[2] of life and literature. As with any Russian doll work of literature, we need to approach it by asking about Nabokov's purposes in combining narrative levels in this novel: What does Kinbote's Commentary add to Shade's poem? What does our reading of Shade's poem bring to our response to Kinbote's creation? How do they combine to produce a work whose meaning arises from that combination?[3]

The glib answer to such questions is that Nabokov's novel is a parody of the sort of annotated texts we have all encountered or heard of, burdened with the notes of an annotator whose hobby horse tramples the poem he claims to illuminate. To be sure, Kinbote's method is familiar and very funny. Still, as Robert Alter insists, "*Pale Fire* is of course both a satire and a parody, but to see it only as that is drastically to reduce its real scope."[4] We are never allowed to forget that Kinbote is a madman, and yet it is his very delusions that provide a key to understanding the contribution his Commentary makes.

There are broad hints in Kinbote's "Foreword" that he is very eccentric, to say the least, but we are likely to forget the "Foreword" as we read the poem. Our first reading of the poem is uninterrupted; there are no numbers or notes on its pages to direct us to the Commentary as we read the poem, and we are likely not to take Kinbote's advice that we read his Commentary before the poem. The Russian doll device comes into play as we begin the Commentary. Despite Kinbote's tendency to use a phrase or line of the poem as the flimsiest pretext to fly off to Zembla, he is also surprisingly capable

of functioning as a learned annotator. As is the case with other Russian doll works, the second story is interrupted by the first. We reread much of Shade's poem in the course of reading Kinbote's notes to it. And on the most obvious level, the answer to the question of what Kinbote's writing adds to Shade's is that Kinbote fills in background information on the poet's life. Kinbote tells us about Hazel Shade's short, unhappy life, he gives us details of the composition of **"Pale Fire,"** and if we read between the lines, he even reveals the identity and motive of Shade's killer. Kinbote is also helpful with linguistic matters, especially puns.

But as we cannot help but notice from the first line onward, Kinbote is crazy. As early as his note to line 42, he reveals his purpose for writing the notes: to tell the story of King Charles the Beloved and his country, Zembla. He intimates very early on that he is King Charles, so we soon learn to distinguish Kinbote the learned commentator from Kinbote the lunatic, obsessed with Zembla and using Shade's poem as an occasion to tell his own story. As with any unreliable narrator, we have to pick our way carefully between truth and delusion, because Kinbote is unable to do so himself.

But what do we make of the Zemblan saga that means so much to Kinbote? Nabokov does not intend us merely to dismiss it. Once we comprehend Kinbote's peculiar perspective on Shade's poem, we begin to read the story of Charles the Beloved and his kingdom as a literary creation in its own right. The story has romance, suspense, adventure, and scenes of beauty—as when Fleur stands before the magic mirror. I find it a curiously compelling story, even if its author is deranged. As we read Kinbote's narrative and move back and forth between it and Shade's poem, we begin to compare the two authors and their creations. Like Shade, Kinbote has the capacity to imagine a world. He can people it with vivid characters like Gradus and Disa, even invent a language for it. As Kinbote's notes reveal, Shade's work may be autobiographical in many ways, but it is shaped by his imagination. Kinbote and Shade do have their similarities as artists.

Kinbote says Shade once remarked at a party that a man "who thought he was God and began redirecting the trains" was "a fellow poet." Kinbote concurs: "We are all, in a sense, poets" (p. 238). This exchange prompts a question for Nabokov's reader with which to approach the comparison of the two as artists: is a madman a poet, or does madness render him incapable of art?

Kinbote may be a kind of artist, but if he is, he is a very different sort of artist from Shade because of his delusions. In his usual inadvertent and perverse way, Kinbote in his Commentary offers a perspective on Shade's poem that enriches our reading of it and shows us how, as in a hall of mirrors, Shade's poem comments on Kinbote's Commentary.

One important difference between a poet like Shade and a madman like Kinbote concerns their degree of control over their stories. In the window of the first stanza of Canto One, Shade sees himself reflected in the windowpane and superimposed on the landscape seen through the window. Shade's vision transforms details and observations from reality into art but never confuses them. Kinbote's vision is limited by his Zemblan delusions. Instead of transforming reality to show its truth in art, Kinbote distorts reality to reveal his own delusions. He cannot make us see things his way, as Shade can. We are always standing back, being reminded that Kinbote is a lunatic. Shade's poem is under his control; he is the god of his literary creation. But Kinbote, a king without a country even in his own fantasy, is out of control in his art as well. We read Kinbote's work differently from Shade's; Shade constructs an artifice to reveal the truth of his existence, whereas Kinbote's artificial construct is a means of escape from inconvenient truths about his existence. Trying to run from reality, Kinbote invents or adopts for himself an identity and a past that he confuses with reality. Ironically, by trying to disappear into this artifice, he reveals himself as he really is instead. His remark to Shade that the story of Zembla needs Shade's artistry to be true is an acknowledgement of this difference between the two. King Charles escapes from Zembla, but Charles Kinbote escapes into it, making it possible for him to avoid the sad and ugly facts of his actual life as an aging homosexual no longer attractive to young men, friendless, ridiculous, reduced to voyeurism, testing the patience of the only man who tolerates him, John Shade.

And yet the comparison between the two men cannot stop with the realization that Kinbote's madness compromises his storytelling. Shade feels some sort of link with the madman, and if we examine his poem with the madman's image in the background, we can see why. "I am the shadow of the waxwing slain / By the false azure in the windowpane;" (ll. 1-2) his poem begins. The bird dies because it cannot distinguish a real from a reflected sky; it dies of a delusion. When he identifies with this bird, Shade resembles Kinbote in his madness. The bird dies because it believes in something that exists only in a mirror, a "crystal land." Kinbote tells us that "crystal land" may refer to Zembla, a land of mirrors. In a way, Kinbote is right—the false azure of the reflected sky, like Zembla, exists only in the imagination of the beholder. If the madman in this book is something of a poet, so is the poet something of a madman.

Kinbote's real name is Botkin, identified in the Index as an "American scholar of Russian descent" (p. 306), a faculty member at Wordsmith College. Apparently his delusions had their genesis in the pain of exile from his homeland. The theme of exile may at first seem not to correspond to anything in Shade's poem, but Shade yearns for a realm first discovered in his childhood trances and revisited when he died temporarily. Julian Moynahan points out that from his first line, Shade "casts his poem as a retrospection from the realm of death."[5] Each canto meditates on death and the possibility of an afterlife for his daughter and himself. We come to realize in reading and then rereading the poem with Kinbote's notes that Shade yearns for death as surely as Kinbote yearns for Zembla. Shade's association with the crackpots at the Institute of Preparation for the Hereafter and his three-hundred-mile trip to visit the woman who also died and was revived are evidence of a man obsessed—not to the point of insanity, to be sure, but driven by grief into some very odd places.

As we follow him in his investigation into the likelihood of life after death, we find another link between Shade and Kinbote: Shade seeks confirmation, in spite of his agnosticism, of order in the universe. As he lies dead of a heart attack, he is aware of "A system of cells interlinked within / Cells interlinked within cells interlinked / Within one stem" (ll. 704-6). Knowledge of the true nature of death is central for him to belief in the "web of sense" he seeks. If death means merely annihilation—and thus the loss forever of his beloved daughter—then there is ultimately no meaning to existence, just a final darkness. But if he can confirm what he felt and saw when briefly dead as something other than a "natural sham," then he has discovered a meaning behind daily life that his poetry reflects. Death must be incorporated into his search for a "correlated pattern in the game" because if it means nothing, there is no pattern.

What is Kinbote's connection to Shade's quest? In part he provides a contrast to Shade's skepticism. Whereas Shade is able to laugh at himself for associating with IPH and enjoy the mountain/fountain misprint, Kinbote is too ready to believe in conspiracies and correspondences without evidence. He knows the poem is not about Zembla, and he expresses his dismay that Shade did not write the poem he wanted, but Kinbote still insists on treating the poem as a kind of code, reading into it "pale phosphorescent hints, and all the many subliminal debts to me" (p. 297), for example his excited discovery of the name Gradus in the middle of one of Shade's variant lines in the words "Tangra dust" (p. 231). He is too ready to believe in what he wants to be true.

However, Nabokov's method in the novel is to complicate such easy comparisons. Shade and Kinbote in their different ways respond to the same human impulse to make sense of things. Kinbote's belief in his secret identity allows him to resist despair. Shade is too sane to invent a country and an identity, but he needs to believe that when he invents a poem, he is reflecting the harmony of the universe:

> I feel I understand
> Existence, or at least a minute part
> Of my existence, only through my art,
> In terms of combinational delight;
> And if my private universe scans right,
> So does the verse of galaxies divine
> Which I suspect is an iambic line.
>
> (ll. 971-77)

Readers of Nabokov's novel engage in a quest similar to that of Kinbote and Shade. Once we understand that Kinbote is unreliable, we respond to Nabokov's juxtaposition of the two literary works by comparing Kinbote and Shade, looking for the connections that will help us harmonize the two and thus discover the meaning of the novel. We read each in terms of the other, exploring delusion, the search for design in the universe, and the fear of and attraction to perfection in death. In so doing, we echo Shade's attempt to uncover the harmony of life in verse and the links between here and hereafter, as well as Kinbote's similarly motivated but doomed attempt to find evidence of his own delusions in the literary invention of his colleague. This enterprise, finding the patterns that unify the parts, is both the subject matter of *Pale Fire* and the experience of linking up its parts as we read, required as we are by the Russian doll device to shuttle between narratives. Thus we participate in the quest for meaning that unifies the novel.

Shade's poem gives an account of his visit with Mrs. Z, the woman who was reported to have seen a fountain when she briefly died. If she saw the fountain too, then Shade has some basis for belief in the objective existence of an afterlife. But as he learns from the reporter who interviewed her, Mrs. Z saw a mountain, not a fountain. Shade would seem to have driven three hundred miles into a dead end. But as he thinks about the misprint, he comes to a conclusion that resonates in Kinbote's account of the poet's death and in our own attempts to unify the narratives:

> But all at once it dawned on me that *this*
> Was the real point, the contrapuntal theme;
> Just this: not text, but texture; not the dream
> But topsy-turvical coincidence,
> Not flimsy nonsense, but a web of sense.
> Yes! It sufficed that I in life could find
> Some kind of link-and-bobolink, some kind
> Of correlated pattern in the game,
> Plexed artistry, and something of the same
> Pleasure in it as they who played it found.
>
> (ll. 806-15)

In this view coincidences are not accidents but emblems of design. Such coincidences are invented by god-like world-makers who take the same pleasure in "Making ornaments / Of accidents and possibilities" (ll. 828-29) as Shade does in making rhymes, Kinbote does in inventing his new identity, and Nabokov does in fashioning the "link-and-bobolink" of *Pale Fire.* This "combinational delight" is shared by Nabokov's readers as we come to see that the presence of Kinbote and his Commentary in the book is just the kind of coincidence Shade celebrates.

By the end of his poem Shade has made his peace with death. He has a "Faint hope" (l. 834) of immortality at the end of Canto Three which waxes in the course of Canto Four. His meditation on his love of poetry and his delight in the way it shapes his days lead Shade to affirm that his "feeling of fantastically planned, / Richly rhymed life" (ll. 969-70) is an echo of the harmony of the cosmos. Thus, "I'm reasonably sure that we survive, / And that my darling somewhere is alive" (ll. 977-78), as sure, he continues, as that he will wake tomorrow. Ironically, his death that day does not preclude the fulfillment of that prediction: he believes that one wakes after death, in a new place. As Julian Moynahan remarks, Kinbote "delivers Shade to a death the elderly poet is fully and hungrily prepared for."[6] In the account of Shade's death that ends Kinbote's Commentary, Nabokov uses the Russian doll device to confirm Shade's conviction that coincidences are meaningful and to justify Kinbote's presence in the book.

Kinbote keeps before us the last stanzas of Shade's poem and the importance of Shade's impending death by following the movements of Gradus in great detail as he closes in on his prey and by directing our attention to a number of specific lines near the end. Kinbote's Commentary includes notes to lines 991, 993-95, 998, and 1000 in the last stanza. As we reread Shade's final lines we know he is ready to die. The poem ends before he can provide what is most likely its final line, a repetition of "I am the shadow of the waxwing slain." By coincidence, he is accompanied on his final walk by an emblem of his wife, the butterfly called Vanessa, his name for his wife Sybil. And he notices a gardener, a man who works for Kinbote, pushing a wheelbarrow, an echo of the toy that he associates with his childhood death-like trances. Nabokov is weaving a web of sense from these coincidences.

The coincidences continue as Kinbote finishes the story. Shade dies because of a case of mistaken identity. We have been informed in passing that Shade resembles Judge Goldsworth, the assassin's intended victim. Shade just happens to be in the wrong place at the wrong time, but for Nabokov's purposes they are the right place and the right time. The killing even makes a kind of sense in Kinbote's terms, as it happens. Kinbote's imagined assassin Gradus wants to kill King Charles to settle a score, to punish him for escaping from Zembla alive. The madman Jack Grey wants to kill Judge Goldsworth as an act of revenge for sending him to prison. Moreover, Kinbote is right to say that the assassin did not kill his intended victim, though he is wrong about the details. Shade's death makes sense in Kinbote's terms and in Shade's own terms—it is a fitting conclusion to his work. And even though we cannot take Kinbote's conspiracy theory at face value, we can understand in the interplay of the narratives that coincidences conspired to kill Shade. Kinbote's delusion about the revolutionaries' conspiracy has provided the "contrapuntal theme" that complements Shade's conclusions about the meaning of coincidences. If the cosmic game-players of Shade's poem exist, they conspire just as surely as Gradus to determine the course of our lives. In the world of the novel, the coincidence that the poem manuscript literally falls into Kinbote's hands not only guarantees Shade literary immortality but ensures that the poem will be published with a Commentary that truly comments on its concern with pattern, harmony, and design in life and death. Nabokov is the god who contrives coincidences which are evidence of his own grand design of correspondences in the novel.

In *Pale Fire,* Nabokov uses each narrative in surprising and subtle ways to deepen our understanding of the other, providing his readers an experience of "combinational delight" peculiar to the reading of a well-wrought Russian doll work. His novel demonstrates some of the great variety of literary effects made possible by the doubling of narrative planes and a reader's efforts to integrate them.

Notes

1. I want to be careful not to insist on the aptness of actual Russian dolls as a symbol of this narrative technique, for several reasons. First, each smaller Russian doll is identical to the one that contains it, as the Russian doll narratives obviously are not. Also, the inner story may be longer and therefore "larger" than the outer, whereas an inner Russian doll of the wooden variety is of necessity smaller than the outer doll that contains it. Finally, most Russian doll novels or plays contain only two narrative planes (although *The White Hotel* is a fascinating exception), while all the actual dolls I have seen are made up of at least four individual dolls.

2. Vladimir Nabokov, *Pale Fire* (New York: Perigee Books, 1980), p. 63, ll. 812-13 of "Pale Fire." Subsequent line and page references in the text are to this edition.

3. The usual emphasis in studies of *Pale Fire* has been on the explication of Nabokov's word games and themes in the novel. One study that focuses on structure is Robert Alter's chapter on *Pale Fire* in *Partial Magic* (Berkeley: University of Califor-

nia Press, 1978), which explains what he calls the circular structure of the novel. The following works have proved helpful in understanding other aspects of Nabokov's technique: H. Grabes, *Fictitious Biographies: Vladimir Nabokov's English Novels,* Studies in American Literature, Vol. 25 (The Hague: Mouton, 1977); Alden Sprowles, "Preliminary Annotation to Charles Kinbote's Commentary on 'Pale Fire,'" in *A Book of Things about Vladimir Nabokov,* ed. Carl R. Proffer (Ann Arbor, Michigan: Ardis, Inc., 1974); Julian Moynahan, *Vladimir Nabokov,* University of Minnesota Pamphlets on American Writers, No. 96 (Minneapolis: University of Minnesota Press, 1971); Page Stegner, *Escape into Aesthetics* (New York: The Dial Press, 1966); Julia Bader, *Crystal Land* (Berkeley: University of California Press, 1972); and Andrew Field, *Nabokov: His Life in Art* (Boston: Little, Brown, 1967).

4. Alter, p. 185.

5. Moynahan, p. 44.

6. Moynahan, p. 43.

Shoshana Knapp (essay date spring 1987)

SOURCE: Knapp, Shoshana. "Hazel Ablaze: Literary License in Nabokov's *Pale Fire*." *Essays in Literature* 14, no. 1 (spring 1987): 105-15.

[*In the following essay, Knapp investigates the literary significance of Hazel Shade, one of the key female figures in Nabokov's novel* Pale Fire.]

Most critical treatments of Nabokov's *Pale Fire* are concerned with the relationship between the poet John Shade, killed by a bullet intended for someone else, and his neighbor Charles Kinbote, who, believing himself to be the exiled king of Zembla, undertakes to explain how Shade's last poem is in fact a disguised biography of Kinbote rather than the idealized autobiography of Shade it appears to be. Nabokov has gleefully and generously supplied the materials for games, speculations, and debates on such subjects as the link between madness and inspiration, the creative infidelity of the commentator who tries to improve upon the original, and the imaginative splendor of an invented world in which one may choose not only to visit, but to live. Before and after the games, however, there remains the character who supplies the emotional and artistic center for the poem and, perhaps, for the entire novel as well: Hazel Shade—misunderstood in life, misrepresented in death, and, as such, the test case for the art of Shade, Kinbote, and Nabokov.

The second canto of John Shade's *Pale Fire* is largely occupied with the nature and fate of his only child, whom he describes as follows:

She hardly ever smiled, and when she did,
It was a sign of pain. She'd criticize
Ferociously our projects, and with eyes
Expressionless sit on her tumbled bed
Spreading her swollen feet, scratching her head
With psoriatic fingernails, and moan,
Murmuring dreadful words in monotone.

([*Pale Fire*] ll. 350-56)[1]

Unattractive, uncongenial, unaccommodating, and unfulfilled—Hazel Shade, according to her father, nonetheless "always nursed a small mad hope" (l. 383) that she might one day find requited love, yet drowned herself in an ice-bound lake when the precipitous departure of a blind date seemed to lay waste to that hope. Her death arouses in the poet pity and grief, but no curiosity: he and his wife know, he says, that the drowning was not an accident, that Hazel "took her poor young life" (l. 493). His yearning to make contact with her ghost fuels his speculations on the afterlife.[2] His questions, such as they are, have to do with her life after death, rather than her life before it. He asks not "Why did she do it?" but "Where is she now?" Charles Kinbote, the author of the commentary on the poem, is similarly confident about his grasp of Hazel's motivations: she "deserved great respect," he writes in his index, "having preferred the beauty of death to the ugliness of life." Neither writer, oddly enough, looks at Hazel's suicide as a grossly disproportionate response to a passing slight; they both claim to understand her and, therefore, to be able to explain her tò the reader.

It is here, though, that the wary reader, trained by Nabokov to distrust the tale as well as the teller, will beg to differ with the poem and the commentary. However we adjudicate the issue of authorship (Did Shade create Kinbote? Did Kinbote invent Shade?), the texts, as they stand, seem to constitute a sanctioned distortion of Hazel Shade—and of other matters as well, for she is not the only subject (or object) of distortion. The literary license that is exercised in the characterization of Hazel may in fact typify, for Shade and Kinbote, the creative process itself.

Shade and Kinbote assume that Hazel equates lack of charm with lack of worth and accordingly suffers. Their assumption is a projection; without direct access to her emotions, they nonetheless claim intimate knowledge. They act as if they were capable of the sort of telepathy Hazel (and Aunt Maud) merely attempted. In the case of Shade and Kinbote, however, their claim to special knowledge can be said to have as its basis no magic talent, but the similarity each perceives between Hazel and himself.

Hazel, apparently, resembles her father, to his pain and regret:

She might have been you [Shade's wife], me, or some
    quaint blend:

Nature chose me so as to wrench and rend
Your heart and mine.

(ll. 293-95)

Both John and Hazel are plump, awkward, unathletic, and untidy (Foreword, ll. 129-30, 296-304, 322, and note to l. 1000).[3] It is worth noting, though, that ugliness is to some extent in the eye of the beholder. Although Kinbote refers explicitly to Shade's "misshapen body" (Foreword) and "broad deformed pelvis" (note to l. 1000), although Shade clearly lacks the lissome slimness Kinbote values in his young companions, the commentator can readily separate the ugliness of surface from the beauty of substance: he is able, for example, to imagine John Shade as a boy, "a physically unattractive but otherwise beautifully developed lad" (note to ll. 1-4). Shade, on the contrary, stresses Hazel's lack of physical attraction and dismisses the value of her achievements: her prizes in French and history are merely "fun," while her appearance in a school pantomime as a bent charwoman is the occasion for tears (ll. 305-14). He assumes, furthermore, that Hazel shares his feelings on this subject, just as he presumes to speak for Sybil. Although Shade reports that Sybil tried to tell him "Good looks / Are not *that* indispensable!" (ll. 324-25), he nonetheless believes that Hazel's plumpness and squint rend his wife's heart as well as his. He has exercised selective focus of attention.

Kinbote's dissimilar treatment of Shade's ugliness shows us that Shade could have chosen otherwise. The poet could have written more of Hazel's qualities of mind and spirit. He could have looked for signs of inherited intelligence and inquisitiveness and not merely inherited clumsiness and homeliness. The resemblances on which the poem focuses, however, testify to Shade's skewed perspective—pity for an irremediable handicap—a perspective that has proved irrelevant to his own physical make-up. The similarity between them, therefore, is a prime example of selective interpretation rather than a source of narrative authority.

The same can be said for the parallels between Hazel and Kinbote. In claiming priority for the uncanny discovery that "redips" is "spider" backwards—an observation that Shade attributes to Hazel (l. 348)—Kinbote points out that "Hazel Shade resembled me in certain respects" (note to ll. 347-48). They share an interest in mirror words, it is true, but this is not an obvious foundation for imaginative sympathy. (It seems, instead, more like the mountain-fountain coincidence in Canto 3, decidedly not to be taken as "a fond / Affinity, a sacramental bond.") Another explicit parallel is similarly debatable. In his note to line 334, Kinbote compares his own anguished waiting for a companion, or for Shade himself, with Hazel's frustrated yearning for "a white-scarfed beau." Although both Hazel and Kinbote indeed meet with rejection, the notion of Hazel's longing for a lover originates in Shade's verse: it is presented, even there, not as a record of Hazel's thoughts, but as the speech of "the demons of our pity" (l. 327). To discern a precise parallel here, one must treat the documents—Shade's poem and Kinbote's commentary—as accurate transcriptions of reality, which they manifestly are not. A final, and seemingly compelling, parallel is the preoccupation with suicide, but even here there is a significant difference. Kinbote thinks about it and writes about it, in terms that mingle a contempt for life with a faith in spiritual survival. Hazel simply commits it. (Although Nabokov has said that Kinbote also kills himself, the act is not within the jurisdiction of *Pale Fire*: no one writes commentaries from beyond the grave.) For both Shade and Kinbote, then, a discussion of the parallels (alleged and actual) between them and Hazel reveals much more about them than it does about her.

One is not surprised, therefore, to find Shade and Kinbote liable to distortion when they speak about her. Shade, to begin with, seems to regard Hazel as an eternal infant; she is not only his child, but a child forever. His first mention of her is a reference to "the phantom of my little daughter's swing" (l. 57). Aunt Maud, he says, "lived to hear the next babe cry" (l. 90); as Kinbote observes, the "babe" was fully sixteen at the time of her great-aunt's death. Shade has preserved "her first toy" (l. 291). He recalls her as "a mere tot" (l. 508). He considers the possibility of seeing a phantom Hazel near the tree where the phantom swing swayed (ll. 650-52), a swing suitable only for a child. When he alludes to Goethe's "The Erl-King," with its reference to a father and his child (l. 664), he is again picturing a younger version of the Hazel who died at twenty-four. He sees her as she once was, but not as she was most recently. (In adapting Goethe's poem to his own purposes, moreover, Shade changes the gender of the child from male to female, mirroring the awkward Zemblan translation of the "pale fire" passage in *Timon of Athens,* in which the male sun becomes female and the female moon becomes male [note to ll. 39-40].) And when he speaks, at the end, of his confidence about her life after death, he may be wrong:

> I'm reasonably sure that we survive
> And that my darling somewhere is alive. . . .
>
> (ll. 977-78)

The following lines undermine this "reasonable" certainty:

> As I am reasonably sure that I
> Shall wake at six tomorrow, on July
> The twenty-second, ninteen fifty-nine.
>
> (ll. 979-81)

It is a day he will not live to see.

Kinbote's distortions are largely editorial exercises of literary license. He nearly removes Hazel from the index; although he records his respect for her suicide, he lists only two of the many references to her. (Kinbote, to be sure, does a much more complete job of obliterating from his index any traces of Sybil Shade.) In one of his notes, furthermore, he says that Shade spends too much poetic space on Hazel, at the expense of "certain other richer and rarer matters [i.e., Zembla] ousted by it" (note to l. 230). Kinbote thus directs the reader to undervalue the material on Hazel. In another note (ll. 403-04), Kinbote denigrates the "synchronization device" by which Shade juxtaposes the steps of Hazel's suicide with the changes of the television channel in the Shade home. (The mode of narration that Shade adopts here, and that Kinbote decries, is one that approximates our procedure in assimilating Kinbote's commentary: we move back and forth between the poem and the annotations.) Again, Kinbote attempts to reduce the impact Shade seems to intend. Kinbote, finally, comes close to excluding Hazel from the poem itself: in the synchronized account of the suicide, Kinbote takes the liberty of italicizing the Hazel theme. Kinbote is even verbally linked with Pete, the young man who rejects Hazel on the night of her death. "My notes and self," he writes at the end of his commentary, "are *petering* out . . ." (emphasis mine). We can, it seems, without departing from the texts, without having recourse to any privileged knowledge, detect the distortion in what Shade and Kinbote say about Hazel.

They presume, furthermore, to speak not only about her, but for her. Shade's account of Hazel's blind date is an imaginative projection, for he did not witness Pete's lame excuse, Hazel's smiling departure, her descent from the bus, her stepping off the bus into the lake. He even quotes Pete, Hazel, and the bus driver; notwithstanding his distance from the events, he renders the Hazel theme specifically, albeit elliptically. His eyewitness for the early part of the evening is Jane, his typist, who is also the source for Kinbote's inventions about Hazel. Her cousin Pete is a liar; she may be, in more ways than one, a near relative.

According to the note for line 347, Jane told Kinbote about Hazel's investigations into the supernatural phenomena she observes in an old barn, investigations that, Kinbote assumes, must have made the Shades fear a recurrence of the "psychokinetic" phenomena that had followed upon Aunt Maud's death and that they interpreted, according to Jane, as "an outward extension or expulsion of insanity" in Hazel (note to l. 230). The three-night investigation itself verged on farce, as far as Kinbote can tell. Jane is his witness for the abortive first night, and Hazel has left a report about the disappointing second. For the third and last, on which Hazel was joined by her parents, no records exist. Kinbote, undaunted, composes a playlet, "The Haunted Barn," which he feels "cannot be too far removed from the truth." His Sybil is sceptical and mirthful, his John tol-

erant and distant, his Hazel hostile, impatient, and ultimately defeated. The scene is plausible, to be sure, but
it is also created practically *ex nihilo,* in an excess of
literary license.

Kinbote's inability to interpret the fruits of Hazel's research on the supernatural is highly revealing. We are
aware that he frequently sees in Shade's poem references to Zembla where anyone else would detect nothing; here he sees nothing where there is in fact something to be seen. Hazel's investigation of the "roundlets"
of "pale light" yielded the following message: "pada ata
lane pad not ogo old wart alan ther tale feur far rant
lant tal told" (note to l. 347). This note is probably the
basis for line 235 of the poem ("Life is a message
scribbled in the dark"), a line Kinbote leaves unexamined. Yet Kinbote confesses that he cannot find any
meaning in Hazel's message. His failure may be due to
the object of his search: something "that might be construed, however remotely, as containing a warning, or
having some bearing on the circumstances of her soon-
coming death."

If we see the note as referring to John Shade's death,
rather than Hazel's, the report can be interpreted as
having more meaning than Kinbote allows it. David
Walker offers the following translation:

> Hazel is telling her father not to cross the lane to Judge
> Goldsworth's house, where she knows he will meet the
> pale fire ("tale feur"?) of Gradus's revolver. And per-
> haps "far rant lant tal told" specifies the time of Shade's
> death, when he has completed telling the tale of Zem-
> bla, that foreign land.[4]

Robert M. Adams offers a slightly different translation:
"Father Atalantis pleads not to go Goldsworth where
tale from foreign land will be told."[5] (Atalantis is the
Red Admirable or Vanessa butterfly, a specimen of
which flutters near Shade shortly before his death.)
Kinbote, though, sees only what he looks for.

If Shade and Kinbote write around Hazel rather than
about her, how, then, can she be apprehended? We can
guess what is wrong with the accounts we have, but
how are we to see what is right? Complete or certain
knowledge is not available in the poem, the commentary, and the novel they compose; to seek it is a patent
absurdity. We can begin, however, by looking closely at
Hazel's name—which is immune to distortion—and by
seeing where it leads us.

The name "Hazel" seems, first of all, to echo the "Haze"
of Dolores Haze, or Lolita. Both Hazel and little Haze
are contemplated by madmen (Kinbote and Humbert)
and artists (Shade and Quilty), and both die after contact with simpler, younger men with faintly phallic first
names (Pete and Dick). The sorrow denoted by the name
"Dolores" is matched by the "tears" (l. 337), the rare

smiles (l. 350), and the "moan" (l. 355) of "morose"
Hazel (l. 357). The nickname "Dolly" may be reflected
in Shade's favorite term for the daughter he nowhere
speaks of by name: "my darling" (ll. 357, 978).

Her last name has received extensive critical treatment
because it is also that of her father; "Shade" and the related words "umbra," "ombre," and "shadow" suggest
ghosts, reflections, the stolen pale fire.[6] But this name
too is an allusion to *Lolita.* The French "ombre" is not
far from the French pronunciation of "Humbert." Humbert Humbert, a double name, comes equipped with its
own reflection, its own shadow. The names of Shade
(ombre) and Humbert have also been said to suggest
"hombre," the Spanish for "man."[7] If Hazel had indeed
been a man, her physical unattractiveness would not
have been perceived as significant. The prizes in French
and history would have been viewed as important rather
than "fun," and homeliness would have handicapped
her no more than it had the father she resembles.

To complete the cycle from *Lolita* to *Pale Fire* and
back, we may observe that the name Hazel Shade represents a combination of Dolores Haze and Humbert
Humbert, a quasi-marriage, albeit, shall we say, in name
only. In this sense Humbert and Dolores—of whose
situation Humbert said that the "refuge of art" was "the
only immortality you and I may share, my Lolita"—can
be said to have found that refuge again by sharing the
name of Hazel Shade.[8]

The full name, as Mary McCarthy has observed, is an
allusion to a line ("In lone Glenartney's hazel shade")
in Scott's *The Lady of the Lake,* a reference echoed in
the Scottish names associated with her place of death.[9]
The reference is ironic (in that Hazel, unlike Ellen Douglas, does not have several suitors fighting for her
favors) and pathetic (in that Hazel's lake is the one in
which she finds death). "Hazel," furthermore, suggests
haze or haziness, mentioned several times in the poem,
in the context of courtship (l. 254) and the afterlife (ll.
580, 756). It is, of course, not surprising to find Hazel's
name associated with the longing for love and the fact
of death. Her name may also be echoed in the reason
given for the burning of the old barn, the site of the supernatural phenomena; it was deemed a "fire *haz*ard"
(note to l. 347—emphasis added).

The hazel tree itself provides additional fruitful associations. The tree is seen as magical and supernatural, as is
the witch hazel shrub. The hazel wand is a divining
rod, the appropriate botanical correlative for a young
woman who wants, among other things, to explore hidden matters. The particular virtue of the hazel wand,
furthermore, depends on its having two forks.[10] These
two forks recall the bifurcation of the highway leading
to Wordsmith University (note to l. 42); Hazel thus becomes part of the landscape. The two forks of the hazel

wand also recall Shade's synchronized account of the night of her death: "And here time forked" (l. 404). Hazel's story, ultimately, ends in death because it is told by means of two forks; if her parents had been with her in fact, and not merely in synchronization, the poem and the plot would have been quite different.

The hint of the hazel wand, a magic rod of divination, recalls another tree with which Hazel can be associated. Mary McCarthy has written of Kinbote's references to "alderwood" and "alderking," with their "overtones of northern forest magic." The German word for "alder" is "Erle." The word "Erle" returns us to Goethe's "Erl-King," to which Shade's poem alludes, and the original "erl-king" in the Danish meant "elf-king" (and was mistranslated by Herder). The word "alder," then, is "touched by the enchanted word elf" and thus "becomes enchanted itself." The alder tree, furthermore, "has the curious property of not rotting under water" and is therefore "a kind of magic tree." After all of McCarthy's ingenious observations,[11] it remains for us to add the one that brings the magic home to Hazel: she is the character who does not rot under water, and she is the child touched by the erl-king. Hazel is magic—alder as well as hazel.

Another meaning of Hazel's name is suggested by the prize she won in French. One translation of "hazel" is "coudrier" with "coudre" as a variant; "coudre" as a verb means: to sew, to connect, to attach, to unite. Hazel ties the work together. Her concerns and her qualities are repeated and embroidered throughout. Consider the following tangled example. Hazel, stepping off the bank, is described as a "blurry shape" (l. 499—the midpoint of the poem). Soon after, Shade imagines dying and seeing his live widow as "a blur" (l. 547). Kinbote remembers seeing a photograph of his father, about to die in a plane accident, "just before the white-blurred shattering crash" (note to l. 71). He also mentions a picture that "once hung in the nursery whose sleepy denizens had always taken it to depict foamy waves in the foreground instead of the blurry shapes of melancholy sheep that it now revealed" (note to l. 130). The nursery recalls Hazel's swing and toy; the waves recall her own blurry shape; and the melancholy sheep recall her own morose nature. Numerous similar connections can be cited.[12]

Hazel, moreover, is a knitter (l. 340), a hobby that links her with the young Baron Mandevil, disguised as an elderly Zemblan knitter (note to l. 149). It is also, perhaps, a hint that she has a touch of the poet, of the ability to perceive what Shade describes as "not text, but texture . . . Not flimsy nonsense, but a web of sense" (ll. 808, 810). Kinbote echoes him: the true artist can "see the web of the world, and the warp and weft of that web" (note to l. 991). Hazel's sewing, knitting, and web-making come to an abrupt end, however, when the thread is cut, "as life snapped" (l. 472). The manner of her end—which can be seen as both a trial and an execution—takes on additional significance in the light of her claim to the title of witch. The word, let it be noted, echoes "wit" and includes among its root meanings "cunning" and "victim." Witch Hazel, winner of prizes in French and history, is as surely clever as she is sadly a victim.

If Hazel is a suspected witch, are we then to interpret her drowning as an example of the well-known trial by water? According to this test, a true witch would be unable to drown, in that the pure element of water would reject the unclean thing; Hazel's sinking, then, would be evidence that she was not a witch.[13] She would be revealed as unexceptional, a person of quirks rather than gifts—and this is in fact the way Kinbote and Shade see her. But the trial by water, often associated in the popular mind with the investigation of witches, was not at all common after the mid-1600's. Increase Mather explicitly denounced the practice as superstitious, as did most other theologians and jurists; "the practice eventually lived on only as an illegal procedure of the mob."[14] The water test for witches is one that the experts abandoned long ago, although it still survives in popular impressions of the witch trials; with reference to Witch Hazel, it stands as the mere semblance or shadow of a test, discredited as are the accounts of Hazel by Zembla's Kinbote and John Shade.

Nabokov had abundant opportunity to learn the truth about the water test. Although he wrote Shade's poem in Nice (where, incidentally, Hazel Shade was conceived in 1933, to be born in 1934, the same year as Nabokov's only son), he "had devised some odds and ends of Zemblan lore" in the late fifties, when he was still at Cornell.[15] The Cornell Library is the home of a Witchcraft Collection that is considered the finest and most important in the world (and one of whose early librarians is the source of the information cited above). Even the physical setting of the collection, at the time Nabokov was there, is suggestive:

> In 1958 the Witchcraft Collection was housed in the vaults of what is now the Uris Undergraduate Library, adjoining the clock tower. To reach it, one undertook a roundabout navigation over shaky iron bridges, through heavy doors, down narrow steel steps.[16]

King Charles the Beloved (Kinbote's alter ego) makes his escape from the South West Tower in August, 1958, through "a stone-paved underground passage."

> [In] its angular and cryptic course it adapted itself to the various structures which it followed, here availing itself of a bulwark to fit in its side like a pencil in the pencil hold of a pocket diary, there running through the cellars of a great mansion too rich in dark passageways to notice the stealthy intrusion.

> (note to l. 130)

In 1958, near the end of his stay at Cornell, it is likely that Nabokov, too, descended the narrow steps of the underground burrow. He could easily have known that only the uninformed see the water test as professional practice. John Shade's daughter, therefore, remains potentially Witch Hazel, and as such vulnerable.

Is her death by drowning, then, a judgment on her, the sentence for witchcraft? Not in the usual sense.

The traditional end for a convicted witch is not a lake of ice, but a stake of fire. In his Foreword, Kinbote refers to that very stake, at the moment when he first mentions pale fire as a physical phenomenon rather than a poetic title. John Shade, says Kinbote, had a habit of destroying imperfect drafts—and who is more imperfect than Hazel?—"burning a whole stack of them in the pale fire of the incinerator before which he stood with bent head like an official mourner among the windborne black butterflies of that backyard auto-da-fe." If Hazel dies not by fire, but by ice, she is destroyed nonetheless. The opposition reminds me of a well-known poem of 1923:

> Some say the world will end in fire,
> Some say in ice.
> From what I've tasted of desire
> I hold with those who favor fire.
> But if it had to perish twice,
> I think I know enough of hate
> To say that for destruction ice
> Is also great
> And would suffice.

The author of that poem, of course, is mentioned in Canto 2 and discussed in the commentary. His name, which could be translated as "pale ice," is (Robert) Frost, and he is the poet with whom John Shade is most often compared.[17]

What does it mean to say that, for purposes of destruction, fire and ice are both "great"? Hazel, who does not manage to taste desire, perishes by ice, rather than by fire, as the poem in some ways leads one to expect. She dies as a "blurry shape," furthermore, because she is not really seen, steadily and whole, by the writers who claim certainty and offer none. But in this she is not alone.

For the artist, the entire world (the subject of Frost's poem) is the object of simultaneous creation and destruction, through the exercise of literary license. Kinbote, in the Foreword, offers a moving description of the artist at work:

> John Shade perceiving and transforming the world, taking it in and taking it apart, re-combining its elements in the very process of storing them up so as to produce at some unspecified date an organic miracle, a fusion of image and music, a line of verse.

But the miracle is also a fraud, as we see when Kinbote likens Shade to a conjurer. And John Shade, while at work, is looking at the distant lake and thinking, perhaps, of its lady, Hazel Shade.

For the miracle, in **Pale Fire,** has been misleading. Both Shade and Kinbote have substituted their creations for the woman herself. Browning's "Prologue" to *Asolando* (1889) contrasts poetic contrivance with the "naked very thing," the "inmost self," that can be found only in clear outlines. Browning's language is suggestive: he asks for "truth ablaze" as an alternative to "falsehood's fancy-haze." It is a warning Shade and Kinbote might well have heeded.

Notes

1. Vladimir Nabokov, *Pale Fire* (New York: Putnam, 1962), p. 45. Subsequent quotations from the novel (composed of the foreword, poem, commentary, and index) are all drawn from this edition and will be identified in the text by the appropriate section of the novel and, when necessary, by line number.

2. The story of the Shade family may have a factual basis. Some years before Nabokov taught at Cornell, an English professor who had lost his daughter brought to the campus Madame Blavatsky, the famous Russian-born spiritualist, who summoned up his daughter's spirit each night of her long visit. Nabokov, not surprisingly, claimed ignorance of these facts. Robert M. Adams comments: "The combination of these distinctive elements (a grieving professor of English, his tragic daughter, a Russian outsider with powerful if discordant vibrations, psychic messages among them) is a spectacular if irrelevant coincidence, for there's no overcoming the author's denial." See *Afterjoyce: Studies in Fiction After Ulysses* (New York: Oxford Univ. Press, 1977), p. 154.

3. Douglas Fowler, *Reading Nabokov* (Ithaca: Cornell Univ. Press, 1974), pp. 108-09. Critics invariably emphasize Hazel's homeliness at the expense of her intelligence, curiosity, and magic propensities. She is typically identified as the "ugly daughter" (Alfred Chester, "Nabokov's Anti-Novel," *Commentary,* 34 [November 1962], 450) or as "Fat, ugly, psoriatic Hazel Shade" (David Walker, "'The Viewer and the View': Chance and Choice in *Pale Fire*," *Studies in American Fiction,* 4 [1976], 206).

4. Walker, p. 213.

5. Adams, p. 153.

6. See, for example, Marilyn Edelstein, "*Pale Fire*: The Art of Consciousness," in *Nabokov's Fifth Arc: Nabokov and Others on His Life's Work,* ed. J. E. Rivers and Charles Nicol (Austin: Univ. of Texas Press, 1982), pp. 216-17.

7. See Edelstein, p. 217, and Jessie Thomas Lokrantz, *The Underside of the Weave: Some Stylistic Devices Used by Vladimir Nabokov,* Studia Anglistica Upsaliensia II (Uppsala, Sweden: Almquist and Wiksell, Acta Universitatis Upsaliensis, 1973), p. 75.

8. Additional correspondences between *Lolita* and *Pale Fire,* as noted by Alfred Appel, include allusions to Dostoevsky's *The Brothers Karamazov,* Goethe's "The Erl-King," and Browning's "Pippa Passes."

9. Mary McCarthy, "Vladimir Nabokov's *Pale Fire,*" *Encounter,* 19 (October 1962), 77.

10. *Encyclopedia Britannica* (1880), XI, 540/1, quoted in *Oxford English Dictionary,* compact edition, "H" volume, p. 138.

11. McCarthy, p. 77.

12. Several additional connections are as follows:

Hazel material	Connections
babe (l. 90)	chubby babe (note to l. 71)
plump (l. 296)	Shade fat (l. 129)
	plump cherubic fist (note to ll. 47-48)
	plump wife (note to l. 149)
riding lessons (l. 301)	Blenda (Kinbote's mother) horsewoman (note to l. 71)
	Blenda is also ghost (note to l. 80), as is Hazel (l. 230)
tennis, badminton (l. 301)	ball, bat (l. 130)
less starch (l. 303)	The grand potato (l. 502)
cute (l. 304)	horribly cute little schoolgirls (note to ll. 47-48)
French (l. 306)	Sybil translates French (l. 678, and note) undeodorized Frenchwoman (note to l. 579)
	Gradus's illness due to French sandwich and French fries (note to l. 949)
	gardener wants to study French (note to l. 998)
history (l. 306)	*Historia Zembla* (note to l. 80)
no doubt (ll. 306, 307)	religious doubts (note to l. 549)
elves (l. 310)	elf-haunted alderwood (note to l. 662)
Mother Time (l. 312)	Father Time (l. 475) (Kinbote gets this one.)
Virgins (l. 323)	virginal-looking daybed (note to l. 12)
	checking a daughter's virginity (note to ll. 597-608)
white-scarfed beau (l. 333)	scarf-skin (l. 194)
chateau in France (l. 336)	Goldsworth chateau (note to l. 62)
	King Charles's castle, *passim*
Korean boy (l. 343)	Korean graduate student (note to l. 181)
Spider, redips (l. 348)	spectral spider (note to l. 80)
	dip or redip, spider (note to l. 181)
pain (l. 351)	Disa, Duchess of Payn (Index)
fingernails (l. 356)	fingernails (l. 186)
	yellow nails (Foreword)

Hazel material	Connections
moan (l. 355)	moaning like doves (note to l. 130)
	Disa, Duchess of Payn, of Great Payn and Mone (Index)
darling (ll. 357, 978)	Darling (l. 831)
furs (l. 360)	fur (notes to ll. 12, 80)
Grim pen (l. 368)	grim shepherd (note to l. 596)
chthonic (l. 370)	underworld (note to ll. 47-48)
sempiternal (l. 372)	many references to eternity
mad (l. 383)	you are insane (Foreword)
"outward extension or expulsion of insanity" (note to l. 230)	
	deranged mind (note to ll. 376-77)
	the madman's fate, lunatic and poet (note to l. 629)
hope (l. 383)	Faint hope (l. 834)
azure entrance [of bar] (l. 397)	false azure (l. 2)
headlights (l. 445)	headlights (l. 431) (Kinbote gets this one.)
Retake, retake! (l. 487)	Retake the fallen snow (l. 13)
death by ice (ll. 498-500)	ice when crossed (note to l. 79)
	drowning in ice-hole of Queen Yaruga (Index)

13. Phyllis Roth of Skidmore College suggested that I pursue the matter of the water test.

14. George Lincoln Burr, ed., *Narratives of the Witchcraft Cases 1648-1706* (New York: Scribner, 1914), p. 21, n. 3.

15. Interview with Robert Hughes, September 1965, in Vladimir Nabokov, *Strong Opinions* (New York: McGraw Hill, 1973), p. 55.

16. Rossell Hope Robbins, *Witchcraft: An Introduction to the Literature of Witchcraft* (Millwood, NY: KTO Press, 1978), p. 2.

17. There are other traces of Frost in Nabokov. The setting of Hazel's death—the "crackling, gulping swamp" (l. 500)—suggests the image of Frost's "Birches" (1916), in which the "sun's warmth" turns the icy branches into "heaps of broken glass. . . . You'd think the inner dome of heaven had fallen." In this poem, the speaker wishes he could "get away from earth awhile" by climbing a tree; in Nabokov's "The Ballad of Longwood Glen" (1957), Art Longwood climbs away and never returns. JoAnn Harvill of Virginia Tech suggested that I look at "Birches."

James F. English (essay date spring 1992)

SOURCE: English, James F. "Modernist Joke-Work: *Pale Fire* and the Mock Transcendence of Mockery." *Contemporary Literature* 33, no. 1 (spring 1992). 74-90.

[*In the following essay, English assesses the role of humor in Nabokov's* Pale Fire.]

The only justification for labeling Vladimir Nabokov's *Pale Fire* a "postmodernist" novel, as so many commentators have done, would be its publication date: 1962. If we are prepared to accept a periodization uncomplicated by any concern with the persistence of residual elements within the dominant culture—a periodization even more absolute than Fredric Jameson's—then we can simply place all postwar or late capitalist cultural production under the rubric of "postmodernism" and be done with it. But from the vantage point of any historicism more nuanced than this, *Pale Fire* shows up clearly as one of the most archetypical texts of modernism, a text in which both the social or ethical aims of modernist fiction and the impediments to their realization appear in unusually pronounced, and hence illuminating, relief.

It is worth reminding ourselves that Nabokov was born the same year as Hemingway (1899), that he established himself as one of the major young émigré writers in the twenties, and that the basic contours of his aesthetic project were fully settled by the end of that decade, remaining constant throughout his subsequent Parisian, American, and Swiss periods. (As Nabokov characteristically put it, "Artistic originality has only its own self to copy" [*Strong Opinions* 95].) It cannot be overstressed that this project, which was as consistent as any with what we can only rather dubiously refer to as "modernist literary production in general," involved a profound, if indirect, commitment to the idea of community. Powerful but reductive Marxist critiques by Raymond Williams (*Culture and Society, The Politics of Modernism*), Terry Eagleton (*Exiles and Emigrés*), and others have accustomed us to a view of modernism as an aesthetic system within which "community" in any positive sense becomes unimaginable. But on this one point at least it seems to me that Marxist critics who are generally more sympathetic to modernism, such as Kenneth Burke, Herbert Marcuse, and Jürgen Habermas, perhaps offer more useful points of departure. Burke argued long ago, in *Counter-Statement* (1931), that the major strain of high modernist aesthetic thought turned not on the self-trivializing pursuit of art for art's sake, but on a more ambitious program of "art for life's sake." The exiles and émigrés who produced modernist literature put forth their doctrine of aesthetic autonomy as a strategic response to prevailing social conditions—conditions of which their own experiences of exile and isolation were of course symptomatic. The need was felt for a "sanctuary" and a "bulwark" against the encroachments of modernization (Marcuse 38), for a realm not simply of "pure art" but of purified social intercourse, where the alienating and divisive effects of the modern lifeworld might be transcended in the direction of, as Habermas puts it, a "happier . . . communicative experience," an "experience of living in solidarity with others" (42).

Nabokov was one of the most determined—and, in a sense, most naive—promoters of this modernist doctrine of art for life's sake. He frequently and notoriously expressed his disdain for "the group, the community, the masses, and so forth," arguing that "what makes a work of fiction safe from larvae and rust is not its social importance but its art, only its art." But he also, and just as frequently, remarked that he did "not care for the slogan 'art for art's sake'" or the "dainty poets" who were its "promoters" (*Strong Opinions* 33). For Nabokov the "refuge of art" (*Lolita* 311) finally justified itself in *social* terms, as a realm in which expressions of tenderness, pity, and fellowship could be freely exchanged. The aesthetic provided means for transcending the constraints on modern social life, for enjoying a more selfless and connected "state of being" (**"On a Book Entitled *Lolita*"** 317) than present conditions would allow. "Pure" artistry was a way of envisioning, and thereby potentially enabling, a more open sociality, a better community.

This is not to say that the many readers and critics who have taken Nabokov's antisocial aestheticist pronouncements at face value—classing him as one of the more extreme instances of the aloof and narcissistic modernist "master," a writer far more concerned with the perfection of his "private universe"[1] than with the needs of community—are simply mistaken. In Nabokov's practice, as in that of other modernist writers, the chosen route to a "happy communicative experience" is impeded by deep contradictions. What I propose to do in this essay is to approach those contradictions by way of the humor in Nabokov's texts, particularly in *Pale Fire*. I take this approach not only because humor figures quite prominently and explicitly in Nabokov's project (the whole of which has been described even by admiring critics as "a joke" [Lilly 88] and "a kind of joke" [Kermode 76]), but because I believe that the study of modernist literature generally has suffered from a lack of any systematic critical analysis of modernist joke-work.

The term "joke-work" comes, of course, from Freud's *Jokes and Their Relation to the Unconscious* (1905). But we should not be misled by the term's psychoanalytic origins into imagining that the work performed through comic exchange is strictly psycho-symbolic in character. As Freud's text itself comes to discover, joking is not finally understandable except as "social process." Without undertaking to elaborate a full-scale theory of humor and laughter here, we can observe, first, that joke-work is best grasped in terms of the subjective repositionings it makes possible along social axes of hierarchy and solidarity, and second, that these repositionings obtain at the level of the group rather than the individual: "our laughter," as Bergson famously expressed it, "is always the laughter of a group" (64).

Stated most generally, the basic social categories on which humor depends are insider and outsider, or better, "in-group" and "out-group" (Martineau); the joke is a kind of highly flexible "dividing practice" (Foucault 208). Whatever else they are doing, the participants in comic exchange—joking subject(s), laughing subject(s), object(s)—are negotiating group boundaries, boundaries of difference. This is not true only for racist, sexist, and other unmistakably "tendentious" jokes (Freud). Even the silliest banter functions as a sort of "understanding test" (Sacks)[2] to mark off recipients who lack certain competencies or, as Pierre Bourdieu would express it, certain pieces of "symbolic capital" (646)—*social* competencies which include not only the ability to make sense but also the ability to make appropriate or acceptable nonsense. When we laugh, some part of our laughter is always directed at the group comprised of real and imagined nonlaughers, at those who aren't "in on it." This is one reason why Freud was ultimately forced to abolish his own distinction between "tendentious" and "non-tendentious" humor, conceding that "jokes . . . are in fact never non-tendentious" (132).

From its fundamentally divisive operation derives humor's great importance to any discourse of exile, alienation, or loneliness—and so to much modernist literature. In the case of Nabokov, all of whose work engages the problematic of exile and belonging both thematically and (through his elaborate narrative tactics or "games" of inclusion and exclusion) strategically, humor plays a characteristically modernist role. Like all humor, Nabokov's turns on the social categories of in-group and out-group; but its distinctive movement is an attempted overturning of these categories, a reordering of the participants by means of a quasi-dialectical deployment of subjects and objects.

A ready example is Jack Cockerell in *Pnin* (1957). Pnin, the hapless émigré Russian professor, makes himself a classic object of in-group laughter through his wild irregularities of speech. As one colleague puts it, "Our friend . . . employs a nomenclature all his own. His verbal vagaries add a new thrill to life. His mispronunciations are mythopeic. His slips of the tongue are oracular. He calls my wife John" (165). Funnier still is Professor Cockerell expertly mimicking these "Pninisms": "It was all built of course around the Pninian gesture and the Pninian wild English, but Cockerell also managed to imitate such things as the subtle degree of difference between the silence of Pnin and the silence of Thayer, as they sat motionlessly ruminating in adjacent chairs at the Faculty Club" (187). But the joke doesn't rest there. The "brilliant" Cockerell becomes so obsessively fond of his mimic routine, trots it out at so many faculty parties, that ultimately his colleagues begin to find *him* more peculiar and ridiculous than "the man he [has] been mimicking for almost ten years" (187). As the narrator remarks, it turns out to be the

kind of joke "which substitutes its own victim for that of the initial ridicule" (189).

The comment is typical of Nabokov, who tends to thematize his humor, calling attention to its movements and progressions. In any comic exchange participants undergo a kind of slippage. As Freud's analysis suggests (and as Samuel Weber's readings of Freud make explicit), the positions of joking subject, laughing subject, and comic object are curiously tenuous and interchangeable in the social economy of the joke. But in Nabokov's practice, such substitutions and reversals are strategically foregrounded, or we might say *simulated,* on the level of the calculated narrative effect. The slippage among subject positions and roles in the exchange is meant to be patterned in a particular way, the jokework anchored to the consciously dialectical purposes of the author.

Consider another comic exchange, a characteristically cock-eyed one from *Pale Fire.* As usual, Dr. Kinbote is being tormented by his colleagues on the Wordsmith faculty, whose aggressively masculine, American-academic style of "jesting and teasing" excludes the eccentric émigré from Zembla (21). One of these men steers the conversation toward the somewhat sensitive matter of two Ping-Pong tables which Kinbote has installed in his basement, and which he is correctly suspected of using to entertain groups of young boyfriends. At any rate, the facetious "tormentor" is obviously probing for some new mark of deviance, some new transgression to mock, when he inquires if Kinbote has in fact acquired these tables. Put on the defensive, Kinbote responds, "Was it a crime?" No, says the other, but why two? "Is *that* a crime?" says Kinbote, who then proudly informs us that "they all laughed" at this clever riposte. "I countered," he explains, "and they all laughed" (22). (At another such moment his comment is, "I turn[ed] it all into a joke" [269].)

There appear to be at least three ways to read this comic exchange. We can read it as Kinbote wants us to, as evidence of his comic mastery, his ability to trade jabs with faculty-lounge wits and come out on top. *He* turns it all into a joke, and *they* all laugh, thereby acceding to his bid for momentary mastery, marking his success as speaking subject of a joke, his in-group status.

It's more likely, of course, that we read the whole transaction ironically, locating the humor in Kinbote's *mis*reading. Kinbote, we would say, is in fact an *un*successful speaking subject here, the subject of a "bad" joke (an utterance that fails to be accorded the status it seeks as "joke"), and consequently the *object* of the "good" joke that amuses us and the professors (with whose ingroup we now become identified). Indeed, Kinbote is doubly the object of this joke, for it is not only his failure to succeed as joker that makes him ridiculous but also his failure to recognize his failure. The joke is not simply that his attempt to make a joke is laughed at, but that he interprets the very laughter that signals his failure and exclusion as the sign of social success, as confirmation that he belongs.

A third reading emerges temporally, as we begin to revise our sense of what Kinbote knows and doesn't know. At some point one sees that Kinbote is in fact aware—quite painfully so—of his subordinate position in such exchanges. Though he puts a good face on things, he knows that when "they all laugh" the laughter is at him, not with him, and that a gay vegetarian immigrant from a Russia-like "distant northern land" will never belong in the clubby world of fifties American academe. From this vantage point, Kinbote is not the proper ironic butt, the naif, but a more complex figure, a tormented outsider, continually punished with laughter for the "crime" of social deviance, of abnormality, but determined to turn his story of exile inside out, to recast even the most humiliating episodes of exclusion as moments of fellowship and mutual recognition. From this third vantage point it is possible to say that Kinbote really does turn the tables on the colleagues who mock him. For, next to his irrepressibly unorthodox negotiation of comic transactions, his wildly fabricated comic "successes," and so forth, their conventional in-group teasing looks rather slow-witted, even ridiculous. They cannot really get the best of Kinbote when the logic of his participation in comic exchange is so much more complex than their own. At least we should say that Kinbote is neither simply the subject of the joke here nor simply its object; like Pnin imitated by Cockerell, he can be seen as a victor as well as a victim of the transaction once its (shifting and negotiable) contextual boundaries are enlarged.

This trilevel comedy, examples of which can be found throughout Nabokov's work, suggests a kind of syllogism. And indeed, in a famous passage of *Laughter in the Dark,* Nabokov (perhaps taking his cue from two writers he admired, Arthur Schopenhauer and Lewis Carroll) links humor to the syllogism quite explicitly:

> Uncle alone in the house with the children said he'd dress up to amuse them. After a long wait, as he did not appear, they went down and saw a masked man putting the table silver into a bag. "Oh Uncle," they cried in delight. "Yes, isn't my make-up good?" said Uncle, taking his mask off. Thus goes the Hegelian syllogism of humor. Thesis: Uncle made himself up as a burglar (a laugh for the children); antithesis: it *was* a burglar (a laugh for the reader); synthesis, it still was Uncle (fooling the reader).
>
> (143)

Nabokov is not just describing the "superhumor" of his diabolical artist-villain, Axel Rex, here. The "Hegelian syllogism" captures the basic movement of Nabokov's

own humor—a movement of the individual comic exchange which is reproduced by the narrative as a whole. Kinbote's attempt to recast the jokes that sustain his exclusion as moments of belonging follows from his larger purpose in writing the foreword and commentary to John Shade's **"Pale Fire"**: that is, to represent a poem that has nothing to do with him, by a poet who at best merely tolerates him, as a poetic version of his own personal history, produced by a "dear friend" in close collaboration with himself. The novel appears at the very outset, at the thetic level, to be a comic imitation; like Uncle, it is "dressed up" to amuse us, in the guise of poem and scholarly commentary. This is the simplest laugh, "a laugh for the children" or for those readers (Dwight MacDonald, for example) who want to read the novel as merely a clever pastiche of academic pedantry. At the antithetic level, the promised imitation appears not to materialize: we are offered a convincingly "serious" poem, but in place of the expected pseudoacademic commentary on this poem we find a series of improbable and impertinent ravings, composed by a sort of mad burglar, an "arrant thief"[3] whose sole purpose lies in appropriating another man's life and work to legitimate his own compensatory émigré fantasies. Here we have the scornful laugh of the knowing and morally superior reader, who sees that Kinbote "really is a burglar," an imposter, a dangerous rule breaker. Finally, at the level of synthesis, we find that we have been mistaken (or misled) as to the true dual nature of the performance: the commentary is both eccentric *and* pertinent, the commentator both a mad parasite or thief of the poem *and* its legitimate guide and authority. The "author's joke," the "super-joke" that counts us, too, among its victims, is that this outsider, this lunatic commentator and chief object of our condescending amusement, is precisely the critical "insider" that we have been looking for and that he has been ("ridiculously") claiming to be all along. For, as a number of critics have observed, Kinbote's seemingly laughable attempts to transform **"Pale Fire"** into a Zemblan epic ultimately reinforce Shade's vision of "plexed artistry" (3.814) and make possible a realization of the "correlated pattern[s]" (3.813) that the poem itself can only describe.

Shade's twin theme is design and death; the fact of mortality becomes bearable to him only when perceived in terms of divine pattern, as a fragment of some supernal tapestry which makes "ornaments / Of accidents and possibilities" and renders "topsy-tervical coincidence" not as "flimsy nonsense" but as "a web of sense":

> Yes! It sufficed that I in life could find
> Some kind of link-and-bobolink, some kind
> Of correlated pattern in the game,
> Plexed artistry, and something of the same
> Pleasure in it as they who played it found.
>
> (3.811-15)

If this reminds us a little of the Enlightenment neoclassicism of Pope (who is the subject of one of Shade's books), it is also very close to Nabokov's modernist aesthetics, which perpetuates the same homology of artistry and divinity, and the same imperative to locate the order underlying apparent chaos and fragmentation. Shade, an "autobiographical" poet in more than one sense of the term, borrows more of this creator's own aesthetic theory and practice than any other artist-character in Nabokov, with the possible exception of Fyodor in *The Gift* (1937).[4] If Nabokov often seems to be playing the divine prankster in his work, it is because, like Shade, he imagines the logic of the human world itself to be that of the practical joke: the "gods" of such a world ("it did not matter who they were") are figured as "aloof" and infinitely devious artists, whose "supernal game" supplies not only the "rules" but the very "texture" of our lives (244). To capture this texture in text the artist must play a similar game in the realm of art. But although Shade accepts the modernist calling to "play God" in an aesthetic heterocosm, **"Pale Fire"** is not in itself a particularly effective representation of "plexed artistry." Whatever its intrinsic interest (and few readers have found it as "beautifully written" as it seems to Kinbote—and, evidently, to Nabokov),[5] the poem lacks the prodigious complexity of design, the interplay of chaos and order, that one would expect from the hand of a self-declared modernist "creator."

But while it is difficult to see **"Pale Fire,"** in isolation, as a game which somehow duplicates the disconcerting but nonrandom logic of poetically lived experience—a logic at once lucid and yet, as Habermas expresses it, "exempt from imperatives of purposive-rationality and giving scope to imagination as well as spontaneity" (42)—the poem begins to suggest this "higher" artistic dimension when read in conjunction with its other-worldly commentary. Through "some kind of correlated pattern in the game," Kinbote's gratuitous supplementary notes turn out to make vital connections with Shade's autobiographical poem. All the comical "accidents" of Kinbote's commentary can be read as "ornaments" of a far more prodigious design than that which the poem itself presents.

This larger design or "web of sense" is what Nabokov's exegetical critics, beginning with Mary McCarthy, have been unraveling since the novel first appeared (indeed, a bit longer than that, since McCarthy's tour-de-force review essay actually beat the novel into print). It comprises a vastly complex system of disguised reflections and submerged hints, each of which establishes a subtle "link or link-and-bobolink" between Kinbote's Zemblan world and the "eminently Appalachian" world of Shade's poem (296). The whole "forest of associations," as McCarthy called it (Page 134), has by now been pretty thoroughly charted, so I will consider just one small branch of it here: Kinbote's fascination with "mirror words" (193), which leads to a good deal of seemingly empty punning and word play in the *Pale Fire* commentary.

Zemblan is known as "the tongue of the mirror" (242), and Kinbote (whose own "real" name may be Botkin) mentions a number of Zemblan figures whose names form reflective pairs, like the assassin Jacob Gradus and the ingenious "Mirror maker" Sudarg of Bokay. But mirror words also find their way into his everyday speech, as when he urges Sybil Shade to "redip, spider" into a volume of Proust (162); they seem not only to reflect the peculiar properties of his native tongue but also the peculiar turns of his unconscious, the "inversions" in his psyche—suggesting, not surprisingly, that the "tongue of the mirror" may have a psychological rather than a geographical point of origin. What links this strange compulsion most directly to **"Pale Fire"** is the fact of its being shared by Hazel Shade, the poet's daughter, another pathetic misfit with "strange fears, strange fantasies, strange force / Of character" (2.344-45). Like Kinbote, Hazel spends her time "mostly alone" and likes to "twist words"; in fact, one pair of twisted words that Shade attributes to her in the poem is "spider" and "redips."

This duplicative "link" of mirror words is just the sort of meaningful coincidence Shade values: it "coordinates" two seemingly "remote events" or contexts (3.827). The conversation in which Kinbote twists "spider" into "redip" occurs in the context of his long, agonized note describing Shade's sixty-first birthday. Kinbote, who spends a good deal of his time tom-peeping on his celebrated next-door neighbor, is in a particularly abject state after having sat up alone all night watching through the usual windows the birthday party to which his "dear friend" neglected to invite him. He proffers the Proust volume, in which he has marked a passage about unkind hostesses, as part of his "sly" "revenge" on the poet's wife next morning (162). Shade quotes these same words from Hazel in the context of her own deep-rooted loneliness and strange outbursts, having a few lines earlier described her as the "one shy . . . guest" who is most apt to be "left out" at "parties" (2.307-8). Though Kinbote's "sly" joke after the birthday party is not explicitly linked to these lines about Hazel (he is commenting on an earlier and quite unrelated passage), a connection is nonetheless perceived as part of a submerged pattern of coincidence. The mirror words, the strange fears and fantasies, the torments of being always the unwanted guest are all links in a schematic of belonging and exile which begins unexpectedly to emerge from the rooted New Englander's autobiographical poem.

Critics have noted that Hazel's suicide, which ends the canto (and is occasioned by yet another instance of being "left out" both socially and sexually), prefigures

Kinbote's own, which implicitly ends the novel. But more significant is the weird and unwitting way in which Kinbote's commentary speaks to this central event of the poem. Shade himself is less able than Kinbote to articulate the pathos of the event; he lacks Kinbote's intimacy with the "cold hard core of loneliness" that makes suicide such an "inviting abyss" (220) for the social outcast. Shade's second canto is formally remarkable (he employs a synchronous arrangement of two themes, blending them together at the moment of Hazel's death), but its language seems to be cut off from the sources of Hazel's distress. Indeed, the sense of being cut off from the unhappiness of one's own child defines the ethos of the canto. Kinbote's commentary manages better to narrow this distance because of the "echoes and spangles of [his own] mind" in Hazel's (297): a special "affinity" (308) exists between the two outsiders. This affinity is marked by their shared trick of using reflective language as an escape from or revenge on the world of the "elected" (162) and thus suggests the serious psychic and social functions of much of the novel's silly Zemblan-style word play, but the connection is not limited to mirror words alone. Throughout Kinbote's wayward commentary, in his many seemingly irrelevant reflections on his own misery, and especially in his lengthy and impassioned apology for suicide—"We who burrow in filth every day may be forgiven perhaps the one sin that ends all sins" (222)—there runs a particular "streak of . . . madness" (296) that leads us, however indirectly, back to the "difficult darling" of Shade's second canto. Paradoxically, it is Kinbote's exclusion from the poet's world that secures for him a viable point of entry to the poem.

Most of Kinbote's comical blunders and scholarly transgressions are freighted with some such hidden relevance. And in this way his shifting position in the narrative reproduces the logic of the Ping-Pong table joke: Kinbote as insider (neighbor, friend, expert reader and critic); Kinbote as outsider (voyeur, crazed admirer, "monstrous parasite of a genius" [172]); Kinbote as both and neither. The strategic function of this quasi-syllogistic humor, as of the larger narrative organization, is plainly to defeat or render inoperable the very categories of insider and outsider, to attain to a "higher" level where everyone, even the most marginal man, even Charles Kinbote, is at the same time an "insider." In this putative realm of comic synthesis the margins don't hold. Through a movement that makes every participant (including the reader) in turn joker, laugher, and victim, one ideally transcends the contingent social realities on which lines of division and exclusion are based and experiences, albeit on the plane of aesthetic pleasure, perfectly open communication, tolerant and noncoercive social practice. The syllogistic movement is meant ultimately to be a movement of the joke be-

yond the joke, a transcending of the social and historical situation that makes a given *énonciation* "jokelike" in the first place.

Though this specific syllogistic movement is not especially common in modernist texts, there is nothing singular about Nabokov's attempt to place humor—the discourse *par excellence* of exclusion—in the service of a yearning for community, for solidary living with others. The modernist recourse to irony, for example, can be seen as an analogous attempt to raise the joke beyond the joke, to attain always to a "higher" seriousness where the cultural dirty work to which joke-work generally assimilates may be disavowed or in some sense sublated. The question is whether the comic transactions of modernism in fact carry out, even on an aesthetic plane, the work they are supposed to. Why, to take the case at hand, is the name *Nabokov* most often invoked in connection with the antisocial, the elite or the private text, and not the text of "happy" communication?

Of course, in a trivial sense, all "difficult" texts such as *Pale Fire* are elitist; their consumption requires cultural capital of a sort that assures exclusion of the "common" reader. But the modernist valorization of difficulty is not really the issue here. It is true that Nabokov saw his syllogistically structured narratives as "diabolical . . . puzzles" which would inevitably leave certain readers (those too clever to accept the "simple 'thetic' solution" but not competent to make out the text's "synthesis") stalled in an "antithetic inferno" of misdirection and delayed disclosure (*Speak Memory* 291-92). He liked to talk about "good" and "bad" readers ("Russian Writers" 11) and to represent the fiercely divided reception of his work—partisans praising his "generous" willingness to "share" experiences and intimations with readers (Updike 245), detractors deploring the manifest self-regard and gratuitous "impenetrability" of his texts (MacDonald 137)—as a simple split between "sophisticated solvers" and "morons" (*Strong Opinions* 288). But the fact is, even the most expert Nabokovian puzzle solvers can see that the attempt to transcend social division through a dialectic of the joke is problematic.

It is not simply that the (bourgeois) conception of the work of art as gateway to an autonomous "higher" realm or refuge from unacceptable social conditions—the conception that has dominated both the production and the reception of the novel as a genre—is no longer entertainable in any form. I have dispensed with a rehearsal of the familiar critiques because it seems to me that we can and should continue to allow for the potential utility of utopia, for the positive social value of at least some attempts to conceive and communicate aesthetically a new and less alienated intersubjectivity. The questions that must be raised concern, rather, the specific character of what might be termed the "utopian comic" in *Pale Fire* and in other modernist texts. According to Marcuse, the "solidarity and community" after which the modernist work yearns "have their basis in the subordination of destructive and aggressive energy to the social emancipation of the life instincts" (17). According to Freud, comic exchange is above all an investment and expenditure of that same destructive and aggressive energy. Thus, insofar as the modernist text seeks to promote solidarity and community (of various sorts) by means of humor (of various sorts), it is attempting not only to develop a self-subordinating comic practice, but to achieve a kind of perfect "forgetting" or erasure of the subordinated joke-work along with its concrete effects. No putative dialectic can save such a project from the contradictions that pervade it.

In Nabokov's case, a paralyzing double bind appears when we consider the authorial insistence, in back of all the wildly mismanaged and misfiring jokes, that humor can be mastered, its movements exactly guided and safely arrested from above. To the extent that Nabokov maintains such a place of mastery it must be disabling to his project, for the ascent to a free and tolerant discursive realm cannot depend on one's assent to an authorial claim to power. A "happy" communicative experience is inconsistent with comic communication of such classically dictatorial character, the reader as it were laughing on cue—passively "enjoying," as Nabokov put it, "what the author meant to be enjoyed" (**"Russian Writers, Censors, and Readers"** 11).

On the other hand, what even Nabokov's own jokes are continually demonstrating is that the author/subject's position is far from a stable seat of power. Nor can such stability be secured by a distinction between primary or "sincere" jokes and secondary or "quoted" ones. Once the process of comic exchange has begun, it defies all efforts to arrest or control it, including those that depend on a boundary between authentic and parasitic comic utterances. Nabokov wants to arrest the humor in *Pale Fire* precisely at the point where the social "work" it performs is most positive, the point at which an *un*doing of the work performed by various "dividing practices" (including humor itself) is effected. The whole comic strategy depends on our accepting this as the final or "serious" authorial position. The author of the "antithetic" stage, positioned to share with his readers a conservative laugh at Kinbote (at the social outcast) must be disregarded—for this is not "seriously" Nabokov joking. The "seriously" joking Nabokov emerges at the synthesis stage, an author positioned to share with Kinbote a laugh at intolerant readers, or rather at intolerance itself: his is the liberating laugh which celebrates the mad and the marginal and ridicules the very conventions that make an "antithetical" laugh possible.

But given the nature of Nabokov's "dialectic," the emancipatory joke cannot simply cancel out or negate the conservative one. Regardless of which jokes are "seriously" intended, *Pale Fire* remains a text that offers a good deal of socially repressive, or exclusionist, comic exchange. Indeed, this is the primary space for comic pleasure in the novel; it is what we refer to when we call the book funny. After all, the simple "thetic" joke of scholarly pastiche wears thin almost immediately, and the "comic synthesis" aims at, to use Nabokov's terms, a kind of "poignant artistic delight" that is presumably distinct from mirth as such (*Speak, Memory* 292). For Nabokov's "good readers" as well as his "bad" ones, the most "successful" moments of comic exchange in *Pale Fire* are likely to operate antitransgressionally, directing laughter at Kinbote for his abnormal and hence unacceptable behavior. Readers who assume the position of laughing recipient in the comic transactions involving Kinbote's sexual deviance, his social gaffes, his impertinent scholarship, and so forth are not mocking the cultural norms that construct the gay, the foreigner, or the unorthodox intellectual as an outsider; they are mocking the outsider himself. At the actual moment of this laughter, at the moment when Nabokov best "succeeds" as subject of comic exchange, the joke-work being performed is resolutely hegemonic. It is conducive to the construction of "community and solidarity" only in the negative sense of reinforcing lines of identification and exclusion that are already firmly established in the social imaginary.

If the "Hegelian dialectic of humor" suggests that Nabokov did not "seriously" endorse this laughter of social constraint and intolerance, nor the narrow conception of community that underlies it, but aimed instead at their transcendence, his success as a hegemonic humorist suggests a contrary (and no less serious) impulse. Nowhere does Nabokov appear more characteristically modernist than in this contradiction: his desire both to secure the happy communicative conditions of a less divisive, more solidary social order, and to be absolute master of the inside joke.

Notes

1. "Pale Fire" 4.975, *Pale Fire* 69. Subsequent references to the poem "Pale Fire" will be given parenthetically by canto and line number only.

2. I am indebted to John B. Thompson, *Studies in the Theory of Ideology* (113-18), for making reference to Sacks's text.

3. According to Dwight MacDonald, the first critic to pin down the reference, Nabokov himself divulged in an interview that his book's title came from *Timon of Athens.* The passage deals with theft and illumination:

> I'll example you with thievery:
> The sun's a thief, and with his great attraction

Robs the vast sea; the moon's an arrant thief,
And her pale fire she snatches from the sun;
The sea's a thief, whose liquid surge resolves
The moon into salt tears.

(4.3.435-40)

MacDonald observed that "Kinbote's academic rape of Shade's poem is, as we say, unmistakable" (140), but he did not note the deliberate irony of Shade's stealing his title from a passage about thievery, nor the far more important reverse irony of the poem's debt to its commentary. Like everything in Shade's poem, the title becomes more fitting and expressive when conjoined with the supposedly gratuitous commentary. A good discussion of the circulation of "pale fire" through *Pale Fire* is found in Robert Alter's influential 1975 essay, "Nabokov's Game of Worlds," 205-7.

4. For Nabokov's comments about Fyodor and Shade see the interview with Martin Esslin in *Strong Opinions* (119). Much of what Shade writes and says in the novel echoes the "strong opinions" of his creator; for example, they are both cultural reactionaries who "loathe . . . jazz . . . progressive schools . . . Freud [and] Marx" ("Pale Fire" 4.924-29). Perhaps the most striking instance of Shade mouthing the aesthetic pronouncements of Nabokov is this one: "I [Shade] am also in the habit of lowering a student's grade catastrophically if he uses 'simple' and 'sincere' in a commendatory sense; examples: 'Shelley's style is always very simple and good'; or 'Yeats is always sincere'" (*Pale Fire* 156). Compare Nabokov in a 1963 interview with Alvin Toffler: "I automatically gave low marks when a student used the dreadful phrase 'sincere and simple'—'Flaubert writes with a style which is always simple and sincere'—under the impression that this was the greatest compliment payable to prose or poetry" (*Strong Opinions* 32).

5. Kinbote says that "Shade could not write otherwise than beautifully" (296). Nabokov has called Shade "by far the greatest of *invented* poets" (*Strong Opinions* 59), and for what it is worth, Shade appears to have been granted the full measure of Nabokov's own capacity to write English verse.

Works Cited

Alter, Robert. "Nabokov's Game of Worlds." *Partial Magic: The Novel as a Self-Conscious Genre*. Berkeley: U of California P, 1975. 180-217.

Bergson, Henri. *Laughter*. 1909. Trans. Wylie Sypher. *Comedy*. Ed. Wylie Sypher. Garden City, NJ: Doubleday-Anchor, 1956. 61-190.

Bourdieu, Pierre. "The Economics of Linguistic Exchanges." *Social Science Information* 16 (1977): 645-68.

Burke, Kenneth. *Counter-Statement*. New York: Harcourt, 1931.

Eagleton, Terry. *Exiles and Emigrés: Studies in Modern Literature*. London: Schocken, 1970.

Foucault, Michel. "The Subject and Power." *Michel Foucault: Beyond Structuralism and Hermeneutics*. Ed. Hubert Dreyfus and Paul Rabinow. Chicago: U of Chicago P, 1982. 208-26.

Freud, Sigmund. *Jokes and Their Relation to the Unconscious*. 1905. Trans. James Strachey. New York: Norton, 1960.

Habermas, Jürgen. "Consciousness Raising or Redemptive Criticism—The Contemporaneity of Walter Benjamin." 1972. Trans. Philip Brewster and Carl Howard Buchner. *New German Critique* 17 (1979): 30-59.

Jameson, Fredric. "Postmodernism, or, the Cultural Logic of Late Capitalism." *New Left Review* 146 (1984): 59-92.

———. "Secondary Elaborations." *Postmodernism, or, the Cultural Logic of Late Capitalism*. Durham: Duke UP, 1991. 297-418.

Kermode, Frank. Rev. of *Bend Sinister*, by Vladimir Nabokov. *Encounter* June 1960: 81-86. Rpt. in Page 75-80.

Lilly, Mark. "Nabokov: Homo Ludens." *Vladimir Nabokov: A Tribute*. Ed. Peter Quennell. New York: Morrow, 1980. 88-102.

MacDonald, Dwight. Rev. of *Pale Fire*, by Vladimir Nabokov. *Partisan Review* Summer 1962: 437-42. Rpt. in Page 137-40.

Marcuse, Herbert. *The Aesthetic Dimension: Toward a Critique of Marxist Aesthetics*. Boston: Beacon, 1978.

Martineau, William H. "A Model of the Social Functions of Humor." *The Psychology of Humor*. Ed. Jeffrey H. Goldstein and Paul E. McGhee. New York: Academic, 1972. 117-25.

McCarthy, Mary. "A Bolt from the Blue." Rev. of *Pale Fire*, by Vladimir Nabokov. *New Republic* 4 June 1962: 21-27. Rpt. in Page 124-36.

Nabokov, Vladimir. *The Gift*. 1938. Trans. Michael Scammell and Vladimir Nabokov. New York: Putnam, 1963.

———. *Laughter in the Dark*. 1933. Trans. Vladimir Nabokov. 1938. New York: New Directions, 1960.

———. *Lolita*. 1955. Annotated ed. Ed. Alfred Appel, Jr. New York: McGraw, 1970.

———. "On a Book Entitled *Lolita*." *Lolita* 312-19.

———. *Pale Fire*. New York: Putnam, 1962.

———. *Pnin*. Garden City, NY: Doubleday, 1957.

———. "Russian Writers, Censors, and Readers." *Lectures on Russian Literature*. Ed. Fredson Bowers. New York: Harcourt, 1981. 1-12.

———. *Speak, Memory: An Autobiography Revisited*. New York: Putnam, 1966.

———. *Strong Opinions*. New York: McGraw, 1973.

Page, Norman, ed. *Nabokov: The Critical Heritage*. Critical Heritage Series. London: Routledge, 1982.

Sacks, Harvey. "Some Technical Considerations of a Dirty Joke." *Studies in the Organization of Conversational Interaction*. Ed. Jim Shenkein. New York: Academic, 1978. 249-69.

Schopenhauer, Arthur. "On the Theory of the Ludicrous." *The World as Will and Idea*. 1819, 1844. Trans. R. B. Haldane and John Kemp. 1896. 3 vols. New York: AMS, 1977. 1: 76-80.

Shakespeare, William. *Timon of Athens*. 1623. *The Riverside Shakespeare*. Ed. G. Blakemore Evans, et al. Boston: Houghton, 1974. 1441-77.

Thompson, John B. *Studies in the Theory of Ideology*. Berkeley: U of California P, 1984.

Updike, John. "Vale, VN." *Hugging the Shore*. New York: Harcourt, 1983. 244-46.

Weber, Samuel. "The Divaricator: Remarks on Freud's *Witz*." *Glyph* 1 (1977): 1-27.

———. "The Shaggy Dog." *The Legend Of Freud*. Minneapolis: U of Minnesota P, 1982. 100-117.

Williams, Raymond. *Culture and Society, 1780-1950*. London: Chatto, 1958.

———. *The Politics of Modernism: Against the New Conformists*. London: Verso, 1989.

Jean Walton (essay date June 1994)

SOURCE: Walton, Jean. "Dissenting in an Age of Frenzied Heterosexualism: Kinbote's Transparent Closet in Nabokov's *Pale Fire*." *College Literature* 21, no. 2 (June 1994): 89-104.

[*In the following essay, Walton examines the way homoerotic desire is represented in Nabokov's* Pale Fire.]

> Kinbote's homosexuality . . . is a metaphor for the artist's minority view of a bad world, of "our cynical age of frantic heterosexualism." If one dared risk a guess at correlative idiosyncrasies in Nabokov himself, one would have to point to his intellectual disgust with Freudianism or remembering that he is a member of the Russian emigre minority, his loathing of Marxism.
>
> (Kermode 671-72)[1]

This remark from Frank Kermode's 1962 review of Vladimir Nabokov's *Pale Fire* typifies the way in which "homosexuality" has functioned in literary critical discourse (if not necessarily in literature itself) until recent years: never as a nexus of experience, a material reality, a specific subject position, but always as a "metaphor" for something else, a signifier for more compelling signifieds, a place marker occupied by nothing and no one of consequence. For what Kermode seems to be suggesting is that, though *Pale Fire* is mediated by an explicitly gay narrator, the more comprehensive issue at hand is the opposition of "artist" to "bad world," and that there are various sub-categories of this opposition, one of which stands, in Nabokov's fiction, as an analogue for the others, which directly concern Nabokov in his life. Thus, the necessarily political conflict between "homosexuality" and "frantic heterosexualism" in *Pale Fire* is not, in Kermode's account, to be considered for what might be its literal implications (implications for gay men in a homophobic culture), but rather to be read as a figure for the more pressing issues of Nabokov's "idiosyncratic" opposition as an "intellectual" to "Freudianism," or as a "Russian emigre" to "Marxism."

Much recent work in the arena of gay and lesbian literary studies has suggested that to read the presence of "homosexuality" in a work of fiction as a figural or metaphorical index to something else is to engage, whether implicitly or explicitly, in avoidance tactics, and to collude with, rather than scrutinize, a prevailing heterocentric imperative. It is scarcely surprising that such reading practices prevail in the case of writers, like Nabokov, who have not been identified as "gay." I would suggest, however, that precisely by exploring *Pale Fire* as being, in some crucial ways, about its protagonist's (proscribed) homoerotic desire, we might see how the novel resists and is complicit with the way sexuality is constructed in twentieth-century Western culture. What do critics have to say, if anything, about the specific sexuality Nabokov has assigned to his apparently insane literary commentator? Or, more importantly, what tone or affect has inflected critical references to Charles Kinbote *as* homosexual? Do they betray a homophobic nervousness, and if so, does it mean that Nabokov's novel encourages such a response?

It might at first seem unreasonable to question such remarks as John Haegert's observation that Kinbote is "Nabokov's incurable pederast and lunatic commentator."[2] *Pale Fire* is, after all, constructed around the gradual revelation of its narrator's insanity, and seems to invite us to link his sexual with his mental "deviance." A brief synopsis will clarify this for readers unfamiliar with the novel. It opens with a preface, in the voice of Charles Kinbote, who introduces to us the first "edition" of a poem by his late friend John Shade. The poem, a four canto lyrical reflection informed by the poet's grief at the suicide of his daughter, Hazel Shade, takes up the next thirty-three pages. The bulk of the book, however, consists of Kinbote's copious commentary on the poem, during the course of which he fills us in on two "stages" of his own autobiography. On the one hand, Kinbote tells us of his life in the academic community of New Wye, where he has come to teach for a year, inhabiting the house next door to John Shade and his wife Sybil. Kinbote, clearly something of a social outcast in New Wye, does his best to foster a friendship with Shade, who is in the process of writing the poem that opens the novel. On the other hand, he tells of his life prior to his arrival in New Wye, a life in which he was the (gay) King of Zembla, where he ruled happily despite unsuccessful attempts to force him to couple with a young lady-in-waiting, Fleur de Fylar, and then with Disa, the woman he is forced to marry. Eventually, however, he is dethroned, and forced to escape to the United States. In New Wye, he understands himself to be living in exile, in disguise, and to be the target of an assassination plot. Little by little, he discloses his "royal past" to John Shade, in the hopes that Shade will immortalize it in the poem he is writing. Inadvertently, Kinbote reveals to us that his delusions of royalty make him an object of ridicule and pity in the New Wye community. By the end of the narrative, we gather that Shade has been mistakenly shot by a local psychopath who has escaped from prison and come in search of the judge who put him there. Kinbote, convinced that the assassin from Zembla has arrived (and missed his mark), takes possession of Shade's poem, and proceeds to write the commentary that will reveal its "true," but hidden, meaning, that is, the story of his life.[3]

As I have suggested, critics have, for the most part, insisted on metaphorizing or pathologizing Kinbote's sexuality. While sketching out some of the typical instances of these critical appraisals, I shall elaborate the parameters of a more culturally specific reading of homoeroticism in the novel, one that treats it for its material rather than its figurative ramifications. My reading of Kinbote is, in this sense, informed by Gayatri Spivak's reading of the Mahasweta Devi story "Stanadayini" ("Breastgiver"). Spivak points out that Devi herself has said she intends the story to function as a "parable of India after decolonization"; this requires that its protagonist, Jashoda, be read not as a realistic character, but as a stand-in for "Mother India" (244). But Spivak wants to resist such a "too neat reading" of Jashoda as place marker for India in order to explore the way in which the story helps to articulate the subject-position of the gendered subaltern in India. Similarly, I shall explore the ways in which readings of Kinbote have de-

pended for their validity on such a "too neat" metaphorization of his character, and a refusal to consider how he functions as another kind of gendered, or what Jonathan Dollimore would call "sexually dissident," subaltern.[4]

HOMOSEXUALITY AS PATHOLOGY

A number of critics have addressed the way in which Kinbote is doubly marginalized in the New Wye community by, on the one hand, his sexuality and on the other, his delusions of royalty. But while the links between Kinbote's sexual orientation and his madness are ambiguous in the novel, they have been variously articulated by critics, depending on how they perceive homoeroticism to participate in the overlapping discourses of pathology, morality, and aesthetics. Generally, Kinbote's insanity has been connected with his homoerotic desire as a sort of interchangeable substitute for it. Indeed, in many cases, Kinbote's mental state is understood to be inseparable from, or synonymous with, his sexual orientation. Such an equivalence is facilitated by the assumption that both insanity and homosexuality belong to the same class of phenomena insofar as they are understood to be pathological disturbances that define the subject as (in this case incurably) ill. Hence, statements like the one I quoted from Haegert earlier: that Kinbote is an "incurable pederast and lunatic commentator" (405).

Although Phyllis A. Roth is one of the few critics to explore Kinbote's sexuality for what she understands to be its particular implications *as* a specific sexuality, her analysis nevertheless adheres too strictly to a pathologizing psychoanalytic conceptualization of the homoerotic. Drawing from Otto Rank's psychoanalytic account of the double or doppelganger in literature, Roth "diagnoses" Kinbote's sexuality as a "neurotic 'adjustment' to an Oedipal situation" (222). According to this scheme, Kinbote treats Shade as a positive father figure, and invents Gradus (the imagined assassin) as a persecuting double (these are the Rankian doppelgangers), thus demonstrating that he "feels guilt for his homosexuality" (225). To be a homosexual is, according to the medical prognosis, to be guilty: "Only by self-destruction," says Roth, "can that guilt be exorcised for him" (227). Naturally, then, homosexuality is inevitably accompanied by a suicidal impulse.

Roth's account is plausible in much of its elaboration of Kinbote's psychic state only because it fails to contextualize that state within the over-arching cultural apparatuses that produce and punish it. To say, as Roth does, that Kinbote cannot "approve of himself" is to say, surely, that he has internalized his culture's homophobia. Roth's reliance on Rank's oedipal "etiology" of homosexuality as a means of "diagnosing" Kinbote, however, portrays that guilt as an essential rather than culturally produced component of a sexual desire that is not strictly hetero-identified. Such an account forecloses the possibility of finding something like a social critique implicit in Kinbote's fantasmatic narrativizing of his sexual history. Roth focuses on how psychoanalysis can illuminate the "disastrous failures" of Nabokov's "central characters." But if this psychoanalytic theory is accompanied by a cultural analysis of the social context for the "psyches" of these central characters, then it is something like the "age of frenzied heterosexualism" that must be understood as a "disastrous failure" in *Pale Fire.*

Kinbote, in his transgression of sexual, literary, social, and rational codes, has challenged the heterosexual imperative insofar as he refuses to occupy the subject position of one who is sick and thereby seeks a cure.[5] If he were the only character in the novel to be abjected by the hetero hegemony in *Pale Fire,* we might assume that the novel does nothing to call this hegemony into question. But surely it is precisely such a hegemony that also annihilates Shade's daughter, Hazel. At least one critic has explored some of the implications of the way in which Hazel Shade suggestively parallels Kinbote, though without, I think, making the necessary next step towards suggesting what their commonality reveals about the culture that marginalizes them. Taking his cue from Roth, David Galef inserts Kinbote into the oedipal family narrative, where he joins Hazel in "a childish bid for [the] attention" of the father (figure), John Shade (430). Also like Roth, Galef emphasizes what he sees as a compelling suicidal impulse in Kinbote—an impulse that finds its analogue in Hazel's suicide. Both "suffer ultimately from a lack of relevance to their surroundings" and are propelled by the "burden of maintaining" their fantasies toward self-annihilation. In this respect, they are both "freaks, in Nabokov's artistic conception and in their own artistic dreams. The author extends his appreciation for their art, sympathy for their lives" (435).

Insofar as both Kinbote and Hazel deviate from certain fairly rigorously prescribed social norms, they can, indeed, be identified as "freaks"; Galef does little to delineate, however, the way in which the frontier between normal and freakish is erected and policed in this novel, beyond implying that to be normal is to be "in touch" with reality, regardless of what that reality entails or how it has been constructed. Thus, though acknowledging that Nabokov feels "tenderness for [his] creatures, particularly those who seem too frail for life" (435), Galef reifies the "normalcy" of that "life," taking for granted the "naturalness" of the heterosexual imperative that plays itself out across the bodies of both Kinbote and Hazel.

John Shade—writing and projecting onto his daughter from firmly within a heterosexual hegemony—can imagine no other future for her than a heterosexually prescribed one. It is a foregone conclusion that her erotic desire will be directed toward men, and since she has never conformed to the ideal of the heterosexually desirable (and desiring) woman, her parents take it for granted that she is doomed to a life of unfulfillment. This is not to imply that Hazel, like Kinbote, is "really" gay, and simply needs to recognize and act upon an attraction to women: such a positivistic account of her sexuality is effectively unavailable to us. Hazel, like Kinbote, is what Judith Butler would call "culturally unintelligible" in the world of *Pale Fire,* insofar as there is a constructed (and suspect) system by which one comes to understand one's (sexual) identity in that world. As Butler has pointed out

> It would be wrong to think that the discussion of "identity" ought to proceed prior to a discussion of gender identity for the simple reason that "persons" only become intelligible through becoming gendered in conformity with recognizable standards of gender intelligibility.
>
> (16)

In a way, Kinbote *as* a gay man and Hazel *as* a (potential) lesbian, are impossible in *Pale Fire* precisely because, in Butler's words,

> The cultural matrix through which gender identity has become intelligible requires that certain kinds of "identities" cannot "exist"—that is, those in which gender does not follow from sex and those in which the practices of desire do not "follow" from either sex or gender. . . . Indeed, precisely because certain kinds of "gender identities" fail to conform to those norms of cultural intelligibility, they appear only as developmental failures or logical impossibilities from within that domain.
>
> (17)

It is important to point out that by and large, the women in *Pale Fire* function primarily as heterosexually prescribed erotic objects (Fleur de Fylar, Disa, and certain coeds for whom other faculty members express lust), or the enforcers of heterosexuality (Fleur de Fylar's mother), or rivals in the pursuit of male sexual objects (Sybil). The only significant female character who falls outside these categories—indeed, who seems herself to be victimized by them—is Hazel, whose sexuality can only be understood by others around her negatively, as a dismally failed heterosexuality. Insofar as there is no positive alternative for her, she is intelligible only as what Butler would call a "developmental failure" or a "logical impossibility." Lesbianism, in the world of New Wye, in the world of *Pale Fire* (and doubtless in the world of 1950s middle America) is invisible—not even on the map of erotic possibilities.

HOMOSEXUALITY AS (COMIC) INVERSION

Following from the assumption that to be homosexual is, by definition, to be a psychological deviant are those discussions of Kinbote's homosexuality that tie it to insanity as a paradigm of a perfect and symmetrical inversion of the norm, which is useful in producing comic literary effects. Andrew Field, for instance, tells us that "[a]s an inversion or direct opposite, homosexuality provides a perfect negative image with which to project normal feeling" (35). We needn't dwell on the fact that, as he says, "[t]he sexuality in *Pale Fire* happens to be pederasty," since "it merely takes the proper positioning of a mirror to translate this into the perversion of Humbert Humbert, or the potentialities inherent in all sexual practice or fantasy" (34). Field's impulse here is to gloss over the specificity of Kinbote's sexuality. This requires that it first be figured as a direct and symmetrical inversion of "normal feeling," and then that the critic perform a mirror trick to translate it into some universally experienced "sexual practice or fantasy," albeit via the questionable, but at least heterosexual, byroad of Humbert Humbert's desire. Moreover, "perverse sexuality by its very nature satisfies one of the most basic precepts of comedy from the time of Aristophanes: the world turned on its head, tragedy and pain softened (but not lessened) by the presence of the absurd and the ludicrous" (35). Homosexuality is primarily, according to Field, an instrument of humor, an "absurd" and "ludicrous" inversion of the norm.

While David Rampton echoes Field's observation about the deployment of homosexuality as a comic literary strategy, he doubts whether a whole novel can rest upon such a device, since for him, homosexuality is a sexuality "arrested at the adolescent stage," and can only give rise to tedious and repetitious jokes at Kinbote's expense "every time a male character is mentioned" (151). What Rampton calls the "welter of sexual detail" in the novel should (if the novel is to have any artistic or epistemological value) "lead us through the twists and turns of the psyche to some truth about the inner self" (151). Kinbote's sexual life—precisely by virtue of its being imbued by the homoerotic—is, according to Rampton, identical to his deranged mental life, and thus constitutes "a fantasy world which has relatively little to do with our own" (154). For this reason, then, it fails to tell us anything about "*the* inner self," which is, after all, presumed to be heterosexual. According to Rampton,

> The imaginary exploits of most of the Commentary . . . identify the world of *Pale Fire* as another version of adolescent wish-fulfillment reconstructed by the over-ripe imagination. [In *Lolita* and *Ada*] other links with the world of common experience give us a sense of solidity and depth that Kinbote's frolics, as funny as they are, do not.
>
> (155)

That it is primarily the homoeroticism in *Pale Fire* that, for Rampton, deprives it of "solidity and depth" is confirmed by the junctures to which he points as restoring

some epistemological value to the novel. He is reassured, it would seem, by Shade's heterosexual presence in the poem, since his life, as Rampton puts it, "simply blows Kinbote's away. . . . [Shade's] earthy humour and robust physical presence break the Kinbote spell and leave him and his paranoid patterns spinning in a self-contained void" (154-55). Elsewhere, Rampton notes

> At some point [Nabokov] must have . . . realized that readers might tire of chuckling at his narcissistic invert. With a view to extending the range of Kinbote's interests, and involving the reader in a more meaningful way, he includes a detailed account of a meeting with Queen Disa on the Riviera and of the reflections occasioned by it.
>
> (152)

As we shall see, Rampton is "involved" as a reader in a "more meaningful way" because he interprets this passage as being primarily about a heterosexual expression of desire. But it is this passage, more than any other perhaps, that marks Charles's desire as uncompromisingly gay, and that demonstrates just the extent to which he will be made, by a homophobic culture, to suffer for this desire.

In the Disa dream passage, Kinbote has just described the nature of their marriage, the result of the efforts of "representatives of the nation" to "persuade him to give up his copious but sterile pleasures and take a wife. It was a matter not of morality but of succession" (173). Whether Zembla is understood to be an invention of Nabokov or of Kinbote, it simultaneously reflects and transforms a system of compulsory heterosexuality in contemporary American culture as inhabited by both Nabokov's characters and his readers. As in American culture, Zembla seems to be made up mostly of an exclusively male homosocial society; the difference is that in Zembla—or in Kinbote's fantasy of Zembla in his childhood and young adulthood—the homoerotic element is explicitly acknowledged, sanctioned, and celebrated. Indeed, acts of gay sexuality are referred to as "manly Zemblan customs," and thus understood to be coextensive not only with accepted models of masculinity, but even with "customary" expressions of national identity. This is partly what makes Zembla a utopian ideal for Kinbote: he seems to participate, by virtue of his sexuality, in a political hegemony, and is linked by that sexuality to others who share it with him. But there is a flaw in this apparent hegemony, and here is where Zembla resembles, after all, its American counterpart. The very perpetuation of the monarchy in Zembla depends upon an institutionalized disruption of its customary system of pleasures: King Charles is compelled to "take a night off" from his erotic life, and "lawfully engender an heir."

This injunction ushers in an altogether different Zembla, one that insists upon a sexuality inseparable from reproduction, which seems to be in the custody of the female half of the population. With an unsuspecting and hopelessly heterosexual Disa, then, King Charles is forced into a marriage that, in turn, translates his mode of erotic pleasure into an instrument of torture. In spite of the optimistic portrayal of his sexuality before the marriage, Charles has internalized the imperatives of the "heterosexualist" law that prescribes his coupling with, and indeed, his loving, Disa, so that the painful dynamics of this marriage look uncannily like those of the closeted gay man's marriage of convenience in contemporary America. What Charles discovers in this marriage is that his sexuality is not negotiable, that he is not bisexual, that he cannot satisfy both his own needs and the needs of his culture (as it is represented by Disa). This would not be so unbearable if the continuation of his sex life outside of the marriage did not, by the internal logic of the marriage itself, constitute the means by which pain should be perpetually inflicted upon Disa. Hence, a series of uneasy pretenses, disclosures, denials, subterfuges, and recriminations is set in motion. At the beginning, he still tries "strenuously to possess her but to no avail" (207). His explanations that he is inexperienced, or that he is incapacitated by "an old riding accident" serve temporarily to keep Disa in the dark about his sexuality, but only until "the inevitable rumors reached her" and she "read books, found out all about our manly Zemblan customs, and concealed her naive distress under a great show of sarcastic sophistication" (208). That Charles now makes an attempt to "give up the practices of his youth" points to the extent to which he has internalized the system of compulsory heterosexuality that has consigned "manly Zemblan customs" to the realm of an adolescent past that must be renounced in adulthood. From then on, his sexuality must stay in the transparent closet that pretends to hide it from his wife, while she, in turn, finds herself in the closet of the long-suffering wife who must hide her dismay in the presence of outsiders. Indeed, what troubles Charles most deeply about these circumstances is the way in which his closeting seems to result in her closeting:

> One might bear—a strong merciless dreamer might bear—the knowledge of her grief and pride but none could bear the sight of her automatic smile as she turned from the agony of the disclosure [of his unfaithfulness] to the polite trivialities required of her.
>
> (211)

Most excruciating of all for Charles is the guilt that has been inculcated in him for his inability to maintain the heterosexual imperative, a guilt so deeply instated that it makes it impossible for him to be reconciled with his own admission to Disa one day that he does not love her as the culture would have him love her. Instead of putting an end to the series of deceptions that have marked their union, this admission, within the logic of

the institution he is now a part of, functions as an agency by which health and well-being are seriously and irrevocably threatened. Disa's sinking "down on the lawn in an impossible gesture" conveys to Charles the unforeseeable import of his confession, so that

> he had taken his words back at once; but the shock had fatally starred the mirror, and thenceforth in his dreams her image was infected with the memory of the confession as with some disease or the secret aftereffects of a surgical operation too intimate to be mentioned.
>
> (210)

These dreams, as a defense mechanism, manufacture for him the love that he imagines he ought to be feeling, which would provide the way for a reconciliation with Disa and an expiation of his monstrous crime against both social and "natural" law.

According to Rampton, however, what we find in the Disa passage are the "old Nabokov themes," which he specifies, curiously, as

> love as a permanently frustrated desire for a still unravished bride; the crudeness of contingency when compared to the fabulous attractions of the past; the difference between a desperate longing to take responsibility for one's actions and an ability to do so.
>
> (153)

What is striking about this characterization of the Disa passage is Rampton's substitution here of a heterosexual for a gay desire, and his reification of a culturally inculcated guilt into a morally charged inability to "take responsibility for one's actions" (as though Kinbote's actions are separable from a certain heterosexually prescribed destiny).

Curiously, it is only in his "Zemblan" existence that Kinbote's is the classic story of the closeted gay man whose marriage helps to preserve that closet. For in the New Wye stage of his life, the closet he inhabits is more explicitly designed to conceal his "secret" identity as King Charles than as a homosexual. It is in the terms of this double closeting that we might most effectively come back to the question I posed earlier about the relationship between Kinbote's sexuality and insanity, and what makes this multi-layered text so rich in the dynamics of what Eve Sedgwick has termed the "epistemology of the closet."

THE TRANSPARENT CLOSET

Through deft readings of earlier modernist novels, Sedgwick investigates the peculiar yet endemic epistemological situation arising from and depending upon the transparent closet inhabited by the man whose homosexuality he believes he has concealed from the public gaze. Proposing that "many of the major nodes of thought and knowledge in twentieth-century Western culture as a whole are structured—indeed, fractured—by a chronic, now endemic crisis of homo/heterosexual definition, indicatively male, dating from the end of the nineteenth century," Sedgwick argues that "an understanding of virtually any aspect of modern Western culture [and by extension, of its literary productions] must be, not merely incomplete, but damaged in its central substance to the degree that it does not incorporate a critical analysis of modern homo/heterosexual definition" (1). Sedgwick brilliantly delineates the politics of the specularization of the gay subject in a homophobic culture, and thus it will be useful to rehearse here a few of the crucial junctures in that delineation, particularly those that so persuasively evoke the positioning of Kinbote in relation to the New Wye community, and to the readers he addresses.

According to Sedgwick, the transparent closet is not simply erected by the gay subject who wishes to remain concealed, but also by those who would be his spectators. This structure of containment, but not concealment, is facilitated by a community of spectators primarily in order to maintain their epistemological superiority over the gay man as inhabitant of the closet. Thus the closeted gay man becomes "that person over whom everyone else in the world has, potentially, an absolute epistemological privilege" (232). As Sedgwick remarks of the Baron de Charlus in Proust's *A la Recherche,*

> if [a gay man's] being in the closet means that he possesses a secret knowledge, it means all the more that everyone around him does; their incessant reading of the plot of his preserving his secret from them provides an all the more eventful plot for them to keep secret from him.

(225-26)

In **Pale Fire,** as in Proust, we find "the establishment of *the spectacle of the homosexual closet* as a presiding guarantor of rhetorical community, of authority—someone else's authority—over world-making discursive terrain that extends vastly beyond the ostensible question of the homosexual" (230).

Indeed, the Baron de Charlus, particularly as he is understood through the lens of Sedgwick's analysis, seems a likely precursor to Charles Kinbote, who devotes an impassioned tirade to what he calls "Proust's rough masterpiece," and seems to object specifically to the self-closeting of its narrator. (He calls the novel "a sexual *travestissement*" containing "an absurd, rubber-and-wire romance between a blond young blackguard [the fictitious Marcel], and an improbable *jeune fille* who has a pasted-on bosom, Vronski's [and Lyovin's] thick neck, and cupid's buttocks for cheeks" [162]. Kinbote belongs, presumably, to the generation of Proust commentators who understand Albertine to be

the transparently gender-reversed stand-in for, among other men, Proust's chauffeur.) As Sedgwick remarks, "in Proust . . . it is the law—that characters in general take on vitality and momentum to the degree that they are mystified about their own involuntary, inauthentic, or unconscious motivations." Kinbote, like Charlus, is "not an exception to the law but its blazing sacrificial embodiment, the burning bush, very flesh of that word" (226). In other words, it is around Kinbote that the New Wye community guarantees its own authority over "world-making discursive terrain" via its preservation and exploitation of the transparent closet that gives its citizens a privileged perspective onto his "secret" existence.

The same goes for readers who align themselves with this community: the pleasure of this kind of reading comes from "seeing through" Kinbote's closet, penetrating it before he voluntarily opens its door to us, indeed, penetrating Kinbote himself as though his identity were transparent to all but himself.

But as I have indicated, the correlation between Kinbote and Charlus is not a direct one. After all, what is concealed and revealed by Kinbote's closet is not primarily his sexual life, but his mental life. Kinbote's secret is not that he is gay (in fact, he frequently refers to events in his erotic life as though he assumes our prior knowledge of, and perhaps even that we share, his sexual orientation. Never does anxiety circulate around the question of whether someone knows he is gay, at least not in his post-Zembla existence) but that he is the deposed and exiled king of Zembla. Since the veracity of that secret is put into question, what is both hidden and displayed by the closet is Kinbote's madness. What the New Wyans know about him, and what we are invited to share with them, is precisely what he cannot know about himself: that he is insane, is living a delusion, is epistemologically exiled from both the world and from himself.

Consider, for example, a scene that offers an almost paradigmatic instance of how this closet is structured. Kinbote, at a party, sees Shade speaking to Mrs. H, and approaches them just in time to hear Shade "object to some remark she had just made" about the "delusion" of an "Exton railway employee":

> "That is the wrong word," he said. "One should not apply it to a person who deliberately peels off a drab and unhappy past and replaces it with a brilliant invention. That's merely turning a new leaf with the left hand."

> I patted my friend on the head and bowed slightly to Eberthella H. The poet looked at me with glazed eyes. She said:

> "You must help us, Mr. Kinbote: I maintain that what's his name, old—the old man, you know at the Exton railway station, who thought he was God and began re-

directing the trains, was technically a loony, but John calls him a fellow poet."

(238)

Shade's "glazed eyes" would seem to indicate that Kinbote is the "loony" in question, but Mrs. H, in what is ostensibly a tactful coverup maneuver, shifts the discourse so that its object becomes something other than it was before, thus effectively denying Kinbote access to the public knowledge of his identity. In this manner, Mrs. H, as member of the New Wye community, retains epistemological superiority over Kinbote, and ensures that he shall not know what she (and everyone else) knows about him. Critics frequently cite this passage as evidence of how Shade's attitude of compassion and pity towards Kinbote contrasts with the disdain and intolerance evinced by the rest of the New Wye community: Kinbote is not a loony, he says, but a fellow poet. Yet, insofar as Shade shares in the diagnostic or evaluative discourse circulating around Kinbote's psyche while simultaneously excluding Kinbote from that discourse (except as its object—never as its subject, or as an interlocutor), he is complicit in maintaining the transparent closet that keeps Kinbote on display.

Thus, though Kinbote is not primarily a closeted *homosexual* in the New Wye community, but a closeted deposed king, the structure of his closet mimics the closet of the Proustian "invert" insofar as it is the mechanism by which subjectivity is denied the inhabitant of the closet. The "secret exile," like Proust's invert, is ignorant, and stands outside the community of shared knowledge. He is ridiculous because he is the one who does not know. And as inhabitant of the transparent closet, he can only be condescended to, never communicated with. But it is not only through the structuring of the closet that homosexuality is invoked by this novel. Because Kinbote is also, literally, himself a gay man, though, as I've suggested, not as explicitly concerned about closeting his sexuality as he is about closeting his royal background.

This double closeting makes Kinbote the focus of a two-pronged persecution in the New Wye community, a persecution perhaps best embodied by Gerald Emerald, who has been portrayed as a tormentor of a specific kind throughout Kinbote's commentary: he is an instructor whom Kinbote has experienced as one who "makes advances and then betrays a noble and naive heart, telling foul stories about his victim and pursuing him with brutal practical jokes" (309). Emerald, then, would seem to be the gay-baiter who, in order to shore up and maintain as stable and normal his own sexual status as hetero, must needle and provoke the gay man, or effectively keep visible and fresh a sexual distinction between himself and Kinbote by seducing Kinbote into revealing his desires, then humiliating him for doing so. Just as he plays with Kinbote's sexual identity, so he

plays with his "royal" identity, never explicitly revealing that he "knows" but threatening, in public situations, to make it known (seemingly inadvertently) to others. The episode in the Faculty Common Room, when a German visitor unwittingly remarks on Kinbote's resemblance to Zembla's King Charles, can, in this sense, be read as a protracted scene of group torment, with Emerald the chief instigator. Emerald turns the visitor's remark into an opportunity to make Kinbote the butt of a private joke for the group, the humor of which will arise over his attempt to hide his anxiety about being exposed. Emerald pushes the joke to its limits as, by going to look up the picture of King Charles in the encyclopedia, he risks blowing Kinbote's "cover." Effectively combining homophobic insult with a sadistic threat to "reveal" Kinbote's royal identity, he remarks of the photo he has found of young King Charles that he was "Quite the fancy pansy," to which Kinbote retorts, "And you . . . are a foul-minded pup in a cheap green jacket" (268).

Kinbote's position as inhabitant of the transparent closet does not remain static. In *Pale Fire,* the narrative depends on the efforts of the inhabitant of the closet to disclose his secret in such a way as to command the proper regard for it by the larger community. Unaware that his closet is transparent, Kinbote's plan is to "come out," indirectly, to the tolerant Shade, a member of the community who already commands considerable discursive authority. Kinbote's hope is that this already respected colleague will, through the power of his authority, perform the public disclosure in such a way as both to ratify and valorize, even consecrate, Kinbote's identity as he would have it constructed through a compelling poeticized biography. In this academic community, truths that are conveyed through literary constructions are more likely to be accepted, valued as universal. The tolerant and pitying humanist must be appealed to as the means by which the alienated outcast will become admired and respected as one who has authority, as a royal, rather than an abject, exception to the common rule.

This attempt to recruit Shade as willing literary ally in the "coming out" process is, from Kinbote's perspective, frustrated when Shade prefers to write about his grief at the death of his daughter while never, ironically, recognizing his own complicity with the system that prohibits her existence as an intelligible subject. When Kinbote, on first reading, can find little trace of his Zemblan narrative in Shade's poem, he must engage in a kind of scholastic guerrilla warfare, waged against a literary critical establishment whose rules are designed to preserve the illusion of pure authorial integrity. In other words, Kinbote transgresses the rules of scholarly commentary that ostensibly seek to render transparent the author's "intentions" via supplementary notes—thus exposing, in the process, the way in which all commentary directs reader response in an interpretive way. Insofar as it functions to preserve the boundaries that define the "body" of the author's work against undesirable incursions from critically deviant "bodies," this literary critical establishment is coextensive with the heterosexual establishment that functions to preserve its ("normal," "healthy") integrity against the undesirable incursions of the sexually deviant body.

KINBOTE AS SEXUAL DISSIDENT?

I suggested above that the reader who shares the perspective of the New Wye community derives her or his pleasure from penetrating Kinbote's closet before he voluntarily opens its door to us. Insofar as Kinbote bears many of the marks of the classically "unreliable narrator," I think that the novel solicits us to read *through* his narrative. Teresa de Lauretis has observed (with special reference to Calvino) that gender binarism has remained much the same in the transition from modernism to postmodernism, insofar as

> woman is still the ground of representation, even in postmodern times. Paradoxically, for all the efforts spent to re-contain real women in the social, whether by economic or ideological means, by threats or by seduction, it is the absent Woman, the one pursued in dreams and found only in memory or in fiction, that serves as the guarantee of masculinity, anchoring male identity and supporting man's creativity and self-representation.
>
> (82)

It could be argued as well that heterosexual identity is similarly anchored, via the deployment of the "homosexual" as the "ground" of novelistic postmodern representation. In this sense, both Kinbote's homosexually desiring body and his deluded psyche become the territory across which we are invited to pleasure in Nabokov's ludic postmodernism. Indeed, the novel is at its most postmodernly titillating when it is impossible to determine the register at which it is operating. When Kinbote is called into Nattochdag's office, for instance, three of the novel's most pervasive social codes are evoked simultaneously, as though they function interchangeably in the policing of Kinbote's behavior. Having called Kinbote into his office, Nattochdag urges him "to be more careful." Kinbote, gathering that he has transgressed some rule, but not sure of the nature of that rule, asks "in what sense, careful?" Nattochdag answers that "a boy had complained to his advisor." But as soon as we understand this private reproval as a warning about inappropriate sexual advances, the register shifts to the realm of professional collegiality—the student's complaint is that Kinbote "criticized a literature course he attended ('a ridiculous survey of ridiculous works, conducted by a ridiculous mediocrity')." When Kinbote laughs at this "in sheer relief" and promises to "never be naughty again," we might suspect that

his relief is at not being chastised about his sexual conduct after all. It is perhaps only retrospectively that we can grasp the third register that is evoked in the next lines as Kinbote salutes Nattochdag because "[h]e always behaved with such exquisite courtesy toward me that I sometimes wondered if he did not suspect what Shade suspected, and what only three people (two trustees and the president of the college) definitely knew" (25). Here, of course, it is not his sexuality that is the focus of what Kinbote imagines others "suspect" or "definitely" know, but his royal identity. And yet, Kinbote is not conscious of his transgression of a third code here: not the (hetero)sexual code, nor the academic collegial code, but only the code that distinguishes the crazy from the sane.

It is his unwitting transgression of the rules of sanity that solicits us to read his narrative like so many symptoms, and that is responsible perhaps for the unrelenting critical diagnoses of his sexuality. And yet, the style and tone of the novel are not always consistent in this sense. There are also passages where a kind of camp libidinal identification is invited—where a reader would have to marshal an army of homophobic defenses not to be seduced by the erotics of the narrative. The paradigmatic example of this is the account of young Charles' discovery and exploration of the hidden passage with his childhood beloved, Oleg.

Oleg is the "regular faunlet" whose "bold virilia" and "girlish grace" has prompted in young Charles an awareness of his sexuality that is at once exhilarating and unnerving. Waiting for Oleg to arrive for a visit on a rainy day, the young Charles decides to look for a toy circus that had amused them the Easter before.

> Less than a fortnight had passed since Oleg's last visit, when for the first time the two boys had been allowed to share the same bed, and the tingle of their misbehavior, and the foreglow of another such night, were now mixed in our young Prince with an embarrassment that suggested refuge in earlier, more innocent games.
>
> (124)

Instead of the circus, however, which would allow the Prince to "take refuge" from his dawning sexuality, he finds the hidden entry to a secret underground passageway that will serve as both prelude to and metaphor for the thrilling and tender second consummation of his affection for Oleg.

Oleg arrives and Charles is reassured by "the downy warmth of [his] crimson ear and by the vivacious nod greeting the proposed investigation, that no change had occurred in his dear bedfellow" (125). Together they enter what Kinbote refers to as the "magical closet"; but this closet, instead of enclosing them, gives access to the "stone-paved underground passage" that is at once separate from and part of the city through which it runs:

in its angular and cryptic course it adapted itself to the various structures which it followed, here availing itself of a bulwark to fit in its side like a pencil in the pencil hold of a pocket diary, there running through the cellars of a great mansion too rich in dark passageways to notice the stealthy intrusion.

(126)

Their entry into and through the "magical closet" has launched them on a sexual journey that allows them to be both inside and outside the official architecture of their culture. Their progress through the long and labyrinthine passageway acts as a suggestive aphrodisiac on them as they become aware of "magic apertures and penetrations, so narrow and deep as to drive one insane" (126). Oleg, leading the way, becomes the focus of Charles' desiring gaze: "his shapely buttocks encased in tight indigo cotton moved alertly, and his own erect radiance, rather than his flambeau, seemed to illume with leaps of light the low ceiling and crowding walls" (126-27).

The tunnel comes to an end at a door that would deliver them once more to the official world, a world characterized apparently by the sounds of an assaultive and violent heterosexuality:

> Two terrible voices, a man's and a woman's, now rising to a passionate pitch, now sinking to raucous undertones, were exchanging insults in Gutnish as spoken by the fisherfolk of Western Zembla. An abominable threat made the woman shriek out in fright. Sudden silence ensued, presently broken by the man's murmuring some brief phrase of casual approval ("Perfect, my dear," or "Couldn't be better") that was more eerie than anything that had come before.

(127)

Rather than entering into this world, the boys "veered in absurd panic" and "raced back the way they had come" (127). The heterosexual imperative, which would seem to entail that a woman's "perfect" compliance be extracted through a man's "abominable" force, has no attraction for Charles and Oleg. They retraverse the passageway rather than pass through it to the official culture of gendered heterosexual oppression. On their return to the palace, their lovemaking, by contrast to the drama at the other end of the passage, is marked by the sounds of a less brutal ecstasy as they find themselves in "a manly state and moaning like doves" (127).

It is in passages like these, where Kinbote delineates the erotics of a desire for which there is no official space in his (and our) culture, a desire that has "adapted itself to the various structures which it followed," a desire that, "running through the cellars" of the "great mansion" of sexuality, has proved that mansion to be "too rich in dark passageways to notice the stealthy intrusion," that something other than an aestheticizing or

a pathologizing response might be elicited by *Pale Fire.* And even if Kinbote appears, nevertheless, as one of the "developmental failures or logical impossibilities" produced by the cultural matrix that defines him, he might also signify, for some readers at least, the locus of a pleasure that begins to challenge, even to alter, that cultural matrix. As Butler points out, the "persistence and proliferation" of subjects like Kinbote "provide critical opportunities to expose the limits and regulatory aims of that [hegemonic] domain of intelligibility and, hence, to open up within the very terms of that matrix of intelligibility rival and subversive matrices of gender disorder" (17).

If a critic like Frank Kermode still searches for the "correlative" in Nabokov's life to the homosexual protagonist of *Pale Fire,* I would suggest that it could be found in the person of the author's gay brother, Sergey. The following passage from Brian Boyd's biography indicates both the ambivalence and the depth of feeling Nabokov experienced with respect to his brother. I quote at length:

> One night at the start of the academic year Nabokov dreamed of his brother Sergey. Although in waking life he supposed Sergey to be safe in the Austrian castle of his lover Hermann, in the dream he saw him in agony on a bunk in a concentration camp. The next day he received a letter from his other brother, Kirill . . . Sergey, Kirill told him, had died of a stomach ailment brought on by malnutrition in a concentration camp near Hamburg. He had been arrested in Berlin in 1943 because of his homosexuality, but five months later his cousin Onya's efforts had secured his release. Hating Berlin, he had managed to find a job in a half-Russian office in Prague. There he openly voiced his contempt for Hitler and Germany and was promptly informed upon and arrested as a British spy. Vexed that Sergey loved not only a man but a German-speaking one, Nabokov had spoken rather harshly of his brother in recent years. Now he was appalled at Sergey's death, filled with admiration at his courageous outspokenness, and mortified that it was too late to make amends.

(88-89)

The heterosexism of Nazi Germany, insofar as it incarcerated its sexual as readily as its religious and political dissidents, was a particularly harrowing reality of which Nabokov was clearly not unaware. And yet, he had participated in this heterosexism by "speaking harshly" of his brother for his sexuality. Though it was too late, after Sergey's death, to "make amends," I would suggest that Nabokov's fictional construction, however ambivalent, of a specifically gay protagonist in *Pale Fire* was the means by which the author could explore his own partial complicity with the cultural imperatives that marginalized and eventually annihilated people like his brother. Whether it was his intention or not, Nabokov, in his perceptive delineation of the structure of the transparent closet, made visible the extent to which the heterosexual imperative of the post-war United States was in many ways consistent with the fascism of Nazi Germany. And while it would be fanciful to characterize Kinbote as some kind of pre-Stonewall gay activist, both the transgressive grafting of his "deviant" narrative onto Shade's hetero lyric and his insistent delineation of the erotics of male-male desire make it possible to read *Pale Fire* as the site of a sexual dissidence that begins to challenge "our cynical age of frenzied heterosexualism."

Notes

1. Kermode slightly misquotes from a passage in *Pale Fire* where Kinbote, the narrator, pays tribute to his dead friend Oswin Bretwit for his "courage . . . integrity, kindness, dignity" and "endearing naivete." Kinbote evokes an image of their clasped hands "across the water over the golden wake of an emblematic sun. . . . Let this lofty handshake be regarded in our cynical age of frenzied heterosexualism as a last, but lasting, symbol of valor and self-abnegation" (176). It is precisely this symbol—insofar as it contrasts with "heterosexualism"—that Kinbote has sought, in vain, in John Shade's poem.

2. I was not the first reader to bristle at Haegert's remark: in the bound periodical where I read the article, a previous reader had written in the margin "?Homophobia: are you an 'incurable heterosexual'?" What is astonishing is that, other than this scrap of unofficial marginalia, I found no other objections, in the reams of Nabokov criticism I read, to the patently heterocentric treatment of his novels.

3. It should be noted that this is only one "version" of the plot. Alternatively, it has been suggested that Zembla really does exist, and is not simply a delusion on the part of Kinbote, or that Kinbote himself does not exist, but is an invention of Shade, who has written both poem and commentary. See Field and Roth for their recapitulations of *Pale Fire*'s plot.

4. In the "complex, often violent, sometimes murderous dialectic between dominant and subordinate cultures, groups and identities" there is a "resistance, operating in terms of gender" that "repeatedly unsettles the very opposition between the dominant and the subordinate," according to Dollimore (21). This resistance is the "sexual dissidence" that I understand to be as politically ramified in Nabokov's text as it is in the texts by Wilde and Gide that Dollimore explores.

5. I borrow here from the language of Monique Wittig:

> All their testimonies emphasize the political significance of the impossibility that lesbians, feminists, and gay men face in the attempt to communicate in heterosexual society, other than with a psychoanalyst. When the general state of things is understood (one is not sick or to be cured, one has an enemy) the result is for the oppressed person to break the psychoanalytical contract. This is what appears in the testimonies along with the teaching that the psychoanalytical contract was not a contract of consent but a forced one.

(52)

Works Cited

Boyd, Brian. *Vladimir Nabokov: The American Years.* Princeton: Princeton UP, 1991.

Butler, Judith. *Gender Trouble.* New York: Routledge, 1990.

De Lauretis, Teresa. *Technologies of Gender: Essays on Theory, Film, and Fiction.* Bloomington: Indiana UP, 1987.

Dollimore, Jonathan. *Sexual Dissidence: Augustine to Wilde, Freud to Foucault.* New York: Oxford UP, 1991.

Field, Andrew. "*Pale Fire*: The Labyrinth of a Great Novel." *Triquarterly* 8 (Winter 1967): 13-36.

Galef, David. "The Self-Annihilating Artists of *Pale Fire*." *Twentieth Century Literature* 31 (1985): 421-37.

Haegert, John. "Author as Reader as Nabokov: Text and Pretext in *Pale Fire*." *Texas Studies in Language and Literature* 26.4 (Winter): 405-24.

Kermode, Frank. "Zemblances." *The New Statesman* 9 November 1962: 671-72.

Nabokov, Vladimir. *Pale Fire.* New York: Putnam's, 1962.

Rampton, David. *Vladimir Nabokov: A Critical Study of the Novels.* Cambridge: Cambridge UP, 1984.

Roth, Phyllis A. "The Psychology of the Double in Nabokov's *Pale Fire*." *Essays in Literature* 2.2 (Fall 1975): 209-29.

Sedgwick, Eve Kosofsky. *The Epistemology of the Closet.* Berkeley: U of California P, 1990.

Spivak, Gayatri Chakravorty. *In Other Worlds: Essays in Cultural Politics.* New York: Routledge, 1988.

Wittig, Monique. "The Straight Mind." *Out There: Marginalization and Contemporary Cultures.* Ed. Russell Ferguson, Martha Gever, Trinh T. Minh-ha, and Cornel West. Cambridge: MIT P, 1990. 51-57.

Brian Boyd (essay date 1999)

SOURCE: Boyd, Brian. "Commentary." In *Nabokov's* Pale Fire: *The Magic of Artistic Discovery,* pp. 37-62. Princeton, N.J.: Princeton University Press, 1999.

[*In the following essay, Boyd offers an in-depth analysis of the four levels of "commentary" in Nabokov's* Pale Fire.]

Martin Amis's observation that Nabokov "does all the usual things better than anybody else" applies with special force to one of the most *un*usual things ever twisted into a tale, the Commentary that occupies most of **Pale Fire.** More than two hundred pages of line-by-line annotations might seem a disastrous recipe for narrative, yet Nabokov here tells three colorfully contrasting stories, one homely, one exotic, one splenetic—Kinbote's intimate friendship with Shade in New Wye, Charles II's escape from Zembla, and Gradus's pursuit of the disguised king—that converge to a climax right in the final note. He simultaneously invents settings that offer both the recognitions of realism (small-town American academia) and the dislocations of romance (the fairyland of Zembla); places in them one of the most original and unforgettable of characters, the preposterously comic, inescapably tragic Charles Kinbote; and, amid all the mayhem Kinbote causes, allows us the pleasures of form, the satisfaction of sensing the author's order everywhere behind the commentator's chaos.

One sustained irony shapes the whole Commentary. Instead of presenting readers of his vast *apparatus criticus* with the result of prodigious labors in labyrinthine libraries, instead of assembling for them identifications they will have no time to make themselves, Kinbote acknowledges that he has "no library in the desolate log cabin where I live like Timon in his cave" ([**Pale Fire**] C. [Commentary] 39-40)[1] and except for one interview has undertaken no research whatever. Unlike *Kinbote's* readers, though, *Nabokov's* are invited to make their own easy and surprising discoveries about what the commentator cannot see. Most of these discoveries demand no infinite Borgesian library—just a good dictionary, a complete Shakespeare, and curiosity, memory, imagination. What we can find in the Commentary depends less on the esoterica of the erudite than simply on an alert assessment of human behavior and character.

NOTE TO LINES 1-4

On a first reading we may not consciously appreciate, but we certainly *feel,* the control Nabokov exerts through the Commentary despite Kinbote's mental disarray. The first note begins with a welcome and elegant paraphrase of the waxwing image that requires us to turn back to the poem itself, so establishing a pattern essential to our enjoyment of the whole Commentary. At the end of the Foreword, Kinbote had claimed: "Let me state that without my notes Shade's text simply has no human reality at all since the human reality of such a poem as his (being too skittish and reticent for an autobiographical work), with the omission of many pithy lines carelessly rejected by him, has to depend entirely on the reality of its author and his surroundings, attachments and so forth, a reality that only my notes can provide. To this statement my dear poet would probably

not have subscribed." Kinbote's first note does indeed provide some of the human reality Shade omits: some of it imagined with the indulgent fancifulness of *biographie romancée* ("We can visualize John Shade in his early boyhood, a physically unattractive but otherwise beautifully developed lad, experiencing his first eschatological shock, as with incredulous fingers he picks up from the turf that compact ovoid body and gazes at the wax-red streaks ornamenting those gray-brown wings"), and some of it mildly helpful, but largely prompted by Kinbote's inability to focus for long on anything but himself:

> When in the last year of Shade's life I had the fortune of being his neighbor in the idyllic hills of New Wye (see Foreword), I often saw those particular birds most convivially feeding on the chalk-blue berries of junipers growing at the corner of his house. (See also lines 181-182.)

> My knowledge of garden Aves had been limited to those of northern Europe but a young New Wye gardener, in whom I was interested (see note to line 998), helped me to identify the profiles of quite a number of tropical-looking little strangers and their comical calls. . . .

Already impossibly egocentric as critical commentary, the note scales new heights of absurdity as he draws our attention to a waxwing-like bird in the heraldic crest "of the Zemblan King, Charles the Beloved (born 1915), whose glorious misfortunes I discussed so often with my friend." The Zemblan theme had been introduced obliquely four times in the Foreword, but only in passing. Now Kinbote seems to feel it cannot be too early to introduce on center stage the real hero of the Commentary, the man whose misfortunes he discussed so often with Shade and who *should* have been the subject of Shade's poem.

The final paragraph of the first note provides one helpful biographical detail ("The poem was begun at the dead center of the year, a few minutes after midnight July 1") only to lapse instantly into Kinbotean self-concern and a hint, already, of another sexual appraisal ("while I played chess with a young Iranian enrolled in our summer school"), and then into a mysterious but clearly outrageous admission: "I do not doubt that our poet would have understood his annotator's temptation to synchronize a certain fateful fact, the departure from Zembla of the would-be regicide Gradus, with that date. Actually, Gradus left Onhava on the Copenhagen plane on July 5." This is the first mention of Gradus, and we are interested to find out how he will have such a "fateful" impact on the story, but the very facts that Kinbote thinks Gradus deserves mention in this first note, that he has been tempted to alter what he believed to be the historical truth of the matter for the sake of symmetry, and that he thinks Shade would have understood this temptation, confirm all the suspicions he engendered in the Foreword. This man who thinks himself in a unique position to present Shade's poem seems to understand neither his own role as commentator nor the man he claims as his friend.

While it offers some helpful paraphrase of the poem and some welcome biographical context, the first note offers us far more of Kinbote's egotism, his incomprehension of Shade, his sexual pursuits, his preoccupation with Zembla, and his fixation on Gradus. Through Kinbote's disordered note Nabokov sounds each of the main themes of the Commentary and invites us to read *through* Kinbote rather than with him, to enjoy the outrageousness of his character and his scholarship.

All it takes to detect most of the ironies is a sense of what one person owes to another. If we remain alert to that, we can read through the heroic story Kinbote projects—his "glorious friendship" with Shade and his singular suitability as the poet's companion, inspiration, and editor, as well as the "glorious misfortunes" in his own past—to see the comedy and pathos of an insane and insufferable self-regard that drives others from him until he is left alone in terror and despair.

There are four major areas of discovery in a first reading of the Commentary. The central discovery, the central joke of the novel, is that Kinbote's notes bear so little relation to Shade's poem. Within that larger surprise are a series of slightly more deferred discoveries, about the true relationships between Kinbote and Shade, between Kinbote and Charles II of Zembla, and between Kinbote and Gradus. Let us examine each of these in turn, in order of increasing distance from Shade's poem.

ONE. KINBOTE AS COMMENTATOR

The gaps between poem and commentary offer us a series of miniature comic discoveries, the simplest of which require no more than flicking back to the poem to see the effrontery, usually the vainglory, sometimes the desperation, of Kinbote's shameless self-concern. "*Line 62*: often," reads one headnote, and Kinbote's gloss opens: "Often, almost nightly, throughout the spring of 1959, I had feared for my life. Solitude is the playfield of Satan . . . ," when the poem in fact reads: "TV's huge paperclip now shines instead / Of the stiff vane so often visited / By the naïve, the gauzy mockingbird." We notice the comedy of Kinbote's failure to explain words (lemniscate); numbers (see note to lines 120-121); natural objects (the Toothwort White); social customs ("*Line 130*: I never bounced a ball or swung a bat": "Frankly I too never excelled in soccer and cricket; I am a passable horseman, a vigorous though unorthodox skier, a good skater, a tricky wrestler, and an enthusiastic rock-climber": European Kinbote fails to see, of course, that American Shade means basketball and base-

ball—*and* that he should keep himself out of this note); and especially literary allusions (the Sherlock Holmes stories, Hardy, Eliot, Frost, Browning, Poe, Shakespeare). While he fails to identify the source of Shade's title, despite the poet's clear hint, the high-churchy Kinbote glosses the Pope in

> I listened to the buzz downstairs and prayed
> For everybody to be always well,
> Uncles and aunts, the maid, her niece Adèle
> Who'd seen the Pope, people in books, and God

with the proud precision of "Pius X, Giuseppe Melchiorre Sarto, 1835-1914; Pope 1903-1914." Unprepared to track down Shade's references, he reroutes the Commentary to his own obsessions and fantasies:

> My own boyhood was too happy and healthy to contain anything remotely like the fainting fits experienced by Shade. It must have been with him a mild form of epilepsy, a derailment of the nerves at the same spot, on the same curve of the tracks, every day, for several weeks, until nature repaired the damage. Who can forget the good-natured faces, glossy with sweat, of copper-chested railway workers leaning upon their spades and following with their eyes the windows of the great express cautiously gliding by?
>
> (C.162)

Here his own incidental metaphor can cause his mind to jump before he guides it into the groove of his own past, his sexual predilections, his craving for admiration. And as so often, Nabokov allows Kinbote a nostalgia and a lyricism inseparable from the absurdity of his irrelevance.

"PALE FIRE"

At each level of the Commentary there seems to be one particular discovery that Nabokov stresses as an opportunity or a problem inviting our special attention. As in the Foreword, Nabokov especially rewards the especially curious, but still leaves a solution open to others.

In Kinbote's second note he records that "The last king of Zembla—partly under the influence of his uncle Conmal, the great translator of Shakespeare (see notes to lines 39-40 and 962), had become, despite frequent migraines, passionately addicted to the study of literature." If we follow both cross-references, we arrive first at Kinbote's comment on a draft couplet that Shade decided against. Citing the discarded lines, Kinbote adds:

> One cannot help recalling a passage in *Timon of Athens* (Act 4, Scene 3) where the misanthrope talks to the three marauders. Having no library in the desolate log cabin where I live like Timon in his cave, I am compelled for the purpose of quick citation to retranslate this passage into English prose from a Zemblan poetical version of *Timon* which, I hope, sufficiently approximates the text, or is at least faithful to its spirit:

The sun is a thief: she lures the sea
and robs it. The moon is a thief:
he steals his silvery light from the sun.
The sea is a thief: it dissolves the moon.

For a prudent appraisal of Conmal's translations of
Shakespeare's works, see note to line 962.

The translation back from the Zemblan should invite
the curious or suspicious reader to look up the Shakespearean original, which offers us not only the expected
comedy of the absurd garbling in the second-generation
translation, but also, unexpectedly, the title of Shade's
poem.[2] If we follow the second cross-reference in the
note to line 12, now backed up by this new cross-
reference, we head for the note to line 962, which turns
out to be Kinbote's gloss on Shade's "But this transparent thingum does require / Some moondrop title. Help
me, Will! *Pale Fire.*" Kinbote correctly deduces that
the poet has lifted a phrase from Shakespeare, but adds:
"But in which of the Bard's works did our poet cull it?
My readers must make their own research. All I have
with me is a tiny vest pocket edition of *Timon of Athens*—in Zemblan! It certainly contains nothing that
could be regarded as an equivalent of 'pale fire' (if it
had, my luck would have been a statistical monster)"
(285).

We can solve the riddle of the title, then, as early as our
reading of the note to line 12, and as a bonus for consulting the cross-references, we return to Kinbote saying that the last king of Zembla "had become . . . passionately addicted to the study of literature." If we have
been consistently curious enough to follow the cross-
references we will know from the Foreword that Kinbote is that "last king" and will see at once the irony
that despite his professed passion for literature he has
too little interest in Shade's poem—as opposed to the
poem he wanted Shade to write and is now forcing on
him in the Commentary—even to search out a Shakespeare concordance.

If however we do not follow those first cross-references
from the note to line 12, we come in the course of a
page-after-page reading to the note to line 39-40, with
its cross-reference to the note to line 962. If we *still* remain incurious, still do not chase down the references,
the next note contains strange echoes of the Zemblan
lines from *Timon* still resounding in Kinbote's mind
from the previous note. He complains that despite all
his pressure on Shade to "recreate in a poem the dazzling Zembla burning in my brain," he now sees how
sadly misplaced were his hopes:

Although I realize only too clearly, alas, that the result,
in its pale and diaphanous final phase, cannot be regarded as a direct echo of my narrative (of which, incidentally, only a few fragments are given in my notes—
mainly to Canto One), one can hardly doubt that the
sunset glow of the story acted as a catalytic agent upon

the very process of the sustained creative effervescence
that enabled Shade to produce a 1000-line poem in
three weeks. There is, moreover, a symptomatic family
resemblance in the coloration of both poem and story. I
have reread, not without pleasure, my comments to his
lines, and in many cases have caught myself borrowing
a kind of opalescent light from my poet's fiery orb, and
unconsciously aping the prose style of his own critical
essays.

(C.42, 81)

The echo of "pale fire" in "pale and diaphanous final
phase," and of the Zemblan *Timon* (unbeknownst to
him, Kinbote's phrase echoes the English *Timon* even
more closely) should trigger our suspicion, if we have
still have not reached for Act IV Scene 3 of *Timon* in
our one-volume Shakespeare.

If even that resonant echo does not make us curious,
there are more references to a copy of the Zemblan *Timon* that the future Charles II discovers in a cupboard
leading to a secret tunnel and that thirty years later, after the Zemblan revolution, he takes with him as a good-
luck talisman as he escapes through the tunnel to
emerge near Timon Alley and Coriolanus Lane. And if
even that insistence does not seem like a problem or a
clue, perhaps all the references to *Timon* and to one
particular passage might be recalled when we come to
the start of Kinbote's note declaring that his tiny vest
pocket edition of the Zemblan *Timon* "certainly contains nothing that could be regarded as an equivalent of
'pale fire.'" At any rate, the problem of the title has at
last clearly been posed, and the alert reader already
given half-a-dozen chances to solve the problem that
Kinbote remains too fixated on his vision of Zembla to
attend to.

I find it staggering that readers can think someone as
playfully generous as Nabokov is out to frustrate them.
He does find incuriosity funny—and sad—but he always rewards the curious.

Two. New Wye: Kinbote and Shade

Kinbote does not bother to stoop to such "humdrum
potterings" (C.747-748) as a serious commentary entails because he thinks he enhances the poem by revealing "the underside of the weave" (F [Foreword], 17),
the much more thrilling story that he pressed Shade so
often to tell, that Shade *should* have told and *would*
have told had he been free. Kinbote assumes without
question that Shade and Shade's readers will naturally
be far more interested in the "glorious misfortunes" of
Charles II of Zembla than in the quiet life of the "gray
poet" (C.12) of New Wye. This leads us naturally to the
second and third levels of the Commentary, to Kinbote
and Shade as neighbors, and to the Zembla Kinbote
thinks they should share.

Kinbote claims that Shade "valued my society above that of all other people." The claim sounded suspect enough in the Foreword, especially when he argued that although they had not known each other long "there exist friendships which develop their own inner duration, their own eons of transparent time, independent of rotating, malicious music" (F, 18-19), or when he admitted that Shade "intentionally concealed" his tenderness toward him when they were not alone, but it looks quite preposterous after Shade's intentionally *revealed* devotion to his wife in **"Pale Fire."** When Kinbote now complains that Professor Hurley's memoir of Shade "contains *not one reference* to the glorious friendship that brightened the last months of John's life" (C.71, 101), he intends it as proof of Hurley's rancorous envy and bias, but even on a first reading, even this short a distance into the Commentary, we have reason to believe that Hurley omits Kinbote because his relationship with Shade was neither glorious nor even friendship. After all, only two notes earlier, lamenting the terrors of his solitude, Kinbote reports that

> it was then, on those dreadful nights, that I got used to consulting the windows of my neighbor's house in the hope for a gleam of comfort (see note to lines 47-48). What would I not have given for the poet's suffering another heart attack (see line 691 and note) leading to my being called over to their house, all windows ablaze, in the middle of the night, in a great warm burst of sympathy, coffee, telephone calls, Zemblan herbal receipts (they work wonders!), and a resurrected Shade weeping in my arms ("There, there, John").
>
> (C.62, 96)

Kinbote also claims to be the "only begetter" (F, 17) of **"Pale Fire,"** but his judgment rests on nothing more than his sense of his own importance: "How persistently our poet evokes images of winter in the beginning of a poem which he started composing on a balmy summer night! The mechanism of the associations is easy to make out (glass leading to crystal and crystal to ice) but the prompter behind it retains his incognito. One is too modest to suppose that the fact that the poet and his future commentator first met on a winter day somehow impinges here on the actual season" (C.34-35). "One is too modest to suppose," he says, with all the pompous impersonality of false modesty, yet he not only supposes, he mentions, he insists: he *is* "the prompter behind."

Although this particular claim merits only ridicule, Nabokov injects into Kinbote's desperate urgency toward Shade a passionate exuberance and enthusiasm that almost convince, even as they amuse: Kinbote's need to thrust Zembla on Shade with a "drunkard's wild generosity," his sexual excitement at filling him with his story ("I knew he was ripe with my Zembla, . . . ready to spurt at the brush of an eyelash"),[3] his uncontrollable urge to spy on Shade at work on a "really big poem"

(C.47-48, 86) that he will not talk about, his sense of stunned betrayal when he realizes that, evening after evening, Shade reads his latest lines out to Sybil, his agony of disappointment when he learns that his visions of Zembla have not after all been fixed forever in the amber of Shade's verse.

Nabokov lets Kinbote express his needs as fervently as Humbert expresses his. Just as Humbert almost persuades some who read **Lolita** without a critical eye to what the urgency of his feelings means for those around him, Kinbote can persuade some into thinking Shade *should* have put the colorful Zembla story in verse. But here lies the main task of readerly discovery in this second, New Wye, level of the Commentary. We are invited to see, behind Kinbote's enthusiasm for his own viewpoint, how insufferable his obsessive behavior is—his thrusting his story at Shade, his shamelessly intrusive and potentially terrifying snooping on his neighbors, his vicious disregard for the man he thinks of as his friend, or indeed for anyone but himself, and his complete failure to understand the unique trust of married love—and how generous and gentle Shade is to his interesting and desperate but deeply disagreeable neighbor.

One scene must suffice. Walking home from church one morning Kinbote has the impression he hears Shade's voice say "Come tonight, Charlie," but there is no one there:

> I at once telephoned. The Shades were out, said the cheeky ancillula, an obnoxious little fan who came to cook for them on Sundays and no doubt dreamt of getting the old poet to cuddle her some wifeless day. I re-telephoned two hours later; got, as usual, Sybil; insisted on talking to my friend (my "messages" were never transmitted), obtained him, and asked him as calmly as possible what he had been doing around noon when I had heard him like a big bird in my garden. He could not quite remember, said wait a minute, he had been playing golf with Paul (whoever that was), or at least watching Paul play with another colleague. I cried that I must see him in the evening and all at once, with no reason at all, burst into tears, flooding the telephone and gasping for breath, a paroxysm which had not happened to me since Bob left me on March 30. There was a flurry of confabulation between the Shades, and then John said: "Charles, listen. Let's go for a good ramble tonight, I'll meet you at eight." It was my second good ramble since July 6 (that unsatisfactory nature talk); the third one, on July 21, was to be exceedingly brief.
>
> Where was I? Yes, trudging along again as in the old days with John, in the woods of Arcady, under a salmon sky.
>
> "Well," I said gaily, "what were you writing about last night, John? Your study window was simply blazing."
>
> "Mountains," he answered.
>
> The Bera Range, an erection of veined stone and shaggy firs, rose before me in all its power and pride. The splendid news made my heart pound, and I felt

that I could now, in my turn, afford to be generous. I begged my friend not to impart to me anything more if he did not wish it. He said yes, he did not, and began bewailing the difficulties of his self-imposed task. He calculated that during the last twenty-four hours his brain had put in, roughly, a thousand minutes of work, and had produced fifty lines (say, 797-847) or one syllable every two minutes. He had finished his Third, penultimate, Canto, and had started on Canto Four, his last (see Foreword, see Foreword, at once), and would I mind very much if we started to go home—though it was only around nine—so that he could plunge back into his chaos and drag out of it, with all its wet stars, his cosmos?

How could I say no? That mountain air had gone to my head: he was reassembling my Zembla!

(C.802)

There are obvious comic ironies to detect here: the discrepancy between Shade's curt "mountains"—the mountain Mrs. Z. sees in her near-death experience, and her "Mont Blanc" in Canto Three of the poem—and Kinbote's assumption that Shade is writing about Charles II's escape over the mountains; the echo of the "fountain"/"mountain" mistake in the poem in the "mountains"/"mountains" mistake here; the narcissistic sexual pride Kinbote takes in his story, in the double entendres of "The Bera Range,[4] an erection of veined stone and shaggy firs." But they are almost a distraction from the more revealing discoveries the attentive reader needs to make about Kinbote the man.

His contempt for the "ancillula, an obnoxious little fan who . . . no doubt dreamt of getting the old poet to cuddle her some wifeless day" reveals how little his self obsession has in common with self-awareness. He too is a Shade fan, derives a sexual charge from his relationship to Shade, and relishes visiting when Sybil is away. His scorn for the ancillula reflects his snobbery, his natural lack of generosity, and his misogyny, his failure to comprehend any kind of claim or attachment between a woman and a man.

Shade, shielded by Sybil at the telephone, rises from his work at Kinbote's insistence, and, unable not to respond to Kinbote's tears, agrees to break the flow of inspiration—he has just been working on the central passage of the poem—to meet Kinbote for a walk. Kinbote cannot imagine that Shade does not look forward to their strolls as passionately as *he* does, or that the poet withstands his incessantly turning any conversation back to Zembla only out of a sense of curiosity, kindness, and pity for someone most people in New Wye reject as insufferable. Once their stroll begins, Kinbote basks in the tranquillity of triumph ("Where was I? Yes, trudging along again as in the old days with John, in the woods of Arcady, under a salmon sky") while Shade diplomatically parries his intrusiveness, and after an hour gently asks Kinbote's leave to return to the con-

centrated fever of his composition. Kinbote agrees without a qualm only because he supposes Shade is today as happily glorying in Charles II as he always does himself.

"PALE LIGHT"

Despite his ridiculous pride in Zembla and in everything from his powerful car and his erect bodily carriage to his imagined social poise, his intimacy with Shade, and his all-round fascination, Kinbote, precisely because of his relentless self-satisfaction, drives away everybody in New Wye apart from Shade and a few passing sexual partners, leaving himself alone, conscious of the dislike he generates, and subject to despair and a dread of persecution. He thinks constantly about the terrors of solitude and darkness, and about suicide as an end to his fears.

For that reason he feels a special affinity for Hazel Shade—although he has never actually asked Shade about either his daughter or his parents (meanwhile telling him all about Charles II's parents, Alfin the Vague and Blenda), and although he complains that there is rather too much of Hazel in Shade's poem and too little of Zembla ("his picture of Hazel is quite clear and complete; maybe a little too complete, architectonically, since the reader cannot help feeling that it has been expanded and elaborated to the detriment of certain other richer and rarer matters ousted by it" [C.230, 164]). The one piece of research Kinbote does undertake is to see Jane Provost, Shade's former secretary, who had arranged Hazel's first and last blind date, and who tells him more about Hazel's poltergeist experiences, not even hinted at in the poem, and her night in "The Haunted Barn," which Shade refers to only in the coyest of terms. From a transcript Jane Provost has made of Hazel's notes in the barn comes the most urgent invitation to discovery in the New Wye element of the Commentary. Like the identification of the *Timon of Athens* passage in the first level, but in a much more mysterious way, it reflects the words "pale fire."

On the one night Hazel visits the Haunted Barn alone, she sees a "roundlet of pale light" darting about the walls. She puts questions to the "luminous circlet," spelling out the alphabet until it seems to give "a small jump of approval" at the right letter, and Kinbote transcribes what she records: "pada ata lane pad not ogo old wart alan ther tale feur far rant lant tal told." (C.347, 188) Because his own thoughts return inexorably to suicide—and he wonders at the end of a note on the subject whether "We who burrow in filth every day may be forgiven perhaps the one sin that ends all sins" (C.493)—Kinbote tries with particular urgency to detect in the message any kind of reference to Hazel's suicide, which took place less than six months after her night in the barn. *His* urgency provokes ours. After trying to construe the line every way he can, he feels he would like to abandon the quest had not a diabolical force urged us to seek a secret design in the abracadabra,

812 Some kind of link-and-bobolink, some kind
813 Of correlated pattern in the game

I abhor such games; they make my temples throb with abominable pain—but I have braved it and pored endlessly, with a commentator's infinite patience and disgust, over the crippled syllables in Hazel's report to find the least allusion to the poor girl's fate. Not one hint did I find. Neither old Hentzner's specter, nor an ambushed scamp's toy flashlight, nor her own imaginative hysteria, express anything here that might be construed, however remotely, as containing a warning, or having some bearing on the circumstances of her soon-coming death.

(C.347, 189)

Kinbote's lingering over the message Hazel records, his throbbing conviction that it *must* have some hidden meaning, and his linking it with the central epiphany of Shade's **"Pale Fire,"** prompt us to try to decipher those "crippled syllables." But if some discoveries come easily, others resist us. If the curious reader can find the source of "pale fire" even before the origin of the title has been posed as a problem, a first-time reader of **Pale Fire** simply cannot at this point detect the source and significance of *this* "pale light." The *re*reader, however, will have the key.

THREE. ZEMBLA: KINBOTE AND CHARLES II

Within the frame of the Commentary and the story of Kinbote and Shade comes the story of Zembla that Kinbote foists on Shade in the hope that he will compose a long poem, "a kind of *romaunt,* about the King of Zembla" (C.1000, 296). For most readers, Zembla is pure enchantment, and its uncertain status adds a shimmer to its radiant crispness. No country at all to us, it seems blandly enough accepted by people in New Wye. What exactly is its shifting relation to Novaya Zemlya or Nova Zembla, to Russia or Scandinavia, to reality and romance?

Kinbote has a boundless enthusiasm for Zembla's cloudless skies and crystal clarities and the reign of its last king. In the first note introducing the subject directly, a note to Shade's "that crystal land," which he suggests is "Perhaps an allusion to Zembla, my dear country," he describes the harmony that was the password of Charles the Beloved's reign: "A small skyscraper of ultramarine glass was steadily rising in Onhava. The climate seemed to be improving. Taxation had become a thing of beauty. The poor were getting a little richer, and the rich a little poorer" (C.12, 75).

Strangest of all the dislocations in Zembla is the sexual inversion that makes male homosexuality if not quite the norm, at least the "manly" Zemblan form of love.

Shade's "my bedroom" (his childhood bedroom in the house he still inhabits) triggers this glorious note from Kinbote that foregrounds the sexual theme:

Our Prince was fond of Fleur as of a sister but with no soft shadow of incest or secondary homosexual complications. She had a small pale face with prominent cheekbones, luminous eyes, and curly dark hair. It was rumored that after going about with a porcelain cup and Cinderella's slipper for months, the society sculptor and poet Arnor had found in her what he sought and had used her breasts and feet for his *Lilith Calling Back Adam*; but I am certainly no expert in these tender matters. Otar, her lover, said that when you walked behind her, and she knew you were walking behind her, the swing and play of those slim haunches was something intensely artistic, something Arab girls were taught in special schools by special Parisian panders who were afterwards strangled. Her fragile ankles, he said, which she placed very close together in her dainty and wavy walk, were the "careful jewels" in Arnor's poem about a *miragarl* ("mirage girl"), for which "a dream king in the sandy wastes of time would give three hundred camels and three fountains."

On ságaren werém tremkín tri stána
Verbálala wod gév ut trí phantána

(I have marked the stress accents).

(C.80)

Right from the start, from the slipperiness of "no soft shadow of incest or secondary homosexual complications," the note defocalizes our response to Zemblan sexuality. The hints of myth and fairy tale in Lilith and Cinderella, the delicious unlikelihood of a "society sculptor" testing the feet and breast size of all Zembla's women, the exoticism of Arab girls and "special Parisian panders who were afterwards strangled," where the gruesome remains harmless behind its veil of remoteness, the suggestion that female beauty is a mere mirage—all this only prepares for the even stranger scene that dominates the note. Pushed by her ambitious mother the Countess, Fleur de Fyler lays siege to the King in his bedroom in the days between his mother's death and his coronation, but she proves "a poor seducer." Fleur's nymphlike, all-but-naked body floating through the scene in a kind of half-hearted and hopeless assault ("The sight of her four bare limbs and three mousepits (Zemblan anatomy) irritated him") makes heterosexual sex seem so bizarre that it thoroughly naturalizes Charles II's "manlier pleasures." Only gradually will Kinbote's guard drop to reveal that the King's homosexuality has a more sordid side in his predilection for young boys.

The major discovery in the Commentary's Zemblan story, *the* first major discovery on a first reading of the novel, is that Charles II of Zembla *is* Kinbote. Kinbote keeps it a secret from all those around him in New Wye and from us until well into the Commentary, and enjoys the secret *as* secret, as something both to be kept and to be bestowed as a priceless reward. He says to Shade on one of their evening rambles: "as soon as your poem is ready, as soon as the glory of Zembla merges with the glory of your verse, I intend to divulge to you an ultimate truth, an extraordinary secret" (C.433-34, 215). Commenting just a little earlier on Shade's dropping from his draft a quotation from Pope ("The sot a hero, lunatic a king"), Kinbote asks: "Or was he afraid of offending an authentic king? In pondering the near past I have never been able to ascertain retrospectively if he really had 'guessed my secret,' as he once observed (see note to line 991)" (C.417-421). There can be few readers who will *not* have guessed the secret by this point, and apart from those who have already followed the cross-reference from the Foreword to the note to line 991, there will be few who will not flick forward now to that note for the pleasure of confirming the hunch. Again the secret is not openly disclosed, yet is all but divulged: Kinbote says to Shade that if he shows him the manuscript of the poem that he has just declared practically finished, "I promise to divulge to you *why* I gave you, or rather *who* gave you, your theme."

If we do not discover that Kinbote is Charles II via the first trail of cross-references from the Foreword, we can still reach his secret through many possible alternative routes. Through Kinbote's strong desire to disclose who he really is, even while preserving his incognito, as in the Foreword's "Imagine a soft, clumsy giant; imagine a historical personage . . .' imagine an exiled prince . . ." (F, 17). Through the slip in his initial eulogy of Charles II's reign: "The poor were getting a little richer, and the rich a little poorer (in accordance with what may be known some day as Kinbote's Law)" (C.12, 75). Through our hunch that someone as narcissistic as Kinbote could be so entranced with Charles II only if he *is* Charles II, a guess we may well make by early in the first long note on Zembla, describing Charles II's parents (C.71). Through the possibility of checking such a hunch at any time by glancing ahead to the Index we saw listed on the Contents page, for there the headnote announces: "The capital letters G, K, and S (which see) stand for the three main characters in this work." (There is no C for Charles II, which already offers a clue; if we follow the "which see" we find "*K*, see Charles II and Kinbote"; if we overlook the headnote and search directly for Charles II, we see at the end of the entry: "See also Kinbote.") Through the vivid detail and charged emotion of certain scenes, like the night the Prince is informed his mother has died (C.71, 105-6), that seem to place the narrator as participant and principal. Through Charles's telling Disa he will go to America to teach literature (C.433-434, 213), where we know Kinbote has recently arrived to do just that. Through Shade's question, after he hears of Charles II's last meeting with his Queen, Disa: "How can you know that all this intimate stuff about your rather appalling

king is true?" (C.433-434, 214). Through the shift of pronoun from third person to first in the note describing the King's arrival by parachute in America (C.691, 247), as if Kinbote feels he can relax his guard now that his story has landed him safely here. Through the letter to Disa that gives his American address as "Dr. C. Kinbote, Kinbote (*not* 'Charles X. Kingbot, Esq.,' as you, or Sylvia, wrote; *please,* be more careful—and more intelligent)" (C.768, 257). The series of clues becomes gradually more unequivocal, so that by this last one surely *every* reader must know what Kinbote still does not say explicitly, so that we *all* have the pleasure of discovering for ourselves Kinbote's "ultimate truth," his "extraordinary secret."

"DIM LIGHT"

Within the Zemblan level of the Commentary, as within the others, there is one special focus of discovery, and like the other special foci, it involves the title of the poem and the image of "pale fire." To Kinbote the high point of his "glorious misfortunes" is his escape through the tunnel and over the mountains. He recounts the tunnel episode in the longest note of all, a note tense with the excitement of discovery and the exultation of escape. Kinbote tells us that the King, imprisoned in a tower of his own palace after the Zemblan revolution, feels himself "the only black piece in what a composer of chess problems might term a king-in-the-corner waiter of the *solus rex* type" (C.130, 118-19). So crucial is this episode to the Zembla saga that Kinbote suggests to Shade he should call his whole poem about Charles II "Solus Rex" (C.1000, 296). The entire tunnel note in fact seems to be constructed as a kind of chess problem for us as well as for the King: can we solve the problem of his escape?

As the King sits in the dismal lumber room to which he has just been transferred, light glints off a key in a closet door and triggers in his mind a thirty-year-old recollection. As a thirteen-year-old looking for a set of toys that he and his special playmate Oleg can play with, he is directed to the lumber room in which he now sits as deposed king. Dislodging a piece of black velvet at the back of the closet with the toys, the boy discovers a secret tunnel. Armed with flashlights, he and Oleg explore the tunnel together, ticking off 1,888 yards on a pedometer, when they reach a door behind which they hear "Two terrible voices, a man's and a woman's, now rising to a passionate pitch, now sinking to raucous undertones, . . . exchanging insults in Gutnish as spoken by the fisherfolk of Western Zembla. An abominable threat made the woman shriek out in fright. Sudden silence ensued, presently broken by the man's murmuring some brief phrase of casual approval ('Perfect, my dear,' or 'Couldn't be better') that was more eerie than anything that had come before" (C.130, 127). They flee in terror back through the tunnel, but once in the palace, they have other discoveries to make: two weeks earlier they had for the first time shared the same bed, and now the "recent thrill of adventure had been superseded already by another sort of excitement. They locked themselves up. The tap ran unheeded. Both were in a manly state and moaning like doves" (127).

The discovery of the tunnel, and the discovery of sex, flash through Charles II's mind as he sits in his prison and realizes he has also discovered his means of escape. He asks to be allowed to play the piano, and is led to the music room, where Odon, an actor and staunch Royalist, poses as an Extremist guard: "'Never heard of any passage,' muttered Odon with the annoyance of a chess player who is shown how he might have saved the game he has lost" (129). Odon asks him to stay put for another day, until he can make arrangements for the escape—he will be busy that night performing an old melodrama at the Royal Theater—but the anxious King, returning to his room, opens the closet door in the dark, pulls on over his pajamas some sportsclothes he finds in a heap on the floor, removes the shelves, takes with him as a talisman a little book he dislodges, a tiny vestpocket version of *Timon Afinsken* he had noticed there thirty years before, enters the tunnel, replaces the shelves, and switches on his flashlight to find that he is now "hideously garbed in bright red" (133). He walks along the remembered tunnel, still not sure where it will come out.

Where *will* he emerge? A plethora of insistent patterns adds an odd urgency to the comparison of the King's imprisonment to a *solus rex* chess problem and of the tunnel to its solution. When the Prince first discovers the tunnel, his tutors Monsieur Beauchamp and Mr. Campbell sit down to a game of chess just as the boys set off to explore and finish just as they emerge; when the King descends into the tunnel, soldiers outside play a game of lansquenet. The lumber room had had a full-length mirror and a green silk sofa when it was the dressing room of the King's grandfather, Thurgus the Third. Above the closet leading to the tunnel hangs a portrait, framed in black velvet, of the actress Iris Acht, whose surname means "eight" in German and who "for several years, ending with her sudden death in 1888," had been Thurgus's mistress. The boys head down green-carpeted steps into the tunnel. Oleg walks in front, and "his shapely buttocks encased in tight indigo cotton moved alertly, and his own erect radiance, rather than his flambeau, seemed to illume with leaps of light the low ceiling and crowding walls. Behind him the young Prince's electric torch played on the ground and gave a coating of flour to the back of Oleg's bare thighs" (126-27). They have tocked off 1,888 yards on their pedometer when they reach a green door to which the key of the closet door fits, but they are startled by that strange argument and by the strange approval it elicits into running back before they find what lies behind that door.

Soon after discovering the secret passage, the Prince almost dies of pneumonia and "in his delirium he would strive one moment to follow a luminous disk probing an endless tunnel and try the next to clasp the melting haunches of his fair ingle" (128). He is sent to the south of Europe to recuperate, and Oleg's death at fifteen helps "to obliterate the reality of their adventure" (128). Now when the King switches on his flashlight inside the tunnel, the

> dim light he discharged at last was now his dearest companion, Oleg's ghost, the phantom of freedom. He experienced a blend of anguish and exultation, a kind of amorous joy, the like of which he had last known on the day of his coronation, when, as he walked to his throne, a few bars of incredibly rich, deep, plenteous music (whose authorship and physical source he was never able to ascertain) struck his ear, and he inhaled the hair oil of the pretty page who had bent to brush a rose petal off the footstool, and by the light of his torch the King now saw that he was hideously garbed in bright red.
>
> (132)

The images of the "luminous disk" and the "dim light" that recalls Oleg so vividly for the King as to seem like his ghost will resonate oddly with the "luminous circlet" and the "roundlet of pale light" we encounter in the Haunted Barn episode, but already have an eeriness of their own. The red garb the King finds himself wearing stands in vivid contrast with the pattern of greens at both ends of the tunnel. What on earth is the point of these patterns, and where will the tunnel lead?

When the King reached the end of the tunnel,

> he unlocked the door and upon pulling it open was stopped by a heavy black drapery. As he began fumbling among its vertical folds for some sort of ingress, the weak light of his torch rolled its hopeless eye and went out. He dropped it: it fell into muffled nothingness. The King thrust both arms into the deep folds of the chocolate-smelling cloth and, despite the uncertainty and the danger of the moment, was, as it were, physically reminded by his own movement of the comical, at first controlled, then frantic undulations of a theatrical curtain through which a nervous actor tries vainly to pass. This grotesque sensation, at this diabolical instant, solved the mystery of the passage even before he wriggled at last through the drapery into the dimly lit, dimly cluttered *lumbarkamer* which had once been Iris Acht's dressing room in the Royal Theater.
>
> (133-34)

At last the problem is solved, at least for the moment. The tunnel had connected Thurgus and his lover; the greens had linked her greenroom[5] and his dressing room; the sounds the boys had heard had been from the rehearsal of an old melodrama, the very melodrama that has just been revived and that Odon now stars in—fortunately, for between scenes Odon encounters the King in his bright red and whisks him away from apprehension.

Now it is possible but extremely unlikely that a first-time reader could guess, before the King does, just where his escape will bring him out, or could recognize all of these patterns. Yet the chess-problem frame, the game of chess and the later game of lansquenet, the doubled names of Beauchamp and Campbell, the doubling of Acht and 1888 and of 1888 as a marker in space and in time, the green and red pattern, the performance then and now of a Gutnish melodrama, the overtones of a descent into the underworld in the description of the tunnel, the references to the flashlight as Oleg's ghost—all accumulate to charge the atmosphere in a way that even a first-time reader can register. But charge with what? A sense of the fates deciding between someone's death or his imminent escape into freedom? A sense that all depends on Charles II making some right move?

A first release comes for us, as for the King, at the moment he finds where that green door leads. The initial mystery stands suddenly solved, but what else lies behind these pervasive patterns? Do they somehow cohere into a single design or a problem we can eventually resolve?

FOUR. KINBOTE AND GRADUS

The fourth level of the Commentary, and the third of its three plot strands, sets out Gradus's approach to his assassination attempt on Charles II. Kinbote, who finds such triumph in the story of the King, exults in a different way in the narrative vengeance he wreaks on his would-be assassin. Always vindictive, whether spontaneously undoing Gerald Emerald's tie as he passes or deliberately wounding Sybil Shade for not inviting him to John's birthday party, Kinbote dedicates a large portion of his Commentary to Gradus in a spirit of unsparing revenge. He vents his animosity through the control he exerts and asserts over Gradus's appearance in the narrative, through recording details that he indicates the unobservant gunman fails to register,[6] through the insatiable insults embedded in his direct descriptions, through his gloating over the misfortunes that befall Gradus—his failed plans, his family woes, his physical ailments.

We glimpse Gradus only in distant summary when he is first introduced, although Kinbote, working from an interview with the killer, conscientiously and contemptuously fills in his background, his birth in Riga, his childhood in Strasbourg, his arrival in Zembla in the 1940s, his first dabblings in Extremism, the botched crimes of his early days as a revolutionary, his selection as assassin, perhaps so that no "son of Zembla" need "incur the dishonor of actual regicide" (C.171, 150). As Gradus reaches Paris, Geneva, Nice, and New York, we see him in tighter and tighter focus, until when he flies from New York to New Wye we watch him in ex-

treme—and extremely unpleasant—close-up, as Kinbote has us peer with superiority and scorn into "his magenta and mulberry insides" as he starts to succumb to food-poisoning, the details of which we are also not spared (C.949/2, 278).

In the last detailed note describing Gradus's approach, Kinbote records that after his explosive discharge in the toilet of a hotel near the New Wye campus, Gradus "was still groaning and grinding his dentures when he and his briefcase re-offended the sun" (C.949/2, 280). He heads for the campus, is directed to the library, asks for Dr. Kinbote. A girl at the main desk suggests he try the Icelandic Collection, but he cannot find it, and when he eventually makes his way back to the main desk, the girl asks, "Didn't you—. . . Oh, there he is!" "Along the open gallery that ran above the hall, parallel to its short side, a tall bearded man was crossing over at a military quick march from east to west. He vanished behind a bookcase but not before Gradus had recognized the great rugged frame, the erect carriage, the high-bridged nose, the straight brow, and the energetic arm swing, of Charles Xavier the Beloved" (281-82). At last Kinbote as storyteller admits in triumph that he is no less a man than the ex-king of Zembla, his identity confirmed by the man who has traveled thousands of miles to put him to death.

But, incompetent as ever, Gradus again loses himself in the library, and on returning to the desk once more is told Dr. Kinbote has left for the day. He is offered a lift to Dulwich Hill by someone passing that way, and dropped off outside the Goldsworth home. "One finds it hard to decide what Gradus alias Grey wanted more at that minute: discharge his gun or rid himself of the inexhaustible lava in his bowels" (283). Gradus remains there, at the end of the second note to line 949, both ominous and odious, this clockwork man under Kinbote's taunting control, while Kinbote in the three notes on the last ten lines of the poem describes the evening atmosphere evoked in Shade's final verses, and his inviting the poet back to his own home to share half a gallon of Tokay.

NOTE TO LINE 1000

In the final note, to line 1000, the four parts of the Commentary (commentary, New Wye, Zembla, Gradus) confront one another as in any classic climax. No cross-references have directed us here in advance, and although the note's events have long been dimly foreshadowed, they come as a complex surprise.

Gradus steps right into the foreground, into the same scene as Kinbote and Shade, only for a moment, only in this last note, as he suddenly shoots at Shade—no, at Kinbote—as they cross from Shade's house to the Goldsworth house Kinbote rents: "His first bullet ripped a sleeve button off my black blazer, another sang past my ear. It is evil piffle to assert that he aimed not at me (whom he had just seen in the library—let us be consistent, gentlemen, ours is a rational world after all), but at the gray-locked gentleman behind me. Oh, he was aiming at me all right but missing me every time, the incorrigible bungler" (294).

Shot through the heart, Shade slumps to the ground as Kinbote's gardener brings a spade crashing down on the gunman. At last we find out how Kinbote comes to be in possession of the poem: leaving Shade lying bleeding on the ground, he spirits the manuscript away, hides it in his closet, and only then calls 11111. The man who had wished his friend might have a heart attack so that he could rush over with his wonder-working Zemblan herbal receipts returns to the garden with no more than a glass of water to find Shade already lying "with open dead eyes directed up at the sunny evening azure" (295).

In the turmoil of that night, Kinbote snatches time to read the poem, only to learn in a fury of disappointment that it contains nothing of the Zemblan lore he had lavished on Shade. When Sybil, hearing the gardener's version of the death scene, and thinking Kinbote has thrown himself between the gunman and Shade, says "There are things for which no recompense . . . is great enough" (298), Kinbote suggests with quick presence of mind that there *is* a recompense, if he be allowed to edit and publish the poem. In her distraction and gratitude she agrees, and Kinbote escapes to record in the Commentary not only his unique friendship with Shade, and the Zembla story he offered him, but also the Gradus story that proves his kingship matters even in New Wye.

GREY SHADOW

Kinbote has wanted us to discover the great secret of the Commentary, that he is no less a personage than King Charles the Beloved of Zembla. What he does not expect is that we will also make another discovery, that the man he calls Jakob Gradus is in fact really an American, Jack Grey, an escapee from an institution for the criminally insane who has come to wreak vengeance on Goldsworth, the judge who sent him there and whom Shade happens to resemble.

Kinbote knows that the police identify the killer only as Grey, but in his sometimes anxious, sometimes cocky attempts to refute that story he only shows how coherent the Jack Grey version is, how consistent with the circumstances, how much more probable than his own account, no matter how painstakingly he has elaborated it. Hints of the version that he wants to suppress occur in one early note (C.47-48), but the first explicit statement that the account he has given of Gradus does not

square with the police's Jack Grey version does not occur until the end of the last long note about Gradus, after he has been dropped off in front of the Shade and Goldsworth homes (C.949/2). Only in the final note, to line 1000, does Kinbote, in attempting to resist the New Wye version of events, inadvertently prompt us to recognize that it makes far more sense than his own. Even his attempt to explain how he knows the details of Gradus's past seems so uncertain as to be self-refuting:

> I did manage to obtain, soon after his detention, an interview, perhaps even two interviews, with the prisoner. He was now much more lucid than when he cowered bleeding on my porch step, and he told me all I wanted to know. By making him believe I could help him at his trial I forced him to confess his heinous crime—his deceiving the police and the nation by posing as Jack Grey, escapee from an asylum, who mistook Shade for the man who sent him there. A few days later, alas, he thwarted justice by slitting his throat with a safety razor blade salvaged from an unwatched garbage container. He died, not so much because having played his part in the story he saw no point in existing any longer, but because he could not live down this last crowning botch—killing the wrong person when the right one stood before him. In other words, his life ended not in a feeble splutter of the clockwork but in a gesture of humanoid despair. Enough of this. Exit Jack Grey.
>
> (299)

"An interview, perhaps even two interviews"—or, far more likely, no interviews at all.

But if Kinbote has invented the regicide Jakob Gradus from the bare name Jack Grey and the fact that he has deliberately shot someone on the property Kinbote rents, then the consequences are momentous. The gunman did not know that Kinbote was "really" Charles II and was not shooting at him at all, as Kinbote so strenuously insists he was. The elaborately orchestrated account of Gradus's approach, which fills almost as much space in the Commentary as the story of the King's escape, disintegrates into fabrication or fantasy. If that circumstantial story, following a trail that begins in Zembla, is entirely unreal, then so too in all probability is Kinbote's claim to be Charles II, and perhaps even the very existence of the country of Zembla.

Kinbote has admitted throughout the Commentary to relentless fears of persecution, and Jack Grey's mistakenly shooting Shade instead of Goldsworth has merely provided our commentator with the occasion to name a persecutor and invent a conspiracy that confirms his own importance. The concerted reactions of those around him in New Wye have given us reason to suspect Kinbote's insanity from as early as the Foreword. We have still more grounds for suspicion in the Commentary, in the extravagance of his claims and his behavior as neighbor and annotator, and in his readiness to see imputations against his sanity even where there are none.[7] Yet he is an intelligent and eloquent man and tells a thoroughly coherent if fabulous story. Only in this last note does the alternative account of Jack Grey clinch our doubts and confirm for us that Kinbote is indeed thoroughly mad.

With Gradus identified as Grey and Kinbote marked as mad, we can diagnose from his behavior and his Commentary that he suffers from classical paranoia in all its three main forms. Those with delusions of grandeur have the rarest and usually the severest kind of paranoia, and their delusions, unlike those of schizophrenia or mania sufferers, tend to be detailed, coherent, stable, and persistent, like Kinbote's conviction that he is the last king of Zembla. That fantasy may well reflect an unbearable nostalgia for a real homeland, perhaps Russia, since he certainly speaks Russian and admits to its being the fashionable language of Zembla when he was a child, and since his story involves deposition by a revolution *à la russe*. Those with erotic paranoia believe themselves loved sexually by someone else, usually famous, who reveals affection through countless small signs, as Kinbote is convinced the celebrated American poet John Shade values his company "above that of all other people" (F, 24). Kinbote has also shown all the traits of the third form of paranoia, persecution mania. At a level beneath his unshakeable self-satisfaction he is aware of the intense dislike he generates around him for his homosexuality and his megalomaniac narcissism.[8] His sense of beleaguered isolation produces terrors, sweats, a panicky dread of solitude at night, in which a fear of assassination and his own strong temptation to escape his despair by killing himself repeatedly fuse: "At times I thought that only by self-destruction could I hope to cheat the relentlessly advancing assassins who were in me, in my eardrums, in my pulse, in my skull, rather than on that constant highway looping up over me and around my heart" (C.62, 97).

Once Shade is shot, once Kinbote sees that Shade's long poem eschews Charles II of Zembla, he hangs on to the manuscript of the poem in order to attach to it a Commentary that will tell the Zembla story and reflect his triple centrality, as Charles the Beloved, as the neighbor and friend whose Zembla saga inspired the creative explosion in which Shade wrote **"Pale Fire,"** and as the intended victim of a vast plot stretching from Zembla across Europe to America. But the very strand of his story that in his final note brings "proof" of his identity all the way to New Wye starts to unravel and to take the whole Commentary with it. Kinbote wants us to discover "an ultimate truth, an extraordinary secret" in the course of the Commentary. We do discover the secret of his true self, but not the one he means us to find (that he is Charles II), but the one that he tries to keep hidden even from himself: that he is a pathetic, lonely paranoid, utterly deluded about himself and his

importance to Shade, to Zembla, to anything outside the desperate compensations in his own mind.

THE LEVELS TILT

But just when we make this unsettling discovery that reveals half of the Commentary to be sheer delusion, and yet allows everything in it to settle into a new kind of stability and sense, the last four paragraphs of the last note tilt and twist in a series of unstable surprises, as Kinbote seems either to lose control completely ("Well, folks, I guess many in this fine hall are as hungry and thirsty as me, and I'd better stop, folks, right there") or to see through the mirages of his madness glimpses of unexpected, inadmissible truths, not only that he is mad, but that he is invented:

> God will help me, I trust, to rid myself of any desire to follow the example of two other characters in this work. I shall continue to exist. I may assume other disguises, other forms, but I shall try to exist. I may turn up yet, on another campus, as an old, happy, healthy, heterosexual Russian, a writer in exile, sans fame, sans future, sans audience, sans anything but his art. I may join forces with Odon in a new motion picture: *Escape from Zembla* (ball in the palace, bomb in the palace square). I may pander to the simple tastes of theatrical critics and cook up a stage play, an old-fashioned melodrama with three principals:[9] a lunatic who intends to kill an imaginary king, another lunatic who imagines himself to be that king, and a distinguished old poet who stumbles by chance into the line of fire, and perishes in the clash between the two figments. Oh, I may do many things! History permitting, I may sail back to my recovered kingdom, and with a great sob greet the gray coastline and the gleam of a roof in the rain. I may huddle and groan in a madhouse. But whatever happens, wherever the scene is laid, somebody, somewhere, will quietly set out—somebody has already set out, somebody still rather far away is buying a ticket, is boarding a bus, a ship, a plane, has landed, is walking toward a million photographers, and presently he will ring at my door—a bigger, more respectable, more competent Gradus.

After all our discoveries in the Commentary, none more startling than those of the last few pages, we leave it with a whole new slew of surprises as we head for the Index.

Notes

1. All reference are to the Vintage edition (New York, 1989), a corrected version of the first edition (New York: Putnam's, 1962). Where the source is not already explicit, citations will be in the form F, P.xxx, C.xxx, I (for Foreword, Poem, Commentary, and Index), so that readers with any edition can locate a reference; page numbers to the Vintage edition are added, if needed, within the Foreword or long notes in the Commentary: "C.130, 125" means "note to line 130; Vintage (or Putnam's) page 125."

Further textual corrections and brief annotations are available in Vladimir Nabokov, *Novels 1955-1962,* ed. Brian Boyd (1996).

2. See above, p. 33. Peter Hutchinson, *Games Authors Play* (1983), 38-39, and Matei Calinescu, *Rereading,* 124-25, 128-29, discuss some of Nabokov's strategy in inviting the reader to trace the source, but without considering the trail he leaves throughout the novel.

3. Nabokov explained to one French translator, Raymond Girard, "*to spurt* vieux dire *to squirt* avec un sens obscène" ("*to spurt* means *to squirt* in an obscene sense," [letter of December 27, 1963, VNA [Vladimir Nabokov Archive, Henry W. and Albert A. Berg Collection, New York Public Library]]) and to another, Maurice-Edgar Coindreau, "le pauvre et dégoûtant Dr. Kinbote se permet ici le triste luxe d'une métaphore obscène" ("poor disgusting Dr. Kinbote allows himself here the sad luxury of an obscene metaphor," [letter of January 14, 1964, VNA]).

4. Ellen Pifer, *Nabokov and the Novel* (1980), 113, notes "Bera" as an anagram of "bare."

5. Greenroom: a room once provided in theaters where actors and actresses could meet or mingle with others between scenes.

6. He takes particular pleasure in girding the loins of Gordon, a fourteen- or fifteen-year-old lad, Charles II's sexual conquest from the previous year, in coverings that keep metamorphosing before our eyes and behind Gradus's back, from "a leopard-spotted loincloth" into ivy "wreathed about the loins," "black bathing trunks," "white tennis shorts," and a "Tarzan brief . . . cast aside on the turf" (C.408).

7. Such as his misconstruing a note saying, "You have hal. . . . s real bad, chum" as referring to "hallucinations" rather than "halitosis" (C.62, 98), the "Poor old man Swift" note (C.231), and the "lunatic a king" note (C.417-21).

8. In *VNAY* [Brian Boyd, *Vladimir Nabokov: The American Years*], 435, I suggest Kinbote's very active homosexuality and extreme paranoia as one of Nabokov's many deliberate counterblasts to Freud, since Freud explains paranoia in terms of *repressed* homosexuality.

9. I have corrected the text's erroneous "principles."

Bibliography

WORKS BY NABOKOV

Pale Fire. New York: Putnam's, 1962; corrected ed., New York: Vintage, 1989.

Poems and Problems. New York: McGraw-Hill, 1970.

SECONDARY SOURCES

Boyd, Brian. *Vladimir Nabokov: The American Years.* Princeton, N.J.: Princeton University Press, 1991.

Calinescu, Matei. *Rereading.* New Haven, Conn.: Yale University Press, 1993.

Hutchinson, Peter. *Games Authors Play.* London: Methuen, 1983.

Pifer, Ellen. *Nabokov and the Novel.* Cambridge, Mass.: Harvard University Press, 1980.

Maurice Couturier (essay date 1999)

SOURCE: Couturier, Maurice. "The Near-Tyranny of the Author: *Pale Fire.*" In *Nabokov and His Fiction: New Perspectives,* edited by Julian W. Connolly, pp. 54-72. Cambridge: Cambridge University Press, 1999.

[*In the following essay, Couturier exposes Nabokov's "tyrannical" desire to prevent readers of* Pale Fire *from interpreting the text.*]

Few contemporary novels have continued to baffle readers for so long as Nabokov's ***Pale Fire,*** an authentic *tour de force.* Joyce's *Ulysses* has, from the start, teased the annotators to elucidate the many linguistic and intertextual enigmas it teems with, and challenged critics from all walks of academia to provide inspired interpretations, but it remains largely open structurally and encourages the reader to appropriate it creatively and to apply to it the methodological grids at his disposal. One might say that *Ulysses,* which has proven to be an inexhaustible source of high-flown gnoses, is reader-friendly, whereas ***Pale Fire,*** more than a generation after its first publication, remains durably reader-resistant. The latest row in 1997-98 on the electronic Nabokov Forum (NABOKV-L) over the question of who invented whom in the novel bears evidence that, no matter how many of its so-called secrets have been cracked, it remains as disturbing as it was when it first came out, as if its author, before departing upon his aeonian crusade on Anti-Terra, had safely locked it in a poetic belt and catapulted the key into inter-galactic space on his way.

Since Mary McCarthy's celebrated "Bolt from the Blue," each new exegete who has tried to tackle this difficult novel, the present one included, has paused more or less as a lucky space-traveler who would have stumbled upon the magic key, until someone came around and told him or her that he or she had obviously brought back the wrong key, since the belt—the text—remained hermetically locked. The first article I published on Nabokov some twenty-three years ago dealt precisely with this novel;[1] and so did, in large part, the paper I read behind the Iron Curtain in 1977.[2] Looking back upon the obstinate research that I have been carrying out on the modern novel these last twenty-five years, I realize that, all the time, I have been trying to find that devilish key, perhaps in a hopeless attempt to outwit Nabokov. This acknowledgment, too painfully reminiscent of Kinbote's arrogance, is unlikely to gain approval among fellow Nabokovians, I fear; but having undertaken to deconstruct the mechanisms of bad faith, I prefer to show my cards (or should I say "my map," both words being translations of the word *"carte"* in French?) right away, especially as the present essay constitutes a report of my latest, hopefully my last, expedition into the intergalactic space separating Kinbote's Zembla from Shade's Sybilland.

Beyond the ludic view of the text promoted by Mary McCarthy, Robert Alter, Julia Bader, and many others, myself included, beyond Page Stegner's Kinbotian interpretation, or Andrew Field or Brian Boyd's Shadean reading of the novel, there is room, I propose, for a third, intratextual (and mildly intersubjective) approach which balances one text, one text-based author, against the other, and allows the reader-critic to free himself from the real author's hold on his text without running the risk of emulating Kinbote's unscholarly stance. This approach, which is in no way based on intentionality,[3] implies that one overlook Nabokov's statements concerning his novel (at first, at least) and test the various reading contracts proposed in the text itself, and that one pay close attention to the various elements of overdetermination which bespeak the desire of the real author as "dictator" and constitute paradoxical and problematic points of contact between real author and real reader, the only genuine subjects, beyond the narrators and characters, involved in textual exchange.

Of the five main functions of literary criticism as I see them—formalist (linguistic, narratological, generic), genetic (biographical, historical), hermeneutic (mimetic, psychoanalytical, didactic, metaphysical, etc.), esthetic, and pragmatic (perlocutionary, affective . . .)[4]—I am aware of putting more emphasis on the first, third, and fifth, than on the other two, though I realize that an intersubjective approach (any approach, perhaps) often leads one to cross borders. Since many of the misunderstandings between the exegetes of this difficult novel come, I am convinced, from a fuzzy definition of one's critical objectives, I felt it necessary to take these methodological precautions before launching upon my textual quest, my eventual goal being to analyze the reader's response to the author's "tyranny," and to propose a possible strategy, based on psychoanalysis (which, in the circumstances, may go all the way back to Aristotle's catharsis), that will enable the reader-critic to free himself with profit and pleasure from the textual belt.[5]

THE READING CONTRACTS

Kinbote proposes a reading contract of the whole book in his "Foreword" when he advises the reader to consult the notes first "and then study the poem with their help, rereading them of course as he goes through its text, and perhaps, after having done with the poem, consulting them a third time so as to complete the picture."[6] Yet, this recommendation appears some sixteen pages into his Foreword in which he has crammed enough damning elements to make us doubt his words and laugh at his presumptions that assume unscholarly proportions when, in an oft-quoted aphorism, he claims that "for better or worse, it is the commentator who has the last word" (29 ["Foreword"]). It is because Kinbote appears as a disagreeable and arrogant character in this Foreword, and also because we tend to obey the law which intimates that we read a book page after page, that we naturally tend to disregard his recommendations and to read the book in the order in which it is presented.

There are a number of data provided by him, however, which have a favorable influence on the way we read the poem: the fact that the poet died the very day he ended or nearly ended his poem, that Kinbote virtually stole the manuscript, that the poet's wife wanted to retrieve it, that a campaign was launched about it on campus, etc. Before we even start reading the poem (at least the first time), we know that it has been the object of a petty feud between people struggling to appropriate it. This "battle of the poem" encourages us to read it with an open mind, without any of the preconceptions or prejudices that Kinbote and, indirectly, his opponents have tried to plant in us. This clever strategy, which contradicts the reading contract Kinbote was trying to impose in his Foreword, must indeed be attributed to a higher narrative instance. That is how, I suggest, the authorial figure appears for the first time in the novel: in the hiatus between Kinbote's restricted (and crazy) reading contract, which gives precedence to the commentary, and the more open contract which gives precedence to the poem, at least for the time being.

The poem does not seem, at first, to raise any problem in terms of narrative reliability: we take on trust everything it says about the poet himself, his parents, his wife, his daughter, his metaphysical views about death, his methods of composition and his esthetic theory. We blissfully absorb its lexical and specular virtuosity, we sympathize with the tortured parents who are painfully aware of their daughter's absence of a love life, with their grief after she commits suicide. As we do so, we totally overlook Kinbote's pretensions, nay his existence even, realizing that we are here in the presence of a highly sincere and sensitive man who needs to exorcize his fear of death and his affliction after his daughter's disappearance. At no time are we tempted to look up the annotations, having realized by now that Kinbote was much too unreliable to be trusted.

Indeed, we may be tempted to consider John Shade as the author's mouthpiece, or rather his ideal self, in view of the accepted fact that lyrical poetry is always the expression of the author's feelings, opinions or emotions. Yet, the poem is not signed "Vladimir Nabokov" but "John Shade," and since its thematics depend so much on the word games this name lends itself to, as in the very first line, for instance ("I was the shadow of the waxwing slain . . ."), we gradually begin to view Shade as another persona, different—to what extent, we don't know—from the real author, but expressing opinions and feelings that the real author (narcissistic at heart, like all authors) would, we assume, readily make his own. Hence the impression that the authorial figure is hovering over the poem more authentically than it does over the Foreword, though that figure remains terribly elusive. So, it is not the text of the poem itself which raises any problem in terms of narrative contract but the fact that it is attributed to an "invented poet." Nabokov crosses the boundaries here (as he also does in *Lolita* and *Ada*) between two literary genres, lyrical poetry on the one hand and the modernist novel on the other: the poem expresses genuine feelings, intense emotions, but we are prompted to believe that those feelings and emotions are not those of the actual poet, Nabokov, but of one of his puppets. The authorial figure, whose hidden purpose and desires still remain inaccessible, looms larger than in the Foreword, because the literary genre involved here leaves less room for lying or simulating than does the critical genre mimicked in the Foreword.

The commentary lends itself to at least three, and probably four, simultaneous reading contracts. The first one, indirectly suggested by the Foreword, consists in identifying the traces of Kinbote's unreliability and megalomania, in viewing the text as a madman's delirious fantasy with no other purpose than to bolster a shaky identity. We take it almost for granted that the commentary has nothing to do, or practically nothing to do, with the poem, that it is the invention of a madman, a parasitic text only tangentially related to Shade's poem—a text somewhat similar to Daniel Paul Schreber's *Denkwürdigkeiten eines nervenkranken* which Freud analyzed in a 1911 article. This reading contract will be given additional legitimacy when Professor Botkin appears in a parenthesis, one step behind Professor Pnin: "Speaking of the Head of the bloated Russian Department, Professor Pnin, a regular martinet in regard to his underlings (happily, Professor Botkin, who taught in another department, was not subordinated to that grotesque 'perfectionist')" (155 [line 172 n.]). The name's spurious etymology had been parenthetically mentioned earlier ("one who makes bottekins, fancy footwear" [100]); it becomes a common noun later in an oblique reference to Shakespeare (220 [line

493 n.]). The autotextual reference (that is, the reference to Nabokov's previous novel) has rarely been exploited in the study of *Pale Fire*. In *Pnin*, there are two conjuring tricks: firstly, the heterodiegetic narrator is supplanted by a homodiegetic one who was once Pnin's rival; and, secondly, the protagonist is supplanted professionally by Cockerell who, despite the fact that he is represented in the third person till the end, seems to be the most likely (and the least likeable because the most prejudiced) homodiegetic narrator. This game of substitution is carried on from *Pnin* to *Pale Fire*; it is in fact one of Nabokov's most consistent narrative ploys, from *Despair* to *The Real Life of Sebastian Knight* and *Lolita.* Amorous rivalry of one kind or the other is often at the root of this game.

The second reading contract turns the commentary into a fable, not unlike a medieval romance, which contains some elements of suspense, not the least of which concerns the dénouement, that is, the way this incredible story will merge with Kinbote's American "reality." From this perspective, the commentary contains a gothic story in reverse. Whereas, in a gothic story, the narrative takes its roots in reality and gradually grades into the supernatural, the story here starts as a sheer fantasy but gradually becomes anchored in reality as the King (and later Gradus himself) leaves implausible Zembla, travels across reality's antechamber (that is, Western Europe), and parachutes down to earthy America. In accordance with this contract, suggested as early as the Foreword ("imagine a historical personage whose knowledge of money is limited to the abstract billions of a national debt; imagine an exiled prince" [17 ("Foreword")]), we believe or feign to believe that Kinbote is indeed Charles Xavier, King of Zembla; after all, romances and novels contain many implausible stories and it does not occur to us to question their "truth" as stories. Paradoxically, it is Shade's poem, firmly anchored as it is in modern-day America, which prevents us from sticking throughout to this reading contract. Kinbote cannot be both Shade's colleague and neighbor and the deposed King of Zembla—unless, of course, we assume that he has invented Shade and written the poem himself, but this reductionist interpretation does not do justice to the virtuosity of the text, as I am trying to show. We are led to conclude that the story told in the commentary cannot be true to facts the way the story told in the poem probably was; nonetheless, we gradually consider that, no matter how implausible it may be, it is far more exciting and imaginative than Shade's own banal story. We are even tempted to consider Kinbote's imagination as stronger than Shade's.

The third reading contract is the one openly proposed by Kinbote himself, namely that the notes offer a more or less enlightening commentary on Shade's poem. Having previously read the foreword, we are now strongly biased against Kinbote who reasserts his pretensions in the first note: "Incidentally, it is curious to note that a crested bird called in Zemblan *sampel* ('silktail') . . ." (73 [lines 1-4 n.]). It is all too obvious that he is trying to foist his Zemblan allegorical interpretation of the poem upon us. In the second note, he avails himself of a variant, unreferenced in the index, to launch the king's story proper; later, however, he will confess that the two lines in the variant "are distorted and tainted by wistful thinking," but he will refuse to erase them, alleging the following reasons: "I could strike them out before publication but that would mean reworking the entire note, or at least a considerable part of it, and I have no time for such stupidities" (227-28 [line 550 n.]). Indeed, striking them out would not simply mean "reworking the entire note" but canceling out the whole saga which largely hangs upon this very tenuous thread.

Kinbote gives us, indeed, enough elements to question his sanity and to consider him as an unscrupulous critic who wants to smuggle the King's story (or his own fantasy) into Shade's poem, stealing the latter in the process. But what if he can prove that the poem is a metaphorical rendering of the King's story? There are indeed plenty of echoes between the poem (not only the variants) and the commentary which the critics have patiently tabulated and which gradually suggest that Kinbote's pretensions may not be as extravagant as they seemed at first. I will take only one example which I analyzed in my 1976 article: the poetic parallel between the opening lines of the poem and the "limpid tintarron" passage of the commentary. Through the waxwing parable, John Shade represents the suicide of Narcissus, the waxwing dying at the very moment when it meets its reflection in the windowpane; the poet, borrowing its wings phoenix-like, pursues the fatal trajectory, and duplicates himself and his furniture outside on the grass or the snow: "The windowpane is no longer a cutting edge: it does not separate life from death, day from night, but makes for greater fluidity of the inside and the outside, of the 'real' and the imaginary."[7] This windowpane, as I suggested then, is more or less a replica of the printed page as an interface between the elusive author and the inquisitive reader who seeks to make contact with him, the dead waxwing representing as it were the absent and dead author who, from his distant nothingness, continues to assert his law upon us and therefore upon Shade as well, though to a lesser degree.

This beautiful opening is magically reflected by Kinbote in his commentary when he describes the King's fleeting confrontation with one of his conniving impersonators:

In its limpid tintarron he saw his scarlet reflection but, oddly enough, owing to what seemed to be at first blush an optical illusion, this reflection was not at his feet but much further; moreover, it was accompanied by the ripple-warped reflection of a ledge that jutted high above his present position. And finally, the strain on the magic of the image caused it to snap as his redsweatered, red-capped doubleganger turned and vanished, whereas he, the observer, remained immobile. He now advanced to the very lip of the water and was met there by a genuine reflection, much larger and clearer than the one that had deceived him.

(143 [line 149 n.])

The word "tintarron," a rare noun in English, is presented as a Zemblan word in the index: "a precious glass stained a deep blue, made in Bokay, a medieval place in the mountains of Zembla" (314 ["Index"]). This passage suggests, indeed, that Zembla is a metaphorical representation of the more ordinary world represented poetically in Shade's poem. This passage as a whole magically reflects the opening lines of the poem, the receding images of the King mirroring the receding images of Shade and his furniture in the poem; it appears in the note to line 171 which refers to the "great conspiracy" concerning "the truth / About survival after death" (39), which suggests that this specular game, like the one described in the opening lines, refers not to death as a tragedy of loss, but to death as the extinction of the self.

Such beautiful passages—and there are many more in the commentary—induce the reader to disregard the referential value of Kinbote's commentary and to privilege its imaginary and poetic value on a par with the poem which, at first, it simply seemed to caricature. This interpretation leads us to adopt a fourth reading contract: to test the commentary against the poem and the poem against the commentary, not only in terms of poetic value, however, but also in terms of reference: if there are so many echoes between the poem and the commentary, is it because Kinbote playfully (poetically?) drew upon the poem's most tenuous suggestions to invent his extravagant saga, or because Shade could not help echoing the story Kinbote was telling him at the time when he was composing his poem? Both interpretations are acceptable, in my view. The first one would probably imply that Kinbote/Botkin, far from being only a megalomaniac or a madman, is also and above all a gifted writer in his own right; the second would naturally be less in his favor. Having no way to decide which of these two interpretations is correct, and being rather inclined to accept them both at the same time, I play one text against the other as if they were mirror images of each other and try to recompose them, to "refigure" them as Paul Ricoeur would put it, as one single text reflecting one single authorial figure.

METATEXTUALITY

This twin-faced interpretation, which eventually conflates all the three reading contracts of the commentary mentioned above, amounts to putting Shade on the same level, both as protagonist and "narrator," as Kinbote himself, and to view **Pale Fire** as a highly elaborate metatextual novel in the tradition of *Pamela, Bleak House,* or *The Sound and the Fury,* to mention only a few. The metatextual novel, like the fragmented novel *à la* Beckett, is a highly daunting text which forces the reader to enter its black box and compels him to try and recompose or refigure it in an attempt to free himself from it. But there are sometimes inconsistencies in the text which providentially allow us to make contact with the author as a fallible craftsman. Such is the case in *Pamela,* for instance. The editor who, in the preface, had listed the reasons which had induced him to publish this collection of letters, does not disappear completely from the text once the exchange of letters begins but continues to intervene throughout the novel. The first time he allows his voice to be heard is in a long footnote following a poem which begins as follows:

> Here it is necessary the reader should know, that when Mr B. found Pamela's virtue was not to be subdued, and he had in vain tried to conquer his passion for her, he had ordered his Lincolnshire coachman to bring his travelling chariot from thence, in order to prosecute his base designs upon the innocent virgin; for he cared not to trust his Bedfordshire coachman, who, with the rest of the servants, so greatly loved and honoured the fair damsel.[8]

As all the letters which had been exchanged since the opening of the book had been written by either Pamela or by her parents, there was apparently no other way for the author to inform the reader of Mr. B.'s evil design and of his intention to sequestrate Pamela. It is in the above footnote that we learn how Mr. B. intercepts Pamela's letters and that we are given to read the letter he sent to her father; after Mr. B.'s letter, the footnote continues with another letter written by Pamela and addressed to Mrs. Jervis. Richardson was unable to stick to the narrative contract he had adopted at the start and felt it necessary to give his reader information no other plausible letter-writer could have provided. Later, the epistolary scheme will turn into a mere diary, Pamela being unable to communicate with her parents anymore.

As this obvious example shows, it is when the narrative contract changes that the authorial figure, the author's desire to guide his reader, appears in the text. In **Pale Fire,** there are indeed many more narrative contracts at work than in *Pamela* but they are so cleverly combined that it is difficult, often impossible, to pinpoint the exact moment when a shift is made. Let us list these contracts again:

—the commentary (Foreword included) is a madman's fantasy with no other purpose than to bolster a shaky identity

—the commentary is a fable, no less extravagant than many medieval romances

—the notes offer a more or less enlightening commentary of Shade's poem

—commentary and poem are mirror images of each other

Each contract implies a different relationship between Shade and Kinbote:

—in the first, Kinbote is the madman and Shade the sane man

—in the second, Kinbote's text is an inflated, referentless fable, whereas Shade's poem is a lyrical text which takes its roots in the poet's life and experience

—in the third, the poem takes precedence over the commentary, and therefore the poet over his commentator

—in the fourth one, which conflates the previous three, poem and commentary, poet and commentator are more or less on the same level, the authorial figure looming prominently over the novel as a whole

In all four readings, the intratextual writers take precedence over their respective texts, defining themselves as they do in terms of their opposition to each other. Here are some of the main points on which they radically differ:

—Kinbote is a homosexual, Shade a heterosexual

—Kinbote is left-handed, Shade right-handed

—Kinbote had many lovers, Shade only one

—Kinbote is childless, Shade has a daughter

—Kinbote is a Christian, Shade an agnostic

—Kinbote is a music lover, Shade is not

—Kinbote is a vegetarian, Shade is not

—Kinbote is tall and erect, Shade short and twisted

—Kinbote is athletic, Shade is clumsy

—Kinbote is bearded, Shade is clean-shaven . . .

On the other hand, they also have many points in common, as Michael Long pointed out: "Shade and Kinbote are both liberal in opinion. Both are haters of violence. Both are lovers of literature. Both are scorners of orthodoxy. Both are scholars of a sort and poets of a sort. Both love wine and word-games. Each has his own kind of arrogance and irascibility, and his own little bundle of Strong Opinions, on trivial matters as well as serious ones."[9] Bringing all these things together, Long concludes: "Their deepest points of contact have to do with the centre of the Nabokovian world," and he points out, for instance, that they both "lost their fathers in infancy."[10] Long, who only refers to the "centre of the Nabokovian world," refrains in part from surrendering to intentional fallacy; his interpretation remains text-based rather than biography-based, but it presupposes that the text contains elements whose roots are grounded in the real author.

If we now put together the many reading contracts that can be applied to the commentary and, indirectly, to the whole novel, as well as the similarities and dissimilarities between Shade and Kinbote, we begin to realize that we have been the victims of an illusion, the illusion that the text is inhabited by two full-fledged subjects who are both endowed with an individual unconscious. In point of fact, I would suggest, these two text-based subjects reflect two complementary facets of one single but schizoid subject who is preoccupied with his sexual identity and with death, and who tries to unburden himself of these obsessions by generating a kind of paranoia in us, hoping to divert our attention from himself, the primary enunciator of the text. It is this partially reconstructed subject with his conflicting desires and inhibitions but also with his virtuosity in composing such a poetic and intricately woven text, that I call the authorial figure. It is the evocation of this figure that allows me to shift from a formalist description of the text in terms of contracts to an interpretation in terms of desire, and thus to get out of the black box of the text. So long as I remain within the text, I am merely describing the novel but remain unable to interpret it. Shade and Kinbote are not the prime enunciators of the text but the author's paradoxical masks. Interpreting the text requires that we identify the author's desire to impose the tyrannical law of his ideal self upon us and his determination to prevent us from having access to his unconscious self.

The Authorial Figure

There is in fact nothing revolutionary in this communication-based approach to fiction and fiction-writing. In *Tristram Shandy,* Sterne humorously explained that writing is a form of conversation:

> Writing, when properly managed (as you may be sure I think mine is) is but a different name for conversation: As no one, who knows what he is about in good company would venture to talk all,—so no author, who understands the just boundaries of decorum and good breeding, would presume to think all. The truest respect which you can pay to the reader's understanding, is to halve this matter amicably, and leave him something to imagine, in his turn, as well as yourself.[11]

There is, perhaps, no better presentation of a truly inter-subjective theory of the novel: the matter must be "halved . . . amicably" between the author and the reader; if the writer is too complacent and does not make sufficient attempts to communicate with his reader, the book will remain a kind of unread and unreadable blank, as some of Beckett's later texts, like "Ping," are; if, on the other hand, the reader does not do his share of the work, the book will remain an intimidating or a boring puzzle. To be sure, there are large differences between oral and literary communication, as Marshall McLuhan and Walter Ong have pointed out, but the similarities are important, too. In daily conversation the speaker can monitor his discourse upon the verbal and non-verbal reactions of his interlocutor; each, though, strives to free himself from the other's law while trying to promote the best possible image of himself in the other's eyes. They both labor under the law of the Lacanian Other of which they, each in turn, claim to be the interpreters when passing judgment on their interlocutor's discourse. In a conversation between two lovers, each speaker addresses the other's ideal ego, an attitude which naturally fosters an illusion of fusion and identification and gives the lovers the impression that they have freed themselves from the law of the Other; they are mistaken, of course, since, as Lacan intimates, the Other also orders the subjects to desire, if only to play their role in the perpetuation of the race.

Textual exchange is, in many respects, a conflation of oral and literary exchange,[12] a form of communication in which the two interlocutors, the author and the reader, both love and hate each other, both passionately depend upon each other but also resent the other's intervention which can lead to dramatic disclosures. They are never face to face, except in such exceptional situations as poetry readings. The author has no other instruments at his disposal than those ciphered into his text to guide or mislead his reader, even though, at times, as we shall later see in the case of Nabokov, he makes belated attempts to put his reader on the "right" or the "wrong" track in his non-fictional pronouncements. And the reader, wary of the intrinsic differences in terms of truth and sincerity between fictional and non-fictional discourse,[13] cannot ask him any question, supposing he was in a position to; neither can he summon biographical data, which, if they might provide a genetic explanation of the text, would not guarantee the legitimacy of one's interpretation of it. The author asserts his superiority over his reader, adopting a one-up position, as Gregory Bateson's disciples' would put it.[14] But, as he tries to indulge his desires, to gain admiration and promote the best possible image of himself (three contradictory priorities, as it were), he unmistakably feels that he is surrendering too much of himself and exposing himself to the analyses that will be proposed by his readers. The complex narrative strategies used in modernist and post-modernist fiction serve all these contradictory purposes at one and the same time: they dazzle the reader and make him wish to commune with the magician who invented them, but they also constitute shrewd denials and indirectly invite the reader to decipher the unwritten, somewhat guilty, pages of the text, and to play the part of the compassionate or complicitous analyst. The reader resents the authorial law ciphered into the text; he would like to appropriate the literary object and use it as the lame depository of his intellectual, aesthetic, or erotic desire, but, if he does not want to be an impostor and purloin the text as Kinbote purloins Shade's text, he must refrain from indulging himself too much in that way. It is in this complex interplay of desires and challenges that the web of the text which Barthes writes about in *The Pleasure of the Text* is woven. A novel is an interface that brings together and keeps apart the author and the reader, compelling them to change places all the time and to enter the black box of the text.

Why speak of the authorial figure, though? And wouldn't it be simpler to speak only of the real author? To me, the real author is a dead subject who once desired and created works of art, and whom the text represents here for me in my act of reading. Biographical criticism attempts to resurrect the dead author and to read the text as he meant it, without taking into acount the fact that the subject is inevitably cleft (he is the subject of his unconscious, to borrow Lacan's theory) and therefore capable of bad faith. Formalist criticism is aware of this bad faith, though it makes little use of it, but it refuses to take into account the author's will to say, seeking to establish the meaning-within-a-given-interpretative-grid of the text; it largely depends, therefore, on the methodological tools it mobilizes: literary conventions, narratology, intertextuality, linguistics, etc.

The two chief anchorings of critical reading are indeed, as Wolfgang Iser claims, the text and the reader as signifying subject.[15] Yet, whereas Iser considers the text as a disembodied signifying object, I consider it as an interface between two subjects, separated temporally and spatially, who passionately desire each other, seeking, and running away from, each other at one and the same time. It is this meshing of desires that I would totally miss were I to propose a purely formalist analysis of the text; the analysis would betray my intellectual desire to master the restive object, but it would speak less of the author's ciphered desire than of the semiotic grid used for the purpose. Meaning, in a literary text, cannot be an ideal, disembodied object: it is necessarily a meaning for a subject who, within the black box of a novel, can temporarily be a character or a narrator. Reading a novel requires therefore that the instances in which the transitional meanings are anchored be identified.

Those instances being themselves embedded at various levels, as I have shown throughout *La Figure de l'auteur*,[16] one eventually reaches the authorial instance which is not at all Booth's implied author. That concept was invented precisely in order to keep the real author totally out of the text: it is invoked mostly in reference to third-person novels where there is no intratextual enunciator; the homodiegetic narrators in novels like *Tristram Shandy,* **Lolita,** or **Pale Fire** are considered therefore as the ultimate enunciators, which, naturally, they are not. It is a fuzzy concept which has neither narratological, nor linguistic, nor psychological foundation. The authorial figure, on the other hand, is an enunciation-based construct: it is the prime enunciator of the text as reconstructed by the reader in the act of reading. This reconstruction depends on various elements of the text: some are linguistic, others narratological, others again thematic. The authorial figure takes its roots in the over-determination of the text on the one hand, and, on the other hand, in the analytic work done by the reader and the chords that the themes of the text strike in him, which naturally (and fortunately) leaves room for misunderstanding. The author's insistence upon over-determining his text and promoting the reader's aesthetic admiration, as well as his need to make of it an efficient screen to keep the reader at a safe distance, lead him to project his ideal self onto the text. It is the ideal self's desire (the ideal self being always to some extent the reversed image of the unconscious, as Freud pointed out) that the reader identifies and that allows him to start constructing the authorial figure - a figure who, from the reader's perhaps limited point of view, stands here and now for the real author who is absent or dead. The authorial figure, being reader-based, can naturally be at variance with the real author, either because, in his reading practice, the reader has overlooked important clues and allowed his desires and fantasies to overrule the text, or because the author managed after all to fool his ideal self. The latter possibility is much less plausible: no matter how imaginative and poetically inventive a writer may be, it is most unlikely that he could project into his work a self and therefore an unconscious totally disconnected from his own, though he can distribute it in various ways among his fictional characters or narrators, as Freud explained in a lecture given in 1907: "The psychological novel in general no doubt owes its special nature to the inclination of the modern writer to split up his ego, by self-observation, into many part-egos, and, in consequence, to personify the conflicting currents of his own mental life in several heroes."[17]

The evocation of the "Viennese witch doctor" may sound sacrilegious, considering Nabokov's countless forays against him, but, in my view, this approach is the only way to get out of the black box of the text, to avoid being forever bogged down in the marshes of description (and annotation), and therefore to free oneself from the author's tyranny. Nabokov was right, of course, to denounce many of the gross simplifications that psychoanalysis has been guilty of, but he shared many of Freud's preoccupations as the superb psychological acumen that he displays throughout his fiction testifies. It is Freud's theory of the unconscious, of course, that he rejected, being passionately convinced that he exerted full control over himself and his literary inventions; and he certainly did, more than most writers, but his obsessions, sexual and otherwise, show that he had a powerful unconscious and a very creative one (thank goodness for that), and that he was using his marvelous talent to cope with it. After dealing with nympholepsy in *Lolita,* he dealt with homosexuality in *Pale Fire,* and with incest in *Ada.* I personally interpret his clever narrative ploy in all three novels both as a strategy to confuse his readers by putting them in a paradoxical situation and as an attempt to blind them to his intense preoccupation with the question of sexual identity, which is central to these three masterpieces and many of his other novels. This interpretation, if it accounts for the complexity of the text as a mask and allows one to free oneself from its black box by cracking the Shade—Kinbote enigma, does not in any way reduce the magnitude of the author's achievement. Nabokov's (near)-tyranny or aesthetic desire was, I presume, proportional to the intensity of his erotic desire, but this conviction, grounded in psychoanalysis as much as in my refusal to surrender to the intentional fallacy, does not entitle me in any way to shout "Eureka!" and to claim that I have discovered *the* meaning of the text, the Shade—Kinbote enigma being only one element—though very important—of this clever novel.[18] The concept of the authorial figure, based on an interactive theory of the text, provides, I think, a useful key to solve some of the problems that the critics have been asking themselves since Forster, Lubbock, Booth, Barthes, Genette, and Stanzel, and that contemporary theoreticians like Iser, Banfield, and Fludernik still attempt to tackle. It does not replace previous theories but neatly complements them by showing that author and reader belong to the same system and try to negotiate their respective places.

POSTSCRIPTS

Indirectly, Nabokov himself demonstrates that the text of his novel is not entirely self-sufficient. Besides the references to poet John Shade elsewhere in his writings, in the unpublished introduction mentioned by Boyd or again in *Ada,* he made a number of declarations about *Pale Fire* in his letters and interviews which confirm his desire to guide or influence his reader further as if he wished to amend or to complete his text. He claimed, for instance, in a letter written a few months before the publication of *Pale Fire,* that the "commentary *is* the novel" (*SL* [*Selected Letters*], 332). How does Shade's poem fit in the book? He does not explain. Perhaps he means that the plot of the book is hatched in the commentary and the commentary only, but, to be sure, it depends a great deal upon the existence of the poem it-

self, as I have tried to show in my presentation of the four reading contracts. This aside suggests that Nabokov himself, Frankenstein-like, was not too sure how to consider his own book and wondered whether his creation had not started to have a life of its own that he could not fully control any longer.

There are two main enigmas in the novel that no one had been able to solve until Nabokov pointed out the solution. To Alfred Appel's question, "Where, please, are the crown jewels hidden?" Nabokov answered tongue in cheek: "In the ruins, sir, of some old barracks near Kobaltana (q.v.); but do not tell it to the Russians" (*SO* [*Strong Opinions*], 92). Kobaltana appears in the index but in a cryptic entry which ends with the words: "not in the text" (310). In this case, the author has clearly been playing a little game with the reader, taking him on a merry-go-round of cross-references, and prompting him to look for "fictitious" jewels as if they were real ones. He is as unreliable in this case as Humbert Humbert was when he discovered from Lolita the name of his rival but flippantly declined to tell us, claiming that we must have guessed long ago. Nabokov clearly wants us to believe that he is the one and only keeper of the book's secret.

The same reasoning would apply in the case of the coded message taken down by Hazel Shade in the barn. Many "translations" had been proposed by the critics but none were as satisfactory as the one given by Nabokov himself to Andrew Field on September 26, 1966:

> As Nabokov has noted privately, the message can be decoded as a garbled warning via Hazel "to her father and hint at the title of the poem to be written many years later. *Padre* should *not go* to the *lane* to be mistaken for *old Goldswart* (worth) after finishing his *tale* (pale) *feur* (fire) [which in Shakespeare is accompanied by] the word 'arrant' (*farant*) [and this] with '*lant*' makes up the Atalanta butterfly in Shade's last scene. It is '*told*' by the spirit in the barn."[19]

Curiously, Field does not communicate this information to his reader as if he were afraid that Nabokov was pulling his leg. The message makes sense, however, but, as far as I know, there is no built-in code in the novel that could have allowed us to decipher it. Of course, we may wonder if the whole passage is not Kinbote's invention rather than Hazel's transcription, which prompts us to resume the annotation game within the black box. Nabokov made another remark concerning Kinbote which projects us outside the limits of the book:

> I think it is so nice that the day on which Kinbote committed suicide (and he certainly did after putting the last touches to his edition of the poem) happens to be both the anniversary of Pushkin's *Lyceum* and that of "poor old man Swift" 's death, which is news to me (but see variant in note to line 231).

> (*SO,* 74-75)

He did not mean to refer to Pushkin or Swift, but he did mean to say that Kinbote committed suicide on October 19, the date on which, we assume, the demented commentator finished his Foreword and his editorial work.

Should Nabokov's statements about his novel be taken seriously? Or wouldn't they constitute another facet of the demented mask games that he plays with us in his fiction? Deception, as he explains to Allene Talmey in one of his interviews, is as essential to his art as it is to nature:

> Deception is practiced even beautifully by that other V. N., Visible Nature. A useful purpose is assigned by science to animal mimicry, protective patterns and shapes, yet their refinement transcends the crude purpose of mere survival. In art, an individual style is essentially as futile and as organic as a fata morgana. The slight-of-hand you mention is hardly more than an insect's sleight-of-wing. A wit might say that it protects me from half-wits. A grateful spectator is content to applaud the grace with which the masked performer melts into Nature's background.
>
> (*SO,* 153)

Shade apparently shares his view on the subject; he says to Kinbote: "when I hear a critic speaking of an author's sincerity I know that either the critic or the author is a fool" (156 [l. 172 n.]).

In all his postscripts to the novel, Nabokov continues to play with us, but he also claims emphatically that the reader will never be able to crack all the novel's secrets without his help, that he is or has the final key that can open all the doors. He obviously wants to make sure that we will never be able to get out of the black box of the text and have access to his desire and his real self behind or beyond the text. These afterthoughts, no matter how much they owe to Nabokov's forethoughts, only confirm the interpretation I have proposed in the present essay: they show the author trying to reassert his authority over us and confirm his total control over his text and his masks; indirectly, also, they betray his doubts about his sanity and his sexual identity. In his last novel, **Look at the Harlequins!,** he was to undertake a last titanic struggle against one of his caricatural doubles, ending his text upon a gaping sentence or a snore.

Notes

1. Maurice Couturier, "Nabokov's *Pale Fire,* or the Purloined Poem," *Revue Française d'Etudes Américaines,* 1 (April 1976): 55-69.

2. See "The Subject on Trial in Nabokov's Novels" in *Proceedings of a Symposium on American Literature,* ed. Marta Sienecka (Poznan University Press, 1980). That symposium, which took place in September 1977, was the first on American literature to be held behind the Iron Curtain.

3. At the second Nice conference on Nabokov, David Lodge accused Brian Boyd of intentional fallacy in his interpretation of *Pale Fire.* See David Lodge, "What Kind of Fiction did Nabokov Write? A Practitioner's View," *Cycnos* 12.2 (1995): 142-43, and *The Practice of Writing* (London: Secker & Warburg, 1996), 162. The problem of "intentionality" is obviously very complex and cannot be as easily shrugged off as it could a generation ago.

4. I am currently preparing a book in which I examine the endless crossovers between these five functions.

5. The title of this article is of course an oblique reference to the subtitle of my second book on Nabokov, *Nabokov ou la tyrannie de l'auteur* (Paris: Ed. du Seuil, "Coll. Poétique," 1993).

6. *Pale Fire* (New York: Vintage International, 1989), 28, ("Foreword"). All subsequent citations appear in the text.

7. Couturier, "Nabokov's *Pale Fire,* or the Purloined Poem," 58.

8. Samuel Richardson, *Pamela* (Harmondsworth: Penguin Books, 1980), 123.

9. Michael Long, *Marvell, Nabokov: Childhood and Arcadia* (Oxford: Clarendon Press, 1984), 181.

10. *Ibid.*

11. Laurence Sterne, *Tristram Shandy* (1760-67; Boston: Houghton Mifflin Co., 1965), 83.

12. Monika Fludernik largely confirms this theory in her recent book, *Towards a 'Natural' Narratology* (London and New York: Routledge, 1996). She does not include the author in the enunciative game, however.

13. A point cleverly analyzed by Peter Lamarque and Stein Haugom Olsen in *Truth, Fiction and Literature* (Oxford: Clarendon Press, 1994), 11-14.

14. See Paul Watzlawick, et al., *Pragmatics of Human Communication* (New York and London: W. W. Norton and Co., 1967), 67ff.

15. Wolfgang Iser, *The Act of Reading* (Baltimore: The Johns Hopkins University Press, 1978), 169.

16. See *La Figure de l'auteur* (Paris: Ed. du Seuil, "Coll. Poétique," 1993).

17. Sigmund Freud, "Creative Writers and Day-Dreaming," *Standard Edition of the Complete Psychological Works of Sigmund Freud,* IX (London: The Hogarth Press, 1959), 150.

18. See Geoffrey Green, *Freud and Nabokov* (Lincoln: University of Nebraska Press, 1988).

19. Quoted by Brian Boyd in *Vladimir Nabokov: The American Years* (Princeton University Press, 1991), 454.

Selected bibliography

Works by Vladimir Nabokov

Ada, or Ardor: A Family Chronicle, 1969; New York: Vintage International, 1990; Harmondsworth: Penguin, 1990.

Despair, 1966; New York: Vintage International, 1989; Harmondsworth: Penguin, 1990.

Lolita, 1955; New York: Vintage International, 1989; Harmondsworth: Penguin, 1995.

Lolita: A Screenplay, 1974; New York: Vintage International, 1997.

Look at the Harlequins! 1974; New York: Vintage International, 1990; Harmondsworth: Penguin, 1991.

Pale Fire, 1962; New York: Vintage International, 1989; Harmondsworth: Penguin, 1991.

Pnin, 1957; New York: Vintage International, 1989; Harmondsworth: Penguin, 1997.

The Real Life of Sebastian Knight, 1941; New York: Vintage International, 1992; Harmondsworth: Penguin, 1995.

Selected Letters, 1940-1977, ed. Dmitri Nabokov and Matthew J. Bruccoli, New York: Harcourt Brace Jovanovich/Bruccoli Clark Layman, 1989.

Work on Vladimir Nabokov

Appel, Alfred, Jr., "Conversations with Nabokov," *Novel* 4 (1971): 209-22.

Boyd, Brian, *Vladimir Nabokov: The American Years,* Princeton University Press, 1991.

Couturier, Maurice, "Nabokov's *Pale Fire,* or the Purloined Poem," *Revue Française d'Etudes Américaines* 1 (1976): 55-69.

Nabokov ou la tyrannie de l'auteur, Paris: Ed. du Seuil, "Coll. Poétique," 1993.

"The Subject on Trial in Nabokov's Novels," in *Proceedings of a Symposium on American Literature,* ed. Marta Sienecka, Poznan University Press, 1980.

Green, Geoffrey, *Freud and Nabokov,* Lincoln: University of Nebraska Press, 1988.

Lodge, David, "What Kind of Fiction did Nabokov Write? A Practitioner's View," *Cycnos* 12.2 (1995): 135-47; repr. in *The Practice of Writing,* London: Secker and Warburg, 1996.

Long, Michael, *Marvell, Nabokov: Childhood and Arcadia,* Oxford University Press, 1984.

McCarthy, Mary, "A Bolt from the Blue," *New Republic,* June 4, 1962, 21-27; repr. in Page (ed.), *Nabokov,* 124-36.

A note on abbreviations

While there is no standard edition of Vladimir Nabokov's works, the publication of a series of his works in the United States under the Vintage International imprint and in the United Kingdom under the Penguin imprint has made the bulk of his fiction available in readily accessible editions. The following is a list of abbreviations used by several of the contributors to this volume. The abbreviations refer to the Vintage International editions of Nabokov's work as well as to a number of other major English-language works by and about Nabokov. The contributors have used the following format: abbreviation of the title followed by the page number; e.g. (*Def,* 36-37). To assist readers with no access to the Vintage editions, the editor has also included the number of the chapter from which the cited material is taken; e.g. (*Def,* 36-37 [ch. 2]). For reference purposes, the date of first publication of the English-language version of a text is included below. A list of the Penguin editions of Nabokov's work is included in the *Selected bibliography* at the end of this book. All works are by Vladimir Nabokov unless otherwise stated.

SL Selected Letters, 1940-1977. Ed. Dmitri Nabokov and Matthew J. Bruccoli. New York: Harcourt Brace Jovanovich/Bruccoli Clark Layman, 1989.

SO Strong Opinions. 1973. New York: Vintage International, 1990.

Neil D. Isaacs (essay date 2002)

SOURCE: Isaacs, Neil D. "The Riddle of/in *Pale Fire.*" *Literature Interpretation Theory* 13, no. 4 (2002): 317-32.

[*In the following essay, Isaacs probes what he refers to as the "riddle" in the poem "Pale Fire," which appears in Nabokov's novel of the same name.*]

I. Riddle me this

The first two couplets of John Shade's **"Pale Fire"**[1] in Vladimir Nabokov's novel of the same name have been subjected to intense analytical and interpretive scrutiny:

> I was the shadow of the waxwing slain / By the false azure in the windowpane; / I was the smudge of ashen fluff—and I / Lived on, flew on, in the reflected sky.

(15)

Critics have exhaustively focused on such essential themes, images, metaphors, and allusions in the passage as the issue of appearance versus reality, the first of many variations on the meanings of "shadow" and "reflect," the nature of art figured forth as fluff on the one hand and eternal on the other, and the first, though oblique, reference to the source of the title in *Timon of Athens*.

But the form of the lines has gone virtually unnoticed. By form I mean neither the metrical format, rhyming pentameter couplets of a Popean or Byronic mode (depending on one's associational/allusive perspective), nor the rhetorical structure (according to whatever interpretive framework guides one's explication). I am referring rather to the generic type of engagement with an audience, in this case an explicit and conventional challenge to readers to "read" or interpret the image(s), thereby "solving" a puzzle or enigma, in order to arrive at an understanding of what is signified. In this sense, the form or genre of these lines is that of a *riddle,* a traditional format the conventional structure of which has persisted from Sophocles and the biblical Amos through Symphosius and Aldhelm to Mallarmé and Tillie Olsen, not to mention Roberto Benigni in *Life Is Beautiful*.[2]

Northrop Frye, in *The Anatomy of Criticism,* discussing "the close relation between the visual and the conceptual in poetry," observes that

> the radical of *opsis* in the lyric is *riddle,* which is characteristically a fusion of sensation and reflection, the use of an object of sense experience to stimulate a mental activity in connection with it. Riddle was originally the cognate object of read, and the riddle seems intimately involved with the whole process of reducing language to visible form, a process which runs through such by-forms of riddle as hieroglyph and ideogram.
>
> (280)

Shade's opening lines illustratively match this description. Moreover, the whole poem could be called a product of what Frye calls "the quiet mind," which,

> if it has a subject beyond recommending itself, attempts to communicate to the reader a private and secret possession, which brings us to the next cardinal point, the riddle.
>
> The idea of the riddle is descriptive containment: the subject is not described but circumscribed, a circle of words drawn around it. In simple riddles, the central subject is an image, and the reader feels impelled to guess, that is, to equate the poem to the name or sign-symbol of its image. A slightly more complicated form of the riddle is the emblematic vision, probably one of the oldest forms in human communication.
>
> (300)

There are two formulas for the presentation of a riddle. The third-person form simply asks "what—or who—is . . . ?" and describes the subject as, for example, black and white and re(a)d all over. The first-person form assumes or describes the identity of the disguised or secret subject, then asks or implies the question "what—or who—am I?" A poem like the Old English "Dream of the Rood" (an "emblematic vision" if there ever was one), with its elaborate use of prosopopoeia, demonstrates the sophisticated potential of this form of riddle (though "Dream of the Rood" is found in the Vercelli Book, not the Exeter Book, that great Anglo-Saxon repository of Riddles, perhaps including the intriguing "Wulf and Eadwacer").

Nabokov himself, composing a review of his own *Speak, Memory* in 1951, says,

> The unravelling of a riddle is the purest and most basic act of the human mind. All thematic lines mentioned are gradually brought together, are seen to interweave or converge, in a subtle but natural form of contact which is as much a function of art as it is a discoverable process in the evolution of personal destiny. Thus, toward the end of the book, the theme of mimicry of the "cryptic disguise" studied by Nabokov in his entomological pursuits, comes to a punctual rendezvous with the riddle theme, with the camouflaged solution of a chess problem, with the piecing together of a design on bits of broken pottery, and with a picture puzzle wherein the eye makes out the contours of a new country. [. . .] The solution of the riddle theme is also the solution of the theme of exile. [. . .] One cannot but respect the amount of retrospective acumen and creative concentration that the author had to summon in order to plan his book according to the way his life had been planned by unknown players of games, and never to swerve from that plan.
>
> (*Conclusive Evidence,* 126)

It is one thing to refer to Nabokov's work with metaphors of game and mirror, puzzle and solution, secret and disguise. It is quite another to find explicit reference to the value of riddle per se as form and function, method and meaning. Indeed, it is hard to read this passage without seeing therein implications for the design of the great novels to come, but especially for that of *Pale Fire.*

I will circle back to the riddle of **"Pale Fire"**—or at least the riddle *in* **"Pale Fire"** if not in *Pale Fire*—and thereby replicate the circling pattern of Shade's poem and of Kinbote's apparatus and of Nabokov's novel themselves. The point of this self-reflecting strategy is to suggest the possible significance of the recognition that the poem begins, quite deliberately, in the riddling format. Solve the riddle of the opening of **"Pale Fire,"** and we may more clearly understand some of the secrets of *Pale Fire* as disguised therein.[3]

II. THE BOYD SOLUTION

Indefatigable and ingenious, Brian Boyd, in *Nabokov's Pale Fire,* has mined the secrets of Nabokov's "plexed artistry" to provide a treasure trove of insights, interconnectedness, and allusive and textural details hitherto unrecognized or insufficiently refined. His explanations have led him, not to a final solution (the connotations of that phrase reinforce its rejection on logical grounds), but to conclusions that are hardly hesitant but barely tentative. In short, he now reads *Pale Fire* as leading the eagerly, devotedly, willingly assiduous reader to believe that, *after death,* Aunt Maud has warned Shade about his death, Hazel Shade has been the inspiration of much of Kinbote's grandiose delusions, and Shade himself has prompted the whole paranoid Gradus component in Kinbote's commentary.[4]

With great admiration for the wealth of Boyd's accomplishments in the study of Nabokov in general and *Pale Fire* in particular, and with respectful temerity, I disagree. Amid the myriad threads woven into Boyd's tapestry, though mosaic or bricolage may be metaphors more apt, I find a few small knots that give me pause. In the light of his considerable contributions, these five items might be dismissed as churlish quibbles. On the other hand, the argument may unravel from these points when they lead to what I see as a major flawed seam in the whole fabric.

First, there is an assumption that line 1000 of the poem **"Pale Fire"** is line 1 repeated; and that assumption is then repeated and relied on as fact. But it is dubious, conjectural at best, and, most important, *not in the poem.* The significant alarms (and jokes) signaled in Kinbote's "heroic couplets, of nine hundred ninety-nine lines" (Boyd 1), point to that absence. Shade's remark about "practically the entire product" (Boyd 194) does not seem to suggest the omission of one closing line repeating the opening one. Not only is that line missing, but Kinbote has described the preceding 51 lines as "extremely rough [. . .] with devastating erasures and cataclysmic insertions" (Boyd 2): Shade never gets the chance for final revisions or line(s) to complete a "Fair Copy" of his poem. It is possible, moreover, to suspect that a symmetry of 1000 lines with the thousandth looping back to the first (like mad Humbert beginning and ending with the trancing name "Lolita") is imposed by a madman whose obsessive-compulsive symptoms contribute to a thorough clinical diagnosis (see below).

Second, once the convincing argument that Kinbote intends to commit suicide is made, Boyd presumes him to *be* dead ("a novel in which four out of five main characters die" [262]). Like the poem's line 1000, Kinbote's suicide is not *in* the book. Thinking outside the box is one thing, reading off the page quite another.

Third, examining the correspondences between the King's escape through the tunnel and a type of chess problem, Boyd observes that the key move is from the square palace to Iris Acht's dressing room. *Iris Acht* (German "eight") thus becomes i8 in chess terminology,

"a king's one-step move, but now off the board" (169). This in turn betokens Kinbote's "ultimate key move" of suicide: off the page and off the board, too (which no chess problem allows in solution), not to mention around the bend.[5]

The fourth and fifth trivial items, minor knots in the weave, are similar to each other. Boyd characterizes Shade's bold reversal of La Fontaine's fable (l. 245 of **"Pale Fire"**) as saying, "while the ant is lifeless, the cicada has flown away from its 'empty emerald case.' It still lives, it can still sing its song" (189-90). But the poem says, "Dead is the mandible, alive the song" (21). Boyd's metonymic substitution of singer for song controverts the tenor of the statement, namely, that the art survives the artist.

At the same point in the argument, Boyd refers to "the waxwing of the poem's opening lines, which he [Shade] imagines flying on after its death, with the cicada still to come, whose song he will declare remains alive" (190). Now the metonymy of cicada/song is dropped, but retroposed upon the waxwing. In those opening lines, however, it is *not* the waxwing that lives on, but the "I" of the riddle, who is the waxwing's shadow and the trace of its remains, living and flying on "in the reflected sky."

As a group, these relatively inconsequential sticking points point toward a flawed seam in the argument, a faultline in its construction. Boyd refers often to Nabokov's taste both for riddles and for chess problems, but in his own usage it is the *problems* in the text that are prominent—whether or not they are modeled on the game and the puzzling delights playfully spun from its rules. In fact, when he does use *riddle,* it is as a synonym for *problem:* "the riddle of the title" (42); "all three riddles" related to the Crown Jewels (102), referring back to "not just one problem [. . .] but three" (101). A possible exception occurs when Boyd asserts, "the book clearly *is* riddling *and* obsessed with the possibility of a life beyond death" (257). In this case he may be punning on the sense "riddled with" along with "puzzle-posing," but I find no instance where the reference is to a riddle in the narrow, strict sense of Riddle.

The problem here is not, of course, a failure to recognize a riddle as a riddle. It is a pattern of accounting off the books, reading a line that isn't there, focusing on an event that never happens in the text, solving a chesslike problem with a move off the board, slipping interchangeably between the tenors and vehicles of metaphors. If we go outside the book, we may at least go to Nabokov for documentation of his delight and expertise in both chess problems and riddles. Boyd himself cites (290) passages in **Strong Opinions** where Nabokov says, "I just like composing riddles with elegant solutions" (16), and, "The solution [. . .] is so simple"

(195). Setting aside the criterion of parsimony, Boyd's solution, for all its brilliant connections and assiduous tracings (shadings?), is hardly simple and arguably inelegant.[6]

Boyd's first chapter, on the poem's Foreword, repeatedly enjoins readers to "trust" Nabokov by following Kinbote's direction to jump through the hoops of his "cross-referencing" notes before returning to the Foreword, never mind beginning the poem. There is an implicit request here to trust *Boyd* to know what Nabokov intends, which is not really all that unreasonable, but let us at least acknowledge that in this case it is *Kinbote* we are being asked to trust, a madman who tells us to read the notes first, then the poem with the notes alongside, and then the notes again.[7]

The point is that **Pale Fire** is not a poem and its *apparatus criticus*. It is a novel. We read a novel from beginning to end, even if one of its characters tells us otherwise, especially if he is insane. Kinbote's mad design is to lead us down a tortured path. To do so is to follow a controversial psychotherapeutic strategy of "entering into the pathology" of a case. I might accept such a perilous proposition, attributing it to the cleverness of an artist who is a masterful disguiser of secrets, except that it is no secret that the book is a novel *containing* a poem and critical apparatus, rather than a poem and/or apparatus *disguising itself* as a novel.

III. Solvitur Ambulando

For the psychoanalytic intervention of entering into the pathology to be effective, the therapist must be firmly rooted in reality. He or she may be very appreciative of the intricate design and elaborated texture of a psychotic patient's projected world—that's how a functional therapeutic bond is forged, after all—but to know a delusion intimately is not necessarily to embrace it. That knowledge will facilitate any possibility of success in the reality-testing required to facilitate the patient's emergence from irrational beliefs.[8]

Not only is it counterintuitive to follow Kinbote's directions on how to read **Pale Fire,** it is also impractical (and questionable practice) to accept some of the delusions as "real," some—the Zembla material—as prompted by a ghostly "voice" (though unheard by *this* schizophrenic, and perhaps in some Keatsian way sweeter therefore), and some—the Gradus material—as prompted by yet another ghostly voice with its own obsessive-compulsive needs.

Kinbote (Botkin) in his paranoid fantasizing is quite capable of exacting all the intricate interrelated details of his grandiose delusions. That is the nature of his condition. Some other aspects of the *apparatus criticus* may be explained by obsessive attention to the observable

minutiae of the manuscript in his possession: that, too, is consistent with his pathology. There remain a few details that are not so clinically appropriate, matters that seem beyond the character's capacities, inconsistent with his delusions, expressed in a voice different in kind and from a perspective different in degree.

There is a bit of confusion in Boyd's diagnosis of Kinbote's condition: "he suffers from classical paranoia in all its three main forms"; "delusions of grandeur [which], unlike those of schizophrenia or mania sufferers, tend to be detailed, coherent, stable, and persistent [. . .]; "erotic paranoia"; and "persecution mania." He also presents a "megalomaniac narcissism" (60) and "insufferable [. . .] obsessive behavior" (45). What Boyd is identifying, however, according to the standard psychiatric taxonomy,[9] are three of the five specific types of delusional disorder: erotomanic, grandiose, and persecutory (no symptoms of the somatic or jealous types are in evidence). But these conditions are diagnosed for *nonbizarre delusions,* whereas Kinbote presents with symptoms that clearly indicate paranoid schizophrenia: grandiose delusions, auditory hallucinations,[10] ideas of reference, and loosened associations or disorganized speech (not prominent, but revealed—in writing—as early as the Foreword). As for axis II diagnoses, the personality disorders, Kinbote shows symptoms of several (obsessive-compulsive, narcissistic, paranoid, and borderline), not at all inconsistent with a primary diagnosis of paranoid schizophrenia.

It is important to separate Nabokov's profound, comprehensive, psychiatric understanding of insanity from his profound, well-documented contempt for Freudian psychology. His portrait of Kinbote is an application of the former, without being a moderation of the latter. And for our attempt to solve the riddle of **Pale Fire,** it is important to separate a mad commentator with posthumous promptings being superimposed upon his elaborated paranoid fantasy (Boyd's solution) from a madman—though Shade rejects the appropriateness of that word—"who deliberately peels off a drab and unhappy past and replaces it with a brilliant invention" (159).[11]

The text allows us to see that Kinbote (Botkin) has intruded, however slightly, upon Shade's consciousness, and that Shade has informed Kinbote's (Botkin's) with powerful if delusional or pretextual force. Moreover, Nabokov has also allowed us to see what he is doing in those regards, in ways that render Boyd's discoveries if not superfluous at least superimposed. Readers may well disagree in identifying specific occasions when Nabokov announces his presence in the text, but few would fail to identify throughout his corpus his characteristic device of speaking *in propria persona* rather than in and through the language, thought, sensibilities, attitudes, and imagination of his created personas.

This part of my argument, it must be said, is hardly original. L.L. Lee, for example, argues that **Pale Fire** "is an order within itself, an esthetic order created by the *whole* novel" (135) and concludes, "Finally, then, we must return to Nabokov, for it is he who is making the art work and so the connections" (142-43). Richard Pearce arrives at a similar conclusion, by way of elaborating on what Nabokov called "the thrill of diabolical pleasure" in artistic creation (28).[12] And Andrew Field says, "[a]bove Shade and Kinbote, the poem and the Commentary is Nabokov himself, who is the most important of the three artists, and who imposes his own pattern upon **Pale Fire** without in any way impinging upon the separate designs of the poet Shade and the madman-artist he has created" (315)—though Field intends Shade, rather than Nabokov, as antecedent for the final pronoun "he."

Boyd acknowledges the point in several passages: "Of couse from outside the world of the novel we know the identity of this ultimate artificer" (235); "[b]ehind the mortal Shade, the dead Hazel, and even the dead Shade, Nabokov in turn places *his* signature" (241); "indeed Nabokov's celebrated personal sign recurs" (241); "[b]eyond Hazel and the other Shades, as designer of their world, is Nabokov himself" (244); "he places the stamp of his own Russianness overtly on Kinbote and his Botkinian shadow and his 'distant northern land,' and covertly on the landscape of New Wye" (288). Most pertinent to the present matter, Boyd says, "Nabokov as the ultimate namer [. . .] seems to be inserting his own signature again and again into Shade's unforgettable opening couplet. [. . .] The creator of the novel's entire fictional world, Nabokov strategically places the butterflies within its maker's marks. [. . .]" (242).

Of the many places in **Pale Fire** where the puppeteer allows himself to be seen behind the curtain, over the heads of Shade and Kinbote (Botkin) as it were, I offer only a few examples. In Kinbote's Foreword, to take an early instance, long after we have realized his insanity, not only in Sybil Shade's pronouncement but more emphatically by his own megalomaniacal grandiosity, ideas of reference, and loosened associations, he interrupts a reverie that focuses on his own exclusive experience of John Shade to describe the poet as

> perceiving and transforming the world, taking it in and taking it apart, re-combining its elements in the very process of storing them up so as to produce at some unspecified date an organic miracle, a fusion of image and music, a line of verse.
>
> (10)

In the context of suspicion, distortion, and occasional forgery, I see the clarity of this vision as far beyond the ocular (or ethical or deranged-mental) capacity of Kinbote looking at a photograph or remembering a fleeting glimpse of the poet—without intruding himself into the frame. Nor can it be read without sophistry as Shade's view of his own art projected through his created commentator. It is Nabokov's own view, expressed in his own voice, as if he were talking about Pushkin.

That voice may just as easily be heard in some of Shade's language in the poem. For example, when Shade at the climax of Canto Three perceives that he could find in life "some kind / of correlated pattern in the game, / Plexed artistry [. . .]" (37), we might hear Nabokov inimitably intoning an epigrammatic emblem of his concept of the relationship between life and art. A better example, perhaps, is the much discussed couplet of lines 939 to 940: "*Man's life as commentary to abstruse / Unfinished poem.* Note for further use" (40). The passage is accurate (written on the last clear-handed card of the Fair Copy) and, though irrelevant in the immediate context, can be accepted as Shade's idea for some future combinational magic. If he is thinking about his present poem, then he imagines it as unfinished. And whether or not one sees that poem as abstruse, the commentary of Kinbote does reveal a man's life—or fantasy-life—and only by indirection his "real" life.

It is extremely unlikely that Shade has deliberately left his poem unfinished in order that the commentary (the life, the novel) fill the prescription of these incidental lines. The italics themselves may provide a clue to the meaning of the passage: passages are italicized in the text of the poem at Kinbote's sole discretion (see note to lines 403-04, p. 131). He could thus be drawing attention, in an offhand remark of Shade's to what *he*, Kinbote, is doing in the Commentary.

But suppose that these lines refer not to *a* man (a poet, a character, a commentator, an editor) but to Man. In that case, here, too, Nabokov announces his presence in an abstract statement of his conception for the book, while teasing us out of other concrete "solutions."[13] Indirectly, Kinbote draws us toward this resolution in his mistaken and misleading note to the couplet.

In the final paragraph of the Commentary, Nabokov takes another occasion to remove his Kinbote mask for a glimpse of himself. As Pearce puts it, there "the narrator distinguishes himself from his fictional personae" (42). "I shall continue to exist," he says, living and flying on like the slain waxwing or its smudged remains:

> I may assume other disguises, other forms, but I shall try to exist. I may turn up yet, on another campus, as an old, happy, healthy, heterosexual Russian, a writer in exile, sans fame, sans fortune, sans audience, sans anything but his art.
>
> (202)

Kinbote goes on to list other possible incarnations, all relating to aspects of the present version, but this one is alertly different. It may suggest Pnin, the protagonist of Nabokov's novel that appeared between *Lolita* and *Pale Fire,* who makes a self-reflexive cameo appearance (190) on the Wordsmith campus (though his name is not found in the Index), but it most clearly represents Nabokov himself, as if Alfred Hitchcock were waving to the camera and saying, "here I am."

Similarly situated is the last sentence of Nabokov's **"On a Book Entitled *Lolita,*"** a kind of afterword that appears in most editions from late 1956 on. He has acknowledged that such an enterprise may be taken "as an impersonation of Vladimir Nabokov talking about his own book," but asserts that "the autobiographic device may induce mimic and model to blend" (313). That ultimate sentence, playfully disingenuous says,

> My private tragedy, which cannot, and indeed should not, be anybody's concern, is that I had to abandon my natural idiom, my untrammeled, rich, and infinitely docile Russian tongue for a second-rate brand of English, devoid of any of those apparatuses—the baffling mirror, the black velvet backdrop, the implied associations and traditions—which the native illusionist, frac-tails flying, can magically use to transcend the heritage in his own way.
>
> (318-19)

Few readers would accept the self-deprecating assessment of limitations in Nabokov's English apparatuses (which include Kinbote's *apparatus criticus,* of course). For me the key terms here are those for the playful, comic, magician-artist: "illusionist, frac-tails flying."[14]

My final example, arguably the strongest for the present enterprise, appears as part of the dialogue on religion, printed in the form of a play:

SHADE:

> There are rules in chess problems: interdiction of dual solutions for instance.

KINBOTE:

> I had in mind diabolical rules likely to be broken by the other party as soon as we come to understand them.
>
> (151)

Where is the voice of Nabokov (composer of chess problems, as well as puzzling fictions) here? Granted the rule that dual solutions are interdicted (Shade's premise); and granted that rules are shifted by a diabolical puzzler (Kinbote's premise); then sequential solutions are demanded (Nabokov's conclusion—for the reader). The concept of sequence is central, because the verb tenses of the riddle must be carefully observed in order to solve the riddle.

Nabokov's game-plan includes drawing attention to the concept of artist as magician or conjuror, to the theme of appearance/reality, and to innovations in points of view, personae, filters, and removes. By employing dual artists and dual lives, interacting and refracting, he newly lights up the old dialectic of life and art, the working out of art as plot, and the concern with artist as subject. In Hyman's phrase, this is the "triumph of artifice" (21), in which Nabokov draws attention to his own presence in the text, a role he enacts by creating two artists who mirror and distort one another—binary satellites, like John Crowe Ransom's "Equilibrists," who twirl "about the clustered night their prison world, [. . .] orbited nice" with flames that are radiant reflections of one another but only really pale fire stolen from the sun of their primary creator—but who maintain their own integrity as secondary artists.

The entire elaborate issue of who is the "primary" artist in *Pale Fire* disappears when the reader, following the clues and the sequential stages of the process, solves the riddle this riddle-fancying author has set for the reader in the opening lines of **"Pale Fire."**

If I *was* the shadow of a bird killed by flying into a window's reflection of blue sky, who was I? Well, I could have been Shade (= shadow); or Kinbote (shadow [stalker, follower] of Shade [poet = bird], who dies colliding with the false reflection of Kinbote's fantasy life); or Jack Grey or Gradus or however we choose to denominate the killer, the shadow who pursues the victim to his death.

If I *was* the smudge of ashen fluff, the material remains of the departed, what was I? Well, I could have been the much edited unfinished poem, the muddled commentary thereon, or the gray perpetrator of either poem or commentary or the would-be assassin of either.

In other words, I could have been either Shade or not-Shade, Kinbote or not-Kinbote, poem or not-poem (i.e., commentary, *apparatus criticus*). These solutions are all dual, diabolically so, but they are preterite. The next sequenced question is, how could I have *lived on* in the reflection? And this question leads to the implied question at the heart of the riddle, implicit in the riddle-form itself: Who *am* "I" as riddled forth in the opening lines of **"Pale Fire"**?

What lives on is the writer as reflected in his work (or the artist *as* his work, in the most universal of metomymies). I am Vladimir Nabokov, keeper of the secret, poser and designer of the riddle, unknown game-player, summoning author, creative planner.

I *was* this, and I *was* that (poem and poet, *apparatus criticus* and commentator/fantasist). The dual solutions are diabolical, interdicted. As the verb forms of the poem modulate from the preterite indicative of the riddle format into the subjunctive, the pluperfect, and the lyric present, so are the initial riddle solutions seen as leading to the singular, masked, playful final solution. It lives on in a reflected sky; it is not a diabolical but a heavenly, divine answer. And how has Nabokov achieved this eternal but "organic miracle"? By "dying into his book."

The phrase is taken from the final section of *Ada* (just after a quotation—and translation!—of a short passage from **"Pale Fire"**), a section when Nabokov most visibly extrudes his face through Van-y-Ada's mask-o'-the-game. There Van and Ada, here Shade and Kinbote, dual, mirrored, twinned, equilibrist artists, in both cases with their creator allowing a glimpse of his flying frock-tails, provide their own implicit ("One can even surmise [. . .]") solution to the riddle of life and art:

> "that if our [. . .] couple ever intended to die they would die, as it were, *into* the finished book, into Eden or Hades, into the prose of the book or the poetry of its blurb."
>
> (587)

And then the final four paragraphs of that novel *are* that blurb.

The disguiser of secrets is at his best when the nature of the very disguises provide *prima facie* intrigue and appreciation. The secrets are no less to be valued for the devices that delay—but do not preclude—their unraveling. The key to the riddle is the riddle; the riddler's triumph is the artifice of flashing the key before our eyes.

Near the end of his *Theories of Play and Postmodern Fiction,* Brian Edwards says,

> Regardless of their intention, texts beckon and dissemble; to think otherwise is to be a dupe of the "game," a poor player whose strutting and fretting may be caused by too ready an acceptance of the role of narratee, implied reader, intended reader, superreader, or some other refinement of *position,* Possibilities for exchange exceed the apparent narrative construction; beyond up-front conceptions of narrator, focaliser, or point of view, any ghostly identikit of the author in the wings has still to contend with the divided operations of reference. There's the rub, and, in play, the opportunities for engagement never end. Revelation is a beginning.
>
> (274-75)

It is in the spirit of playful engagement with a riddling, gameplaying writer, that this tentative "solution" or "revelation" is offered.

Notes

1. For the sake of convenience, citations are to the Berkley edition (New York, 1968), though line numbers of the poem need not be cited by page in text.

2. The word *riddle* appears nearly as often in *Pale Fire* criticism as "puzzle" and "game," perhaps more often than "trick." See, e.g., Michael Wood (277+). Describing the delights of reading *Pale Fire,* Maurice Couturier says, "We are proud of having elaborated all these interpretations which seem to be absent from the text and we tend to supplant the author (as Kinbote supplanted Shade[. . .]). When the riddle is very clever, the solver feels as good an artist as the composer" (121). Here, as elsewhere, "riddle" is metaphor; the present essay speaks, literally, of Riddle.

3. The phrase "Disguise the Secret," according to Robert Graves (54), is the "poetic meaning" of the lapwing in the *Câd Goddeu,* Graves is wrestling with a different sort of riddle, trying to decode the way ancient mythic material is preserved in the bardic traditions and tree alphabets of Western Europe. But the Northern lapwing, *Vanellus vanellus,* is a bird of a different color from Nabokov's (Shade's) waxwing, whether *Bombycilla cedroroum* or *Bombycilla garullus,* both of which are indigenous to the vacinity of the Wordsmith campus in Appalachia, New Wye (for which we may comfortably substitute Cornell and Ithaca, NY). Graves, incidentally, identifies the secret as the key to the sacred king's sovereignty. But if an oblique connection between sacred kingship and bardic genius might suit Kinbote's grandiose fantasy (to which we might add Graves's association of a homosexual priesthood with the legend of Bran), waxwing is the choice of Nabokov (and Shade) as careful naturalist and alliterating poet. We may conclude that sometimes a bird is just a bird.

4. The persistent debate about which character in *Pale Fire* is the "primary author" is neatly summarized and brought up to date by Boyd (114-26), but is rendered moot by his current stance. The present essay supports that conclusion, clearly for different reasons.

5. Accepting Kinbote's gloss of Ferz as "chessqueen" in the index, Boyd adds "Russian *ferz*" (229). In medieval chess, as dramatized by Chaucer's use of the image in *The Book of the Duchess,* the "fers" is the piece next to the king. Once called "wise man" but later queen when its movements were expanded, the word came to English via Old French but was originally the Persian *ferzēn* (wise man).

6. This may seem incautious phrasing, coming from one who winced at Boyd's dismissal of another scholar's work as premised on "a dotty thesis" (269) and his putdown of Andrew Field as "not knowing what more to say" (274).

7. In *The Annotated Lolita,* Alfred Appel, Jr. plays the sedulous ape to Kinbote, of all mentors, when he advises us "to read through a chapter and then read its annotations, or vice versa" (xi). But Appel's annotations are hardly the equivalent of Coleridge's own marginal notes to *The Rime of the Ancient Mariner.*

8. The process is lucidly described and exemplified in a case reported by Frieda Fromm-Reichman (see Bullard, 190, 192+, 196+, 204, 206+, 213. It is the very case reimagined in Joanne Greenberg's autobiographical *I Never Promised You a Rose Garden.* For another, brilliant fictional evocation of the technique at work (though it is not labeled as psychiatric practice), see Christa Wolf's *Cassandra* (61-63).

9. The authoritative text is the American Psychiatric Association's *The Diagnostic and Statistical Manual of Mental Disorders,* now in its fourth edition (DSM-IV). More than a useful reference to guide clinicians to appropriate diagnoses, with its multi-axial concept and its differential diagnoses, it is the required reference for any reporting to insurers.

10. E.g., in his note to 1. 802, Kinbote reports hearing Shade's voice saying, "Come tonight, Charlie," though he discovers, "in awe and wonder," that he is "quite alone." Earlier in the passage he describes being in an "elevated state of mind," like that which precedes or signals the onset of a "fit" or "spell" in a variety of mental illnesses (173).

11. Wood, whose observations on Nobokov are almost always illuminating, unaccountably identifies the subject of this remark as "the old man [. . .] who thought he was God and began redirecting the trains" (179). It is Kinbote/Botkin the group of party-goers is discussing when Kinbote overhears Shade's remark; the mannerly hostess Eberthella Hurley saves embarrassment (Shade's, Kinbote's, her own—it is she who has triggered Shase's quip) by stumblingly referring to an alternative subject. This sort of thing is not uncommon for Kinbote, as in the hallucinations/halitosis confusion (63). Notwithstanding this rare nod, Wood's insights on connections between *Pale Fire* and *Pnin* and with *Ada* are particularly valuable, and I would also specifically credit the sensitive skepticism of the following passage:

> Kinbote has buried Botkin pretty successfully; only a few shreds of his former self cling to his new invention, so his new invention is what we have. Botkin's role in the novel is not to tell the hidden truth, deliver the crown jewels, but to remind us, eerily, that Kinbote's self *is* invented, precarious; that it has a past or has a double.
>
> (178)

The figurative language of this observation itself eerily prefigures some of the literal applications thereof in the present essay.

12. Indeed, Pearce's insistence on the "diabolical" almost identifies Nabokov with Kinbote's response to Shade's comment regarding solutions to chess problems. Pearce pursues a whole series of either—or choices to arrive at his conclusion. The reader may choose, he says, how to read the book. The choice of primary narrator rests on a prior judgment as to whether the poem is good or bad. Finally, he leads us to see such choices as neither rational nor conclusive, finding a "hidden narrator" who is "laughing diabolically" in narrative "black holes" (in *Pale Fire* those which physically separate the foreword from the poem and the poem from the commentary).

13. John Shade, a student of and influenced by Pope, might well be referring here to "Man" in general. It seems to me, however, that Shade's "Pale Fire" is less a Popean "essay" than a spiritual autobiography on the Wordsworthian model. Remembering his childhood, Shade remembers remembering and he thinks of what he thought of; recalling his spells of *petit mal* and comparing the way he sees things now and the way he saw them then, Shade has intimations of immortality.

I would also observe that Shade's preoccupation with Hazel's death has been overstressed in the critical literature at the expense of his equivalent focus on his love for Sybil (she is the constant "you"—the deuteragonist, in John Barth's terms, of his poem and his thoughts). These are probably the two deepest and strongest emotional forces in his life, and his present view of his own life is structured by both: by a comparison of his love for Sybil in his youth with his love for her now, and by his love for Hazel remembered in the attempts to surprise some meaningful pattern in her death.

14. In *The Annotated Lolita,* the final note is to *frac-tails,* beginning:

> Nabokov wittily demonstrates that the "native illusionist" is now an internationalist: *frac* is French for "dress coat." It is just that Nabokov (and this edition) should conclude with a joke [. . .].
>
> (441)

But the homophonous frock-coat is standard American for several garments, including a conventional costume for vaudeville comedians. See, by all means see whenever possible, Irwin Corey or vintage Groucho Marx, frock-tails flying. Perhaps the joke is on Appel. Some of his simple "definitions" are bigger howlers than the predictably fulsome responses to the master putter-on. Apple's notes sometimes seem unwitting adumbrations of Kinbote's, and Nabokov must have taken some devilish pleasure in answering Appel's questions—because he must have divined that Appel would always take the deadpan as gospel.

Works Cited

Appel, Alfred, Jr. See Nabokov, *The Annotated Lolita.*

Boyd, Brian. *Nabokov's Pale Fire: The Magic of Artistic Discovery.* Princeton: Princeton UP, 1999.

Bullard, Dexter M., ed. *Psychoanalysis and Psychotherapy: Selected papers of Frieda Fromm-Reichman.* Chicago: U of Chicago P, 1959.

Couturier, Maurice. "Nabokov's Laughter." *Revue Francaise d'Etudes Americaines* 4 (1977): 115-22.

Diagnostic and Statistical Manual of Mental Disorders. 4th Ed. Washington, D.C.: American Psychiatric Association, 1994.

Edwards, Brian. *Theories of Play and Postmodern Fiction.* New York: Garland, 1998.

Field, Andrew. *Nabokov: His Life in Art.* Boston: Little, Brown, 1967.

Frye, Northrop. *The Anatomy of Criticism.* Princeton: Princeton UP, 1957.

Graves, Robert. *The White Goddess: A Historical Grammar of Poetic Myth.* 1948. New York: Farrar, Straus and Giroux, 1966.

Greenberg, Joanne. *I Never Promised You a Rose Garden.* New York: Holt, Rinehart and Winston, 1964.

Hyman, Stanley Edgar. "Nabokov's Gift." *New Leader* 14 Oct. 1963: 20-21.

Lee, L.L. *Vladimir Nabokov.* Boston: G.K. Hall, 1976.

Nabokov, Vladimir. *Ada.* New York: McGraw-Hill, 1969.

———. *The Annotated Lolita.* Ed. Alfred Appel, Jr. New York: McGraw-Hill, 1970.

———. "Conclusive Evidence.": 1950 *The New Yorker* 28 Dec. 1998: 124-33.

———. *Pale Fire.* New York: Berkley, 1984.

———. *Pnin.* New York: Avon, 1957.

———. *Strong Opinions.* New York: McGraw-Hill, 1973.

Pearce, Richard. "Nabokov's Black (Hole) Humor: *Lolita* and *Pale Fire.*" *Comic Relief: Humor in Contemporary American Literature.* Ed. Sarah Blacher Cohen. Urbana: U of Illinois P, 1978. 28-44.

Ransom, John Crowe. "The Equilibrists". *Selected Poems.* New York: Knopf, 1945.

Wolf, Christa. *Cassandra.* New York: Farrar, Straus and Giroux, 1988.

Wood, Michael. *The Magician's Doubts.* Princeton: Princeton UP, 1995.

FURTHER READING

Criticism

Berberova, Nina. "The Mechanics of *Pale Fire.*" *TriQuarterly* 17 (winter 1970): 147-59.
> Explores the easily recognizable and symbolic aspects of Nabokov's *Pale Fire,* as well as the novel's well-hidden factual layer.

Boyd, Brian. "*Pale Fire*: The Vanessa Atalanta." In *Nabokov at Cornell,* edited by Gavriel Shapiro, pp. 78-90. Ithaca, N.Y.: Cornell University Press, 2003.
> Reveals that the character of Hazel Shade in Nabokov's *Pale Fire* is reincarnated in the image of a Vanessa Atalanta butterfly.

Ciancio, Ralph A. "Nabokov and the Verbal Mode of the Grotesque." *Contemporary Literature* 18, no. 4 (fall 1977): 509-33.
> Observes evidence of the grotesque aesthetic in the language of Nabokov's novels *Lolita* and *Pale Fire.*

Eichelberger, Carl. "Gaming in the Lexical Playfields of Nabokov's *Pale Fire.*" In *Critical Essays on Vladimir Nabokov,* edited by Phyllis A. Roth, pp. 176-85. Boston: G. K. Hall & Co., 1984.
> Explores the various forms of games in Nabokov's *Pale Fire,* including word games, mathematical symbols and patterns, and images related to chess.

Galef, David. "The Self-Annihilating Artists of *Pale Fire.*" *Twentieth Century Literature* 31, no. 4 (winter 1985): 421-37.
> Perceives significant parallels between the character of Hazel Shade and that of the central protagonist, Charles Kinbote, in Nabokov's *Pale Fire.*

Hennard, Martine. "Playing a Game of Worlds in Nabokov's *Pale Fire.*" *MFS* 40, no. 2 (summer 1994): 299-317.
> Applies Jacques Derrida's deconstructionist ideas to Nabokov's *Pale Fire,* arguing that the notion of exile places the novel within the modern and postmodern literary movements.

LeRoy-Frazier, Jill. "'Playing a Game of Worlds': Post-modern Time and the Search for Individual Autonomy in Vladimir Nabokov's *Pale Fire*." *Studies in Twentieth Century Literature* 27, no. 2 (2003): 311-27.

> Assesses previous critical interpretations of Nabokov's *Pale Fire*, claiming that the novel portrays a postmodern world without rules or the possibility of individual autonomy.

McCauley-Myers, Janie. "Sybil and Disa in *Pale Fire*." *The Nabokovian* 23 (fall 1989): 35-9.

> Examines how the central protagonist of Nabokov's novel *Pale Fire*, Charles Kinbote, creates an illusionary wife for himself based upon the image of John Shade's wife.

Oakley, Helen. "Disturbing Design: Nabokov's Manipulation of the Detective Fiction Genre in *Pale Fire* and *Despair*." *Journal of Popular Culture* 36, no. 3 (winter 2003): 480-96.

> Suggests that Nabokov both used and meaningfully misused classic detective fiction archetypes in his novels *Pale Fire* and *Despair*.

Pearce, Richard. "Nabokov's Black (Hole) Humor: *Lolita* and *Pale Fire*." In *Comic Relief: Humor in Contemporary American Literature*, pp. 28-44. Urbana: University of Illinois Press, 1978.

> Proposes that in both *Pale Fire* and *Lolita* Nabokov threatens his readers' sense of judgment by intentionally deconstructing the familiar narrative worlds he created.

Seidel, Michael. "*Pale Fire* and the Art of Narrative Supplement." *ELH* 51, no. 4 (winter 1984): 837-55.

> Acknowledges the way Nabokov allows the fantastic to mingle with the ordinary in his novel *Pale Fire*.

Smith, Herbert F. "The Topology of *Pale Fire*: An Analysis Based on Catastrophe Theory." In *Cross-Cultural Studies: American, Canadian and European Literatures, 1945-1985,* edited by Mirko Jurak, pp. 183-92. Ljubljana, Yugoslavia: Filozofska Fakulteta, Edvard Kardelj University of Ljubljana, 1988.

> Employs elements of "Catastrophe Theory" as a vehicle for analyzing what Smith perceives as the postmodern structure of Nabokov's novel *Pale Fire*.

Strunk, Volker. "Infinity and Missing Links in Nabokov's *Pale Fire*." *English Studies in Canada* 7, no. 4 (December 1981): 456-72.

> Discusses the role of infinity as well as the various "missing links" that complete the puzzle of Nabokov's *Pale Fire*.

Williams, Carol T. "'Web of Sense': *Pale Fire* in the Nabokov Canon." *Critique* 6, no. 3 (winter 1963): 29-45.

> Locates the Hegelian triadic pattern in several of Nabokov's novels, including *Pale Fire*.

Wilson, Robert Rawdon. "Character-Worlds in *Pale Fire*." *Studies in the Literary Imagination* 23, no. 1 (spring 1990): 77-98.

> Interprets the characters in Nabokov's novel *Pale Fire* in terms of Mikail Bakhtin's theory of narrative double-voicedness.

Additional coverage of Nabokov's life and career is contained in the following sources published by Thomson Gale: *American Writers*; *American Writers: The Classics*, Vol. 1; *American Writers Retrospective Supplement*, Vol. 1; *Authors and Artists for Young Adults*, Vol. 45; *Beacham's Encyclopedia of Popular Fiction: Biography & Resources*, Vol. 2; *Concise Dictionary of American Literary Biography: 1941-1968*; *Contemporary Authors*, Vols. 5-8R, 69-72; *Contemporary Authors New Revision Series*, Vols. 20, 102; *Contemporary Literary Criticism*, Vols. 1, 2, 3, 6, 8, 11, 15, 23, 44, 46, 64; *Contemporary Novelists*, Eds. 1, 2; *Contemporary Poets*, Ed. 2; *Dictionary of Literary Biography*, Vols. 2, 244, 278, 317; *Dictionary of Literary Biography Documentary Series*, Vol. 3; *Dictionary of Literary Biography Yearbook*, 1980, 1991; *DISCovering Authors*; *DISCovering Authors: British Edition*; *DISCovering Authors: Canadian Edition*; *DISCovering Authors Modules: Most-studied Authors* **and** *Novelists*; *DISCovering Authors 3.0*; *Encyclopedia of World Literature in the 20th Century*, Ed. 3; *Exploring Short Stories*; *Literature and Its Times Supplement*, Vol. 2; *Literature Resource Center*; *Major 20th-Century Writers*, Eds. 1, 2; *Major 21st-Century Writers*; *Modern American Literature*, Ed. 5; *Nonfiction Classics for Students*, Vol. 4; *Novels for Students*, Vol. 9; *Reference Guide to American Literature*, Ed. 4; *Reference Guide to Short Fiction*, Ed. 2; *Short Stories for Students*, Vols. 6, 15; *Short Story Criticism*, Vols. 11, 86; *Twayne's United States Authors*; *Twentieth-Century Literary Criticism*, Vol. 108; and *World Literature Criticism*, Vol. 4.

Emilia Pardo Bazán
1851-1921

Spanish novelist, short fiction writer, essayist, critic, poet, playwright, and biographer.

INTRODUCTION

Emilia Pardo Bazán is recognized as an important literary figure in modern Spanish fiction. Although she was a prolific writer in multiple genres, she is best remembered for her novels *Los pazos de Ulloa* (1886; *The House of Ulloa*) and *La madre naturaleza* (1887). These as well as other works by Pardo Bazán are considered significant examples of nineteenth-century Spanish Naturalism, and the two novels are often included in anthologies of the Spanish literary canon. Controversy often surrounded Pardo Bazán during her lifetime. Her essays, articles, and stories revealed radical and often unpopular ideas about religion, politics, and issues of gender inequality, especially the lack of educational opportunities for women in her native Spain. Following her death in 1921 and for much of the twentieth century, Pardo Bazán's greater body of work was largely forgotten. In recent decades, however, feminist critics in particular rediscovered her important contribution to women's literature. In addition, scholars began to study her lesser-known essays, novels, and short stories.

BIOGRAPHICAL INFORMATION

Pardo Bazán was born on September 16, 1851, in La Coruña, a prominent town in Galicia, Spain. She was privately educated in La Coruña and then attended a French school in Madrid for three years. In 1868 she married José Quiroga, a law student from a respected family in the region. The couple had three children before separating in 1885. In 1869 Pardo Bazán's family moved to Madrid when her father, Don José Pardo Bazán, became an elected deputy. But Don José soon became disenchanted with Progressive politics, and the family left the country. Pardo Bazán traveled throughout Europe between 1871 and 1874, visiting Paris, Vienna, Venice, and London. During her travels she studied philosophy and theology, as well as the natural sciences. Her first publications were articles on such diverse topics as light, electricity, Charles Darwin, and the poets Dante Alighieri and John Milton. In 1879 Pardo Bazán published her first novel, *Pascual López*.

Many of Pardo Bazán's early novels were influenced by the Naturalism of the French author and thinker Émile Zola, and practiced by such other French writers as Honoré de Balzac and brothers Edmond and Jules de Goncourt. As proposed by Zola, Naturalism as a philosophy and aesthetic promoted careful, realistic, and detailed observations of both the external world and human behavior. Although Pardo Bazán acknowledged the validity of some aspects of Zola's Naturalism, she objected to the philosophy's determinist foundation, as well as its rejection of beauty. In 1881, in an introduction to her second novel, *Un viaje de novios* (*A Wedding Trip*), she criticized the Naturalist movement for dwelling excessively on the sordid details of reality. Despite her concerns with the grimmer aspects of Naturalist fiction, Pardo Bazán employed many of its techniques in her writing. For example, she researched and depicted the inner workings of a cigarette factory in her third novel, *La tribuna* (1883; *The Tribune of the People*). Ironically, the novel was not well received by critics because of its candid descriptions of the working class. Between 1883 and 1885 Pardo Bazán published two more novels, a volume of short stories, and a series of articles concerning the philosophy of Naturalism collected under the title *La cuestión palpitante* (1883). As a result of her views on Naturalism, politics, religion, and women's rights, as well as her rather unconventional lifestyle, Pardo Bazán became a controversial figure in the 1880s and 1890s. In 1886 she published one of her best known novels, *The House of Ulloa*. The following year she produced a sequel to the book titled *La madre naturaleza*. After her father died in 1888, Pardo Bazán inherited his title, but she did not use it until 1908, when King Alfonso XIII honored her as the Countess de Pardo Bazán for her literary achievements. Between 1891 and 1893 Pardo Bazán wrote and produced a monthly literary arts periodical, *El Nuevo Teatro Crítico*. In 1916 she achieved a lifelong ambition when she was appointed a faculty member at the Central University of Madrid. Many students boycotted her class, however, because of her gender, and she was eventually forced to leave her position. She continued to write and publish. Her last three novels, *La quimera* (1905), *La sirena negra* (1908), and *Dulce dueño* (1911), explore issues of religious experience and are considered more spiritual than her earlier work. By the end of her literary career, Pardo Bazán had written twenty novels, twenty-one novellas, seven plays, over five hundred short stories, and sixteen volumes of non-fiction. She died on May 12, 1921, after suffering from complications associated with diabetes.

MAJOR WORKS

The House of Ulloa is frequently praised for its detailed descriptions and realistic portrayal of the language and customs of rural life in Galicia. The principal characters of the story are Don Pedro, Nucha, and Julián. Don Pedro is a bachelor who chooses to marry Nucha, one of his cousins, based partially on the advice of their priest, Julián. Nucha soon gives birth to a daughter, Manuela, but is unable to bear other children. Don Pedro, who expected a male heir, becomes angry at his daughter's birth. Soon after, it is revealed that Perucho, a boy for whom Nucha has maternal feelings, is Don Pedro's illegitimate son. A central theme of the novel is the conflict between religion and nature, which Pardo Bazán conveys primarily through her psychological study of the young priest Julián. As the story unfolds, Julián experiences a growing affection for Nucha and her daughter, as well as a desire to protect them from Don Pedro. These natural inclinations, however, conflict with his obligations and duties as a priest. The struggle between nature and civilization is echoed in the novel's imagery, as well. The manor house itself is in a state of decay, becoming overrun by natural elements of the outside world. Some critics regard *The House of Ulloa* and its sequel, *La madre naturaleza,* as the most accomplished representations of Pardo Bazán's Naturalistic work. Others consider the novels more transitional, employing elements of Naturalism but placing an emphasis on human psychology, a technique which was characteristic of her later, more spiritual writings.

La madre naturaleza continues the storyline of *The House of Ulloa,* depicting the evolving relationship between Perucho and Manuela, who do not know that they are half-brother and sister. Their bond, first established in *The House of Ulloa,* becomes increasingly passionate. The theme of incest is introduced by Pardo Bazán when Gabriel, Nucha's brother, arrives with plans to marry his niece. Through a dream that he experiences, Gabriel comes to associate, and even confuse, his affections for his sister, Nucha, with his amorous feelings for Manuela. Through much of the novel, Gabriel and Perucho compete for Manuela's attention and affection. When Gabriel discloses Perucho's identity to the lovers, Perucho leaves and Manuela becomes ill, though she finally rejects Gabriel's advances. At the close of the novel, Gabriel departs as well. As in its predecessor, *La madre naturaleza* employs elaborate descriptions of nature, many of which have been linked symbolically with the sexual awakening of Manuela and Perucho. In this novel, Pardo Bazán once again examines the tension between natural human inclination and the constraints of civilization.

Although she is most often remembered as a novelist, Pardo Bazán was a prolific short story writer. In recent scholarship, critics have begun to investigate the themes and techniques she employed in her short fiction. *Cuentos de amor* (1898), a collection of forty-three stories, has been noted for its examination of human psychology. Many of the stories are cynical or pessimistic in tone. In one of the first tales, "El amor asesinado," a woman rejects love, personified in the form of a Cupid-like figure. She flees and finally strangles him, unknowingly precipitating her own death. In "Mi suicidio," a widowed man plans to commit suicide until he finds out that his dead wife was unfaithful. Instead of shooting himself, he shoots her portrait. In "Delincuente honrado," a man slaughters his daughter when he mistakes her for his unfaithful wife. Other stories, including "Primer amor," "Sor Aparición," and "Cuento soñado," portray the inevitable fading of youth and beauty as a result of time and old age. Critics have also discussed the feminist themes of many of Pardo Bazán's short stories. In "Champagne" (1898), she challenges traditional ideas with her sympathetic portrayal of a prostitute, and in "Náufragas" (1909), according to some critics, Pardo Bazán critiques the socio-economic system in which women are left uneducated, unskilled, and dependent on men. In this story, three women become refugees, dependent on the goodwill of others, when they are forced to leave their home after the death of the patriarch of the family. These and other stories have led critic Joan M. Hoffman to assert that in her short fiction, as well as in her other work, "Pardo Bazán calls for and champions a new intersection of territory, economics, and morality for women, a re-definition of middle-class decency."

CRITICAL RECEPTION

Because of her extensive contributions to Spanish and women's literature, Pardo Bazán is regarded as one of Spain's most accomplished nineteenth- and early twentieth-century female authors. Although she received only moderate recognition early in her literary career, she achieved both critical and popular acclaim in the 1880s with the publication of her major novels, *The House of Ulloa* and *La madre naturaleza,* and her controversial collection of essays, *La cuestion palpitante,* in which she criticized the pessimism and determinism of French Naturalism. Throughout the next decade, Pardo Bazan found herself the subject of fierce debate, not only for her unwavering Catholic position on Naturalism and strong commitment to feminist concerns, but also because several of her novels employed some of Émile Zola's Naturalist techniques, despite her condemnations of the philosophy. Francisco de Izaca, a literary critic and contemporary of Pardo Bazán, even went so far as to call her a plagiarist, saying that "she translated, adapted, and endowed with her signature the story or the critical article recently read in a foreign book." Despite Pardo Bazán's own claim that she was not "an Idealist, nor a Realist, nor a Naturalist, but an eclectic," criticism of her work both during and after her lifetime focused primarily on her Naturalist themes, especially as demonstrated in such novels as *The Tribune of the People, The House of Ulloa,* and *La madre naturaleza.*

In his 1983 study Maurice Hemingway was among the first critics to question the singular importance of Naturalism in Pardo Bazán's canon. In this study, Hemingway minimized the influence of Naturalism and Zola on Pardo Bazán, arguing instead that her work evolved to reflect her increasing interest in psychology. Similarly, Joyce Tolliver de-emphasized elements of Naturalism and stressed instances of Russian spiritualism in Pardo Bazán's fiction. In recent years, some scholars have begun to examine Pardo Bazán's ideas about art and beauty in her short stories and dramatic works, while others have devoted critical attention to the feminist subtext in her essays and novels. Although criticism of her work has, according to Robert B. Knox, "pursued a tortuous course marked by many vicissitudes and divergent opinions," Pardo Bazán's place in the Spanish literary canon remains secure.

PRINCIPAL WORKS

Estudio crítico de las obras del padre Feijóo (criticism) 1876
Pascual López (novel) 1879
Jaime (poetry) 1881
Un viaje de novios [*A Wedding Trip*] (novel) 1881
San Francisco de Asís (biography) 1882
La cuestión palpitante (criticism) 1883
La tribuna [*The Tribune of the People*] (novel) 1883
Bucólica (novel) 1884
El cisne de Vilamorta [*Swan of Vilamorta*] (novel) 1885
La dama joven (short stories) 1885
Los pazos de Ulloa [*The House of Ulloa*] (novel) 1886
La madre naturaleza (novel) 1887
Insolación (novel) 1889
Morriña (novel) 1889
Una cristiana-La prueba (novel) 1890
El imparcial (short stories) 1891
Obras completas. 43 vols. (novels, novellas, short stories, criticism, essays, plays, and biography) 1891-1926
La piedra angular [*The Angular Stone*] (novel) 1891
Cuentos de Marineda (short stories) 1892
Cuentos nuevos (short stories) 1894
Doña Milagros (novel) 1894
Memorias de un solterón (novel) 1896
El tesoro de Gastón (novel) 1897

Cuentos de amor (short stories) 1898
El saludo de las brujas (novel) 1898
El vestido de boda (play) 1898
Un destripador de antaño (short stories) 1900
En tranvía (short stories) 1901
La suerte (play) 1904
La quimera (novel) 1905
Cuesta abajo (play) 1906
La sirena negra (novel) 1908
Dulce dueño (novel) 1911
La gota de sangre (novella) 1911
Short Stories by Emilia Pardo Bazán (short stories) 1933
Obras completas. 3 vols. (novels, novellas, short stories, and criticism) 1973
Cuentos completos. 4 vols. (short stories) 1990
Torn Lace and Other Stories (short stories) 1996

*This work was partially translated in English as *A Christian Woman.*

CRITICISM

C. C. Glascock (essay date March 1926)

SOURCE: Glascock, C. C. "*La Quimera,* by Emilia Pardo Bazán." *Hispania* 9, no. 2 (March 1926): 86-94.

[*In the following essay, Glascock analyses Pardo Bazán's novel* La quimera *to reveal the author's views on Naturalism, art, and religion.*]

Countess Emilia Pardo Bazán, who died in Madrid on the twelfth of May, 1921, had obtained for herself a place among the foremost modern novelists and critics. **The Chimera (La quimera)** one of the most thoughtful and profound of an extended series of splendid novels, was published in 1905. It embodies the results of a life-long study of psychology (that is to say of character), of art, of religion; nay, of life itself. It sums up the author's experience in life, in art and in faith; it expresses her aesthetic and her religious creeds.

But the book is constructed on and around a central theme, that of man's struggle, often fruitless and destructive, to realize a fond illusion—his chimera, which may prove as deadly to him as the fiery, flaming breath of the Chimera, the monster of Greek mythology. Three illustrations of the vain quest confront us in the work. First and foremost, the failure on the part of a young Galician artist, Silvio Lago, to attain his artistic ideals and become one of the world's great painters. He wears out his fragile frame in the ardent pursuit of artistic perfection, and he dies, a victim of consumption, the result of privation in early years; but not before he is converted to idealism in art and in religion. And then the disappointment and disillusion of two young women who come to love him dearly. The one, a rich and noble young widow of great refinement and culture, Clara Ayamonte, whose exalted ideal of pure and unselfish devotion is shattered rudely by the artist. She finally seeks solace in a convent. She is followed by Espina Porcel, a dashing, arrogant, capricious adventuress who loves him too, in her strange way; she is driven to the use of morphine and to early death by her insatiable and invincible desire to live in a superior atmosphere of exaltation, both aesthetic and sublime.

Emilia Pardo Bazán made a place in this book for many of her best thoughts, the result of her life-long study of art on the one hand, and of the manifold manifestations of the supersensitive and aspiring spirit that clashes with the hard and cruel facts of life and suffers disillusion and defeat. Art then, psychology, and religion are the studies upon which this book is based, in keeping with the author's aesthetic doctrine that a novel should be based on study.

The Chimera embodies many a picture of life in Madrid and Paris among fashionable and aristocratic patrons and devotees of art, among artists and students of art as well, with whom long years of association had made the author perfectly familiar.

The book is a rich repository of the writer's reflections extending over many decades, on the artistic career and its problems, on the artistic temperament and its capricious as well as generous reactions, on the conduct, noble and ignoble, of patrons of art.

Subsidiary characters drawn from the professions of medicine and of music and from the proletariat enable the writer to disclose wide vistas in the province of psychology, normal and abnormal, seen through scientific as well as through artistic eyes. For its wealth of thought alone the book deserves an article, apart from any consideration of fine delineation of character or the technique of storytelling here displayed.

As for technique, attention is at once arrested by the pleasing combination and the variety presented in autobiographical memoirs, correspondence, and the ordinary method of narration from the author's omniscient point of view, in the third person.

Naturalistic pictures and delineations succeed one another, leaving the reader to supply in his imagination gaps, long or short, whose content is often omitted or merely suggested in rapid allusions. Masterful swiftness in dialogue, in narration and in transitions is everywhere a characteristic feature. Pardo Bazán was as gifted in knowing what to omit as she was vigorous in

presenting the essentials. She carried the art of suppression and of omission to a higher degree of perfection than any other Spanish novelist. And thus it is that the reader is spared a vast amount of triviality; there are few lines in *La quimera* that could be excised without a loss. Pereda may be more concise, nay, even deeper at times, but his writing does not convey the impression of marvellous swiftness so peculiar to Pardo Bazán. The reader has to be alert, it is true, but he is gratified at the great saving in time, and at being made to share, as it were, in creative work.

Vigorous indeed is the portrayal of the physical and psychic process that ends in the conversion of the worldly, ambitious, artistic spirit, turning him away from the dream of glory and self-aggrandizement to the humility and submissiveness of a dying Christian. The story grips and moves us, and brings us face to face with death that comes to all. A wonderful setting for the closing regional scenes is furnished in the lovely surroundings of the Galician castle by the sea; and the varying moods of season, sky and landscape are brought in perfect harmony, or contrast, with the suffering soul that hovers on the brink. Regional the story is in its beginning and regional in its conclusion in Galicia. And so it is that Emilia Pardo Bazán is able to pay tribute to her much-loved homeland in all its native beauty, with its mountains and meadows of green, its rivers, its inlets, and its sea. *Heimatkunst,* as the Germans call regional art, is made to play its part too, and variety is deftly provided in the changing scenes of country and of city life, of cosmopolitan and artistic atmosphere, and of charming rural pictures of Galicia by the sea.

Emilia Pardo Bazán has found in the arrangement of this novel a repository for much of the accumulated wisdom and experience gathered in her long and brilliant life. It is a treasury of golden thought; and it casts illuminating flashes of light where often all is dark. But more than a repository for opinions on art, refined by years of reflection and study; more than a careful study of character and of social circles with fashionable and artistic bent; more than a *Bildungs- und Künstlerroman,* as the German may call a novel in which the problems of education and of art in a fuller sense are treated; more than merely a vision of the world through Emilia Pardo Bazán's eyes, it also embodies her confession of faith, in the matter of religion as well as of art, and shows her true to her allegiance to the Roman Catholic church.

But this is not all, for over the whole work there hovers a grand and noble spirit, full of heart and soul, full of love and tenderness for suffering and erring humanity. It is this broad and sympathetic spirit that lends the greatest charm.

It is worth while to consider in some detail the visit made by Silvio to art galleries in Belgium and in Holland, for in the letters that he writes he records impressions that are fraught with meaning.

He visits these art galleries in order to gather impressions, to get direction for his genius; to discover what *genre* is to be his, what master is to exercise the first influence until he overcomes that influence and gains firm ground with its aid. He will begin as a slave but he must end as a king.

In Brussels he is disgusted and repelled by the horrible oddities of the symbolistic, socialistic, and naturalistic painter Anton Wiertz (middle of the Nineteenth Century) who seems grotesque and ridiculous to Silvio when he recalls the serene and luminous beauty of Greek art beneath a bright and floral Christianity as presented by Luini, Perugino, Botticelli; and he flees from the "funereal gallery of spectres and bloody ghosts" where Napoleon is represented as burning in Hell, surrounded by chiding and abusive spirits; where the powerful giants of the earth, as Polyphemus, are crushing the weak ones of earth, the companions of Ulysses; where a man entombed alive raises his demented face out of his coffin and sees on the ground a skull over which a great hairy spider is creeping; and a woman made insane by poverty and hunger is roasting severed portions of her infant, and is fondly clasping the remaining sections to her breast. Can this be art? he says, and he sees very clearly into what errors and weakness an artist may run when he abandons his masters and attempts to develop originality, or follows the bent of crazy ratiocination. He realizes, too, that correctness in the selection of subjects is as important as faithful representation of nature is; in other words, that there is more in art than mere slavish imitation and representation of nature or truth.

We are to witness his gradual conversion from his primitive love of crude realism to that of a romantic idealism or Pre-Raphaelitism, to full appreciation of all that an artist may put of his own soul into his work. This is symbolic in part of the development of Pardo Bazán's own attitude toward naturalism. But whereas Silvio experiences a complete conversion from naturalism to Pre-Raphaelitism, Emilia Pardo Bazán seems to have made of her art a sort of amalgam of naturalism and idealism, observing the truth in both, combining the best things in both, with marked leaning sometimes to one, sometimes to the other, as her mood and as variety may demand, satisfying the alternate longing of the human soul for truth and poetry.

In The Hague Silvio is amazed that so small a country could produce such a swarm of great artists: Cuyp, Van Ostade, Terburg, Rembrandt, Van der Helst, Gerard Dow, Berghem, Ruysdael, Paul Poter, Steen, Van der Neer, Hobbema, Van de Velde and the Wouvermans. They painted only what was around them, because they were not troubled by any ideal. They did not dream; they copied what was put before them, they reproduced without distinction what was pretty and what was ugly, and perhaps more frequently the latter. That was Silvio's first dream: to take a definite region in Spain and depict it with energy and truthfulness.

In Bruges Silvio admits his conversion to Catholicism, in art of course, and he abjures Protestant painting, whether *genre,* civic, national, or anecdotal in character. In a word, it is clear that under the influence of his Swedish friend, Nils Limsoe, he has become a devotee of Pre-Raphaelite art. He now despises himself for his former ideals, for his previous longing to paint a picture of the potato harvest in Galicia. He writes:

> I despise myself, I despise myself, I have sinned, I have sinned!. . . . Now let slender virgins come, let paladins come and a renascence of feeling very near its source, and aristocratic and medieval romanticism! Yes, my lady, all this means that I am gradually becoming a romanticist, for springs are welling within me of which I did not know. If perchance I began to work two years ago in Madrid, with the spirit of a brutal faun in my body, guiding my inexperienced hand, oh, ah! It was nothing! I was mistaken in my vocation.

This is a cry far remote from the crude notions or rude realism that hitherto animated him; it is indicative of the spiritual as well as the artistic reaction that is taking possession of his soul.

It would be interesting to review the stages traversed by Silvio in his artistic if not spiritual regeneration under the guidance of his friend Limsoe, but consideration of it must be limited here to a few of the principles and truths in art that he comes to appreciate. He now sees that art may be elevated and poetic, that it may eschew petty, outrageous, and impure things, that an artist may have respect for the dignity of his art, that it may be a fervid cult, even of the beauty of mysticism, that one may paint in a tender, saintly manner, that art may be saintly and elegant at once. Proof of corruption in the art that follows Raphael and Rubens is seen in Dutch painting that presents coarse and clownish people, men dissecting a corpse, or vomiting wine.

Limsoe urges that to enter the lists of Pre-Raphaelitism one must have conscience, humility, daily communion; one must be pure and beautiful at heart. So Burne-Jones revived the age of chivalry, the dream of humanity with wings. What feeling, what piety, what nobility! What loftiness hidden in this painting that is so delicate! Above all, what variety! Holman Hunt is more religious (although all are religious, and one cannot be a great artist of the ideal without religiousness); Rosetti is a charming poet with Catholic imagination, and he has something of the illumination and of the loving gift of the primitive Franciscan artists.

A current like that of Pre-Raphaelitism produced the inspiration of ineffable Wagner. In art worthy of the name, in art that does not nauseate, there is religiousness only;

religiousness, knight errantry, the soul in search of Heaven. The last word in art, as in love, is ecstacy (i.e., rapture, poetic frenzy). . . . Let the Maelstrom swallow up the descendants of Flaubert and the representations of so-called reason. . . . Such are the ideas advocated with compelling force by Limsoe.

In Bruges Silvio is made acquainted with the work of Memling. He now realizes that Limsoe has completely converted him. With nausea and disgust he recalls Dutch painters with their gluttonous women, their brawls, and festivities, their fairs and wineshops; burgesses bedecked in gala attire, their realism, their tremendous truthfulness. Silvio's soul now asks for something else, and this something else is Memling. What details, what flowering out of feeling, what a chivalry romance is *The Shrine of Saint Ursula*! He cannot tell whether it reveals a devout dreamer or a poet with the heart of a child. Silvio now understands that art may associate religion and chivalry; and religion may be saved by means of art from the impure touches of the multitude. In the figures of Saint Catherine and of Saint Barbara as seen in the *Marriage of Saint Catherine* he discovers the artist's firm resolution to devote his brush only to things that are beautiful, illustrious, rich in form and material; to reproduce only faces that have been redeemed from human misery, virgins that are queens or empresses, under whose feet the miry waves of impurity, bestiality, and violence cannot stir.

Limsoe on looking at Saint Catherine and Saint Barbara remarks to Silvio:

> See what saints those two are! Selected, eh? Do not think that they are here by chance. They are the two sainted, holy philosophers who disdained the low material things in paganism and embraced Christianity for love of purity, but without renouncing their artistic elegance, without ever mingling with coarse ascetics. Saint Barbara in her tower and Saint Catherine in her palace may be imagined, reading a treatise on psychology, crowned with pearls, veiled in gauze, with hands as much like lilies as those that you see here, Saint Catherine's; those that she extends for the Celestial Spouse's ring, hands that are the perfection of beauty in a thing already so beautiful as a woman's beautiful hand!

At this point Silvio bursts into vehement denunciation of his former crude ideals.

Limsoe's final charge to Silvio contains these words:

> Remember that beauty is the depth and the refinement of feeling, and that the flower of beauty is. . . . *ecstasy*. Do not debase your brush, do not besmirch your thought; be chaste, be simple, turn to the art of the Fifteenth Century artists; and if you wish to be free, come and live here with Memling and Van Eyck, keeping your dignity, flying from art and renouncing it if it is to serve in reproducing sensations common to man and to

the hog! Do not allow yourself to be attracted by the bait of nature. Nature does not exist, we create it; Nature is only worthy of attracting our gaze in the mystic hour of communion with the supernatural, when it is caressed by the breath of the spirit. Nature! I would say that it is the great corpse of Paradise, and the swarming worms of sensualism lend the appearance of life to the vast body.

So Limsoe discoursed until they parted at dawn, forever, agreeing never to write each other any letters in order that their friendship might not grow cold amid protestations and lies.

That afternoon Silvio bids eternal adieu to those enchanting gardens of art, to Rembrandt the enigmatic, to Franz Hals the master of secrets, to Rubens the imperial, to Memling the celestial, and all their work. The man who is going to recross the French border is not the same as he who passed it in the direction of Brussels two weeks before.

It seems unquestionable to me that Emilia Pardo Bazán has embodied much of her own experience with naturalism in literary art in the process of conversion that goes on in Silvio's heart in his conversion from naturalism in painting to Pre-Raphaelitism. Not that it is all to be taken literally. Goethe once remarked to Eckermann that everything that he put in his novel *Die Wahlverwandtschaften* (*Elective Affinities*) had been experienced by him, but nothing exactly as it has been experienced by him (*Conversations with Eckermann*, Feb. 17, 1830); so I think we may assume that much truth, but not all the truth, is to be found in the evolution of Silvio's aesthetic notions as representing her own. I think that Emilia Pardo Bazán all her life long was more or less consistent in her love for amplified naturalism as *she* interpreted it, but that she was no less a devotee of things spiritual, elevated, ideal, and divine, that she recognized the true realm and importance of things ideal in our existence, in a word that the world of dreams, of ideals, of aspirations, is in a sense as natural and as much a part of life, as real as the so-called world of actuality. Passages from her prologues demonstrate that she was convinced at an early period in her career of the blindness of Zola and such naturalists as he to the beautiful things in life, to the lofty, spiritual idealism of which man is capable, to the exquisite, nay, even ecstatic emotions and aspirations of the human heart, to religious exaltation; and she condemned explicitly Zola's determinism, obscenity and excesses.

All her life long Pardo Bazán was a lover of truth, not merely of truth as presented in the homely and seamy sides of earthly existence, in its sorrows and in its sufferings, in its drab and dreary monotony, in its hardships, trials, and disappointments, in its disillusions and defeats, even in its ugliest features; but she strove with consistency and steadfastness to portray with equal verity all the loveliness and beauty that we see and that we dream, the glories of the physical and of the spiritual world as well, of the actual and of the ideal. The beautiful world of our imagination and of spiritual and religious aspirations is faithfully revealed by her, and so she gives us *both* sides of the picture of life, and satisfies the longing in our soul for something more than pessimistic delineations of the crudest facts about us, found sometimes in her books.

One of the best things about her work is the just appreciation that she shows of the part played by religion in man's life, of its power to elevate, even to reform, to comfort and console the suffering and the dying, to keep us from the pitfalls and temptations everywhere, to soften and subdue the most rebellious and the fiercest souls. Pardo Bazán was all her life long a communicant of the Roman Catholic church. She was faithful in her adherence to enlightened religion; she was as frank in her acceptance of religious truth as she was open to the facts of science and of history. A more sincere seeker after all that is true and good, a more unprejudiced and honest observer, one freer from all bias and inclination to distort, or one more genuinely sympathetic in dealing with man's frailty, is hard to find. Truly Catholic in her feeling and in her training, in the whole acceptance of the word, she understood and hence she pardoned the frailty of man. Her sympathy was broad and just and was extended to all, or nearly all mankind.

Silvio Lago's conversion is not merely one from crude naturalism to the ethereal and celestial ideals of Pre-Raphaelitism, with all its chivalry and romanticism; but it is also one that takes him finally out of skepticism and indifference, out of material longing for glory and for fame, and compels him in the end, when consumption has wrought its frightful havoc with his body and with his aspirations, to seek the only hope and comfort that remains to such as he, the consolation that religion alone can give in the terrible hours of a lingering and painful death.

This book reveals in no uncertain terms the author's aesthetic and religious creeds, and so it has a value that is great; for it is not merely a comprehensive view of a large and interesting section of society; it points a way for noble aspirations, in the realm of art as well as in the realm of faith. In *La quimera* Emilia Pardo Bazán draws the sum of her experience in art, religion, and in life. It should have been her swan-song; it is fraught with meaning from the first word to the last.

J. Horace Nunemaker (essay date March 1945)

SOURCE: Nunemaker, J. Horace. "Emilia Pardo Bazán as a Dramatist." *Modern Language Quarterly* 6, no. 1 (March 1945): 161-66.

[*In the following essay, Nunemaker assesses Pardo Bazán's accomplishments as a dramatist, focusing on her plays written between 1898 and 1906, especially* El vestido de boda, La suerte, *and* Cuesta abajo.]

The Condesa de Pardo Bazán (1852-1921) stands preëminent as a novelist. Her name and fame have been spread far and wide as symbols of excellence in the novel, realistic and naturalistic. The few critics who have written adversely of her work in that genre are far outnumbered and outweighed by her enthusiastic admirers.

In spite of what seems an almost ominous silence in regard to her dramatic writing, a volume entitled *Teatro* will be found among her *Obras completas*.[1] It may be that her extraordinary success in the novel impelled her to write for the theater, if only experimentally. Her dramas would lead us to believe, rather, that she was in dead earnest in her dramatic writing. She was sure of herself in this new effort,[2] however much her critics were equally sure that she was barking up the wrong tree. But she did not stay with the drama; in fact, the last period of her life was barren in comparison with the almost feverish activity that characterized her early successes. It would not be fair to say that her failure to win favor with her drama was responsible for her literary retirement, but this fact must certainly be taken into account as a contributing factor.

It may almost be said that no one reads her plays or ever read them, and that few persons ever saw them performed, if the dearth of critical opinion of her drama is a fair criterion for judgment. Manuals of literature, special studies of her life and work, and introductions to textbook editions of her work fail even to take notice of her dramatic effort.[3] A few authors and editors of such books and studies do say that she wrote for the theater, but, with the exception of two, no one of them seems to have taken the trouble to examine the work on which he so parsimoniously reports.[4] The question arises as to whether so good a novelist could have been so bad a dramatist, and this without assuming that proficiency in one genre presupposes or guarantees the same in another. It would be obviously impossible to sustain such a premise. The virtues and vices of novelists who write for the theater have been pointed out frequently, particularly in the case of Pardo Bazán's eminent contemporary, Pérez Galdós.

Cejador y Frauca's sparse comment of "silbado" for her dramas, *Verdad* and *Cuesta abajo,* is only an inspiration for the curious to find out why. Similar comments, such as "en el teatro no logró éxito," "obras escritas para el teatro . . . estrenadas con mediana fortuna," and "dos o tres dramas, 'prudentemente cerrados bajo llave apenas concluídos,'" have a like effect. It must be admitted, as González Blanco points out, that Pardo Bazán herself, with amusing modesty if not with the "suprema ironía" that González Blanco attributes to her, uses the word "cometer" to describe her own writing of dramatic works.

The dramatic works of the learned countess form a brief list:

> *El vestido de boda,* monólogo. Escrito expresamente para Balbina Valverde, y estrenado el 1° de Febrero de 1898.
>
> *La suerte,* diálogo dramático. Estrenóse este diálogo con extraordinario aplauso, el día 5 de Marzo de 1904, en el *Teatro de la Princesa,* representando el papel de Ña Bárbara la Sra. Tubau de Palencia, y el de Payo el Sr. Monteagudo.
>
> *Verdad,* drama en cuatro actos, en prosa. Estrenado en el *Teatro Español* el 9 de Enero de 1906.
>
> *Cuesta abajo,*[5] comedia dramática en cinco actos, en prosa. Estrenada en el *Gran Teatro* el 22 de Enero de 1906.
>
> *El becerro de metal,* comedia dramática en tres actos, en prosa, n.d.
>
> *Juventud,* comedia dramática en tres actos, en prosa, n.d.
>
> *Las raíces,* comedia dramática en tres actos, en prosa, n.d.[6]

She thus tried her hand at the monologue and at three-, four-, and five-act plays. Conspicuous success seems to have attended only *El vestido de boda, La suerte,* and *Cuesta abajo.* She herself thought that *Verdad* was a better play than *Cuesta abajo,* but the public disagreed.[7] Luis Morote agreed with her: "Porque *Verdad* es cien veces superior, mil veces superior a *Cuesta abajo,* porque en *Verdad* están Tolstoï y Gorki mejor o peor imitados, mientras que en *Cuesta abajo* se recuerda a Scribe. . . . Pero éstas son las justicias que manda hacer el público y ante sus mandatos hay que doblar la cabeza. . . ."[8] He does say, however, although somewhat cryptically, that *Verdad* was not altogether displeasing to its audience.[9] As he continues, it is evident that his own conditional approval of *Verdad* was not meant to imply satisfaction with it, much less enthusiasm. He even goes so far as to condemn it carefully, along with Santiago Rusiñol's *Buena gente:* "Porque ambos son melodramas, dramones mejor diría, que merecían, en un criterio de perfecta equidad, ser rechazados los dos. . . ."

It is in this last comment that Morote strikes at the heart of all Pardo Bazán's dramatic troubles. Whether intentionally or not, she has given us stark, raving melodrama not unmixed with sentimentality; and for these a Pardo Bazán cannot be forgiven.

Her monologues, *El vestido de boda* and *La suerte,* both beautifully and touchingly written, are full of sentiment and tender feeling. If it may be assumed that Pardo Bazán lacked the warmth of the feminine touch in her novels, such criticism could never be assigned to her monologues. The first gives us a fragment of the life of a Spanish seamstress. *La suerte* is a Galician story of a widow's savings brought to nought at the bottom of a river, when a foundling boy for whom her savings were intended is worsted in a fight and thrown into the river with the money.

Verdad begins with the theme of "nothing but the truth." Irene, the ill-fated semi-protagonist, says in Act I, scene vi: "¿Sigues con la tema de pedir verdades? . . . Mereces, mereces esa verdad que tanto deseas." By Act III, we have progressed to the theme of "your sins will find you out." Martín, the hero, remarks in the first scene of this act: "Siempre asoman a flor de tierra los pies de la verdad, por mucho que la enterremos." The "verdad" theme is worked to death throughout the play, with constant repetition of the word "verdad." We are served up unmitigated and unrelenting tragic atmosphere, spiced with horror throughout. There is an uncompromising insistence on driving home the truth of the truth. This driving home of the theme is in no sense the evangelistic sermonizing of a Fernán Caballero. The play is not meant to be an object lesson to anyone. Pardo Bazán simply goes ahead and tells her story in a straightforward, thoroughgoing manner, as coolly as she did in *Los Pazos de Ulloa* and *La madre naturaleza,* with no punches pulled. The vogue of naturalism had passed, and it would be unfair to classify her drama as anything but the unadulterated realism that was always her ambition. Withal, the characters are well drawn, and the drama seems not to be suffering from that common fault of novelists who write drama, viz., a novelistic portrayal in dramatic form. Pardo Bazán makes one wish he might see a dramatic work of hers written in a calmer mood.

A portion of Morote's report on the *estreno* of *Verdad* will bear quotation:

> El público estuvo cruel, fiero, hosco y hasta grosero con la Pardo Bazán. No le perdonó nada, no tuvo siquiera en cuenta el bagaje literario de la escritora a la que se ha llamado algo irónicamente la eximia. Se juntaron en el Teatro Español todos sus enemigos, dispuestos a devorarla, como en efecto hicieron de un modo implacable. Aquello no era público, era una jauría desatada. En los corredores se escuchaba a jóvenes y a ancianos críticos exclamar: ¡que se vaya a hacer calceta! Ya quisieran muchos de los que censuraban, tener la mitad del talento de *hombre,* no de mujer, que tiene la Pardo Bazán. . . . y nadie pidió el nombre de la autora de *Verdad* al caer el telón. . . .[10]

He concludes his relation of the plot with: "¿Para qué continuar la cuenta? ¡Lástima de drama!"

Pardo Bazán brought all this adverse criticism upon herself by giving us a melodrama with a stupid hero and three assassinations, one of the assassinations being that of the heroine in the first act, and that by strangulation almost in the sight of the audience!

In *Cuesta abajo* she uses the device, often employed by Pérez Galdós, of significant names of characters, e.g., La Marquesa de Castel Quemado, Julio Ambas Castillas, Manolo Lanzafuerte, and Alonso Altacruz. Following the cast of characters, the authoress makes the following unusual suggestion to the impresario:

> Advertencias importantes de la autora.—Si se juzgase oportuno por razones de brevedad o de conveniencia, el cuarto acto de esta obra puede suprimirse en la representación. Los renglones entre asteriscos pueden suprimirse también.

The play begins with the hackneyed device of two servants in the home of the Condes de Castro Real discussing the affairs of the family they serve, as they arrange the room. The burden of the play is the enthronement of traditionalism, in the same uncompromising manner as that used by Ricardo León in *Casta de hidalgos*. The success of this play is as difficult to understand now as it was when Morote saw it on the stage. He writes:

> . . . el triunfo indudable de *Cuesta abajo.* . . . ¡Qué ironías las ironías del público! Poco le faltó en el Teatro Español para silbar *Verdad* y en poco estuvo que no sacaran a la Pardo del Gran Teatro entre vivas y aclamaciones, en una triunfal marcha de las Antorchas para celerar el éxcito de *Cuesta abajo.* ¡Qué injusticia![11]

El becerro de metal is an exaggerated, sentimental play on the Jewish-Spanish theme made famous by Pérez Galdós in *Gloria* and by Fernández Ardavín in *La dama del armiño*. Sentimentality again rules the stage in *Juventud*, and again significant names of characters are used: Socorro, Don Carmelo, and Doña Traspaso. Here we witness the rather unreasonable regeneration of a visionary, idealistic, and somewhat flighty adolescent into the fine, upstanding, and responsible man that we should have recognized in him all along. He is the idealist gone realist and come to his senses, thus being able to marry the girl next door whom he has courted over the back fence. The title is apt, and the reader or audience is not disillusioned. Melodrama comes to the fore again in *Las raíces*. This time the plot revolves around the illicit love affairs of a husband and his wife, each of whom has succeeded in keeping his secret from the other. The death of a sickly child of the wife, the husband's losses in a bank failure, of which bank the wife's paramour is president, and the revelation of forgotten love letters furnish the mental pandemonium of the characters.

Pardo Bazán was not a dramatist, her own convictions, ambitions, and dramatic works to the contrary notwithstanding. It is unfortunate that she ever essayed the drama.[12] The worthy forty-six other volumes of her *Obras completas* will stand as a lasting monument to her prodigious energy and productivity, and to her literary eminence. Her volume of *Teatro* has well deserved the oblivion to which it has been consigned.

Notes

1. Emilia Pardo Bazán, *Obras completas,* 47 vols. (Madrid, 1888-1922). *Teatro* is vol. 35.

2. Undertaken in January, 1906, long after the acclaim with which her *Los Pazos de Ulloa* (1886) and *La madre naturaleza* (1887) were received. Her monologues, however, are earlier: 1898 and 1904.

3. I have examined the following in this connection, none of which even mentions her drama: G. T. Northup, *An Introduction to Spanish Literature* (Chicago, 1925 and 1936); J. D. M. Ford, *Main Currents of Spanish Literature* (New York, 1919); M. Romera-Navarro, *Historia de la literatura española* (Boston, 1928); F. Blanco García, *La literatura española en el siglo XIX,* 3 vols. (Madrid, 1909-1912); A. Salcedo Ruiz, *La literatura española,* 4 vols. (Madrid, 1915-1917); A. González Blanco, *Los Contemporáneos,* 4 vols. (Paris, 1906-1910) and *Historia de la novela en España desde el romanticismo a nuestros días* (Madrid, 1909); F. Vézinet, *Les maîtres du roman espagnol contemporain* (Paris, 1907), pp. 203-31; César Barja, *Libros y autores modernos, siglos XVIII y XIX* (Los Angeles, 1933), pp. 305-22; José León Pagano, *Al través de la España literaria,* 2 vols. (Barcelona, n.d.), II, 113-27; B. Pérez Galdós, *Obras inéditas; arte y crítica,* 2 vols. (Madrid, 1923), pp. 201-08; A. Valbuena Prat, *Historia de la literatura española,* 2 vols. (Barcelona, 1937); José Martínez Ruiz (Azorín), *El paisaje de España visto por los españoles* (Buenos Aires, 1941); Jean Cassou, *Panorama de la littérature espagnole contemporaine* (Paris, 1929); Beatrice Erskine, "Emilia Pardo Bazán," *Contemporary Review,* CXX (1921), 240-44; Luis Ruiz Contreras, *Medio siglo de teatro infructuoso* (Madrid, 1930); Manuel Martínez Espada, *Teatro contemporáneo* (Madrid, 1900); Rubén Darío, *España contemporánea* (Paris, 1921); José Yxart, *El arte escénico en España,* 2 vols. (Barcelona, 1894-1896); Constantino Eguía Ruiz, *Literaturas y literatos* (Madrid, 1914); Julio Casares, *Crítica profana* (Madrid, 1916); Rafael Cansinos-Assens, *La nueva literatura,* 4 vols. (Madrid, 1917-1927) and *Poetas y prosistas del novecientos* (Madrid, 1919); Eduardo Gómez de Baquero, *El renacimiento de la novela en el siglo XIX* (Madrid, 1924); Andrés González Blanco, *Los dramaturgos españoles contemporáneos* (Valencia, 1917); A. Andrade Coello,

La Condesa Emilia Pardo Bazán (Quito, 1922); Margarita Nelken, *Las escritoras españolas* (Barcelona, 1930), pp. 220-26; E. Gómez de Baquero (Andrenio), *De Gallardo a Unamuno* (Madrid, 1926), pp. 145-59; Manuel Gálvez, "Emilia Pardo Bazán," *Nosotros,* XXXVIII (1921), 27-34; José Francés, "Les scénarios du roman espagnol," *Hispania* (Paris), II (1919), 299-306; G. Martínez Sierra, "La feminidad de Emilia Pardo Bazán," *Motivos* (Paris, 1905), pp. 129-41; Boris de Tannenberg, *L'Espagne littéraire, portraits d'hier et d'aujourd'hui,* première série (Paris, 1903), pp. 299-316; A. Canga-Argüelles, "Doña Emilia Pardo Bazán," *La ilustración española y americana* (June 22, 1916); and Manuel de la Cruz, *Estudios literarios* (Madrid, 1924), pp. 277-91.

4. Their brief comment is as follows: Mérimée-Morley, *A History of Spanish Literature* (New York, 1930), p. 550: "As if the laurels of novelist, critic, student, moralist, and publicist were not enough, Sra. Pardo Bazán wished to add to them those of the theater (*Verdad,* 1906) . . . ;" J. Fitzmaurice-Kelly, *Historia de la literatura española* (Madrid, 1921), p. 333: "La condesa de Pardo Bazán . . . ha cultivado el teatro . . ."; José A. Balseiro, *Novelistas españoles modernos* (New York, 1933), p. 326, lists "Tomo 35, 'Teatro'"; A. González Blanco, "Emilia Pardo Bazán," *La Lectura,* VIII (1908), 20-29, 155-66, and 414-21, p. 27: "Ahora [after her prize essay on Feijóo, 1876] es cuando remanece en ella el hervor literario; *comete,* como dice con suprema ironía, dos o tres dramas, 'prudentemente cerrados bajo llave apenas concluídos'"; A. F. G. Bell, *Contemporary Spanish Literature* (New York, 1925), p. 61: "Literary criticism, essays, books of travel, lectures, plays . . ."; J. Hurtado y J. de la Serna y A. González Palencia, *Historia de la literatura española* (Madrid, 1921), p. 1020: "En el teatro no logró éxito; sus obras estrenadas son: *El traje de novia* [*sic* for *El vestido de boda*], *Verdad, Cuesta abajo y La suerte*"; J. Cejador y Frauca, *Historia de la lengua y literatura castellana,* 14 vols. (Madrid, 1915-1922), IX, 285, lists: "*El vestido de boda,* monologo, 1898; *La suerte,* diálogo dramático, 1904; *Verdad,* drama (silbado), 1906; *Cuesta abajo,* comedia (ídem, 1906); *Teatro,* 1909"; *Enciclopedia universal ilustrada* (Espasa), XLI, 1441: "Entre las obras escritas para el teatro figuran *Verdad* y *Cuesta abajo* (1906), estrenadas con mediana fortuna"; E. Gómez de Baquero (Andrenio), *Novelas y novelistas* (Madrid, 1918), p. 297: "Quitando algunos ensayos dramáticos . . ."; C. C. Glascock, "Two Modern Spanish Novelists: Emilia Pardo Bazán and Armando Palacio Valdés," *University of Texas Bulletin,* No. 2625

(Austin, 1926), p. 42: "Her activity extended over a wide range indeed: literary criticism, essays, books on travel, lectures, plays . . ."; and *Short Stories by Pardo Bazán,* ed. A. Shapiro and F. J. Hurley (New York, 1933), Introd., p. vii: "In addition to writing verses, plays. . . ." For the exceptions, see note 7, below. Except for the last work cited above, textbooks do not mention her drama: *Pascual López,* ed. W. I. Knapp (Boston, 1905); *Los mejores cuentos de la Condesa Emilia Pardo Bazán,* ed. W. K. Jones (Garden City, 1931); and *El tesoro de Gastón,* ed. Elizabeth McGuire (New York, 1922).

5. She used this same title for one of her short stories.

6. The title of another work, *Nada,* somewhat ominous, it must be admitted, is given by Mariano Miguel de Val, in *Los novelistas en el teatro* (Madrid, 1906), p. 52: ". . . *Nada,* título éste de su nueva obra, destinada al teatro de la Comedia" (after the performance of *Cuesta abajo*). No work of this title appears in her *Teatro.* Mariano Miguel de Val treats only the first four works in my list.

7. Cf. Luis Morote, *Teatro y novela* (Madrid, 1906), p. 289, where he reports a conversation with the authoress, in which he remarked to her: "Me gusta más *Verdad* con todos sus errores que *Cuesta abajo* con todos sus aplausos. . . ." He goes on to say: "Y la talentuda dama me replicó que pensaba lo mismo, sólo que como no es posible rebelarse contra el público recogía los aplausos tributados a *Cuesta abajo* y mentalmente se los tributaba a su hija predilecta *Verdad.*" The only other critic who seems to have given Pardo Bazán's drama much notice is Mariano Miguel de Val, whose work is cited in note 6, above. This work, *Los novelistas en el teatro,* was written as a result of a polemic sustained with Pardo Bazán in the first issues of the review, *Ateneo.* The polemic is continued in the book, notably pp. 16-55; the treatment is caustic and sinks to name-calling. He says she attacked him only because she thought he attacked her in his *Ateneo* article. The beginnings of this literary feud may be reviewed in *Ateneo,* I (1906), as follows: Mariano Miguel de Val, "Los novelistas en el teatro," 62-65; Emilia Pardo Bazán, "Los novelistas en el teatro," 181-84; and X, "Los novelistas en el. teatro, por Mariano Miguel de Val," 321-22. (The last mentioned is a review of Sr. Val's book before its publication.)

8. *Op. cit.,* p. 288.

9. *Op. cit.,* p. 272: "El drama de la Pardo Bazán, pese a la fama literaria de su autora, o a causa de esa misma fama, fracasó ruidosamente parallel gran público y sólo gustó a contadísimos críticos y hombres de letras."

10. *Op. cit.,* pp. 276-77.

11. *Op. cit.,* p. 288. Mariano Miguel de Val, *op. cit.,* pp. 48-52, cites various periodical reviews of her dramatic work (in *El Imparcial, ABC, Diario Universal, Heraldo de Madrid,* and *Época*), particularly of *Cuesta abajo.*

12. Sr. Val, *op. cit.,* p. 162, quotes her as saying: ". . . he huido del teatro como el diablo de la cruz."

Robert E. Osborne (essay date March 1950)

SOURCE: Osborne, Robert E. "The Aesthetic Ideas of Emilia Pardo Bazán." *Modern Language Quarterly* 11, no. 1 (March 1950): 98-104.

[*In the following essay, Osborne underscores Pardo Bazán's opinions about the nature and purpose of art as displayed in her writings.*]

Emilia Pardo Bazán once wrote, "Todo el que lea mis ensayos críticos comprenderá que no soy idealista, ni realista, ni naturalista, sino ecléctica."[1] If one bears in mind that she is eclectic, and prides herself on so being, one will understand much that otherwise might seem contradictory. Some critics, in their zeal to pigeonhole every writer, have tried to force Doña Emilia into a "school" or into some particular pattern of writing or thinking. To do this, one must ignore certain aesthetic ideas which Doña Emilia professed and—in the main—carried out in her works.

The purpose of art, according to Doña Emilia, and the sole purpose, is to create beauty. She consistently denies that, in her novels, she is defending any particular moral system or that she is trying to teach any special political or social doctrine. Her task is only to create beauty.[2] Whether or not she carries out this principle in practice may be debatable, but, at least in theory, she never abandons it. Nowhere in her writings does Doña Emilia tell us what beauty is. The closest she comes to a definition is when she states, "– la fuente de toda belleza, que es la verdad."[3] The word *verdad* is, of course, vague in meaning, and she never interprets it. Pardo Bazán—who makes no claim to an ordered aesthetic system—rarely defines her terms in a precise manner.

When Doña Emilia speaks of beauty in art, she has no doubt been influenced by her studies on Padre Feijóo. She tells us that the finale of an opera where the tenor sings while dying may be beautiful but not true. A licentious, pagan work of art may be beautiful without being good. It is useless, she continues, to try to rest these conclusions on reason alone because in the perception of beauty there is a certain something, a *no sé qué* which defies logic and cannot be explained.[4]

Pardo Bazán maintains that beauty is, in a certain sense, eternal, but in another is subject to change, renewing and modifying itself as does the atmosphere. For this reason, when prophesying the triumph of realism, she states that she is not under the delusion that this is *the* form of art.[5] There is no definitive form for art, nor, in the strictest sense of the word, is there any progress in art.[6] The purpose of art is the creation of beauty, and man's conception of beauty may vary from age to age and from country to country. She believes that the writer who loses sight of art's purpose will suffer in the same proportion as he has sinned. Even if art should be based on truth, truth is not its principal function—that is the office of science.[7]

Art, says Doña Emilia, cannot be vulgarized. When one tries to place it within reach of the masses, one must put it on a lower plane. At some time in the past there may have existed a popular art, fruit of the social organization of that age, but be that as it may, modern art is not born of the people and indeed scarcely penetrates to them. The people are disinterested in both art and science. They are concerned only by those aspects which seem to be of immediate profit and advantage to them. Towards all else they show a stony indifference. Literary works are judged by how much they may be adapted to support particular political or social opinions or for their value as recreational reading, not by the beauty they may contain or even by what truth they may show. If it were not for that part of society which is perennially becoming aristocratic, and for the *moyenne illustrée* who can spare enough time from the daily search for bread to investigate art and to ponder over it, art would long since have been dead.[8]

Literature is gradually moving further from the people. This movement was greatly accelerated during the nineteenth century. It will lead, Doña Emilia fears, to a complete divorce between the artist and the people, and then to active opposition.[9] Pardo Bazán says that it looks as if the day will arrive when no one will read what the author is trying to say except the author himself.[10] Although considering art to be essentially aristocratic, she is, nevertheless, opposed to these tendencies to dehumanize art. "No puede el arte fundarse sino en la naturaleza, y en la humanidad, y son realidades ambas—inmensas realidades. Hasta la esfera, real también, de lo suprasensible, no la conoce el arte sino al través de la humanidad."[11] When art divorces itself from man and nature, it has no meaning for her, no raison d'être.

Doña Emilia believes, as has been pointed out, that not only is art essentially aristocratic, but that it should not be employed as propaganda. The only time she wavered in her opinion was shortly after the termination of the Spanish-American War. She could not comprehend the impassive attitude of Spanish letters in the face of this terrible blow. In this case, Pardo Bazán the patriot overcame the scruples of Pardo Bazán the artist.

According to Doña Emilia, the highest sign of human nobility is art, in which life, both external and internal, is reflected.[12] Since life is both organic and psychic, Doña Emilia considers that the spiritual effect produced upon her by a picture of the Virgin is just as real as the impression produced by the crude details of a factory. Art must not be mutilated but must be permitted to depict both the material and the spiritual—and by the spiritual she is not referring to that type of writer "—que escribe con agua bendita y a que Barbey llamaba *cretino*—." There are even times when she believes, with Gautier, that art is the only thing which endures. It is the sign of our greatness, of what we have been and the promise of what we may be. It is the archive for the activities of the human soul. *Ars Ionga, vita brevis est.* In many respects art is superior to science, for the art found in the caves of Santillana is as legitimate as that of the latest painter, whereas the science of yesterday may be useless and false today.

Doña Emilia never ceased to wonder over the fact that the artistic creation of man's fantasy could often be more important than the truth itself.[13] The suicide of Werther may be of more significance than that of some unfortunate who threw himself from a bridge last night. The Hamlet of Shakespeare is more important than any real Danish prince. What has just been said should not be interpreted to mean that Doña Emilia thought all works of art should or could live. On the contrary, most of art was doomed to die early if it said little to the generations which followed it. Therefore, she claims, what has been forgotten deserves, in general, to be forgotten.[14]

Art is amoral. That is to say, it is neither immoral nor moral. To be sure, says Doña Emilia, there are words which even the frankest writer does not put down on paper. Parenthetically, she once observed, "Lícito es callar, pero no fingir." Some limits are doubtlessly drawn by good taste. Nevertheless, one cannot condemn Shakespeare because he has passages in some of his works which might be considered immoral. There are, on the other hand, many highly edifying books which do not deserve the name of art. Pardo Bazán scorns that type of English novelist, so common in the nineteenth century, who deemed it his—or frequently her—duty to protect the innocence of the home. Such motives may be noble, but they are not the motives to inspire a true work of art.

Art must not be employed as a means of propaganda, for it is not utilitarian. It is, she says, egoistic, pagan, individual, and so only indirectly useful. It is a grave aesthetic error to place art as an instrument in the service of ethics.[15] She prefers the naturalist who ignores the subject of morals to a Hugo or a Eugène Sue who preaches on every page.

Art reflects the age in which it is born. This is a statement which is found in Doña Emilia's works from *La cuestión palpitante* to her last writings. No one can escape his times, and even the man who revolts against them is only the voice of many others who share the same dissatisfaction.[16] Literature undergoes a ceaseless transformation, adjusting and harmonizing itself with the times. She believes that if all history were lost it could be rather well reconstructed from the literary works of the past. Therefore, Doña Emilia thinks all periods in art are worthy of study.[17]

Since both science and religion do much to determine any age, they have always exerted an influence on art. The religion of a people has a direct bearing on that people's art, as even a superficial observer can tell. The influence of science has been particularly strong during the nineteenth century. Entire systems of art and aesthetics have been based on science. Balzac, Flaubert, Taine, and others proceed as much from the scientific direction as they do from the lyric impulse.[18] Art, thinks Doña Emilia, ought to make use of the sciences. The sculptor should know his anatomy well—but he must aspire to produce more than an anatomical model. That certain something, that *no sé qué* of which Feijóo spoke, must be present, and it is the exclusive patrimony of art. "Quien careciere de esa quisicosa, no pise los umbrales del templo de la belleza, porque será expulsado."[19] The domains of art and science can mutually support one another, but they must not be confused. The principal object of science is truth, while that of art is beauty.

Chronology is deceptive and must always be weighed when speaking of an age. Dumas, Hugo, Vigny, Sainte-Beuve, Gautier, and Stendhal—different from one another in many respects—were all writing in the same period. Pardo Bazán thinks that no period ever possessed complete unity. In former times, powerful general currents may have caused such an illusion, but this unity in reality did not exist. The apparent unity of the eighteenth century, for example, disappears when one remembers that Voltaire doubtlessly thought Rousseau was a fool.

Doña Emilia distrusts schools of writing. She is too eclectic to be tied to any one formula. There is a great difference, she notes, between general principles of aesthetics and the schools which aspire to embody them. Usually the schools are limitations of the principles.[20] No author ought to be scandalized at a new type of writing, for each literary movement is born of the preceding one, and they are linked together with an almost mathematical precision. The caprice of any particular writer is not enough in itself to bring about new artistic forms.

Doña Emilia shows considerable distrust for literary theories. If Shakespeare were to formulate his theory of art, she believes it would not be too different from that of Victor Hugo, and yet how dissimilar the results when put into practice. The theater of Shakespeare is immortal and that of Hugo is alive only as a curiosity, as a document.

Although Doña Emilia believes that no one man can bring about a literary movement, she lays much stress on the importance of the individual in literature. However, she does lament the loss of many of the great collective ideals of the past and deplores the present tendency to make the individual sacred, not because of any value he may have, but merely because he is an individual. As art will always be the exception, she thinks these trends bode ill for its future.[21] Nevertheless, resistance to that which limits and restrains the individual has always been of much import to aesthetics and literature in all ages. Whatever the dogmas of any given school, the individual is always above them. What the naturalists called the *tempérament* is of paramount importance to her. She is opposed to such anti-individualistic views as those held by Taine. Take away Napoleon, and you will change the history of Europe. As to why a group of exceptionally gifted artists should happen to live in the same time and place, thus producing a golden age—as in the case of painters in seventeenth-century Holland—she says she has no explanation. Taine, with his race, environment, and time theory, does not convince her (although she has often used this idea), since opposing conclusions could be drawn from this hypothesis. The only thing that can be said is that it happened. No one explanation is completely satisfactory.

As Pardo Bazán opines that one cannot re-create the past, not so much because of lack of skill or data, but because we do not have the spirit of former times, she places much stress, in literature, on the development of characters. There are, broadly speaking, two types of characters. Tartuffe represents one kind. He is a universal character and stands for or symbolizes something, in this case the hypocrite. Richard III is an individual character. He is an ambitious king, but we see in him things we do not observe in other monarchs, other ambitious leaders, and other men of his time.[22] She prefers the latter type. The individual character is more suited to show that conflict in the human soul which is for her all-important. That conflict, she says, can be summarized under the two headings of sin and repentance.[23] The man who does evil and who does not feel that he is so doing is of little interest to others. Therefore, when the naturalists took away responsibility from the individual, they committed a serious blunder. Here again, one is compelled to note that Doña Emilia did not always carry out in her creative writings what she preached in theory, and some critics, such as Ortega y

Gasset, have said harsh words about her methods of characterizing. But here we are concerned chiefly with her theory.

The question of style was one which often perplexed Doña Emilia. Sometimes a very polished and correct style may place a veil between the reader and the work—perhaps a golden veil, but nevertheless a veil. If the other extreme is taken, the author permits his style to become too relaxed, and he will offend the reader of taste. The style of the work will degenerate into journalism. She herself thinks that when a character speaks for himself, the author should respect the form in which the character would naturally talk and think, but when the author is speaking, then he may show himself in a language which is elegant and if possible perfect. It is on these grounds that she criticizes Valera's characters, saying, "En Valera no hay Sanchos, todos son Valeras."[24] She claims that it is not her intention to mutilate the form of the language under any circumstances, but new words and expressions from everyday speech can be introduced into the literary language whenever they are suitable.[25] Here she has been both impressed and influenced by Hugo's remarks on the subject, remarks which she often quotes.

The literature of the first years of the twentieth century excited considerable comment from Doña Emilia. What is modern in art, she believes, is not the describing of a factory or the cursing of an emperor, but a manner of feeling with that peculiarly modern *sensibilidad*.[26] Here again, Doña Emilia is not so precise in her definition of terms as we might wish. The *Salomé* of Oscar Wilde is very modern, even though the incidents take place almost two thousand years ago in the Near East. Literature, she feels, is not moving toward the simple, but toward the complicated and the *conceptuoso*. With the first World War, she sees the closing of a literary age which began with romanticism and ended with the "disgregación escolástica absoluta" in the first years of the twentieth century. The present moment, said Doña Emilia, is different from others which we know in history, not only because it is materialistic, but because it is so anti-lyrical, so utilitarian.[27] These differences will, of course, be reflected in art.

She is, on the whole, pessimistic about the future of literature. She believes there is a decadence in Spain, noting only a few exceptions such as Maeztu, Baroja, and "Azorín." The same decadence she perceives elsewhere, as in the English novel. She is not certain there will be a renaissance. Perhaps, she told Pagano, the world was growing tired. The conception of the ideal is decaying more and more. There have been Titans, Gods, and Heroes. "Hoy es el Superhombre, mañana será el Hombre."[28]

Notes

1. Emilia Pardo Bazán, *Nuevo teatro crítico*, "Pedro Antonio de Alarcón—las novelas largas," Madrid, November, 1891.

2. *Polémicas y estudios literarios,* in *Obras de Emilia Pardo Bazán* (Pueyo, Madrid, n.d.), Vol. 6, p. 139: "Por centésima vez, el objeto del arte no es defender ni ofender la moral, es realizar la belleza. Para defender la moral, salgan a la palestra los moralistas."

3. *La literatura francesa moderna,* in *Obras,* Vol. 41, III, 224.

4. *La cuestión palpitante* (Madrid, 1883), p. 146.

5. *Ibid.,* pp. 187-88.

6. *La Quimera,* in *Obras,* Vol. 29, p. 352.

7. *La cuestión palpitante,* p. 130.

8. *El lirismo en la poesía francesa,* in *Obras,* Vol. 43, pp. 376-77.

9. *Ibid.,* p. 83: "Desde Lamartine, la poesía, y en general la literatura, van paulatinamente desviándose del público, situándose aparte y fuera de él, hasta llegar a completo divorcio y, más tarde, a oposición."

10. *La literatura francesa moderna,* I, 47.

11. *Ibid.,* III, 24-25.

12. *El lirismo en la poesía francesa,* p. 17.

13. *Ibid.,* p. 16.

14. *La España Moderna,* "Dos cidianistas extranjeros," November, 1890, p. 80.

15. *Nuevo teatro crítico,* "Una polémica entre Valera y Campoamor," February, 1891, Núm. 2, p. 47.

16. *El lirismo en la poesía francesa,* p. 11.

17. *Los poetas épicos cristianos,* Administración (Madrid, 1895), p. 97.

18. *La literatura francesa moderna,* I, 294-95.

19. *La cuestión palpitante,* p. 19.

20. *El lirismo en la poesía francesa,* p. 26.

21. *Ibid.,* p. 240: "El individuo es sagrado, no por valer, sino sencilla y meramente por su condición de individuo, inconfundible con la colectividad. Y claro es que esta suposición es la más incompatible con los derechos del arte: porque el arte será siempre una excepción, y, por tanto, una especialización individual. Así, a medida que los principios del individualismo político y social van avanzando y ganando terreno, el arte pierde su eficacia sobre las colectividades, y pasa a ser patrimonio y bien y pan espiritual solamente de unos pocos, cada vez más distanciados del público."

22. *La literatura francesa moderna,* III, 137.

23. *Ibid.,* III, 204: "Todos los conflictos del alma humana se resumen en el pecado y el arrepentimiento."

24. *La cuestión palpitante,* p. 172.

25. *De mi tierra,* "Feijóo y su siglo," in *Obras,* Vol. 9, pp. 199-200. (This is only one example chosen at random. Many others could be cited.)

26. *La literature francesa moderna,* III, 273.

27. *El lirismo en la poesía francesa,* p. 24.

28. J. L. Pagano, *Al través de la España literaria* (Barcelona, 1904), "Emilia Pardo Bazán," II, 123.

Robert B. Knox (essay date March 1958)

SOURCE: Knox, Robert B. "Artistry and Balance in *La Madre Naturaleza.*" *Hispania* 41, no. 1 (March 1958): 64-70.

[*In the following essay, Knox evaluates the plot, style, tone, and character development in Pardo Bazán's novel* La madre naturaleza.]

Although Emilia Pardo Bazán's place as one of Spain's great novelists appears secure, criticism of her works has pursued a tortuous course marked by many vicissitudes and divergent opinions. Moot points have ranged from the consistency of her literary credo and the trajectory of her development as an author to the character and merits of her style.

What of her personality and its effect on her writings? According to Ronald Hilton, she sees Spain "through the prism of an intellect in which a Catholic upbringing and a Naturalist outlook produce, through their incompatibility, strange distortions,"[1] whereas E. Correa Calderón affirms that "no es la suya una personalidad contradictoria, ni mucho menos."[2] If these pronouncements do not flatly negate one another, they nevertheless seem sharply at variance.

Appraisals of her style also differ widely, and we are left in doubt whether she is "el mejor hablista" among the novelists of her time,[3] wielding "un estilo plástico y certero"[4] or whether, on the other hand, "la prosa de doña Emilia perjudica a sus novelas: al relato, a las descripciones de paisajes, a las sensaciones, al análisis, aun al diálogo."[5]

The very landscape of the Orense region, locale of the Ulloa novels, contributes to the discrepancy of critical reactions. Correa Calderón finds it wilder than the Countess' native coastal area and hence a fitting backdrop for violent passions (p. 37). Not so Emilio González López, who declares that these two districts are much alike in their fertility, placidity, and mild climate and contrasts them with the untamed sections of Galicia that furnished novel settings to Valle-Inclán.[6]

Most of all, however, it is Pardo Bazán's general literary orientation that has been at issue, and for this her stand on naturalism in *La cuestión palpitante* has doubtless been the principal reason. The reservations with which she accepted the French movement have often been cited without much diminishing the vigor of the debate over the extent to which she adopted the literary practices of Zola and his disciples. Discussions of this topic are wont to assume the form of a relative assessment of naturalism and Spanish traditional realism in her stories. If on the one hand there are few critics who regard her as an unmitigated addict of the foreign fashion, there must also be few who would endorse Romera Navarro's reduction of that element in her work to "lo siempre conocido entre nosotros con el nombre de realismo,"[7] or Manuel Gálvez' assertion that "sus novelas . . . apenas se distinguen de las de Pereda, y no vemos en ellas nada semejante a las de Zola" (p. 28).

One portion of Pardo Bazán's fiction which has been most subject to varied judgments in this connection comprises the novel widely regarded as her crowning achievement in that medium, *Los pazos de Ulloa,* and its sequel, *La madre naturaleza.* Declaring that in the latter "el determinismo y fatalismo que a doña Emilia repugnaba en la estética naturalista se ha impuesto por esta vez," César Barja classes both novels among those in which naturalism is predominant, as distinguished from those in which "van a partes iguales . . . el naturalismo y el idealismo o romanticismo—*Un viaje de novios, El cisne de Vilamorta.*"[8] For M. Gordon Brown, on the other hand, the last mentioned novels are among those in which the Countess most closely followed the precepts of Zola, while *Los pazos de Ulloa* and *La madre naturaleza* belong to a transitional phase between them and the more symbolistic later ones.[9]

In all this critical disagreement a lack of uniformity in the use of terminology, with consequent impairment of comprehension, has doubtless played some part. As Correa Calderón remarks, ". . . la polémica sobre el naturalismo, vista a distancia de más de medio siglo, nos parece uno de esos graciosos cuentecillos de sordos, en que cada uno entiende a su manera lo que el otro dijo" (p. 21). Terms like *realism* and *naturalism,* given their checkered history and the intrinsic semantic problems they present, seem made to order for fostering confusion and enlivening controversy.[10]

Nevertheless, a perusal of assorted dicta on the subject reveals some measure of consistency in tracing the boundary between French naturalism and the traditional realism of the Spaniards. Aside from the philosophical foundation in a materialistic determinism, the former is said to be distinguished by pessimistic emphasis, a proclivity for sordid subjects, impersonal tone, and accumulation of detail. And it is the presumed concentration of such characteristics in *Los pazos de Ulloa* and its companion piece that has given rise to the verdict of naturalism brought against them.

Though not unanimous, agreement is rather general on the superiority of *Los pazos de Ulloa* over the rest of Pardo Bazán's fictional output. While *La madre naturaleza* is sometimes included with it as the object of a joint encomium and occasionally receives explicit commendation in its own right, it has usually evoked less critical enthusiasm. Gerald Brenan, who considers the Countess' Galician novels her "only ones worth reading," discusses *Los pazos* in his *Literature of the Spanish People*[11] but does not mention its sequel. Barja rates the latter distinctly below its predecessor and finds it faulty as a novel. "Defecto suele ser en todas las [novelas] de la Condesa de Pardo Bazán la excesiva difusión, y este defecto es exagerado en *La madre naturaleza,* que casi no tiene acción que valga la pena. La novela queda reducida a un rosario de paisajes y de descripciones" (p. 313).

In view of the numerous differences of opinion sampled above, further critical examination of the literary production of Pardo Bazán seems in order; and *La madre naturaleza,* whose reputation remains somewhat unstable, suggests itself as a logical focal point for study—the more so as judgments concerning it have seldom been accompanied by much analysis. Two questions in particular invite consideration: the strength of the plot and its articulation, and the extent to which naturalistic elements are balanced or neutralized by others.

Barja's contention that the work consists of little more than a series of descriptions seems untenable when one recalls the interplay of dramatic forces occasioned by the rivalry of Gabriel and Perucho for Manuela's hand and the emotional crises ignited by that struggle and by the disclosure of the incestuous nature of the young couple's love. These conflicts, which are the main substance of the plot, are gradually and skilfully developed to their climaxes. In the opening chapters the changing nature of the bond between Perucho and Manuela is carefully established and its transformation into an intense passion is foreshadowed. The author then shifts her attention to the major counter force in the person of Gabriel, now approaching the Ulloa estate, his mind occupied with protective and affectionate thoughts about his niece—thoughts which crystallize into a plan to marry her. Certain established techniques for sharpening plot interest come into play here. Centering attention on a traveler en route to a destination where many uncertainties await is one of these. The Romantic device of temporarily concealed identity, dissociated from the absurdities of the *embozo* and the deliberately mysterious look, also proves effective. Moreover, the unrewarded curiosity of the inquisitive Trampeta helps to stimulate that of the reader, as does Gabriel's unexplained interest in matters concerning the Ulloa household.

In the early chapters the main subject of dramatic preparation is the potential competition between Perucho and Gabriel, but the anticipated encounter of the cultivated artillery officer with the primitive social environment of the Ulloa menage likewise stirs forebodings of drama.

As the novel progresses tension grows. Successive outings in which Manuela is attended by each of the rivals in turn draw us toward the major climax: the point at which the contest between the two male leads and the fundamental dilemma of the siblings' double relationship converge in Gabriel's disclosure to Perucho of the youth's identity. Several incidents serve to intensify the suspense in preparation for this climax: Gabriel's insomnia followed by his vain search for Manuela; don Pedro's nearly overt recognition of Perucho's status when he calls for the boy to take his place at the threshing; the discovery that the boy and girl have gone off together at the moment when their absence is most likely to irritate—though for different reasons—the Marquis and Gabriel; the latter's recognition, after a moment of uncertainty, of the two lovers as they return home in the darkness.

Gabriel's revelation to Perucho is the apogee of the plot line and precipitates the denouement. The stormy scene—indirectly presented—in which the boy's father confirms his identity, Perucho's departure, Manuela's illness, and her definitive rejection of her uncle's suit are like the diminuendo of a receding thunderstorm following a devastating bolt close at hand. The departure of Gabriel at the end of the story has the effect of closing the cycle and dropping the keystone into place somewhat as the departure of don Segundo Sombra does in Güiraldes' classic.

Thus, it seems quite inaccurate to regard *La madre naturaleza* as merely a concatenation of landscapes or *cuadros*; and Pardo Bazán's own statement that "en la novela es lo de menos argumento y acción"[12] is applicable to it only if taken to signify a particularly complex sort of plot. Certainly the book offers more than a mere naturalistic slice of life devoid of artistic arrangement.

Furthermore, although descriptions do constitute a major part of the whole, they tend mainly to enhance, rather than to obscure, the plot. The careful depiction of nature, for example, has at least two important related functions with respect to the action: it provides an idyllic setting for some of the scenes of love or intimacy; and in certain passages—notably that devoted to the cave—the emphasis on the promiscuous, genesial ferment symbolizes the budding sexual attraction between Perucho and Manuela and perhaps even stimulates its awakening. "En la gruta, lo que les sacó de su momentáneo embeleso, fué observar la vegetación viciosa y tropical del fondo. . . . Parecía que la naturaleza se revelaba allí más potente y lasciva que nunca, ostentando sus fuerzas genesíacas con libre impudor."[13]

There are several respects in which one can regard this novel as consisting of a balanced blend of naturalistic ingredients with others of a quite different character. Consider the presentation of natural settings. If completely objective, this would presumably consist of a scrupulously accurate and orderly inventory of the details of topography, weather, fauna, and flora uncontaminated by lyricism, symbolism, or stylistic coloring. And it is precisely this sort of description that González López, for one, finds in Doña Emilia's pages: "No hay una sola nota poética en toda su obra; por el contrario su acentuado realismo le lleva a reproducir exactamente, de manera fría e imparcial, las cosas exteriores; para ella le verdad reside en el puro objetivismo, cuyo enemigo es el sentimiento, la sensibilidad, la emoción, en una palabra, todo lo que tenga carácter personal y subjetivo" (p. 105).

We need not seek far in *La madre naturaleza* for a passage with which to test the truth of this assertion. It opens with one: "Las nubes, caliginosas y de un gris amoratado, como de tinta desleída, fueron juntándose, juntándose, atropellándose más bien, en las alturas del cielo, deliberando si se desharían o no se desharían en chubasco. Resueltas finalmente a lo primero, empezaron por soltar goterones anchos, gruesos, legítima lluvia de estío, que doblaba las puntas de las hierbas y resonaba estrepitosamente en los zarzales; luego se apresuraron a porfía, multiplicarón sus esfuerzos, se derritieron en rápidos y oblicuos hilos de agua, empapando la tierra, inundando los matorrales, sumergiendo la vegetación menuda, colándose como podían al través de la copa de los árboles para escurrir después tronco abajo, a manera de raudales de lágrimas por un semblante rugoso y moreno." If the careful observer is at once in evidence here, so is the sensitive artist. Note, for instance, how the scurrying gerunds echo the movements of the clouds, how the simile of tears coursing down a rugged face takes us beyond the purely literal level.

In this downpour Manuela and Perucho turn for shelter to a "magnífico castaño, de majestuosa y vasta copa, abierta con pompa casi arquitectural sobre el ancha y firme columna del tronco, que parecía lanzarse arrogante hacia las desatadas nubes: árbol patriarcal, de

esos que ven con indiferencia desdeñosa sucederse gen-
eraciones de chinches, pulgones, hormigas y larvas, y
les dan cuna y sepulcro en los senos de su rajada
corteza" (p. 6). The sentence is liberally studded with
words unsuited to a strictly botanical description: *magnífico, majestuosa, pompa, arrogante, patriarcal, indiferencia, desdeñosa.*

But there are few passages which better illustrate careful itemization suffused with the glow of sensibility
than that devoted to the rainbow: "No era esbozo de ar-
cada borrosa y próxima a desvanecerse, sino un semi-
círculo delineado con energía, semejante al pórtico de
un palacio celestial, cuyo esmalte formaban los más
bellos, intensos y puros colores que es dado sentir a la
retina humana. El violado tenía la aterciopelada riqueza
de una vestidura episcopal; el añil cegaba con su pro-
funda vibración de zafiro; el azul ostentaba claridades
de agua que refleja el hielo, frías limpideces de noche
de luna; el verde se tornasolaba con el halagüeño matiz
de la esmeralda, en que tan voluptuosamente se recrea
la pupila; y el amarillo, anaranjado y rojo, parecían luz
de bengala encendida en el firmamento, círculos con-
céntricos trazados por un compás celestial con fuego
del que abrasa a los serafines, fuego sin llamas, ascuas,
ni humo" (pp. 12-13).

The author proceeds in orderly analytical fashion to
scrutinize the rainbow band by band, but she also freely
employs words and phrases of a figurative or affective
character. As a matter of fact, unless the rainbows of
Galicia are more vivid and sharply delineated than those
it has been my privilege to see, the very detail may on
reflection seem less the product of painstaking observation than of an industrious imagination.[14]

Sensuous and emotional responsiveness are not alone in
tinting the portrait of nature presented in this novel.
Sometimes it is the filter of literary tradition which does
so: "Caminaban charlando, con tanta alegría como los
mirlos, gorriones, jilgueros, pardillos y demás aves, no
muy pintadas pero asaz parleras, que en setos, viñedos
y árboles cantaban sus trovas a la radiante mañana" (p.
215).

Naturalistic writers have been taken to task for burden-
ing their pages with an excess of tedious minutiae, and
Pardo Bazán has not escaped this reproach. Barja says
that the descriptions in *La madre naturaleza,* as in her
novels generally, "sobre ser muchas, están recargadas
de detalles. O por prurito de escuela o por prurito de
cultura, varias de ellas resultan inventarios, páginas de
un libro de bótanica o de minerología" (p. 313).
González López, who shares this opinion, compares her
unfavorably in this respect with some fellow Galicians:
". . . [Rosalía de Castro, Curros Enríquez, y Valle-
Inclán] captan el paisaje de su tierra en lo esencial y
eterno, prescindiendo de lo anecdótico; en cambio la

escritora realista, con pretensiones de observadora
científica y desinteresada, prefiere el detalle, por estimar que en su abundancia reside el mayor parecido con
el objeto que se pretende representar" (p. 105).

That Pardo Bazán was often generous with detail is undeniable. This can be seen in some of the passages already quoted, and others can easily be found—e.g., in
the pages devoted to the excursion of Gabriel with Manuela. Yet it should be noted that it is not merely the
amount but the kind of detail that gives these scenes
their special character—grass seeds, for instance: ". . .
sus menudas simientes pajizas temblaban, bailaban, os-
cilaban, se encrespaban y bullían como burbujas de aire
moreno, como, gotas de agua enlodada; algunas seme-
jaban bichitos, chinches; otras, como la agrostis, tenían
la vaporosa tenuidad de esas vegetaciones que la fina
punta del pincel de los acuarelistas toca con trazos casi
aéreos, allá al extremo de los países de abanico: una
bruma vegetal, un racimo de menudísimas gotas de
rocío cuajadas" (pp. 173-174). This inspection, if not
precisely microscopic, is certainly attentive. But what is
the effect? Is our response really identical to that elicited by the botany text, which gratifies our desire for
precise knowledge? Or is the artist, by choosing features neglected by the casual passerby and couching
them in evocative language, giving us a fresh vision of
a landscape grown trite from frequent but distrait observation?

It is interesting that minute particulars also abound in
some sections devoted to psychological activity—a
province of reality the naturalists are often said to have
neglected. A case in point is the analysis of Gabriel's
thoughts, feelings, and sensations during the night of
insomnia following the outing with his niece. This account occupies most of a chapter of moderate length
(Ch. XXII). The tempo here can be defended. For the
insomniac himself, without the daytime outlet of physical activity, time creeps; and the sense of its slackened
pace is conveyed to the reader precisely by means of
this protracted report of Gabriel's mental process. It
also prepares more effectively than a few perfunctory
sentences could do for the impact of his discovery next
morning that Manuela has gone off with Perucho.

However, Pardo Bazán does not always proceed in this
fashion but sometimes resorts to narrative economy. An
example is the lean dialogue, virtually without "stage
directions," without even the minimal scaffolding of
such standard verbs of discourse as *decir* and *contestar,*
in the scene where Gabriel announces to don Pedro his
intentions regarding Manuela. Accessory phrases normally supplied by the narrator are stripped away to
quicken the pace of a brisk, almost pugilistic, verbal exchange (pp. 158-160).

It is easy to find in *La madre naturaleza* indications of
the author's scientific interest. They include fragments

like the references to the diastole and systole of Peru-cho's heartbeat or the "vegetación . . . de época ante-diluviana, de capas carboníferas" or the movement of sap in the trees, as well as ideas related to the march of science which enter the thoughts or conversations of the characters. Yet they are hardly so prominent as to estab-lish a dominant tone for the book, nor is their effect necessarily that of exalting science. At one juncture an exposition of Darwinian doctrine is given a pleasantly ironical turn. Gabriel's nocturnal meditation on evolu-tion and its corollary, the struggle for existence, ends in an illustrative skirmish: a mosquito descends on Gabriel and is duly exterminated by the latter's defense (p. 253). Certainly this tempers the seriousness of the pre-sentation of evolutionary theory.

Since the unconsciously incestuous love of Perucho and Manuela, a major theme in the novel, is also a poten-tially sordid one, it may be taken as a distinctly natural-istic feature. In part, the treatment of nature, as men-tioned above, reinforces that aspect of the love theme. To the aforementioned description of the cave can be added the passage wherein Gabriel imagines Mother Nature confiding that ". . . yo jamás he vedado a dos pájaros nacidos en el mismo nido que aniden juntos a su vez en la primavera próxima . . ." (p. 284). Thus, the natural setting of the novel may seem to exude an unwholesome aura corrosive of the morals of the char-acters. Such an impression is in accord with the judg-ment expressed by Ronald Hilton, who draws an inter-esting contrast in this regard with the poet Antonio Machado: "Pardo Bazán differs from Machado in her Catholicism. For her, Mother Nature . . . is essentially sinful. She describes the promiscuously luxuriant nature of Galicia, whereas Machado is thinking of the arid plains of Castile" (p. 329). Yet even in this novel nature is by no means reduced to a simple role of Celestina to a particularly indecent sort of love. In numerous places its beauty emerges untainted by libidinous suggestions, and in the total impression that it leaves on the reader neither somberness nor moral subversiveness stands out.

It is true that the last sentence of the novel is an indict-ment of nature formulated in the mind of Gabriel as he retires from the scene of the action, pausing for a mo-ment to look back: "—Naturaleza, te llaman madre . . . Deberían llamarte madrastra." Yet his feeling toward Mother Nature—"una extraña mezcla de atracción y rencor"—is certainly more equivocal than that unspo-ken sentence might suggest. Moreover, in the descrip-tion of this scene on which he turns a farewell gaze a sense of cleanness and freshness is clearly predominant: "Aquella tarde, el gran ardor de lan canícula daba señales de aplacarse ya, y eran preludio y esperanza de frescura, y acaso de agua, las nubes redondas y los fi-nos *rabos de gallo* que salpicaban caprichosamente el cielo. Una brisa fresca, vivaracha, que columpiaba

partículas de humedad, hacía palpitar el follaje. A lo le-jos chirriaban los carros cargados de mies, y las ranas y los grillos empezaban a elevar su sinfonía vespertina, saludando a la lluvia y al viento antes de que hiciensen su aparición triunfal y refrigerasen la tostada campiña. Todo era vida, vida indiferente, rítmica y serena" (pp. 374-375).

The naturalists are accused of excesses not only in their preoccupation with the sordid and scabrous but also in the mood of unrelieved gloom said to pervade their works. Grimness joins griminess to make such literature repellent. Whether or not this charge could be com-pletely justified even against a novel so central in the movement as *L'assommoir* is not relevant to this study. It is appropriate, however, to consider whether Pardo Bazán, who after all joined in the disapproval of "la pe-renne solemnidad y tristeza, el ceño siempre torvo, la carencia de notas festivas y de gracia y soltura en el es-tilo y en la idea,"[15] disregarded her own critical percepts on this score in *La madre naturaleza.* Anyone who has recently read the novel will recall that it is seasoned with humorous touches which sometimes provide comic relief from high emotional tension. Thus, we turn from Gabriel's recognition of the homeward bound lovers to the *tertulia* presided over by *el Gallo.* This interlude sets the stage for the next crisis: the showdown meeting between the two rivals. Even at the height of their physi-cal struggle we are afforded a fleeting chuckle by a comment on the rocking chair whose collapse changes the course of the fray: "La butaca contra la cual estaba acorralado el comandante era nada menos que una mecedora, mueble que hacía la felicidad del Gallo, por lo mismo que nadie de su familia ni de seis leguas en contorno acertaba a sentarse en ella sino después de re-iterados ensayos, continuas lecciones y fracasos serios" (pp. 305-306).

Not even the final catastrophe—the revelation and its consequences—is utterly unmitigated. Though it pros-trates Manuela, banishes Perucho, and leaves Gabriel severely shaken, none of the three commits suicide, dies of grief, or loses his sanity. The denouement, there-fore, is characterized by a certain moderation, a mod-eration required, in this case, by a genuinely realistic approach. The young people have appeared too sturdy in the course of the novel to succumb readily to emo-tional shock alone, even though Manuela's predisposi-tion to epilepsy complicates matters during the crisis. Moreover, the firmness of their Catholic faith makes suicide a more difficult solution within the internal logic of the story than would otherwise be the case. On first thought, Gabriel, who is not a particularly strong char-acter, might seem easier to dispose of in some definitive manner. However, his experience and sophistication and his penchant for converting emotional crises into sub-jects for intellectual consideration cushion the blow. "En el espíritu de Gabriel batallaban siempre dos tendencias opuestas: la de su imaginación propensa a caldearse y deducir de cada objeto o de cada suceso todo el elemento poético que pueda encerrar, y la de su entendimiento a analizar y calar a fondo todo ese mundo fantástico, destruyéndolo con implacable lucidez" (pp. 289-290). So as he takes his departure from the scene of his frustration he utters an epitaph for his illusion in a tone of "humorística tristeza" rather than one of profound despair: "Otro caballo muerto" (p. 374).

It is my conclusion that **La madre naturaleza,** whose merits as a novel have often been either impugned or ignored, is nevertheless a very good specimen of the novelist's art. Moreover, although criticism has tended to emphasize its naturalistic aspect, or at least its "violent realism," I submit that it consists of a well-balanced blend of varied elements and that naturalism, though an important ingredient, is hardly a dominant one.[16]

Notes

1. Ronald Hilton, "Emilia Pardo-Bazán's Concept of Spain," *Hispania,* XXXIV (Nov. 1951), 329.

2. Universidad de Madrid, Facultad de Filosofía y Letras, *El Centenario de doña Emilia Pardo Bazán* (1952), p. 48. Hereafter called *Centenario.*

3. Eduardo Gómez de Baquero, *De Gallardo a Unamuno* (Madrid, 1926), p. 157.

4. *Centenario,* p. 49.

5. Manuel Gálvez, "Emilia Pardo Bazán," *Nosotros,* XXXVIII (May 1921), 31.

6. Emilio González López, *Emilia Pardo Bazán: Novelista de Galicia* (New York, 1944), pp. 105-108.

7. M. Romera Navarro, *Historia de la literatura española,* 2d ed. (Boston, 1949), p. 591.

8. César Barja, *Libros y autores modernos* (Los Angeles, 1933), pp. 310, 313.

9. "La Condesa de Pardo Bazán y el Naturalismo," *Hispania,* XXXI (May 1948), 156.

10. The richness of the word *realism* as a critical term has been notably placed in relief by the symposium on realism in the Summer, 1951 (Vol. III, no. 3) issue of *Comparative Literature.*

11. Cambridge Univ. Press, 1951, pp. 408-409.

12. *La cuestión palpitante,* 4th ed., *Obras completas,* I (Madrid, 1891), 181.

13. *Obras completas,* IV (Madrid, 1910), p. 11.

14. This treatment of the rainbow is particularly interesting in the light of the focal role played by that gaudy phenomenon in the protracted critical controversy in England over the effects on literature of scientific analysis of nature—a controversy considerably antedating the appearance of the naturalistic movement of the second half of the nineteenth century. See "Newton's Rainbow and the Poet's" in M. H. Abrams, *The Mirror and the Lamp* (Oxford Univ. Press, 1953), pp. 302-312.

15. *Un viaje de novios,* 6th ed. (Madrid, 1919), p. 7. Quoted in *Centenario,* pp. 22-23.

16. It is interesting to note that Gerald Brenan, who recognizes the eclectic technique used in *Los pazos de Ulloa,* does not give it his unqualified approval: ". . . romanticism, realism, naturalism— she has chosen the proportion of each which she thought best suited to her purpose and applied them as a doctor prescribes medicines. This is both the strength of her book and its weakness. *Los Pazos de Ulloa* is a very fine novel, but it does not, I think, quite get hold of us as the works of less competent novelists (Charlotte Brontë, for example) sometimes do. We feel a lack—extraordinary in a Galician—of temperament."

Mary E. Giles (essay date spring 1968)

SOURCE: Giles, Mary E. "Symbolic Imagery in *La Sirena Negra.*" *Papers on Language and Literature* 4, no. 2 (spring 1968): 182-91.

[*In the following essay, Giles examines Pardo Bazán's use of motif, allegory, parallelism of characters, and symbolic imagery in her novel* La sirena negra.]

Emilia Pardo Bazán gradually shifted away from the portrayal of external reality in early novels like **Los pazos de Ulloa** (1886) to the presentation of interior conflict in her final three novels, **La quimera** (1905), **La sirena negra** (1908), and **Dulce Dueño** (1911). These works, the culmination of "el tránsito del naturalismo a un espiritualismo revestido de formas realistas,"[1] resemble contemporary Modernist and *fin de siècle* writing in technique, style, and theme.[2] A specific similarity is the use of symbolist techniques to create mood, develop characters, and enhance theme. The symbolist influence is particularly strong in **La sirena negra,** where it is notable in the symbolic function of imagery and the establishment of image patterns. This study will analyze the nature of imagery in **La sirena negra,** demonstrate how individual images become symbols and part of image patterns, and examine the function of symbolic imagery with respect to the novel's theme, characterization, and tone.

The protagonist, Gaspar de Montenegros, is the typical ennuyé aristocrat of the decadent novel whose tedium, dissatisfaction, and aesthete refinement cause him to disdain the prosaic gratifications of this world and court a perverse fascination with death. He befriends an impoverished, tuberculous woman, Rita Quiñones, because he sees her as one consecrated to death. After she dies, Gaspar adopts her young son, Rafaelín, and engages an English governess and a tutor for the boy. Gaspar's love for his adopted son creates in him a yearning for life that conflicts with his attraction to death. This struggle between the forces of death and life climaxes when the tutor threatens to kill Gaspar for having seduced the governess. Gaspar, refusing to defend himself, succumbs to the fascination of death. Rafaelín, terrified witness to the encounter, runs to intervene, and the shots intended for Gaspar kill the boy instead. Aghast, the tutor shoots himself, while the penitent Gaspar decries his sin: "¡Oh Tú, a quien he ofendido tanto! ¡Dispón de mí; viviré como ordenes, y me llamarás cuando te plazca . . . Pero no me abandones! Tu presencia es ya tu perdón. . . ."[3]

In an effort to capture the enigmatic reality of the spirit, Pardo Bazán emulates other contemporary novelists, like Díaz Rodríguez, Paul Bourget, and J.-K. Huysmans, as she adopts a simple plot line, abandons the detailing of environment, appearance, and secondary characters, and concentrates on the protagonist's emotional conflict. The principal means of describing this conflict is the use of imagery that becomes symbolic through repetition. The reiterated appearance of symbolic images in turn produces an image pattern or system, for "an 'image' may be evoked once as metaphor, but if it persistently recurs both as presentation and representation, it becomes a symbol, may even become part of a symbolic (or mythic) system."[4]

There are three images in *La sirena negra* which become symbols and ultimately part of a pattern: black to signify death, white to represent life in terms of sexual attraction, and the Child Jesus to symbolize life as fraternal love.

The pattern which emerges from the frequent representation of death by black is the most complex because the image is conveyed on three different levels with three modes of expression. The first level is the oneiric representation of death, and the mode of expression, suggested in the novel's title, is the *sirena negra*. The mythological dark siren has appeared to Gaspar in dreams and visions since childhood. While boating on the lake as an adolescent, "unas pupilas oscuras, enormes . . . de asfalto y tinieblas" (p. 114) looked up at him from the waters' depths. Asserting that the eyes were unmistakably those of a woman, he explains the attraction of "aquella criatura de misterio que me arrojaba una mirada magnetizadora; que me invitaba a la sombra y a la paz ya nunca turbada" (p. 114). Later, as an adult, Gaspar recalls that moment when "deprimido por caídas y enfangamiento, apretado del mayor dolor,

que es la vergüenza moral, vi en el fondo del río unos ojos de tinieblas que me llamaban, y estuve a pique de irme hacia ellos, abriendo los brazos y exhalando el '¡Por fin!' de todos los ansiosos amores" (pp. 194-95). When Gaspar returns with Rafaelín to the country estate where he had vacationed as a child, his previous experience on the lake is duplicated. The same dark form rises to meet him out of the obscure waters, and "agarrada a la borda con sus manos de sombra" (p. 229) she fixes upon him the same magnetic eyes. Finally, Gaspar sees her at the moment he welcomes death: "El negro velo en que *ella* se envuelve flotaba ante mis ojos" (p. 249).

The second level of the pattern is the personification of death in the moribund Rita Quiñones, and the descriptions which repeatedly stress the blackness of her hair, eyes, and clothing are the means of expressing the image. The initial description of Rita reveals this emphasis on black: "Para dar idea del tipo de esta mujer, sería preciso evocar las histéricas de Goya, de palidez fosforescente, de pelo enfoscado en erizón, de pupilas como lagos de asfalto, donde duerme la tempestad romántica. El modesto manto de granadina, negro marco de la enflaquecida faz, adquiere garbo de mantilla maja al rodear el crespo tejaroz que deja en sombra la frente" (p. 24). Subsequent references to the woman reinforce the connection between black and death: when Gaspar first visits Rita, she is wearing a "falda de lana negra" (p. 25); she has "la expresión más tétrica en los abismos de asfalto de sus grandes ojos" (p. 27), and as she speaks of her father, "los ojos hondos y calenturientos se velan como de una nube de humo" (p. 27); as they discuss death, she shudders and closes "los pozos de sus ojos" (p. 29); and when she realizes the imminence of death, "le eriza el fosco pelo goyesco" (p. 29); accompanying Gaspar to the theatre, Rita wears "sus acostumbrados trajes de lanilla negra" (p. 30), and as she thrills to the actress' performance, "el agua que duerme en el fondo de sus pupilas tenebrosas salta un momento a la superficie" (pp. 30-31). The final descriptions of the dying woman underscore the quality of blackness: her "cabellera fosca" spreads out on the pillow of her bed, "formando aureola de tinieblas" (p. 51); her pale face moves slightly "entre las tinieblas encrespadas de la cabellera suelta" (p. 56), and her "pupilas de asfalto" (p. 59) are fixed beseechingly on Gaspar. He views the body of the unfortunate Rita after death, and with "sus ojos de sombra" forever closed, she is as usual dressed "de negro paño" (p. 85).

The interpretation of Rita as the personification of death, which is based on the numerous references to the blackness of her features and clothing, is further substantiated by the fact that Gaspar himself admits that he is attracted to her because she represents death. He confesses that he would like to open her skull in order to know "el arcano, único atractivo de este espíritu que, de noche, vaga perdido entre las tinieblas del Miedo y del Mal" (p. 34), and he regards her as the human counterpart of the siren when he compares her eyes with those of his dark temptress: "Y unas pupilas oscuras, enormes—de asfalto y tinieblas, como las de Rita Quiñones la pecadora—me miraban desde el hondón del aqua" (p. 114).

The third level of the image pattern is the darkness of mood around the protagonist, and the mode of expression is the description of tenebrous aspects of people and locale. A funereal atmosphere is established immediately in the novel. In the first chapter, as Gaspar is returning from the theatre late at night, he encounters a poor creature dressed in gray, "de ojeras carbonadas" (p. 9). The night is pregnant with death and misery, and it offers him only "impresiones 'de color sombrío'" (p. 11) that magnify "mi afán de reposo, mi nostalgia de la muerte temporal, mi sed de la nada" (p. 19).

The association of black with death is thus so frequent that the image becomes first symbol and then part of a distinguishable pattern. This pattern is composed of three levels: the oneiric representation of death through the *sirena negra*, the literal description of death through Rita Quiñones, and the evocation of death in descriptions of people and places. Adjectives and nouns of black and darkness link the three levels into a cohesive system.

The two other image patterns result from the symbolic presentation of the forces of life. Two characters possess vitality, and they represent to Gaspar the attraction of life. Miss Annie, the English governess, stands for life in terms of sexual love, and Rafaclín, the adopted child, is life as love for one's fellows. Gaspar recognizes the symbolic role of Miss Annie and Rafaelín when he affirms that "es la salud lo que han de darme las dos supremas representaciones de la existencia: el Niño y la Mujer" (p. 231). The novelist uses white to describe Miss Annie as a force of life, and she compares Rafaelín to the Child Jesus to emphasize his vitality and role as Gaspar's redeemer.

Every description of Miss Annie mentions the lightness of her hair, coloring, or dress. She has "un rubio moño y tez de papel satinado" (p. 136); when she is displeased, she raises "el rubio ceño" (p. 146); and "la tranela blanca de su traje masculino, corto de brazo y pierna, es menos dulce de color que su nuca" (p. 181). When Gaspar sees her swimming from a distance, he notices "la blancura de ondina de los brazos, de las piernas, de la garganta, y la risa silenciosa de la boca emperlada de anchos dientes, otro género de blancura deslumbrante" (pp. 182-83). He refers figuratively to her as a "cándido trozo de nieve solidificada y teñida con el zumo de un pétalo de flor" (p. 186), and when she rides a bicycle, he describes her thus: ". . . nos

sucedía encontrar en las carreteras a la joven, seductoramente masculinizada por los bombachos de paño café y leche, la media escocesa y la gorrilla de tela blanca; sofoquinada por la rápida carrera, alborotadas las guedejas color de cerveza blonda" (p. 193). Gaspar scorns the tutor, Desiderio Solís, for his infatuation with Miss Annie: "¡Eres un mendiguillo, Desiderio! ¡Y todo por un pedazo de carne blanca, donde la naturaleza incrustó dos cuentas de vidrio azul y plantó un matorral de hebras de pelo color cerveza blonda!" (p. 202). Miss Annie comes to Gaspar's room one evening: "La inglesa venía muy guapa, es justo reconocerlo; su pelo de luz, sencilla y hábilmente recogido, y su traje de linó gris, de corte original, exageraban su aire pudibundo y prerrafaelista; era una deslumbradora *girl* de cromo, de ésas en cuya cara la rosa se disuelve en leche y el carmín se afina con transparencias de cristal" (p. 235). Gaspar analyzes the charm of Miss Annie's whiteness: "Jamás me he dado cuenta de este carácter étnico, la blancura de la piel inglesa, como ahora. Es un blanco que será desesperante para un pintor: un blanco tintado imperceptiblemente de rosa té, un blanco virginal, 'carne de doncella' . . . La misma blancura a lo Van-Dick se nota en la pierna larga, esbelta, derecha; en el brazo duro, nada corto; en el pie de mármol, cuyas uñas descubro que están limadas cuidadosamente, y abrillantadas, sin duda, con polvos de coral" (pp. 181-82). Gaspar confesses that the coloring of Miss Annie's skin caused him to seduce her: "Cuando arranqué un jirón de la tela sutil de su corpiño y vi la blancura de su piel, me ofusqué del todo" (p. 238).

As the following introspective remark demonstrates, Gaspar perceives that his attraction to Miss Annie's whiteness is more than a literal interest in her fair coloring: "No cantes victoria, hija de la pérfida Albión, porque notes la eléctrica sacudida que me causa tu presencia. *Yo* no soy esa parte de mi ser a quien tu blancura ha trastornado. *Yo* soy el que piensa, razona, conoce, prevé, diseca. Yo soy el que ama otras cosas muy obscuras, muy sombrías; yo soy el galán de la Negra . . . Soy su trovador, su romántico *minne singer,* capaz de cortarse un dedo, como se lo cortó aquél de la leyenda, para enviárselo a su princesa y dama" (pp. 187-88). Gaspar, then, refuses to be seduced by the life that Miss Annie represents, asserting that even though she may rise from the waves like Aphrodite, she cannot dispel the perverse attraction of death.

Gaspar immediately intuits that only the child, Rafaelín, will save him from his morbid fascination with death. When Gaspar became acquainted with Rita Quiñones, he was so drawn to the boy that his heart "se iba hacia él y le besaba paternalmente" (p. 37), and even then he fancied having him for a son. He soon admits that the lad inspires in him a desire for life sufficient to efface his thoughts on death: "A mí, ese niño me ha dado la grata sorpresa de inspirarme un interés que me . . . me distrae de otros pensamientos . . . algo . . . algo peligroso" (p. 47). After Rita's death, he considers more seriously the possibility of adopting Rafaelín, and he again avows the life-giving power of the child: "Era la engañifa de la vida que volvía a apoderarse de mí con sus seducciones, su persuasión fascinadora de que hay cosas que urge, que importa hacer, y a las cuales debe consagrarse todo nuestro esfuerzo, sin vacilación y sin descanso" (p. 85).[5] Gaspar affirms that another attraction will conquer that of the dark temptress, for "el niño pisará la cabeza de la muerte" (p. 87), and his spirit cries out imploringly to Rafaelín: "¡Oh arcangelito Rafael: haz el milagro de llenarme este abismo que hay en mí; llénamelo con tu monería celeste, con tu mohín murillesco, con tus carnezuelas amasadas de mantequilla y hojas de rosa, con tu mirar donde aún no se ha reflejado la negrura humana! Enamórame de ti, de tu cuerpo santo, sin contaminar, de su pensamiento impoluto, de tus manos sin fuerza, de tus pies corretones" (p. 90).

The frequent comparisons of Rafaelín with the Child Jesus intensify his role as a symbol of life and Gaspar's savior. The first comparison is subtle, for the author mentions only "el reír goyeante, la travesura celeste del chiquillo" (pp. 37-38), but the ensuing references are explicit. Gaspar notes that "sus manizuelas hoyosas tienen el candor amante, el gesto de bendición tierna de las manos del Niño Jesús, que acaricia a San Antonio de Padua" (p. 128), and as the child emerges from bathing, Gaspar states that "su cuerpo es un santuario" (p. 130). When he is sick, "los primeros calores empalidecen las florecientes mejillas de Rafaelín, y su dulzura de Niño Jesús de San Antonio se transforma en abatimiento" (p. 155). The child's temperament is gentle, for he is "dócil, amoroso, poca egoísta" (p. 172). His essential compassion extends to all, particularly to the mendicants and humble people who gather in front of the estate each Sunday. Rafaelín infuses joy into the lives of even the most wretched in a way that is truly reminiscent of Christ: "La presencia de Rafaelín les saca de sus casillas, y ríen más, y exclaman cosas más chuscas y optimistas; vejezuelas desdentadas ríen como niños de pecho; vejezuelos reumáticos, arrastrándose sostenidos en un palo, ríen plegando el rancio cuero de su cara de manzana tabardilla muy madura; un lelo ríe de felicidad al tocarle la manecita del nene, y se olvida de devorar el mendrugo; un ciego es el más jovial, y se empeña en mosconear en la *zanfona* y en dedicarnos coplas alusivas, aduladoras, donde nos llama reyes" (p. 205). Rafaelín fulfills his destiny as Gaspar's redeemer when he, instead of his father, is killed in the climactic confrontation. Gaspar's sorrow is limitless. All day he holds "la víctima" in his arms, begging to stay with his child, "el que dio por mí su vida, sellando el sacrificio con un beso celeste" (p. 252). He acknowledges his debt to the boy: "Se me figura que mi corazón, aquel corazón hastiado, recocido en todos los amargores de mi siglo, curtido en egoísmo, me lo han sacado del pecho. Fuiste tú quien me lo arrancaste de allí, con tus deditos hoyosos, cortos, menudos; me lo quitaste como se quita un insecto venenoso de la ropa de un ser querido" (p. 253). He speaks with the dead child: "¿Qué me dices, niño de mejillas blancas? ¿Qué me sugieren tus labios de rosa tronchada, y tus ojos vidriados, y tu sonrisa graciosa, y tu aspecto de Jesús durmiento sobre la cruz de su martirio?" (pp. 252-53). Gaspar's heart is no longer foul with his desire for death; it is, rather, "virgen, joven, sangrante, limpio como una hostia" (p. 254). Rafaelín's sacrifice guarantees the tranquil purity of grace for Gaspar's soul.

There are three symbolic images that are not extended into definable patterns. The vehicle for each is a color; blue to represent the illusion of happiness; gold, the privileged, moneyed class; and copper to signify the poor class.

Gaspar feels that only a home and family will offer him the slimmest hope for happiness in this life. He associates blue with this dream, as when he states that woman symbolizes "la humareda azul del hogar, garantía de la supervivencia en la familia" (p. 87). Again, pervaded one day with ennui, he acknowledges that "la perspectiva de la humareda azul del hogar" (p. 62) still comes to gladden him.

Desiderio Solís disdainfully calls the privileged class the gilded ones, and he refers to the impoverished many as the copper class. He, "de la casta del cobre" (p. 196) and Gaspar, one of the *dorados,* discuss the differences between the two economic groups. Gaspar asserts that intellectual pleasures and women are among the many things "que lo mismo son de los dorados que de los cobrizos" (p. 196), but Solís refutes equality in either area, particularly with respect to women: "¡Para los cobrizos, las del arroyo! Si tenemos aspiración hacia una mujer bonita, inteligente, delicada . . . allí estará uno de la casta de oro con su oro en la mano, y suya será la victoria!" (pp. 197-98). According to Solís, the poor have an advantage over the rich only in matters of life and death. They are more apt to save another human being because their material interests do not blind them to the value of human life: "En la barca hay sitio para muchos náufragos. ¿Y por qué no darse, antes de partir, un refinado goce? Vea usted: este goce es concedido igual a los cobrizos que a los dorados. No: mejor a los cobrizos, porque los dorados están reblandecidos, y no tienen el valor del gesto supremo" (p. 199). The true opportunity for the copper ones to dominate is murder. Solís' remarks are germane to the development of the plot, for they presage his literal role of the avenging murderer at the climax.[6]

The symbolic function of imagery in *La sirena negra* is artistically appropriate because it emphasizes the theme and is consonant with other symbolic devices.

Pardo Bazán is describing man in spiritual conflict rather than at variance with his environment. When the emphasis was on the description of external reality, as in the early novels of Naturalistic tenor, it was consistent with the theme to treat the world corporeally by appealing to the senses. The reality of *Los pazos de Ulloa,* for example, was presented so that the reader could see, hear, touch, and smell the essence of the decadent rural estate. But the analysis of man's inner struggle, central to *La sirena negra,* evokes a less palpable reality which, by its very nature, escapes direct, sensual perception. Endeavoring to convey the subtleties of mind and spirit, Pardo Bazán rejects the explicitness of the literal phrase and invokes instead the expressiveness of metaphorical language.

The two devices which enhance and complement the novel's symbolic tenor are allegory and the parallelism of characters. The death motif is presented allegorically in a dream that Gaspar has after Rita's death. He dreams that he is horrified spectator at a medieval Dance of Death in which stately rulers, ragged peasants, members of his immediate family, and finally Rita and Rafaelín dance the macabre steps. As an allegorical prefiguration of Rafaelín's death, the dream intensifies the symbolism of the novel.

Parallelism of characters means the description of one character so that he serves only as a symbol of another. Desiderio Solís parallels Gaspar in his ennui, and since this decadent dissatisfaction with life is the only fully described aspect of Desiderio's personality, he never attains the stature of an independent, rounded character. Desiderio is so exclusively the personification of Gaspar's ennui and its attendant fascination with death that when the tutor kills Rafaelín, one feels that he has acted for Gaspar and that the murderer is, in fact, Gaspar. The parallelism of Desiderio with Gaspar and the image of Rafaelín as the redeemer are complementary. In the same way as all mankind, represented by the Jews, killed Jesus Christ and thus was saved, so Gaspar, symbolized by Desiderio, kills Rafaelín and consequently is saved: "Y me pesa, me pesa, me pesa tres veces, y mis lágrimas lo repiten, cayendo como perlas de mansedumbre, sobre la ropa y el cuerpo del Niño que hizo el milagro en mí." (pp. 254-55).

Although the use of symbolic imagery in *La sirena negra* may be consonant with the novel's mood and theme, its success and efficacy are questionable. The very existence of definable image patterns and the fact that established patterns are not disrupted by involving either the signifier or the signified in an unrelated comparison indicate the soundness of the imagery from the point of view of consistency. But the positive value of the imagery's consistency is countered by the damaging effect of the image patterns on characterization. The extension of image first into symbol and then into pattern tends to solidify the characters as symbols and preclude their becoming total, multi-dimensional human beings. This criticism is undoubtedly justified in Rita, Miss Annie, Rafaelín, and Desiderio Solís, and it is even valid to a great extent in Gaspar who, as the personification of *fin de siècle* ennui, is too limited in his role as the stereotyped, decadent hero. Pardo Bazán's effort to portray emotional conflict inspired a metaphorical inventiveness which in itself may be admirable but which may be artistically detrimental in the larger framework of a novel.

Since symbolic images and their resultant image patterns occur in no previous novels, they are definite innovations in Pardo Bazán's later writing. Three interdependent reasons support the conclusion that, as innovations, they were inspired by Modernist and decadent literature: the unquestionable affinity of *La sirena negra* to the contemporary novel in the theme of spiritual conversion, the delineation of an over-refined aristocrat, and the emphasis on psychology; the symbolic intent and use of metaphorical language and image patterns in the Modernist and *fin de siècle* novel;[7] and, finally, the ample evidence in Pardo Bazán's critical writings of her substantial knowledge of current French and Spanish American literature.[8]

Pardo Bazán's symbolist handling of imagery in *La sirena negra* is consistent with her general tendency to draw inspiration for theme, technique, and style from various literary quarters. Her essential literary eclecticism, which she herself admitted frequently,[9] caused her to expand the vision of reality inherited from the realistic Spanish novel of the nineteenth century, and the symbolism of imagery in *La sirena negra* is one means by which she sought to probe the nature of reality in a unique, inventive way and to go beyond the confines of peninsular literary conventions.

Notes

1. Eduardo Gómez de Baquero, "La última manera espiritual de la Sra. Pardo Bazán," *Cultura Española,* X (1908), 399.

2. For specific evidence of the similarities, see my articles: "Impressionist Techniques in Descriptions by Emilia Pardo Bazán," *Hispanic Review,* XXX (Oct. 1962), 304-16; and "Pardo Bazán's Two Styles," *Hispania,* XLVIII (Sept. 1965), 456-62.

3. Emilia Pardo Bazán, *La sirena negra* in *Obras completas,* XLII (Madrid, 1908), 255.

4. René Wellek and Austin Warren, *Theory of Literature* (New York, 1956), p. 178.

5. Further support of Rafaelín's redeeming influence on Gaspar is seen in the following quotations: "La fuerza de vivir ¿no eres tú quien la lleva y la rep-

arte con tus manos horadadas, mártir Nazareno? . . . Por no pedírtela, yo la busco, egoístamente,—en esta criatura" (p. 127); "Una reflexión que me hice contribuyó a suavizar mi gesto; discurrí que el deseo de adherirme a la vida mediante la comedia, o lo que sea, de la paternidad, me impone también la ley de acercarme un poco a mis semejantes, de salir de mi propia caverna, como el oso de las épocas primitivas se echaba fuera de su espelunca a caza de frutos y de miel silvestre" (p. 143); "Si he recogido al niño ha sido por instinto egoísta y de conservación; por no dejarme llevar del atractivo que ejerce sobre mí la Guadañadora" (p. 150).

6. The full significance of the character of Desiderio Solís will be examined later in this study in the discussion of parallelism of characters.

7. Díaz Rodríguez, for example, is generally esteemed for his brilliant symbolic use of the color green in *Sangre Patricia*. Arturo Torres-Ríoseco says: "Podría asegurarse que el *leit motiv* de toda la novela es el color verde, que parece tener una extraña relación con ciertos estados anímicos anunciadores de la locura. Por esto y por ciertas manifestaciones estilísticas hay que insistir en el valor artístico de la novela que nos ocupa y considerar a Díaz Rodríguez como un verdadero simbolista y precursor de maneras estéticas contemporáneas" (*Grandes novelistas de la América Hispana* [Berkeley, 1949], p. 78).

8. Pardo Bazán's knowledge of *fin de siècle* literature is particularly evident in: "La novela novelesca," *Nuevo teatro crítico,* I (junio 1891), 34-44; "Letras y Libros," *Nuevo teatro crítico,* III (diciembre 1893), 256-98; "Ojeada retrospectiva a varias obras francesas de Daudet, Loti, Bourget, Huysmans, Rod y Barrés," *Nuevo teatro crítico,* II (julio 1892), 52-109; "Crónica literaria," *Nuevo teatro crítico,* II (marzo 1892), 84-97; "*Angel Guerra*," *Nuevo teatro crítico,* I (agosto 1891), 19-63. For a substantial examination of Pardo Bazán's attitude to French decadent literature, see John W. Kronik, "Emilia Pardo Bazán and the Phenomenon of French Decadentism," *PMLA,* LXXXI (Oct. 1966), 418-27.

9. "Todo el que lea mis ensayos críticos comprenderá que ni soy idealista, ni realista, ni naturalista, sino ecléctica," *Retratos y apuntes literarios* in *Obras completas* (Madrid, n.d.), XXXII, 190; ". . . en conciencia me encuentro lo que siempre fui: ecléctica y amplísima de criterio . . . ," "Ojeada," p. 73; ". . . el verdadero artista es ante todo ecléctico . . . ," "La novela novelesca," p. 40.

Robert E. Lott (essay date March 1969)

SOURCE: Lott, Robert E. "Observations on the Narrative Method, the Psychology, and the Style of 'Los Pazos de Ulloa'." *Hispania* 52, no. 1 (March 1969): 3-12.

[*In the following essay, Lott divides* The House of Ulloa *into five parts in order to highlight Pardo Bazán's narrative methods in the novel.*]

Structurally *Los Pazos de Ulloa* (1886) is centered around the struggle between the forces of civilization and good and those of nature and evil. The struggle takes place in the *Pazos,* a degenerate mansion which is being overrun, literally and symbolically, from within and without, by rampant nature.[1] The novel's esthetic appeal derives mainly from the masterful interweaving of this simple but often symbolic action with suspenseful or playful moods, from interesting, complex characterizations, particularly those of Nucha and Julián, and from the creation of a believable fictional world, which unobtrusively embodies the author's insights into some of the major concerns of her age, and which authentically evokes rural Galicia in the people, language, and customs. The proper novelistic representation of these effects presupposes, and in this case gets, a narrative method, a style, and literary techniques deeply congenial to the artist's experiences and world-view. This world-view is one of "mitigated naturalism," as I prefer to call it, rather than the "Catholic naturalism" that Donald Fowler Brown speaks of.[2] The author's Catholicism is only one of the factors which attenuate her admiring emulation of Zola. Another is her innate Spanish sense of *pudor,* which prevents her full acceptance of naturalistic material and techniques. Despite the glorification of nature, she does not "demonstrate man's fusion with nature in historical process," as Zola and Blasco Ibáñez do, but reflects instead "a dualistic vision of the world, in which the two forces of good and evil war with each other,"[3] thus at least allowing room for spiritual forces and providing freedom from pseudo-scientific determinism.

I

The action, cast in thirty short chapters of fairly uniform length, can be divided into five parts. A schematic account of the action will serve to elucidate the author's narrative method by revealing significant shifts in mood, pace, center of attention, and point of view.

Part I (chs. i-viii). Exposition. The pace is mainly slow, with detailed treatment of short periods of time. Chapters i-iii treat the afternoon and night of Julián's arrival and the following day. Several days go by in chapter iv. The entire winter passes in chapter v. Chapter vi describes the celebration of St. Julian's Day in Naya. Chapter vii presents Julián's argument with Don Pedro that evening. Chapter viii treats their departure for Santiago the following morning. The mood of hopeless physical and moral decadence is alleviated only by the description of the feast day.

Part II (chs. ix-xiii). Don Pedro, replacing Julián as the center of the author's interest, courts his cousins and finally selects Nucha. The pace is rapid; the rest of that year and the following winter quickly pass. The tone is gay and optimistic, in marked contrast with the gloomy atmosphere at the *Pazos*.

Part III (chs. xiv-xvii). Attention is focused on Nucha's pregnancy, her maternal interest in Perucho, and her visits to "distinguished" neighbors (chs. xiv-xv). Six months go by. Don Pedro's restlessness explodes into resentful anger, when, in October, after a long labor (chs. xvi-xvii) that leaves her unable to have more children, Nucha gives birth to a daughter rather than the male heir he expected.

Part IV (chs. xviii-xxviii). In this, the main action, we see Nucha's unstable convalescence (ch. xviii) and her increasing nervousness and fear, culminating in hysteria, hallucinations, and delusions of persecution (chs. xix-xx, xxiii, xxvi-xxvii). A decisive event is the discovery that Perucho is her husband's son (ch. xxiii). The climax begins with Julián's determination to help Nucha leave the *Pazos* (ch. xxvii).

The tension is broken three times. First, by the change to a *costumbrista* scene, the festive, "epic" preparations for a hunt and the hunt itself (chapters xxi-xxii). Seemingly extraneous, this passage increases our knowledge of this natural, elemental world and of Julián. His utter ineptness, in the midst of primitive manly virtues, makes him the butt of ridicule. The second major interruption concerns the political struggle between the government-sponsored candidate, backed by the violent *Trampeta*, and Don Pedro, whom *Barbacana* supports. Because of Primitivo's betrayal Don Pedro loses the election, thus killing Nucha's faint hope of getting Don Pedro away from the *Pazos*. Afterwards *Barbacana* and his men fight the opposition's supporters in the street. While needlessly detailed, this episode is important for the background and the ironic criticism of another supposedly civilizing force, the local government, which has fallen under Primitivo's expanding influence. It also sets the stage for Nucha's decision to leave and for Primitivo's murder by *Barbacana's* henchman, *El Tuerto*. The tension is broken a third time by the author's totally unexpected and rather contrived shift to Perucho's point of view in the climactic chapter xxviii. While the narrative is still third-person, everything is presented through his eyes. This is done in an interesting, impressionistic way that reflects accurately the boy's psychology and scale of values.[4] Yet the shift seems motivated by the author's avoidance of the melo-

dramatic and violent details of Primitivo's murder and of the angry confrontation of Don Pedro, Julián, and Nucha. These two events are followed by Perucho's brief sequestration of the baby, to protect her from Don Pedro's anger. In this main part of the novel the mood is one of suspenseful dread. As the novel draws to a close, the symbolic meaning is underscored, outside events are brought to bear, and the pace quickens.

Part V (chs. xxix-xxx). These chapters, telling of Julián's enforced departure and subsequent return ten years later, present the pathetic contrast between Primitivo's well-kept tomb and Nucha's shoddy one, as well as the melodramatic appearance of a well-dressed boy (Perucho) and a shabby looking girl (Nucha's daughter), thus constituting an epilogue to this novel and setting the stage for its sequel.

There is a wave-movement in the mood of terror and impending disaster. After each spot of relief the wave surges higher and stronger, finally sweeping everything before it. Religion, virtue, culture, and government are mismatched against nature and evil. Primitivo and Sabel become allpowerful but symbolically shadowy figures, as if they were devilish incarnations of evil forces. In one illuminating scene Julián witnesses the diabolical world of sensualism and evil in the huge kitchen, ruled over by Sabel and her friend, the crone and suspected witch, *La Sabia* (ch. xix). Shortly thereafter, Julián hears a cry and rushes downstairs, thinking that Don Pedro is beating Nucha, although he is only killing a huge spider which caused her to scream. Terror reaches its peak in Julián's and Nucha's search in the dark basement on a stormy day (ch. xx). First Nucha tells Julián:

> Veo cosas muy raras. La ropa que cuelgo me representa siempre hombres ahorcados, o difuntos que salen del ataúd con la mortaja puesta. . . . Hay veces que distingo personas sin cabeza; otras, al contrario, les veo la cara con todas sus facciones, la boca muy abierta y haciendo muecas . . . Esos mamarrachos que hay pintados en el biombo se mueven; y cuando crujen las ventanas con el viento, como esta noche, me pongo a cavilar si son almas del otro mundo que se quejan. . . .[5]

On opening the basement door, Nucha says: "Se me figuró al abrir que estaba ahí dentro un perro muy grande, sentado, y que se levantaba y se me echaba para morderme . . . juraría haberlo visto" (p. 223). She fights this chaotic nether-world, which is guarded over by an imaginary Cerberus, in the lower depths of the horrifying, monstrous mansion. There the confused and deformed objects take on the frightening and macabre aspects of dead figures or parts of the body. She resolutely subdues her fear, but back in her room she is overcome by the first attack of hysteria, which will worsen to the point that she will fear for her child's life and finally succumb.

II

Pardo Bazán, as a good realist should, displays considerable skill in the depiction of her characters. Noteworthy are her keen observation of child psychology, in the case of Perucho, the penetrating details used to describe the care and development of the infant, and the fine secondary characterizations. Of special importance in the structure of the novel is her depiction of Pedro's inadequacies and Nucha's hysteria. But in the interest of brevity and in order not to belabor the obvious, it is preferable to leave these characterizations to the care of the attentive reader and treat instead the excellent portrayal of Julián, who provides the main psychological interest and serves as a catalyst in the novel's action.

Physically Julián is scrupulously clean, blond, of slight frame, and with an otherworldly look. Though very conscientious about his duties, he lacks charity and understanding for others and has excessive pride, which he continually tries to conceal. These defects are seen in his pleasure in Primitivo's murder, his attitude toward the attempted reforming of Don Pedro, and the half-successful effort to Christianize Perucho. In general, Julián's behavior represents an over-reaction to his basic character trait, which is his almost feminine prudishness.

He is also largely responsible for the major error of the characters: Don Pedro's decision to wed Nucha and not the flirtatious Rita, who would have made him a better wife. But Don Pedro heeded Julián's advice and the dictates of an excessively honor-conscious society, which refused to accept any hint of sinfulness in the prospective wife. (Slander and *pundonor* play a great role in the novel. Both the bad marriage and the ending are dependent on it.)

To understand Julián we must interpret the few details given about his childhood. He was the only child, perhaps illegitimate, of a strait-laced, zealous, and domineering housekeeper in Don Manuel's employ. Thus he became accustomed to having a very subordinate role in the household. He was not allowed to play with Don Manuel's daughters, nor is it likely that he had any other opportunity to develop normal heterosexual social relationships. But he was permitted to be with Gabrieliño, several years his junior, and with Nucha, who took very seriously the role of the deceased mother toward the baby boy and even in the household. Temperamentally she was similar to Julián, meticulous and prudish, with a religious bent.

Given the nature of this trio, and Julián's subsequent religious training, we can better understand his constant references to Nucha as the Madonna, the Virgin Mary, in different aspects of her life. As a child she had "miraculously" (in the light of his youthful religiosity) appeared as a mother figure. This would have been an unconscious interpretation; later he made a more conscious one of Nucha and her real child. For this reason Don Pedro was an obstacle; Julián was glad to usurp his place in every way possible. So in a sense he plays Saint Joseph to the Virgin and Her babe.

On a more literal level it is obvious that as a child Julián had repressed his interest in the opposite sex and his love for Nucha. Now he reenacts his childhood fantasy-world with Nucha and suppresses his excessive affection for her. Instead of true sublimation, there is a displacement of his love to a safer object, Nucha's baby daughter. His love for the infant is out of all due proportion to his role as a priest and friend of the family. He is willing to put up with almost anything to maintain this relationship and even has the absurd idea, if Don Pedro is elected, of wanting Nucha to leave the baby at the *Pazos* with him. It is permissible, according to social mores, for him to see the nakedness of the infant as she is bathed, cleaned, and dressed. One day his happiness is supreme. A soft, warm sensation spreads over him as he holds her in his lap. He is henceforth unwilling to forego this pleasure, taking the precaution to wear old trousers. (A Freudian psychologist would perhaps relate this experience to physical and emotional problems derived from enforced celibacy, but such was not the author's intent.)

Another important aspect of Julián's psychological portrayal is the dream he has after witnessing the infernal "witches' kitchen" and fortune-telling scene and the scene in which Don Pedro killed a spider (pp. 214-16). Julián dreamed that the *Pazos* became a feudal castle and that Don Pedro, dressed in armor, dropped a strange weapon on him, a steel boot, but it seemed suspended over him and suddenly turned into an owl, which landed on his shoulder. The disheveled owl was strangely like the witch, *La Sabia*. As he fled her mocking laughter, Nucha, in the form of the *sota de bastos* (English equivalent here: the queen of clubs), lowered herself from a window of the castle. Not the king of clubs (equaling Don Pedro), as it first seemed to be, but St. George (equaling a self-projection of Julián) slowly stuck his lance in the dragon. Oddly enough, Julián felt the pain in his own side, thus revealing his secret guilt. The dream also evinces the duality of his role as a defense against evil and a defender of virtue. His defense of Nucha is reflected in the dream as a frustrated desire for manliness and courage. Outwardly secure in his spiritual strength, especially regarding matters of duty, he is inwardly aware of the shortcomings of his virility.

When, in real life, the artificial nursery world is destroyed and engulfed by the primitive and evil world of the *Pazos,* Julián is forced to flee. When he returns, his mode of living is another form of overreacting: he lives ascetically and detached from his parishioners.

III

Pardo Bazán's prose is sufficiently flexible to achieve stylistic effects ranging from the serious creation of suspense, moods, and terror to irony. The sentence structure is direct and uncluttered, proceeding rapidly and incisively to the conclusion. Without being an impressionist, Pardo Bazán represents an advance from the more traditional prose of her novelistic predecessors and contemporaries (in the 1880's) toward the loosely organized, sketchy, but vivid syntax of impressionists like Blasco Ibáñez and Azorín. The style is frequently nominal, with stress on the nouns in enumerations or, occasionally, even in verbless sentences. Subordinate clauses and parenthetical expressions are quite rare.[6] Often she uses instead run-on phrases separated by a colon to quicken the pace. Three examples of this usage are noted in the first two sentences of the following paragraph, one of the many in which the primary aim is to create a mood of fear.

> Los sueños de las noches de terror suelen parecer risibles apenas despunta la claridad del nuevo día: pero Julián, al saltar de la cama, no consiguió vencer la impresión del suyo. Proseguía el hervor de la imaginación sobreexcitada: miró por la ventana, y el paisaje le pareció tétrico y siniestro: verdad es que entoldaban la bóveda celeste nubarrones de plomo con reflejos lívidos, y que el viento, sordo unas veces y sibilante otras, doblaba los árboles con ráfagas repentinas. El capellán bajó la escalera de caracol con ánimo de decir su misa, que, a causa del mal estado de la capilla señorial, acostumbraba celebrar en la parroquia. Al regresar y acercarse a la entrada de los Pazos, un remolino de hojas secas le envolvió los pies, una atmósfera fría le sobrecogió, y la gran huronera de piedra se le presentó imponente, ceñuda y terrible, con aspecto de prisión, como el castillo que había visto soñando. El edificio, bajo su toldo de negras nubes, con el ruido temeroso del cierzo que lo fustigaba, era amenazador y siniestro. Julián penetró en él con el alma en un puño. Cruzó rápidamente el helado zaguán, la cavernosa cocina, y, atravesando los salones solitarios, se apresuró a refugiarse en la habitación de Nucha, donde acostumbraban servirle el chocolate, por orden de la señorita.
>
> (pp. 216-17)

The mood of foreboding is created not only by the use of themes like "nubarrones" and the wind ("ráfagas," "remolino," and "cierzo"), but especially by well-chosen epithets: "el paisaje . . . tétrico y siniestro," "reflejos lívidos," "edificio . . . amenazador y siniestro," "negras nubes," "ruido temeroso," "helado zaguán," "cavernosa cocina," and "salones solitarios." The use of these and similar emotion-stirring epithets here and throughout the novel certainly constitutes a stylistic dominant.

Especially effective in Pardo Bazán's achieving of a realistic and verisimilar style is her fine representation of the spoken language. She uses the Galician dialect and local and rural expressions, though in such a way that comprehension is not usually impaired. She suggests, rather than reproduces the dialect, except for a few words, the Castilian meanings of which she is careful to make clear. Such is the case when *Bico de Rato (Hocico de Ratón)* includes in a colorful tall tale easily identifiable dialectal forms:

> — . . . Fue un día de San Silvestre . . .
>
> —Andarían las brujas sueltas . . .
>
> —Si eran *meigas* o era el *trasno,* yo no lo sé; pero lo mismo que habemos de dar cuenta a Dios Nuestro Señor de nuestras *auciones,* me pasó lo que les voy a contar. . . .
>
> (p. 227)

In another passage Perucho uses dialect and Galician diminutives in *-iño*: "—Reiniña, mona, *ruliña,* calla, calla, que te he de dar cosas bunitas, bunitas, bunitiñas . . . ¡Si no callas viene un cocón y te come! ¡*Velo,* ahí viene! ¡Calla, soliño, paloma blanca, rosita!" (p. 317). The most typical and extensive example is Perucho's story, in which the author parenthetically explains that *millo* is *maíz, chosco* is *tuerto,* and uses other dialectal forms set in italics, like *presonas, frol, pagarito, árbole,* and *porta* (pp. 320-21), which are easily understood because of the context and the close similarity to Spanish.

Also indicative of Pardo Bazán's realistic style is her occasional graphic representation of emotional speech qualities:

> —Oi-go, siii-seeñoor, oi-go . . . —tartamudeó la moza, comiéndose los sollozos.
>
> (p. 74)

> —Tampoco hay burra—objetó el cazador. . . .
>
> —¿Que . . . no . . . hay . . . bu . . . rraaaaá?—articuló, apretando los puños, D. Pedro.—¿Que no . . . la . . . hayyy? A ver, a ver . . . Repíteme eso, en mi cara.
>
> (p. 84)

Here, as in her use of dialect, Pardo Bazán is moderate and avoids the extremes of Zola or Pereda, who had probably the most naturalistic style among the major Spanish novelists of the 1880's.

Pardo Bazán uses a wide range of colloquial expressions, such as the evidently regional "la carrerita de un can" (p. 8) to indicate a fairly short distance, or the colorfully metaphorical *tocar la guitarra* ("scratching fleas"), which the author explains: "Se oía a los canes *tocar la guitarra,* espulgarse a toda orquesta . . ." (p. 227).[7] Phrases like "Se necesita una vara de correa para vivir entre gentes" (p. 68), "toda esa gavilla que hace de mi casa merienda de negros" (p. 77), and "el señor de los Pazos se llevaría el gato al agua" ("he would win the election," p. 278), if not regional are at least rare enough to be striking. Popular comparisons, while picturesque, tend to be more standard and even stereotyped. Three occur in the following comments about the child's drunkenness:

> Perucho *la tenía*.
>
> —Como un pellejo—gruñó el abad.
>
> —Como una cuba—murmuró el marqués.—A la cama con él en seguida. Que duerma, y mañana estará más fresco que una lechuga.
>
> (p. 23)

Another example: "[Sabel] bailoteando como una descosida" (p. 75). But at times a cliché comparison is revitalized: "Iba el jinete colorado, no como un pimiento, sino como una fresa, encendimiento propio de personas linfáticas" (p. 5). The author sometimes uses colloquial euphemisms: "El cacique añadió, apretando los puños:—¡Me caso con Dios! Mientras no hundamos a Barbacana, no se hará nada en Cebre" (p. 266). There are other colloquial elements, such as proverbs—"más vale asno vivo que doctor muerto" (p. 39)—and tag phrases—"como usted me enseña" (pp. 263 and 267) and "con perdón" (p. 228) or "¡con perdón de las barbas!" (p. 227), of which the latter is used to soften a crude remark, or, as in this case, an unbelievable one.

In short, the style effectively utilizes a large variety of colloquial expressive means. They are especially abundant, of course, in the passages written in a lighthearted or jocular vein and which reflect the novel's equally common and successful ironic style. The irony is produced in a number of ways, primarily by the use of playful colloquial expressions and images:

> No era tortas y pan pintado la limpieza material del archivo; sin embargo, la verdadera obra de romanos fue la clasificación. ¡Aquí te quiero! parecían decir los papelotes así que Julián intentaba separarlos. Un embrollo, una madeja sin cabo, un laberinto sin hilo conductor. No existía faro que pudiese guiar por el piélago insondable: ni libros becerros, ni estados, ni nada.
>
> (p. 37)

> — . . . El marqués no inventó la pólvora. . . . Julián se volvió. . . .
>
> —Pero . . . , el señorito . . . , ¿qué tiene que ver el señorito . . . ?
>
> El cura de Naya saltó, a su vez, sin que ninguna mosca le picase, y prorrumpió en juvenil carcajada.
>
> (p. 69)

> —¡Bah! . . . Esos hijos así, nacidos por detrás de la iglesia. . . .
>
> (p. 70)

Some of the examples above, as well as the following one, also reveal the realist's typically ironical-critical attitude toward his characters: "Fray Venancio, que sólo

había recibido tal cual puntapié o puñada despreciativa, no necesitó más pasaporte para irse al otro mundo, de puro miedo, en una semana . . ." (p. 41).

While realism and irony prevail, one also encounters usages which are not typical of realism, much less of naturalism, such as calling a hunter's pants a "mapamundi de remiendos" (p. 229), or using a Valerian classical-ironical reference, "si Sabel deseaba retener a aquel fugitivo Eneas, no dio de ello la más leve señal . . ." (p. 87), or employing euphemistic images. Also found are generalizations which belie the author's complete impersonality, as in this comment: "Era D. Pedro de los que juzgan muy importantes y dignas de comentarse sus propias acciones y mutaciones—achaque propio de egoístas—y han menester tener siempre cerca de sí algún inferior o subordinado a quien referirla, para que les atribuya también valor extraordinario" (p. 104).

A major element in Pardo Bazán's realistic style, as it is indeed in any thoroughly realistic style in the nineteenth century, is the so-called "free indirect style," by which is meant, in brief, the blurring of the contours between the characters' thoughts and words and the author's narrative style, a technique which responds to the still deeper and stronger current in the nineteenth century toward the integration of the spoken language into literary style. Free indirect style marks the midpoint between direct style (quoting) and indirect style (summing up or talking about) and is a tricky and at times startling way to preserve in the narration the flavor and affective values of the spoken language. Or it may be used to reflect the characters' thoughts, thus deepening the psychological portrayal. Additional advantages are that it gives the author a third way to narrate, is more rapid and less tedious, and provides the perfect stylistic vehicle for the author's irony, or better, critical empathy, because he is thus able to treat ironically the characters' speech and attitudes even while empathically mimicking them.[8]

All these features are seen in *Los Pazos de Ulloa.* Examples of ironical-characterizing usage abound:

> Hechas así las amistades, entablaron el señor de la Lage y su sobrino la imprescindible conversación referente al viaje, sus causas, incidentes y peripecias. No explicaba muy satisfactoriamente el sobrino su impensada venida: pch . . . ganas de *espilirse* . . . Cansa estar siempre solo . . . Gusta la variación . . . No insistió el tío, pensando entre sí:
>
> —Ya Julián me lo contará *todo*.
>
> (p. 93)

> Y en cuanto a lo que de un pueblo antiguo puede enamorar a un espíitu culto, . . . de eso entendía lo mismo don Pedro que de griego o latín. ¡Piedras mohosas! Ya le bastaban las de los Pazos. . . . A pesar de conocer a Orense y haber estado en Santiago cuando

niño, discurría y fantaseaba a su modo lo que debe ser una ciudad moderna: calles anchas, mucha regularidad en las construcciones, todo nuevo y flamante, gran policía, ¿qué menos puede ofrecer la civilización a sus esclavos? Es cierto que Santiago poesía dos o tres edificios espaciosos, la Catedral, el Consistorio, San Martín . . . Pero en ellos existían cosas muy sin razón ponderadas, en concepto del marqués: por ejemplo, la Gloria de la Catedral. ¡Vaya unos santos más mal hechos, y unas santas más larguiruchas y sin forma humana! ¡Unas columnas más raramente esculpidas!

(p. 101)

The above examples reflect a still cautious use of free indirect style: in each case the discursive element is present and the author indicates her intention. But she is bolder in the use of questions, exclamations, and affective values in the depicting of Julián's psychology. A typical example:

> Volvía Julián preocupado a la casa solariega, acusándose de excesiva simplicidad, por no haber reparado en cosas de tanto bulto. El era sencillo como la paloma; sólo que en este pícaro mundo también se necesita ser cauto como la serpiente . . . Ya no podía continuar en los Pazos . . . ¿Cómo volvía a vivir a cuestas de su madre, sin más emolumentos que la misa? ¿Y cómo dejaba así de golpe al señorito D. Pedro, que le trataba tan llanamente? ¿Y la casa de Ulloa, que necesitaba un restaurador celoso y adicto? Todo era verdad; pero ¿y su deber de sacerdote católico?

(p. 71)

A major example, also significant in its use of substitutionary reporting, shows Julián's musings regarding comments his mother had made about Señor de la Lage's daughters (pp. 106-08). Of greater psychological interest is a passage in which Julián debates with himself:

> No, ese guapo no era él. ¡Buena misa sería la que dijese, con la cabeza hecha una olla de grillos! . . .
>
> La cosa era bien clara. Situación: la misma del año penúltimo. Tenía que marcharse. . . . A otra parte, pues, con la música.
>
> Sólo que . . . Vaya, hay cosas más fáciles de proyectar que de hacer. . . . ¿Por qué le disgustaba tanto la perspectiva de salir de los Pazos? Bien mirado, él era un extraño en aquella casa.
>
> Es decir, eso de extraño . . . Extraño, no; pues vivía unido espiritualmente a la familia. . . . Sobre todo la niña, la niña. El acordarse de la niña le dejó como embobado. No podía explicarse a sí mismo el gran sacudimiento interior que le causaba pensar que no volvería a cogerla en brazos. ¡Mire usted que estaba encariñado con la tal muñeca! Se le llenaron de lágrimas los ojos.

(pp. 203-04)

There are two additional important passages, too long to quote, in which Julián's fears and agitation are admirably depicted in a free indirect style, very boldly used (pp. 211-13 and 303-04). The second of these includes a kind of wishful thinking, a short piece of which may be given:

> Se representaba la escena de la escapatoria. Sería al amanecer. Nucha iría envuelta en muchos abrigos. El cargaría con la niña, dormidita y arropadísima también. Por si acaso, llevaría en el bolsillo un tarro con leche caliente. Andando bien, llegarían a Cebre en tres horas escasas. Allí se podían hacer sopas. La nena no pasaría hambre. Tomarían en el coche la berlina, el sitio más cómodo. Cada vuelta de la rueda les alejaría de los tétricos Pazos.

(p. 304)

From this sampling it is evident that Pardo Bazán uses free indirect style with considerable skill and for a variety of purposes, although with some restraint. In the sequel to this novel, she uses it so freely for the characterization of Gabriel that it is but one step from the much discussed interior monologue.

If there is a sense of restraint or mitigation in the use of certain stylistic elements and techniques, the same is true of the images, because in this novel the author suggests, but draws back from a full-fledged utilization of, the anthropomorphic and animizing metaphors typical of naturalists like Zola and Blasco Ibáñez. Among the most effective images are those symbols or symbolical passages regarding the decadence at the *Pazos* and corresponding to the laxity and degradation of its inhabitants, like the overgrowth of vegetation which has destroyed the orderly, civilized aspects of the *Pazos*—as in the overrunning of the symmetrical French garden (pp. 30-32)—and the chaotic state of affairs in the library. Or this serious symbolism may correspond to the fearsomeness of the place (p. 217), to the hell's kitchen scenes, to Julián's and Nucha's fears and hallucinations, and to Julián's dream.

While a classification of the images in ***Los Pazos de Ulloa*** according to provenance is not very helpful, it is of interest to note that one group of images is based on the analogy of plants. They may be serious, as in the overgrowth motif, or only half serious as in Julián's thoughts on Primitivo and Sabel: "¡Horrible familia ilegal, enraizada en el viejo caserón solariego como las parietarias y yedras en los derruídos muros!" (p. 151). Or they may be traditional and openly playful, as in the following passage concerning Perucho: "Parecíale que era providencial el que la señorita cuidase a aquel mal retoño de tronco ruin. Y Nucha entre tanto se divertía infinito con su protegido. . . . Aspiraba a enderezar aquel arbolito tierno, civilizándole a la vez la piel y el espíritu" (p. 157). A similar image: "Parecía que la leñosa corteza se le iba cayendo poco a poco al marqués, y que su corazón bravío y egoísta se inmutaba, dejando asomar, como entre las grietas de una pared florecillas parásitas, blandos afectos de esposo y padre" (p. 168).

It is much more relevant to classify the images by their functions, such as the symbolical, mood-enhancing ones already mentioned. Another important function is the psychological one. So it is that an image giving Julián's impression of Sabel and the old hag reveals his religious training: "Mientras hablaba con la frescachona Sabel, la fantasía de un artista podía evocar los cuadros de tentaciones de San Antonio, en que aparecen juntas una asquerosa hechicera y una mujer hermosa y sensual, con pezuña de cabra" (p. 48). Again we see Julián's attitude in the image used: "La idea . . . de quedarse allí, frente a frente con Sabel, como en obscuro pozo habitado por una sabandija, le era intolerable" (p. 277). Two mystical images reflect Julián's contemplative mood as he views a picture of the *via crucis* in **La imitación de Cristo**: "Parecíale sentir en los hombros una pesadumbre abrumadora y dulcísima a la vez, y una calma honda, como si se encontrase . . . sepultado en el fondo del mar, y el agua le rodease por todas partes, sin ahogarle. Entonces leía párrafos del libro de oro, que se le entraban en el alma a manera de hierro enrojecido en la carne" (p. 295). Anthropomorphic images reveal the fearful reaction to the chaotic basement: "La pata de una mesa parecía un brazo momificado, la esfera de un reloj era la faz blanquecina de un muerto, y unas botas . . . despertaban . . . la idea de un hombre asesinado y oculto allí" (p. 223). Immediately following this passage, the sounds of the storm are animized—thus recalling the legendary "santa compaña" mentioned before (p. 219)—to reflect Julián's and Nucha's quasihallucinatory reaction: "Rugía con creciente ira el viento, y la tronada se había situado sobre los Pazos, oyéndose su estruendo lo mismo que si corriese por el tejado un escuadrón de caballos a galope o si un gigante se entretuviese en arrastrar un peñasco y llevarlo a tumbos por encima de las tejas" (p. 224).

A large number of the images are ironic or playful, and, of course, are clustered in the lighter passages. A few examples follow:

> De los monumentos de Santiago se atenía el marqués a uno de fábrica muy reciente: su prima Rita.
>
> (p. 102)

> Entró allí cierta hechicera más poderosa que la señora María la Sabia: la política. . . .
>
> (p. 247)

> Las ideas no entran en juego, sino solamente las personas, y en el terreno más mezquino: rencores, odios, rencillas, lucro miserable, vanidad microbiológica. Un combate naval en una charca.
>
> (p. 248)

> Ahogándose como ballena encallada en una playa y a quien el mar dejó en seco, entró el Arcipreste, morado de despecho y furor.
>
> (p. 282)

The novel's most strikingly playful images are seen in the idyllic, almost rococo representation of male rabbits blindly following their sexual instinct to death at the hunters' hands as lovesick suitors pursuing a fantastic Dulcinea. At the same time, this image again discloses the author's euphemistic treatment of a perfectly naturalistic theme: biological determinism, in this case.

> Sabe [el cazador] que el fantasma que acaba de cruzar . . . es la hembra, la Dulcinea perseguida y recuestada por innumerables galanes en la época del celo, . . . tras de la cual, desalados y hechos almíbar, corren por lo menos tres o cuatro machos, deseosos de románticas aventuras. Y si se deja pasar delante a la dama, ninguno de los nocturnos rondadores se detendrá en su carrera loca. . . .
>
> No, no se pararán. . . . Al primer hálito de la hembra . . . los fogosos perseguidores se lanzarán de nuevo y con más brío, ciegos de amor, convulsos de deseo, y el cazador que los acecha los irá tendiendo uno por uno a sus pies, sobre la hierba en que soñaron tener el lecho nupcial.
>
> (pp. 237-38)

Most of the images are functional, but a few, like the following ones, are more purely decorative:

> La aurora, que sólo tenía apoyado uno de sus rosados dedos en aquel rincón del orbe, se atrevió a alargar toda la manecita, y un resplandor alegre, puro, bañó las rocas pizarrosas, haciéndolas rebrillar cual bruñida plancha de acero, y entró en el cuarto del capellán, comiéndose la luz amarilla de los cirios.
>
> (p. 187)

> A pesar de haber el pecado original corrompido toda la carne, aquélla que le estaban enseñando era la cosa más pura y santa del mundo: un lirio, una azucena de candor. La cabezuela blanca . . . tenía el olor especial que se nota en los nidos de paloma donde hay pichones implumes todavía; y . . . la boca desdentada y húmeda como coral pálido recién salido del mar. . . .
>
> (pp. 198-99)

In **Los Pazos de Ulloa** there is every indication of a thoroughly realistic narrative method and style. But, because of religious and philosophical beliefs, because of the euphemistic treatment of potentially crude or shocking details and situations, and because of restraint in the use of style features and images, Pardo Bazán falls short of full-fledged naturalism. Yet her artistry is not thereby impaired. The themes, settings, and characterizations are believably and incisively presented and the varying stylistic and imagistic nuances correspond perfectly to the shifts in mood, tone, and point of view.

Notes

1. See Sherman H. Eoff, *The modern Spanish novel* (New York, 1961), pp. 109-15.

2. *The Catholic naturalism of Pardo Bazán* (Chapel Hill, N.C., 1957). Robert E. Osborne, in *Emilia Pardo Bazán: su vida y sus obras* (México, 1964), is essentially in agreement with Brown regarding

Pardo Bazán's naturalism (pp. 69-70), as is Harry L. Kirby, Jr., who studies a little-known essay by her (1877) to show both the emphasis she placed on heredity and environment and "her argument against transformism and the animal origin of man" ("Pardo Bazán, Darwinism and *La madre naturaleza*," *Hispania*, XLVII [1964], 733-37).

3. Eoff, pp. 114 and 119, respectively.

To avoid duplication of Eoff's and Brown's work, I shall refrain from further, general discussion of naturalism as related to Pardo Bazán and concentrate on the more technical aspects. It is, nevertheless, desirable to point out two articles which to some extent corroborate my interpretation.

José Blanco Amor, in "Romanticismo y espíritu de clase en *Los Pazos de Ulloa*," *Cuadernos hispanoamericanos*, Núm. 148 (Abril 1962), calls Pardo Bazán "una posromántica situada entre dos edades literarias: el romanticismo muerto y el naturalismo agonizante" (p. 8). He insists on this romantic-naturalistic duality and on a supposed falsification of the characters: "Los de arriba son buenos, los de abajo son malos. La vileza está en el pueblo; la virtud, en los señores" (p. 10). He is likewise critical of her prejudiced portrayal of the liberal doctor, Máximo Juncal, as "un charlatán, superficial, pedante, inconsciente, tonto" (p. 12). Ronald Hilton's study, "Doña Emilia Pardo Bazán, Neo-Catholicism and Christian socialism," *The Americas*, XI (1954), 3-18, explains Juncal as a M. Homais type and, more importantly, helps us to place *Los Pazos de Ulloa* and its sequel on a trajectory, rather closer to the beginning than the end, between Neo-Catholicism and Christian socialism.

4. It is useful to compare Pardo Bazán's shifts in point of view with Harry Levin's comments on Flaubert: "He developed the technical device that handbooks term point of view by adapting the rhythms of his style to the movement of his character's thoughts. By limiting what has more precisely been termed the center of consciousness to the orbit of a single character . . . purists could intensify the focus of the novel still further" (*The Gates of Horn: A study of five French realists* [New York, 1963], p. 252). Levin goes on to discuss this technique in *Madame Bovary* and its realistic stylistic counterpart, *le style indirect libre*.

5. *Los Pazos de Ulloa, Obras completas*, III (Madrid, n.d. [1891]), p. 219. Subsequent references will be made in the text.

6. In all of this I am at odds with Mary E. Giles. First, in the matter of literary impressionism, which she knows imperfectly, she means themes or motifs—sun through leaves, colors, light, descriptions—not techniques, in her "Impressionist Techniques in Descriptions by Emilia Pardo Bazán," *Hispanic Review*, XXX (1962), 304-16. In a second article ("Pardo Bazán's Two Styles," *Hispania*, XLVIII [1965], 456-62), she unsuccessfully tries to establish a significant distinction between Pardo Bazán's early elaborate and complex style and a later, more modernistic and impressionistic one. Not enough passages are treated, nor do her own examples bear out her theory (which is not to say that there may not be grounds for some distinction—it is simply undocumented).

7. On Pardo Bazán's language, cf. Carmen Bravo-Villasante, *Vida y obra de Emilia Pardo Bazán* (Madrid, 1962), p. 133.

8. For a discussion of the term and its uses and bibliography, see Stephen Ullmann, *Style in the French novel* (New York, 1964), ch. ii.

Currie Kerr Thompson (essay date December 1976)

SOURCE: Thompson, Currie Kerr. "The Use and Function of Dreaming in Four Novels by Emilia Pardo Bazán." *Hispania* 59, no. 4 (December 1976): 856-62.

[*In the following essay, Thompson examines the psychological significance of dream sequences in four of Pardo Bazán's novels, including* The House of Ulloa, La madre naturaleza, A Wedding Trip, *and* Insolación.]

From one point of view the incorporation of dreams in the novels of Emilia Pardo Bazán seems so normal that it scarcely need attract our attention. The dream with its use of symbol and metaphor seems to be a valid literary device and indeed has been so used during the last four thousand years. In his study of the dream in Galdós' novels, Joseph Schraibman gives a brief history of the dream in world literature and regrets that as yet there has been no study of this phenomenon as it affects various periods of Hispanic writing.[1] This lack is particularly unfortunate, I believe, in the study of naturalistic novels of the nineteenth century. The naturalists have always been considered highly science-oriented, and indeed they make this claim for themselves. But nineteenth-century scientific views held that dreams were insignificant from a psychological point of view and merely reflected physiological conditions of the dreamer.[2] This "somatic dispositions" theory held—to give a very simplified example—that a dream of intense heat or cold would actually reflect the body temperature of the dreamer rather than (as is now generally conceded) his ambitions, worries, and experiences. It was not until the publication of Freud's *The Interpretation of Dreams* in 1900 that the physiological theory of dreaming came under close scrutiny, and whereas Freud's ideas ultimately prevailed, it should be noted that this was only after much opposition from the holders of the somatic dispositions theory.

In this light, then, the presence of dreams in the naturalistic narrative seems an interesting paradox. Although the inclusion of dreams in her novels does not distinguish Pardo Bazán from Zola, the initiator of naturalism, an examination of both authors' literary treatises on the naturalistic movement fails to account for their presence. Zola does not examine dreaming in *Le Roman experimental, Les Romanciers naturalistes,* and *Le Naturalisme au théâtre*; and Pardo Bazán likewise disregards this subject in **La cuestión palpitante,** where she recommends adopting Zola's scientific approach to literature—although accommodating this under the broader banner of realism. Does her fictional use of dreams coupled with her failure to mention them in this treatise imply a *lapsus doctrinae*? Is the writer not as scientific as she might like to believe? Clearly several questions are raised, and it will be the intent of this study to contribute to their resolution by an examination of **Los pazos de Ulloa** (1886), **Insolación** (1889), **Un viaje de novios** (1881), and **La madre Naturaleza** (1887). These novels contain a total of six dreams (one of which is a daydream) and are excellent examples of the skill with which Pardo Bazán incorporates dreaming in her narrative technique. In the first two novels, **Los pazos de Ulloa** and **Insolación,** the reader finds clear proof that Pardo Bazán was at least superficially acquainted with the somatic dispositions theory of dreaming.

There are two dreams in **Los pazos de Ulloa.** In the first of these Julián, the dreamer, is a priest who is frightened by the primitive environment of the Galician *pazo* in which he is living. He considers the possibility of escaping but decides against this because of his attachment for Nucha, the wife of the *pazo*'s owner, don Pedro, and the only civilized element in the environment. Julián's dream occurs the night after he has reached his decision to remain at the *pazo.* In his dream, Julián is standing before the *pazo,* which has been transformed into a fortified feudal castle. The *pazo*'s coat of arms, consisting of a pine tree and a pair of wolves, has been animated so that Julián sees it as two live wolves howling in unison with the wind which blows through the pine. In the tower of the castle Julián recognizes don Pedro in armor preparing to drop a steel boot on his head. Julián waits helplessly for the boot to fall and suddenly perceives an owl swooping down toward him. In order to escape he jumps the moat surrounding the castle, and the moat is transformed into the backwater of a mill; likewise, the castle is changed into a painted cardboard tower. A woman is trying to escape from the tower and changes into a card from the tarot deck—the *sota de bastos.* Another tarot figure, the *caballo de es-*

padas, waiting for her beneath the tower, changes into St. George, who is mounted on a spider and attacks Julián with his lance. Julián stands helplessly before the attack and feels the lance pierce his side. He then awakens "resintiéndose de una punzada dolorosa en la mano derecha, sobre la cual había gravitado el peso del cuerpo todo, al acostarse del lado izquierdo, posición favorable a las pesadillas."[3]

It seems obvious that Pardo Bazán is attempting with these words to invoke the somatic dispositions theory in order to explain the occurrence of a nightmare and to equate the stabbing from the lance with the pricking sensation which Julián feels in his arm. However, it seems equally obvious that the bulk of the dream can only be explained psychologically, and the novelist herself intervenes to tell the reader that the basis of dreams "siempre son nociones de lo real, pero barajadas, desquiciadas y revueltas merced al anárquico influjo de la imaginación . . ." (I [**Obras completas**], 241).

The two most prominent elements of the dream—the spider and the tarot cards—can be related to actual events of the previous evening. Before going to bed, Julián stopped by the kitchen to get oil for his reading lamp and saw the servant Sabel using a worn deck of cards to tell fortunes. After returning to his room, he heard a scuffle in the hall and assumed that don Pedro was mistreating Nucha. He ran to defend her but was embarrassed to learn that don Pedro was only chasing a spider which had frightened his wife and that his intervention had allowed the spider to escape. This discovery signals a change in Julián's role from that of rescuer to unwelcome meddler, and this change is reflected by the numerous changes which occur in the dream: moat to backwater (*represa = represión*?); castle to cardboard tower; escaping woman to *sota de bastos; caballo de espadas* to St. George. It is the last change which appears most important. Julián rushes to defend Nucha from her husband and decides not to leave the *pazo,* because he wishes to be her protector (St. George); but this role belongs to her husband. Moreover, by representing Nucha as the *sota de bastos,* Julián seems to recognize subconciously that his attachment for her is not as pure as he might like to think. It must be remembered that *sota,* in addition to referring to one of the cards of the tarot deck (the knave), also means an insolent or shameless woman, and *bastos* (clubs) can easily be associated with the adjective *basto* (crude). The dream represents Julián's passivity by showing him waiting helplessly to be smashed by a falling boot or stabbed by St. George's lance. His one act of jumping the moat precipitates a series of changes, just as his decision to protect Nucha in real life had precipitated a series of role changes in which her husband assumed the protector role coveted by Julián and in which Nucha's role of faithful wife was opened to doubt on the psychological level. It is appropriate, in view of the priest's passivity, that in the dream the inanimate shield becomes alive and that people are represented as lifeless tarot card figures. It should also be observed that this animation of objects and dehumanization of people expresses succinctly a basic theme of naturalism: inanimate objects are alive in the sense that they influence man's actions, and man is made into an object by his inability to act freely. However, the dream is fully justified by its portrayal of Julián's character, without recourse to doctrinal considerations.

The second dream in the novel occurs to Perucho, don Pedro's illegitimate son, who has just witnessed the murder of his grandfather, Primitivo, and has seen don Pedro quarreling with Nucha in the chapel of the *pazo*. These scenes arouse his anxieties and cause him to fear that don Pedro may attack him and Nucha's infant daughter, Manuela. Because of his love for the baby, Perucho hides her in the granary to protect her, and once they are there, the two of them fall asleep and Perucho begins to dream: "Entre las representaciones de una especie de pesadilla angustiosa que agitaba a Perucho, veía el muchacho un animalazo de desmesurado grandor, bestión indómito que se acercaba a él rugiendo, bramando y dispuesto a zampárselo de un bocado o a deshacerlo de una uñada. . . . Se le erizó el cabello, le temblaron las carnes y un sudor frío le empapó la sien. . . . ¡Qué monstruo tan espantoso! Ya se acerca. . . . Ya cierra con Perucho . . . sus garras se hincan en las carnes del rapaz, su cuerpo descomunal le cae encima lo mismo que inmensa roca . . ." (I, 279).

Perucho awakens to discover that the *ama* has found his hiding place and is angrily beating him. Her blows and angry words appear to be the source of Perucho's dream. Thus for the second time we find the author apparently familiar with the somatic dispositions theory of dreaming. However, once again the dream is psychologically significant. Perucho feels threatened and overpowered by his environment, and these fears are symbolized in the dream by the wild animal which attacks him.

In *Insolación*, also, the novelist displays her familiarity with the physiological theory of dreaming while once again making the dream psychologically meaningful. In this novel, the dreamer, Asís, is a Galician widow living in Madrid who has become indecorously involved with Diego Pacheco, a skillful seducer, when she accepts an invitation to attend a *feria* with him and becomes intoxicated from the sun and too much sherry. Frightened by her behavior she decides to leave Madrid and return to Galicia and is in the process of making the necessary preparations for this when she falls asleep and begins to dream. At the beginning of the dream, Pardo Bazán intervenes to announce, "No era la pesadilla que causa la ocupación de estómago, en que tan pronto caemos de altísima torre como volamos por dilatadas zonas ce-

lestes, ni menos el ensueño provocado por la acción del calor del lecho sobre los lóbulos cerebrales, donde, sin permiso de la honrada voluntad, se representan imágenes repulsivas . . ." (I, 467). Having thus paid her respects to the accepted scientific ideas of the day, the novelist then begins to narrate a psychologically meaningful dream. In her dream Asís is on the train with her servant, Diabla, returning to Galicia. The train is passing through Castile and its rocking motion coupled with an unbearable heat and dust cause Asís to wish for water. However, when Diabla gives her a glass of what Asís thinks is water it turns out to be sherry, and this only increases her thirst. Finally, the train enters Galicia and Asís welcomes the tunnels through which the train passes and which seem like baths in a well. As she gazes on the mountain springs she is at first like a fish returned to water. But soon she begins to react to the presence of too much water. The rivers are overflowing and the sky is a dreary gray from which an endless deluge is pouring. Asís feels this water penetrating into her very being "hasta que anegado de tristeza, el corazón empieza también a chorrear agua: primero, gota a gota; luego, a borbotones, con fúnebre ruido de botella que se vacia . . ." (I, 468).

Just as in Julián's dream in *Los pazos de Ulloa,* the elements of Asís' dream come from the dreamer's experiences. Earlier in the novel Asís has heard the theory that the Castilian sun is a stimulus powerful enough to cause Spaniards to cast off their thin veneer of civilization and behave primitively, and she has just learned what a disastrous effect the sun—especially in combination with sherry—can have on her conduct. Thus, in the dream she sees herself fleeing from Castile to escape the sun; the appearance of sherry in the glass that she thinks contains water and the sound of the emptying bottle at the end of the dream are related to the fact that she became inebriated from sherry while at the *feria* with Diego. On the most obvious level, then, the dream communicates that Asís, though preparing to leave Madrid to escape Diego's advances, does not actually wish to leave and secretly realizes that to return to Galicia would not make her happy. Pardo Bazán uses this subconscious realization in order to prepare the reader for what could otherwise be considered paradoxical behavior in the protagonist. That afternoon after leaving the *feria*—still under the influence of the sun and alcohol—Asís was indiscreet enough to allow Diego to take her to an inn, but she resisted his attempt to seduce her (much to the surprise of the servants at the inn, who were listening through an open window). But after her dream, when Diego visits Asís and expresses his desire to spend the night with her the widow submits. The relation of this *volte face* to the dream seems clear in light of the water images used to describe Asís' feelings before yielding to Diego's proposition: "Asís dudó un minuto. Allá dentro percibía, a manera de *in-undación* que todo lo arrolla, un *torrente* de pasión de-satado" (I, 470, italics added).

Since the dream is thus related to a decision regarding Asís' sexual conduct, it would not be inappropriate to investigate the possible presence in it of sexual sym-bols. It should be pointed out, before embarking on this search, that symbols in dreams are usually divided into three classes: accidental, conventional, and universal.[4] An accidental symbol is one which originates in the ex-periences of a particular individual; examples would be the sherry in Asís' dream or the spider in Julián's. Con-ventional symbols are those which are agreed upon by a community; for example, the flag is a conventional sym-bol for a country. Universal symbols are sometimes called "poetic" symbols as they are usually based upon metaphor, synecdoche, or some other poetic figure and hence do not depend upon a knowledge of private expe-riences for their interpretation. Elements from the dream we have just examined which could be so interpreted are: the rocking sensation of the train in motion (the rhythm of the sex act); the penetration of the train (phallic) into the tunnel; the comparison of this to a re-freshing bath in a well (implying a fall = climax); the burning desire for water (a long used symbol for fertility); and finally the culmination of the dream with a spurting liquid.[5]

In *Un viaje de novios,* a novel written eight years be-fore *Los pazos de Ulloa,* Pardo Bazán makes a similar use of a Freudian wish-fulfillment dream in order to foreshadow an otherwise unexpected act by the pro-tagonist. Lucía, the dreamer, is a recently married naive Spanish woman who is spending her honeymoon in France with her older domineering husband, Aurelio Miranda. An accidental separation from Miranda on the train has compelled Lucía to become acquainted with the younger and more sympathetic Ignacio Artegui, whose home is in Paris facing the hotel where the hon-eymooners are staying along with Pedro. The dream oc-curs immediately after Lucía has witnessed the dying Pilar's confession and has gone in a state of emotional exhaustion to rest in the garden facing Artegui's house. In her dream Lucía sees herself in the same garden full of dry sickly banana trees, although the garden is greatly enlarged by the dream. Looking toward Artegui's house, she notices a pale hand extending from one of the win-dows signaling her to come. She tries to run toward the hand but her efforts are vain as the garden grows, pre-venting her from making progress. Finally she decides to fly and takes to the air using a pair of newly ac-quired wings. She is nearing the house when she sud-denly feels a sharp pain and perceives her wings falling to the ground beneath her. She herself falls, not to the ground of the garden, but into the grotto of Lourdes,

where she concentrates on the freshness of the murmur-ing fountain before awakening: "¡Ay, qué fresca y her-mosa era la gruta, con su manantialillo murmurador!" (I, 152).

Lucía has previously associated the grotto of Lourdes with death, which she would welcome as a blessed es-cape from the frustrations caused by her domineering husband, and it appears that the immediate cause of the dream is the impending death of her friend Pilar. It would be possible thus to relate the flight and the wings in the dream to a wish to die and make an angelic as-cent into heaven. However, such an interpretation would overlook the obvious fact that Lucía in her dream wants to go to Artegui's house. This fact is significant, be-cause following the dream, Lucía does indeed go to his house unaccompanied, in spite of the fact that well-bred ladies of her social station are forbidden such conduct. It would appear, then, that this dream, like Asís' in *In-solación,* is used to prepare the reader for an action which might otherwise seem out of character. Using this similarity as a point of departure, we are then struck by other similarities between the two dreams. Both rep-resent a progression from dryness to wetness (the gar-den is dry and sickly at the beginning of Lucía's dream, but there is a fountain in the grotto of Lourdes); both concentrate on rhythmic movement (the rocking train in Asís' case, and in Lucía's, her regular breathing and wing movement); both dreams involve a fall (into a well in Asís' dream, into a grotto with a fountain in Lucía's). In our examination of *Insolación* we saw that these symbols could have a sexual interpretation, and it would not be amiss to suspect that such an interpreta-tion is equally valid for *Un viaje de novios.* We can add to the data already examined the fact that death is fre-quently used in dreams as a symbol of sexual surren-der.[6] There is, of course, in Lucía's dream nothing so explicit as the penetration of the train into the tunnel that we saw in *Insolación,* and this important difference is in keeping with Lucía's character. Incapable of the frankness with which Asís grants Diego permission to spend the night, Lucía feels a strong need to repress her feelings. When she goes alone to Artegui's house she is in a state of hysteria. She does confess her love for him but refuses to escape with him from her overly posses-sive husband. Her confession of love seems to prevent Artegui from committing suicide, and she uses this fact later in order to justify her actions to the priest, Arri-goitia, claiming that her intentions were innocent. How-ever, the dream we have just examined raises signifi-cant questions regarding the alleged innocence of her motives.

A similar use of the dream to add depth to motivation can be found in the character of Gabriel Pardo in *La madre Naturaleza.* In this sequel to *Los pazos de Ulloa* Nucha is dead, and her brother Gabriel, an artillery commander, visits the *pazo* planning to marry his dead sister's daughter, Manuela. The first dream, a daydream, consists of a rather crude six-thousand-word exposition of Gabriel's memories of his sister Nucha (I, 310-19). In this fantasy Gabriel sees Nucha protecting him from his older siblings and encouraging his studies as a young boy. He sees himself saving his money to buy her a ring and sending her a picture of himself in uniform from military school. He sees himself crushed by her death and groping aimlessly through life as he tries to blot her from his mind until the death of his father revives his memories of Nucha and reminds him that her daughter Manuela is now of marriageable age. In this novel, which deals with incest, the reader can hardly overlook the information communicated by this dream: that Gabriel's wish to marry Manuela is really a disguise of a more basic wish to marry his sister, Nucha. This desire is then an incestuous one, and the true nature of it is communicated by Nucha's motherly attitude toward Gabriel in his dream and by the fact that in it he always addresses her as "Mamita."

The impact of this information is felt fully after the second dream of the novel, which occurs on Gabriel's first night at the *pazo*. He is nagged by thirst and has trouble going to sleep in his new environment, but is unable to ask for water as all the other occupants have retired. In order to distract himself he picks up a copy of the *Cantar de los cantares,* translated by Fray Luis de León, and becomes absorbed in reading it. Forgetting his thirst and discomfort, he finally falls asleep and dreams that he is in a landscape which is reminiscent of the *Cantar*: "Gabriel vió viñas y prados, campos de mies opulenta, un mar de mies que no concluía nunca; su sobrina le guiaba al través de él, diciéndole mil ternezas en bíblico estilo y en primorosa lengua castellana; el cura de Ulloa estaba allí, no austero y triste, sino paternal y venerable, con un jarro de agua fresca en la mano. . . . Gabriel pegaba la boca al jarro, bebía, bebía. . . . ¡Qué agua tan delgada, tan refrigerante y deliciosa!" (I, 372).

The central point to understanding this dream is Gabriel's thirst. In the dream his thirst is satisfied by water which the priest gives him to drink, just as before going to sleep his thirst was satisfied by reading the *Cantar de los cantares.* Was Gabriel's soul "thirsting after righteousness" and hence satisfied by Biblical scripture? Actually, an explanation of why the special content of the *Cantar de los cantares* is particularly satisfying is suggested later. On the following day Manuela and Perucho (who are unaware that they are brother and sister) are missing, and while their absence is not disturbing to others, it does bother Gabriel. His worries seem related to the passages from the previous night's reading which flash through his mind "como en placa fotográfica" (I, 379). Gabriel is particularly impressed by the fact that the bride and groom of the *Cantar* are brother and sister, and he dwells on the repetitions of "hermana mía, esposa," used as an endearing form of address through-

out the book. Because of this unique detail of the Biblical selection, Gabriel's suspicions are awakened concerning the missing Manuela's conduct with her half-brother Perucho. But his suspicions also reveal his sensitivity to this aspect of the *Cantar.* In light of this, it seems safe to assume that his pleasure from the previous night's reading was enhanced by the impact of this feature on his suppressed incestuous impulses already seen in the daydream. Receiving water from the priest in the dream should then be examined in light of the previously noted association between water and fertility and the use in various cultures of symbolic imbibing as part of the marriage ceremony (to include the Jewish Orthodox and, in some cases, the Roman Catholic ceremonies). The dream is used in this novel, then, as in *Un viaje de novios,* to add new light to a character's motives. In Gabriel's case, the dream points an ironic finger at his self-righteous indignation when his suspicions concerning Manuela's and Perucho's incestuous relationship are confirmed.

Having completed our examination of the dreams of four novels by Pardo Bazán, we are able to draw the following conclusions. First, it is clear that the novelist was aware of the accepted somatic dispositions theory of dreaming, but that she did not let her knowledge of this theory destroy her own conception of the dream as a psychologically significant phenomenon. Thus two decades prior to the publication of Freud's iconoclastic treatise on the subject we find the Spanish novelist narrating dreams which acquire their full significance when interpreted in light of later theories. It is certain, of course, that Freud's new theories did not emerge from a vacuum in 1900, the year of their publication, but represent the culmination of a formative period during which the ideas he was to develop surely constituted part of the European intellectual atmosphere. In this regard, Lionel Trilling speaks of psychoanalysis as "a science standing upon the shoulders of . . . literature"[7] and notes the importance of literature in the development of Freud's theories. Trilling emphasizes, however, that we are not to look for particular literary influences upon Freud but rather "a whole *Zeitgeist,* a direction of thought."[8] The fact that Pardo Bazán uses psychologically meaningful dreams in her novels shows her to be abreast of this direction of thought and is a credit to her standing as an intellectual. But more important, from an artistic point of view, is the skill with which she used the dream to create subtle nuances in the portrayal of her characters and to add a new dimension to her narrative technique.

Notes

1. Joseph Schraibman, *Dreams in the Novels of Galdós* (New York: Hispanic Institute in the United States, 1960), pp. 13-24.

2. A discussion of the somatic dispositions theory of dreaming and of the changes which occurred fol-

lowing the publication of Freud's work can be found in Eric Fromm, *The Forgotten Language* (New York: Rinehart and Co., 1951) and Medard Boss, *The Analysis of Dreams* (London: Rider and Co., 1957). Freud himself refers to the deficiencies he finds in the somatic dispositions theory in his *The Interpretation of Dreams* in *The Basic Writings of Sigmund Freud* (New York: Random House, 1938), pp. 280-81.

3. Emilia Pardo Bazán, *Obras completas, novelas y cuentos,* 4a ed. (Madrid: Aguilar, 1964), I, 242. All references to Pardo Bazán's works are taken from this edition and will be identified hereafter by inserting the volume and page number in the body of the article.

4. Fromm, op. cit., p. 16.

5. While it is not felt that a substantiation of our interpretation here is needed, the reader wishing to verify our conclusions in this and the following dream may do so by consulting Emile A. Gutheil, *The Language of the Dream* (New York: Macmillan Co., 1939). This work is a lexical arrangement of dream symbols based upon Freudian psychology.

6. Ibid., p. 58.

7. Lionel Trilling, "Freud and Literature" in Hendrick M. Ruitenbeek, *Psychoanalysis and Literature* (New York: E. P. Dutton and Co., 1964), p. 252.

8. Ibid., p. 251.

Thomas Feeny (essay date 1978)

SOURCE: Feeny, Thomas. "Pardo Bazán's Pessimistic View of Love as Revealed in *Cuentos de amor.*" *Hispanófila* 64 (1978): 7-14.

[*In the following essay, Feeny discusses Pardo Bazán's cynical attitude toward love as it is revealed in her short story collection* Cuentos de amor.]

On examining Emilia Pardo Bazán's collection of short stories intitled *Cuentos de amor,*[1] the reader might well wonder at the exceedingly grim view of love the author reveals in these tales. For although the theme of love is touched upon in nearly all of the forty-three stories, it will almost never be that of joyous or blissful love. Rather, Pardo Bazán chooses to write about love unfulfilled (**"El viajero," "Más allá"**); or love betrayed (**"La perla rosa," "Así y todo . . . ," "Sor Aparición," "¿Justicia?"**). She prefers the themes of unrequited love, treated in some depth in **"El dominó verde,"** or aberrant love that inflicts pain and death (**"A secreto**

agravio," "Los buenos tiempos," "Delincuente honrado"**). Though there are starry-eyed lovers, they appear singly, never in pairs. Men and women are, for varying reasons, unable to make each other happy. One cannot, in fact, easily say which sex fares worse in these tales. For while Pardo displays a penchant for etching weak male characters, resounding failures in matters of the heart, she also fancies scheming women who employ their sexual allure solely for personal gain.

Despite her contention that literature, like life, should depict both "lágrimas y risas, el fondo de la eterna tragicomedia del mundo,"[2] within the pages of **Cuentos de amor** one finds Pardo invariably emphasizes the most tragic aspects of love. In an effort to account for the disillusion and cynicism that suffuse these stories, let us examine them in some detail.

The first two tales, **"El amor asesinado"** and **"El viajero"** set the tone of the collection. The former deals with a woman's rejection of love, personified by a Cupid-like child. She flees from him and finally strangles him, only to discover in doing so she has brought about her own death. **"El viajero"** recounts a woman's abandonment by love. Pardo's choice of the traveler to symbolize love indicates the transitoriness she ascribes to that emotion. Although, owing to the fantastic quality of these stories, her pessimism does not strike one as extreme, it increases as she treats more realistic situations. In a few tales, such as **"El corazón perdido"** and **"Mi suicidio,"** the author displays a mildly ironic humor rather rare in her writings. In the first, the narrator attempts to restore a lost heart to the woman who has mislaid it, but though all those he finds are without a heart, none will claim it. When finally a young girl accepts his gift, she dies from an excess of sentiment. Despite Pardo's light touch, the clear implication is that woman, heartless in the literal sense, is equally so in the figurative.

The irony in **"Un corazón perdido"** becomes more evident in **"Mi suicidio."** Here a recent widower, planning suicide because of his grief, discovers his late wife, whom he thought perfect, was unfaithful. Rather than shoot himself, he shoots her portrait. He is but the first of several in **Cuentos de amor** deceived by their wives. Noteworthy, however, is the author's procedure for pointing up the irony of the outcome. Early in the tale, by means of the protagonist's reminiscences while studying his wife's portrait, Pardo leads the reader to understand the dead woman was in all ways a model spouse. Then compromising letters appear, and the reader finds he, like the husband, has been misled. This literary practice of idealizing an initial situation that eventually proves far from ideal, can, of course, lend an ironic twist to the denouement. But in this collection the practice becomes so frequent as to lose its effectiveness. First appearances cease to mislead when they become immediately suspect. More than coincidental, however, is that just as in **"Mi suicidio,"** the initial idealized situation of tales like **"Los buenos tiempos,"** **"El encaje roto,"** **"¿Justicia?"** and **"A secreto agravio,"** depicts the joy of apparently happy couples; that their bliss proves fleeting or illusory reveals Pardo's disillusion with love's permanency. In fact, in **"Los buenos tiempos,"** **"A secreto agravio,"** and **"Así y todo . . ."** one member of the pair ends up slaughtering the other.

The irony that characterizes the author's jaundiced view of love in the early stories turns to bitter cynicism in **"El dominó verde,"** Pardo reveals her thoughts on unrequited love when the protagonist, scorning his former beloved's affection, asserts: "Mas no es culpa nuestra si de este barro nos amasaron, si el sentimiento que no compartimos nos molesta y acaso nos repugna, si las señales de la pasión que no halla eco en nosotros nos incitan a la mofa y al desprecio, y si nos gozamos en pisotear un corazón, por lo mismo que sabemos que ha de verter sangre bajo nuestros crueles pies" ([*Obras completas*] pp. 44-45).

Granted it is possible the character speaks for himself and not for the author; yet the length and acrimony of his attack, not entirely justified by the events of the story, make one suspect Pardo Bazán has let her own skepticism show through. In discussing the importance of observation to a novelist, she writes: "La novela es traslado de la vida, y lo único que el autor pone en ella es su modo peculiar de ver las cosas reales".[3] Although she is talking about analysis and the novel, it would follow that to the short story, as well, an author must bring his particular way of viewing things. And if his view of love and lovers is essentially bleak, then in his treatment of these subjects the pessimistic note will predominate.

Even when a happy outcome would be most plausible, Pardo Bazán purposefully shuns it. Consider **"Martina,"** for example. Though there is no obstacle to the lovers' marriage, almost as an afterthought the author somewhat unconvincingly dispatches the lady off to a convent that she might not die of happiness—"morir de felicidad" (p. 248)—at her beloved's side. When, on rare occasion, Pardo shows herself at all generous to those in love, she does so begrudgingly. In **"Más allá,"** upon the lovers' death their two souls become one. But since his is earmarked for purgatory and hers for heaven, as a single entity they can enter into neither region. Thus they are denied forever the peace of "la eterna bienandanza" (p. 260).

Another thought frequent in Pardo Bazán's writings and doubtlessly related to her disillusion is that time must inexorably take its toll. This is particularly evident in **"Primer amor,"** **"Sor Aparición,"** and **"Cuento soñado."** In the first tale, the repulsive old aunt who sprays her young nephew with spittle as she cackles at him contrasts starkly with the seductive woman in the photo taken years before. Sparing no details in her description, Pardo appears to share the boy's revulsion at time's handiwork. And in **"Sor Aparición,"** the portrait of the withered nun, with her "cara de una amarillez sepulcral, su temblorosa cabeza, su boca consumida" (p. 142) contrasts with the description of her as a young, passionate girl, an "asombro de guapa" (p. 145). In these tales one laments the fading of youthful beauty. Similarly, when the aged queen of **"Cuento soñado,"** worn with the cares and duties of her office, returns to the scenes of her childhood, the author describes her as overwhelmed by the irretrievable loss of "la juventud, la ilusión, la misteriosa energía de los años primaverales" (p. 184), whose passing has left her faded and weary.

In her essays and criticism Pardo Bazán frequently declares her fiction teaches no lesson. "Aborrezco las píldoras de moral rebozadas en una capa de oro literario," she writes in the preface to *Viaje de novios* (p. 10). Yet in a number of her short stories there is a subtle moral, for the author, with obvious relish, repeatedly demonstrates that in matters of love often man's best efforts are doomed to naught. In **"La perla rosa"** the generous husband indulges his unfaithful wife but fails to win her affection. The industrious shopkeeper of **"A secreto agravio,"** on learning of his wife's betrayal, sets fire to his hard-earned business and to his spouse and her lover. And despite his most sincere endeavors to preserve a single illusion about woman's capacity for purely spiritual love, the protagonist of "La última ilusión de Don Juan" ends up totally disenchanted.

Evidence of Maupassant's influence on her short stories appears in *El naturalismo*,[4] one of Pardo's several volumes of criticism on French literature. Admiring his objectivity, she also extols "la forma, . . . lo límpido de la prosa, su naturalidad" (p. 163). In praise of his short stories, she writes: "No son meramente de gorja: hieren otras cuerdas dramáticas, dolorosas, irónicas: la lira humana" (p. 160). As we have seen, the sense of the ironic and emphasis on man's tribulations she admires in Maupassant because they are so much a part of life abound in her own short stories.

Maupassant chose the short story, Pardo Bazán declares, as most suited to his temperament, and in this genre he succeeded in expressing "su concepción de la vida—, pesimista, sensual y cruel" (p. 165). These comments alone may explain why Walter Pattison[5] and other critics attribute much of the pessimism in Pardo Bazán's short stories to Maupassant's influence. It is well, however, to note her remarks in *El naturalismo* concerning other French decadent writers. Having speculated that the early symptoms of Maupassant's ultimate madness had for many years intensified his pessimism, she adds that personal anguish likewise affected the gloomy outlook of a number of his contemporaries: "La tensión e hiperestesia nerviosa de los Goncourt, causa probable de la temprana muerte del menor; la epilepsia de Flaubert; el agotamiento que excesos de la mocedad determinaron en Daudet y que le obligaron a intoxicarse con morfina; la crisis de misticismo modernista de Huysmans, a quien conocí tan enfermo del estómago—y hablo de novelistas únicamente—, arrojan sobre este período, en mis recuerdos, una sombra de desolación íntima, más oscura que la melancolía romántica" (pp. 162-63).

Thus, while Maupassant's influence may well account for much of the disillusion in her short stories, Pardo does acknowledge that the physical and mental sufferings of other French decadents, many personal acquaintances, also worked to cast a grey pall over her recollections of the era.[6]

Although nearly all the tales of *Cuentos de amor* reveal Pardo Bazán's cynical view of love, of special interest are a number that, within the limits the short story allows, present psychological studies of people whose afflictions are related to love; in this category falls **"El dominó verde,"** already discussed. Also included is **"Delincuente honrado,"** whose title character proudly boasts of having redeemed his honor by butchering his young daughter whom, in his madness, he has confused with his unfaithful wife. In **"Un parecido"** the protagonist suddenly realizes that despite the uncanny resemblance between the woman who has rejected him and her half-sister, who loves him, the latter has no appeal since she can exist for him only in her resemblance to his first love. **"El fantasma"** deals with the amorous fantasies of an unstable, sensitive woman wed to a prosaic husband. Her excessively romantic nature has her choose as her fictitious paramour a typical Don Juan figure, "un perdido y un espadachín" (p. 61). The author's attitude toward the wife's hallucinations bears mention; she neither pities nor mocks the woman's delusion but rather maintains a cool detachment while sketching in the details of her illness. Under gentle attack, however, is the foolish sentimentality of the story's narrator. Referring to his "fatuidad de muchacho" (p. 60) and "petulancia juvenil" (p. 61), he feels only embarrassment on recalling his youthful ardor for the wife. Thus, once again, romantic love fares ill at Pardo's hands. The wife's passion is, after all, absurd because her affair is pure illusion; and the young man, in retrospect, views his rapture as mere puerile infatuation. Pardo Bazán's contention, it appears, is that the only genuine sentiment is the stolid husband's devotion to his distraught spouse, an emotion, in the final analysis, more protectively fraternal than conjugal.

In **"La culpable"** Pardo recounts the trials of a loving woman ridden with remorse for having run off with her fiancé before their marriage. Her socially conscious parents, preoccupied with public opinion, never forgive her brief moral lapse. And although, to amend the past, she vows to be a perfect wife, her husband rejects her devotion and plays upon her guilt complex. Magnifying the gravity of her error, she attempts to atone through complete self-effacement. She endures her husband's philandering in silence, convinced she has no moral right to reproach him. In this story Pardo portrays the wife as victim of her "amante corazón" (p. 162), that leads her to risk reputation for love. The author details at length the bitter anguish the woman's sense of unworthiness inflicts upon her. For, though she is guilty in society's eyes and, ironically enough, in the eyes of the man who is the cause of her sorrows, it is her own exaggerated sense of guilt that finally destroys her life.

Although in **"La culpable"** Pardo maintains less detachment than in **"El fantasma,"** and openly sympathizes with the stricken wife, still the author regards the woman's tragedy as inexorable. For it is not merely that she has given her affection to an unworthy man; no one, neither husband nor parent nor child, Pardo implies, could banish the wife's torturous sense of guilt. On her deathbed she receives divine pardon. But, Pardo carefully points out, this does not content the dying woman. She begs her husband's forgiveness. The hypocrisy of his kiss, given as a sign of pardon, illustrates Pardo's contention that man's forgiveness is totally without meaning.

In **"Saga y Agar"** a middle-aged man, his ardor for his wife cooled, becomes involved with his adopted daughter. Here the author traces the evolution of idyllic conjugal love into passionless fraternal affection, as well as the evolution of fatherly love into illicit rapture. Pardo's customary dire view permits those involved no lasting happiness, for the tale ends in abandonment and death.

There are in this collection two tales that show striking similarities in their portrayal of woman's guile and cunning in amatory affairs. In both Pardo shows not only does love often fail to bring anything resembling happiness, but on occasion it leads to crime, disgrace and death. In **"Afra"** what immediately attracts the narrator to the title character is not a conventional beauty but the cold, imperious sexuality she radiates. Inquiring about her, he discovers she is suspected of having murdered her best friend, the fiancé of the man Afra desired. Particularly chilling is her calculating *sang froid*; on learning of her friend's engagement, she conceals her jealousy and helps select the wedding gown. Then the two girls go bathing and though the sea is rough, Afra, an excellent swimmer, urges the other into the surf, where she drowns.

Far more revealing than the bare facts of the tale's plot is Pardo's treatment of her heroine. As a murderess, she must suffer; her punishment is rejection by her beloved, who goes off. Yet, probably because the author is so taken with the woman's determination and capability, qualities Pardo herself possessed in abundance, she really does not treat Afra harshly. On the contrary, there is more than a hint of admiration in the description of Afra's strange power over men and haughty manner shown all would-be suitors.

The title character of "La Bicha," so named for her snake like appearance and evil reputation, draws men to her with a challenging sensuality much like Afra's. Expelled from a society ball as an unwelcome guest, "La Bicha" resolves to seek vengence on the organization's president. Employing all her meretricious allure, within five months she is secretly wed to him. As with Afra, Pardo Bazán seems to revel in depicting the woman's craft and boldness. After her disgrace, feigning remorse, she appears at the president's home to beg his forgiveness. Through tears and flattery, she soon seduces him. With their marriage, her revenge is complete; his young daughter dies and "La Bicha" dominates him ruthlessly.

One finds in the early pages of "La Bicha" explicit evidence of Pardo Bazán's dim view of romantic love's possibilities for happiness. In a quasi-serious tone the author, through her spokesman, an elderly widow, points out the irony that although man seldom complains about parents or children, whom he cannot, after all, choose, he is never content with servant or spouse, his own choices. Then by way of preface to her tale, the widow announces she will recount a story that proves man is quite unable to select a suitable partner, hence his inevitable marital grief.

Pardo's position regarding Afra and "La Bicha" is curious. Like the unfaithful wife of "Así y todo . . ." who, having murdered her husband, weds an "acaudalado caballero" (p. 103) and lives in luxury, Afra and "La Bicha," though portrayed as evil, ultimately conquer. Although Pardo does intimate Afra's disposal of her rival constitutes a bitter victory, "La Bicha" apparently escapes quite unscathed. The author's attitude verges on approval, not of the women themselves, but of their strength and audacity. While Pardo's gentle or submissive female character often must suffer resignedly ("La culpable," "La novia fiel," "Sor Aparición"), the forceful, astute woman frequently wins out over adversity and over man in particular.

Mary E. Giles has written that, at least in Pardo Bazán's latter novels, she shows the influence of the modernists' predilection for "exploring the psychology of their characters."[7] While C. C. Glascock does not relate Pardo's increasing preoccupation with psychological portraits to the modernists, he does find in her latter writing much evidence "she has deeply studied abnormal psychic phenomena," and terms her heroes of this period "schematic, shadowy, unnatural, pathological."[8] These critics are referring primarily to the intense, soul-searching studies of Pardo's last novels (*La quimera,* 1905; *La sirena negra,* 1908; *Dulce dueño,* 1911). But as early as 1891 in "**La novela novelesca**" the author conveys her extreme interest in the psychological novel. She hesitates to undertake that type of work at this time for fear the Spanish public would reject novels that were, in essence, "estudios científicos-psicológicos."[9] She is far more willing, it seems, to experiment within the realm of the short story. Thus, although Pardo's major successes in psychological portraiture appear with the new century, one can find in her *cuentos* of the 1890's a foreshadowing of that later writing.

That Pardo Bazán chose to attempt psychological sketches in her short stories would not, in itself, account for the overriding gloom of *Cuentos de amor.* Hopefully, a psychological study dealing with love need not be dispairing in tone. But as Walter Pattison points out, not only in her three latter novels, but "even as early as *Mother Nature*" (*La madre naturaleza*—1887), Pardo Bazán appears to feel that "compared to divine love, human love is vile . . . Nature, which operates through instincts, draws people together through sex, which we may idealize into Love" (p. 91). Our study of "**La culpable**," I feel, bears out this observation. Unable to take solace in God's pardon, the wife must have the insincere forgiveness of her shallow spouse.

Pardo Bazán's own marriage proved unsuccessful; both Blanca de los Ríos[10] and Carmen Bravo Villasante,[11] perhaps Pardo Bazán's most thorough biographer, intimate she was profoundly disappointed in love. One can, of course, only speculate on the effect the unfortunate outcome of her marriage had upon her view of sensual involvement. Clearly, however, her cynical attitude toward that type of emotion in *Cuentos de amor* may, at least in part, explain that in her final novels it is not love for another human but divine love that will ultimately afford one his salvation.

Notes

1. *O.C. [Obras completas]*, XVI (Madrid: Prieto, [1911]); within the the text I refer in parentheses to pages of this edition and all other works used. The original dates of the various stories in *Cuentos de amor* are uncertain; they were first published as a collection in 1898.

2. Preface to *Un viaje de novios* in *O.C.*, XXX, 6th. ed. (Madrid: Prieto, [1919]), p. 8; first published in 1881.

3. *Ibid.,* p. 7.

4. In *O.C.*, XLI (Madrid: Renacimiento, [1912]).

5. *Emilia Pardo Bazán* (New York: Twayne, 1971), p. 94.

6. For further discussion, see: John Kronik's "Emilia Pardo Bazán and the Phenomenon of French Decadentism," *PMLA,* 81 (1966), 418-27; see also: Cyrus C. Decoster's "Maupassant's *Une Vie* and Pardo Bazán's *Los pasos de Ulloa,*" *Hispanía,* 56, No. 3 (Sept., 1973), 587-92.

7. "Pardo Bazán's Two Styles," *Hispania,* 48 (1965), p. 458. See also: M. Baquero Goyanes' *El cuento español en el siglo XIX* (Madrid: Revista de Filologia Española, anejo L, 1949), for some analysis of several of Pardo's short stories contained in *Cuentos de amor* and elsewhere. Baquero Goyanes also treats the transition from the Romantics' love themes of "libertinaje, seducción, desengaño" (p. 595) to the more psychologically oriented love tales of the late nineteenth century.

8. *Two Modern Spanish Novelists: Emilia Pardo Bazán and Armando Palacio Valdés* (Austin: Univ. of Texas Press, 1926), p. 39.

9. *Nuevo teatro crítico* (Madrid: La España Editorial, 1891), II, p. 42, No. 6.

10. "Elogio de la Condesa de Pardo Bazán," *Raza Española,* XXX (1921), p. 27.

11. *Vida y obra de Emilia Pardo Bazán* (Madrid: Revista de Occidente, 1962).

R. C. Boland (essay date winter 1981)

SOURCE: Boland, R. C. "The Antithesis between Religion and Nature in *Los pazos de Ulloa*: A Different Perspective." *Revista Canadiense de Estudios Hispánicos* 5, no. 2 (winter 1981): 209-15.

[*In the following essay, Boland argues that religion threatens to suppress nature in Pardo Bazán's novel* The House of Ulloa.]

In a recent article, Mariano López views **Los pazos de Ulloa** as Emilia Pardo Bazán's celebration of Catholicism and repudiation of Naturalism.[1] There is no denying that in this, as in other novels, Pardo Bazán rejects the philosophy of Zola's Naturalism, even if she employs its techniques. However, far from writing a celebration of Catholicism, she provides a penetrating, critical analysis of the role of religion in the life of a man. López also argues that Pardo Bazán portrays Nature as a depraving influence: "En **Los pazos de Ulloa** . . . el hombre, al contacto con la naturaleza, no se regenera . . . sino que se degenera."[2] In fact, the contrary is the case: in **Los pazos de Ulloa** Nature emerges as benign and regenerating, the friend and ally of men of good will.

It has been established that in her later novels, Pardo Bazán developed a strong "interest in religious problems and in deeper psychological analysis of charac-

ters."[3] Indeed, as early as in **Los pazos de Ulloa,** published in 1886, she reveals this interest in the portrayal of the Catholic priest, Julián, who constitutes a psychological study showing how a strict, religious upbringing and inflexible religious ideals can stifle the natural impulses in man. Julián is an idealistic priest with a tendency towards mysticism. Imbued with the Catholic theology of the time, he views the world as a battleground for the forces of good and evil, and, whenever in distress, his instinctive recourse is to pray to God for assistance. On the other hand, Julián is also described as "propenso a la ternura, dulce y benigno como las propias malvas" ([**Los pazos de Ulloa** in **Obras completas**] p. 174).[4] The warm-hearted priest develops a deep, personal rapport with Mother Nature, herself gentle and kind. As well as being a servant of God, therefore, he is also a child of nature. There need not be, of course, any contradiction between these two callings. As a Christian, Pardo Bazán regards "la madre Naturaleza" as a manifestation of the wonder and omnipotence of God: in Julián's words, "Dios sobre todo" (p. 191). Nature and religion can play happy, complementary roles in a man's life. The conflict arising in the novel between religion and nature is the result of the former threatening to suppress the latter, as in the case of Julián, whose morbid mysticism strangles his natural impulses, with traumatic psychological and emotional consequences for the young priest.

Early in the novel we learn that Julián has been released from the apron string of a pious, puritanical, possessive mother only to be sent to the seclusion of the Seminary, and that in entering the priesthood he is not fulfilling his own vocation so much as vicariously fulfilling his mother's (p. 174). As a boy, Julián's favourite game had been to play at saying mass; as a man, his childhood game became his profession. Pardo Bazán's suggestion is that Julián's lonely, religious childhood was unnatural in the sense that it was devoid of the fun, games, laughter and friends necessary for a child's healthy psychological and emotional development. It can be argued that the picture of Julián tied to the apron strings of his maternal *beatona* is the other side of the coin to little Perucho's wallowing in compost heaps and sucking cow-teats; Julián's inhibited childhood was in its own way just as unnatural as Perucho's pig-like infancy. That Julián's maternal upbringing was unnatural is testified by some of its legacies: an unhealthy Oedipus complex, a feminine disposition and an abnormal aversion for all physical contact, even with his own body. We learn that his mother is the adult Julián's only confidante, and that he has a purely feminine temperament, which Bazán classifies as "linfático-nervioso" (p. 174). In fact, Julián grows up into a woman in a man's body and even this has a feminine softness and delicacy. Julián's fellow-seminarians consider him a "mummy's boy": "Julián, por su compostura y hábitos de pulcritud—*aprendidos de su madre*

. . . , cogió fama de seminarista 'pollo'" (p. 175; emphasis mine). Julián also exhibits "repulgos de monja" and "pudores de doncella intacta" (p. 174). Not only will he not wash the private parts of the four year old ragamuffin, Perucho, but will not even wash his own. Julián's prudishness, euphemistically described as his "respeto a la carne humana" (p. 183), is evidence of carnal repression, the psychological roots of which can be traced to a dominant mother.

Julián's religious education is completed at the Seminary, from which he emerges as a saintly, idealistic priest whose understanding of the world is derived from pious books. Pardo Bazán engages in a penetrating criticism of Julián's seminary education. The Seminary has produced a young man of dove-like innocence only to cast him into a world crawling with serpents: "El era sencillo como la paloma; sólo que en este pícaro mundo también se necesita ser cauto como la serpiente" (p. 190). Julián cannot cope with the wiles of Primitivo and of his daughter, Sabel, both of whom are constantly described in sinister animal terms, such as "víbora" (p. 275), "escorpión" (p. 262), and "sabandija" (p. 263). In a nightmarish scene, Julián watches mesmerised as don Pedro tramples underfoot a monstrous spider, "un monstruoso vientre columpiado en ocho velludos zancos" (p. 241). In the context of the novel's symbolism, this "feo insecto" represents Primitivo and Sabel, the two monstrous characters conspiring against Julián.[5] However, whereas don Pedro, by nature an aggressive man, can act decisively against the real spider, Julián is impotent against Primitivo and Sabel; all the young priest can do is rage against their wickedness and entertain "ideas feroces" about administering them a sound thrashing (p. 263). Julián's pious books have not taught him to match wits against real evil and he himself eventually realises his ineptitude in dealing with it, his cruel words of self-realisation being "yo no tengo agallas" (p. 238). Pardo Bazán's argument seems to be that if a Seminary is a nursery for docile lambs and innocent doves it should keep them within the confines of its walls; otherwise it should open the eyes of would-be priests to the wickedness they will encounter in the world. A Seminary should equip young priests with the necessary arms to combat the likes of Primitivo and Sabel, the embodiments of the devil and of sin, two theological concepts that Julián understands in the abstract but fails to master when they assume human form.

Pardo Bazán is also critical of the sheer inhumanity of a Seminary education which trains a warm-hearted young man like Julián to suppress his natural emotions. Julián comes out of the Seminary as an austere individual, almost incapable of relating to any human being other than his mother. Once installed as chaplain of *los pazos,* Julián is starved of human contact—a thoroughly unwholesome, unnatural existence. Away from the Seminary and his mother, he has only his pious books and his chapel for solace and company. Under the circumstances, it is not surprising that Julián should become profoundly attached to Nucha's baby girl, for the chaplain's love for the baby is simply helping to satisfy his need to express the warmth and tenderness he has been taught to keep suppressed. In a particularly touching scene, Pardo Bazán evokes the icy barrier against human contact that a Seminary education has erected around Julián. One day, when Julián is nursing the baby, she wets her nappy, and as he feels the "warm wave" penetrate his trousers, he responds with gales of laughter: "Julián brincaba de contento y se cogía la cintura, que le dolía con tantas carcajadas" (p. 236). This is the first and only time in the novel that Julián expresses pure, unadulterated joy—a natural human sentiment that he has been conditioned to keep in cold storage. Significantly, this scene includes a taut, controlled indictment of the unnatural coldness of a Seminary education which freezes the hearts of young men like Julián: "Su contacto derretía no sé qué nieve de austeridad, cuajada sobre un corazón afeminado y virgen allá desde los tiempos del Seminario, desde que se había propuesto renunciar a toda familia y todo hogar en la Tierra entrando en el sacerdocio" (p. 236).

The degree of emotional and psychological repression that the young priest has to endure places an almost unbearable strain upon his heart and conscience. In Julián's own mind the vocations of priest and fatherhood are irreconcilable. He feels that in his paternal affection for Manolita, Nucha's baby, he is being derelict in his duty as a priest: "Hice mal, muy mal, en tomarle tanta afición" (pp. 237-8). Yet the idealistic priest who believes he should be immune to displays of affection cannot bear the thought of being torn away from Manolita. Julián is in fact being torn in two by the opposite callings of Nature and religion. He can only answer one or the other, as he ruefully confesses to himself: "¡Vaya un sacerdote ordenado de misa! Si tengo tal afición a los chiquillos no debí abrazar la carrera que abracé" (p. 237). Pardo Bazán's sugestion is that religion, in the form of the priesthood, is not Julián's true vocation. His natural sensibilities have been harshly represented by the inflexible religious ideal that has been thrust upon him and which he has mistakenly embraced. Nature, in the form of a paternal instinct, is calling out to him, and he yearns to answer its call, but by now it is too late: once a priest, always a priest.

A close reading of *Los pazos de Ulloa* alerts us to Julián's platonic love for Nucha, whom he has known since childhood. To him she is another Virgin Mary, a vessel of purity who should have entered a convent to become a bride of Christ. But Julián also exalts Nucha as the ideal Christian wife, "el tipo ideal de la bíblica esposa" (p. 218) and "una esposa castísima" (p. 238). Julián is instrumental in arranging the marriage between Pedro and Nucha; the chaplain's ideal is for

Pedro to play Saint Joseph to Nucha's Mary, and later, to Manolita's Jesus. What Julián does not realise is that he is asking the degenerate Pedro to play the role for which he, Julián, is ideally cast. After Pedro has failed to live up to the impossible role Julián has conceived for him, the chaplain actually visualises himself as Saint Joseph: "Pues bien: el santo grupo estaba disuelto; allí faltaba San José o le sustituía un clérigo . . ." (p. 237). So possessive is Julián's platonic love, "la veneración que por Nucha sentía" (p. 218), that he cannot bear the thought of a doctor defiling her body with his hands and surgical equipment during childbirth; unconsciously, Julián is thereby expressing his jealousy for the woman he venerates (p. 225). Indeed, during Nucha's agonising childbirth Julián actually experiences sympathetic labour pains (p. 231). The identification between Julián and Nucha during the childbirth scenes goes a long way towards explaining the chaplain's profound attachment to Manolita: unconsciously, he regards Manolita as his daughter, for she was born of his love and pain as much as of Nucha's. Julián in fact emerges as a frustrated father, or more aptly, given his feminine disposition, a frustrated mother. In one of his Hamlet-like interior monologues, Julián himself ponders whether he may not be more suited to the role of mother than to that of a priest: "Bien decían en el Seminario . . . que soy muy apocado y muy . . . , así . . . , como las mujeres . . ." (p. 237). Be this as it may, Julián longs for parenthood and the domestic bliss exemplified in the Holy Family: he sees himself as Saint Joseph, surrounded by his chaste spouse and his holy child. It should be noted that Julián's feminine and celibate disposition is compatible with his role as Saint Joseph who, according to Catholic tradition, was a virgin and Jesus' father by proxy. Julián's highest ideal, chastity, is thus reconciled with his deep-seated longing, parenthood.

So unsuited is Julián in his role as a priest, that he shudders at the thought of having to hear Nucha's confession: "la idea de que (Nucha) se confesase, de ver *desnuda* un alma tan hermosa, le confundía y turbaba" (p. 269; emphasis mine). In Julián's eyes, Nucha's baring her soul in the confessional would be akin to her standing before him naked. The force of *desnuda* in the above quotation is significant, for it is one of the few occasions that a suggestion of sensuality enters Julián's life. Julián flees from the prospect of viewing Nucha's naked soul as he flees from the sight of his own naked body. Julián's trepidation at the prospect of viewing Nucha "naked" may therefore be interpreted as a form of carnal repression. Indeed, immediately after imagining himself alone in the confessional with Nucha, a melodramatic Julián denounces his sinful nature: "Soy tan malo, *tan carnal,* tan ciego, tan inepto" (p. 269; emphasis mine). For Julián, spiritual communion with Nucha would be comparable to deflowering a virgin;

Pardo Bazán's veiled implication seems to be that for the chaplain such spiritual communion would be a substitute for sexual relations.

Julián emerges as a very complex character. Yet this complexity is not inherent in him so much as it is the product of the violent clash between Nature and religion in the heart and mind of a true innocent. Ill-informed religion, in the form of a *beatona* and an inadequate seminary education, have succeeded in wreaking confusion and torment in the life of an individual.

Pardo Bazán also sets up the antithesis between Nature and religion by contrasting a natural ambience with a religious ambience, and by showing the different effects each one has on Julián. When he first arrives at *los pazos,* what Bazán describes as "la ruda y majestuosa soledad de la Naturaleza" fills Julián with "indefinible malestar" (p. 168). However, Julián's initial trepidation in the face of Nature's rugged grandeur is explained by the fact that, having been brought up "en un pueblo tranquilo y soñoliento" (p. 168), he has not yet learned to respond to Nature. But by the time he has experienced the hostility and depravity of the inhabitants of *los pazos,* Julián comes to realize that in Nature he has a wholesome and reassuring friend. After learning that Pedro has fathered a bastard child, the young chaplain is filled with dark and deleterious thoughts. In the midst of his gloom, it is Nature that takes him to her bosom and comforts his troubled spirit: "Era la noche templada y benigna, y Julián apreciaba por primera vez la dulce paz del campo, aquel sosiego que derrama en nuestro combatido espíritu la madre Naturaleza" (p. 191). Significantly, Nature is benign, by contrast with the malignant characters that inhabit *los pazos.* The dense miasma of evil enveloping *los pazos* emanates not from Nature, but from wicked characters like Primitivo, Sabel and the witch-like María *la sabia.* The latter's horrendous goitre, "rostro de visión infernal" (p. 239), symbolises the evil associated with the inhabitants of *los pazos.* Clearly, Pardo Bazán's point is that an evil man is an unnatural growth upon the face of the earth. Mother Nature herself is kind and good, and is even moved to protest at the evil in man. In one of the many scenes with supernatural overtones in the book, thunder and lightning greet Nucha's plaint "¿Por qué serán tan malos cristianos los hombres?" (p. 244). The thunder and lightning constitute the voice of Nature expressing her displeasure at the unnatural evil that lurks in man's heart.

The sweet natural ambience that soothes Julián's uneasy spirit stands in marked contrast with the morbid religious ambience in which he seeks comfort from the "fog" of evil enveloping *los pazos.* The fervid chaplain delights in reading aloud blood-curdling accounts of the torments of Catholic martyrs, from which stores of sadism and masochism he seems to derive some morbid gratification (p. 234). When he feels in need of spiritual sustenance, Julián meditates upon Thomas à Kempis' *The Imitation of Christ,* which has such paradoxical effects upon him as making him feel as if a red-hot poker were entering his soul and as if he were buried alive at the bottom of the sea (p. 270). Julián also seeks refuge in the Ulloa's chapel, where he busies himself feverishly rubbing and polishing the statues "en toda su edificante fealdad" (p. 257); the ironic epithet, "edifying ugliness", is suggestive of the eery cheerlessness surrounding Julián's religious activities—a far cry indeed from the sweet peace he finds in Nature. The oppressive quality of Julián's brand of religion is particularly illustrated in the dramatic chapel scene when the long-suffering Nucha finally cracks under the strain when the chaplain insists on imposing his religious philosophy upon her (p. 271). Without realising it, by enveloping her in his own shroud of mysticism, Julián has only added to the weight of the cross that Nucha has to bear. Only when it is too late for him to halt the tragedy that has been unfolding before him does it dawn upon the well-meaning but misguided Julián that religion, as he conceives it, is of no value in the face of real human suffering such as Nucha's: "Los consuelos místicos que tenía preparados y atesorados, la teoría de abrazarse a la cruz . . . , todo se le había borrado ante aquel dolor voluntarioso, palpitante y desbordado" (p. 271). It is indeed significant that at the end of the book, when Julián visits Nucha's grave ten years after her death, he himself gives way to an outburst of human sorrow that not even his brand of religion can suppress: overwhelmed, the priest falls on knees, kisses Nucha's grave and sobs disconsolately (p. 283). For only the second time in his life, Julián's essential humanity, his "ternura humana expansiva y dulce" (p. 236), wells up inside him and overcomes the austere barrier that his religion has built around him. The first time was when Nucha's baby, Julián's surrogate child, performed that memorable deed that sent the young chaplain into paroxysms of laughter. So unnatural is the religious ideal embraced by Julián that it demands that he suppress his tears and his laughter—two fundamental manifestations of his humanity.

It may be concluded that in *Los pazos de Ulloa* Pardo Bazán sets out to draw a clear-cut antithesis between religion and Nature by employing two strikingly successful techniques: the psychological analysis of Julián, and the contrast between the cloying, oppressive atmosphere of religion and the benign, wholesome atmosphere of Nature. Undoubtedly, the antithesis running through this novel sheds significant light on the philosophical development of Spain's most distinguished Catholic naturalist.

Notes

1. Mariano López, "Naturalismo y espiritualismo en *Los pazos de Ulloa,*" *REH* [*Revista de Estudios Hispánicos*], 12 (1978), 353-71

2. Ibídem, p. 358, n. 9.

3. Carole A. Bradford, "Alienation and the Dual Personality in the Last Three Novels of Emilia Pardo Bazán," *REH,* 12 (1978), 399.

4. All quotations from *Los pazos de Ulloa* in *Obras completas* (Madrid, 1964).

5. In his study of the sexual symbolism in the novel, "Naturalismo y antinaturalismo en *Los pazos de Ulloa,*" *BHS* [*Bulletin of Hispanic Studies*], 48 (1971), 321, Carlos Feal Deibe interprets the spider as a sexual symbol for Nucha. I find it hard to believe, however, that Pardo Bazán regards the innocent, helpless Nucha as an ugly insect.

Lou Charnon-Deutsch (essay date fall 1981)

SOURCE: Charnon-Deutsch, Lou. "Naturalism in the Short Fiction of Emilia Pardo Bazán." *Hispanic Journal* 3, no. 1 (fall 1981): 73-85.

[*In the following essay, Charnon-Deutsch explores Pardo Bazán's use of Naturalist techniques in her short story collection* Cuentos neuvos.]

Naturalism was debated in Spain even before translation of Zola's works appeared, but it was not until Emilia Pardo Bazán published her controversial *La cuestión palpitante* (1882-83) that critics began lining up in earnest on either side of the issue which bore so many sociological and ethical overtones.[1] The series of articles that make up *La cuestión* failed to convince the Spanish readership that the experimentation being carried on by Zola and his followers was of any aesthetic or moral value.[2] What irritated Spanish readers of Zola (and a great deal of non-readers who gathered their secondhand information from periodicals) was the attitude towards determinism which the new school accepted as a cornerstone of its doctrine. Equally distasteful to the Spanish public was the use of vulgar language and accounts of brutality and sexual immorality. The more enlightened prose writers, such as Emilia Pardo Bazán and Leopoldo Alas, succeeded in eliminating what was truly unacceptable for the Spaniard and adopting the style and themes of Zola and his contemporaries while never wholly embracing their ideology.

The subject of my study is a group of Spanish stories which display a marked naturalistic tendency. I hope to show that the naturalist's style was not entirely suited to the story as conceived by nineteenth-century writers. This is so because determinism and notebook realism did not allow for surprise endings, fragmentary and impressionistic techniques and figurative language, or even the *special effect* that storywriters of the last century, beginning with Edgar Allan Poe, sought to achieve at the end of a work.[3] Because of this I will not attempt to formulate a definition of Spanish naturalism as manifested in the short story, although I hope to show how it fits into the evolution of the genre. Rather, I will study in the short story some of the stylistic techniques and ideological premises customarily associated with the novel, where naturalism found its rightful home.

EMILIA PARDO BAZÁN

The countess Pardo Bazán was (until the end of the century when Blasco Ibáñez belatedly took up the cause) the movement's most zealous and outspoken defender and follower, even though both she and Zola understood the gulf that existed between French naturalism and her own particular brand of it, which some critics have since called *Catholic naturalism*.[4] Because she was the self-styled leader of the movement in Spain, critics usually look to her stories for its characteristic manifestation. However, a careful examination of the major collections of stories published between 1885 and 1923 reveals that, despite the fact that many stories do show an unmistakable naturalistic gravity and purpose, she did not have, as some critics maintain, a period which was distinctively naturalistic. She chose instead to adopt an independent position vis-à-vis the French school, for she did not consider the story a proper vehicle to promote social change (although social comment is, in some pieces, very prominent) and she rarely overemphasized subject matter at the expense of technique.

Most critics assume, perhaps because it is so in the case of her longer fiction, that naturalism played a decisive role in Pardo Bazán's short fiction. Porfirio Sánchez claims that between 1879 and 1900 the countess' story publication paralleled that of Galdós and Pereda in its adherence to the «faithful portrayal of everyday reality.»[5] Yet it was during this period that she wrote some of her most romantic stories (see numerous examples in *Cuentos de amor,* 1898). Emilio González López states categorically that the countess is the most prolific writer of naturalistic stories of all times, and he stresses the predominantly naturalistic tone of *Cuentos de Marineda* (1892), *Cuentos nuevos* (1894), *Cuentos de amor* (1896), *En tranvía* (1901) and especially *Un destripador de antaño* (1900), of which he says, «los cuentos son trágicos, con personajes que, movidos por fuertes y primitivos instintos, terminan trágicamente.»[6] It may be that Pardo Bazán wrote more such stories than did her contemporaries, but since she wrote more stories of every kind than most of them, the fact is misleading. Most of the five hundred or more stories she published between 1879 and 1921 are decidedly not naturalistic in any strict sense of the word, and apart from «El destripador,» it cannot even be said that in the above collections naturalism (technically considered) is the style of choice.[7]

In the latter half of the nineteenth century authors of novels and short stories chose to plot the course of the action in contemporary settings with characters selected from the middle or lower classes. This was due partly to the influence of realists and naturalists such as Zola and Flaubert, but to a large extent the shift to a more mimetic fiction was an outgrowth of the *cuadro de costumbres,* whose success as a genre ran concurrent with and then waned as the artistic story's popularity increased in the late decades. Many of Pardo Bazán's stories do end tragically and do deal with contemporary figures and issues, but to call them naturalistic merely because they end in a certain manner is to confuse a plotting device for the literary movement itself and to overlook a basic trait of the nineteenth-century short story.[8] Many artistic stories (whether naturalistic or not) end at the moment a lesson is painfully learned or a test failed, unlike fairytales and folktales which usually end in a manner rewarding to the hero, who profits from his lessons and who is rewarded with wealth, fame or love. In this respect the nineteenth-century story resembles the *exemplum* more than the folktale because it is concerned with the learning of a lesson rather than the reward for its having been learned.

All of Emilia Pardo Bazán's story collections appeared after the *Cuestión palpitante* began to occupy a place in the Spanish literary conscience. It is therefore not possible to judge the effect of the movement by studying collections prior to the 1870s. What I have done instead is to study and compare the individual works of each collection to determine if there was a predominantly naturalistic period in her production. It was found that, while Pardo Bazán wrote her novels in a style which progressed slowly from the strictest naturalism of *Los pazos de Ulloa* and *La madre naturaleza,* to a more spiritualistic period (*La sirena negra*), her stories over the decades show a mixture of romanticism and manners sketch, the starkest naturalism and most fanciful legend, devotional narrations and supernatural accounts. Furthermore, she did not feel it inappropriate to offer her public a mélange of all of these styles and forms in a single collection.

The selections of *Cuentos nuevos* (published in 1894, two years after the publication of *La nueva cuestión palpitante*) provide a perfect example of the eclectic nature of the author's short fiction. «La hierba milagrosa,» as the countess herself explains, is an adaptation of an *exemplum* taken from *Instrucción de la mujer cristiana* by Luis Vives, in which an angelic Albaflor protects her virtue by tricking her would-be seducer into kiling her.[9] **«El tesoro»** begins as a traditional folk-tale: the heroine is happy and gifted in every respect, except that she is cursed «allá en el más escondido ca-marín del pensamiento» with «una curiosidad.»[10] Leav-ing home one day she passes a cave and is confronted by a *brujo* (equivalent to the tale's donor) who gives her a box containing her innocence (the magic agent), as well as a warning (the tale's interdiction):[11] the box is not to be opened under any circumstances. Inés' in-terdiction becomes her test. Unlike the hero of the folk-tale, however, she fails her test, opens the cask only to find it is empty, except for the words which suddenly appear on the cover, «cuando sepas lo que es la inocen-cia, será que la perdiste» ([*Obras completas*] II, 1424). At the end **«El tesoro»** contains a moral that sums up neatly what the argument has already illustrated. It is implied that Inés is now without her «innocence» as a result of her overwhelming curiosity. **«El tesoro»** and **«La hierba milagrosa»** are typical of the moral and re-ligious stories that comprise a large portion of Pardo Bazán's short works. They can in no way be considered naturalistic.

A number of stories in the same collection, perhaps the majority, are peopled wth characters who are not figures of contemporary society, or who suffer spiritual rather than physiological needs. The *niña mártir* (from the story by the same name) is surrounded by every physi-cal comfort imaginable. The narrator states her case by pointing out this fact:

> No se trata de una de estas criaturas cuyas desdichas alborotan de repente la Prensa, de esas que recoge la Policía de las cortes en las altas horas de la noche, ves-tidas de andrajos, escuálidas de hambre, ateridas de frío, acardenaladas y tullidas a golpes, o dislaceradas *[sic]* por el hierro candente que aplicó a sus tiernas carnecitas sañuda madrastra.
>
> (II, 1387)

At issue is a spiritual as opposed to a physical depriva-tion. Society has become too wrapped up in sensation-alism[12] to recognize this type of martyr, as much a vic-tim of her ambience as any other. The *niña* is a prisoner of overbearing love, protective. So complete is the hero-ine's isolation that she regards with envy the «desharra-pados granujas» playing in the street —at least they are healthy and out of doors.

Were the martyr simply to die of her condition, and her death be described in awesome detail, this story might be considered naturalistic, even by a stricter follower of Zola's technique than Emilia Pardo Bazán. But here, as elsewhere in the countess' short works, some of the el-ements which contribute to the effect of the whole would appear hopelessly outdated to a naturalist author. For instance, to emphasize the approaching death of the child-martyr, death itself is personified in a somewhat frivolous manner:

> Entre tanto, la muerte, riéndose con siniestra risa de ca-lavera, se acercaba a la señorial, y cenada mansión. Es de saber que no encontró ni puerta por donde pasar, ni siquiera por donde colarse, y hubo de entrar, aplanán-dose, por debajo de una teja, a la buhardilla.
>
> (II, 1389)

Satisfied the metaphor serves to depict the insidiousness of the stalking foe, the narrator continues on a lighter note, following death through a keyhole, up a flight of stairs and into the doctor's pocket where it remains hid-den behind his *fosforera*.

Thus, the reader is momentarily misled by death's play-fulness, but the story's conclusion is no less tragic for the diversion. Like many a Zola subject, the heroine suffers a slow degeneration (in this case physical, as opposed to moral followed by physical) because she is unable to escape her environment. What is absent from **«La niña mártir»** is the naturalist's attention to detail and technical descriptions, an aseptic view of the situa-tion which would render the stalking death a superflu-ous metaphor. So, while determinism plays a role in the story's outcome, the elaborative techniques do not in any way resemble those used by the naturalists.

Even what could be called Pardo Bazán's most realistic short works are not always devoid of impressionist tech-niques or sentimentality. **«Náufragas»** has barely a note of levity and is written in a direct and matter-of-fact manner, with an argument which fully anticipates the gloomy conclusion. It is also one of the better stories of the **Cuentos nuevos** collection, although not for that reason. But one cannot know from its exposition, an idealized luminous view of Madrid, that **«Náufragas»** will be any different from the romantic **«La paloma negra,»** or the sketch **«Cuatro socialistas»**:

> Era la hora en que las grandes capitales adquieren mis-teriosa belleza. La jornada del trabajo y de la actividad ha concluído; los transeúntes van despacio por las calles, que el riego de la tarde ha refrescado y ya no encharca. Las luces abren sus ojos claros, pero no es aún de noche; el fresa con tonos amatista del crepús-culo envuelve en neblina sonrosada, transparente y ar-dorosa las perspectivas monumentales . . .
>
> (II, 1391)

Prosaic buildings and streets are rendered beautiful when bathed in light. The fragrance of the acacias in-spires languid dreams and the faces of the city women appear evanescent in the dying light of the penumbra. Yet this same Madrid is about to engulf the impover-ished widow and her daughter, who gaze in wonder at its beauty. The concern of the two *náufragas* is the preservation of their dignity in the face of adversity. While the story's ending is not, to a modern audience, terribly pathetic (the heroine's moral downfall is not even depicted), the story itself is so, because the young girl's aspirations are so out of touch with the realities of Madrid life. It is this contrast between ideals and what life has to offer which achieves the special effect of «Náufragas.» In the case of the two country women, the high degree of moral rectitude is not complemented by a well-rounded education or even a native perspicacity: «Muy honradas, sí . . . ; pero con tanta honradez, ¿Qué?, vale más tener gracia, saber desenredarse» (II, 1393). This indirect statement, voicing the sentiments of an erstwhile friend, seems to comprise the hard lesson the *náufragas* face in Madrid.

«Náufragas» is a very short story, with little space to describe the economic organization of the displaced family or detail their degeneration in progressive stages. The author has chosen instead to subordinate descriptions and exposition towards achieving effects of contrast, thereby heightening emotional response in the reader at the story's conclusion. In-this respect it is typical of Emilia Pardo Bazán's stories in that it calls on the reader to imagine only in vague terms the adversity which would surely be documented in a longer narration or a novel, dwelling on the unobtainable good as well as the bleak reality. When the unmarried girl fails to procure a suitable position as a housekeeper, she will, it is implied, sell her favors in a beer hall. But nowhere, not even at the conclusion, is this openly stated. In the end the young girl merely decides to accept work in the beer hall. Resigning herself, she stammers, «En todas partes se puede ser buena» (II, 1394), hiding her fear, and alerting the reader to the fact that the opposite is more likely to be the case. Here, as in so many of her short works, Pardo Bazán avoids the naturalist's tendency to depict the darker side of human relationships.

VICTIMS OF VIOLENCE

While most of Pardo Bazán's stories escape the naturalistic mold for one reason or another, others do not, and although the author shuns the use of pornography and examples of hereditary determinism, she is not above employing low speech and depicting acts of brutal violence and death. Furthermore, her frequent use of environment as a restricting or destructive force demonstrates she lent more credence to Zola's theories than it was her custom to admit when she spoke about determinism. In his careful thematic study of Pardo Bazán's stories Baquero Goyanes reviews several dozen of what are considered the countess' most naturalistic works.[13] Of those which have as a setting the author's native Galicia, he writes, «Son narraciones breves, aguafuertes bárbaros y vigorosos. En casi todos ellos se advierte un clima de angustia muy peculiar en las obras de la autora. [. . .] Existe un personaje latente en estos cuentos que es la barbarie, encarnada en costumbres y tipos.»[14] The description fits the majority of stories mentioned in the section on rural naturalism. The «latent personaje» is better defined as a hostile environment working at counter-purposes to the goals of the protagonist. In most of her naturalistic stories the countess creates an external reality which determines rather than reflects the psychology of the characters. The mode for the action is the relationship between either a victim and an aggressor or aggressors, or a victim and his or her environment which, as Baquero Goynes infers, is bound by social conventions which are shown to cause people physical or psychological harm.

The typical narration depicts (often in scant detail) a series of acts which lead up to and follow an act of extreme violence or submission. Very often the violence is premeditated and results in a character's death, and usually it is perpetrated by one man or a group of men who injure or take the life of another man, although in several cases the victim is a woman (**«Madre gallega,» «La capitana,» «El indulto,» «Ardid de guerra»**). Only rarely does a woman commit an act of violence against another woman (**«El destripador,» «La mayorazga de Bouzas»**) and never is a woman's victim a man. The victim of violence is either a totally innocent person caught between opposing sides of a struggle or one who, because of age, sex, immaturity or some defect, is unable to protect himself or herself from harm. In a few cases the victim is guilty of some incriminating or imprudent deed, but the punishment tends to be unusually severe.

The underlying causes for physical violence and death may be attributed to a large range of emotions and sociological factors, such as murky regional politics (**«El nieto del Cid,» «Ardid de guerra,» «Madre gallega»**), revenge (**«La capitana,» «La corpana»**), superstition (**«El destripador,» «Curado»**) and greed (**«El destino,» «Contratreta»**), to name a few. It is important to note that poverty is rarely the force behind an act of violence or unlawfulness. It is often indirectly involved; for example, the stepparents of **«El destripador»** are poor (though not destitute), but it is greed which is shown to be the force that propels the stepmother to kill her daughter. Poverty may play a role, but characters do not kill or rob because they are hungry. The stories where poverty is the issue have non-violent conclusions: the protagonist may struggle his way out of a difficult situation (**«El mundo»**), recall former poverty (**«El vidrio roto»**), come face to face with poverty (**«El disfraz»**) or succumb to it (**«Las náufragas»**).

Heredity does not play a significant role in determining a character's personality or demeanor. If anything, the author is careful to avoid the issue of physiological determinism, or she indirectly combats it by showing good sons born to bad parents or conversely, bad to good. For example, the foul and greedy parents of **«Los padres de un santo»** are blessed with a son who becomes a priest and afterwards a sainted martyr in Japan, while his parents remain all but indifferent to his plight (II,

1315-17). A hint of a relationship between barbarity of customs and physiognomy occasionally enters a description: when the cruel father of «**Las medias rojas**» notices his daughter wearing a pair of red stockings, his shocked face is described thus: «Una luz de ira cruzó por los ojos pequeños, engarzados en duros párpados, bajo cejas hirsutas, del labrador» (II, 1474). For the most part, however, little comparison is made between personality, deeds and physiological phenomena.

More common is the question of fatality and free will which resolves itself differently from story to story.[15] In *La dama joven* the heroine's decision to select a dull life over an eventful one is entirely determined by social and religious pressures. On the other hand, in *Las desnudas* (from the collection *En tranvía*), the narrator's stated purpose is to demonstrate that «bajo la influencia de un mismo terrible suceso, cada espíritu conserva su espontaneidad y escoge, mediante su iniciativa propia, el camino, bueno o malo, que en esto precisamente estriba la libertad» (I, 1391). The story tells of a misfortune shared by five women, and each one's reaction to her disgrace. As a result of being paraded nude through the streets, one woman dies, another enters the convent, a third becomes a soldier and dies fighting the *liberales,* and a fourth a streetwalker, while the fifth lives «humilde y resignada» with her uncle on whose account she suffered such an outrage. The narrator hopes to show the diversity of reaction to misfortune. However, the story's outcome does not altogether contradict one character's contention that, like a rock obeying laws of physics, we fall inevitably into the *abismo.*[16] It cannot escape the reader, as assuredly it did not the author, that although each woman reacts differently, not one of them obtains in her adult life what she had hoped for. It is implied that the girls are eager to marry: «a pesar de su fe no tenían vocación monástica, y entre los mozos incorporados a la partida del cura, más de una rondaba sus ventanas y pensaba en bodas» (I, 1392). So, while each woman expresses a degree of individuality in her response to tragedy, no one of them rises above her hostile environment. The narrator's conspicuous affirmation, that no one reaction is alike, seems calculated to dispel concern or criticism over Pardo Bazán's naturalistic tendencies. But, a careful examination reveals that, in this case at least, the narrator's rhetoric runs contrary to the fatalistic logic of the text.

LA DAMA JOVEN AND ENVIRONMENTAL DETERMINISM

In the group of short stories reviewed above the characters seem unable to endure or maintain dignity in a harsh environment. But it is only in the longer works such as *La dama joven* that the process of subjugation and determination of will is woven into the narration without violence. Outside of *Viaje de novios,* where environmental circumstances as well as inherited charac-

teristics come into play, *La dama joven* may be Pardo Bazán's most representative example of environmental determinism.[17]

The initial situation resembles the beginning of several of Zola's novels (*Au Bonheur des dames, Le Rêve, L'Assomoir*), which portray the struggle of a woman who has lost the support of her parents or husband. In this case two sisters, Dolores and Concha, orphaned since Dolores was thirteen, struggle to maintain their dignity and dream of an honorable marriage for the younger Concha.[18] The moment of crisis arrives when the latter must choose between a career on the stage and a respectable, if somewhat dull, marriage to a cabinetmaker. Even though Concha herself voices the final consent to the loutish Ramón, her decision is, more than true assent, an acquiescence to the will of her sister, the parish priest and her fiancé, all of whom conspire to convince her to marry. Singly, neither one of the forces at work (the Church in the figure of Dolores' confessor, and social respectability, championed by the combined forces of Dolores and Ramón), would be able to sway Concha who, if left to her own devices, would opt for the theatre. It is implied that the cautious Dolores would have dealt too heavy-handedly with her spirited sister, thereby losing her respect. But behind the well-meaning Dolores, whose attitudes toward morality have themselves been determined by an unhappy experience with men, is the Church—a much stronger, more cunning and experienced force at work to shape Concha's future.

No overt criticism accompanies descriptions of Dolores' confessor-priest, but there are numerous clues to the sinister nature of his function and the probity of his advice in the context of the story. He is always described as an extension of his black confessional, a «jesuita sagaz,» whose pious words cloak the plan that may or may not be leading to Concha's happiness. When from the confessional grate he sees Dolores enter the church, he rushes to dismiss the others who precede her in the confessional line, for he is anxious to play a role in Cocha's future. It is only the tip of the priest's nose that Dolores sees through the grate; he is perceived as a nonperson, whose feelings and thoughts are translated through his nose:

> La punta de la nariz que Dolores veía al través de la reja se contrajo con severidad. Pero dilatóse al punto, como si la llenase el aura de una idea bienhechora. [. . .] La nariz se aguzó, y su fina punta pareció recalcar una suave ironía.
>
> (I, 921, 922)

The priest's plan is to allow Concha an intimate tête-à-tête (her first) with Ramón the very night her impresario is to ask her for a final decision about joining the theatre. It is hoped that the intimacy of the moment will set Concha dreaming of wedding plans. Dolores is skeptical the plan will work, but as always bows to the yoke of her confessor's dictates, expressed once again by his nose:

> Dolores miraba atónita aquella nariz, severa por costumbre, y la desconocía viéndole tan tolerante, tan benignamente entreabierta. Sin embargo, no dudó: no había recibido allí jamás consejo alguno que no probase bien seguir.
>
> (I, 922)

In the last scene of the domestic drama all the forces at work in Concha's life converge to bend her will: Estrella, the *star* of the theatre where Concha works; Gormaz, her would-be agent; Dolores, serene and determined after her session with the priest; and the *novio*, in a position at last to set a wedding date. Added to these is the house Dolores and Concha share, the «habitación arregladita,» beckoning with its «bienestar humilde,» a symbol of duty, familiar protection and comfort.

It is Concha's misfortune that the scene of her decision is to be her home. Had it come in the theatre, there is little doubt she would have chosen to act instead of marry, for earlier, when Ramón threatens to break their engagement if she wears a low-cut dress on stage, she defiantly ignores his wishes. Outside the theatre she is anyting but self-determined. Her complete abnegation of will is reflected in the narrator's total omission of her thoughts and words during the last few scenes of the work. Nothing is directly or indirectly attributable to her until she says quietly, «Qué sé yo, lo que quiera mi hermana» (I, 924). In the end, the defenseless and unpotentialized *Concha* delivers herself into the hands of *Dolores,* to partake of life's sorrows. It is a great victory for moderation and mediocrity. Concha's future with the cabinetmaker seems secure. But the final statement belongs to the actress and agent, and leaves little doubt as to the more sinister consequences of Concha's decision:

> —¡Bah!—murmuró Gormaz—, ¡Y quién sabe si la acierta, hijo! A veces, en la oscuridad, se vive más sosegado . . . Acaso ese novio, que parece un buen muchacho, le dará un felicidad que la gloria no le daría.
>
> —¿Ese?—exclamó Estrella, cortando con las dientes la punta del puro—. Lo que le dará ese bárbaro será un chiquillo por año . . . , y se descuida, un pie de paliza.
>
> (I, 925)

From this it is clear Concha is being manipulated by forces beyond her power to contradict. Her powerlessness is reflected in the very narrative structure of the work. The determinism is carefully masked; Concha's decision is shown to be one which brings with it certain privileges of class and bourgeois security. It is a decision millions of women made every day, and it was probably seen by the majority of Pardo Bazán's readers as the *right* decision. Yet in the context of the story (when all the clues to the pressures of environment come to light after a careful analysis of character function) Concha's decision can only be interpreted as an act of submission and self-denial which will bring more happiness to those around her than to herself.

Information regarding the protagonist's circumstances is never broadly or dogmatically stated, nor documented in close detail. Instead, the pressures brought to bear on her are coded into the narration via a subtle series of clues such as those which divulge the nature of the priest's role. In Emilia Pardo Bazán's novel-length narratives there is proportionately more coding of the type she worked into ***La dama joven,*** as well as more documentation of the type Zola recommended. But among her shorter works literary naturalism seems not to have been the success it was in the novels.

The reasons for this extend beyond the influence of contemporary literary currents and the personal tastes of the author. The economy of the short story required more attention to style than the naturalist was often willing to pay, his primary purpose being to use art as a means of social statement. Only verifiable aspects of life were fit to be part of the *materia novelable.* By its very length the short story, like a poem, calls attention to its form. Pardo Bazán's best stories concern themselves with impressions and fantasies, special effects (in Poe's interpretation of the word) and, above all, the proper expression of these diverse elements in often less-than-straightforward terms. Pardo Bazán's naturalistic pieces are often burdensome because their pessimism does not allow for anticipation, either on the part of the character or the reader. Heroes are not created who wake to a reality which is an illusion or dream contradicted. The world as created in these stories is so bad, so predisposed to evil, that characters seem to work within their circumstances without illusions and therefore without hope. Since the story, as a form, is more end-oriented than the novel,[19] this predictability would be unbearable to most readers of short stories. It is perhaps for this reason that Pardo Bazán chose to offer her readers a mixture of styles when she gathered her stories into collections. To avoid being classified a naturalistic (or any other type) author, she made sure that what was stated or implied in one story was negated or forgotten in the next.

Notes

1. See Gifford Davis' two articles, «The Critical Reception of Naturalism in Spain Before *La cuestión palpitante*» *HR,* 22, 97-108, and «The Spanish Debate over Idealism and Realism before the Impact of Zola's Naturalism» *PMLA,* 84 (1969), 1649-56.

2. Too few recognized above the fury that Zola's aims were humanitarian and that his methods did not have as an end vulgar sensationalism. In his *The Experimental Novel* he defines the novel thus: «And this is what constitutes the experimental novel: to possess a knowledge of the mechanism of the phenomena inherent in man, to show the machinery of his intellectual and sensory manifestations, under the influences of heredity and environment such as physiology shall give them to us, and then finally to exhibit man living in social conditions produced by himself, which he modifies daily, and in the heart of which he himself experiences a continual transformation.» *The Experimental Novel and Other Essays* (New York: Cassell, 1893), p. 21, quoted in *What Was Naturalism?* (New Jersey: Prentice Hall, 1959), p. 56.

3. See Poe's review of Hawthorne's *Twice-Told Tales* in *Discussions of the Short Story.* Hollis Summers, ed. (Boston: D. C. Heath, 1966), pp. 1-4. In the same collection Ray West argues convincingly that the American story was only minimally affected by the event of literary naturalism, which «made less of an impression upon the history of the short story than it did upon the history of the American novel.» «The American Short Story at Mid-Century,» op. cit., p. 33.

4. See Walter T. Pattison, *El naturalismo español* (Madrid: Gredos, 1965), Donald Fowler Brown, *The Catholic Naturalism of Pardo Bazán* (Chapel Hill: University of North Carolina Press, 1957), Donald Fowler Brown, «Pardo Bazán and Zola: Refutation of Some Critics» *Romanic Review,* 27 (1936), 273-78, and Gifford Davis, «Catholicism and Naturalism: Pardo Bazán's Reply to Zola» *MLN,* 90 (1975), 282-87.

5. «How and Why Emilia Pardo Bazán Went from the Novel to the Short Story,» *Rom N,* 11 (1969), 309-14.

6. «Doña Emilia Pardo Bazán y el naturalismo en la narrativa: *Los pazos de Ulloa, La madre naturaleza* y *Un destripador de antaño y otro cuentos,*» *Sin N (Asomante),* 7, 3 (1976), 66.

7. González López omits from his list *Cuentos del terruño* (1907) which contains many such stories, and he places *Cuentos de la tierra* in a group of collections with a more «symbolist» accent. Porfirio Sánchez places the author's realistic period between 1879 and 1900, before either of these collections was published. It is clear that an extensive analysis of the countess' short works is needed.

8. It cannot even be said that naturalism was entirely responsible for the pessimistic view of man that is patent in Pardo Bazán's work. Pessimism is a familiar feature of the Spanish literary tradition.

9. Juan Luis Vives, *Obras morales,* Vol. I of *Obras completas* (Aguilar: Madrid, 1947), 1035-36. The text of the legend reads as follows: «Como Drusila, virgen de la primera noblezade Dinaquio, la cual, viendo que su vencedor cruel amenazaba su castidad, pactó con él que si dejaba su entereza a salvo le daría a conocer una hierba con cuyo zumo, si se untaba con él, sería inviolable todo hierro. Aceptó la condición el soldado. Ella, de una huerta próxima, arrancó una piedra, la primera que le vino a mano, y le invita a probar su virtud en su misma persona, y fregándose con ella la garganta, 'Hiere aquí—le dijo—para hacer experiencia, pues es cosa probada.' El soldado la hirió y mató a la doncella.»

10. *Obras completas,* II (Madrid: Aguilar, 1956), p. 1423. All references to short stories will be to this edition (or to Vol. 1, 1964) and will be parenthetically indicated in the text.

11. The terms donor, magic agent, interdiction and test are functions defined by Vladimir Propp, *Morphologie du conte* (Paris: Seuil, 1970). See chapter 3 «Fonctions des personnages», pp. 35-80.

12. The first-person narrator of Clarín's *Dúo de la tos* has much the same complaint. He is stricken with tuberculosis at a time (post-romantic) when it is no longer a fashionable disease. It is not uncommon for a narrator of the late decades to preface his story with both a denial and a defense of the romantic hero.

13. The majority of these pieces are found in *Cuentos de la tierra* (1923), *Un destripador de antaño* (1900), *En tranvía (Cuentos dramáticos,* 1901), and *El fondo del alma (Cuentos del terruño,* 1907). It is indicative of the gulf that exists between practice and stated theory that all of these collections were published (some of them up to two decades later) after the countess had declared that French naturalism could be considered «un ciclo cerrado» that was giving way to new currents of literary style. Pattison, p. 146.

14. Mariano Baquero Goyannes, *El cuento español en el siglo XIX* (Madrid: Consejo Superior de Investigaciones Científicas, 1949), pp. 367-77. See also the section entitled «Cuentos sociales, naturalistas y postnaturalistas,» pp. 418-20. Naturalism is also treated in the sections «Cuentos de amor» (p. 603), «Cuentos psicológicos y morales» (p. 633), and «Cuentos trágicos y dramáticos» (p. 663).

15. Pardo Bazán did believe in free will and the power of grace to resist temptation. But she explains that her idea of free will is that of a «concepción mixta»: «Si en principio se admite la libertad, hay que suponerla relativa, e incesantemente contras-

tada y limitada por todos los obstáculos que en el mundo encuentra.» *La cuestión palpitante.* Carmen Bravo-Villasante, ed. (Salamanca: Anaya, 1966), p. 36.

16. The countess seems to have given a good deal of thought to Newton's falling rock. In this passage from *La cuestión palpitante* she takes the side of this story's narrator, as opposed to the interlocutor who borrows Newton's law to illustrate adverse determinism: «Tocamos con la mano el vicio capital de la estética naturalista. Someter el pensamiento y la pasión a las mismas leyes que determinan la caída de la piedra; considerar exclusivamente las influencias físico-químicas, prescindiendo hasta de la espontaneidad individual, es lo que se propone el naturalismo . . . lo cual sobre mutilar la realidad, es artificioso y a veces raya en afectación.» *La cuestión palpitante,* op. cit. p. 38.

17. Carmen Bravo Villasante alone recognizes this feature of *La dama joven*: «Emilia quiere dejar patente cómo lo vulgar y mezquino puede ahogar las mejores vocaciones y las cualidades más excelsas.» *Emilia Pardo Bazán,* (Barcelona: Círculo de Lectores, 1971), p. 88.

18. It is this same problem of a *respectable* marriage that torments female protagonists like Angelique *(Le Rêve)* and Denis *(au Bonheur des dames).*

19. For a discussion of this feature of the story see Victor Shklovsky, «La Construction de la nouvelle et du roman» in his *Théorie de la littérature,* trans. Tzvetan Todorov (Paris: Seuil, 1965), pp. 170-96.

Maurice Hemingway (essay date 1983)

SOURCE: Hemingway, Maurice. "*Una cristiana-La prueba.*" In *Emilia Pardo Bazán: The Making of a Novelist,* pp. 64-88. Cambridge: Cambridge University Press, 1983.

[In the following essay, Hemingway probes the psychology, narrative method, and religious content of Pardo Bazán's two-novel set, Una cristiana-La prueba.*]*

> 'Todo el romanticismo es acaso una false concepción de la vida y no otra cosa, y el gran romántico Don Quijote, como sabemos, confirma plenamente esta calificación.'
>
> *El lirismo,* p. 341

Una cristiana and *La prueba* are sequel novels which I shall refer to as one. It centres on the relationship between Salustio, an engineering student, and Carmen, the young wife of his uncle, Felipe. When Salustio visits Galicia for the wedding he falls in love with Carmen, and thereafter he is obsessed with the question of why she is marrying his repulsive uncle. Eventually he discovers that her motive is to escape from the house of her father, whose immoral conduct she cannot condone. Back in Madrid, Salustio goes to live with Felipe and Carmen and takes every opportunity of observing the latter's reactions both to her husband and to himself. At the end of *Una cristiana* Salustio falls ill and Carmen's devoted attention suggests that she loves him. *La prueba* traces the development of Carmen's feelings towards her husband from repugnance to love. He contracts leprosy and she nurses the dying man with tenderness and heroism. The novel ends with Salustio in a state of intellectual and moral confusion.

After the subtlety and detached scrutiny of *Insolación* and *Morriña, Una cristiana—La prueba* is a great disappointment. Pardo Bazán's initial motive for writing about an exemplary Catholic woman was, to judge from her comment to Galdós, apparently trivial: 'Por el camino he pensado una novela, pero no se titula El Hombre; se tiene que titular (a ver si te gusta) *Titi Carmen.* Es la historia de una señora virtuosa e intachable; hay que variar la nota, no se canse el público de tanta cascabelera.'[1] [*Cartas a Benito Pérez Galdós*] With one eye on public response, Pardo Bazán apparently decided that, after the supposedly risqué content of her previous novels, it was time for a change.

Another possible motive was equally inimical to the realisation of a novel with feeling and conviction. At Christmas of 1887 she had visited Rome, where she had had an audience and apparently got on well with Pope Leo XIII, and in July of 1889 she was awarded the decoration of Pro Ecclesia et Pontifice by the Holy Father.[2] One cannot help wondering whether, having been thus honoured, doña Emilia decided to abandon (albeit temporarily) her sense of the complexity of life to preach openly a rather extreme form of the Catholic party-line. For Fr Moreno (the spokesman for Catholicism in *Una cristiana—La prueba*) issues are as cut and dried as they are for Salustio (the spokesman for Positivism). The project of casting doubts on contemporary Positivism leads on from similar projects in *Insolación* and *Morriña,* and there is no reason in principle why it should not be just as telling. But in the earlier novels Pardo Bazán did not attempt to replace one dogma with another, as she does in *Una cristiana—La prueba.* In the following examination of three aspects of this novel (psychology, the first-person narrative and the religious content) it will, I hope, become clear how her temporary lapse into didacticism illustrates her own point that the novelist attempts to preach at his or her peril.

The Psychological Novel

In October of 1889 a Galician newspaper reported that Pardo Bazán 'lleva muy adelantada una novela de costumbres—un estudio psicológico más bien—que se titulará probablemente *Una cristiana*',[3] from which we may deduce that in the novelist's mind *Una cristiana—La prueba* was primarily a psychological novel. The exact meaning of the term 'psychological novel', as discussed in chapter 1 above, is indicated by the narrator, Salustio, when he remarks that although on the surface his story is monotonous and trivial, it is rich in inner details ([*Obras completas*] I, 643b). The novelist is abandoning the conventional reliance on plot and is now attempting to create interest by exploring psychic phenomena. Such an attempt was made possible by a rejection of Zola's schematic psychology, which saw personality as explicable in terms of heredity and environment, in favour of a belief in the essential mysteriousness of human personality.

In the case of *Una cristiana—La prueba* this mysteriousness lies in the concept of the Unconscious, as developed by Schopenhauer and Hartmann.[4] The Unconscious has various meanings, ranging from a simple description of any bodily activity which takes place within an organism without that organ's awareness (for example, digestion) to Schopenhauer's Will as universal force throughout nature,[5] but at both extremes it is an impersonal force which in Eoff's words sets up 'a contrast between the non-rational, embracing the concept of instinct and its relation to the species as a whole, and the rebellious self-consciousness, with which are associated intellect and the sense of personality'.[6] Hartmann identified the Unconscious more particularly with instinct. For him, the realm of instinct was the 'inmost core of every being',[7] whereas the conscious life of the intelligence was a mere accessory.[8]

It is difficult to say whether Pardo Bazán actually read Schopenhauer and Hartmann but, as Whyte and Eoff have shown, their influence in the last third of the nineteenth century was extensive.[9] As we shall see, Pardo Bazán refers to them, directly or indirectly, and the concept of the Unconscious certainly plays an important part in some of her novels from *Una cristiana* to *Memorias de un solterón.*

In *Una cristiana—La prueba* there is an explicit rejection of materialistic psychology when Salustio, in contradiction to those who believe that psychology is as empirical as the natural sciences, points to the fundamental incomprehensibility of human behaviour:

> Pero la repugnancia misteriosa, la sublevación de las profundidades de nuestro ser, ésa no acaba, ni se extirpa, ni se transforma; contra la sinrazón no hay raciocinio, ni lógica contra el instinto, el cual obra en no-

sotros como la Naturaleza, intuitivamente, en virtud de leyes cuya esencia es y será para nosotros, por los siglos de los siglos, indescifrable arcano.

> (I, 612a)

It is easy to see how the rich source of mystery perceived by the novelist in irrational instinct should provide material as promising as that found in any cloak-and-dagger tale or detective thriller.

The story of Salustio's relationship with Carmen is in fact structured upon a series of enigmas, each one, as it is solved, leading to another. His first question concerns Carmen's motive for marrying his disagreeable uncle. Does she love him? (I, 567a) When he discovers that she does not love his uncle, there is left 'la eterna pregunta', why is she marrying him? (I, 580a) To this is added the question: 'Is there an illicit relationship between Carmen and Fr Moreno?' Both of these questions are answered when Salustio overhears the conversation of Carmen and the priest, but then the question is raised of Carmen's feelings in her dreadful situation (I, 593b). After the marriage, Salustio tries to discover whether Carmen loves her husband or not, and whether she is happy (I, 605ab, 610a). Then there is the major question of whether Carmen loves Salustio himself (I, 612b). It is this last question which motivates Salustio's investigations for most of *La prueba,* and until the end the answers are pleasing to him. Carmen hates her husband, is obviously wretched, and loves Salustio. But by the end of the novel, so great is the change in Carmen that the answer to each of these questions has been reversed (she loves her husband, is happy, and feels no passion for Salustio), and Salustio, unlike the classic detective, is left in total confusion.

This is the basic mechanism of the novel and as such it seems perfectly acceptable: the novelist uses a highly motivated narrator to delve into the psychic depths of a woman in a potentially interesting situation and attempts to hold the reader's attention with a series of enigmas. Yet few readers are likely to dispute that the mechanism, as used by Pardo Bazán, fails to interest. Why is this so? The answer surely lies in the character and situation of Carmen herself. In the passage referred to above, in which Salustio refers to the power of irrational instinct, he addresses himself to those dramatists who produce 'espeluznantes creaciones' and asks them 'decidme si hay conflicto más tremendo que aquél cuyas peripecias se desarrollan en el fondo del alma de una mujer unida, sujeta, enlazada día y noche al hombre cuya presencia basta para estremecer de horror todas sus fibras' (I, 611b). Such a project (to study the feelings of a woman married to a man who is repugnant to her) is indeed full of possibilities, but in this work Pardo Bazán fails to realise the potential of Carmen's situation as here described. Salustio is certainly fascinated by her plight but little attempt is made to arouse the reader's interest in it independently of his, or make him search for and ponder the clues along with the detective. As I argue below, when I consider Carmen as a saint-figure, she is never established as a concrete presence in the book and her plight is never presented to us in a concrete way.

There is, moreover, an uneasy duality in the novel which arises from the fact that Salustio, the detective, is more of a psychological mystery than the mystery itself. How is Salustio's psychology presented? Not in the way, for example, Julián's is in *Los pazos de Ulloa,* by an ironic view of his reaction to events: with the exception of the political episode in *La prueba,* little happens to characterise him. The novelist rather imparts to us at the beginning of the novel the basic contradiction in Salustio and this contradiction is then developed through his contact with other characters.

The contradiction lies in the fact that Salustio is, on the one hand, a Rationalist, a radical and a religious sceptic and, on the other a Romantic, a traditionalist and a would-be Catholic. This contradiction is explained, rather unexpectedly, by the idea of the Unconscious: unexpectedly, because it would no doubt have surprised Schopenhauer and Hartmann. The explanation centres on the suggestion that there exists in Spaniards a residue of instinctual attitudes which are autonomous of conscious reason. For example, to begin with the Romantic/Rationalist antinomy, when describing in chapter 1 of *Una cristiana* his fellow boarders in doña Pepa's guesthouse, Salustio compares their lack of common-sense with his own hardheadedness—he is 'más formal y positivo' (I, 542a). This prepares the way for the description in chapter 11 of his enlightened Rationalism. However, despite his sense of superiority over his fellows, he sees that he too shares their Romanticism because it is present in his Spanish blood (I, 542a). Now this is a case of racial heredity familiar in Positivist thinking and by itself makes no allusion to the Unconscious. Nevertheless, Salustio's Romanticism is often associated, particularly by his friend, Luis, with his other anti-Rationalist and reactionary urges, and these are undeniably explained in terms of instinct.

If we take the strong anti-semitism from which his antipathy towards Felipe springs, we find that his rational, Positivistic, progressive formation battles in vain against this 'sinrazón de una antipatía instintiva'.[10] He reflects: 'Extraña cosa [. . .] que lo más íntimo de nuestro ser resista a la voluntad y a los dictados del entendimiento, y que exista en nosotros, a despecho de nosotros, un fondo autónomo, instintivo, donde reina la tradición y triunfa el pasado.' (I, 548a) The words 'un fondo autónomo, instintivo' strongly recall Hartmann's concept of unconscious instinct.

Salustio's attraction to Catholic values is accounted for in the same way: 'Únicamente se explica mi extraña aquiescencia a las palabras del padre Moreno suponiendo que existe en el fondo de nuestro espíritu una tendencia perpetua a la abnegación, a la renunciación, por decirlo así, tendencia que se deriva del subsuelo cristiano sobre el cual reposa nuestro racionalismo superficial.' (I, 593b) Scratch a Spaniard, the novelist is suggesting, and you find a Romantic, a traditionalist and a Catholic. The same idea is later put into the mouth of Salustio's friend, Luis (I, 601b). It is of course a considerable step from stating the commonplace that Spaniards are essentially ('en el fondo') conservative, to postulating the existence of a traditionalist Unconscious peculiar to Spain, but this is precisely what Pardo Bazán is here doing. This idiosyncratic adaptation of the concept of unconscious instinct seems to be based on the following (rather dubious) line of argument. Man's inmost core (to use Hartmann's words) is instinct; now, the Spaniard's inmost core is Romantic, traditionalist and Catholic; therefore these traits are instinctive.

The psychological study of Salustio is based, then, on a contradiction inside him. The technique the novelist uses to present this is to surround Salustio with other characters who bring out in him one or other side of the paradox. So his fellow boarders, don Julián, Botello, Trinidad and Dolfos, bring out the Romantic side in him, and Luis Portal the rational side; Belén the liberated and sensual side, Carmen the moral and spiritual. Luis and Carmen are the most important characters in this respect. The intensity of Salustio's attraction to Carmen's virtue and heroism conveys the intensity of his Romantic yearnings. It also conveys the element of madness or 'quijotismo' contained in his Romanticism. So in reply to Luis's charge that in loving Carmen he is mad and unbalanced he says: '"Déjame a mí. Cada loco con su tema. [. . .] Mi gloria consiste en una quimera, ya lo sé, y quimera extravagante . . ."' (I, 627a) But if Carmen draws him towards the quixotic, Luis is his Sancho Panza, 'moderador de mi fantasía quijotesca' (I, 609b). Between these two characters and the poles they represent Salustio oscillates throughout the novel.

Now, this psychological situation, like Carmen's, is no doubt potentially interesting, but the study of Salustio, if more detailed than that of Carmen, just as surely fails. It fails in the first place because nothing changes in Salustio's mind until the very end, when his experience of Carmen's transformation by grace causes him to lose faith in both Rationalism and Romanticism. For the greater part of the book, however, there is no development. We are told at the beginning of chapter 3 that the traditionalist side of Salustio's personality is deep beneath the surface, but it is not shown to be hidden nor is it gradually revealed, so there is no sense of a mystery unfolding, as is the case in *Memorias de un solterón.* Secondly, the novel lacks a consistent ironic perspective. In *La piedra angular,* Moragas, who is clearly related to Salustio, is treated with a careful combination of irony and seriousness so that the reader knows exactly how far to identify with him and how far to dissociate himself from him. This is not the case in *Una cristiana—La prueba.* In retrospect we can see that Salustio's values are intended to be judged inadequate, but this is by no means obvious as we read the work. This is partly due to the fact that he is the narrator and therefore tends automatically to gain the reader's sympathy, and partly due to the fact that he is so wise. Pardo Bazán seems to have fallen between two stools: by giving up her position as omniscient narrator, she forgoes the privilege of directly discrediting Salustio in the reader's eyes, but she also fails to let him do this unwittingly himself, so that the discrediting of his attitude to life at the end is unconvincing. Again we must return to Carmen; if she had been made a more concrete presence, her behaviour would have challenged Salustio more effectively and rendered his final defeat more acceptable.

It has to be concluded, then, that the psychological analysis in this novel is not successful. We have seen that Pardo Bazán was working from the conviction that the human mind can be absorbing in itself without a primary reliance on plot. But we have also seen that she failed to cope with the technical problems involved in making the psychology of her characters interesting to her reader. The success of the psychological studies in those novels which I shall be examining in the following chapters is therefore the more noteworthy.

THE FIRST-PERSON NARRATIVE METHOD

Parallel to Pardo Bazán's increasing interest in psychological analysis is her exploration of the possibilities of the first-person narrative method. She had used this in her first novel, *Pascual López* (1879), probably because she was writing consciously in the picaresque tradition, and then in the *novela breve, Bucólica* (1884), but did not return to it until the first half of *Insolación,* where it serves to give a very immediate impression of the protagonist's mental confusion. Thereafter, all of those novels, with the exception of *La piedra angular,* which I take to be Pardo Bazán's most important (*Una cristiana—La prueba, Doña Milagros, Memorias de un solterón, La quimera, La sirena negra* and *Dulce dueño*) are narrated wholly or in part in the first person. It is as if the first-person method was, for her, essential to the kind of psychological novel in which the characters reveal the secrets of their inner lives. Two private comments on *Bucólica* show that early on she was interested in experimenting with this method. On 17 May 1884 she wrote to Yxart: 'Tiene la singularidad de ser una novela *por cartas,* método que ya de puro antiguo se va volviendo nuevo.' On 19 July 1884 she wrote to Oller: 'Es un ensayo de un estilo fácil y sencillo, el epistolar. No sé si he logrado vencer algo la personal-

idad del escritor para infundirle la vida del héroe: ¡es tan difícil la empresa!'[11] The implication here is that the first-person method is part of the Realist's attempt at self-effacement aimed in this case at giving the character a life independent of the author's. It may be that already in 1884 Pardo Bazán had misgivings about the third-person method and, when she came to concentrate more exclusively on psychology, she largely abandoned it. I shall be examining her various experiments with the first-person narration during the 1890s in the following chapters.[12]

Bertil Romberg in a study of the first-person narration uses the term 'epic situation' to refer to the narrator's situation when he is telling his story and he identifies three main types: (i) the fictitious memoir; (ii) the diary novel; (iii) the epistolary novel.[13] *Una cristiana—La prueba* is a fictional memoir, although the story covers only the narrator's student years. In the 'Final' Salustio tells Luis that he has written 'una especie de novela o de autobiografía' and then confides to the reader that in the writing of this work he had found a pleasant antidote to his arid studies (I, 703b). The actual moment of composition is some little time after the death of his uncle, Felipe. Salustio has quite recently obtained his diploma, presumably in the summer of the year in which Felipe died, and is now performing his first professional duties. The narrator tells his story, then, soon after the events have occurred, when he is still in a state of confusion following his temporary conversion; his last words are (referring to his feelings about Carmen) 'Ignoro lo que siento . . . Necesito analizar mi espíritu' (I, 706b). This has an important effect on the narration. The traditional type of fictional memoir, exemplified by *Lazarillo de Tormes, Guzmán de Alfarache* and *El buscón,* is told some time after the events are supposed to have occurred, when the narrator is wiser or at least has the benefit of hindsight. Pardo Bazán's first novel, *Pascual López,* is of this type. In this work there is a marked gap between the mature narrator and the protagonist, his younger self. In *Una cristiana—La prueba* and more particularly in the first-person novels which follow it, Pardo Bazán abandoned this traditional form in order to make of the novel the process of the narrator's own self-discovery. On the whole, the narrator of this novel shows no sign of greater wisdom or hindsight than the protagonist. To take the second chapter as an example: he describes his Rationalist's belief in the natural potential of human life without conveying any sense of the disillusionment with this creed experienced at the end of the novel. In fact the story is told throughout with the kind of youthful, Romantic intensity characteristic of Salustio before his traumatic experience. The intention seems to have been to trace his spiritual development towards temporary conversion through the novel, an intention which, as we have seen, was never properly realised.

Pardo Bazán handles the various conventions of the first-person narration (e.g. the perfect memory and the relationship between the narrator and reader) fairly competently, but in the central problem of handing the narration over to the narrator, she fails. The problem involves not just Salustio's literary competence, but also his interests and range of knowledge, both of which are important characterising factors. Needless to say, Salustio could not tell his tale with the same tone of voice as that wise, mature and immensely cultured lady who dominates, say, *Los pazos de Ulloa.* One fundamental difference (fundamental, that is, in nineteenth-century Spain) is his sex. Salustio is a man; yet he notices and comments on things which one would expect to interest only a woman. For example, he describes the clothes and jewellery Carmen is given as wedding presents (I, 572ab) and Belén's clothes (I, 695b) with surprising knowledge. He also seems to know about flower arrangement (I, 637b) and perfume (I, 565b-6a), and remarks on male beauty ('la estética varonil'—I, 624a) in a way more characteristic of a woman, particularly a woman with the aesthetic interests of Pardo Bazán.

Another difference is that Salustio is an unbeliever who has never had any interest in religion (I, 547a); indeed Moreno is the first friar he has ever seen (I, 561b). Yet unaccountably he makes reference to the Bible (I, 649b, 667b, 697b) and Christ's passion (I, 637b), uses the technical liturgical term 'estola' (I, 613a) and compares the character of the mother of Luis's friend, *Mo,* to that of an abbess (I, 648b). He is, moreover, a fairly average engineering student who manages to fail his exams, yet he has an extensive knowledge of such things as religious painting and sculpture (I, 645b, 650b, 652b), medieval triptychs (I, 632b), porcelain figures and Eastern ceramics (I, 632b), poetry (I, 668b), Shakespeare (I, 622a), modern psychology (I, 646a) and medicine (I, 642b). In addition, although he is young and lacking in experience (I, 689a), he possesses an enormous store of wisdom about life and human nature. For example, of Luis he confidently states: 'Era visible que mi amigo estaba en ese período en que las naturalezas, más egoístas que altruístas, ceden al sortilegio de creer en el amor y experimentan una plenitud vanidosa que se parece muchísimo al verdadero entusiasmo.' (I, 623a) And of himself: 'La idea de su forzada convivencia con el leproso me infundió esa pureza o frigidez que se desarrolla a la cabecera de un enfermo grave, al pie de un lecho de muerte, en los supremos instantes penosos de nuestra pobre humanidad.' (I, 684a) How many deathbeds, one wonders, can Salustio have been present at?[14]

Salustio is certainly a very confusing personality. There is even some doubt about his age. Although he tells us that he is twenty-two (I, 566b), and his behaviour and position as a student confirm this, we learn that he reaches puberty only between the end of *Una cristiana* and the beginning of *La prueba* (I, 624a). Even allowing for the later maturity of nineteenth-century youth, this is highly improbable.

It seems clear that the novelist has not come to terms in this work with the change from the third-person omniscient narration to the first-person method. She is unable to hand her story over to her narrator and let him tell it in a way consistent with his character as established independently in the novel, and persistently allows her own erudite self to intrude. Her muddled narrator may well be the result of a muddled view of the psychological novel, for she was perhaps trying to endow her novel with the kind of intelligence she found so impressive in Bourget. She goes about it, however, in a superficial way (by superimposing intelligent comments on the narrative) and in a way disastrous to the first-person technique. Bourget, it should be remembered, like Henry James, nearly always used a third-person narrator in his psychological novels. It was a serious error on the part of the Spanish novelist, and one which contributes largely to the failure of the novel as a whole: I noted above how Salustio's wisdom makes it difficult for the reader to accept that within the norms of the novel he is wrong. It was an error, however, that she was not to repeat.

THE RELIGIOUS CONTENT

I argued in chapter 1 that Pardo Bazán was not greatly impressed by the specifically religious aspect of Spiritual Naturalism. For this reason and because there is nothing particularly religious about the four novels (*Los pazos de Ulloa, La madre naturaleza, Insolación* and *Morriña*) she wrote immediately after reading Tolstoy and Dostoyevsky, it is misleading to speak of a new religious phase in her work.[15] It remains true, however, that in the 1890s she did respond to the trend towards religious subject-matter in the work of certain French novelists. There are religious overtones to both *La piedra angular* and *Doña Milagros,* and *Una cristiana—La prueba* certainly centres on a specifically Christian view of life.

Now, the interest of the French novelists in the 1890s in religious subjects went hand in hand with a return to Catholicism. This was clearly not the case with the life-long Catholic Pardo Bazán. Indeed, even in her most Naturalistic works, *Los pazos de Ulloa* and *La madre naturaleza,* she maintains a perfectly orthodox view of human nature (though not one necessarily shared by all Catholics). In these Ulloa novels certain characters seem to lack the free will to rise above the animals in their behaviour, but this is because the Church in that area is effectively dead and grace is therefore absent. Pardo Bazán excluded the operation of grace from these novels not because she did not believe in it (on the contrary, its reality is affirmed either explicitly or implicitly), but because she wanted to exploit the tragic possibilities of man in a graceless situation, in a state of unredeemed nature.[16] My point is that she is not testing the (undoubtedly heterodox) hypothesis that nature is *necessarily* a stronger force than grace, but simply that nature will assert itself when grace is absent.

Although there is no external evidence that Pardo Bazán intended *Una cristiana—La prueba* to be complementary to *Los pazos de Ulloa* and *La madre naturaleza,* from the point of view of the picture given of man's relationship to nature, it undoubtedly is. It is difficult not to notice that the divergence of views about man and nature between Salustio and Moreno in *Una cristiana—La prueba* exactly reproduces a similar divergence between Gabriel Pardo and Julián in *La madre naturaleza.* The similarity in the situation in both *Una cristiana—La prueba* and *La madre naturaleza* is equally noticeable, with Salustio corresponding to Perucho, Carmen to Manuela, and Felipe to Gabriel. The difference in the final resolution of the two triangular situations gives a clue to the difference between the two novels as a whole. In *La madre naturaleza,* Perucho and Manuela follow their natural inclinations, Gabriel is excluded, and the result is a moral disaster. In *Una cristiana—La prueba,* Carmen overcomes her natural feelings for Salustio, comes to love her husband, and the result is a moral triumph. The former tests the hypothesis that human beings away from the influence of civilisation and religion behave like the animals, by using the case of two young people who, unaware of their kinship and brought up together close to nature, eventually form an incestuous relationship. The latter tests a similar (only more radical) hypothesis, that, whatever the circumstances, natural feelings will inevitably triumph over the restraints of religion and society. The subject of this experiment is a young woman married to a man she finds repugnant and living in close proximity to a young man she apparently likes. But in this case the experiment fails: Carmen does not surrender to her feelings.

Pattison notes the contrast *Una cristiana—La prueba* presents to earlier novels: 'These novels negate the theme of *Mother Nature* and *Sunstroke* where Nature was the victor over society.'[17] However, in stressing the opposition between nature and society, he ignores the important theological content of *Una cristiana—La prueba.* The social law is certainly an element, but the triumph over nature belongs primarily to the supernatural power of grace.

Gabriel Pardo is the spokesman for nature in *La madre naturaleza*; in *Una cristiana—La prueba* this role is assumed by Salustio. Like Gabriel, he is a rationalist. 'Creo que nací racionalista', he states early in the novel and explains how, although not exactly an atheist, he is a natural sceptic (I, 547a). In addition, he shares with Gabriel a belief in the goodness of human nature, a be-

lief which accounts for Salustio's idealistic optimism, which often recalls Gabriel's. He aspires towards freedom which, he feels, will bring personal fulfilment or, in his words, 'vida, vida completa y digna del ser racional, que no ha de reducirse a vegetar ni a golosear los placeres, sino que debe recorrer toda la escala del pensamiento, del sentimiento y de la acción' (I, 544b). These categories of thought, feeling and action recall Auguste Comte's three categories ('Aimer, Penser, Agir') in his 'Tableau systématique de l'âme'.[18] This, together with the fact that Salustio refers to his own 'positivismo científico' (I, 548b) and that Moreno addresses him as 'señor positivista' (I, 687a), places Salustio firmly in the nineteenth-century Positivist tradition. He has a hopeful view of what human beings can do for themselves, by themselves, without, as he says, being a visionary or a dreamer (I, 544b). Moreover, he confidently asserts that human happiness consists in the realisation of the 'true purpose of life' (I, 640b), by which he seems to mean sexual and emotional fulfilment.

This thoroughly modern conviction is the basis of his opposition to Moreno's uncompromising Catholicism, and of his disapproval (albeit, as we shall see, a highly ambiguous one) of Carmen's self-sacrifice. It is this which leads him to tell Moreno at the wedding reception that the marriage between his uncle and Carmen is 'un puro disparate', which will bring dire consequences (I, 596a). Their union cannot possibly be happy because it is not based on love and mutual sympathy; it goes against nature. His conviction becomes a matter of pride and he looks forward, at the end of *Una cristiana,* to nature asserting itself.

The crux of the matter is the question of human happiness. For Salustio, as we have seen, happiness consists in fulfilling one's natural human impulses; in this belief he is assenting to a nineteenth-century Rationalist orthodoxy. In the novel this orthodoxy is challenged by Moreno's arguments and Carmen's sacrifice. A similar challenge has been presented by Julián in *La madre naturaleza,* but in that novel the alternative to a life lived according to the dictates of nature is singularly negative. The only reply Julián can offer to Gabriel's defence of nature and of Manuela's innocence is a bald theological formula about the fall of man, vitiated nature ('la naturaleza enferma'), and grace and redemption (I, 409ab). By contrast, *Una cristiana—La prueba* presents a far more developed version of the religious view on the discursive level, as well as a concrete illustration in Carmen of the redeemed life.

The religious view is conveyed through Moreno in his discussions with Salustio. The introduction of an ideologue separate from Carmen was necessary because she is unable to defend herself from the arguments of Salustio, to whom she is unwilling to admit even the existence of a problem (see I, 614a and 640a). Moreno and Salustio talk alone four times in the novel, twice in *Una cristiana* (chapters 7 and 17) and twice in *La prueba* (chapters 9 and 16). In the first meeting, on the way to El Tejo, the first doubt is cast on Salustio's world-view when he finds that the friar, although living a life of self-abnegation, does not give the impression of being unhappy or unfulfilled. This doubt is intensified in the second conversation during the wedding breakfast. Salustio's disgust at the excesses of the meal and subsequent monkish thoughts of abnegation allow Moreno to question the generally accepted idea of happiness and to offer an alternative. As we know, happiness for Salustio is fulfilment in natural terms: Moreno tells him that precisely by wishing to abandon such fulfilment he is standing at 'the threshold of wisdom and happiness', and that those who possess what the world calls happiness are to be pitied (I, 595b).

The discussion of happiness is taken a step further when Salustio reverts to type and condemns the wedding as 'un horrible desastre' (I, 597a). Moreno concedes that, humanly speaking, the match is a mistake, but then goes on to postulate the existence of the supernatural power of grace (I, 597b). At this point he has said no more than Julián to Gabriel in *La madre naturaleza,* but now he states that grace brings the positive gift of peace of mind: 'La paz del alma es un bien real entre los muchos bienes falsos que ofrece el mundo.' (I, 597b) So to live in the power of grace is not just to repress one's natural feelings; it is also to find 'that peace which the world cannot give'. Unlike Gabriel listening to Julián, Salustio is, for the moment at least, convinced by these arguments, and whether this is due to their intrinsic merit, to the effects of the wine or to Salustio's frustrated passion, the reader is left with a positive impression of Moreno's views.

After the wedding, Moreno disappears from the novel until chapter 9 of *La prueba,* by which stage Carmen's ordeal is well advanced and her unhappiness, as predicted by Salustio, is evident. The third confrontation of Salustio and Moreno, in which the former's idea of happiness is again questioned, is thus strategically placed. In fact it immediately follows the account of what Salustio calls the 'memorable day' on which his conversation with Carmen had convinced him of her aversion to her husband and her love for him (chapter 8). During this third interview Salustio claims that what he had foretold has indeed come about and that Carmen is now 'unhappy and sick with repulsion' (I, 657a). Moreno challenges this on grounds consistent with his previous definition of happiness as peace of mind: Carmen is happy because her conscience and honour are intact (I, 658a).

The final dialogue of any significance between Moreno and Salustio is in chapter 17, when Carmen is tending the stricken Felipe. Here the importance of the title of the novel's second half—*La prueba*—is finally explained. In Salustio's eyes, the fact that Carmen is now having to care for a repulsive leper vindicates his point of view. Moreno replies by again challenging his idea of human happiness: '"Usted cree que la vida ha de componerse de una serie de dichas y venturas, y en eso se equivoca mucho, porque la vida es una prueba, y a veces una sucesión de pruebas que acaban con la muerte."' He adds that, humanly speaking, he would have preferred to see Carmen happy in this life but, as her confessor, he prefers to see her suffer because 'such suffering enhances her spiritual beauty' (I, 686b). This last phrase points to the positive side of the religious view which I have been trying to emphasise. In opposition to Salustio's faith in human life, Moreno is sceptical of terrestrial joys and believes that suffering is the norm. This belief, however, far from leading the Christian to despair, is a means of transformation. *Desengaño,* he suggests, leads to charity and this, together with grace, transforms us and eradicates our natural repugnance for suffering and death (I, 688b). What Moreno is describing is the doctrine of Redemption or the New Creation which proclaims that man is raised, through grace, from his natural fallen state to a new life, characterised by different perspectives and different ways of relating to others.[19]

With these four conversations, then, Pardo Bazán provides the novel with an ideological framework similar to those found in earlier novels, but with a quite different emphasis.

The friar's arguments, however, are by themselves inconclusive because, unlike the ideological content of earlier novels, they are balanced throughout by an opposite view which may possibly be proved correct. Moreno's arguments need to be corroborated by the evidence of Carmen's final triumph. This triumph is conveyed to Salustio in chapter 19 of *La prueba,* where the change in Carmen illustrates what Moreno has said about the power of grace. The illustration lies both in what she says and in the way she says it. Whereas in all her previous encounters with Salustio she has been defensive and obviously struggling with her own feelings, now she is completely at her ease. Salustio, on the other hand, is baffled and wounded by the description she gives of her transformation and the way she accounts for it. The transformation has taken place in her feelings; she now loves her husband, tends him gladly and no longer regrets marrying him. She explains this phenomenon with a simple inference from experience: '"Cuando Dios nos manda la copa de ajenjo, si la bebemos de buena gana, sabe a almíbar . . . ., y si la tomamos con repugnancia, entonces se nota todo el amargor o más aún del amargor que tiene . . ."' (I, 700a) Without using theological terms, Carmen here makes more specific Moreno's theological formulas about the workings of grace, and focuses more clearly on the part played by the human will ('de buena gana' and 'con repugnancia'). She describes her own suffering (the 'copa de ajenjo' of the passage quoted above) and the change in her attitude towards it. Previously she had accepted it with repugnance, out of a sense of obligation. This is the situation dealt with in *Una cristiana* and much of *La prueba,* particularly in the central episode of the yew tree. There Moreno solemnly reminds Carmen that, as a wife, she will be bound to be faithful to her husband, not only in her actions but also in her feelings (I, 587a). Carmen responds with a rather desperate assertion of confidence in her own powers. Whilst paying lip-service to grace, she states emphatically that she herself is strong enough to change her feelings by her own human efforts; but the vehemence of her assertion betrays her self-deception. This deception is clear to the reader until chapter 17 of *La prueba* because, until then, Carmen shows no sign of love for Felipe and many signs of her attachment to Salustio. At the end, as we have seen, she is undeceived. The progression described by Moreno takes place; acceptance of suffering brings love, which in its turn prepares the ground for grace. Through grace, her heart is changed and she comes to love suffering and sickness.[20]

There has indeed taken place in her a New Creation, for, whereas during most of the novel she is acting against her nature by having recourse to duty and obligation, by the end her very nature has changed and to love her husband is no longer to violate her feelings. The sense of freedom she feels contrasts strongly with the way Julián copes with his love for Nucha. In *Los pazos de Ulloa* he deceives himself about the nature of his feelings by thinking of her in terms of the Virgin Mary, and in *La madre naturaleza,* although he has acquired the 'paz de alma' of which Moreno speaks, his melancholy, his daily visits to Nucha's grave and his tight-lipped reticence indicate continual repression rather than the presence of any transforming power in his life. Certainly he does not share Carmen's joy and release, characteristic of the New Creation.

I have examined the opposition between grace and nature in order to establish the exact contrast between *Una cristiana—La prueba* and *Los pazos de Ulloa* and *La madre naturaleza.* The contrast lies in the fact that the Naturalistic experiment in *Una cristiana—La prueba* eventually fails and Carmen does not behave as all the laws of nature decree she must. Her nature is transformed by the supernatural power of grace. But these later novels do not negate, as Pattison says, the earlier ones; on the contrary, the realms of nature and grace, which they dramatise, are complementary. The contrast lies in Pardo Bazán's intention: *Los pazos de Ulloa* and *La madre naturaleza* are tragedies, whereas Carmen's heroic triumph over nature makes *Una cristiana—La prueba* (at least in the novelist's intention) an epic work.

However, the epic heroine herself is singularly elusive. The reason for this, I suggest, is that Pardo Bazán was more concerned with a hagiographical type than a character whom she knows or understands. As Nelly Clémessy's remark that Carmen is 'une sorte de réincarnation de ces saintes de jadis' indicates (p. 584), the hagiographical pattern is central to Pardo Bazán's conception of her character.

Salustio refers to Carmen as a saint on various occasions. On the day of the wedding he writes to Luis that she is 'un ángel', 'un serafín', and 'una santa', and that 'es indudable que en una mujer así hay algo que impone veneración, algo de celestial' (I, 588a). In *La prueba* he describes her as 'santa' (I, 641b, 652a), 'mártir' (I, 637b, 651b, 652a) and 'rosa mística' (I, 670b). That he is thinking specifically of the traditional legends of the saints is clear from his reference to the 'leyenda cristiana' (I, 637b) and the *Año cristiano* (I, 652a) which, together with *Don Quixote,* was standard reading for Spanish middle-class families in the nineteenth century.[21] However, Salustio's comparison of Carmen to a medieval saint is most explicit in the 'Final', where Carmen responds to the dying Felipe's call with an impetuous and heroic sign of love:

> Ella se precipitó al lecho con el rostro transfigurado, con la expresión angelical de la Santa Isabel de Murillo; se desplomó sobre el leproso, murmurando: 'Felipe, alma, corazón mío, si no me voy!' Y sobre aquellos labios, roídos por el asqueroso mal, con una vehemencia que en otra ocasión me hubiese estremecido de rabia hasta los mismos tuétanos, apoyó su boca firme y largamente, y sonó el beso santo . . .
>
> (I, 706a)

The kissing of a leper, together with the reference to St Elizabeth, leaves the reader in no doubt as to Salustio's view of Carmen as a saint figure.

This is his biased opinion of the woman he loves, but it is corroborated by her own behaviour. Carmen, in fact, dismisses the description of herself as a saint figure with the argument that, among other things, the saints used to tend people with repulsive diseases (I, 652b). Moreno uses the same argument but with particular reference to lepers (I, 688b-9a). But these disclaimers are present simply to make clear to the reader that Carmen, by tending a leper (as she does at the end of the novel), is indeed a saint.

This leads us to ask why Pardo Bazán should have been so interested in using a hagiographical model in this novel. The question is particularly important because the novelist consistently drew on hagiography in her writing. Apart from *Una cristiana—La prueba* and *San Francisco de Asís,* it is found in *La piedra angular* (1891), *El tesoro de Gastón* (1897), various short stories, particularly *Cuentos sacro-profanos* (1899),

Cuadros religiosos (1925, but first published 1900-I), *La quimera* (1905), *La sirena negra* (1908) and *Dulce dueño* (1911).[22] In *Una cristiana—La prueba* it can be accounted for in various ways.

First, the saint figure offered Pardo Bazán interesting psychological material. This emerges from one of the *Cuadros religiosos, Santa Teresa, reina,* where the writer implies that one of her tasks in writing about the saints was to 'desentrañar el drama íntimo de su corazón' (II, 1572b). This language strongly resembles Salustio's manner of talking about Carmen. There is also a similarity in the 'drama íntimo' of this particular *cuadro* and that of *Una cristiana—La prueba.* Apart from the fact that St Teresa's obligation to leave her husband is described as 'la prueba' (II, 1574b), there is the general comment Pardo Bazán makes on this category of saints: 'No se desmiente en los santos la condición humana, y acaso interesan más aquellos en quienes observamos la lucha de las pasiones y de la gracia.' (II, 1574a) This conflict between 'pasiones' and 'gracia' is evident in *Una cristiana—La prueba,* where Carmen is intended to be seen not only as a sublime figure but also as a human being (I, 639a).

Secondly, it may be a sign of the influence of the Russian novel. Although this novel as a whole does not have the fervour of a work by, say, Dostoyevsky, in the emphasis laid on suffering as the norm of human life and in the kissing of the leper, Pardo Bazán may have been trying to incorporate into her novel 'la religion de la souffrance' which Vogüé so admired in the Russian novel. This emotional response to suffering is characteristic of popular Russian spirituality. G. P. Fedotov tells us: 'Yet the Russian people hold to the favourite idea of sanctifying suffering. They create saints from pity, showing that pity is one of the strongest roots of their religious life.'[23] Now, some years later, Pardo Bazán compared this aspect of the Russian novel with a painting by Murillo and, by implication, the Spanish Realist tradition: 'Es el naturalismo del pintor español, que hizo vagar las blancas manos de Santa Isabel sobre la tiña y las costras de la cabeza de un mísero, y no infundió repugnancia.'[24] Pardo Bazán seems to be saying that Murillo's picture evokes the same response of pity as the sight of suffering in the Russian novel. The fact that Carmen's face, as she kisses her leprous husband, is compared to the face in the same Murillo suggests that this act too is intended to evoke feelings of pity.

But there appears to be a confusion here in the novelist's mind about the appeal of the lives of the saints. From the outset, and increasingly in her career, it was to their heroism that she was attracted. We find this in, for example, *San Francisco de Asís,* particularly in the chapter 'San Francisco y la mujer', which recounts the stories of various 'heroínas'. In this respect she was following the Western hagiographical tradition of martyr heroes, often young virgins, being torn limb from limb, but bearing their suffering with fortitude. Rivadeneira's *Flos sanctorum,* for example, begins with a hair-raising catalogue of tortures under the title of 'De los tormentos de los martyres'. The intention is to set the 'heroycas virtudes' and 'hazañas tan gloriosas' of the saints at greater relief.[25] The Russian tradition of hagiography, however, places no emphasis on heroism, and martyrs for faith are forgotten. It is the meek sufferer who is canonised.[26]

Now if, as it seems, Pardo Bazán intended through Carmen's ordeal to incorporate into the novel the emotional impact of suffering for religion's sake found in the Russian novel, she clearly fails. Garmen is no meek sufferer. Salustio refers on two occasions to her 'heroísmo' (I, 609a, 698a), and in the final chapters she appears unambiguously as a spiritual heroine. Her sacrifice does not evoke pity because one cannot pity a triumphant hero. My point is that Pardo Bazán's assimilation of this important aspect of the Russian novel is muddled. She seems unaware that 'la religion de la souffrance' and the idea of sanctity which she was perhaps unwittingly taking from it, are completely at odds with her heroic presentation of the saint figure.

However, if the presentation of Carmen's heroism is quite alien to the Russian hagiographical tradition, the challenge which, as a saint figure, she makes to contemporary society is not. This challenge may well be a major reason for Pardo Bazán's interest in hagiography. I am referring to the Russian tradition of the 'holy fool' or the 'fool for Christ's sake', that is a madman or simpleton, feigned or genuine, whose forthright speech and often indecent behaviour, although attributed to his madness, were a cause of scandal to his fellow Christians.[27]

The obvious link between this phenomenon and this novel is the baffling character of the seminarist, Serafin, who in various ways resembles the holy fool. He is a simpleton in that his looks and behaviour are a mixture of the foolish and the infantile. Yet, the nonsensical conversation of this clown or 'naughty monkey' (as he is called) is spiced with such intelligent comments that Salustio wonders whether Serafin is a madman or a cunning rogue (I, 570b). Although no one takes him seriously, he sees through Felipe and Cándida, Carmen's father's mistress (I, 571b), and Galician politicians (I, 591b); but his role as simpleton speaking the truth is most clear during the wedding breakfast when he harangues the politicians present in a violent condemnation of their Liberalism. His harangue ends in an epileptic fit (I, 594ab) and to this extent he is literally mad. He does, then, share several of the characteristics of the holy fool.

Now, it is perfectly true that Pardo Bazán would not have needed to go to Russian spirituality to find this amalgam of holiness and madness, because she was already familiar with the tradition of 'divine folly' in Western Catholic spirituality. Even Spain had its holy fool in St John of God.[28] It is an important element in her biography of St Francis where, for example, the saint informs his brothers in the newly formed order that God has told him to be a fool and to preach the foolishness of the cross.[29]

However, although 'divine folly' is already present in *San Francisco de Asís*, the character of Serafin has none of the sentimental appeal of St Francis and his fellow friars. Serafin bears much more resemblance to the two holy fool figures Pardo Bazán refers to in *La revolución y la novela en Rusia*. The first of these is the main character in Dostoyevsky's novel *The Idiot*, Prince Myshkin. Like Serafin, he is simple and childlike while possessing wisdom. More significantly, he, like Serafin, is an epileptic. St Francis is mad only in a metaphorical sense. Moreover, Pardo Bazán refers to Myshkin as Dostoyevsky's most important character after Raskolnikov in *Crime and Punishment*, and describes him as 'tipo imitado del *Quijote*, enderezador de entuertos, loco, o, mejor dicho, simple sublime' (III, 863a). So it is the holy fool in Myshkin, as described by Vogüé, which she singles out for remark.[30] Soon after this section on *The Idiot*, in a reference to the Franciscan 'madman', Brother Juniper, Pardo Bazán follows Dostoyevsky and describes the friar as 'Fray Junípero *el Idiota*' (III, 866b), thereby associating the Russian and Western traditions of 'divine folly'.

The second holy fool figure referred to in *La revolución* is Grisha, who apears in chapter 5 of Tolstoy's *Childhood Memories*. Grisha, Pardo Bazán says, recounting Tolstoy's description, is 'un vagabundo tuerto y marcado de viruelas, medio idiota, o por mejor decir simple—uno de esos vasos de barro grosero donde, según la literatura rusa contemporánea, gusta de encerrarse la luz divina—' (III, 867b). Again we see the link between madness ('idiota', 'simple') and holiness. Now, although Serafin is not a sublime figure like Grisha, he does share his surface unattractiveness and childlikeness.

I have discussed Serafin's relations to the holy fool tradition, whether Russian or Western, because I believe his function in the novel is to point to an important element in Carmen's status as a saint figure. She is, in a sense, a holy fool, insofar as her behaviour is considered offensive and even lunatic. She is not, of course a simpleton or outrageous in her behaviour, but her values entirely contradict those of the world round her.

Luis, the representative of progressive common-sense, can see nothing virtuous in Carmen's decision to marry Felipe (I, 609a), and describes her because of her actions as 'rather mad' (I, 636a). The modern reader will

no doubt share this reaction. Yet this charge of madness is taken up and fitted into the whole challenge presented by Catholic theology to Rationalist orthodoxy. At the end of the novel Salustio concludes that one can be led only so far by common-sense and reason, that great miracles need love, and sublime deeds madness (I, 700b-1a). Carmen's 'madness', however, differs from Salustio's 'quijotismo' in that it is based not on Romantic illusions, but on the reality of faith (see I, 694a).

The centrality of this point is emphasised by the way the novel ends with a reference to Luis's marriage, an event which itself points to the bankruptcy of 'commonsensology'. Luis has lost his faith in reason, and, in marrying *Mo*, turns explicitly to 'locura': "'Si es locura . . . ¡mejor! Alguna locura se ha de hacer en la vida [. . .]. Estoy convencido de que los locos la aciertan más que los cuerdos. Nuestro siglo está enfermo de sensatez.'" (I, 703a) Luis's reference to 'nuestro siglo' indicates that 'divina locura' is being used here as a critique of contemporary society. Just as the holy fool condemned and even despised the society of his time, so the hagiographical material enables Pardo Bazán to make of her novel a head-on collision with the values of the Rationalism of her own time. It seems to be this collision which was intended to generate power in the novel in a way comparable to the highly controversial views on marriage in Tolstoy's *The Kreutzer Sonata*, which according to Pardo Bazán's own account were the source of power in that novel.[31]

However, I suggest that where Tolstoy succeeded, Pardo Bazán failed. This is because, as I argued above, the reader is invited to see Carmen as a confusing mixture of meek sufferer and triumphant heroine. Another defect is the way Salustio is used as narrator. As we have seen, Carmen is an enigma to him, and in their few unwitnessed encounters she is deliberately uncommunicative. Consequently, the reader is given only Salustio's conjecture about her thoughts and feelings, and has little direct experience of the struggle between passion and grace inside her. Hence she remains a shadowy figure.[32]

Now, a reliable and well-informed narrator is not essential to the success of the first-person narrative technique; indeed, in later novels, notably the *Adán y Eva* cycle and *La sirena negra*, Pardo Bazán was to use the 'unreliable narrator' to great effect. That she was aware of the problems involved in this particular technique is clear from the way she surrounds both Carmen and Salustio with characters and groups of characters who serve to counterbalance the limitations of narrative viewpoint by giving the reader a clear point of comparison. This is why the novel contains so much secondary material. In the case of Carmen, a contrast is made between her and Belén, *Mo*, and the Barrientos sisters, all of whom represent a certain type of womanhood. Belén is the sensual sinner, *Mo* the woman of the future, and the Barrientos sisters typical *cursi* middle-class Spanish girls. To emphasise the contrast the novelist brings these characters in at strategic points. For example, Salustio visits Belén after the humiliating scene where Carmen's heroism is contrasted with his inability to eat at the same table as Felipe; he visits *Mo* and her family at the height of Carmen's ordeal, when she has resumed conjugal relations with Felipe; Camila Barrientos's elopement with her sister's *novio* is placed at the end of the last chapter proper and before the 'Final'. In each case the different women are intended to compare unfavourably with Carmen.

The disadvantage of this device is that it is negative; we learn what Carmen is not, but she herself is not presented as a sufficiently concrete alternative. As a matter of fact, the other women are rather more successful as fictional characters than she. Belén in particular is a lively and engaging personality, whose impetuosity is well drawn in chapters 6 and 18 of *La prueba.* Even *Mo* and the Barrientos sisters, whilst not sympathetic, are at least made interesting by the ironic light in which they are placed. So from an artistic, if not moral, point of view, Carmen compares unfavourably with the very characters whose function it is to set her at relief.

Apart from this failure in narrative technique, there is the failure in the presentment of Carmen's sanctity. Salustio tells us that she is a saint, but this is not shown to be the case in her behaviour. A comparison with the character of Dorothea in *Middlemarch* may help to illustrate this omission. In this novel George Eliot, like Pardo Bazán, set out to create in her protagonist a modern-day saint. The quality which the writer identifies in the novel's 'Prelude' as the distinguishing trait of 'later-born Theresas' is ardour, and this quality is frequently attributed to Dorothea herself. In a comparable way Salustio describes Carmen on a number of occasions (I, 579a, 654b, 664b, 706a) as 'vehemente' (notably in the final scene where she kisses the leper). There is a difference, however, in the fact that we are not simply told that Dorothea is ardent; she is consistently shown to be such. We see it, for example, in her vehement argument with her sister Celia and consequent regret at being too hasty (chapter 1); in that desire to give entirely of herself which leads her foolishly to marry Casaubon (chapters 3 to 10); or in her generous defence of Lydgate when all Middlemarch is against him (chapter 76). Moreover, George Eliot's use of the omniscient third-person narration allows her to take us inside Dorothea's ardent thoughts. So when Ladislaw sees the object of his love as a saint (chapter 22), we are ready on independent evidence to accept his opinion.

This is not the case with *Una cristiana—La prueba.* Apart from Carmen's championing of Cándida in chapter 12 of *La prueba,* we are given little reason for ac-

cepting Salustio's description of her as 'vehemente'. On the contrary, her continual concern with propriety and appearance in the question of her feelings towards her husband and Salustio makes her seem timid and conventional. Furthermore, the specifically theological aspect of sanctity, which is not a feature of George Eliot's work but is central to Pardo Bazán's, is not presented directly to the reader. The fundamental change effected by grace in Carmen takes place, as it were, entirely off-stage somewhere between chapters 14 and 17. As Alas has already put it, 'es lástima que la autora no nos haga asistir al *cómo fue* de la victoria del fraile y de la gracia en el espíritu de Carmen Aldoa'.[33]

So although there is an attempt to dramatise the ideological conflict between grace and nature, the novelist's efforts there are largely neutralised because the subject of the experiment intended to test the rival hypotheses is a confused abstraction. How can the reader feel for, share the triumph of, and accept the lesson of a character whom he scarcely knows?

Conclusion

From the point of view of technique, *Una cristiana—La prueba* is a transitional novel, in which Pardo Bazán's use of the first-person narration displays little of the assurance evident in the third-person novels of the late 1880s as well as in *La piedra angular,* the novel she was writing at the same time as *Una cristiana—La prueba.* As far as psychology in the novel is concerned, she rarely goes beyond the telling to the dramatising of the inner lives of her characters. This defect may be traced back to the fact that the glorifying of a simple, if stirring, ideal is more important to the novelist than the complexity of human life. She uses the novel to refute the Positivist dogma, only to replace it with another. As a result this explicitly religious novel paradoxically conveys none of the mystery of life that such a secular novel as *Insolación* does. In the last resort it does not convince.

The content of this novel points back to the novels of the 1880s and forward to Pardo Bazán's last three published novels. It shares the earlier novels' pessimism about human life, but also, like the later works, suggests the possibility of privileged individuals, such as Carmen, rising above the human condition. Salustio is not such an individual, yet he pursues Romantic chimeras all the same, and the provisional nature of the peace of mind offered by Moreno could never satisfy his fervent longings. Nor, one feels, could it satisfy those of Pardo Bazán. In *La revolución y la novela en Rusia* she confides: 'Y por mi parte, he de confesar francamente que me son simpáticas las locuras de carácter especulativo, sueños que sueña la humanidad de cuando en cuando para convencerse de que no le basta el bienestar material, de que aspira dolorosamente a algo que jamás alcanzará en la tierra (así creemos los espiritualistas).' (III, 805a) The ambiguity in her attitude towards Romantic idealism possibly explains her failure to discredit Salustio's 'quijotismo' in the body of the novel; one has the impression that she is secretly sympathising with him, if only because the refusal of Moreno and Carmen to admit to the existence of a problem, however good their intentions, may strike the reader as dishonest. The most telling features of the epigraph to this chapter are the admiration contained in the epithet 'gran' ('el gran romántico Don Quijote') and the reservation in the adverb 'acaso' ('Todo el romanticismo es acaso una falsa concepción de la vida').

Such an ambiguity was already present in Pardo Bazán's early novels. For example, the disillusionment of the tragic figure of Artegui in *Un viaje de novios* is typical of *fin-de-siècle* Neo-Romanticism,[34] yet the detached observation of this novel makes it very self-consciously Realist. Another example is *La madre naturaleza,* where Pardo Bazán studies the conflict between Gabriel Pardo's progressive formation and his latent Romanticism, and shows his life to be blighted by disillusionment at the failure of all his dreams. Although we are invited to dissociate ourselves from these characters' view of life, our admiration for them makes it difficult for us to do so. In these two novels the ambiguity is probably as unintended as it is in *Una cristiana—La prueba,* but, as we have seen, in *Insolación* Pardo Bazán gives us a deliberately ambiguous perspective on the affair between Asís and Pacheco, so that we cannot finally decide whether there is an element of idealism in their love or not. This uncertainty is even more apparent in Pardo Bazán's last three novels (*La quimera, La sirena negra* and *Dulce dueño*), where she deals with the Decadent characters of Silvio, Clara, Gaspar and Catalina. Her hesitation is most clear in the 'Sinfonía', which precedes *La quimera*: the chimera of foolish illusions is destroyed, but so is all that inspires man's noblest deeds. In these late novels, however, the novelist found a way out of the impasse and resolved the tension between reason and Romanticism by the use, more singleminded than in *Una cristiana—La prueba,* of the ideal of sanctity.[35]

Notes

1. *Cartas a Galdós,* p. 57.

2. See *Mi romería* (Madrid, 1888), and *El eco de Galicia,* XII, 13 July 1889, 6.

3. *El eco de Galicia,* XII, 5 October 1889, 6.

4. L. L. Whyte in his work *The Unconscious before Freud* (London, 1960) shows that the idea of the Unconscious has a history going back at least to the eighteenth century.

5. See Albert Réville, 'Un nouveau système de philosophie allemande, M. von Hartmann et la doc-

trine de l'inconscient', *Revue des deux mondes,* V (1874), 511-51 (p. 521), and Whyte, p. 328.

6. Sherman H. Eoff, *The Modern Spanish Novel* (New York, 1961), p. 92.

7. *Philosophy of the Unconscious,* tr. W. C. Coupland (2nd edn, London, 1893), I, 114.

8. See Réville, p. 521.

9. See Whyte, pp. 163-4, and Eoff, p. 91. U. González Serrano speaks of the great popularity of Hartmann's *Philosophy of the Unconscious* in Spain. See his 'La psicología contemporánea', *Revista de España,* LXVIII (1879), 481-97 (p. 488). Some remarks of the early 1890s show that Pardo Bazán had at least some knowledge of the ideas of Schopenhauer and Hartmann. In 1891 she wrote: 'Si por *instinto* quiere Campoamor significar esa inspiración o actividad de algo sobrehumano, distinto del individuo, que llama Schopenhauer representación *independiente del principio racional,* entonces convendré en que el prosista escribe por instinto.' (III, 948a) See also *Nuevo teatro crítico,* no. 24 (December 1892), 79; III, 1336a and 1198ab. The as yet incomplete catalogue of Pardo Bazán's library, now in the Real Academia Gallega, La Coruña, contains Schopenhauer's *Essay on Free Will* and *The Foundations of Morality* (Paris, 1887 and 1879 respectively).

10. Brian J. Dendle, in 'The Racial Theories of Emilia Pardo Bazán', *Hispanic Review,* XXXVIII (1970), 17-31, assumes that Pardo Bazán shared Salustio's anti-semitism, overlooking the fact that Salustio himself regards it as indefensible in a rational man (I, 548a). This is a view Pardo Bazán herself held (see *Nuevo teatro crítico,* no. 6 (June 1891), 89). Dendle's case is based on quotations which in their context and quoted in full are not at all anti-semitic. For example, Pardo Bazán's remarks on lack of hygiene and prevalence of leprosy are a general comment on the condition of nomadic races, not simply on the Jews. She goes on to say that when the Jews became more sedentary, leprosy decreased and they took pleasure in bathing (*De siglo a siglo* (Madrid, 1902), p. 258).

11. David Torres, 'Veinte cartas inéditas de Emilia Pardo Bazán a José Yxart', *Boletín de la Biblioteca de Menéndez Pelayo,* LIII (1977), 383-409 (pp. 395-6); N.O.-I-1144.

12. See Clémessy's remarks on Pardo Bazán's use of the first-person narration, pp. 672-3.

13. *Studies in the Narrative Technique of the First-Person Novel* (Stockholm, 1962).

14. The movement from the general to the particular seen in the examples quoted here and usually introduced, as in these cases, by a demonstrative ad-

jective is characteristic of Pardo Bazán's third-person omniscient narrative style. See Clémessy, pp. 664-7, and Mariano Baquero Goyanes, 'La novela naturalista española: Emilia Pardo Bazán', *Anales de la Universidad de Murcia,* XIII (1954-5), 157-234, 539-639 (ch. 4).

15. See Correa Calderón, pp. 43-4.

16. [See my article 'Grace, Nature, Naturalism, and Pardo Batán', in *Forum for Modern Language Studies,* XVI (1980), 341-9.]

17. *Emilia Pardo Bazán,* p. 69.

18. *La catéchisme positiviste* (Paris, 1852), p. 135.

19. Grace, according to St Augustine, is 'the sum total of God's free gifts, the purpose of which is to make man's salvation possible in the state of fallen nature'. Etienne Gilson, *The Christian Philosophy of Saint Augustine* (London, 1961), p. 152. See this work, part II, ch. 3 for the effects of grace on the human will.

20. Richard Griffiths, in his study of French Catholic writers of this period (p. 157), emphasises the importance of the voluntary acceptance of suffering: 'In the case of all these forms of expiation, an essential element is the free will of the sufferer [. . .] even if it is God who sends the suffering to the chosen one, that person must both understand the cause of this suffering and willingly accept it, for the suffering to be in any way valid.' The operation of grace is a much disputed question and is part of the wider issue of free will and predestination which was at the centre of the controversy between the Jesuits and the Jansenists. Gilson tells us that 'grace can be irresistible without being constraining, because it is either suited to the free choice of those it has decided to save, or, by transforming from within the will to which it is applied, it causes it to delight freely in things it would otherwise find repugnant' (pp. 155-6). In ch. 6 of *Los pazos de Ulloa* the local clergy argue about this very issue.

21. See the article on Pedro de Rivadeneira in the Espasa-Calpe *Enciclopedia universal ilustrada. Año cristiano* is a generic term referring to a devotional work containing the lives of the saints arranged according to their feasts throughout the year. Rivadeneira's *Flos sanctorum* (1599-1601) was the most important of these in Spain and went through many editions. In the eighteenth century it was augmented by the *Année chrétienne* of Jean Croisset, translated by P. José Francisco de Isla. The collated version became so large that another *Año cristiano* was published by Lorenzo Villanueva in 1790 (see the *Obras escogidas* of Rivadeneira (Madrid, 1952), p. vii). Croisset's work went through various editions (it had reached its ninth edition by 1877) in up to as many as eighteen volumes. It is this work that Julián reads in *Los pazos de Ulloa* (see I, 234ab).

22. There are numerous references to the lives of the saints in her critical and journalistic writings. See for example *Mi romería,* pp. 104-5; *Nuevo teatro crítico,* no. 5 (May 1891), 24; *La ilustración artística,* no. 988 (3 December 1900), 778; *Por la Europa católica* (Madrid, 1902), pp. 247-50. Pardo Bazán shows her love of the lives of the saints in this remark to Narciso Oller: 'Celebro que mi San Francisco le haya aficionado a V. un poco a los Santos. La vida de estos es un tesoro de ternura, gracia, sentido histórico y otras mil cosas buenas. Ardo en deseos de hablar algún día de dos Santos españoles: Santa Teresa y San Juan de la Cruz.—Veremos si Dios me da vida para esta y otras muchas tareas que me he propuesto llevar a cabo.' N.O.-I-1141, 18 November 1883.

23. *The Russian Religious Mind* (Cambridge, Massachusetts, 1966), II, 110.

24. *El Naturalismo,* p. 112.

25. Pedro de Rivadeneira, *Flos sanctorum,* I (Madrid, 1717), i-ii and iv-v. For the Western tradition of martyr heroes see H. Delehaye, *Les origines du culte des martyrs,* 2nd edn (Paris, 1933), p. 1.

26. See Fedotov, pp. 99 and 105.

27. See E. Behr-Sigel, *Prière et sainteté dans l'église russe* (Paris, 1950), ch. 6, and Fedotov, ch. 12.

28. For 'divine folly' see St Paul, I Corinthians 1.18-31, 3.18-19 and 4.10. This last is quoted by Pardo Bazán in her discussion of the Franciscan, Brother Juniper (see note 29 below). For St John of God see Behr-Sigel, p. 93.

29. *San Francisco de Asís,* vol. I, 220. In the same work she describes the childlike behaviour of Brother Juniper and says that in him 'llegó a su colmo la sublime insensatez de la Orden nueva, y se cumplió la enseñanza de Jesús, viéndose al hombre vuelto parvulillo para conquistar el reino de los cielos' (p. 176).

30. Pardo Bazán's remarks on *The Idiot* follow Vogüé closely (see *Le roman russe,* pp. 257-60). Vogüé mentions Myshkin's epilepsy as well as the fact that he is intended by Dostoyevsky to acquire 'les proportions morales d'un saint'. As *The Idiot* was not translated into French until 1887, Pardo Bazán is unlikely to have read it before the composition of *La revolución y la novela en Rusia.* For our purposes, then, what Dostoyevsky wrote is less significant than Vogüé's account of his work.

31. See III, 984a-95b.

32. Alas complained that the characterisation of Carmen was too physical: 'El mérito del artista no aumenta por la magnitud de las hazañas que relata, y la Pardo Bazán, excusándose de estudiar y pintar a su cristiana por dentro y de hacernos ver el conflicto espiritual, no deja de huir las dificultades de su aunto, por muy a lo vivo que nos describa las lacerías bíblicas del leproso y la fuerza de estómago de su legítima esposa.' *Clarín, obra olvidada,* ed. Antonio Ramos-Gascón (Madrid, 1973), p. 86. See also Francisco Pérez Gutiérrez, *El problema religioso en la generación de 1868* (Madrid, 1975), p. 365.

33. *Clarín, obra olvidada,* p. 91.

34. See Clémessy, pp. 553-4, and *Un viaje de novios,* ed. Baquero Goyanes, pp. 39-45.

35. See my article 'The Religious Content of Pardo Bazán's *La sirena negra*', *BHS,* XLIX (1972), 369-82.

Bibliography

Alas, Leopoldo (*Clarín*), *Clarín, obra olvidada.* Ed. Antonio Ramos-Gascón. Madrid, 1973.

Baquero Goyanes, Mariano, 'La novela naturalista española: Emilia Pardo Bazán', *Anales de la Universidad de Murcia,* XIII (1954-5), 157-234, 539-639.

Barroso, Fernando J., *El naturalismo en la Pardo Bazán.* Madrid, 1973.

Behr-Sigel, E., *Prière et sainteté dans l'église russe.* Paris, 1950.

Clémessy, Nelly, *Emilia Pardo Bazán, romancière (la critique, la théorie, la pratique).* Paris, 1973.

Comte, Auguste, *Le catéchisme positiviste.* Paris, 1852.

Correa Calderón, E., 'La Pardo Bazán en su época', in *El centenario de Emilia Pardo Bazán.* Madrid, 1952.

Delehaye, H., *Les origines du culte des martyrs.* 2nd edn. Paris, 1933.

Dendle, Brian J., 'The Racial Theories of Emilia Pardo Bazán', *Hispanic Review,* XXXVIII (1970), 17-31.

Enciclopedia universal ilustrada. Espasa-Calpe. Madrid. 1908-75.

Eoff, Sherman H., *The Modern Spanish Novel.* New York, 1961.

Fedotov, G. P., *The Russian Religious Mind.* Cambridge, Massachusetts, 1966.

Gilson, Etienne, *The Christian Philosophy of Saint Augustine.* London, 1961.

González Serrano, U., 'La psicología contemporánea', *Revista de España,* LXVIII (1879), 481-97.

Griffiths, Richard, *The Reactionary Revolution: The Catholic Revival in French Literature (1870-1914).* London, 1966.

Hartmann, E. von, *Philosophy of the Unconscious.* Tr. W. C. Coupland, 2nd edn. London, 1893.

Hemingway, Maurice, 'Grace, Nature, Naturalism, and Pardo Bazán', *Forum for Modern Language Studies,* XVI (1980), 341-9.

———. 'The Religious Content of Pardo Bazán's *La sirena negra*', *BHS,* XLIX (1972), 369-82.

Pardo Bazán, Emilia, *Cartas a Benito Pérez Galdós (1889-90).* Ed. Carmen Bravo-Villasante. Madrid, 1975.

———. 'Dos sacerdotes se matan', *La ilustración artística,* no. 988 (3 December 1900), 778.

———. *Nuevo teatro crítico.* Madrid, 1891-3.

———. *Obras completas.* Aguilar. I and II, ed. Federico Carlos Sainz de Robles, 3rd edn. Madrid, 1957 and 1964. III, ed. Harry L. Kirby Jr, Madrid, 1973.

———. *Un viaje de novios.* Ed. Mariano Baquero Goyanes. Barcelona, 1971.

Pattison, Walter T., *Emilia Pardo Bazán.* New York, 1971.

Pérez Gutiérrez, Francisco, *El problema religioso en la generación de 1868.* Madrid, 1975.

Réville, Albert, 'Un nouveau système de philosophie allemande, M. von Hartmann et la doctrine de l'inconscient', *Revue des deux mondes,* V (1874), 511-51.

Rivadeneira, Pedro de, *Flos sanctorum,* I. Madrid, 1717.

———. *Obras escogidas.* Ed. Vicente de la Fuente. Madrid, 1952.

Romberg, Bertil, *Studies in the Narrative Technique of the First-Person Novel.* Stockholm, 1962.

Torres, David, 'Veinte cartas inéditas de Emilia Pardo Bazán a José Yxart', *Boletín de la Biblioteca de Menéndez Pelayo,* LIII (1977), 383-409.

Vogüé, Vtc E. M. de, *Le roman russe.* Paris, 1886.

Whyte, L. L., *The Unconscious before Freud.* London, 1960.

Note on Abbreviations

References to works by Pardo Bazán have been made as far as possible to the three volumes of the Aguilar *Obras completas* and have been included in the text abbreviated to a roman numeral (volume), and arabic numeral (page) and a letter, a or b (column on page). The text of the first two volumes of the *Obras completas* is not always accurate. The more glaring errors have been corrected in accordance with the first edition and/or Pardo Bazán's own *Obras completas*. The references to unpublished correspondence from Pardo Bazán to Narciso Oller are the catalogue numbers of the Instituto Municipal de Historia in Barcelona, i.e. the initials of the recipient followed by a roman numeral and an arabic numeral. References to the Giner papers in the Real Academia de la Historia have been abbreviated to RAH, Giner. *Bulletin of Hispanic Studies* has been abbreviated to *BHS*.

Daniel S. Whitaker (essay date spring 1988)

SOURCE: Whitaker, Daniel S. "Power of Persuasion in Pardo Bazán's *La Tribuna*." *Hispanic Journal* 9, no. 2 (spring 1988): 71-80.

[*In the following essay, Whitaker exposes Pardo Bazán's political agenda by examining the textual strategies she employs in her novel* The Tribune of the People.]

Emilia Pardo Bazán was consistent in her opposition to the concept of universal suffrage. Her view was that the common people, both men and women, would be manipulated by those of the upper middle class or the aristocracy. Local *caciques* also had the power to shape the opinions of rural voters, as was the case in the electoral ploys of Barbacana and Trampeta in the closing pages of *Los Pazos de Ulloa*. Doña Emilia's conservative political outlook, shaped by her admiration for the Spanish nobility, led her to urge her fellow countrymen to postpone granting the vote to all Spaniards until they were better educated and understood democratic principles. She wrote, "El caso es huir del radicalismo, dar tiempo al tiempo, no precipitarnos, y dejar para dentro de un siglo lo que podría hacerse en el mes entrante" (**"Con una alemana"** 212-213).[1] In *La Tribuna* (1882), Doña Emilia's third novel, the author makes her most complete statement about what she considered the dangerous results of the Revolution of 1868 (*La Gloriosa*)—the arrival of new democratic institutions to Spain and the control of the Spanish government by a voting public ill prepared for such a calling. This essay will examine the textual strategies employed by Emilia Pardo Bazán as she seeks to convince the contemporary reader of *La Tribuna* of the pitfalls of establishing a republican government in Spain.

The Countess commences her arguments against the excesses of the *Gloriosa* in the prologue of *La Tribuna*, prepared for the first edition of the book in 1882. The custom of writing prologues in general was important for the Countess and served two purposes: to discuss briefly her ideas on literary theory and to comment directly on the text.[2] The prologue of *La Tribuna* follows this pattern. In it the Countess reiterates her desire to describe life realistically, from a point of view midway between the idealism of Fernán Caballero and the naturalism of Zola (this statement reflects a position taken in *La cuestión palpitante,* published shortly before *La Tribuna*). Pardo Bazán is most judgmental when she comments on the text of *La Tribuna.* She clearly states her view that the Spanish people were naive to unthinkingly embrace the new republican form of government: ". . . es absurdo el que un púeblo cifre sus esperanzas de redención y ventura en formas del gobierno que desconoce, y a las cuales por lo mismo atribuye prodigiosas virtudes y maravillosos efectos" (103). The Countess then continues, proposing that novelists should expose the defects of these beliefs: "Como la raza latina practica mucho este género de culto fetichista e idolátrico, opino que, si escritores de más talento que yo lo combatiesen, presentarían señalado servicio a la patria" (103). This statement points out that Pardo Bazán also sees it as a patriotic duty of writers to attack the false worship of misunderstood political tenets.

These declarations are the opening salvos of Doña Emilia's argument to convince the reader of the negative side of the Revolution of 1868. Reinforcing Doña Emilia's authority in the prologue of *La Tribuna* is the statement that the novel is her own world, one in which the author will have complete independence to organize the events as she sees fit—and, we may add, to persuade as she sees necessary: "Este privilegio concedido al novelista de crearse un mundo suyo propio, permite más libre inventiva . . . Tal es el procedimiento que empleo en *La Tribuna* . . ." (103).

Considering these rather strong statements of intent in the prologue, one might expect a thesis novel to follow. Yet this type of overtly didactic fiction was attacked by the Countess, who affirmed in the prologue, to *Un viaje de novios* (1881) that ". . . aborrezco las píldoras de moral rebozadas en una capa de oro literario" (573). Paradoxically, in the same prologue, Doña Emilia confesses that art does provide the opportunity at times to teach and that in her opinion "Yo de mí sé decir que en arte me enamora de la enseñanza indirecta que emana de la hermosura . . ." (573). Clearly, the Countess is walking a fine line in these statements. She is differentiating in what Brian Dendle has described as the distinction, in the minds of many novelists of the Restauration, between the *novela de tesis* (in which the author forces a predetermined ideology on the text) and the *novela tendenciosa* (in which the reader supposedly is left to judge facts for herself or himself). Less overtly didactic than the *novela de tesis,* the *novela tendenciosa,* according to its proponents, could still provide a tactful lesson.

An example of support for the concept of the *novela tendenciosa* is found the prologue to *La quimera,* where Doña Emilia writes, "De la contemplación del destino de Silvio he sacado involuntariamente consecuencias religiosas, hasta místicas, que sin mezquinos respetos humanos vierto en el papel." (9). In similar fashion, returning to the prologue of **La Tribuna,** Pardo Bazán claims that the events themselves will provide what the Countess calls a "propósito docente": "Al escribir **La Tribuna** no quise hacer sátira política . . . Pero así como niego la intención satírica, no sé encubrir que en este libro, casi a pesar mío, entra un propósito que puede llamarse *docente*" (103). Thus, the Countess is setting the stage in her prologue of **La Tribuna** for a *novela tendenciosa* whose artifices of persuasion continue in the text which follows.

Pardo Bazán focuses her critical eye on the female workers of the tobacco factory of Marineda, who are swayed more than any other group to adopt the republican cause as their own. Nine of the thirty eight chapters of **La Tribuna** concentrate on the political events of the day. In these chapters the reader witnesses a text that utilizes satire, parody, irony, exaggeration, and sarcasm to lambast the belief that common people—the *pueblo,* the *vulgo*—could control the destiny of the nation.[3] Amparo, the protagonist of the novel, is the cigarette worker most enamored of the proposed federal republic and is described by the third person narrator as "impresionable, combustible, móvil, y superficial" (123). A key word is *superficial,* which also could apply to Amparo's friends.

As the women read the republican newspapers at the factory in Chapter X, it is clear that the workers are more impressed by the rhetoric of the newspapers than by any concrete ideas of reform. Amparo, who can barely read, even mispronounces key words (*espotismo* 126; *descentraizar* 132; *perficionar* 132). Other scenes from the novel document the foolishness of masculine supporters of the Unión del Norte. Chapter XVIII, the banquet of the visiting republican delegates to Marineda, is a stinging satire on the ineptness of the male leadership. The organizers can not even agree on the menu; the meal begins late. The highest official is more like a senile biblical patriarch who is fond of theatrical gestures ("teatral nobleza de su figura completaba la decoración" 143; "ermitaño de tragedia" 143). The entire dinner is nearly disrupted by the arguments among the delegates and harmony is only restored with the arrival of Amparo and the other women.

Moreover, several different characters echo Doña Emilia's negative opinions in the prologue about the new democratic institutions. In Chapter X an older female supervisor at the factory, after listening to the conversations of the younger women workers about the political events of the day, affirms that Amparo does not know what she is talking about ("pero hablar, hablas sin saber lo que hablas" 127). Perhaps the strongest voice supporting Doña Emilia's views in the prologue is Amparo's friend Carmela in Chapter XVI. After listening to Amparo's generalities about the benefits of the proposed republic, the lace maker asks, "¿Qué más tiene eso que el Gobierno que hay ahora?" (139). Carmela remains skeptical since the *Gloriosa* is now one year old and has not fulfilled its initial promises of governmental reform. In addition, Carmela's advice does carry weight because the young woman also advises Amparo to stay away from Baltasar; by the end of the novel, the events of the text prove that she was correct in both her political and sentimental advice. Rounding out the strategy of utilizing characters to back an author's favored ideological stance is the collective voice of the rural cigarette workers at the tobacco factory. These more conservative women, supporters of a monarchical form of government, oppose Amparo and her republican friends.

Other textual strategies build up Doña Emilia's case against the federalists. Titles of chapters ironically mock their own content: Chapter X, entitled "Estudios históricos y políticos," presents a scene in which ignorant cigarette factory workers try to understand the revolutionary press; Chapter XXXVI, "Ensayo sobre la literatura dramática revolucionaria" describes a badly performed republican propaganda play. On the other hand, humorous scenes point out the cigarette workers' lack of political savvy. When two protestant missionaries attempt to pass out religious material to Amparo and her friends in Chapter XXV, the women repulse them with a barrage of pieces of bread, empanadas, pears, and even handfuls of dirt. The amusing episode underscores the lack of basic understanding of the workers for the democratic institutions they purport to support, namely those of freedom of religion and freedom of speech.

Central to the text's critical view of the republican followers is the third-person reflector in the novel. Far from being a neutral observer, this reflector has an obvious axe to grind. As Germán Gullón has demonstrated, the omniscient narrator is as capable of distorting reality as easily as the *esperpento* description of the poor who encircle the picnicking women in the fiesta of "Las comiditas" ("un elefantiaco," "un fenómeno sin piernas" 158). Amparo, for example, is designated an "oradora demagógica" (132). The narrator compares Amparo's fascination with the ideas of the republicans to those of rural people who are fascinated by the telegraph (124). Mocking the "outrage" of the factory women for the supposed abuses of the old régime, the narrator states, "Era contagiosa la ira, y mujer había allí de corazón más suave que la seda   y capaz a la sazón de pedir cien mil cabezas de los pícaros que viven chupando la sangre del pueblo" (125). As Amparo arrives for the republican banquet, the narrative voice concludes sarcastically that ". . . el Gobierno de

Madrid sabía ya a tal hora que una heroica pitillera marinedina realizaba inauditos esfuerzos para apresurar el triunfo de la federal . . ." (141).

Reinforcing the biased voice used by the third person narrator is that the distance separating this voice from Doña Emilia's own is at times nonexistent. To clarify this aspect of Doña Emilia's persuasive powers the familiar terms of Wayne C. Booth are helpful. In general, we recall that the implied author—that second self of the real flesh-and-blood author—can be at varying distances from the narrator. If the narrator is an undramatized one in the third person, there is little distance between this type of narrator and the implied author (92). Here, I contend, enters the important role of the prologue to *La Tribuna.* In the prologue, as we have seen, Doña Emilia spells out her views clearly on the foolishness of the new converts to republicanism. The prologue is signed by her and the reader knows that these are the Countess' opinions. Therefore, in several passages of *La Tribuna,* the implied author-narrator is overshadowed by the real Doña Emilia because some of the comments of this third-person voice in the text of the novel mirror both the tone and content of what the Countess said in the prologue.

Two examples demonstrate clearly how Doña Emilia gains access to her text to continue the propagation of her views. In Chapter IX the narrative voice outlines the events of the Revolution of 1868. In the north of Spain, the reader is told, the republican form of government was favored, especially the federated republic. Then comes a comment, as if an afterthought, directed at the reader: ". . . tal sólo la federal brindaba al pueblo la beatitud perfecta. ¿Y por qué así? ¡Vaya usted a saber!" (123). The indignation in this comment and the explanation which follows matches perfectly that of Doña Emilia's in the prologue. Later, outraged at the ineptness of the writers of the poorly written articles of the republican newspapers, the narrating voice makes another comment reminiscent of Pardo Bazán: "Daba tanto que hacer la revuelta y absorbente política, que no había tiempo para escribir en castellano!" (124). In this manner the third person narrative voice is not merely an anonymous omniscient voice expressing an opinion but at times a clear echo of Doña Emilia's own voice as she again enters the text to demonstrate her persuasive power.

Up to this point we have seen numerous textual strategies in which Pardo Bazán has skillfully utilized to attack the ideology and followers of republicanism. Yet one more tactic remains: the discrediting of the principal voice for the new form of government in the novel, the protagonist and tobacco factory worker, Amparo. Chapters I–XXIV deal with Amparo's political maneuverings in which, as we have seen, her shortcomings have been underscored. The remainder of the novel,

from Chapters XXV to the conclusion of the novel (Chapter XXXVIII), relates Amparo's sentimental involvement with Baltasar, the son of a rich merchant. In this part of the novel, Amparo's lack of common sense and even egoism match her political inexperience of the first part of the novel. A principal defect in the character of Amparo, initially mentioned in the appropriately named Chapter XXVI, "Lados flacos," is that Amparo is interested in Baltasar not for love but for economic reasons. She desires to advance to the upper middle class and be supported by him. Amparo seems only too ready, after the discouragement of the arrival of Amadeo of Savoy to the throne, to abandon her revolutionary ideals and opt for a safe haven in a large house of the *barrio de arriba.* Rationalizing to herself, Amparo asks, "¿Qué han de hacer las pobres, despreciadas de todo el mundo, sin tener quien mire por ellas, más que perderse?" (162).

Moreover, Amparo's ambition to rise in society is paralleled by her pride in being courted by Marineda's richest and most eligible bachelor. The worker was flattered by Baltasar's attentions: "Lisonjeó mucho a la Tribuna el ver que se habían con ella lo mismo que con las señoritas . . ." (165). In Chapter XXXII ("'La Tribuna' se forja ilusiones") Amparo enjoyed the prestige among her fellow factory workers who knew that Baltasar was courting her; she even wore flowers and claimed—falsely—that they were tokens of his love. In all these actions at the cigarette factory ". . . Amparo disfrutaba viendo la rabia de sus rivales . . ." (177). Also, Amparo seemed to be swayed easily by the counsel of her opportunistic and materialistic friend Ana. In the end, Amparo believes the promise of Baltasar to marry her, is abandoned by him, and at the conclusion of the novel is the mother of his unrecognized son. Thus, as a spokesperson for the federal republic Amparo is doubly discredited in *La Tribuna*: her naivety in the political arena is matched by her incompetence in the field of love. She innocently believes that all men and women are now equal, as she has read in the republican newspapers, and sees no social barriers to her marrying a man from the upper classes. More seriously, in her relations with Baltasar, she is driven by a desire for social gain and not by unselfish love.

While the narrative techniques of *La Tribuna* and the characterization of Amparo match Doña Emilia's assault on the republicans in the prologue, the novel remains a *novela tendenciosa* and not a *novela de tesis.* One of the chief reasons that *La Tribuna* is not a novel of thesis is that its didactic thrust is incomplete. In Alarcón's religious novel of thesis, *El escándalo* (1875), the evils of materialistic society experienced by Fabián Conde are replaced by the norms of Christianity, personified by the wise Jesuit, Father Manrique. The lesson for the reader to learn is neatly polished and stated in text. In *La Tribuna,* on the other hand, the text ruthlessly pans the undigested beliefs of the working class as they grapple with the political changes of the *Gloriosa* but offers no solution or remedy. In fact, the text treats the governing middle class in even harsher terms. In this regard Doña Emilia would earn high marks with Lukács for the critical vision of her own class, just as Scott and Balzac were praised by the Hungarian critic for not failing to note the defects of their own social class in their respective novels.

La Tribuna presents many examples of members from the middle class who lack any sense of social responsibility or even human compassion. Doña Dolores, the mother of Baltasar, is a miser and oblivious to the suffering caused by poverty, as witnessed by the reader in Chapter V when poor children arrive at her house to sing Christmas carols. Baltasar himself, a foreshadowing of the spoiled Juanito Santa Cruz of Galdós' *Fortunata y Jacinta,* has little interest in politics and is chiefly concerned about his own well-being: ". . . prefería los ascensos a la gloria, y a la gloria y a los ascensos reunidos anteponía una buena renta que disfrutar sin moverse de su casa . . ." (137). In comparison to Amparo's interest in politics is the apathy of Josefina, the future wealthy wife of Baltasar, who avoids any discussion of national problems: "pero apenas se tocaban asuntos serios, creíase obligada por su papel de niña elegante y casadera, a encogerse de hombros, obligada por su papel de niña elegante y casadera, a encogerse de hombros, hacer cuatro dengues y mudar de conversación" (134). Likewise, Amadeo is pictured by the text as an ineffective but friendly foreigner who is completely unable to understand the problems of the country.

In contrast to *El escándalo,* where all didactic ends are carefully tied up, *La Tribuna* is silent on the conclusions to be drawn from the events it narrates. To further eliminate any good-bad, white-black contrasts characteristic of the *novela de tesis* is the sympathetic overall view of the working classes and especially of the working-class women in the novel. They are unprepared now for providing remedies to national problems, but the reader has the impression that the optimism and energy of the *pueblo,* if channelled in the proper direction, with the proper education, could in fact in the future regenerate the nation. This aspect of *La Tribuna* returns us to the belief of the Countess that it was necessary to gradually introduce social and political change in her country and "dejar para dentro de un siglo lo que podría hacerse en un mes." If this in fact is the conclusion that the Countess hopes the reader will make, it is not stated directly. *La Tribuna,* following the precepts of the *novela tendenciosa,* thus conforms to Pardo Bazán's belief that although fiction can be didactic it is the reader who ultimately must reflect on the consequences of the events narrated.

One final question is appropriate about this persuasive voice in *La Tribuna.* Is it a male voice or a female voice? Or, if the reader tends to associate the opinions of the narrative voice of the novel with Doña Emilia, because of her statements in the prologue, is the perspective of the Countess more like a woman or a man? The male-female perspective does seem to vary with Pardo Bazán's novels. For example, Carlos Feal Deibe contends that in *Los Pazos de Ulloa* there is an almost androgynous point of view as the narrative perspective is shifted among the omniscient narrative voice, Nucha, the priest Julián, and the boy Perucho. In *La Tribuna,* I believe the case of voice is less ambiguous. In my view, the narrative voice of the novel is primarily masculine.

First of all, in contrast to *Los Pazos de Ulloa,* the narrative voice in *La Tribuna* is not shared with the other characters; the omniscient reflector, as holder of absolute knowledge, is superior to the characters it describes and is careful to protect its privileged position. Similarly, many critics, such as Maurice Hemingway, Robert Osborne, and César Barja have noted the lack of the interior, psychological development of the characters of *La Tribuna.* This indeed is a defect of the novel but can be explained partially by the aggressive narrator-observer who is more concerned with expressing a personal view of reality and thus is uninterested in the thoughts and motives of the people described. In addition, the narrator's concept of control and the unwillingness to compromise seem to echo more the nineteenth-century male Victorian society described in *The Madwoman in the Attic* (Sandra M. Gilbert and Susan Gubar), where men are pictured as anxious to keep women in both the enclosure of the home and of preconceived ideas.

Finally, even the voice's treatment of women is problematic. As Francisca González-Arias has indicated, the text does cry out against the abuse of women in the home as seen in in the case of a female cigarette worker beat constantly by her husband. Also, great is the anger of the female workers who upon learning that Amparo has been abandoned by her wealthy lover swear war against masculine treachery, "contra el eterno enemigo: el hombre" (181). Yet the thrust of these events is to call for better treatment of women within existing social entities, not to actively lobby for a change of the woman's place in the nineteenth-century social, economic, and political institutions.[4]

One explanation of Pardo Bazán's surprisingly conservative view of women in *La Tribuna* is that the novel deals principally with working-class women. In other novels, such as *Memorias de un solterón* (1896) or *La quimera* (1905), female characters do invade masculine space and compete with men on an equal basis with the sympathy and support of the narrating voice. The difference is that these later female characters are women of the upper middle class or of the nobility. In *La Tribuna,* a patriarchal authority that censures rapid political change and that also demands respect for Spanish women within fixed roles is the most notable trait of the novel's power of persuasion.

Notes

1. The Countess maintained that the right to vote should be primarily based on one's aptitude, education, and social standing, as she indicated in 1891: "Yo desearía que el sufragio universal se entendiese así: Fulano (insigne por su saber, sus estudios, sus trabajos), vale diez mil votos. Zutano (ilustre por su integridad, su honrada gestión de los negocios públicos, se elocuencia, sus servicios a la patria), veinte mil. Equis (artista eximio), cinco mil. Zeta (dama opulenta e inteligente, formentadora de la agricultura, de la industria, del arte), quince mil" ("Con una alemana" 209).

2. Many of Emilia Pardo Bazán's prologues form a significant part of her critical writings. The preface to *Un viaje de novios* (1881), for example, foreshadows key ideas the Countess will defend in *La cuestión palpitante* two years later. As a prologue to the first edition of *Los Pazos de Ulloa* (1886), Doã Emilia included an essay entitled "Apuntes autobiográficos," which remains today the most complete commentary Pardo Bazán made on her own life.

3. Brian J. Dendle notes similar strategies in the structure of religious novels of thesis (sarcasm, irony, exaggeration, and characters used as a mouthpiece of the author).

4. Even the preference for men's clothing during the carnival of the female cigarette factory workers does not appear to be a call for a change in the social order. Rather, as the women disguise themselves as country lads, cabin boys, and even gentlemen of the city in the various *comparsas,* the entire event seems to be one of "letting off steam." Natalie Zemon Davis discusses this aspect of the utilization of men's clothing in the fifteenth through eighteenth centuries. Similar acts of defiance by women during those times too represented a safety valve for the system, but ultimately were sources of order and stability (153). See "Women on Top: Symbolic Sexual Inversion and Political Disorder in Early Modern Europe." *The Reversible World.* Ed. Barbara A. Babcock. Ithaca: Cornell University Press, 1978. 147-190.

Works Cited

Barja, César. *Libros y autores modernos.* 2nd ed. New York: Las Américas Publishing Company, 1964.

Booth, Wayne C. "Distance and Point-of-View: An Essay in Classification." *The Theory of the Novel.* Ed. Philip Stevick. New York: The Free Press, 1967. 87-107.

Clemessy, Nelly. *Emilia Pardo Bazán como novelista.* Trans. Irene Gambra. 2 vols. Madrid: Publicaciones de la Fundación Universitaria Española, 1982.

Davis, Natalie Zemon. "Women on Top: Symbolic Sexual Inversion and Political Disorder in Early Modern Europe." *The Reversible World.* Ed. Barbara A. Babcock. Ithaca: Cornell University Press, 1978.

Dendle, Brian J. *The Spanish Novel of Religious Thesis 1876-1936.* Madrid: Editorial Castalia, 1968.

Feal Deibe, Carlos. "La voz femenina en *Los Pazos de Ulloa. Hispania* 70 (1987): 214-221.

Gilbert, Sandra M., and Susan Gubar. *The Madwoman in the Attic: The Woman Writer and the Nineteenth-Century Literary Imagination.* New Haven: Yale University Press, 1979.

González-Arias, Francisca. "A Voice, Not an Echo: Emilia Pardo Bazán and the Modern Novel in Spain and France." Diss. Harvard University, 1985.

Gullón, Germán. *El narrador en la novela del siglo XIX.* Madrid: Taurus, 1976.

Hemingway, Maurice. *Emilia Pardo Bazán: The Making of a Novelist.* New York: Cambridge University Press, 1983.

Osborne, Robert E. *Emilia Pardo Bazán: su vida y sus obras.* México, D. F.: Colección Studium, 1964.

Pardo Bazán, Emilia. "Con una alemana." *La mujer española.* Ed. Leda Schiavo. Madrid: Editora Nacional, 1981. 205-213.

———. Prefacio a *Un viaje de novios. Emilia Pardo Bazán: Obras completas.* Ed. Harry L. Kirby, Jr. Vol III. Madrid: Aguilar, 1973. 571-573.

———. Prólogo. *La quimera.* By Pardo Bazán. Vol. XXIX of *Obras completas de Emilia Pardo Bazán.* Madrid: Administración, n. d.

———. Prólogo. *La Tribuna.* By Pardo Bazán. *Emilia Pardo Bazán: Obras Completas.* Ed. Federico Carlos Sainz de Robles. Vol II. Madrid: Aguilar, 1964. 103-104.

———. *La Tribuna. Emilia Pardo Bazán: Obras Completas.* Ed. Federico Carlos Sainz de Robles. Vol II. Madrid: Aguilar, 1964. 104-196.

Shoemaker, William H. *Los prólogos de Galdós.* México, D. F.: Ediciones de Andrea, 1962.

David Henn (essay date 1988)

SOURCE: Henn, David. "Aspects of Narrative Technique." In *The Early Pardo Bazán: Theme and Narrative Technique in the Novels of 1879-89,* pp. 143-218. Liverpool: Francis Cairns, 1988.

[*In the following excerpt, Henn discusses Pardo Bazán's use of language and dialect in her novels* The Tribune of the People, La madre naturaleza, *and* Insolación.]

In the Prologue to *La Tribuna* Pardo Bazán wrote of "la licencia que me tomo de hacer hablar a mis personajes como realmente se habla en la región en donde los saqué" ([*Obras completas*] II, 104) (the licence which I take in having my characters speak in the way that people do in the region from which I have drawn them). Two years later, in the Prologue to *La dama joven,* she stated that it was unforgivable of writers to "alterar o corregir las formas de la oración popular" (III, 666) (alter or correct popular speech forms) and went on to make the unequivocal pronouncement:

> Aun a costa de exponerme a que censores muy formales me imputen el estilo de mis héroes, insisto en no pulirlo ni arreglarlo, y en dejar a señoritos y curas de aldea, a mujeres del pueblo y amas de cría, que se produzcan como saben y pueden, cometiendo las faltas de lenguaje, barbarismos y provincialismos que gusten.
>
> (III, 666)

(Even at the risk of exposing myself to the danger that very staid critics might blame me for the language of my characters, I refuse to polish or correct it, and instead I allow young gentlemen and country priests, ordinary women and wet-nurses, to talk in the way that they know, coming out with any errors, barbarisms and local expressions that they like.)

However, after another two years Pardo Bazán acknowledged, in the **"Apuntes autobiográficos",** the potential problems in this area: "El campo me gusta tanto, que mi aspiración sería escribir una novela donde sólo figurasen labriegos; pero tropiezo con la dificultad del diálogo" (III, 728) (I'm so fond of the countryside that I would like to write a novel in which only peasants appear; but I'm faced with the problem of the dialogue). At the same time she rejected, at least in the case of her Galician peasants, the possibility of some kind of linguistic hybrid as the solution to the problem: ". . . un libro arlequín, mitad gallego y mitad castellano, sería feísimo engendro" (III, 728) (a harlequin work, half Galician and half Castilian, would be an awful mixture). How, then, does Pardo Bazán approach and tackle in her novels this problem of linguistic authenticity?

The first time that the author presents herself with any kind of linguistic problem is in *Un viaje de novios.* Most of the action of this novel takes place in France, yet there are only occasional single words or snippets of French, often handled in a rather clumsy way:

> —Señor, eso no me concierne . . . (*ce n'est pas mon affaire*)—exclamó la fondista, acudiendo, para mejor explicarse, a su idioma natal—.
>
> (I, 118)

("Sir, that is not my business . . . (*ce n'est pas mon affaire*)," said the hotel owner, reverting to her native language in order to make herself better understood.)

And instead of employing the simple solution of having the French doctor, Duhamel, know Spanish, Pardo Bazán chooses an uneasy—although perhaps realistic—compromise. Thus the reader is informed that Duhamel had been to Brazil and picked up a little Portuguese, which he now passes off as Spanish. His inelegant blend of these two languages is then immediately witnessed as he pronounces on Pilar Gonzalvo's extremely poor state of health. His shaky Portuguese is italicized in the text, although his quaint Spanish is not:

> Ensayaremos un revulsivo enérgico, *forte . . . E um retrocesso ao pulmao . . .* ; veremos de desviarlo . . . ¡Bon Deus!, ¡bailar y beber refrescos! Y ahora tenemos que luchar con el sudor . . . *O suor esgota-a.*
>
> (I, 135)

(We'll attempt a powerful enema, *very strong . . . There is aggravation of the lung . . .* ; we must correct this . . . *Good God!* Dancing and consuming cold drinks! And now we have to stop the sweating . . . *The sweating is exhausting her.*)

On several occasions, parenthetical asides are used to comment on the pronunciation of one of the secondary characters, Perico Gonzalvo: "Pues no sé si cogerá el expreso, el expreso (esta palabra en labios de Gonzalvo sonaba así: 'epés')" (I, 113) (Well, I don't know if he'll catch the express train, the express [Gonzalvo pronounced this word "epess"]). And while such a technique is, of course, thoroughly unsubtle it is also fairly typical of Pardo Bazán's timid and somewhat ungainly efforts in *Un viaje de novios* to address the issue of non-standard speech and pronunciation.

In her next novel, *La Tribuna,* the author prepares her reader for some bolder moves in this area by setting the work in her own native region and city, and also by raising the subject of language and dialogue in the Prologue to the novel. As was noted earlier, she promises that in this novel her characters will speak "in the way that people do in the region from which I have drawn them". But there is really only a modest attempt to fulfil this promise. *La Tribuna* contains a sprinkling of words, frequently italicized, given colloquial pronunciations—yet the indicated pronunciations would be common to most, if not all, regions of Spain. Such words include: *libertá* (II, 125) (liberty); *oficialidá, responsabilidá* (II, 126-27) (officialdom, responsibility); "verdá" (II, 131) (true); "to" (II, 133) (all), and *Madrí, manífica, perficionar* (II, 132) (Madrid, magnificent, to perfect). The occasional grouping also occurs:

Hola, chica . . . , salú y fraternidá . . . ¿Cómo está tu madre? ¿Y la revolusión, cuándo la hasemos? ¿Cuándo me preclamas a mí reina de España?

(II, 166)

(Hello, my girl . . . , 'ealth and fraternity . . . How's your mother? And the revolushun, when are we goin' to 'ave it? When are you goin' to preclaim me queen of Spain?)

But even such modest concentrations are unusual. Other colloquialisms to be found include the misplacing of an object pronoun: ". . . para *te llevar* a la cárcel" (II, 131) (to take you to prison), or a verb such as "aprender" (learn) incorrectly used in the sense of "teach". As is so often the case, italics signal the incorrect usage:

—¡Ay! No me *aprendieron.*

—Pues ¿qué te *aprendieron,* hija? ¿Coser?

(II, 115)

("Oh! They didn't *learn* me."

"Well, what did they *learn* you, dear? To sew?")

When it comes to Galician vocabulary, or Galician contamination of Castilian words and forms, there are even fewer examples to be found. In his edition of *La Tribuna,* Benito Varela Jácome signals, for example, "achinados" (II, 129) (wealthy) as a Galician adjective,[1] and also points out that "indina" (II, 179) (shameless) is the Galician form for "indigna".[2] But "indino"/"indina" is also, of course, a widespread popular form. In addition, Varela Jácome mentions the relationship to Galician of fairly frequently-used verb forms such as "hacedes", "sabedes", "tenedes" (II, 133) (you make, you know, you have), or "Fretirlo" (II, 184) (Fry it).[3] All in all, then, there is evidence in *La Tribuna,* although only a relatively modest amount, to support the suggestion in the Prologue of a general use of local speech forms in the text of the novel.

In Pardo Bazán's next four novels, the two short works *La dama joven* and *Bucólica,* and *El Cisne de Vilamorta* and *Los Pazos de Ulloa*—all of which are set in Galicia—, evidence of, or even reference to, regional speech is exceedingly rare. In one of his letters, the narrator of *Bucólica* mentions that he and Maripepa had been conversing in dialect and he found this very difficult to follow (I, 930). However, there is no attempt at all to give the flavour of such dialogue—perhaps because the narrator did not wish to confuse his correspondent in Madrid! However, no such excuse can apply to either *El Cisne de Vilamorta* or *Los Pazos de Ulloa.* Apart from some colloquialisms and the odd word of dialect neither novel contains any passages of local speech, although the later work does have a reference to the subject in its opening pages. Thus, when Julián asks a local person how far it is to the *pazo,* he

gets a "respuesta ambigua en dialecto:—La carrerita de un can" (I, 168) (an ambiguous answer in dialect: "About as far as a dog runs").

It is not, in fact, until *La madre naturaleza* that the author makes any kind of noticeable attempt to include dialect in one of her rural narratives. And while the extent is still modest, this novel contains appreciably more of the Galician dialect than any of Pardo Bazán's previous works set in the region. In the opening pages there is reference to the fact that Moscoso's daughter, Manuela, uses dialect (I, 289), and much later mention is made of her "marcado acento del país" (I, 342) (strong local accent). However, there is no attempt in the novel to convey this accent. And while Manuela occasionally uses a dialect word, only once is she seen to utter a whole sentence in dialect, and even this is not as part of a dialogue but is, in fact, the local equivalent of "Ladybird, ladybird, fly away home!" (I, 344).

In the later stages of the novel more Galician is presented, but again not as dialogue. This time it is part of a popular song:

A lua vay encuberta
a min pouco se me dá:
a lua que a min m'alumbra
dentro do meu peito está.

(I, 386)

(The moon is veiled by cloud / but it matters little to me: / the moon which lights my way / is here in my breast.)

Dialect words are also scattered, although not thickly, throughout the narrative. Sometimes they are used in descriptions by the narrator and are occasionally italicized. Such words include: "lar", "leito" (I, 291) (fireplace, bed); *meiga* (I, 348) (here used in the sense of "magician") and *cunca* (I, 355) (cup, small drinking-vessel). On other occasions they are to be found in short pieces of dialogue as part of a mishmash of Castilian and Galician. Thus, for example, when Goros suggests to the bone-setter that only God knows the cause of the unhappy events at the *pazo,* Antón replies: "O el diaño, que inda es más listo" (I, 400) (Or the devil, who is even cleverer).

Finally, mention must be made of the narrator's mocking portrayal of Sabel's husband, *Gallo.* One of the notable constituents of the presentation of *Gallo* is the exposure of the kind of language he uses with Gabriel Pardo—a medley of dialect, bad grammar, mispronunciation and general pomposity—when Gabriel enquires after the whereabouts of Perucho:

Señor don Gabriel, no le saberé decir con eusautitú . . . Quizásmente que aún no tendrá voltado, "en atención" a que no se ha visto por aquí su comparecencia.

(I, 386)

(Señor don Gabriel, I cannot be able to tell you exatily . . . Perhapsly he still will not have returned, "having regard to" his appearance not having been seen around here.)

And when Gabriel accuses him of not telling the truth on this matter, *Gallo* responds:

> Adispensando las barbas honradas de usté, señorito don Gabriel, ésas son palabras muy mayores, y mi caballerosidá y mi dicencia, es un decir, no me premiten . . .
>
> (I, 386)

> (Respecting your distinguished self, Señorito don Gabriel, those are very momentous words and my gentlemanliness and my dicorum, if I may say so, won't premit me . . .)

Although Pardo Bazán was well aware—taking into account both author and reader—that there were limits to the extent to which colloquial language and, particularly, dialect could be used in a novel, it is clear that in *La madre naturaleza* she stayed well within these limits. In this respect, the novel is not as linguistically adventurous as some of the author's theoretical statements might have led the reader to expect. Indeed, the tentative steps that she takes in the area of dialect and colloquial language seem to confirm the reservations she had expressed in the **"Apuntes autobiográficos"** on the possibilities of successfully conveying such forms. However, Pardo Bazán's efforts in this sphere were renewed and developed in her next novel, *Insolación,* despite the fact that it was her first novel for eight years to be set outside Galicia. And since the other novel which she published in 1889, *Morriña,* is almost totally bereft of examples of dialect or colloquial language, *Insolación* is the author's last work of the 1879-89 period to pay noticeable attention to the expression of popular speech-forms and the use of non-standard accents.

In *Insolación,* which is set in Madrid, Pardo Bazán concentrates her linguistic attention on a variety of speech-forms heard in and around the capital. However, the first character she scrutinizes in this respect is not a *madrileño* but the dashing young Andalusian, Pacheco. His accent is conveyed as soon as he is introduced to the narrative:

> . . . Haciéndose cargo de la indicación de la duquesa, dijo con acento cerrado y frase perezosa:

> —A cada país le cae bien lo suyo . . . Nuestra tierra no ha dado pruebas de ser nada ruda; tenemos allá de too: poetas, pintores, escritores . . . Cabalmente, en Andalucía la gente pobre es mu fina y mu despabilaa. Protesto contra lo que se refiere a las señoras. Este cabayero convendrá en que toítas son unos ángeles del cielo.
>
> (I, 417)

> (. . . Following up the duchess's point, he said with a strong accent and drawl:

> "Every region is happy with its own ways . . . Ours hasn't shown itself to be at all uncultured; we have evything there: poets, painters, writers . . . What's more, in Andalusia the poor are ver polite and ver lively. I must protest at what has been said about the ladies. This gentleman will surely agree that they are evyone just angels.")

And for the rest of the novel Pardo Bazán attempts to maintain the reader's awareness of Pacheco's accent, almost entirely through use of dialogue.

For her other attempts to convey accent, as well as popular speech, the author turns away from the salon society where Pacheco was first encountered and looks instead at the opposite end of the social scale. Thus, when at the San Isidro fair Pacheco gives a flashy local lad a cigar and asks him if he knows of a suitable place where he and Asís might eat, the response is as follows:

> Se estima . . . Como haber fondas, hay fondas; misté por ahí too alredor, que fondas son; pero tocante a fonda, vamos, según se ice, de comías finas, pa la gente e aquel, me pienso que no hallarán ustés conveniencia; digo, esto me lo pienso yo; ustés verán.
>
> (I, 426)

> (Much obliged . . . As fer restaurants, well there are sorts of restaurants all over; but as fer what you might call a restaurant, you know, wiv nice meals, fer people like yerselves, I meself think that you won't find what suits you; I mean, that's what I meself think; yer'll see.)

And when the couple do find a place to eat, they are soon interrupted by a gypsy fortune-teller who proceeds to examine Asís' hand. Her lengthy predictions begin:

> Una cosa diquelo yo en esta manica, que ha e suseder mu pronto, y nadie saspera que susea . . . Un viaje me vasté a jaser, y no ha e ser para má, que ha e ser pa satisfasión e toos. Una carta me vasté a resibir, y lae alegrá lo que viene escribío en eya.
>
> (I, 428)

> (It says somefin in this nice little 'and, somefin to 'appen real quick, an' nobody 'spects it t'appen. Yer goin' on a journey, but there's no 'arm in it, evryone'll be pleased 'bout it. Yer goin' t'get a letter, an' what's in it'll make yer 'appy.)

Finally, mention should be made of a scene a few days later, when Pacheco and Asís go to eat at an establishment on the outskirts of the city. Here, they are commented on by a group of working girls:

> . . . Hablaban con el seco y recalcado acento de la plebe madrileña, que tiene alguna analogía con lo que pudo ser la parla de Demóstenes, si se le ocurriese escupir a cada frase una de las guijas que llevaba en la boca.

> —¡Ay . . . ! Pus van así como asustaos . . . Ella es guapetona, colorá y blanca.

—Valiente perdía será.

—Se ve caa cosa . . . Hijas, la mar son estos señorones de alcurnia.

—Puee que sea arguna del Circo. Tie pinta de franchuta.

—Que no, que este es un belén gordo, de gente de calidá. Mujer de algún ministro lo menos. ¿Qué vus pensáis? Pus una conicí yo, casaa con un presonaje de los más superfarolíticos . . . , de mucho coche, una casa como el Palacio Rial . . . , y andaba como caa cuala, con su apaño. ¡Qué líos, Virgen!

(I, 461)

(. . . They spoke with the clipped, emphatic accent of the Madrid working classes, which must be similar to how Demosthenes would have spoken if, with every sentence, he spat out one of the pebbles which he had in his mouth.

"Oh . . . ! They look a bit scared . . . She's a lovely one, all rosy'n pale."

"A fine catch she is."

"Don't yer see it all . . . Girls, these great toffs are a real bunch."

"Maybe she's one of 'em from the Circus. She's got that Frenchified look."

"Course not, this is big stuff, 'igh class people. She'll be at least the wife uv some minister. What yer think? I knew one once, married to a real top presonage, 'uge coach, 'ouse like the Royal Palice . . . , she was a crafty one, carried on jiss like the rest uv us. Holy Mother, she 'ad some fun!")

While it could be said that these extracts from *Insolación* suffer from a certain linguistic sameness, they do, nevertheless, reveal a bold attempt to capture the kind of language which Pardo Bazán claimed should be an important aspect of the modern novel—an inescapable and at times crucial part of the world which the novelist was trying to describe.

Up to and including *Los Pazos de Ulloa* Pardo Bazán had, despite her various statements on the topic, largely avoided making any substantial effort to employ colloquial language and dialect in her novels. Certainly, the author's heralded quest in this sphere in *La Tribuna* can only be described as achieving very modest success. Indeed, in her novels with a Galician setting—that is, all those published between 1879 and 1889, with the exception of *Un viaje de novios, Insolación* and *Morriña*—Pardo Bazán never convincingly grasped the appropriate linguistic nettle. Emilio González López suggests that this is because the principal characters in her Galician novels come from the middle classes and above.[4] And while, of course, this observation cannot be said to apply to *La Tribuna*, it is certainly true that very few members of the lower reaches of Galician society figure prominently in Pardo Bazán's Galician

works. Yet at the same time there are still, surely, enough for the author to have injected a substantially greater amount of dialect and popular speech if she had wished to and if she had been able to achieve this with artistic success. *Insolación* would seem to support this contention. As it is, *La Tribuna* and *La madre naturaleza* are, from a linguistic point of view, the most adventurous of her Galician novels. However, both are still modest efforts in this respect and look particularly so when compared to *Insolación.* Ultimately, it is most ironic that in her novels of the first decade Pardo Bazán is linguistically at her boldest not in any of the regional works, but in a novel set in Madrid.

Notes

1. E. Pardo Bazán, *La Tribuna,* ed. Benito Varela Jácome (Madrid: Cátedra, 1975), p. 118.

2. ibid., p. 232.

3. ibid., pp. 127, 243.

4. González López, p. 148.

Select Bibliography

Works by Pardo Bazan

Complete Works

Obras completas, Vols. I & II, ed. Federico Carlos Sainz de Robles, 3rd ed. (Madrid: Aguilar, 1973)

Obras completas, Vol. III, ed. Harry L. Kirby, Jr. (Madrid: Aguilar, 1973)

Critical Editions

Un viaje de novios, ed. Mariano Baquero Goyanes, Textos Hispánicos Modernos, No. 15 (Barcelona: Labor, 1971)

La Tribuna, ed. Benito Varela Jácome (Madrid: Cátedra, 1975)

Mary Lee Bretz (essay date summer 1989)

SOURCE: Bretz, Mary Lee. "Text and Intertext in Emilia Pardo Bazán's *Memorias de un solterón*." *Symposium* 43, no. 2 (summer 1989): 83-93.

[*In the following essay, Bretz offers a feminist reading of* Memorias de un solterón, *noting Pardo Bazán's narrative technique and the intertextual references "that relate to the discussion of marriage."*]

Emilia Pardo Bazán's novel *Memorias de un solterón* has been identified by several critics as an explicitly feminist novel.[1] Recent feminist theorists have demonstrated that a "feminist novel" involves not only a subversion of the patriarchal society on a thematic level, but a subversion and revision of the textual strategies that operate in androcentric literature (Gilbert and Gubar 73; DuPlessis 3-16, Abel 3-19). In this study I will apply feminist narrative theory and the concept of intertextuality to *Memorias de un solterón* in order to illustrate the various textual strategies of narrative discourse that converge to question not only the patriarchal values on a thematic level, but also to challenge the prevailing narrative paradigm (realism/naturalism). The dual focus on the world outside the novel—the social structures of nineteenth-century Spain—and the world of the novel—the narrative canon of the period—is a feature of metafictional discourse and in this sense, *Memorias de un solterón* subverts the very foundation of the realistic/ naturalistic novel. Whereas realism seeks to present the fictional world as "real," *Memorias* examines the interdependence of the fictional and the real, arguing that narrative "scripts" are merely echoes of the social "scripts" that patriarchal society imposes on women both as members of society and as fictional characters.

Memorias de un solterón is the first person account of Mauro Pareja, an inveterate bachelor who falls in love with and marries Feíta Neira, a young feminist. The problem of marriage, its advantages and disadvantages, was much discussed in nineteenth-century Spain.² This discussion and many of the texts that were involved in it constitute an important intertext of Pardo Bazán's novel. The terms "intertext" and "intertextuality" have been defined in different ways by different theorists. Although all refute the view of the text as a closed, self-contained unit and stress the links between a specific textual production and its antecedents, there is disagreement regarding the nature of these relations. Harold Bloom stresses the influence of a specific precursor text or poet on the successor, who continues, refutes, or transforms the inherited text. Julia Kristeva, Roland Barthes, Robert Scholes, and other semioticians offer a broader definition, reaffirming the interdependence of texts and their antecedents, but identifying these antecedents as cultural codes or anonymous traces: "The study of intertextuality is thus not the investigation of sources and influences as traditionally conceived; it casts its net wider to include anonymous discursive practices, codes whose origins are lost, that make possible the signifying of later texts" (Culler 103). Gustavo Pérez Firmat continues this broader definition in his study of intertextuality, pointing out that an intertext is a hinge that links and puts into relation two sign systems. Although the text alluded to, or in Pérez Firmat's terminology "the paratext," is only partially reproduced, the allusion calls to mind the entire paratext as well as the ideology it represents. Furthermore, the paratext is not necessarily a single, concrete text; rather, the intertextual references may well evoke a style or set of conventions canonized by a series of texts (2-3). This is the case of *Memorias,* which makes allusion to a multitude

of nineteenth-century texts and, in this manner, questions the conventions of the realistic/naturalistic novel and the bourgeois ideology that it represents.

There are three different intertextual references in *Memorias* that relate to the discussion of marriage. The first appears in chapter I when Mauro Pareja argues that bachelorhood permits a degree of tranquility and order that marriage and family life preclude. The second occurs when Mauro specifically dissociates himself from Gedeón (450), the protagonist of Pereda's thesis novel, *El buey suelto,* in which bachelorhood is equated with moral and sexual degeneracy. And the third surfaces when Mauro cites Ovid and Feijoo in a discussion of the inevitable disillusionment that occurs when the carefully groomed unmarried woman becomes the tired, haggard, unkempt wife and mother. These three references evoke the various ideologies that contribute to the nineteenth-century discussion of marriage. Pereda voices the archconservative view that marriage serves to control man's libidinous nature. Feijoo, as cited in the narrative, represents a long tradition of misogamistic literature that is tempered but still very evident in nineteenth-century Europe. Mauro Pareja's vision of marriage articulates the ideology of modern bourgeois society, in which order and control receive primary value. There is no specific paratext for this ideology; rather, Pardo Bazán utilizes multiple intertextual references to call to mind the larger text, that is, the cultural codes of the realistic/naturalistic novel as it developed in Spain, particularly as it relates to the problem of women and marriage.

The paratext of any text is identified not by a single allusion but by the accumulation of references (Pérez Firmat 8). The intertextual nature of *Memorias* is signaled by a multitude of references to other authors and texts, by duplication of well-known nineteenth-century literary figures in the names or actions of characters within *Memorias,* and by frequent allusions within the text to its literary character, and thus its dependency on other literary works. The reader is reminded of this dependency from the very beginning, in that the novel is the second and last work in the Adam and Eve cycle, with many of the same characters reappearing and with many references to the events recounted in *Doña Milagros,* the first book in the series. *Memorias* is not, however, a continuation of *Doña Milagros* but rather a contrasting version of the same problem, a sort of rewriting of the antecedent text. Benicio Neira, Feíta's father, was the narrator of *Doña Milagros* but appears as a secondary character in *Memorias.* In the two novels of the series he is both the primary defender of the bourgeois family and the incarnation of all of its deficiencies; but while a more general criticism of bourgeois social structures predominates in *Doña Milagros, Memorias* specifically stresses the link between bourgeois ideology and restrictive social roles for women.

Doña Milagros introduces the reader to Benicio Neira and his wife, the parents of eleven daughters and one son. With a modest income from inherited land, the Neiras cling desperately to a middle-class life style. Once his wife dies, Benicio is left to fend for the family on his own. Within the bourgeois framework, his only hope lies in the financial success of the son or the "successful" marriage of one or more daughters. *Doña Milagros* points out the deficiencies in this stance but offers no other options. *Memorias* investigates new possibilities, suggesting the need for new ideologies, different social structures, and new forms of discourse. In this second novel Benicio's defense of the bourgeois ideology is echoed by Mauro. Both men oppose Feíta's attempts to educate herself and to have a career; and both are scandalized when one of the Neira daughters marries out of her class, preferring a house painter to spinsterhood. But while Benicio defends the bourgeois family in both theory and practice, Mauro steadfastly resists the temptation to marry. Ironically, it is his very insistence on the inalterability of the bourgeois family that shores up his belief in the virtues of bachelorhood. The specter of a dependent wife, numerous children, and the pressures to sustain a middle-class image have prevailed over the appeal of the many young women that he has courted.

Although *Memorias de un solterón* can be read independently of *Doña Milagros,* the many references in the text to the previous novel emphasize the intertextual nature of the second volume in the series. This aspect of *Memorias* is further stressed by the characterization employed in the novel. Benicio, Mauro, and most of the characters that appear in the novel are narrative types that echo, in one form or another, well-known figures of the realistic paratext. For the contemporary reader, the title of the novel, *Memorias de un solterón* would very likely evoke the popular *Memorias de un setentón,* published 16 years earlier by Ramón Mesonero Romanos. The evocation of the Mesonero text continues in the characterization of Mauro Pareja, the narrator. Mesonero Romanos was an extraordinarily popular writer who consistently presented himself in his *artículos de costumbres* as an observer of customs and of types.[3] His works are generally narrated in the first person, and he typically chooses a particular public spot from which he studies the faces and actions of those who pass by, converting this information into a description of the customs of contemporary *madrileños.* For his part, Mauro describes himself early in the novel as a "spectator" or "observer." From his vantage point in the local club he observes the passersby and deciphers their motives and objectives (452-53). In the *tertulia* at Benicio Neira's house, he plays the same role: "La casualidad hizo que yo penetrase en ella en el momento más oportuno para satisfacer mis aficiones de espectador" (465). Both writers employ a jovial, carefree tone and both exalt the bourgeois values of order and decorum. Significantly,

both resist sexual adventure and neither one marries until well into his thirties. Phlegmatic bachelors who resist emotional entanglement and exalt order appear with some frequency in novels of the period: El señor de Albuérniga in Rosalía de Castro's *El caballero de las botas azules,* and Manso in Galdos's *El amigo manso,* to name only two. The henpecked Benicio, with his lack of character and of financial acumen, his rigid moral code, and his gentle demeanor invites comparison with Ramón Villaamil of Pérez Galdós's *Miau,* or Francisco Bringas of *La de Bringas.* Mauro himself sees Benicio as a "type," "el caso más caracterizado de paternidad que entre mis relaciones conozco" (459), and focuses on his misfortune as a reminder of the drawbacks of marriage.

A number of the characters in the novel are described by other characters as types whose actions and words follow a predictable script. Argos, the beautiful and neurotic Neira daughter, is repeatedly associated with the romantic period (465, 489), and her story unfolds in keeping with the romantic paradigm. Her script is so limited that Feíta can predict its outcome early in the novel:

> ¡Y por cierto que se me figura que esta vez . . . Argos . . . le dará que hacer a mi pobre padre! . . . Argos . . . Argos quiere leones; se muere por los audaces, por los insolentes, por los perdidos. Hay bastantes mujeres del temple de Argos. ¿Y usted sabe cómo se llama tal predisposición? Falso romanticismo y telarañas en mollera vacía.

> ([*Obras completas*] 1:489)

Feíta's prediction is fulfilled to the letter. Argos becomes involved with a typical don Juan type, her dishonor precipitates a confrontation between her father and her lover; and in a fit of passion, Benicio Neira runs a sword through his daughter's seducer. A number of paratexts are involved in this subplot. There is obviously an echo of the *folletín* and of the romantic in the dramatic ending. Furthermore, Argos's lover is of mysterious background with hints that he has left an impoverished wife and child in the Philippines—more material from the romantic or feuilletonistic script.[4] Another intertextual reference is to Zorrilla's *Don Juan Tenorio* and also perhaps to Clarín's *La Regenta.* The don Juan of *Memorias* is named Luis Mejía, after Don Juan's rival in Zorrilla's play and significantly similar to Clarín's donjuanesque Alvaro Mesía, which was obviously taken from Zorrilla. Without going into great detail, a few more obvious examples of intertextuality deserve mention. There is the socialist type who sells out to bourgeois comforts, and the reintroduction of characters and themes from Pardo Bazán's earlier novel *La Tribuna.* In addition, there is the example of Rosa, the epitome of nineteenth-century female consumerism, who squanders the family's remaining holdings and becomes the mistress of a man she does not love in order to continue dressing herself in the latest fashion. The parallels with *La de Bringas* are unmistakable. The similarity between the names, Rosa and Rosalía, is also worth noting. Furthermore, both of these fashion conscious women are described as mere "cursis," the ultimate nineteenth-century insult. Mauro Pareja comments that Rosa does not really have a good sense of style:

> Yo comprendía que el supuesto lujo asiático, el boato de la chica de Neira, era en realidad penuria, y que con aquellos cuatro pinguitos, en Madrid, Rosa no pasaría de ser una de las bellas cursis en quienes nadie repara y que desfilan por la ancha y soleada acera de la calle o por las avenidas de Recoletos . . .

(464)

In the well-known scene from Galdós's novel, Refugio Sánchez humiliates Rosalía de Bringas by relating how the Marquesa de Tellería had referred to her as "cursi" (1665).

Semioticians have frequently pointed out the presence of intertextuality in all texts. Kristeva writes that "the poetic text is produced in the complex movement of a simultaneous affirmation and negation of another text" (Culler 107) and, in a similar vein, Robert Scholes comments that "major literary works are all comments on their own form, on the generic tradition or traditions from which they take their being" (33). In **Memorias de un solterón,** Pardo Bazán presents the generic traditions of the realistic/naturalistic novel, which includes residues of the romantic and feuilletonistic paradigms, as familiar scripts with predictable outcomes and types. Furthermore, she points out the restricting character of these scripts, particularly where women are concerned. There is the romantic tragic role of passion and disgrace played by Argos, the traditional retreat to the convent taken by Clara, or the bourgeois obsession with material goods and, in particular, women's clothing exemplified by Rosa.

Against these traditional female scripts, Feíta seeks to elaborate a new role for herself, and in the process she introduces a new type of discourse. Not surprisingly, there is resistance and misinterpretation regarding this new discourse. Typically, characters attempt to interpret Feíta's conduct according to the old, familiar scripts. Her desire to be educated is initially dismissed by both her father and Mauro. This latter calls her a "marisabidilla," a term popular in the eighteenth century that serves to negatively "type" all educated women within a single mold. When Feíta gets a job tutoring several students and insists on walking to work without a chaperone, her father, Mauro, and many local townspeople predict that she will eventually lose her virtue, because according to traditional scripts, only "fallen women" went out without chaperones. Because most profes-

sional women in the nineteenth century were writers, everyone assumes Feíta is a "poetisa," even though her tastes tend toward medicine and the sciences. When she visits Mauro's boarding house to use his landlord's library, Mauro is horrified that someone will see her there and start a scandal; and when the local gossip appears, Mauro insists that Feíta hide so as not to be discovered. Feíta specifically points out the textual precedents for this behavior, refusing to comply with conduct that comes straight out of a "sainete" or comic farce (480).

Although Feíta insists on the importance of her education over all else, Mauro is convinced that she will fall in love with *el compañero Sobrado,* the young socialist. He "reads" the meeting of the two young rebels as if they were characters in a romantic novel: "En el episodio del encuentro con el obrero me pareció que existían encantadores detalles, y mi fantasía empezó a trabajar activamente, como si la inflamase la reciente lectura de alguna novela" (490). However, his attempts to predict her actions and read her character according to preexisting texts fail consistently. Mauro himself compares Feíta with her sisters, whom he has just described according to their respective types, and says that 100 pages would not suffice to portray the unusual Feíta (468). In contrast to the predictability of Rosa and Argos, "con Feíta no estamos nunca dentro de lo previsto y normal, sino que cada día saca ella un resorte nuevo" (469). As Mauro gradually falls in love with her, he finds that his old courting techniques no longer serve. He knows he can play neither knight-errant nor Oliverio de Jalín with Marcela (493). He must learn new ways to speak to her, new narrative techniques, and new forms of discourse because Feíta neither acts nor speaks according to the traditional scripts. Feíta's manner of speech contrasts markedly with Mauro's and with that of the bourgeoisie. In contrast to the proper, ordered language of Mauro and her father, Feíta speaks spontaneously and often incorrectly. On one occasion Mauro refers to her speech as diabolical, the language of Blacks (470). Her language is disordered, illogical, emotionally abrupt (in Kristeva's terminology, it is the semiotic in contrast with the symbolic).[5] The following quotation, with the abrupt transitions from one sentence and topic to another, and the idiosyncratic use of nicknames and sound effects, captures some of its qualities:

> Quedamos en que la salud, inmejorable. Nada de languideces ni de nerviocitos: un sueño de marmota, un apetito de par en par y la cabeza más fresca que una lechuga. Bueno. Pues vamos ahora a lo de dentro . . . que suele ser el corolario de lo otro. Por dentro, maese Abad, ¡me siento tan cambiada! Me he vuelto muy buena y hasta se me ha despertado un deseo atroz de ser útil a mi familia. . . . Los últimos tiempos de mi opresión (patachín, patachín), cuando aún vivía sujeta al ominoso yugo (¡pataratacriiin!), me iba volviendo mala . . . , ¡malísima, infame!

(2:486)

Feíta rejects Mauro's bourgeois discourse, his hypocrisy, and his insistence on protecting appearances. When he lectures her on the importance of feminine self-sacrifice, she accuses him of spouting platitudes (487). Feíta's new discourse is at times incomprehensible to Mauro, as when she rejects his first marriage proposal, saying that she could never "casarse por chiripa." When Mauro asks her to explain the expression, she reverts to the more standard expression: "Bien recordará usted que no entraba en mis planes ir al ara, ¿no se dice así?" (2:509). Mauro is perturbed both by the form and the content of Feíta's discourse. In particular, it irritates him to hear his own ideas on the disadvantages of marriage and the value of self-indulgence in the mouth of a woman (2:487). Feíta herself comments that he is less shocked by the sexual activities of her sisters than by the fact that she discusses them so openly and frankly.

Feíta introduces a new discourse and a new script into the realistic/naturalistic novel. In this respect the use of a male narrator to present Feíta's story is significant. The bourgeois, realistic novel was a male construct, cultivated by male writers who echoed a patriarchal ideology. It enclosed women within the confines of specific spaces and discourses, and female characters who broke out of this confinement were punished in one way or another: madness, death, silence (Gilbert and Gubar 53ff). Feíta's voice and her actions disrupt this construct and require a revision of the texts and scripts that uphold the old order. Mauro, as the author of the text relating Feíta's story, represents the transition from the rejection of this new discourse to its incorporation and even acclamation. Mauro, the bourgeois lover of order and hierarchy, becomes the champion of female liberation and social change. Symbolic of this transformation are the many inversions of sexual roles that Mauro, as narrator, presents without embarrassment in the course of his narration. It is Feíta who decides their future, proposing marriage to him after having initially rejected his proposal. It is Feíta who takes the active role, attempting to pursue a career and seeking to educate herself, while Mauro watches passively from the sidelines. In many respects Mauro is a rather "feminine" figure, with character traits normally associated with women. He is very domestic, attached to his home surroundings and his creature comforts; he loves to gossip, he is worried about gaining weight, and in his reading he prefers novels to economic and scientific treatises. He is fastidious about his clothes and his appearance, and it bothers him that Feíta takes no notice of him as a potential suitor. In ironic inversion, the time that Mauro normally devotes to setting out his clothing and meticulously grooming himself is the time that Feíta, ungroomed and indifferent to her physical appearance, chooses to study science and economics in the library next to Mauro's bedroom.

Mauro's deviation from the patriarchal canon is apparent not only in his characterization but also in the form of his narration. In contrast to the realistic/naturalistic paradigm, with its residue of romantic literary conventions, Mauro's text avoids suspense, passion, and action. The only episodes of these types are textually signaled as belonging to the canonical novel of the day. Such is the case with the confrontation between Benicio Neira and Luis Mejía, linked to the romantic paradigm through the intertextual reference to Zorrilla and through Feíta's prediction of the event, based on her knowledge of her sister's "romantic" character. Unlike many novels of the period, *Memorias* delays the introduction and identification of the central character until well into the novel. Initially the reader assumes that Mauro will be the protagonist, because the first four chapters are devoted to his self-analysis; but after chapter VIII, when Feíta is first introduced, she gradually displaces him as the central figure in the novel.

Although all good novels deviate to some degree from the contemporary canon, *Memorias* foregrounds the breaking of conventions, particularly with respect to the role of observation in the narrative. Since Pardo Bazán's *La cuestión palpitante,* critics have argued regarding the definition of realism and naturalism; but in all definitions the idea of "observation of reality" occupies a central position. Zola's idea of writing as a form of scientific experimentation and Pardo Bazán's own definition of the novel as "el género en que, por altísima prerrogativa, los fueros de la verdad se imponen, la observación desinteresada reina, y la historia positiva de nuestra época ha de quedar escrita con caracteres de oro" (*OC* [*Obras completas*] 3:642) both emphasize this trait as fundamental. The frequency with which writers of the period adopted an omniscient narrator or a narrator who was a disinterested observer of the events reflects their adherence to this central tenet of realism/naturalism.[6] *Memorias* breaks with this tradition in the use of a first person narration and in Mauro's involvement in the events he is describing. In the early chapters, Mauro's insistence on his role as disinterested observer mitigates the use of first-as opposed to third-person narration; however, as it becomes more evident that Mauro is deeply involved in the events narrated, the nature of his narrative and the reader's relation to it change significantly. This change is textually signaled in chapter 16 when Mauro interrupts his narration and addresses the reader directly, concerned that this latter will not know how to interpret his unorthodox narrative:[7]

> Sospecho que antes de llegar aquí habrá dicho cien veces el prudente lector: "Vamos a cuentas, señor memorialista: lo que nos relata usted, ¿son sus memorias, sus verdaderos recuerdos íntimos, o los de la apreciable

familia Neira? ¿Hemos de tomarnos interés por usted, o más bien por Argos, Rosa, Feíta, y demás retoños de ese padre de familia angustiado y maltrecho?

(*OC* 2:492)

In chapter 22, Mauro is even more explicit in distancing his narration from the realistic/naturalistic conventions of disinterested observation. Once again he addresses the reader directly, thus breaking down the division between fiction and reality that is generally observed in the novels of the period. In addition, he stresses the nonnovelistic character of his life, remarking that nothing dramatic or eventful has ever happened to him. Further, he announces that he is changing his procedure and will abandon all efforts to document the sources of his information and will now adopt the narrative strategy of the omniscient narrator, so prevalent in the novels of the day (*OC* 2:511).

Needless to say, by focusing on the narrative techniques being employed and by underscoring the arbitrary shift from one type of narration to another, simply to fit the convenience of the narrator and the level of interest of the reader, **Memorias** destroys the myth of the "disinterested observer" and, consequently, breaks with the central tenet of realism/naturalism. In its final form, Mauro's narration is markedly unrealistic, based more on other texts than on the close observation of external reality. Contemporary critics would point out that this is true of all texts, but whereas other realistic/naturalistic texts strive to hide their intertextual character, in **Memorias de un solterón** it is consciously exhibited. While Pérez Firmat's observation that the realistic novel exhibits only limited incidences of intertextuality is true of other realistic/naturalistic novels, it does not hold for **Memorias.** Furthermore, through Mauro's metafictional discussions of the narrative strategies he is employing, the novel subverts the realistic emphasis on the fictional world as a substitute for the "real" world. Once the process of writing displaces the creation of a fictional reality as the topic of the novel, readers can no longer lose themselves in the substitute reality which realistic fiction offers them. It is not that Pardo Bazán turns her back entirely on the social reality of the world outside of the novel. Rather, she illustrates that new textual strategies and new kinds of discourse are needed precisely because the world of the novel and the world outside the novel have traditionally borrowed from each other and have both been instrumental in enclosing women within certain limiting scripts. New social roles for women are not possible without new modes of writing and speaking. As a feminist novel, **Memorias de un solterón** calls for social change at the same time that it displays literary change, subverting the ideology and the textual strategies of realism/naturalism through a continued and complex play of intertextual references.

Notes

1. See, for example, Nelly Clemmessy 232, Carmen Bravo Villasante 210, and Teresa Cook 150.

2. Among the numerous novelistic texts that discuss this issue are Rosalía de Castro's *El caballero de las botas azules,* José M. de Pereda's *El buey suelto,* and Armando Palacio Valdés's *Marta y María.* Among the essayists who deal with the question in one form or other are Mariano José de Larra, Juan Valera, and Emilia Pardo Bazán.

3. Mesonero Romanos incorporates numerous references to his role as observer in his "artículos de costumbres." See, for example, "La calle de Toledo," "La romería de San Isidro," and "El observatorio de la Puerta del sol," among others, *OC,* I.

4. Both the dramatic ending and the mysterious background bring to mind numerous romantic dramas and, in particular, the duke of Rivas's *Don Alvaro.*

5. Julia Kristeva contrasts the symbolic, ordered, logical language of patriarchy with what she calls the "semiotic" or pre-Oedipal language of marginal groups. For a brief summary of this aspect of Kristeva's work, see Toril Moi.

6. Clearly not every novel written during this period employs an omniscient narrator but the exceptions stand out and are often interpreted as innovative code-breakers, as is the case with Galdós's *El amigo manso.*

7. Bieder points out a confusion in the relation of narrator and narratee in *Memorias.* In combination with the changing narrative technique, this incongruency underscores the "literary" quality of the text, constantly foregrounding those aspects of the novel that are normally camouflaged. Furthermore, through the frequent "inconsistencies" in the relationship of the narrator and the narratee, the novel challenges the canon, inserting instabilities that open the text to other forms of discourse.

Works Cited

Abel, Elizabeth, Marianne Hirsch, and Elizabeth Langland. *The Voyage In.* Hanover, New Hampshire: University Press of New England, 1983.

Bieder, Maryellen. "La comunicación narrativa en *El amigo manso,* de Benito Pérez Galdós." *Actas del VIII Congreso de la Asociación Internacional de Hispanistas.* Vol. 1. Madrid: Istmo, 1986.

Bloom, Harold. *The Anxiety of Influence.* New York: Oxford University Press, 1979.

Bravo Villasante, Carmen. *Vida y obra de Emilia Pardo Bazán.* Madrid: E.M.E.S.A. [Editorial Magisterio Español], 1973.

Clemessy, Nelly. *Emilia Pardo Bazán: Romancière.* Paris: Centre de Recherches Hispaniques, 1973.

Cook, Teresa A. *El feminismo en la novela de la Condesa de Pardo Bazán.* La Coruña: Editorial Gráfica, 1976.

Culler, Jonathan. *The Pursuit of Signs.* Ithaca, New York: Cornell University Press, 1981.

DuPlessis, Rachel. *Writing Beyond the Ending: Narrative Strategies of 20th Century Women Writers.* Bloomington, Indiana: Indiana University Press, 1985.

Gilbert, Susan and Sandra Gubar. *The Madwoman in the Attic.* New Haven, Connecticut: Yale University Press, 1979.

Mesonero Romanos, Ramón. *Memorias de un setentón.* Madrid: Tebas, 1975.

———. *Obras completas.* Madrid: Renacimiento, 1925.

Moi, Toril. *Sexual/Textual Politics.* London: Methuen, 1985.

Pardo Bazán, Emilia. *Obras completas.* Madrid: Aguilar, 1973.

Pérez Firmat, Gustavo. "Apuntes para un modelo de la intertextualidad en literatura." *Romanic Review* 69 (1978):1-14.

Pérez Galdós, Benito. *Obras completas,* IV. Madrid: Aguilar, 1966.

Scholes, Robert. *Semiotics and Interpretation.* New Haven, Connecticut: Yale University Press, 1982.

Francie Cate-Arries (essay date May 1992)

SOURCE: Cate-Arries, Francie. "Murderous Impulses and Moral Ambiguity: Emilia Pardo Bazán's Crime Stories." *Romance Quarterly* 39, no. 2 (May 1992): 205-10.

[*In the following essay, Cate-Arries explores Pardo Bazán's penchant for stories of "violence, deceit, and death," such as her novella* La gota de sangre *and her short stories "En el presidio" and "Crimen libre."*]

In an article published in *La Ilustración Artística* in 1909, Emilia Pardo Bazán writes somewhat wistfully of her secret desire to join the ranks of professional crime solvers: "Todos llevamos dentro algo de instinto policíaco; cuando leo en la prensa el relato de un crimen, experimento deseos de verlo todo, los sitios, los muebles, suponiendo que, de poder hacerlo así, averiguaría mucho y encontraría la pista del criminal verdadero."[1] It is well known that the Condesa confined her restless powers of detection to her armchair; indeed,

criminals and their victims fill a wide range of her short stories and novelettes. In this essay I propose to examine the implications of Pardo Bazán's recurring appropriation of crime as anecdote in her short fiction.

The most logical place to start the investigation is with Pardo Bazán's best-known crime story, the novelette *La gota de sangre,* published in 1911. So begin other critics who have tracked the Galician novelist's incursion into the realm of murder and mystery. Paredes highlights the short novel in his study of doña Emilia's detective fiction (pp. 262-74). Anthony Clarke focuses his 1973 article, "Doña Emilia Pardo Bazán y la novela policíaca," on *La gota,* critiquing the Spanish work according to criteria based on British models of crime-solvers.[2] The narrator-protagonist Selva himself is constantly aware of Sherlock Holmes's influence. Implicated in the murder of a wealthy businessman, Selva is framed in fact by the real assassin. To clear his own name and to bring the guilty party to justice, the accused takes it upon himself to solve the crime. Early on, the narrator acknowledges the pre-existing literary model that generates his own text, and motivates his decision to follow in the footsteps of the fictional amateur detectives that have gone before him: "Quizá me ha sugerido tal propósito la lectura de esas novelas inglesas que ahora están de moda, y en que hay policías de afición, o sea *detectives* por *sport.* Ya sabe Ud. que así como el hombre de la Naturaleza refleja impresiones directas, el de la civilización refleja lecturas."[3] In a quasi-metafictional moment, Selva self-consciously attempts to assume the role he has learned through the mediation of literary forms: "Tenía yo que jugar un poco al *detective* y servirme de medios un tanto extravagantes, con espíritu de novela jurídicopenal" (p. 1178). Later, stumped by the turn of events, he muses, "En mi situación, ¿qué haría un *detective* profesional?" (p. 1179). His answer is lifted directly from the pages of fiction: don a disguise, affect an accent. By the end of the story, the narrator is so captivated by the British model of detection that he announces his intention of setting off to England to pursue his new-found profession, "a tomar lecciones de los maestros" (p. 1187). The narrator's tale concludes with the promise of future escapades to be shared with the reader: "Traeré al descubrimiento de los crímenes elementos novelescos e intelectuales, y acaso un día podré contar al público algo digno de la letra de imprenta" (p. 1187).

The next year, in 1912, the author does offer a similar detective story, **"La cana,"** in which another narrator-protagonist is framed for a murder. Again, using the same powers of deduction, the accused exonerates himself and aids police in the apprehension of the real criminal. But despite the expectations raised in the closing pages of **La gota de sangre,** Pardo Bazán's amateur sleuth Selva never reappears in subsequent publications. In fact, following the appearance of "La cana" in the collection *Cuentos trágicos,* doña Emilia completely abandons this type of detective fiction. In 1916, she refers to her disillusionment with the genre of crime stories which have become so popular in her day: "Fijémonos en que la característica de tales novelas policíacas es la acción, no como resultado de móviles psicológicos, sino por sí misma, como el salto sin finalidad del acróbata de circo."[4] Her rejection of crime literature that focuses on the criminal act itself was prefigured some 25 years earlier in 1894 in a curious prologue to Pardo Bazán's novel *Doña Milagros.* In the short allegorical preface, a convicted murderer meets his Maker, finding to his surprise that he will not be condemned to burn in eternal Hell: "¿Conque no soy asesino? ¿No soy criminal?" The booming voice of the Creator responds: "El hecho descarnado nada significa para mí. . . . El beso de Judás fue asesinato; el tajo de Pedro, que cercenó la oreja a Malco, fue caricia. Cuando Pedro desenvainó la espada, rebosaba amor por mi Hijo. Intenciones, motivos, pensamientos . . . Hechos, no. . . . El hecho es la cáscara de la realidad."[5]

It is at this point that the critic tracking the case of Emilia Pardo Bazán's attraction to murder, mystery, crime and criminals realizes that she has been led down the wrong path by her reading of stories like *La gota de sangre.* By allowing herself to be seduced by the narration of the riveting criminal acts themselves and the ingenious solutions to the murder, she has failed to discover any meaningful clues as to why Pardo Bazán returns time and again to the scene of a crime in her short fiction. The detective Selva's own seduction in *La gota de sangre* by the murderer's beautiful accomplice, la Chulita, may provide the key to understanding the essential common denominator shared by the disparate criminal acts scattered throughout La Condesa's work. Selva gazes into the eyes of la Chulita, and glimpses the very heart and soul of crime reflected there: "No era la mujer y sus ya conocidos lazos y redes lo que causaba mi fascinación maldita; era la idea de que aquella boca estaba macerada en el amargo licor del crimen, en la esencia de la maldad humana, que es también la esencia de nuestro ser decaído y al morderla gustaría la manzana fatal, la de nuestra perdición y nuestra vida miserable . . ." (p. 1181). Questions of original sin, humankind's fall from Grace, the struggle between the forces of good and evil, free will and the power of circumstance: this, then, is the stuff crimes are made of, at least according to Pardo Bazán's confabulation of them.[6]

The Condesa first explored the potential ramifications for literature of the Catholic concept of original sin in her well-known treatise on Naturalism, *La cuestión palpitante*: "Sólo la caída de una naturaleza originariamente pura y libre puede dar la clave de esta mezcla de nobles aspiraciones y bajos instintos, . . . de este *combate* que todos los moralistas, todos los psicólogos, todos los artistas se han complacido en sorprender, analizar y retratar" (*OC [Obras completas]*, 3, 579). The author recognizes that the twin imperative of human nature produces a particularly promising source of grist for the literary mill: "¡Qué horizontes tan vastos abre a la literatura esta concepción mixta de la voluntad humana!" (p. 579). A dozen years later, Pardo Bazán combines for the first time her elaboration of the concept of original sin with theoretical disquisitions about criminality in her *La nueva cuestión palpitante.* The new burning question of this most recent book concerns the legitimacy of current theories propagated by César Lombroso y Max Nordau. Pardo Bazán refers particularly to Lombroso's work—which includes the books *El criminal* and *El crimen político y las revoluciones*—explaining that his research has profoundly modified the concept of penal law. Both Lombroso's and Nordau's studies classify criminal, insane, or "degenerate" behaviour as products of physiological or pathological processes, and largely ignore the factors of free will, circumstance, and intention. Not surprisingly, the Catholic Spanish author dismisses such theories as being simplistic and reductive: "La salud y normalidad intelectual y física, que Lombroso considera como el genio algo concreto, positivo y absoluto, no es más que un estado transitorio, relativo, modificable. . . . Así como no existe hombre enteramente justo—ya sabemos que el mejor cae 7 veces al día—tampoco lo hay enteramente sano ni enteramente cuerdo" (*OC,* 3, 1168). She rejects the proposed notion of the "criminal nato"—"Embriones de iniquidad, de *pecado* . . . no faltan en ningún hijo de Adán" (p. 1168)—and expresses a growing fascination with the external forces capable of producing deviant behaviour: "La embriaguez, el miedo, la cólera, el hambre, el orgullo ofendido, los odios, exaltan el instinto de acometividad y destructividad que reside en las profundidades del ser humano, y hacen de un hombre que parecía normal un insensato y tal vez un asesino" (p. 1168).

In March of 1885, Pardo Bazán had discovered a powerful literary appropriation of this criminal transformation in Dostoyevsky's *Crime and Punishment.* The Spanish writer, by her own admission, was profoundly impressed by the psychological portrait of this "hombre que parecía normal" who acted upon murderous impulses. In *La revolución y la novela en Rusia,* she writes of Dostoyevsky's creation: "Horroriza que aquellos sentimientos tan bien estudiados sean humanos y todos los llevamos ocultos en algún rincón obscuro del alma; no sólo humanos, sino propios de una persona de gran cultura intelectual" (*OC,* 3, 860). In this novel, Pardo Bazán not only finds confirmed the lesson espoused by Catholic doctrine that no one is innocent: "Nadie es puro y perfecto; nadie deja de estar sujeto a flaquezas y miserias de la voluntad y del entendimiento también."[7] What she most admires is Dostoyevsky's masterful manipulation of moral absolutes: "Subvierte las nociones del bien y del mal hasta un grado increíble."[8]

It is in her own crime stories of violence, deceit, and death where Pardo Bazán will consistently call into question conventional notions of good and evil, criminality and socially condoned behavior. The author's ongoing experimentation with these issues in her fiction is especially evident in two radically different stories: **"En el presidio,"** published in 1916, and **"Crimen libre,"** of 1892. The narrator of **"En el presidio"** opens his story by painting a detailed picture of the hulking Juanote, the man convicted of a particularly gruesome murder. The lengthy, heavily naturalistic description of the prisoner appears at first glance to reduce him to little more than a sum of his animalistic parts: "De las orejas y de las manos mucho tendrían que contar los señores que se dedican a estudios criminológicos. . . . En fin, dibujarían el tipo del criminal nato" (*OC,* 3, 99). But the narrator's interlocutor, the prison warden, offers an unexpected twist in the presentation of this brutal murderer. The warden explains that Juanote refused to comply with his accomplices' insistence that he kill the young boy who witnessed the murder. His act of kindness saved the boy's life, but jeopardized his own freedom when the youngster did indeed betray him to the authorities. The irony of Juanote's position is made clear; he is in jail "no por su crimen, sino por su buen sentimiento." The warden concludes his tale to the narrator by affirming the thin line separating criminals from the rest of society: ". . . las acciones de los mayores criminales, en lo habitual, no se diferencian tanto, tanto, de las del hombre normal, de bien" (p. 101).

The narrator of the second story "Crimen libre," meets with two friends in the casino to pass the time by agreeing to "arreglar el Código y reformar la legislación penal." The narrator tells his listeners of a skating accident in which two young boys fall through the ice. A bystander strips and throws himself into the frigid water. He emerges with the boys to find that someone has stolen his trousers. The narrator explains the significance of the anecdote: "Existe un orden de crímenes que no puede estimar como tales la ley, y, sin embargo, revelan en su autor más perversidad, más ausencia de sentido moral que ninguna de las acciones penadas por el Código" (*OC,* 1, 1502). Pardo Bazán's refusal to base a moral judgement solely on the act itself recalls the words of the prologue to **Doña Milagros** cited earlier: "Intenciones, motivos, pensamientos . . . Hechos, no . . . El hecho es la cáscara de la realidad" (*OC,* 2, 353).

The complexity of moral questions raised in Pardo Bazán's crime stories is further exploited by her treatment of "guilty" perpetrators of criminal acts and "innocent" bystanders affected by them. The often blurred boundaries drawn between the two groups are representative of general tendencies in nineteenth-century crime literature. Beth Kalikoff notes in her analysis of the evolution of Victorian murder stories: "Responsibility for murder moves closer and closer to the ordinary citizen or reader. . . . Responsibility for crime moves toward the hearth and, more distressingly, into the mirror."[9] Indeed, both amateur detectives of **La gota de sangre** and **"La cana"** share an unsettling sense of complicity with the murderers that they track. Even as Selva—self-appointed "righter of wrongs"—endeavors to bring the guilty party to justice in **La gota,** he himself feels incriminated by his questionable liaison with the murderer's seductive partner in crime: "Acababa de comprometerme a salvar a la mujer, y mi compromiso me hacía, en cierto modo cómplice de los dos reos. . . . Una parte del pecado me correspondía ya" (*OC,* 1, 1181-82).

The narrator of **"La cana"** is proven innocent of murder at the end of the story. But he is similarly overwhelmed by the disquieting recognition of his own moral shortcomings, and concomitant unwitting role in the crime.[10] His lack of confidence in personal blamelessness echoes in the silence following his closing remarks: "Yo no era asesino ni ladrón pero . . ." (*OC,* 1, 1821). Yet another protagonist of the murder mystery "Nube de paso"—published with **"La cana"** in 1911—refers to the feeling of shared guilt that haunts the most "innocent" witnesses of crime: "Cien testigos afirmaban nuestra inculpabilidad, y, así y todo, nos quedó de aquel lance yo no sé qué: una sombra moral en el espíritu, que ha pesado, creo yo, sobre nuestra vida . . ." (*OC,* 1, 1824).

Pardo Bazán's short story characters are not the only creatures called upon to confront their own moral accountability for others' socially deviant behavior. In various essays—most notably those addressing "crimes of passion"—the author points an accusatory finger at Kalikoff's "ordinary citizen or reader." In one of two such pieces, Pardo Bazán condemns society as a whole for essentially condoning the crime which she most vehemently denounces, the "crimen pasional": "Con este nombre especioso, se cohonestan las acciones más inicuas. . . . Y por esta simpatía, y esta excusa prevenida siempre para el llamado 'delincuente pasional' tiene razón Oliver, cuando titula su drama *El crimen de todos.* La sociedad, al prevenir al individuo la impunidad y hasta la aprobación cuando mata, es tan criminal como él; es, en efecto, cómplice, y casi diré que más culpada que el mismo autor de la fechoría."[11] The Catholic countess reminds her reader in "Coletilla a 'La cuestión palpitante'" that "la naturaleza humana está viciada por el pecado, y que no somos espíritus puros" (*OC,* 3, 658); her meditations on crime are particularly informed by this fundamental belief.

In her study of the nineteenth-century Spanish story, Lou Charnon-Deutsch analyzes the evolution of the genre from its earliest treatment at the hands of the *costumbristas*. The narrator created by these authors, notes Charnon-Deutsch, "assumes that the difference between right and wrong is something graspable and translatable into fiction."[12] The critic characterizes the later generation of Spanish *cuentistas* as writers in search of a dialectic, whose insistence is "less and less on the character's innate goodness or evilness, and more on the process that leads a character from innocence to corruption" (p. 166). For Pardo Bazán, the vehicle that allows her most dramatically to lay bare the often tenuous relationship between right and wrong, good and evil, is certainly the crime story. Here she may detect a glimmer of goodness in the darkest of souls; by the same token, seemingly innocuous acts may be charged with perversity. As armchair detective, la Condesa is hot on the trail of moral ambiguity, retracing the steps to that place where innocence and guilt, criminality and goodness intersect and overlap: at the scene of the crime story.

Notes

1. Quoted by Juan Paredes Nuñez, *Los cuentos de Emilia Pardo Bazán* (Universidad de Granada, 1979), p. 268.

2. *BBMP* [*Boletín de la Biblioteca de Menéndez Pelayo*] 49 (1973): 375-91.

3. Emilia Pardo Bazán, *La gota de sangre, Obras completas,* 1 (Madrid: Aguilar, 1947), 1168.

4. "El porvenir de la literatura después de la guerra," *Obras completas,* 3 (Madrid: Aguilar, 1973), 1547.

5. "Prólogo en el cielo," *Doña Milagros, Obras completas,* 2 (Madrid: Aguilar, 1964), 353. Maurice Hemingway cites this passage as evidence of Pardo Bazán's increasing interest in psychology: "The novel's prologue suggests that the sympathy with which she treats individual psychology and situations owes something to a Christian worldview . . . 'Judge not, that ye be not judged'," *Emilia Pardo Bazán: The Making of a Novelist,* (Cambridge University Press, 1983), p. 132.

6. See Maurice Hemingway's "Grace, Nature, Naturalism and Pardo Bazán," *Forum for Modern Language Studies* 16 (1980): 341-49, for a discussion of these key questions in the context of the novelist's "wider aesthetic intentions" (p. 342).

7. *La nueva cuestión palpitante, OC,* 3, 1168.

8. *La revolución y la novela en Rusia, OC,* 3, 861.

9. *Murder and Moral Decay in Victorian Popular Literature* (Ann Arbor: UMI Research Press, 1986), p. 169.

10. While Clarke notes that "Ni Selva ni X [the protagonist of "La cana"] se presentan sin mancha moral" (p. 390), he fails to offer interpretative commentary of the broader implications of this peculiar "moral contamination" that plagues these and other of Pardo Bazán's characters in the crime stories.

11. Quoted by Paredes Nuñez, p. 257.

12. *The Nineteenth-Century Spanish Story: Textual Strategies of a Genre in Transition* (London: Tamesis Books, 1985), p. 165.

Elizabeth A. Scarlett (essay date 1994)

SOURCE: Scarlett, Elizabeth A. "The Body-as-Text in Emilia Pardo Bazán's *Insolación.*" In *Under Construction: The Body in Spanish Novels,* pp. 10-45. Charlottesville: University Press of Virginia, 1994.

[*In the following essay, Scarlett contends that Pardo Bazán's* Insolación *depicts the female body as a "historical, cultural, biological, and political construct."*]

The "room of one's own" that Virginia Woolf saw as essential to the flourishing of a woman's literary career lay out of reach for the vast majority of Spanish women of the nineteenth century. Widespread illiteracy reached epidemic proportions in the female population, and the Napoleonic Code, imposed in Spain in 1804 and continuing unweakened except for a brief respite from 1868 to 1875, placed married women in a permanent legal infancy. Meanwhile, feminism burgeoned in countries where industrialization and Protestantism coincided. The dominant culture of Spain lacked both a tradition of free thought and a strong industrial base, except in parts of Catalonia and the Basque country.[1] Only women of very high social status who were encouraged from childhood to go a different route—as illustrated by Javier Herrero in his biography of Cecilia Böhl de Faber (1796-1877)—could beat the odds against a woman's gaining access to the forum of literature, carving out a space of their own where none had existed before.[2] Böhl used the pen name Fernán Caballero to publish novels that bridge the gap between romantic *costumbrismo,* a movement that emphasized local custom and "color," and modern realism with a hefty dose of traditional moral didacticism.

In contrast, Emilia Pardo Bazán (1851-1921) took up writing with an explicitly feminist agenda. Her essays demonstrate a more unequivocal championing of feminist causes than do her novels. Among other contributions, she translated John Stuart Mill's *Subjection of Women* (1869) and became the first chaired professor, or *catedrática,* in a Spanish university in 1916. As she did for literary naturalism in *La cuestión palpitante* (1882), Pardo Bazán endeavored to make feminism palatable to the Spanish reading public in a predominantly hostile atmosphere where feminism was viewed "as another heretical legacy of the French Revolution: a hybrid monster unleashed by the enemies of the faith and of Spain with the intention of destroying Spanish national, social, and family life."[3] Her aims allied her with the broader movement toward the Europeanization of Spain, which was gaining momentum among her peers, and for inspiration in lieu of female feminist precursors she could trace her progressivism back to Padre Feijoo (1676-1764), a forebear of Spanish Enlightenment, about whom Pardo Bazán wrote a prizewinning poem and essay in 1876 (the year her first child was born).

While reading for a survey course on Spanish literature twelve years ago, I found that in Pardo Bazán's ***Insolación*** (1889) humor and irony, and a seemingly happy ending, enveloped a subtle, subversive subtext dealing with the heroine's dwelling inside a female body. I agreed with the novelist's most enthusiastic critics in regrading the work as a "small masterpiece," but for reasons other than those already articulated,[4] for I was responding primarily to this subtext rather than to the decorousness and grace for which the book is traditionally recommended. There was something unique in its treatment of a lived-in female body, or what I will call the female body as *vivencia,* as experience. Given the pervasive harnessing of women's physical energies for the purposes of reproduction, it is natural that the pursuit of pleasure for its own sake in this novel leads at first to a negatively charged significance of the body, or the body-turned-against-itself. The refreshing differences I perceived in the inscription of the female body had to do with the way this struggle in the protagonist's inner space turns the body into a main character and with the way the resolution, or lack of one, has the effect of saving the heroine from the fate of the "fallen angel," a fate that was common in novels by the two other paragons of the nineteenth-century realist novel, Pardo Bazán's longtime lover Benito Pérez Galdós and her friend-turned-rejected-suitor-turned-enemy Leopoldo Alas (Clarín).

With Sandra Gilbert and Susan Gubar's notion of an "anxiety of female authorship" in the nineteenth century, the meaning of the body-against-itself broadens. Since the source of anxiety of authorship emanates from gender identification, it follows that for a large part of the work the protagonist's body should be represented as a vulnerability and that when the sexual instinct—Pardo Bazán's naturalist translation of *desire*—located in her body awakens, it should speak at first in a code of pain, fever, nausea, violence, suffocation, paralysis, and sensual overload. Spatial representations in the novel repeat the bodily code of discomfort through a sense of confinement and inescapable heat. The sun acts as a mediator of desire, connecting inner bodily space and outer stimuli; the protagonist's shifting attitudes toward desire chart her progress toward abandoning social norms. The close tie that exists between Asís as transgressing female lover and Pardo Bazán as transgressing female writer is constantly reinforced in both the narratorial voice and the content of the work.

In the language of contemporary French feminism, which in turn is based upon Jacques Lacan's revisionist interpretations of Freudian psychoanalysis, the "law of the Father" reigns over the Symbolic realm, a stage we enter early in life when we realize our separateness from the Mother, who previously was viewed as being in harmonious and perfect union with us. Once we have made this realization, our only access to the lost perfect state is by the substitution of signifiers for what is now perceived as missing. Language then becomes the medium through which our semiotic drive courses in its never-ending quest, and the figure of the Father takes on importance as an intermediary in social intercourse.[5]

So strong is the law of the Father in the work of Emilia Pardo Bazán that the mother-daughter dyad never achieves preeminence; the protagonist has a daughter who is mentioned fleetingly and for this reason seems conspicuously cast aside. This may be one reason why, as Ordóñez points out, contemporary women writers in Spain look, not to past writers, but to foreign counterparts for a sense of community.[6] Perhaps the baggage with which Pardo Bazán must struggle is too great, for she is often found explaining things to, assuaging, and cajoling the Father, as evidenced in her epistolary efforts to persuade her traditionalist friend Menéndez y Pelayo of the wholesomeness of her literary intentions.[7]

What immediately concerns the protagonist Asís Taboada, a widowed marquess in her early thirties who hails from Vigo, Galicia, and resides part of the year in Madrid, is the reaction of her confessor, Father Urdax. His opprobrium will surely be unleashed upon her when she begins to recount to him the previous day's adventures. Whether she has done anything immoral yet or whether her conduct while accompanying a gentleman she had just met at a friend's house to a local festival has been merely unseemly depends upon how one reads some highly ambiguous and elusive passages. Maurice Hemingway finds her first foray blameless, while Donald Shaw recounts that the lady has "seriously compromised herself."[8] This is exactly the undecidable quality cultivated as a hedge against the Father's law. Despite the warnings of her conscience, Asís will continue to see her new acquaintance and soon will spend the night with him. After her brief, unsuccessful attempt at escaping the situation by returning to Galicia, the couple suddenly decides to marry, and the novel abruptly ends.

As she anticipates, her own tale will be filled with circumlocutions, palliatives, ellipses, disclaimers, excuses, and explanatory notes, literary devices to which both she and the author must resort if they are to avoid the wrath of the Father. Urdax is allied with a broader, male-dominated power constellation; when the narrative is not following Asís mentally composing the confession she plans to make to him, it follows the narrator speaking to a group of "señores"—gentlemen and *perhaps* ladies.[9] The confessional mode into which the novel deftly slips places a guilty heroine answering to male authority in a way that is not at all random. Foucault has articulated the power relation inherent by definition in the confession: "One confesses—or one is forced to confess. . . . The confession is a ritual of discourse in which the speaking subject is also the subject of the statement; it is also a ritual that unfolds within a power relationship, for one does not confess without the presence (or virtual presence) of a partner who is not simply the interlocutor but the authority who requires the confession, prescribes and appreciates it, and intervenes in order to judge, punish, forgive, console, and reconcile."[10]

The imagined confession takes up about a third of the novel. Whether this confession, or a similar one, is ever actually uttered by the heroine is not disclosed, for by the end of the story she has succeeded in releasing the hold of the Father's law over her mind and body to the extent that this is no longer a concern. For the duration of the narrator's recording of Asís's planned confession, however, the logocentric gentleman is ever present in the mind of Asís the narrator, and that presence is closely associated with her physical suffering:

> Intentólo en efecto [rezar]; mas si por un lado era soporífera la operación, por otro agravaba las inquietudes y resquemores íntimos de la señora. Bonito se pondría el padre Urdax cuando tocasen a confesarse de aquella cosa inaudita y estupenda. . . . ¿Qué circunloquios serían más adecuados para atenuar la primera impresión de espanto y la primera filípica? ¡Sí, sí, circunloquios al padre Urdax! ¡El, que lo preguntaba todo derecho y claro, sin pararse en vergüenzas ni en reticencias!

> [She did in fact try to pray; but if on the one hand the enterprise made her sleepy, on the other it aggravated the lady's personal doubts and worries. Wouldn't Father Urdax have a fit when the time came to confess that outrageous and spectacular thing. . . . What manner of circumlocutions would be the most adequate for lessening the first frightful impression and the first invective? Yes, indeed, circumlocutions for Father Urdax! He, who asked everything straightforwardly and clearly, without pausing for embarrassment or hesitation!][11]

The hedges Asís plans to use to mitigate the Father's wrath are similar to the devices the third-person narrator will use in the remaining two-thirds of the text to distance herself from the protagonist's actions, which is to say, when the narrator is not playing Asís's accomplice. The narration of the latter part of the novel approximates the protagonist's "inner" thoughts somewhat less closely through the use of *style indirect libre*, which

style occurs whenever the perspective slips almost imperceptibly from an external one to one that copies the character's inner thoughts, without switching from third-person to first-person narration. Hemingway has dealt convincingly with the elusiveness of this second narrator and with the reactions his or her refusal to unambiguously state value judgments elicited among prominent writers and critics of the time; Leopoldo Alas, the old friend turned enemy, who was instrumental in preventing Pardo Bazán's entry into the Real Academia de la Lengua, expressed particular exasperation and disgust.[12] More radical interpretations of the narrator's unmistakable ambivalence toward the opposition of civilization to barbarism and his or her failure to adorn the love affair with the trappings of romantic love are overlooked by Hemingway in favor of two motivations he finds ubiquitous in the author's work: a concern with the tension between romanticism and realism and the goal of portraying human relationships "as ultimately mysterious."[13] While these are undeniable products of the narratorial mode, the political aspect of Pardo Bazán as a writing woman clamors for attention in these obvious examples of conflict with the norms of logocentric and patriarchal narrative authority. In this respect, Tolliver has cited Bakhtin's concept of the hybrid construction, a narrative structure composed of two opposing semantic and axiological belief systems, in an enlightening explanation for the hedges, ambiguities, disclaimers, and ellipses of narration in *Insolación*.[14]

Through moral constraints and the physical suffering the reader assumes to have something to do with her feelings of guilt, Asís's body at the outset is as surely under the Father's control as her consciousness. The more it breaks free, the more problematic it becomes to Asís's mind, which has internalized the Father's law. In this manner, one of the most time-honored of binary oppositions of patriarchal culture, mind/body dualism, is established in the text because of the author's partial adherence to "scientific" naturalism. According to this French offshoot of nineteenth-century positivism, evidently a literary version of the "useful and public discourses" deployed to regulate sexuality, "race, milieu, et moment" are main determinants of human behavior. For this very reason, Pardo Bazán cannot be an uncritical disciple of it; she verbalizes some of her points of contention in *La cuestión palpitante* (1883), while others appear only as they spontaneously occur in her fiction. The body enters the naturalist formula mainly through the first term, *race,* encompassing drives and instincts that flow "in the blood," in addition to the outward physical appearance, or phenotype, of the individual. Readers would not find *Insolación* to be such an engaging narrative of sexual awakening, however, if Pardo Bazán had not gone further than the setting down of the binary opposition of barbaric body to civilized mind, to its ultimate ironizing, subversion, and dissolution. Robert Scari has catalogued the humorous devices that lead to this effect and help to camouflage the lack of an explicit and unflinching moral condemnation of the lovers' premarital affair.[15] The laugh of the Medusa rings audibly in the pervasiveness of humor of various forms, all of which contribute to the defusing and overturning of the predictable messages of dominant discourse.

The reader enters Asís's consciousness just as she reaches wakefulness. Both are greeted with images of throbbing pain, excruciatingly described: drills and red-hot tongs are boring into her temples, and needles stab her scalp. It seems like a scene taken from the Inquisition, or from an Edgar Allan Poe re-creation of the Inquisition. Only later, when the cause for this pain becomes clear, do we realize that its source is far more quotidian. But then it is the excess of the pain, if we consider the incident from which it has resulted, that is striking. For clearly, Asís suffers too much, and in an overly determined way, for this to be an ordinary hangover. The sensual bombardment that characterizes this short novel as a whole likens it to the Victorian sensation novel, known for its performative dimension, or its ability to produce similar states in the reader, and for feminizing nervous distress.[16] The pairing of mental awakening and bodily pain establishes from the very outset the founding of Asís's character "on the indissoluble unity of body and soul."[17] That this pain afflicts areas surrounding the brain signals the conflict between mind and instinct (localized diffusely in the body through the concept of "blood," which comes to signify race). Pardo Bazán's poetics of pain draws on metonymical relationships between parts of the body and their moral functions. Asís's cheeks burn, and her mouth is also affected: its bitterness and aridity almost impede her speech as she mumbles the first utterance to her maid, asking her to soften the arrow of light that has assaulted her eyes. Her punishment fits the crime, and her suffering corresponds neatly to the logic of an eye for an eye, in that each bodily part affected had its role in her transgression of the previous day. The sins of having spoken, seen, and thought evil are translated directly into physical ills. With wry hyperbole, the narrator compares Asís to St. Lorenzo, martyred on the grill. The language of the body becomes textualized as the lived-in body charts Asís's actions and their consequences. Likewise, the text is embodied as it is coopted into following her quest, conscious or otherwise, for sensual pleasure.

The elements of exposure, illness, and intensity of light and heat, all sememes of the one-word title, become a code through which the body speaks throughout much of the work. It is not so much the external phenomenon of a sunburst that is being conveyed (a possible meaning of the title), but its effects on various parts of the body and, inevitably, on Asís's mind, which in this way comes to be viewed as inseparable from her vulnerable body. Her body appears mainly in fragmented form in reaction to pain, as each separate symptom or source of discomfort emerges, and is not represented as a cohesive whole until later in the text, when it assumes an active role. This articulation of the body answers, in symmetrical opposition, to the synecdoche male writers have tended to employ, textually isolating and fetishizing each part of the female form as an object viewed from the outside. Rather than focusing on the sensations each part makes known to the subject or to the totality of body and mind, the mode of representation still predominant among male authors of the time portrays each feminine attribute in a highly stylized manner specific to a particular male-defined aesthetic of femininity.[18]

Gilbert and Gubar describe the tradition of discomfort and disease imagery in writing by nineteenth-century British and American women as symptomatic of their dis-ease with the male-dominated endeavor of writing.[19] If, as Harold Bloom writes of poets, an author (male by default) in the act of literary creation is on some level answering to and seeking to oust a father figure in the guise of preexisting authors,[20] might not the Freudian family drama have a different configuration in the case of women writers, and might this not find expression in the resulting texts? Gilbert and Gubar postulate convincingly—on the basis of close readings of Mary Shelley, the Brontë sisters, George Eliot, Emily Dickinson, and others—that the nineteenth-century woman writer was confronted by something still more formidable than the basic anxiety of influence that challenged male writers. For her there was also the lack of female precursors, persuading her that she herself could not become a literary precursor. In some French feminism we find something similar expressed in the idea that women are deprived of the "phallus," the ultimate sociolinguistic signifier, and hence exist outside of culture, language, and writing.

Furthermore, the dearth of women writers in the nineteenth century stands in contrast to the predominance of women represented in fiction as main characters, often lending their names to the novels that contain them. In Spain this asymmetry was all the more pronounced. On the one hand, novels such as *Pepita Jiménez, La Regenta, Fortunata y Jacinta,* and *La desheredada* display a concern for characterizing the female protagonist in increasing psychological and material detail, in keeping with the aims of fictional realism. Yet among Pardo Bazán's contemporaries, most of those empowered with authorship were male, and female precursors were few and far between. Before Pardo Bazán, the canon admitted few others besides Rosalía de Castro, Gertrudis Gómez de Avellaneda, Fernán Caballero (Cecilia Böhl de Faber), St. Teresa, and María de Zayas. Even in Pardo Bazán's wake, women novelists did not hasten to appear on the scene, and the anomalousness of those who did was reflected in a tongue-in-cheek advice column in the 1940s humor magazine *La Codorniz*:

Curiosa.—Logroño

¿Las escritoras suelen ser simpáticas o atractivas, o no?

Hay de todo. Pero en la mayor parte de los casos muchas escritoras han empezado a escribir simplemente porque no encontraban a nadie con quien hablar.

[Women writers are usually pleasant and attractive, or aren't they?

—Curious in Logroño

There are all sorts. But in most cases many of them began to write simply because they couldn't find anyone to talk to.][21]

Spanish women writers indeed found few others with whom to "speak" on a textual level, and they were isolated from others of their gender if they defined themselves as writers. The concentration of Asís's pain, in the initial pages, in her head functions metonymically to unite her complaints with the constraints placed upon the mind of a woman with the desire to write. The double bind of lacking female precursors and abundant representation of women thereby intensifies the Father's law and creates a specifically feminine "anxiety of authorship," making a woman writer wary of becoming entrapped in the mirror of fiction. Since she has received the cultural message that the only place literature holds for women is as characters imagined by men, her persistence in writing may lead to fears of ceasing to exist, because she has written but cannot "be an author." This last conclusion may be extreme with reference to the intrepid countess who wrote *Insolación*, but Gilbert and Gubar do succeed in finding a prevalence of certain images, which they then relate to the situation of the nineteenth-century woman author: texts abound in silencing, submersion, and containment. In relation to the female body, the imagery often presents itself in scenes of aphasia, unconsciousness, and disease (or disease), which are often followed by flight, solitude, or smokescreens by means of which the author herself appears to vanish. Many of these images and devices show up in *Insolación.*

Asís's amorous transgressions draw her unmistakably close to Pardo Bazán as transgressing female writer. This may be what causes the narrator to seek increasingly to distance him- or herself from the protagonist as the latter grows more willing to ignore the precepts that had held her in check.[22] It may be argued that of all the characters authored by Pardo Bazán, Asís most closely resembles her creator in the incidents of biography, except, of course, for her being portrayed as neither an extraordinary intellect nor an author or even a *literata*. In addition, the incident is based loosely upon the novelist's relationship with José Lázaro Galdiano, to whom the book is dedicated.[23] This enables the transference of the "female author syndrome," so that it occurs more strongly (i.e., more readably) here than in her other works, although *Los pazos de Ulloa* (1886) and *La madre naturaleza* (1887) also present interesting subtexts having to do with female authorship.

As Gilbert and Gubar note, afflictions that incapacitate the mental faculties of female characters in works by women hold a privileged place: "Aphasia and amnesia—two illnesses which symbolically represent (and parody) the sort of intellectual incapacity patriarchal culture has traditionally required of women—appear and reappear in women's writings in frankly stated or disguised forms."[24]

Pardo Bazán battled the stifling patriarchal world that would silence her literary accomplishments: her husband finally left her over his discontent with her literary activities, and her ultimate aim of gaining entry to the Real Academia was stymied by male colleagues and rivals.[25] Asís, in turn, feels instruments of torture at work on her head and drifts in and out of consciousness at the fair. She is referred to alternately as "in a swoon or deceased," "spiritless," and in "syncope" (64, 96, 91). Her ability to reason is simultaneously questioned, as she feels herself to be "annihilated, in the most complete state of idiocy," "not in my right mind," and acting "like a fool" (95, 97, 99). Visual impairment is mentioned several times as another symptom of her distress (66, 67). An inability to speak clearly plagues her throughout the story, as she becomes hoarse or stutters in numerous situations with her male companion and during the morning-after episode. Affliction of the intellect also plagues Asís when she avers that she is incapable of relating her story satisfactorily (addressing her self-deprecating statements to Father Urdax), for lack of either verbal dexterity (41) or memory (96).

The motifs of nausea or seasickness and of suffocation or entrapment are still other forms of the dis-ease and disease that appear to be overdetermined by the femininity of character and author. These two kinds of imagery are surpassed only by heat as unifying elements in the poetics of the feminine mental and physical predicament in *Insolación.* The word *mareo* can refer to an entire spectrum of symptoms, from intoxication to nausea or seasickness. Asís avails herself of its nonspecificity to cloud the true nature and cause of her malaise. The reader infers, however, that her symptoms have much to do with her remaining in the company of an attractive and flirtatious man she does not know very well and finding herself in a throng of lower-class revelers at a festival that should be off-limits to a lady of her social standing. She applies the word *mareo* to the first dizziness, ostensibly caused by exposure to the sun, likening it to "a liquor that goes to one's head" (66), and also to the more vivid seasickness that takes hold when she feels herself adrift on a sea of human bodies:

> Al punto que nos metimos entre aquel bureo se me puso en la cabeza que me había caído en el mar: mar caliente, que hervía a borbotones, y en el cual flotaba yo dentro de un botecillo chico como una cáscara de nuez: golpe va y golpe viene, ola arriba y ola abajo. ¡Sí, era el mar, no cabía duda! ¡El mar, con toda la angustia y desconsuelo del mareo que empieza!

> [The instant we mixed in with the revelry I became convinced that I had fallen into the sea: a boiling hot sea in which I floated inside of a tiny bottle like a nutshell: blow after blow, one wave after another. Yes, it was surely the sea! The sea, with all the anguish and despair of seasickness setting in!]

(84)

In addition to seasickness, nausea, dizziness, and tipsiness, another meaning of *mareo* can be motion sickness, an important meaning when we consider that the protagonist's body, propelled by desire, is in effect traversing a labyrinth consisting of social norms and mores toward a destination unknown to it. The female body in motion acts out what Pardo Bazán would call its acquired shame through this illness, but no degree of motion sickness, not even when it results in unconsciousness, can halt its propulsion.

The illusion of being lost at sea, and hence at the mercy of the elements, is bolstered as the story continues and serves to underline the helplessness of woman in male-dominated society, once again running parallel to the predicament of the woman writer.[26] As the *mareo* worsens, Asís increasingly refers to a sensation of weightlessness: "I didn't even notice the weight of my body" (89). In this context of weakness and illness, the sensation does not bring gratifying freedom from natural laws, but a reinforcement of her body's insignificance and defenselessness: "If I were pushed with one finger, I would fall down and bounce like a ball" (89). All of this occurs tellingly after she has taken hold of her companion's arm for support and glimpsed a revolver in his pocket, an effort on his part to reassure her of safety. This only redoubles her dis-ease and puts her on guard, for she has as much to fear from this stranger as she does from the crowd. To say that it is the phallic quality of the revolver that reminds Asís of her powerlessness would seem banal to some, far-fetched to others. However, here and elsewhere in the novel Pardo Bazán plays half-humorously with phallic imagery to accent her heroine's sense of vulnerability. Ultimately, Asís succumbs to the maternal illusion of being surrounded and rocked by the sea; when she sits with Pacheco beside the Manzanares River, she sees round her the waves of her native Vigo and winds up shouting for the boat to stop, then fainting. An anecdote planted

earlier in the narrative relates that Alexandre Dumas once ceremoniously offered a glass of water as a donation to the trickling Manzanares. Even the reader unfamiliar with Madrid can then appreciate the amusing incongruity of Asís's suffering a fainting spell brought on by such a body of water. Furthermore, suspicion regarding the real cause of her ebbing strength continues to grow. As we learn from a quick flashback, this healthy, fun-loving woman has reached her early thirties without ever satisfying her sensual desires, and now that the possibility of doing so hovers as close as the gleaming revolver, the flaring of crude sexual instinct from within her body threatens to floor her and then succeeds. Out of interest in reclaiming feminine desire, Pardo Bazán couches in delicately humorous terms what she, as a naturalist, should only portray as the most animalistic of passions.

Still more incongruous, and therefore noticeably overdetermined by the subtext of the female-body-turned-against-itself, is the reappearance of torture imagery as Asís sits on the riverbank: "It was as though they were pulling out my stomach and insides with a hook in order to tear them out of my mouth" (91). Pérez Galdós, for example, reserves torture imagery of penetration such as this for Mauricia la Dura undergoing delirium tremens. The use of the third-person plural, an amorphous *they,* is reminiscent of the "legion of enemies" who try to extract her brains on the morning after (34). However humorously these similes are handled in the text, they emphasize the solitude of the female protagonist in her plight, the plurality and nebulosity of the agents of social subjection, and the vital importance of what is at stake. In these and nearly all of the torture images of *Insolación* there is penetration and violation of an inner bodily space, a space that is filled with some of the protagonist's essential organs, whether they be cerebral, digestive, or reproductive in function. The heightening and dramatization of discomfort into a scene of inquisitorial torment contrasts with the mundane or absurd incidents that appear in the story as their immediate provocation: a tame river, a four-legged woman in a sideshow, Asís's own distorted reflection in a funhouse mirror, the consumption of a heavy, hodge-podge lunch.

The seasickness motif will not subside until one final connection emerges. When Asís's first-person narration concludes and the "impersonal" one begins, one of the few retrospections of the text indicates that she lost her mother as a child (aligning her with the vast collection of motherless or orphaned heroines in novels by women from the Brontës to Carmen Martín Gaite) and was raised by her father. The same retrospection also relates that her first romantic interest was a naval officer with whom she corresponded. She broke off relations with the young man when a distant uncle courted and married her. The ensuing marriage is described as benignly affectionate, if lacking in passion; the womanly desire in Asís's body enters a remission of sorts as her avuncular husband keeps her safely within the family fold and she becomes a mother herself. But when her much older husband leaves her a "serene" (but not merry) widow, the affliction of desire is destined to flare up anew, and it carries the embedded nautical motif. The recurrence of seasickness suggests that her marriage never quite succeeded in erasing the memory of "the slender shadow with a white cap and golden anchors" (101).

The heat that oppresses Asís's body begins for the reader with her burning face and body on the morning after, which the narrator likens with irony to a martyrdom scene: "Both bed and body of the guilty one were burning, like St. Lorenzo on the grill" (38). In the plot it goes back to the beginning of her Sunday outing with Pacheco, when she innocently inserts a flower in his lapel and catches a whiff of his heady cologne, provoking in her face "an extraordinary heat" that Pacheco observes as a blush (59). Heat reaches an unbearable crescendo in the dream sequence that has Asís fleeing her lover by train across a parched Castile, her brain fairly simmering, her pleas for water met with offers of dry sherry, and her eyes bursting from their sockets like those of "cats being scalded" (183).

The personification of the agent of desire, suffering, and awakening as the sun god completes the progress toward an exclusively Thetic, Father-dominated stage begun in Pardo Bazán's earlier novels. In the rural environment of *La madre naturaleza* it is a vaguely personified mother nature behind the scenes that attracts two unknowingly incestuous lovers to each other. This label was seen as unsatisfactory by Gabriel Pardo de la Lage, who thought a better name for an entity that caused such tragedy would have been *stepmother*. In *Insolación* we are another step removed from the paradisiacal, rural union of mother and child—Asís grew up motherless, and in the urban landscape of Madrid there is no mother nature, but a ravaging male sun god, whom she and her lover finally greet as their patron deity.[27] Considered in the framework of the semiotic versus the Thetic or the Symbolic state, the urban setting of *Insolación* is clearly more related to the latter, and the Father's law thus emerges as more monolithic in its opposition to the female character. In *La madre naturaleza* there is still evidence of the "free play of drives" characteristic of the semiotic stage viewed in the representation of nature, even though the Father's law, in the form of social tabu against incest, curtails the wild, unbridled situation.

One of Lacan's most resonant writings, for Hispanists as well as feminists, is his analysis of the figure of St. Teresa's ecstasy as sculpted by Bernini. Irigaray also has incorporated this figure into her writings.[28] Lacan's placement of mystics in the schema of relations between the sexes can be applied to males as well, yet he finds in St. Teresa a powerful image of the inexpressible quality of feminine *jouissance* and of its relation to authoritative knowledge: "The male divinity is supported by (and perhaps even dependent on) the pleasure which woman experiences, but cannot express."[29] Feminine *jouissance* is correspondingly elusive in *Insolación*. Much is made of desire (in Lacan's terms, the gap that opens up between demand and need) through the harsh textual events previously described; and indeed for Lacan woman's desire is infinite, fixed as it is upon completion through union with some absolute *Autre,* or Other.

With an overwhelmingly male constellation of figures (the sun god, Father Urdax, the husband's ghost) mediating desire and suffering, only Asís's body is left to speak, in isolated instances, on behalf of the erotic and semiotic drives. Pleasure as well as pain is written upon her textual body. Most commonly this occurs merely as a relief from the discomforts of heat, suffocation, *mareo,* and the like. Relief keeps the body and its sensations ever present in the text and thus engages the reader's sensory imagination continuously in the way of the Victorian sensation novel. In the opening, morning-after passage, pleasant sensations alternate with relapses in rapid succession: her "nice and hot, well-prepared" infusion only causes more waves of nausea when it reaches her lips. Afterwards, she begins to feel a bit better when she lies down "curled up in a shell of cloth," and the association of maternity (in this case, a fetal position) with bodily well-being and pleasure appears for the first time in what will be a recurring cycle in the work. The pleasure principle alternates with bodily discomfort but never equals it in intensity. For there is no explicit moment of *jouissance* or bliss to balance the torment of sunbeaten senses—a curious thing in a novel that has been taken for a very light-hearted, even frivolous, one.[30]

Cleansing also becomes closely associated with relief and well-being. At first only the refreshing effect of water against Asís's face can bring about a respite from headache: "after this, she felt her thoughts become clearer and the tip of the drill withdrew little by little from her brain" (39). Later, bathing takes on the significance of moral cleansing, with the narrator explicitly exposing Asís's self-deception: "With each hygienic operation and each part of her body left clean as a gloss, Asís believed she saw the mark of the day before's immorality disappear, and, unwittingly confusing the physical with the moral, while grooming she thought she regenerated herself" (104).

The young woman slips into her ordinary-looking zinc bathtub, and a passage follows that has been labeled plagiarism by one critic.[31] Zola's *L'Assommoir* (1877) refers to an adulterous lover, Gervaise, who scrubs her hands and shoulders after each tryst as if to remove the moral stigma, and Pardo Bazán uses the essentials of the scene in Asís's toilette above. In its integration, however, it is reworked in a way that significantly differentiates it from Zola, making the charge of plagiarism inappropriate. In the first place, the correspondence between physical and moral cleansing is already a literary universal, as evidenced by Shakespeare's Lady Macbeth. In *Insolación* there is an earnestness of tone, as the narrator continues her gentle mocking of Asís, and an insistence upon material detail that reveals the action as ridiculous from a narratorial viewpoint:

> En el agua clara iban a quedarse la vergüenza, la sofoquina y las inconveniencias de la aventura. . . . ¡Allí estaban escritas con letras de polvo! Polvo doblemente vil, el polvo de la innoble feria! ¡Y cuidado que era pegajoso y espeso! ¡Si había penetrado al través de las medias, de la ropa interior, y en toda su piel lo veía depositado la dama!

> [The shame, discomfort, and improprieties of the affair would be left behind in the clear water. . . . There they were, written in letters of dust! Dust that was doubly vile, dust from the ignoble fair! And watch out, for it was sticky and thick! It had gotten through to the inside of her stockings, her underwear, and the lady saw it deposited all over her skin!]

(104-5)

In *L'Assommoir*, when Gervaise is disgusted with herself at the outset of her affair with Lantier, she succinctly washes her hands, wets a dishrag, and goes about scrubbing her shoulders "as if to rub them off."[32] What lies latent in Zola's text, and what Pardo Bazán develops in her passage with gentle mockery, is the female body as a text that records its transgressions. This is where the primary "writing" of *Insolación* takes place—in letters of dust on the subject's very skin, cutting through the secondary, cultural trappings of clothing. Asís's body comes to bear the marks of the incompleteness of its social subjection. The fundamental unity of body and mind is clear in that only Asís, because of her disconcertion, can read the writing on her body. Then, she is careful to erase her bodily text, as its contents are potentially incriminating.[33]

Still, critics scold Pardo Bazán as though she were an unscrupulous schoolgirl for what is actually an intertextual reference to Zola that adds semiotic value to the "borrowed" material. In so doing they discard the pious tone reserved for male authors. Adding insult to incrimination, Robert E. Osborne offers Pardo Bazán's supposed real-life obsession with personal neatness as an explanation. When she names scores of articles for feminine use that scarcely appear elsewhere in Spanish literature—the *antuca* she mentions (56) is an obscure and specialized item, a sort of parasol—she is following a realist tendency to record the material, and especially the visual, details of everyday life. The difference is that she does so from a female viewpoint, capturing a nearly lost quotidian language that includes words borrowed from other languages that more *castizo* authors avoid, concerned with keeping Spanish pure of foreign influences (the *antuca* derives from *en tout cas*). Just as the realists intended to arrive at the essential by means of the material, Pardo Bazán suggests the severity of feminine codes of conduct with such concrete details as the "bristled glove, softened with almond paste and honey," used to scrub the neck, and the constricting corset, which must be removed when Asís faints. The proliferation of these feminine artifacts serves not so much to provide additional objects for use in visualizing the commodified heroine (as in Galdós and Clarín) as to detail the complicated process of transforming oneself into a socially presentable woman.

While decorum circumvents a textual arrival at full-fledged bliss, ecstasy, *gozo,* or *jouissance* in *Insolación,* there are moments of joy, or *regocijo,* expressed in physical terms. These moments appear when, in the first days of her acquaintance with Pacheco, Asís walks in the open air and responds to the pleasurable effects of the sun and atmosphere before these become overwhelmingly powerful. Specifically, her body responds actively to these sensations, and speaks to "herself" (her consciousness, her soul), across the chasm of the mind/body split:

> Ganas me entraron de correr y brincar como a los quince, y hasta se me figuraba que en mis tiempos de chiquilla no había sentido nunca tal exceso de vitalidad, tales impulsos de hacer extravagancias, de arrancar ramas de árbol y de chapuzarme en el pilón presidido por aquella buena señora de los leones. . . . Nada menos que estas tonterías me estaba pidiendo el cuerpo a mí.

> [I suddenly felt the urge to run and jump like when I was fifteen, and it even seemed to me that as a little girl I had never experienced such an excess of vitality, such impulses to do extravagant things, to pull out tree branches and to splash about in the fountain presided over by that good lady with her lions. . . . My body was asking me for nothing less than this sort of foolishness.]

(52)[34]

Likewise, at the start of the St. Isidro Festival, she finds physical pleasure unexpectedly taking hold, although she purposely checks her impulses and maintains propriety against the effects of alcohol: "All I experienced was a most pleasant liveliness, with my tongue loosened, my senses enhanced, my spirit aflutter, and my heart contented" (81). Her body is vocal once more when a theater date is suggested by a friend: "No: what my body asks of me is exercise" (122). The *cuerpo que pide,* or requesting body, would be hard to encounter in the writings of male authors of the day. As Smith and others have noted, the "commodity fetishism" played upon in works by Galdós sees the female body for its external accountrements only.[35] In *La de Bringas,* for example, there is insistence on clothing and fashion in a way that makes them continuous or synonymous with the body, and blazonlike renderings of the bodily parts. Lou Charnon-Deutsch accounts for this materialist objectification by the influence of serialized novels, illustrated reviews, and other popular literature of mass consumption that recycled old female stereotypes by bringing dress and mannerisms up to date.[36]

In *Insolación* the body exists independently as a desiring subject in its own right. As extensions of the protagonist's inhabited body, four distinct types of space emerge in the course of the novel: the aristocratic domestic interior, the urban thoroughfare, the popular carnival or inn (on the fringes of urban settlement and society), and, finally, the oneiric (here, a train compartment). Except for the last one, all are socially shared in a direct way. All firmly connect with motifs of helplessness and entrapment they elicit in the heroine, causing her body to respond to their influence. Breathlessness or suffocation becomes associated with Asís's suffering from the first passage, where it accompanies her realizations of guilt (38). She loses her breath as a result of hurrying to prepare herself for further encounters with Pacheco, when she feels like a shipwreck victim while alone in her house with Pacheco, when she enters the alcove where she is to dine with Pacheco in a restaurant on the outskirts of Madrid, and when she awakens from her nightmare concerning leaving Madrid.

Loss of breath reminds her urgently and physically that she has lost all control. The heroine fluctuates between a feeling of being cast adrift on the sea and one of being confined and slowly asphyxiated. On the level of spatial representation this dichotomy emerges as the twin poles of exposure and enclosure or entrapment. To a certain extent, the spatial constructions of *Insolación* work as extensions of bodily space; the same forces that propel or repel Asís's body "from within" are equally at work on the mimetic stages of landscape and man-made interiors. In general there is a tendency toward internality: when she is outside, she is continually driven inside by the elements. The narrative style heightens this internal movement, commencing in the first person and hence enclosed within the heroine's consciousness. Even when the narrator changes to the more omniscient third person, Asís's inner "happenings" are always on the very surface of the text. She at times forsakes the safety of interiors in favor of gusts of fresh air, which often provide pleasure or relief. In this respect, the most general spatial tendency in the work can be construed as one that abhors stagnation and finds complete comfort in no single spot. Even though the exteriors prove hostile environments for a

variety of reasons, refuge can turn into entrapment, and she must then escape it as well.

At the Duchess of Sahagún's salon, in the passage in which the mind/body split is articulated and placed in a Spanish context by Gabriel Pardo, there is a conspicuous lack of description of the interior and a disembodiment of Asís that coincides with the stressing of transcendent mind as divorced from the body and its base instincts. Asís's contentious friend Gabriel Pardo happens to be lecturing those present about how in Spain the mind is no match for the body. As he tries to convince the socialites that they are little better than savages, Asís's body is uncharacteristically silent. The introduction of her future lover Pacheco brings on no physical reaction in Asís, but rather a "cold curiosity." The absence of physical inscription coincides with an interior filled with a concentration of her peers listening to a harangue that privileges the mind over the body and implies that Spaniards as a race let the latter get out of hand.

It is not until the following day, on the way to Mass, that the amenity of her outdoor surroundings makes Asís want to run and jump. Outdoor settings serve as enabling conditions of either explicit pleasure or explicit discomfort, keeping the heroine's physical affective state on the surface throughout the work. This is reinforced and determined by the omnipresence of the sun as mediator of desire. Thus, there are instances of the outdoors acting as a refreshment on Asís's senses: "The calm of night and the open air produced the effect of a cold shower on me" (95). These are balanced by instances of oppression in the form of heat, crowds, and the *piropos* of loitering men (customary acclaim for passing women intended to bolster the speaker's consideration among other men). The sidewalks of Madrid are not a place where a woman of her rank can walk unmolested, and when men turn their attention to her she is forced to quicken her pace; rarely in male-authored literature is there an indication of the subtle factors that add up to women's basic lack of liberty on city streets. She resorts to flight in this and other instances that jeopardize her personal safety or social standing.

The interiors afford intimacy in scenes that include Pacheco and shelter her from the excessive heat of the direct sun, but a number of descriptions evidence a sense of entrapment, especially when the heroine is alone or with other women in the house. Her maiden aunts' house, which inspires the most excruciating boredom and a bout of yawning, stands for an entire way of life that cannot satisfy her, no matter how saintly and secure it is. An amusing vignette describes the embarrassing situation of two ladies caught in traffic, so that their carriages force them to face each other, yet they are not sufficiently acquainted to converse and can only smile at each other as they await the end of the awkward encounter (106). The furnishing of her own apartment in Madrid internalizes the labyrinthine entrapment that awaits her on the outside as female character: "Everything intermingled, placed in whatever way created the most obstacles to people passing through, forming an archipelago that could not be navigated without practice" (114). In addition, a masculine figure humorously presides over the maze: "Only the porcelain bulldog, sitting like a sphinx, watched the couple on the sofa with an alarming persistence, displaying an appropriate alertness, as if he were a guard stationed there by the spirit of the respectable deceased marquis" (115).

In the kaleidoscopic landscape of the St. Isidro Fair disparate figures or scenes come one after another into Asís's view. It represents a carnivalesque break with daily life and the usual urban setting, a place outside of social norms where the newly formed couple can take pleasure in "slumming" and in each other's company with relative freedom from the gaze of others of their social circle. In addition to the amusements, the carnival space evidently poses risks to Asís's self-control; excesses of food and drink, exposure to the sun and to Pacheco's attraction, and contact with the lower classes, particularly with marginalized women, threaten her sense of autonomy and her moral behavior. The novel's last utterances consist of Pacheco's joking impersonation of the gypsy fortuneteller at the fair who predicted their ultimate, happy union.

This final crossing of gender boundaries strengthens another feminine subtext activated in the text through the carnival sequence: that of *brujería,* or witchcraft, linked with marginalized women. It begins with Gabriel Pardo's pompous condemnation of the St. Isidro Festival as an *aquelarre,* a witches' sabbath or Walpurgisnacht. The description of the fair itself reinforces what might have seemed an offhand remark. Three gypsy women in succession besiege the couple at their restaurant table. The first one launches into a detailed reading of Asís's palm, predicting good luck in love and an important letter. Besides the letters of shame on her skin and Pacheco's initials on his wallet (which incriminate Asís in the mind of Gabriel Pardo when he glimpses it in her apartment), Asís's palm represents the only significant text that is "read" in the course of the narrative. The final parody of a palm reading executed by Pacheco thus closes the novel with the recurring image of bodily writing. In addition, the mystery of occult practices interweaves itself in this way with the couple's love for each other. This adds to the mystery surrounding human relationships that the novel leaves unresolved;[37] true to the forecasted *aquelarre,* the witchcraft emanates from a feminine source and etches itself on the textual female body.

When the third gypsy in the St. Isidro restaurant is told to depart, she lets loose a string of curses against the waitress. Asís describes all the gypsy *brujas* in animalistic terms: their claws, their serpentine foreheads, how they fight like tigresses or Amazons. In so doing she tries to hold on firmly to the ethnic (Asís would say racial) and class privilege that separates her from these women. Although she perceives them as bestial, their witchcraft does have the power of writing Asís's future for her. Their undefinable characters, inhumanly portrayed bodies, and compelling powers hark back to medieval texts such as the *Celestina,* in which feminine subtexts of witchcraft, prostitution, and virginity restoration, all connected to women's bodies, have a key role in the production of meaning because they are perceived by the reader as intolerable gaps.[38]

As the carnival passage continues, Asís's conception of her own body does not remain altogether divorced from the female witches and monsters she encounters. Immediately after looking at a four-legged woman in a freak show tent, she feels more nauseated than ever. She seeks her own image in a wavy mirror but finds herself reflected in "grotesquely deformed lines" (87). Furthermore, she begins to display her own extrasensory powers, for example, when she senses Pacheco's presence with her eyes closed, although she takes pains to explain it away as a common experience (92), and when she and Pardo feel each other's thoughts through the contact of their arms, "as if via magnetic force" (123). The stereotype of "women's intuition," when exaggerated, is reminiscent of the historical, suspected connection between powerful women and the occult, an area that lies outside of authoritative, logocentric knowledge. Asís has reason to feel haunted by the more marginalized women she encounters at the fair, for they are very close to distortions of her own image. This is why Asís cannot endure the sight of her reflection in a distorting funhouse mirror, having just viewed female "freaks" on display in a sideshow. Carnivalesque themes often force a confrontation with a danger or harsh truth that lies below the surface of merriment. Pardo Bazán takes advantage of this function to dramatize the fear of social disapproval that normally keeps women like Asís in check. Naturally, *Insolación* gives the last word, and the undecidable ending of the text, to the witch (or parody of one). But for readers the story does not end here.

In the absence of the balanced extremes of fire and ice metaphors comparable to those Gilbert and Gubar find prominent in *Jane Eyre,* *Insolación* careens toward the flames, but the flames of what? As we have seen, heat is variously associated throughout the book with punishment and guilt (not unlike El Burlador's final punishment in the original version of Don Juan), as well as with incipient passion. Once the sun god receives his homage, however, he greets the lovers as a beneficent patron. The shifts in significance betray an ambivalent attitude toward sensuality, which is not surprising in one of the first novels that deals straightforwardly with female erotism and neither punishes nor entirely condemns a woman for a premarital affair.

The insistent alternation between pain and pleasure draws the work closer to St. Teresa's *Libro de la vida,* particularly in the light of Smith's relation of her ecstasy to Kristeva's semiotic state. Smith asserts that the mystic state as revealed by St. Teresa's writings fluctuates between exaltation and despair. Aside from this, there are many coincidences on various levels in ***Insolación*** and the *Vida*; Pardo Bazán was continuing a feminine dialogue, consciously or not—it is likely that she had in mind another mystic-influenced heroine, Clarín's Ana Ozores—with one of her rare Spanish precursors. Both texts begin with a confession made to a "father" (their confessors). Both are sprinkled with statements of humility that apologize for the subject's inability to express herself or to behave properly. Irigaray signals the expression of women's desire in a public forum as an important contribution of mystical writing, and ***Insolación*** does nothing if not articulate this desire over and over, using various conceits, including the nautical or seasickness metaphors. The *Vida* also relies heavily on this kind of imagery.[39] Both protagonists describe penetration of an inner space. In St. Teresa's case it is a blissful mystical vision tinged with a burning sensation. For Asís it is a most unpleasant daydream of torture based on actual physical pain. Perhaps Asís does feel a more pleasant kind of penetration as well, but who can say? Certainly not the narrator.

On the level of stylistics, there is also a clear resemblance to St. Teresa's text in the frequency of "paradox, ellipsis, and discontinuity" and other seeming aberrations. Smith opines that these wind up breaking the bonds of male rhetoric, charging that adherence to male literary conventions afforded an insufficient medium for female subjectivity, at least in a Golden Age context.[40] Pardo Bazán's situation is of course different: as a secular author not directly related to any mystical tradition and an aristocrat whose material wealth shields her from the most basic discriminations (she has managed to educate herself), she participates on the same level as male novelists and engages with them in friendships, rivalries, and amorous liaisons. However, the texture of ***Insolación*** is defined by its use of ellipsis, which is executed so perceptibly that Genette's concept of paralipsis, when what is omitted from narration becomes the center of attention for that very reason, is more appropriate.

All novelists of the time were faced with the need to circumvent occurrences in their plots that would violate decorum. As a result, the gaps in their texts take on importance, for the consequences of these scenes for the rest of the story are such that the reader is forced to fill in the gaps. Without whatever Emma Bovary does in-

side her carriage with drawn blinds, for example, the rest of the novel makes little sense. Even though the text does not take us into the compartment, the effect is the same, and all the more compelling for having this sense of mystery, being "where the garment gapes."[41] In *Tristana,* having already introduced the story of Paolo and Francesca de Rimini as an intertext, Galdós can state with a wink that Tristana and Horacio "strolled no more after that day."[42] Pardo Bazán was indeed criticized for not withdrawing sufficiently from the parts where her story line becomes improper. José Maria de Pereda called ***Insolación*** immoral for showing the pair of lovers in concubinage visible to the reader and for including meticulous details about the way they commit sin.[43]

Even when the narration does recede from the scene of the crime, the ornateness of the narratorial "doorways" to these boudoir scenes calls attention to them. The disclaimers offered by the narrator also turn back on themselves in irony, since imagination, and not truth, forces the telling of the tale: "It is painful to have to admit and set down certain things; however, honesty militates against leaving them out of the narration" (117). The feigned obligation to tell historical truth (one of Cervantes's favorite tricks) leaves the author less accountable for having invented, embellished, and published a story of premarital transgression that goes unpunished. This same passage, while keeping its "discreet reticence," lingers very conspicuously in the street outside; where most novelists accelerate, Pardo Bazán decelerates narrative time, describing the tedium of horses and coachmen falling asleep at the curb below and daylight disappearing little by little from the sky.

Whereas discontinuity is apparent among female Golden Age writers, in Pardo Bazán there is narrative intermittence or fluctuation. As Stephen Gilman and Gonzalo Sobejano have noted in different ways, a major transformation of "imported" naturalism was wrought by Spanish novelists, who reflected or retold their plots through a Cervantine mirror of irony and perspectivism.[44] This narration that calls attention to itself often utilizes a fluctuating perspective that is at times omniscient, at times so linked to third-person indirect style that it cannot know information that falls outside of the character's consciousness. Gilman, for example, finds that this is enriching to the reading experience in *Fortunata y Jacinta.* He sees an increasing rapprochement between Galdós as narrator and Fortunata. In Valera, on the other hand, Smith finds that narrative intermittence is handled less effectively, with a resulting obtrusiveness.[45] Hence, fluctuation in general is not exclusive to Pardo Bazán ("Pardo had picked up a newspaper, I believe it was *La Epoca*" [185]). However, in ***Insolación,*** the context of fluctuation makes it overdetermined by the struggle between the Father's law and feminine desire. Narrator at times turns against heroine, at times works as her accomplice, and the twin subjectivities exhibit the "law" articulated with irony by the otherwise hypocritical character Gabriel Pardo: that Woman is a perpetual pendulum swinging between desire and acquired shame. The amused, theatrical narrator often feels obliged to censure the heroine condescendingly for the benefit of gentlemen readers:

> Asís, en la penumbra del dormitorio, entre el silencio, componía mentalmente el relato que sigue, donde claro está que no había de colocarse en el peor lugar, sino paliar el caso: aunque, señores, ello admitía bien pocos paliativos.
>
> No afirmamos que, aun dialogando con su conciencia propia, fuese la marquesa viuda de Andrade perfectamente sincera.
>
> [Asís, in the half-light of her bedroom, in silence, mentally composed the tale that follows, in which she certainly did not want to be displayed in a negative light, but preferred to attenuate the circumstances: although, gentlemen, it allowed for very little attenuation.
>
> We cannot assert that, even in dialogue with her own conscience, the widowed Marquess of Andrade was perfectly honest.]

(40, 100)

As doubt is cast on Asís as narrator, the third-person narrator also claims ignorance about certain key facts: Was Asís really crying? To whom did "the idea" of marriage first occur? An abdication of authority, and thereby of accountability, stems from the refusal to narrate these details, in a way that differs from the more generalized uses of Cervantine narrative fluctuation in male Spanish realists.[46] The overall effect is to confirm the subjectivity of all possible points of view by upholding feminine flexibility against the Father's law.

The resounding declaration made by Asís to the effect that women should be allowed to respond to and comment on the appearances of the men they find handsome throws into relief a contradiction for the contemporary reader. For, indeed, what Asís refers to explicitly in this passage and others concerning Pacheco's attraction is his clothing, grooming, accent, and manners—all of which are tied to culture—when supposedly the offensive aspect of women engaging in *piropos* about men would be their sensuality. Instead, the remarks are usually located one step from the physical: "the favorable impression the Andalusian's personal finery made upon me" (53), "the unstudied elegance of his dress" (111). The "commodity fetishism" noted by Smith (and Marxian critics before him) in *La de Bringas* has a similar effect here, establishing the mannequinlike figure of Pacheco, who is what he wears; the invisibility of the (male) body; and the consequent masquerade of relations between the sexes.

When the references are not so removed, racial characteristics supply the chief code for expressing the Andalusian's appearance. His meridional qualities are insisted upon to the point of setting up a racial difference that complements sexual difference and seems to make Asís's sensual delight in him possible:

> No dejaba de llamarme la atención la mezcla de razas que creía ver en ella [la cara]. Con un pelo negrísimo y una tez quemada del sol, casaban mal aquel bigote dorado y aquellos ojos azules.
>
> ¿Cuándo se verá en ningún inglés un corte de labios sutil, y una sien hundida, y un cuello delgado y airoso como el de Pacheco?
>
> Su rostro, descompuesto por la cólera, perdiendo su expresión indolente, mejoraba infinito: se acentuaban sus enjutas facciones, temblaba el bigote dorado, resplandecían los blancos dientes y los azules ojos, se oscurecían como el agua del Mediterráneo cuando amaga tempestad.
>
> [I couldn't help noticing the mixture of races I perceived in his face. The jet-black hair and sunburned complexion clashed with that golden moustache and blue eyes.
>
> Is there an Englishman who can boast of the finely etched lips, sculpted temples, and graceful, slender neck Pacheco has?
>
> His face, transfixed by rage, losing its indolent expression, improved immeasurably: his lean features were accentuated, the golden moustache trembled, his white teeth glinted, and his blue eyes darkened like the Mediterranean when a storm threatens.]

(60, 60, 177)

The factor of race is essential in the argument of biological determinism versus sociomoral influences that enters the novel in the conversation at the salon where Asís and Pacheco meet, and where Gabriel Pardo holds forth on a number of issues. The recorded dialogue makes the rest of the narrative a naturalist experiment that will prove or disprove one side but insists upon maintaining ambiguity.[47] Gabriel Pardo affirms that Spaniards have African blood coursing through their veins, presumably making them more susceptible to the biological imperatives (41). At the same time, the external forces of nature (sun and heat) are at their most unbridled in Spain, and even more so, one assumes, in Andalusia, leaving Spaniards still more vulnerable to the instincts localized in the body by way of blood. The racial mythology utilized here encodes and shapes bodily discourse. Its comforting effect upon both aristocrats and bourgeois, who looked to the physical for signifiers indicating their belonging to a certain social caste, has been observed by Foucault: "There was a transposition into different forms of the methods employed by the nobility for making and maintaining its caste distinction; for the aristocracy had also asserted the special character of its body, but this was in the form of *blood*, that is, in the form of the antiquity of its ancestry and of the value of its alliances; the bourgeoisie on the contrary looked to its progeny and the health of its organism when it laid claim to a specific body."[48]

What Gabriel Pardo denies is that gender has anything to do with an individual's giving in to baser nature, a position he reaffirms later when he condemns the double standard of morality in sexual behavior applied to women and men in Spanish society: "There are no men, there are no women, there is only humanity, and humanity is *like that*" (204). Pardo's point of view is subverted, however, when he reveals an utterly hypocritical subscription to the double standard in practice. On a textual level, at least, racial difference and gender difference appear linked, as enabling conditions for desire. Pacheco's body is marked in this respect and is harmonized with the natural forces (sun and sea) of his homeland. He too becomes a target for marginalization, which likens his body to the female body, for Pacheco, though male, is a target for the anti-Southern prejudices of Castilians and other Spaniards on account of his features, even if Asís's reactions are quite favorable. As in the nineteenth-century litany of women's body parts, only reference to his facial features, his "silken black hair," and, occasionally his slender hands and neck appear in the text.

When Asís peeks at the skin below the collar of Pacheco's shirt, she finds it to be much lighter in color than she had expected (62). The male body remains a mystery to be glimpsed only furtively in *Insolación,* and her inclination anticipates Roland Barthes's comparison of literary pleasure emanating from intermittence to the seductive flash of skin beneath a garment: "Is not the most erotic portion of the body *where the garment gapes?*"[49] The misplaced signifier of Pacheco's wallet, inscribed with his initials—"one of those unclasped billfolds of English leather, with two entwined initials in silver, an obviously masculine possession" (121)—is immediately recognized by another male, Pardo, as staking the former's claim in Asís's abode. Masculine articles of clothing identify their owner unmistakably, but Pacheco himself is not so unequivocally masculine; he fluctuates in the text between the maternal caretaker of a weakened Asís and, from a feminine viewpoint, a Don Juan figure. The former is another aspect of the gender blurring and role reversals that frequently rise to the surface of *Insolación.* It is as if no other satisfactory model for the true love that must be depicted can be found other than motherly affection, and one is reminded of the prevalence of incest in Pardo Bazán's other novels as well as in this one (Gabriel Pardo's love for his cousin and Asís's marriage to her uncle): "Pacheco held me in silence and with exquisite care, like a sick child" (91); "I was dying for affection, just like a little girl . . . I wanted to be pitied!" (93); "Pacheco rocked her back and forth as one soothes a child" (152). Of course a note of pathos and irony is not lacking from these descriptions, which portray the full-grown aristocrat, a mother herself, as a helpless child. Still, the maternal encoding of mature heterosexual love, often aligned with sea imagery, which acts as a reservoir for both maternal and erotic drives, manifests itself constantly in the works of Pardo Bazán and other women authors.

A transposition of the Don Juan legend also gives shape to the love affair between the heroine and Pacheco. The salon passage in which they are introduced to each other ends with a hint at Pacheco's similarity to the Sevillan *burlador,* or deceiver of women (Pacheco is from nearby Cádiz), including his turbulent relationship with his father and his philandering: "The only thing he had been good at up until then was upsetting women" (51). Upon hearing this the protagonist deems him "a fine example of the Spanish race," setting the tone for the subsuming of his physical representation into the category of race. While he tends more toward the rake than the villain, the parallel is drawn clearly and reinforced, for no other archetypal character has been made to stand so universally for Spanish manhood. Later he admits that he has had hundreds of girlfriends and has even killed a man, yet for Asís (his Doña Inés) he has but the tenderest of sentiments. He cannot be the full-fledged diabolical antihero of drama and poetry; his transposition into the novel and particularly the requirements of the configuration worked up in *Insolación* call for a mitigation of his darker side.

The resemblance to Zorrilla's *Don Juan Tenorio* (1844) is playfully strengthened by his possessing "a lovely kind of romantic sadness" (153), and echoes of the Tenorio are heard in his amatory declarations: "What is it that you have in this mouth, and in these eyes, and in your whole being, that makes me feel this way?" (144). Gabriel Pardo looks down on Pacheco as "an idle cell in the social organism." Foucault finds that Don Juan's very appeal, which has endured for three centuries, is this: his refusal to submit to a productive sexual code, to forsake the fruitless pleasures. More than a mere libertine, he is a sociosexual outlaw, a pervert: "Underneath the great violator of the rules of marriage . . . another personage can be glimpsed: the individual driven, in spite of himself, by the somber madness of sex."[50]

Pardo Bazán was impressed with Galdós's *Fortunata y Jacinta,* published in 1886 and 1887, which also affixes itself to the Don Juan tradition, in the person of Juanito Santa Cruz. Several aspects of *Insolación* noted by Sobejano and González-Arias respond to the innovations of Galdós's monumental novel: the meticulous linguistic imitation of dialogue between lovers (which approximates baby talk in both novels) and of street, gypsy, and *chulo* slang, as well as the novelization of a modern Don Juan figure. To say merely that *Insolación* (in contrast to *Fortunata y Jacinta*) offers a novelized and softened Don Juan legend from a female point of view would be to oversimplify. As Julia Kristeva has observed, the moralistic condemnation of Don Juan implicit or explicit in all texts where he appears shows that he is always viewed through the victim's eyes—the narrator is the seduced woman.[51] Considered with this in view, condemnation of Don Juan behavior is conspicuously mild in *Insolación*. Asís half-affectionately, half-censuringly calls Pacheco a rogue and wonders whether he might be capable of deceiving her (67). The book is mainly concerned with answering one of the three questions Kristeva finds raised by the Don Juan tradition: "What attracts women to him, to a source of unhappiness and rejection?" Galdós's work has more to do with Kristeva's remaining questions: "What makes Don Juan tick? . . . What assembles around Don Juan these men who imagine themselves, who wish themselves, who conduct themselves *as if* they were he?"[52]

Pardo Bazán's answer to what it is about Don Juan that seduces women is not simple or direct. We have seen how desire, and its attendant punishment, is displaced throughout the work, emanating from the natural elements, from Asís's own body, and now from a man cloaked in Southern charm and impeccable attire who bears a resemblance to the archetypal masked man of literature. Their mutual affection shows traces of motherly care, much the same as the relationship between Juanito Santa Cruz and Jacinta. But here the one who "burns" for her sins is not Don Juan but Doña Inés, and the two are united in their being fugitives from the Father's law (Pacheco's father is displeased with him and would have him become a politician against his will; as Kristeva notes regarding nearly all depictions of Don Juan, his mother is never mentioned). The particular transposition of Don Juan Tenorio in *Insolación* shows Asís as the desiring subject not only of her lover but of his power. She feels a surprising inclination to trade places with him, to be permitted his exploits and moral relativism: "Asís felt a stinging curiosity together with unprovoked anger" (146). In another passage Asís puts her hand upon his chest to feel the mysteriously autonomous and varying activity of his vital organ when aroused by her tenderness: "Beneath the lady's palm, Pacheco's heart, like a spirit obeying a spell, erupted in the most violent dance such an organ can execute" (151). The symbolic power of the phallus is thinly veiled beneath the Don Juan persona of Pacheco. The dynamics of Asís's attraction to Pacheco confirm Kristeva's suspicion: "Could the seducer be the phallus itself? The temporary mastership, the timed power, the exhaustion leading to pure loss? The movement itself of erection and detumescence, phantasmally to infinity?"[53]

The resolution of this yearning to trade places with the Don Juan figure finds Asís listening to her own vital organ and enacting a reversal of the cited hand-over-heart sequence with Pacheco. But what is to be felt there is the entanglement of conflicting sensations within the sensationalized body of Asís, not the power concentrated in the heart of Don Juan:

Y a Asís se le revelaba entonces el amor. Poco a poco, sin conciencia de sus actos, acercaba la mano de Diego a su pecho, ansiosa de apretarla contra el corazón y de calmar así el ahogo suave que le oprimía. . . . Sus pupilas se humedecieron, su respiración se apresuró, y corrió por sus vértebras misterioso escalofrío, corriente de aire agitado por las alas del ideal.

[And then love made itself known to Asís. Slowly, unknowingly, she drew Diego's hand toward her chest, yearning to squeeze it against her heart and thus calm the faint breathlessness that afflicted her. . . . Her pupils moistened, her breath quickened, and along her spine ran a mysterious tingling, a gust swept up by the wings of the ideal.]

(189-90)

This final revelation, in which Asís's body speaks its longing and finally convinces her mind, bridges the mind/body split and brings about a hasty conclusion of the plot and the conflicts that set it in motion. There is still, however, no sense of power within that body, no excited beating. The romantic love that has been signified by heat, electricity, pain, and a score of other signifiers remains undecidable. The lovers' decision to marry, referred to euphemistically as *la idea,* no doubt replying in part to Fortunata's *idea blanca,* perpetuates what Lacan calls the "fantasy of reciprocity between the sexes" and allows Asís to reenter the exchange economy, in which her body may be subjected and productive again. As it appears in the text, *la idea* has the ring of euphemism. Yet a euphemism, is generally used to stand for another signifier that is taboo; here, however, it is the conclusion dictated by convention. For this and many other reasons, a sense of unreality hovers over the conclusion. No effort is made to correct its *postizo* (false) quality, and the result is an open text that incites rather than calms the reader's doubts: Don Juan can only enjoy a conquest without possession, and Woman's quest for completion with an absolute Other shows no sign of being fulfilled. For Tolliver, the ending shows Asís's concern with saving face, but at the same time the narrator excites the reader's suspicions with the ironic reference to "something sublime that did not exist" in her lover's eyes. As Spacks observes of eighteenth- and nineteenth-century women writers in general, marriage and family are upheld as avenues to happiness on the surface, with only "subterranean challenges" to their validity.[54] The actual affair on which the story is loosely based did not in fact end in marriage, but blossomed into a long professional relationship, with Galdiano helping Pardo Bazán to direct *La España Moderna.*[55]

Stephen Gilman singles out Fortunata as Galdós's heroine par excellence. He defines her character development as relying very little upon physical detail: her bodily features are never "possessed in memory." She is not seen directly, but "in terms of the overwhelming impression she makes, first on Juanito and then on herself." Gilman holds, on the other hand, that she is a pure presence and that the (presumably male) reader enters her consciousness "in a way we can never know women of flesh and blood—our mothers, our sisters, and our wives."[56] His analysis points to the fundamental gap at the core of Galdós's heroines: they are feminine only in that Woman has come to be the primary signifier for late-nineteenth-century realism. The irreducible, undecidable nature of the figure Woman allows the female character to be a more-than-person. What Tanner writes of the gaps that constitute Emma Bovary applies in good measure to Galdós's heroines: "We have the music of Flaubert's text, and from it and within it we hear and infer the 'motif' of Emma Bovary. But if we search harder and harder for that motif . . . we lose all sense of a founder or 'original' and 'originating person.'"[57]

Whereas Gilman argues that Fortunata transcends the dichotomy of body and mind (to become a "vessel of creative passion"), it could also be argued that the body/mind split is maintained in such a way that a whole person never emerges. For this reason, the difficulty of finding a *vivencia* of the female body in Galdós leaves little room for the kinds of conflicts I have found to be at work in Pardo Bazán's "bodily text." A fascinating passage relevant to this question is "Las Micaelas por dentro," from *Fortunata y Jacinta.* To judge from Mauricia's Napoleonic face, the "manly" inmates, and Fortunata's robustness, one could be visiting a reform school for transvestites instead of a convent sheltering wayward women. In fact, one could well imagine Pedro Almodóvar directing another remake and casting Bibi Anderson in the title role. At any rate, the convent reform school seems to demonstrate that in the absence of men, Galdós's female characters quite naturally take over their role, because their connection to flesh-and-blood women was tenuous in the first place.

Although Pardo Bazán chose to incorporate some of the innovations in dialogue of *Fortunata y Jacinta,* adding to imitation of popular speech the possibilities inherent in a carnival atmosphere, it probably also supplied her with the negative inspiration to pursue her own representation of feminine psychology. Leopoldo Alas, of course, is another matter. Gilman remarks that Galdós lacks the "sensual recollections and libidinal longings that fill the pages of *La Regenta.*"[58] *La Regenta* (1884-85) is indeed sprinkled with the kind of "bodily" markers that abound in *Insolación.* Ana's "nostalgia for her mother's lap" harmonizes perfectly with the tradition of female-authored motherless heroines and the often maternal influence on depictions of mature desire. Clarín looks at the question of honor from the standpoint of its consequences for women, although he consigns Ana to the usual fate of the fallen woman. In addition, fever or heat is used to signify a broad range of emotional reactions: the death of Ana's father, her reading of St. John of the Cross, and the pleasure of being held by Alvaro.[59] Ana also suffers from suffocation, dizziness, and fainting. She feels an affinity for St. Teresa and mysticism in general. But perhaps the greatest difference in the way "the feminine" is conceived of in these two works is that there is no accomplice/censuring narrator—one who acknowledges transgressions and distortions as readily and ironically as the narrator of *Insolación*—in *La Regenta.* Thus, Ana's inner world is another aspect of a chaotic though stagnant provincial world. The narration is not a continuous stream of bodily sensations inciting conscientious objections on the narrator's part.

While more psychologically viable than Galdós heroines, Ana has the second but more essential role of playing a part in the larger mythic substratum of *La Regenta*—on the literary level where honor plays, Don Juan and the mystics interact and clash, and the heroine's body is a battleground. In addition, Ana is portrayed more often from without than from within, as an object of male desire, as when she disrobes and unconsciously strikes an odalisque pose on her bed. Like the odalisque of genre painting, her representation is by and large made for male consumption and casts the reader, whether male or female, as male voyeur.[60]

The inward focus of *Insolación* makes the *vivencia* of the female body of Pardo Bazán's milieu and moment accessible to the reader and also recreates its movement through a variety of social spaces. The panoply of sensations and symptoms to which Asís falls prey brings to mind the hysterization of women, cited by Foucault as one of "the four great strategies [of sexualization] that were deployed in the nineteenth century."[61] There is more at work here than Pardo Bazán loading her heroine with the psychosomatic symptoms that were widely associated with nineteenth-century women of leisure, coming to be regarded as a feminine form of *mal du siècle.* Through insistence upon the internalization of the Father's law practiced by the protagonist—her confessional engagement with Father Urdax, her blaming of herself—and through narration in free indirect style—the oscillation that includes censuring of Asís's actions—*Insolación* does not trap the heroine in a frame labeling her as a hysteric, but reproduces instead the conflict brought on by her pursuit of desire in a patriarchal setting. This in itself—the imperative of a love that satisfies physically as well as emotionally—was revolutionary for the time.[62] The clashing ideologies involved in this conflict include the sexual but do not stop there, as analysis of the carnival and country-inn passages reveals. The Father's law and the feminine semiotic drive develop their own discourses in this short novel, and their skirmishing is facilitated by bodily and spatial codes.

Asís's body is presented as a historical and highly political construct, in addition to being modeled upon a basic biological entity. For this reason, I have chosen to treat its representation in *Insolación* as a chapter of female political anatomy. The particular, historical variety of female subjection at work in the world of Pardo Bazán finds expression in the text, as the protagonist's social situation causes her body to react to the power exercised over it like one of Foucault's soldiers: "Power relations have an immediate hold upon it [the body]; they invest it, mark it, train it, torture it, force it to carry out tasks, to perform ceremonies, to emit signs." Asís's requesting body and the literally physical inscriptions upon it enter into dialogue eloquently with the internalized forces of subjection. The end of these political influences is to render the body a useful force, which is to say, productive and subjected.[63] Hence, the goal is not possession but the exercising of an influence, which ensures an ongoing skirmish rather than complete conquest of the body's forces. In fact, the resolution of the heroine's marriage, which promises to keep her desires in check and productive, is called into question before it even takes place, putting the accent on the ongoing battle.

Similarly, Asís's body is turned into the battleground upon which the Father's law fights a newer ideology of what Luce Irigaray calls "(re)productive earth-mother-nature." The erotic impulse associated with the latter and originating in the semiotic stage of development can be seen both in the lovers' "instinct" and in what fuels narrative and reader and moves them through the text, whereas the narrator's occasional reproaches and the powerful constellation of mainly male figures who stand in the way of desire are concessions made to the former. Undefinable, undecidable, and irreducible to any side of a binary opposition, the female body belongs to Jane Gallop's category of the "remainders" in literature. Thus, the mind/body split is exploded by infinite feminine desire, signified within and without by heat. This is only one of a series of binary oppositions—North/South, educated/uneducated (or rich/poor), male/female, Spain/Europe—on which the novel hinges and which it ultimately undoes. The insistence upon desire, its ravages and punishments, achieves something similar to the excesses of the Marquis de Sade, who, according to Gallop, used images of brutality to show that "the body always exceeds the mind's order."[64]

For this reason, it is not sufficient to cull feminist viewpoints from the text in the form of ideological bits and pieces we might then attribute to the author (e.g., the critique of the double standard), even though Pardo Bazán was an important early feminist.[65] To begin with, the question of a mouthpiece for the author among the main characters of *Insolación* is problematized by the ironization of nearly all viewpoints.[66] In addition, the denigration of lower-class women would contradict any broadly feminist agenda in the work. To assert Pardo Bazán's favoring of a feminist cause by assessing plot occurrences as stacking up in its support also fails to go

the extra but necessary distance. It is on the level of the text, with its coincidences, paradoxes, ellipses, and echoes, that life is breathed into the female body as historical, cultural, biological, and political construct. This novel constitutes, to my knowledge, the first Spanish text in which the inscription of this body reaches the level of protagonization.

Notes

1. Scanlon, *La polémica feminista en la España contemporánea.*

2. Herrero, *Fernán Caballero.*

3. Scanlon, *La polémica feminista en la España contemporánea,* 6.

4. Pattison, *Emilia Pardo Bazán,* 61.

5. I am indebted to the outlines of the work of Jacques Lacan and post-Freudian French feminism provided by Gossy, *The Untold Story,* 130; Smith, *The Body Hispanic*; and Grosz, *Sexual Subversions.* In addition, the first two are invaluable in tracing the intersections of these bodies of knowledge with Hispanism.

6. Ordóñez, "Inscribing Difference," 45.

7. González-Arias, "A Voice, Not an Echo," 49.

8. Hemingway, *Emilia Pardo Bazán,* 42-56; Shaw, *Historia de la literatura española,* 243.

9. The details of this alternating explicit audience, as well as the fluctuating sense of guilt displayed by Asís in her confession and the narrator's equivocally (dis)claimed responsibility for writing down what Asís *would have* confessed if she had chosen to do so, are perceptively analyzed by Joyce Tolliver in "Narrative Accountability and Ambivalence." The present study is an attempt to build upon this gender-based narratological study, adding a *corporeísta* focus.

10. Foucault, *The History of Sexuality,* 1:59-62.

11. Pardo Bazán, *Insolación,* 39; subsequent page references will be cited in the text.

12. Hemingway, *Emilia Pardo Bazán,* 42-56.

13. Ibid., 50.

14. Tolliver, "Narrative Accountability and Ambivalence," 103-18.

15. Scari, "La sátira y otros efectos humorísticos en *Insolación*," 12.

16. Miller, "Sensation and Gender in *The Woman in White.*"

17. Santiáñez-Tió, "Una marquesita 'sandunguera,'" 121.

18. The litany of bodily parts, synecdoche, and fetishization of the female form in contemporaneous English novels is thoroughly treated by Helena Michie in *The Flesh Made Word*.

19. Gilbert and Gubar, *The Madwoman in the Attic*, 45-92.

20. Bloom, *The Anxiety of Influence*.

21. Salcedo, *La Codorniz*, 86.

22. Tolliver, "Narrative Accountability and Ambivalence," 110.

23. González-Arias, "A Voice, Not an Echo," 37. The affair took place in 1888.

24. Gilbert and Gubar, *The Madwoman in the Attic*, 58.

25. Hilton, "Pardo-Bazán and Literary Polemics about Feminism," 41.

26. As part of a Jungian archetypal analysis, Mary E. Giles presents the sun and the sea as poles symbolizing ego and primal unconsciousness, respectively, demonstrating the interpretive resonance of this short novel, in "Feminism and the Feminine in Emilia Pardo Bazán's Novels."

27. The sun god also shows up anomalously as a nude statuette of Apollo among the furnishings of the heroine's prudish aunts (Hemingway, *Emilia Pardo Bazán*, 48).

28. Irigaray treats the relation of Woman and mysticism in "La mystérique," in *Speculum: De l'autre femme*, 238-52, and in "Femmes divines" and "Les femmes, le sacré, l'argent," in *Sexes et parentés*, 67-102.

29. Smith, *The Body Hispanic*, 75.

30. Osborne, *Emilia Pardo Bazán y sus obras*, 72.

31. Ibid., 76.

32. Zola, *L'Assommoir*, 310.

33. Just as the contents of Poe's *Purloined Letter* would be potentially incriminating to its aristocratic female addressee. The letter and Woman are conjoined in this passage, and it is interesting to note that these two terms are Lacan's "irreducibles," or remainders in literature, constituting what, according to Lacan, calls Poe's text into being (Smith, *The Body Hispanic*, 70).

34. The "good lady with her lions" is the goddess Cybeles, an unobtrusive way of introducing an element of aquatic "feminine fecundity," according to Alfred Rodríguez and Saúl Roll, "*Pepita Jiménez* y la creatividad de Pardo Bazán en *Insolación*," 30. It also establishes the presence of a female deity in Madrid.

35. Smith, *The Body Hispanic*, 71.

36. Charnon-Deutsch, *Gender and Representation*, 2. For Blanca Andreu, the concept of feminine virtue exemplified in literature of mass consumption bears a resemblance to the ideology behind some of Galdós's "fallen" heroines—the overly ambitious Amparo of *Tormento* (1884), for example (*Galdós y la literatura popular*, 149).

37. Santiáñez-Tió, "Una marquesita 'sandunguera,'" 126.

38. Gossy, *The Untold Story*, 2.

39. Smith, *The Body Hispanic*, 42.

40. Ibid., 41.

41. Barthes, *The Pleasure of the Text*, 9.

42. Pérez Galdós, *Tristana*, 75.

43. José Maria de Pereda, cited in López-Sanz, *Naturalismo y espiritualismo en Galdós y Pardo-Bazán*, 98.

44. Sobejano, introduction to *La Regenta* by Leopoldo Alas; Gilman, *Galdós and the Art of the European Novel*.

45. Smith, *The Body Hispanic*, 95.

46. Tolliver, "Narrative Accountability and Ambivalence," 116.

47. Hemingway, *Emilia Pardo Bazán*, 49.

48. Foucault, *The History of Sexuality*, 1:124.

49. Barthes, *The Pleasure of the Text*, 9.

50. Foucault, *The History of Sexuality*, 1:39.

51. Kristeva, *Histoires d'amour*, 245.

52. Ibid., 244.

53. Ibid., 249.

54. Tolliver, "Narrative Accountability and Ambivalence," 114; Spacks, *The Female Imagination*, 317.

55. González-Arias, "A Voice, Not an Echo," 3.

56. Gilman, *Galdós and the Art of the European Novel*, 322-23, 320.

57. Tanner, *Adultery in the Novel*, 273.

58. Gilman, *Galdós and the Art of the European Novel*, 352.

59. Alas, *La Regenta*, 736.

60. My views are consonant with those of Fanny Rubio on the female body in Galdós and Clarín. She deems the treatment in the former "unrealized"

and that of the latter both a "desired body" and a totality of sensory references. She has studied the "mutilation" of the female body in some of Pardo Bazán's other novels, but to my knowledge she has not discussed the topic with reference to *Insolación* (77-78).

61. The others Foucault lists are the sexualization of children, the specification of perversions, and the regulation of populations (*The History of Sexuality,* 1:114).

62. Santiáñez-Tió, "Una marquesita 'sandunguera,'" 127.

63. From *Discipline and Punish,* in *The Foucault Reader,* 173.

64. Gallop, *Thinking through the Body,* 4.

65. Teresa A. Cook has attempted this in *El feminismo en la novela de la condesa de Pardo Bazán.*

66. If only because of one of his surnames, Gabriel Pardo de la Lage would be a likely candidate for authorial spokesperson; yet we have seen that his opinions are espoused or discarded according to his vital situation.

Works Cited

Alas, Leopoldo [Clarín, pseud.]. *La Regenta.* 1884. Edited by Gonzalo Sobejano. Barcelona: Noguer, 1976.

Andreu, Alicia. *Galdós y la literatura popular.* Madrid: Sociedad General Española de Librería, 1982.

Barthes, Roland. *The Pleasure of the Text.* 1973. Translated by Richard Miller. New York: Farrar, Straus & Giroux, 1975.

Bloom, Harold. *The Anxiety of Influence.* New York: Oxford Univ. Press, 1973.

Charnon-Deutsch, Lou. *Gender and Representation: Women in Spanish Realist Fiction.* Amsterdam: J. Benjamins, 1990.

Cook, Teresa A. *El feminismo en la novela de la condesa de Pardo Bazán.* La Coruña, Spain: Diputación Principal, 1976.

Foucault, Michel. *The Foucault Reader.* Translated and edited by Paul Rabinow. New York: Pantheon, 1984.

———. *The History of Sexuality.* Vol. 1, *An Introduction.* 1976. Translated by Robert Hurley. New York: Vintage, 1990.

Gallop, Jane. *Thinking through the Body.* New York: Columbia Univ. Press, 1988.

Gilbert, Susan, and Sandra Gubar. *The Madwoman in the Attic: The Woman Writer and the Nineteenth-Century Literary Imagination.* New Haven: Yale Univ. Press, 1979.

Giles, Mary E. "Feminism and the Feminine in Emilia Pardo Bazán's Novels." *Hispania* 63, no. 2 (1980): 357-67.

Gilman, Stephen. *Galdós and the Art of the European Novel: 1867-1887.* Princeton: Princeton Univ. Press, 1981.

González-Arias, Francisca. "A Voice, Not an Echo: Emilia Pardo Bazán and the Novel in Spain and France." Ph. D. diss., Harvard University, 1985.

Gossy, Mary. *The Untold Story: Women and Theory in Golden Age Texts.* Ann Arbor: Univ. of Michigan Press, 1989.

Grosz, Elizabeth. *Sexual Subversions: Three French Feminists.* Sydney: Allen & Unwin, 1989.

Hemingway, Maurice. *Emilia Pardo Bazán: The Making of a Novelist.* Cambridge: Cambridge Univ. Press, 1983.

Herrero, Javier. *Fernán Caballero: Un nuevo planteamiento.* Madrid: Gredos, 1963.

Hilton, Ronald. "Pardo-Bazán and Literary Polemics about Feminism." *Romantic Review* 44 (1953): 40-46.

Irigaray, Luce. *Speculum: De l'autre femme.* Paris: Minuit, 1974.

———. *Sexes et parentés.* Paris: Minuit, 1987.

Kristeva, Julia. *Histoires d'amour.* Paris: Denoël, 1983.

López-Sanz, Mariano. *Naturalismo y espiritualismo en Galdós y Pardo-Bazán.* Madrid: Pliegos, 1985.

Michie, Helena. *The Flesh Made Word: Female Figures and Women's Bodies.* New York: Oxford Univ. Press, 1987.

Miller, D. A. "Sensation and Gender in *The Woman in White.*" Gallagher and Laqueur, *Making of the Modern Body,* 107-36.

Ordóñez, Elizabeth J. "Inscribing Difference: 'L'Écriture Féminine' and New Narrative by Women." *Anales de la literatura española contemporánea* 12, nos. 1-2 (1987): 45-58.

Osborne, Robert E. *Emilia Pardo Bazán y sus obras.* Mexico City: De Andrea, 1964.

Pardo Bazán, Emilia. *Insolación.* 1889. Reprint, Madrid: Taurus, 1980.

Pattison, Walter. *Emilia Pardo Bazán.* New York: Twayne, 1971.

Pérez Galdós, Benito. *Tristana.* 1892. Reprint, Madrid: Alianza, 1992.

Rodríguez, Alfred, and Saúl Roll. "*Pepita Jiménez* y la creatividad de Pardo Bazán en *Insolación.*" *Revista Hispánica Moderna* 44, no. 1 (1991): 29-34.

Rubio, Fanny. "A la busca de un cuerpo (femenino) perdido (esbozo)." In Durán and Rey, *Literatura y vida cotidiana,* 67-90.

Salcedo, José Manuel, ed. *La Codorniz: Antología, 1941-1944.* Madrid: Arnao, 1987.

Santiáñez-Tió, Nil. "Una marquesita 'sandunguera,' o el mito del naturalismo en *Insolación.*" *Revista de Estudios Hispánicos* 23, no. 2 (1989): 119-34.

Scanlon, Geraldine. *La polémica feminista en la España contemporánea (1868-1974).* Translated by Rafael Mazarrasa. Mexico City: Siglo Veintiuno, 1976.

Scari, Robert M. "La sátira y otros efectos humorísticos en *Insolación.*" *Duquesne Hispanic Review* 11, no. 1 (1972): 1-14.

Scarlett, Elizabeth. "*Vinculada a les flors*: Flowers and the Body in *Jardí vora el mar* and *Mirall trencat.*" In McNerny and Vosburg, *The Garden across the Border.* Cranbury, N.J., Susquehannah Univ. Press, in press.

Smith, Paul Julian. *The Body Hispanic: Gender and Sexuality in Spanish and Spanish American Literature.* Oxford: Clarendon, 1989.

Sobejano, Gonzalo. Introduction to *La Regenta,* by Leopoldo Alas, 9-52. 1884. Edited by Gonzalo Sobejano. Barcelona: Noguer, 1976.

Spacks, Patricia Meyer. *The Female Imagination.* New York: Alfred A. Knopf, 1975.

Tanner, Tony. *Adultery in the Novel: Contract and Transgression.* Baltimore: Johns Hopkins Univ. Press, 1979.

Teresa de Jesús. *Libro de su vida.* 1562. Edited by Dámaso Chicharro. Madrid: Cátedra, 1982.

Tolliver, Joyce. "Narrative Accountability and Ambivalence: Feminine Desire in *Insolación.*" *Revista de Estudios Hispánicos* 23, no. 2 (1989): 103-18.

Zola, Émile. *L'Assommoir.* 1877. Reprint, Paris: Presse Pocket, 1978.

Susan McKenna (essay date fall 1998)

SOURCE: McKenna, Susan. "Recalcitrant Endings in the Short Stories of Emilia Pardo Bazán." *Letras Peninsulares* 11, no. 2 (fall 1998): 637-56.

[In the following essay, McKenna offers a feminist critique of Pardo Bazán's short stories, maintaining that they provide a glimpse into the author's experimentations with narrative form and technique.]

A complex and often controversial figure herself, Emilia Pardo Bazán authored essays, novels, short stories, and plays that not only narrate the tumultuous events that occurred in Spain during the second half of the nineteenth century, but document as well the rapid succession of continental literary movements with which she experimented.[1] Walter T. Pattison seconds this view, maintaining that "Doña Emilia is indeed a bundle of conflicting traits, and this is precisely what makes her such a representative figure of her times" (1).[2] Her short stories, rather than the better known corpus of realist and naturalist novels, are the focus of this essay for three closely related reasons. First, despite their qualitative and quantitative wealth, her short stories have not had the same critical attention paid to them as her novels. Unexplored fertile ground, these stories are ripe for feminist critical evaluations of their narrative structures. Second, the great variety of short stories written by Pardo Bazán throughout her career suggests that she used the story as a vehicle for experimentation in narrative form and technique. Accordingly, I examine the innovative narrative structures and strategies of these stories from a feminist theoretical perspective. Third, the formal devices of the short story lend themselves well to structural analysis. Centering my discussion on the formal conventions of narrative closure, my analyses foreground the ways in which the texts themselves work to disrupt closure and thus create alternative endings outside the bounds of traditional narrative design. Pardo Bazán, I contend, breaks with the formal conventions of short-story narrative to allow for the possibility of authentic female subjectivity. Disruptive reappropriation, the term I use to analyze Pardo Bazán's fluid and ever-changing narrative techniques, identifies a trend in her writing that simultaneously exploits and explores the limitations of conventional narrative design. Conflict and contradiction, ambivalence and ambiguity, I conclude, are the salient characteristics of Pardo Bazán's radical expropriation of the short story's narrative conventions.

Closure is one of the most significant narrative structures found in the short story. Characterized by both its brevity, "compression rather than expansion," and its density, "concentration rather than distribution," the short story presupposes the imminence of the ending (May 64). In other words, short stories are highly concentrated toward their conclusions. Like its European and American counterparts, the Spanish short story experienced important changes in its formal conventions of closure in the late nineteenth century. Lou Charnon-Deutsch, for example, ascribes some of these changes to Poe's call for a striking conclusion: "one which would have a special impact on the reader and reinforce the single effect inherent in the story's structure" (130). The *cuentistas,* she continues, "sought to endow their closure with an ironic twist, a shocking last statement or some formal device intended to separate the ending from the body of the text and call attention to the protagonist's ending situation and the narrator's opinion of it" (130). Innovative methods of closure or, in some instances, anti-closure recast the structure of the nineteenth-century Spanish short story. Closure is thus a determining characteristic of the modern Spanish *cuento.*

Short-story theorist Austin M. Wright underscores the significance of the ending to the story in his essay "Recalcitrance in the Short Story." Wright suggests that there are two opposing forces at work in every formed piece of fiction: "the force of a shaping form and the resistance of the shaped materials" (115). The opposing form is that which he calls recalcitrance or, as it resists form, formal recalcitrance. The key to Wright's theory is not to consider the work as "a fully realized entity" but rather as "an emergent hypothesis of reading"—as process (116). Recalcitrance slows down or interferes with the process. The reader is actively engaged in the struggle between unity and the obstruction to that unity. "It is from this point of view," he concludes, "form seen as behavior (constructive in the writer, perceptual in the reader), that the opposition of the two forces appears: the shaping force versus the resisting one" (117). For Wright, then, the lack of temporal, causal or overt thematic links, the rejection of conventional beginnings and endings, the rejection of overt action, and leaving things to inference all represent examples of formal recalcitrance in the short story.

Two types of general recalcitrance common to all short stories, enhanced by or associated with the "shortness" of the story, include inner recalcitrance and final recalcitrance. Inner recalcitrance manifests itself in the "intensity of detail" conferred by the brevity of the short story (121). Words, images, characters, and events stand out more clearly. Recalcitrance, however, is implied in the act of attention required of the reader to comprehend often complicated patterns of behavior, imagery, or structure in a relatively limited amount of time. "Shortness," Wright contends, "intensifies recalcitrance at the ground level of language, even as it loses recalcitrance at the overall level of formal unification" (121). Final recalcitrance involves the challenges presented to the reader at the end of the story. Where one normally assumes resolution, clarification, or explanation, the ending instead aggravates resistance. An enigmatic ending leaves the reader with a feeling of inadequacy—of something left unfinished. He/she is forced to rethink, reexamine, and conclude once again to satisfy his/her expectations of wholeness. "Final recalcitrance," affirms Wright, "forces us to seek the unifying principle subtle enough to bring the details into a single compass" (121). Comprehension requires the reader to put all the pieces together for him/herself.

Five variations of final recalcitrance manifest themselves in Pardo Bazán's short stories. The first, mimetic resistance, occurs when the "story ends in an unresolved contradiction at the level of character or action" (124). Ambiguity or contradiction of motivation forces

the reader to look for deeper motives. The story requires a more complicated interpretation of events than originally perceived. Because the story stops short of explaining what has happened, the reader must do so for him/herself. The second variation of final recalcitrance Wright terms the unexplaining explanation. In this instance, an ending or an event appears to be an explanation (discovery, judgment, clarification), yet fails to actually explain (125). What appears to be the intended explanation provides no assistance to the perplexed reader. He/she must draw his/her own conclusions. The third category arises when the unexplaining explanation itself is suppressed (125).[3] The reader is confronted with an array of disparate materials. No explanation unites them, no connection is made between them. The story ends before any outcome is reached. Sometimes one incident in the story will provide the key to connect the elements. Sometimes the issue is precisely the failure of resolution itself. Once again, it is incumbent upon the reader to determine these answers for him/herself. Wright terms the fourth category symbolic recalcitrance. In this type of final resistance, the "ending leaves unexplained some conspicuous symbolic scheme" (126-7). The reader is given no guidance in how to interpret the symbols found within the fictional world of the story. To apprehend the story's significance, he/she must reorganize the symbolic system for him/herself. Wright's fifth and final category, modal discontinuity, challenges the reader at a more fundamental level. Modal discontinuity takes place when the "resistance is produced by a contradiction in what we may call the 'fictional mode' in the piece—the primary assumptions on which the coherence of the fictional world depends" (127). Two conflicting conceptions of the fictional world remain unresolved. The reader is left to choose between two feasible solutions. It is often the case in these stories that recalcitrance is never fully resolved. In sum, all final recalcitrance depends on the reader to provide coherence and connection: "a work of art becomes a composition that displays a created form in the process of becoming visible" (116).

The five stories examined in this study, **"El indulto," "Voz de la sangre," "La novia fiel," "El comadrón,"** and **"La flor seca"** were published between the years 1883-1895.[4] Rather than study the stories in chronological order, I have ordered them according to Wright's theory of final recalcitrance. As we move from one category to the next, we encounter endings that become progressively more resistant to closure and thus more challenging to the individual reader. Subtle and often elusive, the female subject in these stories emerges through the narrative strategy of final recalcitrance.

Mimetic resistance, Wright's first category, is the method of final recalcitrance used in the tragic story **"El indulto."**[5] An omniscient narrator recounts the story of Antonia, a poor washer-woman terrorized by the notion that her husband will be pardoned for his crime—the murder of his mother-in-law—and return to the village seeking revenge on the wife who helped to convict him. Following two false alarms, the husband indeed returns home, whereupon he demands the recommencement of conjugal duties from a panic-stricken Antonia. Dinner concluded and the child put to bed, Antonia must submit to sleeping with the man who brutally killed her mother. The next morning the village awakens to the cries of the young boy pleading for help. The neighbors find Antonia dying in her bed. The doctor's attempts to bleed her are unsuccessful, for no blood remains in her veins. She dies within twenty-four hours, "de muerte natural, pues no tenía lesión alguna" ([*Cuentos completos*]1:127). The story ends with an unresolved ambiguity at the level of action: Antonia's so-called "natural death." The reader is called upon to resolve this uncertainty for him/herself.

The doctor's inability to draw even one drop of blood from Antonia's body makes little sense without deliberate reconsideration of the story's events. Two previous allusions to blood, easily overlooked upon the first reading, may provide the answer to Antonia's bloodlessness. The first concerns Antonia's memory of her murdered mother: "la herida tenía labios blancos" (1:124). She re-envisions finding her mother's body: "la sangre cuajada al pie del catre" (1:124). Blood drains from her mother's body, leaving her flesh pale and her lips without color. Sliced open like a slaughtered pig, she has been robbed of her life-giving force by her son-in-law. Antonia's dinner with her husband furnishes the scene for the second reference. The husband invites Antonia to share a glass of wine with him but she declines. "Y el vino," remarks the narrator, "al reflejo del candil, se le figuraba un coágulo de sangre" (1:126). Unmoved by her refusal, he drinks the wine, shrugging his shoulders. Antonia is without blood in the final scene because her husband, metaphorically speaking, consumed hers. Like her mother's before her, Antonia's life trickles away from her body, the result of living with fear for many years. The "natural death" suffered by Antonia cannot be understood without consideration of the two episodes just cited. Her death is precipitated by the return of her husband. Although he does not actually murder his wife, Antonia nonetheless dies because of him. Mimetic resistance requires the reader to put these pieces together for him/herself.

"Las cariñosas vecinas," Antonia's fellow washerwomen, play an instrumental role in **"El indulto."** Their prominence in both the beginning and final paragraphs, in addition to their function throughout the narrative, underscores the significance attributed to a community of women in this story. The women offer assistance, solace, companionship, and advice to the desperate Antonia. They stand guard at her home, prepare meals, and help with her washing. When Antonia is too ill to care

for her newborn son, several women feed the infant with milk from their own breasts. Their reception of the child stands in sharp contrast to that of the father's. Upon greeting his son for the first time, the father growls: "¡Qué chiquillo tan feo! Parece que lo chuparon las brujas" (1:126). The child, like his mother, is terrified of the surly intruder. The women also serve as a type of Greek chorus: they voice public opinion and criticize blatant injustices. There is harmony, cooperation, affection, and understanding among the inhabitants of this female microcosm. Despite their poverty and lack of education or worldly sophistication, the women portrayed in this story represent a true community of kindred spirits. Their bonds provide the only means of self-protection in a world controlled by men. Their solidarity is yet another site of female resistance in Pardo Bazán's text.

"El indulto" outwardly condemns the Spanish legal system and its lack of protection for the poor and for women.[6] Antonia and the other villagers blindly put their trust in the law: "esa entidad moral, de la cual Antonia formaba un concepto misterioso y confuso, era sin duda fuerza terrible, pero protectora; mano de hierro que la sostendría al borde del abismo" (1:123). The first time that her husband may be pardoned, Antonia seeks the advice of a lawyer. She is horrified to learn that she is obligated by law to live with the assassin as husband and wife until she can prove mistreatment as grounds for divorce. The neighbors second her dismay, proclaiming: "¡Qué leyes, divino Señor de los cielos! ¡Así los bribones que las hacen las aguantaran!" (1:123). The narrator continues their lament, noting the injustice of all lawsuits: "los pleitos no se acaban nunca, y peor aún si se acaban, porque los pierde siempre el inocente y el pobre" (1:124). Justice is the prerogative of the rich and the powerful, a privilege that by its very nature excludes women. Antonia's helplessness before the law exemplifies the legal status of nineteenth-century women. Instituted and enforced by men, the Spanish legal code was inherently sexist and unjust in its treatment of women as minors before the law. "El indulto" makes clear the inequities of such biased laws. At the end of the story the grandmother is dead, Antonia is dead, the child is orphaned and the husband runs away, unaccountable for his grisly deeds. What *indulto* did the victims receive in this tragic tale? The answer is obvious—justice serves only the interests of men. Those who are vulnerable (women, children, the elderly, and the poor) suffer the consequences.

Final recalcitrance in **"El indulto"** occasions us to search for a more thorough interpretation of the story's motives. Dissatisfied with the doctor's assessment, we return to the text to reexamine certain prevalent issues such as Antonia's plight, the role of women, and the biased legal system in greater detail. An understanding of the significance of these three elements in the events leading up to Antonia's "natural death" provides us with a veritable explanation for her demise. Unable further to withstand the afflictions imposed on her by an insensitive male establishment, Antonia succumbs to death, as she submits to her husband, with "la docilidad fatalista de la esclava." Divested of her life-giving force, Antonia gives up her life. The system wins again.

Final recalcitrance is also a determining factor of narrative resistance in **"Voz de la sangre."**[7] An unexplaining explanation, Wright's second category, leaves the reader feeling dissatisfied with the story's conclusion. Pardo Bazán employs this artifice to encourage her readers to return to the story in pursuit of further narrative disclosure. What we discover upon reconsideration of various textual elements is a story ripe with the interests and concerns of nineteenth-century women. Furthermore, **"Voz de la sangre"** playfully addresses earlier texts from the mythic, Golden Age, Romantic, and Naturalist traditions.[8] This dialogic exchange of intertexts in conjunction with the issues mentioned above allows for the continuous dialogue of male and female modes of discourse so much a part of Pardo Bazán's short fiction. The unexplaining explanation is yet another manifestation of Pardo Buzán's subversion from within.

"Voz de la sangre" recounts the story of Sabino and Leonarda, a childless couple who, despite public opinion, are content with the life God has given them. Leonarda's distraught sister visits them one day, and shortly thereafter the three leave for their country estate and then a year's sojourn to England and France. Upon their return, Sabino and Leonarda proudly display their new daughter, Aurora, born during their stay in Paris, while Leonarda's sister enters a convent. Malicious tongues question the veracity of Leonarda's story, but even they eventually succumb to the child's grace and charm. Many blissful years pass before the family is visited by a mysterious stranger who turns out to be the sister's seducer, Aurora's real father, come to make amends. Unaware of her relation to the *galán,* Aurora falls in love with him. An interview with her parents in the presence of the stranger, who hides behind a curtain in the room, reveals Aurora's true sentiments. Horrified at Aurora's response, the gallant hastily retreats, overwhelmed by sorrow. Attempting to console the man, the compassionate Leonarda suggests that perhaps the attraction Aurora felt for him "sea la voz de la sangre." "Si es voz de la sangre," he responds, "es voz que maldice" (2:204).

The final lines of the story suggest resolution. Reader comprehension, however, remains dissatisfied—the result of an unexplaining explanation. We return instead to the story itself for further clarification. The story begins with a mischievous speculation that questions the existence of happy marriages while simultaneously acknowledging Sabino and Leonarda's contentment with

one another: "Si hubo matrimonios felices, pocos tanto como el de Sabino y Leonarda" (2:201). Similarly, the concluding sentence to this paragraph exonerates Sabino and Leonarda's marriage while condemning those of others: "Ni una sola vez había tenido Leonarda que enjugar esas lágrimas furtivas de rabia y humillación que arrancan a las esposas ciertos reproches de los esposos" (2:202). Present at the story's onset, then, are two subjects salient to a feminist rereading of **"Voz de la sangre"**: marriage and reproduction.

In contrast to the barrenness of Leonarda's marriage, Pardo Bazán juxtaposes the fertility of the unwed sister. Hypocritical social morés, nonetheless, condemn both women: one for not having a child, the other for having one. Public opinion plays an important role in this regulation of the female body and its reproductive capabilities. Numerous references throughout the story, such as "al decir la gente," "lo que comentó," and "las preocupaciones del vulgo," evince society's power to control the individual. Returning from Paris with the child, Leonarda encounters "chismes, murmuraciones, cuentas por los dedos, sonrisitas y hasta indignaciones y 'tole tole' furioso," while her sister "se sepultó en un convento de Carmelitas" (2:202). Word choice here is most revealing, for not only does the sister hide herself away, she literally entombs herself, forsaking the world, pain, and pleasure. The stigma of having lost her honor is too much for the young woman to bear. Instead, she gives up her daughter and seeks refuge in a convent—one of the few outlets available to women at this time (Bonnie Smith 211).

Sabino and Leonarda represent ideal marriage partners. They share similar ages, dispositions, inclinations, and properties. Neither one blames the other for their lack of children. The harmonious *tranquilidad* of their relationship contrasts sharply with that of Leonarda's sister. Pregnant and without the support of the child's father, the desperate young woman seeks the assistance of her family. She arrives at the house pale, disfigured, crying and sad. Years later, her seducer also visits Sabino and Leonarda. He, however, is described as the classic Don Juan: handsome, elegant, wealthy and with an "aire de dominio peculiar de los hombres que han ocupado altos puestos o conseguido grandes triunfos de amor propio, viviendo siempre lisonjeados y felices" (2:203). This bold comparison of appearances makes clear the distinct fate particular to each party: woman as whores, man as gallants. The seducer and the seduced are judged by different moral codes.

Intertextuality also plays a significant role in Pardo Bazán's subversion from within. The gallant compares himself to Midas, the mythical king whose greed for gold nearly caused him to starve to death. In like manner, Aurora's father suffers because of his greed—he is denied the loving affection of his own daughter. It was also Midas, Ovid tells us, whom Apollo once punished by turning his ears into those of an ass. The comparison is noteworthy. Midas, writes classicist Edith Hamilton, "was an example of folly being as fatal as sin, for he meant no harm; he merely did not use any intelligence. His story suggests that he had none" (278). The gullant we now see is a foolish man; an avaricious jackass vanquished by a salacious appetite. Pardo Bazán's subtle inversion of the don Juan story reveals this "tenorio" to be a pathetic figure, a man unable to communicate with women other than as objects to be conquered.[9] An unwitting daughter realizes her mother's revenge. Dejected and defeated, the gallant disappears alone into the night.

In addition to its exaggerated romantic prose, **"Voz de la sangre"** also evokes the Golden Age dramas of honor and love.[10] The scene in which the gallant hides behind the curtain to discover Aurora's true sentiments, for example, is derivative of this seventeenth-century tradition. At the same time, perhaps, it also recalls Leandro Fernández de Moratín's *El sí de las niñas* (1806). Pardo Bazán's ingenious dialogue with earlier texts and traditions evinces the simultaneous appropriation and reinscription synonymous with dialogic discourse. This narrative strategy, enhanced by the text's final recalcitrance, provides the means by which she communicates her critical message without completely alienating her conservative audience. Disruptive reappropriation in **"Voz de la sangre"** is conveyed by the unexplaining explanation. Male and female modes of discourse converse, and meaning is given new form. The reader is left to reconsider patriarchy's cultural institutions and judge for him/herself.

"La novia fiel," the third story analyzed in this essay, represents a synthesis of two of Wright's categories of final recalcitrance.[11] **"La novia fiel"** combines mimetic resistance with the suppression of an unexplaining explanation. Such overlapping strategies of resistance are common to Pardo Bazán's short stories. Her reader must actively engage him/herself in the process of creation. Ellipses permeate the final paragraphs of **"La novia fiel."** Because the story stops short of completing the explanation begun by one of its protagonists, the reader fills in the gaps using clues gleaned from the text. Final recalcitrance requires us to return to the text to search for these clues. In so doing, we rediscover those elements omitted or suppressed by the dominant discourse. Recalcitrance gives rise to dialogue: male and female modes of discourse converge. The unexplaining explanation suppressed in **"La novia fiel"** challenges hypocritical social mores and prescribed gender roles. In the spaces between the unfinished sentences, the female subject emerges.

"La novia fiel" is the story of Amelia and Germán, two young lovers whose protracted engagement endures ten years. While Germán studies law at the university in Santiago de Compostela, Amelia awaits his return while reading, rereading and answering his letters. An "año de prueba para la novia" (1:305) is the result of Germán's decision to continue his education in Madrid. He returns finally to Marineda to look for employment. Initially overjoyed, Amelia becomes increasingly anxious as her diligent fiancé enters the world of local politics, seemingly content with the status quo of the engagement. Her parents, as well as the entire town, grow concerned over the radical decline in Amelia's health during the ninth year. The cause of her ailment remains a mystery at first, but Amelia soon recognizes its source: "su mal no era sino deseo, ansia, prisa, necesidad de casarse" (1:306). Relieved though slightly embarrassed, Amelia attempts to emulate Germán's stalwart patience and forbearance. An abrupt realization, however, shatters this ideal image and Amelia calls off the engagement. No one except her confessor, we are told, knows why.[12] The story ends with Amelia's elliptical declaration to Father Incienso proclaiming her love for Germán but knowing that she must leave him. The reader is left to determine the significance of her words as well as those omitted by the ellipses. Comprehension requires our return to the text.

Germán's year in Madrid proved most difficult for Amelia. He wrote infrequently, his "billetes garrapateados al vuelo, quizá sobre la mesa de un café, concisos, insulsos, sin jugo de ternura" contrast sharply with the "largas y tiernas epístolas" written from Santiago (1:305). Her friends try to distract her, suggesting that she not sit home every night. Germán, they reason, made the most of his time in Madrid: "¡Bien inocente serías si creyeses que no te la pega! . . . A mí me escribe mi primo Lorenzo que vio a Germán muy animado en el teatro con 'unas' . . ." (1:305). Amelia's *sinsabores, dudas,* and *sospechas* are laid to rest with Germán's return. The reader, however, intuits the words which her friends have not spoken. Madrid represents a turning point in the story's trajectory. Amelia's model *novio* may not be so ideal after all.

Amelia's illness and recovery and the subsequent dissolution of her engagement originate with her desire/ yearning/need to marry. Ashamed of these feelings, Amelia vows to hide them from Germán, her parents, and the rest of the world. The subject of Amelia's sudden realization in the next paragraph is obscured by the use of four ellipses. Similarly, elliptical constructions pervade her conversation with the priest. Father Incienso alludes to *esos entretenimientos* typical of men before they marry. Amelia responds that her love for Germán compels her to leave him: "¡Le quería . . . , le quiero . . . , y por lo mismo , . . , por lo mismo, padre! ¡Si no le dejo . . . , le imito! ¡Yo también . . . !" (1:307). The missing pieces of the puzzle become visible as the reader assembles a multitude of disparate clues. Amelia's desire to marry is both spiritual and physical. Germán can afford to be patient and resigned because he has satisfied his sexual needs. Amelia, on the other hand, immersed in the "nociones de honor y honestidad que le inculcaron desde la ninez" (1:306), fears seeking sexual gratification outside the bonds of marriage: ie., imitating Germán. She calls off the engagement as a means of self-protection. By separating herself from Germán, she avoids the perils and the stigma of the "fallen woman." In so doing, she maintains her status as "the faithful fiancée."

Society enforces a distinct moral code for each of the sexes. Though perhaps not condoned, Germán's actions are socially accepted. Even the symbolic voice of the Catholic Church, Father Incienso, excuses Germán's behavior as a male prerogative: "Los hombres . . . , por desgracia. . . . Mientras está soltero habrá tenido esos entretenimientos. . . . Pero usted . . ." (1:307). This lamentable yet acceptable conduct in men does not, of course, pertain also to women. While men are expected to experiment and explore their sexuality, women are taught to suppress it. Germán endures a lengthy engagement because society is willing to overlook his "innocent" male transgressions. Amelia remains celibate and bears the cost both physically and mentally. Deceived by the false pretensions of an unfaithful fiancé, she feels her ten long years of fidelity crash down around her. Although Germán's betrayal initially leaves her *destrozada,* Amelia regains control of her life and breaks off the engagement. Defying the wishes of Germán, her parents, the Church and society, Amelia first rediscovers, then reclaims her self. In the end, the faithful *novia* remains true to herself.

Biased standards of morality and prejudicial societal attitudes are two salient issues explored in Pardo Bazán's **"La novia fiel."** Mimetic resistance and the suppression of the unexplaining explanation combine strategies to present a critical examination of an unjust code of social ethics. Dialogic discourse in the form of elliptical omissions creates the means by which disruptive reappropriation prevails throughout the text: the reader takes part in the creative process, contributing that which has been omitted. Male and female modes of discourse intersect. Final recalcitrance in **"La novia fiel"** gives rise once again to the emergence of a female subject. The voice of female frustration and female desire is distinctly heard.

Likewise, Joyce Tolliver's insightful and provocative reading of this story, based on a linguistic examination of the narrator's discourse, examines not only Pardo Bazán's harsh criticism of socially inscribed attitudes towards sex and sexuality, especially female sexuality, but also explores the emergence of a female subject via an inversion of syntactic symmetry (909). Phrases with

Germán as syntactic subject far outnumber those with Amelia as subject, Tolliver contends, up until the point in the text where Amelia ends the engagement. Then the balance is reversed (910). In this story, concludes Tolliver, Pardo Bazán focuses on "the humiliation associated with Amelia's sudden knowledge of her own sexuality, thus managing both to expose the 'secret' of the power of feminine sexual desire and to acquit herself of any accountability for the exposure of that 'secret'" (916). In short, Pardo Bazán's manipulation of the language itself, in this case the syntax of agency and passivity, results in yet another narrative strategy of disruptive reappropriation. Continuously shifting among and between narrative modes and literary devices, she avoids direct confrontation and thus escapes, to borrow Lacan's terminology, the wrath of the Father.

Variations of mimetic resistance and symbolic recalcitrance, Wright's fourth category, provide the means for subverting dominant male discourse in the story **"El comadrón."** The opening sentence of the story reads like a gothic horror tale.[13] As she does throughout the story, Pardo Bazán creates a series of juxtapositions in the opening paragraph whereby the frightful storm outside contrasts with the tranquility of the midwife's home indoors. Pardo Bazán makes use of certain conventions characteristic of the gothic horror story (the menacing storm, the mysterious stranger, the lengthy journey, the imposing castle, the angelic woman), both to create an enjoyable story and to explore a topic outside the realm of realist/naturalist fiction. **"El comadrón"** recounts the supernatural tale of the birth of *la verdad* and the responses of two men to that truth. The reader is asked to focus his/her attention on the symbolic meaning of events rather than on their plausibility in "real life." The circumstances surrounding the birth and subsequent death of *la verdad* are the focal points of **"El comadrón."**

The story recounts how a male midwife hoping to enjoy a peaceful night's sleep, confides to his wife that only a crazy woman would give birth on such a night, "con este tiempo tan fatal" (2:157). Wicked weather, contrasting elements, ill-timed births, and irrational premonitions set the tone for the rest of the story. Awakened at dawn to assist an inexperienced mother-to-be, the male midwife grudgingly assembles his instruments and greets the mysterious client dressed in black. The client, who is never named, is described by the omniscient narrator as having a wide forehead, burning and imperious eyes, a long grey beard and "un aire indefinible de dignidad y tristeza [que] hacían imponente a aquel hombre" (2:157). The singularity of the situation increases when, after inquiring about the health of the mother and the distance to the client's house, the male midwife receives the strange response that the woman is in grave condition but it is only the child that matters. Determined to save the life of the mother, the compassionate midwife attempts to quicken the pace. His efforts, however, are in vain. The woman is dead by the time the two arrive.

Without having known her, the male midwife experiences a certain sadness upon seeing the beautiful woman's dead body. Her exquisite features are described in detail, in sharp contrast to those of the client mentioned above. Initially the midwife is loathe to cut open the "divine" body, but duty eventually outweighs his aesthetic sensibilities. Meanwhile, the client has become more insistent, using his position and power, addressing the man midwife now as *tú*. The instant the midwife is prepared to cut, the *extraño cliente* grabs his arm and whispers in his ear: "¡Cuidado! Conviene que sepas lo que haces. Este seno que vas a abrir encierra no un ser humano, no una criatura, sino 'una verdad'" (2:158). From this moment on, **"El comadrón"** becomes a full-fledged supernatural story. Disjunctive symbolic elements strewn throughout the story are left for the reader to interpret on his/her own.

The client's warning has a profound effect on the kindly male midwife. Trembling with cowardice and egoism, he vacillates before operating. Arguing with himself he questions: "¿Y quién le había de agradecer que cooperase al feliz nacimiento de una verdad? ¿Qué mayor delito para su mujer, sus amigos, su pueblo, su nación tal vez? ¿Qué crimen se paga tan caro?" (2:158). Nonetheless, the midwife consents, presenting to the client at last "una criatura extraña y repugnante, una especie de escuerzo, de trazas ridículas, negruzco, flaco, informe" (2:158). The ugliness of the *monigote* convinces the midwife that this cannot be a truth. The client, however, insists that it is precisely its unsightliness that makes the creature a truth. When first perceived, he continues, truth horrifies the observer. Only when we have held it in our hearts, given it our life's blood, and affirmed its worth does truth become beautiful.

The orphaned truth requires someone to nurture it. The client declines, explaining that he is truth's announcer, not its caregiver. He challenges the male midwife to take charge of the orphan, that is, if he has the courage to do so. Masculine pride and *viril arrogancia* give rise to the midwife's affirmative response. After a brief respite, the midwife begins his journey home, the child wrapped up in his arms. As dusk settles, he reexamines his charge only to discover that *la verdad* has grown stronger and larger; four white teeth shine from its mouth. Truth bites the midwife and then wails vehemently. Unable to control the deafening noise, the midwife covers truth's mouth with his hand, then with his raincoat, applying pressure until the crying desists. At the river's edge, he unwraps his raincoat and throws the corpse into the current.

The abrupt ending forces the reader to return to the story to seek further clarification and explanation. How do we reconcile the male midwife's final action with his previous efforts? What motivates him to kill the orphan? What is the underlying symbolic scheme uniting the story into a coherent whole? What do these symbols represent? A thorough reexamination of detail prompted by the story's final recalcitrance provides ample material for a feminist rereading of **"El comadrón."** Symbolic recalcitrance combined with mimetic resistance mandate our return to the text.

The introduction to the story, of course, originates with the title **"El comadrón."** The *Real Academia Española* defines a *comadrón* as "el cirujano que asiste a la mujer en el acto de parto." The prefix *co-* signals joint participation, in this case, by both male midwife and mother. In Pardo Bazán's story, however, there is no cooperation, no reciprocity, no mutual participation. Rather, the *comadrón* acts unilaterally, extracting from the dead mother the body of the orphaned truth. The male midwife's final act contradicts everything we previously learned about his compassionate, pious, and kindly nature. We are horrified by truth's suffocation and subsequent disposal in the river. The inversion of conventional role expectations sets the stage for the numerous reversals found throughout the story. What appears to be one thing in this story, we learn, may well be another. Contrasts, contradictions, reversals, and antitheses abound.

The eerie nature of the storm and the client who arrives at dawn create an atmosphere in which indetermination and uncertainty reign. The man midwife experiences *humildad involuntaria* and *respeto inexplicable* before the commanding presence of the enigmatic client. Yet this sovereign client is no more willing to take responsibility for the truth once conceived than the male midwife who abandons his obligations at the first signs of complication. The client's callousness towards truth's mother is another element occasioning distrust in the reader. Why does he dismiss her so readily, concerned only for the welfare of her progeny? Why does he scrutinize the male midwife once the decision has been made to care for the orphan? Again, we return to the text for further clarification.

Human reproduction is the vehicle chosen by Pardo Bazán to represent the inception of truth.[14] Beautiful yet now without life of its own, the woman's body provides the means by which truth is both engendered and delivered into this world.[15] Two men assist in this birth—a parturition that requires not only the death of the mother but also the mutilation of her exquisite form. Ultimately, the child/truth is also stifled—its lifeless body tossed into the waves of the flowing river. Like the nameless mother, the nineteenth-century woman writer who dared to bring forth the product of her own creation often was effectively silenced. Those whose writing engendered truth frequently perished, as writers, attempting to bring that truth to light. As the client tells the male midwife: "Esta, ya lo ves, ha acabado con su madre . . . ¡No se lleva impunemente en las entrañas una verdad!" (2:158). The woman writer suffered at the hands of men whose recognition and assistance she nonetheless required in order to take part, albeit peripherally, in literary circles. Should the writing/child somehow survive the labor that consumed its mother, it too would be silenced, buried beneath the thunderous waves of mainstream (male) public opinion.[16]

A reexamination of **"El comadrón"** clarifies the symbolic framework obscured by the story's final recalcitrance. The difficult task of bringing truths to light, symbolized here by the birthing process, can also be read as the difficult process endured by women writers who attempted to publish their work in an industry dominated and controlled by men. The nameless woman in Pardo Bazán's *cuento* loses command of her creation, delivering *la verdad* into the hands of men. Truth's survival, contingent upon their shifting whims, ultimately results in asphyxiation: the troublesome cries smothered by the depths of the river. Truth's voice, however, continues to be heard above the waves because Pardo Bazán tells truth's story. **"El comadrón"** bears witness to a woman writer's story at the same time as it recounts the creation of another. Disruptive reappropriation, in the form of symbolic recalcitrance, articulates both female desire and subjectivity. The "body-as-text" makes evident these expressions of female desire.

"La flor seca," the fifth and final story examined in this study, illustrates Pardo Bazán's use of modal discontinuity in her short fiction. In this variation of Wright's final recalcitrance, the reader experiences a contradiction in the primary assumptions on which the coherence of the fictional world depends. Two conflicting conceptions of causation are left unresolved; no one answer prevails. The protagonist's version of **"La flor seca"** is distinct from the one the reader perceives. At story's end, however, neither one is conclusive. Did "A" occur or did "B" occur? The reader is never quite certain.

The story is told from the perspective of an omniscient narrator. The conde del Acerolo, seated in his recently deceased wife's private bedroom, reviews her personal items for bestowal on the proper recipients. As the Count examines the contents of her wardrobe, jewelry case and *secrétaire,* the reader is privy to his thoughts and recollections. The scrutinized articles become progressively more intimate as the Count works his way through accessories, clothing, jewelry, and letters. Inside the writing desk's "secret drawer" the count discovers a dried flower delicately wrapped in silk. An un-

familiar handwriting marks the leaves with a specific date: year, month, day, and hour. Consumed with rage, the Count interrogates first the maidservant and then the chauffeur. The maid remembers nothing peculiar about the Countess' activities on that particular day. The chauffeur, on the other hand, readily recalls the date and reminds the Count of his own, not his wife's, indiscretion. The Count remains silent and the servant discreetly exits. The reader is left with two conflicting versions of what occurred on "el día fatal." We return to the text in search of resolution.

The chauffeur's disclosure in the final paragraph is not that startling to the careful reader. The Count's attitude towards women in general and marriage in particular is evident from the first sentence forward. The interjection of reported speech reveals to us his inner thoughts. Having prided himself on behavior that was "cortés, afable y correcto" as a husband, the Count was able to separate "la santa coyunda" from "los devaneos y los amoríos" (1:204). Never, the narrator remarks ironically, did he confuse the two. Examining his conscience while reviewing his wife's clothing and papers, the Count finds reasons only for self-praise and none that explains why the Countess would leave this world "minada por una enfermedad de languidez" (1:204). With one glance, he decides what should go to her maid, what should be boxed and delivered to the bank, and what should be given to her friends—some of whom, he recalls, were very pretty. Hardly the image of the grieving widower, this *expurgo* brings the Count unexplained happiness. Profound egotism, insensitivity and hints of infidelity darken the Count's majestic image of himself. Between the lines the reader encounters the subtle juxtaposition of two contrasting views: the Count's and the narrator's. The final disclosure of his affair by the chauffeur stuns the Count but not the reader. He/she has read both texts.

The subject of the Countess's affair is left open to interpretation. The chauffeur, Manuel, reminds the Count of his visit to the *barrio* on the afternoon in question. He also recalls the excuse he gave to the Countess to account for his master's absence: the Count was hunting hares at the Venta de la Rubia. The Countess retires long before her husband returns from his "hunting" expedition. One could surmise that the Countess recorded the date to mark the loss of her husband's fidelity. The text confirms the date as fairly recent and as anterior to the Countess's illness. This statement immediately follows the description of the dried flower, connecting the two events in the reader's mind. If the Countess indeed left this world sick with languor, then perhaps her unhappiness stemmed from the date inscribed on the yellowed leaves. One mystery, however, remains unsolved: whose handwriting marks the flower? The script on the leaves is described as "letra microscópica y desconocida" (1:205). Yet an earlier description of the Countess's papers characterizes her script as "letra inglesa de prolongado rasgo rectilíneo" (1:205). Contradictory evidence leaves the question unanswered. **"La flor seca"** may signify the Count's betrayal, an amorous liaison for the Countess, neither, or both. The reader must decide for him/herself.

Modal discontinuity in **"La flor seca"** causes the reader to reconsider the assumptions upon which the Count's version of the story is based. The Count prides himself on being a correct and courteous husband. Not once, however, does he question the double standard that grants men both a proper marriage and their idle flirtations and love affairs. Instead, he seethes with rage imagining the same possibility for his wife. Manuel's disclosure at the end of the text may humble the Count momentarily, but the primary assumptions on which his imagined world depends are not altered quite so easily. The reader gains access to other perspectives in the fictional mode through the story's final recalcitrance. Unresolved contradictions motivate us to seek alternative explanations. **"La flor seca"** challenges both the inequitable standards institutionalized in marriage and the attitudes reinforcing these arbitrary structures by appropriating the dried flower as a conventional sign of a lost love or of a cherished memory for its own subversive use. Ultimately, the reader determines these issues for him/herself.

The stories examined in this essay represent five examples of the use of final recalcitrance in the short stories of Emilia Pardo Bazán. By disrupting textual closure, the numerous variations of this strategy allow for the continuous interaction between male and female modes of discourse in Pardo Bazán's fiction. These works both challenge and conform to the dominant discourse. Centripetal and centrifugal forces coexist. Pardo Bazán manipulates final recalcitrance in her short fiction to assert the voice of the female subject. Careful not to exceed certain self-imposed boundaries of permissible radicalism, she nonetheless defies the status quo by taking issue with hegemonic institutions, structures, and attitudes endemic to late nineteenth-century Spanish society. At once combative and conciliatory, these stories exemplify the gendered writing strategies characteristic of women's texts. Disruptive reappropriation through final recalcitrance constitutes one particular version of Pardo Bazán's subversion from within.

The emergence of the female subject in the five stories discussed above takes place both within and without the dominant discourse. This relationship is constituted by dialogue. By manipulating the narrative conventions of closure and/or anticlosure, Pardo Bazán creates a space in which the woman writer's voice becomes audible. Gaps, omissions, deletions, and silences provide the openings through which the author articulates both female frustration and desire. The female subject affirms

her position by simultaneously appropriating and rejecting male tradition. Consequently, she also destabilizes patriarchal notions of a unified whole. Pardo Bazán's distinctly female discursive practice originates from this site.

Notes

1. The author wishes to thank Maryellen Bieder for her incisive reading of an earlier draft of this article.

2. For similar points of view, see Bravo Villasante 207; Clemessy 177; and Shaw 216-217.

3. Rather than entitle this third category, Wright describes its pertinent characteristics (125-6). Accordingly, I will use phrases from his descriptions to denote this category throughout my analyses.

4. Paredes Núñez's four-volume edition of Pardo Bazán's *Cuentos completos* (1990) gives the following bibliographical information: "El indulto" was first published in *La Revista Ibérica,* no. 1, 1883, and later included in *Cuentos de Marineda.* "El comádron" was published in *El Imparcial,* April 2, 1890, and later included in *Cuentos dramáticos.* "La flor seca" appeared in *El Liberal,* August 7, 1893, and was later included in *Cuentos nuevos.* "La novia fiel" was published in *El Liberal,* February 11, 1894, and later included in *Cuentos de amor.* "Voz de la sangre" first appeared in *El Imparcial,* July 29, 1895, and was later included in *Cuentos dramáticos.*

5. For a reading of "El indulto" that examines Pardo Bazán's special blend of naturalism and free will, see Charnon-Deutsch's *The Nineteenth-Century Spanish Story* 83-86. For a reading that examines Pardo Bazán's challenge to Victorian notions of the "angel in the house," see Janet Pérez's "Subversion of Victorian Values and Idea Types: Pardo Bazán and the Angel del Hogar" 38-39.

6. Pérez also underscores Pardo Bazán's exposure of and challenge to the Spanish state's legal biases against women (38-39).

7. In her reading of Pardo Bazán's "feminist stories," Carmen Bravo-Villasante places "Voz de la sangre" among "la serie de estos cuentos atrevidos [donde] hay una condena de la sociedad de su tiempo" (201). "En 'Voz de la sangre,'" she concludes, asistiremos a otra venganza, podríamos decir que providencial: el castigo del tenorio del que se enamora su propia hija" (202).

8. Cervantes' exemplary novel "La fuerza de la sangre," for example, provides not only the symbolic background of physical/spiritual violation (in this case rape) and its Christian resolution, but also the

title from which Pardo Bazán rewrites her own version of the story, self-consciously exchanging "fuerza" for "voz."

9. For an analysis of the divergent literary and critical (re)configurations of the don Juan character as a potent social force in patriarchal society and culture, see James Mandrell's *Don Juan and the Point of Honor: Seduction, Patriarchal Society, and Literary Tradition.*

10. For a feminist reading of Spanish Golden Age texts, see Mary Gossy's *Untold Story: Women and Theory in Golden Age Texts.*

11. Bravo-Villasante considers "La novia fiel" to be one of Pardo Bazán's "most daring and feminist" stories (201). In it, she concludes, "la Pardo exige igualdad de derechos para el hombre y la mujer en las relaciones amorosas, especialmente cuando el noviazgo es largo" (201).

12. In her reading of *Insolación,* Scarlett describes Pardo Bazán's use of the confession as a frequent discursive strategy allowing the body to voice its desire (192). Like Asís, then, Amelia's confession leads to self-justification: a means to fulfilling an end suppressed by the dominant ideology, that is, the articulation of female sexuality and desire.

13. For recent feminist readings of the Gothic tale, see Susan Wolstenholme *Gothic (re)visions: Writing Women as Readers* and Eugenia DeLamotte *Perils of the Night: a Feminist Study of Nineteenth-Century Gothic.*

14. Michel Foucault examines the body as both a biological and historical construct in *The History of Sexuality.* Using Foucault's premises, Delese Wear and Lois La Civita Nixon examine how literature (mis)represents women and medicine in *Literary Anatomies: Women's Bodies and Health in Literature.* For analyses of body politics in Hispanic literature, see Paul Julian Smith's *The Body Hispanic* and Elizabeth Scarlett's *Under Construction.*

15. Scarlett discerns two distinct corporeal divergences from male-oriented norms in Pardo Bazán's writing: the body-as-text and the body-as-process. As protagonist, the female body speaks desire and makes demands of its possessor. This "body-turned-against-itself," concludes Scarlett, expresses "the discomfort, confinement, and simmering pent-up desires" of women who use their bodies for sexual expression, or of women who, like Pardo Bazán, use them for the act of writing (186).

16. Scarlett underscores three points of intersection between feminine physicality and textuality in the works of Pardo Bazán, Rosa Chacel, and Mercè

Rodoreda: the prevalence of the body as text wherein bodily markings or movements take on significance as writing; maternality wherein the empowerment of the female body results in the body as "speaking subject"; and the dissolution of the mind/body dualism wherein the body itself functions as language (7-8).

Works Cited

Bravo-Villasante, Carmen. *Vida y obra de Emilia Pardo Bazán.* Madrid: Novelas y Cuentos, 1987.

Charnon-Deutsch, Lou. *The Nineteenth-Century Spanish Story: Textual Strategies of a Genre in Transition.* London: Tamesis, 1985.

Clemessy, Nelly. *Les contes d'Emilia Pardo Bazán.* 2 vols. Paris: Centre de Recherches Hispaniques, 1971.

Foucault, Michel. *The History of Sexuality.* New York: Pantheon, 1978.

Gossy, Mary. *Untold Story: Women and Theory in Golden Age Texts.* Ann Arbor: U of Michigan P, 1989.

Hamilton, Edith. *Mythology.* New York: Mentor, 1956.

Mandrell, James. *Don Juan and the Point of Honor.* University Park: Penn State UP, 1992.

May, Charles E., ed. *Short Story Theories.* Columbus: Ohio UP, 1976.

Pattison, Walter. "Short Stories and Criticism." *Emilia Pardo Bazán.* New York: Twayne, 1971.

Paredes Núñez, Juan, ed. *Cuentos completos.* Four vols. La Coruña: Galicia, 1990.

Pérez, Janet. "Subversion of Victorian Values and Idea Types: Pardo Bazán and the Angel del Hogar." *Hispanófila* 113 (1995): 31-43.

Scarlett, Elizabeth A. *Under Construction: The Body in Spanish Novels.* Charlottesville: Virginia UP, 1994.

Shaw, Donald. *A Literary History of Spain: The Nineteenth Century.* London: Benn, 1972.

Smith, Bonnie G. *Changing Lives: Women in European History Since 1700.* Lexington, Massachusetts: D.C. Health, 1989.

Smith, Paul Julian. *The Body Hispanic: Gender and Sexuality in Spanish and Spanish American Literature.* Oxford: Claredon, 1989.

Tolliver, Joyce. "Knowledge, Desire, and Syntactic Empathy in Pardo Bazán's 'La novia fiel.'" *Hispania* 72.4 (1989): 103-118.

Wear, Elizabeth and Lois La Civita Nixon. *Literary Anatomies: Women's Bodies and Health in Literature.* Albany: State U of New York P, 1994.

Wright, Austin. "Recalcitrance in the Short Story." Susan Lohafer and Jo Ellyn Clarey, eds., *Short Story Theory at the Crossroads.* Baton Rouge: Louisiana State UP, 1989.

Joyce Tolliver (essay date 1998)

SOURCE: Tolliver, Joyce. "'Masculinity' as Narrative Ventriloquism: '¿Cobardía?'" In *Cigar Smoke and Violet Water: Gendered Discourse in the Stories of Emilia Pardo Bazán,* pp. 90-108. Lewisburg, Pa.: Bucknell University Press, 1998.

[*In the following essay, Tolliver demonstrates how Pardo Bazán uses irony to undercut the masculine narrative voice in her story "¿Cobardía?."*]

Among the numerous novels and novellas that Pardo Bazán composed in the first person, not one of them employs a female narrator. Further, more than a few of her first-person narrators seem to be identified with the most conventional notions of masculinity, even verging at times on misogyny. A cursory examination of even a fraction of her almost six hundred stories reveals the same phenomenon: it is extremely difficult to find a story narrated in an explicitly feminine voice, with the exception of a few stories that make use of framed narration (for example, **"Champagne," "El encaje roto," "Sor Aparición"**) or a narrative voice that could be identified with that of the author, despite the lack of linguistic signs to this effect (**"Piña," "Feminista"**). Given that Pardo Bazán is among those nineteenth-century European authors who most thoroughly and consciously represented the social and affective experiences of women, and especially considering her lifelong commitment to feminism, this aspect of her narrative production seems curious indeed. Nevertheless, critical explorations of this aspect of her work have been limited.

Bauer (1994) has examined what she calls (after Madeleine Kahn 1991) "narrative transvestism" in *Memorias de un solterón* 1896, [*Memoirs of a Confirmed Bachelor*] a work whose very title calls attention to questions of gender, in the obvious differentiation of the author and her fictional voice. In more general terms, Maryellen Bieder (1987, 1989, 1990) has investigated the relationship of gender and genre in *Los pazos de Ulloa* (1886) and *La madre naturaleza* (1887), which, although written in the third person, employ nearly exclusive focalization through the male protagonists. But in general, Pardo Bazán criticism has yet to thoroughly explore the textual, pragmatic, and social functions of the masculine-coded narrative voice, and the apparent resulting silencing of the feminine voice, in this author's works. This may come as no surprise, given that mainstream narratology itself has almost completely ig-

nored the dynamics set into play when a woman writer employs a male narrator—just as it has largely excluded gender issues altogether from its discussions.

As I noted in chapter 3, Pardo Bazán was in many ways hampered by the conceptions still dominant in Spain at the turn of the century about what subject matter, and what style, was appropriate for women writers. Taking into account Lanser's observations (1992) about the historical and cultural contexts surrounding the use of female personal voice, I believe that it is no coincidence that we very often find female personal voice and focalization through female protagonists in the "sentimental little stories with moral pretensions" and the "other weeds and showy flowers of the fallow feminine field" that Pardo Bazán so reviled.[1] I believe that it was partly on account of this desire to dissociate herself from the discredited female literary tradition, and partly because of readers' tendencies to read female-authored narratives written in personal voice through a petty moralizing prism, that Pardo Bazán chose to limit her use of female personal voice in her fiction. The majority of her texts are written in what Lanser calls authorial voice, and when she does write in personal voice, the narrator is almost invariably male. Thus, it is little wonder that a critic such as Robert Osborne should comment that Pardo Bazán wrote her short stories "'as if she were a man'" and that "the reader actually believes that the author is male" [la llevó a escribir relatos breves 'como si fuese un hombre.' Y en verdad el lector cree que el autor es varón (Osborne 1964, 95)].

I would like to suggest that this critical reaction, seen so frequently in readings of Pardo Bazán's works, can be explained by the confluence of at least two separate phenomena. On the one hand, we are accustomed to the voice of authority speaking in deep bass tones; it is, in many cultures, a masculine voice. Logically, then, when we encounter a narrative voice that unequivocally imposes its authority, we "hear" (read) that voice as masculine. But on the other hand, a careful examination of the narrative dynamics of many of Pardo Bazán's stories suggests that there is also something else at work here, something that is not nearly as simple as the assignment of masculine gender to the voice of authority.

It happens frequently that we find, in the narrative works of this author, a masculine narrative voice—or a focalization through the perspective of a male protagonist—in which we detect intonations that are ironic, antagonistic, in Bakhtinian terms, or even fully parodic. In these stories, the deployment of the masculine narrative voice itself results, curiously, in an interrogation of some aspect of masculine discourse. By no means is this phenomenon limited to **"¿Cobardía?"**; as I have discussed elsewhere, (1994a, 1994b) it is set into play both in **"Mi suicidio"** and in **"Sor Aparición,"** among many others.

"**¿Cobardía?**", published in *El Imparcial* in 1891,[2] exemplifies on many levels the way in which this author's utilization of a masculine narrative voice turns the masculine voice against itself, thereby contesting several aspects of conventional notions of what constitutes masculinity. The anonymous narrator relates a conversation he had with several of his acquaintances during the nightly gathering held in a room of Marineda's new club that the members have named La Pecera ["the fishbowl"], for its abundance of imposing windows looking out onto the street. La Pecera is also the setting for several crucial narrative passages of the novel *Memorias de un solterón,* (1896) and in fact the protagonist of that novel, Mauro Pareja, also appears in this story, although here his character is considerably less refined.

The discursive context of this story is explicitly and exclusively masculine, for the story is set during a meeting of the Fishbowl Society [Sociedad la Pecera], composed of what the narrator calls "the toast of male Marineda" [el "todo Marineda" masculino y selecto (118)]; in other words, the "big fish" [los peces gordos (118)] of the town.[3] Their activities correspond to the most conventional, "hegemonic" masculinity:[4] on the night when the events of the story take place, they have, for example, "smoked, gossiped, debated administrative, scientific, and literary programs; told off-color stories, refined some of the thornier questions of the 'erotological' science; picked over the bones of the dozen young ladies who were always upon the dissecting table; touched on local politics and analyzed, for the hundredth time, the operetta company" [se había fumado, murmurado, debatido programas administrativos, científicos y literarios; contado verdores, aquilatado puntos difíciles de la ciencia erotológica; roído algo los zancajos a la docena de señoritas que estaban siempre sobre la mesa de disección; picado en la política local y analizado por centésima vez la compañía de la zarzuela (118)]. The narrator thus represents masculine conversation as one that concerns itself with politics, science, criticism of literature and music, gossip, and above all, sex, given that a third of the nine themes mentioned are related to this realm. The first activity the narrator mentions is smoking, which serves as an obvious masculine-coded cultural sign, thus establishing a clearly gendered frame for the narration that follows. We would expect, then, that the conversation would revolve around conventionally masculine topics, and we are not disappointed. Nevertheless, the narrator presents these topics with an ironic irreverence that highlights the very conventionality of these topics.

The mention of gossip at the beginning of the list, just after the mention of smoking, serves not only to indicate that the conversation that will follow is not of the most serious in nature, but also to undercut the establishment of the exaggeratedly masculine discourse: gossip is an activity normally associated with the frivolous, with the private sphere, and therefore with the feminine.[5] In this way, the narrator prepares us for some play with gender conventions, which will be developed later in the narration, and which I will examine in this chapter.[6] The men's observations on "serious" topics, such as politics, science, and literature, appear to be mixed with the "off-color stories" they tell; and these stories lead to the discussion of what the narrator calls "'erotological' science." The transformation of these "off-color stories" into "science" cannot be anything but ironic. Finally, the narrator suggests that the discussion of "erotology" fuses with malicious gossip through the clinically dehumanizing image of the "dozen young women who were always on the dissecting table" [la docena de señoritas que estaban siempre sobre la mesa de disección (118)]. These are coldblooded fish indeed, as the narrative language emphasizes.

Finally the "big fish" turn to a discussion of what is perhaps the Spanish masculine theme par excellence: "valor and the ways of proving and testing it" [el valor y los modos de probarlo (118)]. Given the context that has been established up to this point of an almost clichéd masculinity, the narratee should not expect subtleties or profound musings on this topic; nor are these to be found, at first, in the conversation of these piscine Marinedans. Mauro Pareja, "a fish of many pounds" [pez de muchas libras (119)], argues in favor of the abolition of the duel, not for humanitarian reasons, but rather because he considers this custom too refined and artificial. He says disputes should be resolved honestly, with fists. Commander Irazu rejects this solution, not for its brutality, but rather because it pertains to an inferior social class: "'Fists are for cartwrights'" [El puño es de carreteros (119)]. When Pareja suggests that in fact it would be more appropriate for the parties in question to fight tooth and nail rather than to duel, the commander scoffs at this idea for its assimilation, not only of manners associated with the proletariat, but even worse, with women: "'Like fishwives!' snorted Irazu. 'Nice system. Any day now we'll be tearing each others' hair out'" ["'Como las verduleras," bufó Irazu. "Bonito sistema. El mejor día nos arrancamos el moño" (119)]. The characters' dialogue thus foregrounds the element of social class and the more obvious element of gender as essential components of the venerable masculine tradition of the duel, as well as of the concept(s) of honor on which this tradition is based.

In fact, "valor and the ways of proving and testing it" form the theme of the conversation, not only in the sense of discourse topic, but also in the way in which it provides a frame for the discussion as a social, extralinguistic event. The participants not only speak of masculine valor, they exhibit it too, through the proliferation of bellicose statements that make up their discourse. They do not exchange opinions; they reject others' opinions in order to impose their own. The entire conversation is dedicated to the struggle of each participant to establish his place in the masculine hierarchy. The sort of masculine conversation that is represented here is, more than an authentic conversation, in the etymological sense of turning together, a manifestation of what Walter Ong (1981) has called ritual combat. Deborah Tannen (1990, 1993, 1994) has helped to popularize Ong's theories about competition in masculine discourse.[7] Tannen, drawing on the work of Ong, proposes that males are linguistically socialized, through interactions with other males, to see conversational interaction as a game in which each man or boy must struggle to maintain the highest possible position relative to other males, in a hierarchy of dominance and control.[8]

It must be noted, however, that this ritual combat does not eliminate the possibility of solidarity among its participants; in fact, it very well could help to create solidarity, as Tannen demonstrates (1993, 1994). Tannen also stresses the importance of considering the diversity of cultural attitudes toward what Ong calls "adversative" interactions; they do not always signal aggression, and at times may signal intimacy or in-group status. Recent studies by Cameron (1997), Pujolar i Cos (1997), Johnson and Finlay (1997), and Kiesling (1997) all highlight this function of verbal competitiveness among men. I do not mean to suggest, then, that the hierarchical ordering of the masculine community that "**¿Cobardía?**" so insistently represents precludes the establishment of solidarity among its members; quite the contrary, as I will show later.

In the passage that reproduces the discussion of the members of the Fishbowl Society, all the participants in the discussion maintain their own status in the hierarchy through the offensive rejection of statements made by others. Cáñamo the attorney depends, appropriately enough, on legal discourse in order to impose his discursive authority. The conversation of Pablito Encinar, who is "the newest little fish" [el pececillo más nuevo] and clearly the member who possesses least status in the society's hierarchy, is marked by the sort of childish pugnacity exemplified in his "Look here, so what!" ["Mire usted, ¡a mí, qué!"]. Even the verbs of diction used throughout by the narrator emphasize the competitive nature of the conversation. The participants do not merely "respond" or "state"; the commander, for example, "argues" and "snorts" [arguye, bufa]; Pablito Encinar "exclaims" [exclama], and Cáñamo "stresses" [recalca], "puffing himself up like a rooster" [engallándose mucho]. And the commander (perhaps the most obvious representative of this aspect of masculine conversational interaction) rejects those ideas proposed by Mauro Pareja with "I swear, now I've heard everything!" [¡Taco, oye uno cada cosa!]. The very use of the word *taco* (literally, swearword) here to euphemistically represent the use of an obscenity by the commander

may mark a certain linguistic boundary that our author will not, or cannot, cross. It may have been licit to fictionally represent masculine discourse, but there are certain things—or certain words—that a lady should not know about, much less repeat, even through the mouth of a fictional character, as Alas's comments about the limitations of women's writing stressed.[9]

It is impossible to forget the importance of the masculine pecking order here. Not only is the conversation one that insistently relies on competition and adversativeness, but the narrator reinforces the importance of this element through evaluative references to the relative "size" of each "fish": Mauro Pareja is a "fish of many pounds"; Pablito is the "newest little fish"; and the Fishbowl Society, as the narrator makes clear, "admits only big fish" [no admite sino peces gordos (118)]. The narrator by no means excludes himself from this hierarchical placement, clearly indicating his relatively high status in the Fishbowl Society by informing us that he is a member of its board of directors (118). In fact this particular school of fish would almost certainly seem to belong to the *Betta spendens* species, the Siamese fighting fish that Ong (1981) mentions as a striking example of the sort of "conspicuous, all-out, one-to-one ritual or ceremonial contest [sometimes] found among conspecific males" (51).

The use of proper names also emphasizes the relative status of each participant: the narrator almost always refers to Mauro Pareja either by his last name or with his full name; he consistently uses either the last name or the titles "Counseler" and "Commander" to refer, respectively, to Arturo Cáñamo and Irazu (whose first name is not even revealed);[10] but poor Pablito Encinar must suffer the humiliation of the diminutive added to his first name, a minimizing morpheme that is almost invariably employed by the narrator in reference to this character.

It is through several aspects of the narrative discourse, then, that the competitive nature of the Fishbowl Society's social interactions is emphasized. But perhaps the textual element that contributes most directly to an ironic presentation of competitive masculine discourse is the use of a technique that some critics have considered classic *esperpentismo*:[11] the narrator, rather than looking directly at the characters and reporting their actions, observes their movements exclusively as images reflected back by the many mirrors that line the walls of the club. The actions and gestures of the characters are thus perceived by the narrator, and subsequently narrativized, as mere reflections, images. More importantly, these gestures are deformed, made grotesque by the multiple reflections in the mirrors: "A cheap illusionist's trick, that produced in me a very curious sort of alienation of the imagination. I had come to fancy that the images reflected in the mirrors were shadows, spectres and *moral caricatures* of the living disputants" [Recreo de ilusionismo barato, que me causaba una especie de extravío imaginativo bastante curioso. Había dado en figurarme que las imágenes reflejadas en los espejos eran sombras, espectros y *caricaturas morales* de los disputadores vivos (119; emphasis added)].

This passage seems to suggest that the discourse that the narrator reflects is not to be perceived as belonging exclusively to the individuals represented in the story. The many mirrors placed on the walls of the club repeat the image of "the toast of male Marineda" in endless succession; there is not just one "big fish," but an infinity of them: "The reproduction in the mirrors of not only the group, but the image of that same group thrown off by the mirrors on the opposite wall, made it seem as if an innumerable crowd were debating in a very long gallery, whose end could not be seen" [Al copiarse en las lunas, no sólo el grupo, sino la imagen del mismo grupo devuelta por las lunas de enfrente, parecía como si discutiese una innumerable muchedumbre en una galería larguísima, a la cual no se le veía el fin (119)]. The movements and postures thus reflected could easily belong to an entire gallery of men, to a great mass of masculinity. The image that is repeated here ad infinitum easily suggests the notion of a long masculine tradition, transmitted through time and through the images that the innumerable men in the endless gallery project of themselves.

This "mirror trick" reveals the essence of the masculine conversational interchange as posture, or image, at the same time that it emphasizes the distance that the narrator imposes between himself and the other members of the society. His role as observer, rather than participant, is emphasized in the explicit criticism of his companions' ridiculous gestures: "Their postures and movements, reproduced by the mirrors, struck me as ironic, dismal, and mocking" [Sus actitudes y movimientos, que reproducían las lunas, me parecían irónicas, lúgubres, y mofadoras (119)]. But the narrator, rather than limiting himself to a criticism of the sincerity and goodwill of the others, includes himself in the criticism by means of a commentary on perception and image whose subtlety is quite striking: "And most certainly it was I who reflected in the mirror the leanings of my own spirit toward so much empty polemic, so much vanity, so much exaggeration, so much vacuity and so much obscenity as was heard there" [Y de fijo era yo quien reflejaba en el espejo la actitud de mi propio espíritu ante tanta polémica huera, tanta vanidad, tanta exageración, tanta vaciedad y tanta palabrota como allí se oía. . . . (119)].

The narrative dynamics of this passage are complex. Pardo Bazán manages to censure stereotypical masculine discourse, and rather mordantly at that. It is significant that this commentary is expressed by a male narrator, for, as Lanser's work (1992) suggests, very likely this same commentary would hold considerably less discursive authority if made by a female character, much less a female narrator. But on the other hand, the force of the commentary seems to be undermined by the narrator's self-criticism: it is not simply the case, as he had imagined, that his colleagues ironically repeat a masculine discourse that has come to seem vulgar, vain, and vacuous, but rather that he himself is projecting his own attitude in response to his peers' interchanges. Just as the mirrors reflect the images of the men, the narrator himself reflects his own response of tedium and surfeit upon perceiving this discourse—and, although he does not say so explicitly, upon narrating it. And of course, Pardo Bazán, in turn, also reflects this discourse; she represents its image and repeats it ironically, just as her narrator does. Thus, while the narrator reduces his own evaluation of the emptiness of this discourse to the projection of his own "spirit," Pardo Bazán simultaneously includes the narrator in her criticism.

But the narrator seems in several ways to reject the traditional concept of masculine valor that his colleagues uphold. In the passage that we have just examined, he offers literally another way to "see" that concept of male valor that is based on aggression. But suddenly, watching the mirrors, he observes the reflection of an occurrence that itself will crystallize and distill all the narrator's skepticism regarding male posturing. Pablito, responding to the claim made by the attorney that the duel is a "barbaric" custom imported by the Teutons, challenges his interlocutor by asking him how he would respond if, at that moment, someone came up to him and slapped him in the face. Would the fact that the Teutons imported this custom serve as any consolation? As he listens to Pablito, the narrator notices that Rodrigo Osorio, a member of the society who has not yet participated in this evening's conversation, is curiously affected by the "littlest fish"'s pugnacious challenge. He turns livid, his face contorts dreadfully, and finally he wordlessly rises and leaves the room.

With the exception of the narrator, all members of the Fishbowl Society seem to understand that it is the newcomer Pablito's tactless comment that has produced this behavior on the part of Osorio, and to further understand precisely why Osorio would interpret the challenge to the attorney as an indirect attack on himself. At the narrator's request, Mauro Pareja deciphers the mystery for him by recounting a narrative in which Osorio serves as protagonist, and which occurred a few years previously, when the narrator was away from Marineda.

At that time, rumors had circulated to the effect that Rodrigo, then barely out of school, was carrying on an affair with the wife of a general who was stationed in Marineda.[12] The general had gotten wind of the rumor, and announced that he refused to duel with a schoolboy, but that if he were to encounter him on the street, he would box his ears and give him a good slapping. Rodrigo's mother had also heard of the rumor, and had responded by taking her son away with her on a long trip. When Rodrigo eventually returned, he did indeed meet the general on the street one day. Rather than avoiding the confrontation, the young Rodrigo marched directly up to the general and said to him, "I know that you would like to slap me, sir. Here I am. You may fulfill your wish" ["Sé que usted desea abofetearme. Aquí estoy. Puede usted cumplir su deseo" (121)]. Naturally the general gave him a resounding slap in the face, and the young Rodrigo retreated, offering no response whatsoever.

The members of the Fishbowl Society find this story quite amusing, and it clearly serves to situate Rodrigo Osorio in the camp of those who swallow insults, those men who have no courage. But the narrator, in contrast, identifies with Osorio, imagining the sting of the slap on his own face. Suddenly, he comprehends the true valor—and value—of his friend, and this comprehension renders him almost speechless with fury at his colleagues' ridicule of Osorio. It is only with great effort that he is able to subdue his rage enough to speak up. When the narrator finally abandons the stance of distanced, ironic observer in order to make his contribution to the discussion, it is in order to offer a radically different view of masculine valor, a view that transforms masculine valor into human valor, through an implicit interrogation of gender roles. In a move that serves to balance the narrative told by Mauro Pareja, both structurally and thematically, he now relates the story of his own friendship with Osorio, a friendship that has remained, to use the narrator's word, "clandestine" ("clandestino") (118). He recounts that it was not in Marineda that he first met Rodrigo, but rather in Madrid, a year previously. At that time, the narrator was gravely ill, suffering from the highly contagious typhoid fever. Rodrigo, who happened to live in the same inn, heard that a fellow Marinedan living there was ill and immediately went to his room to aid him. In spite of the fact that he had never met him, knowing nothing about him except that he was from "back home," Rodrigo nursed the narrator, watching over him constantly and staying in his room with him for over a week. The narrator comments: "He cared for me like a brother, like a sister . . . of Mercy. . . . Now, I'd like to see whoever is braver than Rodrigo Osorio step forward" [Me cuidó como un hermano, como una hermana . . . de la Caridad. . . . Ahora, el que sea más valentón que Rodrigo Osorio, que salga ahí (121)].

In telling this story, the narrator presents a vision of valor that not only dissociates itself from stereotypical masculine notions of this quality, but that further defies gender stereotypes by allying itself explicitly with qualities usually coded as feminine. In case his listeners have not comprehended that, by nursing his countryman through a deadly and highly contagious disease, Rodrigo has demonstrated a type of bravery normally associated with the feminine, the narrator makes this obvious by comparing Rodrigo to a "*sister* of mercy."

With the recounting of the narrator's embedded story about Rodrigo, the homosocial overtones evident in the text from the beginning now begin to take on layers that seem to suggest homosexuality as well as homosociality. Not only is Rodrigo anomalously referred to in feminine terms, but the nature of the friendship between this character and the narrator now seems ambiguous. This friendship began, after all, when Rodrigo willingly undertook to play a quintessentially feminine emotional and social role, that of dedicated nurse; the relationship began, literally, in the intimacy of the narrator's bedside. Further, the narrator has told us that his friendship with Rodrigo was "clandestine," and that their bond was not of the sort that is conventionally considered to characterize "intimate" friendships between men. Rather than cementing their friendship in the more traditionally masculine way of joining constantly in activities together, or by displaying the intimate scribblings that their paramours trusted would remain private, his secret friendship with Rodrigo, the narrator tells us, is established and maintained by a more profound spiritual or sentimental kinship (118). The narrator's mention of this secret spiritual bond serves to set this relationship off as markedly distinct from the aggressive male homosocial relations evoked so vividly by the representation of the interactions among the other members of the Fishbowl Society.

Nevertheless, as if to dispel and counterbalance this passage's suggestion of a homosexual or homophile element in the two men's friendship, the narrator's language simultaneously describes the common perception of male intimate relations in such a way that, in contrast, it is *these* relations that seem to be imbued with an untoward eroticism *not* inherent to the friendship between Rodrigo and the narrator. The popular conception of male intimacy, according to the narrator, involves spending a great deal of time together, in such a "sticky relationship" [trato pegajoso (118)] that a month's separation might signal a dangerous disequilibrium. Clearly this sort of "stickiness," with its implication of unseemly interdependence, is abhorrent to the narrator.

The sharing of intimate letters from female sweethearts, which the narrator implies is typical of this sort of relationship, might itself be seen as an act that partakes of a certain homo-eroticism. For the sharing of these confidential texts transforms what the gullible female letter writer assumes to be an erotic or sentimental relationship shared by two people into a triangular, voyeuristic spectacle in which the truer bond occurs between the two men who simultaneously share an erotic or amorous textuality and ridicule the ingenuous producer of that textuality.[13] The narrator further specifies that, in spite of the spiritual bond shared by the men, they did not feel that they thoroughly understood each other; in fact, he says, their characters and dispositions were so different that there had never been a true mutual understanding, or "compenetración" (119), between them. The choice of this noun cannot be overlooked in this context, for it draws our attention to the potentially homoerotic nature of the relationship by means of a not-so-subtle denial of it. Once the friendship between the two men has been characterized in terms that alternately suggest and deny a homoerotic element, this tension seems to be rather shakily resolved in the representation of Rodrigo in religious terms that serve to desexualize him, in contrast to the narrator's own more heterodox tendencies. Rodrigo's selfless dedication to his sick friend might simply be consistent with the narrator's representation of him as "medio beato" (119), "a bit of a goody-goody." In fact, his unprotesting acceptance of the general's insulting slap in the face suggests a presentation of Rodrigo as a sort of (necessarily desexualized) Christ figure, one who eschews violence and literally turns the other cheek.

But even this move toward a resolution of the ambiguity surrounding the representation of Rodrigo and his relationship with the narrator ultimately collapses. The choice of the word "beato" to describe Rodrigo brings sexual ambiguity to the fore again, for this word is almost always used in its feminine form, "beata," to refer to a very pious woman, often with connotations of hypocrisy or hysteria. Thus the narrator subtly reminds us that, in the masculine value system epitomized by the members of the Fishbowl Society, religious piety is women's sphere. As Pardo Bazán points out in **"The Women of Spain"** [**"La mujer española"**], while men in Spain expect and demand religious devotion of their wives, sisters, daughters, and, above all, mothers, it is entirely dissociated from the masculine sphere: "While women attend Mass, their husbands wait for them outside, leaning against some pillar of the porch. Only women assist at religious exercises such as 'triduos,' 'novenas' and communions. All this is so well known and common that nobody pays any attention to it" [Son hechos tan comunes y repetidos que nadie fija su atención en ellos, el que ínterin las mujeres oyen misa los maridos las esperen recostados en algún pilar del pórtico, y el que a los ejercicios espirituales, triduos, novenas y comuniones apenas asistan más que mujeres, algún sacerdote o algún carlista (1889b, 885; 1890b, 36)].

Rodrigo is thus set apart from other men, his virility already questionable. When the narrator refers to him as a "sister of mercy," then, the seemingly jarring description merely echoes the suggestions of anomalous gender identification that have been present all along in the narrative language referring to this character. While it is significant that Rodrigo's supposed transgression, his rumored affair with the general's wife, was of a (hetero)sexual nature, it seems that this is not enough to gain him full acceptance by the arbiters of masculinity, for whether or not the rumor is true is never made known. Rodrigo's characterization as a "beato" certainly makes him an anomalous sexual rival. Further, Rodrigo's youth deprives him of the power to represent himself as a worthy rival; the general had let it be known that he would never duel with a youngster, but if he were to encounter Rodrigo in public, he would box his ears instead (121). When Rodrigo accepts the general's slap, then, and when he mirrors his previous notorious retreat by again retreating wordlessly at Pablito's elliptical insult, he is simply confirming his "difference," which has already been multiply signalled.

The challenge that the narrator throws out by way of conclusion to his story ("whoever is braver than Rodrigo Osorio, step forward") suggests that this type of private, even intimate valor, devoid of any desire to publicly prove one's virility, is in fact superior to the brand of masculine arrogance that the members of the society mistakenly—and conventionally—take for true courage. Nevertheless, it would seem that this move toward, not only a condemnation of masculine braggadocio but also toward the postulation of a new, feminized value system, might represent rather too great a risk on the narrator's part—and, of course, on the part of the author. This implication that the "feminine" courage shown by nurses is greater than the sort of courage traditionally considered masculine is neutralized by the narrator's observation that Rodrigo had cared for him also like a "brother." The transformation from "brother" to "sister" suggests that the valor that arises from altruistic love is a genderless or androgynous valor, rather than an essentially feminine one. Further, by means of the very way in which the narrator declares the superiority of this type of valor, he inserts himself plainly into the game of conversational competition. He simultaneously proves his own masculinity and challenges that of the others with an incitement to precisely the sort of physical, rather than symbolic, combat that Mauro Pareja had advocated as a definitive demonstration of masculine valor and honor: "Now, whoever is braver than Rodrio Osorio, step forward. Do you hear me? Let's just see if any of you would like me to be the general! Because my hand is itching . . ." ["Ahora, el que sea más valentón que Rodrigo Osorio, que salga ahí. ¿Lo están ustedes oyendo? ¡A ver, a ver si alguno tiene ganas de que yo sea el general! Porque a mí me hormiguea la mano . . ." (121)].

With this display of his own "virile" valor, the narrator allies himself explicitly, not with Rodrigo Osorio, who had the courage to accept a slap in the face without protesting or striking back, but rather with the very man who had slapped him. The identification with Rodrigo that he had experienced as he listened to the story told by Pareja has now disappeared, transforming itself into an identification with the same man who considered it beneath his dignity even to challenge the upstart Rodrigo to a duel. Thus the narrator establishes himself as even braver than Mauro Pareja, sweeping away any doubts about his masculinity that may have occurred to his listeners as he expressed his heterodoxical theories about valor. And, at the same time, of course, traditional concepts of masculinity are firmly restored at the textual level as well. Yet, lest we think the text begins to resolve itself here, it should also be kept in mind that as the narrator itches to play the part of the general, the keeper of the status quo, he also implicitly places the members of the Fishbowl Society he challenges in the place of the "cowardly" and sexually ambiguous Rodrigo.

"¿Cobardía?", then, is made up of a web of ideological and perspectival ambiguities and ambivalences, as dizzying and disorienting as the grotesque masculine images thrown back by the multiple mirrors of the club. The use of narration in the first person contributes to the disorienting effect the story produces. In fact, through a curious metalepsis, or transgression of the boundaries between narrative levels, the text encourages an identification between male narrator and female author, for the narrator introduces the story that forms the substance of "¿Cobardía?" by saying, "the debate that took place on the night to which I am referring developed as you will see, *if you read*" [el de la noche a que me refiero iba por los caminos que ustedes verán, *si leen* (119; my emphasis)]. The narrative voice, then, does not merely *relate* the incident in question, but even usurps the authorial function of writing. He addresses himself, not only to a represented or theoretical narratee, but to the readers themselves, who are positioned within a narrative level parallel to that of author, not to that of narrator. Even without the addition of "if you read," which Pardo Bazán inserted as a revision to the second version of "¿Cobardía?" published in 1892 in *Cuentos de Marineda,* this narratorial self-reference significantly affects the narrative dynamics at work. The direct address to a group of virtual narratees whom the narrator addresses formally, with "ustedes," would already suggest that the narratees in question might form an extension of the Fishbowl Society. Yet the "very best" of Marineda's male population are imaged as fish enclosed in their fishbowls, from which they coldly survey the world outside at the same time that they themselves serve as spectacle, thus reflecting a distorted, grotesque society. Pardo Bazán may seem, at first glance, to be offering a rather tame interrogation of the custom of the duel and traditional concepts of valor. At the same time, however, and more importantly, she parodically reproduces the very discourse that contains and expresses the aggressive, phallic mentality underlying these notions. Like her narrator, then, she displays

considerable valor; but like Rodrigo, she displays her valor in a "different" mode, a mode that embraces contradiction, indirection, and even transvestite disguise. For it is not only in *Memorias de un solterón* that Pardo Bazán "disguises herself" as a man in order to tell her story, and, more importantly, in order to suggest a statement about traditional concepts of masculinity. Here, the narrator's discourse plays subtly with transvestism, in the transformation from "brother" to "sister"—and not merely "sister," but "sister of mercy," which evokes the image of Rodrigo as a sort of nun in drag. The narrator himself displays some qualities that could be called transvestite, quite beyond the play between authorial and narratorial textual levels. He is masculine, at the same time that he marks himself as "other," refusing to embody the conventional sort of masculinity that his companions display. And, as occurs in the transvestite spectacle, he defamiliarizes gender, exposing its nature not only as construction but as image, as performance.[14]

But the gender play present in this and in other stories by Pardo Bazán goes beyond a simple change of clothing and the occultation of the most obvious signs of biological sex. This story, and others such as **"Mi suicidio"** ["My suicide"] and **"La mirada"** [**"The Look"**], for example, explicitly interrogate the conventions and ideologies that underlie masculine linguistic discourse. Pardo Bazán emits a "masculine," or "masculinized," voice, and if we are not attentive, it will seem as it seems to Robert Osborne, "that the author is male" [que el autor es varón (1964, 95)]. In this way, even more than through a narrative transvestism, Pardo Bazán's use of the male narrator is comparable to what I will call narrative ventriloquism.

Brad Epps discusses what he terms the "politics of ventriloquism" in relation to a very different sort of literary text, Juan Goytiloso's 1970 novel *La reivindicación del Conde don Julian.* He comments that "ventriloquism is an uncannily complex speech act. It refers, that is, to the slipperiness of reference, to the mystifying ability to take one thing for another, one's words for another's. Ventriloquism, in other words, is an act of speech that hides its sources and *throws itself, disembodied, into the bodies of others*" (1992, 292; my emphasis). Epps's perception of this act as a linguistic penetration of the bodies of others, one that "requires the dumb compliance, the submissive insignificance, of these other bodies" (292), illuminates his discussion of the ways in which a contemporary male author appropriates and projects feminine speech and silence. The ventriloquist dynamic operant in "¿Cobardía?", however, is substantially different. In contrast to Goytisolo's novel, in which the male author effectively offers his own invention of masculinized or silenced female historical figures, in Pardo Bazán's short story, a female author makes use of stereotypical dominant—masculine—discourse in a way that calls attention to its nature as invention and artifice. Indeed, as Epps himself points out (293, fn 20), Irigaray's exploration (1985a) of the ways in which women linguistically immasculate themselves simply in order to be heard in the patriarchy evokes something quite similar to the notion of ventriloquism—at the same time, I suggest, that the dynamics of this appropriation are radically different from those of masculine appropriation of feminine speech or silence.

While Irigaray's use of the visual metaphor of the "masquerade" to discuss feminine appropriation of masculine discourse draws our attention away from the verbal nature of this phenomenon, the work of Bakhtin insistently returns us to it. Throughout **"¿Cobardía?"**, the narrative discourse is marked by what Bakhtin calls multiple intonations—intonations that combine the bass and the soprano in what we might call a gendered heteroglossia.[15] His analysis of the dynamics of literary authorship, in particular, is vitally relevant to our discussion, in spite of its elision of questions of gender: "A prose writer can . . . make use of language without wholly giving himself up to it, he may treat it as semi-alien or completely alien to himself, while compelling language ultimately to serve all his own intentions. The author . . . speaks, as it were, *through* the language, a language that has somehow more or less materialized, become objectivized, that he merely *ventriloquates*" [sic] (1981, 298-99, emphasis added). In what forms a striking contrast to Epps's projectile, invasive image of ventriloquism, Bakhtin seems to suggest here that it is the author—the ventriloquist—who is positioned to be dominated by language itself, and, further, that this linguistic domination may be resisted by an insistent recognition of the "alien" nature of the language the author-ventriloquist projects. When we alter the gender of the personal pronouns employed in this passage, it suddenly throws new light on the situation of the female writer: "A prose writer can . . . make use of language without wholly giving *herself* up to it, *she* may treat it as semi-alien or completely alien to *herself*, while compelling language ultimately to serve all *her* own intentions."

Just as the mirrors lining the walls of the club throw back the distorted images of the "toast of male Marineda," rendering them "grotesque and dismal," so Pardo Bazán "throws her voice" in this story, reproducing masculine discourse in a way that makes it, too, suddenly grotesque. The author as narrative ventriloquist makes us forget that the masculine voice that she presents as her own and that "has somehow more or less materialized, become objectivized" is actually artifice. She makes us forget the source of the voice that we hear. But the trick of the ventriloquist lies precisely in that moment when we *remember* the source of the projected voice, when we remember that the ventriloquist has transformed her own voice into an alien voice,

which she presents as her own. A ventriloquist's magic is worked, in other words, when we remember that the double voice of the ventriloquist and the dummy emanate from a single source. Ventriloquism "works" when we realize that the projected voice is a voice that another manipulates, that another speaks "through," using it, as Bakhtin suggests, "to serve all [her] own intentions." In **"¿Cobardía?"**, as in many other texts, Pardo Bazán makes use of what Lanser calls personal voice in order to project a masculine narrative voice. But, crucially, this projected masculine voice is saturated with the author's own ironic intonations. Those who hear only the voice of the narrator, without attending to these secondary intonations, are only listening to the voice of a dummy.

Notes

1. "God help me, how tired I was getting of sentimental or stupidly licentious little stories, or those with moral pretensions; and of spiritualist extravagances, along with the other weeds and showy flowers of the fallow feminine field—which I refuse to call *literary* "[así Dios me salve como me iba hartando de historietas sentimentales o tontamente licenciosas, y de pujos morales; y de extravagancias espiritistas, con otras malas hierbas y flores cursis del erial femenino—que no quiero llamar *literario* (Pardo Bazán 1891a, 87-88. Emphasis in the original)].

2. The story first appeared in *El Imparcial,* 16 March 1891, and was included in *Cuentos de Marineda* (1892). All quotes from the original Spanish are from the *Cuentos completos* (1991). Translations are my own.

3. In the choice of the figure of the fish ("pez") to refer to those who frequent the Fishbowl, very possibly we find, not only a play on words—those who are inside the Fishbowl must logically be fish—but also an allusion to the several members of the Pez family who figure in Galdós's novels, characters who incarnate bourgeois vacuity.

4. Connell's notion of "hegemonic masculinity" (1987, 1995) revolves around the very sort of hegemonic, competitive social structure exemplified in the Fishbowl Society.

5. There is ample bibliography on gossip and gender, within which the work of Spacks (1985) assumes primary importance. Within sociolinguistics, Jones 1990 and Coates 1989 are key works, both of them analyzing gossip as a co-operative discourse within all-female groups. Ayim 1994, Code 1994, Collins 1994, and Schein 1994, also reflect this view. Yet more recent scholarship suggests that this association of gossip with the feminine is more indicative of the analyst's own preconcep-

tions about gender than of any empirical truth. This observation is central to Cameron's discussion of gossip in an all-male group (1997). Also see Johnson and Finlay 1997 on gender and gossip.

6. In *Memorias de un solterón* (1896), Pardo Bazán further elaborates the theme of gossip. In that novel as well, it is the male characters who most assiduously and most maliciously dedicate themselves to gossip. See Ragan 1995a for an examination of gossip as both structuring device and theme in *Memorias*.

7. Tannen's *You Just Don't Understand* (1990), written for a general audience, is undoubtedly her most widely read book on gender relations, having met with a commercial success that is unprecedented among books written by linguists about linguistics. Much of the work that she summarizes there is explored with greater detail and subtlety in *Gender and Discourse* (1994), and especially in her essay "The Relativity of Linguistic Strategies: Rethinking Power and Solidarity in Gender and Dominance" (1993), a shorter version of which is included in *Gender and Discourse*.

8. On verbal sparring and competitiveness among contemporary Luso-Iberian men, see Pujolar i Cos 1997 and Vale de Almeida 1996. A related study of interest is that of Neff van Aertselaer 1997, which examines the use of the rhetoric of "hombría" in Spanish political discourse of the 1990s.

9. Alas ["Clarín"] 1887. I discuss Alas's comments extensively in chapter 1.

10. The erasure of the first name here effectively precludes the possibility of solidarity or intimacy with this character—just as Peter Falk's Colombo character always answers queries about his wife's first name with "Mrs.," thus simultaneously protecting his and his spouse's personal privacy and maintaining professional distance between himself and his suspect.

11. Cannon 1980 and Paredes Núñez 1988 are relevant here. Both consider the grotesque effect of the mirror technique employed in this story to be exemplary of *esperpentismo*.

12. This same "Generala" (General's wife) is the protagonist of "El mechón blanco" [The white streak] (1892), whose plot revolves around the general's suspicions of a dalliance between his wife and Rodrigo Osorio. It is notable that neither "El mechón blanco" nor "¿Cobardía?" is explicit about the validity of the general's suspicions. The suspicion itself, and the perceived threat to the general's honor, thus take the central place in the continuing story of the general, his wife, and the young Rodrigo.

13. In fact, this erotic-emotional betrayal for the purpose of cementing solidarity between or among men is very similar in kind, although differing in intensity, to that portrayed in Pardo Bazán's "Sor Aparición," published five years after "¿Cobardía?" I discuss this story at length in Tolliver 1994b.

14. The notion of the "performativity" of gender, developed in Butler 1990, is applied to discourse analysis by Cameron (1997).

15. Epps does mention that the "politics of ventriloquism" that he traces in the Goytisolo novel might be explained through the Bakhtinian notion of a heteroglossia which "by virtue of its extreme complexity, tends to obscure such specifics as gender, class, and race" (1992, 292). But Epps opts not to explore this connection. As many commentators have pointed out, Bakhtin does indeed fail to integrate the elements of gender and race into his analysis, but it is my belief that this blindness on Bakhtin's part by no means precludes our making use of his theories in a way that *does* take these elements into account. The work of Dale Bauer (1988) provides an excellent illustration of this.

Works Cited

By Emilia Pardo Bazán

Short Stories

"Champagne." [1898] 1996. *Cuentos de amor,* Madrid: Prieto. Reprinted in *"El encaje roto" y otros cuentos,* 66-71.

"Champagne." 1996. In *"Torn Lace" and Other Stories,* 68-74.

"¿Cobardía?" [1891] 1990. *El Imparcial* 26 March. Reprinted in *Cuentos completos,* vol. 1, 118-21.

Cuentos completos. 1990. Ed. Juan Paredes Núñez. Coruña: Fundación Pedro Barrie de la Maza Conde de Fenosa. 4 vols.

"El encaje roto." [1897] 1996. *El Liberal,* 19 September. Reprinted. in *"El encaje roto" y otros cuentos,* 58-65.

"Feminist." 1996. In *"Torn Lace" and Other Stories,* 118-25. [Translation of "Feminista."]

"Feminista." [1909] 1996. *Sudexprés.* Madrid: Pueyo. Reprinted in *"El encaje roto" y otros cuentos,* 110-17.

"El mechón blanco." [1892]. *La España Moderna,* Almanaque. Reprinted in *Cuentos completos* vol. 1, 114-17.

"Mi suicidio." [1894] *El Imparcial,* 12 March. Reprinted in *"El encaje roto" y otros cuentos,* 35-40.

"My suicide." 1996. In *"Torn Lace" and Other Stories*. 36-41. [Translation of "Mi suicidio."]

"Piña." [1890] 1996. *La Ilustración Artística* 447. Reprinted in *"El encaje roto" y otros cuentos*, 15-24.

"Sister Aparición." 1996. In *"Torn Lace" and Other Stories*, 42-51. [Translation of "Sor Aparición."]

"Sor Aparición." [1896] 1996. Reprinted in *"El encaje roto" y otros cuentos*, 41-50.

COLLECTIONS AND EDITIONS OF PARDO BAZÁN'S WORKS

Cuentos completos. 1990. Edited by Juan Paredes Núñez. Coruña: Fundación Pedro Barrie de la Maza Conde de Fenosa. 4 vols.

"La mujer española" y otros artículos feministas. 1976. Edited by Leda Schiavo. Madrid: Editora Nacional.

OTHER PARDO BAZÁN WORKS CITED

[1886] 1957. *Los pazos de Ulloa*. In *Obras completas*, vol. 1, 165-284.

[1887] 1957. *La madre naturaleza*. In *Obras completas*, vol. 1, 285-411.

1889b. The Women of Spain. *Fortnightly Review* (1 June): 879-904.

[1890b] 1976. La mujer española. *La España Moderna* 2, no. 7 (May): 101-13. Reprinted in *"La mujer española" y otros artículos feministas*, 25-70.

1891a. Blanca de los Ríos. *Nuevo Teatro Crítico* 1, no. 8 (August): 85-91.

[1896]. 1957. *Memorias de un solterón*. In *Obras completas*, vol. 2, 447-527.

1907a. La mujer española. *Blanco y Negro* 818: 1-2.

OTHER SECONDARY SOURCES

Alas, Leopoldo ["Clarín"]. 1887. Review of *Los pazos de Ulloa*. In *Nueva Campaña*, 219-34. Madrid: Fernando Fé.

Ayim, Maryann. 1994. Knowledge through the Grapevine: Gossip as Inquiry. In Goodman and Ben-Ze'ev, 85-99.

Bakhtin, M. M. 1981. Discourse in the Novel. In *The Dialogic Imagination,* edited by Michael Holquist; translated by Caryl Emerson and Michael Holquist, 259-422. Austin: University of Texas Press.

Bauer, Beth Wietelmann. 1994. Narrative Cross-Dressing: Emilia Pardo Bazán in *Memorias de un solterón*. *Hispania* 77, no. 1: 23-30.

Bauer, Dale M. 1988. *Feminist Dialogics: A Theory of Failed Community*. Albany: SUNY Press.

Bieder, Maryellen. 1987. The Female Voice: Gender and Genre in *La Madre Naturaleza*. *Anales Galdosianos* 22: 103-16.

———. 1989. En-Gendering Strategies of Authority: Emilia Pardo Bazán and the Novel. In Vidal, 473-95.

———. 1990. Between Genre and Gender: Emilia Pardo Bazán and *Los pazos de Ulloa*. In *In the Feminine Mode: Essays on Hispanic Women Writers,* edited by Noël Valis and Carol Maier, 131-45. Lewisburg, PA: Bucknell University Press.

Butler, Judith. 1990. *Gender Trouble: Feminism and the Subversion of Identity*. New York: Routledge.

Cameron, Deborah. 1997. Performing Gender Identity: Young Men's Talk and the Construction of Heterosexual Masculinity. In Johnson and Meinhof, 47-64.

Cannon, Harold. 1980. El esperpentismo en los cuentos de Emilia Pardo Bazán. *Káñina* 4, no. 2: 61-65.

Coates, Jennifer. 1989. Gossip Revisited: Language in All-Female Groups. In *Women in Their Speech Communities: New Perspectives on Language and Sex,* edited by Jennifer Coates and Deborah Cameron, 94-122. New York: Longman.

Code, Lorraine. 1994. Gossip, or in Praise of Chaos. In Goodman and Ben-Ze'ev, 100-105.

Collins, Louise. 1994. Gossip: A Feminist Defense. In Goodman and Ben-Ze'ev, 106-14.

Connell, R. W. 1987. *Gender and Power: Society, the Person, and Sexual Politics*. Stanford: Stanford University Press.

———. 1995. *Masculinities*. Oxford: Polity Press.

Epps, Brad. 1992. The Politics of Ventriloquism: Cava, Revolution and Sexual Discourse in *Conde Julián*. *Modern Language Notes* 107: 274-97.

Goytisolo, Juan. 1970. *La reivindicación del conde Don Julián*. Mexico City: Joaquín Mortiz.

Irigaray, Luce. 1985a. *Speculum of the Other Woman*. Translated by Gillian G. Gill. Ithaca: Cornell University Press.

Johnson, Sally, and Frank Finlay. 1997. Do Men Gossip? An Analysis of Football Talk on Television. In *Language and Masculinity,* Johnson and Meinhof, 130-43. Cambridge, MA: Blackwell.

Jones, Deborah. 1990. Gossip: Notes on Women's Oral Culture. In *The Feminist Critique of Language,* edited by Deborah Cameron, 242-50. London: Routledge.

Kahn, Madeleine. 1991. *Narrative Transvestism: Rhetoric and Gender in the Eighteenth-Century English Novel*. Ithaca: Cornell University Press.

Kiesling, Scott Fabius. 1997. Power and the Language of Men. In *Language and Masculinity,* edited by Sally Johnson and Ulrike Hanna Meinhof, 65-85. Cambridge, MA: Blackwell.

Lanser, Susan Sniader. 1992. *Fictions of Authority: Women Writers and Narrative Voice.* Ithaca: Cornell University Press.

Neff van Aertselaer, JoAnne. 1997. "*Aceptarlo con hombría*": Representations of Masculinity in Spanish Political Discourse. In Johnson and Meinhof, 159-72.

Ong, Walter. 1981. *Fighting for Life: Contest, Sexuality, and Consciousness.* Ithaca: Cornell University Press.

Osborne, Robert E. 1964. *Emilia Pardo Bazán: Su vida y sus obras.* México: Ediciones Andrea.

Paredes Núñez, Juan. 1988. "La visión esperpéntica: De La Pecera marinedina al Callejón del Gato madrileño." In *Homenaje a Alonso Zamora Vicente,* vol. 4, edited by Pedro Peira, Pablo Jauralde, Jesús Sánchez Lobato, and Jorge Urrutia, 287-95. Madrid: Castalia.

Pujolar i Cos, Joan. 1997. Masculinities in a Multilingual Setting. In Johnson and Meinhof 1997, 86-106. Cambridge, MA: Blackwell.

Ragan, Robin. 1995a. Gossip, Gender, and Genre in *Memorias de un solterón* by Emilia Pardo Bazán. *Romance Languages Annual 1995*: 597-603.

Schein, Sylvia. 1994. Used and Abused: Gossip in Medieval Society. In Goodman and Ben-Ze'ev, 139-53.

Spacks, Patricia Meyer. 1985. *Gossip.* New York: Alfred A. Knopf.

Tannen, Deborah. 1990. *You Just Don't Understand.* New York: Ballantine Books.

———. 1993. Rethinking Power and Solidarity in Gender and Dominance. In *Gender and Conversational Interaction,* edited by Deborah Tannen, 165-88. New York: Oxford University Press.

———. 1994. *Gender and Discourse.* New York: Oxford University Press.

Tolliver, Joyce. 1994a. Script Theory, Perspective, and Message in Narrative: The Case of "Mi suicidio." In *The Text and Beyond: Essays in Literary Linguistics,* edited by Cynthia Goldin Bernstein, 97-119. Tuscaloosa: University of Alabama Press.

———. 1994b. "Sor Aparición" and the Gaze: Pardo Bazán's Gendered Reply to the Romantic Don Juan. *Hispania* 77, no. 3: 185-96.

Vale de Almeida, Miguel. 1996. *The Hegemonic Male: Masculinity in a Portuguese Town.* Providence: Berghahn Books.

Elizabeth J. Ordóñez (essay date fall 1999)

SOURCE: Ordóñez, Elizabeth J. "Gender Woes: Refiguring Familial Spheres in Pardo Bazán's *Doña Milagros.*" *Hispanic Journal* 20, no. 2 (fall 1999): 311-25.

[*In the following essay, Ordóñez investigates the role of paternal authority, gender angst, and feminine domesticity in Pardo Bazán's novel* Doña Milagros.]

Doña Milagros (1894) appears to be something less than a remarkable novel. A story about a weak-willed gentleman who upon his wife's death must minister to the needs of his numerous female progeny, ***Doña Milagros*** is redolent of domestic fiction with its focus on the home as a kind of *gynaeceum* for the proper training of girls for womanhood. Family life and economies of domesticity are foregrounded in much of the novel.

Yet more may be at stake here than initially meets the eye. The narrator, unlike those most characteristic of normative nineteenth century domestic fiction, is a father. Furthermore, he is a father obsessed yet dominated by his lack of authority. Intriguingly, he is also a father who, before the body of the text begins, is declared dead. In the Prologue to ***Doña Milagros,*** Benicio Neira, the teetering patriarch of the Neira household, has died and gone to heaven. But an unexpected request awaits him at the threshold to Paradise: the Holy Spirit commands him to write the novel of his life. A quasi-theoretical conversation that takes place after the holy mandate appears to prefigure Unamunian exchanges between character and "author" rather than recall matrilineal exchanges in domestic fiction.[1] Even more suggestively, Benicio's confusion and anxieties about gender seem to announce in another way Unamuno's perplexed male figures.

It is not my intent here to track Benicio Neira's specific influence as a prototype for Augusto Perez or other anguished male figures of Pardo Bazán's young friend, Unamuno. Neira and his adored maternal friend, doña Milagros, may very well have influenced the younger writer and served to generate, some years later, Unamuno's maternity-obsessed male protagonists. What I would like to emphasize is the possibility that Neira's articulation of gender angst ("no estaba seguro de mi virilidad") (***DM*** [***Doña Milagros***] 413), his coinage of the neologism "hembro" to describe his woeful gender status, and his final demise may anticipate Unamuno in a broader sense: Neira may be a harbinger to the crises of modernity that find their way into Unamuno's male protagonists. In this sense, Neira—like Unamuno's characters that succeed him—may have something to do with what Alice Jardine has named, through Lyotard, the nineteenth century "crisis of legitimation" or the "demise of the paternal function in the West" (80).

Tempting though it may be to view Benicio's befuddlement and figurative impotence as simply "modesty and diffidence," as Maurice Hemingway has proposed (110), there is also compelling reason to view our bumbling father figure as an offshoot of what Jardine has called gynesis or "anxiety over the decline of paternal authority" (36). A leitmotiv of Neira's narrative are his complaints and musings, like this one, regarding his lack of authority: "lamenté no haber desplegado . . . el cetro de la autoridad" (*DM* 361). Neira, as well as auguring the gender-linked anxieties of his twentieth century descendants, seems connected to them by the multiple losses that he has sustained—also characteristic of modernity according to Jardine. He has lost legitimacy with the untimely death of his firtborn son and his own ill-favored status as his father's heir; he has lost familial and economic authority; his entire paternal fiction and historical identity is revoked when his wife relocates the family to Marineda: "con el cambio de horizontes . . . me faltó . . . mi vida histórica" (*DM* 360).

A nostalgic lesson that might be gleaned from Benicio's ironically unfolded bewilderment is that if only he could have recaptured legitimate paternal authority and become—as Adolfo Llanos y Alcaráz figured paternal duty in 1864—"el timon de la nave," the problems of his identity and family life could have been resolved (65). But something more than individual psychology or parental effectiveness seems to be implicated here. Benicio's gender and paternal woes appear to rest as much on a discursive as on an individually idiosyncratic level. They suggest that we might do well to regard Neira's crisis as male and father, his loss of familial and historical legitimacy; in short, his anguished status as a paternal subject, as a sign of what Jardine has characterized as late nineteenth century "crises in figurability at the roots of modernity" (80). Neira's unresolved lack of viril authority would point, then, toward a shift in figurative renderings of father, and by extension family and mother, during the waning years of the last century.

The destabilization of Neira's paternal authority places him, as Maryellen Bieder has appropriately noted, in "an ambiguous position with regard to the normative structure which he conveys and within which he functions" ("En-gendering" 481). To this might be added that his paternal crisis, often expressed through self-deprecating lamentations, often positions him outside the contract of "masculine desire to dominate" and "complimentary feminine desire to be dominated" that, as Lou Charnon-Deutsch has demonstrated, underwrites the "tight circle of uneven power relations" in the domestic novel (*Narratives* 61). Indeed, in *Doña Milagros* the tables often appear turned. Nevertheless, Neira also unconsciously acts out other terms of that contract that authorial irony regards as problematic and needful of destabilization, reorganization or refiguration. Pardo Bazán's ironic relationship to the memory of solid paternal authority, and her consciousness of emerging discourses of modernity that undermine it, create a supple

space in *Doña Milagros* wherein tradition can be challenged, contradictions can be exposed, and the potential for refigurations of the family and its constituents can be advanced. Rather than filling in the spaces left by Neira's figural frailties with an absolute reversal of the hapless father's impossible desires, Pardo Bazán instead introduces or implies contesting discourses that continuously question or destabilize normative or dominant discursive positions of parents—father and mother—in their respective familial spheres.[2]

Neira's anxieties (and the novel that they launch) are effectively framed by broad cultural anxieties and shifts (as theorized by Jardine), as well as by more specific, polemical discussions about family life that took place during the waning decades of the nineteenth century. A variety of essayists in the decades preceding Neira's own confrontation with shifting familial dynamics were obsessively engaged in examinations of family life, as that institution faced moral and legal challenges and incursions. Without digressing too much, I would like to identify in broad strokes a more specific contextual basis for my reading. A few exemplary positions should suggest the discursive network into which *Doña Milagros* comes to situate itself. For example, in the Catholic, monarchical *La Margarita,* Patrocinio de Biedma metaphorically envisioned tidal waves of passion sweeping away the supports of family life. A more academically inclined, though nonetheless anxious, Joaquín Sánchez de Toca confronted the same menacing modernity in the more liberal, bourgeois *Revista de España.* Critical of secular constructions of family and marriage, Sánchez de Toca denounced what he called "una teoría funesta" that appeared to claim for paternal authority no more enduring status than that of a human fiction constructed upon ephemeral social convention (84). A more popular echo of Sánchez de Toca's fear (and a striking lexical precursor to Neira's self-defined "momento de crisis . . . en mi existencia de padre" [*DM* 358]) might be F. de Alvaro's dire warning in the women's magazine, *La Guirnalda,* that at that "momento de transición, de crisis, la familia parece extinguirse" (10:11). Exchanges such as these disclose the culture's anguished confrontation with institutional transitions. Whether responding to such changes with appcals to idealized traditional values or with proposals for reform, discourses seeking to manage what Jardine has called an acceleration in "radical upheavals in familial structures" (74) during the latter decades of the nineteenth century are stunning in their testimony—whether directly or indirectly—to the crises that have come to mark modernity.

In the cultural spheres of literary production and consumption, the family also figured prominently as a compelling subject. Indeed, by the 1870s Perez Galdós perceptively noted a strong preoccupation of the middle class with "la organización de la familia" (167), advocated the topic as eminently novelistic, and proved in his own work that it was indeed a fit subject for ironic examination. By the 1890s, however, as Catherine Jagoe has perceptively observed, Galdós reacted to the increasing destabilization of middle-class gender arrangements by narrating a series of nostalgic retreats back to the threatened separate spheres of traditional family life (155).

Near century's end, then, when Benicio Neira confronts the crisis of his own waning paternal status and power, the cultural bases for traditional family life have been shaken, their unproblematic certainties have been disturbed. Neira's individual struggle, and Pardo Bazán's choice to portray or probe it, are therefore effectively read as part of literature's responses to this cultural conflict. For this reason, I would like to focus for the remainder of this essay upon two broadly related issues that I believe are raised by the contextual cultural debate: 1) how *Doña Milagros* refigures—or intimates a need to refigure—paternal, maternal; in short, familial spheres, in response to more traditional or normative discourses on domesticity or family life; 2) how Pardo Bazán's divergence from traditionalist figurations of domesticity and familial spheres results from her position as a critic of normative nineteenth century discourses on gender difference. As a consequence of these discursive and narrative shifts, I believe that we can place Pardo Bazán, and her befuddled paternal protagonist, at the inception of modernity's challenge to traditional family values and their modes of figuration.

The ideal home of domestic fiction, according to Charnon-Deutsch, was a "place where a feminine ideal of intersubjectivity could be striven for if not obtained" (*Narratives* 35). The Neira household swerves from such coziness, and presents itself as a parody of the domestic ideal, by underscoring instead the centrifugal force of its individual components. Daughter Feita's witty comparison of her home to a hen house configures a non-idealized space where females abide, rather oblivious to one another, in self-centered frustration or lassitude: "Tula, por no perder la costumbre, está regañando a la cocinera; Clara, durmiendo la siesta, ¡porque es más comodona!, se ha propuesto ver lo que dura una chica bien cuidada . . . Rosa . . . , colgada de la ventana, a ver no sé qué: los charcos, porque diluvia, y Argos . . . en la plática del padre Incienso. Constanza . . . , papando moscas, por variar . . . , y las otras . . . , las otras, no entienden aún" (*DM* 391). The ideal configuration of domesticity in popular domestic novels or in illustrations for ladies' periodicals, like *La Guirnalda,* would have privileged harmony, domestic productivity, spirituality, and creativity appropriate to the domestic sphere such as drawing or musical performance. Dissimilarly, the Neira household is more likely to be represented as an arena of unmitigated crisis.

Benicio Neira is the object of stern and paternal pastoral censure from Padre Incienso for his part as author of such an imprudent and subversive domestic text: "¡ . . . usted ha permitido que todo se subvierta, que todo se corrompa en su casa de usted! . . . mujeres entregadas a su albedrio no pueden dar al varón prudente sino amarguras" (*DM* 410). Destabilized as "varon prudente," Neira is identified, at least in part, with the vexed status of imprudent male. As a father allowing his daughters to follow their whims, to Padre Incienso he fails to exercise wisely the sort of privileged paternal conduct that Francisco Alonso y Rubio had described a generation earlier: "el padre, que cultiva la razon, . . . se encuentra en condiciones para dirigir la inteligencia de sus hijos, para ser su guia en el mundo, e indicarles los escollos y peligros que deben evitar" (155-156).

To the implied author and more enlighted readers of his instructive predicament, however, Niera suggests lapses in another kind of paternal prudence—that of marital sexuality. As biological father or sire of eighteen pregnancies in his long-suffering wife, Ilduara, Neira has apparently neither engaged with his wife in "límites moderados [en] los placeres del amor . . . para la conservación de la salud" (as advised by contemporary, Amancio Peratoner, [55]), nor has he been cautious and prudent in the augmentation of his family's size (as advocated by Malthusian, Melchor Salvá). Blind to his part in these imprudent excesses, he simply attributes their consequences to his wife's extraordinary fecundity. These various manifestations of paternal imprudence make of Neira an unwitting participant in unequal domestic power relations and, for his part in such apparent contradictions, he is rendered an object of irony as well as censure.

Benicio Neira may be characterized as an engaging, overt narrator, which is to say that though he is likable, he is not altogether trustworthy. As Susan Lanser has summarized the attributes of an overt narrator through Shlomith Rimmon-Kenan, "his chances of being fully reliable are diminished, since his interpretations, judgements, generalizations are not always compatible with the norms of the implied author" (17).[3] Neira's double function as engaging, overt narrator renders him thus an effective site for working out contradictions having to do with conflicting familial discourses. For both traditional and reformist readers/narratees, Benicio Neira is at once attractive and problematic. He presents himself as a gentle spirit, a genuinely good man, so most readers could be expected to sympathize with these engaging qualities. Yet precisely because Benicio Neira fails to conform to normative standards of paternal prudence and authority, and because his generosity and naivete lead him to love not wisely but too much, he fails to inspire complete confidence in either camp of readers. Traditionalists might be inclined to distrust his weak will and lack of authoritative prudence. Similarly, reformists might be exasperated with his naive blindness to more effective ways of managing his domestic crises.

For the latter group—within whose ranks was likely the implied author—Neira characterizes himself as ironically deficient in judgement and vision.

In the gaps of Neira's ironically staged perplexed ruminations lie, then, cultural polemics about the deleterious effects of sexual incontinence. The juxtaposition of cultural and novelistic texts suggest refigurations of the paternal function as something other than that performed by Benicio Neira. Pardo Bazán may even have been influenced by John Stuart Mill in this regard; indeed Neira's excesses appear in bold relief when foiled by Mill's urging of suppression of the sexual impulse as a bourgeois form of population control (Charnon-Deutsch *Narratives* 137). Even in Spain, as we have noted, Malthus and Mill inspired Melchor Salvá to discreetly link sexual incontinence with economic adversity, a condition to which Benicio Neira was indeed not immune (Salvá 263). Neira thus wavers, ironically, outside these more enlightened discourses, capable only of longing nostalgically for greater authority. What remains hidden to Neira's consciousness is his unwitting participation as imprudent paternal educator and inseminator in a tarnished, increasingly questionable figuration of familial practice: that of separate spheres for men and women.

Though a kind man and devoted husband, Neira could avoid biological messes and domestic stresses in his privileged separate sphere of club and casino, while in her domestic sphere his wife, Ilduara, could only deteriorate, rail against her tortured existence, and then ironically escape it only through death. He is clearly aware of the advantage he possesses in these male spheres to "olvidar las penalidades domésticas," and he recognizes (in a rather unsubtle implied authorial critique) that "si las mujeres pudiesen gozar del mismo desahogo, quizá no tomase nunca su carácter la acritud y displicencia que, desgraciadamente, adquirió el de mi esposa" (*DM* 364). *Doña Milagros*'s less-than-rosy portrayal of the figure of separate marital spheres contrasts with its normative representation in more traditional domestic fiction. The latter privileged a cozy private sphere where female bodies could escape threats posed by the world outside, and reproduction was usually "seen in a positive light" (Charnon-Deutsch, "On Desire" 411). Likewise in domestic periodicals, reproduction, motherhood, and the home often came rolled up into idealizing or moralizing platitudes like "un alma maternal no es más que ternura, indulgencia, amor" or "malditos sean aquellos que han despoetizado los goces sagrados del hogar."[4]

Pardo Bazán challenges in *Doña Milagros* fictional and nonfictional discourses of the domestic sphere and idealized maternity in precisely the manner that ladies' magazines and moralists decried: she posits the maternal function as problematic, especially if excessive, and entertains the provocative proposition that reproduction

and nurturing may, indeed, be separate functions. Ilduara, as wife and mother to her prolific brood, seems to rule her domestic roost. Yet, as reproductive body, she is ironically reduced to a "gastado organismo" (*DM* 375), suffering from "diversísimos achaques, unos acabados en *algias* como neuralgias, gastralgias y cefalalgias; otros, en *agias,* como hemorragias; otros, en *emia,* como anemia" (*DM* 360). Of this her narrator husband is obsessively aware. Nonetheless, Benicio is unable to comprehend his wife's hysterical defense of her unceasing reproductive function ("te he parido dieciocho hijos" [*DM* 377]), and her subsequent paroxysm (in which she is heard to "renegar de su maternidad, maldecir la tarea que la dignificaba" [*DM* 381]), as anything but epileptic seizures preceding death. Benicio can assess his wife's rage and rejection of her maternal status only from inside normative discourses that sought to poeticize, idealize, and repress the biological burden of maternity. Moreover, he views the maternal role as essentially disconnected and separate from his paternal one. But the novel cannot settle for an accommodation with either Ilduara's suffering or Benicio's misguided appraisal of it. Beyond idealizing discourses of domesticity lie messy disturbances that demand a refigured response.

Enter the eponymous Doña Milagros who has no biological children yet proves herself absolutely cut out for maternity: "moralmente, ¡qué madre más sublime!" (*DM* 395) rhapsodizes Neira. She may well be the spiritual precursor of Unamuno's Tía Tula with her "me creo que soy la mamá de ellos" (*DM* 424), but Pardo Bazán's biologically sterile maternal woman has none of the acerbic intensity of her successor. Doña Milagros, as her name implies, is sunlight, joy, and life: "parecía crear vida alrededor de sí" (*DM* 393). Redolent of Faustina Saez de Melgar's metaphorical woman writer in her role as sunny presence, she illuminates the troubled Neira household.[5] But she is more than the pure, angelic maternal subject of conventional domestic fiction: she is married, sexy, and moreover Benicio finds himself strongly attracted to this buxom seductive woman who is somebody else's wife. He has to fight his own desire for her and grapple with neighborhood (and his own) suspicion about her implication in another possible amorous plot. Still, by novel's end he performs the ultimate sacrifice of bestowing upon Doña Milagros the priceless gift of his twin infant daughters. Nothing is absolutely neat, nothing is unqualifiedly untainted about the maternal in *Doña Milagros.* Neither Ilduara, with her graceless suffering, nor Doña Milagros with her sensual, barren body, are ever accorded the idealized, elevated status accorded maternal figures in domestic fiction or journalism. This novel's splitting and complicating of the normative maternal figures of idealized domestic discourse instead gestures toward other viable figurations of the family and its functions.

As foils to Benicio's uncertainties and insecurities, Ilduara and doña Milagros, with their exaggerated separation of the reproductive and maternal functions, contest the facile linkage of these roles as a mainstay of traditional nineteenth century fictional and nonfictional discourses on maternal and familial spheres. Clearly, it was far easier to be "un alma maternal [de] no más que ternura" without the heavy—even fatal—burden of excessive reproduction. The maternal as nurturing is accessible even to Feita who, as a mere child, demonstrates a precocious resourcefulness in the care and feeding of her youngest sisters. As Charnon-Deutsch has generalized: "the quality of maternalness as exquisite caregiving does not depend on biological motherhood in Pardo Bazán's fiction" (*Narratives* 124). The vitally sublime yet nonbiological maternity of doña Milagros and the pert efficiency of sister/daughter, Feita, implicitly contest a popular press's veiled insistence on biological mothering and its censure of reluctant practitioners of domestic physiology. As one Dr. Lopez de la Vega counseled and queried readers of *El album de las familias* on reproductive hygiene: "tan sublime la maternidad, ¿por qué muchas de vosotras sois tan frías para el desempeño de los principales deberes de vuestro estado?" (375). If Doña Milagros's and Feita's attentive nonbiological mothering were not sufficient response as alternatives to this earlier rhetoric of medical moralizing, a direct and chilling contestation would clearly lie in the spectre of Ilduara's hysterogenic bondage to her hyperbolic reproductive biology. The predicament of Ilduara's martyred biological maternity seems to contest moralizing precursors like López de la Vega with the simple but formidable notion that maybe these coolly resistant mothers feared for their lives.

Ilduara's hysterical demise becomes part and parcel of this novel's questioning and refiguration of traditionally conceived maternity with its repression of the dark side of the sublime; that is, its risk of premature death and/or hysteria. Along with biological maternity, hysteria was associated with female subjectivity in the figuration of separate spheres advanced by nineteenth century discourses on family life. It was often attributed to essential differences found only in women.[6] In *Doña Milagros,* daughter María Ramona's hysteria raises several more interrelated issues germane to this inquiry. Clearly, it constitutes a crisis for Neira's ongoing paternal anxieties.[7] More implicitly, it challenges normative discourses on the causes, treatments, and possible cures for adolescent female hysteria. Most importantly, proposals for the long term management of María Ramona's hysteria serve to further undermine rather than reinforce figurations of separate spheres produced by discourses of gender difference.

Argos (as María Ramona is affectionately called), because of repressed grieving over her mother's death and similarly repressed desire for the priest, Padre Incienso,

begins to express the typical somatic symptoms of hysteria, including religious mysticism, theatricality, and epileptic-like fits: "Argos se dislocaba, se decoyuntaba, formando su cuerpo arco vibrador" (*DM* 382); "era una actitud digna de una gran trágica" (*DM* 383). When Argos's condition grows so acute as to require treatment, the more enlightened Doctor Moragas just happens to be out of town. The novel's contrived alternative results in a sado-masochistic medical spectacle as the elderly "practicón," don Dioscoro Napelo, applies leeches and lancet to the victim, "crucificada en la espina y el vientre" (*DM* 431).[8]

Ironically, however, the medically antiquated "practicón's" diagnosis of the causes of Argos's condition differs cunningly from his treatment of it. Edged with a subversive modernity, his attempt to sooth Neira's uneasy management of yet another crisis perhaps unwittingly affirms female desire: "El injusto mundo, señor don Benicio, hace a las doncellas responsables de este mal . . . cuando este mal es precisamente un certificado público de vida honesta y de pureza incólume, pues las mujeres que se entregan a desarreglos como el varón apenas conocen tan terrible padecimiento" (*DM* 432). Don Dioscoro's explanation constitutes a curious bit of double-voiced discourse that at once seems to praise feminine virtue to an uncertain father and attribute to that same purity pathological consequences. A subtle contesting and potentially refiguring discourse thus implicates itself here: while some medical tracts of the period might list hysteria as a consequence of unauthorized sexuality—or one kind of sexual "desarreglo" (Pouillet)—, Napelo craftily intimates the effectiveness of "desarreglos" as a prophylactic.

The convictions that guide this implied refiguration of female sexual desire, and, by extension, the construction of gender and the familial in *Doña Milagros,* are theorized in the cycle title to which this novel belongs, *Adán y Eva,* and by an intratextual resonance from Pardo Bazán's 1893 short story, **"Cuento primitivo."** *Doña Milagros,* with its pairings and almost-pairings, affirms the power of sexual attraction and desire felt with equal fervor by woman and man: "Adán y Eva, la primitiva pareja del Edén, el varón y la hembra atraídos el uno hacia el otro merced a instintos que a veces ni saben definir" (*DM* 444). If anyone or anything is incomprehensible or mysterious it is sexual desire irrespective of gender. "Cuento primitivo" concludes with an even more direct affirmation of the sameness of male and female: [Eva] "era de la misma sustancia que el hombre, ni mejor ni peor, sino un poco más fina" (*El encaje* [*El encaje roto y otros cuentos*] 33).

Although Pardo Bazán was a defender of equality in sexual matters, she had a particularly personal stake in the attainment of creative and professional equality. The repeated prescription for Argos's affliction is work, creative work that might allow free expression of her uncommon talents. First Doctor Moragas, then Feita counsel the indecisive Benicio on the talents of his daughter: "Argos es, por vocación, actriz" (*DM* 411); "¡Que cante! ¡Que salga a las tablas!" (*DM* 445). These proposals for the amelioration of Argos's condition articulate an ambitious challenge to normative discourses or practices of gender. In earlier fiction (with more traditionally domestic values), the pursuit of a singing career could have disastrous consequences (as in the case of Böhl de Faber's *La gaviota*). Traditional domestic ideology, as ironically expressed by Neira's most blatant recourse to the figure of separate spheres, constituted "la mujer para la familia, para la maternidad, para la sumisión, para las labores propias de su sexo" (*DM* 429). But Benicio Neira's traditional "default discourse" was not to constitute the last word. Daughter, Feita, articulates and summarizes with aplomb a privileging of equality and a rupturing of the boundaries between the separate spheres of the traditional familial plot: "Cada quisque debe hacer aquello para que tiene disposición" (*DM* 429). Her Latinized, neutral subject pronoun empties duty (normatively associated with the feminine half of the figure of separate spheres) of all gender markings and associations with specific spaces. In a word, she refigures duty as nongender specific.

In view of Argos's refigured spheres of activity, we can speculate that her chances for following her disposition would be better than those of her predecessor in *La gaviota*. La Gaviota's successor has to her advantage Pardo Bazán's quarrel with her culture's normative figurations of gender, a position that ultimately underwrites *Doña Milagros*'s contesting figures of familial discourse. If anything characterized prevalent discourses about gender during the nineteenth century it was their figuration of women as incomprehensibly different, as inscrutable conundrums requiring constant decipherment. As Manuel Cañete bemoaned in 1864, "la mujer es un problema que nunca se resuelve del mismo modo."[9] For her part, Pardo Bazán would subscribe to none of this. Humanity was, to her, "un todo andrógino, indivisible" (Bieder, "Emilia" 24). Pardo Bazán's assertion of the equality of woman and man ultimately destabilizes in her fiction the ideology and resultant figuration of separate spheres.

If Feita's declaration of a non gender specific dedication to duty reflects a discourse of equality privileged by the author, how might this position finally affect the outcome of Benicio's gender woes and anxieties about paternal authority? How do these concerns play themselves out within a broader historical field of cultural discourses? We might recall once more how questions of paternal authority in the family, and about the nature and fate of family life itself, were vigorously debated during the second half of the nineteenth century. Positions regarding authority within the family ranged from

defensive of male privilege to almost egalitarian. In a typical homily to middle-class virtues in separate spheres, Alonso y Rubio counseled male domestic authority, particularly in difficult situations (89). Some decades later, Neira is hard pressed to summon sufficient authority even in demanding circumstances. Sánchez de Toca, conceding in his argument to the semantic affinity between "padres" and "padre," admits a shared authority of father and mother, paternal authority thus issuing from a union of both parents (56). But even this latter, more cautiously egalitarian position eluded the weak willed Neira during his marriage to the strong willed Ilduara.

Within a discursive field marked by decades of concern about paternal authority, Neira struggles near century's end with his hesitations to exercise masculine power. Though prodded at moments of crisis by confessor, conscience, friends, and Feita, Benicio finally relinquishes most of the traditionally normative privileges of his gender and familial status. Into the space he leaves vacant rushes Feita, commanding: "Guíese por mí" (*DM* 444). In this respect the emergence of Feita's growing authority in the face of her father's diminishing powers is akin to family dynamics in the late nineteenth century British domestic novel. Paula Marantz Cohen's generalizations about that context are appropriately illuminating here: "the progressive realization of the daughter's power is destined to be the shaping force behind social organization as the nuclear family breaks down" (23). The Neira family similarly flies apart by novel's end, as Feita inventories and advises her father: "Tula ya hizo la trastada; Clara se buscó la vida a su manera; yo . . . yo . . . soy yo. Mire ahora por Rosa y por Argos" (*DM* 444). After the sacrificial bestowal upon doña Milagros of his twin infant daughters, and after his own suddenly weary aging, Benicio declares himself "un mal padre . . . un viejo chocho" (*DM* 446). Thus at the threshold of modernity's crises, changes, and losses (with their decline and demise of paternal authority and function), Neira's past paternal fiction appears finally exhausted. In its place lies a refigured space for his precocious, determined daughter, Feita; his unremarkable son; and his other diverse, dispersing, and, more often than not, dubiously domesticated daughters.

Notes

1. See Blanco, "The Moral Imperative," for an analysis of matrilineal exchanges in the fiction of María del Pilar Sinués and others.

2. In another context, as Maryellen Bieder has observed, Pardo Bazán also calls "into question the normative definitions of 'male' and 'female'." "Between Genre and Gender" 134.

3. The concept of engaging narrator is from Robyn R. Warhol (31).

4. See F. de Alvaro, "La madre-nodriza" 58 and "Durante nueve meses" 51 respectively.

5. Saez de Melgar described her ideal of the woman writer as "el hermoso sol, que con sus vivificantes y purísimos rayos ilumina y alegra el hogar doméstico" (402).

6. Bridget Aldaraca's research has shown that "the first comprehensive diagnostic manual of mental illness written in Spain reinforces the idea that hysteria is an exaggeration of the basic female nature which is typified by its moral and physical weakness" (409).

7. In another context, Jo Labanyi notes something about youthful hysteria that is suggestive in the context of *Doña Milagros*'s María Ramona: "puberty triggers Ana's mystical and nervous crisis" in *La Regenta,* in part because she lacks a father, who seems "necessary to set boundaries to female existence" (41). In María Ramona's case, her father, Benicio, seems similarly absent and ineffectual.

8. Argos actually fares better than many of her real life contemporaries who, after 1870, routinely received ovariotomies and sometimes even clitoridectomies to relieve hysteria and other behavioral pathologies associated with sexuality. See Lorna Duffin 43, and Thomas Laqueur 176.

9. Manuel Cañete, prologue to Llanos y Alcaráz, *La mujer,* vii.

Works Cited

Aldaraca, Bridget. "The Medical Construction of the Feminine Subject in Nineteenth-Century Spain." *Cultural and Historical Grounding for Hispanic and Luso-Brazilian Feminist Literary Criticism.* Ed. Hernán Vidal. Minneapolis, MN: Institute for the Study of Ideologies and Literature, 1989. 395-413.

Alonso y Rubio, Francisco. *La mujer bajo el punto de vista filosofico, social y moral: sus deberes en relacion con la familia y la sociedad.* Madrid: D. F. Gamayo, 1863.

Alvaro, F. de. "Durante nueve meses." *La Guirnalda* 7 (5 April 1876): 50-51.

———. "La Madre. I. La familia." *La Guirnalda* 10 (20 Jan 1876): 11-12.

———. "La madre-nodriza." *La Guirnalda* 8 (20 April 1876): 58.

Bieder, Maryellen. "Between Genre and Gender: Emilia Pardo Bazán and *Los pazos de Ulloa*." *In the Feminine Mode.* Ed. Noël Valis and Carol Maier. Lewisburg: Bucknell UP, 1990. 131-145.

———. "Emilia Pardo Bazán and Literary Women: Reading Women's Writing in Late 19th-Century Spain." *Revista Hispánica Moderna* 46 (June 1993): 19-33.

———. "En-gendering Strategies of Authority: Emilia Pardo Bazán and the Novel." *Cultural and Historical Grounding for Hispanic and Luso-Brazilian Feminist Literary Criticism.* Ed. Hernán Vidal. Minneapolis: Institute for the Study of Ideologies and Literature, 1989. 473-495.

Biedma, Patrocinio de. "El matrimonio." *La Margarita* 8 (Oct. 1871): 217-219.

Blanco, Alda. "The Moral Imperative for Women Writers." *Indiana Journal of Hispanic Literatures* 2 (Fall 1993): 91-110.

Charnon-Deutsch, Lou. *Narratives of Desire.* University Park: The Pennsylvania State UP, 1994.

———. "On Desire and Domesticity in Spanish Nineteenth-Century Women's Novels." *Revista Canadiense de Estudios Hispánicos* 14 (Spring 1990): 395-414.

Cohen, Paula Marantz. *The Daughter's Dilemma: Family Process and the Nineteenth-Century Domestic Novel.* Ann Arbor: The U of Michigan P, 1991.

Duffin, Lorna. "The Conspicuous Consumptive: Woman as an Invalid." *The Nineteenth-Century Woman: Her Cultural and Physical World.* Ed. Sara Delamont and Lorna Duffin. London: Croom Helm, 1978. 26-56.

Hemingway, Maurice. *Emilia Pardo Bazán.* Cambridge: Cambridge UP, 1983.

Jagoe, Catherine. *Ambiguous Angels. Gender in the Novels of Galdós.* Berkeley: U of California P, 1994.

Jardine, Alice. *Gynesis: Configurations of Woman and Modernity.* Ithaca, NY: Cornell UP, 1985.

Labanyi, Jo. "Mysticism and Hysteria in *La Regenta*: The Problem of Female Identity." *Feminist Readings on Spanish and Latin-American Literature.* Ed. L.P. Condé and S. M. Hart. Lewiston: The Edwin Mellon P, 1991.

Lanser, Susan Sniader. *Fictions of Authority: Women Writers and Narrative Voice.* Ithaca: Cornell UP, 1992.

Laqueur, Thomas. *Making Sex: Body and Gender from the Greeks to Freud.* Cambridge: Harvard UP, 1990.

Llanos y Alcaráz, Adolfo. *La mujer en el siglo diez y nueve.* Madrid: Libreria de San Martin, 1864.

Lopez de la Vega, Dr. "Consejos hijiénicos para las madres." *El album de las familias* 1 (28 Oct. 1866): 374-375.

Pardo Bazán, Emilia. *Doña Milagros.* Obras completas, vol. 2. Ed. Federico Carlos Sainz de Robles. Madrid: Aguilar, 1964.

————. *El encaje roto y otros cuentos.* Ed. Joyce Toliver. New York: MLA, 1996.

Peratoner, Amancio. *La mujer en la alcoba.* Barcelona: Felipe N. Curriols, 1893.

Perez Galdós, Benito. "Noticias literarias." *Revista de España* 15 (1870): 167-169.

Pouillet, et doctor. *Estudio médico-filosófico sobre las formas, las causas, los síntomas, las consecuencias y el tratamiento del onanismo en la mujer* (placeres ilícitos). Madrid: Imprenta de A. Pérez, 1883.

Rimmon-Kenan, Shlomith. *Narrative Fiction: Contemporary Poetics.* London: Methuen, 1983.

Saez de Melgar, Faustina. "La literatura en la mujer." *La violeta* 3 (20 August 1865): 401-402.

Salvá, Melchor. "La mujer bajo el aspecto económico." *Revista de España* 27 (1872): 237-263.

Sanchez de Toca, Joaquín. "El matrimonio: su ley natural, su historia, su importancia social." *Revista de España* 33 (1873): 66-96.

————. "El matrimonio: su ley natural, su historia, su importancia social." *Revista de España* 34 (1873): 53-71.

Warhol, Robyn R. *Gendered Interventions. Narrative Discourse in the Victorian Novel.* New Brunswick: Rutgers UP, 1989.

Joan M. Hoffman (essay date September 2004)

SOURCE: Hoffman, Joan M. "'¡Si no fuese por el decoro!': Emilia Pardo Bazán's Working Girls and the Polite Fiction of the Domestic Ideal." *Hispanofila* 142 (September 2004): 43-54.

[*In the following essay, Hoffman asserts that the short stories "El mundo," "Casi artista," "Náufragas," and "Champagne" illustrate Pardo Bazán's literary subversion of the nineteenth-century domestic ideal.*]

Certainly one of the most stark declarations ever made in print by nineteenth-century author and feminist, Emilia Pardo Bazán, a woman known for not mincing words, is found in her famous essay entitled **"La mujer española"** (1890).[1] Matter-of-factly and without a hint of irony she states that "Hemos convenido en que las señoritas no sirven para cosa alguna" (100-01). Implied in this statement, and long decried by Pardo Bazán, is nothing less than a national conspiracy of sorts, a shared accord (in which the author includes herself) to monitor, manage and control half of the population by a deceptively dangerous confluence of moral, economic, and spatial restraints.

Bridget Aldaraca alludes to this restricted feminine reality in her ground-breaking study of nineteenth-century domesticity in Spain:

> The essence of the ideal woman is not that she is modest, industrious, thrifty and, in the nineteenth century, *ilustrada* (educated), but that she embodies all of these virtues in and only in the house. The ideal woman is ultimately defined not ontologically, not functionally but territorially, by the space which she occupies. The frontier of her existence as a virtuous woman begins and ends at her doorstep.
>
> (27)

And she later elaborates:

> The material preconditions for the realization of the *ángel del hogar* are obviously a house in which the Angel can perform her duties, whether the house of a father, brother or husband, and a man who will support the Angel at a level of middle-class decency throughout her life. For the lady of the house to work, especially given the absence of genteel occupations for women in Spain, is a manifestation of the husband's lack of economic power and, consequently, an overt sign of downward class mobility. Thus the Lady (*la dama*) cannot work if class status is to be maintained; it is her position as Lady [. . .] that ties her to the economic fortunes of the head of the household.
>
> (63)[2]

Clearly, the nineteenth-century recipe for domestic bliss and financial security links spatial concerns with economic and moral status in an indissoluble bond and dictates the presence of a male authority figure to oversee that bond. Society has conspired to agree that a woman can not be decent and genteel—a Lady—unless she remains in the home untainted by contact with the outside world; she is, after all, the "moral anchor" of that home (Tolliver 152). Consequently, confined to this private sphere, ever vigilant of familial virtue and not expected to contribute financially to the household, the Lady is necessarily dependent upon the male in her life to have a good enough position in the public sphere to protect and provide for her in a manner in keeping with her treasured middle-class status; the *señorita*, the *ángel*, the *dama* is useful only as a showpiece of that status.

But what of the countless orphans, widows, and *solteronas,* those would-be *damas* who, through a trick of fate or luck or social custom find themselves fallen from the middle-class pedestal, unable (or unwilling) to count upon the permanence of a home or the support and protection of a man? Are these women who can ill afford to buy into the polite fiction to be denied the cherished mantle of "Lady" merely because they lack a few accouterments? Although the obvious nineteenth-century answer would be a resounding YES, in several of her short stories dealing with middle-class or aspiring middle-class women who must work for a living, Emilia

Pardo Bazán offers a very convincing "No, not necessarily." As is often her way, in such tales as **"El mundo"** (1908), **"Casi artista"** (1908), **"Náufragas"** (1909), and **"Champagne"** (1898), utilizing both positive and negative portrayals of women forced by circumstance into the public sphere, Pardo Bazán succeeds in subverting the domestic ideal. As Joseph Boone would argue, she alters perceptions of social reality by exposing the fictions within that reality (*Tradition* 214); by testing boundaries, challenging limitations, and questioning old definitions, she defies the status quo and champions a new space for women.

As evidenced by the dates of these stories, Pardo Bazán contends that the domestic ideal is nothing more than an antiquated fantasy, unsuitable for a new century. Indeed, as Joyce Tolliver points out, Pardo Bazán "most actively dedicated herself to the short story between about 1890 and 1920, a period that happens to correspond [. . .] to the height of intensity of the European feminist movements" (19). Not unexpectedly, these years also coincide with her most well-known feminist essays, proving that the precarious plight of the middle-class *dama* is of constant concern to the Galician author both before and after the turn of the century in fiction and non-fiction alike (see **"La mujer española"** *y otros escritos* [**"La mujer española"**]).

As recorded in her now famous conversation with an audacious gentleman, Pardo Bazán, the ever-vocal and self-proclaimed "radical feminista" is a tireless champion of equality of the sexes, adamantly believing that "todos los derechos que tiene el hombre debe tenerlos la mujer" (**"Conversación"** [**"Conversación entre Emilia Pardo Bazán y un caballero audaz"**] 330). Further, she repeatedly argues against "el destino relativo de la mujer" and in favor of her "destino propio" (**"La educación"** [**"La educación del hombre y de la mujer"**]153; 169; see also **"Una opinión sobre la mujer"** 194 and **"La educación"** 152). Most importantly, perhaps, Pardo Bazán continually laments the stifling limitations placed upon the Lady by the strict social conventions of her status. Despite the finery and the *fiestas,* hers is a dreary existence devoid of dignity and replete with tedium:

> La mujer se ahoga en las estrechas mallas de una red de moral menuda, menuda. Debercitos: gustar, lucir en un salón. Instruccioncita: música, algo de baile, migajas de historia, nociones superficiales y truncadas. Devocioncilla: prácticas rutinarias, genuflexiones, rezos maquinales, todo enano, raquítico, como los albaricoqueros chinos. Falta el soplo de lo ideal, la línea grandiosa, la majestad, la dignidad, el brío.

> (**"La educación"** 155-6)

According to the reality of this domestic ideal, in Pardo Bazán's view, the *dama* is virtuous, beautiful, dependent, and . . . useless. She can be nothing more than a "mueble de lujo" frantically occupied in a relentless "pesca conyugal," "la única forma de lucha por la existencia permitida a la mujer" (**"La mujer española"** 95; 101).

Ever dependent upon a man, true autonomy and self-reliance in a woman, even out of economic necessity, is unthinkable, immoral. Referring to the same sad *señoritas* of our introductory paragraph, Pardo Bazán asks and answers what she plainly recognizes as rhetorical questions: "¿Qué van a hacer esas niñas? ¿Colocarse detrás de un mostrador? ¿Ejercer una profesión, un oficio, una ocupación cualquiera? ¡Ah! Dejarían de ser señoritas *ipso facto*" (**"La mujer española"** 100). Pardo Bazán further drives home the depressing reality of dependency of the middle-class woman by tracing her restricted trajectory from daughter to wife:

> Quédense en la casa paterna, criando moho, y erigidas en convento de monjas sin vocación: viendo deslizarse su triste juventud, precursora de una vejez cien veces más triste; reducidas a comer mal y poco, a sufrir mil privaciones, para lograr dos objetos en que fundan su única esperanza de mejor porvenir. Primero que tengan carrera los hermanos varones y puedan 'hoy o mañana' servirlas de amparo; segundo, no carecer de cuatro trapitos con que presentarse en público de manera decorosa, a ver si parece el ave fénix, el marido que ha de resolver la situación. Si no parece, ¡qué melancólica existencia la de esa señorita, sentenciada a la miseria y al ocio, o cuando más al trabajo vergonzante, escondido como se esconde un crimen, porque la clase social a que pertenece la expulsaría de sus filas si supiese que cometía la incongruencia de hacer algo más que 'gobernar su casa'!

> (101)

In view of the restrictions placed upon the nineteenth-century Lady by the pervasive domestic ideal, it is not surprising, then, as Pardo Bazán reminds us, that "contadas son las profesiones que la mujer está autorizada para desempeñar en España; pero más contadas aún las mujeres de la clase media que se resuelven a ejercerlas." (101). Faced with a dearth of moral choices, the respectable *burguesa* anxious to guard her virtue and position is fated to a suffocating interior life, a seemingly ironic combination of *miseria* and *ocio*; the public sphere is no place for her: "Una señora, una señorita, no pueden ponerse a hacer esto, aquello ni lo otro; el decoro se lo impide." (**"En favor"** [**"En favor del trabajo de la mujer"**] 302). Awful decorum serves no purpose but to hold back and weigh down a capable woman: "¡Ah! ¡El decoro! ¡Grillo a los pies, esposa a las manos! ¡Soga que se lleva al cuello, sin acertar a desatarla!" (302); Pardo Bazán sees nothing but waste in this system: "se me ocurre que las muchachas, dotadas de inteligencia y con voluntad, podrían (a pesar de las restricciones que las leyes imponen a la actividad de la mujer, vedándole tantos puestos injustamente) obtener colocaciones útiles y fructuosas, a no existir la cortapisa del decoro" (302). Moreover, not only is this ideal moralistic and paternalistic, but also antiquated, as our author points out in yet another context: "Y la mujer de su casa es un anacronismo, que no contribuye al progreso humano" (**"Concepción Arenal"** [**"Concepción Arenal y sus ideas acerca de la mujer"**] 211).[3]

Pardo Bazán can not be more clear in her refusal to accept this restrictive reality for what amounts to "más de medio género humano" (**"Concepción Arenal"** 199): "'La mujer de su casa es un ideal erróneo'" (211). In the name of a new reality, a new ideal; in the name of progress and possibilities, Pardo Bazán presents—in concert with her critical essays—fictional examples of path-finding middle-class *damas,* those *mujeres contadas* who can ill afford to be *muebles de lujo*; women who—at times boldly and at times meekly, but always out of necessity—defy the dictates of decorum to enter heretofore forbidden territory—the public sphere.

Inspired by the territorial concerns of Aldaraca, this study will trace a trajectory from interior space to exterior space, from the more tentative portrayals of Ladies who pursue decent, acceptable public-sphere activities from within their homes to the most daring example of a true public woman. In the process, it is clear that Pardo Bazán challenges her readers' understanding of an entire spectrum of women, from *la mujer en casa, la pierna quebrada* to *la mujer pública.* By so doing, then, she also demands a thoughtful reevaluation of the *ángel del hogar* and the entire domestic ideal.

"El mundo" (1908), perhaps the most cautious of our tales, begins with an all-too-common situation: a family of women alone whose hard times are only exacerbated by the mother's fatal illness: "Estamos completamente arruinadas, y aún peor: estamos alcanzadas en seis mil y pico de duros" (66). Structured on opposition, the tale is driven by the constant interplay of opposing terms—discipline/self-indulgence, truth/fiction, reality/fantasy—and proposes a thoughtful reassessment of both those terms and, ultimately, the entire situation of the nineteenth-century woman.

The oppositions begin with the sisters themselves. As their mother lay dying, faced with the prospect of misery and shame, the two—very different one from the other—exhibit contrary behavior. While the elder and more frivolous Dionisia, reminiscent of her egotistical and emotional Greek namesake, helplessly "lloraba por los rincones," selfishly wishing for a new coach (67); the younger, Germana, only evokes such Teutonic traits as logic and stoicism. Unlike her excitable sister, she quickly accepts the stark reality of their plight: "¿Prefieres pedir limosna?" (67). Just as quickly she refuses to accept, idly, certain fate—"No creas que aguardaré a que mamá se muera, a que nos echen de esta casa y perdamos nuestra única esperanza de salvación"—and devises a bold plan: "Trabajaremos" (66).

Out of necessity, ingenuity, hard work and a bit of falsehood, Germana "fashions" a novel solution. Dressing in her best finery, "con elegancia y coquetería" she sets out to conquer her more-well-off sister *burguesas* with a lure that can not fail (66). Fully aware that present reality does not suit her dire purpose, Germana devises a fiction—"He aceptado la representación de una modista muy elegante de Biarritz."—that, in turn, is transformed into a new reality: "Hemos montado taller" (67). With one curt declaration—"Trabajaremos"—she prys open a new space for herself. By virtue of her own sweat and toil, this girl with the masculine name rejects her helpless sister's response and, in the process, topples the impossible fiction of life as a pampered and protected *ángel del hogar.*

Ironically, the success of her venture is dependent upon exactly those women—the fickle but angelic "parroquianas seguras"—that Germana rejects in herself by mounting it: "Al espejuelo de la elegancia extranjera la mujer acude, y acudió" (67). In fact, throughout, Germana portrays none of the capricious, emotional nature associated with most such women of her time, including her sister. The justification for her apparent ignorance of decorum, for her deception and her supposed lack of proper grief at the death of her mother, comes directly from an amazing perception of the sometimes convoluted ways of the world, as reflected in the tale's title: "Si yo confieso mi verdadera situación [. . .] o me vuelven la espalda o me dan unas 'perras' de limosna . . . Hay que pedir con soberbia y para lujo; no para comer . . ." (68). Germana understands reality just as she understands the needs of her clients; and, like them, she rejects reality—at least the acceptable reality for women like them—as pitiable. While they are content with and convinced by a fantasy of someone else's making, Germana creates a new and more valid truth for herself. Likewise, whereas Dionisia, as if inspired by the mythical Dionysus before her, represents the antiquated myth of the feminine ideal, her younger sister epitomizes fresh logic, a novel truth for a modern time. Stepping out of the protective cocoon of feminine expectation into the public sphere, Germana chooses to become part of **"El mundo,"** to do something both totally necessary and totally unexpected.

Written the same year as **"El mundo," "Casi artista"** is, nevertheless, a more stark portrayal of a woman forced by circumstance into the public sphere.[4] From the outset of the tale, Dolores's class-standing is even more precarious than that of Germana and Dionisia; she, "en chancletas y desgreñada," worked as a seamstress's apprentice before marriage, and her husband is only a carpenter (102). Clearly, however, she aspires to the coveted angel-status, remaining within the home to raise the children; likewise, her husband—"bebedor y holgazán, mujeriego, timbista y perdido" that he is—does perform, if poorly and only temporarily, the duties of a *burgués*: "siempre acompañaba y traía a casa una corteza de pan" (101).

Furthermore, a dark tone is set early on for this protagonist in the simple act of naming. Dolores, la *Cartera,* seems doubly marked by awful fate. In keeping with Pardo Bazán's oft-expressed lament regarding the relative value of women, her inckname positions her only in terms of another, a male, her father the mailman; additionally, her individual identity portends only unhappiness. Accordingly, she finds herself, despite class differences, in the same position as Germana and Dionisia—alone in the world with responsibilities but without the requisite male support. She is desperate and shameful, abandoned by a drunken fortune-hunting husband—Frutos, el *Verderón* (Greenfinch)—who has no difficulty in flying off, in swapping his familial obligations for the promise of the New World.

Dolores's response to her economic dilemma mirrors Germana's as well. Recalling happier times during her apprenticeship at the shop on the *calle* Mayor, she resolves to take up sewing again, "ante la necesidad" (101). Despite the apparent logic of this decision however, her attendant moral dilemma is plainly communicated by this highly critical passage: "A boca de noche, abochornada—¡como si fuera ella quien hubiese el mal!—, se deslizó en el almacén, y en voz baja pidió 'labor para su casa', pues no podía abandonar a las criaturas . . . La retribución, irrisoria; no hay nada peor pagado que 'lo blanco' . . ." (101-02). Clearly, the message is, if a woman alone is to succeed, even out of necessity, she must do so clandestinely and at her own moral peril.

Against all probability, however, Dolores, "una pulcra trabajadora" and "habilísima", does succeed—beyond any level attained by her now-absent husband. She demonstrates that respectability and morality are not incompatible with labor, even in a woman. Moreover, through her work, she gains some partial sense of individual identity, apart, if not from her father, at least from her husband: "En la *Cartera* había desaparecido la csposa del carpintero vicioso" (102). She is a "semiartista" with the needle who understands the "cuerpo femenil" and thus boasts "una clientela de señoras" (102). Consequently, she moves her family to a better home, her son attends school, and she is able to employ several workers, all the while "guarda[ndo] su honra con cuidado religioso" (102). This new Dolores is seemingly the very model of a capable self-sufficient woman, offered up as a viable possibility for a modern age.

Yet, Pardo Bazán does not cnd Dolores's tale here with this achievement as she does "El mundo." We recall that Dolores's very name implies pain; that she, la *Cartera,* is still viewed, despite her accomplishments, relative to a man; and that the title of this tale is less than

fully affirmative. That she *almost* succeeds, that she is only "casi artista" is driven home as el *Verderón* flies back into her newly feathered nest as unexpectedly as he had left. At first, harmony seems possible as Dolores, with her new-found authority, turns the tables on her husband, offering to support him in return for certain considerations: "el *Verderón* comería a cuenta de su mujer, y hasta bebería y fumaría, comprometiéndose a respetar la labor de ella, su negocio, su industria ya fundada, su arte elegante. Y Frutos prometió" (103). But pacts and promises lead only to clients' complaints and threats of eviction as Frutos rejects his new "papel accesorio" (103). Foreshadowing a similar maneuver later in "La punta del cigarro" (1914), here, masculine attempts the destruction of feminine as a cigarette butt is applied to delicate French lace (102); and Dolores is transformed, not by the mere struggle to survive, but by the raw power of something even greater: "La pacífica, la mansa, la sufrida de tantos años había vuelto leona. Defendía su labor, defendía, no ya la corteza para comer, sino el ideal de hermosura cifrado en la obra." (103). Her yardstick is transformed as well, into an "arma terrible" (103); and before she can even process her own fatal actions—"¿Era ella quien había sacudido así?"—it becomes all too clear that "el hombre no se movía, y por su sien, corría un hilo de sangre" (104).

True, the readers' sympathies are with Dolores. Her worthless husband disrupted her little paradise, built on just the right combination of feminine and masculine, of elegance and industry; he may well have deserved to die. But murder is surely punishable; and, just as Dolores stands over the body contemplating her ordeal, so too must we speculate as to her fate. With this openended conclusion, we are left with more questions than answers as Pardo Bazán responds to complexity with complexity, "relating life to plot and plot to life" (Boone, "Wedlock" 72); her purpose is "'unsettle' the reader, who must become a critic of the conventions residing in the [domestic] ideal" (Boone, *Tradition* 151). Far from being a simple approbation of a thoroughly modern arrangement (as evident in **"El mundo"**), **"Casi artista"** presents Dolores, ironically, as a victim of that false ideal; this story is a stark counter-example, a warning, a stalwart wish for something better.

With **"Náufragas"** (1909) Pardo Bazán makes an important spatial shift from interior to exterior.[5] Whereas Germana and Dolores challenge the ideal without leaving the private sphere, the public sphere is the unfortunate arena for the three hapless women of **"Náufragas."** Forced by the death of their husband and father from the middle-class, country home they have always known, they are quickly transformed into outsiders after just "un mes largo de residencia en Madrid" (141). Miserable, unskilled, and homeless, these Ladies of now-diminished status spend their days desperately trying to recuperate what was lost, to replicate the forfeited domestic ideal.

With this portrayal, then, Pardo Bazán offers perhaps her most stinging indictment of the ficticious system that champions a distorted definition of feminine decency over the basic ability to work, even for one's survival; indeed, that not one day of work is completed during the course of the story is a crucial element of this indictment. These poor souls are depicted, like Dolores before them, as victims of a cruel and fallacious system in which "the traditional middle-class woman's socio-economic status, and her limited autonomy, are entirely dependent upon the goodwill and sound financial planning of the men who support her" (Tolliver 153).

Again, as with **"Casi artista,"** Pardo Bazán's aim here is to unsettle the reader to the point of criticism. These "náufragas" are passive, powerless, nameless women, without identity and without agency, against whom every element of the tale conspires, usually to the point of mockery. Initially, their protector, an idealistic and impractical country pharmacist, dies needlessly, "de la más vulgar ictericia," unable to cure himself because he sees no value in any but the most exotic medications (142). This fateful loss only triggers a downward spiral of misery, despair, and debt for the wife and daughters left behind. Even Madrid, that *grande dame* proposed as their savior, seems to plot their downfall; the contrast between the bustling metropolis at the hour of *paseo,* presented in the highly romanticized opening description, and the "lugareñas" could not be more stark (142). Unlike the beautiful women in their shiny coaches, these refugees are far from carefree; they can not be romanticized. Instead, they are at once shipwrecked, "perdidas en el mar madrileño" (141), and thirsting to death in this "desierto cruel" (143). Moreover, whereas these directionless *burguesas* "se veían navegando por las calles, sin techo, sin pan," both the humble flower vendors and their memorable landlady—with her low-class language and her lower-class clientele—mock their helplessness by possessing what the higher-class women sorely lack; the security of a home and an occupation (144).

In addition, the tale's narrator, expertly described by Tolliver as an "urban sophisticate," may wield the harshest blow, conspiring the ruin of these country bumpkins even in the telling of their tale (163). For example, any illusions these hopeful "embobadas" harbor about life in Madrid are quickly dashed as pure fantasy by that unsympathetic, sarcastic narrator:

> La madre entraría en una casa formal, decente, de señores verdaderos, para ejercer las funciones de ama de llaves, propias de una persona seria y 'de respeto';

eso sí, todo antes que perder la dignidad de gente nacida en pañales limpios, de familia 'distinguida', de médicos, farmacéuticos, que no son gañanes . . . La hija mayor se pondría también a servir, pero entendámonos; donde la trataran como corresponde a una señorita de educación, donde no corriese ningún peligro su honra [. . .] En cuanto a la hija menor, de diez años, ¡bah! Nada más natural; la meterían en uno de esos colegios gratuitos que hay [. . .] ¡Ya lo creo!

(142, emphasis mine)[6]

The reality is something else entirely: "Dos lugareñas, que no han servido nunca . . . Muy honradas, sí . . . ; pero con toda honradez, ¿qué?, vale más tener gracia, saber desenredarse . . ." (142). Decorum and respectability be damned; a little sex appeal and street smarts are what is called for in the big city, if one is to survive. Reluctantly, it is the beer-hall or nothing for these defeated Ladies. The polite fiction, the erroneous myth, of domesticity is not to be salvaged. All that remains is a pathetic attempt at optimism: "En todas partes se puede ser buena"; anything is better than begging in the streets (144).

Clearly, these women, raised only to be protected and pampered angels, do not possess the necessary skills for self-sufficiency. That a girl cannot live by honor alone is a bitter pill to swallow; but the ironic attempt to blame a dead man for this predicament—"Si su padre [. . .] hubiera sido *como otros*"—compounds an already passionate system-wide criticism leveled by the author (144). In fact, the pharmacist *was* like all of the others; he was a *burgués,* a willing participant in this impractical and idealistic fiction that keeps women homebound, denying them education and opportunity, creating honorable victims.

With **"Champagne"** (1898), the earliest and most daring story to be examined here, our interior-to-exterior trajectory is complete as a true *mujer pública* tells her own tale in the first person with little narratorial interference.[7] True, the driving force of the tale is career justification, so to speak—"Por haberme casado, ando como me ves" (293)—and, a subsequent indictment of arranged marriage. While I deal with this aspect of the story in another context however, what interests us here is the mere fact that this fallen bride labors as a prostitute at all (Hoffman 242-3); no study of Emilia Pardo Bazán's working women would be complete without a look at **"Champagne."**

Even as he ignores the implications of his own behavior, our protagonist's client, Raimundo Valdés, is prompted to pass swift moral judgment on his nameless "compañera momentánea" (293). Considering the obvious sadness in her eyes, unbefitting "una hembra que hacía profesión de jovialidad"; indeed, a "lujo reservado solamente a las mujeres honradas," he reflects the widespread and unquestioned societal belief that the oldest profession is far from respectable (293); it is certainly not one of Aldaraca's "genteel occupations" (63).

Intriguingly, Pardo Bazán challenges this accepted view of the prostitute by portraying her sympathetically. While she would never recommend such an option, the author is surely more compassionate with the prostitute than with the "náufragas," for example. This courtesan is not Zola-esque; she is not a pathetic, degraded, disease-ridden whore. On the other hand, neither is she a romanticized harlot with the proverbial heart of gold. Falling to neither extreme, this prostitute is real, believable, humanized. If not for the truth of her sad tale calmly told—the handsome young lieutenant, the *cuarentón,* the champagne, the betrayal, the dismissal, the descent into prostitution—she could almost be mistaken for a *dama* enjoying an afternoon cocktail with a gentleman caller in her front parlor.

Far from being that angel, this public woman, nevertheless, has created a new *hogar,* a new life for herself. She is her own head-of-household, self-reliant and successful in her way—despite decorum. Unlike the pure and proper angels, she understands the polite fiction of the domestic ideal and the dangerous power of truth: "creo si todas las mujeres hablasen lo que piensan, como hice yo por culpa del champagne, más de cuatro y más de ocho se verían peor que esta individua." (295). Unrestrained by demure hypocrisy, she knows a certain freedom, tainted to be sure, to speak her own mind and create her own destiny: "Ahora ya puedo beber lo que quiera. No se me escapará ningún secreto" (295). Bring on the champagne!

With **"Champagne,"** as with **"Náufragas," "Casi artista,"** and **"El mundo,"** Pardo Bazán shows that *señoritas* can and should be permitted to serve all manner of useful purposes within society. Be they seamstresses or true public women, small-business owners, individual entrepreneurs, or simply employees, they are capable of self-sufficiency and autonomy, while, at the same time, maintaining their honor and integrity. Women have a right to self-determination; they need and deserve both access to and preparation for the public sphere. To this end, in both essay and fiction, Pardo Bazán calls for and champions a new intersection of territory, economics, and morality for women, a redefinition of middle-class decency. She demands nothing less than the destruction of the *ángel del hogar* and of the polite fiction of the domestic ideal.

Notes

1. The title quote is taken from Emilia Pardo Bazán's 1915 essay, "En favor del trabajo de la mujer" (302). All subsequent references to Pardo Bazán's essays and short stories will appear parenthetically in the text.

2. Aldaraca confirms that the idea of the Lady or *la dama* refers to class origin regardless of the married state (63n18). Following her example, I too capitalize the word "Lady" throughout this study.

3. See also "La galantería y el culto de la mujer": "Error profundo, imaginar que adelantará la raza mientras la mujer se estacione. Al pararse la mujer, párase todo" (309).

4. "El mundo" was first published in 1908 in volume 29 of *La Ilustración Española y Americana*; "Casi artista" was first published in 1908 in volume 919 of *Blanco y Negro*. Both were republished in Pardo Bazán's 1909 collection entitled *Sud-Exprés.*

5. "Náufragas" was first published in 1909 in volume 946 of *Blanco y Negro*. It was republished in the 1910 edition of *Cuentos nuevos.*

6. Tolliver offers several examples of the narrator's conspiracy in her excellent study of narrative discourse in this story that I will not repeat here. See her chapter entitled "'The Negotiation of Difficulties'" (152-70).

7. Probably due to its controversial nature, "Champagne" was one of the few Pardo Bazán short stories not initially published in contemporary journals. It was first included in the collection, *Cuentos de amor* (1898).

Works Cited

Aldaraca, Bridget A. *El ángel del hogar: Galdós and the Ideology of Domesticity in Spain.* North Carolina Studies in the Romance Languages and Literatures 239. Chapel Hill: U of North Carolina P, 1991.

Boone, Joseph Allen. *Tradition Counter Tradition: Love and the Form of Fiction.* Chicago: U of Chicago P, 1987.

———. "Wedlock as Deadlock and Beyond: Closure and the Victorian Marriage Ideal." *For Better or Worse: Attitudes Toward Marriage in Literature.* Ed. Evelyn J. Hinz. Winnipeg: U of Manitoba P, 1985. 65-81.

Hoffman, Joan M. "Torn Lace and Other Transformations: Rewriting the Bride's Script in Selected Stories by Emilia Pardo Bazán." *Hispania* 82 (1999): 238-45.

Pardo Bazán, Emilia. "Casi artista." *Cuentos completos.* Vol. 3. 101-04.

———. "Champagne." *Cuentos completos.* Vol. 1. 293-95.

———. "Concepción Arenal y sus ideas acerca de la mujer." 1893. *"La mujer"* 198-214.

Pardo Bazán, Emilia. "Conversación entre Emilia Pardo Bazán y un caballero audaz." *"La mujer"* 330.

————. *Cuentos completos*. Ed. Juan Paredes Núñez. La Coruña: Fundación Pedro Barrie de la Maza, Conde de Fenosa, 1990. 4 vols.

————. "La educación del hombre y de la mujer." 1892. *"La mujer"* 149-77.

————. "En favor del trabajo de la mujer." 1915. *"La mujer"* 301-03.

————. "La galantería y el culto de la mujer." 1899. *"La mujer"* 308-09.

————. "La mujer española." 1890. *"La mujer"* 83-116.

————. *"La mujer española" y otros escritos* [*"La mujer"*] Ed. Guadalupe Gómez-Ferrer. Feminismos 56. Madrid: Cátedra, 1999.

————. "El mundo." *Cuentos completos*. Vol. 3. 65-68.

————. "Náufragas." *Cuentos completos*. Vol. 1. 141-44.

————. "Una opinión sobre la mujer." 1892. *"La mujer"* 192-7.

————. "La punta del cigarro." *Cuentos completos*. Vol. 3. 398-401.

Tolliver, Joyce. *Cigar Smoke and Violet Water: Gendered Discourse in the Stories of Emilia Pardo Bazán*. Lewisburg: Bucknell UP, 1998.

Kathy Bacon (essay date October 2005)

SOURCE: Bacon, Kathy. "Death and the Virgin Martyr: Re-Writing Hagiography in *Dulce Dueño*." *Forum for Modern Language Studies* 41, no. 4 (October 2005): 375-85.

[*In the following essay, Bacon interprets Pardo Bazán's* Dulce dueño *as a revision of the traditional virgin-martyr tale.*]

According to the logic of virginity evident in medieval hagiography, "the only good virgin—that is, the only true virgin—is a dead virgin" (Bloch, p. 120). The relentless drive of every virgin-martyr legend towards the death of its heroine provokes a variety of critical responses in current hagiographical scholarship. Proponents of what has been called the "rape-pornography reading" (Mills, p. 137), such as Kathryn Gravdal and Simon Gaunt, interpret the tortured female martyr as a passive object for the sadistic male gaze of the author and readership (Gravdal, pp. 21-41; Gaunt, pp. 180-233). Other critics, such as Jocelyn Wogan-Browne and Katherine Lewis, argue that in many texts it is possible to read the virgin martyr as controlling the sequence of events which lead to her torture and death, "scripting"

the action and the interpretation of her own martyrdom.[1] In this reading, the martyr's choice of death confers meaning upon her life, in a move similar to the female suicide described by Elisabeth Bronfen as implying "an authorship with one's own life, a form of writing the self and writing death that is ambivalently poised between self-construction and self-destruction" (Bronfen, p. 142).

This article will examine within this framework not a medieval text, but an early-twentieth-century novel, Emilia Pardo Bazán's *Dulce dueño* (1911),[2] which re-writes the traditional virgin-martyr story in two ways: firstly, in presenting a version of the conversion and martyrdom of St Catherine of Alexandria composed by one of the characters, the priest Carranza; and second, in the life of the protagonist Lina, who narrates the rest of the novel. Whilst Lina appears unlike her patron saint Catherine in her pursuit of a modernist aesthetic of exquisite sensations and her final confinement in a lunatic asylum, she emulates the martyr in her rejection of a series of inferior suitors and her mystical experience of Christ. Carranza's virgin-martyr text occupies most of the first fifth of *Dulce dueño,* and is often interpreted as providing a "script" for the rest of the novel.[3] Such readings, while correctly identifying the importance of the legend for the rest of the novel, have so far neglected to examine the virgin-martyr text itself in detail. By reading Pardo Bazán's restaging of the story of St Catherine in the light of the theoretical debates I have just outlined, I wish to elucidate the text's exploration of the consequences for female subjecthood of the display of death and the writing of death. Lina removes herself from the lethal objectifying gaze of the hagiographer-pornographer only through an act of autothanatography whereby she writes her own symbolic death.

Virgin-martyr legends typically conform to a set pattern, narrating the confrontation between a pagan tyrant and a young woman who refuses to renounce her identity as a Christian virgin, which is under attack either through a command to worship pagan gods, or through the tyrant's sexual advances. The tyrant subjects the virgin to a series of tortures, during which she remains steadfast, and finally succeeds in executing her. One trend in recent hagiographical scholarship argues that these texts should be seen in terms of pornography and rape. Simon Gaunt, for instance, comments that, in hagiographical texts about women, "Certain scenes, when abstracted from their context, have much in common with modern pornography depicting bondage and mutilation" (Gaunt, p. 197), while Kathyrn Gravdal explores what she sees as the centrality of sexual assault in virgin-martyr legends, and asserts that "Hagiography affords a sanctioned space in which [. . .] male voyeurism becomes licit, if not advocated" (Gravdal, p. 24). Such analyses suggest that the male narrator and the implied male readers of such texts are complicit in sadistic voyeurism towards the virgin martyr, and imply that the torture and martyrdom of the virgin constitute a kind of displaced rape.

In another context, Elisabeth Bronfen has developed Laura Mulvey's idea of a voyeuristic male gaze on a fetishised female body by suggesting that the representation of a beautiful *dead* female body functions particularly well as a fetish, stabilising fear and anxiety (Bronfen, pp. 96-8, 123-4). The body of the virgin martyr, imagined as the embodiment of purity, integrity and true beauty, is ideally placed to serve this function. The imagined integrity of her body is enhanced by the fact that it is often miraculously restored to wholeness even after its violation by tortures such as whipping.[4] This body is thus a "safe" target for voyeuristic and sadistic impulses, all the more so because the torture and killing of the virgin martyr may be viewed as theologically necessary for her attainment of sainthood. This reading of the virgin-martyr text, which interprets the male author as writing the violent death of the feminine out of (unconscious) pornographic and sadistic impulses, while by no means the only possible interpretation of virgin-martyr legends, is nonetheless a very productive one for the story of St Catherine as re-told by Carranza in *Dulce dueño.*

In Carranza's re-telling, the martyrdom plot is presented from the beginning as a sexual plot. St Catherine's martyrdom is traditionally depicted as being caused by her defiance of a general proclamation that all must sacrifice to the pagan gods; in many versions it is a result of her own initiative, since she actively seeks out the tyrant in order to remonstrate with him over his idolatry and persecution of Christians.[5] By contrast, in Carranza's re-imagining, the command that the populace must make sacrifices to idols is conceived from the start as a trap for Catherine, after rumours of her conversion, and Gnetes, the villain who suggests this plot to the emperor, is motivated by envy and by frustrated lust: the narrator informs us that "la suposición de lo que sería la posesión de Catalina le había desvelado en su sórdido cubículo" (*Dd* [*Dulce dueño*], p. 75). The threat of sexual violence is explicitly proposed by the same man as the most effective weapon against the saint: "El único modo de reducir a una hembra tan soberbia sería amenazarla con una excursión forzosa al lupanar, o con una fiesta del Panoeum, en que ella hiciese de ninfa y nosotros de capripedes" (*Dd,* p. 97). While the motif of forced prostitution appears in the stories of other virgin martyrs, such as St Agnes and St Agatha (Gravdal, pp. 22-3), it is not a traditional part of the story of St Catherine. Its inclusion here therefore suggests a particular emphasis on the idea of sexual violence. Similarly, the emperor's attitude to Catherine is also portrayed as determined by voyeuristic and sadistic sexuality: while the debate in which she will defend Christianity against

learned pagan philosophers is being arranged, Maximino, "seguro de la derrota de la doncella, proyectaba vengarse con venganza sabrosa," seeing her as "una querida a quien sería grato domeñar" (*Dd,* p. 81).

The portrayal of the legend's villains as driven by perverse sexuality, although particularly clear in Carranza's version, is in some ways typical of the virgin-martyr tradition. Going beyond this, Carranza opens up a space in his text for sadistic voyeurism as a pleasure open to the whole of society, and hence also the reader. When the horrific torture wheel which has been designed for Catherine is displayed, we are told that "el público omitió una exclamación larga, obscura. Quizás protestaban; quizás suspiraban de placer ante la peripecia del drama interesante" (*Dd,* p. 100). The fact that the narrator offers the possible interpretation of the public's reaction as one of pleasure legitimates and even solicits the reader's pleasure in reading about Catherine's torture. Any guilt in the reader over this pleasure can be assuaged by the text's strategy of locating sadistic sexuality in the other, the pagan emperor and, later, the Ethiopian executioner, allowing its Spanish Catholic writer and readers to dissociate themselves from it whilst potentially also enjoying it.

The idea of martyrdom as a displaced rape is strongly signalled in this version of the story. The narrator presents the emperor as ordering the torture and killing of Catherine as a substitute for a sexual assault:

> no tenía ni el arranque brutal necesario para estrechar a la princesa con brazos férreos, para estrujarla con ímpetu de fiera que clava las garras, hinca los dientes y devora el resuello de su presa moribunda. Un vergonzoso temblor, un desmayo de la voluntad lacia y sin nervio le incitaba a la crueldad, a la venganza de los débiles y miserables.
>
> (*Dd,* p. 94)

The association of sexuality with wild beasts evident here is maintained throughout the text. Catherine's Ethiopian executioner is associated through racist stereotyping with bestial sexuality. The execution is described with sexually explicit overtones, evoking the deflowering of the virgin: "el negro se atrevió a separar el velo ya desgarrado por mil partes y a tomar en su izquierda mano, donde apenas cabía, el raudal de la mata de pelo de la princesa, enrollándola y afianzándola vigoroso" (*Dd,* pp. 101-2). The veil functions here as a symbolic substitute for the virgin's hymen, and also combines associations of both the secluded nun and the exotic Oriental veiled woman which make Catherine an exciting focus of sexual interest for Carranza's narrative. Her thick hair, whose sweet smell had previously attracted the emperor's fetishistic interest (*Dd,* p. 91) now plays its part in her punishment, facilitating her beheading.

The hostility towards women which Simon Gaunt suggests is implicit in many hagiographical texts about female virgins (Gaunt, pp. 196-7) becomes almost explicit in Carranza's version of the legend.[6] His text breaks with the tradition which masks hostility to the feminine by depicting the virgin as morally perfect, by consistently describing Catherine as proud, both before and after her conversion. The text reveals a dual impulse to punish and to idealise Catherine:[7] punishment is expressed, for instance, in the bloodthirsty imagining of the effect of the torture wheel: "A la tercer vuelta del infernal artificio, sería la mártir una sanguinolenta masa, y piltrafas de su carne colgarían de las ruedas" (***Dd,*** p. 99). The impulse to punishment is restrained, however, for this is no more than a fantasy within the text: the machine is supernaturally broken before Catherine's body can be brought into this state of disintegration.

The movement towards idealisation in the text leads to fetishistic hyperbole. As Catherine examines herself in the mirror, she sees

> la imagen encantadora de una beldad que evocaba la de las deas antiguas. A su torso escultural faltaba solo el cinturón de Afrodita, y a su cabeza noble, que el oro calcinado con reflejos de miel del largo cabello diademaba, el casco de Palas Atenea.
>
> (***Dd,*** p. 68)

The power of this fetishistic image to capture the gaze is suggested during the debate, during which "se dijera que envolvía a la princesa un fluido luminoso, que una hoguera clara ardía detrás de sus albas vestiduras" (*Dd,* p. 84).

The climactic moment in the staging of the virgin saint as spectacle is her martyrdom. Elisabeth Bronfen argues that the representation of a fetishised, beautiful, dead female body recuperates a sense of stability, and appeases the threat of mortality and of lack of plenitude (Bronfen, p. xii). This function is carried out particularly well by the execution/apotheosis of the virgin martyr which ends her mortal life. Paradoxical though it may seem, the depiction of Catherine's decapitated head and body in Carranza's story corresponds with Bronfen's descriptions of the represented feminine corpse as "a perfect, immaculate aesthetic form" articulating "stillness, wholeness, perfection" (Bronfen, p. 5): in accordance with tradition, Catherine's neck bleeds milk instead of blood, and "El cuerpo de la mártir y su testa pálida, exangüe, perfecta, flotaban en aquel lago" (***Dd,*** p. 102). The miraculous milk, "candidísima, densa leche", forming a "lago de blancor lunar, hecho de claridades de astros y de alburas de nube plateada y plumajes císneos" (ibid.), allows Carranza to replace violent fragmentation with fantasised wholeness, purity and beauty.

This fetishised image of female death nonetheless has an effect of the uncanny, as the virgin's dead eyes return the emperor's gaze in a deathly Medusa-like stare:

> Maximino [. . .] miraba atónito, castañeteando los dientes de terror frío, el puro cuerpo de cisne flotando en el lago de candor, la cabeza sobrenaturalmente aureolada por los cabellos, que en vez de pegarse a las sienes, jugaban alrededor y se expandían, acusando con su halo de sombra la palidez de las mejillas y el vidriado de los ojos ensoñadores de la virgen . . .
>
> (***Dd,*** p. 103)

Catherine's hair here evokes both a saintly halo and Medusa's snakes, pointing out the ambivalence of the hagiographical text towards its female protagonist. The dead virgin becomes the sign of the tyrant's own mortality, and as the text ends he recalls the prophecies of his own overthrow and death.

In presenting the way that Carranza tells the story of St Catherine, Pardo Bazán thus holds out for our inspection the dynamic of the traditional virgin-martyr legend whose text functions as the site of a negotiation between men (Gaunt, pp. 188-9), in which a beautiful young woman is presented as a spectacle for the reader's voyeuristic delectation, and in which a subtext of sexual violence reinforces a dynamic of gender domination. Because the scene of narration is staged for us (rather than being inferred by critics, as in the case of medieval hagiography), this negotiation between men has itself become the object of representation. The text is doubly-oriented, addressed by Carranza to a male scholarly audience, but also addressed by Pardo Bazán to the reader, who is thus invited to demystify the saint's story as a pornographic display of female suffering and death. Pardo Bazán draws our attention to the double-voiced nature of the text by describing it as a transcription of Carranza's reading which may nonetheless have been influenced by the implied author's point of view: "Tal vez al transcribir aquí su lectura se deslicen en ella bastantes arrequives de sentimiento o de estética que el autor reprobaría" (***Dd,*** p. 48).

Carranza reads his text aloud, ostensibly for Lina's benefit, since it is the story of her patron saint (Lina stands for Catalina) and, more importantly, because he hopes that she will pay for its publication. Yet the dry historical style in which the tale begins is clearly aimed not so much at Lina herself as at the other man present: the sceptic and liberal scholar Polilla. The two men use the reading of the text to reinforce their homosocial bond, which is no less strong for being based on their disagreements about religion. For instance, Carranza refers in an aside to what he sees as Polilla's strategy of the subversive mockery of religion, and Polilla is flattered, rather than offended: "se engalló, satisfecho de ser peligroso" (***Dd,*** p. 49). In this scene of staged narration, the interaction between the author and his hearers is never initiated by Lina; Polilla, by contrast, interrupts the reading seven times. Thus it is Polilla who enacts for us the role of the reader who engages with the text and invests affectively in the narration, while Lina, although she insists she wants to hear the story, remains quiet and apparently unresponsive. The virgin-martyr story enables Carranza and Polilla to continue their ongoing argument over the relative merits of Catholicism and liberalism, while at the same time sharing the imagined spectacle of a beautiful young woman being tortured, a pleasure legitimated by the story's status as art, even religious art. In this interaction between the two men, Lina is consigned to the margins.

Raquel Medina argues that Carranza's St Catherine legend functions as "espejo y guía a las acciones de Lina" for the rest of the novel. When critics understand the relation between the embedded martyrdom text and Lina's own story in this way, as one of rigid authority, their almost inevitable conclusion is that the novel ultimately submits Lina to patriarchal discourse. In this understanding of the novel, Lina "reads" and subsequently re-enacts the legend of St Catherine in an entirely passive way; in Medina's words, "transcribe al dictado las palabras pronunciadas por la autoridad patriarcal que representa la figura de Dios" (Medina, p. 301).

In contrast, what I argue is that Lina, as a reader of the story of St Catherine, may be seen as engaging in a "resistant" reading of the legend as it has been presented to her: not merely reproducing, but re-writing it. Here I draw on the work of scholars such as Katherine Lewis and Jocelyn Wogan-Browne, who argue strongly for the recognition of what Lewis calls "the possibility of multiple or resistant readings" of virgin-martyr legends (Lewis, p. 71). Lewis argues that the popularity of such texts among female readers compels us "to consider the ways in which women may have read these texts without lending complicity to the sadism directed against women, or colluding in the patriarchal norms which they produce" (Lewis, p. 74). In this sense, a virgin martyr's staging of her own death can be understood as a practice of autothanatography which has the aim of taking control of her own representation, in a way which resists patriarchal objectification.

Proposing "resistant readings" of virgin-martyr legends does not necessarily mean reading them against the grain. Katherine Lewis provides a detailed discussion of "important text-internal ways of arguing for more nuanced readings" (Lewis, p. 73) of four late-medieval English versions of the torture of St Margaret of Antioch. She shows how, far from being a passive victim, "Margaret arranges the spectacle of her tortured body for the benefit of [the tyrant] Olibrius and the on-looking crowd", "explicitly invit[ing] and instigat[ing] her own torture" (Lewis, p. 75). Furthermore, Margaret engages in a debate with the onlookers as to how her suffering should be understood, seeking to control the interpretation of her bleeding body and thereby turn it into a proof of the truth of Christianity and an opportunity for the salvation of others (Lewis, pp. 76-8). In this way, torture and death become for Margaret "a self-representational act" (Lewis, p. 78), confirming in another context Elisabeth Bronfen's insight into "how an aesthetically staged performance of death may [. . .] signify a moment of control and power" (Bronfen, p. 141).

In ***Dulce dueño,*** Pardo Bazán portrays an initial sadistic and voyeuristic reading of the virgin-martyr text, which reduces its female protagonist to the status of an object. She then follows it with Lina's re-writing of that text. Lina's text erupts disruptively into the novel, with the words "¡Como una bomba, el noticrón!" (***Dd,*** p. 107); its colloquialism and first-person narrator contrast with the formal third-person narrative of both the virgin-martyr legend and its frame. Lina's first-person point of view transforms the dynamic of the virgin-martyr legend. By allowing Lina to narrate her own story, a device never used in traditional virgin-martyr texts, Pardo Bazán positions her as a subject and as a possessor of the gaze, not merely its object, in a further actualisation of the potential described by Katherine Lewis in the texts about St Margaret.

Since Lina is introduced to us first as a reader/hearer of the virgin-martyr story—albeit a marginalised one—, we should understand Lina as writer in the same way that Karen Winstead approaches the authors of virgin-martyr legends, "not only as producers of new narratives but as readers of a larger tradition, engaged in a contest over meaning both with that tradition and with their own readers" (Winstead, p. 4). Lina's rewriting of the story of St Catherine has a dual thrust: firstly, she activates the subversive potential already implicit in virgin-martyr stories; secondly, she re-writes the story by refusing to offer herself as spectacle.

Critical responses to ***Dulce dueño*** take for granted the notion that Lina's story in some way reproduces that of St Catherine. Many readings of the novel trace the parallels of both narrative and character between the two women, including their wealth, pride, love of Beauty, rejection of a series of suitors, and final renunciation of the world for the sake of Christ. The importance of these parallels, however, is not merely that Pardo Bazán is proposing in Lina, to quote Marina Mayoral (p. 32), "una versión actualizada de la santa de Alejandría", but rather that she presents Lina as self-consciously identifying with St Catherine as a strategy for self-definition.

Reading St Catherine subversively enables Lina to embrace rebellious ways of being and behaving. She applies the potential message of the virgin martyr which Jocelyn Wogan-Browne expresses as: "defy authority if it elides you, do not be accommodating and other-determined, do not be socialised only as object of desire and never subject: you do not have to marry"

(Wogan-Browne [1991], p. 323). Her identification with the saint cultivates her feelings of distinction, in the sense of both difference from, and superiority over, those around her. Even as she strives for saintly humility, she appeals to the example of St Catherine to legitimate her own status: "¿He de tenerme por cualquiera? ¿Ignoro lo que soy? [. . .] De seguro que la Alejandrina elegante, mi patrona, no se creía igual a Gnetes. Comprendía de sobra la excelsitud de su propio ánimo" (***Dd,*** p. 282).

Identification with St Catherine legitimates Lina's rejection of marriage and her mockery of men. Lina's humorous reference to her first suitor as a "proco" (***Dd,*** p. 156), the unusual Latinate word used in Carranza's text for St Catherine's rejected admirers, demonstrates her awareness of the model of this Saint's approach to courtship. Jocelyn Wogan-Browne argues that attention to the point of view of a female readership may give us a greater awareness of the comic in hagiography, in particular the deflation of male pretensions (Wogan-Browne [1991], p. 327). Carranza's tale contains little comedy, the emperor being a grotesque rather than strictly comic figure, whereas Lina's acute perception of the foolishness of the men offered to her reinserts this aspect of hagiography into her re-writing of the story. Her highly comic presentation of her first suitor, Hilario Aparicio, in particular, mercilessly mocks supposedly advanced liberal schools of thought which nonetheless assign women a merely domestic and supportive role.

Lina also finds in the virgin-martyr tradition a model of femininity which abolishes sexuality. As Susan Kirkpatrick notes, Lina's rejection of sexuality is related to her understanding of it as "a threat to women's autonomy" (Kirkpatrick, p. 129). Yet underlying Lina's attitude is a more extreme apprehension of sexuality as death and corruption: when she visits a doctor to discover its secrets, she compares him with a gravedigger, and her response to the lurid engravings of his medical textbooks is "¡Qué flora de putrefacción!" (***Dd,*** p. 209). Kirkpatrick rightly links this episode with the fin-desiècle discourses of naturalism which slid "from scientific neutrality into lurid figures of decadence and abnormality" (Kirkpatrick, p. 129); and yet the references to corruption also belong to the medieval discourse of virginity, according to which sexual activity "brings with it the mortal contamination of the fall, the loss of the 'perfect beauty of the white maiden'", while virginity is construed as timeless youth (Wogan-Browne [2001], p. 19).

Lina's association of sexuality with putrid vegetation recalls her disgust at the smell of the flowers placed on the body of "tía Catalina", which she describes as "las flores, envenenadas, en descomposición desde el punto mismo en que las depositamos sobre un cadáver" (***Dd,*** pp. 115-16). Her rejection of sexuality may well be re-

lated to her disdain for this woman, whom she had always believed to be her aunt, but after whose death she deduces to have been her mother. Lina's flight from sexuality can be read as a rejection of what she sees as the abject circumstances of her origin, an extra-marital affair between her mother and the steward Farnesio which, as Lina believes, was concealed by sacrificing her to a life of obscure poverty, ended only by the deaths both of her mother/aunt Catalina and of Catalina's legitimate son. Her disgust at what she sees as a sordid and heartless episode is expressed again in terms of putrefaction:

> Me acuerdo de mi madre, negándome no ya su compañía, sino una caricia, un abrazo; empujándome a un claustro por evitarse rubores en la arrugada frente . . . ¡Miseria todo! [. . .] [M]e asfixio con los vapores de la tierra removida, del craso terruño del cementerio, en que se pudre lo pasado.
>
> (***Dd,*** p. 149)

Her response is to look within herself for purity, in language which again recalls medieval treatises on virginity: "Una necesidad de ilusión, de idealismo inmenso, surge en mí. ¡Azucenas, azucenas! [. . .] ¿Dónde habrá azucenas . . . ? [. . .] En nosotros mismos está, clausurado y recóndito, el jardín virginal" (ibid.). In her re-enactment of the story of the virgin martyr, Lina is therefore seeking a form of femininity which for her will not be abject and corrupted, but high and pure.

Perhaps surprisingly, Lina in this quest does not initially exclude elements traditionally seen as sensuous: perfume, jewels, fine clothes. Her identification with St Catherine legitimates this, since, as Carranza points out, the saint is traditionally portrayed as elegantly dressed (***Dd,*** pp. 52-3). The spectacle of the displayed female body is not excluded from Lina's story; rather, it is transplanted and re-interpreted. Whilst the saint was publicly exposed before the pagans (and, implicitly, the readers), in Lina's story the spectacle of displayed femininity is placed in the intimacy of Lina's boudoir, as she gazes at herself in the mirror. Lina is both object and subject of the gaze in these scenes, as both Susan Kirkpatrick and Maryellen Bieder have pointed out (Kirkpatrick, p. 127; Bieder, p. 12). Lina re-interprets the female body: whilst Carranza's lascivious emperor saw in Catherine "las apretadas nieves de [su] busto" (***Dd,*** p. 91), Lina sees in the mirror a curiously aggressive female form, with obvious phallic overtones: "mi busto brotando del escote como un blanco puñal de su vaina de oro cincelado" (***Dd,*** p. 131). This is a self-sufficient female body, maintaining its virginal integrity and repelling any violation by an other, whether physical or merely visual.

Lina's fetishistic emphasis on her beautifully clothed and jewelled body nonetheless risks entrapment in the same structures of representation that rule the virgin-martyr legend. Lina's most extravagant displays of herself take place without an audience at the level of the fiction; and yet her authoring of the text implies that she is laying out for the reader a dazzling image of female perfection, connoting Mulvey's "*to-be-looked-at-ness*" (Mulvey, p. 19). As the novel progresses, Lina's life becomes increasingly a matter of self-presentation, as not only her clothes but also her furniture and even servants are carefully chosen to display her immaculate taste and distinctive identity.

The difficulty of escaping from these structures of representation is perhaps why Pardo Bazán radically disrupts the virgin-martyr plot, in particular its representation of death, rather than attempting to re-interpret that death, as in the medieval St Margaret texts. Having accepted a proposal of marriage, initially presented to her as a sexless union for the pursuit of power, Lina, like the virgin martyr, begins to court death, possibly in an attempt to avoid the consummation of the marriage with a suitor who has, as she sees it, betrayed her by falling in love with her. Yet it is not her own death but that of her fiancé which results from the dramatic scenario that she scripts by seeking out ever more dangerous adventures. The Swiss lake where he drowns rises "como el hervor de la leche que se desborda" (*Dd,* p. 257), almost as if it is St Catherine's milk-blood that kills him. In a reversal of the virgin-martyr plot, it is thus his death, and not hers, which saves the virgin from the sexual passion with which he threatened, in her terms, to besmirch her.

As the novel draws to a close, Pardo Bazán deliberately denies us the spectacle of the young woman's death which is the climax of the virgin-martyr legend. Refusing eventually to be a signifying object, refusing even to propose her death as meaningful, Lina writes herself into a kind of invisible social death, renouncing her wealth and accepting her incarceration in a lunatic asylum. She effectively withdraws herself from representation, turning herself into an elusive figure, her thoughts constantly present but difficult to interpret, an indeterminate figure of madness and/or mysticism, love and/or egotism. As the novel ends, we are not offered any sense of narrative closure (neither death nor marriage). In contrast with the traditional virgin martyr, whose reified body offers a reassuring aesthetic stillness, Lina preserves what Susan Kirkpatrick calls "the impossible position of the feminine subject" (Kirkpatrick, p. 127) only by disappearing.

In the first part of *Dulce dueño,* Pardo Bazán presents to us the dynamic of the traditional virgin-martyr legend, in its sadistic voyeurism and fetishising fixation of the female body as object, tending inevitably towards death. As her protagonist Lina rewrites this story, she seeks a position for a female subject. Yet this position remains one of death: although the spectacle of death is refused, Lina ultimately writes herself away from representation and into the symbolic death of madness/mysticism which becomes her refuge from objectification.

Notes

1. See e.g. Wogan-Browne (1994) and Lewis.

2. The edition used is E. Pardo Bazán, *Dulce dueño,* ed. M. Mayoral ([1911] Madrid, 1989), references to which will be given in the text as *Dd.*

3. For instance, Susan Kirkpatrick (p. 128) writes that "Lina's story follows *a la moderna* the script set forth by the St. Catherine legend."

4. See Winstead, p. 12.

5. For more traditional versions of St Catherine's passion published around the same time as *Dulce dueño,* see Moreno Durán and Sancho.

6. This is consistent with Carranza's attitude later in the novel, when he confesses "siempre he desconfiado de las hembras . . . Tú me enseñas que el abismo del mal sólo puede llenarlo la malignidad femenil" (*Dd,* p. 266).

7. Cf. Mulvey's discussion of punishment or fetishisation as two possible responses to the feminine in cinema (Mulvey, p. 21).

References

Bieder, M., "Contesting the Body: Gender, Language, and Sexuality. The Modern Woman at the Turn of the Century", in: *Women's Narrative and Film in Twentieth-Century Spain: A World of Difference(s),* ed. O. Ferran & K. M. Glenn, Hispanic Issues 27 (New York & London, 2002), pp. 3-18.

Bloch, R. H., "Chaucer's Maiden Head: 'The Physician's Tale' and the Poetics of Virginity", *Representations* 28 (1989), 113-34.

Bronfen, E., *Over Her Dead Body: Death, Femininity, and the Aesthetic* (Manchester, 1992).

Gaunt, S., *Gender and Genre in Medieval French Literature* (Cambridge, 1995).

Gravdal, K., *Ravishing Maidens: Writing Rape in Medieval French Literature and Law* (Philadelphia, PA, 1991).

Kirkpatrick, S., "Gender and Modernist Discourse: Emilia Pardo Bazán's *Dulce dueño*", in: *Modernism and its Margins: Reinscribing Cultural Modernity from Spain and Latin America,* ed. A. L. Geist & J. B. Monleón, Garland Reference Library of the Humanities 2133/Hispanic Issues 19 (New York & London, 1999), pp. 117-39.

Lewis, K. J., "'Lete Me Suffre': Reading the Torture of St Margaret of Antioch in Late Medieval England", in: *Medieval Women: Text and Contexts in Late Medieval Britain. Essays for Felicity Riddy,* ed. J. Wogan-Browne, R. Voaden et al., Medieval Women: Texts and Contexts 3 (Turnhout, Belgium, 2000), pp. 69-82.

Mayoral, M., Introduction to *Dulce dueño* (Madrid, 1989), pp. 7-41.

Medina, R., "Dulce esclava, dulce histérica: La representación de la mujer en *Dulce dueño* de Emilia Pardo Bazán", *Revista Hispánica Moderna* 51 (1998), 291-303.

Mills, R., "Visions of Excess: Pain, Pleasure and the Penal Imaginary in Late-Medieval Art and Culture" (Ph.D. thesis, University of Cambridge, 2001).

Moreno Durán, T., *Año cristiano y vida de los santos,* 12 vols (Barcelona & Buenos Aires, 1911).

Mulvey, L., "Visual Pleasure and Narrative Cinema", *Screen* 16 (1975), 6-18, reprinted in: *Visual and Other Pleasures* (Basingstoke, 1989), pp. 14-26.

Pardo Bazán, E., *Dulce dueño,* ed. M. Mayoral ([1911] Madrid, 1989).

Sancho, A., *Compendio de la vida de Santa Catalina Virgen y Mártir* ([Valencia: Librería de Pascual M. Villalba, 1914] Facsimile edn, Aras, *c.* 2000).

Winstead, K. A., *Virgin Martyrs: Legends of Sainthood in Late Medieval England* (Ithaca, NY & London, 1997).

Wogan-Browne, J., "Saints' Lives and the Female Reader", *Forum for Modern Language Studies* 27 (1991), 314-32.

———, "The Virgin's Tale", in: *Feminist Readings in Middle English Literature: The Wife of Bath and All her Sect,* ed. R. Evans & L. Johnson (London & New York, 1994), pp. 165-94.

———, *Saints' Lives and Women's Literary Culture c. 1150-1300: Virginity and Its Authorizations* (Oxford, 2001).

FURTHER READING

Criticism

Amago, Samuel. "The Form and Function of Homosocial Desire in *La madre naturaleza.*" *Romance Quarterly* 48, no. 1 (winter 2001): 54-63.

Illustrates the significance of the homoerotic relationship between Juncal and Gabriel, two key characters in Pardo Bazán's *La madre naturaleza.*

Bauer, Beth Wietelmann. "Narrative Cross-Dressing: Emilia Pardo Bazán in *Memorias de un solterón.*" *Hispania* 77, no. 1 (March 1994): 23-30.

Argues that Pardo Bazán speaks through her male narrator in the novel *Memorias de un solterón* in order to question masculine authority.

———. "Catholicism, Feminism, and Anti-Semitism in Pardo Bazán's *Una cristiana-La prueba.*" *Letras Peninsulares* 8, no. 2 (fall 1995): 295-309.

Identifies themes of feminism, Catholic dogma, and hereditary determinism in Pardo Bazán's novel *Una cristiana* and its sequel, *La prueba.*

Berry-Bravo, Judy. "Pardo Bazán's Use of Control as Narrative Device." *Letras Femeninas* 18, nos. 1-2 (spring-fall 1992): 91-6.

Asserts that the theme of control is central to Pardo Bazán's novels *The House of Ulloa* and *La madre naturaleza.*

Bieder, Maryellen. "Emilia Pardo Bazán and Literary Women: Women Reading Women's Writing in Late 19th-Century Spain." *Revista Hispánica Moderna* 46, no. 1 (June 1993): 19-33.

Investigates Pardo Bazán's opinion of and relationship to other Spanish female writers during the first decades of her career.

Bradford, Carole A. "Alienation and the Dual Personality in the Last Three Novels of Emilia Pardo Bazán." *Revista de Estudios Hispánicos* 12, no. 3 (October 1978): 399-417.

Observes the influence of Russian literature on the central themes of Pardo Bazán's last three novels: *La quimera, La sirena negra,* and *Dulce dueño.*

Brown, Donald Fowler. *The Catholic Naturalism of Pardo Bazán,* Chapel Hill: The University of North Carolina Press, 1957, 171 p.

Book-length study defining Emilia Pardo Bazán's relationship to Emile Zola, his theories, and his influence on her work.

DeCoster, Cyrus C. "Pardo Bazán's *Insolación*: A Naturalistic Novel?" *Romance Notes* 13, no. 1 (autumn 1971): 87-91.

Contends that many of the characteristics associated with Naturalism are absent from Pardo Bazán's *Insolación.*

DuPont, Denise. "Decadence, Women Writers, and Literary History in Emilia Pardo Bazán's Late Criticism." *MLN* 117, no. 2 (March 2002): 343-64.

Outlines Pardo Bazán's attitudes toward literary decadence, gender, and romanticism in her critical writings and posthumously published university lectures.

Feeny, Thomas. "The Child as Redeemer and Victim in Pardo Bazán's Short Fiction." *Revista de Estudios Hispánicos* 11, no. 3 (October 1977): 425-32.

Claims that Pardo Bazán represents children as either redeemers or victims in many of her works, including her novel *La sirena negra* and several of the stories in the collection *Cuentos nuevos.*

Gasster, Susan. "Paths Not Taken: The Narrative Finesses of Pardo Bazán." *Letras Femeninas* 17, no. 1-2 (spring-fall 1991): 29-36.

Maintains that the strength of Pardo Bazán's work resides in her use of Naturalism and her creation of morally ambiguous characters.

Giles, Mary E. "Pardo Bazán's Two Styles." *Hispania* 48, no. 3 (September 1965): 456-62.

Provides a detailed analysis of Pardo Bazán's use of language in her novels.

Gilfoil, Anne W. "Progress and Nostalgia in Emilia Pardo Bazán's *El cisne de Vilamorta.*" *Revista de Literatura Española* 19 (April 2001): 21-34.

Explores the cultural, economic, and political environment of nineteenth-century Spain as it is represented by Pardo Bazán in her novel *Swan of Vilamorta.*

Goldin, David. "The Metaphor of Original Sin: A Key to Pardo Bazán's Catholic Naturalism." *Philological Quarterly* 64, no. 1 (winter 1985): 37-49.

Argues that Pardo Bazán employs original sin as a metaphor for deterministic sexual instinct in her novels *La madre naturaleza, Doña Milagros,* and *Memorias de un solterón.*

González-Arias, Francisca. *Portrait of a Woman as Artist: Emilia Pardo Bazán and the Modern Novel in France and Spain,* New York: Garland Publishing, Inc., 1992, 230 p.

Book length study that discusses the relationship between Pardo Bazán and other Naturalist writers, such as Emile Zola, and documents her development as a novelist.

Hemingway, Maurice. "Grace, Nature, Naturalism, and Pardo Bazán." *Forum for Modern Language Studies* 17, no. 2 (April 1981): 341-49.

Analyses the composition of Pardo Bazán's *The House of Ulloa,* noting in particular the point of view of the characters and the structure of the novel.

Henn, David. "Continuity, Change, and the Decadent Phenomenon in Pardo Bazán's Late Fiction." *Neophilologus* 78, no. 3 (July 1994): 395-406.

Traces the development of Pardo Bazán's fiction from the beginning of her career in the 1890s to her last novel in 1911, noting in particular her attention to the phenomenon of decadence.

Hoffman, Joan M. "Torn Lace and Other Transformations: Rewriting the Bride's Script in Selected Stories by Emilia Pardo Bazán." *Hispania* 82, no. 2 (May 1999): 238-45.

Maintains that Pardo Bazán subverts the traditional feminine ideal by depicting independent, autonomous brides in many of her short stories.

Ordóñez, Elizabeth J. "Spirit and Body: Refiguring the Sacred in *Un viaje de novios.*" *Letras Peninsulares* 12, no. 1 (spring 1999): 23-35.

Applies Jacques Lacan's theory of metaphor to an interpretation of Pardo Bazán's *Un viaje de novios.*

Pattison, Walter T. *Emilia Pardo Bazán,* New York: Twayne Publishers, Inc., 1971, 134 p.

Biocritical study of Pardo Bazán's life and works.

Pérez, Janet. "Winners, Losers, and Casualties in Pardo Bazán's Battle of the Sexes." *Letras Peninsulares* 5, no. 3 (winter 1992-1993): 347-56.

Assesses Pardo Bazán's treatment of male-female relationships in her short stories.

Quirk, Ronald J. "Physiognomy in Pardo Bazán's Portrayal of the Human Body." *Anales Galdosianos* 37 (2002): 125-33.

Argues that Pardo Bazán's description of eyes and other facial features in her novels coincides with physiognomic theory.

Rodríguez, Alfred and Joan Lefkoff. "An Aesthetic Use of the Grotesque in Emilia Pardo Bazán's *Los Pazos de Ulloa.*" *Revista de Estudios Hispánicos* 15, no. 2 (May 1981): 275-81.

Examines instances of the grotesque in chapter fifteen of Pardo Bazán's novel *The House of Ulloa.*

Santana, Mario. "An Essay in Feminist Rhetoric: Emilia Pardo Bazán's 'El indulto'." *MLN* 116, no. 2 (March 2001): 250-65.

Offers a feminist reading of Pardo Bazán's story "El indulto," examining in particular the role of the narrator as well as the story's "recalcitrant" ending.

Scanlon, Geraldine M. "Class and Gender in Pardo Bazán's *La Tribuna.*" *Bulletin of Hispanic Studies* 67, no. 2 (April 1990): 137-50.

Probes Pardo Bazán's novel *The Tribune of the People* for ambiguities and contradictions, claiming that they reflect a conflict between the author's conservative ideology and her progressive feminist leanings.

Sherzer, William. "Writing as a Woman or Writing as a Man? The Shifting Perspective Toward Women in Three Short Stories by Emilia Pardo Bazán." *Letras Peninsulares* 14, no. 2 (fall 2001): 195-206.

> Questions whether Pardo Bazán's narrative voice in the short stories "The Warning," "The Red Averages," and "The Mayorazga" is traditional or ironic.

Tolliver, Joyce. "Narrative Accountability and Ambivalence: Feminine Desire in *Insolación*." *Revista de Estudios Hispánicos* 23, no. 2 (May 1989): 103-18.

> Posits that the repressed sexual desires of the female protagonist in Pardo Bazán's *Insolación* mirrors the narrator's perspective of women's role in society.

Urey, Diane F. "Incest and Interpretation in *Los pazos de Ulloa* and *La madre naturaleza*." *Anales Galdosianos* 22 (1987): 117-31.

> Compares the theme of incest in two of Pardo Bazán's novels, *The House of Ulloa* and *La madre naturaleza*.

Wood, Jennifer J. "Quest Narrative as Intertext in *Los pazos de Ulloa*." *Hispanic Journal* 9, no. 2 (spring 1988): 63-9.

> Contends that Pardo Bazán's *The House of Ulloa* both follows the structure of the typical "quest romance" and portrays the Gospel story of a Christ-figure who seeks to redeem humanity from the Fall.

Additional coverage of Pardo Bazán's life and career is contained in the following sources published by Thomson Gale: *Encyclopedia of World Literature in the 20th Century*, Ed. 3; *Feminist Writers*; *Literature Resource Center*; *Reference Guide to Short Fiction*, Ed. 2; *Reference Guide to World Literature*, Eds. 2, 3; and *Short Story Criticism*, Vol. 30.

How to Use This Index

The main references

Calvino, Italo
1923-1985 .... CLC 5, 8, 11, 22, 33, 39,
73; SSC 3, 48

list all author entries in the following Thomson Gale Literary Criticism series:

AAL = Asian American Literature
BG = The Beat Generation: A Gale Critical Companion
BLC = Black Literature Criticism
BLCS = Black Literature Criticism Supplement
CLC = Contemporary Literary Criticism
CLR = Children's Literature Review
CMLC = Classical and Medieval Literature Criticism
DC = Drama Criticism
FL = Feminism in Literature: A Gale Critical Companion
GL = Gothic Literature: A Gale Critical Companion
HLC = Hispanic Literature Criticism
HLCS = Hispanic Literature Criticism Supplement
HR = Harlem Renaissance: A Gale Critical Companion
LC = Literature Criticism from 1400 to 1800
NCLC = Nineteenth-Century Literature Criticism
NNAL = Native North American Literature
PC = Poetry Criticism
SSC = Short Story Criticism
TCLC = Twentieth-Century Literary Criticism
WLC = World Literature Criticism, 1500 to the Present
WLCS = World Literature Criticism Supplement

The cross-references

See also CA 85-88, 116; CANR 23, 61;
DAM NOV; DLB 196; EW 13; MTCW 1, 2;
RGSF 2; RGWL 2; SFW 4; SSFS 12

list all author entries in the following Thomson Gale biographical and literary sources:

AAYA = Authors & Artists for Young Adults
AFAW = African American Writers
AFW = African Writers
AITN = Authors in the News
AMW = American Writers
AMWR = American Writers Retrospective Supplement
AMWS = American Writers Supplement
ANW = American Nature Writers
AW = Ancient Writers
BEST = Bestsellers
BPFB = Beacham's Encyclopedia of Popular Fiction: Biography and Resources
RRW = British Writers
BRWS = British Writers Supplement
BW = Black Writers
BYA = Beacham's Guide to Literature for Young Adults
CA = Contemporary Authors
CAAS = Contemporary Authors Autobiography Series
CABS = Contemporary Authors Bibliographical Series
CAD = Contemporary American Dramatists
CANR = Contemporary Authors New Revision Series
CAP = Contemporary Authors Permanent Series
CBD = Contemporary British Dramatists
CCA = Contemporary Canadian Authors
CD = Contemporary Dramatists
CDALB = Concise Dictionary of American Literary Biography

CDALBS = *Concise Dictionary of American Literary Biography Supplement*
CDBLB = *Concise Dictionary of British Literary Biography*
CMW = *St. James Guide to Crime & Mystery Writers*
CN = *Contemporary Novelists*
CP = *Contemporary Poets*
CPW = *Contemporary Popular Writers*
CSW = *Contemporary Southern Writers*
CWD = *Contemporary Women Dramatists*
CWP = *Contemporary Women Poets*
CWRI = *St. James Guide to Children's Writers*
CWW = *Contemporary World Writers*
DA = *DISCovering Authors*
DA3 = *DISCovering Authors 3.0*
DAB = *DISCovering Authors: British Edition*
DAC = *DISCovering Authors: Canadian Edition*
DAM = *DISCovering Authors: Modules*
  DRAM: *Dramatists Module;* **MST:** *Most-studied Authors Module;*
  MULT: *Multicultural Authors Module;* **NOV:** *Novelists Module;*
  POET: *Poets Module;* **POP:** *Popular Fiction and Genre Authors Module*
DFS = *Drama for Students*
DLB = *Dictionary of Literary Biography*
DLBD = *Dictionary of Literary Biography Documentary Series*
DLBY = *Dictionary of Literary Biography Yearbook*
DNFS = *Literature of Developing Nations for Students*
EFS = *Epics for Students*
EXPN = *Exploring Novels*
EXPP = *Exploring Poetry*
EXPS = *Exploring Short Stories*
EW = *European Writers*
FANT = *St. James Guide to Fantasy Writers*
FW = *Feminist Writers*
GFL = *Guide to French Literature,* Beginnings to 1789, 1798 to the Present
GLL = *Gay and Lesbian Literature*
HGG = *St. James Guide to Horror, Ghost & Gothic Writers*
HW = *Hispanic Writers*
IDFW = *International Dictionary of Films and Filmmakers: Writers and Production Artists*
IDTP = *International Dictionary of Theatre: Playwrights*
LAIT = *Literature and Its Times*
LAW = *Latin American Writers*
JRDA = *Junior DISCovering Authors*
MAICYA = *Major Authors and Illustrators for Children and Young Adults*
MAICYAS = *Major Authors and Illustrators for Children and Young Adults Supplement*
MAWW = *Modern American Women Writers*
MJW = *Modern Japanese Writers*
MTCW = *Major 20th-Century Writers*
NCFS = *Nonfiction Classics for Students*
NFS = *Novels for Students*
PAB = *Poets: American and British*
PFS = *Poetry for Students*
RGAL = *Reference Guide to American Literature*
RGEL = *Reference Guide to English Literature*
RGSF = *Reference Guide to Short Fiction*
RGWL = *Reference Guide to World Literature*
RHW = *Twentieth-Century Romance and Historical Writers*
SAAS = *Something about the Author Autobiography Series*
SATA = *Something about the Author*
SFW = *St. James Guide to Science Fiction Writers*
SSFS = *Short Stories for Students*
TCWW = *Twentieth-Century Western Writers*
WLIT = *World Literature and Its Times*
WP = *World Poets*
YABC = *Yesterday's Authors of Books for Children*
YAW = *St. James Guide to Young Adult Writers*

Literary Criticism Series
Cumulative Author Index

Anand, Mulk Raj 1905-2004 ...... **CLC 23, 93**
See also CA 65-68; CAAS 231; CANR 32, 64; CN 1, 2, 3, 4, 5, 6, 7; DAM NOV; DLB 323; EWL 3; MTCW 1, 2; MTFW 2005; RGSF 2

Anatol
See Schnitzler, Arthur

Anaximander c. 611B.C.-c. 546B.C. .... **CMLC 22**

Anaya, Rudolfo A. 1937- .... **CLC 23, 148; HLC 1**
See also AAYA 20; BYA 13; CA 45-48; 4; CANR 1, 32, 51, 124; CN 4, 5, 6, 7; DAM MULT, NOV; DLB 82, 206, 278; HW 1; LAIT 4; LLW; MAL 5; MTCW 1, 2; MTFW 2005; NFS 12; RGAL 4; RGSF 2; TCWW 2; WLIT 1

Andersen, Hans Christian 1805-1875 .... **NCLC 7, 79; SSC 6, 56; WLC 1**
See also AAYA 57; CLR 6, 113; DA; DA3; DAB; DAC; DAM MST, POP; EW 6; MAICYA 1, 2; RGSF 2; RGWL 2, 3; SATA 100; TWA; WCH; YABC 1

Anderson, C. Farley
See Mencken, H(enry) L(ouis); Nathan, George Jean

Anderson, Jessica (Margaret) Queale 1916- .... **CLC 37**
See also CA 9-12R; CANR 4, 62; CN 4, 5, 6, 7; DLB 325

Anderson, Jon (Victor) 1940- .... **CLC 9**
See also CA 25-28R; CANR 20; CP 1, 3, 4, 5; DAM POET

Anderson, Lindsay (Gordon) 1923-1994 .... **CLC 20**
See also CA 128; CAAE 125; CAAS 146; CANR 77

Anderson, Maxwell 1888-1959 .... **TCLC 2, 144**
See also CA 152; CAAE 105; DAM DRAM; DFS 16, 20; DLB 7, 228; MAL 5; MTCW 2; MTFW 2005; RGAL 4

Anderson, Poul 1926-2001 .... **CLC 15**
See also AAYA 5, 34; BPFB 1; BYA 6, 8, 9; CA 181; 1-4R, 181; 2; CAAS 199; CANR 2, 15, 34, 64, 110; CLR 58; DLB 8; FANT; INT CANR-15; MTCW 1, 2; MTFW 2005; SATA 90; SATA-Brief 39; SATA-Essay 106; SCFW 1, 2; SFW 4; SUFW 1, 2

Anderson, Robert (Woodruff) 1917- .... **CLC 23**
See also AITN 1; CA 21-24R; CANR 32; CD 6; DAM DRAM; DLB 7; LAIT 5

Anderson, Roberta Joan
See Mitchell, Joni

Anderson, Sherwood 1876-1941 ... **SSC 1, 46, 91; TCLC 1, 10, 24, 123; WLC 1**
See also AAYA 30; AMW; AMWC 2; BPFB 1; CA 121; CAAE 104; CANR 61; CDALB 1917-1929; DA; DA3; DAB; DAC; DAM MST, NOV; DLB 4, 9, 86; DLBD 1; EWL 3; EXPS; GLL 2; MAL 5; MTCW 1, 2; MTFW 2005; NFS 4; RGAL 4; RGSF 2; SSFS 4, 10, 11; TUS

Anderson, Wes 1969- .... **CLC 227**
See also CA 214

Andier, Pierre
See Desnos, Robert

Andouard
See Giraudoux, Jean(-Hippolyte)

Andrade, Carlos Drummond de ..... **CLC 18**
See Drummond de Andrade, Carlos
See also EWL 3; RGWL 2, 3

Andrade, Mario de .... **TCLC 43**
See de Andrade, Mario
See also DLB 307; EWL 3; LAW; RGWL 2, 3; WLIT 1

Andreae, Johann V(alentin) 1586-1654 .... **LC 32**
See also DLB 164

Andreas Capellanus fl. c. 1185- .... **CMLC 45**
See also DLB 208

Andreas-Salome, Lou 1861-1937 ... **TCLC 56**
See also CA 178; DLB 66

Andreev, Leonid
See Andreyev, Leonid (Nikolaevich)
See also DLB 295; EWL 3

Andress, Lesley
See Sanders, Lawrence

Andrewes, Lancelot 1555-1626 .... **LC 5**
See also DLB 151, 172

Andrews, Cicily Fairfield
See West, Rebecca

Andrews, Elton V.
See Pohl, Frederik

Andrews, Peter
See Soderbergh, Steven

Andreyev, Leonid (Nikolaevich) 1871-1919 .... **TCLC 3**
See Andreev, Leonid
See also CA 185; CAAE 104

Andric, Ivo 1892-1975 .... **CLC 8; SSC 36; TCLC 135**
See also CA 81-84; CAAS 57-60; CANR 43, 60; CDWLB 4; DLB 147, 329; EW 11; EWL 3; MTCW 1; RGSF 2; RGWL 2, 3

Androvar
See Prado (Calvo), Pedro

Angela of Foligno 1248(?)-1309 .... **CMLC 76**

Angelique, Pierre
See Bataille, Georges

Angell, Roger 1920- .... **CLC 26**
See also CA 57-60; CANR 13, 44, 70, 144; DLB 171, 185

Angelou, Maya 1928- ... **BLC 1; CLC 12, 35, 64, 77, 155; PC 32; WLCS**
See also AAYA 7, 20; AMWS 4; BPFB 1; BW 2, 3; BYA 2; CA 65-68; CANR 19, 42, 65, 111, 133; CDALBS; CLR 53; CP 4, 5, 6, 7; CPW; CSW; CWP; DA; DA3; DAB; DAC; DAM MST, MULT, POET, POP; DLB 38; EWL 3; EXPN; EXPP; FL 1:5; LAIT 4; MAICYA 2; MAICYAS 1; MAL 5; MBL; MTCW 1, 2; MTFW 2005; NCFS 2; NFS 2; PFS 2, 3; RGAL 4; SATA 49, 136; TCLE 1:1; WYA; YAW

Angouleme, Marguerite d'
See de Navarre, Marguerite

Anna Comnena 1083-1153 .... **CMLC 25**

Annensky, Innokentii Fedorovich
See Annensky, Innokenty (Fyodorovich)
See also DLB 295

Annensky, Innokenty (Fyodorovich) 1856-1909 .... **TCLC 14**
See also CA 155; CAAE 110; EWL 3

Annunzio, Gabriele d'
See D'Annunzio, Gabriele

Anodos
See Coleridge, Mary E(lizabeth)

Anon, Charles Robert
See Pessoa, Fernando (Antonio Nogueira)

Anouilh, Jean 1910-1987 ..... **CLC 1, 3, 8, 13, 40, 50; DC 8, 21**
See also AAYA 67; CA 17-20R; CAAS 123; CANR 32; DAM DRAM; DFS 9, 10, 19; DLB 321; EW 13; EWL 3; GFL 1789 to the Present; MTCW 1, 2; MTFW 2005; RGWL 2, 3; TWA

Anselm of Canterbury 1033(?)-1109 .... **CMLC 67**
See also DLB 115

Anthony, Florence
See Ai

Anthony, John
See Ciardi, John (Anthony)

Anthony, Peter
See Shaffer, Anthony; Shaffer, Peter

Anthony, Piers 1934- .... **CLC 35**
See also AAYA 11, 48; BYA 7; CA 200; 200; CANR 28, 56, 73, 102, 133; CLR 118; CPW; DAM POP; DLB 8; FANT; MAICYA 2; MAICYAS 1; MTCW 1, 2; MTFW 2005; SAAS 22; SATA 84, 129; SATA-Essay 129; SFW 4; SUFW 1, 2; YAW

Anthony, Susan B(rownell) 1820-1906 .... **TCLC 84**
See also CA 211; FW

Antiphon c. 480B.C.-c. 411B.C. .... **CMLC 55**

Antoine, Marc
See Proust, (Valentin-Louis-George-Eugene) Marcel

Antoninus, Brother
See Everson, William (Oliver)
See also CP 1

Antonioni, Michelangelo 1912- .... **CLC 20, 144**
See also CA 73-76; CANR 45, 77

Antschel, Paul 1920-1970
See Celan, Paul
See also CA 85-88; CANR 33, 61; MTCW 1; PFS 21

Anwar, Chairil 1922-1949 .... **TCLC 22**
See Chairil Anwar
See also CA 219; CAAE 121; RGWL 3

Anzaldua, Gloria (Evanjelina) 1942-2004 .... **CLC 200; HLCS 1**
See also CA 175; CAAS 227; CSW; CWP; DLB 122; FW; LLW; RGAL 4; SATA-Obit 154

Apess, William 1798-1839(?) .... **NCLC 73; NNAL**
See also DAM MULT; DLB 175, 243

Apollinaire, Guillaume 1880-1918 .... **PC 7; TCLC 3, 8, 51**
See Kostrowitzki, Wilhelm Apollinaris de
See also CA 152; DAM POET; DLB 258, 321; EW 9; EWL 3; GFL 1789 to the Present; MTCW 2; PFS 24; RGWL 2, 3; TWA; WP

Apollonius of Rhodes
See Apollonius Rhodius
See also AW 1; RGWL 2, 3

Apollonius Rhodius c. 300B.C.-c. 220B.C. .... **CMLC 28**
See Apollonius of Rhodes
See also DLB 176

Appelfeld, Aharon 1932- ... **CLC 23, 47; SSC 42**
See also CA 133; CAAE 112; CANR 86, 160; CWW 2; DLB 299; EWL 3; RGHL; RGSF 2; WLIT 6

Appelfeld, Aron
See Appelfeld, Aharon

Apple, Max (Isaac) 1941- .... **CLC 9, 33; SSC 50**
See also CA 81-84; CANR 19, 54; DLB 130

Appleman, Philip (Dean) 1926- .... **CLC 51**
See also CA 13-16R; 18; CANR 6, 29, 56

Appleton, Lawrence
See Lovecraft, H. P.

Apteryx
See Eliot, T(homas) S(tearns)

Apuleius, (Lucius Madaurensis) c. 125-c. 164 .... **CMLC 1, 84**
See also AW 2; CDWLB 1; DLB 211; RGWL 2, 3; SUFW; WLIT 8

Aquin, Hubert 1929-1977 .... **CLC 15**
See also CA 105; DLB 53; EWL 3

Aquinas, Thomas 1224(?)-1274 ..... **CMLC 33**
See also DLB 115; EW 1; TWA

Aragon, Louis 1897-1982 .... **CLC 3, 22; TCLC 123**
See also CA 69-72; CAAS 108; CANR 28, 71; DAM NOV, POET; DLB 72, 258; EW 11; EWL 3; GFL 1789 to the Present; GLL 2; LMFS 2; MTCW 1, 2; RGWL 2, 3

Arany, Janos 1817-1882 .... **NCLC 34**

Aranyos, Kakay 1847-1910
See Mikszath, Kalman

Aratus of Soli c. 315B.C.-c. 240B.C. .... **CMLC 64**
See also DLB 176

Arbuthnot, John 1667-1735 .... **LC 1**
See also DLB 101

Archer, Herbert Winslow
See Mencken, H(enry) L(ouis)

Archer, Jeffrey 1940- .... **CLC 28**
See also AAYA 16; BEST 89:3; BPFB 1; CA 77-80; CANR 22, 52, 95, 136; CPW; DA3; DAM POP; INT CANR-22; MTFW 2005

Archer, Jeffrey Howard
See Archer, Jeffrey

Archer, Jules 1915- .... **CLC 12**
See also CA 9-12R; CANR 6, 69; SAAS 5; SATA 4, 85

Archer, Lee
See Ellison, Harlan

Archilochus c. 7th cent. B.C.- .... **CMLC 44**
See also DLB 176

Arden, John 1930- .... **CLC 6, 13, 15**
See also BRWS 2; CA 13-16R; 4; CANR 31, 65, 67, 124; CBD; CD 5, 6; DAM DRAM; DFS 9; DLB 13, 245; EWL 3; MTCW 1

Arenas, Reinaldo 1943-1990 .. **CLC 41; HLC 1**
See also CA 128; CAAE 124; CAAS 133; CANR 73, 106; DAM MULT; DLB 145; EWL 3; GLL 2; HW 1; LAW; LAWS 1; MTCW 2; MTFW 2005; RGSF 2; RGWL 3; WLIT 1

Arendt, Hannah 1906-1975 .... **CLC 66, 98**
See also CA 17-20R; CAAS 61-64; CANR 26, 60; DLB 242; MTCW 1, 2

Aretino, Pietro 1492-1556 .... **LC 12**
See also RGWL 2, 3

Arghezi, Tudor .... **CLC 80**
See Theodorescu, Ion N.
See also CA 167; CDWLB 4; DLB 220; EWL 3

Arguedas, Jose Maria 1911-1969 .... **CLC 10, 18; HLCS 1; TCLC 147**
See also CA 89-92; CANR 73; DLB 113; EWL 3; HW 1; LAW; RGWL 2, 3; WLIT 1

Argueta, Manlio 1936- .... **CLC 31**
See also CA 131; CANR 73; CWW 2; DLB 145; EWL 3; HW 1; RGWL 3

Arias, Ron 1941- .... **HLC 1**
See also CA 131; CANR 81, 136; DAM MULT; DLB 82; HW 1, 2; MTCW 2; MTFW 2005

Ariosto, Lodovico
See Ariosto, Ludovico
See also WLIT 7

Ariosto, Ludovico 1474-1533 ... **LC 6, 87; PC 42**
See Ariosto, Lodovico
See also EW 2; RGWL 2, 3

Aristides
See Epstein, Joseph

Aristophanes 450B.C.-385B.C. .... **CMLC 4, 51; DC 2; WLCS**
See also AW 1; CDWLB 1; DA; DA3; DAB; DAC; DAM DRAM, MST; DFS 10; DLB 176; LMFS 1; RGWL 2, 3; TWA; WLIT 8

Aristotle 384B.C.-322B.C. .... **CMLC 31; WLCS**
See also AW 1; CDWLB 1; DA; DA3; DAB; DAC; DAM MST; DLB 176; RGWL 2, 3; TWA; WLIT 8

Arlt, Roberto (Godofredo Christophersen) 1900-1942 .... **HLC 1; TCLC 29**
See also CA 131; CAAE 123; CANR 67; DAM MULT; DLB 305; EWL 3; HW 1, 2; IDTP; LAW

Armah, Ayi Kwei 1939- . **BLC 1; CLC 5, 33, 136**
See also AFW; BRWS 10; BW 1; CA 61-64; CANR 21, 64; CDWLB 3; CN 1, 2, 3, 4, 5, 6, 7; DAM MULT, POET; DLB 117; EWL 3; MTCW 1; WLIT 2

Armatrading, Joan 1950- .... **CLC 17**
See also CA 186; CAAE 114

Armin, Robert 1568(?)-1615(?) .... **LC 120**

Armitage, Frank
See Carpenter, John (Howard)

Armstrong, Jeannette (C.) 1948- .... **NNAL**
See also CA 149; CCA 1; CN 6, 7; DAC; SATA 102

Arnette, Robert
See Silverberg, Robert

Arnim, Achim von (Ludwig Joachim von Arnim) 1781-1831 .. **NCLC 5, 159; SSC 29**
See also DLB 90

Arnim, Bettina von 1785-1859 ...... **NCLC 38, 123**
See also DLB 90; RGWL 2, 3

Arnold, Matthew 1822-1888 ..... **NCLC 6, 29, 89, 126; PC 5; WLC 1**
See also BRW 5; CDBLB 1832-1890; DA; DAB; DAC; DAM MST, POET; DLB 32, 57; EXPP; PAB; PFS 2; TEA; WP

Arnold, Thomas 1795-1842 .... **NCLC 18**
See also DLB 55

Arnow, Harriette (Louisa) Simpson 1908-1986 .... **CLC 2, 7, 18**
See also BPFB 1; CA 9-12R; CAAS 118; CANR 14; CN 2, 3, 4; DLB 6; FW; MTCW 1, 2; RHW; SATA 42; SATA-Obit 47

Arouet, Francois-Marie
See Voltaire

Arp, Hans
See Arp, Jean

Arp, Jean 1887-1966 .... **CLC 5; TCLC 115**
See also CA 81-84; CAAS 25-28R; CANR 42, 77; EW 10

Arrabal
See Arrabal, Fernando

Arrabal (Teran), Fernando
See Arrabal, Fernando
See also CWW 2

Arrabal, Fernando 1932- ... **CLC 2, 9, 18, 58**
See Arrabal (Teran), Fernando
See also CA 9-12R; CANR 15; DLB 321; EWL 3; LMFS 2

Arreola, Juan Jose 1918-2001 .... **CLC 147; HLC 1; SSC 38**
See also CA 131; CAAE 113; CAAS 200; CANR 81; CWW 2; DAM MULT; DLB 113; DNFS 2; EWL 3; HW 1, 2; LAW; RGSF 2

Arrian c. 89(?)-c. 155(?) .... **CMLC 43**
See also DLB 176

Arrick, Fran .... **CLC 30**
See Gaberman, Judie Angell
See also BYA 6

Arrley, Richmond
See Delany, Samuel R., Jr.

Artaud, Antonin (Marie Joseph) 1896-1948 .... **DC 14; TCLC 3, 36**
See also CA 149; CAAE 104; DA3; DAM DRAM; DFS 22; DLB 258, 321; EW 11; EWL 3; GFL 1789 to the Present; MTCW 2; MTFW 2005; RGWL 2, 3

Arthur, Ruth M(abel) 1905-1979 ..... **CLC 12**
See also CA 9-12R; CAAS 85-88; CANR 4; CWRI 5; SATA 7, 26

Artsybashev, Mikhail (Petrovich) 1878-1927 .... **TCLC 31**
See also CA 170; DLB 295

Arundel, Honor (Morfydd) 1919-1973 .... **CLC 17**
See also CA 21-22; CAAS 41-44R; CAP 2; CLR 35; CWRI 5; SATA 4; SATA-Obit 24

Arzner, Dorothy 1900-1979 .... **CLC 98**

Asch, Sholem 1880-1957 .... **TCLC 3**
See also CAAE 105; DLB 333; EWL 3; GLL 2; RGHL

Ascham, Roger 1516(?)-1568 .... **LC 101**
See also DLB 236

Ash, Shalom
See Asch, Sholem

Ashbery, John 1927- ... **CLC 2, 3, 4, 6, 9, 13, 15, 25, 41, 77, 125, 221; PC 26**
See Berry, Jonas
See also AMWS 3; CA 5-8R; CANR 9, 37, 66, 102, 132; CP 1, 2, 3, 4, 5, 6, 7; DA3; DAM POET; DLB 5, 165; DLBY 1981; EWL 3; INT CANR-9; MAL 5; MTCW 1, 2; MTFW 2005; PAB; PFS 11; RGAL 4; TCLE 1:1; WP

Ashdown, Clifford
See Freeman, R(ichard) Austin

Ashe, Gordon
See Creasey, John

Ashton-Warner, Sylvia (Constance) 1908-1984 .... **CLC 19**
See also CA 69-72; CAAS 112; CANR 29; CN 1, 2, 3; MTCW 1, 2

Asimov, Isaac 1920-1992 ..... **CLC 1, 3, 9, 19, 26, 76, 92**
See also AAYA 13; BEST 90:2; BPFB 1; BYA 4, 6, 7, 9; CA 1-4R; CAAS 137; CANR 2, 19, 36, 60, 125; CLR 12, 79; CMW 4; CN 1, 2, 3, 4, 5; CPW; DA3; DAM POP; DLB 8; DLBY 1992; INT CANR-19; JRDA; LAIT 5; LMFS 2; MAICYA 1, 2; MAL 5; MTCW 1, 2; MTFW 2005; RGAL 4; SATA 1, 26, 74; SCFW 1, 2; SFW 4; SSFS 17; TUS; YAW

Askew, Anne 1521(?)-1546 .... **LC 81**
See also DLB 136

Assis, Joaquim Maria Machado de
See Machado de Assis, Joaquim Maria

Astell, Mary 1666-1731 .... **LC 68**
See also DLB 252; FW

Astley, Thea (Beatrice May) 1925-2004 .... **CLC 41**
See also CA 65-68; CAAS 229; CANR 11, 43, 78; CN 1, 2, 3, 4, 5, 6, 7; DLB 289; EWL 3

Astley, William 1855-1911
See Warung, Price

Aston, James
See White, T(erence) H(anbury)

Asturias, Miguel Angel 1899-1974 .... **CLC 3, 8, 13; HLC 1; TCLC 184**
See also CA 25-28; CAAS 49-52; CANR 32; CAP 2; CDWLB 3; DA3; DAM MULT, NOV; DLB 113, 290, 329; EWL 3; HW 1; LAW; LMFS 2; MTCW 1, 2; RGWL 2, 3; WLIT 1

Atares, Carlos Saura
See Saura (Atares), Carlos

Athanasius c. 295-c. 373 .... **CMLC 48**

Atheling, William
See Pound, Ezra (Weston Loomis)

Atheling, William, Jr.
See Blish, James (Benjamin)

Atherton, Gertrude (Franklin Horn)
1857-1948 .... **TCLC 2**
See also CA 155; CAAE 104; DLB 9, 78, 186; HGG; RGAL 4; SUFW 1; TCWW 1, 2

Atherton, Lucius
See Masters, Edgar Lee

Atkins, Jack
See Harris, Mark

Atkinson, Kate 1951- .... **CLC 99**
See also CA 166; CANR 101, 153; DLB 267

Attaway, William (Alexander)
1911-1986 .... **BLC 1; CLC 92**
See also BW 2, 3; CA 143; CANR 82; DAM MULT; DLB 76; MAL 5

Atticus
See Fleming, Ian; Wilson, (Thomas) Woodrow

Atwood, Margaret 1939- . **CLC 2, 3, 4, 8, 13, 15, 25, 44, 84, 135, 232; PC 8; SSC 2, 46; WLC 1**
See also AAYA 12, 47; AMWS 13; BEST 89:2; BPFB 1; CA 49-52; CANR 3, 24, 33, 59, 95, 133; CN 2, 3, 4, 5, 6, 7; CP 1, 2, 3, 4, 5, 6, 7; CPW; CWP; DA; DA3; DAB; DAC; DAM MST, NOV, POET; DLB 53, 251, 326; EWL 3; EXPN; FL 1:5; FW; GL 2; INT CANR-24; LAIT 5; MTCW 1, 2; MTFW 2005; NFS 4, 12, 13, 14, 19; PFS 7; RGSF 2; SATA 50, 170; SSFS 3, 13; TCLE 1:1; TWA; WWE 1; YAW

Atwood, Margaret Eleanor
See Atwood, Margaret

Aubigny, Pierre d'
See Mencken, H(enry) L(ouis)

Aubin, Penelope 1685-1731(?) .... **LC 9**
See also DLB 39

Auchincloss, Louis 1917- ..... **CLC 4, 6, 9, 18, 45; SSC 22**
See also AMWS 4; CA 1-4R; CANR 6, 29, 55, 87, 130; CN 1, 2, 3, 4, 5, 6, 7; DAM NOV; DLB 2, 244; DLBY 1980; EWL 3; INT CANR-29; MAL 5; MTCW 1; RGAL 4

Auchincloss, Louis Stanton
See Auchincloss, Louis

Auden, W(ystan) H(ugh) 1907-1973 . **CLC 1, 2, 3, 4, 6, 9, 11, 14, 43, 123; PC 1; WLC 1**
See also AAYA 18; AMWS 2; BRW 7; BRWR 1; CA 9-12R; CAAS 45-48; CANR 5, 61, 105; CDBLB 1914-1945; CP 1, 2; DA; DA3; DAB; DAC; DAM DRAM, MST, POET; DLB 10, 20; EWL 3; EXPP; MAL 5; MTCW 1, 2; MTFW 2005; PAB; PFS 1, 3, 4, 10; TUS; WP

Audiberti, Jacques 1899-1965 .... **CLC 38**
See also CA 252; CAAS 25-28R; DAM DRAM; DLB 321; EWL 3

Audubon, John James 1785-1851 . **NCLC 47**
See also AMWS 16; ANW; DLB 248

Auel, Jean M(arie) 1936- .... **CLC 31, 107**
See also AAYA 7, 51; BEST 90:4; BPFB 1; CA 103; CANR 21, 64, 115; CPW; DA3; DAM POP; INT CANR-21; NFS 11; RHW; SATA 91

Auerbach, Berthold 1812-1882 .... **NCLC 171**
See also DLB 133

Auerbach, Erich 1892-1957 .... **TCLC 43**
See also CA 155; CAAE 118; EWL 3

Augier, Emile 1820-1889 .... **NCLC 31**
See also DLB 192; GFL 1789 to the Present

August, John
See De Voto, Bernard (Augustine)

Augustine, St. 354-430 .... **CMLC 6; WLCS**
See also DA; DA3; DAB; DAC; DAM MST; DLB 115; EW 1; RGWL 2, 3; WLIT 8

Aunt Belinda
See Braddon, Mary Elizabeth

Aunt Weedy
See Alcott, Louisa May

Aurelius
See Bourne, Randolph S(illiman)

Aurelius, Marcus 121-180 .... **CMLC 45**
See Marcus Aurelius
See also RGWL 2, 3

Aurobindo, Sri
See Ghose, Aurabinda

Aurobindo Ghose
See Ghose, Aurabinda

Ausonius, Decimus Magnus c. 310-c. 394 .... **CMLC 88**
See also RGWL 2, 3

Austen, Jane 1775-1817 ...... **NCLC 1, 13, 19, 33, 51, 81, 95, 119, 150; WLC 1**
See also AAYA 19; BRW 4; BRWC 1; BRWR 2; BYA 3; CDBLB 1789-1832; DA; DA3; DAB; DAC; DAM MST, NOV; DLB 116; EXPN; FL 1:2; GL 2; LAIT 2; LATS 1:1; LMFS 1; NFS 1, 14, 18, 20, 21; TEA; WLIT 3; WYAS 1

Auster, Paul 1947- .... **CLC 47, 131, 227**
See also AMWS 12; CA 69-72; CANR 23, 52, 75, 129; CMW 4; CN 5, 6, 7; DA3; DLB 227; MAL 5; MTCW 2; MTFW 2005; SUFW 2; TCLE 1:1

Austin, Frank
See Faust, Frederick (Schiller)

Austin, Mary (Hunter) 1868-1934 . **TCLC 25**
See also ANW; CA 178; CAAE 109; DLB 9, 78, 206, 221, 275; FW; TCWW 1, 2

Averroes 1126-1198 .... **CMLC 7**
See also DLB 115

Avicenna 980-1037 .... **CMLC 16**
See also DLB 115

Avison, Margaret (Kirkland) 1918- .. **CLC 2, 4, 97**
See also CA 17-20R; CANR 134; CP 1, 2, 3, 4, 5, 6, 7; DAC; DAM POET; DLB 53; MTCW 1

Axton, David
See Koontz, Dean R.

Ayckbourn, Alan 1939- ...... **CLC 5, 8, 18, 33, 74; DC 13**
See also BRWS 5; CA 21-24R; CANR 31, 59, 118; CBD; CD 5, 6; DAB; DAM DRAM; DFS 7; DLB 13, 245; EWL 3; MTCW 1, 2; MTFW 2005

Aydy, Catherine
See Tennant, Emma (Christina)

Ayme, Marcel (Andre) 1902-1967 ... **CLC 11; SSC 41**
See also CA 89-92; CANR 67, 137; CLR 25; DLB 72; EW 12; EWL 3; GFL 1789 to the Present; RGSF 2; RGWL 2, 3; SATA 91

Ayrton, Michael 1921-1975 .... **CLC 7**
See also CA 5-8R; CAAS 61-64; CANR 9, 21

Aytmatov, Chingiz
See Aitmatov, Chingiz (Torekulovich)
See also EWL 3

Azorin .... **CLC 11**
See Martinez Ruiz, Jose
See also DLB 322; EW 9; EWL 3

Azuela, Mariano 1873-1952 .. **HLC 1; TCLC 3, 145**
See also CA 131; CAAE 104; CANR 81; DAM MULT; EWL 3; HW 1, 2; LAW; MTCW 1, 2; MTFW 2005

Ba, Mariama 1929-1981 .... **BLCS**
See also AFW; BW 2; CA 141; CANR 87; DNFS 2; WLIT 2

Baastad, Babbis Friis
See Friis-Baastad, Babbis Ellinor

Bab
See Gilbert, W(illiam) S(chwenck)

Babbis, Eleanor
See Friis-Baastad, Babbis Ellinor

Babel, Isaac
See Babel, Isaak (Emmanuilovich)
See also EW 11; SSFS 10

Babel, Isaak (Emmanuilovich)
1894-1941(?) . **SSC 16, 78; TCLC 2, 13, 171**
See Babel, Isaac
See also CA 155; CAAE 104; CANR 113; DLB 272; EWL 3; MTCW 2; MTFW 2005; RGSF 2; RGWL 2, 3; TWA

Babits, Mihaly 1883-1941 .... **TCLC 14**
See also CAAE 114; CDWLB 4; DLB 215; EWL 3

Babur 1483-1530 .... **LC 18**

Babylas 1898-1962
See Ghelderode, Michel de

Baca, Jimmy Santiago 1952- . **HLC 1; PC 41**
See also CA 131; CANR 81, 90, 146; CP 6, 7; DAM MULT; DLB 122; HW 1, 2; LLW; MAL 5

Baca, Jose Santiago
See Baca, Jimmy Santiago

Bacchelli, Riccardo 1891-1985 .... **CLC 19**
See also CA 29-32R; CAAS 117; DLB 264; EWL 3

Bach, Richard 1936- .... **CLC 14**
See also AITN 1; BEST 89:2; BPFB 1; BYA 5; CA 9-12R; CANR 18, 93, 151; CPW; DAM NOV, POP; FANT; MTCW 1; SATA 13

Bach, Richard David
See Bach, Richard

Bache, Benjamin Franklin
1769-1798 .... **LC 74**
See also DLB 43

Bachelard, Gaston 1884-1962 ...... **TCLC 128**
See also CA 97-100; CAAS 89-92; DLB 296; GFL 1789 to the Present

Bachman, Richard
See King, Stephen

Bachmann, Ingeborg 1926-1973 .... **CLC 69**
See also CA 93-96; CAAS 45-48; CANR 69; DLB 85; EWL 3; RGHL; RGWL 2, 3

Bacon, Francis 1561-1626 ..... **LC 18, 32, 131**
See also BRW 1; CDBLB Before 1660; DLB 151, 236, 252; RGEL 2; TEA

Bacon, Roger 1214(?)-1294 .... **CMLC 14**
See also DLB 115

Bacovia, George 1881-1957 .... **TCLC 24**
See Vasiliu, Gheorghe
See also CDWLB 4; DLB 220; EWL 3

Badanes, Jerome 1937-1995 .... **CLC 59**
See also CA 234

Bage, Robert 1728-1801 .... **NCLC 182**
See also DLB 39; RGEL 2

Bagehot, Walter 1826-1877 .... **NCLC 10**
See also DLB 55

Bagnold, Enid 1889-1981 .... **CLC 25**
See also AAYA 75; BYA 2; CA 5-8R; CAAS 103; CANR 5, 40; CBD; CN 2; CWD; CWRI 5; DAM DRAM; DLB 13, 160, 191, 245; FW; MAICYA 1, 2; RGEL 2; SATA 1, 25

Bagritsky, Eduard .... **TCLC 60**
See Dzyubin, Eduard Georgievich

Bagrjana, Elisaveta
See Belcheva, Elisaveta Lyubomirova

Barnes, Julian 1946- .... CLC 42, 141
 See also BRWS 4; CA 102; CANR 19, 54,
 115, 137; CN 4, 5, 6, 7; DAB; DLB 194;
 DLBY 1993; EWL 3; MTCW 2; MTFW
 2005; SSFS 24
Barnes, Julian Patrick
 See Barnes, Julian
Barnes, Peter 1931-2004 .... CLC 5, 56
 See also CA 65-68; 12; CAAS 230; CANR
 33, 34, 64, 113; CBD; CD 5, 6; DFS 6;
 DLB 13, 233; MTCW 1
Barnes, William 1801-1886 .... NCLC 75
 See also DLB 32
Baroja, Pio 1872-1956 .... HLC 1; TCLC 8
 See also CA 247; CAAE 104; EW 9
Baroja y Nessi, Pio
 See Baroja, Pio
Baron, David
 See Pinter, Harold
Baron Corvo
 See Rolfe, Frederick (William Serafino Aus-
 tin Lewis Mary)
Barondess, Sue K(aufman)
 1926-1977 .... CLC 8
 See Kaufman, Sue
 See also CA 1-4R; CAAS 69-72; CANR 1
Baron de Teive
 See Pessoa, Fernando (Antonio Nogueira)
Baroness Von S.
 See Zangwill, Israel
Barres, (Auguste-)Maurice
 1862-1923 .... TCLC 47
 See also CA 164; DLB 123; GFL 1789 to
 the Present
Barreto, Afonso Henrique de Lima
 See Lima Barreto, Afonso Henrique de
Barrett, Andrea 1954- .... CLC 150
 See also CA 156; CANR 92; CN 7; SSFS
 24
Barrett, Michele .... CLC 65
Barrett, (Roger) Syd 1946-2006 .... CLC 35
Barrett, William (Christopher)
 1913-1992 .... CLC 27
 See also CA 13-16R; CAAS 139; CANR
 11, 67; INT CANR-11
Barrett Browning, Elizabeth
 1806-1861 ...... NCLC 1, 16, 61, 66, 170;
 PC 6, 62; WLC 1
 See also AAYA 63; BRW 4; CDBLB 1832-
 1890; DA; DA3; DAB; DAC; DAM MST,
 POET; DLB 32, 199; EXPP; FL 1:2; PAB;
 PFS 2, 16, 23; TEA; WLIT 4; WP
Barrie, J(ames) M(atthew)
 1860-1937 .... TCLC 2, 164
 See also BRWS 3; BYA 4, 5; CA 136;
 CAAE 104; CANR 77; CDBLB 1890-
 1914; CLR 16; CWRI 5; DA3; DAB;
 DAM DRAM; DFS 7; DLB 10, 141, 156;
 EWL 3; FANT; MAICYA 1, 2; MTCW 2;
 MTFW 2005; SATA 100; SUFW; WCH;
 WLIT 4; YABC 1
Barrington, Michael
 See Moorcock, Michael
Barrol, Grady
 See Bograd, Larry
Barry, Mike
 See Malzberg, Barry N(athaniel)
Barry, Philip 1896-1949 .... TCLC 11
 See also CA 199; CAAE 109; DFS 9; DLB
 7, 228; MAL 5; RGAL 4
Bart, Andre Schwarz
 See Schwarz-Bart, Andre
Barth, John (Simmons) 1930- ... CLC 1, 2, 3,
 5, 7, 9, 10, 14, 27, 51, 89, 214; SSC 10,
 89
 See also AITN 1, 2; AMW; BPFB 1; CA
 1-4R; CABS 1; CANR 5, 23, 49, 64, 113;
 CN 1, 2, 3, 4, 5, 6, 7; DAM NOV; DLB
 2, 227; EWL 3; FANT; MAL 5; MTCW
 1; RGAL 4; RGSF 2; RHW; SSFS 6; TUS

Barthelme, Donald 1931-1989 ... CLC 1, 2, 3,
 5, 6, 8, 13, 23, 46, 59, 115; SSC 2, 55
 See also AMWS 4; BPFB 1; CA 21-24R;
 CAAS 129; CANR 20, 58; CN 1, 2, 3, 4;
 DA3; DAM NOV; DLB 2, 234; DLBY
 1980, 1989; EWL 3; FANT; LMFS 2;
 MAL 5; MTCW 1, 2; MTFW 2005;
 RGAL 4; RGSF 2; SATA 7; SATA-Obit
 62; SSFS 17
Barthelme, Frederick 1943- ...... CLC 36, 117
 See also AMWS 11; CA 122; CAAE 114;
 CANR 77; CN 4, 5, 6, 7; CSW; DLB 244;
 DLBY 1985; EWL 3; INT CA-122
Barthes, Roland (Gerard)
 1915-1980 .... CLC 24, 83; TCLC 135
 See also CA 130; CAAS 97-100; CANR
 66; DLB 296; EW 13; EWL 3; GFL 1789
 to the Present; MTCW 1, 2; TWA
Bartram, William 1739-1823 .... NCLC 145
 See also ANW; DLB 37
Barzun, Jacques (Martin) 1907- ..... CLC 51,
 145
 See also CA 61-64; CANR 22, 95
Bashevis, Isaac
 See Singer, Isaac Bashevis
Bashevis, Yitskhok
 See Singer, Isaac Bashevis
Bashkirtseff, Marie 1859-1884 .... NCLC 27
Basho, Matsuo
 See Matsuo Basho
 See also RGWL 2, 3; WP
Basil of Caesaria c. 330-379 .... CMLC 35
Basket, Raney
 See Edgerton, Clyde (Carlyle)
Bass, Kingsley B., Jr.
 See Bullins, Ed
Bass, Rick 1958- .... CLC 79, 143; SSC 60
 See also AMWS 16; ANW; CA 126; CANR
 53, 93, 145; CSW; DLB 212, 275
Bassani, Giorgio 1916-2000 .... CLC 9
 See also CA 65-68; CAAS 190; CANR 33;
 CWW 2; DLB 128, 177, 299; EWL 3;
 MTCW 1; RGHL; RGWL 2, 3
Bastian, Ann .... CLC 70
Bastos, Augusto Roa
 See Roa Bastos, Augusto
Bataille, Georges 1897-1962 .... CLC 29;
 TCLC 155
 See also CA 101; CAAS 89-92; EWL 3
Bates, H(erbert) E(rnest)
 1905-1974 .... CLC 46; SSC 10
 See also CA 93-96; CAAS 45-48; CANR
 34; CN 1; DA3; DAB; DAM POP; DLB
 162, 191; EWL 3; EXPS; MTCW 1, 2;
 RGSF 2; SSFS 7
Bauchart
 See Camus, Albert
Baudelaire, Charles 1821-1867 . NCLC 6, 29,
 55, 155; PC 1; SSC 18; WLC 1
 See also DA; DA3; DAB; DAC; DAM
 MST, POET; DLB 217; EW 7; GFL 1789
 to the Present; LMFS 2; PFS 21; RGWL
 2, 3; TWA
Baudouin, Marcel
 See Peguy, Charles (Pierre)
Baudouin, Pierre
 See Peguy, Charles (Pierre)
Baudrillard, Jean 1929- .... CLC 60
 See also CA 252; DLB 296
Baum, L(yman) Frank 1856-1919 .. TCLC 7,
 132
 See also AAYA 46; BYA 16; CA 133;
 CAAE 108; CLR 15, 107; CWRI 5; DLB
 22; FANT; JRDA; MAICYA 1, 2; MTCW
 1, 2; NFS 13; RGAL 4; SATA 18, 100;
 WCH
Baum, Louis F.
 See Baum, L(yman) Frank

Baumbach, Jonathan 1933- .... CLC 6, 23
 See also CA 13-16R; 5; CANR 12, 66, 140;
 CN 3, 4, 5, 6, 7; DLBY 1980; INT CANR-
 12; MTCW 1
Bausch, Richard (Carl) 1945- .... CLC 51
 See also AMWS 7; CA 101; 14; CANR 43,
 61, 87; CN 7; CSW; DLB 130; MAL 5
Baxter, Charles 1947- .... CLC 45, 78
 See also CA 57-60; CANR 40, 64, 104, 133;
 CPW; DAM POP; DLB 130; MAL 5;
 MTCW 2; MTFW 2005; TCLE 1:1
Baxter, George Owen
 See Faust, Frederick (Schiller)
Baxter, James K(eir) 1926-1972 .... CLC 14
 See also CA 77-80; CP 1; EWL 3
Baxter, John
 See Hunt, E. Howard
Bayer, Sylvia
 See Glassco, John
Bayle, Pierre 1647-1706 .... LC 126
 See also DLB 268, 313; GFL Beginnings to
 1789
Baynton, Barbara 1857-1929 .... TCLC 57
 See also DLB 230; RGSF 2
Beagle, Peter S. 1939- .... CLC 7, 104
 See also AAYA 47; BPFB 1; BYA 9, 10,
 16; CA 9-12R; CANR 4, 51, 73, 110;
 DA3; DLBY 1980; FANT; INT CANR-4;
 MTCW 2; MTFW 2005; SATA 60, 130;
 SUFW 1, 2; YAW
Beagle, Peter Soyer
 See Beagle, Peter S.
Bean, Normal
 See Burroughs, Edgar Rice
Beard, Charles A(ustin)
 1874-1948 .... TCLC 15
 See also CA 189; CAAE 115; DLB 17;
 SATA 18
Beardsley, Aubrey 1872-1898 .... NCLC 6
Beattie, Ann 1947- ..... CLC 8, 13, 18, 40, 63,
 146; SSC 11
 See also AMWS 5; BEST 90:2; BPFB 1;
 CA 81-84; CANR 53, 73, 128; CN 4, 5,
 6, 7; CPW; DA3; DAM NOV, POP; DLB
 218, 278; DLBY 1982; EWL 3; MAL 5;
 MTCW 1, 2; MTFW 2005; RGAL 4;
 RGSF 2; SSFS 9; TUS
Beattie, James 1735-1803 .... NCLC 25
 See also DLB 109
Beauchamp, Kathleen Mansfield 1888-1923
 See Mansfield, Katherine
 See also CA 134; CAAE 104; DA; DA3;
 DAC; DAM MST; MTCW 2; TEA
Beaumarchais, Pierre-Augustin Caron de
 1732-1799 .... DC 4; LC 61
 See also DAM DRAM; DFS 14, 16; DLB
 313; EW 4; GFL Beginnings to 1789;
 RGWL 2, 3
Beaumont, Francis 1584(?)-1616 .. DC 6; LC
 33
 See also BRW 2; CDBLB Before 1660;
 DLB 58; TEA
Beauvoir, Simone de 1908-1986 .... CLC 1, 2,
 4, 8, 14, 31, 44, 50, 71, 124; SSC 35;
 WLC 1
 See also BPFB 1; CA 9-12R; CAAS 118;
 CANR 28, 61; DA; DA3; DAB; DAC;
 DAM MST, NOV; DLB 72; DLBY 1986;
 EW 12; EWL 3; FL 1:5; FW; GFL 1789
 to the Present; LMFS 2; MTCW 1, 2;
 MTFW 2005; RGSF 2; RGWL 2, 3; TWA
Beauvoir, Simone Lucie Ernestine Marie
 Bertrand de
 See Beauvoir, Simone de
Becker, Carl (Lotus) 1873-1945 ..... TCLC 63
 See also CA 157; DLB 17

Becker, Jurek 1937-1997 .... **CLC 7, 19**
See also CA 85-88; CAAS 157; CANR 60, 117; CWW 2; DLB 75, 299; EWL 3; RGHL

Becker, Walter 1950- .... **CLC 26**

Becket, Thomas a 1118(?)-1170 .... **CMLC 83**

Beckett, Samuel 1906-1989 ... **CLC 1, 2, 3, 4, 6, 9, 10, 11, 14, 18, 29, 57, 59, 83; DC 22; SSC 16, 74; TCLC 145; WLC 1**
See also BRWC 2; BRWR 1; BRWS 1; CA 5-8R; CAAS 130; CANR 33, 61; CBD; CDBLB 1945-1960; CN 1, 2, 3, 4; CP 1, 2, 3, 4; DA; DA3; DAB; DAC; DAM DRAM, MST, NOV; DFS 2, 7, 18; DLB 13, 15, 233, 319, 321, 329; DLBY 1990; EWL 3; GFL 1789 to the Present; LATS 1:2; LMFS 2; MTCW 1, 2; MTFW 2005; RGSF 2; RGWL 2, 3; SSFS 15; TEA; WLIT 4

Beckford, William 1760-1844 .... **NCLC 16**
See also BRW 3; DLB 39, 213; GL 2; HGG; LMFS 1; SUFW

Beckham, Barry (Earl) 1944- .... **BLC 1**
See also BW 1; CA 29-32R; CANR 26, 62; CN 1, 2, 3, 4, 5, 6; DAM MULT; DLB 33

Beckman, Gunnel 1910- .... **CLC 26**
See also CA 33-36R; CANR 15, 114; CLR 25; MAICYA 1, 2; SAAS 9; SATA 6

Becque, Henri 1837-1899 .... **DC 21; NCLC 3**
See also DLB 192; GFL 1789 to the Present

Becquer, Gustavo Adolfo
1836-1870 .... **HLCS 1; NCLC 106**
See also DAM MULT

Beddoes, Thomas Lovell 1803-1849 .. **DC 15; NCLC 3, 154**
See also BRWS 11; DLB 96

Bede c. 673-735 .... **CMLC 20**
See also DLB 146; TEA

Bedford, Denton R. 1907-(?) .... **NNAL**

Bedford, Donald F.
See Fearing, Kenneth (Flexner)

Beecher, Catharine Esther
1800-1878 .... **NCLC 30**
See also DLB 1, 243

Beecher, John 1904-1980 .... **CLC 6**
See also AITN 1; CA 5-8R; CAAS 105; CANR 8; CP 1, 2, 3

Beer, Johann 1655-1700 .... **LC 5**
See also DLB 168

Beer, Patricia 1924- .... **CLC 58**
See also CA 61-64; CAAS 183; CANR 13, 46; CP 1, 2, 3, 4, 5, 6; CWP; DLB 40; FW

Beerbohm, Max
See Beerbohm, (Henry) Max(imilian)

Beerbohm, (Henry) Max(imilian)
1872 1956 .... **TCLC 1, 24**
See also BRWS 2; CA 154; CAAE 104; CANR 79; DLB 34, 100; FANT; MTCW 2

Beer-Hofmann, Richard
1866-1945 .... **TCLC 60**
See also CA 160; DLB 81

Beg, Shemus
See Stephens, James

Begiebing, Robert J(ohn) 1946- .... **CLC 70**
See also CA 122; CANR 40, 88

Begley, Louis 1933- .... **CLC 197**
See also CA 140; CANR 98; DLB 299; RGHL; TCLE 1:1

Behan, Brendan (Francis)
1923-1964 .... **CLC 1, 8, 11, 15, 79**
See also BRWS 2; CA 73-76; CANR 33, 121; CBD; CDBLB 1945-1960; DAM DRAM; DFS 7; DLB 13, 233; EWL 3; MTCW 1, 2

Behn, Aphra 1640(?)-1689 .. **DC 4; LC 1, 30, 42, 135; PC 13; WLC 1**
See also BRWS 3; DA; DA3; DAB; DAC; DAM DRAM, MST, NOV, POET; DFS 16; DLB 39, 80, 131; FW; TEA; WLIT 3

Behrman, S(amuel) N(athaniel)
1893-1973 .... **CLC 40**
See also CA 13-16; CAAS 45-48; CAD; CAP 1; DLB 7, 44; IDFW 3; MAL 5; RGAL 4

Bekederemo, J. P. Clark
See Clark Bekederemo, J.P.
See also CD 6

Belasco, David 1853-1931 .... **TCLC 3**
See also CA 168; CAAE 104; DLB 7; MAL 5; RGAL 4

Belcheva, Elisaveta Lyubomirova
1893-1991 .... **CLC 10**
See Bagryana, Elisaveta

Beldone, Phil ''Cheech''
See Ellison, Harlan

Beleno
See Azuela, Mariano

Belinski, Vissarion Grigoryevich
1811-1848 .... **NCLC 5**
See also DLB 198

Belitt, Ben 1911- .... **CLC 22**
See also CA 13-16R; 4; CANR 7, 77; CP 1, 2, 3, 4, 5, 6; DLB 5

Belknap, Jeremy 1744-1798 .... **LC 115**
See also DLB 30, 37

Bell, Gertrude (Margaret Lowthian)
1868-1926 .... **TCLC 67**
See also CA 167; CANR 110; DLB 174

Bell, J. Freeman
See Zangwill, Israel

Bell, James Madison 1826-1902 .... **BLC 1; TCLC 43**
See also BW 1; CA 124; CAAE 122; DAM MULT; DLB 50

Bell, Madison Smartt 1957- ..... **CLC 41, 102, 223**
See also AMWS 10; BPFB 1; CA 183; 111, 183; CANR 28, 54, 73, 134; CN 5, 6, 7; CSW; DLB 218, 278; MTCW 2; MTFW 2005

Bell, Marvin (Hartley) 1937- .... **CLC 8, 31**
See also CA 21-24R; 14; CANR 59, 102; CP 1, 2, 3, 4, 5, 6, 7; DAM POET; DLB 5; MAL 5; MTCW 1; PFS 25

Bell, W. L. D.
See Mencken, H(enry) L(ouis)

Bellamy, Atwood C.
See Mencken, H(enry) L(ouis)

Bellamy, Edward 1850-1898 ..... **NCLC 4, 86, 147**
See also DLB 12; NFS 15; RGAL 4; SFW 4

Belli, Gioconda 1948- .... **HLCS 1**
See also CA 152; CANR 143; CWW 2; DLB 290; EWL 3; RGWL 3

Bellin, Edward J.
See Kuttner, Henry

Bello, Andres 1781-1865 .... **NCLC 131**
See also LAW

Belloc, (Joseph) Hilaire (Pierre Sebastien Rene Swanton) 1870-1953 .... **PC 24; TCLC 7, 18**
See also CA 152; CAAE 106; CLR 102; CWRI 5; DAM POET; DLB 19, 100, 141, 174; EWL 3; MTCW 2; MTFW 2005; SATA 112; WCH; YABC 1

Belloc, Joseph Peter Rene Hilaire
See Belloc, (Joseph) Hilaire (Pierre Sebastien Rene Swanton)

Belloc, Joseph Pierre Hilaire
See Belloc, (Joseph) Hilaire (Pierre Sebastien Rene Swanton)

Belloc, M. A.
See Lowndes, Marie Adelaide (Belloc)

Belloc-Lowndes, Mrs.
See Lowndes, Marie Adelaide (Belloc)

Bellow, Saul 1915-2005 ...... **CLC 1, 2, 3, 6, 8, 10, 13, 15, 25, 33, 34, 63, 79, 190, 200; SSC 14; WLC 1**
See also AITN 2; AMW; AMWC 2; AMWR 2; BEST 89:3; BPFB 1; CA 5-8R; CAAS 238; CABS 1; CANR 29, 53, 95, 132; CDALB 1941-1968; CN 1, 2, 3, 4, 5, 6, 7; DA; DA3; DAB; DAC; DAM MST, NOV, POP; DLB 2, 28, 299, 329; DLBD 3; DLBY 1982; EWL 3; MAL 5; MTCW 1, 2; MTFW 2005; NFS 4, 14; RGAL 4; RGHL; RGSF 2; SSFS 12, 22; TUS

Belser, Reimond Karel Maria de 1929-
See Ruyslinck, Ward
See also CA 152

Bely, Andrey .... **PC 11; TCLC 7**
See Bugayev, Boris Nikolayevich
See also DLB 295; EW 9; EWL 3

Belyi, Andrei
See Bugayev, Boris Nikolayevich
See also RGWL 2, 3

Bembo, Pietro 1470-1547 .... **LC 79**
See also RGWL 2, 3

Benary, Margot
See Benary-Isbert, Margot

Benary-Isbert, Margot 1889-1979 .... **CLC 12**
See also CA 5-8R; CAAS 89-92; CANR 4, 72; CLR 12; MAICYA 1, 2; SATA 2; SATA-Obit 21

Benavente (y Martinez), Jacinto
1866-1954 .... **DC 26; HLCS 1; TCLC 3**
See also CA 131; CAAE 106; CANR 81; DAM DRAM, MULT; DLB 329; EWL 3; GLL 2; HW 1, 2; MTCW 1, 2

Benchley, Peter 1940-2006 .... **CLC 4, 8**
See also AAYA 14; AITN 2; BPFB 1; CA 17-20R; CAAS 248; CANR 12, 35, 66, 115; CPW; DAM NOV, POP; HGG; MTCW 1, 2; MTFW 2005; SATA 3, 89, 164

Benchley, Peter Bradford
See Benchley, Peter

Benchley, Robert (Charles)
1889-1945 .... **TCLC 1, 55**
See also CA 153; CAAE 105; DLB 11; MAL 5; RGAL 4

Benda, Julien 1867-1956 .... **TCLC 60**
See also CA 154; CAAE 120; GFL 1789 to the Present

Benedict, Ruth 1887-1948 .... **TCLC 60**
See also CA 158; CANR 146; DLB 246

Benedict, Ruth Fulton
See Benedict, Ruth

Benedikt, Michael 1935- .... **CLC 4, 14**
See also CA 13-16R; CANR 7; CP 1, 2, 3, 4, 5, 6, 7; DLB 5

Benet, Juan 1927-1993 .... **CLC 28**
See also CA 143; EWL 3

Benet, Stephen Vincent 1898-1943 ..... **PC 64; SSC 10, 86; TCLC 7**
See also AMWS 11; CA 152; CAAE 104; DA3; DAM POET; DLB 4, 48, 102, 249, 284; DLBY 1997; EWL 3; HGG; MAL 5; MTCW 2; MTFW 2005; RGAL 4; RGSF 2; SSFS 22; SUFW; WP; YABC 1

Benet, William Rose 1886-1950 ..... **TCLC 28**
See also CA 152; CAAE 118; DAM POET; DLB 45; RGAL 4

Benford, Gregory (Albert) 1941- .... **CLC 52**
See also BPFB 1; CA 175; 69-72, 175; 27; CANR 12, 24, 49, 95, 134; CN 7; CSW; DLBY 1982; MTFW 2005; SCFW 2; SFW 4

Bengtsson, Frans (Gunnar)
1894-1954 .... **TCLC 48**
See also CA 170; EWL 3

Benjamin, David
See Slavitt, David R(ytman)

Benjamin, Lois
See Gould, Lois

Benjamin, Walter 1892-1940 .... **TCLC 39**
See also CA 164; DLB 242; EW 11; EWL 3

Ben Jelloun, Tahar 1944-
See Jelloun, Tahar ben
See also CA 135; CWW 2; EWL 3; RGWL 3; WLIT 2

Benn, Gottfried 1886-1956 .. **PC 35; TCLC 3**
See also CA 153; CAAE 106; DLB 56; EWL 3; RGWL 2, 3

Bennett, Alan 1934- .... **CLC 45, 77**
See also BRWS 8; CA 103; CANR 35, 55, 106, 157; CBD; CD 5, 6; DAB; DAM MST; DLB 310; MTCW 1, 2; MTFW 2005

Bennett, (Enoch) Arnold
1867-1931 .... **TCLC 5, 20**
See also BRW 6; CA 155; CAAE 106; CD-BLB 1890-1914; DLB 10, 34, 98, 135; EWL 3; MTCW 2

Bennett, Elizabeth
See Mitchell, Margaret (Munnerlyn)

Bennett, George Harold 1930-
See Bennett, Hal
See also BW 1; CA 97-100; CANR 87

Bennett, Gwendolyn B. 1902-1981 .... **HR 1:2**
See also BW 1; CA 125; DLB 51; WP

Bennett, Hal .... **CLC 5**
See Bennett, George Harold
See also CA 13; DLB 33

Bennett, Jay 1912- .... **CLC 35**
See also AAYA 10, 73; CA 69-72; CANR 11, 42, 79; JRDA; SAAS 4; SATA 41, 87; SATA-Brief 27; WYA; YAW

Bennett, Louise 1919-2006 .. **BLC 1; CLC 28**
See also BW 2, 3; CA 151; CAAS 252; CD-WLB 3; CP 1, 2, 3, 4, 5, 6, 7; DAM MULT; DLB 117; EWL 3

Bennett, Louise Simone
See Bennett, Louise

Bennett-Coverley, Louise
See Bennett, Louise

Benoit de Sainte-Maure fl. 12th cent.
- .... **CMLC 90**

Benson, A. C. 1862-1925 .... **TCLC 123**
See also DLB 98

Benson, E(dward) F(rederic)
1867-1940 .... **TCLC 27**
See also CA 157; CAAE 114; DLB 135, 153; HGG; SUFW 1

Benson, Jackson J. 1930- .... **CLC 34**
See also CA 25-28R; DLB 111

Benson, Sally 1900-1972 .... **CLC 17**
See also CA 19-20; CAAS 37-40R; CAP 1; SATA 1, 35; SATA-Obit 27

Benson, Stella 1892-1933 .... **TCLC 17**
See also CA 154, 155; CAAE 117; DLB 36, 162; FANT; TEA

Bentham, Jeremy 1748-1832 .... **NCLC 38**
See also DLB 107, 158, 252

Bentley, E(dmund) C(lerihew)
1875-1956 .... **TCLC 12**
See also CA 232; CAAE 108; DLB 70; MSW

Bentley, Eric 1916- .... **CLC 24**
See also CA 5-8R; CAD; CANR 6, 67; CBD; CD 5, 6; INT CANR-6

Bentley, Eric Russell
See Bentley, Eric

ben Uzair, Salem
See Horne, Richard Henry Hengist

Beranger, Pierre Jean de
1780-1857 .... **NCLC 34**

Berdyaev, Nicolas
See Berdyaev, Nikolai (Aleksandrovich)

Berdyaev, Nikolai (Aleksandrovich)
1874-1948 .... **TCLC 67**
See also CA 157; CAAE 120

Berdyayev, Nikolai (Aleksandrovich)
See Berdyaev, Nikolai (Aleksandrovich)

Berendt, John 1939- .... **CLC 86**
See also CA 146; CANR 75, 83, 151

Berendt, John Lawrence
See Berendt, John

Beresford, J(ohn) D(avys)
1873-1947 .... **TCLC 81**
See also CA 155; CAAE 112; DLB 162, 178, 197; SFW 4; SUFW 1

Bergelson, David (Rafailovich)
1884-1952 .... **TCLC 81**
See Bergelson, Dovid
See also CA 220; DLB 333

Bergelson, Dovid
See Bergelson, David (Rafailovich)
See also EWL 3

Berger, Colonel
See Malraux, (Georges-)Andre

Berger, John (Peter) 1926- .... **CLC 2, 19**
See also BRWS 4; CA 81-84; CANR 51, 78, 117; CN 1, 2, 3, 4, 5, 6, 7; DLB 14, 207, 319, 326

Berger, Melvin H. 1927- .... **CLC 12**
See also CA 5-8R; CANR 4, 142; CLR 32; SAAS 2; SATA 5, 88, 158; SATA-Essay 124

Berger, Thomas 1924- .... **CLC 3, 5, 8, 11, 18, 38**
See also BPFB 1; CA 1-4R; CANR 5, 28, 51, 128; CN 1, 2, 3, 4, 5, 6, 7; DAM NOV; DLB 2; DLBY 1980; EWL 3; FANT; INT CANR-28; MAL 5; MTCW 1, 2; MTFW 2005; RHW; TCLE 1:1; TCWW 1, 2

Bergman, (Ernst) Ingmar 1918- ...... **CLC 16, 72, 210**
See also AAYA 61; CA 81-84; CANR 33, 70; CWW 2; DLB 257; MTCW 2; MTFW 2005

Bergson, Henri(-Louis) 1859-1941 . **TCLC 32**
See also CA 164; DLB 329; EW 8; EWL 3; GFL 1789 to the Present

Bergstein, Eleanor 1938- .... **CLC 4**
See also CA 53-56; CANR 5

Berkeley, George 1685-1753 .... **LC 65**
See also DLB 31, 101, 252

Berkoff, Steven 1937- .... **CLC 56**
See also CA 104; CANR 72; CBD; CD 5, 6

Berlin, Isaiah 1909-1997 .... **TCLC 105**
See also CA 85-88; CAAS 162

Bermant, Chaim (Icyk) 1929-1998 ... **CLC 40**
See also CA 57-60; CANR 6, 31, 57, 105; CN 2, 3, 4, 5, 6

Bern, Victoria
See Fisher, M(ary) F(rances) K(ennedy)

Bernanos, (Paul Louis) Georges
1888-1948 .... **TCLC 3**
See also CA 130; CAAE 104; CANR 94; DLB 72; EWL 3; GFL 1789 to the Present; RGWL 2, 3

Bernard, April 1956- .... **CLC 59**
See also CA 131; CANR 144

Bernard, Mary Ann
See Soderbergh, Steven

Bernard of Clairvaux 1090-1153 .. **CMLC 71**
See also DLB 208

Bernard Silvestris fl. c. 1130-fl. c. 1160 .... **CMLC 87**
See also DLB 208

Berne, Victoria
See Fisher, M(ary) F(rances) K(ennedy)

Bernhard, Thomas 1931-1989 ..... **CLC 3, 32, 61; DC 14; TCLC 165**
See also CA 85-88; CAAS 127; CANR 32, 57; CDWLB 2; DLB 85, 124; EWL 3; MTCW 1; RGHL; RGWL 2, 3

Bernhardt, Sarah (Henriette Rosine)
1844-1923 .... **TCLC 75**
See also CA 157

Bernstein, Charles 1950- .... **CLC 142**
See also CA 129; 24; CANR 90; CP 4, 5, 6, 7; DLB 169

Bernstein, Ingrid
See Kirsch, Sarah

Beroul fl. c. 12th cent. - .... **CMLC 75**

Berriault, Gina 1926-1999 .... **CLC 54, 109; SSC 30**
See also CA 129; CAAE 116; CAAS 185; CANR 66; DLB 130; SSFS 7,11

Berrigan, Daniel 1921- .... **CLC 4**
See also CA 187; 33-36R, 187; 1; CANR 11, 43, 78; CP 1, 2, 3, 4, 5, 6, 7; DLB 5

Berrigan, Edmund Joseph Michael, Jr.
1934-1983
See Berrigan, Ted
See also CA 61-64; CAAS 110; CANR 14, 102

Berrigan, Ted .... **CLC 37**
See Berrigan, Edmund Joseph Michael, Jr.
See also CP 1, 2, 3; DLB 5, 169; WP

Berry, Charles Edward Anderson 1931-
See Berry, Chuck
See also CA 115

Berry, Chuck .... **CLC 17**
See Berry, Charles Edward Anderson

Berry, Jonas
See Ashbery, John
See also GLL 1

Berry, Wendell 1934- .... **CLC 4, 6, 8, 27, 46; PC 28**
See also AITN 1; AMWS 10; ANW; CA 73-76; CANR 50, 73, 101, 132; CP 1, 2, 3, 4, 5, 6, 7; CSW; DAM POET; DLB 5, 6, 234, 275; MTCW 2; MTFW 2005; TCLE 1:1

Berryman, John 1914-1972 ... **CLC 1, 2, 3, 4, 6, 8, 10, 13, 25, 62; PC 64**
See also AMW; CA 13-16; CAAS 33-36R; CABS 2; CANR 35; CAP 1; CDALB 1941-1968; CP 1; DAM POET; DLB 48; EWL 3; MAL 5; MTCW 1, 2; MTFW 2005; PAB; RGAL 4; WP

Bertolucci, Bernardo 1940- ...... **CLC 16, 157**
See also CA 106; CANR 125

Berton, Pierre (Francis de Marigny)
1920-2004 .... **CLC 104**
See also CA 1-4R; CAAS 233; CANR 2, 56, 144; CPW; DLB 68; SATA 99; SATA-Obit 158

Bertrand, Aloysius 1807-1841 .... **NCLC 31**
See Bertrand, Louis oAloysiusc

Bertrand, Louis oAloysiusc
See Bertrand, Aloysius
See also DLB 217

Bertran de Born c. 1140-1215 .... **CMLC 5**

Besant, Annie (Wood) 1847-1933 ..... **TCLC 9**
See also CA 185; CAAE 105

Bessie, Alvah 1904-1985 .... **CLC 23**
See also CA 5-8R; CAAS 116; CANR 2, 80; DLB 26

Bestuzhev, Aleksandr Aleksandrovich
1797-1837 .... **NCLC 131**
See also DLB 198

Bethlen, T. D.
See Silverberg, Robert

Beti, Mongo .... **BLC 1; CLC 27**
See Biyidi, Alexandre
See also AFW; CANR 79; DAM MULT; EWL 3; WLIT 2

Betjeman, John 1906-1984 ...... **CLC 2, 6, 10, 34, 43; PC 75**
See also BRW 7; CA 9-12R; CAAS 112; CANR 33, 56; CDBLB 1945-1960; CP 1, 2, 3; DA3; DAB; DAM MST, POET; DLB 20; DLBY 1984; EWL 3; MTCW 1, 2

Bettelheim, Bruno 1903-1990 .... **CLC 79; TCLC 143**
See also CA 81-84; CAAS 131; CANR 23, 61; DA3; MTCW 1, 2; RGHL

Betti, Ugo 1892-1953 .... **TCLC 5**
See also CA 155; CAAE 104; EWL 3; RGWL 2, 3

Betts, Doris (Waugh) 1932- ..... **CLC 3, 6, 28; SSC 45**
See also CA 13-16R; CANR 9, 66, 77; CN 6, 7; CSW; DLB 218; DLBY 1982; INT CANR-9; RGAL 4

Bevan, Alistair
See Roberts, Keith (John Kingston)

Bey, Pilaff
See Douglas, (George) Norman

Bialik, Chaim Nachman
1873-1934 .... **TCLC 25**
See Bialik, Hayyim Nahman
See also CA 170; EWL 3

Bialik, Hayyim Nahman
See Bialik, Chaim Nachman
See also WLIT 6

Bickerstaff, Isaac
See Swift, Jonathan

Bidart, Frank 1939- .... **CLC 33**
See also AMWS 15; CA 140; CANR 106; CP 5, 6, 7

Bienek, Horst 1930- .... **CLC 7, 11**
See also CA 73-76; DLB 75

Bierce, Ambrose (Gwinett)
1842-1914(?) ..... **SSC 9, 72; TCLC 1, 7, 44; WLC 1**
See also AAYA 55; AMW; BYA 11; CA 139; CAAE 104; CANR 78; CDALB 1865-1917; DA; DA3; DAC; DAM MST; DLB 11, 12, 23, 71, 74, 186; EWL 3; EXPS; HGG; LAIT 2; MAL 5; RGAL 4; RGSF 2; SSFS 9; SUFW 1

Biggers, Earl Derr 1884-1933 .... **TCLC 65**
See also CA 153; CAAE 108; DLB 306

Billiken, Bud
See Motley, Willard (Francis)

Billings, Josh
See Shaw, Henry Wheeler

Billington, (Lady) Rachel (Mary)
1942- .... **CLC 43**
See also AITN 2; CA 33-36R; CANR 44; CN 4, 5, 6, 7

Binchy, Maeve 1940- .... **CLC 153**
See also BEST 90:1; BPFB 1; CA 134; CAAE 127; CANR 50, 96, 134; CN 5, 6, 7; CPW; DA3; DAM POP; DLB 319; INT CA-134; MTCW 2; MTFW 2005; RHW

Binyon, T(imothy) J(ohn)
1936-2004 .... **CLC 34**
See also CA 111; CAAS 232; CANR 28, 140

Bion 335B.C.-245B.C. .... **CMLC 39**

Bioy Casares, Adolfo 1914-1999 ... **CLC 4, 8, 13, 88; HLC 1; SSC 17**
See Casares, Adolfo Bioy; Miranda, Javier; Sacastru, Martin
See also CA 29-32R; CAAS 177; CANR 19, 43, 66; CWW 2; DAM MULT; DLB 113; EWL 3; HW 1, 2; LAW; MTCW 1, 2; MTFW 2005

Birch, Allison .... **CLC 65**

Bird, Cordwainer
See Ellison, Harlan

Bird, Robert Montgomery
1806-1854 .... **NCLC 1**
See also DLB 202; RGAL 4

Birkerts, Sven 1951- .... **CLC 116**
See also CA 176; 133, 176; 29; CAAE 128; CANR 151; INT CA-133

Birney, (Alfred) Earle 1904-1995 .. **CLC 1, 4, 6, 11; PC 52**
See also CA 1-4R; CANR 5, 20; CN 1, 2, 3, 4; CP 1, 2, 3, 4, 5, 6; DAC; DAM MST, POET; DLB 88; MTCW 1; PFS 8; RGEL 2

Biruni, al 973-1048(?) .... **CMLC 28**

Bishop, Elizabeth 1911-1979 ..... **CLC 1, 4, 9, 13, 15, 32; PC 3, 34; TCLC 121**
See also AMWR 2; AMWS 1; CA 5-8R; CAAS 89-92; CABS 2; CANR 26, 61, 108; CDALB 1968-1988; CP 1, 2, 3; DA; DA3; DAC; DAM MST, POET; DLB 5, 169; EWL 3; GLL 2; MAL 5; MBL; MTCW 1, 2; PAB; PFS 6, 12; RGAL 4; SATA-Obit 24; TUS; WP

Bishop, John 1935- .... **CLC 10**
See also CA 105

Bishop, John Peale 1892-1944 ..... **TCLC 103**
See also CA 155; CAAE 107; DLB 4, 9, 45; MAL 5; RGAL 4

Bissett, Bill 1939- .... **CLC 18; PC 14**
See also CA 69-72; 19; CANR 15; CCA 1; CP 1, 2, 3, 4, 5, 6, 7; DLB 53; MTCW 1

Bissoondath, Neil (Devindra)
1955- .... **CLC 120**
See also CA 136; CANR 123; CN 6, 7; DAC

Bitov, Andrei (Georgievich) 1937- ... **CLC 57**
See also CA 142; DLB 302

Biyidi, Alexandre 1932-
See Beti, Mongo
See also BW 1, 3; CA 124; CAAE 114; CANR 81; DA3; MTCW 1, 2

Bjarme, Brynjolf
See Ibsen, Henrik (Johan)

Bjoernson, Bjoernstjerne (Martinius)
1832-1910 .... **TCLC 7, 37**
See also CAAE 104

Black, Benjamin
See Banville, John

Black, Robert
See Holdstock, Robert

Blackburn, Paul 1926-1971 .... **CLC 9, 43**
See also BG 1:2; CA 81-84; CAAS 33-36R; CANR 34; CP 1; DLB 16; DLBY 1981

Black Elk 1863-1950 .... **NNAL; TCLC 33**
See also CA 144; DAM MULT; MTCW 2; MTFW 2005; WP

Black Hawk 1767-1838 .... **NNAL**

Black Hobart
See Sanders, (James) Ed(ward)

Blacklin, Malcolm
See Chambers, Aidan

Blackmore, R(ichard) D(oddridge)
1825-1900 .... **TCLC 27**
See also CAAE 120; DLB 18; RGEL 2

Blackmur, R(ichard) P(almer)
1904-1965 .... **CLC 2, 24**
See also AMWS 2; CA 11-12; CAAS 25-28R; CANR 71; CAP 1; DLB 63; EWL 3; MAL 5

Black Tarantula
See Acker, Kathy

Blackwood, Algernon (Henry)
1869-1951 .... **TCLC 5**
See also CA 150; CAAE 105; DLB 153, 156, 178; HGG; SUFW 1

Blackwood, Caroline (Maureen)
1931-1996 .... **CLC 6, 9, 100**
See also BRWS 9; CA 85-88; CAAS 151; CANR 32, 61, 65; CN 3, 4, 5, 6; DLB 14, 207; HGG; MTCW 1

Blade, Alexander
See Hamilton, Edmond; Silverberg, Robert

Blaga, Lucian 1895-1961 .... **CLC 75**
See also CA 157; DLB 220; EWL 3

Blair, Eric (Arthur) 1903-1950 .... **TCLC 123**
See Orwell, George
See also CA 132; CAAE 104; DA; DA3; DAB; DAC; DAM MST, NOV; MTCW 1, 2; MTFW 2005; SATA 29

Blair, Hugh 1718-1800 .... **NCLC 75**

Blais, Marie-Claire 1939- .... **CLC 2, 4, 6, 13, 22**
See also CA 21-24R; 4; CANR 38, 75, 93; CWW 2; DAC; DAM MST; DLB 53; EWL 3; FW; MTCW 1, 2; MTFW 2005; TWA

Blaise, Clark 1940- .... **CLC 29**
See also AITN 2; CA 231; 53-56, 231; 3; CANR 5, 66, 106; CN 4, 5, 6, 7; DLB 53; RGSF 2

Blake, Fairley
See De Voto, Bernard (Augustine)

Blake, Nicholas
See Day Lewis, C(ecil)
See also DLB 77; MSW

Blake, Sterling
See Benford, Gregory (Albert)

Blake, William 1757-1827 . **NCLC 13, 37, 57, 127, 173; PC 12, 63; WLC 1**
See also AAYA 47; BRW 3; BRWR 1; CD-BLB 1789-1832; CLR 52; DA; DA3; DAB; DAC; DAM MST, POET; DLB 93, 163; EXPP; LATS 1:1; LMFS 1; MAI-CYA 1, 2; PAB; PFS 2, 12, 24; SATA 30; TEA; WCH; WLIT 3; WP

Blanchot, Maurice 1907-2003 .... **CLC 135**
See also CA 144; CAAE 117; CAAS 213; CANR 138; DLB 72, 296; EWL 3

Blasco Ibanez, Vicente 1867-1928 . **TCLC 12**
See Ibanez, Vicente Blasco
See also BPFB 1; CA 131; CAAE 110; CANR 81; DA3; DAM NOV; EW 8; EWL 3; HW 1, 2; MTCW 1

Blatty, William Peter 1928- .... **CLC 2**
See also CA 5-8R; CANR 9, 124; DAM POP; HGG

Bleeck, Oliver
See Thomas, Ross (Elmore)

Blessing, Lee (Knowlton) 1949- .... **CLC 54**
See also CA 236; CAD; CD 5, 6; DFS 23

Blight, Rose
See Greer, Germaine

Blish, James (Benjamin) 1921-1975 . **CLC 14**
See also BPFB 1; CA 1-4R; CAAS 57-60; CANR 3; CN 2; DLB 8; MTCW 1; SATA 66; SCFW 1, 2; SFW 4

Bliss, Frederick
See Card, Orson Scott

Bliss, Gillian
See Paton Walsh, Jill

Bliss, Reginald
See Wells, H(erbert) G(eorge)

Blixen, Karen (Christentze Dinesen)
1885-1962
See Dinesen, Isak
See also CA 25-28; CANR 22, 50; CAP 2; DA3; DLB 214; LMFS 1; MTCW 1, 2; SATA 44; SSFS 20

Bloch, Robert (Albert) 1917-1994 .... **CLC 33**
See also AAYA 29; CA 179; 5-8R, 179; 20; CAAS 146; CANR 5, 78; DA3; DLB 44; HGG; INT CANR-5; MTCW 2; SATA 12; SATA-Obit 82; SFW 4; SUFW 1, 2

Blok, Alexander (Alexandrovich)
1880-1921 .... **PC 21, TCLC 5**
See also CA 183; CAAE 104; DLB 295; EW 9; EWL 3; LMFS 2; RGWL 2, 3

Blom, Jan
See Breytenbach, Breyten

Cade, Toni
See Bambara, Toni Cade
Cadmus and Harmonia
See Buchan, John
Caedmon fl. 658-680 .... **CMLC 7**
See also DLB 146
Caeiro, Alberto
See Pessoa, Fernando (Antonio Nogueira)
Caesar, Julius .... **CMLC 47**
See Julius Caesar
See also AW 1; RGWL 2, 3; WLIT 8
Cage, John (Milton), (Jr.)
1912-1992 .... **CLC 41; PC 58**
See also CA 13-16R; CAAS 169; CANR 9,
78; DLB 193; INT CANR-9; TCLE 1:1
Cahan, Abraham 1860-1951 .... **TCLC 71**
See also CA 154; CAAE 108; DLB 9, 25,
28; MAL 5; RGAL 4
Cain, G.
See Cabrera Infante, G.
Cain, Guillermo
See Cabrera Infante, G.
Cain, James M(allahan) 1892-1977 .. **CLC 3,
11, 28**
See also AITN 1; BPFB 1; CA 17-20R;
CAAS 73-76; CANR 8, 34, 61; CMW 4;
CN 1, 2; DLB 226; EWL 3; MAL 5;
MSW; MTCW 1; RGAL 4
Caine, Hall 1853-1931 .... **TCLC 97**
See also RHW
Caine, Mark
See Raphael, Frederic (Michael)
Calasso, Roberto 1941- .... **CLC 81**
See also CA 143; CANR 89
Calderon de la Barca, Pedro
1600-1681 . **DC 3; HLCS 1; LC 23, 136**
See also DFS 23; EW 2; RGWL 2, 3; TWA
Caldwell, Erskine 1903-1987 ... **CLC 1, 8, 14,
50, 60; SSC 19; TCLC 117**
See also AITN 1; AMW; BPFB 1; CA 1-4R;
1; CAAS 121; CANR 2, 33; CN 1, 2, 3,
4; DA3; DAM NOV; DLB 9, 86; EWL 3;
MAL 5; MTCW 1, 2; MTFW 2005;
RGAL 4; RGSF 2; TUS
Caldwell, (Janet Miriam) Taylor (Holland)
1900-1985 .... **CLC 2, 28, 39**
See also BPFB 1; CA 5-8R; CAAS 116;
CANR 5; DA3; DAM NOV, POP; DLBD
17; MTCW 2; RHW
Calhoun, John Caldwell
1782-1850 .... **NCLC 15**
See also DLB 3, 248
Calisher, Hortense 1911- ..... **CLC 2, 4, 8, 38,
134; SSC 15**
See also CA 1-4R; CANR 1, 22, 117; CN
1, 2, 3, 4, 5, 6, 7; DA3; DAM NOV; DLB
2, 218; INT CANR-22; MAL 5; MTCW
1, 2; MTFW 2005; RGAL 4; RGSF 2
Callaghan, Morley Edward
1903-1990 ..... **CLC 3, 14, 41, 65; TCLC
145**
See also CA 9-12R; CAAS 132; CANR 33,
73; CN 1, 2, 3, 4; DAC; DAM MST; DLB
68; EWL 3; MTCW 1, 2; MTFW 2005;
RGEL 2; RGSF 2; SSFS 19
Callimachus c. 305B.C.-c.
240B.C. .... **CMLC 18**
See also AW 1; DLB 176; RGWL 2, 3
Calvin, Jean
See Calvin, John
See also DLB 327; GFL Beginnings to 1789
Calvin, John 1509-1564 .... **LC 37**
See Calvin, Jean
Calvino, Italo 1923-1985 .... **CLC 5, 8, 11, 22,
33, 39, 73; SSC 3, 48; TCLC 183**
See also AAYA 58; CA 85-88; CAAS 116;
CANR 23, 61, 132; DAM NOV; DLB
196; EW 13; EWL 3; MTCW 1, 2; MTFW
2005; RGHL; RGSF 2; RGWL 2, 3; SFW
4; SSFS 12; WLIT 7

Camara Laye
See Laye, Camara
See also EWL 3
Camden, William 1551-1623 .... **LC 77**
See also DLB 172
Cameron, Carey 1952- .... **CLC 59**
See also CA 135
Cameron, Peter 1959- .... **CLC 44**
See also AMWS 12; CA 125; CANR 50,
117; DLB 234; GLL 2
Camoens, Luis Vaz de 1524(?)-1580
See Camoes, Luis de
See also EW 2
Camoes, Luis de 1524(?)-1580 . **HLCS 1; LC
62; PC 31**
See Camoens, Luis Vaz de
See also DLB 287; RGWL 2, 3
Campana, Dino 1885-1932 .... **TCLC 20**
See also CA 246; CAAE 117; DLB 114;
EWL 3
Campanella, Tommaso 1568-1639 .... **LC 32**
See also RGWL 2, 3
Campbell, John W(ood, Jr.)
1910-1971 .... **CLC 32**
See also CA 21-22; CAAS 29-32R; CANR
34; CAP 2; DLB 8; MTCW 1; SCFW 1,
2; SFW 4
Campbell, Joseph 1904-1987 .... **CLC 69;
TCLC 140**
See also AAYA 3, 66; BEST 89:2; CA 1-4R;
CAAS 124; CANR 3, 28, 61, 107; DA3;
MTCW 1, 2
Campbell, Maria 1940- .... **CLC 85; NNAL**
See also CA 102; CANR 54; CCA 1; DAC
Campbell, (John) Ramsey 1946- ..... **CLC 42;
SSC 19**
See also AAYA 51; CA 228; 57-60, 228;
CANR 7, 102; DLB 261; HGG; INT
CANR-7; SUFW 1, 2
Campbell, (Ignatius) Roy (Dunnachie)
1901-1957 .... **TCLC 5**
See also AFW; CA 155; CAAE 104; DLB
20, 225; EWL 3; MTCW 2; RGEL 2
Campbell, Thomas 1777-1844 .... **NCLC 19**
See also DLB 93, 144; RGEL 2
Campbell, Wilfred .... **TCLC 9**
See Campbell, William
Campbell, William 1858(?)-1918
See Campbell, Wilfred
See also CAAE 106; DLB 92
Campbell, William Edward March
1893-1954
See March, William
See also CAAE 108
Campion, Jane 1954- .... **CLC 95, 229**
See also AAYA 33; CA 138; CANR 87
Campion, Thomas 1567-1620 .... **LC 78**
See also CDBLB Before 1660; DAM POET;
DLB 58, 172; RGEL 2
Camus, Albert 1913-1960 ...... **CLC 1, 2, 4, 9,
11, 14, 32, 63, 69, 124; DC 2; SSC 9,
76; WLC 1**
See also AAYA 36; AFW; BPFB 1; CA 89-
92; CANR 131; DA; DA3; DAB; DAC;
DAM DRAM, MST, NOV; DLB 72, 321,
329; EW 13; EWL 3; EXPN; EXPS; GFL
1789 to the Present; LATS 1:2; LMFS 2;
MTCW 1, 2; MTFW 2005; NFS 6, 16;
RGHL; RGSF 2; RGWL 2, 3; SSFS 4;
TWA
Canby, Vincent 1924-2000 .... **CLC 13**
See also CA 81-84; CAAS 191
Cancale
See Desnos, Robert

Canetti, Elias 1905-1994 .. **CLC 3, 14, 25, 75,
86; TCLC 157**
See also CA 21-24R; CAAS 146; CANR
23, 61, 79; CDWLB 2; CWW 2; DA3;
DLB 85, 124, 329; EW 12; EWL 3;
MTCW 1, 2; MTFW 2005; RGWL 2, 3;
TWA
Canfield, Dorothea F.
See Fisher, Dorothy (Frances) Canfield
Canfield, Dorothea Frances
See Fisher, Dorothy (Frances) Canfield
Canfield, Dorothy
See Fisher, Dorothy (Frances) Canfield
Canin, Ethan 1960- .... **CLC 55; SSC 70**
See also CA 135; CAAE 131; MAL 5
Cankar, Ivan 1876-1918 .... **TCLC 105**
See also CDWLB 4; DLB 147; EWL 3
Cannon, Curt
See Hunter, Evan
Cao, Lan 1961- .... **CLC 109**
See also CA 165
Cape, Judith
See Page, P(atricia) K(athleen)
See also CCA 1
Capek, Karel 1890-1938 .... **DC 1; SSC 36;
TCLC 6, 37; WLC 1**
See also CA 140; CAAE 104; CDWLB 4;
DA; DA3; DAB; DAC; DAM DRAM,
MST, NOV; DFS 7, 11; DLB 215; EW
10; EWL 3; MTCW 2; MTFW 2005;
RGSF 2; RGWL 2, 3; SCFW 1, 2; SFW 4
Capella, Martianus fl. 4th cent. .... **CMLC 84**
Capote, Truman 1924-1984 . **CLC 1, 3, 8, 13,
19, 34, 38, 58; SSC 2, 47, 93; TCLC
164; WLC 1**
See also AAYA 61; AMWS 3; BPFB 1; CA
5-8R; CAAS 113; CANR 18, 62; CDALB
1941-1968; CN 1, 2, 3; CPW; DA; DA3;
DAB; DAC; DAM MST, NOV, POP;
DLB 2, 185, 227; DLBY 1980, 1984;
EWL 3; EXPS; GLL 1; LAIT 3; MAL 5;
MTCW 1, 2; MTFW 2005; NCFS 2;
RGAL 4; RGSF 2; SATA 91; SSFS 2;
TUS
Capra, Frank 1897-1991 .... **CLC 16**
See also AAYA 52; CA 61-64; CAAS 135
Caputo, Philip 1941- .... **CLC 32**
See also AAYA 60; CA 73-76; CANR 40,
135; YAW
Caragiale, Ion Luca 1852-1912 ...... **TCLC 76**
See also CA 157
Card, Orson Scott 1951- .... **CLC 44, 47, 50**
See also AAYA 11, 42; BPFB 1; BYA 5, 8;
CA 102; CANR 27, 47, 73, 102, 106, 133;
CLR 116; CPW; DA3; DAM POP; FANT;
INT CANR-27; MTCW 1, 2; MTFW
2005; NFS 5; SATA 83, 127; SCFW 2;
SFW 4; SUFW 2; YAW
Cardenal, Ernesto 1925- .... **CLC 31, 161;
HLC 1; PC 22**
See also CA 49-52; CANR 2, 32, 66, 138;
CWW 2; DAM MULT, POET; DLB 290;
EWL 3; HW 1, 2; LAWS 1; MTCW 1, 2;
MTFW 2005; RGWL 2, 3
Cardinal, Marie 1929-2001 .... **CLC 189**
See also CA 177; CWW 2; DLB 83; FW
Cardozo, Benjamin N(athan)
1870-1938 .... **TCLC 65**
See also CA 164; CAAE 117
Carducci, Giosue (Alessandro Giuseppe)
1835-1907 .... **PC 46; TCLC 32**
See also CA 163; DLB 329; EW 7; RGWL
2, 3
Carew, Thomas 1595(?)-1640 . **LC 13; PC 29**
See also BRW 2; DLB 126; PAB; RGEL 2
Carey, Ernestine Gilbreth
1908-2006 .... **CLC 17**
See also CA 5-8R; CAAS 254; CANR 71;
SATA 2

Cato, Marcus Porcius
234B.C.-149B.C. .... **CMLC 21**
See Cato the Elder

Cato, Marcus Porcius, the Elder
See Cato, Marcus Porcius

Cato the Elder
See Cato, Marcus Porcius
See also DLB 211

Catton, (Charles) Bruce 1899-1978 . **CLC 35**
See also AITN 1; CA 5-8R; CAAS 81-84;
CANR 7, 74; DLB 17; MTCW 2; MTFW
2005; SATA 2; SATA-Obit 24

Catullus c. 84B.C.-54B.C. .... **CMLC 18**
See also AW 2; CDWLB 1; DLB 211;
RGWL 2, 3; WLIT 8

Cauldwell, Frank
See King, Francis (Henry)

Caunitz, William J. 1933-1996 .... **CLC 34**
See also BEST 89:3; CA 130; CAAE 125;
CAAS 152; CANR 73; INT CA-130

Causley, Charles (Stanley)
1917-2003 .... **CLC 7**
See also CA 9-12R; CAAS 223; CANR 5,
35, 94; CLR 30; CP 1, 2, 3, 4, 5; CWRI
5; DLB 27; MTCW 1; SATA 3, 66; SATA-
Obit 149

Caute, (John) David 1936- .... **CLC 29**
See also CA 1-4R; 4; CANR 1, 33, 64, 120;
CBD; CD 5, 6; CN 1, 2, 3, 4, 5, 6, 7;
DAM NOV; DLB 14, 231

Cavafy, C(onstantine) P(eter) .... **PC 36;**
TCLC 2, 7
See Kavafis, Konstantinos Petrou
See also CA 148; DA3; DAM POET; EW
8; EWL 3; MTCW 2; PFS 19; RGWL 2,
3; WP

Cavalcanti, Guido c. 1250-c.
1300 .... **CMLC 54**
See also RGWL 2, 3; WLIT 7

Cavallo, Evelyn
See Spark, Muriel

Cavanna, Betty .... **CLC 12**
See Harrison, Elizabeth (Allen) Cavanna
See also JRDA; MAICYA 1; SAAS 4;
SATA 1, 30

Cavendish, Margaret Lucas
1623-1673 .... **LC 30, 132**
See also DLB 131, 252, 281; RGEL 2

Caxton, William 1421(?)-1491(?) .... **LC 17**
See also DLB 170

Cayer, D. M.
See Duffy, Maureen (Patricia)

Cayrol, Jean 1911-2005 .... **CLC 11**
See also CA 89-92; CAAS 236; DLB 83;
EWL 3

Cela (y Trulock), Camilo Jose
See Cela, Camilo Jose
See also CWW 2

Cela, Camilo Jose 1916-2002 .... **CLC 4, 13,**
59, 122; HLC 1; SSC 71
See Cela (y Trulock), Camilo Jose
See also BEST 90:2; CA 21-24R; 10; CAAS
206; CANR 21, 32, 76, 139; DAM MULT;
DLB 322; DLBY 1989; EW 13; EWL 3;
HW 1; MTCW 1, 2; MTFW 2005; RGSF
2; RGWL 2, 3

Celan, Paul .... **CLC 10, 19, 53, 82; PC 10**
See Antschel, Paul
See also CDWLB 2; DLB 69; EWL 3;
RGHL; RGWL 2, 3

Celine, Louis-Ferdinand .. **CLC 1, 3, 4, 7, 9,**
15, 47, 124
See Destouches, Louis-Ferdinand
See also DLB 72; EW 11; EWL 3; GFL
1789 to the Present; RGWL 2, 3

Cellini, Benvenuto 1500-1571 .... **LC 7**
See also WLIT 7

Cendrars, Blaise .... **CLC 18, 106**
See Sauser-Hall, Frederic
See also DLB 258; EWL 3; GFL 1789 to
the Present; RGWL 2, 3; WP

Centlivre, Susanna 1669(?)-1723 .... **DC 25;**
LC 65
See also DLB 84; RGEL 2

Cernuda (y Bidon), Luis
1902-1963 .... **CLC 54; PC 62**
See also CA 131; CAAS 89-92; DAM
POET; DLB 134; EWL 3; GLL 1; HW 1;
RGWL 2, 3

Cervantes, Lorna Dee 1954- ..... **HLCS 1; PC**
35
See also CA 131; CANR 80; CP 7; CWP;
DLB 82; EXPP; HW 1; LLW

Cervantes (Saavedra), Miguel de
1547-1616 .... **HLCS; LC 6, 23, 93; SSC**
12; WLC 1
See also AAYA 56; BYA 1, 14; DA; DAB;
DAC; DAM MST, NOV; EW 2; LAIT 1;
LATS 1:1; LMFS 1; NFS 8; RGSF 2;
RGWL 2, 3; TWA

Cesaire, Aime 1913- ..... **BLC 1; CLC 19, 32,**
112; DC 22; PC 25
See also BW 2, 3; CA 65-68; CANR 24,
43, 81; CWW 2; DA3; DAM MULT,
POET; DLB 321; EWL 3; GFL 1789 to
the Present; MTCW 1, 2; MTFW 2005;
WP

Chabon, Michael 1963- ... **CLC 55, 149; SSC**
59
See also AAYA 45; AMWS 11; CA 139;
CANR 57, 96, 127, 138; DLB 278; MAL
5; MTFW 2005; SATA 145

Chabrol, Claude 1930- .... **CLC 16**
See also CA 110

Chairil Anwar
See Anwar, Chairil
See also EWL 3

Challans, Mary 1905-1983
See Renault, Mary
See also CA 81-84; CAAS 111; CANR 74;
DA3; MTCW 2; MTFW 2005; SATA 23;
SATA-Obit 36; TEA

Challis, George
See Faust, Frederick (Schiller)

Chambers, Aidan 1934- .... **CLC 35**
See also AAYA 27; CA 25-28R; CANR 12,
31, 58, 116; JRDA; MAICYA 1, 2; SAAS
12; SATA 1, 69, 108, 171; WYA; YAW

Chambers, James 1948-
See Cliff, Jimmy
See also CAAE 124

Chambers, Jessie
See Lawrence, D(avid) H(erbert Richards)
See also GLL 1

Chambers, Robert W(illiam)
1865-1933 .... **SSC 92; TCLC 41**
See also CA 165; DLB 202; HGG; SATA
107; SUFW 1

Chambers, (David) Whittaker
1901-1961 .... **TCLC 129**
See also CAAS 89-92; DLB 303

Chamisso, Adelbert von
1781-1838 .... **NCLC 82**
See also DLB 90; RGWL 2, 3; SUFW 1

Chance, James T.
See Carpenter, John (Howard)

Chance, John T.
See Carpenter, John (Howard)

Chandler, Raymond (Thornton)
1888-1959 .... **SSC 23; TCLC 1, 7, 179**
See also AAYA 25; AMWC 2; AMWS 4;
BPFB 1; CA 129; CAAE 104; CANR 60,
107; CDALB 1929-1941; CMW 4; DA3;
DLB 226, 253; DLBD 6; EWL 3; MAL
5; MSW; MTCW 1, 2; MTFW 2005; NFS
17; RGAL 4; TUS

Chang, Diana 1934- .... **AAL**
See also CA 228; CWP; DLB 312; EXPP

Chang, Eileen 1921-1995 .... **AAL; SSC 28;**
TCLC 184
See Chang Ai-Ling; Zhang Ailing
See also CA 166

Chang, Jung 1952- .... **CLC 71**
See also CA 142

Chang Ai-Ling
See Chang, Eileen
See also EWL 3

Channing, William Ellery
1780-1842 .... **NCLC 17**
See also DLB 1, 59, 235; RGAL 4

Chao, Patricia 1955- .... **CLC 119**
See also CA 163; CANR 155

Chaplin, Charles Spencer
1889-1977 .... **CLC 16**
See Chaplin, Charlie
See also CA 81-84; CAAS 73-76

Chaplin, Charlie
See Chaplin, Charles Spencer
See also AAYA 61; DLB 44

Chapman, George 1559(?)-1634 . **DC 19; LC**
22, 116
See also BRW 1; DAM DRAM; DLB 62,
121; LMFS 1; RGEL 2

Chapman, Graham 1941-1989 .... **CLC 21**
See Monty Python
See also CA 116; CAAS 129; CANR 35, 95

Chapman, John Jay 1862-1933 .... **TCLC 7**
See also AMWS 14; CA 191; CAAE 104

Chapman, Lee
See Bradley, Marion Zimmer
See also GLL 1

Chapman, Walker
See Silverberg, Robert

Chappell, Fred (Davis) 1936- .... **CLC 40, 78,**
162
See also CA 198; 5-8R, 198; 4; CANR 8,
33, 67, 110; CN 6; CP 6, 7; CSW; DLB
6, 105; HGG

Char, Rene(-Emile) 1907-1988 .... **CLC 9, 11,**
14, 55; PC 56
See also CA 13-16R; CAAS 124; CANR
32; DAM POET; DLB 258; EWL 3; GFL
1789 to the Present; MTCW 1, 2; RGWL
2, 3

Charby, Jay
See Ellison, Harlan

Chardin, Pierre Teilhard de
See Teilhard de Chardin, (Marie Joseph)
Pierre

Chariton fl. 1st cent. (?)- .... **CMLC 49**

Charlemagne 742-814 .... **CMLC 37**

Charles I 1600-1649 .... **LC 13**

Charriere, Isabelle de 1740-1805 .. **NCLC 66**
See also DLB 313

Chartier, Alain c. 1392-1430 .... **LC 94**
See also DLB 208

Chartier, Emile-Auguste
See Alain

Charyn, Jerome 1937- .... **CLC 5, 8, 18**
See also CA 5-8R; 1; CANR 7, 61, 101,
158; CMW 4; CN 1, 2, 3, 4, 5, 6, 7;
DLBY 1983; MTCW 1

Chase, Adam
See Marlowe, Stephen

Chase, Mary (Coyle) 1907-1981 .... **DC 1**
See also CA 77-80; CAAS 105; CAD;
CWD; DFS 11; DLB 228; SATA 17;
SATA-Obit 29

Chase, Mary Ellen 1887-1973 .... **CLC 2;**
TCLC 124
See also CA 13-16; CAAS 41-44R; CAP 1;
SATA 10

Chase, Nicholas
See Hyde, Anthony
See also CCA 1

Churchill, Sir Winston (Leonard Spencer)
1874-1965 .... **TCLC 113**
See also BRW 6; CA 97-100; CDBLB
1890-1914; DA3; DLB 100, 329; DLBD
16; LAIT 4; MTCW 1, 2

Chute, Carolyn 1947- .... **CLC 39**
See also CA 123; CANR 135; CN 7

Ciardi, John (Anthony) 1916-1986 . **CLC 10,
40, 44, 129; PC 69**
See also CA 5-8R; 2; CAAS 118; CANR 5,
33; CLR 19; CP 1, 2, 3, 4; CWRI 5; DAM
POET; DLB 5; DLBY 1986; INT
CANR-5; MAICYA 1, 2; MAL 5; MTCW
1, 2; MTFW 2005; RGAL 4; SAAS 26;
SATA 1, 65; SATA-Obit 46

Cibber, Colley 1671-1757 .... **LC 66**
See also DLB 84; RGEL 2

Cicero, Marcus Tullius
106B.C.-43B.C. .... **CMLC 3, 81**
See also AW 1; CDWLB 1; DLB 211;
RGWL 2, 3; WLIT 8

Cimino, Michael 1943- .... **CLC 16**
See also CA 105

Cioran, E(mil) M. 1911-1995 .... **CLC 64**
See also CA 25-28R; CAAS 149; CANR
91; DLB 220; EWL 3

Cisneros, Sandra 1954- .... **CLC 69, 118, 193;
HLC 1; PC 52; SSC 32, 72**
See also AAYA 9, 53; AMWS 7; CA 131;
CANR 64, 118; CN 7; CWP; DA3; DAM
MULT; DLB 122, 152; EWL 3; EXPN;
FL 1:5; FW; HW 1, 2; LAIT 5; LATS 1:2;
LLW; MAICYA 2; MAL 5; MTCW 2;
MTFW 2005; NFS 2; PFS 19; RGAL 4;
RGSF 2; SSFS 3, 13; WLIT 1; YAW

Cixous, Helene 1937- .... **CLC 92**
See also CA 126; CANR 55, 123; CWW 2;
DLB 83, 242; EWL 3; FL 1:5; FW; GLL
2; MTCW 1, 2; MTFW 2005; TWA

Clair, Rene .... **CLC 20**
See Chomette, Rene Lucien

Clampitt, Amy 1920-1994 .... **CLC 32; PC 19**
See also AMWS 9; CA 110; CAAS 146;
CANR 29, 79; CP 4, 5; DLB 105; MAL 5

Clancy, Thomas L., Jr. 1947-
See Clancy, Tom
See also CA 131; CAAE 125; CANR 62,
105; DA3; INT CA-131; MTCW 1, 2;
MTFW 2005

Clancy, Tom .... **CLC 45, 112**
See Clancy, Thomas L., Jr.
See also AAYA 9, 51; BEST 89:1, 90:1;
BPFB 1; BYA 10, 11; CANR 132; CMW
4; CPW; DAM NOV, POP; DLB 227

Clare, John 1793-1864 .. **NCLC 9, 86; PC 23**
See also BRWS 11; DAB; DAM POET;
DLB 55, 96; RGEL 2

Clarin
See Alas (y Urena), Leopoldo (Enrique
Garcia)

Clark, Al C.
See Goines, Donald

Clark, Brian (Robert)
See Clark, (Robert) Brian
See also CD 6

Clark, (Robert) Brian 1932- .... **CLC 29**
See Clark, Brian (Robert)
See also CA 41-44R; CANR 67; CBD; CD
5

Clark, Curt
See Westlake, Donald E.

Clark, Eleanor 1913-1996 .... **CLC 5, 19**
See also CA 9-12R; CAAS 151; CANR 41;
CN 1, 2, 3, 4, 5, 6; DLB 6

Clark, J. P.
See Clark Bekederemo, J.P.
See also CDWLB 3; DLB 117

Clark, John Pepper
See Clark Bekederemo, J.P.
See also AFW; CD 5; CP 1, 2, 3, 4, 5, 6, 7;
RGEL 2

Clark, Kenneth (Mackenzie)
1903-1983 .... **TCLC 147**
See also CA 93-96; CAAS 109; CANR 36;
MTCW 1, 2; MTFW 2005

Clark, M. R.
See Clark, Mavis Thorpe

Clark, Mavis Thorpe 1909-1999 ...... **CLC 12**
See also CA 57-60; CANR 8, 37, 107; CLR
30; CWRI 5; MAICYA 1, 2; SAAS 5;
SATA 8, 74

Clark, Walter Van Tilburg
1909-1971 .... **CLC 28**
See also CA 9-12R; CAAS 33-36R; CANR
63, 113; CN 1; DLB 9, 206; LAIT 2;
MAL 5; RGAL 4; SATA 8; TCWW 1, 2

Clark Bekederemo, J.P. 1935- . **BLC 1; CLC
38; DC 5**
See Bekederemo, J. P. Clark; Clark, J. P.;
Clark, John Pepper
See also BW 1; CA 65-68; CANR 16, 72;
DAM DRAM, MULT; DFS 13; EWL 3;
MTCW 2; MTFW 2005

Clarke, Arthur C. 1917- .... **CLC 1, 4, 13, 18,
35, 136; SSC 3**
See also AAYA 4, 33; BPFB 1; BYA 13;
CA 1-4R; CANR 2, 28, 55, 74, 130; CLR
119; CN 1, 2, 3, 4, 5, 6, 7; CPW; DA3;
DAM POP; DLB 261; JRDA; LAIT 5;
MAICYA 1, 2; MTCW 1, 2; MTFW 2005;
SATA 13, 70, 115; SCFW 1, 2; SFW 4;
SSFS 4, 18; TCLE 1:1; YAW

Clarke, Austin 1896-1974 .... **CLC 6, 9**
See also CA 29-32; CAAS 49-52; CAP 2;
CP 1, 2; DAM POET; DLB 10, 20; EWL
3; RGEL 2

Clarke, Austin C. 1934- . **BLC 1; CLC 8, 53;
SSC 45**
See also BW 1; CA 25-28R; 16; CANR 14,
32, 68, 140; CN 1, 2, 3, 4, 5, 6, 7; DAC;
DAM MULT; DLB 53, 125; DNFS 2;
MTCW 2; MTFW 2005; RGSF 2

Clarke, Gillian 1937- .... **CLC 61**
See also CA 106; CP 3, 4, 5, 6, 7; CWP;
DLB 40

Clarke, Marcus (Andrew Hislop)
1846-1881 .... **NCLC 19; SSC 94**
See also DLB 230; RGEL 2; RGSF 2

Clarke, Shirley 1925-1997 .... **CLC 16**
See also CA 189

Clash, The
See Headon, (Nicky) Topper; Jones, Mick;
Simonon, Paul; Strummer, Joe

Claudel, Paul (Louis Charles Marie)
1868-1955 .... **TCLC 2, 10**
See also CA 165; CAAE 104; DLB 192,
258, 321; EW 8; EWL 3; GFL 1789 to
the Present; RGWL 2, 3; TWA

Claudian 370(?)-404(?) .... **CMLC 46**
See also RGWL 2, 3

Claudius, Matthias 1740-1815 .... **NCLC 75**
See also DLB 97

Clavell, James 1925-1994 .... **CLC 6, 25, 87**
See also BPFB 1; CA 25-28R; CAAS 146;
CANR 26, 48; CN 5; CPW; DA3; DAM
NOV, POP; MTCW 1, 2; MTFW 2005;
NFS 10; RHW

Clayman, Gregory .... **CLC 65**

Cleaver, (Leroy) Eldridge
1935-1998 .... **BLC 1; CLC 30, 119**
See also BW 1, 3; CA 21-24R; CAAS 167;
CANR 16, 75; DA3; DAM MULT;
MTCW 2; YAW

Cleese, John (Marwood) 1939- .... **CLC 21**
See Monty Python
See also CA 116; CAAE 112; CANR 35;
MTCW 1

Cleishbotham, Jebediah
See Scott, Sir Walter

Cleland, John 1710-1789 .... **LC 2, 48**
See also DLB 39; RGEL 2

Clemens, Samuel Langhorne 1835-1910
See Twain, Mark
See also CA 135; CAAE 104; CDALB
1865-1917; DA; DA3; DAB; DAC; DAM
MST, NOV; DLB 12, 23, 64, 74, 186,
189; JRDA; LMFS 1; MAICYA 1, 2;
NCFS 4; NFS 20; SATA 100; YABC 2

Clement of Alexandria
150(?)-215(?) .... **CMLC 41**

Cleophil
See Congreve, William

Clerihew, E.
See Bentley, E(dmund) C(lerihew)

Clerk, N. W.
See Lewis, C.S.

Cleveland, John 1613-1658 .... **LC 106**
See also DLB 126; RGEL 2

Cliff, Jimmy .... **CLC 21**
See Chambers, James
See also CA 193

Cliff, Michelle 1946- .... **BLCS; CLC 120**
See also BW 2; CA 116; CANR 39, 72; CD-
WLB 3; DLB 157; FW; GLL 2

Clifford, Lady Anne 1590-1676 .... **LC 76**
See also DLB 151

Clifton, Lucille 1936- ... **BLC 1; CLC 19, 66,
162; PC 17**
See also AFAW 2; BW 2, 3; CA 49-52;
CANR 2, 24, 42, 76, 97, 138; CLR 5; CP
2, 3, 4, 5, 6, 7; CSW; CWP; CWRI 5;
DA3; DAM MULT, POET; DLB 5, 41;
EXPP; MAICYA 1, 2; MTCW 1, 2;
MTFW 2005; PFS 1, 14; SATA 20, 69,
128; WP

Clinton, Dirk
See Silverberg, Robert

Clough, Arthur Hugh 1819-1861 .. **NCLC 27,
163**
See also BRW 5; DLB 32; RGEL 2

Clutha, Janet Paterson Frame 1924-2004
See Frame, Janet
See also CA 1-4R; CAAS 224; CANR 2,
36, 76, 135; MTCW 1, 2; SATA 119

Clyne, Terence
See Blatty, William Peter

Cobalt, Martin
See Mayne, William (James Carter)

Cobb, Irvin S(hrewsbury)
1876-1944 .... **TCLC 77**
See also CA 175; DLB 11, 25, 86

Cobbett, William 1763-1835 .... **NCLC 49**
See also DLB 43, 107, 158; RGEL 2

Coburn, D(onald) L(ee) 1938- .... **CLC 10**
See also CA 89-92; DFS 23

Cocteau, Jean 1889-1963 ... **CLC 1, 8, 15, 16,
43; DC 17; TCLC 119; WLC 2**
See also AAYA 74; CA 25-28; CANR 40;
CAP 2; DA; DA3; DAB; DAC; DAM
DRAM, MST, NOV; DLB 65, 258, 321;
EW 10; EWL 3; GFL 1789 to the Present;
MTCW 1, 2; RGWL 2, 3; TWA

Cocteau, Jean Maurice Eugene Clement
See Cocteau, Jean

Codrescu, Andrei 1946- .... **CLC 46, 121**
See also CA 33-36R; 19; CANR 13, 34, 53,
76, 125; CN 7; DA3; DAM POET; MAL
5; MTCW 2; MTFW 2005

Coe, Max
See Bourne, Randolph S(illiman)

Coe, Tucker
See Westlake, Donald E.

Coen, Ethan 1958- .... **CLC 108**
See also AAYA 54; CA 126; CANR 85

Coen, Joel 1955- .... **CLC 108**
See also AAYA 54, CA 126; CANR 119

Conybeare, Charles Augustus
See Eliot, T(homas) S(tearns)

Cook, Michael 1933-1994 .... **CLC 58**
See also CA 93-96; CANR 68; DLB 53

Cook, Robin 1940- .... **CLC 14**
See also AAYA 32; BEST 90:2; BPFB 1;
CA 111; CAAE 108; CANR 41, 90, 109;
CPW; DA3; DAM POP; HGG; INT CA-
111

Cook, Roy
See Silverberg, Robert

Cooke, Elizabeth 1948- .... **CLC 55**
See also CA 129

Cooke, John Esten 1830-1886 .... **NCLC 5**
See also DLB 3, 248; RGAL 4

Cooke, John Estes
See Baum, L(yman) Frank

Cooke, M. E.
See Creasey, John

Cooke, Margaret
See Creasey, John

Cooke, Rose Terry 1827-1892 ...... **NCLC 110**
See also DLB 12, 74

Cook-Lynn, Elizabeth 1930- .... **CLC 93;
NNAL**
See also CA 133; DAM MULT; DLB 175

Cooney, Ray .... **CLC 62**
See also CBD

Cooper, Anthony Ashley 1671-1713 .. **LC 107**
See also DLB 101

Cooper, Dennis 1953- .... **CLC 203**
See also CA 133; CANR 72, 86; GLL 1;
HGG

Cooper, Douglas 1960- .... **CLC 86**

Cooper, Henry St. John
See Creasey, John

Cooper, J. California (?)- .... **CLC 56**
See also AAYA 12; BW 1; CA 125; CANR
55; DAM MULT; DLB 212

Cooper, James Fenimore
1789-1851 .... **NCLC 1, 27, 54**
See also AAYA 22; AMW; BPFB 1;
CDALB 1640-1865; CLR 105; DA3;
DLB 3, 183, 250, 254; LAIT 1; NFS 9;
RGAL 4; SATA 19; TUS; WCH

Cooper, Susan Fenimore
1813-1894 .... **NCLC 129**
See also ANW; DLB 239, 254

Coover, Robert 1932- .. **CLC 3, 7, 15, 32, 46,
87, 161; SSC 15**
See also AMWS 5; BPFB 1; CA 45-48;
CANR 3, 37, 58, 115; CN 1, 2, 3, 4, 5, 6,
7; DAM NOV; DLB 2, 227; DLBY 1981;
EWL 3; MAL 5; MTCW 1, 2; MTFW
2005; RGAL 4; RGSF 2

Copeland, Stewart (Armstrong)
1952- .... **CLC 26**

Copernicus, Nicolaus 1473-1543 .... **LC 45**

Coppard, A(lfred) E(dgar)
1878-1957 .... **SSC 21; TCLC 5**
See also BRWS 8; CA 167; CAAE 114;
DLB 162; EWL 3; HGG; RGEL 2; RGSF
2; SUFW 1; YABC 1

Coppee, Francois 1842-1908 .... **TCLC 25**
See also CA 170; DLB 217

Coppola, Francis Ford 1939- ... **CLC 16, 126**
See also AAYA 39; CA 77-80; CANR 40,
78; DLB 44

Copway, George 1818-1869 .... **NNAL**
See also DAM MULT; DLB 175, 183

Corbiere, Tristan 1845-1875 .... **NCLC 43**
See also DLB 217; GFL 1789 to the Present

Corcoran, Barbara (Asenath)
1911- .... **CLC 17**
See also AAYA 14; CA 191; 21-24R, 191;
2; CANR 11, 28, 48; CLR 50; DLB 52;
JRDA; MAICYA 2; MAICYAS 1; RHW;
SAAS 20; SATA 3, 77; SATA-Essay 125

Cordelier, Maurice
See Giraudoux, Jean(-Hippolyte)

Corelli, Marie .... **TCLC 51**
See Mackay, Mary
See also DLB 34, 156; RGEL 2; SUFW 1

Corinna c. 225B.C.-c. 305B.C. ...... **CMLC 72**

Corman, Cid .... **CLC 9**
See Corman, Sidney
See also CA 2; CP 1, 2, 3, 4, 5, 6, 7; DLB
5, 193

Corman, Sidney 1924-2004
See Corman, Cid
See also CA 85-88; CAAS 225; CANR 44;
DAM POET

Cormier, Robert 1925-2000 .... **CLC 12, 30**
See also AAYA 3, 19; BYA 1, 2, 6, 8, 9;
CA 1-4R; CANR 5, 23, 76, 93; CDALB
1968-1988; CLR 12, 55; DA; DAB; DAC;
DAM MST, NOV; DLB 52; EXPN; INT
CANR-23; JRDA; LAIT 5; MAICYA 1,
2; MTCW 1, 2; MTFW 2005; NFS 2, 18;
SATA 10, 45, 83; SATA-Obit 122; WYA;
YAW

Corn, Alfred (DeWitt III) 1943- .... **CLC 33**
See also CA 179; 179; 25; CANR 44; CP 3,
4, 5, 6, 7; CSW; DLB 120, 282; DLBY
1980

Corneille, Pierre 1606-1684 .. **DC 21; LC 28,
135**
See also DAB; DAM MST; DFS 21; DLB
268; EW 3; GFL Beginnings to 1789;
RGWL 2, 3; TWA

Cornwell, David
See le Carre, John

Cornwell, Patricia 1956- .... **CLC 155**
See also AAYA 16, 56; BPFB 1; CA 134;
CANR 53, 131; CMW 4; CPW; CSW;
DAM POP; DLB 306; MSW; MTCW 2;
MTFW 2005

Cornwell, Patricia Daniels
See Cornwell, Patricia

Corso, Gregory 1930-2001 .... **CLC 1, 11; PC
33**
See also AMWS 12; BG 1:2; CA 5-8R;
CAAS 193; CANR 41, 76, 132; CP 1, 2,
3, 4, 5, 6, 7; DA3; DLB 5, 16, 237; LMFS
2; MAL 5; MTCW 1, 2; MTFW 2005; WP

Cortazar, Julio 1914-1984 ... **CLC 2, 3, 5, 10,
13, 15, 33, 34, 92; HLC 1; SSC 7, 76**
See also BPFB 1; CA 21-24R; CANR 12,
32, 81; CDWLB 3; DA3; DAM MULT,
NOV; DLB 113; EWL 3; EXPS; HW 1,
2; LAW; MTCW 1, 2; MTFW 2005;
RGSF 2; RGWL 2, 3; SSFS 3, 20; TWA;
WLIT 1

Cortes, Hernan 1485-1547 .... **LC 31**

Corvinus, Jakob
See Raabe, Wilhelm (Karl)

Corwin, Cecil
See Kornbluth, C(yril) M.

Cosic, Dobrica 1921- .... **CLC 14**
See also CA 138; CAAE 122; CDWLB 4;
CWW 2; DLB 181; EWL 3

Costain, Thomas B(ertram)
1885-1965 .... **CLC 30**
See also BYA 3; CA 5-8R; CAAS 25-28R;
DLB 9; RHW

Costantini, Humberto 1924(?)-1987 . **CLC 49**
See also CA 131; CAAS 122; EWL 3; HW
1

Costello, Elvis 1954- .... **CLC 21**
See also CA 204

Costenoble, Philostene
See Ghelderode, Michel de

Cotes, Cecil V.
See Duncan, Sara Jeannette

Cotter, Joseph Seamon Sr.
1861-1949 .... **BLC 1; TCLC 28**
See also BW 1; CA 124; DAM MULT; DLB
50

Couch, Arthur Thomas Quiller
See Quiller-Couch, Sir Arthur (Thomas)

Coulton, James
See Hansen, Joseph

Couperus, Louis (Marie Anne)
1863-1923 .... **TCLC 15**
See also CAAE 115; EWL 3; RGWL 2, 3

Coupland, Douglas 1961- .... **CLC 85, 133**
See also AAYA 34; CA 142; CANR 57, 90,
130; CCA 1; CN 7; CPW; DAC; DAM
POP

Court, Wesli
See Turco, Lewis (Putnam)

Courtenay, Bryce 1933- .... **CLC 59**
See also CA 138; CPW

Courtney, Robert
See Ellison, Harlan

Cousteau, Jacques-Yves 1910-1997 .. **CLC 30**
See also CA 65-68; CAAS 159; CANR 15,
67; MTCW 1; SATA 38, 98

Coventry, Francis 1725-1754 .... **LC 46**

Coverdale, Miles c. 1487-1569 .... **LC 77**
See also DLB 167

Cowan, Peter (Walkinshaw)
1914-2002 .... **SSC 28**
See also CA 21-24R; CANR 9, 25, 50, 83;
CN 1, 2, 3, 4, 5, 6, 7; DLB 260; RGSF 2

Coward, Noel (Peirce) 1899-1973 . **CLC 1, 9,
29, 51**
See also AITN 1; BRWS 2; CA 17-18;
CAAS 41-44R; CANR 35, 132; CAP 2;
CBD; CDBLB 1914-1945; DA3; DAM
DRAM; DFS 3, 6; DLB 10, 245; EWL 3;
IDFW 3, 4; MTCW 1, 2; MTFW 2005;
RGEL 2; TEA

Cowley, Abraham 1618-1667 .... **LC 43**
See also BRW 2; DLB 131, 151; PAB;
RGEL 2

Cowley, Malcolm 1898-1989 .... **CLC 39**
See also AMWS 2; CA 5-8R; CAAS 128;
CANR 3, 55; CP 1, 2, 3, 4; DLB 4, 48;
DLBY 1981, 1989; EWL 3; MAL 5;
MTCW 1, 2; MTFW 2005

Cowper, William 1731-1800 ..... **NCLC 8, 94;
PC 40**
See also BRW 3; DA3; DAM POET; DLB
104, 109; RGEL 2

Cox, William Trevor 1928-
See Trevor, William
See also CA 9-12R; CANR 4, 37, 55, 76,
102, 139; DAM NOV; INT CANR-37;
MTCW 1, 2; MTFW 2005; TEA

Coyne, P. J.
See Masters, Hilary

Cozzens, James Gould 1903-1978 . **CLC 1, 4,
11, 92**
See also AMW; BPFB 1; CA 9-12R; CAAS
81-84; CANR 19; CDALB 1941-1968;
CN 1, 2; DLB 9, 294; DLBD 2; DLBY
1984, 1997; EWL 3; MAL 5; MTCW 1,
2; MTFW 2005; RGAL 4

Crabbe, George 1754-1832 .... **NCLC 26, 121**
See also BRW 3; DLB 93; RGEL 2

Crace, Jim 1946- .... **CLC 157; SSC 61**
See also CA 135; CAAE 128; CANR 55,
70, 123; CN 5, 6, 7; DLB 231; INT CA-
135

Craddock, Charles Egbert
See Murfree, Mary Noailles

Craig, A. A.
See Anderson, Poul

Craik, Mrs.
See Craik, Dinah Maria (Mulock)
See also RGEL 2

Deloria, Vine, Jr. 1933-2005 .... **CLC 21, 122;**
  NNAL
    See also CA 53-56; CAAS 245; CANR 5,
    20, 48, 98; DAM MULT; DLB 175;
    MTCW 1; SATA 21; SATA-Obit 171

Deloria, Vine Victor, Jr.
  See Deloria, Vine, Jr.

del Valle-Inclan, Ramon (Maria)
  See Valle-Inclan, Ramon (Maria) del
  See also DLB 322

Del Vecchio, John M(ichael) 1947- .. **CLC 29**
  See also CA 110; DLBD 9

de Man, Paul (Adolph Michel)
  1919-1983 .... **CLC 55**
    See also CA 128; CAAS 111; CANR 61;
    DLB 67; MTCW 1, 2

DeMarinis, Rick 1934- .... **CLC 54**
  See also CA 184; 57-60, 184; 24; CANR 9,
  25, 50, 160; DLB 218; TCWW 2

de Maupassant, (Henri Rene Albert) Guy
  See Maupassant, (Henri Rene Albert) Guy
  de

Dembry, R. Emmet
  See Murfree, Mary Noailles

Demby, William 1922- .... **BLC 1; CLC 53**
  See also BW 1, 3; CA 81-84; CANR 81;
  DAM MULT; DLB 33

de Menton, Francisco
  See Chin, Frank (Chew, Jr.)

Demetrius of Phalerum c.
  307B.C.- .... **CMLC 34**

Demijohn, Thom
  See Disch, Thomas M.

De Mille, James 1833-1880 .... **NCLC 123**
  See also DLB 99, 251

Deming, Richard 1915-1983
  See Queen, Ellery
  See also CA 9-12R; CANR 3, 94; SATA 24

Democritus c. 460B.C.-c. 370B.C. . **CMLC 47**

de Montaigne, Michel (Eyquem)
  See Montaigne, Michel (Eyquem) de

de Montherlant, Henry (Milon)
  See Montherlant, Henry (Milon) de

Demosthenes 384B.C.-322B.C. ...... **CMLC 13**
  See also AW 1; DLB 176; RGWL 2, 3;
  WLIT 8

de Musset, (Louis Charles) Alfred
  See Musset, Alfred de

de Natale, Francine
  See Malzberg, Barry N(athaniel)

de Navarre, Marguerite 1492-1549 ... **LC 61;**
  SSC 85
  See Marguerite d'Angouleme; Marguerite
  de Navarre
  See also DLB 327

Denby, Edwin (Orr) 1903-1983 .... **CLC 48**
  See also CA 138; CAAS 110; CP 1

de Nerval, Gerard
  See Nerval, Gerard de

Denham, John 1615-1669 .... **LC 73**
  See also DLB 58, 126; RGEL 2

Denis, Julio
  See Cortazar, Julio

Denmark, Harrison
  See Zelazny, Roger

Dennis, John 1658-1734 .... **LC 11**
  See also DLB 101; RGEL 2

Dennis, Nigel (Forbes) 1912-1989 ...... **CLC 8**
  See also CA 25-28R; CAAS 129; CN 1, 2,
  3, 4; DLB 13, 15, 233; EWL 3; MTCW 1

Dent, Lester 1904-1959 .... **TCLC 72**
  See also CA 161; CAAE 112; CMW 4;
  DLB 306; SFW 4

De Palma, Brian 1940- .... **CLC 20**
  See also CA 109

De Palma, Brian Russell
  See De Palma, Brian

de Pizan, Christine
  See Christine de Pizan
  See also FL 1:1

De Quincey, Thomas 1785-1859 ..... **NCLC 4,**
  87
  See also BRW 4; CDBLB 1789-1832; DLB
  110, 144; RGEL 2

Deren, Eleanora 1908(?)-1961
  See Deren, Maya
  See also CA 192; CAAS 111

Deren, Maya .... **CLC 16, 102**
  See Deren, Eleanora

Derleth, August (William)
  1909-1971 .... **CLC 31**
    See also BPFB 1; BYA 9, 10; CA 1-4R;
    CAAS 29-32R; CANR 4; CMW 4; CN 1;
    DLB 9; DLBD 17; HGG; SATA 5; SUFW
    1

Der Nister 1884-1950 .... **TCLC 56**
  See Nister, Der

de Routisie, Albert
  See Aragon, Louis

Derrida, Jacques 1930-2004 ...... **CLC 24, 87,**
  225
  See also CA 127; CAAE 124; CAAS 232;
  CANR 76, 98, 133; DLB 242; EWL 3;
  LMFS 2; MTCW 2; TWA

Derry Down Derry
  See Lear, Edward

Dersonnes, Jacques
  See Simenon, Georges (Jacques Christian)

Der Stricker c. 1190-c. 1250 .... **CMLC 75**
  See also DLB 138

Desai, Anita 1937- .... **CLC 19, 37, 97, 175**
  See also BRWS 5; CA 81-84; CANR 33,
  53, 95, 133; CN 1, 2, 3, 4, 5, 6, 7; CWRI
  5; DA3; DAB; DAM NOV; DLB 271,
  323; DNFS 2; EWL 3; FW; MTCW 1, 2;
  MTFW 2005; SATA 63, 126

Desai, Kiran 1971- .... **CLC 119**
  See also BYA 16; CA 171; CANR 127

de Saint-Luc, Jean
  See Glassco, John

de Saint Roman, Arnaud
  See Aragon, Louis

Desbordes-Valmore, Marceline
  1786-1859 .... **NCLC 97**
    See also DLB 217

Descartes, Rene 1596-1650 .... **LC 20, 35**
  See also DLB 268; EW 3; GFL Beginnings
  to 1789

Deschamps, Eustache 1340(?)-1404 .. **LC 103**
  See also DLB 208

De Sica, Vittorio 1901(?)-1974 .... **CLC 20**
  See also CAAS 117

Desnos, Robert 1900-1945 .... **TCLC 22**
  See also CA 151; CAAE 121; CANR 107;
  DLB 258; EWL 3; LMFS 2

Destouches, Louis-Ferdinand
  1894-1961 .... **CLC 9, 15**
    See Celine, Louis-Ferdinand
    See also CA 85-88; CANR 28; MTCW 1

de Tolignac, Gaston
  See Griffith, D(avid Lewelyn) W(ark)

Deutsch, Babette 1895-1982 .... **CLC 18**
  See also BYA 3; CA 1-4R; CAAS 108;
  CANR 4, 79; CP 1, 2, 3; DLB 45; SATA
  1; SATA-Obit 33

Devenant, William 1606-1649 .... **LC 13**

Devkota, Laxmiprasad 1909-1959 . **TCLC 23**
  See also CAAE 123

De Voto, Bernard (Augustine)
  1897-1955 .... **TCLC 29**
    See also CA 160; CAAE 113; DLB 9, 256;
    MAL 5; TCWW 1, 2

De Vries, Peter 1910-1993 ..... **CLC 1, 2, 3, 7,**
  10, 28, 46
  See also CA 17-20R; CAAS 142; CANR
  41; CN 1, 2, 3, 4, 5; DAM NOV; DLB 6;
  DLBY 1982; MAL 5; MTCW 1, 2;
  MTFW 2005

Dewey, John 1859-1952 .... **TCLC 95**
  See also CA 170; CAAE 114; CANR 144;
  DLB 246, 270; RGAL 4

Dexter, John
  See Bradley, Marion Zimmer
  See also GLL 1

Dexter, Martin
  See Faust, Frederick (Schiller)

Dexter, Pete 1943- .... **CLC 34, 55**
  See also BEST 89:2; CA 131; CAAE 127;
  CANR 129; CPW; DAM POP; INT CA-
  131; MAL 5; MTCW 1; MTFW 2005

Diamano, Silmang
  See Senghor, Leopold Sedar

Diamond, Neil 1941- .... **CLC 30**
  See also CA 108

Diaz del Castillo, Bernal c.
  1496-1584 .... **HLCS 1; LC 31**
    See also DLB 318; LAW

di Bassetto, Corno
  See Shaw, George Bernard

Dick, Philip K. 1928-1982 ... **CLC 10, 30, 72;**
  SSC 57
  See also AAYA 24; BPFB 1; BYA 11; CA
  49-52; CAAS 106; CANR 2, 16, 132; CN
  2, 3; CPW; DA3; DAM NOV, POP; DLB
  8; MTCW 1, 2; MTFW 2005; NFS 5;
  SCFW 1, 2; SFW 4

Dick, Philip Kindred
  See Dick, Philip K.

Dickens, Charles (John Huffam)
  1812-1870 .... **NCLC 3, 8, 18, 26, 37, 50,**
  86, 105, 113, 161; SSC 17, 49, 88; WLC
  2
    See also AAYA 23; BRW 5; BRWC 1, 2;
    BYA 1, 2, 3, 13, 14; CDBLB 1832-1890;
    CLR 95; CMW 4; DA; DA3; DAB; DAC;
    DAM MST, NOV; DLB 21, 55, 70, 159,
    166; EXPN; GL 2; HGG; JRDA; LAIT 1,
    2; LATS 1:1; LMFS 1; MAICYA 1, 2;
    NFS 4, 5, 10, 14, 20; RGEL 2; RGSF 2;
    SATA 15; SUFW 1; TEA; WCH; WLIT
    4; WYA

Dickey, James (Lafayette)
  1923-1997 .... **CLC 1, 2, 4, 7, 10, 15, 47,**
  109; PC 40; TCLC 151
    See also AAYA 50; AITN 1, 2; AMWS 4;
    BPFB 1; CA 9-12R; CAAS 156; CABS
    2; CANR 10, 48, 61, 105; CDALB 1968-
    1988; CP 1, 2, 3, 4, 5, 6; CPW; CSW;
    DA3; DAM NOV, POET, POP; DLB 5,
    193; DLBD 7; DLBY 1982, 1993, 1996,
    1997, 1998; EWL 3; INT CANR-10;
    MAL 5; MTCW 1, 2; NFS 9; PFS 6, 11;
    RGAL 4; TUS

Dickey, William 1928-1994 .... **CLC 3, 28**
  See also CA 9-12R; CAAS 145; CANR 24,
  79; CP 1, 2, 3, 4; DLB 5

Dickinson, Charles 1951- .... **CLC 49**
  See also CA 128; CANR 141

Dickinson, Emily (Elizabeth)
  1830-1886 ..... **NCLC 21, 77, 171; PC 1;**
  WLC 2
    See also AAYA 22; AMW; AMWR 1;
    CDALB 1865-1917; DA; DA3; DAB;
    DAC; DAM MST, POET; DLB 1, 243;
    EXPP; FL 1:3; MBL; PAB; PFS 1, 2, 3,
    4, 5, 6, 8, 10, 11, 13, 16; RGAL 4; SATA
    29; TUS; WP; WYA

Dickinson, Mrs. Herbert Ward
  See Phelps, Elizabeth Stuart

DLB 4, 9, 274, 316; DLBD 1, 15; DLBY
1996; EWL 3; MAL 5; MTCW 1, 2;
MTFW 2005; NFS 14; RGAL 4; TUS

Dossage, Jean
See Simenon, Georges (Jacques Christian)

Dostoevsky, Fedor Mikhailovich
1821-1881 .. **NCLC 2, 7, 21, 33, 43, 119,
167; SSC 2, 33, 44; WLC 2**
See Dostoevsky, Fyodor
See also AAYA 40; DA; DA3; DAB; DAC;
DAM MST, NOV; EW 7; EXPN; NFS 3,
8; RGSF 2; RGWL 2, 3; SSFS 8; TWA

Dostoevsky, Fyodor
See Dostoevsky, Fedor Mikhailovich
See also DLB 238; LATS 1:1; LMFS 1, 2

Doty, M. R.
See Doty, Mark

Doty, Mark 1953(?)- .... **CLC 176; PC 53**
See also AMWS 11; CA 183; 161, 183;
CANR 110; CP 7

Doty, Mark A.
See Doty, Mark

Doty, Mark Alan
See Doty, Mark

Doughty, Charles M(ontagu)
1843-1926 .... **TCLC 27**
See also CA 178; CAAE 115; DLB 19, 57,
174

Douglas, Ellen .... **CLC 73**
See Haxton, Josephine Ayres; Williamson,
Ellen Douglas
See also CN 5, 6, 7; CSW; DLB 292

Douglas, Gavin 1475(?)-1522 .... **LC 20**
See also DLB 132; RGEL 2

Douglas, George
See Brown, George Douglas
See also RGEL 2

Douglas, Keith (Castellain)
1920-1944 .... **TCLC 40**
See also BRW 7; CA 160; DLB 27; EWL
3; PAB; RGEL 2

Douglas, Leonard
See Bradbury, Ray

Douglas, Michael
See Crichton, Michael

Douglas, (George) Norman
1868-1952 .... **TCLC 68**
See also BRW 6; CA 157; CAAE 119; DLB
34, 195; RGEL 2

Douglas, William
See Brown, George Douglas

Douglass, Frederick 1817(?)-1895 ..... **BLC 1;
NCLC 7, 55, 141; WLC 2**
See also AAYA 48; AFAW 1, 2; AMWC 1;
AMWS 3; CDALB 1640-1865; DA; DA3;
DAC; DAM MST, MULT; DLB 1, 43, 50,
79, 243; FW; LAIT 2; NCFS 2; RGAL 4;
SATA 29

Dourado, (Waldomiro Freitas) Autran
1926- .... **CLC 23, 60**
See also CA 25-28R, 179; CANR 34, 81;
DLB 145, 307; HW 2

Dourado, Waldomiro Freitas Autran
See Dourado, (Waldomiro Freitas) Autran

Dove, Rita 1952- .. **BLCS; CLC 50, 81; PC 6**
See also AAYA 46; AMWS 4; BW 2; CA
109; 19; CANR 27, 42, 68, 76, 97, 132;
CDALBS; CP 5, 6, 7; CSW; CWP; DA3;
DAM MULT, POET; DLB 120; EWL 3;
EXPP; MAL 5; MTCW 2; MTFW 2005;
PFS 1, 15; RGAL 4

Dove, Rita Frances
See Dove, Rita

Doveglion
See Villa, Jose Garcia

Dowell, Coleman 1925-1985 .... **CLC 60**
See also CA 25-28R; CAAS 117; CANR
10; DLB 130; GLL 2

Dowson, Ernest (Christopher)
1867-1900 .... **TCLC 4**
See also CA 150; CAAE 105; DLB 19, 135;
RGEL 2

Doyle, A. Conan
See Doyle, Sir Arthur Conan

Doyle, Sir Arthur Conan
1859-1930 ..... **SSC 12, 83, 95; TCLC 7;
WLC 2**
See Conan Doyle, Arthur
See also AAYA 14; BRWS 2; CA 122;
CAAE 104; CANR 131; CDBLB 1890-
1914; CLR 106; CMW 4; DA; DA3;
DAB; DAC; DAM MST, NOV; DLB 18,
70, 156, 178; EXPS; HGG; LAIT 2;
MSW; MTCW 1, 2; MTFW 2005; RGEL
2; RGSF 2; RHW; SATA 24; SCFW 1, 2;
SFW 4; SSFS 2; TEA; WCH; WLIT 4;
WYA; YAW

Doyle, Conan
See Doyle, Sir Arthur Conan

Doyle, John
See Graves, Robert

Doyle, Roddy 1958- .... **CLC 81, 178**
See also AAYA 14; BRWS 5; CA 143;
CANR 73, 128; CN 6, 7; DA3; DLB 194,
326; MTCW 2; MTFW 2005

Doyle, Sir A. Conan
See Doyle, Sir Arthur Conan

Dr. A
See Asimov, Isaac; Silverstein, Alvin; Silverstein, Virginia B(arbara Opshelor)

Drabble, Margaret 1939- ...... **CLC 2, 3, 5, 8,
10, 22, 53, 129**
See also BRWS 4; CA 13-16R; CANR 18,
35, 63, 112, 131; CDBLB 1960 to Present;
CN 1, 2, 3, 4, 5, 6, 7; CPW; DA3; DAB;
DAC; DAM MST, NOV, POP; DLB 14,
155, 231; EWL 3; FW; MTCW 1, 2;
MTFW 2005; RGEL 2; SATA 48; TEA

Drakulic, Slavenka 1949- .... **CLC 173**
See also CA 144; CANR 92

Drakulic-Ilic, Slavenka
See Drakulic, Slavenka

Drapier, M. B.
See Swift, Jonathan

Drayham, James
See Mencken, H(enry) L(ouis)

Drayton, Michael 1563-1631 .... **LC 8**
See also DAM POET; DLB 121; RGEL 2

Dreadstone, Carl
See Campbell, (John) Ramsey

Dreiser, Theodore 1871-1945 .... **SSC 30;
TCLC 10, 18, 35, 83; WLC 2**
See also AMW; AMWC 2; AMWR 2; BYA
15, 16; CA 132; CAAE 106; CDALB
1865-1917; DA; DA3; DAC; DAM MST,
NOV; DLB 9, 12, 102, 137; DLBD 1;
EWL 3; LAIT 2; LMFS 2; MAL 5;
MTCW 1, 2; MTFW 2005; NFS 8, 17;
RGAL 4; TUS

Dreiser, Theodore Herman Albert
See Dreiser, Theodore

Drexler, Rosalyn 1926- .... **CLC 2, 6**
See also CA 81-84; CAD; CANR 68, 124;
CD 5, 6; CWD; MAL 5

Dreyer, Carl Theodor 1889-1968 ...... **CLC 16**
See also CAAS 116

Drieu la Rochelle, Pierre
1893-1945 .... **TCLC 21**
See also CA 250; CAAE 117; DLB 72;
EWL 3; GFL 1789 to the Present

Drieu la Rochelle, Pierre-Eugene 1893-1945
See Drieu la Rochelle, Pierre

Drinkwater, John 1882-1937 ...... **TCLC 57**
See also CA 149; CAAE 109; DLB 10, 19,
149; RGEL 2

Drop Shot
See Cable, George Washington

Droste-Hulshoff, Annette Freiin von
1797-1848 .... **NCLC 3, 133**
See also CDWLB 2; DLB 133; RGSF 2;
RGWL 2, 3

Drummond, Walter
See Silverberg, Robert

Drummond, William Henry
1854-1907 .... **TCLC 25**
See also CA 160; DLB 92

Drummond de Andrade, Carlos
1902-1987 .... **CLC 18; TCLC 139**
See Andrade, Carlos Drummond de
See also CA 132; CAAS 123; DLB 307;
LAW

Drummond of Hawthornden, William
1585-1649 .... **LC 83**
See also DLB 121, 213; RGEL 2

Drury, Allen (Stuart) 1918-1998 .... **CLC 37**
See also CA 57-60; CAAS 170; CANR 18,
52; CN 1, 2, 3, 4, 5, 6; INT CANR-18

Druse, Eleanor
See King, Stephen

Dryden, John 1631-1700 ..... **DC 3; LC 3, 21,
115; PC 25; WLC 2**
See also BRW 2; CDBLB 1660-1789; DA;
DAB; DAC; DAM DRAM, MST, POET;
DLB 80, 101, 131; EXPP; IDTP; LMFS
1; RGEL 2; TEA; WLIT 3

du Bellay, Joachim 1524-1560 .... **LC 92**
See also DLB 327; GFL Beginnings to
1789; RGWL 2, 3

Duberman, Martin (Bauml) 1930- ..... **CLC 8**
See also CA 1-4R; CAD; CANR 2, 63, 137;
CD 5, 6

Dubie, Norman (Evans) 1945- .... **CLC 36**
See also CA 69-72; CANR 12, 115; CP 3,
4, 5, 6, 7; DLB 120; PFS 12

Du Bois, W(illiam) E(dward) B(urghardt)
1868-1963 ..... **BLC 1; CLC 1, 2, 13, 64,
96; HR 1:2; TCLC 169; WLC 2**
See also AAYA 40; AFAW 1, 2; AMWC 1;
AMWS 2; BW 1, 3; CA 85-88; CANR
34, 82, 132; CDALB 1865-1917; DA;
DA3; DAC; DAM MST, MULT, NOV;
DLB 47, 50, 91, 246, 284; EWL 3; EXPP;
LAIT 2; LMFS 2; MAL 5; MTCW 1, 2;
MTFW 2005; NCFS 1; PFS 13; RGAL 4;
SATA 42

Dubus, Andre 1936-1999 ..... **CLC 13, 36, 97;
SSC 15**
See also AMWS 7; CA 21-24R; CAAS 177;
CANR 17; CN 5, 6; CSW; DLB 130; INT
CANR-17; RGAL 4; SSFS 10; TCLE 1:1

Duca Minimo
See D'Annunzio, Gabriele

Ducharme, Rejean 1941- .... **CLC 74**
See also CAAS 165; DLB 60

du Chatelet, Emilie 1706-1749 .... **LC 96**
See Chatelet, Gabrielle-Emilie Du

Duchen, Claire .... **CLC 65**

Duclos, Charles Pinot- 1704-1772 .... **LC 1**
See also GFL Beginnings to 1789

Ducornet, Erica 1943-
See Ducornet, Rikki
See also CA 37-40R; CANR 14, 34, 54, 82;
SATA 7

Ducornet, Rikki .... **CLC 232**
See Ducornet, Erica

Dudek, Louis 1918-2001 .... **CLC 11, 19**
See also CA 45-48; 14; CAAS 215; CANR
1; CP 1, 2, 3, 4, 5, 6, 7; DLB 88

Duerrenmatt, Friedrich 1921-1990 ... **CLC 1,
4, 8, 11, 15, 43, 102**
See Durrenmatt, Friedrich
See also CA 17-20R; CANR 33; CMW 4;
DAM DRAM; DLB 69, 124; MTCW 1, 2

Duffy, Bruce 1953(?)- .... **CLC 50**
See also CA 172

Ellis, Trey 1962- .... **CLC 55**
See also CA 146; CANR 92; CN 7

Ellison, Harlan 1934- .... **CLC 1, 13, 42, 139;
SSC 14**
See also AAYA 29; BPFB 1; BYA 14; CA
5-8R; CANR 5, 46, 115; CPW; DAM
POP; DLB 8; HGG; INT CANR-5;
MTCW 1, 2; MTFW 2005; SCFW 2;
SFW 4; SSFS 13, 14, 15, 21; SUFW 1, 2

Ellison, Ralph 1914-1994 . **BLC 1; CLC 1, 3,
11, 54, 86, 114; SSC 26, 79; WLC 2**
See also AAYA 19; AFAW 1, 2; AMWC 2;
AMWR 2; AMWS 2; BPFB 1; BW 1, 3;
BYA 2; CA 9-12R; CAAS 145; CANR
24, 53; CDALB 1941-1968; CN 1, 2, 3,
4, 5; CSW; DA; DA3; DAB; DAC; DAM
MST, MULT, NOV; DLB 2, 76, 227;
DLBY 1994; EWL 3; EXPN; EXPS;
LAIT 4; MAL 5; MTCW 1, 2; MTFW
2005; NCFS 3; NFS 2, 21; RGAL 4;
RGSF 2; SSFS 1, 11; YAW

Ellmann, Lucy 1956- .... **CLC 61**
See also CA 128; CANR 154

Ellmann, Lucy Elizabeth
See Ellmann, Lucy

Ellmann, Richard (David)
1918-1987 .... **CLC 50**
See also BEST 89:2; CA 1-4R; CAAS 122;
CANR 2, 28, 61; DLB 103; DLBY 1987;
MTCW 1, 2; MTFW 2005

Elman, Richard (Martin)
1934-1997 .... **CLC 19**
See also CA 17-20R; 3; CAAS 163; CANR
47; TCLE 1:1

Elron
See Hubbard, L. Ron

El Saadawi, Nawal 1931- .... **CLC 196**
See al'Sadaawi, Nawal; Sa'adawi, al-
Nawal; Saadawi, Nawal El; Sa'dawi,
Nawal al-
See also CA 118; 11; CANR 44, 92

Eluard, Paul .... **PC 38; TCLC 7, 41**
See Grindel, Eugene
See also EWL 3; GFL 1789 to the Present;
RGWL 2, 3

Elyot, Thomas 1490(?)-1546 .... **LC 11**
See also DLB 136; RGEL 2

Elytis, Odysseus 1911-1996 .... **CLC 15, 49,
100; PC 21**
See Alepoudelis, Odysseus
See also CA 102; CAAS 151; CANR 94;
CWW 2; DAM POET; DLB 329; EW 13;
EWL 3; MTCW 1, 2; RGWL 2, 3

Emecheta, Buchi 1944- .... **BLC 2; CLC 14,
48, 128, 214**
See also AAYA 67; AFW; BW 2, 3; CA 81-
84; CANR 27, 81, 126; CDWLB 3; CN
4, 5, 6, 7; CWRI 5; DA3; DAM MULT;
DLB 117; EWL 3; FL 1:5; FW; MTCW
1, 2; MTFW 2005; NFS 12, 14; SATA 66;
WLIT 2

Emerson, Mary Moody
1774-1863 .... **NCLC 66**

Emerson, Ralph Waldo 1803-1882 . **NCLC 1,
38, 98; PC 18; WLC 2**
See also AAYA 60; AMW; ANW; CDALB
1640-1865; DA; DA3; DAB; DAC; DAM
MST, POET; DLB 1, 59, 73, 183, 223,
270; EXPP; LAIT 2; LMFS 1; NCFS 3;
PFS 4, 17; RGAL 4; TUS; WP

Eminem 1972- .... **CLC 226**
See also CA 245

Eminescu, Mihail 1850-1889 .. **NCLC 33, 131**

Empedocles 5th cent. B.C.- .... **CMLC 50**
See also DLB 176

Empson, William 1906-1984 ... **CLC 3, 8, 19,
33, 34**
See also BRWS 2; CA 17-20R; CAAS 112;
CANR 31, 61; CP 1, 2, 3; DLB 20; EWL
3; MTCW 1, 2; RGEL 2

Enchi, Fumiko (Ueda) 1905-1986 ..... **CLC 31**
See Enchi Fumiko
See also CA 129; CAAS 121; FW; MJW

Enchi Fumiko
See Enchi, Fumiko (Ueda)
See also DLB 182; EWL 3

Ende, Michael (Andreas Helmuth)
1929-1995 .... **CLC 31**
See also BYA 5; CA 124; CAAE 118;
CAAS 149; CANR 36, 110; CLR 14;
DLB 75; MAICYA 1, 2; MAICYAS 1;
SATA 61, 130; SATA-Brief 42; SATA-
Obit 86

Endo, Shusaku 1923-1996 ..... **CLC 7, 14, 19,
54, 99; SSC 48; TCLC 152**
See also CA 29-32R; CAAS 153; CANR
21, 54, 131; DA3; DAM NOV; MTCW 1,
2; MTFW 2005; RGSF 2; RGWL 2, 3

Endo Shusaku
See Endo, Shusaku
See also CWW 2; DLB 182; EWL 3

Engel, Marian 1933-1985 .... **CLC 36; TCLC
137**
See also CA 25-28R; CANR 12; CN 2, 3;
DLB 53; FW; INT CANR-12

Engelhardt, Frederick
See Hubbard, L. Ron

Engels, Friedrich 1820-1895 .. **NCLC 85, 114**
See also DLB 129; LATS 1:1

Enright, D(ennis) J(oseph)
1920-2002 .... **CLC 4, 8, 31**
See also CA 1-4R; CAAS 211; CANR 1,
42, 83; CN 1, 2; CP 1, 2, 3, 4, 5, 6, 7;
DLB 27; EWL 3; SATA 25; SATA-Obit
140

Ensler, Eve 1953- .... **CLC 212**
See also CA 172; CANR 126; DFS 23

Enzensberger, Hans Magnus
1929- .... **CLC 43; PC 28**
See also CA 119; CAAE 116; CANR 103;
CWW 2; EWL 3

Ephron, Nora 1941- .... **CLC 17, 31**
See also AAYA 35; AITN 2; CA 65-68;
CANR 12, 39, 83, 161; DFS 22

Epicurus 341B.C.-270B.C. .... **CMLC 21**
See also DLB 176

Epsilon
See Betjeman, John

Epstein, Daniel Mark 1948- .... **CLC 7**
See also CA 49-52; CANR 2, 53, 90

Epstein, Jacob 1956- .... **CLC 19**
See also CA 114

Epstein, Jean 1897-1953 .... **TCLC 92**

Epstein, Joseph 1937- .... **CLC 39, 204**
See also AMWS 14; CA 119; CAAE 112;
CANR 50, 65, 117

Epstein, Leslie 1938- .... **CLC 27**
See also AMWS 12; CA 215; 73-76, 215;
12; CANR 23, 69; DLB 299; RGHL

Equiano, Olaudah 1745(?)-1797 . **BLC 2; LC
16**
See also AFAW 1, 2; CDWLB 3; DAM
MULT; DLB 37, 50; WLIT 2

Erasmus, Desiderius 1469(?)-1536 ..... **LC 16,
93**
See also DLB 136; EW 2; LMFS 1; RGWL
2, 3; TWA

Erdman, Paul E(mil) 1932- .... **CLC 25**
See also AITN 1; CA 61-64; CANR 13, 43,
84

Erdrich, Karen Louise
See Erdrich, Louise

Erdrich, Louise 1954- .... **CLC 39, 54, 120,
176; NNAL; PC 52**
See also AAYA 10, 47; AMWS 4; BEST
89:1; BPFB 1; CA 114; CANR 41, 62,
118, 138; CDALBS; CN 5, 6, 7; CP 6, 7;
CPW; CWP; DA3; DAM MULT, NOV,

POP; DLB 152, 175, 206; EWL 3; EXPP;
FL 1:5; LAIT 5; LATS 1:2; MAL 5;
MTCW 1, 2; MTFW 2005; NFS 5; PFS
14; RGAL 4; SATA 94, 141; SSFS 14,
22; TCWW 2

Erenburg, Ilya (Grigoryevich)
See Ehrenburg, Ilya (Grigoryevich)

Erickson, Stephen Michael
See Erickson, Steve

Erickson, Steve 1950- .... **CLC 64**
See also CA 129; CANR 60, 68, 136;
MTFW 2005; SFW 4; SUFW 2

Erickson, Walter
See Fast, Howard

Ericson, Walter
See Fast, Howard

Eriksson, Buntel
See Bergman, (Ernst) Ingmar

Eriugena, John Scottus c.
810-877 .... **CMLC 65**
See also DLB 115

Ernaux, Annie 1940- .... **CLC 88, 184**
See also CA 147; CANR 93; MTFW 2005;
NCFS 3, 5

Erskine, John 1879-1951 .... **TCLC 84**
See also CA 159; CAAE 112; DLB 9, 102;
FANT

Eschenbach, Wolfram von
See von Eschenbach, Wolfram
See also RGWL 3

Eseki, Bruno
See Mphahlele, Ezekiel

Esenin, S.A.
See Esenin, Sergei
See also EWL 3

Esenin, Sergei 1895-1925 .... **TCLC 4**
See Esenin, S.A.
See also CAAE 104; RGWL 2, 3

Esenin, Sergei Aleksandrovich
See Esenin, Sergei

Eshleman, Clayton 1935- .... **CLC 7**
See also CA 212; 33-36R, 212; 6; CANR
93; CP 1, 2, 3, 4, 5, 6, 7; DLB 5

Espada, Martin 1957- .... **PC 74**
See also CA 159; CANR 80; CP 7; EXPP;
LLW; MAL 5; PFS 13, 16

Espriella, Don Manuel Alvarez
See Southey, Robert

Espriu, Salvador 1913-1985 .... **CLC 9**
See also CA 154; CAAS 115; DLB 134;
EWL 3

Espronceda, Jose de 1808-1842 ..... **NCLC 39**

Esquivel, Laura 1950(?)- ... **CLC 141; HLCS
1**
See also AAYA 29; CA 143; CANR 68, 113,
161; DA3; DNFS 2; LAIT 3; LMFS 2;
MTCW 2; MTFW 2005; NFS 5; WLIT 1

Esse, James
See Stephens, James

Esterbrook, Tom
See Hubbard, L. Ron

Estleman, Loren D. 1952- .... **CLC 48**
See also AAYA 27; CA 85-88; CANR 27,
74, 139; CMW 4; CPW; DA3; DAM
NOV, POP; DLB 226; INT CANR-27;
MTCW 1, 2; MTFW 2005; TCWW 1, 2

Etherege, Sir George 1636-1692 . **DC 23; LC
78**
See also BRW 2; DAM DRAM; DLB 80;
PAB; RGEL 2

Euclid 306B.C.-283B.C. .... **CMLC 25**

Eugenides, Jeffrey 1960(?)- .... **CLC 81, 212**
See also AAYA 51; CA 144; CANR 120;
MTFW 2005; NFS 24

Euripides c. 484B.C.-406B.C. .... **CMLC 23, 51; DC 4; WLCS**
See also AW 1; CDWLB 1; DA; DA3; DAB; DAC; DAM DRAM, MST; DFS 1, 4, 6; DLB 176; LAIT 1; LMFS 1; RGWL 2, 3; WLIT 8

Evan, Evin
See Faust, Frederick (Schiller)

Evans, Caradoc 1878-1945 ... **SSC 43; TCLC 85**
See also DLB 162

Evans, Evan
See Faust, Frederick (Schiller)

Evans, Marian
See Eliot, George

Evans, Mary Ann
See Eliot, George
See also NFS 20

Evarts, Esther
See Benson, Sally

Everett, Percival
See Everett, Percival L.
See also CSW

Everett, Percival L. 1956- .... **CLC 57**
See Everett, Percival
See also BW 2; CA 129; CANR 94, 134; CN 7; MTFW 2005

Everson, R(onald) G(ilmour) 1903-1992 .... **CLC 27**
See also CA 17-20R; CP 1, 2, 3, 4; DLB 88

Everson, William (Oliver) 1912-1994 .... **CLC 1, 5, 14**
See Antoninus, Brother
See also BG 1:2; CA 9-12R; CAAS 145; CANR 20; CP 2, 3, 4, 5; DLB 5, 16, 212; MTCW 1

Evtushenko, Evgenii Aleksandrovich
See Yevtushenko, Yevgeny (Alexandrovich)
See also CWW 2; RGWL 2, 3

Ewart, Gavin (Buchanan) 1916-1995 .... **CLC 13, 46**
See also BRWS 7; CA 89-92; CAAS 150; CANR 17, 46; CP 1, 2, 3, 4, 5, 6; DLB 40; MTCW 1

Ewers, Hanns Heinz 1871-1943 ..... **TCLC 12**
See also CA 149; CAAE 109

Ewing, Frederick R.
See Sturgeon, Theodore (Hamilton)

Exley, Frederick (Earl) 1929-1992 .... **CLC 6, 11**
See also AITN 2; BPFB 1; CA 81-84; CAAS 138; CANR 117; DLB 143; DLBY 1981

Eynhardt, Guillermo
See Quiroga, Horacio (Sylvestre)

Ezekiel, Nissim (Moses) 1924-2004 .. **CLC 61**
See also CA 61-64; CAAS 223; CP 1, 2, 3, 4, 5, 6, 7; DLB 323; EWL 3

Ezekiel, Tish O'Dowd 1943- .... **CLC 34**
See also CA 129

Fadeev, Aleksandr Aleksandrovich
See Bulgya, Alexander Alexandrovich
See also DLB 272

Fadeev, Alexandr Alexandrovich
See Bulgya, Alexander Alexandrovich
See also EWL 3

Fadeyev, A.
See Bulgya, Alexander Alexandrovich

Fadeyev, Alexander .... **TCLC 53**
See Bulgya, Alexander Alexandrovich

Fagen, Donald 1948- .... **CLC 26**

Fainzil'berg, Il'ia Arnol'dovich
See Fainzilberg, Ilya Arnoldovich

Fainzilberg, Ilya Arnoldovich 1897-1937 .... **TCLC 21**
See Il'f, Il'ia
See also CA 165; CAAE 120; EWL 3

Fair, Ronald L. 1932- .... **CLC 18**
See also BW 1; CA 69-72; CANR 25; DLB 33

Fairbairn, Roger
See Carr, John Dickson

Fairbairns, Zoe (Ann) 1948- .... **CLC 32**
See also CA 103; CANR 21, 85; CN 4, 5, 6, 7

Fairfield, Flora
See Alcott, Louisa May

Fairman, Paul W. 1916-1977
See Queen, Ellery
See also CAAS 114; SFW 4

Falco, Gian
See Papini, Giovanni

Falconer, James
See Kirkup, James

Falconer, Kenneth
See Kornbluth, C(yril) M.

Falkland, Samuel
See Heijermans, Herman

Fallaci, Oriana 1930-2006 .... **CLC 11, 110**
See also CA 77-80; CAAS 253; CANR 15, 58, 134; FW; MTCW 1

Faludi, Susan 1959- .... **CLC 140**
See also CA 138; CANR 126; FW; MTCW 2; MTFW 2005; NCFS 3

Faludy, George 1913- .... **CLC 42**
See also CA 21-24R

Faludy, Gyoergy
See Faludy, George

Fanon, Frantz 1925-1961 ... **BLC 2; CLC 74; TCLC 188**
See also BW 1; CA 116; CAAS 89-92; DAM MULT; DLB 296; LMFS 2; WLIT 2

Fanshawe, Ann 1625-1680 .... **LC 11**

Fante, John (Thomas) 1911-1983 .... **CLC 60; SSC 65**
See also AMWS 11; CA 69-72; CAAS 109; CANR 23, 104; DLB 130; DLBY 1983

Far, Sui Sin .... **SSC 62**
See Eaton, Edith Maude
See also SSFS 4

Farah, Nuruddin 1945- ...... **BLC 2; CLC 53, 137**
See also AFW; BW 2, 3; CA 106; CANR 81, 148; CDWLB 3; CN 4, 5, 6, 7; DAM MULT; DLB 125; EWL 3; WLIT 2

Fargue, Leon-Paul 1876(?)-1947 .... **TCLC 11**
See also CAAE 109; CANR 107; DLB 258; EWL 3

Farigoule, Louis
See Romains, Jules

Farina, Richard 1936(?)-1966 .... **CLC 9**
See also CA 81-84; CAAS 25-28R

Farley, Walter (Lorimer) 1915-1989 .... **CLC 17**
See also AAYA 58; BYA 14; CA 17-20R; CANR 8, 29, 84; DLB 22; JRDA; MAI-CYA 1, 2; SATA 2, 43, 132; YAW

Farmer, Philip Jose 1918- .... **CLC 1, 19**
See also AAYA 28; BPFB 1; CA 1-4R; CANR 4, 35, 111; DLB 8; MTCW 1; SATA 93; SCFW 1, 2; SFW 4

Farquhar, George 1677-1707 .... **LC 21**
See also BRW 2; DAM DRAM; DLB 84; RGEL 2

Farrell, J(ames) G(ordon) 1935-1979 .... **CLC 6**
See also CA 73-76; CAAS 89-92; CANR 36; CN 1, 2; DLB 14, 271, 326; MTCW 1; RGEL 2; RHW; WLIT 4

Farrell, James T(homas) 1904-1979 . **CLC 1, 4, 8, 11, 66; SSC 28**
See also AMW; BPFB 1; CA 5-8R; CAAS 89-92; CANR 9, 61; CN 1, 2; DLB 4, 9, 86; DLBD 2; EWL 3; MAL 5; MTCW 1, 2; MTFW 2005; RGAL 4

Farrell, Warren (Thomas) 1943- ...... **CLC 70**
See also CA 146; CANR 120

Farren, Richard J.
See Betjeman, John

Farren, Richard M.
See Betjeman, John

Fassbinder, Rainer Werner 1946-1982 .... **CLC 20**
See also CA 93-96; CAAS 106; CANR 31

Fast, Howard 1914-2003 .... **CLC 23, 131**
See also AAYA 16; BPFB 1; CA 181; 1-4R, 181; 18; CAAS 214; CANR 1, 33, 54, 75, 98, 140; CMW 4; CN 1, 2, 3, 4, 5, 6, 7; CPW; DAM NOV; DLB 9; INT CANR-33; LATS 1:1; MAL 5; MTCW 2; MTFW 2005; RHW; SATA 7; SATA-Essay 107; TCWW 1, 2; YAW

Faulcon, Robert
See Holdstock, Robert

Faulkner, William (Cuthbert) 1897-1962 .... **CLC 1, 3, 6, 8, 9, 11, 14, 18, 28, 52, 68; SSC 1, 35, 42, 92, 97; TCLC 141; WLC 2**
See also AAYA 7; AMW; AMWR 1; BPFB 1; BYA 5, 15; CA 81-84; CANR 33; CDALB 1929-1941; DA; DA3; DAB; DAC; DAM MST, NOV; DLB 9, 11, 44, 102, 316, 330; DLBD 2; DLBY 1986, 1997; EWL 3; EXPN; EXPS; GL 2; LAIT 2; LATS 1:1; LMFS 2; MAL 5; MTCW 1, 2; MTFW 2005; NFS 4, 8, 13, 24; RGAL 4; RGSF 2; SSFS 2, 5, 6, 12; TUS

Fauset, Jessie Redmon 1882(?)-1961 .. **BLC 2; CLC 19, 54; HR 1:2**
See also AFAW 2; BW 1; CA 109; CANR 83; DAM MULT; DLB 51; FW; LMFS 2; MAL 5; MBL

Faust, Frederick (Schiller) 1892-1944 .... **TCLC 49**
See Brand, Max; Dawson, Peter; Frederick, John
See also CA 152; CAAE 108; CANR 143; DAM POP; DLB 256; TUS

Faust, Irvin 1924- .... **CLC 8**
See also CA 33-36R; CANR 28, 67; CN 1, 2, 3, 4, 5, 6, 7; DLB 2, 28, 218, 278; DLBY 1980

Fawkes, Guy
See Benchley, Robert (Charles)

Fearing, Kenneth (Flexner) 1902-1961 .... **CLC 51**
See also CA 93-96; CANR 59; CMW 4; DLB 9; MAL 5; RGAL 4

Fecamps, Elise
See Creasey, John

Federman, Raymond 1928- .... **CLC 6, 47**
See also CA 208; 17-20R, 208; 8; CANR 10, 43, 83, 108; CN 3, 4, 5, 6; DLBY 1980

Federspiel, J.F. 1931- .... **CLC 42**
See also CA 146

Federspiel, Juerg F.
See Federspiel, J.F.

Feiffer, Jules 1929- .... **CLC 2, 8, 64**
See also AAYA 3, 62; CA 17-20R; CAD; CANR 30, 59, 129, 161; CD 5, 6; DAM DRAM; DLB 7, 44; INT CANR-30; MTCW 1; SATA 8, 61, 111, 157

Feiffer, Jules Ralph
See Feiffer, Jules

Feige, Hermann Albert Otto Maximilian
See Traven, B.

Feinberg, David B. 1956-1994 .... **CLC 59**
See also CA 135; CAAS 147

Feinstein, Elaine 1930- .... **CLC 36**
See also CA 69-72; 1; CANR 31, 68, 121; CN 3, 4, 5, 6, 7; CP 2, 3, 4, 5, 6, 7; CWP; DLB 14, 40; MTCW 1

Flanagan, Thomas (James Bonner)
1923-2002 .... **CLC 25, 52**
See also CA 108; CAAS 206; CANR 55;
CN 3, 4, 5, 6, 7; DLBY 1980; INT CA-
108; MTCW 1; RHW; TCLE 1:1
Flaubert, Gustave 1821-1880 .... **NCLC 2, 10,**
19, 62, 66, 135, 179; SSC 11, 60; WLC
2
See also DA; DA3; DAB; DAC; DAM
MST, NOV; DLB 119, 301; EW 7; EXPS;
GFL 1789 to the Present; LAIT 2; LMFS
1; NFS 14; RGSF 2; RGWL 2, 3; SSFS
6; TWA
Flavius Josephus
See Josephus, Flavius
Flecker, Herman Elroy
See Flecker, (Herman) James Elroy
Flecker, (Herman) James Elroy
1884-1915 .... **TCLC 43**
See also CA 150; CAAE 109; DLB 10, 19;
RGEL 2
Fleming, Ian 1908-1964 .... **CLC 3, 30**
See also AAYA 26; BPFB 1; CA 5-8R;
CANR 59; CDBLB 1945-1960; CMW 4;
CPW; DA3; DAM POP; DLB 87, 201;
MSW; MTCW 1, 2; MTFW 2005; RGEL
2; SATA 9; TEA; YAW
Fleming, Ian Lancaster
See Fleming, Ian
Fleming, Thomas 1927- .... **CLC 37**
See also CA 5-8R; CANR 10, 102, 155;
INT CANR-10; SATA 8
Fleming, Thomas James
See Fleming, Thomas
Fletcher, John 1579-1625 .... **DC 6; LC 33**
See also BRW 2; CDBLB Before 1660;
DLB 58; RGEL 2; TEA
Fletcher, John Gould 1886-1950 .... **TCLC 35**
See also CA 167; CAAE 107; DLB 4, 45;
LMFS 2; MAL 5; RGAL 4
Fleur, Paul
See Pohl, Frederik
Flieg, Helmut
See Heym, Stefan
Flooglebuckle, Al
See Spiegelman, Art
Flora, Fletcher 1914-1969
See Queen, Ellery
See also CA 1-4R; CANR 3, 85
Flying Officer X
See Bates, H(erbert) E(rnest)
Fo, Dario 1926- .... **CLC 32, 109, 227; DC 10**
See also CA 128; CAAE 116; CANR 68,
114, 134; CWW 2; DA3; DAM DRAM;
DFS 23; DLB 330; DLBY 1997; EWL 3;
MTCW 1, 2; MTFW 2005; WLIT 7
Foden, Giles 1967- .... **CLC 231**
See also CA 240; DLB 267; NFS 15
Fogarty, Jonathan Titulescu Esq.
See Farrell, James T(homas)
Follett, Ken 1949- .... **CLC 18**
See also AAYA 6, 50; BEST 89:4; BPFB 1;
CA 81-84; CANR 13, 33, 54, 102, 156;
CMW 4; CPW; DA3; DAM NOV, POP;
DLB 87; DLBY 1981; INT CANR-33;
MTCW 1
Follett, Kenneth Martin
See Follett, Ken
Fondane, Benjamin 1898-1944 ..... **TCLC 159**
Fontane, Theodor 1819-1898 . **NCLC 26, 163**
See also CDWLB 2; DLB 129; EW 6;
RGWL 2, 3; TWA
Fonte, Moderata 1555-1592 .... **LC 118**
Fontenot, Chester .... **CLC 65**
Fonvizin, Denis Ivanovich
1744(?)-1792 .... **LC 81**
See also DLB 150; RGWL 2, 3

Foote, Horton 1916- .... **CLC 51, 91**
See also CA 73-76; CAD; CANR 34, 51,
110; CD 5, 6; CSW; DA3; DAM DRAM;
DFS 20; DLB 26, 266; EWL 3; INT
CANR-34; MTFW 2005
Foote, Mary Hallock 1847-1938 .. **TCLC 108**
See also DLB 186, 188, 202, 221; TCWW
2
Foote, Samuel 1721-1777 .... **LC 106**
See also DLB 89; RGEL 2
Foote, Shelby 1916-2005 .... **CLC 75, 224**
See also AAYA 40; CA 5-8R; CAAS 240;
CANR 3, 45, 74, 131; CN 1, 2, 3, 4, 5, 6,
7; CPW; CSW; DA3; DAM NOV, POP;
DLB 2, 17; MAL 5; MTCW 2; MTFW
2005; RHW
Forbes, Cosmo
See Lewton, Val
Forbes, Esther 1891-1967 .... **CLC 12**
See also AAYA 17; BYA 2; CA 13-14;
CAAS 25-28R; CAP 1; CLR 27; DLB 22;
JRDA; MAICYA 1, 2; RHW; SATA 2,
100; YAW
Forche, Carolyn 1950- .. **CLC 25, 83, 86; PC**
10
See also CA 117; CAAE 109; CANR 50,
74, 138; CP 4, 5, 6, 7; CWP; DA3; DAM
POET; DLB 5, 193; INT CA-117; MAL
5; MTCW 2; MTFW 2005; PFS 18;
RGAL 4
Forche, Carolyn Louise
See Forche, Carolyn
Ford, Elbur
See Hibbert, Eleanor Alice Burford
Ford, Ford Madox 1873-1939 ... **TCLC 1, 15,**
39, 57, 172
See Chaucer, Daniel
See also BRW 6; CA 132; CAAE 104;
CANR 74; CDBLB 1914-1945; DA3;
DAM NOV; DLB 34, 98, 162; EWL 3;
MTCW 1, 2; RGEL 2; TEA
Ford, Henry 1863-1947 .... **TCLC 73**
See also CA 148; CAAE 115
Ford, Jack
See Ford, John
Ford, John 1586-1639 .... **DC 8; LC 68**
See also BRW 2; CDBLB Before 1660;
DA3; DAM DRAM; DFS 7; DLB 58;
IDTP; RGEL 2
Ford, John 1895-1973 .... **CLC 16**
See also AAYA 75; CA 187; CAAS 45-48
Ford, Richard 1944- .... **CLC 46, 99, 205**
See also AMWS 5; CA 69-72; CANR 11,
47, 86, 128; CN 5, 6, 7; CSW; DLB 227;
EWL 3; MAL 5; MTCW 2; MTFW 2005;
RGAL 4; RGSF 2
Ford, Webster
See Masters, Edgar Lee
Foreman, Richard 1937- .... **CLC 50**
See also CA 65-68; CAD; CANR 32, 63,
143; CD 5, 6
Forester, C(ecil) S(cott) 1899-1966 . **CLC 35;**
TCLC 152
See also CA 73-76; CAAS 25-28R; CANR
83; DLB 191; RGEL 2; RHW; SATA 13
Forez
See Mauriac, Francois (Charles)
Forman, James
See Forman, James D(ouglas)
Forman, James D(ouglas) 1932- .... **CLC 21**
See also AAYA 17; CA 9-12R; CANR 4,
19, 42; JRDA; MAICYA 1, 2; SATA 8,
70; YAW
Forman, Milos 1932- .... **CLC 164**
See also AAYA 63; CA 109

Fornes, Maria Irene 1930- .... **CLC 39, 61,**
187; DC 10; HLCS 1
See also CA 25-28R; CAD; CANR 28, 81;
CD 5, 6; CWD; DLB 7; HW 1, 2; INT
CANR-28; LLW; MAL 5; MTCW 1;
RGAL 4
Forrest, Leon (Richard)
1937-1997 .... **BLCS; CLC 4**
See also AFAW 2; BW 2; CA 89-92; 7;
CAAS 162; CANR 25, 52, 87; CN 4, 5,
6; DLB 33
Forster, E(dward) M(organ)
1879-1970 ...... **CLC 1, 2, 3, 4, 9, 10, 13,**
15, 22, 45, 77; SSC 27, 96; TCLC 125;
WLC 2
See also AAYA 2, 37; BRW 6; BRWR 2;
BYA 12; CA 13-14; CAAS 25-28R;
CANR 45; CAP 1; CDBLB 1914-1945;
DA; DA3; DAB; DAC; DAM MST, NOV;
DLB 34, 98, 162, 178, 195; DLBD 10;
EWL 3; EXPN; LAIT 3; LMFS 1; MTCW
1, 2; MTFW 2005; NCFS 1; NFS 3, 10,
11; RGEL 2; RGSF 2; SATA 57; SUFW
1; TEA; WLIT 4
Forster, John 1812-1876 .... **NCLC 11**
See also DLB 144, 184
Forster, Margaret 1938- .... **CLC 149**
See also CA 133; CANR 62, 115; CN 4, 5,
6, 7; DLB 155, 271
Forsyth, Frederick 1938- .... **CLC 2, 5, 36**
See also BEST 89:4; CA 85-88; CANR 38,
62, 115, 137; CMW 4; CN 3, 4, 5, 6, 7;
CPW; DAM NOV, POP; DLB 87; MTCW
1, 2; MTFW 2005
Forten, Charlotte L. 1837-1914 .... **BLC 2;**
TCLC 16
See Grimke, Charlotte L(ottie) Forten
See also DLB 50, 239
Fortinbras
See Grieg, (Johan) Nordahl (Brun)
Foscolo, Ugo 1778-1827 .... **NCLC 8, 97**
See also EW 5; WLIT 7
Fosse, Bob 1927-1987
See Fosse, Robert L.
See also CAAE 110; CAAS 123
Fosse, Robert L. .... **CLC 20**
See Fosse, Bob
Foster, Hannah Webster
1758-1840 .... **NCLC 99**
See also DLB 37, 200; RGAL 4
Foster, Stephen Collins
1826-1864 .... **NCLC 26**
See also RGAL 4
Foucault, Michel 1926-1984 . **CLC 31, 34, 69**
See also CA 105; CAAS 113; CANR 34;
DLB 242; EW 13; EWL 3; GFL 1789 to
the Present; GLL 1; LMFS 2; MTCW 1,
2; TWA
Fouque, Friedrich (Heinrich Karl) de la
Motte 1777-1843 .... **NCLC 2**
See also DLB 90; RGWL 2, 3; SUFW 1
Fourier, Charles 1772-1837 .... **NCLC 51**
Fournier, Henri-Alban 1886-1914
See Alain-Fournier
See also CA 179; CAAE 104
Fournier, Pierre 1916-1997 .... **CLC 11**
See Gascar, Pierre
See also CA 89-92; CANR 16, 40
Fowles, John 1926-2005 .... **CLC 1, 2, 3, 4, 6,**
9, 10, 15, 33, 87; SSC 33
See also BPFB 1; BRWS 1; CA 5-8R;
CAAS 245; CANR 25, 71, 103; CDBLB
1960 to Present; CN 1, 2, 3, 4, 5, 6, 7;
DA3; DAB; DAC; DAM MST; DLB 14,
139, 207; EWL 3; HGG; MTCW 1, 2;
MTFW 2005; NFS 21; RGEL 2; RHW;
SATA 22; SATA-Obit 171; TEA; WLIT 4
Fowles, John Robert
See Fowles, John

Fox, Paula 1923- .... **CLC 2, 8, 121**
  See also AAYA 3, 37; BYA 3, 8; CA 73-76;
  CANR 20, 36, 62, 105; CLR 1, 44, 96;
  DLB 52; JRDA; MAICYA 1, 2; MTCW
  1; NFS 12; SATA 17, 60, 120, 167; WYA;
  YAW

Fox, William Price (Jr.) 1926- .... **CLC 22**
  See also CA 17-20R; 19; CANR 11, 142;
  CSW; DLB 2; DLBY 1981

Foxe, John 1517(?)-1587 .... **LC 14**
  See also DLB 132

Frame, Janet .. **CLC 2, 3, 6, 22, 66, 96; SSC
  29**
  See Clutha, Janet Paterson Frame
  See also CN 1, 2, 3, 4, 5, 6, 7; CP 2, 3, 4;
  CWP; EWL 3; RGEL 2; RGSF 2; TWA

France, Anatole .... **TCLC 9**
  See Thibault, Jacques Anatole Francois
  See also DLB 123, 330; EWL 3; GFL 1789
  to the Present; RGWL 2, 3; SUFW 1

Francis, Claude .... **CLC 50**
  See also CA 192

Francis, Dick
  See Francis, Richard Stanley
  See also CN 2, 3, 4, 5, 6

Francis, Richard Stanley 1920- ... **CLC 2, 22,
  42, 102**
  See Francis, Dick
  See also AAYA 5, 21; BEST 89:3; BPFB 1;
  CA 5-8R; CANR 9, 42, 68, 100, 141; CD-
  BLB 1960 to Present; CMW 4; CN 7;
  DA3; DAM POP; DLB 87; INT CANR-9;
  MSW; MTCW 1, 2; MTFW 2005

Francis, Robert (Churchill)
  1901-1987 .... **CLC 15; PC 34**
  See also AMWS 9; CA 1-4R; CAAS 123;
  CANR 1; CP 1, 2, 3, 4; EXPP; PFS 12;
  TCLE 1:1

Francis, Lord Jeffrey
  See Jeffrey, Francis
  See also DLB 107

Frank, Anne(lies Marie)
  1929-1945 .... **TCLC 17; WLC 2**
  See also AAYA 12; BYA 1; CA 133; CAAE
  113; CANR 68; CLR 101; DA; DA3;
  DAB; DAC; DAM MST; LAIT 4; MAI-
  CYA 1, 2; MAICYAS 1; MTCW 1, 2;
  MTFW 2005; NCFS 2; RGHL; SATA 87;
  SATA-Brief 42; WYA; YAW

Frank, Bruno 1887-1945 .... **TCLC 81**
  See also CA 189; DLB 118; EWL 3

Frank, Elizabeth 1945- .... **CLC 39**
  See also CA 126; CAAE 121; CANR 78,
  150; INT CA-126

Frankl, Viktor E(mil) 1905-1997 ...... **CLC 93**
  See also CA 65-68; CAAS 161; RGHL

Franklin, Benjamin
  See Hasek, Jaroslav (Matej Frantisek)

Franklin, Benjamin 1706-1790 .. **LC 25, 134;
  WLCS**
  See also AMW; CDALB 1640-1865; DA;
  DA3; DAB; DAC; DAM MST; DLB 24,
  43, 73, 183; LAIT 1; RGAL 4; TUS

Franklin, (Stella Maria Sarah) Miles
  (Lampe) 1879-1954 .... **TCLC 7**
  See also CA 164; CAAE 104; DLB 230;
  FW; MTCW 2; RGEL 2; TWA

Franzen, Jonathan 1959- .... **CLC 202**
  See also AAYA 65; CA 129; CANR 105

Fraser, Antonia 1932- .... **CLC 32, 107**
  See also AAYA 57; CA 85-88; CANR 44,
  65, 119; CMW; DLB 276; MTCW 1, 2;
  MTFW 2005; SATA-Brief 32

Fraser, George MacDonald 1925- ...... **CLC 7**
  See also AAYA 48; CA 180; 45-48, 180;
  CANR 2, 48, 74; MTCW 2; RHW

Fraser, Sylvia 1935- .... **CLC 64**
  See also CA 45-48; CANR 1, 16, 60; CCA 1

Frayn, Michael 1933- .... **CLC 3, 7, 31, 47,
  176; DC 27**
  See also AAYA 69; BRWC 2; BRWS 7; CA
  5-8R; CANR 30, 69, 114, 133; CBD; CD
  5, 6; CN 1, 2, 3, 4, 5, 6, 7; DAM DRAM,
  NOV; DFS 22; DLB 13, 14, 194, 245;
  FANT; MTCW 1, 2; MTFW 2005; SFW
  4

Fraze, Candida (Merrill) 1945- .... **CLC 50**
  See also CA 126

Frazer, Andrew
  See Marlowe, Stephen

Frazer, J(ames) G(eorge)
  1854-1941 .... **TCLC 32**
  See also BRWS 3; CAAE 118; NCFS 5

Frazer, Robert Caine
  See Creasey, John

Frazer, Sir James George
  See Frazer, J(ames) G(eorge)

Frazier, Charles 1950- .... **CLC 109, 224**
  See also AAYA 34; CA 161; CANR 126;
  CSW; DLB 292; MTFW 2005

Frazier, Ian 1951- .... **CLC 46**
  See also CA 130; CANR 54, 93

Frederic, Harold 1856-1898 ... **NCLC 10, 175**
  See also AMW; DLB 12, 23; DLBD 13;
  MAL 5; NFS 22; RGAL 4

Frederick, John
  See Faust, Frederick (Schiller)
  See also TCWW 2

Frederick the Great 1712-1786 .... **LC 14**

Fredro, Aleksander 1793-1876 .... **NCLC 8**

Freeling, Nicolas 1927-2003 .... **CLC 38**
  See also CA 49-52; 12; CAAS 218; CANR
  1, 17, 50, 84; CMW 4; CN 1, 2, 3, 4, 5,
  6; DLB 87

Freeman, Douglas Southall
  1886-1953 .... **TCLC 11**
  See also CA 195; CAAE 109; DLB 17;
  DLBD 17

Freeman, Judith 1946- .... **CLC 55**
  See also CA 148; CANR 120; DLB 256

Freeman, Mary E(leanor) Wilkins
  1852-1930 .... **SSC 1, 47; TCLC 9**
  See also CA 177; CAAE 106; DLB 12, 78,
  221; EXPS; FW; HGG; MBL; RGAL 4;
  RGSF 2; SSFS 4, 8; SUFW 1; TUS

Freeman, R(ichard) Austin
  1862-1943 .... **TCLC 21**
  See also CAAE 113; CANR 84; CMW 4;
  DLB 70

French, Albert 1943- .... **CLC 86**
  See also BW 3; CA 167

French, Antonia
  See Kureishi, Hanif

French, Marilyn 1929- .. **CLC 10, 18, 60, 177**
  See also BPFB 1; CA 69-72; CANR 3, 31,
  134; CN 5, 6, 7; CPW; DAM DRAM,
  NOV, POP; FL 1:5; FW; INT CANR-31;
  MTCW 1, 2; MTFW 2005

French, Paul
  See Asimov, Isaac

Freneau, Philip Morin 1752-1832 .. **NCLC 1,
  111**
  See also AMWS 2; DLB 37, 43; RGAL 4

Freud, Sigmund 1856-1939 .... **TCLC 52**
  See also CA 133; CAAE 115; CANR 69;
  DLB 296; EW 8; EWL 3; LATS 1:1;
  MTCW 1, 2; MTFW 2005; NCFS 3; TWA

Freytag, Gustav 1816-1895 .... **NCLC 109**
  See also DLB 129

Friedan, Betty 1921-2006 .... **CLC 74**
  See also CA 65-68; CAAS 248; CANR 18,
  45, 74; DLB 246; FW; MTCW 1, 2;
  MTFW 2005; NCFS 5

Friedan, Betty Naomi
  See Friedan, Betty

Friedlander, Saul 1932- .... **CLC 90**
  See also CA 130; CAAE 117; CANR 72;
  RGHL

Friedman, B(ernard) H(arper)
  1926- .... **CLC 7**
  See also CA 1-4R; CANR 3, 48

Friedman, Bruce Jay 1930- ...... **CLC 3, 5, 56**
  See also CA 9-12R; CAD; CANR 25, 52,
  101; CD 5, 6; CN 1, 2, 3, 4, 5, 6, 7; DLB
  2, 28, 244; INT CANR-25; MAL 5; SSFS
  18

Friel, Brian 1929- .... **CLC 5, 42, 59, 115; DC
  8; SSC 76**
  See also BRWS 5; CA 21-24R; CANR 33,
  69, 131; CBD; CD 5, 6; DFS 11; DLB
  13, 319; EWL 3; MTCW 1; RGEL 2; TEA

Friis-Baastad, Babbis Ellinor
  1921-1970 .... **CLC 12**
  See also CA 17-20R; CAAS 134; SATA 7

Frisch, Max 1911-1991 ...... **CLC 3, 9, 14, 18,
  32, 44; TCLC 121**
  See also CA 85-88; CAAS 134; CANR 32,
  74; CDWLB 2; DAM DRAM, NOV; DLB
  69, 124; EW 13; EWL 3; MTCW 1, 2;
  MTFW 2005; RGHL; RGWL 2, 3

Fromentin, Eugene (Samuel Auguste)
  1820-1876 .... **NCLC 10, 125**
  See also DLB 123; GFL 1789 to the Present

Frost, Frederick
  See Faust, Frederick (Schiller)

Frost, Robert 1874-1963 . **CLC 1, 3, 4, 9, 10,
  13, 15, 26, 34, 44; PC 1, 39, 71; WLC 2**
  See also AAYA 21; AMW; AMWR 1; CA
  89-92; CANR 33; CDALB 1917-1929;
  CLR 67; DA; DA3; DAB; DAC; DAM
  MST, POET; DLB 54, 284; DLBD 7;
  EWL 3; EXPP; MAL 5; MTCW 1, 2;
  MTFW 2005; PAB; PFS 1, 2, 3, 4, 5, 6,
  7, 10, 13; RGAL 4; SATA 14; TUS; WP;
  WYA

Frost, Robert Lee
  See Frost, Robert

Froude, James Anthony
  1818-1894 .... **NCLC 43**
  See also DLB 18, 57, 144

Froy, Herald
  See Waterhouse, Keith (Spencer)

Fry, Christopher 1907-2005 ... **CLC 2, 10, 14**
  See also BRWS 3; CA 17-20R; 23; CAAS
  240; CANR 9, 30, 74, 132; CBD; CD 5,
  6; CP 1, 2, 3, 4, 5, 6, 7; DAM DRAM;
  DLB 13; EWL 3; MTCW 1, 2; MTFW
  2005; RGEL 2; SATA 66; TEA

Frye, (Herman) Northrop
  1912-1991 .... **CLC 24, 70; TCLC 165**
  See also CA 5-8R; CAAS 133; CANR 8,
  37; DLB 67, 68, 246; EWL 3; MTCW 1,
  2; MTFW 2005; RGAL 4; TWA

Fuchs, Daniel 1909-1993 .... **CLC 8, 22**
  See also CA 81-84; 5; CAAS 142; CANR
  40; CN 1, 2, 3, 4, 5; DLB 9, 26, 28;
  DLBY 1993; MAL 5

Fuchs, Daniel 1934- .... **CLC 34**
  See also CA 37-40R; CANR 14, 48

Fuentes, Carlos 1928- .. **CLC 3, 8, 10, 13, 22,
  41, 60, 113; HLC 1; SSC 24; WLC 2**
  See also AAYA 4, 45; AITN 2; BPFB 1;
  CA 69-72; CANR 10, 32, 68, 104, 138;
  CDWLB 3; CWW 2; DA; DA3; DAB;
  DAC; DAM MST, MULT, NOV; DLB
  113; DNFS 2; EWL 3; HW 1, 2; LAIT 3;
  LATS 1:2; LAW; LAWS 1; LMFS 2;
  MTCW 1, 2; MTFW 2005; NFS 8; RGSF
  2; RGWL 2, 3; TWA; WLIT 1

Fuentes, Gregorio Lopez y
  See Lopez y Fuentes, Gregorio

Fuertes, Gloria 1918-1998 .... **PC 27**
  See also CA 178, 180; DLB 108; HW 2;
  SATA 115

Fugard, (Harold) Athol 1932- . **CLC 5, 9, 14, 25, 40, 80, 211; DC 3**
See also AAYA 17; AFW; CA 85-88; CANR 32, 54, 118; CD 5, 6; DAM DRAM; DFS 3, 6, 10; DLB 225; DNFS 1, 2; EWL 3; LATS 1:2; MTCW 1; MTFW 2005; RGEL 2; WLIT 2

Fugard, Sheila 1932- .... **CLC 48**
See also CA 125

Fujiwara no Teika 1162-1241 .... **CMLC 73**
See also DLB 203

Fukuyama, Francis 1952- .... **CLC 131**
See also CA 140; CANR 72, 125

Fuller, Charles (H.), (Jr.) 1939- .... **BLC 2; CLC 25; DC 1**
See also BW 2; CA 112; CAAE 108; CAD; CANR 87; CD 5, 6; DAM DRAM, MULT; DFS 8; DLB 38, 266; EWL 3; INT CA-112; MAL 5; MTCW 1

Fuller, Henry Blake 1857-1929 .... **TCLC 103**
See also CA 177; CAAE 108; DLB 12; RGAL 4

Fuller, John (Leopold) 1937- .... **CLC 62**
See also CA 21-24R; CANR 9, 44; CP 1, 2, 3, 4, 5, 6, 7; DLB 40

Fuller, Margaret
See Ossoli, Sarah Margaret (Fuller)
See also AMWS 2; DLB 183, 223, 239; FL 1:3

Fuller, Roy (Broadbent) 1912-1991 ... **CLC 4, 28**
See also BRWS 7; CA 5-8R; 10; CAAS 135; CANR 53, 83; CN 1, 2, 3, 4, 5; CP 1, 2, 3, 4, 5; CWRI 5; DLB 15, 20; EWL 3; RGEL 2; SATA 87

Fuller, Sarah Margaret
See Ossoli, Sarah Margaret (Fuller)

Fuller, Sarah Margaret
See Ossoli, Sarah Margaret (Fuller)
See also DLB 1, 59, 73

Fuller, Thomas 1608-1661 .... **LC 111**
See also DLB 151

Fulton, Alice 1952- .... **CLC 52**
See also CA 116; CANR 57, 88; CP 5, 6, 7; CWP; DLB 193; PFS 25

Furphy, Joseph 1843-1912 .... **TCLC 25**
See Collins, Tom
See also CA 163; DLB 230; EWL 3; RGEL 2

Fuson, Robert H(enderson) 1927- .... **CLC 70**
See also CA 89-92; CANR 103

Fussell, Paul 1924- .... **CLC 74**
See also BEST 90:1; CA 17-20R; CANR 8, 21, 35, 69, 135; INT CANR-21; MTCW 1, 2; MTFW 2005

Futabatei, Shimei 1864-1909 .... **TCLC 44**
See Futabatei Shimei
See also CA 162; MJW

Futabatei Shimei
See Futabatei, Shimei
See also DLB 180; EWL 3

Futrelle, Jacques 1875-1912 .... **TCLC 19**
See also CA 155; CAAE 113; CMW 4

Gaboriau, Emile 1835-1873 .... **NCLC 14**
See also CMW 4; MSW

Gadda, Carlo Emilio 1893-1973 ...... **CLC 11; TCLC 144**
See also CA 89-92; DLB 177; EWL 3; WLIT 7

Gaddis, William 1922-1998 ... **CLC 1, 3, 6, 8, 10, 19, 43, 86**
See also AMWS 4; BPFB 1; CA 17-20R; CAAS 172; CANR 21, 48, 148; CN 1, 2, 3, 4, 5, 6; DLB 2, 278; EWL 3; MAL 5; MTCW 1, 2; MTFW 2005; RGAL 4

Gage, Walter
See Inge, William (Motter)

Gaiman, Neil 1960- .... **CLC 195**
See also AAYA 19, 42; CA 133; CANR 81, 129; CLR 109; DLB 261; HGG; MTFW 2005; SATA 85, 146; SFW 4; SUFW 2

Gaiman, Neil Richard
See Gaiman, Neil

Gaines, Ernest J. 1933- .. **BLC 2; CLC 3, 11, 18, 86, 181; SSC 68**
See also AAYA 18; AFAW 1, 2; AITN 1; BPFB 2; BW 2, 3; BYA 6; CA 9-12R; CANR 6, 24, 42, 75, 126; CDALB 1968-1988; CLR 62; CN 1, 2, 3, 4, 5, 6, 7; CSW; DA3; DAM MULT; DLB 2, 33, 152; DLBY 1980; EWL 3; EXPN; LAIT 5; LATS 1:2; MAL 5; MTCW 1, 2; MTFW 2005; NFS 5, 7, 16; RGAL 4; RGSF 2; RHW; SATA 86; SSFS 5; YAW

Gaitskill, Mary 1954- .... **CLC 69**
See also CA 128; CANR 61, 152; DLB 244; TCLE 1:1

Gaitskill, Mary Lawrence
See Gaitskill, Mary

Gaius Suetonius Tranquillus
See Suetonius

Galdos, Benito Perez
See Perez Galdos, Benito
See also EW 7

Gale, Zona 1874-1938 .... **TCLC 7**
See also CA 153; CAAE 105; CANR 84; DAM DRAM; DFS 17; DLB 9, 78, 228; RGAL 4

Galeano, Eduardo (Hughes) 1940- . **CLC 72; HLCS 1**
See also CA 29-32R; CANR 13, 32, 100; HW 1

Galiano, Juan Valera y Alcala
See Valera y Alcala-Galiano, Juan

Galilei, Galileo 1564-1642 .... **LC 45**

Gallagher, Tess 1943- .... **CLC 18, 63; PC 9**
See also CA 106; CP 3, 4, 5, 6, 7; CWP; DAM POET; DLB 120, 212, 244; PFS 16

Gallant, Mavis 1922- ..... **CLC 7, 18, 38, 172; SSC 5, 78**
See also CA 69-72; CANR 29, 69, 117; CCA 1; CN 1, 2, 3, 4, 5, 6, 7; DAC; DAM MST; DLB 53; EWL 3; MTCW 1, 2; MTFW 2005; RGEL 2; RGSF 2

Gallant, Roy A(rthur) 1924- .... **CLC 17**
See also CA 5-8R; CANR 4, 29, 54, 117; CLR 30; MAICYA 1, 2; SATA 4, 68, 110

Gallico, Paul (William) 1897-1976 ..... **CLC 2**
See also AITN 1; CA 5-8R; CAAS 69-72; CANR 23; CN 1, 2; DLB 9, 171; FANT; MAICYA 1, 2; SATA 13

Gallo, Max Louis 1932- .... **CLC 95**
See also CA 85-88

Gallois, Lucien
See Desnos, Robert

Gallup, Ralph
See Whitemore, Hugh (John)

Galsworthy, John 1867-1933 .... **SSC 22; TCLC 1, 45; WLC 2**
See also BRW 6; CA 141; CAAE 104; CANR 75; CDBLB 1890-1914; DA; DA3; DAB; DAC; DAM DRAM, MST, NOV; DLB 10, 34, 98, 162, 330; DLBD 16; EWL 3; MTCW 2; RGEL 2; SSFS 3; TEA

Galt, John 1779-1839 .... **NCLC 1, 110**
See also DLB 99, 116, 159; RGEL 2; RGSF 2

Galvin, James 1951- .... **CLC 38**
See also CA 108; CANR 26

Gamboa, Federico 1864-1939 .... **TCLC 36**
See also CA 167; HW 2; LAW

Gandhi, M. K.
See Gandhi, Mohandas Karamchand

Gandhi, Mahatma
See Gandhi, Mohandas Karamchand

Gandhi, Mohandas Karamchand 1869-1948 .... **TCLC 59**
See also CA 132; CAAE 121; DA3; DAM MULT; DLB 323; MTCW 1, 2

Gann, Ernest Kellogg 1910-1991 ..... **CLC 23**
See also AITN 1; BPFB 2; CA 1-4R; CAAS 136; CANR 1, 83; RHW

Gao Xingjian 1940- .... **CLC 167**
See Xingjian, Gao
See also MTFW 2005

Garber, Eric 1943(?)-
See Holleran, Andrew
See also CANR 89

Garcia, Cristina 1958- .... **CLC 76**
See also AMWS 11; CA 141; CANR 73, 130; CN 7; DLB 292; DNFS 1; EWL 3; HW 2; LLW; MTFW 2005

Garcia Lorca, Federico 1898-1936 ...... **DC 2; HLC 2; PC 3; TCLC 1, 7, 49, 181; WLC 2**
See Lorca, Federico Garcia
See also AAYA 46; CA 131; CAAE 104; CANR 81; DA; DA3; DAB; DAC; DAM DRAM, MST, MULT, POET; DFS 4, 10; DLB 108; EWL 3; HW 1, 2; LATS 1:2; MTCW 1, 2; MTFW 2005; TWA

Garcia Marquez, Gabriel 1928- .... **CLC 2, 3, 8, 10, 15, 27, 47, 55, 68, 170; HLC 1; SSC 8, 83; WLC 3**
See also AAYA 3, 33; BEST 89:1, 90:4; BPFB 2; BYA 12, 16; CA 33-36R; CANR 10, 28, 50, 75, 82, 128; CDWLB 3; CPW; CWW 2; DA; DA3; DAB; DAC; DAM MST, MULT, NOV, POP; DLB 113, 330; DNFS 1, 2; EWL 3; EXPN; EXPS; HW 1, 2; LAIT 2; LATS 1:2; LAW; LAWS 1; LMFS 2; MTCW 1, 2; MTFW 2005; NCFS 3; NFS 1, 5, 10; RGSF 2; RGWL 2, 3; SSFS 1, 6, 16, 21; TWA; WLIT 1

Garcia Marquez, Gabriel Jose
See Garcia Marquez, Gabriel

Garcilaso de la Vega, El Inca 1539-1616 .... **HLCS 1; LC 127**
See also DLB 318; LAW

Gard, Janice
See Latham, Jean Lee

Gard, Roger Martin du
See Martin du Gard, Roger

Gardam, Jane (Mary) 1928- .... **CLC 43**
See also CA 49-52; CANR 2, 18, 33, 54, 106; CLR 12; DLB 14, 161, 231; MAICYA 1, 2; MTCW 1; SAAS 9; SATA 39, 76, 130; SATA-Brief 28; YAW

Gardner, Herb(ert George) 1934-2003 .... **CLC 44**
See also CA 149; CAAS 220; CAD; CANR 119; CD 5, 6; DFS 18, 20

Gardner, John, Jr. 1933-1982 ... **CLC 2, 3, 5, 7, 8, 10, 18, 28, 34; SSC 7**
See also AAYA 45; AITN 1; AMWS 6; BPFB 2; CA 65-68; CAAS 107; CANR 33, 73; CDALBS; CN 2, 3; CPW; DA3; DAM NOV, POP; DLB 2; DLBY 1982; EWL 3; FANT; LATS 1:2; MAL 5; MTCW 1, 2; MTFW 2005; NFS 3; RGAL 4; RGSF 2; SATA 40; SATA-Obit 31; SSFS 8

Gardner, John (Edmund) 1926- .... **CLC 30**
See also CA 103; CANR 15, 69, 127; CMW 4; CPW; DAM POP; MTCW 1

Gardner, Miriam
See Bradley, Marion Zimmer
See also GLL 1

Gardner, Noel
See Kuttner, Henry

Gardons, S. S.
See Snodgrass, W.D.

Garfield, Leon 1921-1996 .... **CLC 12**
See also AAYA 8, 69; BYA 1, 3; CA 17-
20R; CAAS 152; CANR 38, 41, 78; CLR
21; DLB 161; JRDA; MAICYA 1, 2;
MAICYAS 1; SATA 1, 32, 76; SATA-Obit
90; TEA; WYA; YAW

Garland, (Hannibal) Hamlin
1860-1940 .... **SSC 18; TCLC 3**
See also CAAE 104; DLB 12, 71, 78, 186;
MAL 5; RGAL 4; RGSF 2; TCWW 1, 2

Garneau, (Hector de) Saint-Denys
1912-1943 .... **TCLC 13**
See also CAAE 111; DLB 88

Garner, Alan 1934- .... **CLC 17**
See also AAYA 18; BYA 3, 5; CA 178; 73-
76, 178; CANR 15, 64, 134; CLR 20;
CPW; DAB; DAM POP; DLB 161, 261;
FANT; MAICYA 1, 2; MTCW 1, 2;
MTFW 2005; SATA 18, 69; SATA-Essay
108; SUFW 1, 2; YAW

Garner, Hugh 1913-1979 .... **CLC 13**
See Warwick, Jarvis
See also CA 69-72; CANR 31; CCA 1; CN
1, 2; DLB 68

Garnett, David 1892-1981 .... **CLC 3**
See also CA 5-8R; CAAS 103; CANR 17,
79; CN 1, 2; DLB 34; FANT; MTCW 2;
RGEL 2; SFW 4; SUFW 1

Garnier, Robert c. 1545-1590 .... **LC 119**
See also DLB 327; GFL Beginnings to 1789

Garrett, George (Palmer, Jr.) 1929- . **CLC 3,
11, 51; SSC 30**
See also AMWS 7; BPFB 2; CA 202; 1-4R,
202; 5; CANR 1, 42, 67, 109; CN 1, 2, 3,
4, 5, 6, 7; CP 1, 2, 3, 4, 5, 6, 7; CSW;
DLB 2, 5, 130, 152; DLBY 1983

Garrick, David 1717-1779 .... **LC 15**
See also DAM DRAM; DLB 84, 213;
RGEL 2

Garrigue, Jean 1914-1972 .... **CLC 2, 8**
See also CA 5-8R; CAAS 37-40R; CANR
20; CP 1; MAL 5

Garrison, Frederick
See Sinclair, Upton

Garrison, William Lloyd
1805-1879 .... **NCLC 149**
See also CDALB 1640-1865; DLB 1, 43,
235

Garro, Elena 1920(?)-1998 .. **HLCS 1; TCLC
153**
See also CA 131; CAAS 169; CWW 2;
DLB 145; EWL 3; HW 1; LAWS 1; WLIT
1

Garth, Will
See Hamilton, Edmond; Kuttner, Henry

Garvey, Marcus (Moziah, Jr.)
1887-1940 ... **BLC 2; HR 1:2; TCLC 41**
See also BW 1; CA 124; CAAE 120; CANR
79; DAM MULT

Gary, Romain .... **CLC 25**
See Kacew, Romain
See also DLB 83, 299; RGHL

Gascar, Pierre .... **CLC 11**
See Fournier, Pierre
See also EWL 3; RGHL

Gascoigne, George 1539-1577 .... **LC 108**
See also DLB 136; RGEL 2

Gascoyne, David (Emery)
1916-2001 .... **CLC 45**
See also CA 65-68; CAAS 200; CANR 10,
28, 54; CP 1, 2, 3, 4, 5, 6, 7; DLB 20;
MTCW 1; RGEL 2

Gaskell, Elizabeth Cleghorn
1810-1865 .... **NCLC 5, 70, 97, 137; SSC
25, 97**
See also BRW 5; CDBLB 1832-1890; DAB;
DAM MST; DLB 21, 144, 159; RGEL 2;
RGSF 2; TEA

Gass, William H. 1924- . **CLC 1, 2, 8, 11, 15,
39, 132; SSC 12**
See also AMWS 6; CA 17-20R; CANR 30,
71, 100; CN 1, 2, 3, 4, 5, 6, 7; DLB 2,
227; EWL 3; MAL 5; MTCW 1, 2;
MTFW 2005; RGAL 4

Gassendi, Pierre 1592-1655 .... **LC 54**
See also GFL Beginnings to 1789

Gasset, Jose Ortega y
See Ortega y Gasset, Jose

Gates, Henry Louis, Jr. 1950- ... **BLCS; CLC
65**
See also BW 2, 3; CA 109; CANR 25, 53,
75, 125; CSW; DA3; DAM MULT; DLB
67; EWL 3; MAL 5; MTCW 2; MTFW
2005; RGAL 4

Gatos, Stephanie
See Katz, Steve

Gautier, Theophile 1811-1872 .. **NCLC 1, 59;
PC 18; SSC 20**
See also DAM POET; DLB 119; EW 6;
GFL 1789 to the Present; RGWL 2, 3;
SUFW; TWA

Gay, John 1685-1732 .... **LC 49**
See also BRW 3; DAM DRAM; DLB 84,
95; RGEL 2; WLIT 3

Gay, Oliver
See Gogarty, Oliver St. John

Gay, Peter 1923- .... **CLC 158**
See also CA 13-16R; CANR 18, 41, 77,
147; INT CANR-18; RGHL

Gay, Peter Jack
See Gay, Peter

Gaye, Marvin (Pentz, Jr.)
1939-1984 .... **CLC 26**
See also CA 195; CAAS 112

Gebler, Carlo 1954- .... **CLC 39**
See also CA 133; CAAE 119; CANR 96;
DLB 271

Gee, Maggie 1948- .... **CLC 57**
See also CA 130; CANR 125; CN 4, 5, 6,
7; DLB 207; MTFW 2005

Gee, Maurice 1931- .... **CLC 29**
See also AAYA 42; CA 97-100; CANR 67,
123; CLR 56; CN 2, 3, 4, 5, 6, 7; CWRI
5; EWL 3; MAICYA 2; RGSF 2; SATA
46, 101

Gee, Maurice Gough
See Gee, Maurice

Geiogamah, Hanay 1945- .... **NNAL**
See also CA 153; DAM MULT; DLB 175

Gelbart, Larry
See Gelbart, Larry (Simon)
See also CAD; CD 5, 6

Gelbart, Larry (Simon) 1928- .... **CLC 21, 61**
See Gelbart, Larry
See also CA 73-76; CANR 45, 94

Gelber, Jack 1932-2003 ...... **CLC 1, 6, 14, 79**
See also CA 1-4R; CAAS 216; CAD;
CANR 2; DLB 7, 228; MAL 5

Gellhorn, Martha (Ellis)
1908-1998 .... **CLC 14, 60**
See also CA 77-80; CAAS 164; CANR 44;
CN 1, 2, 3, 4, 5, 6 7; DLBY 1982, 1998

Genet, Jean 1910-1986 .. **CLC 1, 2, 5, 10, 14,
44, 46; DC 25; TCLC 128**
See also CA 13-16R; CANR 18; DA3;
DAM DRAM; DFS 10; DLB 72, 321;
DLBY 1986; EW 13; EWL 3; GFL 1789
to the Present; GLL 1; LMFS 2; MTCW
1, 2; MTFW 2005; RGWL 2, 3; TWA

Genlis, Stephanie-Felicite Ducrest
1746-1830 .... **NCLC 166**
See also DLB 313

Gent, Peter 1942- .... **CLC 29**
See also AITN 1; CA 89-92; DLBY 1982

Gentile, Giovanni 1875-1944 .... **TCLC 96**
See also CAAE 119

Geoffrey of Monmouth c.
1100-1155 .... **CMLC 44**
See also DLB 146; TEA

George, Jean
See George, Jean Craighead

George, Jean Craighead 1919- .... **CLC 35**
See also AAYA 8, 69; BYA 2, 4; CA 5-8R;
CANR 25; CLR 1; 80; DLB 52; JRDA;
MAICYA 1, 2; SATA 2, 68, 124, 170;
WYA; YAW

George, Stefan (Anton) 1868-1933 . **TCLC 2,
14**
See also CA 193; CAAE 104; EW 8; EWL
3

Georges, Georges Martin
See Simenon, Georges (Jacques Christian)

Gerald of Wales c. 1146-c. 1223 ... **CMLC 60**

Gerhardi, William Alexander
See Gerhardie, William Alexander

Gerhardie, William Alexander
1895-1977 .... **CLC 5**
See also CA 25-28R; CAAS 73-76; CANR
18; CN 1, 2; DLB 36; RGEL 2

Gerson, Jean 1363-1429 .... **LC 77**
See also DLB 208

Gersonides 1288-1344 .... **CMLC 49**
See also DLB 115

Gerstler, Amy 1956- .... **CLC 70**
See also CA 146; CANR 99

Gertler, T. .... **CLC 34**
See also CA 121; CAAE 116

Gertsen, Aleksandr Ivanovich
See Herzen, Aleksandr Ivanovich

Ghalib .... **NCLC 39, 78**
See Ghalib, Asadullah Khan

Ghalib, Asadullah Khan 1797-1869
See Ghalib
See also DAM POET; RGWL 2, 3

Ghelderode, Michel de 1898-1962 ..... **CLC 6,
11; DC 15; TCLC 187**
See also CA 85-88; CANR 40, 77; DAM
DRAM; DLB 321; EW 11; EWL 3; TWA

Ghiselin, Brewster 1903-2001 .... **CLC 23**
See also CA 13-16R; 10; CANR 13; CP 1,
2, 3, 4, 5, 6, 7

Ghose, Aurabinda 1872-1950 .... **TCLC 63**
See Ghose, Aurobindo
See also CA 163

Ghose, Aurobindo
See Ghose, Aurabinda
See also EWL 3

Ghose, Zulfikar 1935- .... **CLC 42, 200**
See also CA 65-68; CANR 67; CN 1, 2, 3,
4, 5, 6, 7; CP 1, 2, 3, 4, 5, 6, 7; DLB 323;
EWL 3

Ghosh, Amitav 1956- .... **CLC 44, 153**
See also CA 147; CANR 80, 158; CN 6, 7;
DLB 323; WWE 1

Giacosa, Giuseppe 1847-1906 .... **TCLC 7**
See also CAAE 104

Gibb, Lee
See Waterhouse, Keith (Spencer)

Gibbon, Edward 1737-1794 .... **LC 97**
See also BRW 3; DLB 104; RGEL 2

Gibbon, Lewis Grassic .... **TCLC 4**
See Mitchell, James Leslie
See also RGEL 2

Gibbons, Kaye 1960- .... **CLC 50, 88, 145**
See also AAYA 34; AMWS 6; CA 151;
CANR 75, 127; CN 7; CSW; DA3; DAM
POP; DLB 292; MTCW 2; MTFW 2005;
NFS 3; RGAL 4; SATA 117

Gibran, Kahlil 1883-1931 . **PC 9; TCLC 1, 9**
See also CA 150; CAAE 104; DA3; DAM
POET, POP; EWL 3; MTCW 2; WLIT 6

Gibran, Khalil
See Gibran, Kahlil

Gibson, Mel 1956- .... **CLC 215**

Gibson, William 1914- .... **CLC 23**
  See also CA 9-12R; CAD; CANR 9, 42, 75, 125; CD 5, 6; DA; DAB; DAC; DAM DRAM, MST; DFS 2; DLB 7; LAIT 2; MAL 5; MTCW 2; MTFW 2005; SATA 66; YAW

Gibson, William 1948- .... **CLC 39, 63, 186, 192; SSC 52**
  See also AAYA 12, 59; AMWS 16; BPFB 2; CA 133; CAAE 126; CANR 52, 90, 106; CN 6, 7; CPW; DA3; DAM POP; DLB 251; MTCW 2; MTFW 2005; SCFW 2; SFW 4

Gibson, William Ford
  See Gibson, William

Gide, Andre (Paul Guillaume)
  1869-1951 ...... **SSC 13; TCLC 5, 12, 36, 177; WLC 3**
  See also CA 124; CAAE 104; DA; DA3; DAB; DAC; DAM MST, NOV; DLB 65, 321, 330; EW 8; EWL 3; GFL 1789 to the Present; MTCW 1, 2; MTFW 2005; NFS 21; RGSF 2; RGWL 2, 3; TWA

Gifford, Barry (Colby) 1946- .... **CLC 34**
  See also CA 65-68; CANR 9, 30, 40, 90

Gilbert, Frank
  See De Voto, Bernard (Augustine)

Gilbert, W(illiam) S(chwenck)
  1836-1911 .... **TCLC 3**
  See also CA 173; CAAE 104; DAM DRAM, POET; RGEL 2; SATA 36

Gilbert of Poitiers c. 1085-1154 .... **CMLC 85**

Gilbreth, Frank B(unker), Jr.
  1911-2001 .... **CLC 17**
  See also CA 9-12R; SATA 2

Gilchrist, Ellen (Louise) 1935- .. **CLC 34, 48, 143; SSC 14, 63**
  See also BPFB 2; CA 116; CAAE 113; CANR 41, 61, 104; CN 4, 5, 6, 7; CPW; CSW; DAM POP; DLB 130; EWL 3; EXPS; MTCW 1, 2; MTFW 2005; RGAL 4; RGSF 2; SSFS 9

Giles, Molly 1942- .... **CLC 39**
  See also CA 126; CANR 98

Gill, Eric .... **TCLC 85**
  See Gill, (Arthur) Eric (Rowton Peter Joseph)

Gill, (Arthur) Eric (Rowton Peter Joseph)
  1882-1940
  See Gill, Eric
  See also CAAE 120; DLB 98

Gill, Patrick
  See Creasey, John

Gillette, Douglas .... **CLC 70**

Gilliam, Terry 1940- .... **CLC 21, 141**
  See Monty Python
  See also AAYA 19, 59; CA 113; CAAE 108; CANR 35; INT CA-113

Gilliam, Terry Vance
  See Gilliam, Terry

Gillian, Jerry
  See Gilliam, Terry

Gilliatt, Penelope (Ann Douglass)
  1932-1993 .... **CLC 2, 10, 13, 53**
  See also AITN 2; CA 13-16R; CAAS 141; CANR 49; CN 1, 2, 3, 4, 5; DLB 14

Gilligan, Carol 1936- .... **CLC 208**
  See also CA 142; CANR 121; FW

Gilman, Charlotte (Anna) Perkins (Stetson)
  1860-1935 ...... **SSC 13, 62; TCLC 9, 37, 117**
  See also AAYA 75; AMWS 11; BYA 11; CA 150; CAAE 106; DLB 221; EXPS; FL 1:5; FW; HGG; LAIT 2; MBL; MTCW 2; MTFW 2005; RGAL 4; RGSF 2; SFW 4; SSFS 1, 18

Gilmour, David 1946- .... **CLC 35**

Gilpin, William 1724-1804 .... **NCLC 30**

Gilray, J. D.
  See Mencken, H(enry) L(ouis)

Gilroy, Frank D(aniel) 1925- .... **CLC 2**
  See also CA 81-84; CAD; CANR 32, 64, 86; CD 5, 6; DFS 17; DLB 7

Gilstrap, John 1957(?)- .... **CLC 99**
  See also AAYA 67; CA 160; CANR 101

Ginsberg, Allen 1926-1997 .... **CLC 1, 2, 3, 4, 6, 13, 36, 69, 109; PC 4, 47; TCLC 120; WLC 3**
  See also AAYA 33; AITN 1; AMWC 1; AMWS 2; BG 1:2; CA 1-4R; CAAS 157; CANR 2, 41, 63, 95; CDALB 1941-1968; CP 1, 2, 3, 4, 5, 6; DA; DA3; DAB; DAC; DAM MST, POET; DLB 5, 16, 169, 237; EWL 3; GLL 1; LMFS 2; MAL 5; MTCW 1, 2; MTFW 2005; PAB; PFS 5; RGAL 4; TUS; WP

Ginzburg, Eugenia .... **CLC 59**
  See Ginzburg, Evgeniia

Ginzburg, Evgeniia 1904-1977
  See Ginzburg, Eugenia
  See also DLB 302

Ginzburg, Natalia 1916-1991 .... **CLC 5, 11, 54, 70; SSC 65; TCLC 156**
  See also CA 85-88; CAAS 135; CANR 33; DFS 14; DLB 177; EW 13; EWL 3; MTCW 1, 2; MTFW 2005; RGHL; RGWL 2, 3

Giono, Jean 1895-1970 .... **CLC 4, 11; TCLC 124**
  See also CA 45-48; CAAS 29-32R; CANR 2, 35; DLB 72, 321; EWL 3; GFL 1789 to the Present; MTCW 1; RGWL 2, 3

Giovanni, Nikki 1943- ...... **BLC 2; CLC 2, 4, 19, 64, 117; PC 19; WLCS**
  See also AAYA 22; AITN 1; BW 2, 3; CA 29-32R; 6; CANR 18, 41, 60, 91, 130; CDALBS; CLR 6, 73; CP 2, 3, 4, 5, 6, 7; CSW; CWP; CWRI 5; DA; DA3; DAB; DAC; DAM MST, MULT, POET; DLB 5, 41; EWL 3; EXPP; INT CANR-18; MAICYA 1, 2; MAL 5; MTCW 1, 2; MTFW 2005; PFS 17; RGAL 4; SATA 24, 107; TUS; YAW

Giovene, Andrea 1904-1998 .... **CLC 7**
  See also CA 85 88

Gippius, Zinaida (Nikolaevna) 1869-1945
  See Hippius, Zinaida (Nikolaevna)
  See also CA 212; CAAE 106

Giraudoux, Jean(-Hippolyte)
  1882-1944 .... **TCLC 2, 7**
  See also CA 196; CAAE 104; DAM DRAM; DLB 65, 321; EW 9; EWL 3; GFL 1789 to the Present; RGWL 2, 3; TWA

Gironella, Jose Maria (Pous)
  1917-2003 .... **CLC 11**
  See also CA 101; CAAS 212; EWL 3; RGWL 2, 3

Gissing, George (Robert)
  1857-1903 .... **SSC 37; TCLC 3, 24, 47**
  See also BRW 5; CA 167; CAAE 105; DLB 18, 135, 184; RGEL 2; TEA

Gitlin, Todd 1943- .... **CLC 201**
  See also CA 29-32R; CANR 25, 50, 88

Giurlani, Aldo
  See Palazzeschi, Aldo

Gladkov, Fedor Vasil'evich
  See Gladkov, Fyodor (Vasilyevich)
  See also DLB 272

Gladkov, Fyodor (Vasilyevich)
  1883 1958 .... **TCLC 27**
  See Gladkov, Fedor Vasil'evich
  See also CA 170; EWL 3

Glancy, Diane 1941- .... **CLC 210; NNAL**
  See also CA 225; 136, 225; 24; CANR 87; DLB 175

Glanville, Brian (Lester) 1931- .... **CLC 6**
  See also CA 5-8R; 9; CANR 3, 70; CN 1, 2, 3, 4, 5, 6, 7; DLB 15, 139; SATA 42

Glasgow, Ellen (Anderson Gholson)
  1873-1945 .... **SSC 34; TCLC 2, 7**
  See also AMW; CA 164; CAAE 104; DLB 9, 12; MAL 5; MBL; MTCW 2; MTFW 2005; RGAL 4; RHW; SSFS 9; TUS

Glaspell, Susan 1882(?)-1948 ..... **DC 10; SSC 41; TCLC 55, 175**
  See also AMWS 3; CA 154; CAAE 110; DFS 8, 18; DLB 7, 9, 78, 228; MBL; RGAL 4; SSFS 3; TCWW 2; TUS; YABC 2

Glassco, John 1909-1981 .... **CLC 9**
  See also CA 13-16R; CAAS 102; CANR 15; CN 1, 2; CP 1, 2, 3; DLB 68

Glasscock, Amnesia
  See Steinbeck, John (Ernst)

Glasser, Ronald J. 1940(?)- .... **CLC 37**
  See also CA 209

Glassman, Joyce
  See Johnson, Joyce

Gleick, James (W.) 1954- .... **CLC 147**
  See also CA 137; CAAE 131; CANR 97; INT CA-137

Glendinning, Victoria 1937- .... **CLC 50**
  See also CA 127; CAAE 120; CANR 59, 89; DLB 155

Glissant, Edouard (Mathieu)
  1928- .... **CLC 10, 68**
  See also CA 153; CANR 111; CWW 2; DAM MULT; EWL 3; RGWL 3

Gloag, Julian 1930- .... **CLC 40**
  See also AITN 1; CA 65-68; CANR 10, 70; CN 1, 2, 3, 4, 5, 6

Glowacki, Aleksander
  See Prus, Boleslaw

Gluck, Louise 1943- .... **CLC 7, 22, 44, 81, 160; PC 16**
  See also AMWS 5; CA 33-36R; CANR 40, 69, 108, 133; CP 1, 2, 3, 4, 5, 6, 7; CWP; DA3; DAM POET; DLB 5; MAL 5; MTCW 2; MTFW 2005; PFS 5, 15; RGAL 4; TCLE 1:1

Glyn, Elinor 1864-1943 .... **TCLC 72**
  See also DLB 153; RHW

Gobineau, Joseph-Arthur
  1816-1882 .... **NCLC 17**
  See also DLB 123; GFL 1789 to the Present

Godard, Jean-Luc 1930- .... **CLC 20**
  See also CA 93-96

Godden, (Margaret) Rumer
  1907-1998 .... **CLC 53**
  See also AAYA 6; BPFB 2; BYA 2, 5; CA 5-8R; CAAS 172; CANR 4, 27, 36, 55, 80; CLR 20; CN 1, 2, 3, 4, 5, 6; CWRI 5; DLB 161; MAICYA 1, 2; RHW; SAAS 12; SATA 3, 36; SATA-Obit 109; TEA

Godoy Alcayaga, Lucila 1899-1957 .. **HLC 2; PC 32; TCLC 2**
  See Mistral, Gabriela
  See also BW 2; CA 131; CAAE 104; CANR 81; DAM MULT; DNFS; HW 1, 2; MTCW 1, 2, MTFW 2005

Godwin, Gail 1937- ...... **CLC 5, 8, 22, 31, 69, 125**
  See also BPFB 2; CA 29-32R; CANR 15, 43, 69, 132; CN 3, 4, 5, 6, 7; CPW; CSW; DA3; DAM POP; DLB 6, 234; INT CANR-15; MAL 5; MTCW 1, 2; MTFW 2005

Godwin, Gail Kathleen
  See Godwin, Gail

Godwin, William 1756-1836 .. **NCLC 14, 130**
  See also CDBLB 1789-1832; CMW 4; DLB 39, 104, 142, 158, 163, 262; GL 2; HGG; RGEL 2

Gracian y Morales, Baltasar
1601-1658 .... **LC 15**

Gracq, Julien .... **CLC 11, 48**
See Poirier, Louis
See also CWW 2; DLB 83; GFL 1789 to
the Present

Grade, Chaim 1910-1982 .... **CLC 10**
See also CA 93-96; CAAS 107; DLB 333;
EWL 3; RGHL

Grade, Khayim
See Grade, Chaim

Graduate of Oxford, A
See Ruskin, John

Grafton, Garth
See Duncan, Sara Jeannette

Grafton, Sue 1940- .... **CLC 163**
See also AAYA 11, 49; BEST 90:3; CA 108;
CANR 31, 55, 111, 134; CMW 4; CPW;
CSW; DA3; DAM POP; DLB 226; FW;
MSW; MTFW 2005

Graham, John
See Phillips, David Graham

Graham, Jorie 1950- .... **CLC 48, 118; PC 59**
See also AAYA 67; CA 111; CANR 63, 118;
CP 4, 5, 6, 7; CWP; DLB 120; EWL 3;
MTFW 2005; PFS 10, 17; TCLE 1:1

Graham, R(obert) B(ontine) Cunninghame
See Cunninghame Graham, Robert
(Gallnigad) Bontine
See also DLB 98, 135, 174; RGEL 2; RGSF
2

Graham, Robert
See Haldeman, Joe

Graham, Tom
See Lewis, (Harry) Sinclair

Graham, W(illiam) S(ydney)
1918-1986 .... **CLC 29**
See also BRWS 7; CA 73-76; CAAS 118;
CP 1, 2, 3, 4; DLB 20; RGEL 2

Graham, Winston (Mawdsley)
1910-2003 .... **CLC 23**
See also CA 49-52; CAAS 218; CANR 2,
22, 45, 66; CMW 4; CN 1, 2, 3, 4, 5, 6,
7; DLB 77; RHW

Grahame, Kenneth 1859-1932 ...... **TCLC 64,
136**
See also BYA 5; CA 136; CAAE 108;
CANR 80; CLR 5; CWRI 5; DA3; DAB;
DLB 34, 141, 178; FANT; MAICYA 1, 2;
MTCW 2; NFS 20; RGEL 2; SATA 100;
TEA; WCH; YABC 1

Granger, Darius John
See Marlowe, Stephen

Granin, Daniil 1918- .... **CLC 59**
See also DLB 302

Granovsky, Timofei Nikolaevich
1813-1855 .... **NCLC 75**
See also DLB 198

Grant, Skeeter
See Spiegelman, Art

Granville-Barker, Harley
1877-1946 .... **TCLC 2**
See Barker, Harley Granville
See also CA 204; CAAE 104; DAM
DRAM; RGEL 2

Granzotto, Gianni
See Granzotto, Giovanni Battista

Granzotto, Giovanni Battista
1914-1985 .... **CLC 70**
See also CA 166

Grass, Guenter
See Grass, Gunter
See also CWW 2; DLB 330; RGHL

Grass, Gunter 1927- .. **CLC 1, 2, 4, 6, 11, 15,
22, 32, 49, 88, 207; WLC 3**
See Grass, Guenter
See also BPFB 2; CA 13-16R; CANR 20,
75, 93, 133; CDWLB 2; DA; DA3; DAB;
DAC; DAM MST, NOV; DLB 75, 124;
EW 13; EWL 3; MTCW 1, 2; MTFW
2005; RGWL 2, 3; TWA

Grass, Gunter Wilhelm
See Grass, Gunter

Gratton, Thomas
See Hulme, T(homas) E(rnest)

Grau, Shirley Ann 1929- .... **CLC 4, 9, 146;
SSC 15**
See also CA 89-92; CANR 22, 69; CN 1, 2,
3, 4, 5, 6, 7; CSW; DLB 2, 218; INT CA-
89-92; CANR-22; MTCW 1

Gravel, Fern
See Hall, James Norman

Graver, Elizabeth 1964- .... **CLC 70**
See also CA 135; CANR 71, 129

Graves, Richard Perceval
1895-1985 .... **CLC 44**
See also CA 65-68; CANR 9, 26, 51

Graves, Robert 1895-1985 ... **CLC 1, 2, 6, 11,
39, 44, 45; PC 6**
See also BPFB 2; BRW 7; BYA 4; CA 5-8R;
CAAS 117; CANR 5, 36; CDBLB 1914-
1945; CN 1, 2, 3; CP 1, 2, 3, 4; DA3;
DAB; DAC; DAM MST, POET; DLB 20,
100, 191; DLBD 18; DLBY 1985; EWL
3; LATS 1:1; MTCW 1, 2; MTFW 2005;
NCFS 2; NFS 21; RGEL 2; RHW; SATA
45; TEA

Graves, Valerie
See Bradley, Marion Zimmer

Gray, Alasdair 1934- .... **CLC 41**
See also BRWS 9; CA 126; CANR 47, 69,
106, 140; CN 4, 5, 6, 7; DLB 194, 261,
319; HGG; INT CA-126; MTCW 1, 2;
MTFW 2005; RGSF 2; SUFW 2

Gray, Amlin 1946- .... **CLC 29**
See also CA 138

Gray, Francine du Plessix 1930- ..... **CLC 22,
153**
See also BEST 90:3; CA 61-64; 2; CANR
11, 33, 75, 81; DAM NOV; INT CANR-
11; MTCW 1, 2; MTFW 2005

Gray, John (Henry) 1866-1934 ...... **TCLC 19**
See also CA 162; CAAE 119; RGEL 2

Gray, John Lee
See Jakes, John

Gray, Simon (James Holliday)
1936- .... **CLC 9, 14, 36**
See also AITN 1; CA 21-24R; 3; CANR 32,
69; CBD; CD 5, 6; CN 1, 2, 3; DLB 13;
EWL 3; MTCW 1; RGEL 2

Gray, Spalding 1941-2004 .... **CLC 49, 112;
DC 7**
See also AAYA 62; CA 128; CAAS 225;
CAD; CANR 74, 138; CD 5, 6; CPW;
DAM POP; MTCW 2; MTFW 2005

Gray, Thomas 1716-1771 .... **LC 4, 40; PC 2;
WLC 3**
See also BRW 3; CDBLB 1660-1789; DA;
DA3; DAB; DAC; DAM MST; DLB 109;
EXPP; PAB; PFS 9; RGEL 2; TEA; WP

Grayson, David
See Baker, Ray Stannard

Grayson, Richard (A.) 1951- .... **CLC 38**
See also CA 210; 85-88, 210; CANR 14,
31, 57; DLB 234

Greeley, Andrew M. 1928- .... **CLC 28**
See also BPFB 2; CA 5-8R; 7; CANR 7,
43, 69, 104, 136; CMW 4; CPW; DA3;
DAM POP; MTCW 1, 2; MTFW 2005

Green, Anna Katharine
1846-1935 .... **TCLC 63**
See also CA 159; CAAE 112; CMW 4;
DLB 202, 221; MSW

Green, Brian
See Card, Orson Scott

Green, Hannah
See Greenberg, Joanne (Goldenberg)

Green, Hannah 1927(?)-1996 .... **CLC 3**
See also CA 73-76; CANR 59, 93; NFS 10

Green, Henry .... **CLC 2, 13, 97**
See Yorke, Henry Vincent
See also BRWS 2; CA 175; DLB 15; EWL
3; RGEL 2

Green, Julian .... **CLC 3, 11, 77**
See Green, Julien (Hartridge)
See also EWL 3; GFL 1789 to the Present;
MTCW 2

Green, Julien (Hartridge) 1900-1998
See Green, Julian
See also CA 21-24R; CAAS 169; CANR
33, 87; CWW 2; DLB 4, 72; MTCW 1, 2;
MTFW 2005

Green, Paul (Eliot) 1894-1981 .... **CLC 25**
See also AITN 1; CA 5-8R; CAAS 103;
CAD; CANR 3; DAM DRAM; DLB 7, 9,
249; DLBY 1981; MAL 5; RGAL 4

Greenaway, Peter 1942- .... **CLC 159**
See also CA 127

Greenberg, Ivan 1908-1973
See Rahv, Philip
See also CA 85-88

Greenberg, Joanne (Goldenberg)
1932- .... **CLC 7, 30**
See also AAYA 12, 67; CA 5-8R; CANR
14, 32, 69; CN 6, 7; NFS 23; SATA 25;
YAW

Greenberg, Richard 1959(?)- .... **CLC 57**
See also CA 138; CAD; CD 5, 6

Greenblatt, Stephen J(ay) 1943- ...... **CLC 70**
See also CA 49-52; CANR 115

Greene, Bette 1934- .... **CLC 30**
See also AAYA 7, 69; BYA 3; CA 53-56;
CANR 4, 146; CLR 2; CWRI 5; JRDA;
LAIT 4; MAICYA 1, 2; NFS 10; SAAS
16; SATA 8, 102, 161; WYA; YAW

Greene, Gael .... **CLC 8**
See also CA 13-16R; CANR 10

Greene, Graham 1904-1991 .. **CLC 1, 3, 6, 9,
14, 18, 27, 37, 70, 72, 125; SSC 29;
WLC 3**
See also AAYA 61; AITN 2; BPFB 2;
BRWR 2; BRWS 1; BYA 3; CA 13-16R;
CAAS 133; CANR 35, 61, 131; CBD;
CDBLB 1945-1960; CMW 4; CN 1, 2, 3,
4; DA; DA3; DAB; DAC; DAM MST,
NOV; DLB 13, 15, 77, 100, 162, 201,
204; DLBY 1991; EWL 3; MSW; MTCW
1, 2; MTFW 2005; NFS 16; RGEL 2;
SATA 20; SSFS 14; TEA; WLIT 4

Greene, Robert 1558-1592 .... **LC 41**
See also BRWS 8; DLB 62, 167; IDTP;
RGEL 2; TEA

Greer, Germaine 1939- .... **CLC 131**
See also AITN 1; CA 81-84; CANR 33, 70,
115, 133; FW; MTCW 1, 2; MTFW 2005

Greer, Richard
See Silverberg, Robert

Gregor, Arthur 1923- .... **CLC 9**
See also CA 25-28R; 10; CANR 11; CP 1,
2, 3, 4, 5, 6, 7; SATA 36

Gregor, Lee
See Pohl, Frederik

Gregory, Lady Isabella Augusta (Persse)
1852-1932 .... **TCLC 1, 176**
See also BRW 6; CA 184; CAAE 104; DLB
10; IDTP; RGEL 2

Gregory, J. Dennis
See Williams, John A(lfred)

Gregory of Nazianzus, St.
329-389 .... **CMLC 82**

Grekova, I. .... **CLC 59**
See Ventsel, Elena Sergeevna
See also CWW 2

Grendon, Stephen
See Derleth, August (William)

Grenville, Kate 1950- .... **CLC 61**
See also CA 118; CANR 53, 93, 156; CN
7; DLB 325

Hamilton, (Robert) Ian 1938-2001 . **CLC 191**
See also CA 106; CAAS 203; CANR 41,
67; CP 1, 2, 3, 4, 5, 6, 7; DLB 40, 155

Hamilton, Jane 1957- .... **CLC 179**
See also CA 147; CANR 85, 128; CN 7;
MTFW 2005

Hamilton, Mollie
See Kaye, M.M.

Hamilton, (Anthony Walter) Patrick
1904-1962 .... **CLC 51**
See also CA 176; CAAS 113; DLB 10, 191

Hamilton, Virginia 1936-2002 ...... **CLC 26**
See also AAYA 2, 21; BW 2, 3; BYA 1, 2,
8; CA 25-28R; CAAS 206; CANR 20, 37,
73, 126; CLR 1, 11, 40; DAM MULT;
DLB 33, 52; DLBY 2001; INT CANR-
20; JRDA; LAIT 5; MAICYA 1, 2; MAI-
CYAS 1; MTCW 1, 2; MTFW 2005;
SATA 4, 56, 79, 123; SATA-Obit 132;
WYA; YAW

Hammett, (Samuel) Dashiell
1894-1961 .... **CLC 3, 5, 10, 19, 47; SSC
17; TCLC 187**
See also AAYA 59; AITN 1; AMWS 4;
BPFB 2; CA 81-84; CANR 42; CDALB
1929-1941; CMW 4; DA3; DLB 226, 280;
DLBD 6; DLBY 1996; EWL 3; LAIT 3;
MAL 5; MSW; MTCW 1, 2; MTFW
2005; NFS 21; RGAL 4; RGSF 2; TUS

Hammon, Jupiter 1720(?)-1800(?) .... **BLC 2;
NCLC 5; PC 16**
See also DAM MULT, POET; DLB 31, 50

Hammond, Keith
See Kuttner, Henry

Hamner, Earl (Henry), Jr. 1923- ...... **CLC 12**
See also AITN 2; CA 73-76; DLB 6

Hampton, Christopher 1946- .... **CLC 4**
See also CA 25-28R; CD 5, 6; DLB 13;
MTCW 1

Hampton, Christopher James
See Hampton, Christopher

Hamsun, Knut .... **TCLC 2, 14, 49, 151**
See Pedersen, Knut
See also DLB 297, 330; EW 8; EWL 3;
RGWL 2, 3

Handke, Peter 1942- .... **CLC 5, 8, 10, 15, 38,
134; DC 17**
See also CA 77-80; CANR 33, 75, 104, 133;
CWW 2; DAM DRAM, NOV; DLB 85,
124; EWL 3; MTCW 1, 2; MTFW 2005;
TWA

Handy, W(illiam) C(hristopher)
1873-1958 .... **TCLC 97**
See also BW 3; CA 167; CAAE 121

Hanley, James 1901-1985 ..... **CLC 3, 5, 8, 13**
See also CA 73-76; CAAS 117; CANR 36;
CBD; CN 1, 2, 3; DLB 191; EWL 3;
MTCW 1; RGEL 2

Hannah, Barry 1942- .. **CLC 23, 38, 90; SSC
94**
See also BPFB 2; CA 110; CAAE 108;
CANR 43, 68, 113; CN 4, 5, 6, 7; CSW;
DLB 6, 234; INT CA-110; MTCW 1;
RGSF 2

Hannon, Ezra
See Hunter, Evan

Hansberry, Lorraine (Vivian)
1930-1965 ... **BLC 2; CLC 17, 62; DC 2**
See also AAYA 25; AFAW 1, 2; AMWS 4;
BW 1, 3; CA 109; CAAS 25-28R; CABS
3; CAD; CANR 58; CDALB 1941-1968;
CWD; DA; DA3; DAB; DAC; DAM
DRAM, MST, MULT; DFS 2; DLB 7, 38;
EWL 3; FL 1:6; FW; LAIT 4; MAL 5;
MTCW 1, 2; MTFW 2005; RGAL 4; TUS

Hansen, Joseph 1923-2004 .... **CLC 38**
See Brock, Rose; Colton, James
See also BPFB 2; CA 29-32R; 17; CAAS
233; CANR 16, 44, 66, 125; CMW 4;
DLB 226; GLL 1; INT CANR-16

Hansen, Karen V. 1955- .... **CLC 65**
See also CA 149; CANR 102

Hansen, Martin A(lfred)
1909-1955 .... **TCLC 32**
See also CA 167; DLB 214; EWL 3

Hanson, Kenneth O(stlin) 1922- .... **CLC 13**
See also CA 53-56; CANR 7; CP 1, 2, 3, 4,
5

Hardwick, Elizabeth 1916- .... **CLC 13**
See also AMWS 3; CA 5-8R; CANR 3, 32,
70, 100, 139; CN 4, 5, 6; CSW; DA3;
DAM NOV; DLB 6; MBL; MTCW 1, 2;
MTFW 2005; TCLE 1:1

Hardy, Thomas 1840-1928 .... **PC 8; SSC 2,
60; TCLC 4, 10, 18, 32, 48, 53, 72, 143,
153; WLC 3**
See also AAYA 69; BRW 6; BRWC 1, 2;
BRWR 1; CA 123; CAAE 104; CDBLB
1890-1914; DA; DA3; DAB; DAC; DAM
MST, NOV, POET; DLB 18, 19, 135, 284;
EWL 3; EXPN; EXPP; LAIT 2; MTCW
1, 2; MTFW 2005; NFS 3, 11, 15, 19; PFS
3, 4, 18; RGEL 2; RGSF 2; TEA; WLIT
4

Hare, David 1947- . **CLC 29, 58, 136; DC 26**
See also BRWS 4; CA 97-100; CANR 39,
91; CBD; CD 5, 6; DFS 4, 7, 16; DLB
13, 310; MTCW 1; TEA

Harewood, John
See Van Druten, John (William)

Harford, Henry
See Hudson, W(illiam) H(enry)

Hargrave, Leonie
See Disch, Thomas M.

**Hariri, Al- al-Qasim ibn 'Ali Abu
Muhammad al-Basri**
See al-Hariri, al-Qasim ibn 'Ali Abu Mu-
hammad al-Basri

Harjo, Joy 1951- ..... **CLC 83; NNAL; PC 27**
See also AMWS 12; CA 114; CANR 35,
67, 91, 129; CP 6, 7; CWP; DAM MULT;
DLB 120, 175; EWL 3; MTCW 2; MTFW
2005; PFS 15; RGAL 4

Harlan, Louis R(udolph) 1922- .... **CLC 34**
See also CA 21-24R; CANR 25, 55, 80

Harling, Robert 1951(?)- .... **CLC 53**
See also CA 147

Harmon, William (Ruth) 1938- .... **CLC 38**
See also CA 33-36R; CANR 14, 32, 35;
SATA 65

Harper, F. E. W.
See Harper, Frances Ellen Watkins

Harper, Frances E. W.
See Harper, Frances Ellen Watkins

Harper, Frances E. Watkins
See Harper, Frances Ellen Watkins

Harper, Frances Ellen
See Harper, Frances Ellen Watkins

Harper, Frances Ellen Watkins
1825-1911 ..... **BLC 2; PC 21; TCLC 14**
See also AFAW 1, 2; BW 1, 3; CA 125;
CAAE 111; CANR 79; DAM MULT,
POET; DLB 50, 221; MBL; RGAL 4

Harper, Michael S(teven) 1938- ... **CLC 7, 22**
See also AFAW 2; BW 1; CA 224; 33-36R,
224; CANR 24, 108; CP 2, 3, 4, 5, 6, 7;
DLB 41; RGAL 4; TCLE 1:1

Harper, Mrs. F. E. W.
See Harper, Frances Ellen Watkins

Harpur, Charles 1813-1868 .... **NCLC 114**
See also DLB 230; RGEL 2

Harris, Christie
See Harris, Christie (Lucy) Irwin

Harris, Christie (Lucy) Irwin
1907-2002 .... **CLC 12**
See also CA 5-8R; CANR 6, 83; CLR 47;
DLB 88; JRDA; MAICYA 1, 2; SAAS 10;
SATA 6, 74; SATA-Essay 116

Harris, Frank 1856-1931 .... **TCLC 24**
See also CA 150; CAAE 109; CANR 80;
DLB 156, 197; RGEL 2

Harris, George Washington
1814-1869 .... **NCLC 23, 165**
See also DLB 3, 11, 248; RGAL 4

Harris, Joel Chandler 1848-1908 ..... **SSC 19;
TCLC 2**
See also CA 137; CAAE 104; CANR 80;
CLR 49; DLB 11, 23, 42, 78, 91; LAIT 2;
MAICYA 1, 2; RGSF 2; SATA 100; WCH;
YABC 1

**Harris, John (Wyndham Parkes Lucas)
Beynon** 1903-1969
See Wyndham, John
See also CA 102; CAAS 89-92; CANR 84;
SATA 118; SFW 4

Harris, MacDonald .... **CLC 9**
See Heiney, Donald (William)

Harris, Mark 1922- .... **CLC 19**
See also CA 5-8R; 3; CANR 2, 55, 83; CN
1, 2, 3, 4, 5, 6, 7; DLB 2; DLBY 1980

Harris, Norman .... **CLC 65**

Harris, (Theodore) Wilson 1921- .... **CLC 25,
159**
See also BRWS 5; BW 2, 3; CA 65-68; 16;
CANR 11, 27, 69, 114; CDWLB 3; CN 1,
2, 3, 4, 5, 6, 7; CP 1, 2, 3, 4, 5, 6, 7; DLB
117; EWL 3; MTCW 1; RGEL 2

Harrison, Barbara Grizzuti
1934-2002 .... **CLC 144**
See also CA 77-80; CAAS 205; CANR 15,
48; INT CANR-15

Harrison, Elizabeth (Allen) Cavanna
1909-2001
See Cavanna, Betty
See also CA 9-12R; CAAS 200; CANR 6,
27, 85, 104, 121; MAICYA 2; SATA 142;
YAW

Harrison, Harry (Max) 1925- .... **CLC 42**
See also CA 1-4R; CANR 5, 21, 84; DLB
8; SATA 4; SCFW 2; SFW 4

Harrison, James
See Harrison, Jim

Harrison, James Thomas
See Harrison, Jim

Harrison, Jim 1937- .... **CLC 6, 14, 33, 66,
143; SSC 19**
See also AMWS 8; CA 13-16R; CANR 8,
51, 79, 142; CN 5, 6; CP 1, 2, 3, 4, 5, 6;
DLBY 1982; INT CANR-8; RGAL 4;
TCWW 2; TUS

Harrison, Kathryn 1961- .... **CLC 70, 151**
See also CA 144; CANR 68, 122

Harrison, Tony 1937- .... **CLC 43, 129**
See also BRWS 5; CA 65-68; CANR 44,
98; CBD; CD 5, 6; CP 2, 3, 4, 5, 6, 7;
DLB 40, 245; MTCW 1; RGEL 2

Harriss, Will(ard Irvin) 1922- .... **CLC 34**
See also CA 111

Hart, Ellis
See Ellison, Harlan

Hart, Josephine 1942(?)- .... **CLC 70**
See also CA 138; CANR 70, 149; CPW;
DAM POP

Hart, Moss 1904-1961 .... **CLC 66**
See also CA 109; CAAS 89-92; CANR 84;
DAM DRAM; DFS 1; DLB 7, 266; RGAL
4

Harte, (Francis) Bret(t)
1836(?)-1902 ... **SSC 8, 59; TCLC 1, 25;
WLC 3**
See also AMWS 2; CA 140; CAAE 104;
CANR 80; CDALB 1865-1917; DA;
DA3; DAC; DAM MST; DLB 12, 64, 74,
79, 186; EXPS; LAIT 2; RGAL 4; RGSF
2; SATA 26; SSFS 3; TUS

Hofmannsthal, Hugo von 1874-1929 ... **DC 4; TCLC 11**
See also CA 153; CAAE 106; CDWLB 2; DAM DRAM; DFS 17; DLB 81, 118; EW 9; EWL 3; RGWL 2, 3

Hogan, Linda 1947- ..... **CLC 73; NNAL; PC 35**
See also AMWS 4; ANW; BYA 12; CA 226; 120, 226; CANR 45, 73, 129; CWP; DAM MULT; DLB 175; SATA 132; TCWW 2

Hogarth, Charles
See Creasey, John

Hogarth, Emmett
See Polonsky, Abraham (Lincoln)

Hogarth, William 1697-1764 .... **LC 112**
See also AAYA 56

Hogg, James 1770-1835 .... **NCLC 4, 109**
See also BRWS 10; DLB 93, 116, 159; GL 2; HGG; RGEL 2; SUFW 1

Holbach, Paul-Henri Thiry
1723-1789 .... **LC 14**
See also DLB 313

Holberg, Ludvig 1684-1754 .... **LC 6**
See also DLB 300; RGWL 2, 3

Holcroft, Thomas 1745-1809 .... **NCLC 85**
See also DLB 39, 89, 158; RGEL 2

Holden, Ursula 1921- .... **CLC 18**
See also CA 101; 8; CANR 22

Holderlin, (Johann Christian) Friedrich
1770-1843 .... **NCLC 16; PC 4**
See also CDWLB 2; DLB 90; EW 5; RGWL 2, 3

Holdstock, Robert 1948- .... **CLC 39**
See also CA 131; CANR 81; DLB 261; FANT; HGG; SFW 4; SUFW 2

Holdstock, Robert P.
See Holdstock, Robert

Holinshed, Raphael fl. 1580- .... **LC 69**
See also DLB 167; RGEL 2

Holland, Isabelle (Christian)
1920-2002 .... **CLC 21**
See also AAYA 11, 64; CA 181; 21-24R; CAAS 205; CANR 10, 25, 47; CLR 57; CWRI 5; JRDA; LAIT 4; MAICYA 1, 2; SATA 8, 70; SATA-Essay 103; SATA-Obit 132; WYA

Holland, Marcus
See Caldwell, (Janet Miriam) Taylor (Holland)

Hollander, John 1929- .... **CLC 2, 5, 8, 14**
See also CA 1-4R; CANR 1, 52, 136; CP 1, 2, 3, 4, 5, 6, 7; DLB 5; MAL 5; SATA 13

Hollander, Paul
See Silverberg, Robert

Holleran, Andrew .... **CLC 38**
See Garber, Eric
See also CA 144; GLL 1

Holley, Marietta 1836(?)-1926 .... **TCLC 99**
See also CAAE 118; DLB 11; FL 1:3

Hollinghurst, Alan 1954- .... **CLC 55, 91**
See also BRWS 10; CA 114; CN 5, 6, 7; DLB 207, 326; GLL 1

Hollis, Jim
See Summers, Hollis (Spurgeon, Jr.)

Holly, Buddy 1936-1959 .... **TCLC 65**
See also CA 213

Holmes, Gordon
See Shiel, M(atthew) P(hipps)

Holmes, John
See Souster, (Holmes) Raymond

Holmes, John Clellon 1926-1988 ...... **CLC 56**
See also BG 1:2; CA 9-12R; CAAS 125; CANR 4; CN 1, 2, 3, 4; DLB 16, 237

Holmes, Oliver Wendell, Jr.
1841-1935 .... **TCLC 77**
See also CA 186; CAAE 114

Holmes, Oliver Wendell
1809-1894 .... **NCLC 14, 81; PC 71**
See also AMWS 1; CDALB 1640-1865; DLB 1, 189, 235; EXPP; PFS 24; RGAL 4; SATA 34

Holmes, Raymond
See Souster, (Holmes) Raymond

Holt, Victoria
See Hibbert, Eleanor Alice Burford
See also BPFB 2

Holub, Miroslav 1923-1998 .... **CLC 4**
See also CA 21-24R; CAAS 169; CANR 10; CDWLB 4; CWW 2; DLB 232; EWL 3; RGWL 3

Holz, Detlev
See Benjamin, Walter

Homer c. 8th cent. B.C.- .... **CMLC 1, 16, 61; PC 23; WLCS**
See also AW 1; CDWLB 1; DA; DA3; DAB; DAC; DAM MST, POET; DLB 176; EFS 1; LAIT 1; LMFS 1; RGWL 2, 3; TWA; WLIT 8; WP

Hongo, Garrett Kaoru 1951- .... **PC 23**
See also CA 133; 22; CP 5, 6, 7; DLB 120, 312; EWL 3; EXPP; PFS 25; RGAL 4

Honig, Edwin 1919- .... **CLC 33**
See also CA 5-8R; 8; CANR 4, 45, 144; CP 1, 2, 3, 4, 5, 6, 7; DLB 5

Hood, Hugh (John Blagdon) 1928- . **CLC 15, 28; SSC 42**
See also CA 49-52; 17; CANR 1, 33, 87; CN 1, 2, 3, 4, 5, 6, 7; DLB 53; RGSF 2

Hood, Thomas 1799-1845 .... **NCLC 16**
See also BRW 4; DLB 96; RGEL 2

Hooker, (Peter) Jeremy 1941- .... **CLC 43**
See also CA 77-80; CANR 22; CP 2, 3, 4, 5, 6, 7; DLB 40

Hooker, Richard 1554-1600 .... **LC 95**
See also BRW 1; DLB 132; RGEL 2

Hooker, Thomas 1586-1647 .... **LC 137**
See also DLB 24

hooks, bell 1952(?)- .... **CLC 94**
See also BW 2; CA 143; CANR 87, 126; DLB 246; MTCW 2; MTFW 2005; SATA 115, 170

Hooper, Johnson Jones
1815-1862 .... **NCLC 177**
See also DLB 3, 11, 248; RGAL 4

Hope, A(lec) D(erwent) 1907-2000 .... **CLC 3, 51; PC 56**
See also BRWS 7; CA 21-24R; CAAS 188; CANR 33, 74; CP 1, 2, 3, 4, 5; DLB 289; EWL 3; MTCW 1, 2; MTFW 2005; PFS 8; RGEL 2

Hope, Anthony 1863-1933 .... **TCLC 83**
See also CA 157; DLB 153, 156; RGEL 2; RHW

Hope, Brian
See Creasey, John

Hope, Christopher (David Tully)
1944- .... **CLC 52**
See also AFW; CA 106; CANR 47, 101; CN 4, 5, 6, 7; DLB 225; SATA 62

Hopkins, Gerard Manley
1844-1889 .... **NCLC 17; PC 15; WLC 3**
See also BRW 5; BRWR 2; CDBLB 1890-1914; DA; DA3; DAB; DAC; DAM MST, POET; DLB 35, 57; EXPP; PAB; RGEL 2; TEA; WP

Hopkins, John (Richard) 1931-1998 .. **CLC 4**
See also CA 85-88; CAAS 169; CBD; CD 5, 6

Hopkins, Pauline Elizabeth
1859-1930 .... **BLC 2; TCLC 28**
See also AFAW 2; BW 2, 3; CA 141; CANR 82; DAM MULT; DLB 50

Hopkinson, Francis 1737-1791 .... **LC 25**
See also DLB 31; RGAL 4

Hopley-Woolrich, Cornell George 1903-1968
See Woolrich, Cornell
See also CA 13-14; CANR 58, 156; CAP 1; CMW 4; DLB 226; MTCW 2

Horace 65B.C.-8B.C. .... **CMLC 39; PC 46**
See also AW 2; CDWLB 1; DLB 211; RGWL 2, 3; WLIT 8

Horatio
See Proust, (Valentin-Louis-George-Eugene) Marcel

Horgan, Paul (George Vincent
O'Shaughnessy) 1903-1995 .. **CLC 9, 53**
See also BPFB 2; CA 13-16R; CAAS 147; CANR 9, 35; CN 1, 2, 3, 4, 5; DAM NOV; DLB 102, 212; DLBY 1985; INT CANR-9; MTCW 1, 2; MTFW 2005; SATA 13; SATA-Obit 84; TCWW 1, 2

Horkheimer, Max 1895-1973 .... **TCLC 132**
See also CA 216; CAAS 41-44R; DLB 296

Horn, Peter
See Kuttner, Henry

Horne, Frank (Smith) 1899-1974 ...... **HR 1:2**
See also BW 1; CA 125; CAAS 53-56; DLB 51; WP

Horne, Richard Henry Hengist
1802(?)-1884 .... **NCLC 127**
See also DLB 32; SATA 29

Hornem, Horace Esq.
See Byron, George Gordon (Noel)

Horney, Karen (Clementine Theodore
Danielsen) 1885-1952 .... **TCLC 71**
See also CA 165; CAAE 114; DLB 246; FW

Hornung, E(rnest) W(illiam)
1866-1921 .... **TCLC 59**
See also CA 160; CAAE 108; CMW 4; DLB 70

Horovitz, Israel (Arthur) 1939- .... **CLC 56**
See also CA 33-36R; CAD; CANR 46, 59; CD 5, 6; DAM DRAM; DLB 7; MAL 5

Horton, George Moses
1797(?)-1883(?) .... **NCLC 87**
See also DLB 50

Horvath, odon von 1901-1938
See von Horvath, Odon
See also EWL 3

Horvath, Oedoen von -1938
See von Horvath, Odon

Horwitz, Julius 1920-1986 .... **CLC 14**
See also CA 9-12R; CAAS 119; CANR 12

Horwitz, Ronald
See Harwood, Ronald

Hospital, Janette Turner 1942- .... **CLC 42, 145**
See also CA 108; CANR 48; CN 5, 6, 7; DLB 325; DLBY 2002; RGSF 2

Hostos, E. M. de
See Hostos (y Bonilla), Eugenio Maria de

Hostos, Eugenio M. de
See Hostos (y Bonilla), Eugenio Maria de

Hostos, Eugenio Maria
See Hostos (y Bonilla), Eugenio Maria de

Hostos (y Bonilla), Eugenio Maria de
1839-1903 .... **TCLC 24**
See also CA 131; CAAE 123; HW 1

Houdini
See Lovecraft, H. P.

Houellebecq, Michel 1958- .... **CLC 179**
See also CA 185; CANR 140; MTFW 2005

Hougan, Carolyn 1943- .... **CLC 34**
See also CA 139

Household, Geoffrey (Edward West)
1900-1988 .... **CLC 11**
See also CA 77-80; CAAS 126; CANR 58; CMW 4; CN 1, 2, 3, 4; DLB 87; SATA 14; SATA-Obit 59

Housman, A(lfred) E(dward)
1859-1936 .... PC 2, 43; TCLC 1, 10;
WLCS
See also AAYA 66; BRW 6; CA 125; CAAE
104; DA; DA3; DAB; DAC; DAM MST,
POET; DLB 19, 284; EWL 3; EXPP;
MTCW 1, 2; MTFW 2005; PAB; PFS 4,
7; RGEL 2; TEA; WP

Housman, Laurence 1865-1959 .... TCLC 7
See also CA 155; CAAE 106; DLB 10;
FANT; RGEL 2; SATA 25

Houston, Jeanne Wakatsuki 1934- .... AAL
See also AAYA 49; CA 232; 103, 232; 16;
CANR 29, 123; LAIT 4; SATA 78, 168;
SATA-Essay 168

Howard, Elizabeth Jane 1923- ..... CLC 7, 29
See also BRWS 11; CA 5-8R; CANR 8, 62,
146; CN 1, 2, 3, 4, 5, 6, 7

Howard, Maureen 1930- .... CLC 5, 14, 46,
151
See also CA 53-56; CANR 31, 75, 140; CN
4, 5, 6, 7; DLBY 1983; INT CANR-31;
MTCW 1, 2; MTFW 2005

Howard, Richard 1929- .... CLC 7, 10, 47
See also AITN 1; CA 85-88; CANR 25, 80,
154; CP 1, 2, 3, 4, 5, 6, 7; DLB 5; INT
CANR-25; MAL 5

Howard, Robert E 1906-1936 .... TCLC 8
See also BPFB 2; BYA 5; CA 157; CAAE
105; CANR 155; FANT; SUFW 1;
TCWW 1, 2

Howard, Robert Ervin
See Howard, Robert E

Howard, Warren F.
See Pohl, Frederik

Howe, Fanny (Quincy) 1940- .... CLC 47
See also CA 187; 117, 187; 27; CANR 70,
116; CP 6, 7; CWP; SATA-Brief 52

Howe, Irving 1920-1993 .... CLC 85
See also AMWS 6; CA 9-12R; CAAS 141;
CANR 21, 50; DLB 67; EWL 3; MAL 5;
MTCW 1, 2; MTFW 2005

Howe, Julia Ward 1819-1910 .... TCLC 21
See also CA 191; CAAE 117; DLB 1, 189,
235; FW

Howe, Susan 1937- .... CLC 72, 152; PC 54
See also AMWS 4; CA 160; CP 5, 6, 7;
CWP; DLB 120; FW; RGAL 4

Howe, Tina 1937- .... CLC 48
See also CA 109; CAD; CANR 125; CD 5,
6; CWD

Howell, James 1594(?)-1666 .... LC 13
See also DLB 151

Howells, W. D.
See Howells, William Dean

Howells, William D.
See Howells, William Dean

Howells, William Dean 1837-1920 ... SSC 36;
TCLC 7, 17, 41
See also AMW; CA 134; CAAE 104;
CDALB 1865-1917; DLB 12, 64, 74, 79,
189; LMFS 1; MAL 5; MTCW 2; RGAL
4; TUS

Howes, Barbara 1914-1996 .... CLC 15
See also CA 9-12R; 3; CAAS 151; CANR
53; CP 1, 2, 3, 4, 5, 6; SATA 5; TCLE 1:1

Hrabal, Bohumil 1914-1997 ...... CLC 13, 67;
TCLC 155
See also CA 106; 12; CAAS 156; CANR
57; CWW 2; DLB 232; EWL 3; RGSF 2

Hrabanus Maurus 776(?)-856 .... CMLC 78
See also DLB 148

Hrotsvit of Gandersheim c. 935-c.
1000 .... CMLC 29
See also DLB 148

Hsi, Chu 1130-1200 .... CMLC 42

Hsun, Lu
See Lu Hsun

Hubbard, L. Ron 1911-1986 .... CLC 43
See also AAYA 64; CA 77-80; CAAS 118;
CANR 52; CPW; DA3; DAM POP;
FANT; MTCW 2; MTFW 2005; SFW 4

Hubbard, Lafayette Ronald
See Hubbard, L. Ron

Huch, Ricarda (Octavia)
1864-1947 .... TCLC 13
See also CA 189; CAAE 111; DLB 66;
EWL 3

Huddle, David 1942- .... CLC 49
See also CA 57-60; 20; CANR 89; DLB
130

Hudson, Jeffrey
See Crichton, Michael

Hudson, W(illiam) H(enry)
1841-1922 .... TCLC 29
See also CA 190; CAAE 115; DLB 98, 153,
174; RGEL 2; SATA 35

Hueffer, Ford Madox
See Ford, Ford Madox

Hughart, Barry 1934- .... CLC 39
See also CA 137; FANT; SFW 4; SUFW 2

Hughes, Colin
See Creasey, John

Hughes, David (John) 1930-2005 ..... CLC 48
See also CA 129; CAAE 116; CAAS 238;
CN 4, 5, 6, 7; DLB 14

Hughes, Edward James
See Hughes, Ted
See also DA3; DAM MST, POET

Hughes, (James Mercer) Langston
1902-1967 ..... BLC 2; CLC 1, 5, 10, 15,
35, 44, 108; DC 3; HR 1:2; PC 1, 53;
SSC 6, 90; WLC 3
See also AAYA 12; AFAW 1, 2; AMWR 1;
AMWS 1; BW 1, 3; CA 1-4R; CAAS 25-
28R; CANR 1, 34, 82; CDALB 1929-
1941; CLR 17; DA; DA3; DAB; DAC;
DAM DRAM, MST, MULT, POET; DFS
6, 18; DLB 4, 7, 48, 51, 86, 228, 315;
EWL 3; EXPP; EXPS; JRDA; LAIT 3;
LMFS 2; MAICYA 1, 2; MAL 5; MTCW
1, 2; MTFW 2005; NFS 21; PAB; PFS 1,
3, 6, 10, 15; RGAL 4; RGSF 2; SATA 4,
33; SSFS 4, 7; TUS; WCH; WP; YAW

Hughes, Richard (Arthur Warren)
1900 1976 .... CLC 1, 11
See also CA 5-8R; CAAS 65-68; CANR 4;
CN 1, 2; DAM NOV; DLB 15, 161; EWL
3; MTCW 1; RGEL 2; SATA 8; SATA-
Obit 25

Hughes, Ted 1930-1998 . CLC 2, 4, 9, 14, 37,
119; PC 7
See Hughes, Edward James
See also BRWC 2; BRWR 2; BRWS 1; CA
1-4R; CAAS 171; CANR 1, 33, 66, 108;
CLR 3; CP 1, 2, 3, 4, 5, 6; DAB; DAC;
DLB 40, 161; EWL 3; EXPP; MAICYA
1, 2; MTCW 1, 2; MTFW 2005; PAB;
PFS 4, 19; RGEL 2; SATA 49; SATA-
Brief 27; SATA-Obit 107; TEA; YAW

Hugo, Richard
See Huch, Ricarda (Octavia)

Hugo, Richard F(ranklin)
1923 1982 .... CLC 6, 18, 32; PC 68
See also AMWS 6; CA 49-52; CAAS 108;
CANR 3; CP 1, 2, 3; DAM POET; DLB
5, 206; EWL 3; MAL 5; PFS 17; RGAL 4

Hugo, Victor (Marie) 1802-1885 .... NCLC 3,
10, 21, 161; PC 17; WLC 3
See also AAYA 28; DA; DA3; DAB; DAC;
DAM DRAM, MST, NOV, POET; DLB
119, 192, 217; EFS 2; EW 6; EXPN; GFL
1789 to the Present; LAIT 1, 2; NFS 5,
20; RGWL 2, 3; SATA 47; TWA

Huidobro, Vicente
See Huidobro Fernandez, Vicente Garcia
See also DLB 283; EWL 3; LAW

Huidobro Fernandez, Vicente Garcia
1893-1948 .... TCLC 31
See Huidobro, Vicente
See also CA 131; HW 1

Hulme, Keri 1947- .... CLC 39, 130
See also CA 125; CANR 69; CN 4, 5, 6, 7;
CP 6, 7; CWP; DLB 326; EWL 3; FW;
INT CA-125; NFS 24

Hulme, T(homas) E(rnest)
1883-1917 .... TCLC 21
See also BRWS 6; CA 203; CAAE 117;
DLB 19

Humboldt, Alexander von
1769-1859 .... NCLC 170
See also DLB 90

Humboldt, Wilhelm von
1767-1835 .... NCLC 134
See also DLB 90

Hume, David 1711-1776 .... LC 7, 56
See also BRWS 3; DLB 104, 252; LMFS 1;
TEA

Humphrey, William 1924-1997 .... CLC 45
See also AMWS 9; CA 77-80; CAAS 160;
CANR 68; CN 1, 2, 3, 4, 5, 6; CSW; DLB
6, 212, 234, 278; TCWW 1, 2

Humphreys, Emyr Owen 1919- .... CLC 47
See also CA 5-8R; CANR 3, 24; CN 1, 2,
3, 4, 5, 6, 7; DLB 15

Humphreys, Josephine 1945- ..... CLC 34, 57
See also CA 127; CAAE 121; CANR 97;
CSW; DLB 292; INT CA-127

Huneker, James Gibbons
1860-1921 .... TCLC 65
See also CA 193; DLB 71; RGAL 4

Hungerford, Hesba Fay
See Brinsmead, H(esba) F(ay)

Hungerford, Pixie
See Brinsmead, H(esba) F(ay)

Hunt, E. Howard 1918-2007 .... CLC 3
See also AITN 1; CA 45-48; CANR 2, 47,
103, 160; CMW 4

Hunt, Everette Howard, Jr.
See Hunt, E. Howard

Hunt, Francesca
See Holland, Isabelle (Christian)

Hunt, Howard
See Hunt, E. Howard

Hunt, Kyle
See Creasey, John

Hunt, (James Henry) Leigh
1784-1859 .... NCLC 1, 70; PC 73
See also DAM POET; DLB 96, 110, 144;
RGEL 2; TEA

Hunt, Marsha 1946- .... CLC 70
See also BW 2, 3; CA 143; CANR 79

Hunt, Violet 1866(?)-1942 .... TCLC 53
See also CA 184; DLB 162, 197

Hunter, E. Waldo
See Sturgeon, Theodore (Hamilton)

Hunter, Evan 1926-2005 .... CLC 11, 31
See McBain, Ed
See also AAYA 39; BPFB 2; CA 5-8R;
CAAS 241; CANR 5, 38, 62, 97, 149;
CMW 4; CN 1, 2, 3, 4, 5, 6, 7; CPW;
DAM POP; DLB 306; DLBY 1982; INT
CANR-5; MSW; MTCW 1; SATA 25;
SATA-Obit 167; SFW 4

Hunter, Kristin
See Lattany, Kristin (Elaine Eggleston)
Hunter
See also CN 1, 2, 3, 4, 5, 6

Hunter, Mary
See Austin, Mary (Hunter)

Hunter, Mollie 1922- .... CLC 21
See McIlwraith, Maureen Mollie Hunter
See also AAYA 13, 71; BYA 6; CANR 37,
78; CLR 25; DLB 161; JRDA; MAICYA
1, 2; SAAS 7; SATA 54, 106, 139; SATA-
Essay 139; WYA; YAW

Kristeva, Julia 1941- .... **CLC 77, 140**
See also CA 154; CANR 99; DLB 242;
EWL 3; FW; LMFS 2

Kristofferson, Kris 1936- .... **CLC 26**
See also CA 104

Krizanc, John 1956- .... **CLC 57**
See also CA 187

Krleza, Miroslav 1893-1981 .... **CLC 8, 114**
See also CA 97-100; CAAS 105; CANR
50; CDWLB 4; DLB 147; EW 11; RGWL
2, 3

Kroetsch, Robert (Paul) 1927- .... **CLC 5, 23,
57, 132**
See also CA 17-20R; CANR 8, 38; CCA 1;
CN 2, 3, 4, 5, 6, 7; CP 6, 7; DAC; DAM
POET; DLB 53; MTCW 1

Kroetz, Franz
See Kroetz, Franz Xaver

Kroetz, Franz Xaver 1946- .... **CLC 41**
See also CA 130; CANR 142; CWW 2;
EWL 3

Kroker, Arthur (W.) 1945- .... **CLC 77**
See also CA 161

Kroniuk, Lisa
See Berton, Pierre (Francis de Marigny)

Kropotkin, Peter (Aleksieevich)
1842-1921 .... **TCLC 36**
See Kropotkin, Petr Alekseevich
See also CA 219; CAAE 119

Kropotkin, Petr Alekseevich
See Kropotkin, Peter (Aleksieevich)
See also DLB 277

Krotkov, Yuri 1917-1981 .... **CLC 19**
See also CA 102

Krumb
See Crumb, R.

Krumgold, Joseph (Quincy)
1908-1980 .... **CLC 12**
See also BYA 1, 2; CA 9-12R; CAAS 101;
CANR 7; MAICYA 1, 2; SATA 1, 48;
SATA-Obit 23; YAW

Krumwitz
See Crumb, R.

Krutch, Joseph Wood 1893-1970 ..... **CLC 24**
See also ANW; CA 1-4R; CAAS 25-28R;
CANR 4; DLB 63, 206, 275

Krutzch, Gus
See Eliot, T(homas) S(tearns)

Krylov, Ivan Andreevich
1768(?)-1844 .... **NCLC 1**
See also DLB 150

Kubin, Alfred (Leopold Isidor)
1877-1959 .... **TCLC 23**
See also CA 149; CAAE 112; CANR 104;
DLB 81

Kubrick, Stanley 1928-1999 .... **CLC 16;
TCLC 112**
See also AAYA 30; CA 81-84; CAAS 177;
CANR 33; DLB 26

Kumin, Maxine 1925- .... **CLC 5, 13, 28, 164;
PC 15**
See also AITN 2; AMWS 4; ANW; CA
1-4R; 8; CANR 1, 21, 69, 115, 140; CP 2,
3, 4, 5, 6, 7; CWP; DA3; DAM POET;
DLB 5; EWL 3; EXPP; MTCW 1, 2;
MTFW 2005; PAB; PFS 18; SATA 12

Kundera, Milan 1929- . **CLC 4, 9, 19, 32, 68,
115, 135, 234; SSC 24**
See also AAYA 2, 62; BPFB 2; CA 85-88;
CANR 19, 52, 74, 144; CDWLB 4; CWW
2; DA3; DAM NOV; DLB 232; EW 13;
EWL 3; MTCW 1, 2; MTFW 2005; NFS
18; RGSF 2; RGWL 3; SSFS 10

Kunene, Mazisi 1930-2006 .... **CLC 85**
See also BW 1, 3; CA 125; CAAS 252;
CANR 81; CP 1, 6, 7; DLB 117

Kunene, Mazisi Raymond
See Kunene, Mazisi

Kunene, Mazisi Raymond Fakazi Mngoni
See Kunene, Mazisi

Kung, Hans .... **CLC 130**
See Kung, Hans

Kung, Hans 1928-
See Kung, Hans
See also CA 53-56; CANR 66, 134; MTCW
1, 2; MTFW 2005

Kunikida Doppo 1869(?)-1908
See Doppo, Kunikida
See also DLB 180; EWL 3

Kunitz, Stanley 1905-2006 ..... **CLC 6, 11, 14,
148; PC 19**
See also AMWS 3; CA 41-44R; CAAS 250;
CANR 26, 57, 98; CP 1, 2, 3, 4, 5, 6, 7;
DA3; DLB 48; INT CANR-26; MAL 5;
MTCW 1, 2; MTFW 2005; PFS 11;
RGAL 4

Kunitz, Stanley Jasspon
See Kunitz, Stanley

Kunze, Reiner 1933- .... **CLC 10**
See also CA 93-96; CWW 2; DLB 75; EWL
3

Kuprin, Aleksander Ivanovich
1870-1938 .... **TCLC 5**
See Kuprin, Aleksandr Ivanovich; Kuprin,
Alexandr Ivanovich
See also CA 182; CAAE 104

Kuprin, Aleksandr Ivanovich
See Kuprin, Aleksander Ivanovich
See also DLB 295

Kuprin, Alexandr Ivanovich
See Kuprin, Aleksander Ivanovich
See also EWL 3

Kureishi, Hanif 1954- .. **CLC 64, 135; DC 26**
See also BRWS 11; CA 139; CANR 113;
CBD; CD 5, 6; CN 6, 7; DLB 194, 245;
GLL 2; IDFW 4; WLIT 4; WWE 1

Kurosawa, Akira 1910-1998 ..... **CLC 16, 119**
See also AAYA 11, 64; CA 101; CAAS 170;
CANR 46; DAM MULT

Kushner, Tony 1956- .... **CLC 81, 203; DC 10**
See also AAYA 61; AMWS 9; CA 144;
CAD; CANR 74, 130; CD 5, 6; DA3;
DAM DRAM; DFS 5; DLB 228; EWL 3;
GLL 1; LAIT 5; MAL 5; MTCW 2;
MTFW 2005; RGAL 4; RGHL; SATA 160

Kuttner, Henry 1915-1958 .... **TCLC 10**
See also CA 157; CAAE 107; DLB 8;
FANT; SCFW 1, 2; SFW 4

Kutty, Madhavi
See Das, Kamala

Kuzma, Greg 1944- .... **CLC 7**
See also CA 33-36R; CANR 70

Kuzmin, Mikhail (Alekseevich)
1872(?)-1936 .... **TCLC 40**
See also CA 170; DLB 295; EWL 3

Kyd, Thomas 1558-1594 .. **DC 3; LC 22, 125**
See also BRW 1; DAM DRAM; DFS 21;
DLB 62; IDTP; LMFS 1; RGEL 2; TEA;
WLIT 3

Kyprianos, Iossif
See Samarakis, Antonis

L. S.
See Stephen, Sir Leslie

Labe, Louise 1521-1566 .... **LC 120**
See also DLB 327

Labrunie, Gerard
See Nerval, Gerard de

La Bruyere, Jean de 1645-1696 .... **LC 17**
See also DLB 268; EW 3; GFL Beginnings
to 1789

LaBute, Neil 1963- .... **CLC 225**
See also CA 240

Lacan, Jacques (Marie Emile)
1901-1981 .... **CLC 75**
See also CA 121; CAAS 104; DLB 296;
EWL 3; TWA

Laclos, Pierre-Ambroise Francois
1741-1803 .... **NCLC 4, 87**
See also DLB 313; EW 4; GFL Beginnings
to 1789; RGWL 2, 3

Lacolere, Francois
See Aragon, Louis

La Colere, Francois
See Aragon, Louis

La Deshabilleuse
See Simenon, Georges (Jacques Christian)

Lady Gregory
See Gregory, Lady Isabella Augusta (Persse)

Lady of Quality, A
See Bagnold, Enid

**La Fayette, Marie-(Madelaine Pioche de la
Vergne)** 1634-1693 .... **LC 2**
See Lafayette, Marie-Madeleine
See also GFL Beginnings to 1789; RGWL
2, 3

Lafayette, Marie-Madeleine
See La Fayette, Marie-(Madelaine Pioche
de la Vergne)
See also DLB 268

Lafayette, Rene
See Hubbard, L. Ron

La Flesche, Francis 1857(?)-1932 ...... **NNAL**
See also CA 144; CANR 83; DLB 175

La Fontaine, Jean de 1621-1695 .... **LC 50**
See also DLB 268; EW 3; GFL Beginnings
to 1789; MAICYA 1, 2; RGWL 2, 3;
SATA 18

LaForet, Carmen 1921-2004 .... **CLC 219**
See also CA 246; CWW 2; DLB 322; EWL
3

LaForet Diaz, Carmen
See LaForet, Carmen

Laforgue, Jules 1860-1887 . **NCLC 5, 53; PC
14; SSC 20**
See also DLB 217; EW 7; GFL 1789 to the
Present; RGWL 2, 3

Lagerkvist, Paer (Fabian)
1891-1974 ..... **CLC 7, 10, 13, 54; TCLC
144**
See Lagerkvist, Par
See also CA 85-88; CAAS 49-52; DA3;
DAM DRAM, NOV; MTCW 1, 2; MTFW
2005; TWA

Lagerkvist, Par .... **SSC 12**
See Lagerkvist, Paer (Fabian)
See also DLB 259, 331; EW 10; EWL 3;
RGSF 2; RGWL 2, 3

Lagerloef, Selma (Ottiliana Lovisa)
.... **TCLC 4, 36**
See Lagerlof, Selma (Ottiliana Lovisa)
See also CAAE 108; MTCW 2

Lagerlof, Selma (Ottiliana Lovisa)
1858-1940
See Lagerloef, Selma (Ottiliana Lovisa)
See also CA 188; CLR 7; DLB 259, 331;
RGWL 2, 3; SATA 15; SSFS 18

La Guma, Alex 1925-1985 .. **BLCS; CLC 19;
TCLC 140**
See also AFW; BW 1, 3; CA 49-52; CAAS
118; CANR 25, 81; CDWLB 3; CN 1, 2,
3; CP 1; DAM NOV; DLB 117, 225; EWL
3; MTCW 1, 2; MTFW 2005; WLIT 2;
WWE 1

Lahiri, Jhumpa 1967- .... **SSC 96**
See also AAYA 56; CA 193; CANR 134;
DLB 323; MTFW 2005; SSFS 19

Laidlaw, A. K.
See Grieve, C(hristopher) M(urray)

Lainez, Manuel Mujica
See Mujica Lainez, Manuel
See also HW 1

Laing, R(onald) D(avid) 1927-1989 . **CLC 95**
See also CA 107; CAAS 129; CANR 34;
MTCW 1

Lawler, Raymond Evenor 1922- .... **CLC 58**
See Lawler, Ray
See also CA 103; CD 5, 6; RGEL 2

Lawrence, D(avid) H(erbert Richards)
1885-1930 .... **PC 54; SSC 4, 19, 73;
TCLC 2, 9, 16, 33, 48, 61, 93; WLC 3**
See Chambers, Jessie
See also BPFB 2; BRW 7; BRWR 2; CA
121; CAAE 104; CANR 131; CDBLB
1914-1945; DA; DA3; DAB; DAC; DAM
MST, NOV, POET; DLB 10, 19, 36, 98,
162, 195; EWL 3; EXPP; EXPS; LAIT
3; MTCW 1, 2; MTFW 2005; NFS 18;
PFS 6; RGEL 2; RGSF 2; SSFS 2, 6;
TEA; WLIT 4; WP

Lawrence, T(homas) E(dward)
1888-1935 .... **TCLC 18**
See Dale, Colin
See also BRWS 2; CA 167; CAAE 115;
DLB 195

Lawrence of Arabia
See Lawrence, T(homas) E(dward)

Lawson, Henry (Archibald Hertzberg)
1867-1922 .... **SSC 18; TCLC 27**
See also CA 181; CAAE 120; DLB 230;
RGEL 2; RGSF 2

Lawton, Dennis
See Faust, Frederick (Schiller)

Layamon fl. c. 1200- .... **CMLC 10**
See also DLB 146; RGEL 2

Laye, Camara 1928-1980 ..... **BLC 2; CLC 4,
38**
See Camara Laye
See also AFW; BW 1; CA 85-88; CAAS
97-100; CANR 25; DAM MULT; MTCW
1, 2; WLIT 2

Layton, Irving 1912-2006 ..... **CLC 2, 15, 164**
See also CA 1-4R; CAAS 247; CANR 2,
33, 43, 66, 129; CP 1, 2, 3, 4, 5, 6, 7;
DAC; DAM MST, POET; DLB 88; EWL
3; MTCW 1, 2; PFS 12; RGEL 2

Layton, Irving Peter
See Layton, Irving

Lazarus, Emma 1849-1887 ...... **NCLC 8, 109**

Lazarus, Felix
See Cable, George Washington

Lazarus, Henry
See Slavitt, David R(ytman)

Lea, Joan
See Neufeld, John (Arthur)

Leacock, Stephen (Butler)
1869-1944 .... **SSC 39; TCLC 2**
See also CA 141; CAAE 104; CANR 80;
DAC; DAM MST; DLB 92; EWL 3;
MTCW 2; MTFW 2005; RGEL 2; RGSF
2

Lead, Jane Ward 1623-1704 .... **LC 72**
See also DLB 131

Leapor, Mary 1722-1746 .... **LC 80**
See also DLB 109

Lear, Edward 1812-1888 ..... **NCLC 3; PC 65**
See also AAYA 48; BRW 5; CLR 1, 75;
DLB 32, 163, 166; MAICYA 1, 2; RGEL
2; SATA 18, 100; WCH; WP

Lear, Norman (Milton) 1922- .... **CLC 12**
See also CA 73-76

Leautaud, Paul 1872-1956 .... **TCLC 83**
See also CA 203; DLB 65; GFL 1789 to the
Present

Leavis, F(rank) R(aymond)
1895-1978 .... **CLC 24**
See also BRW 7; CA 21-24R; CAAS 77-
80; CANR 44; DLB 242; EWL 3; MTCW
1, 2; RGEL 2

Leavitt, David 1961- .... **CLC 34**
See also CA 122; CAAE 116; CANR 50,
62, 101, 134; CPW; DA3; DAM POP;
DLB 130; GLL 1; INT CA-122; MAL 5;
MTCW 2; MTFW 2005

Leblanc, Maurice (Marie Emile)
1864-1941 .... **TCLC 49**
See also CAAE 110; CMW 4

Lebowitz, Fran(ces Ann) 1951(?)- ... **CLC 11,
36**
See also CA 81-84; CANR 14, 60, 70; INT
CANR-14; MTCW 1

Lebrecht, Peter
See Tieck, (Johann) Ludwig

le Carre, John 1931- .... **CLC 9, 15**
See also AAYA 42; BEST 89:4; BPFB 2;
BRWS 2; CA 5-8R; CANR 13, 33, 59,
107, 132; CDBLB 1960 to Present; CMW
4; CN 1, 2, 3, 4, 5, 6, 7; CPW; DA3;
DAM POP; DLB 87; EWL 3; MSW;
MTCW 1, 2; MTFW 2005; RGEL 2; TEA

Le Clezio, J. M.G. 1940- .... **CLC 31, 155**
See also CA 128; CAAE 116; CANR 147;
CWW 2; DLB 83; EWL 3; GFL 1789 to
the Present; RGSF 2

Le Clezio, Jean Marie Gustave
See Le Clezio, J. M.G.

Leconte de Lisle, Charles-Marie-Rene
1818-1894 .... **NCLC 29**
See also DLB 217; EW 6; GFL 1789 to the
Present

Le Coq, Monsieur
See Simenon, Georges (Jacques Christian)

Leduc, Violette 1907-1972 .... **CLC 22**
See also CA 13-14; CAAS 33-36R; CANR
69; CAP 1; EWL 3; GFL 1789 to the
Present; GLL 1

Ledwidge, Francis 1887(?)-1917 .... **TCLC 23**
See also CA 203; CAAE 123; DLB 20

Lee, Andrea 1953- .... **BLC 2; CLC 36**
See also BW 1, 3; CA 125; CANR 82;
DAM MULT

Lee, Andrew
See Auchincloss, Louis

Lee, Chang-rae 1965- .... **CLC 91**
See also CA 148; CANR 89; CN 7; DLB
312; LATS 1:2

Lee, Don L. .... **CLC 2**
See Madhubuti, Haki R.
See also CP 2, 3, 4, 5

Lee, George W(ashington)
1894-1976 .... **BLC 2; CLC 52**
See also BW 1; CA 125; CANR 83; DAM
MULT; DLB 51

Lee, Harper 1926- ... **CLC 12, 60, 194; WLC
4**
See also AAYA 13; AMWS 8; BPFB 2;
BYA 3; CA 13-16R; CANR 51, 128;
CDALB 1941-1968; CSW; DA; DA3;
DAB; DAC; DAM MST, NOV; DLB 6;
EXPN; LAIT 3; MAL 5; MTCW 1, 2;
MTFW 2005; NFS 2; SATA 11; WYA;
YAW

Lee, Helen Elaine 1959(?)- .... **CLC 86**
See also CA 148

Lee, John .... **CLC 70**

Lee, Julian
See Latham, Jean Lee

Lee, Larry
See Lee, Lawrence

Lee, Laurie 1914-1997 .... **CLC 90**
See also CA 77-80; CAAS 158; CANR 33,
73; CP 1, 2, 3, 4, 5, 6; CPW; DAB; DAM
POP; DLB 27; MTCW 1; RGEL 2

Lee, Lawrence 1941-1990 .... **CLC 34**
See also CAAS 131; CANR 43

Lee, Li-Young 1957- .... **CLC 164; PC 24**
See also AMWS 15; CA 153; CANR 118;
CP 6, 7; DLB 165, 312; LMFS 2; PFS 11,
15, 17

Lee, Manfred B. 1905-1971 .... **CLC 11**
See Queen, Ellery
See also CA 1-4R; CAAS 29-32R; CANR
2, 150; CMW 4; DLB 137

Lee, Manfred Bennington
See Lee, Manfred B.

Lee, Nathaniel 1645(?)-1692 .... **LC 103**
See also DLB 80; RGEL 2

Lee, Shelton Jackson
See Lee, Spike
See also AAYA 4, 29

Lee, Spike 1957(?)- .... **BLCS; CLC 105**
See Lee, Shelton Jackson
See also BW 2, 3; CA 125; CANR 42;
DAM MULT

Lee, Stan 1922- .... **CLC 17**
See also AAYA 5, 49; CA 111; CAAE 108;
CANR 129; INT CA-111; MTFW 2005

Lee, Tanith 1947- .... **CLC 46**
See also AAYA 15; CA 37-40R; CANR 53,
102, 145; DLB 261; FANT; SATA 8, 88,
134; SFW 4; SUFW 1, 2; YAW

Lee, Vernon .... **SSC 33, 98; TCLC 5**
See Paget, Violet
See also DLB 57, 153, 156, 174, 178; GLL
1; SUFW 1

Lee, William
See Burroughs, William S.
See also GLL 1

Lee, Willy
See Burroughs, William S.
See also GLL 1

Lee-Hamilton, Eugene (Jacob)
1845-1907 .... **TCLC 22**
See also CA 234; CAAE 117

Leet, Judith 1935- .... **CLC 11**
See also CA 187

Le Fanu, Joseph Sheridan
1814-1873 .... **NCLC 9, 58; SSC 14, 84**
See also CMW 4; DA3; DAM POP; DLB
21, 70, 159, 178; GL 3; HGG; RGEL 2;
RGSF 2; SUFW 1

Leffland, Ella 1931- .... **CLC 19**
See also CA 29-32R; CANR 35, 78, 82;
DLBY 1984; INT CANR-35; SATA 65;
SSFS 24

Leger, Alexis
See Leger, (Marie-Rene Auguste) Alexis
Saint-Leger

**Leger, (Marie-Rene Auguste) Alexis
Saint-Leger** 1887-1975 .. **CLC 4, 11, 46;
PC 23**
See Perse, Saint-John; Saint-John Perse
See also CA 13-16R; CAAS 61-64; CANR
43; DAM POET; MTCW 1

Leger, Saintleger
See Leger, (Marie-Rene Auguste) Alexis
Saint-Leger

Le Guin, Ursula K. 1929- ...... **CLC 8, 13, 22,
45, 71, 136; SSC 12, 69**
See also AAYA 9, 27; AITN 1; BPFB 2;
BYA 5, 8, 11, 14; CA 21-24R; CANR 9,
32, 52, 74, 132; CDALB 1968-1988; CLR
3, 28, 91; CN 2, 3, 4, 5, 6, 7; CPW; DA3;
DAB; DAC; DAM MST, POP; DLB 8,
52, 256, 275; EXPS; FANT; FW; INT
CANR-32; JRDA; LAIT 5; MAICYA 1,
2; MAL 5; MTCW 1, 2; MTFW 2005;
NFS 6, 9; SATA 4, 52, 99, 149; SCFW 1,
2; SFW 4; SSFS 2; SUFW 1, 2; WYA;
YAW

Lehmann, Rosamond (Nina)
1901-1990 .... **CLC 5**
See also CA 77-80; CAAS 131; CANR 8,
73; CN 1, 2, 3, 4; DLB 15; MTCW 2;
RGEL 2; RHW

Leiber, Fritz (Reuter, Jr.)
1910-1992 .... **CLC 25**
See also AAYA 65; BPFB 2; CA 45-48;
CAAS 139; CANR 2, 40, 86; CN 2, 3, 4,
5; DLB 8; FANT; HGG; MTCW 1, 2;
MTFW 2005; SATA 45; SATA-Obit 73;
SCFW 1, 2; SFW 4; SUFW 1, 2

Lewis, Matthew Gregory
    1775-1818 .... **NCLC 11, 62**
    See also DLB 39, 158, 178; GL 3; HGG;
    LMFS 1; RGEL 2; SUFW

Lewis, (Harry) Sinclair 1885-1951 . **TCLC 4,**
    13, 23, 39; WLC 4
    See also AMW; AMWC 1; BPFB 2; CA
    133; CAAE 104; CANR 132; CDALB
    1917-1929; DA; DA3; DAB; DAC; DAM
    MST, NOV; DLB 9, 102, 284, 331; DLBD
    1; EWL 3; LAIT 3; MAL 5; MTCW 1, 2;
    MTFW 2005; NFS 15, 19, 22; RGAL 4;
    TUS

Lewis, (Percy) Wyndham
    1884(?)-1957 .. **SSC 34; TCLC 2, 9, 104**
    See also BRW 7; CA 157; CAAE 104; DLB
    15; EWL 3; FANT; MTCW 2; MTFW
    2005; RGEL 2

Lewisohn, Ludwig 1883-1955 .... **TCLC 19**
    See also CA 203; CAAE 107; DLB 4, 9,
    28, 102; MAL 5

Lewton, Val 1904-1951 .... **TCLC 76**
    See also CA 199; IDFW 3, 4

Leyner, Mark 1956- .... **CLC 92**
    See also CA 110; CANR 28, 53; DA3; DLB
    292; MTCW 2; MTFW 2005

Lezama Lima, Jose 1910-1976 .... **CLC 4, 10,**
    101; HLCS 2
    See also CA 77-80; CANR 71; DAM
    MULT; DLB 113, 283; EWL 3; HW 1, 2;
    LAW; RGWL 2, 3

L'Heureux, John (Clarke) 1934- ...... **CLC 52**
    See also CA 13-16R; CANR 23, 45, 88; CP
    1, 2, 3, 4; DLB 244

Li Ch'ing-chao 1081(?)-1141(?) .... **CMLC 71**

Liddell, C. H.
    See Kuttner, Henry

Lie, Jonas (Lauritz Idemil)
    1833-1908(?) .... **TCLC 5**
    See also CAAE 115

Lieber, Joel 1937-1971 .... **CLC 6**
    See also CA 73-76; CAAS 29-32R

Lieber, Stanley Martin
    See Lee, Stan

Lieberman, Laurence (James)
    1935- .... **CLC 4, 36**
    See also CA 17-20R; CANR 8, 36, 89; CP
    1, 2, 3, 4, 5, 6, 7

Lieh Tzu fl. 7th cent. B.C.-5th cent.
    B.C. .... **CMLC 27**

Lieksman, Anders
    See Haavikko, Paavo Juhani

Lifton, Robert Jay 1926- .... **CLC 67**
    See also CA 17-20R; CANR 27, 78, 161;
    INT CANR-27; SATA 66

Lightfoot, Gordon 1938- .... **CLC 26**
    See also CA 242; CAAE 109

Lightfoot, Gordon Meredith
    See Lightfoot, Gordon

Lightman, Alan P(aige) 1948- .... **CLC 81**
    See also CA 141; CANR 63, 105, 138;
    MTFW 2005

Ligotti, Thomas (Robert) 1953- ...... **CLC 44;**
    SSC 16
    See also CA 123; CANR 49, 135; HGG;
    SUFW 2

Li Ho 791-817 .... **PC 13**

Li Ju-chen c. 1763-c. 1830 .... **NCLC 137**

Lilar, Francoise
    See Mallet-Joris, Francoise

Liliencron, Detlev
    See Liliencron, Detlev von

Liliencron, Detlev von 1844-1909 .. **TCLC 18**
    See also CAAE 117

Liliencron, Friedrich Adolf Axel Detlev von
    See Liliencron, Detlev von

Liliencron, Friedrich Detlev von
    See Liliencron, Detlev von

Lille, Alain de
    See Alain de Lille

Lillo, George 1691-1739 .... **LC 131**
    See also DLB 84; RGEL 2

Lilly, William 1602-1681 .... **LC 27**

Lima, Jose Lezama
    See Lezama Lima, Jose

Lima Barreto, Afonso Henrique de
    1881-1922 .... **TCLC 23**
    See Lima Barreto, Afonso Henriques de
    See also CA 181; CAAE 117; LAW

Lima Barreto, Afonso Henriques de
    See Lima Barreto, Afonso Henrique de
    See also DLB 307

Limonov, Eduard
    See Limonov, Edward
    See also DLB 317

Limonov, Edward 1944- .... **CLC 67**
    See Limonov, Eduard
    See also CA 137

Lin, Frank
    See Atherton, Gertrude (Franklin Horn)

Lin, Yutang 1895-1976 .... **TCLC 149**
    See also CA 45-48; CAAS 65-68; CANR 2;
    RGAL 4

Lincoln, Abraham 1809-1865 .... **NCLC 18**
    See also LAIT 2

Lind, Jakov .... **CLC 1, 2, 4, 27, 82**
    See Landwirth, Heinz
    See also CA 4; DLB 299; EWL 3; RGHL

Lindbergh, Anne Morrow
    1906-2001 .... **CLC 82**
    See also BPFB 2; CA 17-20R; CAAS 193;
    CANR 16, 73; DAM NOV; MTCW 1, 2;
    MTFW 2005; SATA 33; SATA-Obit 125;
    TUS

Lindsay, David 1878(?)-1945 .... **TCLC 15**
    See also CA 187; CAAE 113; DLB 255;
    FANT; SFW 4; SUFW 1

Lindsay, (Nicholas) Vachel
    1879-1931 ...... **PC 23; TCLC 17; WLC 4**
    See also AMWS 1; CA 135; CAAE 114;
    CANR 79; CDALB 1865-1917; DA;
    DA3; DAC; DAM MST, POET; DLB 54;
    EWL 3; EXPP; MAL 5; RGAL 4; SATA
    40; WP

Linke-Poot
    See Doeblin, Alfred

Linney, Romulus 1930- .... **CLC 51**
    See also CA 1-4R; CAD; CANR 40, 44,
    79; CD 5, 6; CSW; RGAL 4

Linton, Eliza Lynn 1822-1898 .... **NCLC 41**
    See also DLB 18

Li Po 701-763 .... **CMLC 2, 86; PC 29**
    See also PFS 20; WP

Lipsius, Justus 1547-1606 .... **LC 16**

Lipsyte, Robert 1938- .... **CLC 21**
    See also AAYA 7, 45; CA 17-20R; CANR
    8, 57, 146; CLR 23, 76; DA; DAC; DAM
    MST, NOV; JRDA; LAIT 5; MAICYA
    1, 2; SATA 5, 68, 113, 161; WYA; YAW

Lipsyte, Robert Michael
    See Lipsyte, Robert

Lish, Gordon 1934- .... **CLC 45; SSC 18**
    See also CA 117; CAAE 113; CANR 79,
    151; DLB 130; INT CA-117

Lish, Gordon Jay
    See Lish, Gordon

Lispector, Clarice 1925(?)-1977 .... **CLC 43;**
    HLCS 2; SSC 34, 96
    See also CA 139; CAAS 116; CANR 71;
    CDWLB 3; DLB 113, 307; DNFS 1; EWL
    3; FW; IIW 2; LAW; RGSF 2; RGWL 2,
    3; WLIT 1

Littell, Robert 1935(?)- .... **CLC 42**
    See also CA 112; CAAE 109; CANR 64,
    115; CMW 4

Little, Malcolm 1925-1965
    See Malcolm X
    See also BW 1, 3; CA 125; CAAS 111;
    CANR 82; DA; DA3; DAB; DAC; DAM
    MST, MULT; MTCW 1, 2; MTFW 2005

Littlewit, Humphrey Gent.
    See Lovecraft, H. P.

Litwos
    See Sienkiewicz, Henryk (Adam Alexander
    Pius)

Liu, E. 1857-1909 .... **TCLC 15**
    See also CA 190; CAAE 115; DLB 328

Lively, Penelope 1933- .... **CLC 32, 50**
    See also BPFB 2; CA 41-44R; CANR 29,
    67, 79, 131; CLR 7; CN 5, 6, 7; CWRI 5;
    DAM NOV; DLB 14, 161, 207, 326;
    FANT; JRDA; MAICYA 1, 2; MTCW 1,
    2; MTFW 2005; SATA 7, 60, 101, 164;
    TEA

Lively, Penelope Margaret
    See Lively, Penelope

Livesay, Dorothy (Kathleen)
    1909-1996 .... **CLC 4, 15, 79**
    See also AITN 2; CA 25-28R; 8; CANR 36,
    67; CP 1, 2, 3, 4, 5; DAC; DAM MST,
    POET; DLB 68; FW; MTCW 1; RGEL 2;
    TWA

Livy c. 59B.C.-c. 12 .... **CMLC 11**
    See also AW 2; CDWLB 1; DLB 211;
    RGWL 2, 3; WLIT 8

Lizardi, Jose Joaquin Fernandez de
    1776-1827 .... **NCLC 30**
    See also LAW

Llewellyn, Richard
    See Llewellyn Lloyd, Richard Dafydd Viv-
    ian
    See also DLB 15

Llewellyn Lloyd, Richard Dafydd Vivian
    1906-1983 .... **CLC 7, 80**
    See Llewellyn, Richard
    See also CA 53-56; CAAS 111; CANR 7,
    71; SATA 11; SATA-Obit 37

Llosa, Jorge Mario Pedro Vargas
    See Vargas Llosa, Mario
    See also RGWL 3

Llosa, Mario Vargas
    See Vargas Llosa, Mario

Lloyd, Manda
    See Mander, (Mary) Jane

Lloyd Webber, Andrew 1948-
    See Webber, Andrew Lloyd
    See also AAYA 1, 38; CA 149; CAAE 116;
    DAM DRAM; SATA 56

Llull, Ramon c. 1235-c. 1316 .... **CMLC 12**

Lobb, Ebenezer
    See Upward, Allen

Locke, Alain (Le Roy)
    1886-1954 .... **BLCS; HR 1:3; TCLC 43**
    See also AMWS 14; BW 1, 3; CA 124;
    CAAE 106; CANR 79; DLB 51; LMFS
    2; MAL 5; RGAL 4

Locke, John 1632-1704 .... **LC 7, 35, 135**
    See also DLB 31, 101, 213, 252; RGEL 2;
    WLIT 3

Locke-Elliott, Sumner
    See Elliott, Sumner Locke

Lockhart, John Gibson 1794-1854 .. **NCLC 6**
    See also DLB 110, 116, 144

Lockridge, Ross (Franklin), Jr.
    1914-1948 .... **TCLC 111**
    See also CA 145; CAAE 108; CANR 79;
    DLB 143; DLBY 1980; MAL 5; RGAL
    4; RHW

Lockwood, Robert
    See Johnson, Robert

Lugones, Leopoldo 1874-1938 .... **HLCS 2; TCLC 15**
See also CA 131; CAAE 116; CANR 104; DLB 283; EWL 3; HW 1; LAW

Lu Hsun .... **SSC 20; TCLC 3**
See Shu-Jen, Chou
See also EWL 3

Lukacs, George .... **CLC 24**
See Lukacs, Gyorgy (Szegeny von)

Lukacs, Gyorgy (Szegeny von) 1885-1971
See Lukacs, George
See also CA 101; CAAS 29-32R; CANR 62; CDWLB 4; DLB 215, 242; EW 10; EWL 3; MTCW 1, 2

Luke, Peter (Ambrose Cyprian)
1919-1995 .... **CLC 38**
See also CA 81-84; CAAS 147; CANR 72; CBD; CD 5, 6; DLB 13

Lunar, Dennis
See Mungo, Raymond

Lurie, Alison 1926- ..... **CLC 4, 5, 18, 39, 175**
See also BPFB 2; CA 1-4R; CANR 2, 17, 50, 88; CN 1, 2, 3, 4, 5, 6, 7; DLB 2; MAL 5; MTCW 1; NFS 24; SATA 46, 112; TCLE 1:1

Lustig, Arnost 1926- .... **CLC 56**
See also AAYA 3; CA 69-72; CANR 47, 102; CWW 2; DLB 232, 299; EWL 3; RGHL; SATA 56

Luther, Martin 1483-1546 .... **LC 9, 37**
See also CDWLB 2; DLB 179; EW 2; RGWL 2, 3

Luxemburg, Rosa 1870(?)-1919 ..... **TCLC 63**
See also CAAE 118

Luzi, Mario (Egidio Vincenzo)
1914-2005 .... **CLC 13**
See also CA 61-64; CAAS 236; CANR 9, 70; CWW 2; DLB 128; EWL 3

L'vov, Arkady .... **CLC 59**

Lydgate, John c. 1370-1450(?) .... **LC 81**
See also BRW 1; DLB 146; RGEL 2

Lyly, John 1554(?)-1606 .... **DC 7; LC 41**
See also BRW 1; DAM DRAM; DLB 62, 167; RGEL 2

L'Ymagier
See Gourmont, Remy(-Marie-Charles) de

Lynch, B. Suarez
See Borges, Jorge Luis

Lynch, David 1946- .... **CLC 66, 162**
See also AAYA 55; CA 129; CAAE 124; CANR 111

Lynch, David Keith
See Lynch, David

Lynch, James
See Andreyev, Leonid (Nikolaevich)

Lyndsay, Sir David 1485-1555 .... **LC 20**
See also RGEL 2

Lynn, Kenneth S(chuyler)
1923-2001 .... **CLC 50**
See also CA 1-4R; CAAS 196; CANR 3, 27, 65

Lynx
See West, Rebecca

Lyons, Marcus
See Blish, James (Benjamin)

Lyotard, Jean-Francois
1924-1998 .... **TCLC 103**
See also DLB 242; EWL 3

Lyre, Pinchbeck
See Sassoon, Siegfried (Lorraine)

Lytle, Andrew (Nelson) 1902-1995 ... **CLC 22**
See also CA 9-12R; CAAS 150; CANR 70; CN 1, 2, 3, 4, 5, 6; CSW; DLB 6; DLBY 1995; RGAL 4; RHW

Lyttelton, George 1709-1773 .... **LC 10**
See also RGEL 2

Lytton of Knebworth, Baron
See Bulwer-Lytton, Edward (George Earle Lytton)

Maas, Peter 1929-2001 .... **CLC 29**
See also CA 93-96; CAAS 201; INT CA-93-96; MTCW 2; MTFW 2005

Mac A'Ghobhainn, Iain
See Smith, Iain Crichton

Macaulay, Catherine 1731-1791 .... **LC 64**
See also DLB 104

Macaulay, (Emilie) Rose
1881(?)-1958 .... **TCLC 7, 44**
See also CAAE 104; DLB 36; EWL 3; RGEL 2; RHW

Macaulay, Thomas Babington
1800-1859 .... **NCLC 42**
See also BRW 4; CDBLB 1832-1890; DLB 32, 55; RGEL 2

MacBeth, George (Mann)
1932-1992 .... **CLC 2, 5, 9**
See also CA 25-28R; CAAS 136; CANR 61, 66; CP 1, 2, 3, 4, 5; DLB 40; MTCW 1; PFS 8; SATA 4; SATA-Obit 70

MacCaig, Norman (Alexander)
1910-1996 .... **CLC 36**
See also BRWS 6; CA 9-12R; CANR 3, 34; CP 1, 2, 3, 4, 5, 6; DAB; DAM POET; DLB 27; EWL 3; RGEL 2

MacCarthy, Sir (Charles Otto) Desmond
1877-1952 .... **TCLC 36**
See also CA 167

MacDiarmid, Hugh .... **CLC 2, 4, 11, 19, 63; PC 9**
See Grieve, C(hristopher) M(urray)
See also BRWS 12; CDBLB 1945-1960; CP 1, 2; DLB 20; EWL 3; RGEL 2

MacDonald, Anson
See Heinlein, Robert A.

Macdonald, Cynthia 1928- .... **CLC 13, 19**
See also CA 49-52; CANR 4, 44, 146; DLB 105

MacDonald, George 1824-1905 .... **TCLC 9, 113**
See also AAYA 57; BYA 5; CA 137; CAAE 106; CANR 80; CLR 67; DLB 18, 163, 178; FANT; MAICYA 1, 2; RGEL 2; SATA 33, 100; SFW 4; SUFW; WCH

Macdonald, John
See Millar, Kenneth

MacDonald, John D. 1916-1986 .. **CLC 3, 27, 44**
See also BPFB 2; CA 1-4R; CAAS 121; CANR 1, 19, 60; CMW 4; CPW; DAM NOV, POP; DLB 8, 306; DLBY 1986; MSW; MTCW 1, 2; MTFW 2005; SFW 4

Macdonald, John Ross
See Millar, Kenneth

Macdonald, Ross ..... **CLC 1, 2, 3, 14, 34, 41**
See Millar, Kenneth
See also AMWS 4; BPFB 2; CN 1, 2, 3; DLBD 6; MAL 5; MSW; RGAL 4

MacDougal, John
See Blish, James (Benjamin)

MacDougal, John
See Blish, James (Benjamin)

MacDowell, John
See Parks, Tim(othy Harold)

MacEwen, Gwendolyn (Margaret)
1941-1987 .... **CLC 13, 55**
See also CA 9-12R; CAAS 124; CANR 7, 22; CP 1, 2, 3, 4; DLB 53, 251; SATA 50; SATA-Obit 55

Macha, Karel Hynek 1810-1846 .... **NCLC 46**

Machado (y Ruiz), Antonio
1875-1939 .... **TCLC 3**
See also CA 174; CAAE 104; DLB 108; EW 9; EWL 3; HW 2; PFS 23; RGWL 2, 3

Machado de Assis, Joaquim Maria
1839-1908 .... **BLC 2; HLCS 2; SSC 24; TCLC 10**
See also CA 153; CAAE 107; CANR 91; DLB 307; LAW; RGSF 2; RGWL 2, 3; TWA; WLIT 1

Machaut, Guillaume de c.
1300-1377 .... **CMLC 64**
See also DLB 208

Machen, Arthur .... **SSC 20; TCLC 4**
See Jones, Arthur Llewellyn
See also CA 179; DLB 156, 178; RGEL 2; SUFW 1

Machiavelli, Niccolo 1469-1527 ... **DC 16; LC 8, 36; WLCS**
See also AAYA 58; DA; DAB; DAC; DAM MST; EW 2; LAIT 1; LMFS 1; NFS 9; RGWL 2, 3; TWA; WLIT 7

MacInnes, Colin 1914-1976 .... **CLC 4, 23**
See also CA 69-72; CAAS 65-68; CANR 21; CN 1, 2; DLB 14; MTCW 1, 2; RGEL 2; RHW

MacInnes, Helen (Clark)
1907-1985 .... **CLC 27, 39**
See also BPFB 2; CA 1-4R; CAAS 117; CANR 1, 28, 58; CMW 4; CN 1, 2; CPW; DAM POP; DLB 87; MSW; MTCW 1, 2; MTFW 2005; SATA 22; SATA-Obit 44

Mackay, Mary 1855-1924
See Corelli, Marie
See also CA 177; CAAE 118; FANT; RHW

Mackay, Shena 1944- .... **CLC 195**
See also CA 104; CANR 88, 139; DLB 231, 319; MTFW 2005

Mackenzie, Compton (Edward Montague)
1883-1972 .... **CLC 18; TCLC 116**
See also CA 21-22; CAAS 37-40R; CAP 2; CN 1; DLB 34, 100; RGEL 2

Mackenzie, Henry 1745-1831 .... **NCLC 41**
See also DLB 39; RGEL 2

Mackey, Nathaniel 1947- .... **PC 49**
See also CA 153; CANR 114; CP 6, 7; DLB 169

Mackey, Nathaniel Ernest
See Mackey, Nathaniel

MacKinnon, Catharine A. 1946- .... **CLC 181**
See also CA 132; CAAE 128; CANR 73, 140; FW; MTCW 2; MTFW 2005

Mackintosh, Elizabeth 1896(?)-1952
See Tey, Josephine
See also CAAE 110; CMW 4

Macklin, Charles 1699-1797 .... **LC 132**
See also DLB 89; RGEL 2

MacLaren, James
See Grieve, C(hristopher) M(urray)

MacLaverty, Bernard 1942- .... **CLC 31**
See also CA 118; CAAE 116; CANR 43, 88; CN 5, 6, 7; DLB 267; INT CA-118; RGSF 2

MacLean, Alistair (Stuart)
1922(?)-1987 .... **CLC 3, 13, 50, 63**
See also CA 57-60; CAAS 121; CANR 28, 61; CMW 4; CP 2, 3, 4, 5, 6, 7; CPW; DAM POP; DLB 276; MTCW 1; SATA 23; SATA-Obit 50; TCWW 2

Maclean, Norman (Fitzroy)
1902-1990 .... **CLC 78; SSC 13**
See also AMWS 14; CA 102; CAAS 132; CANR 49; CPW; DAM POP; DLB 206; TCWW 2

MacLeish, Archibald 1892-1982 ... **CLC 3, 8, 14, 68; PC 47**
See also AMW; CA 9-12R; CAAS 106; CAD; CANR 33, 63; CDALBS; CP 1, 2; DAM POET; DFS 15; DLB 4, 7, 45; DLBY 1982; EWL 3; EXPP; MAL 5; MTCW 1, 2; MTFW 2005; PAB; PFS 5; RGAL 4; TUS

Author Index

Nakos, Lilika 1903(?)-1989 .... **CLC 29**
Napoleon
See Yamamoto, Hisaye
Narayan, R.K. 1906-2001 ...... **CLC 7, 28, 47,**
121, 211; SSC 25
See also BPFB 2; CA 81-84; CAAS 196;
CANR 33, 61, 112; CN 1, 2, 3, 4, 5, 6, 7;
DA3; DAM NOV; DLB 323; DNFS 1;
EWL 3; MTCW 1, 2; MTFW 2005; RGEL
2; RGSF 2; SATA 62; SSFS 5; WWE 1
Nash, (Frediric) Ogden 1902-1971 . **CLC 23;**
PC 21; TCLC 109
See also CA 13-14; CAAS 29-32R; CANR
34, 61; CAP 1; CP 1; DAM POET; DLB
11; MAICYA 1, 2; MAL 5; MTCW 1, 2;
RGAL 4; SATA 2, 46; WP
Nashe, Thomas 1567-1601(?) .... **LC 41, 89**
See also DLB 167; RGEL 2
Nathan, Daniel
See Dannay, Frederic
Nathan, George Jean 1882-1958 .... **TCLC 18**
See Hatteras, Owen
See also CA 169; CAAE 114; DLB 137;
MAL 5
Natsume, Kinnosuke
See Natsume, Soseki
Natsume, Soseki 1867-1916 .... **TCLC 2, 10**
See Natsume Soseki; Soseki
See also CA 195; CAAE 104; RGWL 2, 3;
TWA
Natsume Soseki
See Natsume, Soseki
See also DLB 180; EWL 3
Natti, (Mary) Lee 1919-
See Kingman, Lee
See also CA 5-8R; CANR 2
Navarre, Marguerite de
See de Navarre, Marguerite
Naylor, Gloria 1950- ..... **BLC 3; CLC 28, 52,**
156; WLCS
See also AAYA 6, 39; AFAW 1, 2; AMWS
8; BW 2, 3; CA 107; CANR 27, 51, 74,
130; CN 4, 5, 6, 7; CPW; DA; DA3;
DAC; DAM MST, MULT, NOV, POP;
DLB 173; EWL 3; FW; MAL 5; MTCW
1, 2; MTFW 2005; NFS 4, 7; RGAL 4;
TCLE 1:2; TUS
Neal, John 1793-1876 .... **NCLC 161**
See also DLB 1, 59, 243; FW; RGAL 4
Neff, Debra .... **CLC 59**
Neihardt, John Gneisenau
1881-1973 .... **CLC 32**
See also CA 13-14; CANR 65; CAP 1; DLB
9, 54, 256; LAIT 2; TCWW 1, 2
Nekrasov, Nikolai Alekseevich
1821-1878 .... **NCLC 11**
See also DLB 277
Nelligan, Emile 1879-1941 .... **TCLC 14**
See also CA 204; CAAE 114; DLB 92;
EWL 3
Nelson, Willie 1933- .... **CLC 17**
See also CA 107; CANR 114
Nemerov, Howard 1920-1991 .... **CLC 2, 6, 9,**
36; PC 24; TCLC 124
See also AMW; CA 1-4R; CAAS 134;
CABS 2; CANR 1, 27, 53; CN 1, 2, 3;
CP 1, 2, 3, 4, 5; DAM POET; DLB 5, 6;
DLBY 1983; EWL 3; INT CANR-27;
MAL 5; MTCW 1, 2; MTFW 2005; PFS
10, 14; RGAL 4
Nepos, Cornelius c. 99B.C.-c.
24B.C. .... **CMLC 89**
See also DLB 211
Neruda, Pablo 1904-1973 .. **CLC 1, 2, 5, 7, 9,**
28, 62; HLC 2; PC 4, 64; WLC 4
See also CA 19-20; CAAS 45-48; CANR
131; CAP 2; DA; DA3; DAB; DAC;
DAM MST, MULT, POET; DLB 283,

331; DNFS 2; EWL 3; HW 1; LAW;
MTCW 1, 2; MTFW 2005; PFS 11;
RGWL 2, 3; TWA; WLIT 1; WP
Nerval, Gerard de 1808-1855 ... **NCLC 1, 67;**
PC 13; SSC 18
See also DLB 217; EW 6; GFL 1789 to the
Present; RGSF 2; RGWL 2, 3
Nervo, (Jose) Amado (Ruiz de)
1870-1919 .... **HLCS 2; TCLC 11**
See also CA 131; CAAE 109; DLB 290;
EWL 3; HW 1; LAW
Nesbit, Malcolm
See Chester, Alfred
Nessi, Pio Baroja y
See Baroja, Pio
Nestroy, Johann 1801-1862 .... **NCLC 42**
See also DLB 133; RGWL 2, 3
Netterville, Luke
See O'Grady, Standish (James)
Neufeld, John (Arthur) 1938- .... **CLC 17**
See also AAYA 11; CA 25-28R; CANR 11,
37, 56; CLR 52; MAICYA 1, 2; SAAS 3;
SATA 6, 81, 131; SATA-Essay 131; YAW
Neumann, Alfred 1895-1952 .... **TCLC 100**
See also CA 183; DLB 56
Neumann, Ferenc
See Molnar, Ferenc
Neville, Emily Cheney 1919- .... **CLC 12**
See also BYA 2; CA 5-8R; CANR 3, 37,
85; JRDA; MAICYA 1, 2; SAAS 2; SATA
1; YAW
Newbound, Bernard Slade 1930-
See Slade, Bernard
See also CA 81-84; CANR 49; CD 5; DAM
DRAM
Newby, P(ercy) H(oward)
1918-1997 .... **CLC 2, 13**
See also CA 5-8R; CAAS 161; CANR 32,
67; CN 1, 2, 3, 4, 5, 6; DAM NOV; DLB
15, 326; MTCW 1; RGEL 2
Newcastle
See Cavendish, Margaret Lucas
Newlove, Donald 1928- .... **CLC 6**
See also CA 29-32R; CANR 25
Newlove, John (Herbert) 1938- .... **CLC 14**
See also CA 21-24R; CANR 9, 25; CP 1, 2,
3, 4, 5, 6, 7
Newman, Charles 1938-2006 .... **CLC 2, 8**
See also CA 21-24R; CAAS 249; CANR
84; CN 3, 4, 5, 6
Newman, Charles Hamilton
See Newman, Charles
Newman, Edwin (Harold) 1919- ...... **CLC 14**
See also AITN 1; CA 69-72; CANR 5
Newman, John Henry 1801-1890 . **NCLC 38,**
99
See also BRWS 7; DLB 18, 32, 55; RGEL
2
Newton, (Sir) Isaac 1642-1727 ...... **LC 35, 53**
See also DLB 252
Newton, Suzanne 1936- .... **CLC 35**
See also BYA 7; CA 41-44R; CANR 14;
JRDA; SATA 5, 77
New York Dept. of Ed. .... **CLC 70**
Nexo, Martin Andersen
1869-1954 .... **TCLC 43**
See also CA 202; DLB 214; EWL 3
Nezval, Vitezslav 1900-1958 .... **TCLC 44**
See also CAAE 123; CDWLB 4; DLB 215;
EWL 3
Ng, Fae Myenne 1957(?)- .... **CLC 81**
See also BYA 11; CA 146
Ngema, Mbongeni 1955- .... **CLC 57**
See also BW 2; CA 143; CANR 84; CD 5,
6
Ngugi, James T(hiong'o) . **CLC 3, 7, 13, 182**
See Ngugi wa Thiong'o
See also CN 1, 2

Ngugi wa Thiong'o
See Ngugi wa Thiong'o
See also CD 3, 4, 5, 6, 7; DLB 125; EWL 3
Ngugi wa Thiong'o 1938- ... **BLC 3; CLC 36,**
182
See Ngugi, James T(hiong'o); Ngugi wa
Thiong'o
See also AFW; BRWS 8; BW 2; CA 81-84;
CANR 27, 58; CDWLB 3; DAM MULT,
NOV; DNFS 2; MTCW 1, 2; MTFW
2005; RGEL 2; WWE 1
Niatum, Duane 1938- .... **NNAL**
See also CA 41-44R; CANR 21, 45, 83;
DLB 175
Nichol, B(arrie) P(hillip) 1944-1988 . **CLC 18**
See also CA 53-56; CP 1, 2, 3, 4; DLB 53;
SATA 66
Nicholas of Cusa 1401-1464 .... **LC 80**
See also DLB 115
Nichols, John 1940- .... **CLC 38**
See also AMWS 13; CA 190; 9-12R, 190;
2; CANR 6, 70, 121; DLBY 1982; LATS
1:2; MTFW 2005; TCWW 1, 2
Nichols, Leigh
See Koontz, Dean R.
Nichols, Peter (Richard) 1927- .... **CLC 5, 36,**
65
See also CA 104; CANR 33, 86; CBD; CD
5, 6; DLB 13, 245; MTCW 1
Nicholson, Linda .... **CLC 65**
Ni Chuilleanain, Eilean 1942- .... **PC 34**
See also CA 126; CANR 53, 83; CP 5, 6, 7;
CWP; DLB 40
Nicolas, F. R. E.
See Freeling, Nicolas
Niedecker, Lorine 1903-1970 ..... **CLC 10, 42;**
PC 42
See also CA 25-28; CAP 2; DAM POET;
DLB 48
Nietzsche, Friedrich (Wilhelm)
1844-1900 .... **TCLC 10, 18, 55**
See also CA 121; CAAE 107; CDWLB 2;
DLB 129; EW 7; RGWL 2, 3; TWA
Nievo, Ippolito 1831-1861 .... **NCLC 22**
Nightingale, Anne Redmon 1943-
See Redmon, Anne
See also CA 103
Nightingale, Florence 1820-1910 ... **TCLC 85**
See also CA 188; DLB 166
Nijo Yoshimoto 1320-1388 .... **CMLC 49**
See also DLB 203
Nik. T. O.
See Annensky, Innokenty (Fyodorovich)
Nin, Anais 1903-1977 ..... **CLC 1, 4, 8, 11, 14,**
60, 127; SSC 10
See also AITN 2; AMWS 10; BPFB 2; CA
13-16R; CAAS 69-72; CANR 22, 53; CN
1, 2; DAM NOV, POP; DLB 2, 4, 152;
EWL 3; GLL 2; MAL 5; MBL; MTCW 1,
2; MTFW 2005; RGAL 4; RGSF 2
Nisbet, Robert A(lexander)
1913-1996 .... **TCLC 117**
See also CA 25-28R; CAAS 153; CANR
17; INT CANR-17
Nishida, Kitaro 1870-1945 .... **TCLC 83**
Nishiwaki, Junzaburo 1894-1982 .... **PC 15**
See Junzaburo, Nishiwaki
See also CA 194; CAAS 107; MJW; RGWL
3
Nissenson, Hugh 1933- .... **CLC 4, 9**
See also CA 17-20R; CANR 27, 108, 151;
CN 5, 6; DLB 28
Nister, Der
See Der Nister
See also DLB 333; EWL 3

Niven, Larry 1938-
See Niven, Laurence VanCott
See also CA 207; 21-24R, 207; 12; CANR 14, 44, 66, 113, 155; CPW; DAM POP; MTCW 1, 2; SATA 95, 171; SFW 4

Niven, Laurence VanCott .... **CLC 8**
See Niven, Larry
See also AAYA 27; BPFB 2; BYA 10; DLB 8; SCFW 1, 2

Nixon, Agnes Eckhardt 1927- .... **CLC 21**
See also CA 110

Nizan, Paul 1905-1940 .... **TCLC 40**
See also CA 161; DLB 72; EWL 3; GFL 1789 to the Present

Nkosi, Lewis 1936- .... **BLC 3; CLC 45**
See also BW 1, 3; CA 65-68; CANR 27, 81; CBD; CD 5, 6; DAM MULT; DLB 157, 225; WWE 1

Nodier, (Jean) Charles (Emmanuel)
1780-1844 .... **NCLC 19**
See also DLB 119; GFL 1789 to the Present

Noguchi, Yone 1875-1947 .... **TCLC 80**

Nolan, Christopher 1965- .... **CLC 58**
See also CA 111; CANR 88

Noon, Jeff 1957- .... **CLC 91**
See also CA 148; CANR 83; DLB 267; SFW 4

Norden, Charles
See Durrell, Lawrence (George)

Nordhoff, Charles Bernard
1887-1947 .... **TCLC 23**
See also CA 211; CAAE 108; DLB 9; LAIT 1; RHW 1; SATA 23

Norfolk, Lawrence 1963- .... **CLC 76**
See also CA 144; CANR 85; CN 6, 7; DLB 267

Norman, Marsha (Williams) 1947- . **CLC 28, 186; DC 8**
See also CA 105; CABS 3; CAD; CANR 41, 131; CD 5, 6; CSW; CWD; DAM DRAM; DFS 2; DLB 266; DLBY 1984; FW; MAL 5

Normyx
See Douglas, (George) Norman

Norris, (Benjamin) Frank(lin, Jr.)
1870-1902 .... **SSC 28; TCLC 24, 155**
See also AAYA 57; AMW; AMWC 2; BPFB 2; CA 160; CAAE 110; CDALB 1865-1917; DLB 12, 71, 186; LMFS 2; MAL 5; NFS 12; RGAL 4; TCWW 1, 2; TUS

Norris, Leslie 1921-2006 .... **CLC 14**
See also CA 11-12; CAAS 251; CANR 14, 117; CAP 1; CP 1, 2, 3, 4, 5, 6, 7; DLB 27, 256

North, Andrew
See Norton, Andre

North, Anthony
See Koontz, Dean R.

North, Captain George
See Stevenson, Robert Louis (Balfour)

North, Captain George
See Stevenson, Robert Louis (Balfour)

North, Milou
See Erdrich, Louise

Northrup, B. A.
See Hubbard, L. Ron

North Staffs
See Hulme, T(homas) E(rnest)

Northup, Solomon 1808-1863 ...... **NCLC 105**

Norton, Alice Mary
See Norton, Andre
See also MAICYA 1; SATA 1, 43

Norton, Andre 1912-2005 .... **CLC 12**
See Norton, Alice Mary
See also AAYA 14; BPFB 2; BYA 4, 10, 12; CA 1-4R; CAAS 237; CANR 2, 31, 68, 108, 149; CLR 50; DLB 8, 52; JRDA; MAICYA 2; MTCW 1; SATA 91; SUFW 1, 2; YAW

Norton, Caroline 1808-1877 .... **NCLC 47**
See also DLB 21, 159, 199

Norway, Nevil Shute 1899-1960
See Shute, Nevil
See also CA 102; CAAS 93-96; CANR 85; MTCW 2

Norwid, Cyprian Kamil
1821-1883 .... **NCLC 17**
See also RGWL 3

Nosille, Nabrah
See Ellison, Harlan

Nossack, Hans Erich 1901-1977 .... **CLC 6**
See also CA 93-96; CAAS 85-88; CANR 156; DLB 69; EWL 3

Nostradamus 1503-1566 .... **LC 27**

Nosu, Chuji
See Ozu, Yasujiro

Notenburg, Eleanora (Genrikhovna) von
See Guro, Elena (Genrikhovna)

Nova, Craig 1945- .... **CLC 7, 31**
See also CA 45-48; CANR 2, 53, 127

Novak, Joseph
See Kosinski, Jerzy

Novalis 1772-1801 .... **NCLC 13, 178**
See also CDWLB 2; DLB 90; EW 5; RGWL 2, 3

Novick, Peter 1934- .... **CLC 164**
See also CA 188

Novis, Emile
See Weil, Simone (Adolphine)

Nowlan, Alden (Albert) 1933-1983 ... **CLC 15**
See also CA 9-12R; CANR 5; CP 1, 2, 3; DAC; DAM MST; DLB 53; PFS 12

Noyes, Alfred 1880-1958 ...... **PC 27; TCLC 7**
See also CA 188; CAAE 104; DLB 20; EXPP; FANT; PFS 4; RGEL 2

Nugent, Richard Bruce
1906(?)-1987 .... **HR 1:3**
See also BW 1; CA 125; DLB 51; GLL 2

Nunn, Kem .... **CLC 34**
See also CA 159

Nussbaum, Martha Craven 1947- .. **CLC 203**
See also CA 134; CANR 102

Nwapa, Flora (Nwanzuruaha)
1931-1993 .... **BLCS; CLC 133**
See also BW 2; CA 143; CANR 83; CD-WLB 3; CWRI 5; DLB 125; EWL 3; WLIT 2

Nye, Robert 1939- .... **CLC 13, 42**
See also BRWS 10; CA 33-36R; CANR 29, 67, 107; CN 1, 2, 3, 4, 5, 6, 7; CP 1, 2, 3, 4, 5, 6, 7; CWRI 5; DAM NOV; DLB 14, 271; FANT; HGG; MTCW 1; RHW; SATA 6

Nyro, Laura 1947-1997 .... **CLC 17**
See also CA 194

Oates, Joyce Carol 1938- .. **CLC 1, 2, 3, 6, 9, 11, 15, 19, 33, 52, 108, 134, 228; SSC 6, 70; WLC 4**
See also AAYA 15, 52; AITN 1; AMWS 2; BEST 89:2; BPFB 2; BYA 11; CA 5-8R; CANR 25, 45, 74, 113, 129; CDALB 1968-1988; CN 1, 2, 3, 4, 5, 6, 7; CP 5, 6, 7; CPW; CWP; DA; DA3; DAB; DAC; DAM MST, NOV, POP; DLB 2, 5, 130; DLBY 1981; EWL 3; EXPS; FL 1:6; FW; GL 3; HGG; INT CANR-25; LAIT 4; MAL 5; MBL; MTCW 1, 2; MTFW 2005; NFS 8, 24; RGAL 4; RGSF 2; SATA 159; SSFS 1, 8, 17; SUFW 2; TUS

O'Brian, E. G.
See Clarke, Arthur C.

O'Brian, Patrick 1914-2000 .... **CLC 152**
See also AAYA 55; BRWS 12; CA 144; CAAS 187; CANR 74; CPW; MTCW 2; MTFW 2005; RHW

O'Brien, Darcy 1939-1998 .... **CLC 11**
See also CA 21-24R; CAAS 167; CANR 8, 59

O'Brien, Edna 1932- ..... **CLC 3, 5, 8, 13, 36, 65, 116; SSC 10, 77**
See also BRWS 5; CA 1-4R; CANR 6, 41, 65, 102; CDBLB 1960 to Present; CN 1, 2, 3, 4, 5, 6, 7; DA3; DAM NOV; DLB 14, 231, 319; EWL 3; FW; MTCW 1, 2; MTFW 2005; RGSF 2; WLIT 4

O'Brien, Fitz-James 1828-1862 ..... **NCLC 21**
See also DLB 74; RGAL 4; SUFW

O'Brien, Flann .... **CLC 1, 4, 5, 7, 10, 47**
See O Nuallain, Brian
See also BRWS 2; DLB 231; EWL 3; RGEL 2

O'Brien, Richard 1942- .... **CLC 17**
See also CA 124

O'Brien, Tim 1946- .... **CLC 7, 19, 40, 103, 211; SSC 74**
See also AAYA 16; AMWS 5; CA 85-88; CANR 40, 58, 133; CDALBS; CN 5, 6, 7; CPW; DA3; DAM POP; DLB 152; DLBD 9; DLBY 1980; LATS 1:2; MAL 5; MTCW 2; MTFW 2005; RGAL 4; SSFS 5, 15; TCLE 1:2

Obstfelder, Sigbjoern 1866-1900 .... **TCLC 23**
See also CAAE 123

O'Casey, Sean 1880-1964 .... **CLC 1, 5, 9, 11, 15, 88; DC 12; WLCS**
See also BRW 7; CA 89-92; CANR 62; CBD; CDBLB 1914-1945; DA3; DAB; DAC; DAM DRAM, MST; DFS 19; DLB 10; EWL 3; MTCW 1, 2; MTFW 2005; RGEL 2; TEA; WLIT 4

O'Cathasaigh, Sean
See O'Casey, Sean

Occom, Samson 1723-1792 .... **LC 60; NNAL**
See also DLB 175

Occomy, Marita (Odette) Bonner
1899(?)-1971
See Bonner, Marita
See also BW 2; CA 142; DFS 13; DLB 51, 228

Ochs, Phil(ip David) 1940-1976 .... **CLC 17**
See also CA 185; CAAS 65-68

O'Connor, Edwin (Greene)
1918-1968 .... **CLC 14**
See also CA 93-96; CAAS 25-28R; MAL 5

O'Connor, (Mary) Flannery
1925-1964 ..... **CLC 1, 2, 3, 6, 10, 13, 15, 21, 66, 104; SSC 1, 23, 61, 82; TCLC 132; WLC 4**
See also AAYA 7; AMW; AMWR 2; BPFB 3; BYA 16; CA 1-4R; CANR 3, 41; CDALB 1941-1968; DA; DA3; DAB; DAC; DAM MST, NOV; DLB 2, 152; DLBD 12; DLBY 1980; EWL 3; EXPS; LAIT 5; MAL 5; MBL; MTCW 1, 2; MTFW 2005; NFS 3, 21; RGAL 4; RGSF 2; SSFS 2, 7, 10, 19; TUS

O'Connor, Frank .... **CLC 23; SSC 5**
See O'Donovan, Michael Francis
See also DLB 162; EWL 3; RGSF 2; SSFS 5

O'Dell, Scott 1898-1989 .... **CLC 30**
See also AAYA 3, 44; BPFB 3; BYA 1, 2, 3, 5; CA 61-64; CAAS 129; CANR 12, 30, 112; CLR 1, 16; DLB 52; JRDA; MAICYA 1, 2; SATA 12, 60, 134; WYA; YAW

Odets, Clifford 1906-1963 ..... **CLC 2, 28, 98; DC 6**
See also AMWS 2; CA 85-88; CAD; CANR 62; DAM DRAM; DFS 3, 17, 20; DLB 7, 26; EWL 3; MAL 5; MTCW 1, 2; MTFW 2005; RGAL 4; TUS

O'Doherty, Brian 1928- .... **CLC 76**
See also CA 105; CANR 108

O'Donnell, K. M.
See Malzberg, Barry N(athaniel)

O'Donnell, Lawrence
See Kuttner, Henry

O'Donovan, Michael Francis
1903-1966 .... **CLC 14**
See O'Connor, Frank
See also CA 93-96; CANR 84

Oe, Kenzaburo 1935- .. **CLC 10, 36, 86, 187;
SSC 20**
See Oe Kenzaburo
See also CA 97-100; CANR 36, 50, 74, 126;
DA3; DAM NOV; DLB 182, 331; DLBY
1994; LATS 1:2; MJW; MTCW 1, 2;
MTFW 2005; RGSF 2; RGWL 2, 3

Oe Kenzaburo
See Oe, Kenzaburo
See also CWW 2; EWL 3

O'Faolain, Julia 1932- .... **CLC 6, 19, 47, 108**
See also CA 81-84; 2; CANR 12, 61; CN 2,
3, 4, 5, 6, 7; DLB 14, 231, 319; FW;
MTCW 1; RHW

O'Faolain, Sean 1900-1991 ...... **CLC 1, 7, 14,
32, 70; SSC 13; TCLC 143**
See also CA 61-64; CAAS 134; CANR 12,
66; CN 1, 2, 3, 4; DLB 15, 162; MTCW
1, 2; MTFW 2005; RGEL 2; RGSF 2

O'Flaherty, Liam 1896-1984 .... **CLC 5, 34;
SSC 6**
See also CA 101; CAAS 113; CANR 35;
CN 1, 2, 3; DLB 36, 162; DLBY 1984;
MTCW 1, 2; MTFW 2005; RGEL 2;
RGSF 2; SSFS 5, 20

Ogai
See Mori Ogai
See also MJW

Ogilvy, Gavin
See Barrie, J(ames) M(atthew)

O'Grady, Standish (James)
1846-1928 .... **TCLC 5**
See also CA 157; CAAE 104

O'Grady, Timothy 1951- .... **CLC 59**
See also CA 138

O'Hara, Frank 1926-1966 .... **CLC 2, 5, 13,
78; PC 45**
See also CA 9-12R; CAAS 25-28R; CANR
33; DA3; DAM POET; DLB 5, 16, 193;
EWL 3; MAL 5; MTCW 1, 2; MTFW
2005; PFS 8, 12; RGAL 4; WP

O'Hara, John (Henry) 1905-1970 . **CLC 1, 2,
3, 6, 11, 42; SSC 15**
See also AMW; BPFB 3; CA 5-8R; CAAS
25-28R; CANR 31, 60; CDALB 1929-
1941; DAM NOV; DLB 9, 86, 324; DLBD
2; EWL 3; MAL 5; MTCW 1, 2; MTFW
2005; NFS 11; RGAL 4; RGSF 2

O'Hehir, Diana 1929- .... **CLC 41**
See also CA 245

Ohiyesa
See Eastman, Charles A(lexander)

Okada, John 1923-1971 .... **AAL**
See also BYA 14; CA 212; DLB 312

Okigbo, Christopher 1930-1967 .... **BLC 3;
CLC 25, 84; PC 7; TCLC 171**
See also AFW; BW 1, 3; CA 77-80; CANR
74; CDWLB 3; DAM MULT, POET; DLB
125; EWL 3; MTCW 1, 2; MTFW 2005;
RGEL 2

Okigbo, Christopher Ifenayichukwu
See Okigbo, Christopher

Okri, Ben 1959- .... **CLC 87, 223**
See also AFW; BRWS 5; BW 2, 3; CA 138;
CAAE 130; CANR 65, 128; CN 5, 6, 7;
DLB 157, 231, 319, 326; EWL 3; INT
CA-138; MTCW 2; MTFW 2005; RGSF
2; SSFS 20; WLIT 2; WWE 1

Olds, Sharon 1942- .. **CLC 32, 39, 85; PC 22**
See also AMWS 10; CA 101; CANR 18,
41, 66, 98, 135; CP 5, 6, 7; CPW; CWP;
DAM POET; DLB 120; MAL 5; MTCW
2; MTFW 2005; PFS 17

Oldstyle, Jonathan
See Irving, Washington

Olesha, Iurii
See Olesha, Yuri (Karlovich)
See also RGWL 2

Olesha, Iurii Karlovich
See Olesha, Yuri (Karlovich)
See also DLB 272

Olesha, Yuri (Karlovich) 1899-1960 . **CLC 8;
SSC 69; TCLC 136**
See Olesha, Iurii; Olesha, Iurii Karlovich;
Olesha, Yury Karlovich
See also CA 85-88; EW 11; RGWL 3

Olesha, Yury Karlovich
See Olesha, Yuri (Karlovich)
See also EWL 3

Oliphant, Mrs.
See Oliphant, Margaret (Oliphant Wilson)
See also SUFW

Oliphant, Laurence 1829(?)-1888 .. **NCLC 47**
See also DLB 18, 166

Oliphant, Margaret (Oliphant Wilson)
1828-1897 .... **NCLC 11, 61; SSC 25**
See Oliphant, Mrs.
See also BRWS 10; DLB 18, 159, 190;
HGG; RGEL 2; RGSF 2

Oliver, Mary 1935- ... **CLC 19, 34, 98; PC 75**
See also AMWS 7; CA 21-24R; CANR 9,
43, 84, 92, 138; CP 4, 5, 6, 7; CWP; DLB
5, 193; EWL 3; MTFW 2005; PFS 15

Olivier, Laurence (Kerr) 1907-1989 . **CLC 20**
See also CA 150; CAAE 111; CAAS 129

Olsen, Tillie 1912-2007 .... **CLC 4, 13, 114;
SSC 11**
See also AAYA 51; AMWS 13; BYA 11;
CA 1-4R; CANR 1, 43, 74, 132;
CDALBS; CN 2, 3, 4, 5, 6, 7; DA; DA3;
DAB; DAC; DAM MST; DLB 28, 206;
DLBY 1980; EWL 3; EXPS; FW; MAL
5; MTCW 1, 2; MTFW 2005; RGAL 4;
RGSF 2; SSFS 1; TCLE 1:2; TCWW 2;
TUS

Olson, Charles (John) 1910-1970 .. **CLC 1, 2,
5, 6, 9, 11, 29; PC 19**
See also AMWS 2; CA 13-16; CAAS 25-
28R; CABS 2; CANR 35, 61; CAP 1; CP
1; DAM POET; DLB 5, 16, 193; EWL 3;
MAL 5; MTCW 1, 2; RGAL 4; WP

Olson, Toby 1937- .... **CLC 28**
See also CA 65-68; 11; CANR 9, 31, 84;
CP 3, 4, 5, 6, 7

Olyesha, Yuri
See Olesha, Yuri (Karlovich)

Olympiodorus of Thebes c. 375-c.
430 .... **CMLC 59**

Omar Khayyam
See Khayyam, Omar
See also RGWL 2, 3

Ondaatje, Michael 1943- ..... **CLC 14, 29, 51,
76, 180; PC 28**
See also AAYA 66; CA 77-80; CANR 42,
74, 109, 133; CN 5, 6, 7; CP 1, 2, 3, 4, 5,
6, 7; DA3; DAB; DAC; DAM MST; DLB
60, 323, 326; EWL 3; LATS 1:2; LMFS
2; MTCW 2; MTFW 2005; NFS 23; PFS
8, 19; TCLE 1:2; TWA; WWE 1

Ondaatje, Philip Michael
See Ondaatje, Michael

Oneal, Elizabeth 1934-
See Oneal, Zibby
See also CA 106; CANR 28, 84; MAICYA
1, 2; SATA 30, 82; YAW

Oneal, Zibby .... **CLC 30**
See Oneal, Elizabeth
See also AAYA 5, 41; BYA 13; CLR 13;
JRDA; WYA

O'Neill, Eugene (Gladstone)
1888-1953 ... **DC 20; TCLC 1, 6, 27, 49;
WLC 4**
See also AAYA 54; AITN 1; AMW; AMWC
1; CA 132; CAAE 110; CAD; CANR 131;
CDALB 1929-1941; DA; DA3; DAB;

DAC; DAM DRAM, MST; DFS 2, 4, 5,
6, 9, 11, 12, 16, 20; DLB 7, 331; EWL 3;
LAIT 3; LMFS 2; MAL 5; MTCW 1, 2;
MTFW 2005; RGAL 4; TUS

Onetti, Juan Carlos 1909-1994 ... **CLC 7, 10;
HLCS 2; SSC 23; TCLC 131**
See also CA 85-88; CAAS 145; CANR 32,
63; CDWLB 3; CWW 2; DAM MULT,
NOV; DLB 113; EWL 3; HW 1, 2; LAW;
MTCW 1, 2; MTFW 2005; RGSF 2

O Nuallain, Brian 1911-1966
See O'Brien, Flann
See also CA 21-22; CAAS 25-28R; CAP 2;
DLB 231; FANT; TEA

Ophuls, Max
See Ophuls, Max

Ophuls, Max 1902-1957 .... **TCLC 79**
See also CAAE 113

Opie, Amelia 1769-1853 .... **NCLC 65**
See also DLB 116, 159; RGEL 2

Oppen, George 1908-1984 ..... **CLC 7, 13, 34;
PC 35; TCLC 107**
See also CA 13-16R; CAAS 113; CANR 8,
82; CP 1, 2, 3; DLB 5, 165

Oppenheim, E(dward) Phillips
1866-1946 .... **TCLC 45**
See also CA 202; CAAE 111; CMW 4; DLB
70

Oppenheimer, Max
See Ophuls, Max

Opuls, Max
See Ophuls, Max

Orage, A(lfred) R(ichard)
1873-1934 .... **TCLC 157**
See also CAAE 122

Origen c. 185-c. 254 .... **CMLC 19**

Orlovitz, Gil 1918-1973 .... **CLC 22**
See also CA 77-80; CAAS 45-48; CN 1;
CP 1, 2; DLB 2, 5

O'Rourke, Patrick Jake
See O'Rourke, P.J.

O'Rourke, P.J. 1947- .... **CLC 209**
See also CA 77-80; CANR 13, 41, 67, 111,
155; CPW; DAM POP; DLB 185

Orris
See Ingelow, Jean

Ortega y Gasset, Jose 1883-1955 ...... **HLC 2;
TCLC 9**
See also CA 130; CAAE 106; DAM MULT;
EW 9; EWL 3; HW 1, 2; MTCW 1, 2;
MTFW 2005

Ortese, Anna Maria 1914-1998 .... **CLC 89**
See also DLB 177; EWL 3

Ortiz, Simon J(oseph) 1941- ... **CLC 45, 208;
NNAL; PC 17**
See also AMWS 4; CA 134; CANR 69, 118;
CP 3, 4, 5, 6, 7; DAM MULT, POET;
DLB 120, 175, 256; EXPP; MAL 5; PFS
4, 16; RGAL 4; SSFS 22; TCWW 2

Orton, Joe ...... **CLC 4, 13, 43; DC 3; TCLC
157**
See Orton, John Kingsley
See also BRWS 5; CBD; CDBLB 1960 to
Present; DFS 3, 6; DLB 13, 310; GLL 1;
RGEL 2; TEA; WLIT 4

Orton, John Kingsley 1933-1967
See Orton, Joe
See also CA 85-88; CANR 35, 66; DAM
DRAM; MTCW 1, 2; MTFW 2005

Orwell, George ...... **SSC 68; TCLC 2, 6, 15,
31, 51, 128, 129; WLC 4**
See Blair, Eric (Arthur)
See also BPFB 3; BRW 7; BYA 5; CDBLB
1945-1960; CLR 68; DAB; DLB 15, 98,
195, 255; EWL 3; EXPN; LAIT 4, 5;
LATS 1:1; NFS 3, 7; RGEL 2; SCFW 1,
2; SFW 4; SSFS 4; TEA; WLIT 4; YAW

Osborne, David
See Silverberg, Robert

Peckinpah, David Samuel
See Peckinpah, Sam
Peckinpah, Sam 1925-1984 .... **CLC 20**
See also CA 109; CAAS 114; CANR 82
Pedersen, Knut 1859-1952
See Hamsun, Knut
See also CA 119; CAAE 104; CANR 63;
MTCW 1, 2
Peele, George 1556-1596 .... **DC 27; LC 115**
See also BRW 1; DLB 62, 167; RGEL 2
Peeslake, Gaffer
See Durrell, Lawrence (George)
Peguy, Charles (Pierre)
1873-1914 .... **TCLC 10**
See also CA 193; CAAE 107; DLB 258;
EWL 3; GFL 1789 to the Present
Peirce, Charles Sanders
1839-1914 .... **TCLC 81**
See also CA 194; DLB 270
Pellicer, Carlos 1897(?)-1977 .... **HLCS 2**
See also CA 153; CAAS 69-72; DLB 290;
EWL 3; HW 1
Pena, Ramon del Valle y
See Valle-Inclan, Ramon (Maria) del
Pendennis, Arthur Esquir
See Thackeray, William Makepeace
Penn, Arthur
See Matthews, (James) Brander
Penn, William 1644-1718 .... **LC 25**
See also DLB 24
PEPECE
See Prado (Calvo), Pedro
Pepys, Samuel 1633-1703 ... **LC 11, 58; WLC
4**
See also BRW 2; CDBLB 1660-1789; DA;
DA3; DAB; DAC; DAM MST; DLB 101,
213; NCFS 4; RGEL 2; TEA; WLIT 3
Percy, Thomas 1729-1811 .... **NCLC 95**
See also DLB 104
Percy, Walker 1916-1990 .... **CLC 2, 3, 6, 8,
14, 18, 47, 65**
See also AMWS 3; BPFB 3; CA 1-4R;
CAAS 131; CANR 1, 23, 64; CN 1, 2, 3,
4; CPW; CSW; DA3; DAM NOV, POP;
DLB 2; DLBY 1980, 1990; EWL 3; MAL
5; MTCW 1, 2; MTFW 2005; RGAL 4;
TUS
Percy, William Alexander
1885-1942 .... **TCLC 84**
See also CA 163; MTCW 2
Perec, Georges 1936-1982 .... **CLC 56, 116**
See also CA 141; DLB 83, 299; EWL 3;
GFL 1789 to the Present; RGHL; RGWL
3
**Pereda (y Sanchez de Porrua), Jose Maria
de** 1833-1906 .... **TCLC 16**
See also CAAE 117
Pereda y Porrua, Jose Maria de
See Pereda (y Sanchez de Porrua), Jose
Maria de
Peregoy, George Weems
See Mencken, H(enry) L(ouis)
Perelman, S(idney) J(oseph)
1904-1979 .. **CLC 3, 5, 9, 15, 23, 44, 49;
SSC 32**
See also AITN 1, 2; BPFB 3; CA 73-76;
CAAS 89-92; CANR 18; DAM DRAM;
DLB 11, 44; MTCW 1, 2; MTFW 2005;
RGAL 4
Peret, Benjamin 1899-1959 .... **PC 33; TCLC
20**
See also CA 186; CAAE 117; GFL 1789 to
the Present
Peretz, Isaac Leib
See Peretz, Isaac Loeb
See also CA 201; DLB 333

Peretz, Isaac Loeb 1851(?)-1915 ...... **SSC 26;
TCLC 16**
See Peretz, Isaac Leib
See also CAAE 109
Peretz, Yitzkhok Leibush
See Peretz, Isaac Loeb
Perez Galdos, Benito 1843-1920 ..... **HLCS 2;
TCLC 27**
See Galdos, Benito Perez
See also CA 153; CAAE 125; EWL 3; HW
1; RGWL 2, 3
Peri Rossi, Cristina 1941- .. **CLC 156; HLCS
2**
See also CA 131; CANR 59, 81; CWW 2;
DLB 145, 290; EWL 3; HW 1, 2
Perlata
See Peret, Benjamin
Perloff, Marjorie G(abrielle)
1931- .... **CLC 137**
See also CA 57-60; CANR 7, 22, 49, 104
Perrault, Charles 1628-1703 .... **LC 2, 56**
See also BYA 4; CLR 79; DLB 268; GFL
Beginnings to 1789; MAICYA 1, 2;
RGWL 2, 3; SATA 25; WCH
Perry, Anne 1938- .... **CLC 126**
See also CA 101; CANR 22, 50, 84, 150;
CMW 4; CN 6, 7; CPW; DLB 276
Perry, Brighton
See Sherwood, Robert E(mmet)
Perse, St.-John
See Leger, (Marie-Rene Auguste) Alexis
Saint-Leger
Perse, Saint-John
See Leger, (Marie-Rene Auguste) Alexis
Saint-Leger
See also DLB 258, 331; RGWL 3
Persius 34-62 .... **CMLC 74**
See also AW 2; DLB 211; RGWL 2, 3
Perutz, Leo(pold) 1882-1957 .... **TCLC 60**
See also CA 147; DLB 81
Peseenz, Tulio F.
See Lopez y Fuentes, Gregorio
Pesetsky, Bette 1932- .... **CLC 28**
See also CA 133; DLB 130
Peshkov, Alexei Maximovich 1868-1936
See Gorky, Maxim
See also CA 141; CAAE 105; CANR 83;
DA; DAC; DAM DRAM, MST, NOV;
MTCW 2; MTFW 2005
Pessoa, Fernando (Antonio Nogueira)
1888-1935 ..... **HLC 2; PC 20; TCLC 27**
See also CA 183; CAAE 125; DAM MULT;
DLB 287; EW 10; EWL 3; RGWL 2, 3;
WP
Peterkin, Julia Mood 1880-1961 ...... **CLC 31**
See also CA 102; DLB 9
Peters, Joan K(aren) 1945- .... **CLC 39**
See also CA 158; CANR 109
Peters, Robert L(ouis) 1924- .... **CLC 7**
See also CA 13-16R; 8; CP 1, 5, 6, 7; DLB
105
Petofi, Sandor 1823-1849 .... **NCLC 21**
See also RGWL 2, 3
Petrakis, Harry Mark 1923- .... **CLC 3**
See also CA 9-12R; CANR 4, 30, 85, 155;
CN 1, 2, 3, 4, 5, 6, 7
Petrarch 1304-1374 .... **CMLC 20; PC 8**
See also DA3; DAM POET; EW 2; LMFS
1; RGWL 2, 3; WLIT 7
Petronius c. 20-66 .... **CMLC 34**
See also AW 2; CDWLB 1; DLB 211;
RGWL 2, 3; WLIT 8
Petrov, Evgeny .... **TCLC 21**
See Kataev, Evgeny Petrovich
Petry, Ann (Lane) 1908-1997 .. **CLC 1, 7, 18;
TCLC 112**
See also AFAW 1, 2; BPFB 3; BW 1, 3;
BYA 2; CA 5-8R; 6; CAAS 157; CANR
4, 46; CLR 12; CN 1, 2, 3, 4, 5, 6; DLB

76; EWL 3; JRDA; LAIT 1; MAICYA 1,
2; MAICYAS 1; MTCW 1; RGAL 4;
SATA 5; SATA-Obit 94; TUS
Petursson, Halligrimur 1614-1674 .... **LC 8**
Peychinovich
See Vazov, Ivan (Minchov)
Phaedrus c. 15B.C.-c. 50 .... **CMLC 25**
See also DLB 211
Phelps (Ward), Elizabeth Stuart
See Phelps, Elizabeth Stuart
See also FW
Phelps, Elizabeth Stuart
1844-1911 .... **TCLC 113**
See Phelps (Ward), Elizabeth Stuart
See also CA 242; DLB 74
Philips, Katherine 1632-1664 . **LC 30; PC 40**
See also DLB 131; RGEL 2
Philipson, Ilene J. 1950- .... **CLC 65**
See also CA 219
Philipson, Morris H. 1926- .... **CLC 53**
See also CA 1-4R; CANR 4
Phillips, Caryl 1958- ..... **BLCS; CLC 96, 224**
See also BRWS 5; BW 2; CA 141; CANR
63, 104, 140; CBD; CD 5, 6; CN 5, 6, 7;
DA3; DAM MULT; DLB 157; EWL 3;
MTCW 2; MTFW 2005; WLIT 4; WWE
1
Phillips, David Graham
1867-1911 .... **TCLC 44**
See also CA 176; CAAE 108; DLB 9, 12,
303; RGAL 4
Phillips, Jack
See Sandburg, Carl (August)
Phillips, Jayne Anne 1952- .... **CLC 15, 33,
139; SSC 16**
See also AAYA 57; BPFB 3; CA 101;
CANR 24, 50, 96; CN 4, 5, 6, 7; CSW;
DLBY 1980; INT CANR-24; MTCW 1,
2; MTFW 2005; RGAL 4; RGSF 2; SSFS
4
Phillips, Richard
See Dick, Philip K.
Phillips, Robert (Schaeffer) 1938- .... **CLC 28**
See also CA 17-20R; 13; CANR 8; DLB
105
Phillips, Ward
See Lovecraft, H. P.
Philostratus, Flavius c. 179-c.
244 .... **CMLC 62**
Piccolo, Lucio 1901-1969 .... **CLC 13**
See also CA 97-100; DLB 114; EWL 3
Pickthall, Marjorie L(owry) C(hristie)
1883-1922 .... **TCLC 21**
See also CAAE 107; DLB 92
Pico della Mirandola, Giovanni
1463-1494 .... **LC 15**
See also LMFS 1
Piercy, Marge 1936- .... **CLC 3, 6, 14, 18, 27,
62, 128; PC 29**
See also BPFB 3; CA 187; 21-24R, 187; 1;
CANR 13, 43, 66, 111; CN 3, 4, 5, 6, 7;
CP 1, 2, 3, 4, 5, 6, 7; CWP; DLB 120,
227; EXPP; FW; MAL 5; MTCW 1, 2;
MTFW 2005; PFS 9, 22; SFW 4
Piers, Robert
See Anthony, Piers
Pieyre de Mandiargues, Andre 1909-1991
See Mandiargues, Andre Pieyre de
See also CA 103; CAAS 136; CANR 22,
82; EWL 3; GFL 1789 to the Present
Pilnyak, Boris 1894-1938 . **SSC 48; TCLC 23**
See Vogau, Boris Andreyevich
See also EWL 3
Pinchback, Eugene
See Toomer, Jean

Quoirez, Francoise 1935-2004 .... **CLC 9**
See Sagan, Francoise
See also CA 49-52; CAAS 231; CANR 6, 39, 73; MTCW 1, 2; MTFW 2005; TWA
Raabe, Wilhelm (Karl) 1831-1910 . **TCLC 45**
See also CA 167; DLB 129
Rabe, David (William) 1940- .. **CLC 4, 8, 33, 200; DC 16**
See also CA 85-88; CABS 3; CAD; CANR 59, 129; CD 5, 6; DAM DRAM; DFS 3, 8, 13; DLB 7, 228; EWL 3; MAL 5
Rabelais, Francois 1494-1553 .... **LC 5, 60; WLC 5**
See also DA; DAB; DAC; DAM MST; DLB 327; EW 2; GFL Beginnings to 1789; LMFS 1; RGWL 2, 3; TWA
Rabi'a al-'Adawiyya c. 717-c. 801 .... **CMLC 83**
See also DLB 311
Rabinovitch, Sholem 1859-1916
See Sholom Aleichem
See also CAAE 104
Rabinyan, Dorit 1972- .... **CLC 119**
See also CA 170; CANR 147
Rachilde
See Vallette, Marguerite Eymery; Vallette, Marguerite Eymery
See also EWL 3
Racine, Jean 1639-1699 .... **LC 28, 113**
See also DA3; DAB; DAM MST; DLB 268; EW 3; GFL Beginnings to 1789; LMFS 1; RGWL 2, 3; TWA
Radcliffe, Ann (Ward) 1764-1823 ... **NCLC 6, 55, 106**
See also DLB 39, 178; GL 3; HGG; LMFS 1; RGEL 2; SUFW; WLIT 3
Radclyffe-Hall, Marguerite
See Hall, Radclyffe
Radiguet, Raymond 1903-1923 ...... **TCLC 29**
See also CA 162; DLB 65; EWL 3; GFL 1789 to the Present; RGWL 2, 3
Radnoti, Miklos 1909-1944 .... **TCLC 16**
See also CA 212; CAAE 118; CDWLB 4; DLB 215; EWL 3; RGHL; RGWL 2, 3
Rado, James 1939- .... **CLC 17**
See also CA 105
Radvanyi, Netty 1900-1983
See Seghers, Anna
See also CA 85-88; CAAS 110; CANR 82
Rae, Ben
See Griffiths, Trevor
Raeburn, John (Hay) 1941- .... **CLC 34**
See also CA 57-60
Ragni, Gerome 1942-1991 .... **CLC 17**
See also CA 105; CAAS 134
Rahv, Philip .... **CLC 24**
See Greenberg, Ivan
See also DLB 137; MAL 5
Raimund, Ferdinand Jakob 1790-1836 .... **NCLC 69**
See also DLB 90
Raine, Craig (Anthony) 1944- .. **CLC 32, 103**
See also CA 108; CANR 29, 51, 103; CP 3, 4, 5, 6, 7; DLB 40; PFS 7
Raine, Kathleen (Jessie) 1908-2003 .. **CLC 7, 45**
See also CA 85-88; CAAS 218; CANR 46, 109; CP 1, 2, 3, 4, 5, 6, 7; DLB 20; EWL 3; MTCW 1; RGEL 2
Rainis, Janis 1865-1929 .... **TCLC 29**
See also CA 170; CDWLB 4; DLB 220; EWL 3
Rakosi, Carl .... **CLC 47**
See Rawley, Callman
See also CA 5; CAAS 228; CP 1, 2, 3, 4, 5, 6, 7; DLB 193
Ralegh, Sir Walter
See Raleigh, Sir Walter
See also BRW 1; RGEL 2; WP

Raleigh, Richard
See Lovecraft, H. P.
Raleigh, Sir Walter 1554(?)-1618 .... **LC 31, 39; PC 31**
See Ralegh, Sir Walter
See also CDBLB Before 1660; DLB 172; EXPP; PFS 14; TEA
Rallentando, H. P.
See Sayers, Dorothy L(eigh)
Ramal, Walter
See de la Mare, Walter (John)
Ramana Maharshi 1879-1950 .... **TCLC 84**
Ramoacn y Cajal, Santiago 1852-1934 .... **TCLC 93**
Ramon, Juan
See Jimenez (Mantecon), Juan Ramon
Ramos, Graciliano 1892-1953 .... **TCLC 32**
See also CA 167; DLB 307; EWL 3; HW 2; LAW; WLIT 1
Rampersad, Arnold 1941- .... **CLC 44**
See also BW 2, 3; CA 133; CAAE 127; CANR 81; DLB 111; INT CA-133
Rampling, Anne
See Rice, Anne
See also GLL 2
Ramsay, Allan 1686(?)-1758 .... **LC 29**
See also DLB 95; RGEL 2
Ramsay, Jay
See Campbell, (John) Ramsey
Ramuz, Charles-Ferdinand 1878-1947 .... **TCLC 33**
See also CA 165; EWL 3
Rand, Ayn 1905-1982 ...... **CLC 3, 30, 44, 79; WLC 5**
See also AAYA 10; AMWS 4; BPFB 3; BYA 12; CA 13-16R; CAAS 105; CANR 27, 73; CDALBS; CN 1, 2, 3; CPW; DA; DA3; DAC; DAM MST, NOV, POP; DLB 227, 279; MTCW 1, 2; MTFW 2005; NFS 10, 16; RGAL 4; SFW 4; TUS; YAW
Randall, Dudley (Felker) 1914-2000 . **BLC 3; CLC 1, 135**
See also BW 1, 3; CA 25-28R; CAAS 189; CANR 23, 82; CP 1, 2, 3, 4, 5; DAM MULT; DLB 41; PFS 5
Randall, Robert
See Silverberg, Robert
Ranger, Ken
See Creasey, John
Rank, Otto 1884-1939 .... **TCLC 115**
Ransom, John Crowe 1888-1974 .. **CLC 2, 4, 5, 11, 24; PC 61**
See also AMW; CA 5-8R; CAAS 49-52; CANR 6, 34; CDALBS; CP 1, 2; DA3; DAM POET; DLB 45, 63; EWL 3; EXPP; MAL 5; MTCW 1, 2; MTFW 2005; RGAL 4; TUS
Rao, Raja 1908-2006 .... **CLC 25, 56; SSC 99**
See also CA 73-76; CAAS 252; CANR 51; CN 1, 2, 3, 4, 5, 6; DAM NOV; DLB 323; EWL 3; MTCW 1, 2; MTFW 2005; RGEL 2; RGSF 2
Raphael, Frederic (Michael) 1931- ... **CLC 2, 14**
See also CA 1-4R; CANR 1, 86; CN 1, 2, 3, 4, 5, 6, 7; DLB 14, 319; TCLE 1:2
Raphael, Lev 1954- .... **CLC 232**
See also CA 134; CANR 72, 145; GLL 1
Ratcliffe, James P.
See Mencken, H(enry) L(ouis)
Rathbone, Julian 1935- .... **CLC 41**
See also CA 101; CANR 34, 73, 152
Rattigan, Terence (Mervyn) 1911-1977 .... **CLC 7; DC 18**
See also BRWS 7; CA 85-88; CAAS 73-76; CBD; CDBLB 1945-1960; DAM DRAM; DFS 8; DLB 13; IDFW 3, 4; MTCW 1, 2; MTFW 2005; RGEL 2

Ratushinskaya, Irina 1954- .... **CLC 54**
See also CA 129; CANR 68; CWW 2
Raven, Simon (Arthur Noel) 1927-2001 .... **CLC 14**
See also CA 81-84; CAAS 197; CANR 86; CN 1, 2, 3, 4, 5, 6; DLB 271
Ravenna, Michael
See Welty, Eudora
Rawley, Callman 1903-2004
See Rakosi, Carl
See also CA 21-24R; CAAS 228; CANR 12, 32, 91
Rawlings, Marjorie Kinnan 1896-1953 .... **TCLC 4**
See also AAYA 20; AMWS 10; ANW; BPFB 3; BYA 3; CA 137; CAAE 104; CANR 74; CLR 63; DLB 9, 22, 102; DLBD 17; JRDA; MAICYA 1, 2; MAL 5; MTCW 2; MTFW 2005; RGAL 4; SATA 100; WCH; YABC 1; YAW
Ray, Satyajit 1921-1992 .... **CLC 16, 76**
See also CA 114; CAAS 137; DAM MULT
Read, Herbert Edward 1893-1968 ..... **CLC 4**
See also BRW 6; CA 85-88; CAAS 25-28R; DLB 20, 149; EWL 3; PAB; RGEL 2
Read, Piers Paul 1941- .... **CLC 4, 10, 25**
See also CA 21-24R; CANR 38, 86, 150; CN 2, 3, 4, 5, 6, 7; DLB 14; SATA 21
Reade, Charles 1814-1884 .... **NCLC 2, 74**
See also DLB 21; RGEL 2
Reade, Hamish
See Gray, Simon (James Holliday)
Reading, Peter 1946- .... **CLC 47**
See also BRWS 8; CA 103; CANR 46, 96; CP 5, 6, 7; DLB 40
Reaney, James 1926- .... **CLC 13**
See also CA 41-44R; 15; CANR 42; CD 5, 6; CP 1, 2, 3, 4, 5, 6, 7; DAC; DAM MST; DLB 68; RGEL 2; SATA 43
Rebreanu, Liviu 1885-1944 .... **TCLC 28**
See also CA 165; DLB 220; EWL 3
Rechy, John 1934- ..... **CLC 1, 7, 14, 18, 107; HLC 2**
See also CA 195; 5-8R, 195; 4; CANR 6, 32, 64, 152; CN 1, 2, 3, 4, 5, 6, 7; DAM MULT; DLB 122, 278; DLBY 1982; HW 1, 2; INT CANR-6; LLW; MAL 5; RGAL 4
Rechy, John Francisco
See Rechy, John
Redcam, Tom 1870-1933 .... **TCLC 25**
Reddin, Keith 1956- .... **CLC 67**
See also CAD; CD 6
Redgrove, Peter (William) 1932-2003 .... **CLC 6, 41**
See also BRWS 6; CA 1-4R; CAAS 217; CANR 3, 39, 77; CP 1, 2, 3, 4, 5, 6, 7; DLB 40; TCLE 1:2
Redmon, Anne .... **CLC 22**
See Nightingale, Anne Redmon
See also DLBY 1986
Reed, Eliot
See Ambler, Eric
Reed, Ishmael 1938- ..... **BLC 3; CLC 2, 3, 5, 6, 13, 32, 60, 174; PC 68**
See also AFAW 1, 2; AMWS 10; BPFB 3; BW 2, 3; CA 21-24R; CANR 25, 48, 74, 128; CN 1, 2, 3, 4, 5, 6, 7; CP 1, 2, 3, 4, 5, 6, 7; CSW; DA3; DAM MULT; DLB 2, 5, 33, 169, 227; DLBD 8; EWL 3; LMFS 2; MAL 5; MSW; MTCW 1, 2; MTFW 2005; PFS 6; RGAL 4; TCWW 2
Reed, John (Silas) 1887-1920 .... **TCLC 9**
See also CA 195; CAAE 106; MAL 5; TUS
Reed, Lou .... **CLC 21**
See Firbank, Louis
Reese, Lizette Woodworth 1856-1935 .... **PC 29; TCLC 181**
See also CA 180; DLB 54

Reeve, Clara 1729-1807 .... **NCLC 19**
See also DLB 39; RGEL 2

Reich, Wilhelm 1897-1957 .... **TCLC 57**
See also CA 199

Reid, Christopher (John) 1949- .... **CLC 33**
See also CA 140; CANR 89; CP 4, 5, 6, 7;
DLB 40; EWL 3

Reid, Desmond
See Moorcock, Michael

Reid Banks, Lynne 1929-
See Banks, Lynne Reid
See also AAYA 49; CA 1-4R; CANR 6, 22,
38, 87; CLR 24; CN 1, 2, 3, 7; JRDA;
MAICYA 1, 2; SATA 22, 75, 111, 165;
YAW

Reilly, William K.
See Creasey, John

Reiner, Max
See Caldwell, (Janet Miriam) Taylor
(Holland)

Reis, Ricardo
See Pessoa, Fernando (Antonio Nogueira)

Reizenstein, Elmer Leopold
See Rice, Elmer (Leopold)
See also EWL 3

Remarque, Erich Maria 1898-1970 . **CLC 21**
See also AAYA 27; BPFB 3; CA 77-80;
CAAS 29-32R; CDWLB 2; DA; DA3;
DAB; DAC; DAM MST, NOV; DLB 56;
EWL 3; EXPN; LAIT 3; MTCW 1, 2;
MTFW 2005; NFS 4; RGHL; RGWL 2, 3

Remington, Frederic S(ackrider)
1861-1909 .... **TCLC 89**
See also CA 169; CAAE 108; DLB 12, 186,
188; SATA 41; TCWW 2

Remizov, A.
See Remizov, Aleksei (Mikhailovich)

Remizov, A. M.
See Remizov, Aleksei (Mikhailovich)

Remizov, Aleksei (Mikhailovich)
1877-1957 .... **TCLC 27**
See Remizov, Alexey Mikhaylovich
See also CA 133; CAAE 125; DLB 295

Remizov, Alexey Mikhaylovich
See Remizov, Aleksei (Mikhailovich)
See also EWL 3

Renan, Joseph Ernest 1823-1892 . **NCLC 26,
145**
See also GFL 1789 to the Present

Renard, Jules(-Pierre) 1864-1910 .. **TCLC 17**
See also CA 202; CAAE 117; GFL 1789 to
the Present

Renart, Jean fl. 13th cent. - .... **CMLC 83**

Renault, Mary .... **CLC 3, 11, 17**
See Challans, Mary
See also BPFB 3; BYA 2; CN 1, 2, 3;
DLBY 1983; EWL 3; GLL 1; LAIT 1;
RGEL 2; RHW

Rendell, Ruth 1930- .... **CLC 28, 48**
See Vine, Barbara
See also BPFB 3; BRWS 9; CA 109; CANR
32, 52, 74, 127; CN 5, 6, 7; CPW; DAM
POP; DLB 87, 276; INT CANR-32;
MSW; MTCW 1, 2; MTFW 2005

Rendell, Ruth Barbara
See Rendell, Ruth

Renoir, Jean 1894-1979 .... **CLC 20**
See also CA 129; CAAS 85-88

Resnais, Alain 1922- .... **CLC 16**

Revard, Carter 1931 .... **NNAL**
See also CA 144; CANR 81, 153; PFS 5

Reverdy, Pierre 1889-1960 .... **CLC 53**
See also CA 97-100; CAAS 89-92; DLB
258; EWL 3; GFL 1789 to the Present

Rexroth, Kenneth 1905-1982 .... **CLC 1, 2, 6,
11, 22, 49, 112; PC 20**
See also BG 1:3; CA 5-8R; CAAS 107;
CANR 14, 34, 63; CDALB 1941-1968;
CP 1, 2, 3; DAM POET; DLB 16, 48, 165,
212; DLBY 1982; EWL 3; INT CANR-
14; MAL 5; MTCW 1, 2; MTFW 2005;
RGAL 4

Reyes, Alfonso 1889-1959 .... **HLCS 2; TCLC
33**
See also CA 131; EWL 3; HW 1; LAW

Reyes y Basoalto, Ricardo Eliecer Neftali
See Neruda, Pablo

Reymont, Wladyslaw (Stanislaw)
1868(?)-1925 .... **TCLC 5**
See also CAAE 104; DLB 332; EWL 3

Reynolds, John Hamilton
1794-1852 .... **NCLC 146**
See also DLB 96

Reynolds, Jonathan 1942- .... **CLC 6, 38**
See also CA 65-68; CANR 28

Reynolds, Joshua 1723-1792 .... **LC 15**
See also DLB 104

Reynolds, Michael S(hane)
1937-2000 .... **CLC 44**
See also CA 65-68; CAAS 189; CANR 9,
89, 97

Reznikoff, Charles 1894-1976 .... **CLC 9**
See also AMWS 14; CA 33-36; CAAS 61-
64; CAP 2; CP 1, 2; DLB 28, 45; RGHL;
WP

Rezzori, Gregor von
See Rezzori d'Arezzo, Gregor von

Rezzori d'Arezzo, Gregor von
1914-1998 .... **CLC 25**
See also CA 136; CAAE 122; CAAS 167

Rhine, Richard
See Silverstein, Alvin; Silverstein, Virginia
B(arbara Opshelor)

Rhodes, Eugene Manlove
1869-1934 .... **TCLC 53**
See also CA 198; DLB 256; TCWW 1, 2

R'hoone, Lord
See Balzac, Honore de

Rhys, Jean 1890-1979 .... **CLC 2, 4, 6, 14, 19,
51, 124; SSC 21, 76**
See also BRWS 2; CA 25-28R; CAAS 85-
88; CANR 35, 62; CDBLB 1945-1960;
CDWLB 3; CN 1, 2; DA3; DAM NOV;
DLB 36, 117, 162; DNFS 2; EWL 3;
LATS 1:1; MTCW 1, 2; MTFW 2005;
NFS 19; RGEL 2; RGSF 2; RHW; TEA;
WWE 1

Ribeiro, Darcy 1922-1997 .... **CLC 34**
See also CA 33-36R; CAAS 156; EWL 3

Ribeiro, Joao Ubaldo (Osorio Pimentel)
1941- .... **CLC 10, 67**
See also CA 81-84; CWW 2; EWL 3

Ribman, Ronald (Burt) 1932- .... **CLC 7**
See also CA 21-24R; CAD; CANR 46, 80;
CD 5, 6

Ricci, Nino (Pio) 1959- .... **CLC 70**
See also CA 137; CANR 130; CCA 1

Rice, Anne 1941- .... **CLC 41, 128**
See Rampling, Anne
See also AAYA 9, 53; AMWS 7; BEST
89:2; BPFB 3; CA 65-68; CANR 12, 36,
53, 74, 100, 133; CN 6, 7; CPW; CSW;
DA3; DAM POP; DLB 292; GL 3; GLL
2; HGG; MTCW 2; MTFW 2005; SUFW
2; YAW

Rice, Elmer (Leopold) 1892-1967 ...... **CLC 7,
49**
See Reizenstein, Elmer Leopold
See also CA 21-22; CAAS 25-28R; CAP 2;
DAM DRAM; DFS 12; DLB 4, 7; IDTP;
MAL 5; MTCW 1, 2; RGAL 4

Rice, Tim(othy Miles Bindon)
1944- .... **CLC 21**
See also CA 103; CANR 46; DFS 7

Rich, Adrienne 1929- ..... **CLC 3, 6, 7, 11, 18,
36, 73, 76, 125; PC 5**
See also AAYA 69; AMWR 2; AMWS 1;
CA 9-12R; CANR 20, 53, 74, 128;
CDALBS; CP 1, 2, 3, 4, 5, 6, 7; CSW;
CWP; DA3; DAM POET; DLB 5, 67;
EWL 3; EXPP; FL 1:6; FW; MAL 5;
MBL; MTCW 1, 2; MTFW 2005; PAB;
PFS 15; RGAL 4; RGHL; WP

Rich, Barbara
See Graves, Robert

Rich, Robert
See Trumbo, Dalton

Richard, Keith .... **CLC 17**
See Richards, Keith

Richards, David Adams 1950- .... **CLC 59**
See also CA 93-96; CANR 60, 110, 156;
CN 7; DAC; DLB 53; TCLE 1:2

Richards, I(vor) A(rmstrong)
1893-1979 .... **CLC 14, 24**
See also BRWS 2; CA 41-44R; CAAS 89-
92; CANR 34, 74; CP 1, 2; DLB 27; EWL
3; MTCW 2; RGEL 2

Richards, Keith 1943-
See Richard, Keith
See also CA 107; CANR 77

Richardson, Anne
See Roiphe, Anne

Richardson, Dorothy Miller
1873-1957 .... **TCLC 3**
See also CA 192; CAAE 104; DLB 36;
EWL 3; FW; RGEL 2

**Richardson (Robertson), Ethel Florence
Lindesay** 1870-1946
See Richardson, Henry Handel
See also CA 190; CAAE 105; DLB 230;
RHW

Richardson, Henry Handel .... **TCLC 4**
See Richardson (Robertson), Ethel Florence
Lindesay
See also DLB 197; EWL 3; RGEL 2; RGSF
2

Richardson, John 1796-1852 .... **NCLC 55**
See also CCA 1; DAC; DLB 99

Richardson, Samuel 1689-1761 ...... **LC 1, 44;
WLC 5**
See also BRW 3; CDBLB 1660-1789; DA;
DAB; DAC; DAM MST, NOV; DLB 39;
RGEL 2; TEA; WLIT 3

Richardson, Willis 1889-1977 .... **HR 1:3**
See also BW 1; CA 124; DLB 51; SATA 60

Richler, Mordecai 1931-2001 .... **CLC 3, 5, 9,
13, 18, 46, 70, 185**
See also AITN 1; CA 65-68; CAAS 201;
CANR 31, 62, 111; CCA 1; CLR 17; CN
1, 2, 3, 4, 5, 7; CWRI 5; DAC; DAM
MST, NOV; DLB 53; EWL 3; MAICYA
1, 2; MTCW 1, 2; MTFW 2005; RGEL 2;
RGHL; SATA 44, 98; SATA-Brief 27;
TWA

Richter, Conrad (Michael)
1890-1968 .... **CLC 30**
See also AAYA 21; BYA 2; CA 5-8R;
CAAS 25-28R; CANR 23; DLB 9, 212;
LAIT 1; MAL 5; MTCW 1, 2; MTFW
2005; RGAL 4; SATA 3; TCWW 1, 2;
TUS; YAW

Ricostranza, Tom
See Ellis, Trey

Riddell, Charlotte 1832-1906 .... **TCLC 40**
See Riddell, Mrs. J. H.
See also CA 165; DLB 156

Riddell, Mrs. J. H.
See Riddell, Charlotte
See also HGG; SUFW

Saint-Exupery, Antoine Jean Baptiste Marie Roger de
  See Saint-Exupery, Antoine de

St. John, David
  See Hunt, E. Howard

St. John, J. Hector
  See Crevecoeur, Michel Guillaume Jean de

Saint-John Perse
  See Leger, (Marie-Rene Auguste) Alexis Saint-Leger
  See also EW 10; EWL 3; GFL 1789 to the Present; RGWL 2

Saintsbury, George (Edward Bateman) 1845-1933 .... **TCLC 31**
  See also CA 160; DLB 57, 149

Sait Faik .... **TCLC 23**
  See Abasiyanik, Sait Faik

Saki .... **SSC 12; TCLC 3; WLC 5**
  See Munro, H(ector) H(ugh)
  See also BRWS 6; BYA 11; LAIT 2; RGEL 2; SSFS 1; SUFW

Sala, George Augustus 1828-1895 . **NCLC 46**

Saladin 1138-1193 .... **CMLC 38**

Salama, Hannu 1936- .... **CLC 18**
  See also CA 244; EWL 3

Salamanca, J(ack) R(ichard) 1922- .. **CLC 4, 15**
  See also CA 193; 25-28R, 193

Salas, Floyd Francis 1931- .... **HLC 2**
  See also CA 119; 27; CANR 44, 75, 93; DAM MULT; DLB 82; HW 1, 2; MTCW 2; MTFW 2005

Sale, J. Kirkpatrick
  See Sale, Kirkpatrick

Sale, John Kirkpatrick
  See Sale, Kirkpatrick

Sale, Kirkpatrick 1937- .... **CLC 68**
  See also CA 13-16R; CANR 10, 147

Salinas, Luis Omar 1937- ... **CLC 90; HLC 2**
  See also AMWS 13; CA 131; CANR 81, 153; DAM MULT; DLB 82; HW 1, 2

Salinas (y Serrano), Pedro 1891(?)-1951 .... **TCLC 17**
  See also CAAE 117; DLB 134; EWL 3

Salinger, J.D. 1919- . **CLC 1, 3, 8, 12, 55, 56, 138; SSC 2, 28, 65; WLC 5**
  See also AAYA 2, 36; AMW; AMWC 1; BPFB 3; CA 5-8R; CANR 39, 129; CDALB 1941-1968; CLR 18; CN 1, 2, 3, 4, 5, 6, 7; CPW 1; DA; DA3; DAB; DAC; DAM MST, NOV, POP; DLB 2, 102, 173; EWL 3; EXPN; LAIT 4; MAICYA 1, 2; MAL 5; MTCW 1, 2; MTFW 2005; NFS 1; RGAL 4; RGSF 2; SATA 67; SSFS 17; TUS; WYA; YAW

Salisbury, John
  See Caute, (John) David

Sallust c. 86B.C.-35B.C. .... **CMLC 68**
  See also AW 2; CDWLB 1; DLB 211; RGWL 2, 3

Salter, James 1925- .. **CLC 7, 52, 59; SSC 58**
  See also AMWS 9; CA 73-76; CANR 107, 160; DLB 130

Saltus, Edgar (Everton) 1855-1921 . **TCLC 8**
  See also CAAE 105; DLB 202; RGAL 4

Saltykov, Mikhail Evgrafovich 1826-1889 .... **NCLC 16**
  See also DLB 238:

Saltykov-Shchedrin, N.
  See Saltykov, Mikhail Evgrafovich

Samarakis, Andonis
  See Samarakis, Antonis
  See also EWL 3

Samarakis, Antonis 1919-2003 .... **CLC 5**
  See Samarakis, Andonis
  See also CA 25-28R; 16; CAAS 224; CANR 36

Sanchez, Florencio 1875-1910 .... **TCLC 37**
  See also CA 153; DLB 305; EWL 3; HW 1; LAW

Sanchez, Luis Rafael 1936- .... **CLC 23**
  See also CA 128; DLB 305; EWL 3; HW 1; WLIT 1

Sanchez, Sonia 1934- .... **BLC 3; CLC 5, 116, 215; PC 9**
  See also BW 2, 3; CA 33-36R; CANR 24, 49, 74, 115; CLR 18; CP 2, 3, 4, 5, 6, 7; CSW; CWP; DA3; DAM MULT; DLB 41; DLBD 8; EWL 3; MAICYA 1, 2; MAL 5; MTCW 1, 2; MTFW 2005; SATA 22, 136; WP

Sancho, Ignatius 1729-1780 .... **LC 84**

Sand, George 1804-1876 ..... **NCLC 2, 42, 57, 174; WLC 5**
  See also DA; DA3; DAB; DAC; DAM MST, NOV; DLB 119, 192; EW 6; FL 1:3; FW; GFL 1789 to the Present; RGWL 2, 3; TWA

Sandburg, Carl (August) 1878-1967 . **CLC 1, 4, 10, 15, 35; PC 2, 41; WLC 5**
  See also AAYA 24; AMW; BYA 1, 3; CA 5-8R; CAAS 25-28R; CANR 35; CDALB 1865-1917; CLR 67; DA; DA3; DAB; DAC; DAM MST, POET; DLB 17, 54, 284; EWL 3; EXPP; LAIT 2; MAICYA 1, 2; MAL 5; MTCW 1, 2; MTFW 2005; PAB; PFS 3, 6, 12; RGAL 4; SATA 8; TUS; WCH; WP; WYA

Sandburg, Charles
  See Sandburg, Carl (August)

Sandburg, Charles A.
  See Sandburg, Carl (August)

Sanders, (James) Ed(ward) 1939- .... **CLC 53**
  See Sanders, Edward
  See also BG 1:3; CA 13-16R; 21; CANR 13, 44, 78; CP 1, 2, 3, 4, 5, 6, 7; DAM POET; DLB 16, 244

Sanders, Edward
  See Sanders, (James) Ed(ward)
  See also DLB 244

Sanders, Lawrence 1920-1998 .... **CLC 41**
  See also BEST 89:4; BPFB 3; CA 81-84; CAAS 165; CANR 33, 62; CMW 4; CPW; DA3; DAM POP; MTCW 1

Sanders, Noah
  See Blount, Roy (Alton), Jr.

Sanders, Winston P.
  See Anderson, Poul

Sandoz, Mari(e Susette) 1900-1966 .. **CLC 28**
  See also CA 1-4R; CAAS 25-28R; CANR 17, 64; DLB 9, 212; LAIT 2; MTCW 1, 2; SATA 5; TCWW 1, 2

Sandys, George 1578-1644 .... **LC 80**
  See also DLB 24, 121

Saner, Reg(inald Anthony) 1931- .... **CLC 9**
  See also CA 65-68; CP 3, 4, 5, 6, 7

Sankara 788-820 .... **CMLC 32**

Sannazaro, Jacopo 1456(?)-1530 .... **LC 8**
  See also RGWL 2, 3; WLIT 7

Sansom, William 1912-1976 . **CLC 2, 6; SSC 21**
  See also CA 5-8R; CAAS 65-68; CANR 42; CN 1, 2; DAM NOV; DLB 139; EWL 3; MTCW 1; RGEL 2; RGSF 2

Santayana, George 1863-1952 .... **TCLC 40**
  See also AMW; CA 194; CAAE 115; DLB 54, 71, 246, 270; DLBD 13; EWL 3; MAL 5; RGAL 4; TUS

Santiago, Danny .... **CLC 33**
  See James, Daniel (Lewis)
  See also DLB 122

Santillana, Inigo Lopez de Mendoza, Marques de 1398-1458 .... **LC 111**
  See also DLB 286

Santmyer, Helen Hooven 1895-1986 .... **CLC 33; TCLC 133**
  See also CA 1-4R; CAAS 118; CANR 15, 33; DLBY 1984; MTCW 1; RHW

Santoka, Taneda 1882-1940 .... **TCLC 72**

Santos, Bienvenido N(uqui) 1911-1996 ... **AAL; CLC 22; TCLC 156**
  See also CA 101; CAAS 151; CANR 19, 46; CP 1; DAM MULT; DLB 312; EWL; RGAL 4; SSFS 19

Sapir, Edward 1884-1939 .... **TCLC 108**
  See also CA 211; DLB 92

Sapper .... **TCLC 44**
  See McNeile, Herman Cyril

Sapphire
  See Sapphire, Brenda

Sapphire, Brenda 1950- .... **CLC 99**

Sappho fl. 6th cent. B.C.- .. **CMLC 3, 67; PC 5**
  See also CDWLB 1; DA3; DAM POET; DLB 176; FL 1:1; PFS 20; RGWL 2, 3; WLIT 8; WP

Saramago, Jose 1922- ..... **CLC 119; HLCS 1**
  See also CA 153; CANR 96; CWW 2; DLB 287, 332; EWL 3; LATS 1:2; SSFS 23

Sarduy, Severo 1937-1993 .... **CLC 6, 97; HLCS 2; TCLC 167**
  See also CA 89-92; CAAS 142; CANR 58, 81; CWW 2; DLB 113; EWL 3; HW 1, 2; LAW

Sargeson, Frank 1903-1982 ..... **CLC 31; SSC 99**
  See also CA 25-28R; CAAS 106; CANR 38, 79; CN 1, 2, 3; EWL 3; GLL 2; RGEL 2; RGSF 2; SSFS 20

Sarmiento, Domingo Faustino 1811-1888 .... **HLCS 2; NCLC 123**
  See also LAW; WLIT 1

Sarmiento, Felix Ruben Garcia
  See Dario, Ruben

Saro-Wiwa, Ken(ule Beeson) 1941-1995 .... **CLC 114**
  See also BW 2; CA 142; CAAS 150; CANR 60; DLB 157

Saroyan, William 1908-1981 ... **CLC 1, 8, 10, 29, 34, 56; SSC 21; TCLC 137; WLC 5**
  See also AAYA 66; CA 5-8R; CAAS 103; CAD; CANR 30; CDALBS; CN 1, 2; DA; DA3; DAB; DAC; DAM DRAM, MST, NOV; DFS 17; DLB 7, 9, 86; DLBY 1981; EWL 3; LAIT 4; MAL 5; MTCW 1, 2; MTFW 2005; RGAL 4; RGSF 2; SATA 23; SATA-Obit 24; SSFS 14; TUS

Sarraute, Nathalie 1900-1999 .... **CLC 1, 2, 4, 8, 10, 31, 80; TCLC 145**
  See also BPFB 3; CA 9-12R; CAAS 187; CANR 23, 66, 134; CWW 2; DLB 83, 321; EW 12; EWL 3; GFL 1789 to the Present; MTCW 1, 2; MTFW 2005; RGWL 2, 3

Sarton, May 1912-1995 ... **CLC 4, 14, 49, 91; PC 39; TCLC 120**
  See also AMWS 8; CA 1-4R; CAAS 149; CANR 1, 34, 55, 116; CN 1, 2, 3, 4, 5, 6; CP 1, 2, 3, 4, 5, 6; DAM POET; DLB 48, DLBY 1981; EWL 3; FW; INT CANR-34; MAL 5; MTCW 1, 2; MTFW 2005; RGAL 4; SATA 36; SATA-Obit 86; TUS

Sartre, Jean-Paul 1905-1980 . **CLC 1, 4, 7, 9, 13, 18, 24, 44, 50, 52; DC 3; SSC 32; WLC 5**
  See also AAYA 62; CA 9-12R; CAAS 97-100; CANR 21; DA; DA3; DAB; DAC; DAM DRAM, MST, NOV; DFS 5; DLB 72, 296, 321, 332; EW 12; EWL 3; GFL 1789 to the Present; LMFS 2; MTCW 1, 2; MTFW 2005; NFS 21; RGHL; RGSF 2; RGWL 2, 3; SSFS 9; TWA

Shirley, James 1596-1666 .... **DC 25; LC 96**
See also DLB 58; RGEL 2

Sholokhov, Mikhail (Aleksandrovich)
1905-1984 .... **CLC 7, 15**
See also CA 101; CAAS 112; DLB 272,
332; EWL 3; MTCW 1, 2; MTFW 2005;
RGWL 2, 3; SATA-Obit 36

Sholom Aleichem 1859-1916 .... **SSC 33;
TCLC 1, 35**
See Rabinovitch, Sholem
See also DLB 333; TWA

Shone, Patric
See Hanley, James

Showalter, Elaine 1941- .... **CLC 169**
See also CA 57-60; CANR 58, 106; DLB
67; FW; GLL 2

Shreve, Susan
See Shreve, Susan Richards

Shreve, Susan Richards 1939- .... **CLC 23**
See also CA 49-52; 5; CANR 5, 38, 69, 100,
159; MAICYA 1, 2; SATA 46, 95, 152;
SATA-Brief 41

Shue, Larry 1946-1985 .... **CLC 52**
See also CA 145; CAAS 117; DAM DRAM;
DFS 7

Shu-Jen, Chou 1881-1936
See Lu Hsun
See also CAAE 104

Shulman, Alix Kates 1932- .... **CLC 2, 10**
See also CA 29-32R; CANR 43; FW; SATA
7

Shuster, Joe 1914-1992 .... **CLC 21**
See also AAYA 50

Shute, Nevil .... **CLC 30**
See Norway, Nevil Shute
See also BPFB 3; DLB 255; NFS 9; RHW;
SFW 4

Shuttle, Penelope (Diane) 1947- .... **CLC 7**
See also CA 93-96; CANR 39, 84, 92, 108;
CP 3, 4, 5, 6, 7; CWP; DLB 14, 40

Shvarts, Elena 1948- .... **PC 50**
See also CA 147

Sidhwa, Bapsi 1939-
See Sidhwa, Bapsy (N.)
See also CN 6, 7; DLB 323

Sidhwa, Bapsy (N.) 1938- .... **CLC 168**
See Sidhwa, Bapsi
See also CA 108; CANR 25, 57; FW

Sidney, Mary 1561-1621 .... **LC 19, 39**
See Sidney Herbert, Mary

Sidney, Sir Philip 1554-1586 .... **LC 19, 39,
131; PC 32**
See also BRW 1; BRWR 2; CDBLB Before
1660; DA; DA3; DAB; DAC; DAM MST,
POET; DLB 167; EXPP; PAB; RGEL 2;
TEA; WP

Sidney Herbert, Mary
See Sidney, Mary
See also DLB 167

Siegel, Jerome 1914-1996 .... **CLC 21**
See Siegel, Jerry
See also CA 169; CAAE 116; CAAS 151

Siegel, Jerry
See Siegel, Jerome
See also AAYA 50

Sienkiewicz, Henryk (Adam Alexander Pius)
1846-1916 .... **TCLC 3**
See also CA 134; CAAE 104; CANR 84;
DLB 332; EWL 3; RGSF 2; RGWL 2, 3

Sierra, Gregorio Martinez
See Martinez Sierra, Gregorio

Sierra, Maria de la O'LeJarraga Martinez
See Martinez Sierra, Maria

Sigal, Clancy 1926- .... **CLC 7**
See also CA 1-4R; CANR 85; CN 1, 2, 3,
4, 5, 6, 7

Siger of Brabant 1240(?)-1284(?) . **CMLC 69**
See also DLB 115

Sigourney, Lydia H.
See Sigourney, Lydia Howard (Huntley)
See also DLB 73, 183

Sigourney, Lydia Howard (Huntley)
1791-1865 .... **NCLC 21, 87**
See Sigourney, Lydia H.; Sigourney, Lydia
Huntley
See also DLB 1

Sigourney, Lydia Huntley
See Sigourney, Lydia Howard (Huntley)
See also DLB 42, 239, 243

Siguenza y Gongora, Carlos de
1645-1700 .... **HLCS 2; LC 8**
See also LAW

Sigurjonsson, Johann
See Sigurjonsson, Johann

Sigurjonsson, Johann 1880-1919 ... **TCLC 27**
See also CA 170; DLB 293; EWL 3

Sikelianos, Angelos 1884-1951 .... **PC 29;
TCLC 39**
See also EWL 3; RGWL 2, 3

Silkin, Jon 1930-1997 .... **CLC 2, 6, 43**
See also CA 5-8R; 5; CANR 89; CP 1, 2, 3,
4, 5, 6; DLB 27

Silko, Leslie 1948- ...... **CLC 23, 74, 114, 211;
NNAL; SSC 37, 66; WLCS**
See also AAYA 14; AMWS 4; ANW; BYA
12; CA 122; CAAE 115; CANR 45, 65,
118; CN 4, 5, 6, 7; CP 4, 5, 6, 7; CPW 1;
CWP; DA; DA3; DAC; DAM MST,
MULT, POP; DLB 143, 175, 256, 275;
EWL 3; EXPP; EXPS; LAIT 4; MAL 5;
MTCW 2; MTFW 2005; NFS 4; PFS 9,
16; RGAL 4; RGSF 2; SSFS 4, 8, 10, 11;
TCWW 1, 2

Sillanpaa, Frans Eemil 1888-1964 ... **CLC 19**
See also CA 129; CAAS 93-96; DLB 332;
EWL 3; MTCW 1

Sillitoe, Alan 1928- .. **CLC 1, 3, 6, 10, 19, 57,
148**
See also AITN 1; BRWS 5; CA 191; 9-12R,
191; 2; CANR 8, 26, 55, 139; CDBLB
1960 to Present; CN 1, 2, 3, 4, 5, 6; CP 1,
2, 3, 4, 5; DLB 14, 139; EWL 3; MTCW
1, 2; MTFW 2005; RGEL 2; RGSF 2;
SATA 61

Silone, Ignazio 1900-1978 .... **CLC 4**
See also CA 25-28; CAAS 81-84; CANR
34; CAP 2; DLB 264; EW 12; EWL 3;
MTCW 1; RGSF 2; RGWL 2, 3

Silone, Ignazione
See Silone, Ignazio

Silver, Joan Micklin 1935- .... **CLC 20**
See also CA 121; CAAE 114; INT CA-121

Silver, Nicholas
See Faust, Frederick (Schiller)

Silverberg, Robert 1935- .... **CLC 7, 140**
See also AAYA 24; BPFB 3; BYA 7, 9; CA
186; 1-4R, 186; 3; CANR 1, 20, 36, 85,
140; CLR 59; CN 6, 7; CPW; DAM POP;
DLB 8; INT CANR-20; MAICYA 1, 2;
MTCW 1, 2; MTFW 2005; SATA 13, 91;
SATA-Essay 104; SCFW 1, 2; SFW 4;
SUFW 2

Silverstein, Alvin 1933 .... **CLC 17**
See also CA 49-52; CANR 2; CLR 25;
JRDA; MAICYA 1, 2; SATA 8, 69, 124

Silverstein, Shel 1932-1999 .... **PC 49**
See also AAYA 40; BW 3; CA 107; CAAS
179; CANR 47, 74, 81; CLR 5, 96; CWRI
5; JRDA; MAICYA 1, 2; MTCW 2;
MTFW 2005; SATA 33, 92; SATA-Brief
27; SATA-Obit 116

Silverstein, Virginia B(arbara Opshelor)
1937- .... **CLC 17**
See also CA 49-52; CANR 2; CLR 25;
JRDA; MAICYA 1, 2; SATA 8, 69, 124

Sim, Georges
See Simenon, Georges (Jacques Christian)

Simak, Clifford D(onald) 1904-1988 . **CLC 1,
55**
See also CA 1-4R; CAAS 125; CANR 1,
35; DLB 8; MTCW 1; SATA-Obit 56;
SCFW 1, 2; SFW 4

Simenon, Georges (Jacques Christian)
1903-1989 .... **CLC 1, 2, 3, 8, 18, 47**
See also BPFB 3; CA 85-88; CAAS 129;
CANR 35; CMW 4; DA3; DAM POP;
DLB 72; DLBY 1989; EW 12; EWL 3;
GFL 1789 to the Present; MSW; MTCW
1, 2; MTFW 2005; RGWL 2, 3

Simic, Charles 1938- .... **CLC 6, 9, 22, 49, 68,
130; PC 69**
See also AMWS 8; CA 29-32R; 4; CANR
12, 33, 52, 61, 96, 140; CP 2, 3, 4, 5, 6,
7; DA3; DAM POET; DLB 105; MAL 5;
MTCW 2; MTFW 2005; PFS 7; RGAL 4;
WP

Simmel, Georg 1858-1918 .... **TCLC 64**
See also CA 157; DLB 296

Simmons, Charles (Paul) 1924- .... **CLC 57**
See also CA 89-92; INT CA-89-92

Simmons, Dan 1948- .... **CLC 44**
See also AAYA 16, 54; CA 138; CANR 53,
81, 126; CPW; DAM POP; HGG; SUFW
2

Simmons, James (Stewart Alexander)
1933- .... **CLC 43**
See also CA 105; 21; CP 1, 2, 3, 4, 5, 6, 7;
DLB 40

Simms, William Gilmore
1806-1870 .... **NCLC 3**
See also DLB 3, 30, 59, 73, 248, 254;
RGAL 4

Simon, Carly 1945- .... **CLC 26**
See also CA 105

Simon, Claude 1913-2005 ... **CLC 4, 9, 15, 39**
See also CA 89-92; CAAS 241; CANR 33,
117; CWW 2; DAM NOV; DLB 83, 332;
EW 13; EWL 3; GFL 1789 to the Present;
MTCW 1

Simon, Claude Eugene Henri
See Simon, Claude

Simon, Claude Henri Eugene
See Simon, Claude

Simon, Marvin Neil
See Simon, Neil

Simon, Myles
See Follett, Ken

Simon, Neil 1927- .... **CLC 6, 11, 31, 39, 70,
233; DC 14**
See also AAYA 32; AITN 1; AMWS 4; CA
21-24R; CAD; CANR 26, 54, 87, 126;
CD 5, 6; DA3; DAM DRAM; DFS 2, 6,
12, 18; DLB 7, 266; LAIT 4; MAL 5;
MTCW 1, 2; MTFW 2005; RGAL 4; TUS

Simon, Paul 1941(?)- .... **CLC 17**
See also CA 153; CAAE 116; CANR 152

Simon, Paul Frederick
See Simon, Paul

Simonon, Paul 1956(?)- .... **CLC 30**

Simonson, Rick .... **CLC 70**

Simpson, Harriette
See Arnow, Harriette (Louisa) Simpson

Simpson, Louis 1923- ... **CLC 4, 7, 9, 32, 149**
See also AMWS 9; CA 1-4R; 4; CANR 1,
61, 140; CP 1, 2, 3, 4, 5, 6, 7; DAM
POET; DLB 5; MAL 5; MTCW 1, 2;
MTFW 2005; PFS 7, 11, 14; RGAL 4

Simpson, Mona 1957- .... **CLC 44, 146**
See also CA 135; CAAE 122; CANR 68,
103; CN 6, 7; EWL 3

Simpson, Mona Elizabeth
See Simpson, Mona

Simpson, N(orman) F(rederick)
1919- .... **CLC 29**
See also CA 13-16R; CBD; DLB 13; RGEL
2

Snodgrass, W.D. 1926- .... **CLC 2, 6, 10, 18, 68; PC 74**
See also AMWS 6; CA 1-4R; CANR 6, 36, 65, 85; CP 1, 2, 3, 4, 5, 6, 7; DAM POET; DLB 5; MAL 5; MTCW 1, 2; MTFW 2005; RGAL 4; TCLE 1:2

Snorri Sturluson 1179-1241 .... **CMLC 56**
See also RGWL 2, 3

Snow, C(harles) P(ercy) 1905-1980 ... **CLC 1, 4, 6, 9, 13, 19**
See also BRW 7; CA 5-8R; CAAS 101; CANR 28; CDBLB 1945-1960; CN 1, 2; DAM NOV; DLB 15, 77; DLBD 17; EWL 3; MTCW 1, 2; MTFW 2005; RGEL 2; TEA

Snow, Frances Compton
See Adams, Henry (Brooks)

Snyder, Gary 1930- . **CLC 1, 2, 5, 9, 32, 120; PC 21**
See also AAYA 72; AMWS 8; ANW; BG 1:3; CA 17-20R; CANR 30, 60, 125; CP 1, 2, 3, 4, 5, 6, 7; DA3; DAM POET; DLB 5, 16, 165, 212, 237, 275; EWL 3; MAL 5; MTCW 2; MTFW 2005; PFS 9, 19; RGAL 4; WP

Snyder, Zilpha Keatley 1927- .... **CLC 17**
See also AAYA 15; BYA 1; CA 252; 9-12R, 252; CANR 38; CLR 31; JRDA; MAI-CYA 1, 2; SAAS 2; SATA 1, 28, 75, 110, 163; SATA-Essay 112, 163; YAW

Soares, Bernardo
See Pessoa, Fernando (Antonio Nogueira)

Sobh, A.
See Shamlu, Ahmad

Sobh, Alef
See Shamlu, Ahmad

Sobol, Joshua 1939- .... **CLC 60**
See Sobol, Yehoshua
See also CA 200; RGHL

Sobol, Yehoshua 1939-
See Sobol, Joshua
See also CWW 2

Socrates 470B.C.-399B.C. .... **CMLC 27**

Soderberg, Hjalmar 1869-1941 ...... **TCLC 39**
See also DLB 259; EWL 3; RGSF 2

Soderbergh, Steven 1963- .... **CLC 154**
See also AAYA 43; CA 243

Soderbergh, Steven Andrew
See Soderbergh, Steven

Sodergran, Edith (Irene) 1892-1923
See Soedergran, Edith (Irene)
See also CA 202; DLB 259; EW 11; EWL 3; RGWL 2, 3

Soedergran, Edith (Irene) 1892-1923 .... **TCLC 31**
See Sodergran, Edith (Irene)

Softly, Edgar
See Lovecraft, H. P.

Softly, Edward
See Lovecraft, H. P.

Sokolov, Alexander V(sevolodovich) 1943-
See Sokolov, Sasha
See also CA 73-76

Sokolov, Raymond 1941- .... **CLC 7**
See also CA 85-88

Sokolov, Sasha .... **CLC 59**
See Sokolov, Alexander V(sevolodovich)
See also CWW 2; DLB 285; EWL 3; RGWL 2, 3

Solo, Jay
See Ellison, Harlan

Sologub, Fyodor .... **TCLC 9**
See Teternikov, Fyodor Kuzmich
See also EWL 3

Solomons, Ikey Esquir
See Thackeray, William Makepeace

Solomos, Dionysios 1798-1857 .... **NCLC 15**

Solwoska, Mara
See French, Marilyn

Solzhenitsyn, Aleksandr I. 1918- .. **CLC 1, 2, 4, 7, 9, 10, 18, 26, 34, 78, 134, 235; SSC 32; WLC 5**
See Solzhenitsyn, Aleksandr Isayevich
See also AAYA 49; AITN 1; BPFB 3; CA 69-72; CANR 40, 65, 116; DA; DA3; DAB; DAC; DAM MST, NOV; DLB 302, 332; EW 13; EXPS; LAIT 4; MTCW 1, 2; MTFW 2005; NFS 6; RGSF 2, RGWL 2, 3; SSFS 9; TWA

Solzhenitsyn, Aleksandr Isayevich
See Solzhenitsyn, Aleksandr I.
See also CWW 2; EWL 3

Somers, Jane
See Lessing, Doris

Somerville, Edith Oenone 1858-1949 .... **SSC 56; TCLC 51**
See also CA 196; DLB 135; RGEL 2; RGSF 2

Somerville & Ross
See Martin, Violet Florence; Somerville, Edith Oenone

Sommer, Scott 1951- .... **CLC 25**
See also CA 106

Sommers, Christina Hoff 1950- ...... **CLC 197**
See also CA 153; CANR 95

Sondheim, Stephen (Joshua) 1930- . **CLC 30, 39, 147; DC 22**
See also AAYA 11, 66; CA 103; CANR 47, 67, 125; DAM DRAM; LAIT 4

Sone, Monica 1919- .... **AAL**
See also DLB 312

Song, Cathy 1955- .... **AAL; PC 21**
See also CA 154; CANR 118; CWP; DLB 169, 312; EXPP; FW; PFS 5

Sontag, Susan 1933-2004 ... **CLC 1, 2, 10, 13, 31, 105, 195**
See also AMWS 3; CA 17-20R; CAAS 234; CANR 25, 51, 74, 97; CN 1, 2, 3, 4, 5, 6, 7; CPW; DA3; DAM POP; DLB 2, 67; EWL 3; MAL 5; MBL; MTCW 1, 2; MTFW 2005; RGAL 4; RHW; SSFS 10

Sophocles 496(?)B.C.-406(?)B.C. .... **CMLC 2, 47, 51, 86; DC 1; WLCS**
See also AW 1; CDWLB 1; DA; DA3; DAB; DAC; DAM DRAM, MST; DFS 1, 4, 8; DLB 176; LAIT 1; LATS 1:1; LMFS 1; RGWL 2, 3; TWA; WLIT 8

Sordello 1189-1269 .... **CMLC 15**

Sorel, Georges 1847-1922 .... **TCLC 91**
See also CA 188; CAAE 118

Sorel, Julia
See Drexler, Rosalyn

Sorokin, Vladimir .... **CLC 59**
See Sorokin, Vladimir Georgievich

Sorokin, Vladimir Georgievich
See Sorokin, Vladimir
See also DLB 285

Sorrentino, Gilbert 1929-2006 .... **CLC 3, 7, 14, 22, 40**
See also CA 77-80; CAAS 250; CANR 14, 33, 115, 157; CN 3, 4, 5, 6, 7; CP 1, 2, 3, 4, 5, 6, 7; DLB 5, 173; DLBY 1980; INT CANR-14

Soseki
See Natsume, Soseki
See also MJW

Soto, Gary 1952- ... **CLC 32, 80; HLC 2; PC 28**
See also AAYA 10, 37; BYA 11; CA 125; CAAE 119; CANR 50, 74, 107, 157; CLR 38; CP 4, 5, 6, 7; DAM MULT; DLB 82; EWL 3; EXPP; HW 1, 2; INT CA-125; JRDA; LLW; MAICYA 2; MAICYAS 1; MAL 5; MTCW 2; MTFW 2005; PFS 7; RGAL 4; SATA 80, 120, 174; WYA; YAW

Soupault, Philippe 1897-1990 .... **CLC 68**
See also CA 147; CAAE 116; CAAS 131; EWL 3; GFL 1789 to the Present; LMFS 2

Souster, (Holmes) Raymond 1921- .... **CLC 5, 14**
See also CA 13-16R; 14; CANR 13, 29, 53; CP 1, 2, 3, 4, 5, 6, 7; DA3; DAC; DAM POET; DLB 88; RGEL 2; SATA 63

Southern, Terry 1924(?)-1995 .... **CLC 7**
See also AMWS 11; BPFB 3; CA 1-4R; CAAS 150; CANR 1, 55, 107; CN 1, 2, 3, 4, 5, 6; DLB 2; IDFW 3, 4

Southerne, Thomas 1660-1746 .... **LC 99**
See also DLB 80; RGEL 2

Southey, Robert 1774-1843 .... **NCLC 8, 97**
See also BRW 4; DLB 93, 107, 142; RGEL 2; SATA 54

Southwell, Robert 1561(?)-1595 .... **LC 108**
See also DLB 167; RGEL 2; TEA

Southworth, Emma Dorothy Eliza Nevitte 1819-1899 .... **NCLC 26**
See also DLB 239

Souza, Ernest
See Scott, Evelyn

Soyinka, Wole 1934- .. **BLC 3; CLC 3, 5, 14, 36, 44, 179; DC 2; WLC 5**
See also AFW; BW 2, 3; CA 13-16R; CANR 27, 39, 82, 136; CD 5, 6; CDWLB 3; CN 6, 7; CP 1, 2, 3, 4, 5, 6 ,7; DA; DA3; DAB; DAC; DAM DRAM, MST, MULT; DFS 10; DLB 125, 332; EWL 3; MTCW 1, 2; MTFW 2005; RGEL 2; TWA; WLIT 2; WWE 1

Spackman, W(illiam) M(ode) 1905-1990 .... **CLC 46**
See also CA 81-84; CAAS 132

Spacks, Barry (Bernard) 1931- .... **CLC 14**
See also CA 154; CANR 33, 109; CP 3, 4, 5, 6, 7; DLB 105

Spanidou, Irini 1946- .... **CLC 44**
See also CA 185

Spark, Muriel 1918-2006 .... **CLC 2, 3, 5, 8, 13, 18, 40, 94; PC 72; SSC 10**
See also BRWS 1; CA 5-8R; CAAS 251; CANR 12, 36, 76, 89, 131; CDBLB 1945-1960; CN 1, 2, 3, 4, 5, 6, 7; CP 1, 2, 3, 4, 5, 6, 7; DA3; DAB; DAC; DAM MST, NOV; DLB 15, 139; EWL 3; FW; INT CANR-12; LAIT 4; MTCW 1, 2; MTFW 2005; NFS 22; RGEL 2; TEA; WLIT 4; YAW

Spark, Muriel Sarah
See Spark, Muriel

Spaulding, Douglas
See Bradbury, Ray

Spaulding, Leonard
See Bradbury, Ray

Speght, Rachel 1597-c. 1630 .... **LC 97**
See also DLB 126

Spence, J. A. D.
See Eliot, T(homas) S(tearns)

Spencer, Anne 1882-1975 ...... **HR 1:3; PC 77**
See also BW 2; CA 161; DLB 51, 54

Spencer, Elizabeth 1921- .... **CLC 22; SSC 57**
See also CA 13-16R; CANR 32, 65, 87; CN 1, 2, 3, 4, 5, 6, 7; CSW; DLB 6, 218; EWL 3; MTCW 1; RGAL 4; SATA 14

Spencer, Leonard G.
See Silverberg, Robert

Spencer, Scott 1945- .... **CLC 30**
See also CA 113; CANR 51, 148; DLBY 1986

Spender, Stephen 1909-1995 ..... **CLC 1, 2, 5, 10, 41, 91; PC 71**
See also BRWS 2; CA 9-12R; CAAS 149; CANR 31, 54; CDBLB 1945-1960; CP 1, 2, 3, 4, 5, 6; DA3; DAM POET; DLB 20; EWL 3; MTCW 1, 2; MTFW 2005; PAB; PFS 23; RGEL 2; TEA

Spengler, Oswald (Arnold Gottfried) 1880-1936 .... **TCLC 25**
See also CA 189; CAAE 118

Spenser, Edmund 1552(?)-1599 ...... **LC 5, 39, 117; PC 8, 42; WLC 5**
See also AAYA 60; BRW 1; CDBLB Before 1660; DA; DA3; DAB; DAC; DAM MST, POET; DLB 167; EFS 2; EXPP; PAB; RGEL 2; TEA; WLIT 3; WP

Spicer, Jack 1925-1965 .... **CLC 8, 18, 72**
See also BG 1:3; CA 85-88; DAM POET; DLB 5, 16, 193; GLL 1; WP

Spiegelman, Art 1948- .... **CLC 76, 178**
See also AAYA 10, 46; CA 125; CANR 41, 55, 74, 124; DLB 299; MTCW 2; MTFW 2005; RGHL; SATA 109, 158; YAW

Spielberg, Peter 1929- .... **CLC 6**
See also CA 5-8R; CANR 4, 48; DLBY 1981

Spielberg, Steven 1947- .... **CLC 20, 188**
See also AAYA 8, 24; CA 77-80; CANR 32; SATA 32

Spillane, Frank Morrison .... **CLC 3, 13**
See Spillane, Mickey
See also BPFB 3; CMW 4; DLB 226; MSW

Spillane, Mickey 1918-2006
See Spillane, Frank Morrison
See also CA 25-28R; CAAS 252; CANR 28, 63, 125; DA3; MTCW 1, 2; MTFW 2005; SATA 66; SATA-Obit 176

Spinoza, Benedictus de 1632-1677 .. **LC 9, 58**

Spinrad, Norman (Richard) 1940- ... **CLC 46**
See also BPFB 3; CA 233; 37-40R, 233; 19; CANR 20, 91; DLB 8; INT CANR-20; SFW 4

Spitteler, Carl 1845-1924 .... **TCLC 12**
See also CAAE 109; DLB 129, 332; EWL 3

Spitteler, Karl Friedrich Georg
See Spitteler, Carl

Spivack, Kathleen (Romola Drucker) 1938- .... **CLC 6**
See also CA 49-52

Spivak, Gayatri Chakravorty 1942- .... **CLC 233**
See also CA 154; CAAE 110; CANR 91; FW; LMFS 2

Spofford, Harriet (Elizabeth) Prescott 1835-1921 .... **SSC 87**
See also CA 201; DLB 74, 221

Spoto, Donald 1941- .... **CLC 39**
See also CA 65-68; CANR 11, 57, 93

Springsteen, Bruce 1949- .... **CLC 17**
See also CA 111

Springsteen, Bruce F.
See Springsteen, Bruce

Spurling, Hilary 1940- .... **CLC 34**
See also CA 104; CANR 25, 52, 94, 157

Spurling, Susan Hilary
See Spurling, Hilary

Spyker, John Howland
See Elman, Richard (Martin)

Squared, A.
See Abbott, Edwin A.

Squires, (James) Radcliffe 1917-1993 .... **CLC 51**
See also CA 1-4R; CAAS 140; CANR 6, 21; CP 1, 2, 3, 4, 5

Srivastava, Dhanpat Rai 1880(?)-1936
See Premchand
See also CA 197; CAAE 118

Stacy, Donald
See Pohl, Frederik

Stael
See Stael-Holstein, Anne Louise Germaine Necker
See also EW 5; RGWL 2, 3

Stael, Germaine de
See Stael-Holstein, Anne Louise Germaine Necker
See also DLB 119, 192; FL 1:3; FW; GFL 1789 to the Present; TWA

Stael-Holstein, Anne Louise Germaine Necker 1766-1817 .... **NCLC 3, 91**
See Stael; Stael, Germaine de

Stafford, Jean 1915-1979 .. **CLC 4, 7, 19, 68; SSC 26, 86**
See also CA 1-4R; CAAS 85-88; CANR 3, 65; CN 1, 2; DLB 2, 173; MAL 5; MTCW 1, 2; MTFW 2005; RGAL 4; RGSF 2; SATA-Obit 22; SSFS 21; TCWW 1, 2; TUS

Stafford, William (Edgar) 1914-1993 .... **CLC 4, 7, 29; PC 71**
See also AMWS 11; CA 5-8R; 3; CAAS 142; CANR 5, 22; CP 1, 2, 3, 4, 5; DAM POET; DLB 5, 206; EXPP; INT CANR-22; MAL 5; PFS 2, 8, 16; RGAL 4; WP

Stagnelius, Eric Johan 1793-1823 . **NCLC 61**

Staines, Trevor
See Brunner, John (Kilian Houston)

Stairs, Gordon
See Austin, Mary (Hunter)

Stalin, Joseph 1879-1953 .... **TCLC 92**

Stampa, Gaspara c. 1524-1554 .. **LC 114; PC 43**
See also RGWL 2, 3; WLIT 7

Stampflinger, K. A.
See Benjamin, Walter

Stancykowna
See Szymborska, Wislawa

Standing Bear, Luther 1868(?)-1939(?) .... **NNAL**
See also CA 144; CAAE 113; DAM MULT

Stanislavsky, Constantin 1863(?)-1938 .... **TCLC 167**
See also CAAE 118

Stanislavsky, Konstantin
See Stanislavsky, Constantin

Stanislavsky, Konstantin Sergeievich
See Stanislavsky, Constantin

Stanislavsky, Konstantin Sergeivich
See Stanislavsky, Constantin

Stanislavsky, Konstantin Sergeyevich
See Stanislavsky, Constantin

Stannard, Martin 1947- .... **CLC 44**
See also CA 142; DLB 155

Stanton, Elizabeth Cady 1815-1902 .... **TCLC 73**
See also CA 171; DLB 79; FL 1:3; FW

Stanton, Maura 1946- .... **CLC 9**
See also CA 89-92; CANR 15, 123; DLB 120

Stanton, Schuyler
See Baum, L(yman) Frank

Stapledon, (William) Olaf 1886-1950 .... **TCLC 22**
See also CA 162; CAAE 111; DLB 15, 255; SCFW 1, 2; SFW 4

Starbuck, George (Edwin) 1931-1996 .... **CLC 53**
See also CA 21-24R; CAAS 153; CANR 23; CP 1, 2, 3, 4, 5, 6; DAM POET

Stark, Richard
See Westlake, Donald E.

Staunton, Schuyler
See Baum, L(yman) Frank

Stead, Christina (Ellen) 1902-1983 ... **CLC 2, 5, 8, 32, 80**
See also BRWS 4; CA 13-16R; CAAS 109; CANR 33, 40; CN 1, 2, 3; DLB 260; EWL 3; FW; MTCW 1, 2; MTFW 2005; RGEL 2; RGSF 2; WWE 1

Stead, William Thomas 1849-1912 .... **TCLC 48**
See also CA 167

Stebnitsky, M.
See Leskov, Nikolai (Semyonovich)

Steele, Richard 1672-1729 .... **LC 18**
See also BRW 3; CDBLB 1660-1789; DLB 84, 101; RGEL 2; WLIT 3

Steele, Timothy (Reid) 1948- .... **CLC 45**
See also CA 93-96; CANR 16, 50, 92; CP 5, 6, 7; DLB 120, 282

Steffens, (Joseph) Lincoln 1866-1936 .... **TCLC 20**
See also CA 198; CAAE 117; DLB 303; MAL 5

Stegner, Wallace (Earle) 1909-1993 .. **CLC 9, 49, 81; SSC 27**
See also AITN 1; AMWS 4; ANW; BEST 90:3; BPFB 3; CA 1-4R; 9; CAAS 141; CANR 1, 21, 46; CN 1, 2, 3, 4, 5; DAM NOV; DLB 9, 206, 275; DLBY 1993; EWL 3; MAL 5; MTCW 1, 2; MTFW 2005; RGAL 4; TCWW 1, 2; TUS

Stein, Gertrude 1874-1946 .... **DC 19; PC 18; SSC 42; TCLC 1, 6, 28, 48; WLC 5**
See also AAYA 64; AMW; AMWC 2; CA 132; CAAE 104; CANR 108; CDALB 1917-1929; DA; DA3; DAB; DAC; DAM MST, NOV, POET; DLB 4, 54, 86, 228; DLBD 15; EWL 3; EXPS; FL 1:6; GLL 1; MAL 5; MBL; MTCW 1, 2; MTFW 2005; NCFS 4; RGAL 4; RGSF 2; SSFS 5; TUS; WP

Steinbeck, John (Ernst) 1902-1968 ... **CLC 1, 5, 9, 13, 21, 34, 45, 75, 124; SSC 11, 37, 77; TCLC 135; WLC 5**
See also AAYA 12; AMW; BPFB 3; BYA 2, 3, 13; CA 1-4R; CAAS 25-28R; CANR 1, 35; CDALB 1929-1941; DA; DA3; DAB; DAC; DAM DRAM, MST, NOV; DLB 7, 9, 212, 275, 309, 332; DLBD 2; EWL 3; EXPS; LAIT 3; MAL 5; MTCW 1, 2; MTFW 2005; NFS 1, 5, 7, 17, 19; RGAL 4; RGSF 2; RHW; SATA 9; SSFS 3, 6, 22; TCWW 1, 2; TUS; WYA; YAW

Steinem, Gloria 1934- .... **CLC 63**
See also CA 53-56; CANR 28, 51, 139; DLB 246; FL 1:1; FW; MTCW 1, 2; MTFW 2005

Steiner, George 1929- .... **CLC 24, 221**
See also CA 73-76; CANR 31, 67, 108; DAM NOV; DLB 67, 299; EWL 3; MTCW 1, 2; MTFW 2005; RGHL; SATA 62

Steiner, K. Leslie
See Delany, Samuel R., Jr.

Steiner, Rudolf 1861-1925 .... **TCLC 13**
See also CAAE 107

Stendhal 1783-1842 .... **NCLC 23, 46, 178; SSC 27; WLC 5**
See also DA; DA3; DAB; DAC; DAM MST, NOV; DLB 119; EW 5; GFL 1789 to the Present; RGWL 2, 3; TWA

Stephen, Adeline Virginia
See Woolf, (Adeline) Virginia

Stephen, Sir Leslie 1832-1904 .... **TCLC 23**
See also BRW 5; CAAE 123; DLB 57, 144, 190

Stephen, Sir Leslie
See Stephen, Sir Leslie

Stephen, Virginia
See Woolf, (Adeline) Virginia

Stephens, James 1882(?)-1950 .... **SSC 50; TCLC 4**
See also CA 192; CAAE 104; DLB 19, 153, 162; EWL 3; FANT; RGEL 2; SUFW

Stephens, Reed
See Donaldson, Stephen R(eeder)

Stephenson, Neal 1959- .... **CLC 220**
See also AAYA 38; CA 122; CANR 88, 138; CN 7; MTFW 2005; SFW 4

Steptoe, Lydia
See Barnes, Djuna
See also GLL 1

Sterchi, Beat 1949- .... **CLC 65**
See also CA 203

Sterling, Brett
See Bradbury, Ray; Hamilton, Edmond

Sterling, Bruce 1954- .... **CLC 72**
  See also CA 119; CANR 44, 135; CN 7;
  MTFW 2005; SCFW 2; SFW 4

Sterling, George 1869-1926 .... **TCLC 20**
  See also CA 165; CAAE 117; DLB 54

Stern, Gerald 1925- .... **CLC 40, 100**
  See also AMWS 9; CA 81-84; CANR 28,
  94; CP 3, 4, 5, 6, 7; DLB 105; RGAL 4

Stern, Richard (Gustave) 1928- ... **CLC 4, 39**
  See also CA 1-4R; CANR 1, 25, 52, 120;
  CN 1, 2, 3, 4, 5, 6, 7; DLB 218; DLBY
  1987; INT CANR-25

Sternberg, Josef von 1894-1969 .... **CLC 20**
  See also CA 81-84

Sterne, Laurence 1713-1768 .... **LC 2, 48;**
  WLC 5
  See also BRW 3; BRWC 1; CDBLB 1660-
  1789; DA; DAB; DAC; DAM MST, NOV;
  DLB 39; RGEL 2; TEA

Sternheim, (William Adolf) Carl
  1878-1942 .... **TCLC 8**
  See also CA 193; CAAE 105; DLB 56, 118;
  EWL 3; IDTP; RGWL 2, 3

Stevens, Margaret Dean
  See Aldrich, Bess Streeter

Stevens, Mark 1951- .... **CLC 34**
  See also CA 122

Stevens, Wallace 1879-1955 . **PC 6; TCLC 3,**
  12, 45; WLC 5
  See also AMW; AMWR 1; CA 124; CAAE
  104; CDALB 1929-1941; DA; DA3;
  DAB; DAC; DAM MST, POET; DLB 54;
  EWL 3; EXPP; MAL 5; MTCW 1, 2;
  PAB; PFS 13, 16; RGAL 4; TUS; WP

Stevenson, Anne (Katharine) 1933- .. **CLC 7,**
  33
  See also BRWS 6; CA 17-20R; 9; CANR 9,
  33, 123; CP 3, 4, 5, 6, 7; CWP; DLB 40;
  MTCW 1; RHW

Stevenson, Robert Louis (Balfour)
  1850-1894 ...... **NCLC 5, 14, 63; SSC 11,**
  51; WLC 5
  See also AAYA 24; BPFB 3; BRW 5;
  BRWC 1; BRWR 1; BYA 1, 2, 4, 13; CD-
  BLB 1890-1914; CLR 10, 11, 107; DA;
  DA3; DAB; DAC; DAM MST, NOV;
  DLB 18, 57, 141, 156, 174; DLBD 13;
  GL 3; HGG; JRDA; LAIT 1, 3; MAICYA
  1, 2; NFS 11, 20; RGEL 2; RGSF 2;
  SATA 100; SUFW; TEA; WCH; WLIT 4;
  WYA; YABC 2; YAW

Stewart, J(ohn) I(nnes) M(ackintosh)
  1906-1994 .... **CLC 7, 14, 32**
  See Innes, Michael
  See also CA 85-88; 3; CAAS 147; CANR
  47; CMW 4; CN 1, 2, 3, 4, 5; MTCW 1,
  2

Stewart, Mary (Florence Elinor)
  1916- .... **CLC 7, 35, 117**
  See also AAYA 29, 73; BPFB 3; CA 1-4R;
  CANR 1, 59, 130; CMW 4; CPW; DAB;
  FANT; RHW; SATA 12; YAW

Stewart, Mary Rainbow
  See Stewart, Mary (Florence Elinor)

Stifle, June
  See Campbell, Maria

Stifter, Adalbert 1805-1868 .. **NCLC 41; SSC**
  28
  See also CDWLB 2; DLB 133; RGSF 2;
  RGWL 2, 3

Still, James 1906-2001 .... **CLC 49**
  See also CA 65-68; 17; CAAS 195; CANR
  10, 26; CSW; DLB 9; DLBY 01; SATA
  29; SATA-Obit 127

Sting 1951-
  See Sumner, Gordon Matthew
  See also CA 167

Stirling, Arthur
  See Sinclair, Upton

Stitt, Milan 1941- .... **CLC 29**
  See also CA 69-72

Stockton, Francis Richard 1834-1902
  See Stockton, Frank R.
  See also AAYA 68; CA 137; CAAE 108;
  MAICYA 1, 2; SATA 44; SFW 4

Stockton, Frank R. .... **TCLC 47**
  See Stockton, Francis Richard
  See also BYA 4, 13; DLB 42, 74; DLBD
  13; EXPS; SATA-Brief 32; SSFS 3;
  SUFW; WCH

Stoddard, Charles
  See Kuttner, Henry

Stoker, Abraham 1847-1912
  See Stoker, Bram
  See also CA 150; CAAE 105; DA; DA3;
  DAC; DAM MST, NOV; HGG; MTFW
  2005; SATA 29

Stoker, Bram . **SSC 62; TCLC 8, 144; WLC**
  6
  See Stoker, Abraham
  See also AAYA 23; BPFB 3; BRWS 3; BYA
  5; CDBLB 1890-1914; DAB; DLB 304;
  GL 3; LATS 1:1; NFS 18; RGEL 2;
  SUFW; TEA; WLIT 4

Stolz, Mary 1920-2006 .... **CLC 12**
  See also AAYA 8, 73; AITN 1; CA 5-8R;
  CANR 13, 41, 112; JRDA; MAICYA 1,
  2; SAAS 3; SATA 10, 71, 133; YAW

Stolz, Mary Slattery
  See Stolz, Mary

Stone, Irving 1903-1989 .... **CLC 7**
  See also AITN 1; BPFB 3; CA 1-4R; 3;
  CAAS 129; CANR 1, 23; CN 1, 2, 3, 4;
  CPW; DA3; DAM POP; INT CANR-23;
  MTCW 1, 2; MTFW 2005; RHW; SATA
  3; SATA-Obit 64

Stone, Oliver 1946- .... **CLC 73**
  See also AAYA 15, 64; CA 110; CANR 55,
  125

Stone, Oliver William
  See Stone, Oliver

Stone, Robert 1937- .... **CLC 5, 23, 42, 175**
  See also AMWS 5; BPFB 3; CA 85-88;
  CANR 23, 66, 95; CN 4, 5, 6, 7; DLB
  152; EWL 3; INT CANR-23; MAL 5;
  MTCW 1; MTFW 2005

Stone, Ruth 1915- .... **PC 53**
  See also CA 45-48; CANR 2, 91; CP 5, 6,
  7; CSW; DLB 105; PFS 19

Stone, Zachary
  See Follett, Ken

Stoppard, Tom 1937- ... **CLC 1, 3, 4, 5, 8, 15,**
  29, 34, 63, 91; DC 6; WLC 6
  See also AAYA 63; BRWC 1; BRWR 2;
  BRWS 1; CA 81-84; CANR 39, 67, 125;
  CBD; CD 5, 6; CDBLB 1960 to Present;
  DA; DA3; DAB; DAC; DAM DRAM,
  MST; DFS 2, 5, 8, 11, 13, 16; DLB 13,
  233; DLBY 1985; EWL 3; LATS 1:2;
  MTCW 1, 2; MTFW 2005; RGEL 2;
  TEA; WLIT 4

Storey, David (Malcolm) 1933- . **CLC 2, 4, 5,**
  8
  See also BRWS 1; CA 81-84; CANR 36;
  CBD; CD 5, 6; CN 1, 2, 3, 4, 5, 6; DAM
  DRAM; DLB 13, 14, 207, 245, 326; EWL
  3; MTCW 1; RGEL 2

Storm, Hyemeyohsts 1935- ... **CLC 3; NNAL**
  See also CA 81-84; CANR 45; DAM MULT

Storm, (Hans) Theodor (Woldsen)
  1817-1888 .... **NCLC 1; SSC 27**
  See also CDWLB 2; DLB 129; EW; RGSF
  2; RGWL 2, 3

Storni, Alfonsina 1892-1938 . **HLC 2; PC 33;**
  TCLC 5
  See also CA 131; CAAE 104; DAM MULT;
  DLB 283; HW 1; LAW

Stoughton, William 1631-1701 .... **LC 38**
  See also DLB 24

Stout, Rex (Todhunter) 1886-1975 ..... **CLC 3**
  See also AITN 2; BPFB 3; CA 61-64;
  CANR 71; CMW 4; CN 2; DLB 306;
  MSW; RGAL 4

Stow, (Julian) Randolph 1935- ... **CLC 23, 48**
  See also CA 13-16R; CANR 33; CN 1, 2,
  3, 4, 5, 6, 7; CP 1, 2, 3, 4; DLB 260;
  MTCW 1; RGEL 2

Stowe, Harriet (Elizabeth) Beecher
  1811-1896 ..... **NCLC 3, 50, 133; WLC 6**
  See also AAYA 53; AMWS 1; CDALB
  1865-1917; DA; DA3; DAB; DAC; DAM
  MST, NOV; DLB 1, 12, 42, 74, 189, 239,
  243; EXPN; FL 1:3; JRDA; LAIT 2;
  MAICYA 1, 2; NFS 6; RGAL 4; TUS;
  YABC 1

Strabo c. 64B.C.-c. 25 .... **CMLC 37**
  See also DLB 176

Strachey, (Giles) Lytton
  1880-1932 .... **TCLC 12**
  See also BRWS 2; CA 178; CAAE 110;
  DLB 149; DLBD 10; EWL 3; MTCW 2;
  NCFS 4

Stramm, August 1874-1915 .... **PC 50**
  See also CA 195; EWL 3

Strand, Mark 1934- .. **CLC 6, 18, 41, 71; PC**
  63
  See also AMWS 4; CA 21-24R; CANR 40,
  65, 100; CP 1, 2, 3, 4, 5, 6, 7; DAM
  POET; DLB 5; EWL 3; MAL 5; PAB;
  PFS 9, 18; RGAL 4; SATA 41; TCLE 1:2

Stratton-Porter, Gene(va Grace) 1863-1924
  See Porter, Gene(va Grace) Stratton
  See also ANW; CA 137; CLR 87; DLB 221;
  DLBD 14; MAICYA 1, 2; SATA 15

Straub, Peter 1943- .... **CLC 28, 107**
  See also BEST 89:1; BPFB 3; CA 85-88;
  CANR 28, 65, 109; CPW; DAM POP;
  DLBY 1984; HGG; MTCW 1, 2; MTFW
  2005; SUFW 2

Straub, Peter Francis
  See Straub, Peter

Strauss, Botho 1944- .... **CLC 22**
  See also CA 157; CWW 2; DLB 124

Strauss, Leo 1899-1973 .... **TCLC 141**
  See also CA 101; CAAS 45-48; CANR 122

Streatfeild, (Mary) Noel
  1897(?)-1986 .... **CLC 21**
  See also CA 81-84; CAAS 120; CANR 31;
  CLR 17, 83; CWRI 5; DLB 160; MAI-
  CYA 1, 2; SATA 20; SATA-Obit 48

Stribling, T(homas) S(igismund)
  1881-1965 .... **CLC 23**
  See also CA 189; CAAS 107; CMW 4; DLB
  9; RGAL 4

Strindberg, (Johan) August
  1849-1912 ... **DC 18; TCLC 1, 8, 21, 47;**
  WLC 6
  See also CA 135; CAAE 104; DA; DA3;
  DAB; DAC; DAM DRAM, MST; DFS 4,
  9; DLB 259; EW 7; EWL 3; IDTP; LMFS
  2; MTCW 2; MTFW 2005; RGWL 2, 3;
  TWA

Stringer, Arthur 1874-1950 .... **TCLC 37**
  See also CA 161; DLB 92

Stringer, David
  See Roberts, Keith (John Kingston)

Stroheim, Erich von 1885-1957 ..... **TCLC 71**

Strugatskii, Arkadii (Natanovich)
  1925-1991 .... **CLC 27**
  See Strugatsky, Arkadii Natanovich
  See also CA 106; CAAS 135; SFW 4

Strugatskii, Boris (Natanovich)
  1933- .... **CLC 27**
  See Strugatsky, Boris (Natanovich)
  See also CA 106; SFW 4

Strugatsky, Arkadii Natanovich
  See Strugatskii, Arkadii (Natanovich)
  See also DLB 302

T. O., Nik
See Annensky, Innokenty (Fyodorovich)

Tabori, George 1914- .... **CLC 19**
See also CA 49-52; CANR 4, 69; CBD; CD 5, 6; DLB 245; RGHL

Tacitus c. 55-c. 117 .... **CMLC 56**
See also AW 2; CDWLB 1; DLB 211; RGWL 2, 3; WLIT 8

Tagore, Rabindranath 1861-1941 .... **PC 8; SSC 48; TCLC 3, 53**
See also CA 120; CAAE 104; DA3; DAM DRAM, POET; DLB 323, 332; EWL 3; MTCW 1, 2; MTFW 2005; PFS 18; RGEL 2; RGSF 2; RGWL 2, 3; TWA

Taine, Hippolyte Adolphe
1828-1893 .... **NCLC 15**
See also EW 7; GFL 1789 to the Present

Talayesva, Don C. 1890-(?) .... **NNAL**

Talese, Gay 1932- .... **CLC 37, 232**
See also AITN 1; CA 1-4R; CANR 9, 58, 137; DLB 185; INT CANR-9; MTCW 1, 2; MTFW 2005

Tallent, Elizabeth 1954- .... **CLC 45**
See also CA 117; CANR 72; DLB 130

Tallmountain, Mary 1918-1997 .... **NNAL**
See also CA 146; CAAS 161; DLB 193

Tally, Ted 1952- .... **CLC 42**
See also CA 124; CAAE 120; CAD; CANR 125; CD 5, 6; INT CA-124

Talvik, Heiti 1904-1947 .... **TCLC 87**
See also EWL 3

Tamayo y Baus, Manuel
1829-1898 .... **NCLC 1**

Tammsaare, A(nton) H(ansen)
1878-1940 .... **TCLC 27**
See also CA 164; CDWLB 4; DLB 220; EWL 3

Tam'si, Tchicaya U
See Tchicaya, Gerald Felix

Tan, Amy 1952- ...... **AAL; CLC 59, 120, 151**
See also AAYA 9, 48; AMWS 10; BEST 89:3; BPFB 3; CA 136; CANR 54, 105, 132; CDALBS; CN 6, 7; CPW 1; DA3; DAM MULT, NOV, POP; DLB 173, 312; EXPN; FL 1:6; FW; LAIT 3, 5; MAL 5; MTCW 2; MTFW 2005; NFS 1, 13, 16; RGAL 4; SATA 75; SSFS 9; YAW

Tandem, Carl Felix
See Spitteler, Carl

Tandem, Felix
See Spitteler, Carl

Tanizaki, Jun'ichiro 1886-1965 ... **CLC 8, 14, 28; SSC 21**
See Tanizaki Jun'ichiro
See also CA 93-96; CAAS 25-28R; MJW; MTCW 2; MTFW 2005; RGSF 2; RGWL 2

Tanizaki Jun'ichiro
See Tanizaki, Jun'ichiro
See also DLB 180; EWL 3

Tannen, Deborah 1945- .... **CLC 206**
See also CA 118; CANR 95

Tannen, Deborah Frances
See Tannen, Deborah

Tanner, William
See Amis, Kingsley

Tante, Dilly
See Kunitz, Stanley

Tao Lao
See Storni, Alfonsina

Tapahonso, Luci 1953- .... **NNAL; PC 65**
See also CA 145; CANR 72, 127; DLB 175

Tarantino, Quentin (Jerome)
1963- .... **CLC 125, 230**
See also AAYA 58; CA 171; CANR 125

Tarassoff, Lev
See Troyat, Henri

Tarbell, Ida M(inerva) 1857-1944 . **TCLC 40**
See also CA 181; CAAE 122; DLB 47

Tarkington, (Newton) Booth
1869-1946 .... **TCLC 9**
See also BPFB 3; BYA 3; CA 143; CAAE 110; CWRI 5; DLB 9, 102; MAL 5; MTCW 2; RGAL 4; SATA 17

Tarkovskii, Andrei Arsen'evich
See Tarkovsky, Andrei (Arsenyevich)

Tarkovsky, Andrei (Arsenyevich)
1932-1986 .... **CLC 75**
See also CA 127

Tartt, Donna 1964(?)- .... **CLC 76**
See also AAYA 56; CA 142; CANR 135; MTFW 2005

Tasso, Torquato 1544-1595 .... **LC 5, 94**
See also EFS 2; EW 2; RGWL 2, 3; WLIT 7

Tate, (John Orley) Allen 1899-1979 .. **CLC 2, 4, 6, 9, 11, 14, 24; PC 50**
See also AMW; CA 5-8R; CAAS 85-88; CANR 32, 108; CN 1, 2; CP 1, 2; DLB 4, 45, 63; DLBD 17; EWL 3; MAL 5; MTCW 1, 2; MTFW 2005; RGAL 4; RHW

Tate, Ellalice
See Hibbert, Eleanor Alice Burford

Tate, James (Vincent) 1943- ..... **CLC 2, 6, 25**
See also CA 21-24R; CANR 29, 57, 114; CP 1, 2, 3, 4, 5, 6, 7; DLB 5, 169; EWL 3; PFS 10, 15; RGAL 4; WP

Tate, Nahum 1652(?)-1715 .... **LC 109**
See also DLB 80; RGEL 2

Tauler, Johannes c. 1300-1361 ...... **CMLC 37**
See also DLB 179; LMFS 1

Tavel, Ronald 1940- .... **CLC 6**
See also CA 21-24R; CAD; CANR 33; CD 5, 6

Taviani, Paolo 1931- .... **CLC 70**
See also CA 153

Taylor, Bayard 1825-1878 .... **NCLC 89**
See also DLB 3, 189, 250, 254; RGAL 4

Taylor, C(ecil) P(hilip) 1929-1981 .... **CLC 27**
See also CA 25-28R; CAAS 105; CANR 47; CBD

Taylor, Edward 1642(?)-1729 . **LC 11; PC 63**
See also AMW; DA; DAB; DAC; DAM MST, POET; DLB 24; EXPP; RGAL 4; TUS

Taylor, Eleanor Ross 1920- .... **CLC 5**
See also CA 81-84; CANR 70

Taylor, Elizabeth 1912-1975 ..... **CLC 2, 4, 29**
See also CA 13-16R; CANR 9, 70; CN 1, 2; DLB 139; MTCW 1; RGEL 2; SATA 13

Taylor, Frederick Winslow
1856-1915 .... **TCLC 76**
See also CA 188

Taylor, Henry (Splawn) 1942- .... **CLC 44**
See also CA 33-36R; 7; CANR 31; CP 6, 7; DLB 5; PFS 10

Taylor, Kamala 1924-2004
See Markandaya, Kamala
See also CA 77-80; CAAS 227; MTFW 2005; NFS 13

Taylor, Mildred D. 1943- .... **CLC 21**
See also AAYA 10, 47; BW 1; BYA 3, 8; CA 85-88; CANR 25, 115, 136; CLR 9, 59, 90; CSW; DLB 52; JRDA; LAIT 3; MAICYA 1, 2; MTFW 2005; SAAS 5; SATA 135; WYA; YAW

Taylor, Peter (Hillsman) 1917-1994 .. **CLC 1, 4, 18, 37, 44, 50, 71; SSC 10, 84**
See also AMWS 5; BPFB 3; CA 13-16R; CAAS 147; CANR 9, 50; CN 1, 2, 3, 4, 5; CSW; DLB 218, 278; DLBY 1981, 1994; EWL 3; EXPS; INT CANR-9; MAL 5; MTCW 1, 2; MTFW 2005; RGSF 2; SSFS 9; TUS

Taylor, Robert Lewis 1912-1998 .... **CLC 14**
See also CA 1-4R; CAAS 170; CANR 3, 64; CN 1, 2; SATA 10; TCWW 1, 2

Tchekhov, Anton
See Chekhov, Anton (Pavlovich)

Tchicaya, Gerald Felix 1931-1988 .. **CLC 101**
See Tchicaya U Tam'si
See also CA 129; CAAS 125; CANR 81

Tchicaya U Tam'si
See Tchicaya, Gerald Felix
See also EWL 3

Teasdale, Sara 1884-1933 .... **PC 31; TCLC 4**
See also CA 163; CAAE 104; DLB 45; GLL 1; PFS 14; RGAL 4; SATA 32; TUS

Tecumseh 1768-1813 .... **NNAL**
See also DAM MULT

Tegner, Esaias 1782-1846 .... **NCLC 2**

Teilhard de Chardin, (Marie Joseph) Pierre
1881-1955 .... **TCLC 9**
See also CA 210; CAAE 105; GFL 1789 to the Present

Temple, Ann
See Mortimer, Penelope (Ruth)

Tennant, Emma (Christina) 1937- .. **CLC 13, 52**
See also BRWS 9; CA 65-68; 9; CANR 10, 38, 59, 88; CN 3, 4, 5, 6, 7; DLB 14; EWL 3; SFW 4

Tenneshaw, S. M.
See Silverberg, Robert

Tenney, Tabitha Gilman
1762-1837 .... **NCLC 122**
See also DLB 37, 200

Tennyson, Alfred 1809-1892 ... **NCLC 30, 65, 115; PC 6; WLC 6**
See also AAYA 50; BRW 4; CDBLB 1832-1890; DA; DA3; DAB; DAC; DAM MST, POET; DLB 32; EXPP; PAB; PFS 1, 2, 4, 11, 15, 19; RGEL 2; TEA; WLIT 4; WP

Teran, Lisa St. Aubin de .... **CLC 36**
See St. Aubin de Teran, Lisa

Terence c. 184B.C.-c. 159B.C. ...... **CMLC 14; DC 7**
See also AW 1; CDWLB 1; DLB 211; RGWL 2, 3; TWA; WLIT 8

Teresa de Jesus, St. 1515-1582 .... **LC 18**

Teresa of Avila, St.
See Teresa de Jesus, St.

Terkel, Louis .... **CLC 38**
See Terkel, Studs
See also AAYA 32; AITN 1; MTCW 2; TUS

Terkel, Studs 1912-
See Terkel, Louis
See also CA 57-60; CANR 18, 45, 67, 132; DA3; MTCW 1, 2; MTFW 2005

Terry, C. V.
See Slaughter, Frank G(ill)

Terry, Megan 1932- .... **CLC 19; DC 13**
See also CA 77-80; CABS 3; CAD; CANR 43; CD 5, 6; CWD; DFS 18; DLB 7, 249; GLL 2

Tertullian c. 155-c. 245 .... **CMLC 29**

Tertz, Abram
See Sinyavsky, Andrei (Donatevich)
See also RGSF 2

Tesich, Steve 1943(?)-1996 .... **CLC 40, 69**
See also CA 105; CAAS 152; CAD; DLBY 1983

Tesla, Nikola 1856-1943 .... **TCLC 88**

Teternikov, Fyodor Kuzmich 1863-1927
See Sologub, Fyodor
See also CAAE 104

Tevis, Walter 1928-1984 .... **CLC 42**
See also CA 113; SFW 4

Tey, Josephine .... **TCLC 14**
See Mackintosh, Elizabeth
See also DLB 77; MSW

Tolkien, J(ohn) R(onald) R(euel)
1892-1973 .... **CLC 1, 2, 3, 8, 12, 38;**
TCLC 137; WLC 6
See also AAYA 10; AITN 1; BPFB 3;
BRWC 2; BRWS 2; CA 17-18; CAAS 45-
48; CANR 36, 134; CAP 2; CDBLB
1914-1945; CLR 56; CN 1; CPW 1;
CWRI 5; DA; DA3; DAB; DAC; DAM
MST, NOV, POP; DLB 15, 160, 255; EFS
2; EWL 3; FANT; JRDA; LAIT 1; LATS
1:2; LMFS 2; MAICYA 1, 2; MTCW 1,
2; MTFW 2005; NFS 8; RGEL 2; SATA
2, 32, 100; SATA-Obit 24; SFW 4; SUFW;
TEA; WCH; WYA; YAW

Toller, Ernst 1893-1939 .... **TCLC 10**
See also CA 186; CAAE 107; DLB 124;
EWL 3; RGWL 2, 3

Tolson, M. B.
See Tolson, Melvin B(eaunorus)

Tolson, Melvin B(eaunorus)
1898(?)-1966 .... **BLC 3; CLC 36, 105**
See also AFAW 1, 2; BW 1, 3; CA 124;
CAAS 89-92; CANR 80; DAM MULT,
POET; DLB 48, 76; MAL 5; RGAL 4

Tolstoi, Aleksei Nikolaevich
See Tolstoy, Alexey Nikolaevich

Tolstoi, Lev
See Tolstoy, Leo (Nikolaevich)
See also RGSF 2; RGWL 2, 3

Tolstoy, Aleksei Nikolaevich
See Tolstoy, Alexey Nikolaevich
See also DLB 272

Tolstoy, Alexey Nikolaevich
1882-1945 .... **TCLC 18**
See Tolstoy, Aleksei Nikolaevich
See also CA 158; CAAE 107; EWL 3; SFW
4

Tolstoy, Leo (Nikolaevich)
1828-1910 . **SSC 9, 30, 45, 54; TCLC 4,**
11, 17, 28, 44, 79, 173; WLC 6
See Tolstoi, Lev
See also AAYA 56; CA 123; CAAE 104;
DA; DA3; DAB; DAC; DAM MST, NOV;
DLB 238; EFS 2; EW 7; EXPS; IDTP;
LAIT 2; LATS 1:1; LMFS 1; NFS 10;
SATA 26; SSFS 5; TWA

Tolstoy, Count Leo
See Tolstoy, Leo (Nikolaevich)

Tomalin, Claire 1933- .... **CLC 166**
See also CA 89-92; CANR 52, 88; DLB
155

Tomasi di Lampedusa, Giuseppe 1896-1957
See Lampedusa, Giuseppe (Tomasi) di
See also CAAE 111; DLB 177; EWL 3;
WLIT 7

Tomlin, Lily 1939(?)-
See Tomlin, Mary Jean
See also CAAE 117

Tomlin, Mary Jean .... **CLC 17**
See Tomlin, Lily

Tomline, F. Latour
See Gilbert, W(illiam) S(chwenck)

Tomlinson, (Alfred) Charles 1927- .... **CLC 2,**
4, 6, 13, 45; PC 17
See also CA 5-8R; CANR 33; CP 1, 2, 3, 4,
5, 6, 7; DAM POET; DLB 40; TCLE 1:2

Tomlinson, H(enry) M(ajor)
1873-1958 .... **TCLC 71**
See also CA 161; CAAE 118; DLB 36, 100,
195

Tonna, Charlotte Elizabeth
1790-1846 .... **NCLC 135**
See also DLB 163

Tonson, Jacob fl. 1655(?)-1736 .... **LC 86**
See also DLB 170

Toole, John Kennedy 1937-1969 ..... **CLC 19,**
64
See also BPFB 3; CA 104; DLBY 1981;
MTCW 2; MTFW 2005

Toomer, Eugene
See Toomer, Jean

Toomer, Eugene Pinchback
See Toomer, Jean

Toomer, Jean 1894-1967 .. **BLC 3; CLC 1, 4,**
13, 22; HR 1:3; PC 7; SSC 1, 45;
TCLC 172; WLCS
See also AFAW 1, 2; AMWS 3, 9; BW 1;
CA 85-88; CDALB 1917-1929; DA3;
DAM MULT; DLB 45, 51; EWL 3; EXPP;
EXPS; LMFS 2; MAL 5; MTCW 1, 2;
MTFW 2005; NFS 11; RGAL 4; RGSF 2;
SSFS 5

Toomer, Nathan Jean
See Toomer, Jean

Toomer, Nathan Pinchback
See Toomer, Jean

Torley, Luke
See Blish, James (Benjamin)

Tornimparte, Alessandra
See Ginzburg, Natalia

Torre, Raoul della
See Mencken, H(enry) L(ouis)

Torrence, Ridgely 1874-1950 .... **TCLC 97**
See also DLB 54, 249; MAL 5

Torrey, E. Fuller 1937- .... **CLC 34**
See also CA 119; CANR 71, 158

Torrey, Edwin Fuller
See Torrey, E. Fuller

Torsvan, Ben Traven
See Traven, B.

Torsvan, Benno Traven
See Traven, B.

Torsvan, Berick Traven
See Traven, B.

Torsvan, Berwick Traven
See Traven, B.

Torsvan, Bruno Traven
See Traven, B.

Torsvan, Traven
See Traven, B.

Tourneur, Cyril 1575(?)-1626 .... **LC 66**
See also BRW 2; DAM DRAM; DLB 58;
RGEL 2

Tournier, Michel 1924- .... **CLC 6, 23, 36, 95;**
SSC 88
See also CA 49-52; CANR 3, 36, 74, 149;
CWW 2; DLB 83; EWL 3; GFL 1789 to
the Present; MTCW 1, 2; SATA 23

Tournier, Michel Edouard
See Tournier, Michel

Tournimparte, Alessandra
See Ginzburg, Natalia

Towers, Ivar
See Kornbluth, C(yril) M.

Towne, Robert (Burton) 1936(?)- ..... **CLC 87**
See also CA 108; DLB 44; IDFW 3, 4

Townsend, Sue .... **CLC 61**
See Townsend, Susan Lilian
See also AAYA 28; CA 127; CAAE 119;
CANR 65, 107; CBD; CD 5, 6; CPW;
CWD; DAB; DAC; DAM MST; DLB
271; INT CA-127; SATA 55, 93; SATA-
Brief 48; YAW

Townsend, Susan Lilian 1946-
See Townsend, Sue

Townshend, Pete
See Townshend, Peter (Dennis Blandford)

Townshend, Peter (Dennis Blandford)
1945- .... **CLC 17, 42**
See also CA 107

Tozzi, Federigo 1883-1920 .... **TCLC 31**
See also CA 160; CANR 110; DLB 264;
EWL 3; WLIT 7

Tracy, Don(ald Fiske) 1905-1970(?)
See Queen, Ellery
See also CA 1-4R; CAAS 176; CANR 2

Trafford, F. G.
See Riddell, Charlotte

Traherne, Thomas 1637(?)-1674 .. **LC 99; PC**
70
See also BRW 2; BRWS 11; DLB 131;
PAB; RGEL 2

Traill, Catharine Parr 1802-1899 .. **NCLC 31**
See also DLB 99

Trakl, Georg 1887-1914 .... **PC 20; TCLC 5**
See also CA 165; CAAE 104; EW 10; EWL
3; LMFS 2; MTCW 2; RGWL 2, 3

Trambley, Estela Portillo .... **TCLC 163**
See Portillo Trambley, Estela
See also CA 77-80; RGAL 4

Tranquilli, Secondino
See Silone, Ignazio

Transtroemer, Tomas Gosta
See Transtromer, Tomas (Goesta)

Transtromer, Tomas (Gosta)
See Transtromer, Tomas (Goesta)
See also CWW 2

Transtromer, Tomas (Goesta)
1931- .... **CLC 52, 65**
See Transtromer, Tomas (Gosta)
See also CA 129; 17; CAAE 117; CANR
115; DAM POET; DLB 257; EWL 3; PFS
21

Transtromer, Tomas Gosta
See Transtromer, Tomas (Goesta)

Traven, B. 1882(?)-1969 .... **CLC 8, 11**
See also CA 19-20; CAAS 25-28R; CAP 2;
DLB 9, 56; EWL 3; MTCW 1; RGAL 4

Trediakovsky, Vasilii Kirillovich
1703-1769 .... **LC 68**
See also DLB 150

Treitel, Jonathan 1959- .... **CLC 70**
See also CA 210; DLB 267

Trelawny, Edward John
1792-1881 .... **NCLC 85**
See also DLB 110, 116, 144

Tremain, Rose 1943- .... **CLC 42**
See also CA 97-100; CANR 44, 95; CN 4,
5, 6, 7; DLB 14, 271; RGSF 2; RHW

Tremblay, Michel 1942- .... **CLC 29, 102, 225**
See also CA 128; CAAE 116; CCA 1;
CWW 2; DAC; DAM MST; DLB 60;
EWL 3; GLL 1; MTCW 1, 2; MTFW
2005

Trevanian .... **CLC 29**
See Whitaker, Rod

Trevor, Glen
See Hilton, James

Trevor, William .. **CLC 7, 9, 14, 25, 71, 116;**
SSC 21, 58
See Cox, William Trevor
See also BRWS 4; CBD; CD 5, 6; CN 1, 2,
3, 4, 5, 6, 7; DLB 14, 139; EWL 3; LATS
1:2; RGEL 2; RGSF 2; SSFS 10; TCLE
1:2

Trifonov, Iurii (Valentinovich)
See Trifonov, Yuri (Valentinovich)
See also DLB 302; RGWL 2, 3

Trifonov, Yuri (Valentinovich)
1925-1981 .... **CLC 45**
See Trifonov, Iurii (Valentinovich); Tri-
fonov, Yury Valentinovich
See also CA 126; CAAS 103; MTCW 1

Trifonov, Yury Valentinovich
See Trifonov, Yuri (Valentinovich)
See also EWL 3

Trilling, Diana (Rubin) 1905-1996 . **CLC 129**
See also CA 5-8R; CAAS 154; CANR 10,
46; INT CANR-10; MTCW 1, 2

Trilling, Lionel 1905-1975 ..... **CLC 9, 11, 24;**
SSC 75
See also AMWS 3; CA 9-12R; CAAS 61-
64; CANR 10, 105; CN 1, 2; DLB 28, 63;
EWL 3; INT CANR-10; MAL 5; MTCW
1, 2; RGAL 4; TUS

3; EXPS; HGG; LAIT 3; MAL 5; MBL;
MTCW 1, 2; MTFW 2005; NFS 13, 15;
RGAL 4; RGSF 2; RHW; SSFS 2, 10;
TUS

Welty, Eudora Alice
See Welty, Eudora

Wen I-to 1899-1946 .... **TCLC 28**
See also EWL 3

Wentworth, Robert
See Hamilton, Edmond

Werfel, Franz (Viktor) 1890-1945 ... **TCLC 8**
See also CA 161; CAAE 104; DLB 81, 124;
EWL 3; RGWL 2, 3

Wergeland, Henrik Arnold
1808-1845 .... **NCLC 5**

Wersba, Barbara 1932- .... **CLC 30**
See also AAYA 2, 30; BYA 6, 12, 13; CA
182; 29-32R, 182; CANR 16, 38; CLR 3,
78; DLB 52; JRDA; MAICYA 1, 2; SAAS
2; SATA 1, 58; SATA-Essay 103; WYA;
YAW

Wertmueller, Lina 1928- .... **CLC 16**
See also CA 97-100; CANR 39, 78

Wescott, Glenway 1901-1987 .. **CLC 13; SSC
35**
See also CA 13-16R; CAAS 121; CANR
23, 70; CN 1, 2, 3, 4; DLB 4, 9, 102;
MAL 5; RGAL 4

Wesker, Arnold 1932- .... **CLC 3, 5, 42**
See also CA 1-4R; 7; CANR 1, 33; CBD;
CD 5, 6; CDBLB 1960 to Present; DAB;
DAM DRAM; DLB 13, 310, 319; EWL
3; MTCW 1; RGEL 2; TEA

Wesley, Charles 1707-1788 .... **LC 128**
See also DLB 95; RGEL 2

Wesley, John 1703-1791 .... **LC 88**
See also DLB 104

Wesley, Richard (Errol) 1945- .... **CLC 7**
See also BW 1; CA 57-60; CAD; CANR
27; CD 5, 6; DLB 38

Wessel, Johan Herman 1742-1785 .... **LC 7**
See also DLB 300

West, Anthony (Panther)
1914-1987 .... **CLC 50**
See also CA 45-48; CAAS 124; CANR 3,
19; CN 1, 2, 3, 4; DLB 15

West, C. P.
See Wodehouse, P(elham) G(renville)

West, Cornel 1953- .... **BLCS; CLC 134**
See also CA 144; CANR 91, 159; DLB 246

West, Cornel Ronald
See West, Cornel

West, Delno C(loyde), Jr. 1936- .... **CLC 70**
See also CA 57-60

West, Dorothy 1907-1998 ...... **HR 1:3; TCLC
108**
See also BW 2; CA 143; CAAS 169; DLB
76

West, (Mary) Jessamyn 1902-1984 ... **CLC 7,
17**
See also CA 9-12R; CAAS 112; CANR 27;
CN 1, 2, 3; DLB 6; DLBY 1984; MTCW
1, 2; RGAL 4; RHW; SATA-Obit 37;
TCWW 2; TUS; YAW

West, Morris L(anglo) 1916-1999 ..... **CLC 6,
33**
See also BPFB 3; CA 5-8R; CAAS 187;
CANR 24, 49, 64; CN 1, 2, 3, 4, 5, 6;
CPW; DLB 289; MTCW 1, 2; MTFW
2005

West, Nathanael 1903-1940 .. **SSC 16; TCLC
1, 14, 44**
See also AMW; AMWR 2; BPFB 3; CA
125; CAAE 104; CDALB 1929-1941;
DA3; DLB 4, 9, 28; EWL 3; MAL 5;
MTCW 1, 2; MTFW 2005; NFS 16;
RGAL 4; TUS

West, Owen
See Koontz, Dean R.

West, Paul 1930- .... **CLC 7, 14, 96, 226**
See also CA 13-16R; 7; CANR 22, 53, 76,
89, 136; CN 1, 2, 3, 4, 5, 6, 7; DLB 14;
INT CANR-22; MTCW 2; MTFW 2005

West, Rebecca 1892-1983 ... **CLC 7, 9, 31, 50**
See also BPFB 3; BRWS 3; CA 5-8R;
CAAS 109; CANR 19; CN 1, 2, 3; DLB
36; DLBY 1983; EWL 3; FW; MTCW 1,
2; MTFW 2005; NCFS 4; RGEL 2; TEA

Westall, Robert (Atkinson)
1929-1993 .... **CLC 17**
See also AAYA 12; BYA 2, 6, 7, 8, 9, 15;
CA 69-72; CAAS 141; CANR 18, 68;
CLR 13; FANT; JRDA; MAICYA 1, 2;
MAICYAS 1; SAAS 2; SATA 23, 69;
SATA-Obit 75; WYA; YAW

Westermarck, Edward 1862-1939 . **TCLC 87**

Westlake, Donald E. 1933- .... **CLC 7, 33**
See also BPFB 3; CA 17-20R; 13; CANR
16, 44, 65, 94, 137; CMW 4; CPW; DAM
POP; INT CANR-16; MSW; MTCW 2;
MTFW 2005

Westlake, Donald Edwin
See Westlake, Donald E.

Westmacott, Mary
See Christie, Agatha (Mary Clarissa)

Weston, Allen
See Norton, Andre

Wetcheek, J. L.
See Feuchtwanger, Lion

Wetering, Janwillem van de
See van de Wetering, Janwillem

Wetherald, Agnes Ethelwyn
1857-1940 .... **TCLC 81**
See also CA 202; DLB 99

Wetherell, Elizabeth
See Warner, Susan (Bogert)

Whale, James 1889-1957 .... **TCLC 63**
See also AAYA 75

Whalen, Philip (Glenn) 1923-2002 .... **CLC 6,
29**
See also BG 1:3; CA 9-12R; CAAS 209;
CANR 5, 39; CP 1, 2, 3, 4, 5, 6, 7; DLB
16; WP

Wharton, Edith (Newbold Jones)
1862-1937 ... **SSC 6, 84; TCLC 3, 9, 27,
53, 129, 149; WLC 6**
See also AAYA 25; AMW; AMWC 2;
AMWR 1; BPFB 3; CA 132; CAAE 104;
CDALB 1865-1917; DA; DA3; DAB;
DAC; DAM MST, NOV; DLB 4, 9, 12,
78, 189; DLBD 13; EWL 3; EXPS; FL
1:6; GL 3; HGG; LAIT 2, 3; LATS 1:1;
MAL 5; MBL; MTCW 1, 2; MTFW 2005;
NFS 5, 11, 15, 20; RGAL 4; RGSF 2;
RHW; SSFS 6, 7; SUFW; TUS

Wharton, James
See Mencken, H(enry) L(ouis)

Wharton, William (a pseudonym)
1925- .... **CLC 18, 37**
See also CA 93-96; CN 4, 5, 6, 7; DLBY
1980; INT CA-93-96

Wheatley (Peters), Phillis
1753(?)-1784 ... **BLC 3; LC 3, 50; PC 3;
WLC 6**
See also AFAW 1, 2; CDALB 1640-1865;
DA; DA3; DAC; DAM MST, MULT,
POET; DLB 31, 50; EXPP; FL 1:1; PFS
13; RGAL 4

Wheelock, John Hall 1886-1978 .... **CLC 14**
See also CA 13-16R; CAAS 77-80; CANR
14; CP 1, 2; DLB 45; MAL 5

Whim-Wham
See Curnow, (Thomas) Allen (Monro)

Whisp, Kennilworthy
See Rowling, J.K.

Whitaker, Rod 1931-2005
See Trevanian
See also CA 29-32R; CAAS 246; CANR
45, 153; CMW 4

White, Babington
See Braddon, Mary Elizabeth

White, E. B. 1899-1985 .... **CLC 10, 34, 39**
See also AAYA 62; AITN 2; AMWS 1; CA
13-16R; CAAS 116; CANR 16, 37;
CDALBS; CLR 1, 21, 107; CPW; DA3;
DAM POP; DLB 11, 22; EWL 3; FANT;
MAICYA 1, 2; MAL 5; MTCW 1, 2;
MTFW 2005; NCFS 5; RGAL 4; SATA 2,
29, 100; SATA-Obit 44; TUS

White, Edmund 1940- .... **CLC 27, 110**
See also AAYA 7; CA 45-48; CANR 3, 19,
36, 62, 107, 133; CN 5, 6, 7; DA3; DAM
POP; DLB 227; MTCW 1, 2; MTFW
2005

White, Elwyn Brooks
See White, E. B.

White, Hayden V. 1928- .... **CLC 148**
See also CA 128; CANR 135; DLB 246

White, Patrick (Victor Martindale)
1912-1990 ...... **CLC 3, 4, 5, 7, 9, 18, 65,
69; SSC 39; TCLC 176**
See also BRWS 1; CA 81-84; CAAS 132;
CANR 43; CN 1, 2, 3, 4; DLB 260, 332;
EWL 3; MTCW 1; RGEL 2; RGSF 2;
RHW; TWA; WWE 1

White, Phyllis Dorothy James 1920-
See James, P. D.
See also CA 21-24R; CANR 17, 43, 65,
112; CMW 4; CN 7; CPW; DA3; DAM
POP; MTCW 1, 2; MTFW 2005; TEA

White, T(erence) H(anbury)
1906-1964 .... **CLC 30**
See also AAYA 22; BPFB 3; BYA 4, 5; CA
73-76; CANR 37; DLB 160; FANT;
JRDA; LAIT 1; MAICYA 1, 2; RGEL 2;
SATA 12; SUFW 1; YAW

White, Terence de Vere 1912-1994 ... **CLC 49**
See also CA 49-52; CAAS 145; CANR 3

White, Walter
See White, Walter F(rancis)

White, Walter F(rancis) 1893-1955 ... **BLC 3;
HR 1:3; TCLC 15**
See also BW 1; CA 124; CAAE 115; DAM
MULT; DLB 51

White, William Hale 1831-1913
See Rutherford, Mark
See also CA 189; CAAE 121

Whitehead, Alfred North
1861-1947 .... **TCLC 97**
See also CA 165; CAAE 117; DLB 100,
262

Whitehead, Colson 1970- .... **CLC 232**
See also CA 202

Whitehead, E(dward) A(nthony)
1933- .... **CLC 5**
See Whitehead, Ted
See also CA 65-68; CANR 58, 118; CBD;
CD 5; DLB 310

Whitehead, Ted
See Whitehead, E(dward) A(nthony)
See also CD 6

Whiteman, Roberta J. Hill 1947- ...... **NNAL**
See also CA 146

Whitemore, Hugh (John) 1936- .... **CLC 37**
See also CA 132; CANR 77; CBD; CD 5,
6; INT CA-132

Whitman, Sarah Helen (Power)
1803-1878 .... **NCLC 19**
See also DLB 1, 243

Whitman, Walt(er) 1819-1892 .. **NCLC 4, 31,
81; PC 3; WLC 6**
See also AAYA 42; AMW; AMWR 1;
CDALB 1640-1865; DA; DA3; DAB;
DAC; DAM MST, POET; DLB 3, 64,

224, 250; EXPP; LAIT 2; LMFS 1; PAB;
PFS 2, 3, 13, 22; RGAL 4; SATA 20;
TUS; WP; WYAS 1

Whitney, Isabella fl. 1565-fl. 1575 ..... **LC 130**
See also DLB 136

Whitney, Phyllis A(yame) 1903- .... **CLC 42**
See also AAYA 36; AITN 2; BEST 90:3;
CA 1-4R; CANR 3, 25, 38, 60; CLR 59;
CMW 4; CPW; DA3; DAM POP; JRDA;
MAICYA 1, 2; MTCW 2; RHW; SATA 1,
30; YAW

Whittemore, (Edward) Reed, Jr.
1919- .... **CLC 4**
See also CA 219; 9-12R, 219; 8; CANR 4,
119; CP 1, 2, 3, 4, 5, 6, 7; DLB 5; MAL
5

Whittier, John Greenleaf
1807-1892 .... **NCLC 8, 59**
See also AMWS 1; DLB 1, 243; RGAL 4

Whittlebot, Hernia
See Coward, Noel (Peirce)

Wicker, Thomas Grey 1926-
See Wicker, Tom
See also CA 65-68; CANR 21, 46, 141

Wicker, Tom .... **CLC 7**
See Wicker, Thomas Grey

Wideman, John Edgar 1941- ... **BLC 3; CLC
5, 34, 36, 67, 122; SSC 62**
See also AFAW 1, 2; AMWS 10; BPFB 4;
BW 2, 3; CA 85-88; CANR 14, 42, 67,
109, 140; CN 4, 5, 6, 7; DAM MULT;
DLB 33, 143; MAL 5; MTCW 2; MTFW
2005; RGAL 4; RGSF 2; SSFS 6, 12, 24;
TCLE 1:2

Wiebe, Rudy 1934- .... **CLC 6, 11, 14, 138**
See also CA 37-40R; CANR 42, 67, 123;
CN 1, 2, 3, 4, 5, 6, 7; DAC; DAM MST;
DLB 60; RHW; SATA 156

Wiebe, Rudy Henry
See Wiebe, Rudy

Wieland, Christoph Martin
1733-1813 .... **NCLC 17, 177**
See also DLB 97; EW 4; LMFS 1; RGWL
2, 3

Wiene, Robert 1881-1938 .... **TCLC 56**

Wieners, John 1934- .... **CLC 7**
See also BG 1:3; CA 13-16R; CP 1, 2, 3, 4,
5, 6, 7; DLB 16; WP

Wiesel, Elie 1928- ...... **CLC 3, 5, 11, 37, 165;
WLCS**
See also AAYA 7, 54; AITN 1; CA 5-8R; 4;
CANR 8, 40, 65, 125; CDALBS; CWW
2; DA; DA3; DAB; DAC; DAM MST,
NOV; DLB 83, 299; DLBY 1987; EWL
3; INT CANR-8; LAIT 4; MTCW 1, 2;
MTFW 2005; NCFS 4; NFS 4; RGHL;
RGWL 3; SATA 56; YAW

Wiesel, Eliezer
See Wiesel, Elie

Wiggins, Marianne 1947- .... **CLC 57**
See also AAYA 70; BEST 89:3; CA 130;
CANR 60, 139; CN 7

Wigglesworth, Michael 1631-1705 .... **LC 106**
See also DLB 24; RGAL 4

Wiggs, Susan .... **CLC 70**
See also CA 201

Wight, James Alfred 1916-1995
See Herriot, James
See also CA 77-80; SATA 55; SATA-Brief
44

Wilbur, Richard 1921- .. **CLC 3, 6, 9, 14, 53,
110; PC 51**
See also AAYA 72; AMWS 3; CA 1-4R;
CABS 2; CANR 2, 29, 76, 93, 139;
CDALBS; CP 1, 2, 3, 4, 5, 6, 7; DA;
DAB; DAC; DAM MST, POET; DLB 5,
169; EWL 3; EXPP; INT CANR-29;
MAL 5; MTCW 1, 2; MTFW 2005; PAB;
PFS 11, 12, 16; RGAL 4; SATA 9, 108;
WP

Wilbur, Richard Purdy
See Wilbur, Richard

Wild, Peter 1940- .... **CLC 14**
See also CA 37-40R; CP 1, 2, 3, 4, 5, 6, 7;
DLB 5

Wilde, Oscar (Fingal O'Flahertie Wills)
1854(?)-1900 .... **DC 17; SSC 11, 77;
TCLC 1, 8, 23, 41, 175; WLC 6**
See also AAYA 49; BRW 5; BRWC 1, 2;
BRWR 2; BYA 15; CA 119; CAAE 104;
CANR 112; CDBLB 1890-1914; CLR
114; DA; DA3; DAB; DAC; DAM
DRAM, MST, NOV; DFS 4, 8, 9, 21;
DLB 10, 19, 34, 57, 141, 156, 190; EXPS;
FANT; GL 3; LATS 1:1; NFS 20; RGEL
2; RGSF 2; SATA 24; SSFS 7; SUFW;
TEA; WCH; WLIT 4

Wilder, Billy .... **CLC 20**
See Wilder, Samuel
See also AAYA 66; DLB 26

Wilder, Samuel 1906-2002
See Wilder, Billy
See also CA 89-92; CAAS 205

Wilder, Stephen
See Marlowe, Stephen

Wilder, Thornton (Niven)
1897-1975 .. **CLC 1, 5, 6, 10, 15, 35, 82;
DC 1, 24; WLC 6**
See also AAYA 29; AITN 2; AMW; CA 13-
16R; CAAS 61-64; CAD; CANR 40, 132;
CDALBS; CN 1, 2; DA; DA3; DAB;
DAC; DAM DRAM, MST, NOV; DFS 1,
4, 16; DLB 4, 7, 9, 228; DLBY 1997;
EWL 3; LAIT 3; MAL 5; MTCW 1, 2;
MTFW 2005; NFS 24; RGAL 4; RHW;
WYAS 1

Wilding, Michael 1942- ...... **CLC 73; SSC 50**
See also CA 104; CANR 24, 49, 106; CN
4, 5, 6, 7; DLB 325; RGSF 2

Wiley, Richard 1944- .... **CLC 44**
See also CA 129; CAAE 121; CANR 71

Wilhelm, Kate .... **CLC 7**
See Wilhelm, Katie
See also AAYA 20; BYA 16; CA 5; DLB 8;
INT CANR-17; SCFW 2

Wilhelm, Katie 1928-
See Wilhelm, Kate
See also CA 37-40R; CANR 17, 36, 60, 94;
MTCW 1; SFW 4

Wilkins, Mary
See Freeman, Mary E(leanor) Wilkins

Willard, Nancy 1936- .... **CLC 7, 37**
See also BYA 5; CA 89-92; CANR 10, 39,
68, 107, 152; CLR 5; CP 2, 3, 4, 5; CWP;
CWRI 5; DLB 5, 52; FANT; MAICYA 1,
2; MTCW 1; SATA 37, 71, 127; SATA-
Brief 30; SUFW 2; TCLE 1:2

William of Malmesbury c. 1090B.C.-c.
1140B.C. .... **CMLC 57**

William of Ockham 1290-1349 ..... **CMLC 32**

Williams, Ben Ames 1889-1953 ..... **TCLC 89**
See also CA 183; DLB 102

Williams, Charles
See Collier, James Lincoln

Williams, Charles (Walter Stansby)
1886-1945 .... **TCLC 1, 11**
See also BRWS 9; CA 163; CAAE 104;
DLB 100, 153, 255; FANT; RGEL 2;
SUFW 1

Williams, C.K. 1936- .... **CLC 33, 56, 148**
See also CA 37-40R; 26; CANR 57, 106;
CP 1, 2, 3, 4, 5, 6, 7; DAM POET; DLB
5; MAL 5

Williams, Ella Gwendolen Rees
See Rhys, Jean

Williams, (George) Emlyn
1905-1987 .... **CLC 15**
See also CA 104; CAAS 123; CANR 36;
DAM DRAM; DLB 10, 77; IDTP;
MTCW 1

Williams, Hank 1923-1953 .... **TCLC 81**
See Williams, Hiram King

Williams, Helen Maria
1761-1827 .... **NCLC 135**
See also DLB 158

Williams, Hiram Hank
See Williams, Hank

Williams, Hiram King
See Williams, Hank
See also CA 188

Williams, Hugo (Mordaunt) 1942- ... **CLC 42**
See also CA 17-20R; CANR 45, 119; CP 1,
2, 3, 4, 5, 6, 7; DLB 40

Williams, J. Walker
See Wodehouse, P(elham) G(renville)

Williams, John A(lfred) 1925- . **BLC 3; CLC
5, 13**
See also AFAW 2; BW 2, 3; CA 195; 53-
56, 195; 3; CANR 6, 26, 51, 118; CN 1,
2, 3, 4, 5, 6, 7; CSW; DAM MULT; DLB
2, 33; EWL 3; INT CANR-6; MAL 5;
RGAL 4; SFW 4

Williams, Jonathan (Chamberlain)
1929- .... **CLC 13**
See also CA 9-12R; 12; CANR 8, 108; CP
1, 2, 3, 4, 5, 6, 7; DLB 5

Williams, Joy 1944- .... **CLC 31**
See also CA 41-44R; CANR 22, 48, 97

Williams, Norman 1952- .... **CLC 39**
See also CA 118

Williams, Roger 1603(?)-1683 .... **LC 129**
See also DLB 24

Williams, Sherley Anne 1944-1999 ... **BLC 3;
CLC 89**
See also AFAW 2; BW 2, 3; CA 73-76;
CAAS 185; CANR 25, 82; DAM MULT;
POET; DLB 41; INT CANR-25; SATA
78; SATA-Obit 116

Williams, Shirley
See Williams, Sherley Anne

Williams, Tennessee 1911-1983 . **CLC 1, 2, 5,
7, 8, 11, 15, 19, 30, 39, 45, 71, 111; DC
4; SSC 81; WLC 6**
See also AAYA 31; AITN 1, 2; AMW;
AMWC 1; CA 5-8R; CAAS 108; CABS
3; CAD; CANR 31, 132; CDALB 1941-
1968; CN 1, 2, 3; DA; DA3; DAB; DAC;
DAM DRAM, MST; DFS 17; DLB 7;
DLBD 4; DLBY 1983; EWL 3; GLL 1;
LAIT 4; LATS 1:2; MAL 5; MTCW 1, 2;
MTFW 2005; RGAL 4; TUS

Williams, Thomas (Alonzo)
1926-1990 .... **CLC 14**
See also CA 1-4R; CAAS 132; CANR 2

Williams, William C.
See Williams, William Carlos

Williams, William Carlos
1883-1963 ..... **CLC 1, 2, 5, 9, 13, 22, 42,
67; PC 7; SSC 31; WLC 6**
See also AAYA 46; AMW; AMWR 1; CA
89-92; CANR 34; CDALB 1917-1929;
DA; DA3; DAB; DAC; DAM MST,
POET; DLB 4, 16, 54, 86; EWL 3; EXPP;
MAL 5; MTCW 1, 2; MTFW 2005; NCFS
4; PAB; PFS 1, 6, 11; RGAL 4; RGSF 2;
TUS; WP

Williamson, David (Keith) 1942- ..... **CLC 56**
See also CA 103; CANR 41; CD 5, 6; DLB
289

Williamson, Ellen Douglas 1905-1984
See Douglas, Ellen
See also CA 17-20R; CAAS 114; CANR 39

Williamson, Jack .... **CLC 29**
See Williamson, John Stewart
See also CA 8; DLB 8; SCFW 1, 2

Williamson, John Stewart 1908-2006
See Williamson, Jack
See also CA 17-20R; CANR 23, 70, 153;
SFW 4

Willie, Frederick
   See Lovecraft, H. P.
Willingham, Calder (Baynard, Jr.)
   1922-1995 .... CLC 5, 51
   See also CA 5-8R; CAAS 147; CANR 3;
   CN 1, 2, 3, 4, 5; CSW; DLB 2, 44; IDFW
   3, 4; MTCW 1
Willis, Charles
   See Clarke, Arthur C.
Willy
   See Colette, (Sidonie-Gabrielle)
Willy, Colette
   See Colette, (Sidonie-Gabrielle)
   See also GLL 1
Wilmot, John 1647-1680 .... LC 75; PC 66
   See Rochester
   See also BRW 2; DLB 131; PAB
Wilson, A.N. 1950- .... CLC 33
   See also BRWS 6; CA 122; CAAE 112;
   CANR 156; CN 4, 5, 6, 7; DLB 14, 155,
   194; MTCW 2
Wilson, Andrew Norman
   See Wilson, A.N.
Wilson, Angus (Frank Johnstone)
   1913-1991 . CLC 2, 3, 5, 25, 34; SSC 21
   See also BRWS 1; CA 5-8R; CAAS 134;
   CANR 21; CN 1, 2, 3, 4; DLB 15, 139,
   155; EWL 3; MTCW 1, 2; MTFW 2005;
   RGEL 2; RGSF 2
Wilson, August 1945-2005 .. BLC 3; CLC 39,
   50, 63, 118, 222; DC 2; WLCS
   See also AAYA 16; AFAW 2; AMWS 8; BW
   2, 3; CA 122; CAAE 115; CAAS 244;
   CAD; CANR 42, 54, 76, 128; CD 5, 6;
   DA; DA3; DAB; DAC; DAM DRAM,
   MST, MULT; DFS 3, 7, 15, 17; DLB 228;
   EWL 3; LAIT 4; LATS 1:2; MAL 5;
   MTCW 1, 2; MTFW 2005; RGAL 4
Wilson, Brian 1942- .... CLC 12
Wilson, Colin (Henry) 1931- .... CLC 3, 14
   See also CA 1-4R; 5; CANR 1, 22, 33, 77;
   CMW 4; CN 1, 2, 3, 4, 5, 6; DLB 14, 194;
   HGG; MTCW 1; SFW 4
Wilson, Dirk
   See Pohl, Frederik
Wilson, Edmund 1895-1972 .. CLC 1, 2, 3, 8,
   24
   See also AMW; CA 1-4R; CAAS 37-40R;
   CANR 1, 46, 110; CN 1; DLB 63; EWL
   3; MAL 5; MTCW 1, 2; MTFW 2005;
   RGAL 4; TUS
Wilson, Ethel Davis (Bryant)
   1888(?)-1980 .... CLC 13
   See also CA 102; CN 1, 2; DAC; DAM
   POET; DLB 68; MTCW 1; RGEL 2
Wilson, Harriet
   See Wilson, Harriet E. Adams
   See also DLB 239
Wilson, Harriet E.
   See Wilson, Harriet E. Adams
   See also DLB 243
Wilson, Harriet E. Adams
   1827(?)-1863(?) .... BLC 3; NCLC 78
   See Wilson, Harriet; Wilson, Harriet E.
   See also DAM MULT; DLB 50
Wilson, John 1785-1854 .... NCLC 5
Wilson, John (Anthony) Burgess 1917-1993
   See Burgess, Anthony
   See also CA 1-4R; CAAS 143; CANR 2,
   46; DA3; DAC; DAM NOV; MTCW 1,
   2; MTFW 2005; NFS 15; TEA
Wilson, Katharina .... CLC 65
Wilson, Lanford 1937- .. CLC 7, 14, 36, 197;
   DC 19
   See also CA 17-20R; CABS 3; CAD; CANR
   45, 96; CD 5, 6; DAM DRAM; DFS 4, 9,
   12, 16, 20; DLB 7; EWL 3; MAL 5; TUS

Wilson, Robert M. 1941- .... CLC 7, 9
   See also CA 49-52; CAD; CANR 2, 41; CD
   5, 6; MTCW 1
Wilson, Robert McLiam 1964- .... CLC 59
   See also CA 132; DLB 267
Wilson, Sloan 1920-2003 .... CLC 32
   See also CA 1-4R; CAAS 216; CANR 1,
   44; CN 1, 2, 3, 4, 5, 6
Wilson, Snoo 1948- .... CLC 33
   See also CA 69-72; CBD; CD 5, 6
Wilson, William S(mith) 1932- .... CLC 49
   See also CA 81-84
Wilson, (Thomas) Woodrow
   1856-1924 .... TCLC 79
   See also CA 166; DLB 47
Winchilsea, Anne (Kingsmill) Finch
   1661-1720
   See Finch, Anne
   See also RGEL 2
Winckelmann, Johann Joachim
   1717-1768 .... LC 129
   See also DLB 97
Windham, Basil
   See Wodehouse, P(elham) G(renville)
Wingrove, David 1954- .... CLC 68
   See also CA 133; SFW 4
Winnemucca, Sarah 1844-1891 .... NCLC 79;
   NNAL
   See also DAM MULT; DLB 175; RGAL 4
Winstanley, Gerrard 1609-1676 .... LC 52
Wintergreen, Jane
   See Duncan, Sara Jeannette
Winters, Arthur Yvor
   See Winters, Yvor
Winters, Janet Lewis .... CLC 41
   See Lewis, Janet
   See also DLBY 1987
Winters, Yvor 1900-1968 .... CLC 4, 8, 32
   See also AMWS 2; CA 11-12; CAAS 25-
   28R; CAP 1; DLB 48; EWL 3; MAL 5;
   MTCW 1; RGAL 4
Winterson, Jeanette 1959- .... CLC 64, 158
   See also BRWS 4; CA 136; CANR 58, 116;
   CN 5, 6, 7; CPW; DA3; DAM POP; DLB
   207, 261; FANT; FW; GLL 1; MTCW 2;
   MTFW 2005; RHW
Winthrop, John 1588-1649 .... LC 31, 107
   See also DLB 24, 30
Wirth, Louis 1897-1952 .... TCLC 92
   See also CA 210
Wiseman, Frederick 1930- .... CLC 20
   See also CA 159
Wister, Owen 1860-1938 .... TCLC 21
   See also BPFB 3; CA 162; CAAE 108;
   DLB 9, 78, 186; RGAL 4; SATA 62;
   TCWW 1, 2
Wither, George 1588-1667 .... LC 96
   See also DLB 121; RGEL 2
Witkacy
   See Witkiewicz, Stanislaw Ignacy
Witkiewicz, Stanislaw Ignacy
   1885-1939 .... TCLC 8
   See also CA 162; CAAE 105; CDWLB 4;
   DLB 215; EW 10; EWL 3; RGWL 2, 3;
   SFW 4
Wittgenstein, Ludwig (Josef Johann)
   1889-1951 .... TCLC 59
   See also CA 164; CAAE 113; DLB 262;
   MTCW 2
Wittig, Monique 1935-2003 .... CLC 22
   See also CA 135; CAAE 116; CAAS 212;
   CANR 143; CWW 2; DLB 83; EWL 3;
   FW; GLL 1
Wittlin, Jozef 1896-1976 .... CLC 25
   See also CA 49-52; CAAS 65-68; CANR 3;
   EWL 3

Wodehouse, P(elham) G(renville)
   1881-1975 . CLC 1, 2, 5, 10, 22; SSC 2;
   TCLC 108
   See also AAYA 65; AITN 2; BRWS 3; CA
   45-48; CAAS 57-60; CANR 3, 33; CD-
   BLB 1914-1945; CN 1, 2; CPW 1; DA3;
   DAB; DAC; DAM NOV; DLB 34, 162;
   EWL 3; MTCW 1, 2; MTFW 2005; RGEL
   2; RGSF 2; SATA 22; SSFS 10
Woiwode, L.
   See Woiwode, Larry (Alfred)
Woiwode, Larry (Alfred) 1941- ... CLC 6, 10
   See also CA 73-76; CANR 16, 94; CN 3, 4,
   5, 6, 7; DLB 6; INT CANR-16
Wojciechowska, Maia (Teresa)
   1927-2002 .... CLC 26
   See also AAYA 8, 46; BYA 3; CA 183;
   9-12R, 183; CAAS 209; CANR 4, 41;
   CLR 1; JRDA; MAICYA 1, 2; SAAS 1;
   SATA 1, 28, 83; SATA-Essay 104; SATA-
   Obit 134; YAW
Wojtyla, Karol (Jozef)
   See John Paul II, Pope
Wojtyla, Karol (Josef)
   See John Paul II, Pope
Wolf, Christa 1929- .... CLC 14, 29, 58, 150
   See also CA 85-88; CANR 45, 123; CD-
   WLB 2; CWW 2; DLB 75; EWL 3; FW;
   MTCW 1; RGWL 2, 3; SSFS 14
Wolf, Naomi 1962- .... CLC 157
   See also CA 141; CANR 110; FW; MTFW
   2005
Wolfe, Gene 1931- .... CLC 25
   See also AAYA 35; CA 57-60; 9; CANR 6,
   32, 60, 152; CPW; DAM POP; DLB 8;
   FANT; MTCW 2; MTFW 2005; SATA
   118, 165; SCFW 2; SFW 4; SUFW 2
Wolfe, Gene Rodman
   See Wolfe, Gene
Wolfe, George C. 1954- .... BLCS; CLC 49
   See also CA 149; CAD; CD 5, 6
Wolfe, Thomas (Clayton)
   1900-1938 ...... SSC 33; TCLC 4, 13, 29,
   61; WLC 6
   See also AMW; BPFB 3; CA 132; CAAE
   104; CANR 102; CDALB 1929-1941;
   DA; DA3; DAB; DAC; DAM MST, NOV;
   DLB 9, 102, 229; DLBD 2, 16; DLBY
   1985, 1997; EWL 3; MAL 5; MTCW 1,
   2; NFS 18; RGAL 4; SSFS 18; TUS
Wolfe, Thomas Kennerly, Jr.
   1931- .... CLC 147
   See Wolfe, Tom
   See also CA 13-16R; CANR 9, 33, 70, 104;
   DA3; DAM POP; DLB 185; EWL 3; INT
   CANR-9; MTCW 1, 2; MTFW 2005; TUS
Wolfe, Tom .... CLC 1, 2, 9, 15, 35, 51
   See Wolfe, Thomas Kennerly, Jr.
   See also AAYA 8, 67; AITN 2; AMWS 3;
   BEST 89:1; BPFB 3; CN 5, 6, 7; CPW;
   CSW; DLB 152; LAIT 5; RGAL 4
Wolff, Geoffrey 1937- .... CLC 41
   See also CA 29-32R; CANR 29, 43, 78, 154
Wolff, Geoffrey Ansell
   See Wolff, Geoffrey
Wolff, Sonia
   See Levitin, Sonia (Wolff)
Wolff, Tobias 1945- .... CLC 39, 64, 172; SSC
   63
   See also AAYA 16; AMWS 7; BEST 90:2;
   BYA 12; CA 117; 22; CAAE 114; CANR
   54, 76, 96; CN 5, 6, 7; CSW; DA3; DLB
   130; EWL 3; INT CA 117; MTCW 2;
   MTFW 2005; RGAL 4; RGSF 2; SSFS 4,
   11
Wolitzer, Hilma 1930- .... CLC 17
   See also CA 65-68; CANR 18, 40; INT
   CANR-18; SATA 31; YAW

Literary Criticism Series
Cumulative Topic Index

Topic Index

This index lists all topic entries in Thompson Gale's *Children's Literature Review* (CLR), *Classical and Medieval Literature Criticism* (CMLC), *Contemporary Literary Criticism* (CLC), *Drama Criticism* (DC), *Literature Criticism from 1400 to 1800* (LC), *Nineteenth-Century Literature Criticism* (NCLC), *Short Story Criticism* (SSC), and *Twentieth-Century Literary Criticism* (TCLC). The index also lists topic entries in the Gale Critical Companion Collection, which includes the following publications: *The Beat Generation* (BG), *Feminism in Literature* (FL), *Gothic Literature* (GL), and *Harlem Renaissance* (HR).

Topic Index

Topic Index

Topic Index

TCLC Cumulative Nationality Index

JAMAICAN

De Lisser, H(erbert) G(eorge) **12**
Garvey, Marcus (Moziah Jr.) **41**
Mais, Roger **8**
Redcam, Tom **25**

JAPANESE

Abé, Kōbō **131**
Akutagawa Ryunosuke **16**
Dazai Osamu **11**
Endō, Shūsaku **152**
Futabatei, Shimei **44**
Hagiwara, Sakutaro **60**
Hayashi, Fumiko **27**
Ishikawa, Takuboku **15**
Kunikida, Doppo **99**
Masaoka, Shiki **18**
Mishima, Yukio **161**
Miyamoto, (Chujo) Yuriko **37**
Miyazawa, Kenji **76**
Mizoguchi, Kenji **72**
Mori Ogai **14**
Nagai, Kafu **51**
Nishida, Kitaro **83**
Noguchi, Yone **80**
Santoka, Taneda **72**
Shiga, Naoya **172**
Shimazaki Toson **5**
Suzuki, Daisetz Teitaro **109**
Yokomitsu, Riichi **47**
Yosano Akiko **59**

LATVIAN

Berlin, Isaiah **105**
Rainis, Jānis **29**

LEBANESE

Gibran, Kahlil **1, 9**

LESOTHAN

Mofolo, Thomas (Mokopu) **22**

LITHUANIAN

Kreve (Mickevicius), Vincas **27**

MARTINIQUE

Fanon, Frantz **188**

MEXICAN

Azuela, Mariano **3**
Gamboa, Federico **36**
Garro, Elena **153**
Gonzalez Martinez, Enrique **72**
Ibargüengoitia, Jorge **148**
Nervo, (Jose) Amado (Ruiz de) **11**
Reyes, Alfonso **33**
Romero, José Rubén **14**
Villaurrutia, Xavier **80**

NEPALI

Devkota, Laxmiprasad **23**

NEW ZEALANDER

Mander, (Mary) Jane **31**
Mansfield, Katherine **2, 8, 39, 164**

NICARAGUAN

Darío, Rubén **4**

NIGERIAN

Okigbo, Christopher **171**
Tutuola, Amos **188**

NORWEGIAN

Bjoernson, Bjoernstjerne (Martinius) **7, 37**
Bojer, Johan **64**
Grieg, (Johan) Nordahl (Brun) **10**

Hamsun, Knut **151**
Ibsen, Henrik (Johan) **2, 8, 16, 37, 52**
Kielland, Alexander Lange **5**
Lie, Jonas (Lauritz Idemil) **5**
Obstfelder, Sigbjoern **23**
Skram, Amalie (Bertha) **25**
Undset, Sigrid **3**

PAKISTANI

Iqbal, Muhammad **28**

PERUVIAN

Arguedas, José María **147**
Palma, Ricardo **29**
Vallejo, César (Abraham) **3, 56**

POLISH

Asch, Sholem **3**
Borowski, Tadeusz **9**
Conrad, Joseph **1, 6, 13, 25, 43, 57**
Herbert, Zbigniew **168**
Peretz, Isaac Loeb **16**
Prus, Boleslaw **48**
Przybyszewski, Stanislaw **36**
Reymont, Wladyslaw (Stanislaw) **5**
Schulz, Bruno **5, 51**
Sienkiewicz, Henryk (Adam Alexander Pius) **3**
Singer, Israel Joshua **33**
Witkiewicz, Stanislaw Ignacy **8**

PORTUGUESE

Pessoa, Fernando (António Nogueira) **27**
Sa-Carniero, Mario de **83**

PUERTO RICAN

Hostos (y Bonilla), Eugenio Maria de **24**

ROMANIAN

Bacovia, George **24**
Caragiale, Ion Luca **76**
Rebreanu, Liviu **28**

RUSSIAN

Adamov, Arthur **189**
Aldanov, Mark (Alexandrovich) **23**
Andreyev, Leonid (Nikolaevich) **3**
Annensky, Innokenty (Fyodorovich) **14**
Artsybashev, Mikhail (Petrovich) **31**
Babel, Isaak (Emmanuilovich) **2, 13, 171**
Bagritsky, Eduard **60**
Bakhtin, Mikhail **160**
Balmont, Konstantin (Dmitriyevich) **11**
Bely, Andrey **7**
Berdyaev, Nikolai (Aleksandrovich) **67**
Bergelson, David **81**
Blok, Alexander (Alexandrovich) **5**
Bryusov, Valery Yakovlevich **10**
Bulgakov, Mikhail (Afanas'evich) **2, 16, 159**
Bulgya, Alexander Alexandrovich **53**
Bunin, Ivan Alexeyevich **6**
Chekhov, Anton (Pavlovich) **3, 10, 31, 55, 96, 163**
Der Nister **56**
Eisenstein, Sergei (Mikhailovich) **57**
Esenin, Sergei (Alexandrovich) **4**
Fadeyev, Alexander **53**
Gladkov, Fyodor (Vasilyevich) **27**
Gumilev, Nikolai (Stepanovich) **60**
Gurdjieff, G(eorgei) I(vanovich) **71**
Guro, Elena **56**
Hippius, Zinaida **9**
Ilf, Ilya **21**
Ivanov, Vyacheslav Ivanovich **33**
Kandinsky, Wassily **92**
Khlebnikov, Velimir **20**
Khodasevich, Vladislav (Felitsianovich) **15**
Klimentov, Andrei Platonovich **14**
Korolenko, Vladimir Galaktionovich **22**

Kropotkin, Peter (Aleksieevich) **36**
Kuprin, Aleksander Ivanovich **5**
Kuzmin, Mikhail **40**
Lenin, V. I. **67**
Mandelstam, Osip (Emilievich) **2, 6**
Mayakovski, Vladimir (Vladimirovich) **4, 18**
Merezhkovsky, Dmitry Sergeyevich **29**
Nabokov, Vladimir (Vladimirovich) **108, 189**
Olesha, Yuri **136**
Pasternak, Boris **188**
Pavlov, Ivan Petrovich **91**
Petrov, Evgeny **21**
Pilnyak, Boris **23**
Prishvin, Mikhail **75**
Remizov, Aleksei (Mikhailovich) **27**
Rozanov, Vassili **104**
Shestov, Lev **56**
Sologub, Fyodor **9**
Stalin, Joseph **92**
Stanislavsky, Konstantin **167**
Tolstoy, Alexey Nikolaevich **18**
Tolstoy, Leo (Nikolaevich) **4, 11, 17, 28, 44, 79, 173**
Trotsky, Leon **22**
Tsvetaeva (Efron), Marina (Ivanovna) **7, 35**
Zabolotsky, Nikolai Alekseevich **52**
Zamyatin, Evgeny Ivanovich **8, 37**
Zhdanov, Andrei Alexandrovich **18**
Zoshchenko, Mikhail (Mikhailovich) **15**

SCOTTISH

Barrie, J(ames) M(atthew) **2, 164**
Brown, George Douglas **28**
Buchan, John **41**
Cunninghame Graham, Robert (Gallnigad) Bontine **19**
Davidson, John **24**
Doyle, Arthur Conan **7**
Frazer, J(ames) G(eorge) **32**
Lang, Andrew **16**
MacDonald, George **9, 113**
Muir, Edwin **2, 87**
Murray, James Augustus Henry **117**
Sharp, William **39**
Tey, Josephine **14**

SLOVENIAN

Cankar, Ivan **105**

SOUTH AFRICAN

Bosman, Herman Charles **49**
Campbell, (Ignatius) Roy (Dunnachie) **5**
La Guma, Alex **140**
Mqhayi, S(amuel) E(dward) K(rune Loliwe) **25**
Paton, Alan **165**
Plaatje, Sol(omon) T(shekisho) **73**
Schreiner, Olive (Emilie Albertina) **9**
Smith, Pauline (Urmson) **25**
Vilakazi, Benedict Wallet **37**

SPANISH

Alas (y Urena), Leopoldo (Enrique Garcia) **29**
Aleixandre, Vicente **113**
Barea, Arturo **14**
Baroja (y Nessi), Pio **8**
Benavente (y Martinez), Jacinto **3**
Blasco Ibáñez, Vicente **12**
Echegaray (y Eizaguirre), Jose (Maria Waldo) **4**
García Lorca, Federico **1, 7, 49, 181**
Jiménez (Mantecón), Juan Ramón **4, 183**
Machado (y Ruiz), Antonio **3**
Martinez Sierra, Gregorio **6**
Martinez Sierra, Maria (de la O'LeJarraga) **6**
Miro (Ferrer), Gabriel (Francisco Victor) **5**
Onetti, Juan Carlos **131**
Ortega y Gasset, José **9**
Pardo Bazán, Emilia **189**

TCLC-189 Title Index

ISBN-13: 978-0-7876-9964-2
ISBN-10: 0-7876-9964-0